THE AFGHAN CAMPAIGNS OF 1878-1880.

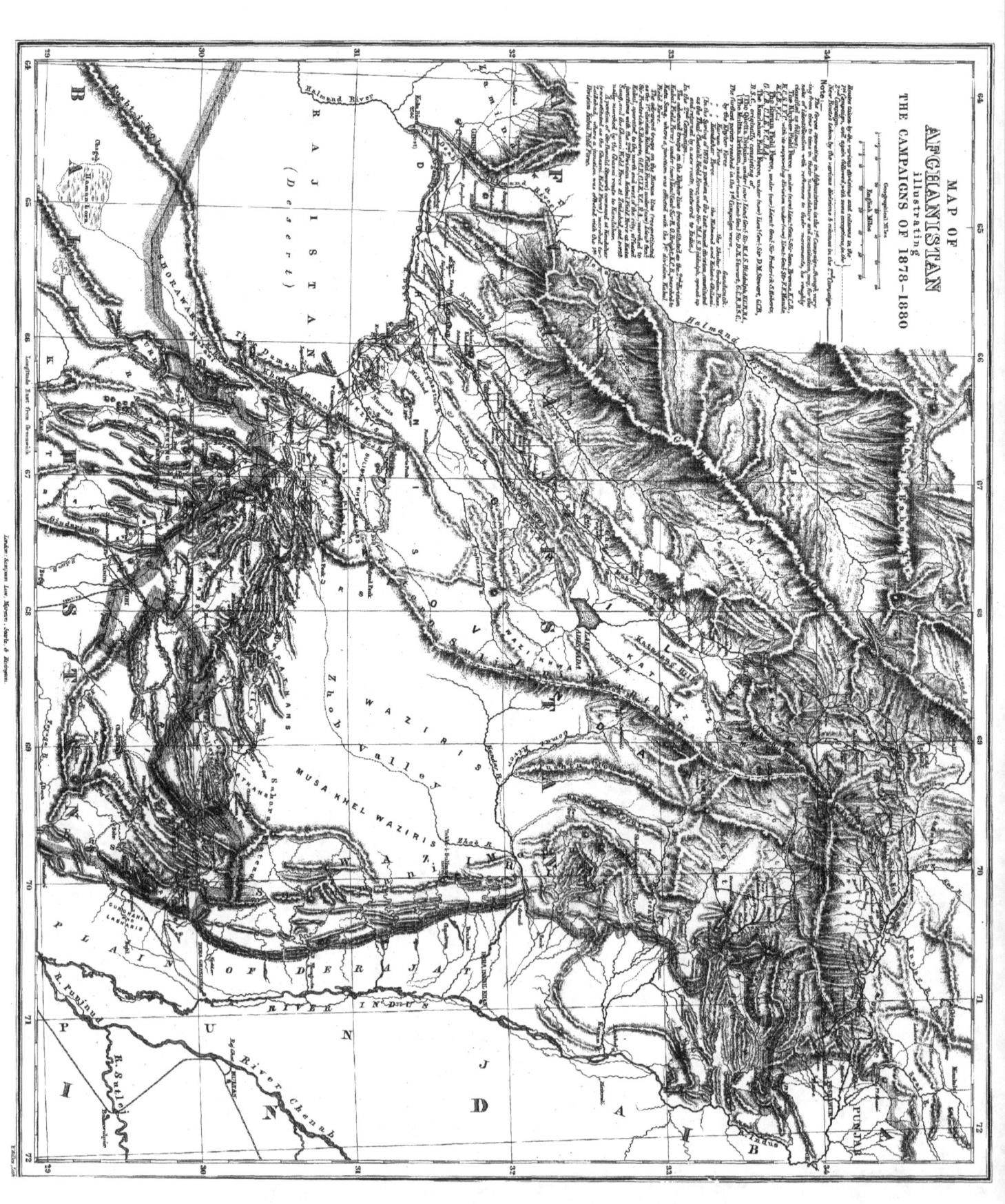

THE AFGHAN CAMPAIGNS
OF 1878—1880,

COMPILED FROM OFFICIAL AND PRIVATE SOURCES.

BY

SYDNEY H. SHADBOLT,

OF THE INNER TEMPLE, BARRISTER-AT-LAW;

Joint Author of "The South African Campaign of 1879."

𝔇𝔢𝔡𝔦𝔠𝔞𝔱𝔢𝔡, 𝔟𝔶 𝔭𝔢𝔯𝔪𝔦𝔰𝔰𝔦𝔬𝔫, 𝔱𝔬

LIEUT.-GENERAL SIR F. S. ROBERTS, BART., G.C.B., C.I.E., V.C., R.A.
COMMANDER-IN-CHIEF OF THE MADRAS ARMY.

COMPRISING HISTORICAL AND BIOGRAPHICAL DIVISIONS, AND CONTAINING A RAPID SKETCH OF THE WAR,
MAPS ILLUSTRATING THE OPERATIONS AND THE MOVEMENTS OF THE FORCES, ONE HUNDRED AND FORTY
PERMANENT PHOTOGRAPHS OF OFFICERS WHO LOST THEIR LIVES IN THE CAMPAIGNS AND OF
RECIPIENTS OF THE VICTORIA CROSS, WITH MEMOIRS PREPARED FROM MATERIALS
FURNISHED BY THEIR RELATIONS AND SURVIVING COMRADES, SUMMARIES
OF THE MOVEMENTS IN THE FIELD OF THE VARIOUS REGIMENTS
WHICH WERE ENGAGED, AND SEPARATE RECORDS OF THE
SERVICES OF EVERY BRITISH OFFICER WHO
WAS EMPLOYED IN THE WAR.

𝔥𝔦𝔰𝔱𝔬𝔯𝔦𝔠𝔞𝔩 𝔇𝔦𝔳𝔦𝔰𝔦𝔬𝔫.

Τεθνάμεναι γὰρ καλὸν ἐπὶ προμάχοισι πεσόντα
ἄνδρ' ἀγαθόν, περὶ ᾗ πατρίδι μαρνάμενον.
TYRTÆUS, *Gnom. eleg.* iv., 1, 2.

The Naval & Military Press Ltd

Published by

The Naval & Military Press Ltd
Unit 5 Riverside, Brambleside
Bellbrook Industrial Estate
Uckfield, East Sussex
TN22 1QQ England

Tel: +44 (0)1825 749494

www.naval-military-press.com
www.nmarchive.com

Author:
Sydney H. Shadbolt was a London barrister and the author of works on imperial subjects.

Cover image:
72nd Duke of Albany's Own Highlanders advancing at Peiwar Kotal, 1878
by Richard Simkin

The 72nd Highlanders was one of Major-General Frederick Roberts' most trusted regiments in the Kurram Valley Field Force. As the latter advanced along the Kurram Valley towards Kabul, their route was blocked at Peiwar Kotal by an enemy force of 18,000 men with 11 artillery pieces. While a feint attack was made on the Afghans, Roberts commanded a turning movement by the 72nd, the 5th Goorkha Regiment (the Hazara Goorkha Battalion) and other troops, which succeeded in dislodging the enemy, inflicting heavy casualties and capturing all their artillery.

Roberts lost fewer than 100 killed and wounded. This defeat resulted in the flight of the Amir, Sher Ali, and his replacement by Yakub Khan, who signed the Treaty of Gandamak, ending the first phase of the 2nd Afghan War (1878-1880).

In reprinting in facsimile from the original, any imperfections are inevitably reproduced and the quality may fall short of modern type and cartographic standards.

Published by

The Naval & Military Press Ltd
Unit 5 Riverside, Brambleside
Bellbrook Industrial Estate
Uckfield, East Sussex
TN22 1QQ England

Tel: +44 (0)1825 749494

www.naval-military-press.com
www.nmarchive.com

In reprinting in facsimile from the original, any imperfections are inevitably reproduced and the quality may fall short of modern type and cartographic standards.

CONTENTS OF HISTORICAL DIVISION.

	PAGES
SKETCH OF THE WAR	1—111
MAPS ILLUSTRATING THE MOVEMENTS OF THE FORCES AND VARIOUS ENGAGEMENTS	*Facing* 1, 23, 55, 81, 97, 103
RECORDS OF SERVICE:—	
STAFF, &C.	117—149
BRITISH REGIMENTS	150—242
ARMY MEDICAL DEPARTMENT	243—250
INDIAN NATIVE REGIMENTS	251—341
INDIAN MEDICAL DEPARTMENT	342—352

LIEUT.-GENERAL SIR F. S. ROBERTS, BART.,
G.C.B., C.I.E., V.C., R.A.,
COMMANDER-IN-CHIEF OF THE MADRAS ARMY.

Produced by permanent photo-process by the London Stereoscopic Company.

SKETCH OF THE WAR.

I.

INTRODUCTORY.

IN the closing months of the year 1875 an opinion was formed by Her Majesty's Government that it had become desirable, in consequence of the possibility of danger to India resulting from the rapid and unchecked advances of Russia in the East, to place the British relations with Afghanistan on a more definite and satisfactory footing than had hitherto subsisted; and that for the attainment of this object the first favourable opportunity should be taken to reopen amicable negotiations with the Amir of Kabul, Shere Ali Khan.

At this time the only formal obligation existing between the British Government and the Barakzai rulers of Afghanistan was a treaty which had been entered into in March, 1855, establishing perpetual peace and friendship between the East India Company and the Amir Dost Muhammad Khan—the father of Shere Ali—and his heirs, binding each party to the contract to respect, reciprocally, the territories of the other, and pledging the Afghan ruler to be the friend of the East India Company's friends, and the enemy of its enemies. This compact had been supplemented, two years afterwards, by a more complete engagement, limited, however, to take effect only during the continuance of the war then being waged with the Shah of Persia. Dost Muhammad received a large grant of treasure and arms, a stipulation being at the same time made that British representatives should be permitted to reside at Kabul, Kandahar, and Herat. In compliance with the earnest solicitations of the Amir, the fulfilment of this condition, in so far as it had reference to the nationality and number of these residents, was not exacted; but an arrangement was substituted by which the Government was permanently represented at Kabul by a Vakeel or Native Agent.

In 1863 the eventful career of Dost Muhammad Khan was brought to a close by death, and Afghanistan became rent by internal dissensions. Shere Ali, alone and unaided, after varying fortunes and many reverses, eventually regained the throne bequeathed to him by his father, and while exhibiting some trace of resentment for the neutral attitude which had been observed towards him in his hour of need, expressed a desire, without loss of time, to bring himself into close relations with the British Government. The consistent aim of the latter during a series of years had been to establish on the North-Western border of India a strong, friendly, and independent State, with interests in unison with its own, and ready to act, in certain eventualities, as an auxiliary in the protection of the frontier from foreign intrigue or aggression; and this object, it had been considered, was best attained by abstaining from active interference in the internal affairs of Afghanistan, and by the friendly recognition of its *de facto* rulers, without undertaking inconvenient liabilities on their behalf. Shere Ali's advances were, however, responded to, a somewhat closer political connection being entered into. In 1868 a free grant of money and arms was made to him by Lord Lawrence; and the following year, at a conference held at Umballa between the Amir and Lord Mayo, Lord Lawrence's successor in the Viceroyalty, a written assurance was given him that assistance in strengthening his government would be extended as circumstances might require, and that any attempt on the part of his rivals to disturb his position as ruler of Kabul, would be viewed with severe displeasure.

Rendered, as time progressed, distrustful in a high degree of the intentions of Russia by the complete disregard of the assurances given by the Government of that country to refrain from interference within the recently defined boundaries of Afghanistan, and becoming more immediately apprehensive in consequence of the subjugation of the Khanate of Khiva by the forces of the Czar, in the spring of 1873, Shere Ali deputed to Lord Northbrook, Lord Mayo's successor, during the succeeding summer, a special envoy, charged with the duty of applying for money and arms with a view to the preparation of defensive works on the Northern border of his territories, and ascertaining to what further extent he might rely, under the circumstances, on the assistance of the British Government. In the conference which ensued he was given to understand that though, under certain conditions, the Government would assist him in repelling unprovoked aggression, it did not, at the time, share his apprehensions; and he was ultimately informed that the discussion of the question would be best postponed to a more convenient season. The effect of this announcement on the Amir was not favourable. He took no notice of a proposal made by the Viceroy to depute a British officer to examine the Northern frontier of Afghanistan; he subsequently refused permission to a British envoy, who had been sent on a friendly mission to Kashgar, to return to India through Kabul; he left untouched a gift of money which had been lodged to his credit; and he assumed towards the Indian Government, generally, an attitude of extreme reserve. Thus matters stood when, in 1875, the Home Government arrived at the conclusion that it would be desirable to place the relations with Afghanistan on a more definite and satisfactory footing.

Conformably with the views entertained by Her Majesty's advisers, the Indian Government availed itself of the opportunity for re-opening negotiations which was afforded by the accession of Lord Lytton to the Viceroyalty, and by the assumption by the Queen of her Imperial title, and invited Shere Ali to receive a temporary mission at Kabul in order that he might be conferred with on what was taking place, assured of the readiness of Her Majesty's Government to give an explicit pledge of material support in the event of his territories being subjected to unprovoked foreign aggression, and induced to permit British agents to be placed on the Afghan frontier to watch the course of events beyond it.

Lord Lytton's overtures were not met by Shere Ali with the cordial reception which it was expected would be accorded them. Declining to receive the proposed Mission at Kabul, on the ground that he desired no change in his relations with the Government, and for the additional reasons that he could not guarantee the safety of a British envoy, and that if he were to admit the mission he could not refuse to receive a Russian one, he subsequently deputed the Native Agent of the Indian Government to proceed to Simla to suggest that, if the terms of a treaty were to be discussed, the conference should be held between envoys of the respective Governments on Indian, and not Afghan territory. The Agent was also entrusted to recapitulate various grievances which were weighing on His Highness's mind: notably a communication he had received from the late Viceroy in 1874 on behalf of his rebellious son Yakub Khan, whom he had imprisoned; and the repeated rejection of his previous requests for an alliance and a formal recognition of the order of succession as established by him in the person of his son Abdulla Jan.

The proposition concerning the reception of the Afghan envoy, with a view to the formulation of terms for a treaty, was acceded to by the Indian Government, which intimated its willingness to recognize the proposed order of succession, and its desire to clear up past misunderstandings and remove all cause of complaint; but although the Amir was informed in writing that the concessions which the Government was ready to grant to him were dependent on his compliance with the condition that accredited British officers should be located upon those points of the Afghan frontier from whence intelligence could be obtained by no other means, and which were most exposed to the attacks against which the Government was asked to defend it; and although, at the same time, it was signified to him that it would be of no avail for him to send his envoy unless he were prepared to agree to this condition as the basis of the proposed treaty, it became apparent in the course of the conference, which was subsequently held at Peshawar, that his minister had received no specific authority to accept it. As, moreover, the conduct of the Amir, in encouraging Russian intrigue, became more and more openly inimical, the British representative, Sir Lewis Pelly, took advantage of the sudden death of the Afghan envoy to discontinue negotiations, the basis of which had been practically rejected.

Early in 1868, two years after declining to receive a British envoy, even temporarily, within his territory, on the ground that he could not guarantee his safety, nor thereafter be left with any excuse for declining to receive a Russian mission, Shere Ali, well knowing that the cabinet of St. Petersburg stood pledged by engagements with England to regard Afghanistan as completely beyond the sphere of Russian influence, welcomed with every appearance of ostentation an embassy from the Czar, despatched to his Court at a time when there were indications that an interruption of friendly relations between Great Britain and Russia was imminent. Under these circumstances it was decided by Her Majesty's Government to insist on the reception of a British mission at Kabul.

In a letter carried to the Afghan capital by the Nawab Ghulam Hussain Khan, C.S.I., formerly British Agent at Kabul, Shere Ali was informed of the projected departure of the mission on a specified date, which would give adequate time for the issue of orders to the local Afghan officials for its reception; and that it was to be headed by an officer of rank in the person of Sir Neville Chamberlain, whose name and family were held in high esteem by the Amir.

On the 21st Sept., 1878, the mission eventually left Peshawar, and moving to Jamrud, encamped there for the day. Major Cavagnari, of the envoy's staff, who was specially charged with the conduct of the intercourse of the mission with Kabul, was deputed to ride forward with a small escort to Ali Musjid to demand from the Amir's officials permission for its advance through the Khyber Pass. The passage of the mission was, however, refused; it being announced by Faiz Muhammad Khan, the Governor of the Fort, that it was his intention to oppose, by force of arms, its further progress, and that but for his personal friendship for Major Cavagnari he would have fired on him and his party.

A demand was now addressed to Shere Ali consisting of three requisitions: that a full and suitable apology should be made within a given time for the affront which he had offered to the British Government; that a permanent British mission should be received within his territories; and that reparation should be made for any injury inflicted by him on the Afridi tribesmen who had attended Sir Neville Chamberlain and Major Cavagnari into the Khyber Pass, as well as an undertaking not to molest them hereafter; and the Amir was informed that unless a clear and satisfactory reply were received from him by the 20th Nov., 1878, his intentions would be considered as hostile, and he would be treated as a declared enemy. To this manifesto no satisfactory reply was returned within the specified period during which its receipt would have averted the threatened recourse to arms.

In the meantime the military authorities were not idle, and for weeks the trans-Indus was alive with troops and supplies streaming on towards Peshawar, Thal, and Quetta, the three points from which the British forces were to cross the frontier into Afghanistan in the event of war being declared. The plan of operations eventually decided on was, to launch three columns of invasion simultaneously from these positions, one through the Khyber Pass, one through the Kuram Valley, and one into the Pishin Valley, the two Northern divisions being intended to advance, respectively, to Daka and the Peiwar Pass as their objectives, and the Southern division, after being reinforced with a large body of troops in course of concentration at Multan, to march on Kandahar. Originally, no operations up the Khyber Pass were contemplated, though the Corps of Guides had been retained at Jamrud after the repulse of Sir Neville Chamberlain's mission, and had since been strengthened by the advent of the Hazara Mountain Battery and the 1st Sikhs. In the early days of October, 1878, a proposition that this force, supported by 1,000 Infantry and three heavy guns, should by a sudden movement effect the surprise and capture of Ali Musjid, was made, and accepted by Government; but intelligence being received that the garrison of the Fort had been largely augmented, the projected attempt was abandoned.

The antecedents of the Generals to whom the various commands were allotted, bear witness that the selection of the authorities was not ill exercised. To Lieut.-General Sir Sam. Browne, K.C.S.I., C.B., V.C., was entrusted the command of the advanced column at Peshawar, subsequently designated the Peshawar Valley Field Force, which consisted of some 10,000 men and thirty guns; to Major-General F. S. Roberts, C.B., V.C., the command of the advanced column at Thal, subsequently designated the Kuram Valley Field Force, which consisted of some 5,500 men and twenty-four guns; and to Major-General M. A. S. Biddulph, C.B., the command of the advanced column at Quetta, which consisted of some 6,250 men with eighteen guns. A strong reinforcement for the latter, consisting of some

7,300 men, with a large proportion of artillery, had assembled under the command of Lieut.-General D. M. Stewart, C.B., at Multan, and was advancing to Quetta by the Dera Bughti and Bolan route. General Stewart, on arrival, was to take over the command of the whole Quetta army, which, when eventually made up to its full strength, was organized in two divisions, designated the 1st and 2nd Division Kandahar Field Force, the immediate command of the latter of which was retained by General Biddulph. The Peshawar Valley Force was based upon Peshawar; the Kuram Force, upon Kohat; and the Kandahar Force, when completed, was to rest on Quetta. In addition to these columns, reserve divisions were being formed at Hassan Abdal, and Sukkur: one, under the command of Major-General F. F. Maude, C.B., V.C., to consist of some 6,000 men, and to act in support of the Peshawar Valley Force; the other, under the command of Major-General J. M. Primrose, C.S.I., composed of Bombay and Madras troops, and also to consist of some 6,000 men, to act in support of the Kandahar Force. A contingent, too, consisting of some 5,000 men, with artillery, was placed at the disposal of Government by the Sikh Feudatory States, and was to be employed, under the command of Colonel J. Watson, C.B., V.C., on the lines of communication. In consequence of the wide extent of the field of the contemplated operations precluding the possibility of rapid intercommunication, the Generals commanding the various columns were to act independently of one another, and take their instructions direct from the head-quarters of the Army and of Government.

At the time of the outbreak of the war, the Army of Invasion was constituted approximately as follows:—

PESHAWAR VALLEY FIELD FORCE, Lieut.-General Sir Sam. Browne, K.C.S.I., C.B., V.C., commanding: *Cavalry Brigade*—10th Hussars (two squadrons), 11th Bengal Cavalry, and Guide Cavalry, Brigadier-General C. J. S. Gough, C.B., V.C., commanding; *Artillery*—I/C, R.H.A., E/3, 11/9, and 13/9, R.A., No. 4 Mountain Battery Punjab Frontier Force, and Ordnance Field Park, Col. W. J. Williams, C.B., R.A., commanding; *Engineers*—Head-quarters and four companies Bengal Sappers and Miners, and Engineers Field Park, Col. F. R. Maunsell, C.B., R.E., commanding; *1st Infantry Brigade*—4th Battalion Rifle Brigade, 20th Bengal N.I., and 4th Goorkhas, Brigadier-General H. T. Macpherson, C.B., V.C., commanding; *2nd Infantry Brigade*—1st Battalion 17th Foot, Guide Infantry and 1st Sikhs, Brigadier-General J. A. Tytler, C.B., V.C., commanding; *3rd Infantry Brigade*—81st Foot, 14th Bengal N.I., and 27th Bengal N.I., Brigadier-General F. E. Appleyard, commanding; *4th Infantry Brigade*—51st Foot, 6th Bengal N.I., and 45th Bengal N.I., Brigadier-General W. B. Browne, 81st Foot, commanding.

KURAM VALLEY FIELD FORCE, Major-General F. S. Roberts, C.B., V.C., commanding: *Cavalry Brigade*—10th Hussars (one squadrons), 12th Bengal Cavalry, and 5th Punjab Cavalry, Brigadier-General H. H. Gough, C.B., V.C., commanding; *Artillery*—F/A, R.H.A., G/3, R.A., Nos. 1 and 2 Mountain Batteries Punjab Frontier Force, and Ordnance Field Park, Lt.-Col. A. H. Lindsay, R.A., commanding; *Engineers*—one company Bengal Sappers and Miners, and Engineer Field Park, Lt.-Col. Æ. Perkins, R.E., commanding; *1st Infantry Brigade*—2nd Battalion 8th Foot, 29th Bengal N.I., and 5th Punjab Infantry, Brigadier-General A. H. Cobbe, 17th Foot, commanding; *2nd Infantry Brigade*—72nd Highlanders, 21st Bengal N.I., 2nd Punjab Infantry, and 5th Goorkhas, Brigadier-General J. B. Thelwall, C.B., commanding; 23rd and 28th Bengal N.I., not brigaded.

KANDAHAR FIELD FORCE, Lieut.-General D. M. Stewart, C.B., commanding : 1ST (MULTAN) DIVISION : *Cavalry Brigade*—15th Hussars, 8th Bengal Cavalry, and 19th Bengal Cavalry, Brigadier-General W. Fane, C.B., commanding ; *Artillery*— A/B, R.H.A., I/1, D/2, G/4, 13/8, 16/8, 5/11, 6/11, 8/11, 11/11, R.A., Siege Train, and Ordnance Field Park, Brigadier-General C. G. Arbuthnot, C. B., R.A., commanding ; *Engineers*—two companies Bengal Sappers and Miners, and Engineer Field Park, Col. R. H. Sankey, R.E., commanding ; *1st Infantry Brigade*—2nd Battalion 60th Rifles, 15th Bengal N.I., and 25th Bengal N.I., Brigadier-General R. Barter commanding ; *2nd Infantry Brigade*—59th Foot, 1st Goorkhas, and 3rd Goorkhas, Brigadier-General R. J. Hughes, commanding. 2ND (QUETTA) DIVISION, Major-General M. A. S. Biddulph, C.B., R.A., commanding : *Cavalry Brigade*—1st Punjab Cavalry, 2nd Punjab Cavalry, and 3rd Sind Horse, Brigadier-General C. H. Palliser, C.B., commanding ; *Artillery*—E/4, R.A., No. 3 Mountain Battery Punjab Frontier Force, No. 2 Bombay Mountain Battery, and Ordnance Field Park, Lt.-Col. C. B. Le Mesurier, R.A., commanding ; *Engineers*—one company Bengal Sappers and Miners, and Engineer Field Park, Lt.-Col. W. Hichens, R.E., commanding ; *1st Infantry Brigade*—70th Foot, 19th Bengal N.I., and 30th Bombay N.I., Brigadier-General R. Lacy commanding ; *2nd Infantry Brigade*—26th Bengal N.I., 1st. Punjab Infantry, and 29th Bombay N.I., Brigadier-General T. Nuttall ; 32nd Bengal N.I. and 2nd Sikhs, not brigaded.

II.

THE FIRST CAMPAIGN.

THE period allowed for the acceptance by Shere Ali of the terms of the ultimatum having expired at sunset on the 20th Nov., 1878, without any satisfactory reply having been received by the Indian Government, telegrams were despatched from Army head-quarters setting the various columns of invaaion in motion.

The capture of Ali Musjid, the formidable fortress that had figured so prominently in the repulse of the British mission, was appropriately decided on, though only at the last moment, as the initiatory measure of the campaign, the duty of carrying it out devolving on the Peshawar Valley Field Force, which was by this time assembled at Jamrud, a small fort on the extreme frontier of British India, four miles distant from the entrance to the Khyber Pass, and separated by a stream from the Afghan frontier. Sir Sam. Browne's plan of operations, which was explained in detail to the brigadiers and staff officers of the division, and which was based upon information gleaned from reconnaissances that had been made by himself and by detachments of the Corps of Guides up the Khyber Pass, was, to send forward the 1st and 2nd Brigades under Brigadier-General Macpherson—the latter under the immediate command of Brigadier-General Tytler—to work their way to the rear of Ali Musjid : the one to proceed cautiously along the Rhotas heights in quest of a point commanding the fort itself, from which a flank attack might be delivered ; the other to make a wide détour, and to take up a position near the village of Kata Kushtia, commanding the débouchure of the defile through which it was expected the garrison might attempt to escape in the event of defeat ; and with the remainder of the division, commanded by himself in person, it was the General's purpose to storm the enemy's position from the front.

In accordance with this plan, Tytler's brigade, consisting of the 1st Battalion 17th Foot, the Guide Infantry, and the 1st Sikhs, commenced its march at 6 p.m. on the 20th Nov., Macpherson's, consisting of the 4th Battalion Rifle Brigade, the 4th Goorkhas, the 20th Native Infantry, and the Hazara Mountain Battery following some eight hours later. It being anticipated that they would reach their assigned positions by 1 p.m. on the 21st, it was intended that about that hour the front and flank attacks should be simultaneously delivered.

Counting on the co-operation of the 1st Brigade, which, as it eventually turned out, was prevented by the insuperable obstacles of the country from reaching its destination, Sir Sam. Browne, with the remainder of the force, marched from Jamrud at 7 a.m. on the 21st Nov. The advance guard, commanded by Brigadier-General Appleyard, consisting of 250 of all ranks of the 14th Sikhs, 250 of the 81st Foot, two companies Sappers and Miners, 40 of the 11th Bengal Lancers, and I/C, R.H.A., was followed by 11/9, R.A., the remainder of the 14th Sikhs, and the Engineer Field Park, and, at an interval of half a mile, by the remainder of the 81st Foot, the 27th Native Infantry, and Batteries E/3 and 13/9, R.A., the rear being brought up by the 4th Infantry Brigade, under Brigadier-General W. B. Browne.

Almost immediately after the leading companies had entered the Khyber Pass, a picquet of the enemy's cavalry was seen, which gradually retired as the British force advanced, and eventually, after being fired upon, galloped off in the direction of Ali Musjid.

At 11 a.m. the head of the advance guard reached the Shagai heights, and was halted while the remainder of the troops came up. From these heights Ali Musjid and its defences, distant some 2,500 yards, were distinctly visible. The enemy's extreme right rested on a ridge connected with an extensive range of hills behind Ali Musjid; and a line of breastworks, broken by three peaks commanding the fort and separated from it by a deep gorge, extended at an angle of 45° from this range due east. The fort itself is on a detached hill commanding the defile, and immediately opposite, across the Khyber stream, is a cliff. From this point a sort of covered way and entrenchments were continued along the face of another very precipitous cliff under the Rhotas mountain, and extended some 600 yards, completing the defences on the enemy's left; and above this line, on the highest points of the spurs from the Rhotas mountain, Afghan irregular troops were posted. On all these positions guns of various calibre were mounted; and the defences, on the whole, were of a most formidable character.

Large numbers of the enemy being assembled on the Rhotas heights, to the British right, a portion of the 4th Brigade was directed to occupy the intervening ridges; and at the same time the advance guard threw out parties to its right and left, one of 100 rifles also being moved forward to occupy a rocky acclivity some 200 yards in front, and to cover a working party employed in making the descent towards it from the Shagai ridge passable for guns.

About noon the enemy opened fire, and the ranges being well known to them, made excellent practice, though the advanced parties, being well sheltered, suffered but slightly. Battery I/C, R.H.A., was the first to reply. Within the next hour all the British artillery had entered into action, and from various positions remained engaged throughout the day.

At 2.25 p.m., in view of the probability of the 1st and 2nd Brigades having reached their destinations, Sir Sam. Browne ordered a general advance, Brigadier-General Appleyard, who was entrusted with the attack on the enemy's right, being directed to cross the Khyber stream with two companies 81st Foot, 100 rifles 14th Sikhs, and six companies 27th Punjab Native Infantry at a place called Lala China, and availing himself of the shelter of an intervening spur, to work round towards the three peaks already referred to as commanding the fort. Sir Sam. Browne himself at the same time led the 51st Foot, the 6th Native Infantry, the 45th Sikhs, and various detachments on to the ridge in front of Shagai to attack the enemy's left, Battery 11/9, R.A., being ordered also to advance on to this ridge, and open fire, and Battery I/C, R.H.A., to descend with an escort of the 10th Hussars into the Khyber stream, and take up the most suitable position to aid in silencing the enemy's guns. The place of the latter battery, which, after making its way down from the heights, went into action at a range of 1,000 yards, was taken by the heavy battery and E/3, R.A., and a heavy and effective fire was kept up on the enemy's position till dusk.

About 3.30 p.m. the troops under Sir Sam. Browne's immediate command were in sharp conflict with the enemy's left, which was strongly posted along the face of a precipitous cliff, against which no further advance could be made. In the meantime the troops under Brigadier-General Appleyard had reached the indicated spur, and about 4 p.m. were ordered forward to attack the enemy's position beyond it, two companies of the 27th Native Infantry being directed to hold a hill to the left, to prevent the flank of the attacking force being turned, the 100 men of the 14th Sikhs to skirmish in advance, the four remaining companies of the 27th Native Infantry to act in support of the 14th Sikhs, and the two companies of the 81st Foot to remain temporarily in reserve.

Day was now closing in, and as yet there was no evidence, either by the abatement of the enemy's fire, or by signs of confusion, that Macpherson's brigade had accomplished its task, and carried the Rhotas hill, or that Tytler had worked round so as to threaten the communications. Until these operations were effected, it would evidently have involved a useless loss of life for the 3rd and 4th Brigades to press on the front attack up to the fort. The order to cease firing was therefore given, word being sent to Brigadier-General Appleyard to postpone further operations till the following morning, and to hold during the night the ridge under cover of which he had effected his advance. By this time, however, his skirmishers were hotly engaged with the enemy behind their successive lines of entrenchment, and before the order to retire could be carried out, Major Birch and Lieut. Fitzgerald of the 27th Native Infantry had met their death while gallantly leading on their men, Captain Maclean, 14th Sikhs, had been wounded, and many other casualties in the two leading detachments had taken place.

During the night Sir Sam. Browne decided to reinforce General Appleyard with the mountain battery and some infantry, in view of a renewed attack on the enemy's right the following morning. At daybreak on the 22nd it was noticed, however, that while the battery, conformably with this decision, was crossing an exposed portion of the Khyber stream, it failed to draw the enemy's fire; and other indications that Ali Musjid had been abandoned by the Amir's troops under cover of the night were observed, and subsequently verified.

While the 3rd and 4th Brigades had been engaged in the front attack, the 1st and 2nd Brigades were encountering almost insuperable difficulties in carrying out the flanking operations with which they had been entrusted. Tytler's column, after a most laborious march, had bivouacked during the night of the 20th at a broad and sandy part of the bed of the Khyber stream, called Lashura, and from thence had made its way up a precipitous hill to a spur of the Tartara mountains known as Panipat, where it arrived, utterly exhausted, at 1 p.m. on the 21st. It being then found impossible for the whole column to reach Kata Kushtia that night, General Tytler directed the Guides and the 1st Sikhs, under Colonel Jenkins, to press forward in advance and descend into the Khyber defiles, the European battalion remaining at Panipat to bring on the supplies, which were being convoyed up by Macpherson's brigade. Starting at 2.30 p.m., Colonel Jenkins' troops, clambering with hands and knees, leaping from rock to rock, and sliding down water-worn declivities, succeeded by great efforts in reaching Kata Kushtia at dusk. Hardly had the companies been placed in position in the rocky hills overhanging the Pass before a body of the enemy's cavalry appeared, and receiving a volley, scattered and fled. After a brief interval they were followed by parties of infantry, and these, being surrounded, threw down their arms, and were taken prisoners. Early on the 22nd General Tytler arrived on the scene with the 17th Foot, in time to render aid in taking more prisoners—the total capture amounting to 5 officers and 255 Sepoys.

Macpherson's column, which had started at 2 a.m. on the 21st, followed as far as Panipat the route traversed by Tytler, encountering the same difficulties, and being further impeded by the duty of convoying rations for the advanced brigade. From Panipat the route pursued by the 1st Brigade diverged from that taken by the 2nd, and thenceforward the advance became still more laborious. When, about noon on the 22nd, the position on the Rhotas mountains was at length reached by the exhausted troops, it was found to have been evacuated; and it being ascertained, on examination, that there was no track leading from it to Ali Musjid, General Macpherson was compelled to retrace his steps and seek the Khyber by the Tor Tong defile, through which part of the column passed on the night of the 22nd, and the remainder the following morning. A small force of the 20th Native Infantry, under Major Gordon of that regiment, had been detached from the brigade at Tubai while *en route*, and coming across a party of the enemy on Rhotas, had driven them before them, some 50 being captured by a few men under Captain W. H. Meiklejohn of the same regiment.

Though, in consequence of the imperfect nature of the information obtainable, the distances to be traversed and the difficulties to be overcome by the 1st and 2nd Brigades had been under-estimated, the movements of those columns being observed by the enemy, had had the effect relied on, causing the Amir's troops to commence the retreat which Brigadier-General Appleyard's attack on the entrenchments on the British left materially accelerated.

The strength of the enemy—the greater number of whom, finding their direct line of retreat cut off, had fled by the Pesh Bolak track, which lay through their right entrenchments—was ascertained to have been, in cavalry, 200 men; artillery, 24 guns; infantry, 3,000 regulars and 600 irregulars. The defensive works proved, on examination, to be most skilfully and formidably designed. Had they been manned by a sufficient force, and had measures been taken to counteract flanking movements, the position would have been almost impregnable, and an attack in front alone could only have been successful at the cost of an immense loss of life. As it was, the casualties of the attacking force were comparatively light, 2 officers and 13 men being killed, and 1 officer and 34 men being wounded.

After the defeat of the enemy at Ali Musjid, the bulk of the Peshawar Valley Force, preceded by the General with some detachments of cavalry, made its way leisurely through the Khyber Pass to Daka, Brigadier-General Appleyard's brigade being detached *en route* to hold Landi Khana. The advance was uncontested, the attitude of the tribes being very friendly, and several of the headmen of the villages coming in to proffer their services. At Daka, a miserable village on the southern bank of the Kabul river, situated in a level plain surrounded by wild and rocky hills, it was found that no supplies were procurable; so all carriage had to be sent back to Peshawar, to bring up such as were to be obtained at the base. To relieve the immediate pressure on the commissariat department, a portion of the force, under Brigadier-General Macpherson, was moved on to Basawal, one march in advance.

On the departure of the main body of the division from Ali Musjid, the camp had been left in charge of Brigadier-General W. B. Browne's brigade, on which devolved the arduous duty of holding the country between Shagai and Kata Kushtia, a tract infested with Afridi robbers and assassins. In this portion of the Pass raids on convoys, thefts of telegraph wire, and similar depredations, were of daily and nightly occurrence, these offences at length culminating, about 8 p.m. on the 27th Nov., in an organized attack on the camp and the outlying picquets. After an hour's severe fighting the attack was repelled; but the enemy mustered in such force that they subsequently succeeded in closing the Khyber Pass for two days. Two regiments of infantry and some artillery, under Brigadier-General Appleyard, were despatched from Landi Khana to Brigadier-General Browne's assistance; and with the help of this reinforcement, communication with Jamrud was reopened. No further organized opposition was offered, though desultory firing into camp at night was continued.

During the period the head-quarters of the 1st Division remained at Daka, numerous reconnaissances and several unopposed expeditions were conducted into the surrounding country, one of the latter being led by Major Cavagnari, the chief Political officer with the Division, against the Zaka Khel, a section of the Afridi tribe, for recently committed depredations; another being led by General Macpherson from Basawal to Pesh Bolak in pursuit of the Amir's Master of Horse, who, however, succeeded in making his escape; and a third, to Chiari, against the Mirzan Khel, a section of the Shinwari tribe, who had cut off and killed four native camp followers. In each case punishment was inflicted by the destruction of towers and villages.

In the second week in December, 1878, Sir Sam. Browne received orders to push on to Jalalabad—the scene of General Sale's stubborn defence in the winter of 1841-1842—instead of returning to Peshawar, as had been originally intended; and after being detained till the morning of the 17th of that month, for want of supplies, the Cavalry Brigade, the 1st Infantry Brigade, and a portion of the 2nd Infantry Brigade commenced their march, the remainder of the 2nd Brigade, under General Tytler, being left *en route* at Basawal. Jalalabad was reached on the 20th idem, no opposition being encountered; and after marching through the town, which, with the fort, was found to be in a state of rapid decay, the force encamped outside the walls. It was now ascertained that Shere Ali, panic-stricken with the news of the reverses which had been sustained by his arms both at Ali Musjid and on the Kuram line of invasion, had handed over the Government to his son, Yakub Khan, whom he had released from prison for the purpose, and had quitted Kabul for Turkestan, in order, as he asserted, that he might seek Russian protection, and lay his case for consideration before a congress of the European Powers.

By the end of the first week in December, the 2nd or Reserve Division of the Peshawar Valley Force was moving forward from Hassan Abdal to Peshawar, and General Maude, on arrival, took over the command of the troops at that station and in the Khyber Pass. A redistribution of brigade commands was also made, the 4th Brigade, which was the junior one of the 1st Division, being broken up, and the regiments composing it being absorbed into Brigadier-General Appleyard's brigade, which returned to Landi Khana. General Maude's division, when completed, included a Cavalry Brigade, consisting of the 9th Lancers and the 10th and 13th Bengal Cavalry, commanded by Brigadier-General J. E. Michell, C.B.; a 1st Infantry Brigade, consisting of the 1st Battalion 25th Foot, the 24th Native Infantry, and the Bhopal Battalion, commanded by Brigadier-General H. S. Blyth; and a 2nd Infantry Brigade, consisting of the 1st Battalion 5th Foot, the 2nd Goorkhas, and the Mhairwara Battalion, commanded by Brigadier-General Doran, together with three batteries of Artillery and two companies of Sappers.

The sections of the Afridi tribe mainly implicated in the recent attacks on the camp at Ali Musjid, and in the perpetration of numerous minor raids in the Khyber Pass, were the Zaka Khels of Bazar and Bara, valleys lying to the south of the Pass, and separated from it by a lofty range of mountains. The almost total immunity from punishment which these predatory clans had long enjoyed had served to encourage them in the belief that the fastnesses they occupied were practically inaccessible to the operations of regular troops; and the necessity for disabusing them of this conviction became every day more apparent. It was accordingly decided to send out an expeditionary force, under the command of General Maude, to surround their stronghold, and effect, by means of a surprise, the capture of their headmen; and, with this object in view, arrangements were made for the simultaneous advance of mutually supporting columns from Ali Musjid and Daka. The Ali Musjid column, which consisted of three guns D/A, R.H.A., troops of the 11th and 13th Bengal Lancers, 300 of all ranks of the 1st Battalion 5th Foot, 200 of the 51st Foot, the 2nd Goorkhas, and the Mhairwara Battalion, under Brigadier-General Doran, and was accompanied by General Maude, commenced its march during the night of the 19th Dec., and making its way southwards by ill-defined mountain tracks, bivouacked near the village of Chura. The following day the column pursued its course along the bed of the Chura river without meeting with any hostile demonstration other than an occasional shot from the hills, the heights on both sides being crowned with flanking parties, and frequent reconnaissances being pushed forward. Wallai, the first of the Bazar villages, was reached about noon, but was found to be deserted: here the force remained for the rest of the day, and bivouacked for the night. At 9 a.m. on the 21st, the troops were paraded, it having been decided that if certain terms which had been offered to the people of the district by Captain Tucker, the political officer accompanying the force, were not by that time complied with, the work of destroying their villages and towers should be commenced. Exactly at that hour

Brigadier-General Tytler, the officer in command of the co-operating column from Daka, arrived upon the scene, and by his opportune appearance excited in no small degree the admiration of a number of headmen of the friendly Malikdin Khel, who had accompanied General Maude from Chura. His column, consisting of two guns 11/9, R.A., 300 of all ranks of the 1st Battalion 17th Foot, a company of Sappers, 263 of the 27th Native Infantry, and 114 of the 45th Sikhs, had started from Daka, in successive sections, on the 19th Dec., and about 4 p.m. on the following day, after protracted marches over very mountainous country, had reached a cave village at the eastern end of the Bazar plain. Halts had been made *en route* at the villages of Chunar and Sitsobi, the headmen of which had proffered their submission, and had been made use of as guides. During the night of the 20th the column had bivouacked at the eastern end of the plain, and shortly after daybreak on the 21st, the cave village, which, like Wallai, was found to have been deserted, together with two others in its neighbourhood, had been destroyed. General Tytler was now directed to move on Nekai, another village, and after burning it to return to Daka. Chinar, Halwai, and every other village of any importance in the Valley were then visited by Doran's column, and their towers razed to the ground. From each and all of these the enemy had escaped with their cattle and other moveable property.

After firing Nekai, on the 21st, Brigadier-General Tytler found that it was too late to reach the Sitsobi Pass before dark; but learning that there was water and a camping ground some few miles off in the Tubai Pass, another defile by which Daka could be reached, he resolved to pass the night there, and proceed by the new route next day. On nearing the camping ground, it became evident that the enemy were gathering in the neighbourhood; and the rear-guard, coming up the valley, was sharply attacked, one man of the 17th Foot being wounded. During the night the column was undisturbed, and the following morning, at 8.30 a.m., it moved on its way, the usual order of march, in view of the notorious predilection of the Afridis for attacking the baggage-guard, being varied, each corps carrying its own baggage, the Artillery and Sappers, being most encumbered, following close behind the advance-guard, and a strong rear-guard being told off to resist pressure from behind. The heights on the right of the Pass were occupied by flanking parties of the 45th Sikhs, under Lieut. McRae, and two companies of the 27th Native Infantry, under Captain Cook, were sent forward to secure the highest point of the road, which was both steep and tortuous. The main body of the column had hardly started when a brisk fire was opened upon it from a high hill to the left. Captain Cook, who had by this time gained the crest of the Pass, directed Lieut. Leach, R.E., with a half-company of Sappers, together with a party of the 27th Native Infantry, under Lieut. Williams, to take the summit of the hill, an order which was rapidly and effectively carried out. General Tytler and his staff remained with the rear of the column to superintend the advance, and did not reach the top of the Pass till 9.45 a.m. Before this time the rear-guard, consisting of a company of the 27th Native Infantry, under Captain Lonsdale, 17th Foot, had become hotly engaged, and was now reinforced by a company of the 17th Foot, under Captain Gamble, which, at the commencement of the march, had been sent forward to clear the hills. Captain Lonsdale was at this time directed to hold the crest of the Pass with two companies 27th Native Infantry and one company of his own regiment until the flanking parties should be withdrawn, and then to follow the remainder of the troops. The whole column, during its progress, was more or less molested; and near the termination of the

Pass a number of the enemy, who had concealed themselves in a deep gorge, succeeded in killing two men and wounding a third. From this position the enemy were dislodged by a half-company of the 17th Foot, under Lieut. Creed, and the gorge was held by a force of 30 Sikhs under Captain Rogers, 4th Goorkhas, during the egress of the rear-guard, which had been engaged in a continuous skirmish from the top of the Pass. After open country was gained, all opposition ceased, and the column continued its advance. Daka was eventually reached about 11.30 p.m. the same day, after a very trying march of fifteen hours' duration, during the greater number of which the troops had been more or less under fire. The casualties of the column during the day's fighting were, 2 men killed and 7 wounded. Brigadier-General Doran's column also reached its point of departure, Ali Musjid, on the 22nd Dec.

In consequence of the information which the enemy had gained of the intended attack, enabling them to escape with their cattle and other moveable goods, the expedition was to some extent a failure; and notwithstanding that a certain amount of punishment had been inflicted on them by the destruction of their huts and towers, and the fallacy of their belief in the inaccessibility of their mountain fastnesses had been clearly demonstrated, they continued to give considerable trouble after the return of the expeditionary force to the Khyber Pass.

For some time after the arrival of the head-quarters of the 1st Division at Jalalabad, the troops were actively employed in improving the sanitary condition of the place, in erecting a new fort, with barracks and store accommodation, and in spanning the Kabul river with a bridge capable of bearing field artillery. During the same period the road through the Khyber Pass was being brought into excellent condition by General Maude's division, while camps for winter quarters were being formed, and hospitals and supply depôts established along the whole line of communications. By both divisions numerous reconnaissances were conducted into a wide extent of surrounding country, and from time to time various expeditions were despatched to break up hostile gatherings, and inflict punishment on refractory tribes.

On the 1st Jan., 1879, an imposing durbar was held at Jalalabad by Sir Sam. Browne, which was attended by most of the local Khans and other influential men of the neighbourhood. Major Cavagnari, addressing them, commented on recent events as manifesting the strength of the British Government and the failure of the Amir's resistance, and at the same time assured them that the Government had no quarrel with the people of Afghanistan. The principal Khan expressed his contentment with the change of authority, and the services of all were freely proffered.

A number of murders and robberies having been committed by a section of the Mohmand tribe in Kama, a district on the north side of the Kabul river, under the rule of a well-affected chief, a force under Brigadier-General Jenkins, consisting of 50 of the Guide Cavalry, under Captain Battye, 250 of the Guide Infantry, under Major Campbell, and two guns of the Mountain Battery, under Captain de Lautour, was sent out from Jalalabad before daybreak on the 11th Jan., with the object of surprising the fort of Shergash, a village in which, it was believed, the marauders were being sheltered. The expedition was accompanied by Major Cavagnari, and guided by Khalik Khan, the chief of Besud. After fording the Kabul and Kunar rivers, and marching some ten miles, the force reached Shergash about 11 a.m., and the headmen of the village, finding their retreat cut off, came out and surrendered. While they were being secured, a band of ninety Mohmands emerged from a small fort hard by, and made off rapidly for the hills. Though they were too far off to be intercepted, Captain de Lautour was able to throw two or three well-directed shells into their midst after they had gained the heights, killing three and wounding one. The column then moved on to a large village called Serai, and after passing the night there, made its way back by the ford of the river opposite Ali Boghan, the men suffering keenly from the icy coldness of the water, which rendered several of them quite insensible. The object of the expedition was successfully attained, its good effects becoming immediately manifest. A party of 25 sabres of the 10th Hussars and 100 rifles of the 20th Native Infantry were sent out beyond Ali Boghan as a support, but their help was not needed.

The road between Ali Musjid and Jamrud having been on one occasion temporarily closed by the Afridis, and the attacks on outposts and picquets, the raiding on convoys, and the cutting up of camp followers in the Khyber Pass being carried on with unabated vigour, it was considered that a salutary effect might be produced by despatching a second expeditionary force under General Maude to temporarily occupy the Bazar Valley, and visit in rotation a number of villages in which both thieves and stolen property were known to have been harboured. With this object in view, arrangements were made for sending out, towards the latter end of January, three columns, one from Jamrud, one from Ali Musjid, and one from Basawal, the two former, after effecting a junction, to join the latter at the head of the Bazar Valley; and it being considered desirable that a more accurate topographical knowledge of the district should be obtained, two surveying parties were detailed to accompany the expedition. The Jamrud Column, consisting of two guns D/A, R.H.A., two guns 11/9, R.A., 313 of all ranks of the 5th Fusiliers, 316 of the 25th Foot, 145 of the 13th Bengal Lancers, 356 of the 24th Native Infantry, and 55 of the Madras Sappers, under Brigadier-General Blyth, and the Ali Musjid Column, consisting of two guns 11/9, R.A., 213 of all ranks of the 51st Foot, 312 of the 2nd Goorkhas, 320 of the Mhairwara Battalion, 31 Sappers, and (from Landi Kotal) 31 of the 6th Native Infantry, under Brigadier-General Appleyard, marched from their respective points of departure on the 25th Jan., and after destroying the towers of various villages, effected a junction, on the 26th, at Burj. From that place, the towers of which were likewise blown up, an advance was made to the Bazar Valley, the enemy attacking the tail of a detached portion of the Jamrud Column *en route*, but being repelled by two companies of the 2nd Goorkhas marching in the extreme rear, ably handled by Major Battye of that regiment. During the night of the 26th there was considerable firing upon the picquets, one private of the 25th Foot being killed, and two wounded. At daybreak on the 27th 300 men under Colonel Ruddell, 25th Foot, were sent by General Maude to scour the Chinar hill, and a detachment of cavalry under Lt.-Colonel Low, 13th Bengal Lancers, to cut off the retreat of the enemy, seven or eight of whom were killed. The same afternoon the Basawal Column, consisting of two guns 11/9, R.A., 413 of all ranks of the 17th Foot, 210 of the 4th Battalion Rifle Brigade, 32 of the Guide Cavalry, 43 Sappers, 201 of the 4th Goorkhas, 104 of the 27th Native Infantry, and 257 of the 45th Sikhs, under Brigadier-General Tytler, arrived in camp.

On the 28th Jan. General Maude proceeded to make a personal reconnaissance of the Bokhar Pass, leading towards Bara, the movement being covered by a force of 1,000 men, with two guns of the Mountain Battery, under Brigadier-General

SKETCH OF THE WAR.

Tytler. On the arrival of this force opposite Halwai, two miles from camp, the Afridis opened fire from a hill opposite that village; and from there to within 1,100 yards of the top of the Bokhar Pass, every hill-top was contested. By the judicious advance of Brigadier-General Tytler, the enemy was forced to abandon each successive position; and after observations had been taken, the force returned to camp, the retirement being carried out in the same careful manner as the advance. The British loss on this occasion was, 1 man killed, and 1 officer and 3 men wounded, that of the enemy being allowed to have been 15 killed. On the same day a detachment under Captain Atkins, 6th Native Infantry, while taking back camels to Ali Musjid for supplies, was attacked near the Prang Darah heights; but owing to the able dispositions of the officer in command, not a man or animal was touched, while four of the enemy were seen to fall. On the 29th, 450 men under Colonel Thompson, 6th Native Infantry, were detached by General Maude to blow up the towers of Halwai, where fire had been first opened on the reconnoitring force the previous day. The enemy showed in great force; and on the return of Colonel Thompson through the low hills to the south of the camp, after effecting the object of his advance, their numbers became largely augmented. A sharp skirmish ensued, 1 man of Colonel Thompson's force being killed, and 5 wounded, while a loss estimated at 20 killed was inflicted on the enemy. On the same day Lt.-Colonel Low, 13th Bengal Lancers, while reconnoitring towards the Sasobai Pass, also found the enemy occupying the hills in great force.

The duration of the expedition had been strictly limited by the military authorities to ten days, of which six had already elapsed: and it was now rapidly becoming evident that the hostility of many other sections of the Afridi tribe besides the Zaka Khel was being aroused. Bearing in mind that war had been declared not against the people of Afghanistan, but against the Amir and his troops, and finding that, by forcing his way to Bara in the face of the determined opposition he was likely to meet with, the commencement of an Afridi war was almost certain to develope itself, General Maude directed Captain Tucker, the political officer accompanying the force, to endeavour to break up the hostile combination, and at the same time applied for further instructions as to the course which, under the circumstances, he was to pursue. On the 31st, whilst negotiations were proceeding, an additional complication arose from the receipt of a telegram from Sir Sam. Browne calling for the return of Tytler's column in view of a threatened attack by Mohmands and Bajwaris on Jalalabad and Daka. Just at this time it fortunately transpired, however, that the enemy had suffered severely in the skirmishes of the last few days, and that, in consequence of the protracted occupation of the Valley, they were well disposed to accede to reasonable conditions. A deputation from all the sections of the Bara Zaka Khel was received in camp; the restitution of a number of stolen camels was accepted as an earnest of future good behaviour; and terms which were considered satisfactory were rapidly arranged. The columns were thus enabled to leave the Valley on the 3rd Feb., Brigadier-General Tytler's proceeding by the Sitsobi Pass to Daka, and Brigadier-Generals Blyth and Appleyard's by Chura to Ali Musjid and Jamrud respectively, each reaching its original point of departure the following day.

The threat of an attack on Jalalabad and Daka, which had prompted the recall of Brigadier-General Tytler's column, was not carried into effect, the hostile attitude of a force of some 8,000 Mohmands, Bajwaris, and Utman Khels, who had assembled on the north side of the Kabul river opposite Chardeh, in the territory of a Chief under British protection, resulting merely in a raid on a cluster of villages in Kama, which were partly destroyed. On the 7th Feb., the day after the perpetration of this outrage, a force under Brigadier-General Macpherson, consisting of detachments of the Rifle Brigade, 20th Native Infantry, 4th Goorkhas, and 1st Sikhs, with a mountain battery, a troop of the 10th Hussars, and a squadron of the 11th Bengal Lancers, crossed the Kabul river by the bridge at Jalalabad with the object of breaking up the hostile combination, a force under Brigadier-General Tytler, consisting of 300 rifles 17th Foot, two mountain guns, and a squadron of Guide Cavalry being detailed to co-operate from Basawal. After making his way for some distance eastwards, and fording the Kunar river, in the passage of which he lost three camp followers, General Macpherson found the enemy had already retreated to the hills; but succeeding in coming within long range of them, he dispersed a few scattered parties by Artillery fire. In the meantime General Tytler had moved to Chardeh, and endeavoured to cross the Kabul river at a neighbouring ford; but finding the water near the northern shore of the river too deep for the passage of his infantry and guns, he had drawn up the bulk of his force on an island, with the intention of enfilading any of the enemy who might be driven past by the Guide Cavalry, which, under Major Battye, succeeded in reaching the opposite bank. By a reconnaissance which was made by this squadron to the foot of a range of hills three miles north of the river, it was ascertained, however, that the district had been evacuated. The two columns shortly afterwards retraced their steps, and within a few days all excitement in the district had subsided.

In consequence of the attitude taken up by the Sirdar Azmatallah Khan of Lughman, who, influenced by the intrigues of Yakub Khan, had steadily refused to tender his submission, and had carried his hostility to the extent of incarcerating two brothers of the native Governor of Jalalabad, it was decided to despatch an expedition into his territory, to overawe the inhabitants, and take measures for obtaining the release of the prisoners. With this object in view, a force under Brigadier-General Jenkins, consisting of a troop of the 10th Hussars, a squadron of the Guide Cavalry, two guns of the Mountain Battery, 200 of the Rifle Brigade, 250 of the Guide Infantry, and 250 of the 1st Sikhs, accompanied by Major Cavagnari, marched from Jalalabad at daybreak on the 22nd Feb., with four days' supplies, and making its way across the Lughman river on the 23rd, continued its advance up a fertile and populous valley to the confluence of the Alingar and Alishang rivers, opposite Tingari. The expedition was most successful, not a shot being fired, and most of the headmen tendering their submission. After hostages for the release of the imprisoned Sirdars were taken, the column returned on the 25th.

On the 28th Feb. a letter arrived at Jalalabad from Yakub Khan, couched in friendly terms, and conveying the important announcement that his father, Shere Ali, who, it was known, had for some time been suffering from a mortal malady, had died on the 21st of that month at a place called Mazar-i-Sharif, near Balkh, in Turkestan.

In view of the unsettled condition of political affairs, orders were now issued for a forward concentration of the 1st Division at Jalalabad, and for the 2nd Division to move up and occupy the positions vacated by Sir Sam. Browne's troops as far westward as Daka. This forward concentration was completed on the 28th of March. By that date nine months' supplies had been accumulated between Daka and Jalalabad, ammunition was abundant, the transport service, though the mortality amongst the camels was excessive, was in fair working order, and preparations generally had been made to meet the contingent necessity for a further advance.

Meanwhile, on the 28th Feb., an attack had been made by a large number of Afridis on a party of twenty men of the 4th Native Infantry under Mr. Scott, of the Survey Department, who was collecting topographical data in the neighbourhood of Michni. Mr. Scott eventually succeeded in fighting his way through his assailants, almost forfeiting his life, while doing so, in a most heroic attempt to save one of his sepoys, who was wounded, from falling into their hands. A few weeks afterwards, on the 17th of March, a similar attack was made by a force of 200 Shinwaris on Captain Leach, R.E., while carrying on surveying operations in the neighbourhood of Maidanak, near Jalalabad, with an escort of 30 sabres of the Guide Cavalry, under Lieut. Hamilton, and 40 rifles of the 45th Sikhs, under Lieut. Barclay. The onslaught was very successfully repelled, a loss of 9 killed and 6 wounded being inflicted on the enemy. Of the Survey party, Captain Leach—who for his gallant behaviour on the occasion was decorated with the Victoria Cross—was severely wounded, Lieut. Barclay was shot through the lungs, and died shortly afterwards, and one native officer was killed. To obtain satisfaction for this attack, a force under Brigadier-General Tytler, consisting of 100 of the Guide Cavalry and 11th Bengal Lancers, 500 of the 17th Foot, 4th Goorkhas, 27th Native Infantry, and 45th Native Infantry, four mountain guns, and 100 Sappers, marched from Barikab at midnight on the 21st towards Ghilzai, and being there joined by a force under Lieut.-Colonel Ball Acton, 51st Foot, consisting of 30 of the 11th Bengal Cavalry, 100 of the 17th Foot, and 300 of the 51st Foot, advanced up the valley towards Maidanak and Girdi Kas. The objects of the expedition were accomplished without bloodshed, the Shinwaris, who assembled to the number of 2,000, accepting General Tytler's terms, which were, that the interrupted survey should be carried out on the spot, that a fine of 1,500 rupees should be paid, and twelve hostages given for its liquidation, and that seven of the towers in the valley should be destroyed. In the meantime, on the 18th March, the day following the attack on Captain Leach and his escort near Maidanak, a detachment of the 27th Native Infantry under Jemadar Gunesha, which was protecting some camels and mules sent out to bring in supplies, had been attacked by another section of the tribe, the Shinwaris of Deh Sarak. The Jemadar covered the retirement of his convoy without loss, killing one and wounding two of the enemy. The duty of inflicting punishment on the villages which had furnished the attacking party was again entrusted to Brigadier-General Tytler, who, with a force consisting of two guns, 11/9, R.A., 90 sabres 11th Bengal Cavalry, 60 sabres 13th Bengal Cavalry, 150 rifles 5th Fusiliers, 250 of the 17th Foot, 50 of the 27th Native Infantry, and 50 of the 2nd Goorkhas, started at 1 a.m. on the 24th of March from Basawal. The march was tedious; and day beginning to break before the column had reached its destination, General Tytler trotted forward with the cavalry in order to prevent the escape of the enemy from a large fortified village called Mausam, which was situated on high ground sloping down to the Pesh Bolak plain, and was found to be protected by deep nullahs on either side. At the bottom of this slope, about half a mile distant from Mausam, were three smaller villages; and near these the cavalry were halted. The people of Mausam, who had by this time become cognizant of their proximity, were now seen to crowd the walls of the village and occupy the ground in front, while others were observed collecting in one of the nullahs, to General Tytler's right, and on a level plateau beyond it; and from each of these positions, as also from the most distant of the three smaller villages, which were situated on the British right rear, a heavy fire was almost immediately opened. General Tytler dismounted a portion of his cavalry, and extended them to reply to this fire, and for about half-an-hour held his position against increasing numbers of the enemy, who were gradually pushing closer. The infantry, meantime, hurried up at the double with the guns; and as the leading companies arrived, they took the place of the cavalry skirmishers. The guns were now ordered to shell the village of Mausam, and the infantry to advance in skirmishing order, the cavalry, under Captain Thompson, 13th Bengal Lancers, being at the same time directed to cross the nullah to the right to prevent a flank attack, and to charge the enemy in the event of a favourable opportunity presenting itself. These movements met with the most complete success. The enemy holding Mausam were overwhelmed by the fire of the artillery and the skirmishers, and abandoned the village, which was taken by the infantry with a rush, while those on the plateau across the nullah, occupied with the attack of the infantry, did not observe the approach of the cavalry till too late. Captain Thompson, as soon as he came in sight of them, ordered the charge, and rushed upon them with a line of 100 lances. The enemy, numbering about 300, met the onslaught with a volley at close range, which emptied two saddles; but in a moment more the whole of them were dispersed, pursued by the Lancers, and from 50 to 60 were left dead on the plain. The enemy now retreated in every direction, and General Tytler occupied a position in advance of Mausam, seizing two other villages a few hundred yards to the left, and sending infantry picquets to hold the high ground on either side beyond the nullahs. After a number of towers had been blown up, and the villages given to the flames, a leisurely retirement was commenced by alternate lines of skirmishers, halts being occasionally made to open fire with the guns against large masses of the enemy, over 3,000 of whom had again collected, and who began to press on the rear of the column and on either flank, sometimes approaching to within eighty or a hundred yards of the skirmishers, and making demonstrations of attacking sword in hand. Their shooting was, fortunately, very wild, and their efforts to charge, perfectly futile; for whenever they exposed themselves, which they freely did, the deadly fire which was poured into them by the infantry caused them to recoil. After open country was reached, the retirement was covered by the cavalry in alternate squadrons, and the force ultimately made its way back to camp. In this admirably managed affair only 2 men of General Tytler's force were killed, and 12 wounded, while the loss suffered by the enemy was upwards of 160 in killed alone.

During the next few days numerous small raids continued to be made by the tribesmen along the line of communications, while disturbances in the contiguous districts—supposed to be the result of the intrigues of emissaries from Kabul—were from time to time reported. At the latter end of March a second expedition to the Lughman Valley was organized with the object of effecting the capture of the refractory chief Azmatallah Khan, who was believed to be inciting the inhabitants of that district to rise. With this purpose in view a force under Brigadier-General Macpherson, consisting of 300 of all arms of the Rifle Brigade, 300 of the 20th Native Infantry, 300 of the 4th Goorkhas, and four guns of the Hazara Mountain

SKETCH OF THE WAR.

Battery, marched from Jalalabad at 9 a.m. on the 30th of that month, a force of cavalry under Lieut.-Colonel Wood, 10th Hussars, being detailed to co-operate on the north side of the Kabul river. After crossing the Siah Koh range of mountains, General Macpherson ascertained that Azmatallah had made good his escape; so the column retraced its steps. In the meantime the co-operating force under Lieut.-Colonel Wood, consisting of a squadron of the 10th Hussars and a squadron of the 11th Bengal Lancers, had quitted Jalalabad, marching down at 10 p.m. on the 31st to the Kala-i-Sakh ford of the Kabul river, distant about a mile from camp. The stream was here divided by a large island, beyond which flowed the main channel, between two and three hundred feet broad. Descending into the water by the light of the moon, the Lancers, headed by Col. Wood, were followed by the mules carrying their supplies, the immediate rear being brought up by the 10th Hussars. The Lancers, with the baggage animals, reached the northern shore of the river in safety, but owing to the uncertainty of the light and the great velocity of the current, which was running at about nine miles an hour, the tail of the squadron had unconsciously diverged down stream, a tendency which more and more affected the files in the rear. In the rapidly deepening water the horses became restive and lost their footing, the lamentable result being, that nearly the whole of the squadron of Hussars was swept away—a struggling mass of heavily accoutred men and animals—to the rapids below. Of the seventy officers, non-commissioned officers, and men who had marched from Jalalabad, no less than forty-six were consigned by this accident, in the space of a few minutes, to a common grave. The remainder of the squadron returned to Jalalabad the same night, the rest of the force, on it becoming known that Azmatallah Khan had fled, retracing their steps the following day.

On the day after the departure of the force under Brigadier-General Macpherson for the Lughman Valley, the 31st March, a column under Brigadier-General C. Gough, consisting of three troops of the 10th Hussars, three troops of the Guide Cavalry, 400 men of the 17th Foot, 210 of the 27th Native Infantry, 300 of the 45th Native Infantry, four guns, I/C, R.H.A., and a company of Sappers, was pushed forward by Sir Sam. Browne towards Gandamak, a village some thirty miles in advance of Jalalabad, on the Kabul road. After advancing fifteen miles, the force encamped near the village of Futtehabad. About 1 p.m. on the 2nd of April, the look-out picquets reported the proximity and hostile movements of large bodies of Kugianis, a tribe of Durani Afghans, whose lands lie between those of the Shinwaris and Ghilzais, and from whom some opposition had been anticipated. The troops were immediately ordered under arms, and preparations made for an attack. The position taken up by the enemy, who numbered between four and five thousand, was on an elevated plateau, protected by breastworks, and commanding the Gandamak road; their front extended about a mile, each flank resting on a steep declivity, from the base of which the ground fell gradually towards the British camp. Leaving the camp in charge of Lieut.-Colonel M'Pherson, 17th Foot, with 300 infantry and two troops of cavalry, and directing the rest of the infantry to follow, General Gough galloped forward, with the bulk of the cavalry and the horse artillery, to within 1,200 yards of the plateau, and opened fire. The enemy throwing out lines of skirmishers from their right, General Gough gradually retired his cavalry and guns, with the object of drawing the main body out of their very strong position. The movement was completely successful, the enemy streaming forth with flags flying, drums beating, and every demonstration of making an attack. As the cavalry fell back, the infantry came up, and were immediately brought into action on the left, being ordered to make a continuous advance: the 17th Foot and the 27th Native Infantry in the front line, with the 45th Native Infantry in reserve. During this advance, which was resisted with great determination, a gallant charge was made by a few men of the 17th Foot under Lieut. Wiseman, who, unhappily at the cost of his life, captured the enemy's standard. The resistance now beginning slightly to slacken, the cavalry, on the right, swept forward to the charge—three troops of the Guides, under Major Wigram Battye, and three troops of the 10th Hussars, under Lieut.-Colonel Lord Ralph Kerr—breaking upon the wavering masses with irresistible impetuosity, riding through their ranks, rallying, and again falling upon them. The enemy fled in every direction, endeavouring to reach the numerous forts which dotted the richly cultivated valleys surrounding the plateau; but the cavalry, again let loose, pursued them with great slaughter, the guns at the same time being brought to bear with effect on groups wherever cohesion manifested itself. Between three and four hundred dead were left upon the plain, the British loss being 6 killed and 40 wounded. The victory was dimmed by the death of Major Wigram Battye, a gallant and revered officer of the Corps of Guides, who was severely wounded immediately after the first charge was ordered, but who, with the life-blood pouring from his body, continued to lead his men till a second bullet pierced his heart. For the gallantry he displayed in this action, another young officer of the Guides, Lieut. Hamilton, who led the troops of his regiment in the pursuit, was subsequently awarded the Victoria Cross.

After remaining two days at Futtehabad, General Gough's column, which was reinforced by a detachment from General Macpherson's brigade in the Lughman Valley, and by the bulk of the 2nd Brigade under General Tytler, continued its march on Gandamak, which was reached without further opposition on the 6th April. Its advance was followed by the gradual forward concentration of the 1st Division, the head-quarters of which were eventually located in a camp formed at Safed Sang, an elevated position three miles from Gandamak, on the Jalalabad side.

On the 21st April a somewhat regrettable collision with a section of the Mohmand tribe occurred in the neighbourhood of Daka. The headmen of Kam Daka, a village on the right bank of the Kabul river, having expressed their sympathy with the British cause, and their fear to display their friendship openly lest such an exhibition might draw down upon them the displeasure of their fellow tribesmen on the north side of the river, it was determined, through some misconception of their requirements, to send over from Daka a small force to give confidence to the inhabitants of the village; and a party of 150 men of the Mhairwara Battalion, under Captain Creagh, were detailed for this duty. On his arrival at Kam Daka, Captain Creagh was informed that the presence of so small a force would, of a certainty, prove an irresistible temptation to the tribesmen to the north of the river to cross over and annihilate it; and entreaties and threats were alternately used to induce him to leave. His orders were, however, absolute, and he encamped for the night; the result being that, by daybreak on the 21st, a force of 2,000 Mohmands had crossed the river, and more were rapidly following. Captain Creagh now endeavoured to withdraw to Daka, but found, after he had proceeded about two miles, that his retreat was cut off. He then made the best disposition of his little force that was possible, intrenching himself in a graveyard, where he was immediately surrounded. A gallant sowar of the 10th Bengal Lancers ran the gauntlet of the enemy's position, carrying a message to the officer commanding at Daka, explaining the situation, particulars of which were telegraphed on to General Maude at Landi Kotal. Captain Tucker, the political officer in charge of the Jalalabad section of the line, who happened to be on the spot, was at once despatched with twenty-five troopers of the 10th Bengal Lancers, under Captain Strong, and a company of the 5th Fusiliers, under Captain Ormond, to render assistance, a further reinforcement, consisting of two guns of a mountain battery, escorted by 100 men of the 12th Foot, being ordered on immediately afterwards. When the first reinforcement arrived upon the scene, Captain Creagh's situation had become critical, his ammunition being nearly expended. Up to this time he had lost one man killed, and four or five wounded; but within the next few minutes three more were killed and seven or eight wounded. The Bengal Lancers now gallantly charged the enemy, while the Mhaiwaras, under Captains Creagh and Tucker, fell back by alternate companies, the Fusiliers holding the line of retreat, and the Mohmands occupying each successive position as it was vacated. The second reinforcement was met with, hurrying forward, shortly afterwards, and the retreat, now covered by the company of the 12th Foot, was continued to Daka, which was reached about 10 p.m. The British loss on this day amounted to 5 killed and 24 wounded. For the gallantry of his defence, Captain Creagh was subsequently awarded the Victoria Cross.

While Sir Sam. Browne's division of the Army of Invasion had been engaged in the forcing of the Khyber Pass and the advance to Jalalabad, successes no less significant had been achieved by the column under General Roberts on the Kuram line. Pushing forward a squadron of the 10th Hussars and two companies of the 29th Native Infantry to intercept the escape of the garrison of Kapigong, the General crossed the frontier with the main body of the division on the 21st Nov., 1878, a few hours after permission had been accorded to commence hostile operations, and advanced upon the fort, which was found to have been quite recently evacuated. On the 23rd and 24th Nov. the column, preceded by the General with detachments of cavalry, continued its progress over very broken ground to Ahmadshana and Hazar Pir, and during the three succeeding days to Muhammad Azim's fort, which was occupied without opposition. The inhabitants of the country showed a friendly disposition, the Turis bringing up their flocks for disposal, and the tribesmen of the Khost district sending in a deputation to proffer their allegiance.

After reconnoitring with the 12th Bengal Cavalry to Habib Kila, in the direction of the Peiwar Kotal, and finding the enemy posted in force, General Roberts ordered an advance of the division in two columns from Muhammad Azim's fort, at 3 a.m. on the 28th November; one column, under Brigadier-General Cobbe, consisting of one squadron 12th Bengal Cavalry, two guns No. 1 Mountain Battery, a wing of the 8th King's, the 5th Punjab Infantry, the 23rd Pioneers, the 29th Native Infantry, and two guns, F/A, R.H.A., mounted on elephants, taking a path leading along the foot of the hills which bound the plain to the north; the other column, under Brigadier-General Thelwall, consisting of one squadron 12th Bengal Cavalry, two guns No. 1 Mountain Battery, a wing of the 72nd Highlanders, the 2nd Punjab Infantry, the 5th Goorkhas, and two guns, F/A, R.H.A., marching by the direct road. At Habib Kila, which was reached about 10 a.m., it was reported that the enemy were flying in confusion up the eastern side of the Peiwar Kotal, having abandoned twelve guns. To ascertain the real state of the case, a reconnaissance in force, consisting of two guns No. 1 Mountain Battery, the 8th King's, the 5th Punjab Infantry, the 29th Native Infantry, and the 23rd Pioneers, subsequently reinforced by the 5th Goorkhas, was passed up the south-eastern flanks of the mountain. A hot skirmish rapidly ensued, the fact being elicited that so far from the enemy having abandoned any guns, they had taken up an extremely strong position on the Pass, and that they were well provided with artillery judiciously placed. The object of the reconnaissance being accomplished, the detached troops were withdrawn, and rejoined the main body of the division. In the fighting on this day one sepoy was killed, and one British officer (Lieut. Reid, 29th N.I.), one native officer, and eight sepoys, were wounded.

Sufficient having been seen of the Afghan defences to convince General Roberts that they could not be carried by a direct attack without incurring severe loss, he resolved to halt a few days: first, with the view of recruiting the men's strength, which had been severely taxed by the recent marching; and secondly, to gain time to ascertain, by further reconnaissances, whether the position could not be turned, or, failing that, in what manner a front attack might be most advantageously conducted.

The defences were found to extend along the crest of a lofty and rugged range of mountains from the Spin Gawai Kotal, on the Afghan left, to some commanding heights a mile south of the Peiwar Kotal, and to have a front of about four miles, facing east, the Peiwar Kotal forming the right centre. These mountains, which were mostly covered with dense pine forests, rose almost precipitously from the plain on the eastern or Kuram side, but were known to descend westwards in a succession of upland meadows stretching away towards the valley of the Hariab.

After carefully supplementing, by successive reconnaissances, the information he had already obtained, General Roberts formulated his plan of operations, which was explained in detail to commanding officers as darkness was closing in on the 1st of December. His intention was, by a secret night march on the Spin Gawai Kotal, to throw the bulk of the troops at his disposal on the enemy's flank, with the object of turning it, while the remainder of his force, left temporarily in camp, were to co-operate with the main body of the division by a direct attack on the enemy's position as soon as the turning movement should be developed. The 29th Native Infantry, the 5th Goorkhas, and No. 1 Mountain Battery, under Colonel Gordon, 29th N.I.; the 72nd Highlanders, the 2nd Punjab Infantry, and the 23rd Pioneers, under Brigadier-General Thelwall, together with four guns, F/A, R.H.A., mounted on elephants, the whole under General Roberts' immediate command, were detailed to form the turning force, and were to march the same night, without noise or bugle sound, and leaving camps standing; while the 5th Punjab Infantry, the 12th Bengal Cavalry, two guns, F/A, R.H.A., and three guns, G/3, R.A., together with a number of Turi and other levies commanded by Major Palmer, the whole under Brigadier-General Cobbe, were to remain temporarily in camp. Brigadier-General Cobbe received general instructions to open fire upon the enemy about 6 a.m.; to get his troops into position in front of the Peiwar Kotal by 8.30 a.m.; and to storm the place when the flank attack should have shaken the enemy's defence.

At 10 p.m. the troops under General Roberts marched silently out of camp, and after reaching the village of Peiwar, commenced a long and intensely laborious ascent of the mountain side. It was the General's intention to halt the column en route for a three hours' rest during the night; but an unforeseen breach of faith

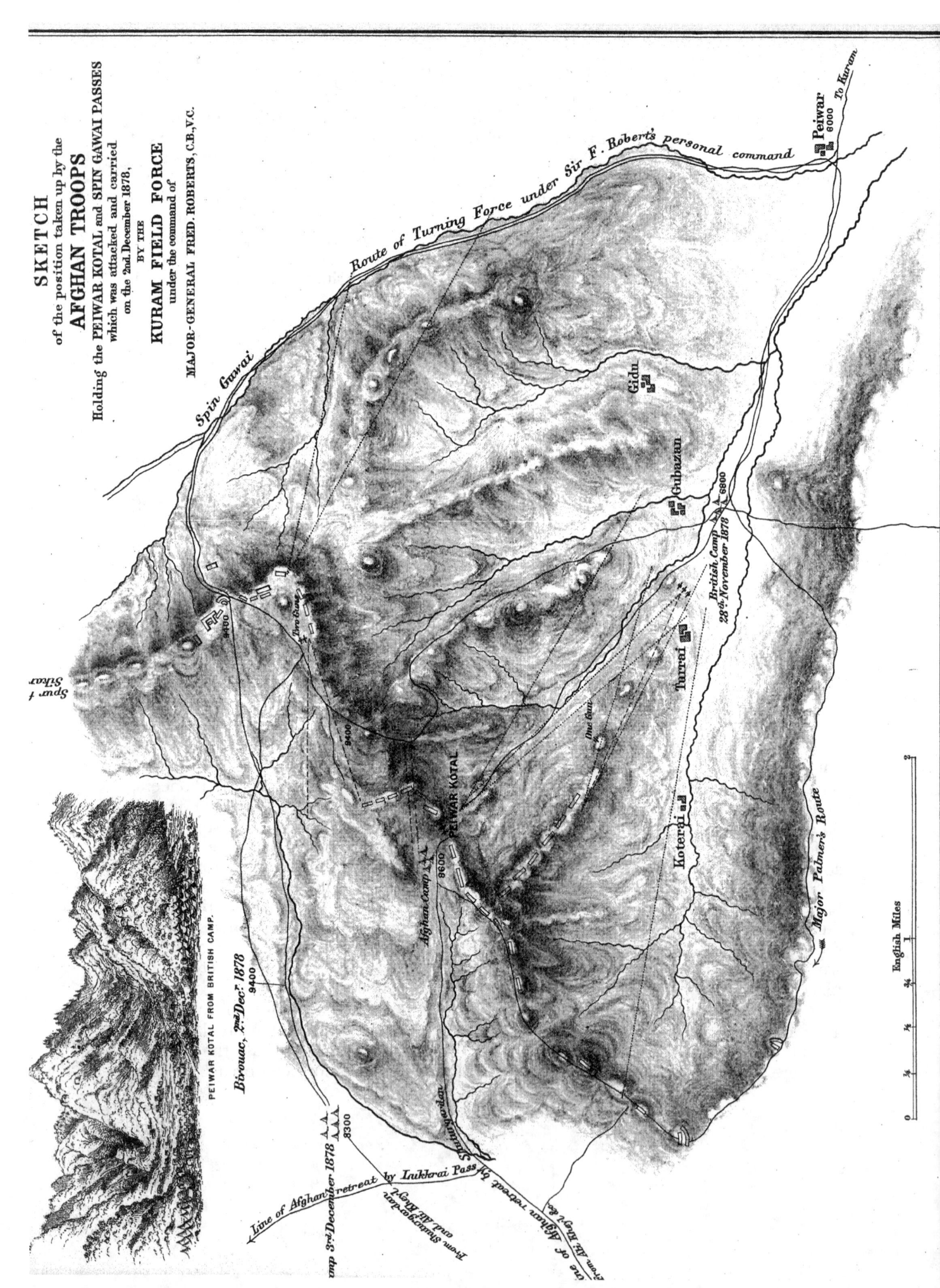

frustrated this arrangement. Knit by ties of kindred with the race against whom they were being led, some Pathans in the ranks of the 29th Native Infantry, the leading battalion, at first manifested their disaffection by impeding the progress of the rest of the force by their slow and straggling advance, and at length, within an hour of dawn, their treachery culminated, at a most critical juncture, in an attempt to warn the enemy of the approach of the column by firing, in the intense stillness of the night, two shots from their rifles. Fortunately, these shots were unheard, or, if heard, were unheeded. The regiment was at once halted, and sent to the rear, its place being taken by the 5th Goorkhas and 72nd Highlanders. After this change had been effected in the order of march, the advance was quickly pushed forward, and at length, about 6 a.m. on the 2nd of December, the head of the column, thus far unobserved, reached the foot of the Spin Gawai Kotal. The alarm being given at this moment by musket shots from the enemy's sentries, the advanced company of the 5th Goorkhas rapidly formed up, and led by Major Fitz Hugh and Captain Cook, and closely followed by the leading company of the 72nd Highlanders under Colonel Brownlow, rushed straight at the first barricade, which now became apparent about fifty yards to the front. The remainder of the 5th Goorkhas extended, and swarmed round the flanks of the obstacle, which was carried in brilliant style, its defenders firing one volley into the attacking force, and being nearly all bayoneted at their posts. Goorkhas and Highlanders, vying with one another in their eager desire to close with the enemy, continued to fight their way up the steep side of the Kotal, carrying, in brilliant succession, stockade after stockade, each of which was most obstinately defended. During this advance, No. 1 Mountain Battery, whose gallant commander, Captain Kelso, R.A., was shot through the head just after passing the first barricade, rendered the greatest assistance, the guns being fought in the most determined manner well up in the front line. The 29th Native Infantry, acting as a support, rapidly demonstrated the fact that the disloyalty which had been manifested was confined to isolated companies, and performed valuable service in repelling an attempted attack by the enemy on the right flank. By half-past six o'clock the whole of the Spin Gawai barricades and stockades had been captured, the line of the enemy's defence being completely turned; and an hour later communication by visual signalling was established with Brigadier-General Cobbe, who was instructed to co-operate vigorously from below in attacking the Kotal. Orders were now given for the turning force to continue its direct advance on the enemy's left flank, along the crest of the Peiwar towards the Pass leading over its centre, and General Roberts himself led on the 29th Native Infantry to clear the intervening woods and heights. About this time the guns in the British camp below opened fire upon the enemy's position, and shortly afterwards considerable execution was wrought by the four guns, F/A, R.H.A., which had been brought up on elephants.

Continuing its advance along the crest of the Peiwar ridge, and being subjected at every yard to a more and more severe fire, the 29th Native Infantry at length reached a precipitous-sided gully, on the farther side of which the enemy were posted in great force. Supported by small detachments of the 23rd Pioneers and 2nd Punjab Infantry, the regiment at once descended into the ravine, and made two gallant but unsuccessful attempts to scale the opposite heights, the enemy contesting the position with the greatest determination, continually bringing up fresh reinforcements, and at times assuming the offensive. Here Major Anderson, of the 23rd Pioneers, was killed while charging up the hill-side at the head of his men. The 72nd Highlanders, the 5th Goorkhas, and the remainder of the 23rd Pioneers were now brought into the front line, but the fight continued for some time without any perceptible advantage being gained by either side, till at length the enemy retired to their original position. The 5th Punjab Infantry, which, originally left behind in camp, had worked its way up over the slopes in front of the enemy's left centre, now appeared upon the scene, and proved a welcome addition to the turning force. About this time intimation was received of the discovery of a position on the ridge from which the Afghan camp behind the Kotal was within range of the artillery; and two guns of the Mountain Battery being sent to the spot, a number of shells were thrown from them with such precision as to fire the enemy's tents, and cause a hasty stampede.

It having now become apparent that the Kotal was practically inaccessible from the northern side, on which he was operating, General Roberts resolved to withdraw the troops from this line of attack altogether, and, by making another turning movement, to attempt to penetrate to the rear of the enemy's centre. With this object in view it was arranged that the 2nd Punjab Infantry should hold the crest of the hill to which the advance had already been pushed, that the 29th Native Infantry should occupy the heights overlooking the Spin Gawai, and protect the field hospital which had been established there, and that the remainder of the force, consisting of the 5th Goorkhas, the 5th Punjab Infantry, the 23rd Pioneers, the 72nd Highlanders, the four guns, F/A, R.H.A., and the Mountain Battery, under Brigadier-General Thelwall, should march under the immediate command of General Roberts in the Zabardast Kila direction, so as to threaten the enemy's line of retreat. By this time, about 1 p.m., the men, who had been marching continuously since 10 p.m. the previous day, and fighting since 6 a.m., were in a state of great exhaustion. A short rest was therefore ordered, and a hurried meal partaken of, before the second turning movement was commenced.

Conformably with the orders he had received prior to the departure of the main body of the division from camp, and with the supplementary directions which had subsequently been signalled to him from the Spin Gawai Kotal, Brigadier-General Cobbe had moved his artillery into position before daybreak, about a mile up the Peiwar Valley, under escort of a company of the 8th King's, and at 6.15 a.m. had opened fire, at a range of about 1,700 yards, upon a gun placed on a crag which commanded the lower part of the Pass, the infantry of his force being at the same time extended slightly in advance, and under cover. About 7 a.m. the fire of a portion of the artillery was turned upon the Kotal batteries, which were at the time being vigorously served, and an hour later a further advance was ordered, two companies of the 8th King's and the 5th Punjab Infantry occupying a ridge 350 yards nearer the enemy's position. For the next three hours an incessant and well-directed artillery fire was kept up on both sides, with the result that two of the enemy's guns, situated to the left of the summit of the Pass, were silenced at about 11 o'clock. The infantry simultaneously advanced from ridge to ridge, and by noon had approached to within 1,400 yards of the top of the Kotal. About this time Brigadier-General Cobbe was severely wounded, and the command of the troops devolved upon Colonel F. Barry Drew, of the 8th Foot. The 5th Punjab Infantry, who had made considerable progress to the right front, and were close under the main ridge of which the Kotal forms the lowest part, now established communication with, and joined the force under General Roberts' immediate command. Shortly after 1 o'clock the remaining infantry, consisting of five companies of the 8th King's, gained the crest of an extremely steep and difficult hill, from which they were able to open fire, at a range of 800 yards, upon the guns on the Kotal, and also to clear the opposite side of the valley. The Afghan artillerymen continued to serve their guns for some time with the greatest gallantry, but the withering fire which was poured upon them at length compelled them to abandon their batteries.

By 2 p.m. the second turning movement of the troops under General Roberts' immediate command was in part developed, and its effect became immediately apparent; the enemy, subjected to a galling fire in front, and finding their line of retreat simultaneously threatened, beginning to waver in their defence. Colonel Drew now resolved to deliver his attack. As his infantry, the 8th King's, were making their way across two deep and precipitous-sided ravines to gain the road which led up to the side of the Kotal, they were subjected to a dropping fire; but once on the road, all opposition ceased, and shortly before half-past two o'clock the troops entered the Afghan position without further loss. The enemy had fled with the greatest precipitation, leaving behind them a number of their dead, besides eighteen pieces of ordnance, and vast quantities of stores and ammunition which had evidently been accumulated with a view to the occupation of the position throughout the winter. The 12th Bengal Cavalry, under Colonel Hugh Gough, were now sent in pursuit, and captured several more guns which had been abandoned by the enemy in their rapid flight.

The native levies under Major Palmer had been detached, earlier in the day, to operate on the Afghan right flank, with the design of diverting the enemy's attention, and committing the Turis and other tribes to the British cause. It was with the utmost difficulty that they could be induced, during the action, to expose themselves to fire, or restrained, after the Afghan position was carried, from mutilating the dead.

During the night the Peiwar Kotal was garrisoned by the 8th King's, the troops under General Roberts' immediate command bivouacking near the village of Zabardast Kila.

An examination of the Peiwar Kotal proved the place to be one of enormous natural strength, and that the dispositions for repelling any attack on it from the front were very complete and judicious. The enemy's strength was reliably ascertained to have been 3,500 regulars and large numbers of irregulars; while that of the British consisted of 43 officers and 2,220 men, forming the turning force, and 30 officers and 838 men, forming the co-operating column. Of these, 21, including 2 officers, were killed, and 72 wounded. The losses of the enemy throughout the day must have been heavy, over 70 of their dead having been counted on the Spin Gawai Kotal alone.

The sick and wounded being sent back to Fort Kuram, and a wing of the 8th King's and three guns left at Peiwar, with the 29th Native Infantry to act as a support in the valley below, the main body of the division advanced on the 5th and 6th of December to Zabardast Kila and Ali Khel, large quantities of ammunition and grain, which had been stored by the Afghan army, being secured *en route*. During the succeeding week General Roberts, with detachments of the 72nd Highlanders and 5th Goorkhas, and two guns of the Mountain Battery, conducted an unopposed reconnaissance to the Shutargardan Pass, the object of which was, to ascertain the extent of the defeat which had been administered to the Amir's forces, and the capability of the Pass for being held as a defensive position against troops moving from the Kuram Valley on Kabul. It was found that though the summit of the Pass was 11,200 feet high, no insuperable difficulties were presented by it to the advance of an opposing army; and the complete nature of the defeat of the Afghan forces on the 2nd of December was evidenced by the Jagi and Ghilzai tribesmen, who were supposed to have been very loyal to the Amir's cause, coming forward with warm protestations of welcome.

It being important to obtain an exact knowledge of the lines of communication between the Kuram Valley and the trans-Peiwar district of Hariab, in which Ali Khel is situated, General Roberts marched from the latter post on the 12th of December with a brigade of troops consisting of No. 1 Mountain Battery, a wing of the 72nd Highlanders, the 5th Goorkhas, and the 23rd Pioneers, and following a route which cuts off the angle formed by the junction of the Hazardarakht stream and the Kuram river, encamped the same night near the hamlet of Sapari. At 2 a.m. on the 13th of December, in consequence of a warning which had been received from friendly Ghilzai villagers that the force would probably be obstructed by the Mangal tribe when passing through the defile which lies between Sapari and Kharaiah, the next halting-place, the baggage of the column, in charge of Captain F. T. Goad, Assistant Superintendent of Transport, was sent on in advance, with a view to its reaching the summit of the Pass before the tribesmen might have time to collect. The difficulties of the ascent, however, proved to be greater than had been anticipated; and it was not till 11 a.m. that the last of the camels had passed over the highest point of the Pass. The strength of the brigade was insufficient to admit of the surrounding hills, which were broken and precipitous, being crowned with effect; and a lamentable loss of life was the result. As the long column of animals was descending the steep and narrow valley into which the defile opened, the Mangals, of whom nearly a hundred had collected, and whose numbers were subsequently considerably increased, commenced firing into the baggage-guard, and pressing the 5th Goorkhas in the extreme rear. From this time till nearly 4 p.m., when the column at length cleared the heights, the enemy never ceased annoying the rear-guard, sometimes becoming so bold in their attacks as to oblige the Goorkhas to use their bayonets. Early in the day Captain Goad, who had been most active in keeping order in the baggage-train, was mortally wounded, and while lying helpless on the ground was defended with great gallantry against a horde of the Mangals by Sergeant Greer and four men of the 72nd Highlanders. Besides Captain Goad, three Goorkha Sepoys were killed, and Captain Powell and eleven Goorkha Sepoys wounded, the former mortally. So successfully was the rear-guard duty performed by the 5th Goorkhas, that not a single baggage-animal or load was lost. For the gallantry of their behaviour under very trying circumstances, a warm tribute was paid to the officers and men of this regiment by the General in his despatch.

The Field Force head-quarters moved forward to Fort Kuram on the 14th of December, and were shortly afterwards followed by the remainder of the brigade. During the next fortnight, a period throughout which the Afridis were giving great trouble on the Khyber line, the tribesmen of the Kuram Valley were no less active, numerous raids being made on convoys moving between Kohat and Peiwar.

Retaliatory measures were taken where the offences could be brought home to the inhabitants of specific villages; and a salutary effect was produced by executing, in the presence of the principal headmen of the valley, four marauders who had been taken in the act of cutting up camp followers in the Darwaza Pass.

On the 26th of December an important Durbar was held by General Roberts at Fort Kuram, which was attended by all the Khans and principal inhabitants of the valley and the neighbouring districts. The General, addressing them, formally announced the annexation of the valley by the British Government, and informed them that they were henceforth to look to the Empress of India as their Sovereign, for the rule of the Amir had passed away for ever. The following day the head-quarters camp at Kuram was broken up, and the troops distributed, the 5th Goorkhas and a company of the 72nd Highlanders remaining to garrison the fort, a wing of the 72nd being sent back to Habib Kila, and General Roberts, with his staff and the remainder of the brigade, proceeding to Hazar Pir, a small village on the Kuram river, situated midway between the fort and Thal.

It being considered that a satisfactory result might be produced by the temporary occupation of the hitherto comparatively unexplored district of Khost, and that the topographical information attainable by this means might prove of value, a flying column was organized for the purpose at the latter end of December, and on the 2nd of January, 1879, commenced its march from Hazir Pir. Muhammad Akram Khan, the Afghan Deputy Governor of the district, a functionary with whom General Roberts had been for some time in communication, had agreed, on the condition that his own personal safety should be guaranteed, to maintain order until the arrival of the column, and then to make over possession of the important fort of Matun. It was therefore hoped that the objects of the expedition might be effected without bloodshed.

The force was commanded by General Roberts in person, and consisted of a squadron of the 10th Hussars, a wing of the 72nd Highlanders, three troops of the 5th Punjab Cavalry, Nos. 1 and 2 Mountain Batteries, and the 21st and 28th Native Infantry, Colonel Barry Drew being in command of the Infantry, Colonel Hugh Gough of the Cavalry, and Lieut.-Colonel Lindsay of the Artillery. During the 3rd, 4th, and 5th of January the march was continued through generally fertile and populous country, and on the 6th the village of Matun was reached, and possession taken of the fort. Hitherto, no opposition had been met with, though indications were not wanting that the presence of the column in the valley was unwelcome. Some of the most influential of the headmen had refrained from coming in to pay their respects until they were sent for, while others who were met with on the road asked for permission to return before they had entered the camp. This attitude of the inhabitants was attributable, it would seem, to the influence of the religious teachers, of whom that district possessed a large number famed for their learning and fanaticism. On the day on which possession was taken of the fort, intelligence was received of a projected attack by the Mangal tribe, and a reconnaissance sent out early the following morning was fired on, and elicited the fact that the enemy, to the number of several thousands, had collected round three sides of the camp.

General Roberts decided that the time had now arrived when prompt and vigorous action was required to insure the safety of the column, separated, as it was, from its nearest support by many miles of country; and with the object of inflicting speedy and severe punishment on the tribes who had ventured to organize the attack, he proceeded to make his dispositions. While the Cavalry, under Colonel Hugh Gough, supported by six companies of the 28th Native Infantry and No. 2 Mountain Battery were moved out to operate to the north-west of the camp, where the enemy appeared to have the greatest strength, the remainder of the Infantry and Artillery were temporarily retained for purposes of defence, a wing of the 21st Native Infantry and two guns of No. 1 Mountain Battery being detailed to protect the right or eastern flank of the camp, the other wing of the 21st Native Infantry and the remaining two guns of No. 1 Mountain Battery to cover the rear, and the wing of the 72nd Highlanders to take care of the front and left flank. The whole of the troops in and around the camp were placed under the command of Colonel Barry Drew, who was directed merely to hold his own until Colonel Gough should have disposed of the enemy in his front. For the consummation of this task Colonel Drew had not long to wait. Dismounting part of his force, Colonel Gough engaged the enemy, drove him up into the higher ranges of the hills, and kept him well in check until his supports arrived. He then assumed command of all the troops in that part of the field, retired his cavalry under cover of the Infantry and Artillery fire, and formed them up in the plain ready to cover, in turn, the withdrawal of the Infantry. Each arm ably performed the duty entrusted to it, the result being that the enemy on the north-west side were completely repulsed.

General Roberts now directed Colonel Drew to carry a number of villages to the right and rear of the camp, from which fire had been opened, and to burn them as a punishment to the inhabitants for having given shelter to the enemy. During this operation, which was rapidly performed, a troop of the 5th Punjab Cavalry, which had been taken from Colonel Gough's command, made a very effective charge on a number of the Mangals who were escaping from the rear of a village on which the infantry were advancing, killing about twenty of them. Before it was dark, all the troops had been withdrawn to camp, and so completely had the enemy been beaten, that they did not attempt to follow up the retirement, according to the usual Pathan custom.

During the night of the 8th, a number of prisoners who had been taken made a desperate attempt, by preconcerted signal, to escape. To prevent themselves being overwhelmed, their guard was compelled to fire upon them, and eight were killed before order could be restored. The following day the remainder were released, some being fined, others merely admonished.

For the next three weeks the expeditionary force remained in occupation of the district, which was exhaustively explored and surveyed. The lesson which had been administered on the 7th of January was not without effect, representatives of tribes dwelling in territory beyond the limits of Khost, as well as the head men of the various villages, coming in to make their submission. A small force was detached by General Roberts to garrison the fort of Matun; but in view of the more pressing requirements of the advanced posts on the main line of communications, it was subsequently withdrawn, and replaced by 600 Turi levies under a native Assistant Commissioner, Shahzada Sultan Jan.

After the installation of the native representative, which took place on the 26th of January, camp was struck, and the troops commenced their return march to the Kuram Valley. The column had not, however, proceeded beyond Sabari, some twelve miles on the road, when reports were brought in that the Mangals were again threatening Matun. On receiving this news General Roberts, with the bulk of his force, at once hurried back to rescue the Shahzada, and arrived just in time to avert an attack on the fort by large bodies of the hill-men, who were found to have assembled round it. It was now decided, in view of the impossibility of adequately garrisoning the fort, to abandon it altogether. The native Assistant Commissioner and the levies were accordingly removed, and a quantity of grain and other stores which could not be carried away were destroyed. The column then returned to Sabari, the cavalry, which covered the rear during the march, engaging the Mangals in a slight skirmish, and killing several. From Sabari the whole of the troops forming the expeditionary force continued their march to Hazar Pir, and ultimately arrived at their destination on the 31st of January.

Immediately prior to his departure from Khost, General Roberts received news from the front of considerable political significance. Captain Rennick, the Political Officer of the Hariab, who, with a small escort, had been holding his own in the midst of a hostile and fanatical population at the isolated village of Ali Khel, thirteen miles in advance of the British outposts, had succeeded in detaching from the Amir's cause the influential Ghilzai chief, Pashah Khan; and almost immediately afterwards the same officer reported that the Sirdar Wali Muhammad, Governor of Kuram and Khost, a half-brother of Shere Ali, and a man of considerable importance in Afghanistan, had also come in, and wished for an interview. His request was at once complied with, General Roberts receiving him in durbar at Hazar Pir on the 1st of February. It being deemed desirable, however, that he should be placed in direct communication with the political officers on the Khyber line, merely formal courtesies were exchanged, and a few days afterwards the Sirdar started with an escort of the 10th Hussars for Jalalabad. About this time, too, the welcome intelligence was received that the Punjab Chiefs' Contingent, under General Watson, had been ordered up to Kohat and Thal: a measure urgently needed, as the Kuram Valley Force was at the time distributed over a vast area, and not only were its communications far too extended for its strength, but its base had been almost entirely denuded of troops.

During the absence of General Roberts in the Khost Valley the advanced troops under Brigadier-General Thelwall in the neighbourhood of the Peiwar Kotal were busily employed in constructing defensive works and improving their quarters. The position was again and again seriously threatened by hostile combinations of the tribes—notably, on the nights of the 3rd, 4th, and 5th of January by the Mangals and Jagis, who assembled in the neighbourhood in immense numbers. Every preparation was made for their reception; but the actual attack was in each instance averted, either by the diplomatic skill of Captain Rennick, the Political officer at Ali Khel, or by dissensions between the tribes arising from mutual jealousy and distrust, and without external stimulus.

With the exception of a series of raids on the line of communications and on the frontier, with which the Mahsud Waziris followed up an incursion they had made into British territory in the first week in January, no disturbances occurred in the Kuram Valley or its neighbourhood for some little time, the operations of the Field Force during the remainder of the winter being mainly confined to strengthening the outposts, improving the quarters, and passing up supplies to the front, while minor redistributions of the troops from time to time took place. The

23rd Pioneers and the Sappers had been long actively employed in road-making, and by the middle of February there were two excellent routes available for wheeled traffic between Thal and Kuram. For some weeks the snow, which first made its appearance at the latter end of January, lay several feet deep on the Peiwar and Shutargardan passes, and the cold was intense; but the troops were comfortably hutted before the first fall, and notwithstanding the rigorous nature of the climate, enjoyed excellent health.

At the latter end of March, the Peiwar Kotal and the intermediate posts on the Kuram line were visited by His Excellency the Commander-in-Chief, who had recently inspected the Peshawar Valley army, and shortly afterwards a forward concentration of the Field Force towards Ali Khel, almost contemporaneously with the advance of Sir Sam. Browne's division on the Khyber line, was ordered. Arrangements were at the same time made for the Punjab Chiefs' Contingent, under Brigadier-General Watson, the greater part of which had arrived at Thal in the middle of February, to move up and occupy the different stations vacated by the advanced troops. In the meantime the Pioneers and Sappers, having completed their work between Thal and Kuram, had been sent on to Peiwar, and were actively employed in preparing the road beyond that post. The excitement amongst the tribes had now abated, and the more important sections of the Mangals and Jagis had sent in representatives and tendered their submission.

For the next few weeks the forward concentration steadily progressed, the whole of the infantry of the division moving up to Ali Khel, though the cavalry and artillery still remained at Kuram in consequence of the larger quantity and better quality of the fodder obtainable there. Besides large quantities of stores and ammunition, 4,000 camels were collected at the front, and there was a sufficiency of transport for the troops and fifteen days' supplies. By the end of April the snow had melted from the passes, and the Kuram column, like the 1st Division of the Peshawar Valley Army, stood ready to advance.

To turn to the movements of the forces on the southern line of invasion. By the 21st of November, 1878, two of the regiments of cavalry and seven of the regiments of infantry which had been detailed to General Biddulph's command had arrived at Quetta, while the troops under General Stewart destined for the reinforcement of the Quetta division were pushing forward as rapidly as possible on their long march of 250 miles from Sukkar through Dadar and the Bolan Pass. On that date the nucleus of General Biddulph's column commenced its advance northwards from Quetta, the march being carried out for convenience of organization and supply by successive detachments, and concentration being afterwards made at suitable points. On the 27th Nov. the divisional head-quarters, having entered Afghanistan, reached Haikalzai in the Pishin Valley without encountering opposition, and there remained till the 8th Dec., large quantities of supplies, during the interval, being collected, numerous reconnaissances into the surrounding country and to the entrances of the passes over the Khoja Amran Mountains being conducted, a route through the Gazaband Pass for the artillery of General Stewart's force being prepared by native labour, and the organization of the division being gradually rendered more complete by the arrival of the brigadiers. During the same period a detachment at Dadar marched to Oramzai, on the Kalat border, and another detachment occupied Sibi, in Afghan territory. From Haikalzai the main body of General Biddulph's force moved forward to Kila Abdula, a post being formed at the same time at the foot of the Khojak Pass—the route eventually adopted for the passage of General Biddulph's division in its advance on Kandahar. The reconstruction of the road over the pass was now commenced, the other passes over the Khoja Amram range, including the Ghwaja, the route subsequently adopted for the passage of General Stewart's division, being thoroughly examined.

On the evening of the 14th Dec. the Khojak Pass was reported fit for the passage of infantry, cavalry, and mountain guns; and on the 15th Colonel Kennedy, 2nd Punjab Infantry, moved the advance guard to Chaman, on the farther side. On this day General Stewart arrived and assumed supreme command of the troops, General Biddulph retaining command of the advance column, which was constituted as the 2nd Division. About this time reports were received that the Amir did not intend to defend Kandahar in the event of the British advance being continued as far as that city.

The passage of the Khojak Pass by the 2nd Division continued from the 19th Dec. to the end of that month without intermission, every path and zigzag being thronged with streams of troops, and laden and unladen camels passing to and fro. From a pinnacle hard by, a complicated correspondence was carried on by heliograph with five stations: two, occupied by the cavalry brigade, in the Kadani plain, one at Chaman, one at Khojak camp, and one at Kila Abdula, which, in turn, was connected with Gulistan Karez, where General Stewart's head-quarters were situated. At the latter end of January the passage of the Ghwaja Pass by the 1st Division presented a scene of similar activity, it having been decided to adopt both routes for the advance of the troops on Kandahar. After the passage of the Khoja Amran range should be completed, the two divisions were to continue their march by separate routes converging towards Takht-i-pul, where, on arrival, they were to concentrate.

The forward movement of the head-quarters of the 1st Division was commenced on the 2nd Jan., 1879, and that of the head-quarters of the 2nd Division on the following day. The Cavalry Brigade of the 2nd Division, under Brigadier-General Palliser, led the advance on each road, Brigadier-General Palliser, on the Ghwaja road, commanding in person the Left Column of the advanced troops, which consisted of a squadron of the 15th Hussars, two guns, A/B, R.H.A., two squadrons 1st Punjab Cavalry, the 25th Punjab N.I., the 32nd Pioneers, a wing of the 2nd Baluchis, and two companies of Sappers; and Colonel Kennedy, 2nd Punjab Cavalry, on the Khojak road, being in command of the Right Column, which consisted of one troop 15th Hussars, two guns, A/B, R.H.A., 200 sabres 2nd Punjab Cavalry, and 30 sabres 3rd Sind Horse. The leading troops of General Biddulph's division on the Khojak road, following Colonel Kennedy, were one company 2nd Battalion 60th Rifles, a wing of the 70th Foot, the 26th Native Infantry, a wing of the 2nd Baluchis, E/4, R.A., a company of Sappers, and the Engineer Field Park. The most advanced troops on the Ghwaja route following Brigadier-General Palliser, were D/2, R.A., and a detachment of the 2nd Battalion 60th Rifles. These were followed by the whole of the 1st Division, with the exception of A/B, R.H.A., I/1, and 11/11, R.A., and the 15th Hussars, which, with the 2nd Division, moved by the Khojak route. A moveable column, consisting of a squadron of the 8th Bengal Cavalry, two guns of the Peshawar Mountain Battery, and the 1st Punjab Infantry, remained for duty in the Pishin Valley. The fort of Chaman was held by two companies of the 2nd Sikhs, two guns of the

Jacobabad Battery, and 40 sabres of the 3rd Sind Horse; and a wing of the 30th Bombay N.I., was detached to Kalat.

On the morning of the 4th Jan., the Right and Left columns of the advance, under Brigadier-General Palliser, the former under the immediate command of Colonel Kennedy, while marching by separate routes across the Mel Valley—the one to encamp at the entrance to the Ghlo Pass, and the other at Saif-u-din—came into contact with some regiments of Afghan cavalry which had been sent out from Kandahar with the object, apparently, of intercepting their progress. About 1 p.m., Major Luck, 15th Hussars, who was in command of a reconnoitring party consisting of 100 sabres 15th Hussars and 28 sabres 1st Punjab Cavalry, which had been despatched through the Konna Pass (Palliser's line of route) into the Takht-i-pul Valley, sent a message to the effect that he had exchanged shots with the enemy's scouts, and that they were retiring before him. General Palliser at once ordered a reconnaissance in force from both columns through the passes respectively in front of them, and taking all his available cavalry and the two guns, A/B, R.H.A., pushed forward and joined Major Luck. An advance was now made by the Left column parallel to the course of the Kadani river, over very broken ground, and presently detached groups of the enemy were sighted on ridges a mile distant. About the same time the cavalry and horse artillery, under Colonel Kennedy, came across another party of the Amir's horsemen, and bringing an effective fire to bear on them, succeeded in emptying several saddles. The groups which had been sighted by the Left column retiring as the force moved forward, and the fire of Kennedy's guns now becoming audible from the south of the Ghlo Pass, to the right, General Palliser changed the direction of the advance of his cavalry towards the northern débouchure of the pass, with the object of falling upon the rear of the portion of the enemy with which the Right column was engaged. At the same time orders were given for the two guns, A/B, R.H.A., to continue their march along the route originally pursued; for the 32nd Pioneers to enter the Konna Pass and hold it; and for the remainder of the infantry to close up to the artillery. After proceeding a distance of some three miles, the cavalry neared the northern entrance to the Ghlo Pass from the Kandahar direction, and found the enemy, to the number of not less than 300, débouching from it in a leisurely retirement before the advance of Colonel Kennedy's force. The two troops of the 15th Hussars and detachments of the 1st Punjab Cavalry, led by Major Luck, at once swept forward to the charge, and were received with a volley from the carbines of the Afghan horsemen, who, after a short hand-to-hand encounter turned and fled, and were pursued for some distance along the base of the hills. Very shortly afterwards, Colonel Kennedy's cavalry and guns emerged from the pass, and a junction having been effected between the two columns, General Palliser returned towards Saif-u-din with the intention of selecting ground for encamping. In the meantime the guns and infantry had been placed in position by Colonel Moore, C.I.E., who had assumed temporary command, and bodies of the enemy's cavalry were reported to General Palliser on his arrival as being some distance in front, firing occasional shots at the detachment of the 1st Punjab Cavalry—the gun escort—which had advanced to drive them back. At these groups two or three rounds were fired by the Horse Artillery after the camping ground had been selected, and subsequently a few shots by four companies of the 2nd Baluchis, supported by the 25th Native Infantry, which were moved forward for the purpose. Darkness now coming on, the whole force, with the exception of a strong picquet, was retired to camp, and the following morning it was ascertained, from a reconnaissance, that the Afghan horsemen had fallen back towards Kandahar. The number of the enemy engaged was estimated to have been 1,000 to 1,200, and their loss in killed and wounded, 100. The casualties of the British forces during the day were 11 officers and men wounded, and 10 horses killed, wounded, or missing.

On the 6th Jan., the 1st and 2nd Divisions effected their junction at Abdul Rahman in the Takht-i-pul district, and from thence continued their march, still by separate roads, on Kandahar. At Kushab, a village seven miles south of that city, information was received by General Stewart to the effect that the Governor of Kandahar, and most of the other officials, together with the Afghan cavalry, had fled towards Herat; and on the afternoon of the 7th Jan., a letter from the Deputy Governor, tendering submission and professing his readiness to hand over the city, was sent into camp.

At 3.30 p.m., on the 8th January, 1879, the Shikarpur Gate of Kandahar was reached by General Stewart with his staff and escort, and a ceremonial march was made by the 1st Infantry Brigades of the two divisions through the streets of the city. The attitude of the population—with the exception of the large Hindoo colony, the members of which crowded round the troops with every manifestation of delight—was purely apathetic, the greater number of the shopkeepers plying their trades, and the artificers their crafts, as if nothing unusual were happening. After arriving at the centre of the city, the column made its way out by the Kabul Gate, and encamped in a plain by the side of the Kabul road, where it was eventually joined by the remainder of the force. The following day the troops entered Kandahar freely; and no measures of a precautionary nature, further than the occupation of the central square of the city by a half battalion of infantry, and the placing of guards at each of the city gates, were considered necessary.

Kandahar having fallen without serious opposition, it was now determined that the Field Force, separated into divisions as formerly, should advance laterally to the North-East and North-West, the 1st Division, under General Stewart's immediate command, moving on Kalat-i-Ghilzai, about ninety miles distant on the Ghazni and Kabul road, and the 2nd Division, under General Biddulph, having for its objective the Halmand river and Girishk, about eighty miles distant on the Herat road, while a force consisting of detachments from each division should remain behind, under the command of Brigadier-General Nuttall, to form the garrison of Kandahar. Preparations for the march were at once pushed forward, superfluous native followers being sent back to India, and the commissariat and transport services being more perfectly organized. Captain Bisset, R.E., was left behind to undertake the serious task of putting the fort and palace, which were in a state of dirt, decay, and confusion, into a condition suitable for hospitals and the many requirements of an army. The garrison of Kandahar, on the departure of the columns consisted of Batteries E/4, 5/11, and 6/11, R.A., the 1st Punjab Cavalry, a wing of the 59th Foot, a wing of the 12th Native Infantry, and the 26th Native Infantry, the troops moving from camp, and taking up their quarters in the citadel. Major St. John, R.E., remained at Kandahar as Political Officer, and the Nawab Ghulam Hussan as Civil Commandant.

On the 15th January the 1st Division commenced its advance on Kalat-i-Ghilzai, the scene of the memorable defence of 1841-42, Brigadier-General Hughes'

Brigade, which was accompanied by General Stewart, being preceded by the Cavalry Brigade under Brigadier-General Fane, by one march, and followed by Brigadier-General Barter's brigade, one day's march in the rear. The country traversed was generally barren, but interspersed with patches of irrigated cultivation; and the inhabitants, who were found to be friendly, brought in their supplies freely. On the Cavalry Brigade arriving at the village of Pul-i-Sang, which was reached on the 20th, Colonel Browne, the Political Officer accompanying the force, at once pushed forward with a small escort to Kalat-i-Ghilzai and entered the fort, which was found to have been quite recently vacated, the garrison having left behind them a quantity of ammunition and grain. The Cavalry Brigade arrived on the 21st, and encamped hard by, General Stewart, with Brigadier-General Hughes' brigade, moving up the following day, while Brigadier-General Barter's brigade was halted at Jaldak, a village on the Kandahar road some fourteen miles distant.

General Stewart, with the Cavalry and 2nd Infantry Brigades, remained at Kalat-i-Ghilzai for eleven days, during which the troops were regularly employed in improving the sanitary condition of the fort, and preparing it generally for a more lengthened occupation. Foraging parties were sent out daily; and difficulty being experienced in obtaining supplies, a system of requisitioning the neighbouring villages to produce specific quantities was successfully inaugurated. During this period reconnaissances were pushed into the Argandab and Arghesan Valleys, which were thoroughly explored. On the 2nd of February General Stewart fell back on Kandahar with the Cavalry and 1st Infantry Brigade, leaving Brigadier-General Hughes in temporary occupation; and on the 22nd idem the 2nd Brigade was also withdrawn, the fort being handed over to a Native official who had been selected to take charge of the place when it might be vacated.

Almost simultaneously with the advance of the Column under General Stewart's immediate command from Kandahar for Kalat-i-Ghilzai, General Biddulph's column, consisting of the 2nd Punjab Cavalry, the 3rd Sind Horse, Battery I/1, R.A., two guns, 11/11, R.A., four guns No. 3 Mountain Battery, the 70th Foot, a wing of the 19th Native Infantry, the 2nd Baluchis, and the 32nd Pioneers commenced its march for the Halmand, the head-quarters and main body of the force moving on the 16th of January to Kokaran. Brigadier-General Palliser commanded the Cavalry, and fell into command of the advance column, while Brigadier-General Lacy commanded the Infantry, and ultimately the rear column. The objects of the expedition being to reduce the consumption of the products of the immediate neighbourhood of Kandahar and the provisions brought from India, and there being no pressure with regard to time, the movements of the force were conducted in a leisurely manner, which admitted of the collection of supplies without seriously inconveniencing or producing unnecessary excitement among the people, halts of one or two days being made according to the productive capacity of the country traversed. The days of halting were fully occupied in reconnoitring, surveying, and foraging. No opposition was met with en route, and on the 29th of January General Biddulph reconnoitred in force across the Halmand, visited the castle of Girishk, which was found to be in a somewhat dilapidated condition, and selected sites for camps. These were subsequently formed on both sides of the river, and occupied by the troops, the accommodation of the fort being also utilized. The passage of the Halmand by boat and pontoon raft was rapidly reduced to a system, and in a short time the ferry became a busy scene of traffic from daybreak to nightfall.

After a time the construction of a bridge across the river, formed of rough timber procurable in the valley, was commenced. Heliographic communication provided a means of correspondence by day, and signal lights were used by night. During this period reconnaissances were pushed for two or three marches towards Herat, and careful surveys were made up the valley of the Halmand to the border of Zamindawar, and to the south, to Kala Bist. In the work of completing the passages of the river, in survey and reconnaissance duties, and in collecting supplies, every officer, soldier, follower, and animal of the force were engaged day by day.

The force maintained its position on the Halmand till the 23rd of February, when the return march to Kandahar was commenced. It was part of the plan of the retirement that, while the main body of the division was gaining the road leading to the village of Khushk-i-Nakhud, a force under Colonel Malcolmson, 3rd Sind Horse, should watch the fords from Zamindawar, where, it was expected, an attack might be made by the warlike Alizai tribe, sections of which had taken up, within the last few days, a somewhat hostile attitude. The passage of the river was effected, however, without opposition, and the force under Colonel Malcolmson, now acting as rear-guard, followed General Palliser's Column at an interval of one day's march. On the 25th of February an attack by the Alizais on the main body of the column, then at Khushk-i-Nakhud, again seemed imminent, but was not carried into effect. The following morning the village was vacated, and the rear-guard moved up and encamped there. The force at Colonel Malcolmson's disposal consisted of only 283 of all ranks of his own regiment, the 3rd Sind Horse, 2 Lance-Duffadars of the 2nd Punjab Cavalry, and 121 Native officers and men of the 2nd Baluch Regiment, under Lieut.-Colonel O. V. Tanner, and under the impression, apparently, that it might be easily overwhelmed, the Alizais determined to deliver their long-deferred attack. About 4.30 p.m. large numbers of them were seen, with flags flying, advancing over the crest of some rising ground about a mile and a half from the left front of the camp. Dispositions were at once made for their reception. With a view to drawing the enemy on to some open ground which extended about a mile to the front and left of the camp, upon which the cavalry might act with effect, Colonel Tanner was directed by Colonel Malcolmson to take forward the infantry, and after making a demonstration, gradually to fall back. Keeping up a heavy fire, the enemy continued to advance rapidly on the camp till the Baluchis opened a lively fusillade upon them at a range of about 500 yards, when they began to diverge slightly to their right, with the intention, apparently, of gaining some huts and enclosures on the British left flank. A few minutes afterwards, judging that they were sufficiently in the open to be dealt with effectively, Colonel Malcolmson led the 3rd Sind Horse against their left centre, the most formidable portion of their line. A fierce hand-to-hand fight ensued, which lasted for about ten minutes: the enemy then gave way, and dividing into two portions, commenced a rapid retreat, still, however, continuing to contest the ground. While Colonel Malcolmson, collecting a few of his men, endeavoured to intercept a number of fugitives who were making for a village near the camp, the remainder of the 3rd Sind Horse, under Major Reynolds, were let loose in pursuit of the right wing of the routed enemy, numbers of whom were sabred. In this pursuit, Major Reynolds, who, though he had been severely wounded early in the day, nevertheless continued to discharge with the utmost gallantry the duties of his command, was thrown from his horse, and was instantly set upon and slain. In the meantime Colonel Tanner, with the infantry, had followed up and dealt very effectively with the left wing of the retreating force, and only desisted from pursuit when darkness closed in. The enemy were computed to have numbered over 1,500, of whom 163 were counted dead on the plain, many more being killed in the enclosures, and many wounded. The British loss was 5 killed and 24 wounded. The severe lesson taught by this action was taken to heart, and the troops arrived at Kandahar without further molestation.

During the absence of Generals Stewart and Biddulph from Kandahar, a few isolated outrages had been perpetrated in the city by fanatics, but on the whole affairs had been quiet.

Meanwhile, early in January, Major-General Primrose had been ordered up from India to take command of the 1st Division, and Brigadier-General Phayre was placed in command of the troops between Sukkur and Dadar. Towards the end of that month General Phayre was charged with the difficult duty of convoying six months' supplies for 30,000 men to Dadar and Quetta before the end of April: a task which, in the sequel, was successfully accomplished, notwithstanding the fact that the route between Jacobadad and Dadar which had hitherto been used had become totally unsuitable for wheeled traffic, and a new one had to be selected and prepared.

The retirement of the columns from Kalat-i-Ghilzai and Girishk proved to be part of a scheme for the material reduction of the numbers of the troops in Southern Afghanistan before the hot weather should set in, a measure determined on by the authorities in the expectation that matters were about to be permanently settled. Orders were accordingly given to General Stewart to retain for disposal at Kandahar, Pishin, and Quetta, a force consisting of only seven batteries of artillery, three regiments of native cavalry, two battalions of British infantry, seven of native infantry, and two companies of Sappers, while the remainder of the troops, under General Biddulph, were to open up and return to India by a new route—known as the Thal-Chotiali route—leading through the hitherto unexplored country lying to the east of the Pishin valley. On the 1st of March General Biddulph reached Kandahar, and immediately afterwards broke up his division and set the various corps in motion towards Khushdil Khan, the selected point of departure.

The Thal-Chotiali Field Force was organized in three columns, which quitted Khushdil Khan, successively, on the 11th, 21st, and 22nd of March. The 1st Column, consisting of a squadron of the 8th Bengal Cavalry, a squadron of the 2nd Sind Horse, two guns of the Jacobabad Mountain Battery, two guns of the Peshawar Mountain Battery, and the 1st Punjab Infantry, was commanded by Major Keen, 1st Punjab Infantry, and accompanied by Major Sandeman, the Governor-General's Agent in Kalat, an officer to whose great personal influence the sympathy and goodwill which had hitherto been shown by the Baluch tribes were mainly attributable; the 2nd Column, consisting of the 15th Hussars, two guns of the Peshawar Mountain Battery, the 32nd Pioneers, and the 1st Goorkhas, was commanded by Colonel Sale Hill, 1st Goorkhas, and accompanied by General Biddulph and the head-quarters staff; and the 3rd Column, consisting of two squadrons of the 8th Bengal Cavalry, six companies of the 70th Foot, a wing of the 12th Native Infantry, and a company of Sappers, was commanded by Brigadier-General Nuttall. Another column, consisting of two squadrons of the 15th Bengal Cavalry, 400 of the 21st Madras Native Infantry, 200 of the 30th Madras Native Infantry, and 100 of the Rawalpur Contingent, under the command of Colonel

Prendergast, 15th Bengal Cavalry, constituted as the Dera Ghazi Column, marched from the Indus for Legari Barkhan, with supplies for the columns advancing eastward. Besides a general survey being taken, the country traversed was to be carefully examined with a view to the construction of a military road and railway, and choice was to be made of a suitable military post.

The movement was carried out without serious opposition until the advance column, under Major Keen, had marched about a hundred miles from its original point of departure. While it was leisurely making its way through the Smallan Valley, on the 22nd of March, the rear-guard was attacked by some 2,000 marauders. This attack was effectively repulsed by Captain Lorne Campbell, 1st Punjab Infantry, with the loss of one Sepoy killed. Two days afterwards, on the 24th of March, the same column was again attacked at a place called Baghao by the combined tribal forces of Zhob, Bori, and the vicinity. Notice of the enemy's approach was given by the videttes about 3 p.m., and orders were immediately issued to the troops to fall in. Leaving the two guns of the Peshawar Mountain Battery, a squadron of the 2nd Sind Horse, and four companies of the 1st Punjab Infantry, under Major G. U. Prior, Assistant Quartermaster-General, to protect the camp, Major Keen set out with the two guns of the Jacobabad Mountain Battery, the squadron of the 8th Bengal Cavalry, and four companies of the 1st Punjab Infantry, in the direction from which the tribesmen were advancing. After proceeding a short distance, a party of the 1st Punjab Infantry, under Major Vallings, was directed to move forward in skirmishing order against the enemy's line, the two guns at the same time being brought into action, and a party of the 8th Bengal Cavalry, under Major Chapman, detailed to protect the left flank of the advance. After two or three rounds had been fired, the enemy were seen to halt, and immediately afterwards a number of them were observed to make their way up some hills to the right. Major Keen now ordered Major Higginson and Captain Campbell, of the 1st Punjab Infantry, with two companies of that regiment, to carry these heights at the point of the bayonet, a feat which was gallantly performed in the face of a determined opposition, a heavy loss being inflicted. At the same time Major Vallings, advancing rapidly to the left, drove another portion of the enemy's force before him, and subsequently took up a position from which he was able to co-operate with the companies clearing the hills. While these operations were progressing, both the guns of the Jacobabad Mountain Battery, one accompanying Major Chapman, and the other moving to somewhat higher ground, made excellent practice. Major Vallings next cleared a number of caves and rocks; and the enemy being now completely routed, further pursuit was stopped, and the troops were ordered to return to camp. The enemy were estimated to have numbered 3,000, of whom some 150 were killed, and many wounded. Major Keen's loss was 2 killed and 5 wounded.

The march of the Thal-Chotiali Field Force was concluded without any misadventure, and the columns, after incessant watchfulness and much hard work, found a few days' repose in the peaceful Barkhan Plain. From this district, being in a country absolutely peaceful and friendly, the corps were moved singly by two routes, a proportion of them being left at Barkhan with the view of establishing a camp at Vitakri. In the meantime Colonel Prendergast's Column, which had started from Dera Ghazi Khan on the 23rd February, reached Vitakri on the 6th of March, and continuing its advance from thence, on the 30th idem, through the Han

Pass, effected a junction with Major Keen and Major Sandeman. The column was threatened, but was not attacked.

For some time after the departure of the troops under General Biddulph for India, affairs at Kandahar remained generally quiet, and by the middle of April many of the chiefs who had fled from the city had returned and given in their adhesion to the British cause. Raids on foraging parties and assassinations of camp followers along the line of communications were of occasional occurrence, but these grew less and less frequent as time wore on. The only active operation in Southern Afghanistan of any importance within this period was the defeat of a large body of Barechi Pathans at Syud But, in Shorawak, by a party of 30 of the 1st Punjab Cavalry and 176 of Jacob's Rifles, under Major F. T. Humfrey, of the latter regiment, who were attacked while escorting Mr. O. T. Duke, Assistant Agent for the Governor-General, from Kalat to Pishin. About 8 a.m. on the 27th of March reports were received by Major Humfrey of the advance of 3,000 of the tribesmen on his camp. He at once ordered out the cavalry, under Ressaldar Mir Alam Khan, accompanied by Mr. Duke, to reconnoitre; and after the latter had proceeded some four miles, the enemy were sighted, moving forward under the protection of a range of sand-hills, about sixty feet in height. By the judicious withdrawal of the cavalry, the enemy were induced to temporarily abandon their cover; but on fire being opened upon them by a company of infantry under Subadar Hyder Khan, which was moved forward for the purpose, they again sought shelter. Major Humfrey hereupon determined to assault their position on two sides; and entrusting Subadar Hyder Khan, in command of his company of the Rifles, with the front attack, moved under a heavy fire with the remainder of the infantry in skirmishing order to the left, round the base of the sand-hills, the cavalry also taking up a position in the same direction. After working their way forward for a short distance under cover, the files detailed for the left attack rapidly ascended the hills, and gaining the summit of the ridge, found the enemy posted upon it in masses, about 300 yards distant. A heavy and effective fire was at once opened, the front attack being developed about the same time. The enemy, finding their position enfiladed, retreated fighting. In a few minutes their retreat was turned into a complete rout, the cavalry, led by Mr. Duke, charging over a spur of the hills, and falling upon them with great execution. In this affair 90 of the Pathans were killed, and many wounded, while the loss of the escort was only 7 wounded. The whole of the enemy's baggage was captured. The following day the headmen of the district came in and surrendered unconditionally.

The political effects of the successful military operations which have been thus far briefly chronicled had long since begun to make themselves apparent, and while the troops of the northern divisions of the Army of Invasion were being concentrated at the most advanced posts on the Khyber and Kuram lines for an advance on Kabul, should such a movement become necessary, the difficulties in the way of a peaceful settlement were being rapidly removed. The reverses sustained by the Afghan army at Ali Musjid and the Peiwar Kotal had resulted, as has been already recorded, in the flight of the Amir from Kabul, which, in turn, had been followed by wholesale desertions from the garrisons of the capital. The assumption of authority by Shere Ali's long incarcerated son, the Sirdar Yakub Khan, had afforded the Indian Government an opportunity for addressing to him, through Major Cavagnari, a letter which, though couched in general terms, was friendly in its tone, and such as to afford His Highness an opportunity of separating himself, were he so minded, from the policy which had proved so disastrous to his father. But Yakub Khan was not at this time regarded either by himself or his fellow-subjects as a free agent; and the reply he returned to Major Cavagnari's letter expressed no desire on his own behalf or that of the Amir to come to terms. Early in February, 1879, however, a spontaneous communication was received from the Sirdar, containing distinct overtures for the reconciliation which had been suggested, and an offer of his good offices, as an intermediary between the British Government and the Amir, for the removal of differences which he regarded as susceptible of adjustment; and a few days afterwards another letter was received from him, announcing the death of his father and his own accession to the throne. These communications were received by Major Cavagnari, who was authorized to respond to the latter by a suitable expression of the Viceroy's condolences, and to the former, by a plain statement of the terms on which His Excellency in Council was prepared to entertain negotiations for peace. After some discussion of these conditions, Yakub Khan, accelerated in his decision, apparently, by the defection from his cause of the Wali Muhammad, Padshah Khan, and others, announced his intention, within a few days after the occupation of Gandamak by the British troops, of proceeding to that place for the purpose of entering into a personal conference with Major Cavagnari. The latter was accordingly instructed to arrange with Sir Sam. Browne for the honourable reception of His Highness, and was invested with full powers to represent the Government in negotiations, respecting which he had previously been furnished with detailed oral instructions by the Viceroy at Lahore.

From the hour when war with Shere Ali had been declared, and the various columns of invasion had been set in motion, the efforts of the Government had been directed not only to the punishment of what was considered to have been an unprovoked affront, but also to the prompt and complete attainment of the following objects: firstly, the exclusion of all foreign influence from Afghanistan; and secondly, a rectification of the frontier sufficient to render impossible for the future the exclusion of British influence from that State. Such a result, it was considered, would be obtained by locating a British representative at Kabul, and by permanently securing the command of those passes which, piercing the extreme edge of the vast mountain tract which rises immediately above the plains of India, constitute the only practicable approaches to the Empire beyond its northern and western confines. In draughting the terms of the proposed treaty, Major Cavagnari was instructed to hold these objects of the Government carefully in view.

Yakub Khan reached Gandamak on the 8th of May, 1879, and was received there by the British authorities with all possible honour and hospitality. After the formal ceremonies of his reception, negotiations were opened by His Highness, and continued without interruption till the 26th of May. On that date a treaty was signed in the British camp by the Amir, and by Major Cavagnari on behalf of the British Government. By this treaty, which was formally ratified by the Viceroy at Simla on the 30th of May, the objects held to be of paramount importance by the Government in prosecuting the war were very amply secured. Its more important clauses provided in detail not only for the exercise of adequate control by the British Government over the Amir's external relations, and for the location of a British representative at Kabul, but also for the cession by the Amir, under an assignment, of the districts of Pishin, Sibi, and Kuram, and the retention by the

British Government of the control of the Khyber and Michni Passes. With the exception of the assigned districts, which were not to be considered as permanently severed from the Afghan kingdom, and the revenues of which, less the charges of civil administration, were to be handed over to the Amir, all the territory in possession of the British armies was to be restored. On the part of the British Government, obligations were contracted to assist the Amir against foreign aggression, and to pay to His Highness and his successors an annual subsidy of six lakhs of rupees. Provision was also made in the treaty for the publication by the Amir of a complete amnesty, absolving all his subjects from responsibility for intercourse with the British forces during the war; for the protection and encouragement of commerce between India and Afghanistan; and for the immediate construction of a line of telegraph between Kabul and Kuram.

After the ratification of the treaty the Amir returned to Kabul, and orders were immediately issued for the withdrawal of the troops of the two Northern divisions from most of the positions lying beyond the newly-defined British frontier, though the evacuation of Kandahar was postponed, for sanitary reasons, till the ensuing autumn. This retirement, which was conducted in the burning heat of summer, and through territory notoriously unhealthy, was not effected without an appalling loss of life, cholera in its most virulent form breaking out, and together with heat apoplexy, literally decimating the ranks of regiments weakened by the exposure to which they had long been subjected, and the arduous nature of the duties they had been called upon to perform. By the middle of June the evacuation of Northern Afghanistan was practically complete, and the garrisons of the various posts in the Khyber Pass and the Kuram Valley were reduced to a peace footing.

THE SECOND CAMPAIGN.

A FEW weeks after the ratification of the Peace of Gandamak, Major Cavagnari —who, for his recent eminent services was created a Knight Commander of the Order of the Bath—proceeded to Kabul as Envoy and Minister Plenipotentiary of the British Government at the Court of His Highness the Amir Yakub Khan. He was accompanied by Mr. William Jenkins, of the Punjab Civil Service, as Political Assistant, and Dr. Ambrose Kelly, of the Indian Medical Department, as Medical Officer to the Embassy, and was escorted by twenty-five Sowars and fifty Sepoys of the Corps of Guides, under the command of Lieut. W. R. P. Hamilton, V.C.

The Mission arrived at Kabul on the 24th of July, 1879, and was accorded a brilliant reception. As early as the 6th of August, however, indications of hostility towards it on the part of a section of the army and the people were to be observed. On that day large bodies of turbulent soldiery, who had recently returned to Kabul from Herat, paraded the streets, and followed by a disorderly crowd of townspeople, manifested their disaffection by loudly abusing the Ambassador by name.

As time wore on the relations subsisting between the Embassy and the Amir appear to have become somewhat strained, and indications of the menacing attitude

SKETCH OF THE WAR.

of the populace, to have multiplied. In the Kabul diaries allusion is more than once made to the prevalence of insubordination amongst the Afghan regiments, and street fights between the Amir's troops and the soldiers of the Envoy's escort were not of unfrequent occurrence. Notwithstanding this, no cause for immediate alarm seems to have been felt at the Residency, and a telegram despatched by Sir Louis Cavagnari to the Viceroy of India as late as the 2nd of September contained the announcement that all was well with the Embassy. That this confidence was misplaced, the sequel disastrously proved. The cheerfully-worded message had barely reached its destination before the hand which had written it was closed in death, and the labours of the Mission had been brought to an untimely and tragical close.

The buildings occupied by the British Ambassador and his retinue were situated within the Bala Hissar, the citadel of Kabul, and were erected on two sides of a spacious courtyard, distant but a stone's throw from the Amir's palace. Here, on the morning of the 3rd of September, were collected the Envoy, his suite, and sixty-eight Sepoys and troopers of the escort, seven of the latter being absent on duty with grass-cutters on the plains beyond the city. About 8 a.m. on that day some unarmed Afghan regiments were paraded in the Bala Hissar to receive their pay, and began clamouring for arrears. Upon these being refused, a riot broke out. While some of the mutinous troops hurried off to fetch their arms and to loot the magazine of the Upper Bala Hissar, others made their way across to the Envoy's stables, and commenced to stone the syces and unfasten the horses. The gates of the courtyard were at once closed. In a short time the Residency was regularly besieged, the mutinous troops being joined by the townspeople, and the mob being every minute augmented by fresh accessions from the city. A message, despatched by Sir Louis Cavagnari to the Amir at the very beginning of the fray, was safely delivered into his hands; but beyond sending out the Commander-in-Chief of his Forces, Daud Shah, and subsequently his son, to remonstrate with the rabble, he made no effort to avert the impending catastrophe. With devoted gallantry, the defence of the Residency was conducted by the little garrison for hour after hour, in spite of the fact that their numbers were rapidly diminishing, and of the conviction which must have early forced itself upon them that all hope of succour was at an end. Three of the British officers, it is reported, charged out of the building, a little before noon, at the head of twenty-five of the Guide Sowars and Sepoys; and when charged, the Afghans—according to the testimony of an eye-witness—ran like sheep before a wolf. Later in the day, another sally was made by a party with two officers leading; and subsequently a third, and a fourth, the last charge being led by a gallant Sikh Jemadar, every British officer being by that time killed. About noon the gates of the courtyard were burst open, and the Residency was fired; but it was some time before the flames made any appreciable impression upon the building in which the members of the Mission made their final stand. At length the walls fell in, and the rabble, streaming through, completed their work of devastation. The first shot had been fired shortly before 8 o'clock in the morning, and it was nearly 8 o'clock in the evening before the last of the garrison was killed. Besides Sir Louis Cavagnari and his suite, the gallant Guide Sowars and Sepoys forming the Envoy's escort perished almost to a man.

The first intelligence of the attack on the Embassy to reach India, which was received by the Government on the morning of the 5th of September through Captain Conolly, the Assistant Political Officer at Ali Khel, left room for hope that the members of the Mission had not yet perished, and that if the defence of the Residency could be maintained for a short time longer, the lives of its inmates might still be saved. To that end, strenuous efforts were at once directed. Captain Conolly was instructed to inform the Amir by letter that he would be held responsible for the safety of Sir Louis Cavagnari and his companions. At the same time, as a preliminary measure, Brigadier-General Dunham Massy, commanding the advanced troops at Ali Khel, was ordered to seize and hold the Shutargardan Pass, while General Stewart, who was still commanding in Southern Afghanistan, was directed to stand fast at Kandahar, concentrating there all the troops previously under orders to return to India. During the night of the 5th of September supplementary information was received from Captain Conolly which dissipated all hope of saving the lives of the members of the Mission; but the occupation of, and complete domination over Kabul, within the very shortest period possible, was nevertheless regarded by Government to be a measure of paramount importance. To attain this object it was decided that a strong column should move forward with all speed from the Shutargardan, and that preparations should be made for the maintenance of its communications by two routes, the Khyber as well as the Kuram, in view of the necessity for abandoning the latter at an early date in consequence of the closing of the passes by the first winter snowfall.

The general arrangements for carrying out these operations were as follows. The column destined for the advance on Kabul was to consist of three batteries of artillery, one squadron of British cavalry, two regiments of Native cavalry, three of British infantry, four of Native infantry, and one company of Sappers, in all about 6,500 men. It was to be commanded by Major-General Sir F. S. Roberts, V.C., K.C.B., and was to be divided into three brigades, one of cavalry, under Brigadier-General W. G. D. Massy, and two of infantry, under Brigadier-Generals H. T. Macpherson, V.C., C.B., and T. D. Baker. The country between the Shutargardan and Thal was to be held by two batteries of artillery, two regiments of Native cavalry, one of British infantry, and five of Native infantry, in all about 4,000 men, under Brigadier-Generals T. E. Gordon, C.S.I., and J. A. Tytler, V.C., C.B., Brigadier-General Hugh Gough, V.C., C.B., being placed in charge of the communications. In addition to the Peshawar garrison and the troops already holding the Khyber Pass as far as Landi Kotal, a force consisting of five batteries of artillery, two regiments of British cavalry, four of Native cavalry, five of Native infantry, and two companies of Sappers, in all about 6,600 men, under the command of Major-General R. O. Bright, was detailed for operations on the Jalalabad line. This force, it was intended, should protect the road from Peshawar to Gandamak, and provide a moveable column for holding Jagdalak and establishing communications with Kabul. At the same time measures were taken for securing an efficient reserve of 5,500 men between Peshawar and Rawal Pindi. Major-General J. Ross, C.B., was to command the Reserve Division, Brigadier-General J. Doran, C.B., the section of the line from Peshawar to Basawal, Brigadier-General C. G. Arbuthnot, C.B., from Basawal to Jalalabad and Gandamak, and Brigadier-General Charles Gough, V.C., C.B., from thence onwards. The Khyber and Kuram forces, as thus constituted, would represent a division having its head-quarters at Kabul, with its army line base at Peshawar, and a secondary line across the Shutargardan until that pass should be closed. It was considered that it would be capable of crushing any resistance that was likely to be opposed to it. The Kandahar force, composed mainly of the troops which had recently evacuated the city and were échelonded along the line from Kokaran to Quetta, was to consist of eight batteries of artillery, four regiments of Native cavalry, two of British infantry, seven of Native infantry, and two companies of Sappers, in all about 9,000 men, and was to be commanded by Lieut.-General Sir D. M. Stewart, K.C.B., with Brigadier-Generals C. H. Palliser, C.B., R. J. Hughes, and R. Barter commanding brigades. By this force Kalat-i-Ghilzai was to be re-occupied without delay, and Ghazni threatened besides. In addition to these troops there was a small force at Vitakri, consisting of a mountain battery, one regiment of Native cavalry, and two of Native infantry, about 1,080 men, under the command of Colonel J. C. Georges, and also a reserve of the Kandahar force on the communications from Quetta to Sukkur, composed of Bombay troops, and consisting of one regiment of Native cavalry, three of Native infantry, and four companies of Sappers, about 2,000 men in all, under the command of Brigadier-General R. Phayre, C.B.

Many of the transport animals of the Kuram force had suffered severely from sickness during the previous months, and the remainder had to a great extent been dispersed to graze where they were not immediately available beyond the Shutargardan. To expedite the advance of the entire force under General Roberts, it was consequently necessary to collect at that point carriage and supply for 6,500 men. This operation General Massy successfully completed on the evening of the 11th of September, though it could only be done, with a minimum of difficulty and delay, by denuding the Peshawar Valley force of all its available transport. To supply within the shortest possible period the deficiency thus created, all parts of the Empire were subsequently placed under requisition. In view of the anticipated difficulties in collecting and organizing transport for operations which might be indefinitely extended, a new office was called into being, separated from the Military Department, and placed in immediate communication with the Commander-in-Chief, on the one hand, and the head of the Civil Government, on the other. The direct control of this office was entrusted to Lieut.-General Sir Michael Kennedy, R.E., K.C.S.I., who was invested with special powers for the expeditious conduct of its business. As Comptroller-General of the Commissariat, this officer was to be responsible for the supply of transport to the various columns detailed for field operations; but on their receipt of the transport thus supplied, it was to be treated as regimental equipment, for the supervision and organization of which the responsibility was to rest exclusively upon the commanding officers concerned.

During the second and third week in September the forward concentration of the troops detailed for the advance on Kabul was continued with the greatest activity. On the 11th of that month the Shutargardan Pass was occupied by the 23rd Pioneers, the 5th Goorkhas, and No. 2 Mountain Battery, the position taken up being strongly intrenched. The following day Sir Frederick Roberts, with Brigadier-Generals Macpherson and Baker, arrived at Ali Khel, from whence the latter proceeded onward to take command of the advanced troops. On the 14th the Nawab Sir Ghulam Hussan Khan, who had been sent from Kandahar to join Sir Louis Cavagnari as Native Assistant at Kabul, and concerning whose safety great anxiety had been felt, arrived in the British camp, having heard of the outbreak at the capital when within a few miles of his destination, and having at once made for the Shutargardan. Several letters were now received by General Roberts from the Amir, expressing his regret for what had happened, his intention to punish the mutineers, and his unabated confidence in the friendship of the Viceroy; but the simultaneous receipt of reports that His Highness was making every effort in his power to induce the tribes to oppose the impending advance of the British forces cast some doubt on the sincerity of these professions.

With the exception of occasional shots being fired at night, no hostility was shown by the tribes in the neighbourhood of the Shutargardan till the 22nd of September, when a convoy of telegraph stores, escorted by eleven Sepoys of the 5th Punjab Infantry, was attacked near Karatiga by a body of two or three hundred Mangals and Ghilzais. In this affair six Sepoys and about twenty mule-drivers were killed, and the whole of the stores looted. A detachment of the 72nd Highlanders was immediately sent out to the scene of the encounter, but the tribesmen had made off, and pursuit proved useless.

By the 24th September the supply of transport and the progress made up the Kuram Valley by the successive reinforcements had placed the column in a position to advance. On that day the troops under Brigadier-General Baker moved down from the Shutargardan, and crossing the Shinkai Kotal, reached Kushi, a village distant only forty-eight miles from Kabul, the same evening. On the 27th General Roberts moved his head-quarters from Ali Khel for the Shutargardan, in company with the head-quarters of the Cavalry Brigade, a squadron of the 9th Lancers, the 5th Punjab Cavalry, the 28th Native Infantry, and a detachment of the 5th Punjab Infantry, the infantry being directed to bring up the rear of the force during the march, whilst the cavalry and staff were to push forward and endeavour to reach the Shutargardan before dark. About 10.30 a.m. the head of the column was joined by twenty-five men of the 92nd Highlanders, who had been sent from Karatiga to act as an advance guard in consequence of a rumour that the Mangals and Ghilzais were gathering in the Hazardarakht defile. The rumour proved to be well founded. About 11 a.m. it was ascertained by a reconnoitring party under Captain Vousden, 5th Punjab Cavalry, who had his horse shot under him, that some 2,000 of the tribesmen were assembled on either side of the ravine, about half a mile beyond a ruined fort called Jagi Thana. The detachment of the 92nd Highlanders, supported by a dismounted troop of the 9th Lancers, speedily cleared the northern side of the gorge, but the enemy clung obstinately to some precipitous heights to the south; they were, however, eventually dislodged, and on the arrival of the 28th Native Infantry, a commanding hill was held till the rear-guard had passed, A volley fired at close quarters at Sir F. Roberts and his staff took effect, Surgeon-General Townsend being severely wounded in the face. A small detachment of the 92nd Highlanders and 3rd Sikhs, which had been sent out from Karatiga to meet the column, now appeared in sight, with large numbers of the enemy in full flight before it. This detachment, ably handled by Colour-Sergeant Hector Macdonald, and Jemadar Sher Muhammad, had been for some hours hotly engaged, and though consisting of only 63 rifles all told, had succeeded in inflicting a loss on the Mangals of 30 killed, its own casualties being 1 Havildar and 3 Sepoys killed.

Sir Frederick Roberts continued his advance, on the 28th September, to Kushi. At that place the Amir Yakub Khan, after sending forward to make inquiries as to whether he could be received, had arrived in General Baker's camp the previous day, attended by his eldest son and several influential Sirdars, including Daud Shah, the Afghan Commander-in-Chief, together with a suite of forty-five members and an escort of two hundred men. The Amir had apparently proceeded in some haste from Kabul on hearing that the Sirdar Wali Muhammad and other influential personages were about to join the British force. Sir Frederick Roberts now received general instructions to secure his Highness's personal safety, and at the same time to retain adequate control over his movements until the question as to his complicity in the recent outrage at Kabul could be solved.

On the 29th of September another attack was made near Karatiga by the Mangals and Ghilzais on a wing of the 67th Foot, forming the rear-guard of a force convoying stores and reserve ammunition through the Hazardarakht defile. The attack was effectively repulsed, the only casualties on the British side being two men wounded.

To avoid leaving small parties along the road while it was still insecure, and being desirous of reaching Kabul with as strong a force as possible, General Roberts now arranged to evacuate Kushi until he should be firmly in possession of the Bala Hissar, when it was his intention to establish a military postal service between the capital and the Shutargardan Pass. The whole column accordingly moved to Zargunshahr on the 2nd of October, and the following morning marched on to Zaidabad. Here it was compulsorily halted for a day, owing to the lack of transport, the insufficiency of which had long been keenly felt. On the morning of the 5th of October the march was resumed, a force consisting of two guns No. 2 Mountain Battery, one squadron 5th Punjab Cavalry, a wing of the 67th Foot, and the 28th Native Infantry, under the command of Brigadier-General Macpherson, being left behind to escort the reserve ammunition and commissariat stores. The passage of the Logar river at Zaidabad was attended with considerable difficulty, partly in consequence of the bridge being unequal to the weight of artillery or laden animals, and partly in consequence of the hostility evinced by the tribesmen, large numbers of whom assembled in the neighbourhood, and at times showed so determined a front as to necessitate their being driven off at the point of the bayonet by covering parties of the 72nd Highlanders and 5th Goorkhas. The village of Charasiab was reached the same afternoon, and opposition being expected, reconnoitring parties of cavalry were pushed forward along three roads leading towards the city of Kabul, eleven miles distant. A few shots were fired at these parties from villages and walled enclosures, but no traces were visible of any large body of the enemy.

That night strong picquets were thrown out all round the camp, which was pitched to the south of the village, and cavalry patrols were ordered to proceed at daybreak to feel for the enemy. At the same time General Roberts determined to seize, as soon as possible after dawn, the crest of the pass known as the Sang-i-Nawishta, about six miles in advance of the camp, on the road by which he had decided to continue his march towards Kabul. With the purpose of preparing this road, which, it had been reported, was unfit for the passage of artillery, the 23rd Pioneers, accompanied by a wing of the 92nd Highlanders, and two guns No. 2 Mountain Battery, were sent forward from camp shortly after daybreak on the 6th.

Almost before any report could be received from the cavalry patrols, all doubts as to the intentions of the enemy were dissipated. Troops could be seen in large numbers and regular formation crowning the crest line of the hills, which extended from the narrow defile of the Sang-i-Nawishta—both sides of which were held—on their extreme left, to the heights above the Chardeh Valley, which formed their right; other bodies were observed assembling on the heights on either side of the camp, with the obvious intention of attacking it on the first favourable opportunity; while reports were brought in that the road in the rear was blocked, and that the march of Macpherson's brigade, with its long string of baggage, would be contested. Behind the heights extending from the Sang-i-Nawishta to the Chardeh Valley lay the densely crowded city of Kabul, the scarcely less crowded suburbs of Chardeh and Deh-i-Afghan, and numerous villages clustered all over the Kabul Valley. Each and all of these had contributed their quota of men to assist the troops collected to oppose the advance on the capital, and it was certain that the numbers already assembled would be still further augmented if they were allowed to remain in possession of their stronghold a single night. Under these circumstances Sir Frederick Roberts determined not to postpone the engagement which had now become inevitable; and sending notice to General Macpherson to keep a keen look out, and to reach Charasiab, if possible, before dark, he proceeded to make his preparations for dislodging the enemy from the very strong position they had taken up.

The party which had been sent out to improve the road had been halted, about a mile in front of the camp, as soon as it was ascertained that the Sang-i-Nawishta defile and the heights on either side of it were strongly held. Apprehending, from the direction which had been taken by this party and by the cavalry patrols, that an attack was about to be made on their left, the enemy were now seen to be rapidly concentrating their forces in the vicinity of the gorge. General Roberts determined, however, merely to hold them in check in that quarter, and by an outflanking movement to throw the main body of his column on their extreme right, with the object of taking them in reverse.

The conduct of these operations was entrusted to Brigadier-General Baker, under whose command was placed a force consisting of four guns No. 2 Mountain Battery, under Captain Swinley, R.A., two Gatling guns, under Captain Broadfoot, R.A., the 7th Company Sappers and Miners, under Lieut. Nugent, R.E., the 72nd Highlanders, under Lieut.-Colonel Clarke, six companies 5th Goorkhas, under Major Fitz Hugh, and 200 rifles 5th Punjab Infantry, under Captain Hall, in all about 2,000 men, in addition to the party which had already advanced towards the Sang-i-Nawishta, whilst the force left to protect the camp, exclusive of the 5th Punjab Infantry, which was shortly afterwards sent forward to guard General Baker's reserve ammunition and field hospital, was reduced to about 450 cavalry, 9 guns, and between 600 and 700 infantry.

After assembling his little column in the wooded enclosures of the Charasiab village, General Baker made his dispositions for the attack. The party which had first left camp, and which consisted of three guns G/3, R.A., under Major Parry, two squadrons of cavalry made up of detachments 9th Lancers, 5th Punjab Cavalry, and 12th Bengal Cavalry, under Major Hammond, 5th Punjab Cavalry, a wing 92nd Highlanders under Major Hay, and 100 rifles 23rd Pioneers under Captain Patterson, the whole under the command of Major White, 92nd Highlanders, was entrusted with the operations on the right, Major White being directed to continue threatening the Sang-i-Nawishta; to prevent the enemy occupying any portion of the Charasiab village; to advance within artillery range of the enemy's main position; and when the outflanking movement should be thoroughly developed, and the enemy in retreat, to push the cavalry through the pass and pursue. With the remainder of his force General Baker moved off to the left, to attack the extreme right of the enemy's position, his line of advance lying through the Charasiab village and over a series of bare undulating hills rising to the left or west of the plain through which the road led to the Sang-i-Nawishta gorge.

The strength of the enemy's position now became fully apparent, their front being found to extend in the form of a crescent for a distance of nearly three miles, and to rest on a succession of commanding ridges extremely difficult of access. The most elevated of these ridges rose to a height of over 2,000 feet, about half a mile distant from, and to the proper right of the Sang-i-Nawishta gorge, towards which it gradually fell away, but again rose to terminate in a steep hill immediately to the right of the gorge. To the left of the gorge, and bounding the plain, three steep hills formed a continuation of the range. Each horn of the crescent terminated in a high peak, on both of which detached parties of the enemy were posted.

On emerging from the village, which was cleared about 11.30 a.m., the troops under General Baker's immediate command continued to move forward, in the face of some opposition, to the first low range of hills held by the enemy in force. After the advance had been continued for about a mile, a flanking company of the 72nd Highlanders, under Captain Brooke Hunt, was directed to crown some heights to the British left, in front of the peak which formed the extreme advanced point on the right of the enemy's position, and which dominated the elevations all round it. At the same time the remainder of the 72nd, led by Lieut.-Colonel Clarke, swept forward under a heavy fire to attack a strongly-held ridge—termed, from its colour, the Red Ridge—which extended from this peak to the enemy's centre, and in a few minutes were hotly engaged. So obstinate was the resistance offered in both these quarters that it became necessary to move up reinforcements, two companies of the 5th Goorkhas, under Major Cook, V.C., being pushed forward to assist Captain Brooke Hunt, and two more companies of the 5th Goorkhas, under Major Fitz Hugh, together with 200 men of the 5th Punjab Infantry, under Captain Hall, being at the same time advanced to strengthen the direct attack.

In the meantime it had become evident to the enemy that the real attack was being directed against their right, and their troops had for some time been observed hurrying down from their main position in the centre of the crescent to reinforce that quarter. The attacking battalions were, however, not to be denied, and by 2 p.m., after two hours' fighting, the Highlanders, Goorkhas, and Punjab Infantry, admirably covered in their advance by the fire of the Mountain Battery, had carried both the Red Ridge and the Left Peak, the defenders of the latter, in their retreat, suffering heavy loss from the cross-fire which was directed upon them.

The Afghans now took up a second position on a higher ridge some 600 or 700 yards to the rear of that from which they had been driven, but still well in advance of their centre. Against this new position General Baker's troops advanced in rushes, covered by the fire of the Mountain Battery. After making a stand for half an hour, the enemy again fell back, the attack made by a company of the 23rd Pioneers under Lieut. Chesney, supported by the 72nd Highlanders, the 5th Goorkhas, and two companies of the 92nd Highlanders, proving irresistible. The two companies of the 92nd, under Captain Oxley, had been detached by Major

White from the right attack earlier in the day, and had performed excellent service while working their way round to join the outflanking force.

The troops now advanced rapidly at the double in order to keep the enemy on the move, and to prevent them from making a further stand; all the available artillery being at the same time brought to bear upon them. The result quickly made itself manifest. By 3.45 p.m. the main ridge was carried, the Afghan regiments which had held it breaking and flying in disorder in the direction of Chardeh. The defence of this ridge was almost their last effort, for very shortly afterwards they commenced to evacuate their position on the immediate right of the Sang-i-Nawishta gorge.

While these operations were progressing, the troops under Major White, entrusted with the right attack, had not been idle. The enemy's left was found to be very strongly posted on the advanced detached hill, with cavalry and infantry picquets occupying a series of ridges on their right front. Two companies of the 92nd, under Captain Oxley, were detached to drive in these picquets. This they quickly accomplished, and subsequently working their way across to General Baker's force, joined the left attack. Major Parry, commanding G/3, R.A., was now directed to shell the detached hill: but notwithstanding the excellent practice made by the guns, the enemy refused to quit their entrenchments. Major White therefore ordered Captain Cotton, with two companies of the 92nd, to carry the position, a feat which was performed with great gallantry, the Afghans rushing forward to repel the advance, but being forced back by the Highlanders, and driven headlong down the reverse slopes of the hill. After a halt of some duration had been made to await the development of the left attack, the other heights on the left of the gorge were carried in succession, the Highlanders and Pioneers meeting with but feeble resistance. From the last hill a battery of four guns, stationed at the entrance to the gorge, was taken in flank and captured. The plain was then crossed, and the hill immediately on the right of the gorge, and commanding it, fell to Captain Gordon's company of the 92nd Highlanders, who captured twelve mountain guns in position on its summit. The cavalry, in the meantime, entered the gorge, supported by detachments of the Pioneers and Highlanders, under Major Hay. After proceeding, however, for about half a mile over very broken ground, and occasionally dismounting to reply to a brisk fire which was opened upon them from either side, they found their further progress barred by the enemy, large numbers of whom had posted themselves in a fort built in the middle of the pass, and completely commanding the road.

By this time, about 4.30 p.m., the troops under General Baker's immediate command, encountering little resistance after having turned the enemy's main position, had worked round to the immediate vicinity of the gorge. On the situation of the cavalry becoming apparent, the guns of the Mountain Battery were at once brought into action from a position on the heights above, the 23rd Pioneers and the 5th Punjab Infantry being at the same time directed to descend into the valley at the double, and to engage the remains of the enemy's force. These orders were rapidly carried out. The artillery fire proved most effective, and together with the infantry advance, crushed the last vestige of opposition.

It was subsequently ascertained that thirteen regular regiments of the enemy had been engaged in the action, besides large contingents from the Kabul city and neighbouring villages. Their loss was estimated to have been upwards of 300 killed, and many wounded, while that of General Baker's force was 20 killed and 67 wounded. All the guns, twenty in number, which had been brought out from Kabul to assist in the defence were captured. During the engagement the camp at Charasiab had been threatened, but not attacked.

That night a portion of General Baker's force bivouacked on the Kabul side of the Sangi-Nawishta, and the following day the remainder of the Division moved through the defile and encamped at Ben-i-Shahr.

On the morning of the 8th, the Cavalry Brigade under General Massy was sent out to cut off the retreat of a number of the Afghan troops who, it was ascertained, had not yet dispersed to their homes, and who seemed likely to offer further resistance. After making his way northwards over the Siah Sang heights and across the Kabul River, General Massy, finding the Sherpur cantonment had been abandoned, proceeded to take possession of it, 76 pieces of ordnance of various calibre falling into his hands. From this place the enemy were observed in great force on the Asmai heights, to the westward, provided with artillery, and occupying a position commanding the city of Kabul. Heliographing this information to Sir F. Roberts, General Massy moved off in a westerly direction towards the Chardeh Valley, and placed himself in the enemy's direct line of retreat. On being made acquainted with the situation, General Roberts at once despatched from camp a force of infantry and artillery under General Baker to assault the enemy's position. After a very arduous march, the neighbourhood of Asmai was reached by this force just as darkness was closing in, and the attack had consequently to be postponed till the following morning; during the night, however, it was ascertained that the enemy had abandoned the position, and their camp, together with 18 pieces of artillery, fell into General Baker's hands. At daybreak on the 9th, the cavalry scoured the neighbouring villages and a wide area of the surrounding country, but with the exception of a few small parties who were overtaken and cut up by the 5th Punjab Cavalry, the enemy had made good their escape. During the day, several of the horses of the Cavalry Brigade died of exhaustion and privation. Before nightfall the whole of the troops had returned to camp, General Massy, with the cavalry, having passed through the city of Kabul on the way without mishap.

On the 9th of October the camp of the whole division was moved from Ben-i-Shahr to the heights of Siah Sang, an elevated and commanding plateau less than a mile to the east of the Bala Hissar, and dominating the city of Kabul. The two following days were devoted by Sir Frederick Roberts to visiting the Sherpur cantonment and the Bala Hissar, and making an examination of the buildings which had been occupied by the late Envoy and his suite and escort.

General Roberts took formal possession of the Bala Hissar on the 12th of October. The Amir did not accompany him, but the Heir Apparent and a large number of the most influential Sirdars of Kabul were in attendance, and special care was taken that the proceedings should be impressive. After the Amir's garden was reached, General Roberts made known, by proclamation, the intentions of the British Government, announcing that a heavy penalty would be inflicted on the city for the murder of the Envoy and his companions, and that rewards would be given for the surrender of persons implicated in the attack on the Residency. Notification was also given of the arrangements which would be made for the repression of disorder, and the restrictions which would be imposed as to bearing arms. The assembled Sirdars were then dismissed, four of their number, however, being detained on suspicion, pending a detailed inquiry into their conduct. The following day the whole of the Field Force marched through the leading thoroughfares of Kabul, no opposition being encountered, and the inhabitants maintaining a respectful demeanour. The city and the surrounding country to a distance of ten miles was placed under martial law, Major-General Hills, V.C., C.B., taking over the office of Military Governor, and the Nawab Sir Ghulam Hussan Khan being appointed to assist him in his duties, while for the investigation of the circumstances of the late outbreak, and the trial of persons suspected of participation in the attack on the Embassy, commissions under the presidency, respectively, of Colonel C. M. Macgregor, C.B., C.S.I., C.I.E., and Brigadier-General Dunham Massy, were nominated.

Besides vast stores of ammunition, eighty-five guns, mortars, and howitzers were found in the Bala Hissar, making a total capture of over two hundred pieces of ordnance. In consequence of immense quantities of gunpowder lying loose within the fortress, various precautions were taken against accidents; but on the 16th of October a terrific explosion occurred, followed, several hours afterwards, by a succession of minor detonations. Twenty lives, including that of Captain Shafto, R.A., were lost by this accident. The conflagration which ensued was not extinguished till the morning of the 18th, the profoundest anxiety being felt, during the interim, for the safety of the magazine, which was known to contain upwards of two hundred tons of gunpowder. As it appeared probable that the Bala Hissar had been undermined, it was now determined to destroy the fortification, partly as a precaution against further accidents, and partly by way of a national punishment, which would fall with peculiar severity on the Sirdars and other influential personages of Kabul, nearly all of whom possessed houses within its walls. A short time afterwards the work of demolition was commenced.

On the day on which Sir Frederick Roberts had made his formal entry into the Bala Hissar, the Amir Yakub Khan, prompted, apparently, by the conviction of his inability to control the Afghan people, by weariness of a life of incessant trouble and intrigue, and possibly in part by the suspicion which had been thrown upon his action and motives, had announced to the Lieutenant-General his intention to abdicate. His Highness was requested by Sir Frederick Roberts to take time to reconsider his decision, but a few hours afterwards he stated that the determination he had come to was final. This unexpected declaration had been communicated to the Indian Government, and transmitted by the Viceroy to England for the consideration of Her Majesty's advisers, who, after due deliberation, had decided that the government of Afghanistan should be temporarily carried on under the immediate supervision of General Roberts, without the declared aid of any Afghan Chief or Sirdar. On the 28th of October a proclamation to that effect, announcing the abdication of the Amir, was issued at Kabul, and the various functionaries engaged in the administration of the country were bidden to continue to maintain order in their several districts.

On the 17th of October Brigadier-General Hugh Gough quitted Kabul with a force consisting of the 5th Punjab Cavalry, the 5th Punjab Infantry, and four guns of the Mountain Battery, for Kushi, with the object of opening communication with, and if necessary reinforcing, the troops holding the Shutargardan Pass and Ali Khel, who were at the time being threatened by an extensive combination of the neighbouring tribes. On the advance of the main body of the Field Force from the Shutargardan on Kabul, an intrenched force consisting of the 3rd Sikhs, the 21st Native Infantry, and four guns No. 1 Mountain Battery, under the command of Lieut.-Colonel Noel Money, 3rd Sikhs, had been left by General Roberts as a permanent garrison to hold the pass, the command of the line of communications from Ali Khel eastward to Kohat having been previously handed over to Brigadier-General T. E. Gordon, C.S.I., whose head-quarters were now at Ali Khel. With the exception of a murderous attack which had been made near Thal by a party of Zaimushts on a British officer—Lieut. Kinloch, of the Bengal Cavalry—proceeding through the valley to join his regiment at the front, the hostile operations of the tribes on the Kuram line had been confined, during the last few weeks, to the neighbourhood of the more advanced posts. Shortly after daybreak on the 2nd of October, the independent Ghilzais, emboldened by the departure of the Field Force from the Shutargardan, began to make their appearance on the hills which overlook the crest of the pass. Although their intentions were evidently hostile, and they were actually within range of the mountain guns, Colonel Money refrained for a time from attacking them, as it was represented to him by the officer in political charge of the Shutargardan that Allahudin Khan, a brother of Padshah Khan, the head of the Ghilzais, who was momentarily expected in camp, would probably have sufficient influence to induce the hostile tribes to come to friendly terms, and withdraw without bloodshed. Accepting this suggestion, but deeming it of importance to secure the crest of the Kotal in order that heliographic communication with the Field Force should not be interrupted, Lieut.-Colonel Money sent 100 rifles 3rd Sikhs, under Major Griffiths, together with a signalling party, to occupy it. Before they were far from camp, however, the enemy, in considerable numbers and with several standards flying, appeared on the very spot it was intended to hold. One hundred more rifles of the 3rd Sikhs, under Captain Aislabie, were immediately despatched in support of Major Griffiths, who was directed to halt for a short time in the hope that Allahudin Khan might yet arrive.

Rendered confident by the apparent hesitation of the British troops, the enemy, who by this time had increased to some 1,500 in number, and held a position strong in itself and further strengthened by breastworks in front and on the flanks, began firing upon the advanced party, thus annulling all hope of intervention. Colonel Money judged that the time had now arrived for a prompt and vigorous attack, and directing fire to be opened by the four guns of the Mountain Battery, which were posted in divisions on the right and left, ordered Major Griffiths, 3rd Sikhs, with 200 rifles of his regiment and 50 rifles of the 21st Native Infantry under Lieut. Dyce, to storm the enemy's position, 150 rifles 21st Native Infantry being held temporarily in reserve. The assault was delivered in the most spirited manner, and was perfectly successful, the Ghilzais being forced to take to precipitate flight, and being pursued for a considerable distance down the opposite slopes of the hills. Their loss was estimated to have been heavy, the practice of the mountain guns having been excellent throughout. The casualties of Colonel Money's force on this day were 1 British officer and 6 non-commissioned officers and Sepoys wounded.

Despite the punishment administered to them on the 2nd of October, the tribes in the neighbourhood of Ali Khel and the Shutargardan continued for some time to give considerable trouble. At daybreak on the 14th large numbers of Mangals, Spegwals, and Jagis surrounded and made a bold attack on Brigadier-General Gordon's camp at Ali Khel, which was at the time held by the 8th King's, the 11th and 29th Native Infantry, and three guns, C/4, R.A., together with detachments of the 12th Bengal Cavalry and 5th Punjab Cavalry, which were passing through to join the head-quarters of those regiments at the front. The attack was repulsed on all sides; and a counter-attack made by a detachment of the 29th Native Infantry, under Lieut. Picot, supported by parties of the 8th King's and the 11th Native Infantry, resulted in the complete rout of the enemy, numbers of whom were effectively dealt with by the cavalry details and the artillery during their retreat. The casualties of Brigadier-General Gordon's force were only 6 wounded. The enemy numbered between 1,500 and 2,000, and twenty-three of their dead were counted in the immediate vicinity of the camp.

While these operations were progressing at Ali Khel, a heavy engagement was being carried on in the neighbourhood of the Shutargardan, between Colonel Money's force and the Ghilzais, large numbers of whom had assembled about the pass before daybreak on the 14th. In view of their threatening demeanour, the precaution was taken of augmenting the ordinary relief of the garrison of a block-house on the Surkai Kotal, above Karatiga, which was held by a detachment of Colonel Money's force, under the command of a British officer. About 7 a.m. Major Collis, 21st Native Infantry, left camp in command of 90 men of the 3rd Sikhs, 100 of the 21st Native Infantry, and two guns of the Mountain Battery, and made his way towards the block-house. On arriving at the Surkai Kotal he found the post being actually attacked, and his own force immediately afterwards became engaged with the enemy. Receiving intimation of this, Colonel Money sent forward a further reinforcement of 100 men of the 3rd Sikhs, under Major Griffiths of that regiment, who, on arriving upon the scene, found Major Collis attacking large bodies of the Ghilzais on the hills to the north of the Kotal. These were in a short time routed, and pursued for some distance with considerable slaughter. Meanwhile other bodies of the enemy had assembled on some heights to the south of the block-house, and made demonstrations of again taking the offensive. Against these Major Griffiths advanced with a company of the 21st, supported by a flanking company of the 3rd Sikhs and the two guns. The enemy were rapidly driven back, but reaching some broken ground, rallied, and made another stand on a steep ridge fortified with breastworks. Major Collis, who had been collecting his men after the pursuit of the enemy to the north, now came up, and the advance was resumed in full strength. The Ghilzais were forced out of their defences by a bayonet charge, and gave way along the whole line, being subsequently pursued for a distance of two miles. Fifty of their number were killed. The loss sustained by Major Griffiths was 2 Sepoys killed, and 1 British officer and 5 Sepoys wounded.

Though the enemy were totally routed, they did not wholly disperse, but took up a position on the Spegah road, some five miles distant from the camp on the Shutargardan. Here they received daily large accessions to their numbers, till their total strength amounted to upwards of 17,000 men. In view of this vast gathering, Colonel Money deemed it advisable to withdraw the garrison of the Surkai Kotal. On the 16th of October the Shutargardan was completely invested by the enemy, and on the 18th, after the little garrison had been called upon to surrender, a determined attack was commenced upon the position, the Ghilzai sharp-shooters pushing up to within a short distance of the advanced picquets. The following day the force under Brigadier-General Gough, which had been sent out from Kabul, arrived at Kushi, and established heliographic communication with the garrison. Colonel Money at once resumed the offensive, the result being that the enemy, disheartened by the failure of their attacks and the near approach of reinforcements, broke and dispersed. About this time a successful demonstration from Kuram along the Chakmani valley dispersed the Chakmanis, Mangals, and Jagis, who were again assembling and threatening Ali Khel.

By the end of October the opening up of the Khyber line was sufficiently far advanced to justify General Roberts in closing the Ali Khel line of supply, and abandoning the Shutargardan for the winter. The post was accordingly vacated on the 30th of that month, the bulk of the garrison returning with Brigadier-General Hugh Gough's force to Kabul.

In the meantime the military commissions at the capital had been steadily prosecuting their inquiries, and, though considerable difficulty was experienced in obtaining evidence, many cases had been clearly proved. The general who commanded the parade of the Afghan troops in the Bala Hissar on the 3rd of September was convicted and hanged, and by the end of October eleven criminals had been executed. During this period the cantonment of Sherpur was being rapidly prepared for occupation by the British troops, and it was now decided to abandon the camp at Siah Sang. The neighbouring tribes had by this time quieted down, and supplies were coming in plentifully.

On the 1st of November a force consisting of the 12th Bengal Cavalry, two guns, F/A, R.H.A., No. 2 Mountain Battery, the 67th Foot, the 23rd Pioneers, and the 28th Native Infantry, under the command of Brigadier-General Macpherson, marched from Kabul towards Jagdalak, with the object of establishing communication between General Roberts's force and the Khyber column. The following day Sir Frederick Roberts joined General Macpherson at Butkhak, and carefully reconnoitred the Chinari, Khurd Kabul, and Lataband passes. The junction between the two columns was effected on the 6th, at a place called Kata Sang, the advance brigade of the Khyber column being commanded by Brigadier-General Charles Gough, and accompanied by General Bright in person. The following day General Gough fell back towards Gandamak, while General Macpherson proceeded northward, and crossing the Kabul River at Sirobi, conducted a reconnaissance up the Lughman Valley. On the 10th of November, while the brigade was encamped at Naghlu, on the left bank of the river, a foraging party, under the command of Captain Poole, 67th Foot, was attacked by several hundreds of the Safis of Tagao, near the village of Doaba. The little force made a gallant resistance, and managed to hold the enemy in check, inflicting a heavy loss upon them, till relief arrived from Camp. Three men of the foraging party were killed, and Captain Poole and four men were wounded. The same evening the brigade recrossed the Kabul River, and after remaining encamped at various places en route, returned, towards the end of the month, to Sherpur, having furnished posts at Butkhak and Lataband. In the meantime working parties of the 23rd Pioneers and 28th Native Infantry were actively engaged in making a road through the Lataband Pass, the route ultimately adopted as the line of communication towards Jalalabad.

On the 21st of November a force of all arms, under the command of Brigadier-General Baker, was sent into the Maidan district, with the dual object of drawing supplies and at the same time ascertaining the movements of the aged head Mulla, the Mushk-i-Alam, a priest famed for his learning and fanaticism, who, it was reported, was inciting the tribes to rise. The following day information reached General Baker to the effect that a number of the tribesmen, instigated by the Mulla, had assembled in the north of the Wardak district with the intention of crossing over into the Nirkh valley, immediately to the west of Maidan, and at the same time Bahadur Khan, headman of a section of the Ghilzais of that valley, refused to respond to a summons to appear in camp. General Roberts, who had ridden over from Sherpur on the 23rd, ordered Captain Turner, the Political Officer with General Baker's force, to proceed on that day with two squadrons of cavalry to Nirkh, and bring in, if necessary by force, the refractory Chief. On nearing Bahadur Khan's village, which was found to be strongly fortified, the cavalry were received with a heavy fire, the Ghilzais appearing in force on all sides. The following morning the remainder of the brigade arrived upon the scene, and the village and fort, which were found to have been deserted, were destroyed. On the 27th of November, while reconnoitring with his cavalry near Beni Badam, General Baker fell in with a small body of the insurgents, with whom shots were exchanged, and on whom punishment was inflicted. After gathering in the forage requisitioned from the district, the brigade made its way back to Sherpur, where it arrived on the 1st of December. On that day the ex-Amir, Yakub Khan, who for some days had been kept a close prisoner, left Sherpur under a strong guard for India, it having been discovered that the night before the action of Charasiab he was visited in his tent by Nek Muhammad, who commanded the enemy the following day, and also that a plan for his escape from the British camp had been matured. His deportation was followed, shortly afterwards, by that of Yahya Khan, Zakaria Khan, and the Wazir Shah Muhammad, his ministers, who had all been placed under arrest on suspicion of complicity in the outbreak of the 3rd of September, and whose influence, it was considered, was likely to be adversely employed, so long as they were permitted to remain in the country.

For some time both before and after the return of General Baker's force from Maidan, the disaffection of the tribes in the neighbourhood of Kabul, quickened by the fervent addresses to Mahommedan religious feeling made by the Mushk-i-Alam and his following, by the appeals of the ladies of Yakub Kahn's family to the popular sympathies, and by the distribution of large quantities of concealed treasure, was rapidly gaining ground. It appears probable that, after the rapid march of events terminating in the occupation of Kabul, the general expectation amongst the Afghans had been that the British Government, following the course which had been pursued by it forty years previously under similar circumstances, would withdraw its army, after exacting a heavy retribution from the nation and the city for the murder of its representative. The spectacle of the prolonged occupation of the capital; the measures which had been taken to dismantle the Bala Hissar, the historical fortress of the nation and the residence of its kings and principal nobles; and finally the imprisonment and deportation to India of the ex-Amir, Yakub Khan, and his leading ministers, had conspired to inflame to a high degree the natural antipathies felt towards a foreign invader. Under these circumstances the Mullas were able to succeed in subordinating private quarrels to hatred of the common foe, and the movement they set on foot, after passing through the phase of religious enthusiasm, at length culminated

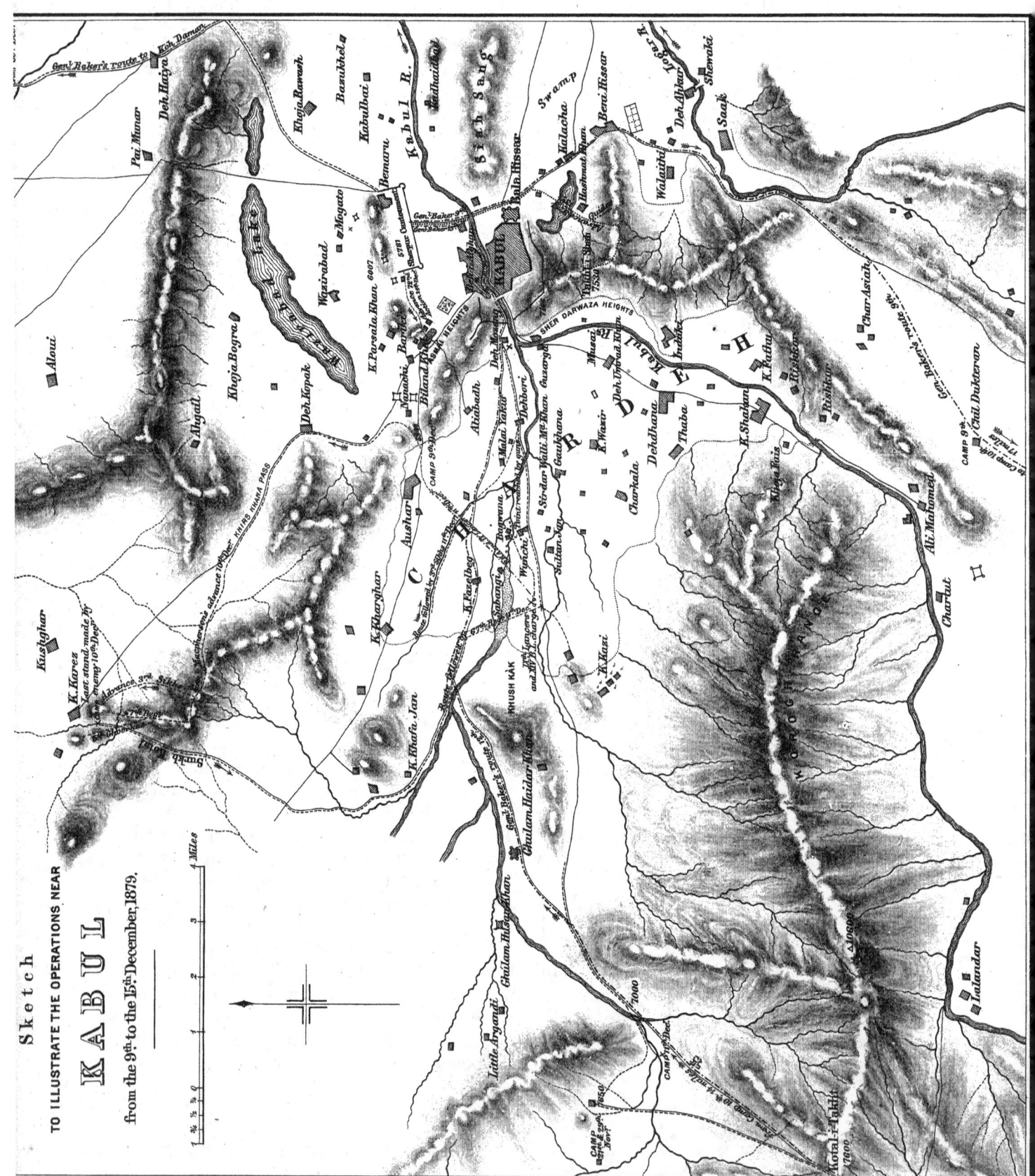

in nothing less than a national uprising against the English invader. Musa Khan, the heir of Yakub, was with the insurgents, and Muhammad Jan, a Wardak general of some note, appeared as the military head of the combination of the tribes.

It was now ascertained that with the object of gaining possession of the city and Bala Hissar, and after occupying the numerous forts and villages in the neighbourhood of Sherpur, of surrounding the cantonments, a general plan of operations had been matured, by which the Afghan forces from the south—viz., from Logar, Zurmat, and the Mangal and Jadran districts—should seize the range of hills which extends from Kabul to Charasiab; while the Kohistans should occupy the Asmai heights and the hills to the north, and the Maidan and Wardak troops move upon the city from the westward.

As it was evident that if these several bodies once concentrated on Kabul they would be joined by the disaffected portion of the people of the city and the neighbouring villages, Sir Frederick Roberts took measures to deal with the advancing forces in detail. With this intent a column consisting of four guns, F/A, R.H.A., four guns No. 1 Mountain Battery, 401 men of the 67th Foot, 509 of the 3rd Sikhs, 393 of the 5th Goorkhas, one squadron 9th Lancers, and two squadrons 14th Bengal Lancers, under the command of Brigadier-General Macpherson, was despatched from Sherpur on the 8th of December towards the west, by way of Killa Aushar and Argandi, in order to meet the enemy and force him back on Maidan. The following day Brigadier-General Baker was ordered to proceed with a force consisting of two and a half squadrons 5th Punjab Cavalry, four guns No. 2 Mountain Battery, 25 men of the Sappers and Miners, 450 of the 92nd Highlanders, and 450 of the 5th Punjab Infantry, by way of Charasiab, towards Maidan, and thus place himself across the line by which the enemy, in the event of defeat by General Macpherson, would have to retire. To give time for the completion of this movement, and to draw the Afghans forward by an appearance of hesitation, General Macpherson was halted on the 9th at Killa Aushar. It being ascertained, however, that large numbers of the enemy were moving up from Argandi and Paghman towards Kohistan, and that a considerable body of Kohistanis had collected at Karez Mir, about ten miles north of Kabul, Macpherson's line of advance was changed, in order that he might deal with the latter before a junction between the two forces could be effected. Quitting Killa Aushar at 7 a.m. on the 10th of December, and leaving behind him the bulk of the cavalry and the horse artillery of his force in consequence of the country being unsuitable to the operations of those arms, he now continued his march in a north-westerly direction. On reaching the Surkh Kotal, about two miles short of Karez Mir, he found that his arrival was well timed, the enemy advancing from the west being still below him in the Paghman Valley. About 10.30 a.m. reports were brought in by the cavalry (a squadron of the 14th Bengal Lancers which had accompanied the main body of the column from Killa Aushar) that the Kohistanis, to the number of over 2,000, were occupying a position on three conical hills at Karez Mir, having a front extending about three-quarters of a mile. At the same time a large body of the enemy was observed advancing from this direction towards the Surkh Kotal. With the object of effecting a surprise, General Macpherson had concealed his force under the crest of the ridge, and his dispositions were so far successful that about noon the advancing Kohistanis arrived within striking distance without, apparently, being aware of its juxtaposition. Two companies of the 67th Foot, under Major Baker, and two companies of the 5th Goorkhas, under Captain Cook, were now moved rapidly and silently forward, and bursting suddenly upon the foe, drove them helter-skelter down the reverse slopes of the hill to the plain which lay between the Kotal and their main position. A general advance was now ordered, Lieut.-Colonel Money, 3rd Sikhs, with five companies of his own regiment, one company of the 67th, and two guns, being left to hold the ridge. Sweeping forward at the double—the 5th Goorkhas to the left, the 67th Foot in the centre, and the 3rd Sikhs, in support of the cavalry, on the right—the main body of the column kept the retreating enemy incessantly on the move, preventing them from rallying till they reached their intrenched position at Karez Mir. So complete was their demoralization that even behind their breastworks they were able to offer but a half-hearted resistance, and after a momentary pause the infantry, covered by a well-directed fire from the mountain guns, which, throughout the advance had made excellent practice, carried the main position with a rush. The casualties of Macpherson's force during this engagement were 7 wounded. The enemy advancing from Maidan seemed inclined at first to ascend the Surkh Kotal from the Paghman Valley and assist the Kohistanis, but on seeing that the British troops held all the commanding positions, and probably hearing of the defeat of their allies, they retreated towards Argandi. With the object of cutting in on their line of retreat, the horse artillery and cavalry were ordered out from Killa Aushar, but as soon as it made its appearance the enemy took shelter in the villages and on the skirts of the high hills which surround Paghman. The troops consequently retraced their steps.

General Macpherson encamped on the night of the 10th at Karez Mir, and General Baker, who had steadily pursued his march by a very difficult road, halted a short distance to the west of Maidan. Meantime orders were sent to General Macpherson to follow up, as early as possible on the 11th, the enemy who had been observed retreating south and west by the Paghman Valley, and endeavour to drive them towards General Baker; he was informed at the same time that the horse artillery and cavalry at Killa Aushar, under the command of Brigadier-General Massy, would leave that place at 9 a.m., and he was directed to join them later in the day on the Argandi road.

On the morning of the 11th of December General Massy moved out from Killa Aushar with four guns, F/A, R.H.A., two squadrons 9th Lancers, and one squadron 14th Bengal Lancers, his orders being to advance cautiously along the main Ghazni road towards Argandi, feeling for the enemy, but not committing himself to an engagement until he should have placed himself in communication with General Macpherson, to the movements of whose force he was to subordinate those of his own. Misunderstanding, however, the directions which had been laid down for his guidance, General Massy, to avoid the wide détour which would have been involved in adhering to the route indicated, struck across country, with the object of gaining the main Ghazni road beyond the village of Killa Kazi. The mistake was attended with disastrous consequences, the projected junction between the two forces never being effected. The hills on either side of the main road some distance beyond the village were found to be strongly held, and as Massy continued to advance, the enemy moved down in overwhelming strength to attack him. To check their advance, the guns were three times moved forward, and on each occasion went into action; no appreciable effect was, however, produced by them, and the same lack of result attended the efforts of a troop of the Lancers who were dismounted to open fire as soon as carbine range was reached.

About this time General Roberts, who had started from Sherpur with the object of taking command of Macpherson and Massy's united forces, arrived upon the ground, and seeing the inutility of continuing a cavalry and horse artillery action against an enemy in such overwhelming strength, ordered General Massy to retire slowly, to find a road by which the artillery could be safely withdrawn, and to watch for an opportunity for the cavalry to charge, so that time might be gained for extricating the guns. Orders were at the same time sent back by the Lieutenant-General to Brigadier-General Hugh Gough, commanding at Sherpur, to despatch 200 of the 72nd Highlanders with the least possible delay to hold the Deh Mozang gorge, in order to prevent the enemy from gaining possession of the city. Towards this point the retirement was now directed.

A cavalry charge, gallantly led by Lieut.-Colonel Cleland, who was dangerously wounded, and by Captain Bloomfield Gough on the flank, was brilliantly delivered and wrought considerable execution, but did not succeed in checking the enemy for more than a few minutes, and was attended with great loss. Shortly afterwards the artillery found their further movement in retirement stopped by a deep and narrow channel. Here, whilst searching for a passage across, General Roberts ordered another cavalry charge as a last hope of saving the guns; but this had still less effect than the first, the enemy coming rapidly forward, outflanking the troops on both sides, and maintaining a destructive fire. It being found impossible to get the guns across the deep channel, it became absolutely necessary to spike and abandon them. This was done, after which General Roberts fell back towards Deh Mozang with the greater part of the cavalry, who, by manœuvring in front of the enemy and keeping them in check, enabled the 72nd Highlanders to arrive at the gorge just in time to hold it, and bar the passage of the on-coming hordes. The retirement throughout was conducted with admirable steadiness and coolness. Many of the troopers lost their horses in the charges, and instances of saving wounded and dismounted men from falling into the hands of the enemy were numerous.

Finding they were unable to enter the city, the enemy took ground on their right and occupied the Takht-i-Shah, the slopes leading up to it, and the large walled villages of Chardeh, thereby threatening the Bala Hissar.

While these events were in progress, General Macpherson, who had marched from the Surkh Kotal at 8 a.m., moved in a south-westerly direction towards Argandi, but observing large bodies of the enemy crossing his front and proceeding towards Kabul, and hearing the firing of General Massy's guns on his left, he brought his right forward, and at 12.30 p.m., or about an hour after the cavalry and artillery had commenced retiring, found himself very nearly on the ground where General Massy's action had been fought. Here he came across the rear of the enemy, who were speedily dispersed, some making for the hills above Killa Kazi, others for the Chardeh Valley; during the afternoon General Macpherson withdrew his force, conformably with an order received from Sherpur, to Deh Mozang, arriving at 7 a.m., and thus still further securing the approach to the city.

When Sir Frederick Roberts retired the main portion of General Massy's cavalry to Deh Mozang, Colonel MacGregor, Deputy Adjutant and Quartermaster-General, who had accompanied him to Killa Kazi, thinking that the infantry that had been ordered from Sherpur might take the road by the Kotal to the north of Killa Aushar, went in that direction to meet them. Observing from this point that the ground where the abandoned horse artillery guns were lying had been partially cleared of the enemy by the advance of General Macpherson's troops, he collected a small party of the 9th Lancers, 14th Bengal Lancers, and artillerymen who had remained with him, retraced his steps, and picking up, on the way, a few soldiers belonging to Macpherson's baggage-guard, succeeded in recovering the guns and bringing them into cantonments.

On the morning of this day, the 11th, General Baker had started early from his encampment in the neighbourhood of Maidan, and found the enemy in considerable force, occupying the hills on either side of the Argandi road. The main body of General Baker's force was allowed to proceed unmolested, but his rear-guard and baggage were somewhat hotly attacked; owing, however, to the able manner in which the rear-guard was commanded by Captain M'Callum, 92nd Highlanders, and to the energy of the officers in charge of the Transport, the whole of the baggage was brought through in safety. The advance guard had in the meantime reached Argandi, and found the enemy in possession of both sides of the gorge through which the road runs into the Chardeh Valley. Although late in the afternoon, it was deemed necessary to dislodge them at once from their position, commanding, as it did, the road to Kabul. This was effected in a brilliant manner by a portion of the 92nd Highlanders under the command of Major White, gallantly led by Lieut. Scott Napier. That night General Baker encamped at Argandi. Though attempts had been made during the day to open communication with him by heliograph, it was not until the following morning that he learnt that the enemy were threatening the city in very considerable strength, and that he was required to return to the neighbourhood of Sherpur.

The casualties of the British force during the 11th of December were—of General Massy's brigade, 27 killed and 25 wounded, together with 51 horses killed and 16 wounded; of General Macpherson's brigade, 2 killed and 7 wounded; and of General Baker's brigade, 1 killed and 12 wounded.

Feeling that the enemy could not be permitted to retain their commanding position on the Takht-i-Shah, Sir Frederick Roberts directed General Macpherson, on the morning of the 12th of December, to endeavour to drive them from it by an attack from the Bala Hissar and Deh Mozang directions. Lieut.-Colonel Money, of the 3rd Sikhs, was deputed to undertake this operation, the force placed at his disposal consisting of two guns No. 1 Mountain Battery, 215 rifles of the 67th and 72nd Regiments, 150 of the 3rd Sikhs, and 195 of the 5th Goorkhas.

The position which had been taken up by the enemy on the Takht-i-Shah was a most formidable one, the slopes of the mountain, which were extremely steep, being strewn with jagged masses of rock and intercepted with scarps, and the natural impediments with which the assaulting party had to contend being still further increased by breastworks, which had been thrown up at various points on the ascent to the peak. Behind these the enemy were strongly posted, and fought resolutely. After many gallant attempts had been made to carry the position, it at last became evident that, to insure success without very serious loss, and to prevent the enemy relieving and reinforcing the party holding the peak, as they had been doing during the day, it was necessary not only to attack them in front, but also to operate on their line of retreat. The assault was consequently ordered by the Lieutenant-General to be deferred, General Macpherson being directed to hold the ground of which he had already gained possession, and informed that on the following morning General Baker would co-operate with him from the Ben-i-Shahr side.

During this day, the 12th of December, General Baker's brigade returned to Sherpur. The enemy showed themselves in considerable force in his rear and on both flanks, and the rear-guard, which was ably commanded by Major Pratt, 5th Punjab Infantry, was at first closely pressed. On the march the little column was skilfully protected and covered by the 5th Punjab Cavalry, who, under the command of Lieut.-Colonel Williams, missed no opportunity of inflicting loss on the enemy. The casualties on the 12th were—of Macpherson's brigade, 4 killed and 12 wounded; of Baker's brigade, 1 killed and 2 wounded.

Conformably with the intentions formed on the previous day, a force consisting of four guns G/3, R.A., four guns No. 2 Mountain Battery, one squadron 9th Lancers, the 5th Punjab Cavalry, six companies 92nd Highlanders, seven companies Guide Infantry, and 300 rifles 3rd Sikhs, afterwards reinforced by 150 rifles 5th Punjab Infantry, marched from Sherpur on the morning of the 13th of December, under the command of Brigadier-General Baker, with orders to proceed by the Bala Hissar road in the direction of Ben-i-Shahr, to seize the heights above that village, and to operate on the enemy's position on the Takht-i-Shah from the south-east. General Macpherson was at the same time directed to act in conjunction with General Baker from the north.

Soon after passing the Bala Hissar, General Baker observed the enemy streaming out of the villages immediately below the Ben-i-Shahr Ridge, the centre of which he seized by a bold and rapid movement, and thus cut the enemy's forces in two. The 92nd Highlanders led the advance, which was covered by a heavy and well-directed fire from the eight guns. The attack on the enemy's first position was gallantly headed by Lieut. Forbes, who, together with the Colour-Sergeant of his company, James Drummond, was killed in a hand-to-hand fight. The leading men of the 92nd Highlanders were most resolutely charged by the enemy, who had a very considerable advantage both in numbers and position. For the gallantry he displayed on this occasion Lieut. Dick-Cunyngham, who had taken Lieut. Forbes's place, was awarded the Victoria Cross.

After the first position was carried, the 92nd Highlanders and Guides, covered by the fire of Swinley's guns, which had by this time gained the summit of the lower ridge, and aided by that of G/3, R.A., from the plain below, continued the advance on the Takht-i-Shah, fighting for some distance every foot of the way. The position the enemy had taken up on the heights was enormously strong, but by 11.30 a.m. the 92nd and the Guides had reached the summit. Here they were met by some of the 72nd Highlanders, 3rd Sikhs, and 5th Goorkhas, under the command of Major Sym, 5th Goorkhas, from Macpherson's force, who had ascended a few minutes before. Colour-Sergeant John Yule, 72nd Highlanders—a gallant non-commissioned officer who lost his life the following day—was the first man up, and succeeded in capturing two standards.

During the main attack the reserve of Baker's force in the valley below became engaged with large bodies of the enemy who had débouched from the city during the advance, and occupied positions on both flanks and in the rear, while the cavalry of the force was occupied in disposing of reinforcements coming up from the direction of the Khurd Khyber. To assist General Baker in dealing with so many detached parties, General Massy was sent out by Sir Frederick Roberts from Sherpur with one squadron 9th Lancers, two squadrons 14th Bengal Lancers, and the Guide Cavalry, and proceeded first in the direction of the Siah Sang heights, where large numbers of the enemy had collected. In the operations which ensued, most efficient service was rendered by the cavalry, brilliant charges being again and again delivered, and large numbers of the enemy slain. In the evening General Baker was recalled to cantonments, and General Macpherson was directed to move from Deh Mozang and occupy the Bala Hissar heights, leaving the 5th Goorkhas to retain possession of the Takht-i-Shah. The casualties of the Infantry during this day were 6 killed, and 26 wounded; of the Cavalry, 8 killed and 19 wounded.

The successes on the 13th of December had been so decided, and the losses inflicted on the enemy so heavy, that it was anticipated by the Lieutenant-General that the hostile combination would have broken up, and that the various sections would have scattered and returned to their homes. But at daylight on the 14th very large numbers of men, with numerous standards, were seen to be occupying a high hill on the Kohistan road, about a mile north of the Asmai range, and as the day advanced they passed in great numbers from this hill, and also along the road from Kohistan, to the crest of the Asmai heights, where they were joined by many others from the direction of Chardeh and the city. It then became apparent that, foiled in their operations in the west and south, the Afghans had concentrated to the north-west, and were about to deliver an attack in great strength from that quarter.

In view of this new aspect of affairs, Sir Frederick Roberts determined to drive the enemy off the Asmai heights, to cut their communications with the north, and to carry out the same plan of operations, modified in detail, as that which had been so successfully applied on the previous day in dealing with the combinations to the south.

Brigadier-General Baker was accordingly sent out from Sherpur at 9 a.m. on the 14th of December towards the eastern slope of the Asmai range to attack the heights, the force placed at his disposal consisting of four guns, G/3, R.A., four guns No. 2 Mountain Battery, the 14th Bengal Lancers, 192 rifles 72nd Highlanders, 100 rifles 92nd Highlanders, 460 rifles Guides Infantry, and 470 rifles 5th Punjab Infantry. His first object was to seize a small conical hill which forms the northern shoulder of the Aliabad Kotal, and thus to place himself on the enemy's line of communication, and prevent the force on Asmai receiving support either from the large bodies on the hill to the north or from those on the Kohistan road.

The attack was commenced, under cover of the fire of the field and mountain guns, by 194 rifles 72nd Highlanders, under Lieutenant-Colonel Brownlow, 70 rifles 92nd Highlanders, under Captain Gordon, and 422 rifles Guides Infantry, under Colonel Jenkins, and after a short conflict, the conical hill fell into the hands of the British troops. Leaving 64 men of the 72nd Highlanders, and 60 of the Guides Infantry, under the command of Lieutenant-Colonel Clarke, 72nd Highlanders, who had led the successful assault upon this point, to secure the hill against reoccupation, Colonel Jenkins, who was in immediate command of the advance, pushed on with the remainder of the force to dislodge the enemy from the position on Asmai, the 72nd Highlanders, under the command of Lieutenant-Colonel Brownlow, now leading, and the Guides Infantry on the right affording assistance by continually operating on the enemy's flank. The advance was covered by four guns, F/A, R.H.A., under Captain Pipon, which were brought into action near the south-west corner of the Sherpur cantonment, in addition to the four guns, G/3, R.A., under Major Craster, which were with General Baker; and the attack was further assisted by the fire of four guns of No. 1 Mountain Battery, under Captain Morgan, attached to Brigadier-General Macpherson's column, from the Bala Hissar hill, as also by two companies of the 67th Foot, under Major Baker, which crossed the Kabul river, and acting on the enemy's left rear, contributed to render their position on the Asmai heights untenable. The ground was most difficult, and the enemy fought with the greatest obstinacy; the Highlanders and Guides were, however, not to be denied, and eventually reached the highest peak of the range, where a number of Ghazis stood fast, determined to die. Here a great struggle took place, several of the Highlanders distinguishing themselves by great personal gallantry. By 12.30 p.m. the British troops were in possession of the whole of the Asmai heights.

As soon as the extreme eastern point of the enemy's position had been carried, General Baker had directed four guns of No. 2 Mounted Battery, escorted by 100 rifles of the 5th Punjab Infantry, to reinforce the party which had been left on the conical hill, with a view of supporting the main advance by engaging the enemy in the Chardeh and Kohistan directions. Shortly after the highest peak of Asmai had been carried, very large bodies of the enemy were observed moving northwards from Indiki, with the apparent intention of effecting a junction with the hostile force that still held the hills in the Kohistan direction, and of endeavouring to retake the original position, and a few minutes later it was noticed that the little force holding the conical hill was being hotly pressed. A party of the 5th Punjab Infantry was at once sent to their assistance by General Baker, and at the same time Sir Frederick Roberts moved up 200 rifles of the 3rd Sikhs from Sherpur, likewise to render aid. Unfortunately, before either of the reinforcements could reach the threatened position, the enemy had gained possession of it. Their numbers were overwhelming, and though the Highlanders, Guides, and 5th Punjab Infantry made a most stubborn defence, and Captain Spens, of the 72nd Highlanders, sacrificed his life in a heroic attempt to stem the advance of the enemy, it was of no avail: the British troops retreated quietly and steadily down the eastern slope of the hill, unable to bring away two guns—which were, however, eventually recovered—of the Mountain Battery, that had been served with the utmost gallantry up to the very last moment.

Whilst these events were in progress, numbers of the enemy were observed to be collecting, as during the previous day, on the Siah Sang heights, and proceeding round the eastern flank of the cantonments in the direction of Kohistan. A small force of cavalry and two guns, F/A, R.H.A., under the command of Brigadier-General Hugh Gough, was thererefore sent out by Sir F. Roberts to disperse them; but the ground was found to be so intersected by deep watercourses that the advance of the artillery was necessarily slow, and by the time the obstacles were overcome the enemy had got so far on the road towards Kohistan, and so close to the hills, that pursuit was hopeless. A party of the 5th Punjab Cavalry, which regiment was quartered in the King's Garden, between Sherpur and the city, met, however, with better success. About 1 p.m. some three or four hundred of the enemy were observed by Captain Vousden—who, with one troop, was out reconnoitring—moving along the left bank of the Kabul river. Captain Vousden most gallantly charged into the middle of them, and notwithstanding that only twelve of his men, six of whom were wounded, were able to follow him, the remainder being stopped by a heavy fire which was opened upon them from behind some walls, he succeeded in dispersing the enemy, and inflicting severe loss upon them, killing five men with his own hand.

Up to this time there had been no reason to apprehend that the Afghans were in sufficient force to successfully cope with disciplined troops; but the determined manner in which the conical hill had been recaptured, and the fact that large masses of the enemy were still advancing from the north, south, and west, made it evident that the numbers who had combined were too overwhelming to admit of the comparatively small force at the Lieutenant-General's disposal meeting them, especially on ground which still further increased the advantages they possessed from their vast numerical superiority. Sir Frederick Roberts therefore determined to withdraw from all isolated positions, and to concentrate the whole force at Sherpur, thus securing the safety of the large cantonments, and avoiding what had now become a useless sacrifice of life. Involving, as it did, the temporary abandonment of the city and the Bala Hissar, a loss serious in itself and likely to produce a bad effect on the country at large, the measure was one which was most reluctantly decided on. Under the circumstances, however, it was clear that no other course was open but to remain for a time on the defensive, and wait until the arrival of reinforcements, or the growing confidence of the enemy, should present a favourable opportunity for delivering an attack. Orders to retire were accordingly issued.

The withdrawal from the Bala Hissar and the Asmai heights was accomplished in a manner highly creditable to the officers in command and to the discipline of the troops. General Macpherson's brigade had to pass through a portion of the city and the suburb of Deh Afghan. His rear-guard was harassed, and his troops were subjected to a heavy fire as they moved along the narrow streets and through the numerous gardens and orchards; but the Brigadier-General brought off his men and baggage in perfect order, and with comparatively little loss. By the evening of the 14th all the troops were within cantonments, and that night the Afghan army occupied the City and the Bala Hissar. The casualties of the British force on this day were—of Brigadier-General Baker's brigade, 29 killed and 89 wounded; of Brigadier-General Macpherson's brigade, 5 killed and 11 wounded; and of the Cavalry Brigade, 8 wounded, 1 mortally.

The Sherpur cantonment, a large fortified enclosure built by Shere Ali, is in form a rectangular parallelogram, about a mile and a half long, and three-quarters of a mile broad. Its northern side is formed by the Bemaru heights, a range of steep isolated hills, and its southern face and western flank consist of a massive and continuous mud wall, some sixteen feet in height, which has also been carried round on the eastern side, but not completed, rising here only to a height of seven feet. Although the perimeter was large for the force at the Lieutenant-General's disposal, still its defensive powers, both natural and artificial, were so great that it was confidently anticipated that it might be successfully held against any attack.

The possible necessity for withdrawing into Sherpur had been foreseen by Sir Frederick Roberts and provided for; and besides supplies, medicine, and hospital comforts, there was a sufficient store of ammunition to last the entire British force for at least four months. The defences of the place were, however, in parts very defective, and throughout the period of the investment, afforded incessant employment for the troops.

Early on the morning of the 15th of December the telegraph wire was cut by the enemy, but not before a message had been despatched communicating the situation at Kabul to the Commander-in-Chief and the Government of India, and requesting that reinforcements might be sent up as speedily as possible. At the same time orders were sent by Sir Frederick Roberts to Major-General Bright, at Jalalabad, to move Brigadier-General Charles Gough's brigade from Gandamak to Kabul without loss of time, and also to send forward another brigade of the Khyber Line Force as soon as fresh troops should reach Jalalabad from India.

It had been decided by the Lieutenant-General to recall to Sherpur the garrison of Butkhak, which was in an exposed and isolated position, and not sufficiently strong to defend itself against serious attack. The expediency had been considered of also withdrawing the force at Lataband, which consisted of two mountain guns, the 28th Punjab Native Infantry, and a wing of the 23rd Pioneers, the whole commanded by Colonel J. Hudson, of the former regiment; but as the position was a strong one, ammunition plentiful, and supplies in hand sufficient to last over the probable date of Brigadier-General Charles Gough's arrival, and as, moreover, it was in direct communication with Kabul, it was decided to maintain the post. So long as Lataband was held, no serious opposition, it was anticipated, could be offered to General Gough's advance. It was, in fact, the most important link in the chain of communications; and though its occupation materially diminished the force at Sherpur, its retention was considered to be worth the sacrifice.

On the 16th of December a body of the enemy numbering about 1,000 threatened the camp at Lataband. Colonel Hudson, however, attacked and dispersed them, inflicting considerable loss both in killed and wounded. Owing to the excellent manner in which the attack was covered both by artillery and infantry fire, there were no casualties in Colonel Hudson's force.

During the interval between the 14th and 21st of December the enemy daily took up positions in the forts and gardens surrounding Sherpur, and their fire from behind cover caused a few casualties in the camp. Each day cavalry reconnaissances were made, and some portion of the force moved out to dislodge the Afghans from any place where they could cause special annoyance. Some of the forts and other cover in the immediate neighbourhood of Sherpur were destroyed, but only minor operations of this description were undertaken, sorties on a large scale with the object of gaining possession of portions of the enemy's positions being avoided, as the British force was insufficient to admit of acquisitions thus acquired being retained.

Every night information was received that an attack was contemplated, but it was not until the 21st of December that the enemy showed signs of special activity. On that and the following day large numbers of them moved from the city, and passing round to the eastward of Sherpur, occupied the numerous forts beyond it in very great force. It became apparent that this movement was preparatory to an attack from that quarter. At the same time intelligence was received that the enemy were preparing a number of ladders, with the intention of attacking the southern and western walls by escalade.

The night of the 22nd of December passed without disturbance, but the songs and cries of the enemy could be heard in the surrounding villages. Information had been received that the 23rd was the day fixed upon for their great effort, and it had also been ascertained that the aged Mushk-i-Alam would with his own hand light the beacon-fire at dawn on the Asmai heights, which was to be the signal for the commencement of the attack. Possessing this knowledge, and being also aware that the feelings of the people had been worked to the highest pitch of excitement by the preachings of the Mullas, General Roberts directed all troops to be under arms at a very early hour on that date.

The information which had been received proved correct, and the appearance of the signal-fire on the Asmai heights, shortly before daybreak on the 23rd, announced the beginning of the assault. Heavy firing almost immediately commenced against the southern and eastern faces of the cantonment, and by 7 a.m. an attack in force against the eastern side was fully developed, whilst a very large number of the enemy, provided with scaling ladders, were drawn up under cover of the walls to the south. From 7 a.m. until 10 a.m. the fight was carried on vigorously: repeated attempts were made to carry the low eastern wall by escalade, but though the enemy on several occasions reached the abattis, they were each time repulsed, and many dead marked the spots where the assault had been most determinedly pressed home. Soon after 10 a.m. a lull took place, as though the attacking force had recoiled before the breechloader, but at 11 a.m. the fight again grew hot, although it was not marked by the determination of the former period.

Finding that it was impossible to dislodge the enemy by any fire that could be brought to bear upon them from the defences, General Roberts determined to attack them in flank, and for this purpose directed four guns of G/3, R.A., and the 5th Punjab Cavalry, under the command of Major Craster, R.A., and Lieut.-Colonel Williams, 5th Punjab Cavalry, respectively, to move out through the gorge in the Bemaru heights. This counterstroke at once told. The Afghans wavered, and shortly afterwards broke. By 1 p.m. all vigour had passed from the attack, and the time for the action of cavalry having arrived, Brigadier-General Massy was directed to proceed with every available man and horse and do his utmost against the enemy. At the same time a party of infantry and sappers moved out to destroy some villages to the south, which had caused considerable annoyance, and which it was necessary to clear in order to facilitate the arrival of Brigadier-General Charles Gough's brigade from Jagdalak, which was expected to reach Kabul the following day. This work was successfully accomplished, though, unhappily, at the cost of the lives of two gallant officers—Captain Dundas, V.C., R.E., and Lieut. Nugent, R.E.—who were killed by the premature explosion of a mine. Meanwhile a party of the cavalry had worked round to the base of Siah Sang, and succeeded in rendering a good account of the enemy in that quarter, whilst the Guides Cavalry and a squadron of the 14th Bengal Lancers, who had been manœuvring more to the eastward, had been equally fortunate. By evening firing had nearly ceased, and daylight on the 24th showed that the enemy, abandoning all hope of success, had dispersed, not a man being found in the neighbouring villages, or being visible on the surrounding hills. The city, too, was clear of them, and so precipitate was their flight that, leaving their dead unburied where they fell, many parties of fugitives were by mid-day upwards of twenty-five miles from Kabul, the rapidity of their retreat being doubtless accelerated by the knowledge that reinforcements were near at hand. At 5 o'clock in the morning a party of the 72nd Highlanders occupied without opposition the fort of Muhammad Sharif, and later a force under Brigadier-

General Macpherson moved out to cover, and if necessary aid, the entry of Brigadier-General Charles Gough's column, which had halted the previous evening about six miles from Sherpur. The cavalry, divided into two parties commanded respectively by Brigadier-Generals Dunham Massy and Hugh Gough, proceeded by Ben-i-Shahr and the Chardeh Valley in pursuit; but the squadrons were retarded by a heavy snow-storm, and no success attended their efforts, though neither party returned to Sherpur until after nightfall.

Thus broke up the most extensive and formidable combination which had ever opposed British arms in Afghanistan. The united forces of the enemy are said to have exceeded 100,000, and it has been computed that of these, as many as 60,000 at one time took the field. Their losses from first to last were considerable, not less than 3,000 having been killed or wounded.

Commenting on the services of the troops under his command, Sir Frederick Roberts dwells in warm terms, in his despatch, on the spirit by which they were animated. All night and every night, in most severe weather, officers and men were at their posts or sleeping with their arms in the immediate vicinity of the trenches, and hardships and exposure were throughout cheerfully borne by all. The casualties between the 15th and 24th of December were 18 killed and 68 wounded, including camp followers.

During the time the enemy had occupied the city and the Bala Hissar they had committed some excesses, maltreating the inhabitants whose relations with the British force had been friendly, and looting their houses. About one hundred and thirty tons of gunpowder, which it had been found impossible to destroy before the retirement within the lines of Sherpur became necessary, had been left in the large magazine, and the whole of this was either carried off by the Afghans, or expended in accidental explosions. In one of these, which were of common occurrence, upwards of one hundred of the enemy were killed.

On the 27th of December a force of all arms, under General Baker, was sent into Kohistan, with a view of ascertaining whether the inhabitants of that district had dispersed to their homes. Everything was found to be quiet, and on the 31st of December the column re-entered Kabul after a somewhat harassing march consequent on the country being covered with snow. In the meantime affairs at the capital were rapidly settling down, the shops in the bazaars were being re-opened, and the inhabitants generally were resuming their ordinary avocations.

Up to the time of the concentration of the Field Force under the command of Sir Frederick Roberts at Ali Khel and the Shutargardan immediately prior to the advance on Kabul, all available transport and supplies had been diverted from Peshawar to facilitate the projected operations of that column. As soon, however, as the dispositions for the forward movement on the capital had been completed, it became a matter of paramount importance to mobilize the Khyber Force, and by the latter end of September every effort was being directed towards that end, though the difficulties to contend with were stupendous.

On the 13th of September General Bright had arrived at Peshawar and assumed command of the troops, his arrival being followed during the succeeding week by that of Brigadier-Generals Charles Gough and Arbuthnot. Brigadier-General Doran, commanding at Landi Kotal, had for some days previously been pushing forward reconnaissances towards Daka, and had ascertained that there was little likelihood of the advance of the British troops being opposed.

At this time many of the corps detailed for the operations on the Khyber line were still *en route* to the front, while many more had not even left their stations far down country. It was several weeks, therefore, before the brigade organization of the force could become anything like complete. Orders, however, that a demonstration should be made in the direction of Jalalabad were pressing, and with this object in view a force under Brigadier-General Charles Gough was with some difficulty equipped by the end of the month. General Gough left Peshawar on the 27th of September, and on the 29th arrived at Landi Kotal. On the same day Colonel Jenkins, C.B., with the Guides Cavalry and two guns of the Hazara Mountain Battery, pushed on to Daka, whither he was followed on the 30th by General Gough with a regiment of cavalry and a regiment of infantry. The fort was occupied without opposition. There had been rumours of a gathering of the Mohmands in the neighbourhood, but none were met with, and the only sign of hostility was the removal of women and children from Lalpura, on the opposite bank of the Kabul river. The Khan of that place who was in power during the British occupation of the country in the spring, had been removed by the Amir, and his successor at first declined to aid the advance of the British troops, alleging that he had received no orders from Kabul to do so; but upon it becoming known to him that Yakub Khan had gone to meet General Roberts at Kushi, supplies were freely promised.

On the 2nd of October General Gough marched with a portion of his brigade through the Kurd Khyber, though transport was still so scarce that it was only by utilizing the baggage-animals of the force left behind that he was able to do so. Shortly after Basawal was reached, a messenger arrived bearing a letter from the Governor of Jalalabad, who wrote that he had been ordered by the Amir to afford every assistance in supplies and transport, and that he had enjoined the tribes to refrain from acts of hostility. On the 4th the Governor of Jalalabad himself, accompanied by the Khan of Lalpura, visited General Gough in camp, and supplies shortly afterwards began to come in freely. The sickness amongst the troops in the Peshawar Valley and Khyber Pass had for some time been unusually great, no less than twenty-five per cent. of the entire force being under medical treatment. The health of the men at the more advanced posts had recently improved, but at Ali Musjid the condition of some of the corps was deplorable, the returns of one battalion, the 29th Native Infantry, showing 470 sick out of a total of 556.

During the next few weeks the forward movement along the whole line was continued without opposition, and post after post was occupied as the means of transport and supply gradually improved. Jalalabad was entered by the Corps of Guides —which acted throughout as the advance guard of Gough's brigade—on the 12th of October, and Gandamak on the 23rd, Divisional Head-quarters moving up to Jalalabad on the 24th. On the 2nd of November General Bright reached Gandamak, and the following day the advance brigade, under Brigadier-General Gough, carrying seven days' provisions, started for Jagdalak, to meet the force under Brigadier-General Macpherson, which had been sent out from the capital to open communication between the Kabul and Khyber columns, The junction, as has been already recorded, was effected at Kata Sang on the 6th of November. After an interview with General Macpherson, Generals Bright and Gough fell back, from want of supplies, towards Gandamak, leaving at Jagdalak Colonel Jenkins with the Guides, the 2nd Goorkhas, and two guns of No 4 Mountain Battery.

On the 19th of November telegraphic communication between Kabul and

India was completed. Posts held by the Guides were established at Pezwan, Jagdalak, and Kata Sang, and by the end of the month convoys to and from Kabul were passing continually without interruption. During this period the construction of new cantonments at Gandamak was being proceeded with, and the troops along the line were settling down into winter quarters. Conformably with orders received from Sir Frederick Roberts, the Corps of Guides was sent forward from Jagdalak to Kabul on the 9th of December, and arrived at its destination in time to render distinguished service in the stirring operations with which the year was brought to a close.

For some weeks after the return of the column which established communication with the capital, nothing of importance occurred on the Khyber line till the middle of December, when it became known that Sir Frederick Roberts's force was being attacked by immense numbers of the enemy, and orders were received for the 1st Brigade of General Bright's Division to hold itself in readiness for an advance at any moment to Kabul. The flame of insurrection rapidly spread eastwards along the line of communications, the first symptom of coming hostility appearing in the relinquishment by the Ghilzai labourers of their work upon the road.

At this time Brigadier-General Gough was at Gandamak with an effective strength of 150 cavalry, 935 infantry, and a battery of Horse Artillery, and the three outposts on the Kabul side of Gandamak, viz., Pezwan, Jagdalak Kotal, and Jagdalak Fort, were somewhat weakly held—Pezwan, by 50 of the 10th Bengal Lancers, four guns of the Hazara Mountain Battery, a company of Sappers, and 187 of the 2nd Goorkhas; the Kotal, by a company of Sappers and 40 of the 2nd Goorkhas; and the Fort, by 90 of the 10th Bengal Lancers, two guns of the Hazara Mountain Battery, and 180 of the 2nd Goorkhas. On the 14th of December General Gough, taking with him two of the headmen of the Kugianis as hostages for the good behaviour of the tribe, moved on to Jagdalak, his force now consisting of 140 lances 10th Bengal Lancers, 73 rifles Sappers and Miners, 487 rifles 2nd Battalion 9th Foot, and 375 rifles 4th Goorkhas. At Pezwan he was joined by two guns of the Mountain Battery, to replace which he left at that post 280 rifles of the 9th Foot and 187 rifles of the 4th Goorkhas. These parties, under the command of Lieut.-Colonel Daunt, 9th Foot, rejoined the main body of the brigade the following day, their rear-guard being attacked, during the march to Jagdalak, by a number of the Ghilzais, who were repulsed with comparatively little trouble, and suffered some loss. Early on the morning of the 15th the telegraph wire was cut on both sides of Jagdalak, but not before General Gough received from Sir Frederick Roberts orders to advance as soon as he possibly could to Kabul, and to bring on with him the detachment under Colonel Hudson, which was holding the isolated post at Lataband. That evening crowds of men with standards were observed from camp assembling on all the surrounding hills, and information was received that the Ghilzai chief, Azmatallah Khan, had advanced from Lughman with a large gathering, and purposed to attack Jagdalak, in conjunction with the Hissarak section of the tribe. Later on, as it was getting dark, the enemy came pouring down from the hill-tops, and opened a desultory and long-range fire from all sides upon the camp, fortunately, however, without inflicting loss. As they continued to harass the position from behind cover on the hills, after daybreak on the 16th, Lieut. Mayne, of the 9th Foot, with a small party of his regiment, was sent out to dislodge them, a duty which was effectually performed. On the 17th of December Major Macnaghten, 10th Bengal Lancers, was sent out towards Pezwan with two companies of infantry and forty lances of his own regiment to clear the road, and reopen communications with Gandamak, Major Thackeray, V.C., R.E., commanding at Jagdalak Kotal, being directed to co-operate. Major Macnaghten vigorously attacked over a thousand of the enemy, whom he found posted across the road about two miles south of the Kotal, and dispersed them with loss. Colonel Norman, 24th Native Infantry, had also moved out from Pezwan and attacked the enemy in the rear, but in consequence of the divergent retreat of the Ghilzais the co-operating forces did not meet. On the 18th the road was again cleared by forces advancing simultaneously from the two posts, one under Major Rowcroft, 4th Goorkhas, and the other under Colonel Norman. The latter officer was now directed to move up to Jagdalak on the 19th, with two guns of the Mountain Battery, the 24th Native Infantry, a wing of the 2nd Goorkhas, and as large a convoy of supplies as he could obtain, the arrival of reinforcements at Pezwan setting these troops free; and in order to assist his advance, a force consisting of two mountain guns, 80 cavalry, and 300 infantry, under the command of Major Roberts, 9th Foot, was sent out from Jagdalak to act against the Ghilzais, who had again assembled on the road. Major Roberts found the enemy posted near the spot they had previously occupied, and a sharp encounter ensued, the Ghilzais attempting to outflank the British force, but being successfully repelled. Colonel Norman now arrived upon the scene from Pezwan, and bringing his guns into action, enfiladed the enemy's whole line, causing them to retire with considerable loss, their leader, Syud Khan, and his son, being amongst the wounded. Major Roberts then covered the passage of Colonel Norman's convoy, which was brought into camp without the loss of a single animal, a daring attempt made to get at it whilst it was making its way through a pass to the west of the Kotal being defeated by the steadiness of the rear-guard.

The arrival of Colonel Norman's party increased the strength of the brigade at Jagdalak to six mountain guns, 242 cavalry, and 1,752 infantry, and together with a convoy of supplies which came in on the 20th, placed General Gough in a position to carry out an order he received from Sir Frederick Roberts on that day to advance with all speed to Kabul. Garrisoning Jagdalak with two guns of the Hazara Mountain Battery, the 24th Native Infantry, and 224 of the 10th Bengal Lancers, the whole under the command of Colonel Norman, General Gough commenced his march with the remainder of the brigade on the 21st of December, and reaching Lataband the following day, united his force with that of Colonel Hudson, and with the 12th Bengal Cavalry, which regiment, under the command of Major J. H. Green, had moved out from Sherpur before daybreak on the 22nd, and had rendered gallant service in running the gauntlet of the hordes investing the cantonments. On the 23rd of December the entire column halted on the right bank of the Logar river, protecting the bridge which lies half-way between Kabul and Butkhak, and on the 24th marched into Sherpur without a shot being fired.

During the afternoon of the 23rd of December a very determined attack was made on the fortified post at Jagdalak Kotal, distant about three and a half miles from Jagdalak, and held by two companies of Sappers and Miners, and a company of the 24th Punjab Native Infantry, under the command of Major E. T. Thackeray, V.C., R.E. The small garrison gallantly held their own, and dispersed the enemy, though the latter numbered between two and three thousand. Major Thackeray was severely wounded, and three of his men were killed. Of the enemy, twelve were killed, and many more wounded. Colonel Norman, commanding at Jagdalak Fort, hearing that the enemy were about to renew their attack, reached the Kotal the following morning, and having strengthened the post there, proceeded a short distance towards Pezwan, to meet a force under Lieut.-Colonel Ball Acton, 51st Light Infantry, which had been directed to march from thence to co-operate with the Jagdalak troops. After effecting a junction, the two columns retraced their steps, Colonel Norman, on his way back to the fort, coming into contact with the enemy, who partly blocked the pass. The fire of the guns, and the rifle fire of two parties, commanded, respectively, by Captain Barrow, 10th Bengal Lancers, and Jemadar Bidhi Chand, a young Dogra officer of the 24th Punjab Native Infantry, quickly overcame resistance, and the force reached Jagdalak in the evening with a loss of three men wounded. The enemy's casualties were twenty-five killed and wounded.

Early on the morning of the 29th of December the enemy again began to show in large numbers round the camp at Jagdalak. A detachment of the 51st Light Infantry under Captain Smyth, and 100 men of the 24th Punjab Native Infantry under Captain Stedman, were sent by Colonel Norman to clear some heights to the left, while Captain Money-Simons, of the 24th Punjab Native Infantry, with 100 rifles of his regiment, advanced upon a somewhat similar position to the right. Captain Stedman quickly carried the hill for which he had made, and perceiving that the enemy were in considerable force on the hill against which the right attack was being directed, despatched the party of the 51st Light Infantry to Captain Simons' aid, a further reinforcement of 25 men of the 9th Foot, under Lieut. Ommanney, being at the same time sent up by Colonel Norman. The two guns of the Hazara Mountain Battery, with some dismounted men of the 10th Bengal Lancers acting as escort, were now moved from the camp, whence they had been firing, to a position which enabled them to enfilade the enemy, and went into action with good effect. At 1 o'clock p.m. a heliogram was received by Colonel Norman stating that Lieut.-Colonel Ball Acton was moving up from Pezwan with four guns 11/9, R.A., three companies of the 51st Light Infantry, and six companies of the 45th Native Infantry, and as there were signs that the enemy were changing their position in order to enable them to assail this force when it was making its way through the pass, Major Macnaghten, with 50 Sowars of the 10th Bengal Lancers, was sent to meet Lieut.-Colonel Ball Acton and acquaint him with the position. By 4 p.m. the Pezwan column had reached Norman's right, and fire was opened by the four guns of 11/9, R.A., Lieut. I. D. Wright, of the Battery, being shortly afterwards killed. The enemy now began to retire, but as darkness was coming on, and the baggage of the Pezwan column had not come in, Colonel Norman considered that it would not be safe to withdraw from the hills which covered its passage, and engage his troops in pursuit. About an hour after the last shot had been fired, the baggage and rear-guard arrived safely in camp, and the troops were then withdrawn. Azmatallah Khan, of Lughman, on this day commanded in person, and the number of the enemy engaged was not short of 2,000 men. Their loss was heavy, and their defeat complete. The casualties of Colonel Norman's force were comparatively light, one officer and one man being killed, and three non-commissioned officers and men being wounded.

On the 28th of December Captain Tucker, S.C., who had accompanied Brigadier-General Charles Gough's brigade to Sherpur on political duty, was despatched by Sir Frederick Roberts from Kabul, escorted by one squadron of cavalry, to re-open communications with Jagdalak, a duty which was very efficiently performed. Seh Baba was reached on the 30th, and Jagdalak on the 31st. Azmatallah Khan, already disheartened by his defeat by Colonel Norman, receiving exaggerated reports of the strength of Captain Tucker's escort, and believing that troops were being sent against him from Kabul, on that day quitted the neighbourhood of Jagdalak, and returned with his following to the Lughman Valley. Seh Baba and Lataband were now permanently re-occupied, but the drain of reinforcements towards the advanced posts had considerably weakened the lower portion of the line of communications and the base, and an addition to the strength of the Khyber column became urgently requisite. The crisis, while it lasted, had been severe, and the Government of India had deemed it necessary not only to delay the return home of those battalions which would have embarked for England as soon as their places were filled by the annual reliefs, but also to obtain a regiment for service from the Cape.

With the exception of an unimportant raid made by a party of Shinwaris upon a post near Ali Boghan, no further disturbances occurred along the line of communications before the year closed. Lieut.-Colonel Fryer, 6th Dragoon Guards, was sent out with a few troops of cavalry from Jalalabad on the 26th of December to obtain information concerning this attack; and on the 29th a mixed force under Lieut.-Colonel Mackenzie, 3rd Bengal Cavalry, marched to Barikab, and effecting the surprise of a cluster of villages some ten miles distant, which were supposed to have given shelter to the marauders, secured a number of hostages for the future good behaviour of the inhabitants.

A few days after the withdrawal of the Shutargardan garrison to Kabul at the latter end of October, and the closing of the Ali Khel line of supply, the Hariab Valley was also evacuated, the Peiwar Kotal becoming the most advanced post held by the troops of the Kuram Division. In the meantime Brigadier-General John Watson, V.C., C.B., had arrived and assumed command of the Field Force, *vice* Brigadier-General Gordon, whose services were required in India.

Preparations had for some weeks been in progress for an expedition against the Zaimushts, a tribe occupying territory to the North and East of the British communications between Kuram and Kohat, who, in addition to being guilty of the murder of a British officer while travelling to join his regiment at the front, had recently been committing numerous minor outrages. With the object of inflicting punishment upon them, a column consisting of four guns, 1/8, R.A., two guns No. 1 Mountain Battery, a company of Sappers, detachments of the 1st, 13th, and 18th Bengal Cavalry, the 85th Foot, and detachments of the 8th Foot, the 13th, 20th, and 29th Bengal Native Infantry, and the 4th Punjab Native Infantry, in all about 250 sabres and 2,560 bayonets, under the command of Brigadier-General Tytler, marched from Bulesh Khel on the 8th of December, eleven days' supplies being taken. Destroying a number of towers *en route*, and meeting with little organized opposition, the expeditionary force arrived on the 12th of December at the village of Chinarak, and the same afternoon reconnaissances were pushed forward towards the Zaimusht stronghold of Zawa, General Tytler's objective point. This fastness, deemed by the enemy to be impregnable, consists of a group of five villages, lying in a hollow plateau or basin, approachable from Chinarak through a ravine six or seven miles long, winding between high hills, and narrowing gradually until the cliffs on either side meet at the top.

Leaving a small force under Colonel Rogers, C.B., 20th Native Infantry, to protect the camp at Chinarak, General Tytler marched with the remainder of the troops at daybreak on the 13th of December towards the village of Ragha, situated at the entrance of the ravine. From an elevated plateau immediately in front of this village, the two guns of 1/8, R.A., went into action, at a range of about 800 yards, against detached bodies of the Zaimushts crowning the opposite heights to the right. Under cover of the fire of the guns, a force under Colonel J. H. Gordon, C.B., consisting of four companies of the 85th Foot and four companies of the 29th Native Infantry forming the right attack, advanced against the enemy, and after rapidly carrying the first position, continued to push forward over a succession of ravines and ridges, each of the latter higher than the one preceding it, and all defended by stone breast-works. As soon as Colonel Gordon's attack was sufficiently developed, General Tytler descended from the plateau fronting Ragha, and led the main body of his column, consisting of two guns, 1/8, R.A., two guns No. 1 Mountain Battery, one company of the 85th Light Infantry, the 4th Punjab Infantry, and the 20th Native Infantry, up the ravine. As he advanced, the enemy opened a desultory fire from the rocks above. To drive them from the heights the guns were brought into action on the sides of the gorge, firing across it. A few shells were on each occasion sufficient to dislodge them, and the infantry, occupying the positions they vacated, worked steadily from crest to crest until they reached the village of Bagh, about three miles and a half from Chinarak. Here picquets were thrown out, and the troops bivouacked, communication being maintained with the column on the right. In the meantime Colonel Gordon, after clearing the hills to the right of Ragha, had advanced against a strong position taken up by the enemy on a rocky ridge to the east of the village of Bagh, from which all attempts to dislodge him by a direct attack failed. A flanking movement by the 29th Native Infantry resulted, however, after a fierce hand-to-hand fight, in the capture of a hill from which the ridge could be enfiladed; and the two guns No. 1 Mountain Battery, which had worked round to the left, now coming into action, the opportunity was seized by the 85th Foot and 29th Native Infantry for delivering a simultaneous attack on the enemy's main position. By 4 p.m. the whole of the ridge had been carried. There Gordon's column bivouacked for the night, the enemy having taken up a new position about a mile distant, to the north. Early on the morning of the 14th the advance of both columns was continued, and by 11 a.m Colonel Gordon's force commanded the approaches to Zawa from the eastward, the Zaimushts having retired from that direction as the troops moved forward. Meanwhile the force under General Tytler's immediate command was moving with difficulty along the bed of the ravine, parties of the 4th Punjab Infantry and the 20th Native Infantry crowning the hills to the right, and an effective fire being opened by the two guns, 1/8, R.A., aided by the two guns No. 1 Mountain Battery with Colonel Gordon's force, upon masses of the enemy occupying the heights in front. The column continued to move forward, under a plunging fire and a shower of rocks from above, through the defile opening out upon Zawa itself, the crest of the pass being at length gained with the loss of one British officer and two Sepoys of the 4th Punjab Infantry mortally wounded. Here a brief halt was ordered, after which, all opposition having ceased, the villages were given to the flames. The column then returned unmolested to Bagh; and a few days afterwards the whole force quitted Zaimusht territory and made its way to Thal, the objects of the expedition having been successfully attained.

During the latter half of the month of December the Peiwar Kotal and some other of the advanced posts were threatened by gatherings of the tribes, but these dispersed after news of the British re-occupation of Kabul became circulated, and in the Kuram district, as on the Khyber line, the year closed quietly.

With the exception of occasional operations undertaken in consequence of hostile demonstrations along the Khyber line of communications, the earlier months of the year 1880 were marked by little of military interest in Northern Afghanistan. At the capital the troops were actively engaged in perfecting the defences of the British position, and by the middle of February these were well advanced. All walled enclosures within 1,000 yards of Sherpur were demolished, and amongst other works a good military road was constructed round the walls of the cantonments, while another led to Siah Sang over a strong bridge practicable for artillery. The Ghilzai Chief, Padshah Khan, together with several leading men from Kohistan and Lughman, reassured by the terms of a general amnesty which had been proclaimed, were received in durbar by Sir Frederick Roberts, and shortly afterwards the Sirdar Wali Muhammad was appointed Governor of Kabul, the office of Military Governor, the duties of which had been ably discharged by General Hills, being at the same time abolished. During this period reports were from time to time received of attempts on the part of Muhammad Jan, Mir Butcha—the leader of the force which had sustained defeat at the hands of General Macpherson at Karez Mir—and the Mushk-i-Alam to incite a rising amongst the tribes of Logar, and of renewed disturbances in Koh Daman.

About the middle of March Mr. Lepel Griffin arrived at Kabul on a special political mission; but hitherto there had been no indication of the provisional government of Afghanistan being superseded, though some political interest had begun to attach to the movements of Abdul Rahman Khan, the son of Mir Afzul and a grandson of Dost Muhammad, who had the reputation of being an able soldier, and a man possessed of greater influence than any other chief in Afghanistan.

This prince had taken a prominent part in the hostile operations conducted by his father against Shere Ali; but when the latter had crushed all opposition, Abdul Rahman had retired into exile, and had since been supported by Russian bounty. News was now received that he was collecting men and raising money with a view to prosecuting his claim to the throne of Kabul, and that his emissaries were being well received in Kohistan.

On the 11th of April a number of maliks of Ghazni, Maidan, and Logar, and minor chiefs of the Ghilzai, Wardak, and neighbouring tribes, were induced to come in from the disaffected districts to the capital, and give expression to their views and wishes, and on the 13th of that month they were received in durbar to hear an announcement of the intentions of the British Government with regard to the future settlement of the country. In the course of an address delivered in Persian Mr. Lepel Griffin informed them that the province of Kandahar would be severed from Kabul, and placed under the independent rule of a Barakzai prince; that for the administration of the provinces remaining attached to Kabul the Government was anxious to appoint an Amir who should be strong enough to govern his people and be steadfast in his friendship to the British; that if only these qualifications were secured the wishes of the Afghan people and their tribal chiefs would be recognized, and an Amir of their choice nominated, though no prayer for the restoration of Yakub Khan would be considered, and that when the country should have become settled, and a friendly ruler selected, the British forces would be withdrawn from Afghanistan. The assembled maliks were then dismissed.

In the neighbourhood of the advanced posts on the Khyber line the Ghilzais continued, during the month of January, to give trouble. Masulla Khan, Chief of the Hissarak section of the tribe, in return for a free pardon for past misdemeanours, had sworn to protect the postal and telegraph communications; but injuries to the wires between Pezwan and Jagdalak, and petty raids along the line, were of frequent occurrence, and a punitory expedition into the Hissarak district, as well as into the Lughman Valley, was only delayed until such time as the arrival of reinforcements might enable troops to be spared for the duty.

During the second week of January reports were received of large gatherings of the Mohmand tribe on the north side of the Kabul river opposite Ali Boghan, and in the neighbourhood of Palosi and Reina, opposite Kam Daka. On the 12th of that month a party of the enemy under Moghal Khan of Goshta crossed over to the south side of the river and attacked the post of Ali Boghan, but were beaten off by the garrison, and returned. Early the following morning 100 sabres of the 3rd Bengal Cavalry and 500 rifles drawn from the 12th Foot and 27th and 45th Native Infantry, under Colonel Walker, 12th Foot, were sent from Jalalabad to reinforce the post, and it being intimated that the enemy, to the number of several thousands, were about to cross the river, a second reinforcement, consisting of two guns, D/A, R.H.A., and two troops of the Carabineers, under Lieut.-Colonel Fryer, of that regiment, were also despatched by General Bright to the scene of the threatened attack. On arriving at his destination, Colonel Fryer found the Mohmands drawn up in three bodies, one of which had partly forded the river. Fire was opened upon them by the two guns with such good effect that the gathering almost at once broke up. Meanwhile large numbers of the force which had assembled opposite Kam Daka had crossed the river and blocked the road between Landi Khana and Daka. With the object of dispersing them a column under Brigadier-General Doran, consisting of two guns, 11/9, R.A., 200 bayonets 5th Fusiliers, 200 of the 25th Foot, 30 of the 17th Bengal Cavalry, 32 of the Sappers and Miners, 300 of the 31st Punjab Native Infantry, 300 of the 1st Madras Native Infantry, and 200 of the 4th Madras Native Infantry, marched from Landi Khana before daybreak on the 15th of January, a co-operating column under Colonel Boisragon, consisting of four guns, I/C, R.H.A., 60 sabres of the Carabineers, 50 of the 17th Bengal Cavalry, and 550 bayonets of the 8th and 30th Native Infantry, moving out from Daka some hours later. About 10 a.m. Colonel Boisragon came across masses of the enemy occupying the Gara hills, and under cover of a well-directed fire from the guns, the Native Infantry, led by Captains Webb and Halkett, swarmed up the heights and carried the enemy's position with a rush, the Mohmands retreating towards Kam Daka. About this time the main body of Doran's column, after a very difficult march, arrived upon a large open plain below Kam Daka, across which large numbers of the enemy were flying; and pushing forward rapidly, the troops succeeded in intercepting and inflicting loss upon them. At nightfall both columns moved on to Kam Daka and bivouacked without food and without bedding, the baggage, owing to the extremely difficult nature of the country traversed, not arriving till midday on the 16th. On the 17th the Daka force crossed the Kabul river on rafts, and the following morning burnt the village of Reina, after which it returned, and the two columns made their way back to their respective points of departure.

Towards the end of January the arrival of reinforcements at the base had progressed sufficiently to admit of the concentration between Barikab and Lataband of the troops hitherto distributed along the whole line of communications. General Ross's command was now extended to Daka, the Reserve Division being broken up into three new brigades commanded, respectively, by Brigadier-Generals Roberts, Sale Hill, and Gib, the 1st of which remained at Peshawar, while the 2nd moved up to Jamrud, and the 3rd to Landi Kotal, the latter furnishing posts up to and including Daka and Basawal, and a moveable column at Landi Kotal. Moveable columns at Jalalabad and Gandamak were also furnished by General Bright's division.

The forward concentration of these reinforcements along the line of communications at length set free a sufficient number of troops to enable General Bright to make preparations for the long projected expedition into the Lughman Valley, a fertile tract of country to the west of Jalalabad, watered by the Kabul river. The eastern entrance to the division of the valley lying south of the river is by the Lakai Pass, which crosses the Siah Koh about eight miles to the west of Fort Sale, while the northern division, or Lughman Valley proper, is accessible from the south-east by the Daranta ford. Prior to its improvement by working parties sent out for the purpose from Jalalabad, the Lakai Pass was a mere goat-track, and it had been customary to effect the entrance to the southern division of the valley with laden animals by first fording the river at Daranta, and subsequently re-crossing it by another ford farther to the westward. It was considered that, besides restraining the movements of the freebooter Azmatallah Khan, a force occupying the valley would hold in check the Safis of Tagao on the west, as well as the dwellers in the valley of the Kunar, and Moghul Khan, the hostile chief of Goshta, and farther east, the powerful tribe of the Mohmands, as also the people of Kama, east of the Kunar river.

On the 27th of January the expeditionary force, consisting of two squadrons of the Carabineers, one squadron 17th Bengal Cavalry, two guns, C/3, R.A., two guns, 11/9, R.A., two guns Hazara Mountain Battery, four companies 12th Foot, four companies 25th Foot, two companies Madras Sappers and Miners, 300 bayonets 27th Native Infantry, and the 30th Native Infantry, the whole under the command of Colonel Walker, 12th Foot, and accompanied by General Bright and his staff, marched from Jalalabad, and entering the valley the following day, remained in occupation of it for some seven weeks. During this period the whole district, both south and north of the Kabul river, was thoroughly explored and mapped, reconnaissances being pushed to the borders of Kafiristan. Seventy of the head men of the Valley in all, came in and tendered their submission, and with the exception of a few shots being fired upon one of the reconnoitring parties, the columns into which the force was broken up were permitted to conduct their various operations without molestation. After the objects of the expedition had been accomplished, the valley was evacuated, and by the 16th of March the last of the troops had returned to Jalalabad.

SKETCH OF THE WAR.

By this time an entirely new distribution of the forces in Northern Afghanistan, and of the divisional and brigade commands, had been decided on, and on the 13th of March a general order had been issued notifying the changes which were to take place. The 2nd Division of the Kabul Field Force under Major-General Bright, and the Reserve Division under Major-General Ross, were to be broken up, and the latter absorbed on the line of communications. The force at Kabul was to be divided into two divisions, the 1st to be under the immediate command of Sir Frederick Roberts, the 2nd under that of Major-General Ross. Major-General Bright was to be Inspector-General of the Line of Communications, commanding all troops thereon. The Peshawar District Force lately commanded by Major-General Ross was to be temporarily commanded by Brigadier-General Hankin, 4th Bengal Cavalry. The line of communications was to be divided into three sections, the 1st from Jamrud to Basawal, under Brigadier-General Gib, the 2nd from Barikab to Fort Battye, under Brigadier-General Doran, and the 3rd from Safed Sang to Butkhak, under Brigadier-General Hill. Brigadier-General Arbuthnot was to command the moveable columns at Jalalabad and Safed Sang, and Brigadier-General Roberts a brigade of the 2nd Division at Kabul. The whole force at Kabul was to be henceforth styled the Kabul Field Force, and that on the line of communications, the Khyber Line Force. The movements of the troops consequent upon these changes in the organization, and the equipment of the moveable columns, were now rapidly proceeded with.

During the latter half of the month of March the raiding on convoys and thefts of telegraph wire beyond Jalalabad were carried on with unabated activity, and on the 22nd of that month a British officer, Lieut. Thurlow, 51st Foot, was fired upon and killed by a party of Hissarak Ghilzais while riding between Jagdalak and Jagdalak Kotal. On the 26th a small force under Colonel Hodding, 4th Madras Native Infantry, moved out from Jalalabad to the support of the friendly chief Azim Khan, against a threatened attack by Moghal Khan of Goshta; but the latter took to flight on hearing of the approach of the British troops. The same day the Kugianis and Shinwaris assembled in force in the neighbourhood of Futtehabad, and during the night made a determined attack on Fort Battye, which was held by small detachments of the 4th Bengal Cavalry, 31st Bengal Native Infantry, and 4th Madras Native Infantry, under Major Blenkinsop, of the latter regiment. After a brief hand-to-hand conflict, the enemy were beaten off with considerable loss, the casualties of the garrison being 8 killed, including Lieut. Angelo, 31st Madras Native Infantry, and 19 wounded. In this attack two sections of the Kugiani tribe were concerned. The head men of one section were at once seized, and a fine of 5,000 rupees extracted from them, by Captain Tucker, the Political Officer at Gandamak. The leaders of the other section, the Wazir Kugianis, trusting to the inaccessibility of their position under the Safed Koh, refused, however, to pay a fine of like amount, and with the object of compelling them to do so, the two moveable columns, which were now fully equipped, were set in motion to visit the implicated districts. On the 3rd of April the No. 1 Column, consisting of four guns, I/A, R.H.A., a squadron of the 6th Dragoon Guards, a squadron of the 4th Bengal Cavalry, 400 rifles 12th Foot, the 31st Native Infantry, and the 1st Goorkhas, under the command of Brigadier-General Arbuthnot, commenced its march from Safed Sang, being subsequently joined by General Bright with a company of the Madras Sappers and Miners, and the same day No. 2 Column, consisting of two guns, C/3, R.A., two guns, 11/9, R.A., a squadron of the 6th Dragoon Guards, head-quarters 25th Foot, and the 4th Madras Native Infantry, under the command of Brigadier-General Doran, started from Jalalabad. On the evening of the 5th both columns encamped at Kailagu, on the borders of Wazir territory, and the following day advanced up the valley. Several towers were blown up, and four villages concerned in the recent attack were burnt. On the 6th the Waziris sent in a deputation with promises to pay the fine which had been inflicted, and the object of the expedition being gained, the columns returned. General Doran's column shortly afterwards moved up to Safed Sang in relief of Arbuthnot's force, which was now ordered into the Hissarak Valley to inflict punishment on the Ghilzais under Mazulla Khan for the recent murder of Lieut. Thurlow near Jagdalak, the troops detailed for this duty being 50 sabres 6th Dragoon Guards, 50 sabres 4th Bengal Cavalry, two guns, I/A, R.H.A., two guns, 11/9, R.A., two guns No. 1 Mountain Battery, the 51st Foot, the 8th and 31st Native Infantry, the 1st Goorkhas, one company of Bengal Sappers and Miners, and one company Madras Sappers and Miners. This column, accompanied by General Bright, commenced its march on the 12th of April, and after crossing the Kar Kacha river, came upon a number of the Ghilzais posted on the Nasar ridge. These were quickly dislodged by skirmishing parties of the 51st Foot, 8th Native Infantry, and 1st Goorkhas, covered by the fire of the mountain guns, and the same evening the brigade reached Mazulla Khan's fort, which was found to be deserted. The neighbouring villages, which had been implicated in Lieut. Thurlow's murder, were given to the flames, and the troops bivouacked for the night within a short distance of the fort, a reconnaissance having previously been pushed forward some six miles, and having drawn the fire of the enemy. On the 14th a reconnoitring party of 600 rifles and two mountain guns, under Colonel Ball Acton, 51st Foot, accompanied by General Bright, found the enemy holding a strongly entrenched position on either side of the Awazangani gorge. A brisk encounter ensued, the parties on the west side being forced from behind their breast-works; but it being found that further attempts to carry the position on the eastern side of the gorge would entail a useless loss of life, Colonel Acton was directed to withdraw his force. Though the retirement was ably conducted, it was not effected without loss, one British officer being killed, and two officers and two men wounded. By a counter attack delivered within a mile of the camp, the enemy were dispersed. On the 15th another fort and some villages were destroyed, and the following day the valley was evacuated, the enemy following up the retirement, harrying the rear-guard of the column the whole way, and inflicting on it a loss of six wounded. After the return of the column, the posts on the line were fired into at night, the telegraph wire was constantly cut, and some levies which had been raised to help to protect the road disbanded themselves and disappeared. To remedy this condition of affairs it was found necessary to locate two regiments between Hissarak and Pezwan, and as the position occupied flanked the road, and was a standing menace to Hissarak, its tenure had a good effect.

While the divisions in Northern Afghanistan had been engaged in establishing British supremacy at Kabul and along the Kuram and Khyber lines of communication, the forces in Southern Afghanistan, under Sir Donald Stewart's command, had likewise been discharging their allotted duties in accordance with the general plan of operations. After the receipt of the news of the massacre of the British Envoy at Kabul, all the troops north of Pishin had been immediately recalled to

Kandahar, and by the third week in September, 1879, General Stewart was in a position to carry out the orders he had received to aid the movement of Sir Frederick Roberts on Kabul by demonstrating towards Ghazni. The Sirdar Shere Ali, Governor of Kandahar, had expressed his devotion to the British cause; the Khan of Kalat had offered to render assistance to the Government to the utmost of his power; and the disposition of the Baluch tribes remained friendly.

On the 23rd of September, 1879, a column consisting of two guns, G/4, R.A., two guns, 6/11, R.A., three guns, 11/11, R.A., the 2nd Punjab Cavalry, a wing of the 59th Foot, a wing of the 3rd Goorkhas, and six companies of the 29th Bombay Native Infantry, under the command of Brigadier-General Hughes, marched from Kandahar for Kalat-i-Ghilzai, and on the 25th Major St. John, who accompanied the force on political duty, received a letter from the Afghan Governor of that place, Sirdar Tahir Khan, expressing pleasure at the approach of the British troops, and promising assistance in obtaining supplies. The march was conducted without difficulty, the Sirdar Shere Ali Khan having made excellent arrangements for supplies along the road, and no opposition being met with. Kalat-i-Ghilzai was reached on the 30th of September, the Afghan Governor meeting the British commander outside the fort. Grain was found to be abundant, but forage and fuel were scarce. The surrounding country was apparently quiet, and caravans were arriving unmolested from Kabul.

Leaving the two guns, 6/11, R.A., with two companies of the 59th Foot and four companies of the 29th Bombay Native Infantry, under the command of Colonel Lacy, 59th Foot, to garrison the fortress, General Hughes moved forward with the remainder of his column, on the 3rd of October, to Naorak, and from thence to Tazi, thirty-two miles from Kalat-i-Ghilzai, on the Ghazni road. Here the force remained encamped for some weeks. About the middle of October reports were received that the Taraki Ghilzais, under the leadership of Sahib Jan, a notorious freebooter, were assembling in force at Shah Jui, some twelve miles farther on the Ghazni road, and it was subsequently ascertained that an attack on the camp was meditated. Deciding to anticipate this movement, General Hughes sent out a small force consisting of two squadrons of the 2nd Punjab Cavalry, two guns, 11/11, R.A., 80 rifles 59th Foot, and 100 rifles 29th Bombay Native Infantry, under the command of Colonel Kennedy, 2nd Punjab Cavalry, shortly after midnight on the 23rd of October, to reconnoitre in the direction from whence hostilities were expected, and with the remainder of the brigade himself moved forward early on the morning of the 24th. Arriving within two miles of Shah Jui as day broke, Colonel Kennedy surprised and drove in the enemy's outlying picquets. The alarm being given, the Ghilzais came streaming out of the village to the attack, but being checked by the fire of the mountain guns and the breech-loaders, diverged towards the left in their advance, and sought cover behind some hillocks on a ridge which separates the Tarnak and Argandab valleys. Dislodged from this position by a turning movement of the 59th Foot, they were met in front and taken in flank by the two squadrons of the 2nd Punjab Cavalry. After a fierce hand-to-hand conflict the main body of the enemy turned and fled, and were hotly pursued by the cavalry. A number of Ghazis still remaining posted on the summit of a precipitous-sided hill, the position they had taken up was stormed and brilliantly carried by Captain Sartorius, 59th Foot, with five or six men of his regiment, two standards being captured, and seven of the enemy being bayoneted where they stood. For the gallantry he displayed on this occasion, Captain Sartorius, who was severely wounded with sword-cuts, was awarded the Victoria Cross. Of the enemy, whose strength was estimated at 200 horse and 700 foot, Sahib Jan himself and 41 others were found dead on the field, and many were wounded. Colonel Kennedy's losses on this day were 2 killed and 27 wounded. After the cavalry had returned from the pursuit, the troops rejoined the remainder of the force under General Hughes, which had in the meantime moved up to Shah Jui. Here a halt was made for two days, after which the column made its way back to Kalat-i-Ghilzai. On the 2nd of November General Hughes, in accordance with orders he had received, withdrew the main portion of his column to Kandahar, which was reached on the 8th of that month, a small force consisting of a squadron of the 2nd Punjab Cavalry, two guns, G/4, R.A., two guns, 11/11, R.A., two companies of the 59th Foot, and the 29th Bombay Native Infantry, the whole under Colonel Tanner, of the latter regiment, being left as a winter garrison at Kalat-i-Ghilzai.

The proclamation issued by Sir Frederick Roberts at Kabul, commanding all Afghan authorities to continue their functions and to preserve order, was read in full durbar at Kandahar on the 4th of November, and an announcement was then made that in consideration of the peaceable behaviour of the Duranis and the loyal conduct of the Sirdar Shere Ali Khan, the British Government had been pleased to appoint the latter Governor of the province, including Pusht-i-Rud and Kalat-i-Ghilzai, till the new arrangements alluded to in the proclamation should be made. Both the terms of the proclamation and the confirmation of the Sirdar's authority were well received by the mass of the people.

For some length of time after the return of General Hughes's column from Kalat-i-Ghilzai no further movements of importance were undertaken in Southern Afghanistan, and throughout the winter the country remained in a state of almost unbroken tranquillity. To the north of Kalat-i-Ghilzai, however, complete anarchy prevailed, and at Herat, where the Sirdar Ayub Khan, the brother of Yakub Khan, was endeavouring to consolidate his rule, disturbances were also rife. During the latter part of the reign of his father, Shere Ali, this prince had been living in exile; but on the flight of the Amir from Kabul he had returned to and made himself master of Herat, which he had formerly governed conjointly with his brother Yakub. So early as November, 1879, it was rumoured that two Kabul regiments which were in that city were clamouring to be led against Kandahar, and that they had since mutinied and seized a considerable amount of revenue which had been recently collected. Early in December Ayub actually did move a few miles out of Herat, presumably with the object of advancing on Kandahar, but an opposing faction seized the city and closed the gates upon him, whereupon a conflict ensued between the Kabuli and Herati regiments, ending in the defeat of the latter. This misadventure induced Ayub to abandon for the time his projected expedition.

Towards the end of January, 1880, it was directed that, in view of renewed operations in the spring, the Bengal troops under Sir Donald Stewart's command should be held in readiness to move as a division from Kandahar on Ghazni, and open up communications with Kabul, and that they should be relieved in the Pishin Valley, at Kandahar, and at Kalat-i-Ghilzai by General Phayre's brigade (hitherto employed to the eastward of Quetta), strengthened by reinforcements from Bombay, which, in turn, should be relieved by another Bombay contingent. On the 18th of March it was notified that Major-General Primrose, C.S.I., was to command the

Bombay division of the Kandahar Field Force, and that Brigadier-Generals G. R. S. Burrows and H. F. Brooke were to command brigades of the same, while Brigadier-General Phayre was given command of the line of communications. In the meantime the forward concentration of the Bombay troops was actively pushed on, and by the latter end of March had progressed sufficiently to enable the Bengal division to commence its advance.

On the 29th of March the 1st Infantry Brigade of Sir Donald Stewart's Division, consisting of the 1st Punjab Cavalry, 11/11, R.A., the 2/60th Foot, the 15th Sikhs, and the 25th Punjab Native Infantry, under the command of Brigadier-General Barter, accompanied by Major Clifford, 2nd Punjab Cavalry, as political officer, started from Kandahar, and pursued its march towards Ghazni by way of the Arghastan and Kushkirud valleys; its departure was followed on the 30th by that of the Cavalry Brigade under Brigadier-General Palliser, which was accompanied by divisional head-quarters, and consisted of the 19th Bengal Lancers, A/B, R.H.A., 6/11, R.A., the 19th Punjab Native Infantry, the Engineer Field Park, one company 2/60th, and one company 25th Native Infantry, the route adopted lying through the Tarnak valley; and the Cavalry Brigade was in turn followed on the 31st by the 2nd Infantry Brigade, consisting of the 2nd Punjab Cavalry, G/4, R.A., the 59th Foot, the 3rd Goorkhas, the 2nd Sikhs, and the Ordnance Field Park, under the command of Brigadier-General Hughes.

The head-quarters of the Ghazni Field Force arrived at Kalat-i-Ghilzai on the 6th of April. The following day the march was continued, the Bengal troops forming part of the garrison of that place being absorbed into the division and taken on. Until Shah Jui was reached supplies were plentiful, but beyond that place all villages were found to have been forsaken, the inhabitants having carried off to the hills the bulk of their moveable property, and having either destroyed or buried the grain they could not take away. The marches were long and trying, and the difficulty of procuring supplies was very great. Foraging parties, which were sent out daily, were compelled to proceed long distances, and in many instances had to resort to turning over freshly-dug ground for concealed grain, to prevent themselves from returning empty-handed. Beyond Kalat-i-Ghilzai large bodies of Hazaras, taking advantage of the opportunity afforded by the advance of the division for wreaking vengeance on their hereditary foes, followed in the rear of the Cavalry Brigade, and at night fired many villages and committed some atrocities. No opposition was met with till Ghazni was neared, though for some time previously a hostile gathering had been observed marching on the British right flank at a distance of about eight miles.

On the 19th of April the Field Force moved at dawn from the halting-ground of Mushaki in the following order:—Under the command of Brigadier-General Palliser—300 sabres 19th Bengal Lancers, six guns, A/B, R.H.A., 470 rifles 19th Punjab Native Infantry, Field Force head-quarters, 63 rifles 2/60th Foot, 85 rifles 25th Punjab Native Infantry, 50 sabres 19th Bengal Lancers, and 80 rifles Bengal Sappers and Miners; under the command of Brigadier-General Hughes—436 rifles 59th Foot, 289 rifles 3rd Goorkhas, 367 rifles 2nd Sikh Infantry, six guns, G/4, R.A., four guns, 6/11, R.A., and 349 sabres 2nd Punjab Cavalry; Field Hospitals, Ordnance and Engineer Field Parks, Treasure, Commissariat, and Baggage; under the command of Brigadier-General Barter—443 rifles 2/60th Foot, 570 rifles 15th Sikhs, 380 rifles 25th Punjab Native Infantry, six guns, 11/11, R.A., and 316 sabres

1st Punjab Cavalry. The length of the entire column in order of march was about six miles.

About an hour after the camp had been vacated the enemy were observed in great strength about three miles in advance of the head of the column, holding a position on a range of hills at Ahmad Khel, some twenty-three miles south of Ghazni. In view of an impending attack, General Stewart at once proceeded to make his dispositions. The three batteries of artillery being in column of route upon the road, the infantry of Brigadier-General Hughes's brigade was advanced to the left, in line with the leading battery, one troop of the 19th Bengal Lancers being detached to scout on the left flank, along a range of low hills terminating in the enemy's position; the remainder of the cavalry was formed to the right of the guns in flat country stretching for some three miles as far as the Ghazni river; and the 19th Punjab Native Infantry, the two companies of Sappers and Miners, with the Lieutenant-General's escort—one troop 19th Bengal Lancers, one company 2/60th Rifles, and one company 25th Punjab Native Infantry—were placed in reserve. At 7.45 a.m. orders were sent to Brigadier-General Barter to bring forward one-half of the infantry of his brigade, and to release two squadrons of the 1st Punjab Cavalry to join Palliser, who assumed command of the cavalry.

In this formation the advance was continued at 8 o'clock. When the column was within a mile and a half of the enemy's line, A/B, R.H.A., and G/4, R.A., moved out to positions immediately to the right of the road, 6/11, R.A., coming into action from a knoll 1,500 yards in rear, the infantry under the command of Brigadier-General Hughes (59th Foot, 3rd Goorkhas, and 2nd Sikh Infantry) being formed for attack on the left of the field batteries, while the 19th Punjab Infantry furnished one company as escort to G/4, R.A., and the 19th Bengal Lancers detached a squadron as escort to A/B, R.H.A. At 9 o'clock, and before the intended attack was developed, the crest of the range of hills occupied by the enemy was observed to be swarming with men along a front of nearly two miles, a body of horsemen who formed the enemy's right outflanking the left of the British line. The guns had scarcely opened fire when an enormous mass of the Afghan troops, with standards flying, formed on the crest of the hills, a considerable number of horsemen riding along the ridge with the intention of sweeping to the rear of the British line to attack the baggage. From the central mass out rushed successive waves of swordsmen on foot, stretching out right and left, and seeking to envelope General Stewart's position. The horsemen succeeded in turning the British left, which had been recently strengthened by a squadron of the 19th Bengal Lancers, and pouring down two ravines, struck the troopers before they could charge, forcing back the leading squadron on to a knoll occupied by the head-quarters staff. The 3rd Goorkhas, the infantry of the left, formed rallying squares, and by a withering fire temporarily stemmed the rush of the oncoming horde; but the situation was critical, as the Lancers could not be rallied till they had passed to the rear of the right of the line of infantry, which itself was hotly pressed, and beginning to give way.

The onslaught of fanatic swordsmen was at this time so rapid, and was pushed with such desperation, that during the few minutes which followed it became necessary to place every man of the reserve in the firing line—the two Sapper companies with a half battalion of the 19th Punjab Infantry reinforcing the left, while the other half battalion of the 19th, with the two companies serving on the Lieutenant-

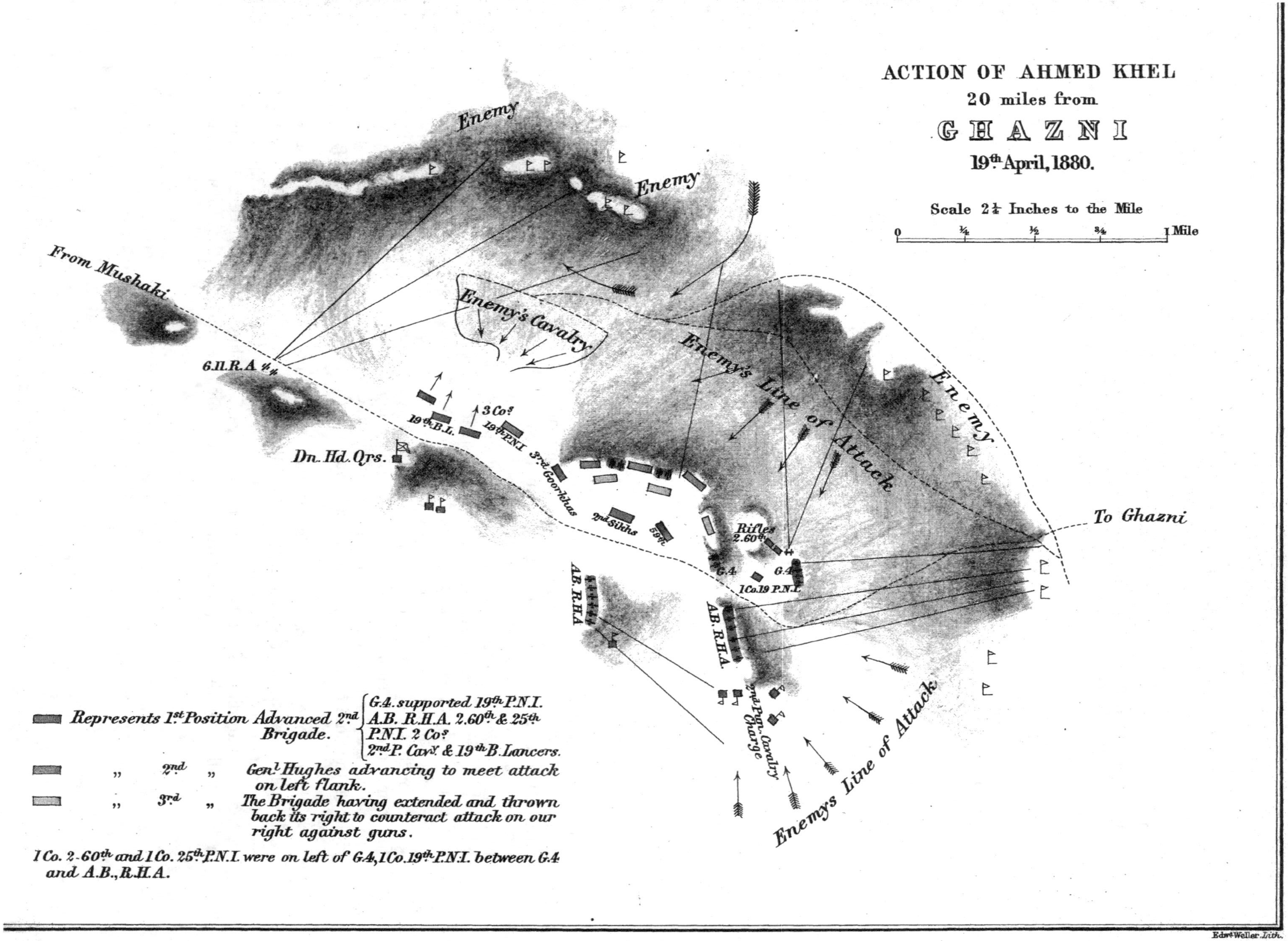

ACTION OF AHMED KHEL
20 miles from
GHAZNI
19th April, 1880.

Scale 2¼ Inches to the Mile

From Mushaki

To Ghazni

Enemy

Enemy's Line of Attack

Enemy's Cavalry

Enemy's Line of Attack

2nd Pun. Cavalry Charge

Dn. Hd. Qrs.

6 II R.A.

19th B.I.

3 Cos

1st P.N.I. 3rd Goorkhas

2nd Sikhs

59th

G.4.

Rifles 2.60th

1 Co.19 P.N.I.

A.B. R.H.A.

A.B. R.H.A.

■ Represents 1st Position Advanced 2nd Brigade.
„ „ 2nd „ { G.4. supported 19th P.N.I. / A.B. R.H.A. 2.60th & 25th / P.N.I. 2 Cos / 2nd P. Cav^y & 19th B. Lancers.
„ „ 3rd „ Genl Hughes advancing to meet attack on left flank.
„ „ „ The Brigade having extended and thrown back its right to counteract attack on our right against guns.

1 Co. 2. 60th and 1 Co. 25th P.N.I were on left of G.4, 1Co. 19th P.N.I. between G.4 and A.B., R.H.A.

London: Sampson Low, Marston, Searle, & Rivington.

Edwd Weller, lith.

General's escort, supported the guns on their left. The enemy, however, continued to push on, and approached within a few yards of the guns. The whole of their case-shot being expended, both batteries, the guns of which were served with the utmost gallantry till the last, were withdrawn a distance of two hundred yards, two of the 9-pounders of G/4 being detached to the left centre, where they were shortly afterwards followed by the remainder of the battery. The infantry of the right was at the same time forced back by sheer weight of numbers, but took up a fresh position with its right thrown back to meet any further attack on the guns. Two troops of the 2nd Punjab Cavalry now relieved the escort of A/B, R.H.A., and the remainder of the regiment moved to the left of the line, the 19th Bengal Lancers and two squadrons of the 1st Punjab Cavalry being pushed to the right, towards the river, while some well-directed shell from the 40-pounders of 6/11, R.A., checked the forward movement of the enemy's horsemen round the British left flank.

The fighting lasted till 10 o'clock, the troops under General Barter coming up towards the close of the engagement and reinforcing the British left centre. At that hour the order to cease fire was sounded, the enemy's attack having been effectually defeated, their entire body spreading broadcast over the country, and considerable numbers of them being cut up by the cavalry on the right. The pursuit was, however, checked by the necessity for retaining the greater portion of that arm to protect the large parks and baggage-train formed in the rear of the column.

The enemy's strength was estimated at 1,000 horse and from 12,000 to 15,000 foot. More than a thousand of their dead were counted on the field, and their total loss was computed to have been between 2,000 and 3,000. The casualties of the British force during the engagement were 17 killed and 124 wounded. Testimony is borne by General Stewart, in his report of the action, to the admirable spirit which animated all ranks under very trying conditions.

After halting for two hours, during which time the dead were buried and the wounded attended to, the entire force moved forward and passed over the enemy's position, completing a march of seventeen miles to Nani, where camp was pitched. The following day the advanced cavalry entered Ghazni without opposition, and on the 21st the whole Division moved up and encamped to the north-east of that place. Here the force remained halted for three days, communication being opened with a column under Major-General Ross, which had been sent out from Kabul for the purpose.

On the 22nd of April the presence of a force of the enemy occupying a position on some high ground about six miles to the south-east of Sir Donald Stewart's camp, was reported by the cavalry patrols, and an hour before daybreak on the 23rd a column consisting of A/B, R.H.A., 11/11, R.A., 525 rifles 2/60th Foot, 578 rifles 15th Sikhs, 458 rifles 25th Punjab Native Infantry, and 424 rifles 2nd Sikhs, under the command of Brigadier-General Palliser, and 647 sabres 1st and 2nd Punjab Cavalry, under Brigadier-General Barter, were sent out to dislodge them. On nearing the position the enemy had taken up, General Palliser found it too strong, however, to attack with the troops at his disposal, and heliographed to that effect to Field Force head-quarters. General Stewart at once reinforced Palliser with a half battalion of the 59th Foot and six companies of the 3rd Goorkhas, and shortly afterwards himself moved forward with G/4, R.A., a half battalion 59th

Foot, a half battalion 19th Punjab Native Infantry, and the 19th Bengal Lancers, leaving Major Tillard, R.A., with 6/11, R.A., two companies of Sappers and Miners, and two companies of the 3rd Goorkhas, together with the usual standing guards, to protect the camp. General Palliser had meanwhile taken up a position on a ridge some 2,500 yards short of the villages of Arzu and Shatez, which were held by the enemy. Here General Stewart arrived at 11 o'clock, and resuming command of the entire force, formed the troops for the attack, the horse artillery and cavalry, with the 1st Infantry Brigade, being disposed on the right, from which side the attack on the village of Shatez was delivered, the remainder of the troops moving on Arzu from the left, and taking Shatez in flank. The advance was ordered at 11.40, and by 12.30 all was over, the enemy, after slight resistance, having fled precipitately, pursued by the cavalry and horse artillery. Four hundred of their number were computed to have been killed and wounded, while the casualties of the Field Force were only two killed and eight wounded.

On the 28th of April Sir Donald Stewart took leave of the Division, and proceeded by way of Shekabad to Kabul to assume supreme command of the forces in Northern Afghanistan. The Ghazni Field Force, shortly afterwards reconstituted as the 3rd Division Kabul Field Force, then entered the Logar Valley, and remained in occupation of that district, under the commands, successively, of Brigadier-General Hughes and Major-General Hills, C.B., V.C., till the troops were eventually concentrated at Kabul, prior to the evacuation of Northern Afghanistan.

Meanwhile Major-General Ross, C.B., who had arrived at Kabul and assumed command of the 2nd Division, had started on the 16th of April for Shekabad, with a force consisting of one squadron 9th Lancers, the 3rd Bengal Cavalry, two squadrons 3rd Punjab Cavalry, four guns, 6/8, R.A., No. 4 Mountain Battery, the 2/9th Foot, the 23rd Pioneers, the 24th Native Infantry, the 4th Goorkhas, and a company of Sappers to join hands with the Division advancing from Kandahar, and to open up the roads leading from the grain-growing districts towards Kabul. After this column had entered the Maidan Valley, and was engaged in collecting supplies and reconnoitring the surrounding country, reports were received that serious opposition to its further progress was likely to be offered from the direction of Logar. Considering a counter-movement in anticipation of this threatened hostile action desirable, Sir Frederick Roberts sent out from Sherpur, on the 20th of April, a small force consisting of the Guides Cavalry, two guns, F/A, R.H.A., a wing of the 92nd Highlanders, and the Guides Infantry, in all 873 men, under the command of Colonel Jenkins, C.B., with orders to march towards Logar and keep the tribes of the district in check.

On the 21st of April Colonel Jenkins encamped near the village of Chihildaltaran, beyond Charasiab, and there learned that Muhammad Hassan Khan, the ex-Governor of Jalalabad, with a large following, had arrived in the neighbourhood with the intention of attacking General Ross's column. Nothing of importance occurred, however, till the night of the 24th, when intelligence was received that Muhammad Hassan had moved forward to a position on the Logar river, within seven miles of the camp. Information to this effect was sent back to Sherpur, and at the same time Colonel Jenkins ordered his infantry under arms, and sent a party of the Guides Cavalry down the Logar road, in the direction from which an attack was to be expected. As day broke, the enemy were seen to be advancing in force

SKETCH OF THE WAR.

over the hills to the south-east of the camp, and also from the westward, while the party of Guides cavalry, which had been sent out a short time previously, were already engaged with and retiring slowly before a third body moving forward along the Logar road. Without hurry or confusion, the tents were at once struck and the baggage parked under a small hill in rear of the site of the camp, where it was protected by a half company of the 92nd Highlanders and a company of the Guides; detachments of the latter regiment were also sent to occupy two small ruined forts close at hand, one of which afforded shelter to a troop of the cavalry; and at the same time two companies of the 92nd, under Captain Robertson, were extended in line with two companies of the Guides, under Captain Battye, to cover the front, while three companies of the Guides, under Captain Hammond, covered the left flank, and the two guns, F/A, R.H.A., under Lieut. Wodehouse, went into action a few hundred yards to the rear.

The enemy, at first about 3,000 strong, but afterwards reinforced, advanced against the front and both flanks of Colonel Jenkins's position simultaneously, pouring in a heavy fire from their Martinis and Sniders, which was replied to with good effect by the British Infantry and the guns. As soon as the sun was sufficiently high, an intimation that the camp was attacked was sent by heliograph to the station on the Shahr Darwaza, and a reply was shortly afterwards received to the effect that Brigadier-General Macpherson had started with reinforcements from Sherpur. An unequal fight was sustained by Colonel Jenkins till about 1.30 p.m. During this period the casualties amongst the horses of the artillery were so many that the guns had to be withdrawn 400 yards; but in consequence of the small number of the infantry available for stemming a sudden onslaught, it was necessary to keep the Guides Cavalry, whose horses suffered equally severely, exposed to fire throughout the day. As the attack developed, the enemy brought up their standards to within one and two hundred yards of the troops extended on the front and right; but the fire of the British infantry was so effective that they could not be induced by their leaders to make an effective charge.

About 1.30 p.m. General Macpherson, who had left two companies of the 45th Sikhs *en route* to hold the Sang-i-Nawishta pass, and thus secure the road to Kabul, arrived upon the scene with one troop 3rd Punjab Cavalry, two guns, 6/8, R.A., four guns No. 2 Mountain Battery, 278 rifles 92nd Highlanders, six companies 45th Sikhs, and 104 rifles 2nd Goorkhas, and at once made preparations for attacking the enemy's left, shortly afterwards detaching three companies of the 45th Sikhs, under Lieut.-Colonel Armstrong, to reinforce Colonel Jenkins, who, it was arranged, should deliver a counter-attack on the enemy's centre as soon as the operations on the right were developed. The two companies of the 2nd Goorkhas, under Captain Hill, and the head-quarters wing of the 92nd Highlanders, under Lieut.-Colonel Parker, covered by the fire of the four guns of the Mountain Battery under Major Swinley, moved forward at the double, and quickly became engaged, some rising ground upon which was planted the enemy's principal standard having been indicated to Captain Hill as his objective. In spite of the opposition offered to their further advance, the companies continued steadily to push forward, the guns of Swinley's battery, and the horse-artillery guns under Lieut. Wodehouse, at the same time making excellent practice. In a short time the Highlanders were able to enfilade the enemy, and the Goorkhas, supported on their extreme right by a detachment of the 45th Sikhs, had forced their way to within 400 yards of their objective point. General Macpherson now directed Captain Hill to assault the position without firing, and responding to the order with a cheer, the Goorkhas sprang forward to the attack, and captured the standard. This was the signal for a general falling back of the Afghans. A fire, however, being opened by them from the orchards of Charasiab, these were at once rushed, and the enemy, after suffering severely, abandoned the whole of the left of their position, making for the hills to the north under a telling fire from the guns. At this juncture Colonel Jenkins, finding their centre exposed, delivered the left attack with great spirit, the infantry carrying a position which had been taken up by the enemy on a high hill in front, and the cavalry and horse artillery, let loose in pursuit, following the flying foe for four miles in the direction of Logar. While the pursuit on the left was being continued, Macpherson's infantry cleared the hills to the north and west, until not a man was visible. At 4 p.m. the whole force re-formed on the site of the camp, and commenced their return march to Sherpur. The enemy's loss was estimated at 200 killed, while that of the united columns under Macpherson was 4 killed and 34 wounded.

In the meantime General Ross, on the 20th of April, had succeeded in opening heliographic communication with the advance guard of the Ghazni Field Force, and had received intelligence of Sir Donald Stewart's victory at Ahmad Khel, which was forwarded on by special messenger to Sherpur. On the 23rd the column had reached Zaidabad and halted, no serious opposition having been thus far met with, though reconnoitring parties had been occasionally fired upon, and numbers of the tribesmen had been observed during the last march gathering in the direction of Langar. On the 24th of April a company of Sappers employed in improving the road near Shekabad was threatened by a party of the enemy, and during the night numerous beacon-fires were observed on some high ridges distant four or five miles north-west of the camp, where, it was subsequently ascertained, large bodies of the tribesmen had assembled under the leadership of Abdul Gafur, of Langar, and Atkai Biland, of Rustam Khel. Early on the morning of the 25th groups of men with several standards became visible on these spurs and ridges, and later in the day, General Ross's picquets were fired upon. At 11 a.m. a force consisting of two guns of the Hazara Mountain Battery, two companies of the 2/9th Foot, a wing of the 4th Goorkhas, and a troop of the 3rd Bengal Cavalry, under the command of Lieut.-Colonel Rowcroft, 4th Goorkhas, was sent out from camp to dislodge the enemy from the position they had taken up, and at the same time another party, consisting of three companies of the 24th Punjab Native Infantry and a half troop of the 3rd Punjab Cavalry, under the command of Major Combe, Deputy Assistant Quartermaster-General, was directed to proceed along the Shekabad road and operate on the enemy's left as soon as the direct attack should have developed itself. Colonel Rowcroft's party engaged the enemy at 11.45 a.m., and though they clung tenaciously to several strong positions, and the ground was rugged and difficult, they were driven from point to point till they retired to positions on the ridge so distant that further pursuit was considered useless. At 1 p.m. two companies of the 24th Native Infantry were despatched to Rowcroft's support, while two other companies of that regiment, and two guns, 6/8, R.A., were sent out to hold a gorge some miles to the west of the camp, in the neighbourhood of which parties of the tribesmen were assembling with the apparent intention of cutting off or harassing his retreat. In the meantime the Shekabad party, under Major Combe, had turned into the hills and attacked the enemy on the right, and soon succeeded in driving them back to the higher ridges. While these operations were progressing, two more guns of 6/8, R.A., and the remaining wing of the 4th Goorkhas, had been sent out to ascend the slopes of a high hill lying to the west of the camp, and from this position they succeeded—aided by the fire of the guns from the valley below—in dispersing several groups of the tribesmen who had gathered in this direction on a ridge leading from the gorge already indicated towards the camp. The enemy having got beyond range, the troops were gradually withdrawn, no attempt being made to follow them up; and by 6 p.m. all had returned to camp. The enemy's total strength was computed to have been between 1,200 and 1,500 men; but many of these being on peaks and ridges well out of range, were never engaged. Forty of their dead were counted on the ground, and their loss was believed to have amounted to 150 killed and wounded. The casualties of General Ross's column on this day were singularly small, one Goorkha Sepoy only having been killed, and four other men slightly wounded.

The night of the 25th passed quietly, but early the following morning intimation was received that the enemy were again assembling on the ridges beyond the high hill to the west of the camp. Two guns of the Hazara Mountain Battery were at once sent out in that direction to occupy the hill, whilst Brigadier-General Charles Gough moved rapidly up the valley beyond it with two guns, 6/8, R.A., a wing of the 2/9th Foot, and a wing of the 23rd Pioneers. A few well-directed shells from the guns soon dispersed the enemy, who retired along the ridge bordering the valley on the south towards the pass at its western end. Crossing the gorge, they then ascended a rocky slope leading towards a high peak on its north side. From this position also they were quickly dislodged by the fire of the guns, and the acclivity was shortly afterwards occupied by Gough's force without opposition. The enemy having now completely dispersed, the troops returned to camp. The practice of the guns had been very accurate, and nine dead bodies and several wounded were found amongst the hills. The following day it was found that Abdul Gafur had decamped from Langar.

On the 27th of April a junction was effected between General Ross's column and the Ghazni Field Force, after which, while the latter proceeded into the Logar Valley, the former, accompanied by Sir Donald Stewart, made its way back to Kabul, where it arrived on the 2nd of May, a small force under Brigadier-General Charles Gough having been detached *en route* to destroy Abdul Gafur's forts in Langar.

For some time after the crushing defeat of the enemy by Sir Donald Stewart at Ahmad Khel, and the successes attending the operations of the columns under Generals Ross and Macpherson, affairs in the immediate vicinity of Kabul remained comparatively quiet, and though disturbances continued to occur in the outlying districts, and it was found necessary on occasions to occupy them with British columns in order to restore tranquillity, this result was effected, generally speaking, with little or no bloodshed. The conviction of their powerlessness to expel the British troops from the country by force appeared to be gradually gaining ground amongst the people of Northern Afghanistan, and by the end of June affairs seemed generally to point to a speedy pacification and the consequent evacuation of Kabul, in accordance with the terms of Mr. Lepel Griffin's speech of the 12th of April.

Early in May Sir Frederick Roberts started from Sherpur for the Logar

Valley with a column of all arms under the immediate command of Brigadier-General Baker, with the object of easing the pressure on supplies, and of opening communications with the Ghazni Field Force. After visiting General Hughes in camp and remaining in and about Logar for some three weeks, the Lieutenant-General returned with a portion of the column to the capital, the main body moving to Maidan, where General Baker continued to collect supplies and make explorations of the district till the 8th of June.

About a week after the return of General Baker's column to Kabul, Brigadier-General Charles Gough moved out with his brigade towards Pughman. No opposition was met with by this force till the 20th of June, on which day Colonel Norman, 24th Native Infantry, was sent into the Maidan district with a few cavalry and infantry details to disperse a gathering in the direction of Argandab, and a slight skirmish ensued in the neighbourhood of the Kotal-i-Takht between a detached party of the 3rd Bengal Cavalry under Lieut. Lumsden—afterwards reinforced from Gough's camp by another squadron of the 3rd Bengal Cavalry, a wing of the 4th Goorkhas, and two guns of No. 4 Mountain Battery, under Colonel Mackenzie, 3rd Bengal Cavalry—and a large body of the enemy who appeared from the direction of Ghazni. On the arrival of the reinforcements, these were quickly put to flight. Again on the 29th of June a small detached force under Colonel Mackenzie encountered and drove off from Sofian and Baba-Kuch-Kar about 200 of the tribesmen who had some days previously fired upon a reconnoitring party.

At the latter end of June the late Ghazni Field Force—now reconstituted as the 3rd Division Northern Afghanistan Field Force, and commanded by Major-General Hills, C.B., V.C.—moved up from Hissarak to Charasiab, and from thence, on the 30th of that month, to Zargunshahr. Here information was received that some 1,000 or 1,500 Zermuttis were assembled at the village of Patkao Shana, under the command of Sirdar Hassan Khan, and were in hourly expectation of reinforcements reaching them under Muhammad Jan. To operate against this gathering Brigadier-General Palliser started from camp at 3.30 a.m. on the 1st of July with 226 sabres 1st Punjab Cavalry, 155 sabres 2nd Punjab Cavalry, and 183 sabres 19th Bengal Lancers; but on nearing Patkao Shana he found that the enemy had received timely notice of his approach, and were in full retreat. Ascertaining, however, the direction of their retirement, and hearing that the greater number of them had only proceeded a short distance, General Palliser left a squadron of the 2nd Punjab Cavalry under Captain Broome to watch the village, and pressed on with the rest of the brigade. After advancing about three miles, the squadrons succeeded in overtaking some 1,500 of the Zermuttis. This force General Palliser at once attacked, and with such vigour that, although the enemy offered resistance wherever the nature of the ground favoured them, they were again and again broken by the cavalry, and by 9.30 a.m. had disappeared, utterly demoralized, amongst the high hills opposite Altimor, leaving 200 dead and wounded behind them in their retreat. The casualties of Palliser's force in this engagement were 3 killed and 29 wounded, together with 8 horses killed and 25 wounded. The day's work was long and trying, the cavalry covering nearly forty miles of country before they returned to camp.

The political events in Northern Afghanistan during this period were highly important. After the capture of Kabul and the infliction of punishment on the perpetrators of the crime which had been committed there, the British Government had been anxious to withdraw the troops as soon as possible from all points beyond the frontier settled by the treaty of Gandamak, and had only refrained from doing so for two reasons : firstly, because of the continued disturbances in the vicinity of the capital, and the presence of armed gatherings in the neighbourhood of Ghazni ; and secondly, in consequence of the inability of the Kabul Sirdars to agree amongst themselves on the selection of a ruler strong enough to maintain order after the evacuation. With the successes attending the operations of the armies under Sir Frederick Roberts and Sir Donald Stewart, the first of these objections had ceased to exist ; and with the appearance of Abdul Rahman as a candidate for the throne of Kabul, together with the probability of his being supported by at least a majority of the population, the second objection seemed likely also to be speedily removed. Under these circumstances it was definitely decided to withdraw the troops from Kabul before the month of October ; and conformably with this decision Mr. Lepel Griffin was directed to depute a mission to Afghan Turkestan to invite Abdul Rahman to declare his intentions, and to inform him that the Government were disposed to consider favourably any representations that he might have to make. The invitation was not, however, to be given, as a preliminary to forming any alliance with him, and thus contracting fresh liabilities, but chiefly in order that, by transferring the administration to a competent ruler, the Government might be spared the necessity of leaving the country in a state of anarchy. Two Native gentlemen attached to Mr. Griffin's staff were accordingly despatched from Kabul to Turkestan on the 2nd of May, 1880, with a brief written communication addressed to the Sirdar, the contents of which were to be supplemented orally. On arriving at their destination they were received with every manifestation of welcome ; but a letter written by Abdul Rahman in response to the invitation which had been addressed to him contained nothing beyond general expressions of friendship and hope for support, and it shortly afterwards became evident that he was merely temporizing. In the meantime the purport of the communications which were passing became known throughout Northern Afghanistan. The general uncertainty as to the result of this correspondence, the rumours prevalent regarding the Sirdar's real dispositions and plans, and the jealousies of opposing factions, caused much fermentation among the people ; while this uneasiness was increased and extended by letters, purporting to emanate from Abdul Rahman, and bidding the tribes to be armed and ready, which circulated through the country. Some of these letters were intercepted and brought to Kabul, and the Sirdar was simultaneously reported to be in close correspondence with Muhammad Jan, who was known to be levying forces with hostile intentions. A peremptory letter was now addressed to him by the chief Political Officer, desiring him to proceed to Kabul and take immediate measures for controlling the tribal gatherings ; and though the prospect of a solution of the difficulties which had arisen appeared at one time slight, the Sirdar was induced to cross the Hindu Kush with friendly intentions, and the negotiations with him were at length carried by Mr. Griffin to a successful issue. On the 20th of July Abdul Rahman reached Charikar. A large number of leading chiefs and other personages, including Mushk-i-Alam and some of the principal men of the Ghilzai and Wardak tribes having signified their adhesion to his cause, and many of them having gone to meet him, Sir Donald Stewart and Mr. Griffin considered that, under the circumstances, it was advisable that his public recognition as Amir should no longer be deferred ; and the Sirdar himself, who was consulted, expressed much satisfaction at the proposal. On the 22nd of July, accordingly, an imposing durbar, which was attended by a large number of chiefs and other influential personages, and by a deputation from Charikar, was held at the capital; and Abdul Rahman was then and there formally and publicly recognized on the part of Her Majesty's Government as Amir of Kabul.

During the spring and early summer of 1880 the general restlessness of the tribes occupying territory contiguous to the Khyber line of communications continued to prevail after the return of the moveable columns from the expeditions against the Wazir Kugianis and Hissarak Ghilzais: isolated posts were fired into at night, rumours of projected attacks were frequent, and raids on convoys and thefts of telegraph wire were of almost daily occurrence; and in order to quell disturbances and disperse gatherings it was found necessary to despatch expeditionary columns of considerable strength into the districts of Besud, Kama, Mazina, and Lughman.

At the latter end of April rumours of a projected attack on Seh Baba by the Khan of Tagao caused that post to be considerably strengthened, and on the 25th of the same month reports of hostile movements in Tezin led to the concentration of Arbuthnot's column at Jagdalak. During the night of the 5th of May a raid was made from the Lughman Valley on a herd of commissariat cattle collected at Jalalabad, a large number of which were driven off. The 5th Foot, under Colonel Rowland, were at once sent out in pursuit of the marauders, and after a very rapid march succeeded in coming up with, and inflicting some loss upon, their rear-guard, in the Daranta pass; the cattle, however, were not recovered.

Reports being received during the second week in May that the district of Besud, on the north side of the Kabul river, opposite Jalalabad, was being threatened by a large gathering of Safis and men from the Kunar Valley under the leadership of Mulla Khalil, a force consisting of two guns No. 1 Mountain Battery, 200 rifles 5th Fusiliers, 200 rifles 12th Foot, two troops Central India Horse, and 200 rifles 1st and 4th Madras Native Infantry, crossed over to the left bank on the 14th, 15th, and 18th of that month, and bivouacked in the fort of Dabila Kila. At daybreak on the 19th of May this force, under the command of Brigadier-General Doran, moved out to the northward, and shortly afterwards came upon upwards of 2,000 of the enemy, who had débouched from the hills, and were about to seize on the Besud villages. General Doran's troops, under the immediate command of Colonel Dawson, Madras Native Infantry, the senior regimental officer present, at once formed in order of attack—the 5th Fusiliers on the left, the 1st Madras Native Infantry in the centre, and the 12th Foot on the right, while the cavalry were drawn up to the left rear of the Fusiliers, and the guns were held in reserve in rear of the centre of the line. In this formation the column advanced until within 900 yards of the enemy's centre, and 600 yards from a fort on which their right rested, a heavy fire being opened on both sides, and the mountain guns entering into action. Unable for long to face the deadly fusilade which was directed upon them, the main body of the enemy fell back upon the village of Beninga; but upon a few shells being thrown into their midst, they rapidly quitted this position and retreated to rising ground in their rear, there making a temporary stand until the infantry again moved forward to attack them, when they fled in disorder towards the Kunar Valley. In the meantime, on the first position being abandoned, the Central India Horse, under Lieut.-Colonel Martin, had swept forward between the fort and the hills on which the second position had been taken up, and succeeded in rendering a good account of the enemy in this part of the field. Some of the defenders of the fort, seeing their retreat cut off, stood their ground to the last. The guns having been brought up, and several shots fired, a number of the enemy made a sortie, but were cut down to a man by a small party of the 5th Fusiliers under Colonel Rowland. Immediately afterwards Captain Kilgour and Colour-Sergeant Wood, of that regiment, gallantly charged into the building, and after a desperate conflict disposed of the remainder, five in number, who still stood their ground. The pursuit was carried on by the cavalry to the banks of the Kunar river, several of the Safis being forced into its waters, and many slain. In this affair 70 of the enemy were killed, and a large number wounded, while the casualties of General Doran's force were only seven wounded, one of whom subsequently died. After remaining in the district for the next three days, and destroying the forts of Abdul Khel and Kila Banaras Khan, the troops re-crossed the Kabul river and returned to Jalalabad—an operation which, in consequence of the river being at high flood, was attended with some loss, one Sepoy and four horses being swept away and drowned.

While the force under Brigadier-General Doran was engaged in operating against the Safis in Besud, a moveable column, under the command of Brigadier-General Gib, consisting of one squadron 8th Hussars, one squadron 5th Bengal Cavalry, two guns, L/5, R.A., 400 rifles 14th Foot, and 400 rifles 32nd Pioneers, had marched out from Pesh Bolak on the 18th of May to break up a large gathering of the Shinwaris under the leadership of Ghulam Ahmad. On the 20th of that month General Gib encountered and defeated with heavy loss between 2,000 and 3,000 of the enemy, who occupied an entrenched position on high ground in the neighbourhood of Mazina. In this action more than 100 of the enemy were computed to have been slain.

On the 31st of May the moveable column under Brigadier-General Arbuthnot, consisting of one squadron 6th Dragoon Guards, one squadron 4th Bengal Cavalry, two guns, 11/9, R.A., the 51st Foot, the 1st Goorkhas, and the 31st Punjab Native Infantry, in all 1,605 rifles and 226 sabres, marched from Jagdalak for Pezwan, to inflict punishment on the Mulla Fakir for several recently-committed outrages. After the column had started, however, it was found necessary to change its destination for the Lughman Valley, in consequence of the threatening attitude assumed by the tribes under Azmatallah Khan. One of the objects of the expedition was to bring away the Governor of the district, Azaf Khan, who was at the time in a very anomalous position—nominally the servant of the British Government, but unsupported, and quite unable to hold his own. After proceeding to a place opposite the fortified village of Sali Kali, the bulk of the force crossed the Kabul river by raft, on the 8th and 9th of June, into the Upper Lughman, Azaf Khan coming into camp on the 8th, and remaining with Captain Tucker, the Political Officer accompanying the column. The next two days were devoted to destroying the forts of the principal offenders, seizing cattle, and cutting the green crops for fodder, this being the only possible method of realizing a fine, as the inhabitants had all disappeared. On the morning of the 11th of June the troops commenced to re-cross the river, picquets being posted, for the purpose of covering the embarkation, on a semicircle of low mounds forming a natural *tête de pont* to the ferry which had been selected. By evening the whole of the column, with the exception of some 60 or 70 men, had reached the right bank of the river, and the picquets were withdrawn. Just as they were about to embark, however, the position they had hitherto held was suddenly occupied by the Lughmanis, who opened a heavy fire upon them. During the next half-hour the situation of the detached party on the north side of the river was a critical one; but General Arbuthnot eventually succeeded, by the exercise of admirable coolness and fertility of resource, in getting them across without mishap, the Brigadier himself being the last to quit the shore.

While preparations were being made for General Arbuthnot's expedition into the Lughman Valley, one squadron Central India Horse, two guns, C/3, R.A., two guns, L/5, R.A., two guns No. 1 Mountain Battery, and detachments of the 1/5th and 2/14th Foot, 9th and 32nd Bengal Native Infantry, and 14th and 15th Madras Native Infantry were concentrating from Jalalabad and Pesh Bolak at Girdi Kas for an expedition into Kama, the object of which was to inflict punishment on Mulla Khalil and other refractory chiefs who had assembled in that district. On the 2nd of June General Doran arrived and assumed command of the troops, and on the 3rd and 4th of that month the main body of the force crossed over to the north side of the Kabul river, which was at the time in high flood. On the approach of the troops, Mulla Khalil and his following took to flight, and after several strong forts had been blown up, and a cavalry reconnaissance conducted into Goshta, the column re-crossed the river without having encountered any opposition, and was broken up.

After the return of the Lughman Valley expeditionary force, the raiding on the line between Pezwan and Jagdalak was continued with unabated vigour. On the 29th of June, four men were killed and two wounded while on convoy duty, and the following day an officer of the 51st Foot was wounded. At the instigation of Captain Tucker, the Political Officer in charge of this section of the line, an expedition was organized with the object of retaliating on the perpetrator of these outrages, a Ghilzai chief who had established himself at Jokan, a village near Hissarak, and who had hitherto enjoyed immunity from punishment for his misdemeanours. At 11 p.m. on the 4th of July a force consisting of 40 sabres 4th Bengal Cavalry, two guns, 11/9, R.A., 200 rifles 1/25th Foot, 196 rifles 51st Foot, and 94 rifles 31st Native Infantry, under the command of Colonel Ball Acton, 51st Foot, moved out from Pezwan towards Ishpan, south of the Surkhab river, there to co-operate with two squadrons of the Carabineers under Lieut.-Colonel Fryer, which were ordered to advance simultaneously from Safed Sang. As the column neared Jokan, the enemy's outlook picquets sprang up and disappeared in the darkness, and the neighbouring village of Nargusai was reached at daybreak without a shot having been fired. Here the Pezwan and Safed Sang parties effected a junction, and shortly afterwards the enemy were found posted in strength on a ridge a little to the east of the village. After a few shots had been fired, the western part of the enemy's position was carried with a rush by the 1/25th Foot, and shortly afterwards the whole of the ground which had been occupied was cleared. Nargusai and two small adjacent villages were then given to the flames, some arms were captured, some cattle lifted, and a large quantity of grain was destroyed, after which the troops returned without molestation. In this affair 58 of the enemy were killed and 5 wounded, the British casualties being 2 killed and 2 wounded. The result of the summary punishment which was inflicted became immediately apparent, the raiding on the advanced section of the line entirely ceasing.

During the month of July the troops along the whole of the Khyber line of communications were busily employed on duties connected with the return to India of the large accumulations of superfluous stores. A system of raft service was successfully inaugurated, but more than once had to be suspended in consequence of the difficulty of protecting the parties on the river from the hostile action of the tribes. On the 12th of July a most determined attack was made near Lachipur on a number of rafts conveying invalids; it was, however, effectively repulsed by Captain Fenwick, 1st Madras Native Infantry, commanding at that place, with detachments of his own regiment and the Central India Horse; and though the rafts continued to be molested from time to time in many other parts of the river, the service was maintained with fair regularity, and proved of immense value as a means of transit.

In the Kuram district little of military interest occurred during the spring and summer of 1880, the operations of the troops employed in the Valley being confined to such small expeditions as were rendered necessary by disturbances on or near the line of communications, and to the occasional infliction of punishment on the tribes for raids committed on the border. Throughout April the Waziris gave considerable trouble, raiding on convoys, murdering native labourers employed on the roads, and cutting and stealing telegraph wire. On the 6th of that month large numbers of the Mahsud section of the tribe were reported to be collecting near Jandola, to the north-west of Tank, while other bodies were threatening the Gumal Valley, more to the southward. A few days afterwards an isolated post in the Gumal Valley was attacked, but the enemy were gallantly repulsed by a few Sowars of the 4th Punjab Cavalry. On the 13th of April a squadron of the 18th Bengal Cavalry, under the command of Captain Richardson, which had been sent out from Thal to the south-west to reconnoitre, encountered and put to flight some 600 Waziris at Biland Khel, killing four and wounding eight of their number. The only occasion on which loss of life was inflicted on British troops was a night surprise which was effected on the 1st of May by a body of Khostwals on the post of Chapri, a small fort and courtyard situated some eight miles distant from Thal, and four from Mandoria. The sentry, who was presumably asleep, together with an officer of the Commissariat Department and ten men, were killed, and sixteen wounded. Armed parties were sent out the following morning from Thal and Mandoria to scour the country in search of the enemy, but their efforts were unsuccessful. During the next few weeks rumours were current of gatherings of the Khostwals in the neighbourhood of Thal, and of the Mahsud Waziris in the vicinity of Tank, but these broke up without any attempt at concerted action.

News being received at Peiwar on the 22nd of May of the presence at Karmanna of the Malik Nanak Shamu Khel, a notorious intriguer and enemy of the British, a small force of all arms marched out with the object of effecting his capture. The village, which is situated some three miles beyond Ali Khel, was surrounded before daybreak on the 23rd, but the Malik was found to have effected his escape. After blowing up his forts, the column retraced its steps.

Throughout the month of June the country was comparatively quiet, and in July, though raiding on the part of the tribes was renewed, it was carried on with less zest than heretofore. A number of camels having been carried off near Biland Khel, a party of the 18th Bengal Cavalry under Captain Richardson was sent out from Thal in pursuit, and surrounded the village of Fatteh Khel. Several of the camels were seized, and hostages taken, and the following day the stolen animals were restored by the inhabitants.

During this period various changes took place in the organization of the Field Force. On the 14th of February the services of a gallant and revered soldier were lost to Government by the death of Brigadier-General Tytler, who succumbed to pneumonia within a few weeks after his return from the Zaimusht expedition. On the 18th of March Major-General Watson proceeded on a tour of inspection to Rawal Pindi, Brigadier-General Gordon, C.B., who had been appointed to command a brigade, *vice* Brigadier-General Tytler, deceased, assuming temporary command of the Upper Kuram. At the latter end of March Brigadier-General H. R. L. Newdigate, C.B., was appointed to command a brigade in the Kuram Valley, and on the 31st of that month General Watson returned and resumed command of the line.

Shortly after the departure of the Bengal troops under Sir Donald Stewart for Ghazni, General Primrose arrived at Kandahar and took over the command of the Bombay Division from General Phayre, who proceeded to assume charge of the communications. Throughout April, May, and June the defences of the city were strengthened, the sanitation improved, and the surrounding country cultivated. Occasional raids along the line of communications and disturbances in some of the outlying districts from time to time necessitated punitory measures being taken against the tribes implicated; but it was the hostile preparations of Ayub Khan at Herat to which during this period attention was chiefly directed.

On the 17th of April telegraphic communication with Chaman was interrupted, and shortly afterwards information was received that Dabrai, a small post in the Kadanai Valley, some twenty-five miles beyond Chaman on the Kandahar road, which was held by native levies, had been sacked and burnt. It was subsequently ascertained that on the previous day Major Waudby, 19th Bombay Native Infantry, Road Commandant, with two Sowars of the 3rd Sind Horse and two Sepoys of his own regiment, had halted at Dabrai while returning to Kandahar from a tour of inspection, and a few hours afterwards had received intelligence that large numbers of Kakar Pathans were gathering in the neighbourhood with hostile intentions. About 10 p.m. over three hundred of the enemy were observed by the garrison advancing over some hills to the eastward, and shortly afterwards the post was surrounded. For several hours a most heroic defence was maintained by Major Waudby and his party, but their ammunition at length failing them, they were overwhelmed and slain. One Sowar, who escaped, carried news of the catastrophe to Chaman, and General Brooke, who was at Kila Abdulla, at once hastened up with a detachment of the 3rd Sind Horse and a wing of the 30th Native Infantry to the scene of the encounter. The assailants had, however, in the meantime made off. The duty of exacting retribution for this outrage was entrusted to Sirdar Shere Ali Khan, the Governor of Kandahar. On the 26th of April some cavalry and infantry details drawn from Chaman and Gatai, with two mountain-guns, the whole under the command of Major Singleton, 28th Native Infantry, proceeded to co-operate with the Sirdar's troops against Abu Said, a Kadanai Malik, who was believed to be implicated in the attack. Abu Said himself was taken prisoner, and his fort destroyed.

On the 1st of May Colonel Tanner, commanding at Kalat-i-Ghilzai, marched from that place with five companies of the 29th Native Infantry and a signalling party of the 66th Foot to Kaj Baj, to exact retribution from the inhabitants for a recently-committed raid, and to pay a punitory visit to the villages of Jaldak and

Tirandaz, on the left bank of the Tarnak river, opposite Pul-i-Sang, for sheltering marauders. The following morning these villages were surrounded, and a quantity of stolen property was recovered, hostages being taken for the payment of a fine which was inflicted. On returning to Kalat-i-Ghilzai, Colonel Tanner found a considerable body of Achakzais posted on a high hill known as the Shah Bolan, and after a brisk encounter, defeated and dispersed them, killing fourteen of their number, including their leader, and wounding eight.

During the month of May the reports of Ayub's movements and intentions continued to be uncertain and conflicting. Affairs at Herat were described as being in a state of disorder, while Ayub's preparations for departure were supposed to be dictated by a desire to escape from his own troops. On the 29th of May intelligence was received that a body of horsemen were already on the Kandahar road; but this was shortly afterwards denied, and up to the 17th of June messengers from Herat reported that no attempt had been made to advance beyond planting the standards outside the gates of the city. On the 21st of June, however, the Wali Shere Ali Khan, who had been at Girishk with his troops since the 10th of that month, sent word to Colonel St. John, the Resident at Kandahar, that the rumours previously received were correct; that Ayub himself was advancing with the main body of his troops; and that he had sent forward one of his colonels, the Luinab Khushdil Khan, with 2,000 horsemen, towards the Kandahar frontier, to raise the country in his favour.

In the meantime earnest representations had been made by Shere Ali Khan of the desirability of his being supported by the presence of a British Brigade at Girishk, to enable him to advance with confidence in the direction of Herat; and trustworthy information was now received to the effect that if the Wali were to meet Ayub's army without support, he would almost certainly be defeated. His own regular troops, it was reported, were wavering in their allegiance to him; while a contingent of Alizais from Zamindawar, who had recently joined him, were said to be merely awaiting a favourable opportunity to desert to Ayub's camp. Under these circumstances, it was decided to despatch a British brigade from Kandahar to the Halmand, and to push up reinforcements as quickly as possible from the line of communications and the reserves in Sind; and it was hoped that its presence would not only help to confirm the allegiance of the Wali's wavering troops, and overawe the Zamindawaris, but also that its departure on such a mission would have a favourable effect on the population of the city and the surrounding country. By the 26th of June Ayub's advance guard had reached Farah, 164 miles from Herat, and Ayub himself, with the main body of his troops, was only a march or two in rear of it. The strength of the British forces in Southern Afghanistan at this time was approximately as follows: Under Colonel Tanner at Kalat-i-Ghilzai, 1,050 of all ranks; under General Primrose at Kandahar, 4,700 of all ranks; under General Phayre on the line of communications and in the outlying districts, 5,270 of all ranks.

On the 2nd of July a force consisting of E/B, R.H.A., six companies of the 66th Foot, 500 sabres of the 3rd Bombay Light Cavalry and 3rd Sind Horse, and the 1st and 30th Bombay Native Infantry, in all about 2,300 of all ranks and arms, under the command of Brigadier-General Burrows, the cavalry under the immediate command of Brigadier-General Nuttall, was accordingly detailed for an immediate advance to the Halmand; and on the 4th and 5th of that month the brigade quitted Kandahar, instructions having been issued to the effect that it was on no account to cross the river, beyond which boundary the Wali would have to rely on his own resources. The cavalry and artillery, under General Nuttall, which preceded the infantry throughout by one march, arrived at the Halmand on the 11th of July, and encamped on the left bank of the river, opposite Girishk, where it was joined by the remainder of the brigade the following day. Forage was plentiful, and supplies had been collected in abundance by the Wali, the main body of whose force was on the right bank a little south of Girishk, his advanced troops occupying a position about twenty miles distant, to the north-east. On this day news reached Colonel St. John, the political officer with General Burrows's force, that the advanced portion of Ayub Khan's army was at Washir, sixty miles west of Girishk, and that Ayub himself was not far in rear.

On the 13th of July it became evident that the infantry in the service of the Wali, about 2,000 strong, were in such an unsatisfactory state, and so untrustworthy, that General Burrows and Colonel St. John deliberated on the question of disarming them; and it was decided to test their loyalty the following day by ordering them to cross the river. Directions were issued accordingly on the morning of the 14th, and in a short time the cavalry were seen marching down from their camp, under the immediate command of the Wali; the infantry, however, began to move off in the opposite direction, and it soon became evident that they were deserting *en masse*, taking with them a battery of smooth-bore guns, which had been recently presented to Shere Ali Khan by the British Government. Almost immediately afterwards a portion of the cavalry, about 2,500 strong, which had in the meantime reached the left bank of the river, began streaming off in the direction of Kandahar.

Leaving two companies of the 66th Foot, the 1st Grenadiers, and five companies of Jacob's Rifles, to protect the camp, General Burrows, with the remainder of his force, crossed the bed of the Halmand, which was here some two miles in width, and in parts dry, and started in pursuit of the mutinous infantry, with the hope of recovering the guns. On reaching the right bank of the river, the cavalry and horse artillery, under General Nuttall, pushed on in advance to feel for the enemy and hold him in check until the infantry could be brought up; but the country being irrigated, the guns were somewhat delayed in their progress, and the 3rd Sind Horse, under Colonel Malcolmson, were passed rapidly forward. After proceeding some little distance, Colonel Malcolmson came upon the rebels, formed up on a rocky ridge, with their left resting on the right bank of the Halmand. The nature of the ground was such as to preclude the possibility of a charge being delivered, but by demonstrating with his cavalry, Malcolmson succeeded in drawing the enemy's fire, and holding him in check for upwards of half an hour. Before the guns and infantry could be brought up, however, the mutineers moved off in a direction parallel to the river, but being followed up and threatened by the cavalry, again halted and opened fire with their artillery. A few minutes afterwards Major Blackwood, commanding E/B, R.H.A., succeeded in bringing four of his guns into action, and in half an hour completely silenced the enemy's fire, causing the gunners to abandon their position. The cavalry at once charged forward and seized the guns, but were met by a sharp fusillade from masses of the enemy posted on the reverse slopes of the hill; on the approach of the horse artillery and infantry, however, the Afghan troops completely abandoned their position, dispersing and flying in all directions, under a heavy fire from the guns and breech-loaders, and leaving sixty of their dead on the field. Besides the battery, which consisted of four 6-pounder smooth-bore guns and two 12-pounder howitzers, the whole of the enemy's baggage and ammunition was captured. The British casualties on this day were four wounded.

As the mutinous troops had plundered the stores of supplies collected at Girishk by Shere Ali Khan, and as reports reached Colonel St. John that it was Ayub Khan's intention, if he were to cross the Halmand at all, to do so at a point to the north of Girishk, General Burrows determined to abandon the position he had hitherto occupied, and retire to Khushk-i-Nakhud, distant thirty miles from Girishk and forty-five from Kandahar, where several roads from the Halmand to Kandahar converge, and where supplies were plentiful. This retirement was effected during the night of the 15th, and on the morning of the 16th the troops occupied their old camping-ground. On the 18th a more favourable site, two miles nearer to Mir-Karez, was selected, the stores being collected in an enclosure, and arrangements made to leave the baggage with a small guard, should it be necessary to move out to meet the enemy. This camp was held till the morning of the 27th of July. Reliable information concerning Ayub's movements was meagre in the extreme, and was mainly derived from spies sent out by Colonel St. John, under the auspices of Shere Ali Khan; for some days little was ascertained beyond the bare fact that Ayub had reached the Halmand, and moving from Girishk, had distributed his troops along the river bed, south of the ford at Haidarabad. Cavalry patrols were sent out daily, but nothing of the enemy was seen until the 21st. On that day a reconnoitring party encountered a small force at Sangbar, a village situated about midway between Khushk-i-Nakhud and Girishk, and after exchanging a few shots, retired. On the 22nd, Sangbar was again found to be occupied, and the following day a reconnaissance in force towards that place found about 600 of Ayub's horsemen in the plain below the Garmao hills. Shortly afterwards the enemy retired, pursued by the cavalry and shelled by the horse-artillery guns at long ranges for some miles.

During this period the brigade received some small accessions to its strength from Kandahar, and General Burrows was kept fully advised by General Primrose of the instructions which were being transmitted to him from Army Head-Quarters. The most important of these was contained in a communication despatched from Simla on the 21st of July, by which General Burrows was given full liberty to attack Ayub in the event of his considering himself strong enough to do so, and by which he was informed that Government considered it of the greatest political importance that Ayub's force should be dispersed, and prevented from passing on to Ghazni.

Vague reports daily found their way into camp concerning the strength of the enemy; the regular troops, however, were believed to number 4,000 cavalry, and 4,000 to 5,000 infantry, and to have at their disposal thirty guns. In addition to these there were the deserters from the Wali's army, another 2,000, besides an irregular force composed of malcontents from all the unsettled districts north of the Halmand. Of the number of the latter it was impossible to form any estimate. At Kandahar at this time, great uneasiness prevailed in the city, and large numbers of families were leaving daily, ostensibly for fear of Ayub's approach.

On the afternoon of the 26th of July important information reached camp at

Khushk-i-Nakhud. 2,000 of the enemy's cavalry and a large number of Ghazis, it was reported, had arrived at Garmao and Maiwand, and were to be followed immediately by Ayub Khan with the main body of his army, his intention being, it was said, to make his way into the Argandab Valley by the Maiwand Pass. It thus became necessary, in order to carry out the directions which had been received with reference to preventing him from slipping past towards Ghazni, to arrest his further progress without delay; and it was believed that by a rapid advance on the village of Maiwand his force might be cut in two; and his advanced cavalry at Garmao driven to the northward before aid could reach it.

At 6.30 a.m. on the 27th of July camp was struck, and the brigade—now consisting of E/B, R.H.A., the smooth-bore battery captured from the mutineers, 516 of all ranks of the 66th Foot, 316 of the 3rd Light Cavalry, 260 of the 3rd Sind Horse, 45 of the Sappers and Miners, 648 of the 1st Grenadiers, and 625 of Jacob's Rifles, in all 2,599 of all ranks and arms, inclusive of 34 Europeans and 50 natives in hospital—commenced its march on Maiwand. The hostile state of the country rendered it impossible to leave anything behind in safety, and the column was consequently encumbered by an enormous quantity of ordnance and commissariat stores and baggage.

The advance lay through a belt of cultivated land, along the right bank of the Khushk-i-Nakhud river, which was at this season perfectly dry. At 8 a.m. the village of Mushak was reached, and a halt was made to allow the baggage to close up. Half an hour later a move was made to Karezak, eight miles distant from the Khushk-i-Nakhud camp, and four miles south-east of Maiwand. Here it was reported that Ayub Khan's whole army, including his artillery, was in the immediate vicinity, and marching on Maiwand; but the information which had been recently derived from native sources had proved so untrustworthy, that little heed was given to the rumour. About 10 a.m., however, a brief reconnaissance disclosed large masses of the enemy's cavalry moving across the left front towards Maiwand. As the brigade continued to advance, these bodies were observed to incline in a northerly direction towards Garmao. A thick haze which shrouded the surrounding country precluded the possibility, however, of forming any correct estimate of their disposition and numbers.

About 10 a.m. the advanced cavalry occupied without opposition the village of Mundabad, three miles to the south-west of Maiwand, it being General Burrows' intention to avail himself of the walled enclosures of the village for relieving the brigade of the heavy baggage train with which it was encumbered, and then to make his dispositions for attacking the enemy. While the arrival of the baggage was awaited, General Nuttall proceeded with two of the guns of E/B, R.H.A., under Major Blackwood, to reconnoitre the enemy's position from the edge of a broad and deep ravine, running north and south, in front of the village.

To the west of Mundabad, and separated from the village by the ravine already alluded to, stretched a waterless stony plain, bounded on its northern and north-western extremity by three parallel ranges of hills, which, extending in a north-easterly direction, enclose between them the Garmao and Maiwand Valleys. Beyond, and opening into the Maiwand Valley—the more easterly of the two—is the Khakrez Valley, through the eastern barrier of which, north of the Maiwand Pass, are roads leading towards Kandahar and the Upper Argandab. It was across this stony plain to the westward that Ayub Khan's army, almost entirely hidden from

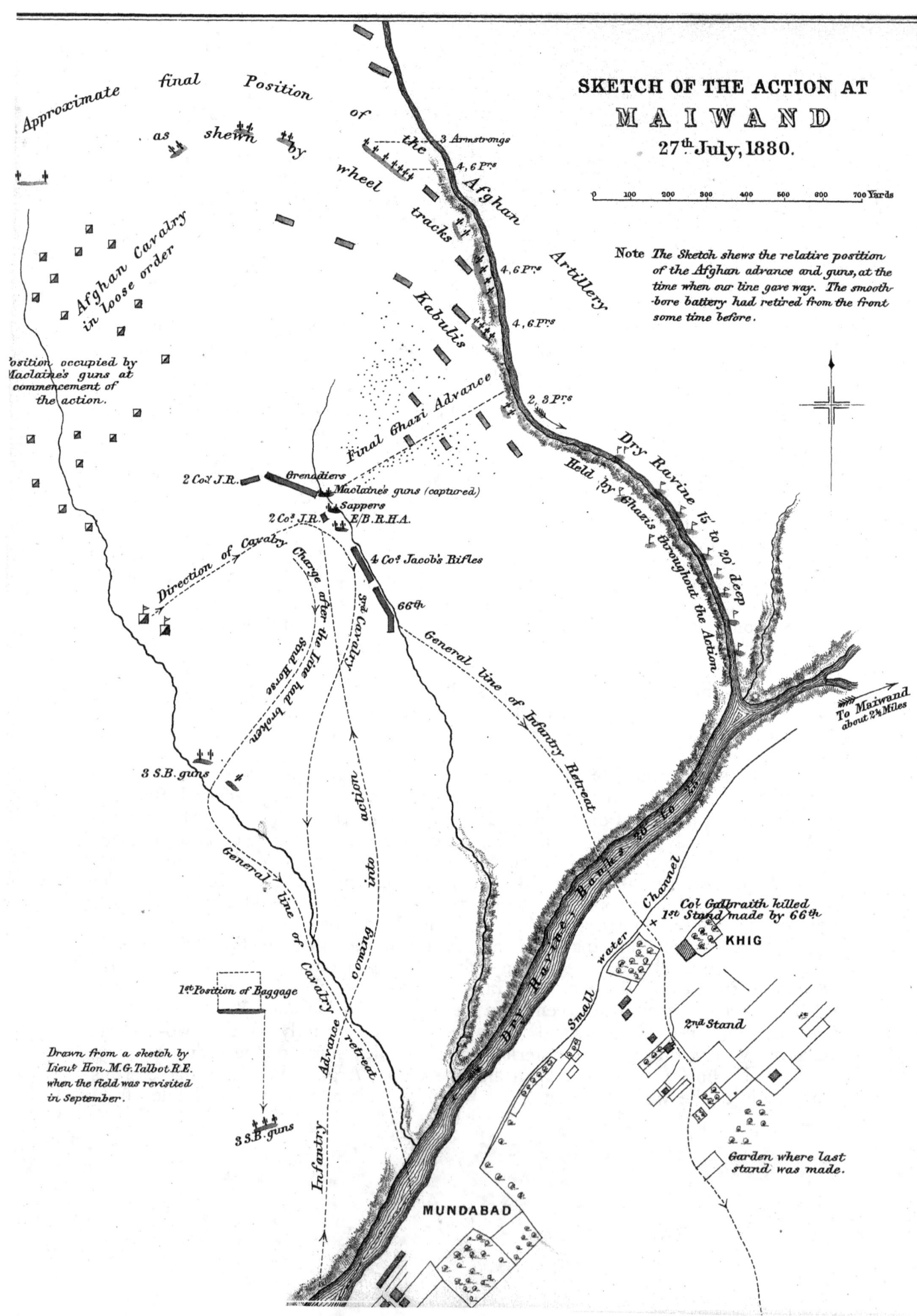

view by the dense haze, was moving in an easterly direction towards the village of Maiwand, which, lying a little to the west of the pass of the same name, covers its entrance as well as the approaches to the valuable water-supply in that neighbourhood. Had General Burrows desired to remain on the defensive, the position he now occupied offered many advantages. The village of Mundabad would have afforded protection for the baggage; a number of low walled enclosures which connected its various parts would have given admirable cover for the infantry; and there was abundance of water. But acting under the erroneous impression that the enemy had no guns, and that their force, whatever its strength might be, would very possibly retire without risking an encounter, General Burrows considered that a favourable opportunity had arrived for taking the initiative, and determined on delivering an attack without further delay.

An incident now occurred which at once precipitated the commencement of the action. While General Nuttall and Major Blackwood were observing the movements of groups of the enemy who were visible from the edge of the broad nullah, two of the four advanced guns of E/B, R.H.A., under the command of Lieut. Maclaine, escorted by a troop of the 3rd Sind Horse under Lieut. Monteith, had crossed the ravine somewhat lower down, and advancing rapidly across the plain on the extreme left opened fire at a range of 1,800 yards on a large mass of Afghan horsemen who had just become visible. Failing in his attempts to recall this detachment before the guns had entered into action, General Nuttall sent back orders for two guns of the same battery, under Lieut. Osborne, which were with the rear-guard, to hasten up to the front, and crossing the ravine with the 3rd Sind Horse, and Blackwood's two remaining guns, advanced to within 800 yards of the position which had been taken up by Lieut. Maclaine. Here a halt was made to await the arrival of the infantry, Maclaine being at the same time directed to move down nearer the main body.

In the meantime the infantry under General Burrows, with the smooth-bore guns under Captain Slade, had crossed the nullah and deployed in the following order :—the 66th Foot on the right, the smooth-bore guns in the centre, the 1st Grenadiers on the left, and the 30th Native Infantry (Jacob's Rifles), with the Sappers, in support. Immediately on the left of the infantry line were the four guns of E/B, R.H.A., under Major Blackwood and Lieut Osborne, supported by 130 sabres of the 3rd Light Cavalry under Major Currie, who, with Captain Mayne of that regiment, also watched the right flank; the two remaining guns of E/B, R.H.A., under Lieut. Maclaine, supported by a troop of the 3rd Sind Horse, were on the extreme left; and in rear, écheloned outside the guns, but with its left thrown back, was a troop of the 3rd Light Cavalry under Lieut. Reid, formed thus to watch a large body of the enemy's cavalry who were threatening the British left flank. Protecting the baggage, which had followed in rear at an interval of about 1,000 yards, were Colonel Malcolmson and Lieut. Geoghegan, the former with 96 sabres 3rd Sind Horse, and the latter with 50 sabres 3rd Light Cavalry.

By the time this disposition was effected, the enemy had assumed more definite formations, but nothing had yet occurred to unmask their real strength. Their numbers, however, rapidly developed, and in a short time an advance was made by a large number of Ghazis from the direction of Maiwand upon the British right flank. To meet this movement, the right of the infantry line (the 66th Foot) was thrown back, and the front extended by ordering up two companies of Jacob's

Rifles to the extreme left, and filling the gap between the guns and the 66th with the other four companies of Jacob's Rifles and the little party of Sappers. Two of the smooth-bore guns were at the same time withdrawn from the centre to the right, while Lieut. Maclaine, recalled from the extreme left, formed up in the centre with the other four guns of E/B, R.H.A. The whole of the fighting strength was thus in line, ten of the twelve guns being massed in the centre, and two on the extreme right.

For the first half-hour the enemy's artillery had made no sign, but by degrees battery after battery was unmasked, till eventually the fire of thirty guns was concentrated on the British position. The infantry were ordered to lie down, but there was little or no cover for the artillery and cavalry, nor could the latter be withdrawn out of range, as it was necessary to demonstrate continuously against the swarm of Afghan horsemen, which from the first began circling round both flanks and threatening the baggage. The Ghazis on the right advanced to within 500 yards of the infantry, but recoiling before the Martini fire of the 66th, sought cover in a small watercourse and remained stationary.

For two hours the artillery duel was continued with little change in the disposition of the British troops, two of the smooth-bore guns, under Captain Slade, being temporarily withdrawn to the left, however, to check an advance in that quarter. During this period the numbers of the enemy on either flank were continually augmented, and though General Nuttall's force succeeded in preventing the Afghan horsemen establishing themselves in the immediate rear of the British infantry, its strength was totally inadequate to control the more extended flanking operations, and in a short time the brigade was all but surrounded, the rear-guard being hotly engaged in protecting the baggage. By 2 o'clock p.m. the cavalry had lost 14 per cent. of the men in the front line and 149 horses, and though the infantry, lying on the ground, had not suffered so severely, they had not escaped punishment. The day was unusually hot and sultry, and want of water had soon began to tell upon the Sepoys, who were continually leaving the ranks and falling to the rear to assuage their thirst.

About 2.30 p.m., the smooth-bore guns ran short of ammunition, and a few minutes later were ordered to the rear to replenish. Their withdrawal was followed by a general move along the enemy's front, the Afghan horsemen on the British left spreading out in loose order and endeavouring to complete the cordon around the British troops, the right rear of the column having been already turned by large bodies of mounted and dismounted irregulars, who had taken possession of the village of Mundabad. The fire of the enemy's guns now momentarily slackened, and swarms of Ghazis appeared to be preparing to rush upon the British centre and left. At this critical juncture the two companies of Jacob's Rifles on the extreme left fell back in disorder, the men, who had been suffering severely from want of water, being completely cowed by the heavy artillery fire to which they had been subjected, and the casualties which had occurred in their ranks. Unsteadied by the Rifles, the 1st Grenadiers, which had twice successfully checked the advance of the enemy, also gave way, and a few moments afterwards the collapse on the left flank was complete, the Native Infantry rolling up like a wave towards the right, the Sepoys, surrounded and mixed up with the Ghazis, being swept back on the guns of E/B, R.H.A. A very gallant stand was here made by the artillery, who had throughout borne the brunt of the enemy's fire, the gunners, ably seconded

SKETCH OF THE WAR.

by the little detachment of Sappers under Lieut. Henn, R.E., fighting the Ghazis with handspikes, sponge-rods, and other improvised weapons. When the order to limber up and retire was reluctantly given, there was barely sufficient time to carry it out, and the two guns under Lieut. Maclaine, which occupied a position a little in advance of the rest of the battery, remaining behind to fire one more round, fell into the enemy's hands. The Ghazis now threw the whole of their strength on the retreating Native Infantry, who, in one hopelessly confused mass were falling back upon the 66th Foot. The havoc which ensued was appalling. Officers and men were carried back by sheer weight of numbers, the Sepoys, making little attempt to defend themselves, in many instances, being literally dragged out of the ranks and massacred. A cavalry charge was now ordered as a last resource to cover the infantry retirement, but cavalry, as well as infantry, were demoralized by the terrible artillery fire to which they had been subjected, and in consequence of a considerable detachment being absent on duty with the baggage in rear, and of many horses having been killed or disabled, General Nuttall had only 255 sabres at his disposal. With these numbers a charge was made in the direction of the captured guns, but not being driven home, it failed, and the troopers retired in disorder. All subsequent attempts made at this time to induce the men to rally were unsuccessful, and the squadrons were withdrawn to the east side of the main ravine immediately in front of the village of Mundabad, where, covered by the horse artillery guns, they again formed up facing the enemy. In the meantime the infantry, hemmed in by the Ghazis on all sides, retired laboriously towards the village of Khig, situated about a mile and a half north-east of Mundabad. After crossing the ravine the scattered remnants of the Native Infantry streamed away to the eastward. All General Burrows's efforts to rally them were unavailing; discipline was utterly gone, and in spite of every endeavour to induce them to close on the cavalry and artillery, the fugitives persisted in inclining away in a direction which carried them farther and farther from water. A small number had, however, joined a body of the 66th, which, rallying round its colours, made a gallant stand, with a small party of the Sappers, in a garden enclosure near Khig. Here, amongst others, several officers of the 66th, including Colonel Galbraith, were killed, and the little force becoming rapidly outflanked, again retired, making stand after stand, until at last only eleven men survived. So valiantly did these eleven bear themselves that it was not till the last man was disabled that the Ghazis dared to advance on them. Amongst this band were Major Blackwood, R.H.A., Lieut. Henn, R.E., and Lieut. Hinde, 1st Grenadiers.

Whilst the infantry was thus hotly engaged in the enclosures of the village of Khig, the cavalry, covered by the guns, and now in proper formation, moved on after the baggage, which was by this time stretching away for miles in the direction of Kandahar. One or more of the enemy's guns opened fire upon this portion of the force, but a single troop was sufficient to hold the irregular horse, who attempted to follow, completely in check. The majority of the men wounded early in the day were at this time well in advance with the smooth-bore battery, but others, less fortunate, had fallen behind, and were picked up and carried on. At 5 p.m. the bed of the Khushk-i-Nakhud river, about four miles from the scene of action, was reached, and the two lines of stragglers effected a junction. The retreat was then continued, a troop of cavalry covering the rear as before, with the aid of the horse artillery guns, the limbers of which were now crowded with wounded. Pursuit had by this time practically ceased, and although groups of the enemy's horse were seen on the opposite side of the river-bed, they were kept at a distance by the fire of the dismounted troopers.

The line of baggage and wounded officers and men formed a straggling column upwards of six miles in length, and were following a route which, after passing within a short distance of the camping-ground previously occupied at Khushk-i-Nakhud, crossed a bare and waterless expanse to Hanz-i-Madat, sixteen miles distant. Shortly before nightfall General Burrows pushed forward with the main body of the cavalry by a divergent route towards Ata Karez for water, and an orderly was sent forward to turn the retreating line in that direction; the rout, however, had become so general, and the remnants of the brigade were so widely scattered, that this was found to be impossible, and the greater number of the fugitives, suffering agonies of thirst, and impelled onward by alarms which were constantly raised that the enemy were in close pursuit, struggled painfully on to Hanz-i-Madat, which was at length reached shortly before midnight. After a long search, a well was found, and water was obtained for the first time after leaving the battle-field. The first care was for the wounded on the guns, and at the end of an hour every one had drunk. Stragglers were continually coming in, and at once hurried to the water, each succeeding quarter of an hour adding largely to the numbers; happily, however, the noisy gathering, struggling angrily for precedence, was completely unmolested, although the barking of watch-dogs gave warning that a village was not far distant. After half an hour's rest the troops struggled on to Asu Khan, where the cultivated portion of the Argandab was entered, and numerous villages had to be passed through. The news of the defeat had been spread by the retainers of the Wali Shere Ali Khan, who had sought safety in flight from the battle-field early in the day, and as soon as it grew light large numbers of armed villagers, greedy for loot, turned out and harassed the retreat. Hovering around the line, they made dashes wherever a gap occurred, and numbers of followers fell victims to their knives. The troops had to fight, more or less, all the way to Kokaran, from whence a small force under Brigadier-General Brooke, which had been sent to their aid, covered the further retirement to Kandahar, and was instrumental in saving a large number of followers from destruction. Between Asu Khan and Sinjiri, Lieut. Whitby, 1st Grenadiers, was killed, and Lieut. Maclaine, R.H.A., taken prisoner, both officers having been surprised while in search of water. Besides the two horse artillery guns captured by the enemy, five of the smooth-bore guns had to be abandoned, one after the other, during the retreat, four of the horses in one team alone dying of exhaustion. About noon on the 28th the remnants of the brigade reached Kandahar. Out of a total of 2,476 of all ranks, engaged on this disastrous day, 964, including 20 officers, were killed, and 167, including 9 officers, wounded; 331 regimental followers and 201 horses were also killed, and 7 followers and 68 horses wounded.

The first news of the reverse which had been sustained reached Kandahar at 1.30 a.m., on the 28th of July, and with a view to covering the retreat of the defeated troops, Brigadier-General Brooke started from cantonments at 5 a.m. with 40 sabres Poona Horse, two guns, C/2, R.A., 70 rifles 7th Fusiliers, and 100 rifles 28th Native Infantry, and pushed forward along the Herat road. Rapidly clearing the village of Abasabad, the gardens of which were full of armed men, the little column emerged into the open country beyond, continually meeting small bodies of fugitives, each of whom imagined that they were the last survivors of the ill-fated brigade. At 9 a.m., after dislodging the enemy from a strong position they had taken up, the force reached the eastern outskirts of Kokaran, and took up a position commanding the village and the Herat road, while a small body of cavalry under Captain Anderson went forward to communicate with General Burrows, who, with the remnants of his brigade, was seen halted about one mile west of the village. Large numbers of armed men, who had for some time been cutting off and killing stragglers from the retiring force, were now observed streaming out of the fortified enclosure of Kokaran, and taking up a strong position on the right flank of General Brooke's column; a few shells and a rapid demonstration, however, soon put them to flight. After the retreating force had passed through the village, General Brooke withdrew his cavalry, which had meantime been watching a ford of the Argandab river a mile in advance. During their retirement the enemy, emboldened by the preparations for departure, suddenly rushed down from the neighbouring heights in great numbers to cut them off; but Captain Anderson succeeded in cutting his way through their midst, with the loss of only one man killed. The whole force then moved on towards Kandahar, General Brooke covering the retirement, which was unmolested for three miles, when a message was received from the front that the village of Abasabad and the hills immediately above it were strongly occupied by the enemy. The two guns of C/2, R.A., under Captain Law, and the cavalry under Captain Anderson, were at once pushed through Burrows's halted force, followed by Brooke's infantry. A well-directed artillery fire soon cleared the hills, after which the skirmishers, a second time that day, swept the garden enclosures of the village. General Burrows then moved on without further molestation to the cantonments, from whence a company of the 7th Fusiliers under Captain Adderley was despatched to hold the eastern outskirts of Abasabad during the retirement of Brooke's column. On arriving at the cantonments all the wounded and sick were sent into the citadel, whither they were followed by the remainder of the force the same evening.

In the meantime, at Kandahar preparations for a siege had been commenced. It being considered impossible to retain the cantonments, which, besides having no military defences of any kind, and being commanded on one side by two low hills, were also without an independent water supply, it was decided to concentrate the British force in and near the citadel; but as this could not possibly have been held against an enemy in possession of the city, it became necessary to adopt the only alternative, and to occupy the latter also.

The city of Kandahar is in form quadrilateral, with a total perimeter of 6,286 yards, its walls being built of solid sun-dried masonry, varying from eighteen to twenty-five feet in height. The citadel is a square of 268 yards, its northern face lying seventy-three yards within the northern wall of the city, to meet which the eastern and western faces are prolonged.

By dusk on the 28th of July the whole force was withdrawn from the cantonments, and told off for duty on the city walls. The effective garrison on the night of the 28th, including the survivors of General Burrows's force, numbered 4,360 of all ranks and arms. A detachment of the 19th Native Infantry and Poona Horse at Mandi Hissar was recalled to Kandahar, while the garrisons of Abdul Rahman, Mel Karez, Dabrai, and Gatai were ordered to fall back on Chaman.

A cavalry reconnaissance sent out on the morning of the 29th of July, found the abandoned cantonment looted and partly burnt, and the whole country covered with armed men. The following day orders were issued that the whole of the Pathan population, whose presence in Kandahar was considered to be a source of the utmost danger, should leave the city, and that in the afternoon search parties would go round to ascertain that the order was being obeyed. This eventually resulted in about 12,000 persons moving out, no opposition having been offered. The next care was to improve and strengthen the existing fortifications both inside and out. Numerous walls and houses which had been built up to the city gate were destroyed, free communication along the entire length of the walls was arranged, platforms for mounting guns in important positions were constructed and repaired, an entanglement of telegraph wire was drawn round the city, abattis were placed in front of all the entrances and weak portions of the walls, and numerous other works undertaken. Though every available man was employed on work all day, it was not until the 13th of August that the Commanding Royal Engineer reported that he had no further need of military labour. During this period covering parties were daily engaged with the enemy, and in a sharp skirmish on the 12th of August inflicted severe loss upon them, killing, amongst others, the Governor of Farah.

Early on the morning of the 8th of August, the enemy opened artillery fire on the citadel from Picquet Hill, an eminence behind the old cantonment, which Ayub Khan had chosen for the site of his camp, and shortly afterwards brought guns to bear on the city from the villages of Deh Khoja and Deh Khati. This fire, though it was sustained regularly for many days, did little or no harm, excellent cover being found for both men and animals behind the walls of the citadel.

The enemy having clearly shown his intention of making a complete and careful investment of Kandahar, by occupying and fortifying the adjacent villages, under cover of which batteries could at any time be unmasked, and there being no reliable information regarding his actual dispositions, General Primrose decided on making a sortie to force him to show his hand. The village of Deh Khoja, situated about half a mile east of the city, was selected as the point of attack, and in accordance with arrangements made on the afternoon of the previous day, a force consisting of four companies each of the 7th Fusiliers, 19th and 28th Native Infantry, in all 800 rifles, together with a detachment of Sappers, the whole under the command of Brigadier-General Brooke, proceeded at dawn on the 16th of August to clear the village, and, if possible, destroy any works the enemy might have constructed under cover of the walls, while Brigadier-General Nuttall co-operated with 100 sabres each of the 3rd Light Cavalry, the Poona Horse, and the 3rd Sind Horse. The infantry were divided into three columns—the 1st under Lieut.-Colonel Daubeny, 7th Fusiliers, consisting of two companies 7th Fusiliers and two companies 19th Native Infantry; the 2nd, under Lieut.-Col. Nimmo, 28th Native Infantry, consisting of one company 7th Fusiliers and three companies 28th Native Infantry; and the 3rd, under Colonel Heathcote, 19th Native Infantry, consisting of one company 7th Fusiliers, two companies 19th Native Infantry, and one company 28th Native Infantry.

At 4.30 a.m., the cavalry emerged from the city by the Idgah Gate and trotted round to the east of Deh Khoja, to keep the ground clear in that direction and prevent the arrival of reinforcements; at 4.45 a.m., one of the 40-pounders, two 9-pounders, and two 8-inch mortars opened fire on the village from the city walls; and at 5 a.m. the first two parties of infantry, under Colonels Daubeny and Nimmo,

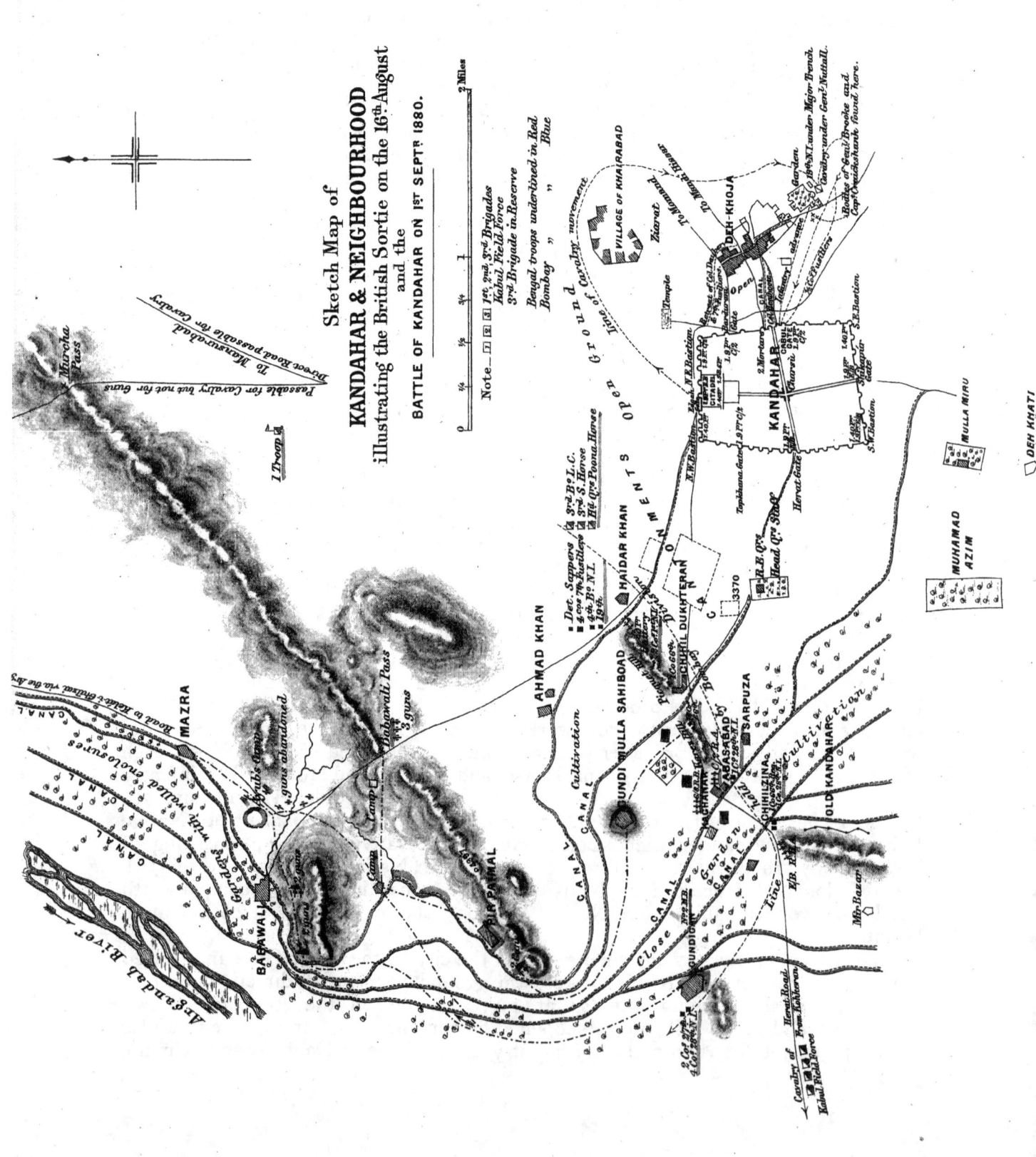

débouched from the Kabul Gate, and made for the south of the village, which they entered, under a heavy fire, half an hour later.

At this time large numbers of Ghazis were seen making for Deh Khoja, across the open ground to the south; a well-delivered charge by a troop of the 3rd Light Cavalry, under Lieut. Geoghegan, however, drove them back, with heavy loss, into broken ground, where further pursuit was hopeless. A few minutes afterwards they again collected in large numbers, and attempted to cross from the south; but Major Trench, 19th Native Infantry, who had seized a position on the extreme British right, with two companies of his regiment, met them with three well-directed volleys, and General Nuttall, falling upon them with the 3rd Light Cavalry and Poona Horse, cut up many of their number, and forced the remainder to seek shelter a second time in the broken ground.

In the meantime the two attacking columns forced their way, under a heavy fire, through the southern portion of the village; but it soon became evident that the force at General Brooke's disposal was quite inadequate in strength to perform the heavy task which had been allotted to it. Every door was blockaded, every wall loop-holed, every loop-hole occupied by a rifle, and all that could be done was to press on and seize, if possible, one or more houses in rear of the village, whence to work back, clearing the walls and enclosures *en route*, and so giving the sappers an opportunity of demolishing the outer wall facing the Kabul Gate. The 3rd column, under Colonel Heathcote, supported the movement by lining the walls in the fields, close to the south and east of the village, and succeeded, to some extent, in drawing the fire of its defenders. Every minute the troops within the village itself were getting spread over a wider and wider area, it being necessary to guard the cross streets, as they were passed, to prevent the columns being taken in rear. General Brooke now reported his position as untenable, and General Primrose, who was watching the progress of affairs from Kandahar, ordered the troops to be recalled, the movement to be covered by artillery and rifle fire from the city walls. On receiving this order, Brooke sent to Nuttall, requesting him to cover the retirement of the infantry, which were still south of the village; and the supporting column, with Trench's companies, then fell back to the Kabul Gate, followed by the cavalry, whose withdrawal was the signal for the advance of every Afghan who had hitherto been held in check by them. Every wall in the fields and gardens was immediately lined by the enemy's skirmishers, who kept up a crushing fire, from which the cavalry suffered heavily before reaching the city walls.

By this time General Brooke's troops, broken up into small detachments, had penetrated to the north of Deh Khoja, where, under cover of some high walls, they obtained a brief respite; but finding it impossible to make good their hold, they endeavoured shortly afterwards to make their way back through the village. The enemy's reinforcements were, however, arriving in swarms, and the fire from the loop-holes was terribly severe; three bodies of the British troops, at last, extricated themselves, two by the north and one by the west, and rallied, to a certain extent, behind walls in the fields. Brigadier-General Brooke, while supporting Captain Cruickshank, R.E., who was severely wounded, was himself shot down, Captain Cruickshank being killed immediately afterwards. The disastrous retirement was at length completed about 7 a.m., when the firing ceased, and the enemy were seen carrying away their dead, some being evidently leaders of consequence. The total number of British troops engaged in this sortie was 1,556, of whom 106, including 8 British officers, were killed, and 117 wounded. The troops behaved with the utmost gallantry throughout, and many individual acts of heroism were performed.

Whilst the fighting was going on in Deh Khoja, the enemy opened artillery fire on the city from Picquet Hill and from a gun in position about 1,200 yards from the west face of the city wall. They also attempted to form up their infantry in the old cantonments; but the answering fire from the city effectually prevented them carrying out their intention, and within an hour their guns were silenced, one of them on Picquet Hill being dismounted.

During this day a messenger arrived from Kalat-i-Ghilzai, reporting that a large British force was being collected at Quetta, and that a strong division, under Sir Frederick Roberts, had left Kabul for Kandahar on the 7th instant.

In reporting on the events of the 16th of August, General Primrose stated his opinion that although disastrous as regards the heavy British losses, the sortie had a good effect on the spirits and *morale* of his troops, which had been considerably shaken by the results of the action of Maiwand; and further, that by it the confidence of the enemy received a shock from which it never recovered, hardly another shot being fired till the garrison of Kandahar was relieved.

On the receipt of news in India of the reverse which had been sustained at Maiwand, and of the subsequent investment of Kandahar by the Afghan forces, measures for the relief of the beleaguered garrison were immediately decided on, orders being issued for the formation and equipment of two strong divisions destined to advance simultaneously from the north and east and co-operate in the overthrow of Ayub Khan: the one, under the command of Sir Frederick Roberts, from Kabul, and the other, under the command of General Phayre, from Quetta. It was also determined that the events which had happened should not be permitted to interfere with the projected evacuation of Northern Afghanistan, and that while General Roberts moved southwards on Kandahar to raise the siege of that city, General Stewart should retire the remainder of the troops in Northern Afghanistan by the Khyber route to India. Conformably with this decision, the detached brigades were recalled to Kabul from the outlying districts, and the equipment of a division for special service under the command of Sir Frederick Roberts was hastened forward with all speed. At the beginning of the second week in August this force quitted Kabul on its march southwards, and the remainder of the troops, combined in one division under the command of Major-General Hills, and consisting of three brigades commanded respectively by Brigadier-Generals C. Gough, R. Hughes, and W. Daunt, made preparations for immediately evacuating the capital.

At 7 a.m. on the 11th of August, 1880, the new Amir was received in Durbar outside the western gate of Sherpur by Sir Donald Stewart, Major-General Hills, and other officers, as well as by many of the political staff under Mr. Griffin, and about 7.30, a.m., the whole of the British troops in Kabul moved off in three parallel columns to Butkhak, after the Bala Hissar and the cantonments had been handed over to Abdul Rahman's representatives. During the next few weeks the gradual retirement of the Khyber Line Force was continued in conjunction with the movements of the Kabul brigades, and by the second week in September, 1880, the last of the troops destined for India had reached Burj Hari Singh, four miles west of Peshawar, where a standing camp had been formed. The frontier of the treaty of Gandamak was again adopted on the Peshawar-Jalalabad line, and the military situation in the Khyber was almost identical with that which had existed at the moment of the Kabul outbreak of the 3rd September, 1879.

The force which had been placed at Sir Frederick Roberts's disposal for the relief of Kandahar comprised three brigades of infantry, one brigade of cavalry, and three batteries of mountain guns—the 1st Infantry Brigade consisting of the 92nd Highlanders, 23rd Pioneers, 45th Punjab Native Infantry, and 2nd Goorkhas; the 2nd Infantry Brigade consisting of the 72nd Highlanders, 2nd Sikh Infantry, 3rd Sikh Infantry, and 5th Goorkhas; the 3rd Infantry Brigade consisting of the 2/60th Rifles, 15th Sikhs, 25th Punjab Native Infantry, and 4th Goorkhas; the Cavalry Brigade consisting of the 9th Lancers, 3rd Bengal Cavalry, 3rd Punjab Cavalry, and Central India Horse; and the Artillery Division consisting of Battery 6/8, R.A., 11/9, R.A., and No. 2 Mountain Battery: in all, 2,562 British troops, 7,151 Native troops, 273 British officers, and 18 guns. Major-General Ross commanded the Infantry Division, the 1st, the 2nd, and 3rd Brigades of which were commanded respectively by Brigadier-Generals Macpherson, Baker, and MacGregor; Brigadier-General Hugh Gough commanded the Cavalry Brigade, and Colonel A. C. Johnson the Artillery; Colonel Æ. Perkins held the position of Commanding Royal Engineer, and Deputy Surgeon-General Hanbury that of Principal Medical Officer. The object of the expedition being to reach Kandahar in the shortest possible time, and it being not improbable that the main road would have to be left should the Afghan army endeavour to make its way towards Ghazni and Kabul by the valleys of the Argandab and Arghastan, it was decided that no wheeled guns or transport should accompany the force, that the baggage should be lightened as much as possible, that the supplies carried should be reduced to a minimum, and that the baggage-animals should not include camels.

The Kabul-Kandahar Field Force moved into camp by brigades on the 8th of August in the vicinity of Kabul, and the following morning commenced its march. The route lay through the fertile Logar Valley, that line being chosen instead of the usual road by Maidan, on account of the facilities it offered for collecting supplies. Ghazni, ninety-eight miles distant from Kabul, was reached on the seventh day of the march, and the force encamped on the east side of the city, the keys of which were handed over by the Governor to Sir F. Roberts. Though the inhabitants of the Wardak country were unfriendly to the new Amir, no hostilities had been attempted, and Major Hastings, the principal political officer accompanying the force, had found no great difficulty in managing the various headmen. Supplies, forage, wood, and water had been plentiful. The march had commenced daily about 4 a.m., and wherever possible had been carried out in two or three parallel lines; the troops were encamped by 1 or 2 p.m., the baggage being usually reported all in by 5 p.m.; the road, though difficult, had been generally good; the thermometer by day had varied between 84° and 92° in the shade. No further tidings of the beleaguered garrison having been as yet received, the Lieutenant-General determined to push on with all speed, and some hours before daybreak on the 16th of August the Field Force was again in motion.

On the 20th of August, shortly after reaching Panjak, General Roberts received a letter from Colonel Tanner, 29th Bombay Native Infantry, commanding at Kalat-i-Ghilzai, written on the 18th, intimating that all was well with his garrison, that the neighbourhood of Kalat-i-Ghilzai was quiet, and that General Phayre, writing from Quetta on the 12th of August, had stated that he hoped to be in Kandahar on the 2nd of September at latest. The following day heliographic communication was opened with Kalat-i-Ghilzai, and by this means news was heard of the welfare of the garrison of Kandahar: that they were in no straits for supplies for troops and followers, that they were all in good health and spirits, and that they had forage sufficient to hold out for some little time. Under these circumstances it was decided to push on, and give the troops a well-earned rest of one day at Kalat-i-Ghilzai; here the Field Force arrived on the 23rd, the distance from Ghazni, one hundred and thirty-four miles, having been marched in eight days, an average daily rate of sixteen miles and three-quarters having been sustained.

Being of opinion that it would be inconvenient to keep open communication with Kalat-i-Ghilzai for some time to come, and seeing no immediate advantage in continuing its occupation, General Roberts determined to withdraw the garrison and take it on to Kandahar. All the necessary arrangements for this purpose were made during the day the force halted, the 24th of August; and the charge of the fort was handed over to Muhammad Sadik Khan, a Toki Ghilzai, who had possession of it when the British troops under Sir Donald Stewart reached Kalat-i-Ghilzai in January, 1879. The following day the march was resumed.

On the 26th of August, at Tirandaz, news was received from General Primrose, commanding at Kandahar, that on the 23rd Ayub Khan had abandoned the villages to the east and west of Kandahar; and that on the 24th he had struck his camp and taken up a position in the Argandab Valley between Baba Wali and Mazra, due north of the city—thus practically abandoning the investment of Kandahar.

With the object of opening communication with General Primrose, and if possible, with General Phayre, who was advancing from Quetta, Brigadier-General Hugh Gough was despatched, on the morning of the 27th of August, with two regiments of cavalry to Robat, a distance of thirty-four miles, the remainder of the force moving forward the same day about half-way to that village. At Robat General Gough was met by Lieut-Colonel St. John, the Resident, and Major Adam, Assistant Quartermaster-General at Kandahar, and information was received to the effect that Ayub Khan was strengthening his position, which was said to extend from Gandizan to Kotal-i-Murcha, and would probably make a stand. Upon receipt of this news it was determined by the Lieutenant-General to halt one day at Robat, and to divide the remaining distance to Kandahar, nineteen miles, into two short marches. Soldiers, followers, and transport animals had been severely taxed by the long and continuous marching, and were beginning to feel the effects of the now daily increasing heat; it was desirable, moreover, that the troops should be brought into Kandahar in as fresh a state as possible, and fit for any work that might be required of them.

During the halt at Robat on the 29th, General Roberts received a letter from General Phayre stating that he was in hopes that his division, which had been retarded in its movements for want of transport, would be assembled at Kila Abdulla on the 28th, and be able to march for Kandahar on the 30th—a date which, it was apparent, would preclude the possibility of its arrival in time to co-operate with the Kabul force.

On the 31st of August the Field Force marched at 3.30 a.m. from Mohmand, whither it had advanced the previous day, for Kandahar. Sir Frederick Roberts, who had been ailing for some time, was carried in a dhoolie till within two miles of the city, when he mounted his horse in time to meet General Primrose and his brigadiers, a little to the east of Deh Khoja. By 8.30 a.m., the whole force had piled arms under the southern face of the city in front of the Shikarpur gate, where breakfast had been prepared for them by the garrison. All the baggage-animals were here unloaded and fed, as it was not improbable that the troops might have to fight for their camping-ground, a site for which was selected north of the city, the right resting on the cantonments—commanded by the Karez Hill—and the left on Old Kandahar. The Karez Hill was, however, unoccupied by the enemy, and together with the Picquet Hill was held by the 1st and 3rd Brigades, while the 2nd Brigade and the Cavalry were engaged on baggage and rear-guard duties. A few distant shots were fired at the advance guard, but no decided opposition was met with, and by 3 p.m. the whole force was tented. The total distance from Kalat-i-Ghilzai was eighty-eight miles, which had been traversed in seven days, including the halt at Robat.

Thus was brought to a successful issue one of the most memorable marches of modern times, an operation that had been unopposed throughout, owing, possibly, to the good offices of the new Amir, and had fortunately been greatly assisted by the favourable condition of the standing crops of autumn corn, which served as the principal means of feeding the numerous animals. On the other hand, it had been carried out through a hostile country by a force which had no base, and no assured line of retreat in the event of a reverse from the southward; and which was entirely dependent upon the country for its daily supply of meat, flour, and corn.

From the encampment of the Field Force, on the morning of the 31st of August, large bodies of the enemy were seen occupying the Baba Wali Kotal, distant two miles and a half from the north-west bastion of Kandahar, while working parties were observed to be engaged in constructing shelter-trenches along the crests of its under-features on the south-east, and by a cursory examination it at once became evident that a direct attack on Ayub Khan's position would be attended with severe loss. Under these circumstances, Sir Frederick Roberts—who, on arriving at Kandahar had assumed supreme command of the troops in Southern Afghanistan—decided on a turning movement by the enemy's right, and with a view of ascertaining how this operation could best be carried out, ordered General Gough to proceed with the 3rd Bengal Cavalry, 3rd Sikhs, and two guns of 11/9, R.A., to make as complete a reconnaissance as possible.

Starting at 1 p.m. on the 31st, General Gough made his way towards the high ground immediately above the village of Gandizan, and halting his infantry and guns, advanced about two miles farther with the cavalry to the front of the village of Pir Paimal, where it was found the enemy were strongly entrenched. As soon as the fire of the Afghan troops along this line had been drawn, the cavalry fell slowly back, the guns in rear being meantime brought into action; partly to test the range, and also to check the enemy, who now advanced in such numbers that eventually the whole of the 3rd Brigade, and part of the 1st Brigade, were ordered under arms. The required information having been obtained, the retirement was completed by dusk, not, however, without the loss of 4 killed, and 10 wounded. During the night occasional sharp bursts of musketry fire took place along the line of picquets to the westward, which were accordingly strengthened.

In the meantime General Roberts's plan of operations had been matured, and was personally explained by him at 6 a.m. to commanding officers. This plan, briefly, was to threaten the enemy's centre and left (the Baba Wali Kotal), and to attack in force his right by the village of Pir Paimal. The troops were to breakfast at 7 a.m., and to be in position soon after 8 a.m.

The whole of the infantry of the Kabul-Kandahar Field Force, to whom was entrusted the duty of carrying the enemy's position, were formed up in rear of the low hills which covered the front of the British camp, the right being at Picquet Hill, and the left resting on Chilzani, while the cavalry, under the command of Brigadier-General Hugh Gough, was held in readiness, in rear of the left, to operate by Gandizan towards the bed of the Argandab river, so as to threaten the rear of Ayub Khan's camp, and endanger his line of retreat towards Girishk and Khakrez. Four guns of E/B, R.H.A., two companies of the 2/7th Fusiliers, and four companies of the 28th Native Infantry, were placed at the disposal of General Gough to take up a position near Gandizan, and when opportunity might offer to support his advance. Small detachments of the 2/7th Fusiliers, 66th Foot, and 1st and 30th Bombay Native Infantry were detailed for the protection of the city, the remaining troops of General Primrose's command being ordered to be distributed as follows:—
A force under Brigadier-General Daubeny, composed of four companies 66th Foot, and two companies each of the 1st and 28th Bombay Native Infantry to hold the ground from which the Kabul force would advance to the attack; a force under Brigadier-General Burrows, consisting of C/2, R.A., four guns 5/11 R. A. (40-pounders), four companies 2/7th Foot, and the 4th and 19th Bombay Native Infantry, together with all the available cavalry, viz., the Poona Horse, 3rd Sind Horse, and 3rd Bombay Light Cavalry, under Brigadier-General Nuttall, to take up a position north of the cantonment, from which the 40-pounders might be brought to bear directly on the Baba Wali Pass: the cavalry being instructed to watch the pass called Kotal-i-Murcha, and to cover the city.

It was clear from a very early hour in the morning that an offensive movement was contemplated by the enemy. The villages of Gandizan and Gandi Mullah Sahibdab were held in strength; and a desultory fire was brought to bear upon the British front from the orchards connecting these two villages, while an ill-directed shell fire was opened from the Baba Wali Kotal, which was held by the enemy in force during the greater part of the day's operations.

At 9.30 a.m. fire was opened from the 40-pounders upon the Baba Wali Pass, and shortly afterwards the brigades of the Kabul-Kandahar Field Force were ordered to the attack, the 1st Brigade being on the right, the 2nd on the left, and the 3rd in reserve. Two batteries of artillery, viz., C/2, R.A., and 6/8, R.A., had meanwhile been placed in position to cover the advance of the infantry, and commenced shelling the village of Gandi Mullah Sahibdad. The instructions given by General Ross to General Macpherson were, to make his first attack on that village, and afterwards to clear the enemy from the enclosures which lay between the village and a low spur of the hill short of Pir Paimal. He further ordered General Baker to advance in a westerly direction, keeping touch with the 1st Brigade on his right, and clearing the gardens and orchards in his immediate front.

The attack upon the village of Gandi Mullah Sahibdad was made by the 2nd Goorkhas and 92nd Highlanders, under the respective commands of Lieut.-Colonels Battye and Parker, the remaining two regiments of the 1st Infantry Brigade being in support. The village was carried in the most dashing style, Goorkhas and Highlanders vying with each other in the rapidity of their advance. By 10.33 a.m. the enemy had withdrawn sullenly and leisurely, a considerable number remaining to the last in the village to receive a bayonet charge.

During the advance of the 1st Brigade on the village of Gandi Mullah Sahibdad, the 2nd Brigade had been threading its way through lanes and walled enclosures towards Gandizan, the first line being formed by the 72nd Highlanders on the left, and the 2nd Sikhs on the right, supported respectively by the 5th Goorkhas, with No. 2 Mountain Battery, and the 3rd Sikhs. The resistance encountered was most stubborn, the enemy being well protected by high loop-holed walls, and the leading battalions had frequently to fix bayonets to carry different points in the position, or to check determined rushes. The left wing of the 72nd, under Major Guinness, supported by the 5th Goorkhas, under Lieut.-Colonel Fitz-Hugh, soon carried the village, while the right wing, under Major Stockwell, cleared orchard after orchard, at one time being exposed to a terrible enfilading fire from a loop-holed wall which the 2nd Sikhs, on the right, were trying to turn. Here Colonel Brownlow and Captain Frome, of the former regiment, were killed. A few minutes later the wall was carried, and Baker's right reached some rather more open ground, where it was exposed to the fire of three guns from the Pir Paimal ridge, and to the rush of large masses of Ghazis, who, however, could make but little impression on the firm front presented by the 2nd Sikhs, under Colonel Boswell. A counter-attack at the point of the bayonet, by Stockwell's Highlanders, soon dispersed these bodies, and the brigade obtained a short breathing-time.

By this time the leading troops of the 1st Brigade were in alignment with Baker's right, and the moment had arrived for a final rush round the southern face of the ridge. The 92nd Highlanders and 2nd Goorkhas, rounding the face of the hill, soon carried the village, while Baker's troops, sweeping round to the left, cleared the closely-wooded gardens and orchards covering the western slopes of the ridge.

It was now noon, and up to this time the 3rd Brigade had taken no active part in the operations. This brigade had been drawn up in front of the village of Abasabad, with the double object of forming a reserve to the leading brigades, and of meeting a possible counter-stroke from the Baba Wali Kotal; but the capture of Pir Paimal had brought the leading British troops in rear of the pass, and seeing that nothing was now to be feared from the enemy's left centre and left, the Lieutenant-General ordered Brigadier-General MacGregor to advance to the support of Major-General Ross.

Meanwhile, however, Major White, commanding the advanced portion of the 92nd in Pir Paimal, found himself face to face with masses of the enemy, who seemed determined to make a final stand about their guns to the south-west of the Baba Wali Kotal; reinforcements also were hurrying up from the northward, and the guns on the Kotal itself were turned round to increase the heavy artillery fire brought to bear on the British advance. It became, therefore, necessary to storm this position without waiting for reinforcements, and, covered by the fire of 6/8, R.A., and supported by Becher's Goorkhas and the 23rd Pioneers, which had worked up into the front line, the 92nd, led by Major White, made a gallant rush and carried the two guns on the more easterly entrenchment. The enemy (said to have numbered about 8,000 at this point) were hopelessly broken by this advance;

the 92nd pressing forward like a wedge between him and the slopes of the ridge on his left as far as the western débouchure of the Baba Wali Kotal, drove him down towards the river, where Baker's brigade swept away numbers who tried to cling to the cover afforded by the lower watercourses to the westward, while a wing of the 3rd Sikhs, under Lieut.-Colonel Money, charged a body of men on the extreme British left, and succeeded in capturing three guns.

The enemy were now completely routed, the first stream of fugitives making for the Argandab in the Kokaran direction, where they fell into the hands of Gough's cavalry, and a second stream making off northwards to Ayub Khan's main camp at Mazra. Owing to the conformation of the ground, it was impossible, however, for General Ross, who was commanding in the front line, to realize the extent of his success; and expecting the enemy to take up a fresh position farther on, and to continue their resistance, he halted the 1st and 2nd Brigades, and ordered them to replenish with ammunition. When this had been done, the advance was continued, when, on rounding a spur which had hitherto hid Mazra from view, the leading troops came in sight of Ayub's chief camp, standing deserted, and apparently just as it had been left by the enemy in the morning. A little after 3 p.m. it was occupied by the two brigades, which then moved forward to Mazra, where they were shortly afterwards joined by the 3rd Brigade.

With his camp Ayub Khan lost all his artillery, numbering thirty-two pieces, including the two guns of E/B, R.H.A., which had been captured by his troops at Maiwand. The success of the day was clouded by the barbarous murder of Lieutenant Maclaine, R.H.A., who, having been a prisoner of war in Ayub's camp since the 27th of July, was now found with his throat cut, close to Ayub's tent.

The operations of the cavalry were continued throughout the day; while General Gough, crossing the Argandab river and pushing beyond the line of the enemy's retreat towards Kakrez, succeeded in cutting up some 350 fugitive Ghazis and irregulars, General Nuttall, taking his squadrons across the Baba Wali Kotal and up the left bank of the river, rendered a good account of the enemy in that direction. With the exception of the 1st Brigade, which remained halted at Mazra for the night, all the troops returned to Kandahar before dark.

The number of the Kabul-Kandahar Field Force engaged on this day was 8,392 of all ranks, and the casualties, 35 killed, including 3 British officers, and 213 wounded, including 9 British officers; of the Kandahar garrison—who, by setting free the whole of the Bengal troops, contributed materially to the success of the day—4,110 of all ranks were under arms, 1 of whom was killed, and 5 wounded. The strength of the enemy was computed to have been 4,800 regulars and 8,000 irregulars; and his estimated loss was 1,200 killed, of whom 600 were counted and buried between Kandahar and Pir Paimal alone.

After toiling through Sind and the Bolan Pass at the very hottest time of the year, the troops under General Phayre destined for the relief of Kandahar from the south, had been retarded in their further advance, not only by formidable difficulties in connection with transport and supplies, but also by having to take serious precautions, in view of the hostile attitude assumed by the Marris and other tribes, for the safety of the line of communications, by which alone supplies could be furnished for the garrison of Kandahar and the Kabul-Kandahar Field Force. Though great exertions were put forth to overcome these obstacles, the division was only able to reach Abdul Rahman, twenty-six miles distant from Kandahar, by the 3rd of

September, on which date Sir Frederick Roberts's despatches were received announcing the crushing defeat of the forces of Ayub Khan two days previously.

With the battle of Kandahar the second Afghan War was brought to a close. The recent accession of a Liberal Government to office resulted in a complete reversal of the policy which had been pursued by their predecessors, and it was now determined to abandon the advanced military positions on the north-west frontier which had been acquired by the treaty of Gandamak, and to restore Kandahar, as soon as arrangements could be made for doing so, to the dominion of Afghanistan. Conformably with this intention, the Kuram Valley and Khyber Pass were successively evacuated by the British troops during the winter of 1880-1881, the independence of the Turis of the Kuram Valley, and the tribes inhabiting the Khyber Pass and contiguous country, being recognized, and arrangements being made with the latter for keeping the road through the Pass open and free from interference. In the meantime an early opportunity had been taken to inform the Amir that the Government were disposed to reconsider the arrangements which had been made with reference to Southern Afghanistan, and during the succeeding summer, after brief negotiation, the province of Kandahar was transferred to his rule, the districts of Sibi and Pishin being thus the only portion of the territory assigned to India by the treaty of Gandamak which was still retained, and this only as a temporary measure. The apprehensions which had disturbed both India and England in and before 1878 were dispelled; and with the present Amir of Kabul established without a rival in the country, and closely bound by his interests, if not by his gratitude, to the Power to which he owes his throne, there appeared ground for hope that the danger of foreign interference in the affairs of Afghanistan was at an end.

RECORDS OF SERVICE.

THE AFGHAN WAR-MEDAL AND CLASPS.

LL troops who served over the Afghan frontier between the 22nd November, 1878, and the 26th May, 1879, and between the 3rd September, 1879, and the 15th August, 1880, on the Khyber and Kuram lines, and the 20th September, 1880, in Southern Afghanistan, are entitled to receive the Medal.

Clasps have been granted for the battles or actions of "Peiwar Kotal," "Ali Musjid," "Charasia," "Kabul," "Ahmed Kheyl," and "Kandahar," and a bronze decoration for the march from Kabul to the relief of Kandahar.

STAFF, TRANSPORT, COMMISSARIAT, &c.,

Being the Services of Officers who were employed during the War exclusively on other than regimental duty.

LT.-COLONEL *H. R. Abadie, 9th Lancers.* (For services see 9th Lancers.)

Capt. A. K. Abbott, B.S.C., served with the Transport Corps, Kuram Valley F.F., from 14 Jan. till 7 Apl., 1879, and with the Punjab Chiefs' Contingent from 6 May, 1879, till conclusion of first campaign. Was appointed to the command of various posts on the line of communication. Conducted the Kapur Thala troops to their State.

Major F. J. S. Adam, Bo.S.C., served during the second campaign as Assistant Quartermaster-General, Kandahar Field Force, being present throughout the defence of Kandahar, and at the battle of Kandahar. (Mentioned in despatches.)

Lieut. J. C. Addison, R.E., served during the second campaign as Assistant Field Engineer, Khyber Line Force.

Lieut. W. Adye, Royal Irish Rifles, served throughout the second campaign, first as Transport Officer on the Kandahar line, having charge, for six months, of the stations of Dozan and Darwaza in the Bolan Pass, and afterwards as Brigade Transport Officer, 1st Division, Kandahar F.F., at Kandahar. Performed garrison duty throughout the siege. During the retirement of the troops from the sortie to Deh Khwaja distinguished himself by carrying, under a heavy fire, two of the wounded to places of safety. Was present at the reconnaissance of 31 Aug., 1880, and the battle of Kandahar. Proceeded to India in Nov., 1880, to rejoin his regiment prior to embarkation to Natal. (Recommended by H.E. the Commander-in-Chief, and by General Primrose, for the Victoria Cross.)

Lieut. A. Adye, B.S.C. (For services see 5th Bengal L.I.)

Surgeon-General F. F. Allen, M.D., Q.H.P., C.B., late Bengal Med. Dept., served as Principal Medical Officer, Kuram F.F., from Oct., 1878, till Nov., 1879, being present at the assault and capture of the Peiwar Kotal. (Mentioned in despatches.)

Lieut. F. E. Allsopp, R.A. (For services see R.A.)

Major M. A. Alves, R.E., served with the 1st Division, Kabul F.F., during the second campaign, being present at the action of Charasiab, 25 April, 1880. (Mentioned in despatches.)

Capt. A. D. Anderson, R.A., served throughout the first campaign as Brigade Major of R.A., under Brigadier-General Arbuthnot, commanding R.A. in S. Afghanistan, and on the head-quarter Staff of General Stewart, commanding S. Afghanistan F.F., taking part in the original advance on, and occupation of, Kandahar and Kalat-i-Ghilzai.

Major W. C. Anderson, B.S.C. (For services see 3rd Punjab Cavalry.)

Capt. J. W. Andrews, Devonshire Regt., served during the second campaign as Brigade Major, 2nd Division, Kandahar F.F.

Capt. J. Angus, York and Lancashire Regt., served with the Transport Dept. in the first campaign.

Colonel F. E. Appleyard, C.B., commanded, with rank of Brigadier-General, the 3rd Brigade, 1st Divis., Peshawar Valley F.F., from the date of its formation on the outbreak of the war, till it was broken up on the 3rd Dec., 1878, taking part in the front attack on Ali Musjid. From 3 Dec., 1878, till 24 March, 1879, was in command of all troops on the line extending from Ali Musjid to Landi Kotal. Took part, in command of the Ali Musjid Column, in the second Bazar Valley expedition, and commanded the rear and flank guards (which extended over three miles) of the expeditionary force during its return march. Commanded the 3rd Brigade, 1st Divis., Peshawar Valley F.F., from 24 March, 1879, till after peace was signed, being in command at Jalalabad after the departure of the other units of the Division for Gandamak on the 12th April, 1879. After returning to India, assumed command, 19 June, 1879, of the Multan Division. (Three times mentioned in despatches.)

Colonel Sir C. G. Arbuthnot, K.C.B., R.A., commanded the R.A., 1st Division, Kandahar F.F., during the first campaign, taking part in the advance on and occupation of Kandahar. During the second campaign commanded the 2nd Brigade of the Khyber Division and subsequently a moveable column of the Khyber Line Force. Commanded a column of the expeditionary force in the operations against the Wazir Kugianis, the operations in the Hissarak District, and operations in the Lughman Valley. (Mentioned in despatches.)

Bt. Lieut.-Colonel A. R. Badcock, C.B., B.S.C., joined the Kuram F.F. as Chief Commissariat Officer, Sep., 1878, and served throughout all operations until Aug., 1879, when sent to England on sick leave. On services being called for, returned to India, and rejoined at Kabul 15 Nov., 1879. Appointed Depy. Commissary-General, Kabul F.F., and served throughout all operations round Kabul; also accompanied the Kabul-Kandahar F.F. on its march to Kandahar, and served with it as Depy. Commissary-General until it was broken up in Oct., 1880. (Three times mentioned in despatches, and services twice specially brought to the notice of the Govt. of India; Brevet of Major and of Lt.-Colonel; C.B.)

Lieut. J. M. T. Badgley, R.E.

Lieut. C. H. Bagot, R.E.

Capt. J. E. Baines, Royal Warwickshire Regt., joined the Transport Corps at Kohat, 9 Jan., 1879, and was employed at that station and at Thal in raising and organizing the local carriage. Performed both Commissariat and Transport duty at Kohat during the equipment of General Roberts' Force for its advance on Kabul. On 14th Oct., 1879, marched with General Tytler's Force as Transport Officer and Provost Marshal to Kuram. Appointed Asst.-Genl. Transport Officer at Thal, 6 Nov., 1879, an appointment he resigned for that of Brigade Transport Officer with General Tytler's Force about to proceed on the Zaimusht expedition, but was invalided on the day the expeditionary force departed. Was subsequently again posted to Kohat, where he served till invalided to England in May, 1880.

Major G. Baker, Hampshire Regt. (For services see 67th Foot.)

Colonel Sir T. D. Baker, K.C.B., A.D.C., commanded a brigade of the Kabul and Kabul-Kandahar Field Forces from the date of its formation in Sept., 1879, when it formed the advance guard on the Shutargardan, till Oct., 1880. Was in command of the whole force engaged at the actions of Charasiab, Takht-i-Shah, Asmai Heights, and the repulse of the enemy at Sherpur on the 23rd Dec., 1879; of the force employed in the expeditions into Maidan and Kohistan, and in the various operations in connection therewith; and of the brigade in the march from Kabul to the relief of Kandahar, and at the battle of Kandahar. (Several times mentioned in despatches; K.C.B.)

Capt. E. A. Ball, Royal Warwickshire Regt., served during the second campaign as Transport Officer, Khyber Line.

Lieut. R. A. Bannatine, R.H.A., arrived at Kandahar, April, 1879, and served there with a field battery till the conclusion of the first campaign. Was appointed Adjutant of Field Artillery, S. Afghanistan, 27 Sep., 1879. Accompanied Brigadier-General Hughes' Brigade beyond Kalat-i-Ghilzai, and was present at the affair at Shahjui. Was appointed Adjutant of Artillery, S. Afghanistan F.F., and subsequently of the Ghazni and of the 3rd Divis., N. Afghanistan F.F. Marched with Sir D. Stewart's Division from Kandahar to Kabul, and was present at the battle of Ahmad Khel and the action of Arzu. As Orderly Officer to Col. Johnson, commanding R.A. Kabul-Kandahar F.F., took part in the advance to the relief of Kandahar, and was present at the reconnaissance of the 31st Aug., 1880, and the battle of Kandahar, in which his horse was wounded. (Twice mentioned in despatches.)

Capt. A. T. Banon, B.S.C., served with the Transport Dept. in the first campaign, from March till July, 1879.

Lieut. C. P. Barchard, P.W.O. West Yorkshire Regt., served as Brigade Transport Officer, 2nd Brigade, Reserve Division, Khyber Force, from 10 Feb., till 16 March, 1880, and as Orderly Officer to Brigadier-General R. Sale Hill, from the latter date till the conclusion of the campaign.

Lieut. E. A. Barclay, Bo.S.C., served with the Commissariat Dept. throughout the second campaign.

RECORDS OF SERVICE.

Major J. H. Barnard, C.M.G., Royal Munster Fusiliers, served during the first and throughout the second campaign as Aide-de-Camp to General Bright, in N. Afghanistan, being present at the operations in the Lughman Valley, the operations against the Wazir Kugianis, and the operations in the Hissarak District. (Mentioned in despatches; Brevet of Major.)

Lieut. H. H. Barnet, R.E., served as Asst. Field Engineer with the force under General Phayre's command during Sept. and Oct., 1879, and was subsequently employed till invalided home in March, 1880, on the preliminary and ordinary survey for the railway through the hills above Sibi.

Lt.-Colonel J. Barras, Bo.S.C., served during the second campaign as chief Transport Officer with General Phayre's Division, taking part in the advance from Quetta to Kandahar in the autumn of 1880. (Mentioned in despatches.)

Bt.-Major S. D. Barrow, B.S.C. (For services see 10th D. C. O. Bengal Lancers.)

Major T. A. A. Barstow, Seaforth Highlanders, served in the Kuram F.F. as Orderly Officer to Brigadier-General Cobbe and Col. Drew from the commencement of the war till Aug., 1879, with the exception of a period during which he acted as Superintendent of Army Signalling. Was present at the front attack and capture of the Peiwar Kotal, took part in the Khost Valley expedition, and was present at the action of Matun. (Mentioned in despatches.)

Colonel R. Barter, C.B., B.S.C., served as Brigadier-General in command of the 1st Brigade of Sir Donald Stewart's Division during both campaigns, taking part in the advance on and occupation of Kandahar and Kolat-i-Ghilzai, and the advance on Ghazni and to Kabul, and being present at the battle of Ahmad Khel, the action of Arzu, and the operations in the Logar Valley and about Kabul till Aug., 1880, when, being compelled by sickness to resign his command, he returned to India by the Khyber Pass. (Mentioned in despatches; C.B.)

Bt. Lt.-Colonel H. J. Barton, B.S.C., served with the Commissariat Dept. in S. Afghanistan during the second campaign. (Mentioned in despatches; Brevet of Lt.-Colonel.)

Capt. G. W. Bartram, R.E., served with the 1st Division, Peshawar Valley F.F. throughout the first campaign, during the greater part of the time in charge of the Field Park. Was present at the assault and capture of Ali Musjid, and took part in the first Bazar Valley expedition.

Lieut. F. Beauclerk, R.E.

Major R. Beaven, B.S.C., served during the first campaign in charge of the Survey operations with General Biddulph's Division, carrying a route-survey through the Dera Bugti country, the Bolan Pass, from Quetta to Kandahar, by the Khojak Pass, and to Girishk, and mapping the country round Kandahar. During the second campaign served in charge of the Survey operations in Baluchistan. (Mentioned in despatches.)

Lieut. A. C. Becker, Norfolk Regt. (For services see 9th Foot.)

Major A. W. R. Becker, Bengal Cavalry, served during both campaigns as Superintendent of Transport, Kandahar line.

Lt.-Colonel S. W. Bell, Retired, late Border Regt., served with the Transport Dept. in the first campaign.

Surgeon-Major H. W. Bellew, C.S.I., I.M.D., served on the Political Staff with the Kabul F.F. during the second campaign, from 19th Sept., 1879, till 4th Jan., 1880, being present at the defence of Ali Khel in Oct., 1879, and the operations round Kabul and defence of Sherpur in Dec., 1879. (Mentioned in despatches.)

Capt. Lord W. L. de la P. Beresford, V.C., 9th Lancers. (For services see 9th Lancers.)

Capt. W. J. de la P. Beresford-Peirse, Berkshire Regt. (For services see 66th Foot.)

Lt.-Colonel G. F. Beville, Bo.S.C., commanded the Sind Frontier Force at Sukkur during the first campaign. During the second campaign served as Deputy Judge Advocate, Kandahar Field Force, and also performed the duties of Provost Marshal, being present throughout the defence of Kandahar, and at the battle of Kandahar. (Mentioned in despatches.)

Lt.-General Sir. M. A. S. Biddulph, K.C.B., R.A., commanded the Quetta Division Kandahar Field Force, and the Thal-Chotiali Field Force, respectively, from the dates of their formation until they were broken up, taking part in the original advance on and occupation of Kandahar and Girishk, being present at the repulse of the rear-guard attack near Atta Karez, and opening up the new Thal-Chotiali route to India. (Received the thanks of both Houses of Parliament for his services; mentioned in despatches; K.C.B.)

Capt. M. W. Biddulph, Northumberland Fusiliers, served in Southern Afghanistan during the second campaign as Superintendent of Army Signalling, accompanying General Phayre's Division in its advance from Quetta to Kandahar.

Lieut. S. F. Biddulph, Border Regt., served as Aide-de-Camp to Major-General Biddulph throughout the period of his service in the war, taking part in the original advance on and occupation of

Kandahar and Girishk, being present at the repulse of the rear-guard attack near Atta Karez, and returning with the Thal-Chotiali F.F. to India. (Mentioned in despatches.)

Capt. E. H. Bingham, B.S.C. (For services see 13th Regt. B.N.I.)

Lt.-Colonel A. J. C. Birch, B.S.C., served with the Transport Dept. in the first campaign.

Bt. Lt.-Colonel G. C. Bird, M.S.C. (For services see 1st Punjab Cavalry.)

Lieut. W. S. Birdwood, Bo.S.C., served during the second campaign with the Transport Train S. Afghanistan Field Force.

Bt. Lt.-Colonel W. W. Biscoe, Bengal Cavalry. (For services see 19th Bengal Lancers.)

Bt. Major E. B. Bishop, B.S.C. (For services see 3rd Goorkhas.)

Bt. Major L. T. Bishop, B.S.C. (For services see 2nd Punjab Cavalry.)

Bt. Major W. S. S. Bisset, R.E., served as Field Engineer, 2nd Division, Kandahar F.F., during the first campaign, taking part in the advance on and occupation of Kandahar. (Mentioned in despatches; Brevet of Major.)

Bt. Lt.-Colonel H. F. Blair, R.E., served during the first campaign as Field Engineer, 1st Division, Peshawar Valley F.F., being present at the action of Futtehabad. (Mentioned in despatches; Brevet of Lt.-Colonel.)

Capt. E. Blaksley, R.A., served as Brigade Major, R.A., General Phayre's Division, from Aug. till the end of Nov., 1880, taking part in the advance to Kandahar; and as Adjutant, R.A., at Kandahar till the evacuation. (Mentioned in despatches.)

Major F. H. Blanshard, Bo.S.C., served with the Commissariat Dept. in the second campaign.

Lieut. E. Blunt, R.E., served during both campaigns as Superintendent of Army Signalling, Khyber line.

Major-General F. S. Blyth, C.B., commanded the 1st Brigade, 2nd Division, Peshawar Valley F.F. during the first campaign. Commanded the Jamrud Column in the second Bazar Valley expedition. (Mentioned in despatches; C.B.)

Major-General T. W. R. Boisragon (retired). (For services see 30th P.N.I.)

Bt.-Colonel J. Bonus, R.E., was employed during the second campaign as Engineer-in-Chief on the Peshawar-Jalalabad Railway Survey.

Lieut. L. E. B. Booth, West Riding Regt., served in the Transport Train, 1st Division, Kabul F.F., and Kabul-Kandahar F.F.; during the second campaign, being present at the action of Charasiab, taking part in the advance from Kabul to the relief of Kandahar, and being present at the battle of Kandahar. (Twice mentioned in despatches.)

Lieut. C. E. Borton, Norfolk Regt. (For services see 2nd Battn. 9th Foot.)

Capt. G. F. O. Boughey, R.E., served as Field Engineer, Kuram F.F., during the second campaign.

Capt. A. Bowles, East Yorkshire Regt., served in S. Afghanistan from May till Sept., 1880, as Transport Officer, Kandahar line.

Lieut. W. G. Bowyer, R.E.

Lt.-Colonel J. M. Boyd, Bo.S.C., served as Executive Commissariat Officer throughout the second campaign, taking part in the advance of General Phayre's Division from Quetta to Kandahar. (Mentioned in despatches.)

Major W. J. Boyes, late 12th Foot, served as Assistant Adjutant-General to General Bright's Division from Oct., 1879, till the conclusion of the campaign. (Mentioned in despatches; Brevet of Major.)

Bt. Major J. P. Brabazon, 10th Hussars. (For services see 10th Hussars.)

Capt. M. C. Brackenbury, R.E., served as Field Engineer with the Kabul and Kabul-Kandahar Field Forces, taking part in the advance from Kabul to the relief of Kandahar, and being present at the battle of Kandahar. (Mentioned in despatches.) Subsequently took part in the Marri expedition.

Capt. W. Bradish, Dorsetshire Regt., served with the Commissariat Dept., in the second campaign.

Capt. A. J. Brander, B.S.C., served with the Commissariat Dept. in the 2nd Division Peshawar Valley F.F. during the first campaign.

Bt. Colonel M. J. Brander, B.S.C., served with the Transport Corps, S. Afghanistan, throughout the first campaign.

Lt.-General Sir R. O. Bright, K.C.B., commanded, first, the Rawal Pindi Division, and afterwards the 2nd Division, Peshawar Valley F.F. during the first campaign. Throughout the second campaign commanded the Khyber Division, commanded the expeditionary forces in the operations in the Lughman Valley, the operations against the Wazir Kugianis, and the operations in the Hissarak district. (Received the thanks of both Houses of Parliament; K.C.B.)

Major Sir B. P. Bromhead, Bart., B.S.C., served during both campaigns as Assistant General Transport Officer, Khyber line. (Mentioned in despatches.)

Brigadier-General H. F. Brooke. (Killed in action. See Biographical Division.)

Capt. R. O'S. Brooke, A.P.D., served during the second campaign as Provost Marshal, Khyber Division, Kabul F.F. (Mentioned in despatches.)

Major A. P. Broome, Bengal Infantry. (For services see 12th Bengal Cavalry.)

Lieut. R. H. Brown, R.E., served during the second campaign as Assistant Field Engineer, Khyber Line Force, being present at the operations at Besud. (Mentioned in despatches.)

Colonel T. S. Brown (retired). Commanded a brigade in the 2nd Division, Kandahar F.F., during the second campaign.

Bt. Colonel James Browne, C.S.I., R.E., served during the first campaign as Political Officer with the Kandahar F.F., and Thal-Chotiali F.F., taking part in the advance on and occupation of Kandahar, the advance to the Halmand, and the opening up of the new route to India.

Lieut. L. J. Browne, B.S.C., served as a Transport Officer in the first campaign.

Lt.-General Sir S. J. Browne, K.C.B., K.C.S.I., V.C., B.S.C., commanded the 1st Division Peshawar Valley F.F. from the date of its formation, and the whole of the troops in N. Afghanistan during the latter phase of the first campaign. Was present in personal command at the front attack on Ali Musjid, the forcing of the Khyber Pass, and the advance to Daka, Jalalabad, and Gandamak. (Received the thanks of the Government of India and of both Houses of Parliament; K.C.B.)

Colonel T. S. Brown, h.p. (retired), commanded, with rank of Brigadier-General, the 2nd Brigade of General Phayre's Division during the second campaign, taking part in the advance from Quetta to Kandahar. (Mentioned in despatches.)

Colonel W. B. Browne (retired), commanded, with rank of Brigadier-General, the 4th Brigade, 1st Division, Peshawar Valley F.F., from the date of its formation on the outbreak of the war, till it was broken up on the 5th Dec., 1878, taking part in the front attack on Ali Musjid, and the forcing of the Khyber Pass. (Mentioned in despatches.)

Major W. H. Browne, B.S.C., served with the Transport Train, Kandahar line, during both campaigns.

Major H. S. Brownrigg, Rifle Brigade, served during the first campaign as Deputy Assistant Quartermaster-General, 2nd Division, Peshawar Valley F.F., was present at the operations in the Shiliman Valley. (Mentioned in despatches; Brevet of Major.)

Lieut. A. C. Bruce, R.E., served from April, 1879, till the conclusion of the first campaign as Asst. Field Engineer, 2nd Division, Peshawar Valley F.F., and subsequently with the Khyber Brigade at Landi Kotal; in the second campaign served in the same capacity with the Khyber Line Force, principally as Fort Engineer at Daka, till invalided in May, 1880. (Mentioned in despatches.)

Major E. A. Bruce, M.S.C., served during both campaigns from Dec., 1878, till June, 1880, as Executive Commissariat Officer with the Vitakri and Kuram Field Forces, respectively.

Colonel E. J. Bruce, R.A., served during the first campaign in command of the Siege Train, Kandahar F.F. (Since deceased.)

Deputy Surgeon-General L. S. Bruce, served as Principal Medical Officer, 2nd Division, S. Afghanistan F.F., throughout the second campaign, performing the whole of the administrative work of the Med. Dept., European and Native, along the line of communication from Sibi to Kandahar, and arranging for the medical requirements of Kandahar itself. After the relief of Kandahar, took over, in addition to his own duties, those of Depy. Surg.-Gen. Hanbury, and supervised the Med. Dept. of the S. A. F.F., till the arrival of Dr. Simpson from Bengal. (Mentioned in despatches.)

Mr. R. I. Bruce, C.I.E., C.S., served during the first campaign as Assistant Commissioner with the Quetta Division, Kandahar F.F.

Lieut. P. A. Buckland, B.S.C., served during the war in the Commissariat Dept., Kuram Valley F.F.

Major W. R. Bunbury, B.S.C., served during the war in the Commissariat Dept., Kuram F.F.

Lt.-Colonel H. M. B. Burlton, B.S.C., performed Political duty in Afghanistan during the war.

Lt.-Colonel N. R. Burlton, B.S.C., served during the second campaign as Principal Commissariat Officer of the Khyber line of communications.

Lieut. A. Burlton-Bennet, B.S.C. (Deceased. See Biographical Division.)

Capt. J. R. Burlton-Bennet, B.S.C., served throughout the first campaign as Personal Assistant to the Chief Commissariat Officer, and Executive Commissariat Officer, 1st Division, Peshawar Valley F.F., being present at the capture of Ali Musjid, the forcing of the Khyber Pass, and the advance to Jalalabad and Safed Sang. On the return of the troops to India was deputed to collect and arrange the Afghan Campaign account. Organized and supervised a new Field Accounts Office for the second campaign, and remained in charge of it till invalided to England in Nov., 1880.

Bt. Lt.-Colonel C. J. Burnett, East Yorkshire Regt., served during 1879 as Brigade Major to the Sind Reserve Brigade. (Thanked in orders and minutes.) Served as Asst. Adjutant-General to the Kandahar F.F. from March, 1880, till the conclusion of the war, taking part in the defence of Kandahar, the sortie to Deh Khwaja, and the battle of Kandahar. (Twice mentioned in despatches; Brevet of Lt.-Colonel.)

Capt. H. Burnley, 6th Dragoon Guards. (For services see 6th Dragoon Guards.)

Lieut. J. Burn-Murdoch, R.E., served in the first campaign as Asst. Field Engineer, and subsequently as Adjutant, R.E., Kuram F.F. In the second campaign took part in the advance of Sir F. Roberts' force on Kabul, proceeding in charge of the R.E. Park over the Shutargardan, and being present at the action of Charasiab. Was present at the fighting round Kabul in Dec., 1879, the defence of Sherpur, and the action of the 23rd Dec., in which he was wounded. (Twice mentioned in despatches.)

Lieut. E. Burrell, Shropshire Regt., served as Deputy Assistant Quartermaster-General, Kuram Force, from 15 Oct., 1879, till the conclusion of the campaign, taking part in the Zaimusht expedition, and being present at the storming of Zawa. (Mentioned in despatches.)

Major-General G. R. S. Burrows, Bombay Infantry, commanded, during the second campaign, first, a brigade at Jacobabad, afterwards the assigned district of Sibi, and eventually, from March, 1880, a brigade of the Kandahar F.F. Commanded the brigade which marched from Kandahar in July, 1880, for Girishk: at the defeat of the Wali Shere Ali Khan's mutinied troops on the 14th July, at the battle of Maiwand, and throughout the defence of Kandahar. Commanded a mixed force at the battle of Kandahar. (Four times mentioned in despatches.)

Bt. Major F. C. Burton, B.S.C., commanded the Kapurthala Contingent, consisting of a mixed force of 2,000 men, on the line of communications in the Kuram Valley from Thal to Bulesh Khel, during the first campaign. Appointed Political Officer on line of communications from Landi Kotal to Kabul. Raised and organized the Native Levies. Appointed Political Officer of the Eastern Ghilzais from Jagdalak to Kabul. Accompanied Col. Mackenzie's force as Political Officer and Guide when the surprise and capture of Badda, in the Shinwari country, was effected, for which the thanks of the Viceroy were received. Recovered from the Stanizai Ghilzais Rs. 80,000, in gold, raided from the Kokhand merchants. Recovered 21 bags looted mails during the operations around Jagdalak in Dec., 1879, for which he received the thanks of Sir F. Roberts. Was placed in political charge of the rear-guard on the withdrawal of the troops from Kabul. (Received the thanks of Government; Brevet of Major.)

Captain G. S. Burton, Norfolk Regt. (For services see 2nd Battn., 9th Foot.)

Bt. Lt.-Colonel F. J. Caldecott, R.A., served during the second campaign as Commissary of Ordnance, Kandahar F.F., being present in Kandahar throughout the siege. (Mentioned in despatches; Brevet of Lt.-Colonel.)

Bt. Major C. F. Call, R.E., served during the first campaign as Assistant Field Engineer, 1st Division, Kandahar F.F., taking part in the advance on and occupation of Kandahar, and being present at the action of Saif-u-din. During the second campaign served, first as Field Engineer, Kandahar Force, and afterwards as Brigade Major, Ghazni and Kabul-Kandahar Field Forces, taking part in the advance from Kandahar on Ghazni and into the Logar Valley, and the advance from Kabul to the relief of Kandahar, and being present at the battle of Ahmad Khel, the action of Arzu, and the battle of Kandahar. (Twice mentioned in despatches; Brevet of Major.)

Lieut. G. T. Campbell, King's Royal Rifle Corps, served during the first campaign as Aide-de-Camp to Sir Sam. Browne, Commanding 1st Division Peshawar Valley F.F.

Lieut. J. C. Campbell, R.E. (For services see R.E.)

Bt. Lt.-Colonel W. M. Campbell, R.E., from March, 1879, till Nov., 1879, had charge, as Senior Officer of the Dept., of the whole of the Survey operations in Southern Afghanistan. On the renewal of hostilities accompanied Brigadier-General Hughes' force to Kalat-i-Ghilzai. (Brevet of Lt.-Colonel.)

Lieut. W. B. Capper, Shropshire Regt. (For services see 85th Foot.)

Major S. Cargill, R.A., served during the second campaign in charge of the Ordnance Field Park, Khyber Division, Kabul F.F.

Major F. S. Carr, Bengal Infantry. (For services see 5th Punjab Cavalry.)

Capt. C. A. Carchew, B.S.C. (Deceased. See Biographical Division.)

Major C. Case, B.S.C., served in the Commissariat Dept., in S. Afghanistan, during the war.

Lieut. T. P. Cather, R.E., served during the second campaign as Adjutant, R.E., Kabul F.F. and Kabul-Kandahar F.F., taking part in the operations round Kabul and defence of Sherpur in Dec., 1879, the advance from Kabul to the relief of Kandahar, and being present at the battle of Kandahar. (Twice mentioned in despatches.)

Major Sir P. L. N. Cavagnari, K.C.B., C.I.E., B.S.C. (Deceased. See Biographical Division.)

Major R. Chalmer, King's Royal Rifle Corps, served in Afghanistan from Feb., 1879, till March, 1880: first as Brigade Major to Brigadier-General Barter, being present at the battle of Ahmad Khel, the surrender of Ghazni, and the action of Arzu; afterwards marched with Sir F. Roberts' force from Kabul to the relief of Kandahar, as Brigade Major to Brigadier-General MacGregor, and was present at the battle of Kandahar. (Three times mentioned in despatches; Brevet of Major.) Subsequently served as Brigade Major to Brigadier-General MacGregor in the Marri expedition. (Mentioned in despatches.)

Lieut. N. F. F. Chamberlain, B.S.C., served during the first campaign as Orderly Officer to General Roberts, being present at the assault and capture of the Peiwar Kotal, and during the second campaign as Assistant Political Officer, 1st Division Kabul F.F., taking part in the advance on and occupation of Kabul, and being present at the action of Charasiab, and operations round Kabul and defence of Sherpur in Dec., 1879. (Three times mentioned in despatches.)

Bt. Colonel E. F. Chapman, A.D.C., C.B., R.A., served throughout both campaigns: first as Assistant Quartermaster-General of Sir D. Stewart's Division, taking part in the advance on and occupation of Kandahar and Kolat-i-Ghilzai; afterwards as D.A. and Q.M.G. of the Ghazni and N. Afghanistan Field Forces, and as Chief of the Staff Kabul-Kandahar F.F., taking part in the advance on Ghazni and into the Logar Valley, and the advance from Kabul to the relief of Kandahar, and being present at the battle of Ahmad Khel, the action of Arzu, and the battle of Kandahar. (Twice mentioned in despatches; Brevet of Lt.-Colonel; C.B.)

Lt.-Colonel F. S. Cherry, Madr. Cav., served during the first campaign as Asst. Supt. of Tr., P.V.F.F.

Lieut. E. S. E. Childers, R.E., served during the first campaign as Assistant Field Engineer, 1st Division, Kandahar F.F., taking part in the advance on and occupation of Kandahar and Kalat-i-Ghilzai, and being present at the action of Takht-i-pul. Served during the second campaign as Orderly Officer to General Macpherson, taking part in the advance on and occupation of Kabul, and the advance from Kabul to the relief of Kandahar, and being present at the action of Charasiab, the operations round Kabul, and defence of Sherpur in Dec., 1879, and the battle of Kandahar. (Mentioned in despatches.)

Lieut. W. H. Chippendall, R.E., served at Quetta and the neighbourhood from Dec., 1878, till invalided home in Aug., 1880, performing various duties as Executive and Assistant Engineer. Was Executive Engineer in the Pishin Valley during March and April, 1880.

Mr. A. Christie, C.S., served during the first campaign as Assistant Commissioner with the Kuram Valley F.F., and during the second campaign with the Kabul F.F.

Mr. James Christie, C.I.E., C.S., accompanied Mr. Griffin, as Head of the Intelligence Dept., on his special Political Mission to Kabul.

Lieut. P. R. S. Churchward, North Lancashire Regt. (For services see 81st Foot.)

Mr. E. H. Clarke accompanied Mr. Griffin, as personal assistant, on his special Political Mission to Kabul.

Major S. C. Clarke, R.E., was employed during the second campaign on the Peshawar-Jalalabad Railway Survey.

Major R. C. R. Clifford, B.S.C. (For services see 2nd Punjab Cavalry.)

Brigadier-General A. H. Cobbe, C.B., commanded the 1st Brigade Kuram Valley F.F. from 29th Oct., 1878, till 2nd Dec., 1878. Was present, in command of the front attack, at the storming of the Peiwar Kotal, on which occasion he was severely wounded. Resumed command of the brigade on the 1st March, 1879, and retained it till the 26th June, 1879, when he was appointed to the command of the Agra district. (Twice mentioned in despatches; C.B.)

Capt. E. B. Coke, R.H.A., served during the second campaign as Assistant Road Commandant, Khyber line of communications.

Capt. E. H. H. Collen, B.S.C., served during the second campaign as Assistant to the Controller-General of Transport and Supply. Was deputed by that officer to proceed on a tour of inspection to Kabul in the Spring of 1880.

Lt.-Colonel H. Collett, C.B., B.S.C. (For services see 23rd P.N.I.)

Bt. Lieut.-Colonel J. F. Fitz G. Cologan, B.S.C., served during the second campaign as Transport Officer and Offg. Transport Staff Officer, Khyber Line. (Mentioned in despatches; Brevet of Lt.-Colonel.)

Major J. A. S. Colquhoun, R.A., served with the Kuram F.F. as Commissary of Ordnance in charge of the Ordnance Field Park from the end of Nov., 1878, till the end of July, 1879, being present at the left attack on the Peiwar Kotal, and the operations in the Khost district, including the action of Matun. (Mentioned in despatches.)

Lt.-Colonel W. B. Colvin, Royal Fusiliers, served during the second campaign as Assistant Quartermaster-General, 2nd Division, Kandahar F.F.

Bt. Lieut.-Colonel B. A. Combe, 10th Hussars, served throughout the first campaign as Brigade Major of the Cavalry Brigade, 1st Division, Peshawar Valley F.F., being present at the capture of Ali Musjid and the action of Futtehabad. Joined the force assembled in Sep., 1879, under the orders of Sir F. Roberts, and served as D.A.Q.M.G. throughout the second campaign, taking part in the advance on Kabul, the action of Charasiab and subsequent operations, the relief of the Shutargardan, the occupation of the Maidan Valley and skirmishes in Nov., 1879, the actions round Sherpur in Dec., 1879, and near Shekabad (under General Ross) in April, 1880, the march from Kabul to the relief of Kandahar (with the Cavalry Brigade), the reconnaissance of the 31st Aug., 1880, and the battle of Kandahar. (Five times mentioned in despatches; Brevets of Major and Lt.-Colonel.)

Bt. Lt.-Colonel A. Conolly, B.S.C., was employed on political duty during the second campaign, and was present at the action of Ali Khel and the storming of Zawa. (Mentioned in despatches; Brevet of Lt.-Colonel.)

Major E. R. Conolly, B.S.C., served during the first campaign as Officiating Judicial Assistant at Dera Ismail Khan. During the second campaign served as Assistant Political Agent, Kuram Division, Kabul F.F., from the renewal of hostilities till Jan., 1880, when proceeded to Peshawar to assume the duties of Judicial Assistant. Was present at the action of Deh Sarak. (Mentioned in despatches.)

Major James Cook, B.S.C. (For services see 14th P.N.I.)

Major John Cook, V.C., B.S.C. (Killed in action. See Biographical Division).

Capt. L. A. C. Cook, B.S.C. (For services see 10th Bengal Lancers.)

Capt. W. Cooke, M.S.C., served from May till Sept., 1879, with the Kuram Valley Force, in charge of Commissariat. Was present at the repulse of the enemy at Ali Khel; and accompanying the Advance Brigade of General Roberts' force, in Commissariat charge, from the Shutargardan to Kushi, took part in the advance on and occupation of Kabul, and was present at the action of Charasiab, and subsequently at the operations round Kabul and defence of Sherpur in Dec., 1879. Remained with the N. Afghanistan F.F. until the return of the troops to India in Sept., 1880.

Capt. W. Cooke-Collis, Royal Irish Rifles, served during the second campaign as Brigade Major, on the Kandahar line of communications, and as Assistant Adjutant-General with General Phayre's Division, taking part in the advance from Quetta to Kandahar. (Mentioned in despatches.)

Lieut. A. F. Cotton, B.S.C., served during the second campaign as a Transport Officer with the Kuram Division, Kabul F.F., taking part in the advance on and occupation of Kabul, and being present at the action of Charasiab, and the operations round Kabul and defence of Sherpur in Dec., 1879. (Twice mentioned in despatches.)

Major G. J. Coulson, Bo.S.C., served with the Transport Dept. in the first campaign, part of the time as Assistant Superintendent of Transport at Shikarpur.

Lieut. H. V. Cowan, R.H.A. (For services see R.A.)

Bt. Lt.-Colonel Crombie Cowie, R.A., served throughout both campaigns, continuously, in charge of the Ordnance Field Park of the Kandahar F.F., the Ghazni F.F., the N. Afghanistan F.F., and the Kabul-Kandahar F.F., taking part in the advance from Quetta to Kandahar, the advance from Kandahar to Ghazni and Kabul, and the advance from Kabul to the relief of Kandahar, and being present at the battles of Ahmad Khel and Kandahar. (Twice mentioned in despatches; Brevet of Lt.-Colonel.)

Bt. Colonel J. B. Cox, B.S.C., served during the second campaign as Principal Commissariat Officer, Kuram Valley Force.

Lt.-Colonel John Creagh (retired). (For services see 5th Foot.)

Bt. Major O'M. Creagh, V.C., Bo.S.C. (For services see Biographical Division.)

Major-General W. Creagh (retired). (For services see 19th Bo.N.I.)

Capt. E. W. H. Crofton, King's Royal Rifle Corps. (Deceased. See Biographical Division.)

Capt. G. F. M. Cruickshank, R.E. (Deceased. See Biographical Division.)

Capt. H. F. G. Cruickshank, R.A., served during the first campaign as Adjutant R.A., 2nd Division, Kandahar F.F., taking part in the advance on and occupation of Kandahar.

Capt. C. S. Cumberland, Dorsetshire Regt., served with the Transport Dept. in both campaigns.

Major F. H. T. G. Cumming, Bo.S.C., served during the second campaign as Brigade Superintendent of Transport, Khyber Line Force, being present at the operations in the Kama district and the action of Kam Daka. (Mentioned in despatches.)

Major J. T. Cummins, M.S.C., served during the first campaign as Transport Officer, 2nd Division, Peshawar Valley F.F., taking part in the Bazar Valley operations. During the second campaign served as Staff Officer, Kuram Valley Transport. (Brevet of Major.)

Major C. A. Cuningham, Bo.S.C., served during the second campaign as Assistant Adjutant-General, 2nd Division, Kandahar F.F.

Mr. A. F. D. Cunningham, C.I.E., C.S., during the first campaign was Assistant Commissioner with the Peshawar Valley F.F., and during the second campaign accompanied Mr. Griffin, as First Assistant, on his special Political Mission to Kabul.

Capt. W. H. Dick Cunyngham, V.C., Gordon Highlanders. (For services see Biographical Division.)

Lieut. A. Currie, Norfolk Regt., was specially employed as Superintendent of Army Signalling to the

1st Division Peshawar Valley F.F., from the outbreak of the war till the 14th Dec., 1878, being present at the taking of Ali Musjid.

Lieut. F. B. G. D'Aguilar, R.E., served during the second campaign as Assistant Field Engineer with the S. Afghanistan F.F.

Depy. Surgeon-General A. J. Dale, M.B., Bengal Med. Dept., served as Principal Medical Officer Kuram F.F., from Sept., 1879, till Nov., 1880.

Lieut. H. L. Daly, 15th Hussars. (For services see 15th Hussars.)

Mr. M. L. Dames, C.S., served during the first campaign as Assistant Commissioner with the Quetta Division Kandahar F.F.

Capt. C. C. W. Dandridge, King's Own Borderers. (For services see 25th Foot.)

Lt.-Colonel W. Daunt, C.B., Norfolk Regt. (For services see 9th Foot).

Lieut. A. Davidson, King's Royal Rifle Corps. (For services see 60th Foot.)

Lieut. G. Davidson, R.E.

Bt. Major J. Davidson, B.S.C., served as Deputy Assistant Quartermaster-General with the 1st Division Peshawar Valley F.F., throughout the first campaign; being present at the capture of Ali Musjid, and the action of Futtehabad. (Mentioned in despatches; Brevet of Major.)

Colonel A. H. Dawson, R.A., served in command of the Heavy Batteries, Quetta Division, during the first campaign.

Lieut. J. G. Day, R.E.

Honorary Surgeon-Major J. R. Deane, served in Medical Charge of the Punjab Chiefs' Contingent during the first campaign.

Capt. T. Deane, B.S.C., was officially attached by the Government of India to the Staff of the Controller-General of Transport and Supply during his tour of inspection to Kabul, and was present at the operations in the neighbourhood of that city, and the defence of Sherpur, in Dec., 1879. (Mentioned in despatches.)

Capt. D. C. Dean-Pitt, R.A., served as Aide-de-Camp to General Phayre during the first campaign.

Lieut. J. E. Dickie, R.E., took part, as Asst. Field Engineer, in the original advance on Kandahar, being present at the affair at Saif-u-din. Subsequently served as Supt. Army Signalling with the 2nd Division Kandahar F.F., during the operations on the Halmand, with the S. Afghanistan F.F., during the occupation of Kandahar, and with the Ghazni F.F., during the advance on Ghazni. Acted as Orderly Officer to Sir D. Stewart at the battle of Ahmad Khel and the action of Arzu. (Mentioned in despatches.)

Capt. F. R. Ditmas, B.S.C., served as Staff Officer, Vitakri F.F., during the second campaign.

Capt. H. G. Dixon, King's Own Borderers. (For services see 25th Foot.)

Capt. G. C. Dobbs, Bo.S.C., served with the Commissariat Dept., Kandahar Force, during the second campaign, taking part in the advance of General Burrows' Brigade from Kandahar to Girishk, and being present at the battle of Maiwand. (Mentioned in despatches.)

Colonel John Doran, C.B., B.S.C., commanded, with rank of Brigadier-General, a brigade of the 2nd Division Peshawar Valley F.F., from Nov., 1878, till the force was broken up on the 9th June, 1879. Was appointed early in Sep., 1879, to the command of the Khyber Brigade at Landi Kotal, a command which was subsequently, on the renewal of hostilities, emerged into that of a brigade in the Khyber Line Force, and held till Sep., 1880, when the troops returned to India. Was employed as 2nd in command of a column under General Maude, in the first Bazar Valley Expedition, 19 to 23 Dec., 1878; commanded the Landi Kotal column in the operations against the Mohmands at Kam Daka, 15 to 18 Jan., 1880; a column in the operations against the Wazir Kugianis, 4 to 6 April, 1880; a column in the operations against the Mohmands in Besud, 18 to 21 May, 1880; and a column in the operations in Kama, 3 to 7 June, 1880. (Mentioned in despatches.)

Capt. C. F. J. Douglas, 15th Hussars. (For services see 15th Hussars.)

Major T. F. Dowden, R.E., served as Superintending Engineer in Baluchistan, during the second campaign, and accompanied General Phayre's Division in its advance from Quetta to Kandahar in the autumn of 1880. (Mentioned in despatches.)

Capt. C. V. S. Downes, East Lancashire Regt., served with the Transport Train, 1st Division Kabul F.F., during the second campaign.

Colonel F. B. Drew, C.B., West Yorkshire Regt. (For services see 8th Foot.)

Lieut. F. H. R. Drummond, B.S.C. (For services see 10th Bengal Lancers.)

Surgeon-Major O. T. Duke, I.M.D. (For services see Indian Medical Dept.)

Major H. L. Dundas, East Yorkshire Regt., served as Brigade Major, 2nd Brigade, 2nd Division Kandahar F.F., during its march to Kandahar, Aug. to Sept., 1880. Appointed A.A.G. S. Afghanistan F.F., Nov., 1880.

Capt. J. Dundas, V.C., R.E. (Deceased. See Biographical Division.)

Lieut. J. W. Dunlop, R.A. (For services see R.A.)

Lieut. H. W. Duperier, R.E., served during the second campaign, from Oct., 1879, till Oct., 1880, as Field Engineer with the Kuram Force, being employed on various duties along the whole line from Thal to the Peiwar Kotal.

Mr. H. M. Durand, C.S., served as Political Secretary to Sir F. Roberts during the second campaign, taking part in the advance on and occupation of Kabul, and being present at the action of Charasiab, the operations round Kabul, and defence of Sherpur in Dec., 1879. (Twice mentioned in despatches.)

Major the Hon. C. Dutton, Shropshire Regt., served during the second campaign as Assistant Quartermaster-General, 2nd Division, Kabul and N. Afghanistan Field Forces, being present at the action of Shekabad. (Mentioned in despatches; Brevet of Major.)

Major J. D. Dyson-Laurie, Border Regt., served during the first campaign superintending communications on the Khyber line.

Colonel S. de B. Edwardes, C.B., Bombay Infantry, served as Director of Transport, Kandahar Force, during the second campaign, being present at Kandahar throughout the siege. (Mentioned in despatches; C.B.)

Capt. G. L. Eliot, B.S.C., served with the Commissariat Dept., Kuram F.F., during the second campaign.

Capt. G. H. Elliott, B.S.C. (For services see 3rd Bengal Cavalry.)

Major W. V. Ellis, B.S.C. (For services see 25th P.N.I.)

Lieut. F. B. Elmslie, R.A., served with the Ordnance Field Park, Peshawar Valley F.F., during the first campaign.

Capt. H. J. Elverson, Royal West Surrey Regt., served in the Transport Department throughout both campaigns, being employed on the line of communications between Sukkur and Kandahar till July, 1879, when he was appointed Brigade Transport Officer to General Hughes' Brigade, Kandahar F.F., and took part in the advance on and occupation of Kalat-i-Ghilzai. Accompanied Sir D. Stewart's Division, in charge of transport of 2nd Brigade, in its advance on Ghazni, and to Kabul, being present at the battle of Ahmad Khel (during which he acted as Orderly Officer to General Hughes), the action of Arzu, and the subsequent operations in the Logar Valley. Accompanied the Kabul-Kandahar F.F. in its advance to the relief of Kandahar, and was present at the battle of Kandahar. (Mentioned in despatches.)

Lieut. A. D. Enriquez, B.S.C. (For services see 16th B.N.I.)

Capt. F. J. W. Eustace, R.A., served as Adjutant Horse and Field Artillery, 1st Division Kandahar F.F., from Jan. till Dec., 1879. He joined Sir D. Stewart at Kabul, Mar., 1880, and served as his A.D.C. from that date till the conclusion of the campaign, being present at the action of Charasiab, in April, 1880.

Brigadier-General C. R. O. Evans, R.A., commanded the R.A., Khyber Division, Kabul F.F., from the outbreak of the second campaign; subsequently succeeded to the command of the R.A. of both divisions of the Field Force, and continued in command of it until 28 June, 1880, when he quitted Kabul to take up a Brigade command in India.

Colonel F. V. Eyre, late R.A., served in charge of the Ordnance Field Park, 2nd Division, Kandahar F.F., during the first campaign.

Capt. V. G. L. Eyre, B.S.C. (For services see 23rd Punjab Pioneers.)

Major J. L. Fagan, Bo.S.C., served with the Commissariat Dept. in S. Afghanistan during both campaigns, taking part in the advance of General Phayre's Division from Quetta to Kandahar. (Mentioned in despatches.)

Major-General W. Fane, C.B. (retired), commanded the Cavalry Brigade of Sir D. Stewart's Division during the first advance on and occupation of Kandahar and Kalat-i-Ghilzai.

Lt.-Colonel M. C. Farrington, South Yorkshire Regt., served as Assistant Adjutant-General, 2nd Division, Peshawar Valley F.F., during the first campaign.

Major W. C. Farwell, Bengal Infantry, served during the first campaign as Brigade Major, 3rd, and subsequently 1st, Brigade, 1st Division Peshawar Valley F.F., being present at the capture of Ali Musjid, and during the second campaign as Brigade Major in the Kabul and Kabul-Kandahar Field Forces; taking part in the advance on and occupation of Kabul, and the advance from Kabul to the relief of Kandahar, and being present at the action of Charasiab, the operations round Kabul, and defence of Sherpur in Dec., 1879, and the battle of Kandahar.

Capt. H. J. Fergusson, The Buffs, served in the first campaign with the 1st Division Kandahar F.F., taking part, as Transport Officer, in the advance on and occupation of Kandahar and Kalat-i-Ghilzai.

Lieut. J. A. Ferrier, R.E., served in the first campaign as Asst. Field Engineer, 2nd Division

Peshawar Valley F.F., and, after the conclusion of peace, was placed in charge of the water supply at Landi Kotal. During the second campaign served as Asst. Field Engineer in and about the Khyber Pass.

Lieut. H. Finnis, R.E.

Lieut. R. B. W. Fisher, 10th Hussars. (For services see 10th Hussars.)

Lieut. C. M. Fitzgerald, B.S.C. (For services see 21st P.N.I.)

Lieut. A. C. Foley, R.E., served as Assistant Field Engineer with the Kandahar Field Force during the first campaign.

Major F. W. Foord, M.S.C., served with the Transport Dept. in the first campaign.

Major-General Hamilton Forbes (retired). (For services see Bhopaul Battn.)

Capt. W. E. G. Forbes, Royal Warwickshire Regt., served during the second campaign, first with the Commissariat Dept. in S. Afghanistan, and afterwards as Orderly Officer to Brigadier-General Palliser in the Ghazni and 3rd Division Kabul Field Force, taking part in the advance from Kandahar on Ghazni, and into the Logar Valley, and being present at the battle of Ahmad Khel, and the actions of Arzu and Palkao Shana. (Twice mentioned in despatches.)

Lieut. A. Foster, East Yorkshire Regt., served during the second campaign as Transport Officer on the Kandahar line. (Mentioned in despatches.)

Lieut. T. F. T. Fowle, R.A. (For services see R.A.)

Colonel E. S. Fox (retired), served with the Transport Dept. in the first campaign.

Lieut. J. C. Francis, Bo.S.C., served with the Commissariat Dept. in S. Afghanistan during the second campaign.

Lieut. A. D. Fraser, Gordon Highlanders. (For services see 92nd Highlanders.)

Major-General the Hon. D. M. Fraser, C.B., R.A., commanded the Royal Artillery, 2nd Division, Peshawar Valley F.F., during the first campaign, accompanying the Bazar Valley expedition. (Mentioned in despatches.)

Colonel G. W. Fraser, B.S.C. (For services see 39th B.N.I.)

Major-General W. French, C.B. (retired), commanded the Royal Artillery, Kandahar F.F., during the second campaign, including the defence of Kandahar, the sortie to Deh Khwaja, and the battle of Kandahar. (Mentioned in despatches.)

Lieut. G. Frend, Northumberland Fusiliers. (For services see 5th Fusiliers.)

Mr. F. W. Fryer, C.S., as Officiating Deputy Commissioner of Dera Ismail Khan, accompanied General Biddulph through the Dera Bughli country, and subsequently served as Political Officer with Col. Prendergast's Column to Legari Barkhan.

Capt. C. F. Fuller, R.E., served during the second campaign as Asst. Field Engineer in the South Afghanistan Column under General Phayre, taking part in the advance of that force to Kandahar.

Lieut. H. S. A. Fuller, Bo.S.C., served with the Commissariat Dept. in S. Afghanistan during the second campaign.

Capt. G. Gaisford, B.S.C. (For services see 5th Punjab Infantry.)

Lt.-Colonel W. Galbraith, Shropshire Regt. (For services see 85th Foot.)

Major P. F. G. Gallwey, R.A., served from Dec., 1878, till the conclusion of the first campaign as Ordnance Officer in charge of the Field Parks of the 1st and 2nd Divisions, Peshawar Valley F.F., on the Khyber line between Gandamak and Jamrud, taking part in the second Bazar Valley expedition.

Lieut. R. F. Gartside-Tipping, B.S.C. (For services see 1st Bengal Cavalry.)

Bt.-Major A. Gaselee, B.S.C., served throughout both campaigns as D.A.Q.M.G. with the Divisions under Sir D. Stewart and Sir F. Roberts, taking part in the advance on and occupation of Kandahar and Kalat-i-Ghilzai, the advance from Kandahar on Ghazni and to Kabul, and the advance from Kabul to the relief of Kandahar; and being present at the action of Shahjui, the battle of Ahmad Khel, the affair at Arzu, the reconnaissance of the 31st Aug., 1880, and the battle of Kandahar. (Three times mentioned in despatches; Brevet of Major.)

Lieut. G. F. A. Gavin, B.S.C., served as Asst. Road Commandant, S. Afghanistan F.F., from Aug., 1880, till the conclusion of the war.

Colonel F. C. Georges, M.S.C. (For services see 30th M.N.I.)

Bt. Lieut-Colonel M. G. Gerard, B.S.C., served during the first campaign as Brigade Major, Cavalry Brigade, 2nd Division, Peshawar Valley F.F., taking part in the Bazar Valley expedition; and during the second campaign as Brigade Major in the Khyber Division Kabul F.F., the 1st Division Kabul F.F., and the Kabul-Kandahar F.F., taking part in the advance of General Gough's Brigade to Sherpur, and the advance from Kabul to the relief of Kandahar, and being present at the battle of Kandahar. (Three times mentioned in despatches; Brevet of Lt.-Colonel.)

Colonel W. A. Gib, C.B., M.S.C., served during the second campaign, with the rank of Brigadier-General, first in command of the 3rd Brigade, Reserve Division, at Peshawar, and afterwards, from

13 March, 1880, in command of the 1st Section, Khyber Line Force. Commanded the force in the operations in the Mazina Valley, including the action of Mazina. (Mentioned in despatches; C.B.)

Depy. Surgeon-General J. Gibbons, C.B., A.M.D., served during the first campaign as Principal Medical Officer, 1st Division, Peshawar Valley F.F., being present at the capture of Ali Musjid, and the forcing of the Khyber Pass. (Mentioned in despatches; C.B.)

Lt.-Colonel H. H. F. Gifford, 13th Hussars, served during the first campaign as Brigade Major, Cavalry Brigade, General Stewart's Division, taking part in the advance on and occupation of Kandahar and Kalat-i-Ghilzai; afterwards as Brigade Major, 2nd Column, Thal-Chotiali F.F. (Mentioned in despatches; Brevet of Major.)

Lieut. H. E. Godwyn, R.E.

Colonel A. R. Gloag, R.A., served during the latter part of the first campaign in command of the Artillery of the Haidarabad Subsidiary Force.

Capt. F. T. Goad, B.S.C. (Killed in action. See Biographical Division.)

Colonel C. J. Godby, B.S.C.

Lieut. R. E. Golightly, King's Royal Rifle Corps. (For services see 60th Rifles.)

Bt. Lt.-Colonel A. H. A. Gordon, York and Lancaster Regt., served throughout the first campaign as Brigade Major, 2nd Brigade, 1st Division, Peshawar Valley F.F., and subsequently, till invalided home in June, 1879, as Brigade Major, Khyber Brigade. Took part with the 2nd Brigade in the capture of Ali Musjid, and with the columns under Brigadier-General Tytler in the first and second Bazar Valley expeditions, the expedition to Chardeh, and the operations against the Shinwaris in the neighbourhood of Pesh Bolak. (Mentioned in despatches; Brevet of Lt.-Colonel.)

Bt. Colonel B. L. Gordon, C.B., R.H.A., commanded the R.A. of the Division under Sir F. Roberts from the date of the advance on Kabul in Sep., 1879, till the end of April, 1880, being present at the action of Charasiab, the operations round Kabul in Dec., 1879, including the action of Killa Kazi, and the defence of Sherpur. Commanded the R.A. of the 2nd Division N. Afghanistan F.F. from the end of April till the 28th June, 1880, when he was invalided home. (Twice mentioned in despatches; C.B.)

Capt. C. S. Gordon, West Yorkshire Regt. (For services see 14th Foot.)

Major-General John Gordon, C.B., Bengal Infantry, served during the second campaign, first in temporary command, and, subsequently to the death of General Tytler, in permanent command, of the Upper Kuram Brigade.

Bt. Colonel T. E. Gordon, C.B., C.S.I., served on special political duty with the Kuram Valley F.F. during the latter part of the first campaign, and commanded, with rank of Brigadier-General, the Kuram line of communications, and subsequently a brigade of the Kuram Division, during the earlier part of the second campaign. Repulsed the enemy in their attack on Ali Khel, 14 Oct., 1879. (Mentioned in despatches; C.B.)

Lieut. St. G. C. Gore, R.E., served during both campaigns as Survey Officer to the force under Sir D. Stewart, being employed during 1879 in surveying and making reconnaissances of the hitherto unknown country in the neighbourhood of Pishin, taking part in the advance from Kandahar to Kabul, and being present at the battle of Ahmad Khel.

Bt. Lt.-Colonel C. A. Gorham, R.A., served on the Staff of Sir F. Roberts as Deputy Judge Advocate from 30 Oct., 1879, till the conclusion of the war, being present at the action of Ali Khel, 15 Oct., 1879, whilst *en route* to take up his appointment, and subsequently at the affairs round Kabul and the defence of Sherpur in Dec., 1879, during which he had charge of, and commanded in action, the captured guns; accompanied the advance from Kabul to the relief of Kandahar, and was present at the battle of Kandahar. (Twice mentioned in despatches; Brevet of Lt.-Colonel.)

Bt. Major Bloomfield Gough, 9th Lancers. (For services see 9th Lancers.)

Brigadier-General Sir C. J. S. Gough, K.C.B., V.C., commanded the Cavalry Brigade, 1st Division, Peshawar Valley F.F., throughout the first campaign, being present at the taking of Ali Musjid and the forcing of the Khyber Pass, leading the advance from Jalalabad to Gandamak, and defeating and cutting up the enemy at Futtehabad. During the second campaign commanded first the advanced brigade, and afterwards a moveable column, of the Khyber Division, a brigade of the Kabul and of the N. Afghanistan F.F., a brigade of the troops returning from Kabul on the evacuation of that city, and eventually the Khyber Brigade. Effected the junction of the Khyber Division with the Kabul Force in Nov., 1879, and the following month marched to Sherpur, which was at the time in a state of siege, and conducted operations against the enemy in the neighbourhood of Jagdalak, *en route*. Proceeded with General Ross's Force from Kabul to open up communications with the Ghazni F.F., and was present at the action of Shekabad. Subsequently conducted various operations with his brigade in the Logar and Maidan districts. (Three times mentioned in despatches; K.C.B.)

RECORDS OF SERVICE.

Colonel Sir H. H. Gough, K.C.B., V.C., commanded the Cavalry of the Kuram Valley F.F., as senior officer of the branch, throughout the first campaign, being present at the capture of the Peiwar Kotal and subsequent pursuit, the affair in the Mangior defile, and the operations in Khost, including the action of Matun. Was appointed Brigadier-General in charge of communications, Kuram Division, Kabul F.F., on the renewal of hostilities in Sep., 1879, and Brigadier-General Commdg. the Cavalry Brigade at Kabul, 1st March, 1880. Was present at the action of Charasiab, and the operations round Kabul and defence of Sherpur in Dec., 1879. (Wounded.) In command of the Cavalry Brigade took part in the advance from Kabul to the relief of Kandahar, and was present at the reconnaissance of the 31st Aug., 1880, in command of the troops engaged, and in the Cavalry pursuit at the battle of Kandahar. (Six times mentioned in despatches; K.C.B.)

Major H. S. Gough, 10th Hussars, served during the war as Aide-de-Camp to H.E. the Commander-in-Chief. Was on special duty at the assault and capture of Ali Musjid.

Mr. J. A. Grant, C.S., was employed during the second campaign on Political duty on the Kuram line.

Bt. Major H. G. Grant, Seaforth Highlanders, served during the second campaign as Brigade Major, Kuram F.F., being present at the repulse of the enemy at Ali Khel, and the operations in Zaimusht territory, including the surprise and capture of Zawa. (Mentioned in despatches; Brevet of Major.)

Lieut. S. Grant, R.E., served during the first campaign as Assistant Field Engineer, Kuram Valley F.F., being present, acting as Orderly Officer to Brigadier-General Thelwall, at the assault and capture of the Peiwar Kotal. In the second campaign served in the same capacity with the 1st Division, Kabul F.F., being present at the action of Charasiab, 25 April, 1880. (Twice mentioned in despatches.)

Capt. H. A. Graves, B.S.C., served with the Transport Dept. in the first campaign.

Lieut W. du G. Gray, M.S.C., served as Transport Officer, Khyber line, in the second campaign.

Sir Lepel H. Griffin, K.C.S.I., C.S., was deputed in February, 1880, by H.E. the Viceroy of India, to proceed on a special Political mission to Kabul, and from that date till the evacuation of N. Afghanistan had entire and independent control of all political work in Northern and Eastern Afghanistan, conducting the negotiations and arrangements which resulted in the Amir Abdul Rahman Khan being placed upon the throne. (Received on many occasions the thanks of the Government of India; K.C.S.I.)

Major J. G. E. Griffith, Bo.S.C., served during the first campaign as Superintendent of Transport with the Bombay Column and on the line of communications, from Dec., 1878, till June, 1879, organizing the camel train and superintending operations across the desert from Jacobabad to Bagh; subsequently succeeded Col. Hogg as Superintendent at the base of operations. (Twice mentioned in despatches.)

Bt. Colonel G. C. E. Grogan, Liverpool Regt. (For services see 8th Foot.)

Capt. C. E. Gubbins, B.S.C., served as Transport Officer, Kuram Valley, in the second campaign.

Lt.-Colonel C. W. N. Guinness, Seaforth Highlanders. (For services see 72nd Highlanders.)

Brigade-Surgeon A. Guthrie, M.D., A.M.D., served as Principal Medical Officer to the Reserve Division at Peshawar from Jan. till Feb., 1880, when he was posted to the Medical charge of the Field Hospital at Landi Kotal and to act as P.M.O. of the 1st section Khyber Line Force, in which capacity he continued to serve till the close of the operations in Sep., 1880. (Mentioned in despatches.)

Lt.-Colonel N. X. Gwynne, Manchester Regt., served during the first campaign as Brigade Major, 2nd Brigade, 2nd Division, Peshawar Valley F.F., taking part, with the Jamrud column, in the first Bazar Valley expedition.

Capt. G. R. Hadaway, R.A., served with the Ordnance Field Park, Peshawar Valley F.F. during the first campaign.

Capt. W. Hailes, B.S.C., served as Deputy Assistant Quartermaster-General, Reserve Division, Peshawar, and on the Khyber Line extending to Basawal, from Sep., 1879, till the Division was broken up. Subsequently served as D.A.Q.M.G. at Peshawar, continuing in the tenure of the appointment during the return of the troops from Kabul. (Mentioned in despatches.)

Major G. W. M. Hall, Berkshire Regt., was appointed to the Kandahar Transport Train, Nov., 1879, and placed in charge of the contingent sent by order of Sir R. Temple to assist in the construction of the Kandahar State Railway and carry forward stores and material through the Put Desert to Sibi and thence by the Nari Gorge into the Marri country. (Twice mentioned in reports.)

Capt. C. E. Hallett, B.S.C., served with the Commissariat Dept., S. Afghanistan, during the war.

Lt.-Colonel H. J. Hallowes, East Yorkshire Regt., conducted the whole of the arrangements of Brigadier-General C. Gough's Brigade, as Superintendent, in its advance to Kabul in Dec., 1879, being present at the minor engagements *en route*. Returned from Kabul, after the country had quieted down, to take up his appointment of Inspector of Gymnasia in India. (Mentioned in despatches.)

Lieut. B. M. Hamilton, East Yorkshire Regt. (For services see 15th Foot.)

Capt. C. H. Hamilton, R.A., served during the second campaign as Adjutant, R.A., Reserve Division, Peshawar, and Khyber Line Force.

Lieut. E. O. F. Hamilton, Royal West Surrey Regt., served during the second campaign as Aide-de-Camp to General Primrose, being present at Kandahar throughout the siege, and at the battle of Kandahar. (Mentioned in despatches.)

Lieut. G. H. C. Hamilton, 14th Hussars, served during the first campaign, from 15th Dec., 1878, till 4th June, 1879, as Aide-de-Camp to Sir Sam. Browne, being present at the affair at Maidanak; during the second campaign was attached to the 9th Lancers from the 6th Jan., 1880, and served at Kabul as Orderly Officer to Brigadiers-General Massy and Hugh Gough, successively, till invalided in August, 1880.

Lieut. I. S. M. Hamilton, Gordon Highlanders. (For services see 92nd Highlanders.)

Deputy Surgeon-General J. A. Hanbury, M.B., C.B., A.M.D., served during the first campaign as Principal Medical Officer, 2nd Division, Peshawar Valley F.F., taking part in both the first and second Bazar Valley expeditions. (Several times mentioned in despatches; specially thanked by Government for services in connection with the cholera epidemic during the return march of the troops through the Khyber.) During the second campaign served as P.M.O. of General Bright's Division, and subsequently of the 2nd Division Kabul F.F., and the Kabul-Kandahar F.F., taking part in the advance to the relief of Kandahar, and being present at the battle of Kandahar. Was eventually appointed P.M.O. of the entire S. Afghanistan F.F. (Mentioned in despatches; C.B.)

Bt. Lt.-Colonel A. G. Handcock, B.S.C., served during the first campaign as Brigade Major, 2nd Brigade, 1st Division, Kandahar F.F., and during the second campaign as Assistant Adjutant-General, Kandahar, Ghazni, and 3rd Division Kabul Field Forces, taking part in the advance from Kandahar on Ghazni and into the Logar Valley, and being present at the battle of Ahmad Khel and the action of Arzu. (Mentioned in despatches; Brevet of Lt.-Colonel.)

Colonel G. C. Hankin, B.S.C., served during the second campaign, first as Brigadier-General in command of the Cavalry Brigade, Reserve Division, Khyber Line, and subsequently in command of the Peshawar District, discharging the duties involved in the command of the Base of operations of the army at the front from the beginning of March, 1880, till the conclusion of the campaign. (Mentioned in despatches.)

Bt. Lt.-Colonel H. B. Hanna, B.S.C., served during the first campaign as Deputy Assistant Quartermaster-General, 2nd Division, Kandahar F.F., taking part in the advance on and occupation of Kandahar, and the advance to the Halmand, and subsequently accompanying to India, as Survey Officer, the Thal-Chotiali F.F. During the second campaign accompanied the Controller-General of Transport and Supply on his tour of inspection to Kabul, and was present at the operations in the neighbourhood of that city, and the defence of Sherpur, in Dec., 1879. (Mentioned in despatches; Brevet of Lt.-Colonel.)

Lieut. E. Hanstock, East Yorkshire Regt. (For services see 15th Foot.)

Lieut. W. F. J. Hardisty, B.S.C., served with the Commissariat Dept. in the second campaign.

Capt. G. J. Hare, B.S.C. (Died at Safed Sang, 5 Jan., 1880.)

Lieut. J. H. C. Harrison, R.E., was employed, during the second campaign, on the Peshawar-Jalalabad Railway Survey.

Lieut. S. K. Harris, Devonshire Regt., served with the Transport Dept. in the first campaign.

Capt. T. Harris, Berkshire Regt. (For services see 66th Foot.)

Capt. R. C. Hart, V.C., R.E. (For services see Biographical Division.)

Major E. Harvey, R.E., was employed during the first campaign in charge of the bridge of boats over the Indus at Khushilgarh, and in constructing and repairing the road forming the line of communication of the Kuram Valley F.F., from the Indus to Thal. Served in the second campaign as Field Engineer on the Khyber line, being most of the time in charge of the fort-works and roads near Gandamak. (Brevet of Major.)

Depy. Surgeon-General H. B. Hassard, C.B., A.M.D., served during the second campaign as Principal Medical Officer, Khyber Division, Kabul F.F. (C.B.)

Bt. Lt.-Colonel E. G. G. Hastings, C.B., Bengal Cavalry, served during the first campaign, from April, 1879, in Political charge of the Khyber Pass, and during the second campaign as Chief Political Officer with the Kuram Division Kabul F.F., senior Political Officer in general charge of the city and district of Kabul, and Chief Political Officer of the Kabul-Kandahar F.F., taking part in the advance on and occupation of Kabul, and the advance from Kabul to the relief of Kandahar, and being present at the action of Charasiab, the operations round Kabul and the defence of Sherpur in Dec., 1879, and the battle of Kandahar. (Three times mentioned in despatches; C.B.; Brevet of Lt.-Colonel.)

Mr. C. G. Hastings, C.S., served on the Staff of Mr. Griffin during his special Political mission at Kabul.

Lieut. H. M. Hatchell, Royal Irish Regt. (For services see 18th Foot.)

Lieut. H. M. P. Hawkes, B.S.C., served with the Commissariat Dept. in the Kabul and Kabul-

Kandahar Field Forces, taking part in the advance from Kabul to the relief of Kandahar, and being present at the battle of Kandahar. (Mentioned in despatches.)

Capt. W. H. Haydon, R.E., served as Field Engineer, S. Afghanistan F.F., from 29th Jan., 1881. (Mentioned in despatches.)

Bt. Lt.-Colonel C. Hayter, M.S.C., served throughout the second campaign as Director of Transport, first to the second Division, N. Afghanistan F.F., taking part in General Ross's expedition from Kabul through the Maidan Valley to co-operate with the Ghazni F.F., and being engaged in the operations of the Division near Zaidabad, and the operations of General Gough's Brigade, and subsequently as Director of Transport to the whole force returning by the Khyber route to India. (Mentioned in despatches; Brevet of Lt.-Colonel.)

Capt. W. W. Haywood, West Yorkshire Regt. (For services see 14th Foot.)

Capt. P. C. Heath, B.S.C. (Killed in action. See Biographical Division.)

Lt.-Colonel M. H. Heathcote, C.B., B.S.C., served during the first campaign, first as Assistant Quartermaster-General, 2nd Division, Peshawar Valley F.F., in which capacity he took part in the Bazar Valley expedition, and afterwards as Road Commandant. During the second campaign served first as Director of Transport, Kuram Division, Kabul F.F., and afterwards as Road Commandant. Took part in the advance on and occupation of Kabul, and was present at the action of Charasiab. (Three times mentioned in despatches; C.B.)

Major W. J. Heaviside, R.E., served in the Survey Dept. with the Kandahar F.F. during the first campaign, carrying a route-survey from Quetta to Kandahar, mapping the Kadanai district, and accompanying the Thal-Chotiali Force in opening up the new route to India. (Mentioned in despatches; Brevet of Major.

Bt. Major F. W. Hemming, 5th Dragoon Guards, served throughout the first campaign as Aide-de-Camp to General Maude, taking part in the first and second Bazar Valley expeditions, and minor operations. (Mentioned in despatches; Brevet of Major.)

Colonel J. H. Henderson, Bo.S.C. (For services see 24th Bo.N.I.)

Deputy Surgeon-General J. Hendley, C.B., A.M.D., served during the first campaign as Principal Medical Officer, 2nd Division, Kandahar F.F., taking part in the advance on Kandahar and to the Halmand, and accompanying the Thal-Chotiali Force in opening up the new route to India. (Mentioned in despatches; C.B.)

Lieut. T. R. Henn, R.E. (Killed in action. See Biographical Division.)

Major R. Hennell, Bombay Infantry, served with the Commissariat Dept. in the second campaign.

Capt. G. Henry, R.E.

Lieut. G. C. B. Hervey, B.S.C., served with the Commissariat Dept. in the second campaign.

Major A. R. Heyland, Bo.S.C., served during the second campaign as Deputy Assistant Quartermaster-General, 2nd Division, Kandahar F.F. (Mentioned in despatches.)

Major J. Hibbert, Bombay Infantry, served with the Commissariat Dept. in both campaigns.

Major-General W. Hichens, C.B., R.E., was Commanding Royal Engineer, 2nd Division, Kandahar F.F. during the first campaign, taking part in the advance on and occupation of Kandahar, and served in the same capacity with the Kandahar F.F. during the second campaign. (Mentioned in despatches; C.B.)

Lieut. S. A. E. Hickson, R.E., was employed on the Kandahar Railway during the second campaign.

Major A. Hill, R.E.

Capt. E. C. Hill, Wiltshire Regt., served as Transport Officer, Khyber Line, during the second campaign.

Colonel R. S. Hill, C.B., B.S.C. (For services see 1st Goorkhas, L.I.)

Bt. Lt.-Colonel G. S. Hills, R.E., served during the second campaign as Commanding R.E., Khyber Line Force. (Brevet of Lt.-Colonel.)

Major-General Sir James Hills, K.C.B., V.C., R.A., served during the first campaign as Assistant Adjutant-General, 1st Division, Kandahar F.F., taking part in the advance on and occupation of Kandahar. During the second campaign accompanied the Division under Sir F. Roberts in the advance on and occupation of Kabul, being present at the action of Charasiab. Was appointed Military Governor of Kabul, and subsequently held command of the 1st Division Kabul F.F., being present at the operations round Kabul and defence of Sherpur in Dec., 1879. Accompanied General Ross from Kabul to effect a junction with the Ghazni F.F., and was subsequently appointed to the command of that force, reconstituted as the 3rd Division, Kabul F.F. Defeated the enemy at Patkao Shana. On the departure of Sir D. Stewart to India, commanded the whole of the N. Afghanistan F.F. returning by the Khyber route. (Several times mentioned in despatches; thanked by both Houses of Parliament; K.C.B.)

Colonel John Hills, C.B., R.E. (For services see Royal Engineers.)

Bt. Major F. T. Hobday, B.S.C., served with the Commissariat Dept. in S. Afghanistan during the first campaign. (Brevet of Major.)

Captain J. R. Hobday, B.S.C., served in the Survey Dept. in S. Afghanistan during the first campaign, and till invalided in Aug., 1880, carrying a route-survey from Chainan to Kandahar, and mapping the country in the neighbourhood of that city.

Brigadier-General A. G. F. Hogg, Bo.S.C., served during the first campaign as Director of Transport with the Bombay Reserve Brigade on the Kandahar line. During the second campaign served as Assistant to the Controller-General of Transport and Supply, and was present with that officer at the operations round Kabul and defence of Sherpur in Dec., 1879. (Mentioned in despatches; Brevet of Colonel.)

Major G. C. Hogg, Bombay Cavalry. (For services see Poona Horse.)

Bt. Major T. H. Holdich, R.E., was specially employed during the first campaign on survey duty in S. Afghanistan, in the neighbourhood of Kandahar and with the Thal-Chotiali Force *en route* to India. Throughout the second campaign had charge of all the survey operations in N. Afghanistan. Was present at all the engagements fought in and around Kabul in Dec., 1879, and was employed as a Field Engineer in the defence of Sherpur. (Twice mentioned in despatches; Brevet of Major.) Subsequently served in the Mahsud Waziri expedition of 1881.

Lieut. E. C. F. Holland, R.H.A., served with the Transport Dept. in the first campaign.

Bt. Lt.-Colonel W. B. Holmes, R.E., served as Commanding R.E., Kuram F.F., from the 19th Oct., 1879, till the conclusion of the war, proceeding with the force into the Chamkani country in Nov., 1879, and with the detached brigade under General Tytler on the Zaimusht expedition, and being present at the storming of Zawa. (Mentioned in despatches; Brevet of Lt.-Colonel.)

Major S. B. Home, Bengal Infantry, served as Brigade Major, 1st Brigade Reserve Division, and 1st Brigade 2nd Division, N. Afghanistan F.F., from Jan. to Sept., 1880.

Major W. C. Hood, Royal West Surrey Regt., served from April, 1880, in the second campaign, as Brigade Major, Lower Kuram Brigade.

Capt. C. Hoskyns, R.E., served in both campaigns as Asst. Field Engineer with the force under Sir D. Stewart's command. Was present at the battle of Ahmad Khel, in which he acted as Orderly Officer to Brigadier-General Palliser. (Mentioned in despatches.)

Major C. F. Hughes, Bo.S.C., served in the Commissariat Dept. in both campaigns, accompanying the Ghazni F.F. in its advance from Kandahar on Ghazni and into the Logar Valley, and being present at the battle of Ahmad Khel and the action of Arzu. (Mentioned in despatches; Brevet of Major.)

Brigadier-General R. J. Hughes, C.B., H.P., commanded, during the first campaign, the 2nd Brigade, 1st Division, Kandahar F.F., taking part in the advance on and occupation of Kandahar and Kalat-i-Ghilzai. On the renewal of hostilities in September, 1879, advanced a second time, in command of a column, on Kolat i-Ghilzai and to Tazi, returning to Kandahar in November after defeating the enemy at Shahjui. Commanded the 2nd Brigade, Ghazni F.F., in the advance on Ghazni and into the Logar Valley, at the battle of Ahmad Khel, and at the action of Arzu. Was in temporary command of the Ghazni F.F., in the Logar Valley, after the departure of General Stewart to Kabul. Eventually commanded the 2nd Brigade of General Hill's Division during the return march from Kabul by the Kyber route to India. (Several times mentioned in despatches; C.B.).

Captain J. C. T. Humfrey, A.P.D., served throughout the first campaign in charge of the Field Treasure Chest, 1st Division Peshawar Valley F.F.; subsequently, in charge of the Treasure Chest at Landi Kotal; and in charge of the Field Treasure Chest, Kyber Line Force, from the renewal of hostilities till the return of the Division to India, holding, in addition, the appointment of Divisional Provost Marshal from 15 Jan., 1880.

Bt. Major H. V. Hunt, B.S.C., served with the Commissariat Dept., 1st Division, Kabul F.F., during the second campaign, being present at the operations round Kabul and defence of Sherpur in Dec., 1879. (Mentioned in despatches; Brevet of Major.)

Colonel J. V. Hunt, C.B., B.S.C., served during the first campaign as Principal Commissariat Officer, 1st Division, Peshawar Valley F.F., being present at the capture of Ali Musjid; and during the second campaign served in the same capacity with the Kuram Division. (Mentioned in despatches; C.B.)

Major H. McL. Hutchinson, West Yorkshire Regt., served as Brigade Major, 3rd Brigade, Reserve Division, from the date of its formation in Dec., 1879, and subsequently, in the same capacity, to the 3rd Section Khyber Line Force. Appointed D.A.A.G. to the Chief of the Staff at Kabul, June, 1880. Took part, as Orderly Officer to General Macgregor, in the advance from Kabul to the relief of Kandahar, and was present at the reconnaissance of the 31st Aug., 1880, and the battle of Kandahar. (Mentioned in despatches; Brevet of Major.) Subsequently served as D.A.Q.M.G. to the force under General Macgregor in the Marri expedition. (Mentioned in despatches.)

Major J. W. Inge, R.A., served during the second campaign as Adjutant R.A., 1st Division, Kabul F.F., until invalided.

Capt. S. L. Jacob, R.E.

Major A. J. A. Jackson, Royal Irish Regt. (For services see 18th Foot.)

Bt. Colonel H. H. James, B.S.C., commanded, with rank of Brigadier-General, the 1st Brigade of General Phayre's Division during the second campaign, taking part in the advance from Quetta to Kandahar. (Mentioned in despatches.)

Bt. Major R. E. C. Jarvis, Hampshire Regt. (For services see 67th Foot.)

Colonel F. H. Jenkins, C.B., B.S.C. (For services see Q.O. Corps of Guides.)

Colonel R. Jenkins, B.S.C. (Deceased. For services see 1st Bengal Cavalry.)

Mr. W. Jenkins, C.S.I., C.S. (Deceased. See Biographical Division.)

Major S. W. Jenner, R.E., served during the second campaign as Field Engineer, Khyber Division, Kabul F.F.

Lieut. R. Jennings, R.E., served from Dec., 1878, till April, 1879, on the Sukkur-Dadar Railway Survey; from April to Sept., 1879, as Assistant Field Engineer with the Bombay Reserve Brigade; during Sept. and Dec., 1879, on the Baluchistan Public Works; and from Dec., 1879, on Political duty in Southern Afghanistan, having charge during part of the time of the Thal-Chotiali, Pishin, and other districts, and accompanying, as Political Officer, the Thal-Pishin, the Kowas, and the Marri expeditions. (Mentioned in despatches; Thanked in orders.)

Colonel A. C. Johnson, C.B., R.A., joined the force under General Stewart on its way back from Kalat-i-Ghilzai, and commanded the R.A. at Kandahar from 15 Feb., 1879, till 19 March, 1880. Commanded the R.A. Ghazni F.F., in the march from Kandahar, and was present at the battle of Ahmad Khel and the action of Arzu, subsequently remaining in command of the R.A. of the Division in the Logar Valley till the end of Aug., 1880. Commanded the R.A., Kabul-Kandahar F.F., in the advance to the relief of Kandahar, and was present at the battle of Kandahar. (Three times mentioned in despatches; C.B.)

Captain E. A. Johnson, R.A., served during the second campaign with General Phayre's Division (Mentioned in despatches.)

Lieut. G. S. Jones, R.A., served with the Transport Dept., Kandahar F.F., during the second campaign, being present with General Burrows' Brigade at the action of Girishk, in which he acted as Galloper to General Nuttall, the battle of Maiwand, the defence of Kandahar, and the battle of Kandahar. (Twice mentioned in despatches.)

Lt.-Colonel H. T. Jones, H.P., served throughout both campaigns, first as Brigade Major, 1st Brigade, 1st Division, Peshawar Valley F.F., being present at the capture of Ali Musjid, and taking part in the expeditions into the Bazar and Lughman Valleys, and afterwards as Brigade Major, Kuram Division, taking part in the Zaimusht expedition, and being present at the storming of Zawa. (Mentioned in despatches; Brevet of Lt.-Colonel.)

Major J. Jopp, Bo.S.C. served during the second campaign as Assistant Quartermaster-General with General Phayre's Division, taking part in the advance from Quetta to Kandahar in the autumn of 1880. (Mentioned in despatches.)

Major K. A. Jopp, R.E., was employed during the second campaign on the Peshawar-Jalalabad Railway Survey.

Lt.-Colonel C. N. Judge, late R.E. (retired), served during the first campaign as Field Engineer with the 2nd Division Peshawar Valley F.F., being employed in the construction of fortified camps at Landi Kotal and Ali Musjid; subsequently with the Khyber Brigade, making a chain of outposts to connect Ali Musjib with Jamrud. During the second campaign was attached as Field Engineer to Sir O. Bright's Division, and constructed the fortified camp at Pezwan. Accompanied the punitory expedition despatched into the Hissarak Valley. (Mentioned in despatches.)

Bt. Major M. N. G. Kane, Seaforth Highlanders. (For services see 72nd Highlanders.)

Lt.-Colonel F. J. Keen, B.S.C. (For services see 1st Punjab Infantry.)

Captain C. M. Keighley, B.S.C., served with the Commissariat Dept., Kabul F.F., during the second campaign.

Captain James Keith, R.A. (For services see R.A.)

General Sir M. K. Kennedy, K.C.S.I., R.E., served as Controller-General of Transport and Supply throughout the second campaign, was present at the operations round Kabul and defence of Sherpur in Dec., 1879. (Mentioned in despatches.)

Bt. Lt.-Colonel R. G. Kennedy, B.S.C., served as Deputy Assistant Quartermaster-General, Kuram Valley F.F., throughout the first campaign, being present at the assault and capture of the Peiwar Kotal and minor operations. During the second campaign served in the same capacity with the Kabul

F.F., and as Assistant Quartermaster-General, Kabul-Kandahar F.F., taking part in the advance on and occupation of Kabul, and the advance from Kabul to the relief of Kandahar, and being present at the skirmish with the enemy near Zaidabad during the crossing of the Logar River (in which he was wounded), the action of Charasiab, the operations round Kabul and defence of Sherpur in Dec., 1879, the second action of Charasiab, and the battle of Kandahar. (Several times mentioned in despatches; Brevet of Major and Lt.-Colonel.) (Since deceased.)

Colonel T. G. Kennedy, B.S.C. (For services see 2nd Punjab Cavalry.)

Lieut. A. H. Kenney, R.E., served throughout the second campaign, first, till Dec., 1879, as Asst. Field Engineer, Kuram Force, and afterwards in the same capacity, with the 1st Division Kabul F.F. Was employed on various sections of the line, extending to the Peiwar Kotal, in road-making, and at Kabul in the works for the defence of the Bala Hissar. Accompanied, with a section of the R.E. Field Park, the force under General Ross, which marched through Maidan and the Wardak country, in April, 1880, and was present at the fighting at Zaidabad, and in numerous minor operations.

Captain C. H. M. Kensington, R.E., served as Assistant Field Engineer, Khyber Line Force, during the second campaign.

Bt. Lt.-Colonel A. A. A. Kinloch, King's Royal Rifle Corps, served as Deputy Assistant Quartermaster-General with the Khyber Column throughout both campaigns. During the first, was present, with General Macpherson's Brigade, at the taking of Ali Musjid, and the repulse of the attack by Afridis; took part in both expeditions into the Bazar Valley (mentioned in despatches on the occasion of the forcing of the Tubbai Pass); and after the advance of the 1st Division to Jalalabad, served for the remainder of the campaign with the 2nd Division, to which he was transferred, as senior officer of the Q.M.G. Dept., under General Maude. During the period between the first and second campaign, served as D.A.Q.M.G. with the Khyber Brigade at Landi Kotal. In the second campaign, served as D.A.Q.M.G. with General C. Gough's advanced Brigade, and was engaged in the operations at Jagdalak and subsequent march to Sherpur; accompanied General Ross on his march to co-operate with the Ghazni F.F.; and was with General C. Gough throughout the period of his occupation of the Koh Daman. (Mentioned in despatches; Brevets of Major and Lt.-Colonel.)

Lieut. F. W. Kitchener, West Yorkshire Regt. (For services see 14th Foot.)
Colonel C. B. Knowles, C.B., Hampshire Regt. (For services see 67th Foot.)
Bt. Major W. G. Knox, R.A. (For services see R.A.)
Colonel R. Lacy (retired). (For services see 59th Foot.)
Lieut. W. Lambert, B.S.C. (For services see 3rd Punjab Cavalry.)

Major A. Landon, Bengal Infantry, served in charge of the Treasure Chest, Kuram F.F., during the second campaign.

Colonel C. S. Lane, B.S.C., served as Principal Commissariat Officer, 2nd Division, Kandahar F.F. during the first campaign. (Mentioned in despatches).

Lieut. C. R. Lang, Manchester Regt., served with the Commissariat Dept. in S. Afghanistan during the second campaign.

Capt. R. A. Lanning, R.A., served during the first campaign as Adjutant Siege Train, Kandahar F.F., and during the second campaign as Adjutant R.A., Khyber Division, Kabul F.F., and 2nd Division, Kabul F.F. (Twice mentioned in despatches.)

Bt. Major E. M. Larmine, R.E., served as Brigade Major of R.E. at Kandahar, from the autumn of 1879 till April, 1880; afterwards accompanied General Stewart's force, as Commanding R.E., to Ghazni (of which he made a special survey), being present at the battle of Ahmad Khel and the action of Arzu, and subsequently remained with the Division in the Logar Valley till July, 1880, when he returned to India by the Khyber Pass. (Mentioned in despatches; Brevet of Major.)

Major A. F. Laughton, M.S.C., served during both campaigns, from April, 1879, till April, 1880, as Executive Commissariat Officer, Reserve Division, Rawal Pindi.

Capt. W. Law, R.A., served during the second campaign as Brigade Major, 1st Infantry Brigade, Kandahar F.F., accompanying General Brooke's force sent out to cover the retreat of the fugitives from Maiwand, being present in Kandahar throughout the siege, and being present at the sortie to Deh Khwaja and the battle of Kandahar. (Mentioned in despatches.)

Lieut. E. E. M. Lawford, M.S.C. (For services see 1st Madras Light Cavalry.)

Bt. Lt.-Colonel W. A. Lawrence, B.S.C., served as Transport Officer to the Cavalry Brigade of General Biddulph's Division from the outbreak of the war till June, 1879, taking part in the advance on Kandahar and Girishk, and accompanying the force under General Palliser into the Khakrez Valley; in July, 1879, marched to the Khojak and back to Kandahar; where he remained, as General Transport Officer, till March, 1880; took part, as Director of Transport, in the advance of the Ghazni F.F. from Kandahar, being present at the battle of Ahmad Khel, and remained with the Division in the Logar

Valley throughout the summer; eventually accompanied, in the same capacity, the Division under General Hills in its march through the Khyber to India. (Mentioned in despatches; Brevet of Lt.-Colonel.)

Bt. Lt.-Colonel E. P. Leach, V.C., R.E. (For services see Biographical Division.)

Capt F. W. V. Leckie, Bo. S.C., served during the second campaign as Brigade Major, Kandahar F.F., accompanying General Brooke's force sent out to cover the retreat of the fugitives from Maiwand, being present in Kandahar throughout the siege, and being present at the battle of Kandahar. (Mentioned in despatches.)

Bt. Lt.-Colonel A. Le Mesurier, R.E., served as Brigade Major, R.E., 1st Division, Kandahar F.F., during the first campaign, from Nov., 1878, till Oct., 1879, taking part in the advance on and occupation of Kandahar and Kalat-i-Ghilzai, and being present at the action of Saif-u-din. (Mentioned in despatches; Brevet of Lt.-Colonel.)

Colonel C. B. Le Mesurier, R.A., commanded the R.A.. 2nd Division, Kandahar F.F., during the first campaign, taking part in the advance on and occupation of Kandahar.

Lieut. C. M. Lester, West Yorkshire Regt. (For services see 14th Foot)

Bt. Major T. L. Lewis, B.S.C., served with the Commissariat Dept., 1st Division, Kandahar F.F., during the second campaign, being present at the operations round Kabul and defence of Sherpur in Dec., 1879. (Mentioned in despatches; Brevet of Major.)

Bt. Colonel D. Limond, C.B., R.E., served during the first campaign as Commanding Royal Engineer, 2nd Division, Peshawar Valley F.F., and during the second campaign as Commanding Royal Engineer, Khyber Division, Kabul F.F., and N. Afghanistan F.F., took part in the operations in the Hissarak district. (Mentioned in despatches; C.B.)

Major-General A. H. Lindsay, C.B., R.A. (retired), commanded the Royal Artillery, Kuram Valley F.F. during the first campaign, being present at the assault and capture of the Peiwar Kotal, and taking part in the Khost Valley operations, including the action of Matun. (Mentioned in despatches.)

Lt.-Colonel J. G. Lindsay, R.E., served during the second campaign as Engineer-in-Chief, Jacobabadad, Sukkur, and Quetta Railway Survey, and subsequently as Commanding Engineer with General Phayre's Division, taking part in the march from Quetta to Kandahar in the autumn of 1880, and being present at the destruction of Abusaid's Fort. (Mentioned in despatches.)

Lieut. P. B. Lindsell, Royal Irish Regt., served in the Transport Train, Kuram Valley and Kabul Field Forces during both campaigns.

Major F. E. Lloyd (retired). (For services see 25th Foot.)

Capt. W. Loch, Bo.S.C. (For services see 2nd Sind Horse).

Lt.-Colonel W. S. A. Lockhart, C.B., Bengal Infantry, served as Road Commandant, Khyber Line, from Sep. to Dec., 1879; as A.Q.M.G., 1st Division, Kabul F.F., from Dec., 1879, to May, 1880, being present at the operations round Kabul and defence of Sherpur in Dec., 1879, including the actions of Karez Mir, 10 Dec., Chardeh, 11 Dec., and Takht-i-Shah, 12 and 13 Dec.; was subsequently detached as Staff Officer to General Baker in his raid on the village of Baba-Kusk-Kar; from May to Aug., 1880, during the operations in the Logar Valley, was A.Q.M.G. to General Hill's Division; and in Aug., 1880, joined Sir Donald Stewart as Chief Staff Officer in the withdrawal from Kabul by the Khyber route. (Several times mentioned in despatches; C.B.)

Capt. W. F. Longbourne, A.P.D. (For services see 5th Fusiliers.)

Lieut. F. B. Longe, R.E. (For services see R.E.)

Bt. Lt.-Colonel B. Lovett, C.S.I., R.E., served during the first campaign as Brigade Major R.E., 1st Division, Peshawar Valley F.F., being present at the capture of Ali Musjid and the forcing of the Khyber Pass. (Mentioned in despatches; Brevet of Lt.-Colonel).

Lieut. P. Low, East Yorkshire Regt., served with the Commissariat Dept., S. Afghanistan, during the second campaign.

Lt.-Colonel R. C. Low, C.B., Bengal Cavalry. (For services see 13th Bengal Lancers.)

Capt. H. C. E. Lucas, Bo.S.C., served with the Commissariat Dept. in the first campaign.

Bt. Lt.-Colonel W. Luckhardt, Bo.S.C., served with the Commissariat Dept., Kandahar F.F., during the first and latter part of the second campaign, taking part in the advance on and occupation of Kandahar, and accompanying as Principal Commissariat Officer, 2nd Division, Kandahar F.F. in the advance to the Halmand, and in the same capacity with the Thal-Chotiali F.F., in the return march to India. (Brevet of Lt.-Colonel).

Bt. Major H. T. Lugard, R.A. (For services see R.A.)

Colonel Sir P. S. Lumsden, K.C.B., C.S.I., A.D.C., served as Chief of the Headquarter Staff during the second campaign. (K.C.B.)

Capt. E. E. Lushington, 8th Hussars, served with the Transport Train in the Kuram Valley from May till July, 1879, and again from Oct., 1879, till May, 1880.

Lieut. H. F. Lyons-Montgomery, B.S.C. (For services see 28th P.N.I.)

Capt. W. H. Lyster, Bo.S.C. (For services see 24th Bo.N.I.)

Major M. J. Macartney, R.E., served from Oct., 1879, till July, 1880, on the Kandahar Railway Survey; subsequently, from July till Nov., 1880, as Executive Engineer of the Pishni Districts, during which period General Phayre's relieving force marched through the Valley to Kandahar; and finally as Superintending Engineer and Secretary to the Agent for the Governor-General, Baluchistan.

Colonel G. S. Macbean, C.B., B.S.C., served as Principal Commissariat Officer, Khyber Line F.F., during the second campaign. (Mentioned in despatches; C.B.)

Lieut. J. B. M'Donell, Suffolk Regt. (For services see 12th Foot.)

Lt.-Colonel R. B. McEwen, h.p. (For services see 92nd Highlanders.)

Bt. Major A. D. McGregor, Gordon Highlanders. (For services see 92nd Highlanders).

Major-General Sir C. M. MacGregor, K.C.B., C.S.I., C.I.E., V.C., B.S.C., served during the first campaign as Deputy Adjutant and Quartermaster-General 1st Division Peshawar Valley F.F., taking part in the operations in the Bazar and Jalalabad Valleys. During the second campaign served, first, as Director of Transport, Khyber Division, subsequently as D.A. and Q.M.G., afterwards as Chief of the Staff, Kabul F.F., and eventually in command of the 3rd Brigade, Kabul-Kandahar F.F., taking part in the advance on and occupation of Kabul, and the advance from Kabul to the relief of Kandahar, and being present at the actions of Charasiab, the operations round Kabul in Dec., 1879, including the recovery of the guns at Killa Kazi, the defence of Sherpur, and the battle of Kandahar. Subsequently commanded the Marri F.F. in the operations against the Marris. (Four times mentioned in despatches; C.B.; K.C.B.)

Bt. Major C. R. Macgregor, B.S.C., served during the second campaign with the Transport Corps, 1st Division, Kabul F.F., and Kabul-Kandahar F.F., taking part in the advance from Kabul to the relief of Kandahar, and being present at the battle of Kandahar. Subsequently served in the operations against the Marris. (Mentioned in despatches; Brevet of Major.)

Major W. Mackie (retired), served during the first campaign with the Transport Corps, Kandahar Line, part of the time as Assistant Superintendent of Transport at Sukkur.

Mr. Donald C. Macnabb, C.S.I., C.S., was Commissioner of Peshawar during the first campaign. Accompanied, with full political powers, the second Bazar Valley expedition.

Bt. Colonel H. McLeod, R.A., served in charge of the Ordnance Field Park, 2nd Division, Kandahar F.F., during the first campaign.

Lt.-Colonel E. J. M'Nair, Bengal Infantry, served during the second campaign as Director of Transport, Kuram Force. (Mentioned in despatches.)

Capt. J. L. Macpherson, R.E., served from Oct., 1879, till Sept., 1880, as Field Engineer with the Kuram F.F. under General Watson.

Major-General Sir H. T. Macpherson, K.C.B., V.C., B.S.C., throughout the first campaign commanded the 1st Brigade, 1st Division, Peshawar Valley F.F.; at the capture of Ali Musjid, and in the expeditions to Kama and the Lughman Valley. During the second campaign commanded the 1st Brigade Kabul and Kabul-Kandahar Field Forces, in the advance on and occupation of Kabul, the advance from Kabul to the relief of Kandahar, the action of Charasiab, and the battle of Kandahar. Commanded variously constituted forces in the operations round Kabul in Dec., 1879, including the defeat of the Kohistanis at Karez Mir, and the assault of the Takht-i-Shah, and in numerous minor operations and expeditions. (Five times mentioned in despatches; K.C.B.)

Lieut. F. G. L. Mainwaring, B.S.C. (For services see 30th P.N.I.)

Bt. Colonel W. G. Mainwaring, C.I.E., Bo.S.C. (For services see 30th Bo.N.I.)

Lieut. F. C. Maisey, B.S.C., served throughout the first campaign as Asst. Superintendent of Transport, Kuram Valley F.F., being in charge of the transport of the 2nd Brigade during the assault and capture of the Peiwar Kotal. Served from Oct., 1879, till June, 1880, as Deputy Assistant Quartermaster-General, Khyber Line Force, accompanying the expedition against the Mohmands of Kam Daka, the expedition into the Lughman Valley, the expedition against the Wazir Kugianis, and the expedition to Kama. (Mentioned in despatches.) From July to Oct., 1880, served as D.A.Q.M.G., Kuram Force.

Capt. P. J. Maitland, Bo.S.C. (For services see 3rd Sind Horse.)

Lieut. J. W. Malet, Northumberland Fusiliers. (For services see 5th Fusiliers.)

Colonel J. H. P. Malcolmson, C.B., Bo.S.C. (For services see 3rd Sind Horse).

Capt. F. G. Maltby, B.S.C., served with the Transport Corps, Khyber Line, during both campaigns.

Bt. Major J. D. Mansel, Rifle Brigade, served throughout the first campaign as Aide-de-Camp to

Brigadier-General Macpherson, in which capacity he was present at the taking of Ali Musjid, and accompanied the Kunar and Lughman Valley expeditions. Served in the second campaign as Aide-de-Camp to General Ross, and in that capacity accompanied the force under Sir F. Roberts from Kabul to the relief of Kandahar, and was present at the battle of Kandahar. (Mentioned in despatches; Brevet of Major.)

Lieut. H. Mansfield, B.S.C., served during the first campaign with the 27th P.N.I. and 1st Sikhs, taking part in the front attack on Ali Musjid; and in the second campaign, with the Commissariat Dept., Kuram line, accompanying the Zaimusht expedition, and being present at the storming of Zawa. (Mentioned in despatches.)

Lieut. H. R. Marrett, B.S.C. (For services see 24th P.N.I.)

Major E. M. L. Marriott, Bengal Infantry, served with the Commissariat Dept., Kuram F.F., during the second campaign.

Capt. G. W. Martin, B.S.C., served in the Survey Dept. with the Kabul F.F. during the second campaign, being present at the operations round Kabul and defence of Sherpur in Dec., 1879. (Mentioned in despatches.)

Capt. G. W. Martin, B.S.C., served in the Survey Dept., with the Kuram Valley F.F. during the first campaign, and with the Kabul F.F. during the second campaign, being present at the operations round Kabul and the Defence of Sherpur (temporarily serving in the Field Engineer's Dept.) in Dec., 1879, and accompanying Brigadier-General C. Gough's Brigade into the Koh Daman. (Mentioned in despatches.)

Capt. M. K. Martin, B.S.C., served with the Transport Corps in the first campaign.

Brigadier-General W. G. Dunham Massy, h.p., commanded the Cavalry Brigade, Kuram Division, Kabul F.F., during the second campaign, till March, 1880; in the advance on and occupation of Kabul, at the action of Charasiab and subsequent operations, and in the operations round Kabul and defence of Sherpur in Dec., 1879. (Twice mentioned in despatches.)

Lieut.-General Sir F. F. Maude, K.C.B., V.C., commanded the 2nd Division Peshawar Valley F.F., from the date of its formation till it was broken up on the conclusion of the first campaign. Commanded the first and second expeditions into the Bazar Valley. (Received the thanks of both Houses of Parliament; K.C.B.)

Major-General F. R. Maunsell, C.B., R.E., served as Commanding Royal Engineer, 1st Division, Peshawar F.F., during the first campaign, being present at the capture of Ali Musjid, and the forcing of the Khyber Pass. (Mentioned in despatches.)

Lieut. N. F. A. Maunsell, Royal Warwickshire Regt., served during the second campaign as Transport Officer, Khyber F.F., at Barikab.

Lieut. R. C. Maxwell, R.E., served during the second campaign as Assistant Engineer, Peshawar-Jalalabad Railway Survey.

Lieut. A. L. Mein, R.E., served during the second campaign as Assistant Field Engineer, Kabul F.F.

Capt. Howard Melliss, Bo.S.C., served during the second campaign as Deputy Assistant Quartermaster-General, 2nd Division, Kandahar F.F.

Mr. W. R. H. Merk, C.S., served as Assistant Political Officer, Khyber line, from April, 1879, with an interval of one month's absence, till Nov., 1880, when he was transferred to Kandahar, and continued in that district till March, 1881. Was present at the actions of Daka and Mazina, and accompanied the expedition to Kama and Brigadier-General Wilkinson's brigade to Maiwand. (Mentioned in despatches and minutes; received on two occasions the thanks of the Government of India.)

Major-General J. E. Michell, C.B., R.A., commanded the Cavalry Brigade, 2nd Division, Peshawar Valley F.F., during the first campaign, taking part in the the Bazar Valley expedition. (Mentioned in despatches.)

Bt. Major C. F. W. Moir, Leicestershire Regt. (For services see 17th Foot.)

Major E. Molloy, B.S.C. (For services see 5th Goorkha Regt.)

Capt. G. E. Money, B.S.C., served with the Transport Train in the Kuram Valley during the first campaign.

Capt. J. J. Money-Simons, B.S.C. (For services see 24th P.N.I.)

Lieut. E. J. Montagu-Stuart-Wortley, King's Royal Rifle Corps, served as Transport Officer, Kuram Force, previous to the advance of Sir F. Roberts from Kushi, and from 1 Dec., 1879, until invalided in Aug., 1880, as Superintendent and Assistant Superintendent of Army Signalling, Kuram Force, with the exception of a brief interval during which he again performed Transport duties. Accompanied General Tytler in the Zaimusht expedition. (Mentioned in despatches.)

Lieut. J. Monteith, Bo.S.C. (For services see 2nd Sind Horse.)

Lieut. B. T. G. Montgomery, King's Royal Rifle Corps, served from Oct., 1878, till Sept., 1879, as

Orderly Officer to Brigadier-General Barker, commanding 1st Brigade 1st Division Kandahar F.F., taking part in the advance on and occupation of Kandahar and Kalat-i-Ghilzai.

Colonel H. Moore, C.B., C.I.E., Bo.S.C., served during the first campaign as Assistant Quartermaster-General, 2nd Division, Kandahar F.F., taking part in the advance on and occupation of Kandahar, being present at the action of Saif-u-din, and accompanying, as Political Officer, the expedition to the Halmand. (Mentioned in despatches; C.B.)

Capt. R. F. Moore, R.E., served as Assistant Field Engineer, Khyber Line Force, during the second campaign.

Lieut. G. H. More-Molyneux, B.S.C., commanded the Khyber Levies from June till Sept., 1880, holding the Pass during the retirement of the army under Sir Donald Stewart.

Capt. W. More-Molyneux, B.S.C., served with the Transport Train in S. Afghanistan during the first campaign. (Died at Shahpur, Baluchistan, 9 Dec., 1878.)

Lt.-Colonel M. P. Moriarty, B.S.C. (retired), served in charge of the Transport, Kuram Valley F.F., from the outbreak of the war till 31 Dec., 1878. Was appointed to the charge of the Treasury attached to the force, 1 Jan., 1879, and in that capacity took part in the advance of the Division under Sir F. Roberts on Kabul, being present at the action of Charasiab. Was a member of the Military Commission for the trial of those who were implicated in the massacre of the British Embassy. Took part in the operations round Kabul and defence of Sherpur in Dec., 1879. Had charge of the Kabul Treasury during the whole period of the British occupation, and of that of the army under Sir D. Stewart during the final retirement. (Mentioned in despatches.)

Major F. de L. Morison, Lothian Regt., served with the Transport Corps, Kuram Valley F.F., during the first campaign, being present at the assault and capture of the Peiwar Kotal, and accompanying the reconnaissance to the Shutargardan Pass.

Capt. E. C. Morris, North Lancashire Regt., served as Transport Officer, Peshawar Valley F.F., from 2 April till 19 June, 1879.

Lieut. P. A. Morshead, Royal Irish Regt. (For services see 18th Foot.)

Bt. Lt.-Colonel G. de C. Morton, Royal Warwickshire Regt., served throughout both campaigns: as Brigade Major, 2nd Brigade, Kuram F.F., from the outbreak of the war till 12 Sep., 1879; as Brigade Major, 1st Brigade, Kabul F.F. till 1 Dec., 1879; as A.A.G., Kabul F.F., till 3 April, 1880; as A.A.G., 1st Division, Kabul F.F., till 5 Aug., 1880; and as A.A.G., Infantry Division, Kabul-Kandahar F.F., till 14 Oct., 1880. Was present at the assault and capture of the Peiwar Kotal, and the action of Charasiab and subsequent pursuit; accompanied the 1st Brigade Kabul F.F. to open up communications with the Khyber Force; was present at the affair at Doaba, 10 Nov., 1879, and the operations round Kabul and defence of Sherpur in Dec., 1879; accompanied the force under Sir F. Roberts, which marched through the Logar, Wardak, and Maidan Valleys in May, 1880; took part in the advance from Kabul to the relief of Kandahar, and was present at the battle of Kandahar. (Four times mentioned in despatches; Brevets of Major and Lt.-Colonel.)

Major C. W. Murray, Gloucester Regt., in the Spring of 1880 was attached for duty to the 72nd Highlanders at Kabul. Was appointed Orderly Officer to Brigadier-General Baker, and accompanied his column, in that capacity, in the expedition into the Logar Valley in May and June, 1880.

Capt. J. W. Murray, R.A., served with the Transport Dept. in the first campaign.

Bt. Colonel W. C. R. Mylne, B.S.C., served as Principal Commissariat Officer, 2nd Division, Peshawar Valley F.F., during the first campaign, accompanying the expedition into the Bazar Valley. (Mentioned in despatches.)

Lieut. J. Nagle, East Surrey Regt. (For services see 70th Foot.)

Bt. Major the Hon. J. S. Napier, Gordon Highlanders. (For services see 92nd Highlanders.)

Lieut. E. M. Nedham, B.S.C., served with the Transport Dept. in the first campaign.

Major A. H. S. Neill, B.S.C., served in the Kuram Valley during the second campaign, first as Aide-de-Camp to General Watson, and subsequently as Road Commandant. (Mentioned in despatches; Brevet of Major.)

Lieut. J. Neville, R.E., served during the second campaign as Assistant Field Engineer with General Phayre's Division, taking part in the advance from Quetta to Kandahar. (Mentioned in despatches.)

Bt. Colonel H. R. L. Newdigate, C.B., Rifle Brigade. (For services see Rifle Brigade.)

Bt. Major W. G. Nicholson, R.E., served throughout the first campaign as Field Engineer, Kandahar F.F., from 10 Oct. 1878, till 5 March, 1879, and as Commanding R.E., Thal-Chotiali F.F., from 6 March till 30 April, 1879. Served throughout the second campaign, first as Field Engineer, 1st Division, Kabul F.F., from 23 Sep., 1879, till 7 Aug., 1880, being present at the action near Surkai Kotal, 14 Oct., 1879, the defence of the Shutargardan, Oct., 1879, and the defence of the Lataband,

Dec., 1879; then as Field Engineer, Kabul-Kandahar F.F., taking part in the advance to the relief of Kandahar, and being present at the battle of Kandahar. (Four times mentioned in despatches; Brevet of Major.)

Lt.-Colonel M. H. Nicolson, Bombay Infantry, served during the first campaign as Brigade Major, 1st Brigade, 2nd Division, Kandahar F.F., taking part in the advance on and occupation of Kandahar; and during the second campaign as Brigade Major with the Division under Sir D. Stewart, taking part in the advance on Ghazni and into the Logar Valley, being present at the battle of Ahmad Khel and the action of Arzu, and eventually returning to India by the Khyber route. (Mentioned in despatches; Brevet of Lt.-Colonel.)

Lieut. J. E. Nixon, B.S.C. (For services see 18th Bengal Cavalry.)

Lieut. N. I. Noble, Gloucestershire Regt., served with the Commissariat Dept. in S. Afghanistan during the second campaign.

Major W. H. Noble, R.A., served as Staff Officer of the Siege Train, Kandahar F.F., from 1 Nov., 1878, till 1 Oct., 1879.

Lieut. W. P. Noon, Devonshire Regt., served from Jan. till Sept., 1879, as Transport Officer, in Baluchistan and the Pishin Valley; from Sept., 1879, till March, 1880, as Transport Officer at Quetta and Kandahar; and subsequently as Brigade Transport Officer, 1st Brigade, Ghazni F.F., taking part in the advance on Ghazni and into the Logar Valley, being present at the battle of Ahmad Khel, and the night attack in the Logar Valley, 13th May, 1880 (during which he acted as Orderly Officer to Brigadier-General Barter), and eventually returning to India from Kabul by the Khyber route.

Bt. Lt.-Colonel W. North, R.E. (For services see "Royal Engineers.")

Capt. A. W. Noyes, West Yorkshire Regt. (For services see 14th Foot.)

Lieut. C. Nugent, R.E. (Deceased. See Biographical Division.)

Bt. Colonel T. Nuttall, Bo.S.C., during the first campaign, commanded the 2nd Brigade, 2nd Division, Kandahar F.F., taking part in the advance on and occupation of Kandahar; commanded at Kandahar on the departure of Generals Stewart and Biddulph for Kalat-i-Ghilzai and the Halmand; and commanded the 3rd Column Thal-Chotiali F.F. on the return march to India, and subsequently the Vitakri F.F. Took part in the Naga Hills expedition, and was wounded at the action of Konoma. During the second campaign commanded the Cavalry Brigade, Bombay Division, Kandahar F.F., taking part in the advance of General Burrows' force to Girishk, defeating the Wali Shere Ali Khan's mutinied troops 14 July, 1880, and being present at the battle of Maiwand, the defence of Kandahar, the sortie to Deh Khwaja, and the battle of Kandahar. (Five times mentioned in despatches.)

Major C. O'Donel, B.S.C., served with the Commissariat Dept. in S. Afghanistan during the second campaign.

Deputy Surgeon-General J. O'Nial, C.B., A.M.D., served during the second campaign as Principal Medical Officer, Bombay Division, Kandahar F.F., being present at the defence of Kandahar, the sortie to Deh Khwaja, and the battle of Kandahar. (Mentioned in despatches.)

Lieut. G. C. P. Onslow, R.E., served with the Kuram Valley F.F. from the 11th Jan., 1879, until after peace was signed. Accompanied the 23rd Pioneers and Goorkhas in their advance from Shalozan to seize the Shutargardan immediately after news was received of the massacre of the British Embassy, and roughly fortified the Pass and prominent positions on the road from Ali Khel. Advanced with the force under Sir F. Roberts to Kabul, being present at the action of Charasiab and subsequent pursuit. Took part in the operations round Kabul in Dec., 1879, holding a village on General Baker's right during the fighting on the 14th, and being engaged in blowing up villages after the repulse of the enemy's attack on the 23rd. Returned to India with a portion of the R.E. Park in July, 1880. (Mentioned in despatches.)

Major W. C. Ormand (retired). (For services see 5th Fusiliers.)

Capt. R. T. Orpen, R.E., was employed during the first campaign in selecting and marking out the new line of communications between Jacobabad and Dadar for the force under General Phayre's command.

Capt. W. J. Orr, Bo.S.C., served with the Commissariat Dept. in S. Afghanistan during the second campaign.

Lt.-Colonel R. D. Osborn (retired, late B.S.C.), served in charge of the Field Treasure Chest, Quetta Division, Kandahar F.F., during the first campaign.

Lieut. E. G. Osborne, R.A. (Killed in action. See Biographical Division.)

Brigadier-General Sir C. H. Palliser, K.C.B., B.S.C., as Brigadier-General of Cavalry commanded the advanced troops of General Stewart's force in the advance on Kandahar, and defeated the enemy in the Takht-i-pul Valley and at Saif-u-din, 4th Jan., 1879; in the same capacity took part in General Biddulph's advance to the Halmand; commanded an expedition into the Khakrez Valley, April, 1879;

commanded the Kokaran outpost during the summer of 1879, and subsequently remained with the S. Afghanistan F.F. at Kandahar till the end of March, 1880; commanded the Cavalry Brigade in the advance on Ghazni and into the Logar Valley, at the battle of Ahmad Khel, and the action of Arzu, and repulsed and cut up the enemy at Patkao Shana, 1 July, 1880, with the Cavalry Brigade of the 3rd Division, N. Afghanistan F.F. Eventually returned to India by the Khyber route on the retirement of the troops from Kabul. (Repeatedly mentioned in despatches; K.C.B.)

Bt. Lt.-Colonel A. P. Palmer, B.S.C., served thoughout the first and during the second campaign. Commanded the Levies raised in the Kuram Valley at the assault and capture of the Peiwar Kotal, and during the remainder of the first campaign was the Chief Officer of the Transport Dept., Kuram F.F. (Received the thanks of Government; Brevet of Lt.-Colonel.) In the second campaign served first as Road Commandant in charge of communications in the Kuram Valley, and afterwards as Assistant Adjutant and Quartermaster-General, Kuram Force.

Lieut. S. S. Parkyn, Royal Irish Regt., served with the Transport Dept. in the first campaign.

Capt. W. Peacocke, R.E., served as Assistant Field Engineer, 1st Division, Peshawar Valley F.F., during the first campaign. Accompanied General Tytler's Column, as Survey Officer, in the Bazar Valley expedition. (Mentioned in despatches.)

Lieut. T. C. Pears, B.S.C. (For services see 1st Punjab Infantry.)

Capt. A. J. Pearson, R.A., served during the first campaign, first as Adjutant, R.A., and subsequently as Brigade Major, R.A., with the Punjab Chiefs' Contingent.

Bt. Lt.-Colonel H. P. Pearson, Suffolk Regt., was Deputy Assistant Quartermaster-General in command of the Signallers of Sir S. Browne's Division at the capture of Ali Musjid, and the forcing of the Khyber Pass; and was Brigade Major in the Khyber F.F. from June, 1879, till July, 1880, being present in that capacity at the defeat of the Mohmands at Kam Daka, and the operations in the Besud district, including the action of Beninga. (Mentioned in despatches; Brevet of Lt.-Colonel.)

Lieut. F. Peel, R.E., served as Assistant Field Engineer with General Watson's force in the Kuram Valley from April, 1880, till invalided to India in Aug., 1880.

Major S. E. Pemberton, R.A., served during the first campaign in charge of the Ordnance Field Park, Kuram Valley F.F., and during the second campaign in charge of the Ordnance Field Park, Kuram Division, Kabul F.F.

Lieut. A. L. Pennington, Northumberland Fusiliers. (For services see 5th Fusiliers.)

Bt. Colonel Æ. Perkins, C.B., A.D.C., R.E., served during the first campaign as Commanding Royal Engineer, Kuram Valley F.F., being present at the assault and capture of the Peiwar Kotal; and during the second campaign as Commanding Royal Engineer, Kuram Division Kabul F.F., 1st Division, Kabul F.F., and Kabul-Kandahar F.F., taking part in the advance on and occupation of Kabul, and the advance from Kabul to the relief of Kandahar, and being present at the action of Charasiab, the operations round Kabul in Dec., 1879, constructing the defences of Sherpur, and being present at the battle of Kandahar. (Four times mentioned in despatches; C.B.)

Capt. E. W. Perry, 40th Foot. (Deceased. See Biographical Division.)

Major E. N. Peters, R.E., served on the Kandahar Railway Survey, during the second campaign.

Captain Richard Phayre, North Yorkshire Regt., served during the second campaign as Aide-de-Camp to General Phayre, taking part in the advance from Quetta to Kandahar in the autumn of 1880. (Mentioned in despatches.)

Lt.-General Sir Robert Phayre, K.C.B., A.D.C., Bo.S.C., assumed command of the Bombay Reserve Brigade and the Sukkur-Quetta line of communications in Dec., 1878, and during the first and earlier part of the second campaign was mainly engaged in the construction of several hundreds of miles of road, and in the development of an extensive system of Transport, between Sukkur and the base of the Divisions operating in S. Afghanistan; in the Spring of 1880, marched with his Brigade to Kandahar, to relieve the Division under Sir D. Stewart; in April, 1880, was appointed to command the lines of communication between Kandahar and the base, and shortly afterwards organized a Field Column and accompanied Sir R. Sandeman in his expedition to traverse and tranquillize part of the newly acquired frontier districts; on the receipt of the news of the disaster at Maiwand, concentrated the Bombay troops, and secured the Khojak Pass; commanded the column destined for the relief of Kandahar, which reached its destination shortly after the defeat of Ayub Khan's army by the Division under Sir F. Roberts; and eventually commanded in S. Afghanistan until relieved by General Hume, C.B. (Thanked by both Houses of Parliament and the Government of India; mentioned in despatches; K.C.B.)

Major H. Pipon, R.A. (For services see R.A.)

Lieut. W. A. Plant, R.A. (For services see R.A.)

Lieut. F. G. Pogson, East Yorkshire Regt., served in S. Afghanistan during the second campaign as Transport Officer, Kandahar Line. (Mentioned in despatches.)

Capt. R. Pole-Carew, Coldstream Guards, served during the second campaign as Aide-de-Camp to Sir F. Roberts, taking part in the advance on and occupation of Kabul, and the advance from Kabul to the relief of Kandahar, and being present at the action of Charasiab, the operations round Kabul and defence of Sherpur in Dec., 1879, and the battle of Kandahar. (Three times mentioned in despatches.)

Lieut. G. M. Porter, R.E.

Surgeon-Major J. Porter, A.M.D. (Deceased. See Biographical Division.)

Capt. J. R. Povah, Royal Dublin Fusiliers, served as Transport Officer, 2nd Brigade, 1st Division, Kandahar F.F., throughout the first campaign, being present at the occupation of Kandahar and Kalat-i-Ghilzai; after the Treaty of Gandamak served with General Palliser's Flying Column in the Argandab Valley; and in the second campaign, till Feb., 1880, with Sir D. Stewart's head-quarters at Kandahar.

Major C. L. Prendergast, Bengal Infantry, served during the second campaign as Deputy Judge-Advocate, Reserve Division, Peshawar, and Khyber Line Force.

Colonel G. A. Prendergast, B.S.C. (For services see 15th Bengal Cavalry.)

Bt. Lt.-Colonel G. T. Pretyman, R.A., served as Aide-de-Camp to General Roberts throughout the first campaign. Was present at the operations preceding, and at the capture of the Peiwar Kotal, when he accompanied the General on the flank march, and assisted at the storming of the barricades of the Spingawi Kotal; accompanied the reconnaissance to the top of the Shutargardan Pass; was present at the affair in the Sapari defile; and took part in the Khost Valley operations, including the action of Matun. In July, 1879, accompanied General Roberts when he escorted Sir L. Cavagnari to the Shutargardan. On the renewal of hostilities was again appointed A.D.C. to Sir F. Roberts, and taking part in the advance on Kabul, was present at the action of Charasiab and the subsequent occupation of the capital. Was invalided to India, Nov., 1879, till March, 1880, when he rejoined Sir F. Roberts' head-quarters as A.D.C., and served in that capacity till the conclusion of the war. Took part in the advance from Kabul to the relief of Kandahar, and was present at the battle of Kandahar, acting as Commandant of the Head-quarter Camp. (Three times mentioned in despatches; Brevets of Major and Lt.-Colonel.)

Lt.-General J. M. Primrose, C.S.I., commanded the Reserve Division, Kandahar F.F., in Dec., 1878, and in Jan., 1879, proceeded to Kandahar to take over the command of the 1st Division; but the reduction of the forces employed in S. Afghanistan having been in the meantime decided on by Government, he returned to Sind shortly after reaching his destination. During the second campaign commanded the Kandahar F.F. from March, 1880. Commanded the Kandahar Force throughout the siege, and at the battle of Kandahar.

Bt. Lt.-Colonel G. U. Prior, Leinster Regt., served during the first campaign, first as Deputy Assistant Quartermaster-General to the Division commanded by Sir D. Stewart, taking part in the advance on and occupation of Kandahar; subsequently as D.A.Q.M.G. to the Cavalry Brigade, taking part in the advance on and occupation of Kalat-i-Ghilzai; afterwards, in the same capacity, to a column ordered to reconnoitre the Arghesan Valley; and finally as D.A.Q.M.G. to the Advance Column of the Division opening up and returning by the Thal-Chotiali route to India, being present at the action of Baghao. (Mentioned in despatches; Brevet of Lt.-Colonel.)

Bt. Lt.-Colonel M. Protheroe, C.S.I., C.B., M.S.C., served during the first campaign, from March, 1879, as extra Aide-de-Camp to Sir D. Stewart, commanding at Kandahar. During the second campaign served as Political Officer with the Khyber Line Force, the Kabul F.F., and the Kabul-Kandahar F.F., being present at the operations in the Kama and Besud Districts, taking part in the advance from Kabul to the relief of Kandahar, and being present at the battle of Kandahar. (Mentioned in despatches; C.S.I.)

Capt. R. R. Pulford, R.E., served during the second campaign as Transport Staff Officer on the Khyber Line.

Colonel H. M. G. Purvis, R.A., commanded the Royal Artillery of the Reserve Division, Peshawar, and Khyber Line Force, during the second campaign.

Lieut. H. L. Ramsay, B.S.C., served during the second campaign as Assistant Political Officer, Kabul F.F., being present at the operations round Kabul and defence of Sherpur in Dec., 1879. (Mentioned in despatches.)

Capt. St. G. J. Rathbone, Berkshire Regt., served as Transport Officer with the Kuram Valley F.F. during the second campaign, from Sep., 1879, till Oct., 1880, taking part in the Zaimusht expedition.

Capt. A. A. Rawlinson, 8th Hussars. (For services see 8th Hussars.)

Lieut. F. W. Reader, Leicestershire Regt., served as Orderly Officer to Brigadier-General Cobbe, C.B., Commanding 1st Brigade, Kuram Valley F.F., from 19 Oct., 1878, till 2 Dec., 1879, being present at the assault and capture of the Peiwar Kotal. (Mentioned in despatches.)

Capt. B. L. P. Reilly, Bo.S.C., served with the Commissariat Dept. throughout both campaigns, taking part with General Biddulph's Division in the advance on and occupation of Kandahar and the advance to the Halmand, and the advance of the Ghazni F.F. on Ghazni and into the Logar Valley, being present at the affair at Khushk-i-Nakhud, the battle of Ahmad Khel, and the action of Arzu. (Twice mentioned in despatches.)

Major R. H. F. Rennick, B.S.C. (For services see 29th P.N.I.)

Lieut. J. T. Rice, R.E. (Deceased. See Biographical Division.)

Bt. Lt.-Colonel J. W. Ridgeway, Bengal Infantry, served during the second campaign as Political Assistant, Kabul and Kabul-Kandahar Field Forces, accompanying brigades under Generals Ross and C. Gough into the Maidan, Wardak, and Koh Daman Districts, taking part in the advance from Kabul to the relief of Kandahar, and being present at the battle of Kandahar. (Twice mentioned in despatches; Brevet of Lt.-Colonel.)

Bt. Major A. T. S. A. Rind, B.S.C., served with the Commissariat Dept., Kabul and Kabul-Kandahar Field Forces, during the second campaign, taking part in the advance from Kabul to the relief of Kandahar, and being present at the battle of Kandahar. (Mentioned in despatches; Brevet of Major.)

Major V. Rivaz, B.S.C., served as Deputy Assistant Adjutant and Quartermaster-General, Punjab Chiefs' Contingent, during the first campaign. (Mentioned in despatches.)

Lt.-General Sir F. S. Roberts, Bart., G.C.B., C.I.E., V.C., R.A., commanded the Kuram Valley F.F. throughout the first campaign: in the assault and capture of the Peiwar Kotal, the reconnaissance to the summit of the Shutargardan Pass, the repulse of the Mangals in the Sapari defile, and the occupation of and operations in the Khost District, including the action of Matun. (Received the thanks of both Houses of Parliament; K.C.B.) During the second campaign commanded the Kabul F.F. in the advance on and occupation of Kabul in the autumn of 1879, at the action of Charasiab and subsequent operations, and in the operations round Kabul and defence of Sherpur in Dec., 1879. (C.I.E.) Commanded the Kabul-Kandahar F.F. which marched from Kabul to Kandahar in Aug., 1880, relieved the Kandahar garrison, and on the 1st Sept. defeated and dispersed the army under Ayub Khan. (Received the thanks of both Houses of Parliament.) Nominated G.C.B., and created a Baronet for his distinguished services in India. Has been twenty-three times mentioned in despatches before the Afghan War, during which he was eight times thanked for his services by the Viceroy and Commander-in-Chief in India.

Major-General W. Roberts, late 5th Fusiliers, held brigade commands in India during the first campaign. In Dec., 1879, was appointed to the command of a brigade of the Khyber Line Force. In March, 1880, proceeded to Kabul, and commanded a brigade in the Bala Hissar. (Mentioned in despatches.)

Lieut. C. G. Robertson, Liverpool Regt. (For services see 8th Foot.)

Capt. W. W. Robinson, R.E., joined the Kandahar Ry. Survey, 9th Dec., 1879, and was employed in surveying for the line over the Amran Mountains, the Pishin district, and the Kakar country until Aug., 1880. Served with General Phayre's Division as Asst. Field Engineer from Aug. till Oct., 1880, when he resumed survey work for the Kandahar line through the Kakar country, and continued thus employed till Dec., 1880.

Major J. C. Robson, R.A., served during the second campaign as Adjutant R.A., 2nd Division, Kandahar F.F. (Since deceased.)

Major P. Roddy, V.C., Bengal Infantry, served during the first campaign, from March till June, 1879, with the 20th P.N.I., 1st Division Peshawar Valley F.F., and also with the Transport Corps on the Khyber Line.

Major G. W. Rogers, B.S.C. (For services see 4th Goorkha Regt.)

Bt. Major M. W. Rogers, R.E., served throughout the first campaign, and till August, 1879, in charge of the Survey operations with Sir D. Stewart's Division, carrying a route-survey from Quetta by way of the Gwaja Pass to Kandahar, and from Kandahar to Kalat-i-Ghilzai. (Brevet of Major.)

Major-General Sir J. Ross, K.C.B., commanded, during the second campaign, first, the Peshawar Reserve Division, from the date of its formation till it was broken up, subsequently the 2nd Division Kabul F.F., and finally, the Infantry Division of the Kabul-Kandahar F.F. Commanded the force which effected the junction with the Ghazni F.F., and defeated the enemy at Shekabad, took part, as second in command, in the advance from Kabul to the relief of Kandahar, and the battle of Kandahar. (Thanked by both Houses of Parliament; K.C.B.)

Major G. W. C. Rothe, R.A., served as Adjutant of Artillery, 1st Division, Peshawar Valley F.F., from the outbreak of the war till promotion in Jan., 1879, being present as the only Artillery Staff Officer at the capture of Ali Musjid and the forcing of the Khyber. (Mentioned in despatches.)

Lt.-Colonel H. Rowland, Bengal Infantry, served with the Commissariat Dept. in N. Afghanistan during the war.

Capt. the Hon. W. C. Rowley, R.A., served during the second campaign as Orderly Officer to Sir F. Roberts, taking part in the advance from Kabul to the relief of Kandahar, and being present at the battle of Kandahar. (Mentioned in despatches.)

Capt. A. Ruttledge, West Yorkshire Regt., served as Transport Officer on the Khyber line during the first campaign.

Bt. Lt.-Colonel O. B. C. St. John, R.E., was appointed to the Mission under Sir N. Chamberlain in Aug. and Sept., 1878, and on its failure, was selected to accompany Sir Donald Stewart as Chief Political Officer with the Kandahar F.F. (Mentioned in despatches; C.S.I.; Brevet of Lt.-Colonel.) On Sir D. Stewart's departure from Kandahar with the Ghazni F.F., was appointed Resident in Southern Afghanistan. Accompanied the force under General Burrows to the Halmand, and was present at the recapture of the mutineers' guns, 14 July, 1880, and the battle of Maiwand, in which his horse was wounded. Was at Kandahar during the investment, and was present at the sortie to Deh Khwaja, the reconnaissance of 31 Aug., and the battle of Kandahar. Continued in charge of the civil government of Kandahar till the evacuation in April, 1881. (Mentioned in despatches.)

Major T. A. St. Quintin, 10th Hussars. (For services see 10th Hussars.)

Lieut. P. Saltmarshe, R.H.A. (For services see R.A.)

Bt. Lt.-Colonel Sir R. G. Sandeman, K.C.S.I., B.S.C., who had held the appointment of Governor-General's Agent for Baluchistan, from the time the Agency was established, performed Political duty with the Quetta Army from the outbreak of the war. Assisted in organizing the Thal-Chotiali expedition, and accompanying the 1st Column of the Field Force as Political Officer, was present at the action of Baghao. Accompanied General Phayre's Division in its advance to Kandahar. Commanded an expedition against the Achakzai tribes. (Mentioned in despatches; K.C.S.I.; Brevet of Lt.-Colonel.)

Major T. W. Sanders, Bo.S.C., served with the Commissariat Dept. in S. Afghanistan during the second campaign. (Since deceased.)

Lieut. E. C. C. Sandys, B.S.C., served with Commissariat Dept., Khyber Line Force, during the second campaign, accompanying the expedition into the Mazina Valley, and being present at the action of Mazina. (Mentioned in despatches.)

Bt. Lt.-Colonel G. E. L. S. Sanford, R.E., served as Assistant Quartermaster-General, 1st Division Peshawar Valley F.F., from its formation till the conclusion of the first campaign, being present at the capture of Ali Musjid and the forcing of the Khyber Pass, and finally conducting the ferrying operations across the Indus at Attock. (Mentioned in despatches; Brevet of Lt.-Colonel.)

Colonel R. H. Sankey, C.B., R.E., served as Commanding Royal Engineer, 1st Division, Kandahar F.F., during the first campaign, taking part in the advance on and occupation of Kandahar, and being present at the action of Saif-u-din. (Mentioned in despatches; C.B.)

Lt.-Colonel R. W. Sartorius, V.C., C.M.G., Bengal Infantry, served as Superintendent of Transport, 1st Division, Peshawar Valley F.F., during the first campaign.

Capt. G. R. R. Savage, R.E., served on the Staff of Sir D. Stewart as Officer in charge of the advanced Field Telegraphs and Army Signalling during the advance on Kandahar and Kalat-i-Ghilzai in 1878-1879.

Capt. W. H. Sawyer, Royal Lancaster Regt., served with the Transport Dept. in the first campaign.

Lieut. E. E. S. Schuyler, West Yorkshire Regt. (For services see 14th Foot.)

Major Andrew Scott, V.C., B.S.C., served as Brigade Major, 1st Infantry Brigade, Kuram Valley F.F., from the outbreak of the war until invalided in June, 1879, being present at the front attack and capture of the Peiwar Kotal, and the operations in the Khost Valley, including the action of Matun. (Mentioned in despatches; Brevet of Major.)

Lieut. B. Scott, R.E.

Lieut. D. A. Scott, R.E., served during the first campaign, from Feb. to Sept., 1879, with the 2nd Division Peshawar Valley F.F.

Lieut. G. K. Scott-Moncrieff, R.E., served during the first campaign in the 1st Division Peshawar Valley F.F., being present at the assault and capture of Ali Musjid, and being subsequently employed at Jalalabad, as Garrison Engineer, served during the second campaign in the 1st Division Kabul Field Force, taking part in the operations round Kabul and defence of Sherpur in Dec., 1879. (Mentioned in despatches.)

Lieut. C. H. Seddon, Bo.S.C., served with the Commissariat Dept. in S. Afghanistan during the second campaign.

Capt. H. O. Selby, R.E., served during the second campaign as Superintendent of Army Signalling, with the South Afghanistan Column under General Phayre, taking part in the advance of that force from Quetta to Kandahar in the autumn of 1880. (Mentioned in despatches.)

Major H. W. H. Senior, B.S.C., served with the Transport Dept. in the first campaign.

Major M. C. Seton, Hampshire Regt. (For services see 67th Foot.)

Capt. W. B. Seton, Bo.S.C., served with the Commissariat Dept. in the first campaign.

RECORDS OF SERVICE.

Lieut H. W. Seymonr, Bo.S.C. (For services see 16th Bo.N.I.)

Capt. E. D. Shafto, R.A. (Deceased. See Biographical Division.)

Major H. Shaw, V.C., Royal Irish Regt. (For services see 18th Foot.)

Major C. E. Shepherd, B.S.C., served on the Kandahar Railway Survey during the second campaign.

Lieut. M. L. Shepley, Royal Fusiliers, served in the Reserve Division, Kandahar F.F., at Quetta, during the second campaign.

Capt. C. H. Sheppard, M.S.C., served as Transport Officer, Basawal, Khyber line, during the second campaign.

Lieut. R. C. Sherard, M.S.C., served from Aug., 1880, till the conclusion of the war, as Assistant to the Chief Commissariat Officer at Quetta.

Lieut. J. Sherston, Rifle Brigade, served as Aide-de-Camp to Sir F. Roberts during the latter part of the first and throughout the second campaign, taking part in the advance on and occupation of Kabul, and the advance from Kabul to the relief of Kandahar, and being present at the action of Charasiab, the operations round Kabul and defence of Sherpur in Dec., 1879, and the battle of Kandahar. (Twice mentioned in despatches.)

Lt.-Colonel A. M. Shewell, M.S.C. (Deceased. See Biographical Division.)

Lieut. W. T. Shone, R.E.

Major H. W. Shoubridge, B.S.C., served from the outbreak of the war till April, 1879, as Brigade Major, 1st Brigade, 2nd Division, Peshawar Valley F.F., taking part in the second Bazar Valley expedition as Brigade Major to the Jamrud Column.

Major-General T. H. Sibley (retired), served as Principal Commissariat Officer, Kandahar F.F., during both campaigns.

Lieut. G. H. Sim, R.E.

Bt. Major J. R. Slade, C.B., R.A. (For services see R.A.)

Surgeon-General A. Smith, M.D., C.B., A.M.D., served during both campaigns as Principal Medical Officer Kandahar, Ghazni, and Kabul Field Forces, taking part in the advance on and occupation of Kandahar and Kalat-i-Ghilzai, the advance from Kandahar on Ghazni and into the Logar Valley, and the return march to India by the Khyber route, and being present at the battle of Ahmad Khel and the action of Arzu. (Mentioned in despatches; C.B.)

Bt. Lt.-Colonel C. B. Euan Smith, C.S.I., Madras Infantry, served during the second campaign, first as Political Assistant at Kandahar, and afterwards as Chief Political Officer with the Ghazni, 3rd Division Kabul, and Kabul-Kandahar Field Forces, taking part in the advance from Kandahar on Ghazni and into the Logar Valley, and the advance from Kabul to the relief of Kandahar, and being present at the battle of Ahmad Khel, the actions of Arzu and Patkao Shana, and the battle of Kandahar. (Four times mentioned in despatches ; Brevet of Lt.-Colonel.)

Lieut. C. H. M. Smith, B.S.C. (For services see 3rd Sikh Infantry.)

Major G. W. Smith, Shropshire Regt., served throughout the first campaign as Assistant Adjutant-General, 1st Division, Peshawar Valley F.F., being present at the capture of Ali Musjid and the forcing of the Khyber Pass. (Mentioned in despatches ; Brevet of Major.)

Lieut. H. W. Smith, R.E., served throughout both campaigns in Northern Afghanistan as Superintendent of Army Signalling: from Nov., 1878, till June, 1879, with the 1st Division Peshawar Valley F.F., being present at the assault and capture of Ali Musjid; from Sep., 1879, till March, 1880, with the Khyber Line Force; from March till Aug., 1880, with the 2nd Division and Head-quarters Northern Afghanistan F.F.

Bt. Lt.-Colonel J. B. Smith, B.S.C., served with the Commissariat Dept., Khyber Line Force, in the second campaign. (Brevet of Lt.-Colonel.)

Bt. Colonel T. Parkyns Smith, R.H.A., commanded the Royal Artillery of General Phayre's Division during the second campaign, taking part in the advance from Quetta to Kandahar in the autumn of 1880. (Mentioned in despatches.)

Major R. E. S. Smyth, Bengal Infantry. (For services see 15th B.N.I.)

Col. B. Soady, B.S.C., served with the Transport Dept. in the first campaign.

Lieut. the Hon. G. F'R. H. Somerset, Grenadier Guards, served during the second campaign as Orderly Officer to General Phayre, taking part in the advance from Quetta to Kandahar in the autumn of 1880. (Mentioned in despatches.)

Lieut. E. K. E. Spence, South Lancashire Regt., served with Transport Dept., Kandahar line, during the first campaign.

Capt. F. T. N. Spratt, R.E., served throughout the first campaign as Adjutant of R.E., Kuram Valley F.F., being present at the assault and capture of the Peiwar Kotal, the passage of the Mangior Pass, and minor operations. Served during the second campaign: first, as Deputy Assistant Quartermaster-General Kabul F.F., taking part in the advance on and occupation of Kabul, and being present at the action of Charasiab; afterwards accompanying the Kabul-Kandahar F.F., as D.A.Q.M.G., 2nd Brigade, in the advance to the relief of Kandahar, and being present at the battle of Kandahar. (Three times mentioned in despatches.)

Lieut. W. F. H. Stafford, R.E. (For services see "Royal Engineers.")

Major W. Stainforth, Madras Infantry. (For services see 21st M.N.I.)

Major D. J. Stewart, Bengal Infantry, served with the Transport Dept. in the first campaign.

General Sir D. M. Stewart, Bart., G.C.B., C.I.E., Commander-in-Chief in India, commanded first the Multan Division, and subsequently the forces in Southern Afghanistan, from the outbreak of the war till April, 1880, advancing on and occupying Kandahar and Kalat-i-Ghilzai. Commanded the Ghazni F.F. in the advance on Ghazni, at the battle of Ahmad Khel, and the action of Arzu. Was in chief command of the forces in Northern Afghanistan from May, 1880, until the evacuation of Kabul in Aug., 1880. (Received the thanks of the Governor-General and Government of India, and of both Houses of Parliament; K.C.B., G.C.B.; created a Baronet.)

Bt. Major N. R. Stewart, B.S.C., served as Aide-de-Camp to Sir Donald Stewart from the outbreak of the war till 23 May, 1880, and from that date till the return of the troops to India in Sept., 1880, as Brigade Major, 3rd Section, Khyber Line Force; took part in the advance on and occupation of Kandahar and Kalat-i-Ghilzai, the advance of the Ghazni F.F. on Ghazni and into the Logar Valley, from whence he proceeded to Kabul, and the return march to India through the Khyber Pass; and was present at the battle of Ahmad Khel and the action of Arzu. (Mentioned in despatches; Brevet of Major.)

Major R. M'G. Stewart, R.A., served during the first campaign as Assistant Quartermaster-General, 2nd Division, Kandahar F.F., and Thal-Chotiali F.F., taking part in the advance on and occupation of Kandahar, the advance to the Halmand, and the return-march by the new route to India. (Mentioned in despatches; Brevet of Major.)

Major H. J. Stock, Bo.S.C., served during the second campaign as Brigade Major, 2nd Division, Kandahar F.F.

Major C. M. Stockley, Norfolk Regt. (For services see 9th Foot.)

Capt. C. H. Stoddart, B.S.C., served as Assistant Road Commandant, Khyber line, during the second campaign.

Capt. A. B. Stopford, R.A., was employed during the first campaign in selecting the new line of communications from Jacobabad to Dabar for the troops under General Phayre's command, and during the second campaign as Deputy Assistant Quartermaster-General, 2nd Division, Kandahar F.F.

Major C. Strahan, R.E., served in the Survey Dept. with the Peshawar Valley F.F. during the first campaign, being mainly engaged in mapping the country in the neighbourhood of Safed Sang. (Brevet of Major.)

Capt. E. Straton, 22nd Foot. (Deceased. See Biographical Division.)

Major R. W. Studdy, Manchester Regt., served with the Transport Train, Khyber Line, in 1879, until invalided home from Jalalabad.

Lt.-Colonel C. Swinhoe, Bo.S.C., served with the Commissariat Dept. as Administrative Officer, S. Afghanistan F.F., from Sept., 1880, till the final evacuation of Kandahar.

Capt. J. J. Swinton, R.A., served with the Transport Dept. in the first campaign.

Lieut. the Hon. M. G. Talbot, R.E. (For services see R.E.)

Lt.-Colonel H. C. B. Tanner, Bo.S.C., served throughout the first campaign in charge of the Survey operations with the 1st Division, Peshawar Valley F.F., being present at the capture of Ali Musjid, and carrying a continuous route-survey through the Khyber and to Jalalabad. In May, 1879, started on an expedition into Kafiristan, which he was compelled to abandon in consequence of a complete breakdown in health. (Mentioned in despatches; Brevet of Lt.-Colonel.)

Colonel O. V. Tanner, C.B., B.S.C. (For services see 29th Bo.N.I.)

Lt.-Colonel H. H. Taylor (retired). (For services see 5th Fusiliers.)

Major F. S. Terry, h.p. (For services see 25th Foot.)

Lieut. C. G. R. Thackwell, South Yorkshire Regt. (For services see 51st K.O.L.I.)

Major-General J. B. Thelwall, C.B. (retired), commanded the 2nd Brigade, Kuram Valley F.F., from the outbreak of the war till invalided to England in Feb., 1879, being present at the assault and capture of the Peiwar Kotal, and in command at Peiwar during the absence of General Roberts on the Khost Valley expedition. (Mentioned in despatches.)

Major W. G. Thomas, King's Own Borderers, served with the Transport Train, Kandahar F.F., during the first campaign, taking part in the advance on and occupation of Kandahar, and in the advance of General Biddulph's force to the Halmand.

Lt.-Colonel H. Thompson, B.S.C., served during the second campaign as Assistant Adjutant-General, Reserve Division, Kabul F.F., and subsequently in the same capacity with the Khyber Line Force.

Capt. J. W. Thurburn, R.E.

Major R. P. Tickell, R.E., served from Nov., 1879, as Field Engineer, Khyber Division, having charge of works in the Khyber Pass; subsequently, from Jan., 1880, as Field Engineer, 1st Division, Kabul F.F., carrying on the duties of Commanding R.E. during the absence of that officer from Kabul in May, 1880. Accompanied General Ross's force to Zaidabad in April, 1880. Took part in the advance from Kabul to the relief of Kandahar, and was present, on General Macpherson's staff, at the battle of Kandahar. Accompanied General Macpherson's brigade, as Field Engineer, on march back to India, and until it left the field. (Mentioned in despatches.)

Brigade Surgeon A. M. Tippetts, A.M.D., served with the 5th Fusiliers during the first campaign. Was temporarily P.M.O. of General Maude's Division in the Khyber, and officiated in that capacity in the first Bazar Valley expedition. Was afterwards employed on General Michell's committee on the defences of the Khyber. On the renewal of hostilities was appointed to the charge of Field Hospital, 2nd Section, Khyber Division, and P.M.O. to Brigadier-General Arbuthnot's Brigade. In Feb., 1880, was appointed P.M.O. to General Bright's Division, with officiating rank of Deputy Surgeon-General, and accompanied the expedition to Hissarak. Made all the arrangements for the transport of the sick and wounded of the Kabul army to India previous to the evacuation. (Mentioned in despatches.)

Surgeon-General S. C. Townsend, C.B., I.M.D., served during the second campaign as Principal Medical Officer, Kuram Division, Kabul F.F. Was severely wounded at the affair at Jagi Thana. (Mentioned in despatches.)

Bt. Lt.-Colonel J. O. Travers, Leicestershire Regt., served during the first campaign as Aide-de-Camp to Brigadier-General Macpherson, being present in that capacity at the taking of Ali Musjid and the operations in the Lughman Valley. Served in the second campaign as General Transport Officer, Kuram Division, and subsequently in the same capacity with the Khyber Line Force. (Mentioned in despatches.)

Lt.-Colonel E. W. Trevor, Bo.S.C., served during the second campaign as Director of Transport, Kuram Force.

Major L. H. E. Tucker, Bengal Infantry, was employed on Political duty on the Khyber line throughout the first campaign, being in charge of the Pass from Nov., 1878, till April, 1879, and subsequently of the Jalalabad district. Was present at the capture of Ali Musjid, the affair at Kam Daka, and minor operations, and accompanied both the expeditions into the Bazar Valley. During the second campaign served, first, as Political Assistant with General C. Gough's Brigade, accompanying it to Kata Sang and to Kabul, and afterwards in charge of sections of the Khyber line. Escorted by a squadron of Cavalry, left Kabul 28 Dec., 1879, and restored interrupted communications with Jagdalak. Accompanied the expeditions against the Wazir Kugianis and to Hissarak in April, the Lughman Valley expedition in June, and the raid on the Ghilzai villages in July, 1880. (Mentioned in despatches; received on two occasions the thanks of the Government of India.)

Lt.-Colonel H. St. G. Tucker, C.B., Bengal Infantry, served during the first campaign as Director of Transport with Sir D. Stewart's force, and throughout the second campaign as Chief Director of Transport, Khyber Line Force. (C.B.)

Capt. S. D. Turnbull, B.S.C., served during the first campaign as Aide-de-Camp to General Watson, commanding the Punjab Chiefs' Contingent, and during the second, as Transport Officer, Vitakri F.F.

Major A. H. Turner, B.S.C. (For services see 2nd Punjab Infantry.)

Bt. Lt.-Colonel W. Tweedie, C.S.I., B.S.C., served during the second campaign, first as Senior Political Officer, Khyber Column, and subsequently as Political Secretary to Sir F. Roberts; eventually, after the arrival of Mr. Griffin at Kabul on a special political mission, returned to the Khyber line of communications, and exercised chief political and administrative control between the Peshawar and Kabul political jurisdictions. (C.S.I.)

Major E. D'O. Twemlow, R.E., served during the second campaign, first on the Sukkur-Quetta Railway, and subsequently with General Phayre's Division, taking part in the advance from Quetta to Kandahar in the autumn of 1880. (Mentioned in despatches.)

Bt. Lt.-Colonel R. F. C. A. Tytler, Bengal Infantry, served during both campaigns as Deputy Judge Advocate, with General Stewart's force, taking part in the advance on and occupation of Kandahar and Kalat-i-Ghilzai, and the advance on Ghazni and into the Logar Valley, and being present at the battle of Ahmad Khel and the action of Arzu. (Mentioned in despatches; Brevet of Lt.-Colonel.)

Brigadier-General J. A. Tytler, C.B., V.C., B.S.C. (Deceased. See Biographical Division.)

Lieut.-General J. L. Vaughan, C.B., B.S.C., was present at the operations round Kabul and defence of Sherpur in Dec., 1879. (Mentioned in despatches.)

Lieut. E. P. Ventris, The Buffs. (Deceased. See Biographical Division.)

Major T. E. Verner, Wiltshire Regt., served as Transport Officer on the line of communications between Kandahar and the base from the outbreak of the war till March, 1880, being part of the time in charge of the Transport at Quetta. Subsequently served in charge of the Transport of the Artillery Brigade, Ghazni F.F., taking part in the advance on Ghazni and into the Logar Valley, and being present at the battle of Ahmad Khel and the action of Arzu. Eventually returned from Kabul to India by the Khyber.

Bt. Colonel the Hon. G. P. H. Villiers, Grenadier Guards, served during the first campaign in general charge of the outposts of the Kuram Valley F.F. Was present at the assault and capture of the Peiwar Kotal. (Mentioned in despatches.)

Bt. Major W. J. Vousden, V.C., Bo.S.C. (For services see Biographical Division.)

Lieut. C. F. Vyse, B.S.C. (For services see 41st B.N.I.)

Bt. Lt.-Colonel E. S. Walcot, Bombay Infantry, served during the second campaign with the Commissariat Dept., Kandahar F.F., being present in Kandahar throughout the siege. (Mentioned in despatches; Brevet of Lt.-Colonel.)

Mr. G. C. Walker, C.S., was attached to the Head-quarters Staff of Mr. Griffin, as 2nd Assistant, on his special Political Mission to Kabul.

Colonel G. F. Walker, Suffolk Regt. (For services see 12th Foot.)

Major W. A. J. Wallace, R.E.

Lieut. E. A. Waller, R.E., served as Asst. Field Engineer in the Bolan and on the Nari route from Jan., 1879, till June, 1880, and at Kandahar from July, 1880, till May, 1881. (Mentioned in despatches, and recommended for the Victoria Cross, and a Brevet Majority on obtaining his Captaincy, for gallant conduct during the siege of Kandahar.)

Capt. J. Walsh, Seaforth Highlanders. (For services see 72nd Highlanders.)

Major R. Warburton, B.S.C., served during the second campaign, first as Assistant Political Officer in the Khyber; afterwards, from Oct., 1879, till invalided to England in May, 1880, at Jalalabad (Brevet of Major.)

Lieut. H. B. Warden, Bo.S.C., served with the Kandahar F.F. as Commissariat Officer from Oct., 1879, till May, 1880, when he was invalided to England. Returned to Afghanistan in Nov., 1880, and served from that date in charge of the commissariat arrangements on the Harnai route till the evacuation.

Capt. D. M. D. Waterfield, R.A., served with the Transport Corps, Kuram Valley Force, during the first campaign, and with the Kuram Force during the second campaign, being present, and severely wounded, at the repulse of the enemy at the Sirkai Kotal, Shutargardan. (Mentioned in despatches.)

Lt.-Colonel W. G. Waterfield, C.S.I., B.S.C., served during the first campaign as Political Officer with the Kuram Valley F.F., being present at the assault and capture of the Peiwar Kotal, accompanying the Khost Valley expedition; and being present at the action of Matun. (Twice mentioned in despatches; C.S.I.)

Major J. T. Watling, Bo.S.C., served during the second campaign as Deputy Assistant Quartermaster-General with General Phayre's Division, taking part in the advance from Quetta to Kandahar in the autumn of 1880. (Mentioned in despatches.)

Major-General John Watson, C.B., V.C., A.D.C., Bo.S.C., served during the first campaign, first in command of the Punjab Chiefs' Contingent, and afterwards as Inspector-General of the line of communications, Kuram Valley F.F. During the second campaign commanded the Kuram District Force. (Received the thanks of both Houses of Parliament.)

Major R. J. Watson, Worcestershire Regt. (For services see 59th Foot.)

Lt.-Colonel R. A. Wauchope, B.S.C. (For services see 14th B.N.I.)

Lieut. H. E. C. Way, East Yorkshire Regt., served in S. Afghanistan as Transport Officer, Kandahar Line, from Aug., 1880, till the final evacuation.

Major A. J. T. Welchman, Bengal Infantry, served with the Transport Dept. in the first campaign.

Major H. R. E. Wellesley, late 2nd Madras Cavalry, served with the Transport Dept. in the first campaign.

Capt. H. L. Wells, R.E., on the outbreak of the war raised and commanded the Ghilzai Coolie Corps, and was mainly employed in constructing roads through the Gazaband and Khojak Passes. Commanded the 33 sabres Sind Horse and Punjab Cavalry which surprised the camp of the marauder Lushka Khan, and killed him and his nephews. (Wounded.) Was attached, as a Survey Officer, in command of the Ghilzais, to the 1st Column Thal-Chotiali F.F., and during the return march by the new route to India was present at the action of Baghao. During the second campaign served from Jan., 1880, with the Khyber Force, accompanying, as Aide-de-Camp and D.A.Q.M.G., General Gib's expedition against the Shinwaris in May, 1880, and being present at the action of Mazina, and in June, 1880, taking part in the Kama expedition. (Three times mentioned in despatches.)

Colonel H. M. Wemyss, C.B., B.S.C., served during the first campaign in command of the 39th B.N.I., at Ali Musjid in March and April, 1879, and afterwards in command of the Bhopal Battalion, at Landi Kotal. Commanded a reconnaissance of cavalry and infantry to Kam Shiliman to watch the movements of the Mohmands. Served throughout the second campaign as D.A. and Q.M.G., Khyber Line Force. Accompanied the 1st Brigade in its advance to effect a junction with the Kabul troops at Kata Sang, and took part in the Lughman expedition, Jan. and Feb., 1880, the expedition against the Wazir Kugianis, and the expedition into the Hissarak Valley, April, 1880. (Mentioned in despatches; C.B.)

Major R. Westmacott, Bo.S.C., served from Oct., 1879, as General Transport Officer in charge of the Transport arrangements in the Bolan Pass, and from Feb., 1880, in charge from Quetta to Chaman. Held the appointment of Road Commandant from Kandahar to Chaman, and subsequently to Quetta, from April, 1880, till the evacuation of Kandahar. Commanded the Cavalry on the line of communications during the siege of Kandahar, and was frequently engaged with the enemy in the Khojak Pass to prevent its being closed. Advanced with General Phayre's Division on Kandahar, and arranged for its foraging *en route*, and for that of Sir F. Roberts' force on its return. Was detailed, with political powers, with a brigade to blow up Abu Seyd's Fort. (Mentioned in despatches.)

Capt. F. J. Whalley, Liverpool Regt. (For services see 8th Foot.)

Capt. R. Whalley, Dorsetshire Regt., served throughout the first campaign as Transport Officer with 1st Division Peshawar Valley F.F., and during the second campaign, in the same capacity, with the Khyber and N. Afghanistan F.F., being employed at Daka, Butkhak, Seh Baba, and the Bala Hissar, and returning to India, on the final retirement from Kabul, as Transport Officer, 2nd Brigade. Acted as Orderly Officer to General Doran in the affair with the Mohmands, 17 Jan., 1880. (Mentioned in despatches.)

Lieut. W. H. White, R.E., was employed, during the second campaign, on the Peshawar-Jalalabad Railway Survey.

Capt. W. W. B. Whiteford, R.E. (For services see " Royal Engineers.")

Capt. C. B. Wickham, R.A., served with the Transport Dept. in the first campaign.

Colonel H. C. Wilkinson, h.p., late 16th Lancers, commanded, with rank of Brigadier-General, the Cavalry Brigade of General Phayre's Division during the second campaign, taking part in the advance from Quetta to Kandahar. (Mentioned in despatches.)

Lieut. J. Willcocks, Leinster Regt., served as Transport Officer, Khyber line, during the first campaign.

Lieut. G. F. Willes, B.S.C., served with the Transport Dept. in the first campaign.

Lt.-Colonel Ben. Williams, B.S.C. (For services see 5th Bengal Cavalry.)

Colonel W. J. Williams, C.B., R.A., commanded the Royal Artillery, 1st Division, Peshawar Valley F.F., during the first campaign, being present at the capture of Ali Musjid. (Mentioned in despatches.)

Capt. H. P. Willoughby, R.A., served from the commencement of the war till invalided to England in April, 1879, as Commissary of Ordnance with the Ordnance Field Park, 2nd Division, S. Afghanistan F.F. During the second campaign, from Nov., 1879, till Aug., 1880, served in the same capacity in charge of the Ordnance Field Park, Kuram Division.

Lieut. R. H. F. W. Wilson, 10th Hussars. (For services see 10th Hussars.)

Major W. H. St. A. Wilton, Madras Infantry, served with the Commissariat Dept. in S. Afghanistan during the second campaign.

Capt. A. T. Wintle, R.A., served as Brigade Superintendent of Transport, Advanced Brigade, Khyber Line, during the second campaign.

Bt. Lt.-Colonel G. B. Wolseley, York and Lancaster Regt., served as Assistant Adjutant-General, Kandahar and Thal-Chotiali Field Forces, during the first campaign, taking part in the advance on and occupation of Kandahar, the advance to the Halmand, and the return-march by the new route to India. (Mentioned in despatches; Brevet of Lt.-Colonel.)

Major-General H. H. A. Wood, C.B., Bo.S.C., commanded a Brigade of General Phayre's Division during the second campaign.

Lieut. H. St. L. Wood, East Yorkshire Regt., served as a Brigade Transport Officer with the Kandahar F.F., from the outbreak of the war till Nov., 1880. Was present at Kandahar throughout the siege, and acted as Orderly Officer to Brigadier-General Brooke at the sortie to Deh Khwaja, in which he was dangerously wounded, and his horse was killed. (Gratuity. Wound pension.)

Bt. Lt.-Colonel R. G. Woodthorpe, R.E., served as Senior Survey Officer with the Kuram Valley F.F. throughout the first campaign, carrying a route-survey from the frontier to the Shutargardan Pass, accompanying the expedition into the Khost Valley, and mapping the district, and being present at the skirmish of the 28th Nov., 1878, the assault and capture of the Peiwar Kotal (during which his pistol-stock was smashed by an Afghan bullet), and the action of Matun. On the renewal of hostilities was appointed to the charge of Survey operations with the Kuram Force, and joined Sir F. Roberts in Kabul 4 Nov., 1879. Was present at the operations round Kabul and the defence of Sherpur (serving temporarily in the Field Engineer's Dept.), in Dec., 1879. Accompanied Sir F. Roberts into the Logar Valley, and General Ross towards Ghazni, and was present at the action of Shekabad. (Three times mentioned in despatches, and several times in reports; Brevets of Major and Lt.-Colonel.)

Major D. R. F. Wooldridge, Bo.S.C., served during the first campaign as Assistant Superintendent of Transport at Jacobabad, and during the second campaign as Superintendent of Transport, first of General Creagh's Brigade, and afterwards of General Phayre's, taking part in the advance from Quetta to Kandahar in the autumn of 1880. (Mentioned in despatches.)

Lt.-Colonel H. C. Wright, M.S.C., served in the war from 10 May till 14 Dec., 1879. Was employed first as Executive and subsequently as Chief Commissariat Officer, Kuram F.F. Accompanied the Kabul F.F. as Chief Commissariat Officer in the advance on and occupation of Kabul, and was present at the action of Charasiab. (Mentioned in despatches.)

Capt. G. T. Wright, R.E.

Major H. Wylie, C.S.I., Bengal Infantry, served during the second campaign, first as Assistant Political Officer in S. Afghanistan, and afterwards as Chief Political Officer with General Phayre's Division, taking part in the advance from Quetta to Kandahar in the autumn of 1880. (Mentioned in despatches.)

Capt. R. J. H. Wyllie, B.S.C., served with the Commissariat Dept. in the Kuram Valley during the first campaign.

Capt. W. H. C. Wyllie, C.I.E., B.S.C., accompanied General Phayre's Division, as Assistant Political Officer, in its advance from Quetta to Kandahar in the autumn of 1880. (Mentioned in despatches.)

Major C. J. Wyndham, Royal Irish Rifles, served with the Commissariat Dept., Kandahar line, during the first campaign.

Major A. S. Wynne, South Yorkshire Regt., served during the first campaign as Superintendent of Army Signalling, Kuram Valley F.F., being present at the assault and capture of Peiwar Kotal, the affair in the Mangior Pass, and the operations in the Khost district, including the action of Matun. (Mentioned in despatches; Brevet of Major.)

Major W. A. Wynter (late 33rd Foot, retired), served with the Transport Dept. in the Kabul and Kabul-Kandahar Field Forces, taking part in the advance on and occupation of Kabul, and the advance from Kabul to the relief of Kandahar, and being present at the action of Charasiab, the operations round Kabul and defence of Sherpur in Dec., 1879, and the battle of Kandahar. (Three times mentioned in despatches; Brevet of Major.)

Capt. A. G. Yaldwyn, B.S.C., served with the Commissariat Dept., Peshawar Valley F.F., during the first campaign.

Capt. H. A. Yorke, R.E., served as Assistant Field Engineer, Khyber Line Force, during the second campaign.

Lieut. C. L. Young, R.E., served as Assistant Field Engineer with the Quetta Division from Jan. till May, 1881, and subsequently as Adjutant R.E., Quetta Division.

Capt. H. P. Young, Bo.S.C., served with the Transport Dept. in the first campaign.

Capt. W. A. Yule, Royal Scots Fusiliers, was appointed Transport Officer, 4th Brigade, 1st Division, Peshawar Valley F.F., 14th Nov., 1878, and was present at Ali Musjid during the night attacks by the Khyber tribes after the capture of the Fort. Served as Transport Officer at Camp Basawar 3 Jan. till 20 March, 1879, accompanying General Tytler's column in the second Bazar Valley expedition; as Staff Officer of the Transport, 1st Division, at Jalalabad and Gandamak till 17 May, 1879; and accompanied the Rear-guard Brigade as a Transport Officer on the evacuation of Gandamak. (Mentioned in despatches.)

CAVALRY.

6th DRAGOON GUARDS (CARABINIERS).

IN September, 1879, on receipt of news of the massacre of H.M.'s Envoy and escort at Kabul, the regiment received orders to take the field, and on the 30th Sept., and 1st Oct., left Umballa, where it was then stationed, for the front.

The Carabiniers, under the command of Lieut.-Col. John Fryer, C.B., arrived at Peshawar on the 23rd Oct., 1879, and on the following day crossed the frontier into Afghanistan, with orders to push on to join the 2nd Brigade Jalalabad Field Force, under Br.-Genl. C. G. Arbuthnot, C.B.,—the whole of the Khyber Divis. being under command of Lieut.-Genl. Sir R. O. Bright, K.C.B.

Leaving *en route* one squadron under command of Capt. Hardin Burnley to garrison Basawal, the regiment marched into Jalaladad on the 31st Oct., and joined the Hd.-Qrs. of the 2nd Brigade. Its duties now consisted in escorting convoys, mails, &c., and patrolling along the line of communications.

The Carabiniers formed the escort of the ex-Amir Yakub Khan, with Lieut.-Col. Fryer, C.B., in personal charge, when His Highness was sent to India as a state prisoner; the regiment also escorted, at different times, several other state prisoners to India, amongst them the ex-Amir's father-in-law, and Daud Shah, the late Commander-in-Chief of the Afghan army.

On the 13th Jan., 1880, Capts. D. C. Graham and T. C. Porter's troops of the Carabiniers formed part of a brigade of Cavalry and R.H.A., under command of Lieut.-Col. Fryer, C.B., which attacked and repulsed with heavy loss a force of about 4,000 Mohmands, under Sirdar Moghul Khan, who were in the act of crossing the Kabul River to attack the British post at Ali Boghan. On the 15th of the same month the squadron under Capt. H. Burnley, employed as escort to four guns I/C, R.H.A., and forming part of the small mixed force under Col. Boisragon, 30th P.N.I., took part in the engagement with the Mohmands at Daka.

The Hd.-Qrs. of the Carabiniers, with Capts. A. G. Fife and T. C. Porter's troops, proceeded with the expeditionary force under Lieut.-Genl. Sir R. O. Bright, which marched into the Lughman Valley, and penetrated as far as the borders of Kaffiristan. The objects of the expedition were successfully obtained without opposition. On the return of the force to Jalalabad, two moveable columns were formed along the line of communications, and the Carabiniers furnished a squadron for each. Of another expeditionary force against the Mohmands, sent into the Chardeh Valley under Lieut.-Col. G. Hodding, 4th M.N.I., and operating from the 24th to 31st March, 1880, Capt. H. B. Hamilton's troop formed part.

Both moveable columns under Br.-Genl. C. G. Arbuthnot, C.B., marched against the Wazir Kugianis on the 4th and 5th Apl., 1880, and inflicted heavy punishments for raids the tribe had committed on British posts. A few days afterwards, Capts. D. C. Graham and T. C. Porter's troops accompanied a force under Lieut.-Genl. Sir R. O. Bright, K.C.B., into the Hissarak Valley, returning to Safed Sang on the 18th April, where the whole of the regt. was then concentrated for the first time since Oct., 1879.

Capt. H. B. Hamilton and W. C. Calvert's troops formed part of the expeditionary force under Br.-Genl. C. G. Arbuthnot, C.B., which proceeded into the Lughman Valley on the 2nd, and returned on the 14th June. On the 5th July, two squadrons of the regiment, and a detachment of the 4th Bengal

RECORDS OF SERVICE.

Cavalry, under the command of Lieut.-Col. Fryer, marched from Safed Sang, and co-operated with a force under Col. Ball-Acton, C.B., 51st K.O.L.I., from Pezwan, against the Ghilzai villages of Nargozi, Arab Khel, and Jokan, which were destroyed as punishments for various raids committed by the tribes on convoys, &c.

The Carabiniers left Safed Sang for India on the conclusion of negotiations with Abdul Rahman, commencing its march on the 11th Aug., and arriving at Sialkot, Punjab, on the 25th Sept., 1880.

The total number of non-comm. officers and men who died during the campaign was thirty-six.

SERVICES IN AFGHANISTAN OF OFFICERS OF THE 6TH DRAGOON GUARDS (CARABINIERS).

Bt. Colonel John Fryer, C.B., commanded the regiment throughout the period it was employed in the war; the brigade which defeated the enemy at Ali Boghan; the Cavalry in the Lughman Valley and Wazir Kugiani expeditions; and the Cavalry force from Safed Sang at the destruction of the Ghilzai villages. (Mentioned in despatches; C.B.)

Major C. F. Marriott served with the regiment from Oct., 1879, till July, 1880; *Major H. B. Hamilton* from March till Sept., 1880; *Major H. Burnley, Captains W. C. Calvert, D. A. G. C. Graham, A. G. Fife, T. C. Porter, Lieuts. A. Sprot, A. Weston* (as Adjutant), *B. N. Heywood-Jones, C. R. S. Douglas-Hamilton, R. G. W. Long, H. M. Owen, F. H. A. Des Vœux*, and *Quartermaster J. W. Tomlinson*, throughout the period it was employed in the war; *Lieut. P. H. H. Massy*, from Dec., 1879, till July, 1880; *Lieut. H. C. Hanbury*, from March till Sept., 1880; *Lieut. F. S. Garratt*, from Oct., 1879, till May, 1880; *Lieut. M. Cradock*, from Dec., 1879, till Sept., 1880, and *Vet. Surg.* (1st Class) *R. Poyser*, from Oct., 1879, till July, 1880. *Major Marriott* took part in the Wazir Kugiana expedition; *Major Hamilton* commanded the detachment in the operations against the Mohmands in the Chardeh Valley, commanded the detached squadron in the Lughman Valley expedition, and was present at the destruction of the Ghilzai villages; *Major Burnley* commanded a detached squadron from Oct., 1879, till Feb., 1880, being present at the defeat of the enemy near Daka, accompanied the Kabul-Kandahar F.F. from Kabul to the relief of Kandahar as Orderly Officer to Brigadier-General H. Gough, and was present at the reconnaissance in force, 31st Aug., 1880 (horse shot), the battle of Kandahar, and the final Cavalry pursuit (mentioned in despatches); *Capt. Calvert* took part in the Lughman Valley expedition, and was present at the destruction of the Ghilzai villages; *Capt. Graham* was present at the defeat of the enemy at Ali Boghan, and took part in the Wazir Kugiani and Hissarak Valley expeditions; *Capt. Fife*, and *Lieuts. Long* and *Des Vœux*, took part in the Lughman Valley and Wazir Kugiani expeditions, and were present at the destruction of the Ghilzai villages; *Capt. Porter* was present at the defeat of the enemy at Ali Boghan, took part in the Lughman Valley, Wazir Kugiani, and Hissarak Valley expeditions, and was present at the destruction of the Ghilzai villages; *Lieut. Sprot* was present at the defeat of the enemy near Daka, and proceeded from Safed Sang to Kabul in charge of a convoy in April, 1880; *Lieut. Weston* took part in the Lughman Valley and Wazir Kugiani expeditions, was present at the destruction of the Ghilzai villages, and acted as Staff Officer and Provost Marshal of the 2nd Moveable Column, Khyber Line Force, from May till Aug., 1880; *Lieut. Massy* took part in the Wazir Kugiani expedition; *Lieut. Hanbury* was present at the destruction of the Ghilzai villages; *Lieut. Heywood-Jones* was present at the defeat of the enemy at Ali Boghan, and the destruction of the Ghilzai villages; *Lieut. Douglas-Hamilton* was present at the defeat of the enemy at Ali Boghan, and took part in the Lughman Valley and Wazir Kugiani expeditions; *Lieut. Owen* was present at the defeat of the enemy at Daka, and took part in the Wazir Kugiani expedition; and *Lieut. Cradock* and *Vet. Surg. Poyser* took part in the Lughman Valley and Wazir Kugiani expeditions.

8TH (KING'S ROYAL IRISH) HUSSARS.

IN December, 1879, reinforcements being required in Northern Afghanistan in consequence of the serious aspect of affairs in the neighbourhood of Kabul, the 8th Hussars, then stationed at Muttra, was ordered to the front.

Proceeding to Peshawar, the regiment—with the exception of the 1st Squadron, under Major

Burke, with Captain Sutton and Lieut. Fell, which was sent forward to Basawal, detaching a small party under Lieut. Duff at Fort Daka—remained at that station till February, 1880, when it was moved up to Jamrud: here the Head-quarters and remaining two squadrons were encamped till the latter end of March, when they advanced to Basawal, and were there rejoined by the 1st Squadron. For the next few weeks the duties of the regiment consisted mainly in escorting convoys and patrolling the line of communications.

In the middle of April the 8th Hussars marched to Pesh Bolak, and there remained, forming part of the Flying Column under the command of Brigadier-General Gib, for a period of five weeks. At the latter end of May orders were received for the regiment to return to India, and in pursuance of these directions, Head-quarters and the right wing marched down to Basawal, the left wing remaining behind to follow on the next day: before it started, however, telegraphic instructions were received by General Gib to proceed on his expedition against the Shinwaris; and marching with the expeditionary force, the left wing took part in the action of Mazina.

After being stationed for a short time at Naushahra, and afterwards at Campbellpur, the regiment eventually made its way, at the latter end of September, 1880, to Rawal Pindi.

The undermentioned officers served with the 8th Hussars during the period the regiment was employed in the war, and are in possession of the medal:—

Lt.-Colonel J. W. Chaplin, V.C., in command; *Majors H. P. Burke* (since deceased), *R. N. Sutton*, and *A. M. Crofton*; *Captains G. A. de Visme* (since deceased), *A. A. Rawlinson* (also served as Assistant Road Commandant, Khyber F.F., from Oct., 1879, till Feb., 1880) (mentioned in despatches), *G. S. Williams*, and *E. J. Fell*; *Lieuts. P. L. Clowes* (was sent up to Kabul from Peshawar in charge of transport animals, and whilst *en route* took part in the expedition against the Wazir Kugianis, under Brigadier-General Arbuthnot, to whom he acted as Aide-de-Camp) (mentioned in despatches), *D. E. Wood* (also served with the 13th Bengal Lancers from Oct., 1879, till Jan., 1880, taking part in the Zaimusht expedition), *J. R. Lecky*, *B. Grant*, *W. K. Mitford*, *T. H. Farrer*, *E. Christy* (since deceased), *F. J. Carandini* (as Adjutant), and *C. E. Duff*; and *Quartermaster J. A. Hefferson*.

For services of *Major E. E. Lushington*, see "Staff."

9TH (QUEEN'S ROYAL) LANCERS.

AT the latter end of December, 1878, the 9th Lancers were stationed at Taru, in the neighbourhood of Peshawar, where, having been warned for active service, it had recently arrived from Sialkot. It was not until the 13th March, 1879, that a forward concentration of the 2nd Division Peshawar Valley Field Force, to which the regiment had been detailed, caused it to be moved into hostile territory. Entering the Khyber on that date, the 9th Lancers—with the exception of one squadron which had been detached from Taru to Kohat—was employed mainly in holding the Pass from Jamrud to Basawal till the conclusion of the first campaign. After the signing of the peace of Gandamak the regiment returned to India, suffering during the march, in common with the rest of the troops, from the epidemic of cholera which was raging in the Khyber, and losing a quantity of baggage, on the 6th June, in an attack made by hill-men on the transport waggons.

The squadron which was detached to Kohat left Taru for that station under the command of Captain Apperley, on the 14th Jan., 1879, and reaching its destination on the 18th idem, remained encamped there till the 6th March, when it proceeded to join General Roberts' Head-quarters in the Kuram Valley.

At the time of the massacre of the Kabul Embassy, the detached squadron of the 9th Lancers under the command of Captain Apperley was stationed, with the rest of the advanced troops of the late Kuram Division, at Ali Khel. Quitting that post on the 27th September with the Head-quarters of the newly-constituted Division, it marched across the Shutargardan to Kushi, being engaged *en route* in the encounter with the Mangals at Jagi Thana in the Hazardarakht defile, and taking part in the continued advance of the Cavalry Brigade under Br.-Genl. Massy, on Kabul, it was present at the action of Charasiab on the 6th October (in which it suffered a casualty of one man and horse wounded), the pursuit of the enemy in the direction of Maidan on the 8th idem, and the subsequent occupation of the capital.

On the day on which the advanced troops quitted Ali Khel for the Shutargardan, the 27th Sept., 1879, the Head-quarters and two squadrons 9th Lancers, under the command of Lt.-Colonel Cleland, left Rawal Pindi, *en route*, to join them at the front. Reaching Ali Khel on the 26th Oct., the regiment proceeded, after a short halt, to Kushi, and eventually arrived at Kabul on the 4th Nov., when it was rejoined by the detached squadron.

At the latter end of November, one squadron of the regiment took part in the advance of the force under Brigadier-General Baker into the Maidan district, and in the operations which ensued, including the affair on the Bamian road on the 22nd, and the subsequent destruction of Bahadur Khan's Fort.

In the operations round Kabul in the month of December, the 9th Lancers played a prominent part. At the action of Killa Kazi on the 11th, in which the Horse Artillery guns had to be temporarily abandoned, Head-quarters and three troops, under Lt.-Colonel Cleland, were present, and in a series of brilliant charges, facing again and again what appeared to be certain death, succeeded in temporarily staying the advance of the overwhelming numbers of the enemy. In this engagement 2 officers (Lieuts. Hearsey and Richards), 16 non-commissioned officers and men, and 36 horses of the regiment were killed, and 2 officers (Lt.-Colonel Cleland and Captain Stewart-Mackenzie), 8 non-commissioned officers and men, and 10 horses, were wounded. For their distinguished gallantry on this occasion, Lt.-Colonel Cleland (who subsequently died from the effects of his wound), Captains Stewart-Mackenzie and Bloomfield Gough, Lieuts. Trower, McInnis, and Hunter, Qr.-Mr.-Sergt. Finn, Troop Sergt.-Majors England, Young (by whose exertions Col. Cleland's life was saved), and Spittle (since killed in action), and Privates Lougheed, Haisent, Oakes, and Druce, were mentioned in warm terms in despatches. The assault and capture of the Siah Sang Heights on the 13th, in which one squadron of the 9th Lancers was engaged, again heavily increased the regimental casualty roll, Captain Butson (in command), Sergt.-Major Spittle, and 3 men, losing their lives, and 2 officers (Captain Scott-Chisholme and Lieutenant Trower), and 8 men being wounded, in addition to 12 horses killed and wounded, in a splendidly-delivered charge, in which the enemy were effectually routed. The squadron was brought out of action by Captain Scott Chisholme, who, notwithstanding the severity of his wound, remained in the saddle. On the 14th the regiment retired, with the rest of the Division, into Sherpur, and took part in the defence of the cantonment; and on the 23rd, after the repulse of the enemy's attack, it was engaged in the Cavalry pursuit.

From the 1st Jan. till the 7th Aug., 1880, the 9th Lancers served in the 1st Division Northern Afghanistan Field Force; from the 8th Aug. till the 7th Sept., 1880, in the Kabul-Kandahar Field Force; and from the 8th Sept. till the 2nd Dec., 1880, in the 3rd Division Southern Afghanistan Field Force.

One squadron of the regiment marched from Kabul on the 16th April, 1880, in the force under Major-General Ross, which advanced along the Ghazni road to co-operate with the troops *en route* from Kandahar under Sir D. M. Stewart, and was present at the action of Zaidabad on the 26th idem. In the interval another squadron proceeded with the column under Brigadier-General Macpherson to the support of the troops under Colonel F. H. Jenkins at the action in the neighbourhood of Charasiab on the 25th April.

On the 8th May Head-quarters and three troops accompanied the force under Sir Frederick Roberts, which proceeded to Maidan and the Logar Valley. One troop returned to Kabul on the 29th of the same month, and the two remaining troops on the 8th June.

On the 29th July one squadron of the regiment marched from Sherpur to join the force under Brigadier-General C. Gough, and on the 31st July and 1st Aug. accompanied the chief Political Officer to Zimma, where a meeting took place each day with the Amir Abdul Rahman. This squadron rejoined Head-quarters at Kabul on the 4th Aug.

When the news of the siege of Kandahar caused a reorganization of the troops in Northern Afghanistan, the 9th Lancers was one of the regiments selected to form part of the force under Sir Frederick Roberts destined for the relief of that city. With the rest of the Cavalry Brigade it quitted Kabul on the 8th Aug., 1880, and after participating in the memorable march to Kandahar, took part, on the 1st September, in the crowning defeat of the enemy, being engaged in the pursuit which was continued throughout the day.

In the month of December, 1880, the 9th Lancers returned to India, and went into quarters at Umballa.

SERVICES IN AFGHANISTAN OF OFFICERS OF THE 9TH (QUEEN'S ROYAL) LANCERS.

Colonel H. Marshall (retired) joined the regiment at Basawal on the 18th May, 1879, from England (where he had been absent on sick leave), and commanded it till the conclusion of the first campaign.

Lt.-Colonel R. S. Cleland. (Deceased. See Biographical Division.)

Lt.-Colonel H. A. Bushman, C.B., commanded the regiment in the second campaign from Feb., 1880, till the conclusion of hostilities, taking part in the march from Kabul to the relief of Kandahar, and being present at the battle of Kandahar. (Mentioned in despatches; C.B.)

Lt.-Colonel H. R. Abadie served throughout the first campaign as Brigade Major, Quetta Division, Kandahar F.F., taking part in the advance on and occupation of Kandahar and Girishk, and being present at the action of Saif-u-din. Rejoined the regiment at Kabul during the second campaign, took part in the march from Kabul to the relief of Kandahar, and was present at the battle of Kandahar. (Mentioned in despatches; Brevet of Major.)

Major the Hon. H. Legge served with the regiment in the second campaign from March, 1880, till the conclusion of hostilities. Commanded the squadron which was present at the action of Zaidabad, and the squadron which accompanied the chief Political Officer to Zimma on the occasion of his interviews with the Amir. Took part in the march from Kabul to the relief of Kandahar, and was present at the battle of Kandahar.

Major H. W. Apperley served with the regiment in both campaigns. Accompanied, as a volunteer, the first expedition into the Bazar Valley in Dec., 1878. Commanded the detached squadron of the regiment in the Kuram Valley from 17 March till 27 Sept., 1879, and subsequently in the advance on and occupation of Kabul, being present at the actions of Jagi Thana and Charasiab, and taking part in the pursuit of the enemy on the 9th Oct. Left Kabul for India on the 14th Nov. *en route* to the regimental depôt, but was recalled on reaching Rawal Pindi, and returned to Kabul on 4th Jan., 1880. Served with the regiment till the conclusion of the war, taking part in the march from Kabul to the relief of Kandahar, and being present at the battle of Kandahar. (Twice mentioned in despatches; Brevet of Major.)

Major J. A. F. H. Stewart-Mackenzie served with the regiments in both campaigns. Accompanied, as a volunteer, the first expedition into the Bazar Valley in Dec., 1878. Took part in the expedition to Maidan, the operations around Kabul in December, 1879, including the action of Killa Kazi on the 11th (in which he was severely wounded, and on which occasion he brought the regiment out of action), the defence of Sherpur, and the action of the 23rd. Took part in the march from Kabul to the relief of Kandahar, and was present at the battle of Kandahar. (Twice mentioned in despatches; Brevet of Major.)

Captain Lord W. L. de la P. Beresford, V.C., served in the first campaign as Aide-de-Camp to Sir Sam. Browne, Commdg. Peshawar Valley Field Force, and was present at the taking of Ali Musjid. Left Afghanistan for South Africa, and after taking part in the Zulu war and earning the Victoria Cross, rejoined the 9th Lancers in Kabul, and served with the regiment from Dec., 1879, till Feb., 1880. (Mentioned in despatches.)

Captain S. G. Butson. (Killed in action. See Biographical Division.)

Bt. Major J. J. Scott Chisholme served with the regiment in both campaigns. Was present as a volunteer at the taking of Ali Musjid. Took part in the operations around Kabul in Dec., 1879, including the action of Siah Sang on the 13th (in which he was severely wounded, and on which occasion he brought the regiment out of action), the defence of Sherpur, and the action of the 23rd. In consequence of his wound, was invalided to England, leaving Kabul 5 Jan., 1880. (Mentioned in despatches; Brevet of Major.)

Bt. Major Bloomfield Gough served in the first campaign as Aide-de-Camp to Brigadier-General C. Gough, Commdg. the Cavalry Brigade, 1st Division, Peshawar Valley Field Force, and was present at the taking of Ali Musjid. Served with the 9th Lancers in the second campaign, being engaged in the operations around Kabul in Dec., 1879, including the actions of Killa Kazi and Siah Sang, the defence of Sherpur, the repulse of the enemy's attack on the 23rd, and the subsequent pursuit, taking part in the march from Kabul to the relief of Kandahar, and being present at the battle of Kandahar. (Twice mentioned in despatches; Brevet of Major.)

Captain E. E. Shearburn served with the regiment in both campaigns, taking part in the operations around Kabul in Dec., 1879.

Captain G. A. P. Evans served with the regiment in the first campaign.

Captain C. J. W. Trower served with the regiment in both campaigns. Was present as a volunteer at the taking of Ali Musjid, and in the first Bazar Valley expedition. Was engaged in the operations around Kabul in Dec., 1879, including the actions of Killa Kazi and Siah Sang (in which he was wounded), and the defence of Sherpur, took part in the march from Kabul to the relief of Kandahar, and was present at the battle of Kandahar. (Mentioned in despatches.)

Captain E. B. McInnis served with the regiment as Adjutant in both campaigns. Was engaged in the operations around Kabul in Dec., 1879, including the actions of Killa Kazi and Siah Sang, the defence of Sherpur, and the pursuit of the enemy on the 23rd, took part in the march from Kabul to the relief of Kandahar, and was present at the battle of Kandahar. (Twice mentioned in despatches.)

Lieut. H. C. Hopkins served with the regiment in both campaigns. Took part in the march from Kabul to the relief of Kandahar, and was present at the battle of Kandahar.

Lieut. C. J. R. Hearsey. (Killed in action. See Biographical Division.)

Lieut. J. H. Lamont served with the regiment in the second campaign, being engaged in the operations around Kabul in Dec., 1879, including the action of Siah Sang, the defence of Sherpur, and the pursuit of the enemy on the 23rd, taking part in the march from Kabul to the relief of Kandahar, and being present at the battle of Kandahar.

Lieut. J. Hunter served with the regiment in both campaigns. Was present as a volunteer at the taking of Ali Musjid. Was with the detached squadron in the Kuram Valley from 17 March till 27 Sept., 1879, and subsequently in the advance on and occupation of Kabul, being present at the actions of Jagi Thana and Charasiab, and taking part in the pursuit of the enemy on the 9th Oct. Was engaged in the operations around Kabul in Dec., 1879, including the actions of Killa Kazi and Siah Sang, the defence of Sherpur, and the pursuit of the enemy on the 23rd; took part in the march from Kabul to the relief of Kandahar, and was present at the battle of Kandahar. (Mentioned in despatches.)

Lieut. W. P. Ricardo. (Killed in action. See Biographical Division.)

Lieut. E. H. de T. G. Bell-Martin served with the regiment in both campaigns. Took part in the expedition to Maidan, the operations around Kabul in December, 1879, the defence of Sherpur, the march from Kabul to the relief of Kandahar, and the battle of Kandahar.

Lieut. M. O. Little served with the regiment in both campaigns. Took part in the expedition to Maidan, the operations around Kabul in Dec., 1879 (including the action of Siah Sang, the defence of Sherpur, and the pursuit of the enemy on the 23rd), the march from Kabul to the relief of Kandahar, and was present at the battle of Kandahar, in which he acted as Orderly Officer to Brigadier-General Hugh Gough. (Mentioned in despatches.)

Lieuts. H. R. Alston and C. St. C. Cameron served with the regiment in the second campaign from March, 1880, till the conclusion of hostilities, taking part in the march from Kabul to the relief of Kandahar, and being present at the battle of Kandahar.

Riding-Master J. Marshall served with the regiment in both campaigns, taking part in the operations around Kabul in Dec., 1879, including the action of Siah Sang, the defence of Sherpur, and the pursuit of the enemy on the 23rd.

Qr.-Mr. J. Forsythe and Vet.-Surg. J. A. Woods served with the regiment in both campaigns, taking part in the operations round Kabul in Dec., 1879, the defence of Sherpur, the march from Kabul to the relief of Kandahar, and the battle of Kandahar.

10TH (P. W. O. ROYAL) HUSSARS.

ON the breaking out of hostilities with Afghanistan in the autumn of 1878, Head-quarters and two squadrons of the 10th Hussars, under the command of Lt.-Col. (then Major) E. A. Wood, formed part of the Cavalry Brigade of the Peshawar Valley Field Force, one squadron of the regiment, under the command of Captain T. J. W. Bulkeley, being detached, and forming part of the Cavalry Brigade of the Kuram Valley Field Force.

Taking part in the advance of Sir Sam. Browne's Division into the Khyber Pass, Head-quarters and two squadrons were present, on the 21st Nov., 1878, at the first attack on Ali Musjid. After the flight of the enemy and the capture of the fort, the regiment participated in the forward movement of the Division to Daka, and eventually to Jalalabad, which was reached on the 20th December.

Various small detachments of the regiment were now employed in the reconnaissances which were conducted into the surrounding country, including those which proceeded respectively to Sultanpur, on the 29th Dec., 1878, and Daulatzai on the 10th Jan., 1879.

On the 11th Jan., 1879, twenty-five sabres were sent out beyond Ali Boghan as a support to the force under Brigadier-General Jenkins, which was engaged in the destruction of the village of Shirgarh.

One troop of the regiment accompanied the column under the command of Brigadier-General Macpherson, which proceeded, on the 7th Feb., 1879, across the Kabul River into the Kunar Valley, against a body of Mohmands, and which, after dispersing them, returned to divisional Head-quarters on the 11th idem. Another troop formed part of the expeditionary force under the command of Brigadier-General Jenkins, which crossed the Lughman River on the 22nd Feb., 1879, and after penetrating a distance of thirty miles into new country, returned to Jalalabad on the 25th idem.

The detached squadron of the regiment under the command of Captain Bulkeley, which had been detailed to the Cavalry Brigade of the Kuram Valley Field Force, crossed the frontier on the 20th Nov., 1878, and after taking part, as a portion of the advance guard, in the movements of General Roberts' Division on Kapigong and Ahmadshana, was present, on the 2nd Dec., at the assault and capture of the Peiwar Kotal.

As a portion of the advance guard of the expeditionary force under the command of General Roberts which proceeded into the Khost Valley, the detached squadron marched from Hazar Pir on the 2nd Jan., 1879. At the action of Matun, on the 7th of that month, it was the first unit of the force which engaged the enemy, delivering an effective charge to the left front of the camp, and subsequently taking part in the pursuit. In the skirmishing with the Mangals on the 29th—the day on which General Roberts temporarily reoccupied Matun before finally abandoning it—the squadron was also engaged. After taking part, during the occupation of the Khost district throughout the month, in the numerous reconnaissances which were conducted into the surrounding country, it returned with the rest of the force, on the 30th Jan., to Hazar Pir.

On reaching Divisional Head-quarters, the detached squadron received orders to proceed to Jalalabad as escort to the Sirdar Wali Muhammad, half-brother of Shere Ali. Starting on the 4th Feb., 1879, it marched to its destination by way of Kohat, and rejoining Head-quarters, served in the Peshawar Valley Field Force during the remainder of the campaign.

On the 31st March, 1879, three troops of the regiment took part in the advance of the force under the command of Brigadier-General C. Gough towards Gandamak. In the action of Futtehabad on the 2nd April, they contributed, by a well-delivered charge to the right front, to the crushing defeat of the enemy, subsequently taking part in the pursuit, which was continued almost up to the walls of the village of Khuja.

On the same day on which Brigadier-General Gough's column marched from Jalalabad—the 31st March—a force of cavalry under the command of Lt.-Colonel Wood, 10th Hussars, which included one squadron of the regiment, was directed to cross the Kabul River to co-operate with a column under Brigadier-General Macpherson, which, earlier in the day, left divisional Head-quarters on the second expedition into the Lughman Valley. Making its way across the river on the night of the 31st, the squadron, in the uncertain light of the moon, was caused by the velocity and weight of the current to diverge from the ford, and was swept away—a struggling mass of heavily-accoutred men and horses—to the rapids below. Of the seventy officers, non-commissioned, officers and men who had left Jalalabad, no less than forty-six—including Lieut. Harford—were consigned by this accident in the space of a few minutes to a common grave.

During the month of May, five troops of the 10th Hussars were stationed at Gandamak, and one troop at Landi Kotal. Here they remained till the 1st June, when, the evacuation of the Northern line having been ordered, they commenced the return march to India. In the burning heat and the pestilential atmosphere in which the retrogressive movement was conducted, the regiment suffered heavily, cholera and heat-apoplexy swelling the casualty-roll by some eighty-five deaths before Head-quarters recrossed the frontier.

SERVICES IN AFGHANISTAN OF THE 10TH (P. W. O. ROYAL) HUSSARS.

Colonel Lord Ralph Kerr, C.B., joined the Head-quarters and service troops at Jalalabad in March, 1879, and commanded the regiment during the remainder of the campaign. Commanded the Cavalry Brigade at the action of Futtehabad. (Mentioned in despatches; C.B.)

Lt.-Col. E. A. Wood commanded the regiment from the date of the breaking out of hostilities till March, 1879, and served with it during the remainder of the campaign. Was present at the taking of Ali Musjid. (Mentioned in despatches; Brevet of Lt.-Colonel.)

RECORDS OF SERVICE.

Major T. J. W. Bulkeley (*retired*) commanded the detached squadron of the regiment in the Kuran Valley Field Force from the date of the breaking out of hostilities till Feb., 1879. Was present on orderly duty at the assault and capture of the Peiwar Kotal, and with the squadron in the operations in the Khost Valley, including the action of Matun. Subsequently served with the Head-quarters till the conclusion of the campaign, being present at the action of Futtehabad. (Mentioned in despatches; Brevet of Major.)

Major T. A. St. Quintin served with the regiment throughout the campaign, being present at the taking of Ali Musjid and the action of Futtehabad, in which he acted as aide-de-camp to Brigadier-General C. Gough. (Mentioned in despatches; Brevet of Major.)

Bt. Lt.-Colonel B. A. Combe. (For services see "Staff.")

Major R. C. D'E. Spottiswoode joined the head-quarters and service troops of the regiment at Jalalabad from England 15 March, 1879, and served with them until April, when he was sent to command the Depôt at Rawal Pindi. Was present at the fording of the Kabul River on the night of the 31st March, 1879.

Major H. S. Gough. (For services see "Staff.")

Captain W. B. Barker. (Deceased. See Biographical Division.)

Captain M. E. Wood joined the Head-quarters and service troops of the regiment at Jalalabad from England 29 Jan., 1879, and served with them during the remainder of the campaign. Was present at the action of Futtehabad. (Mentioned in despatches.)

Captain M. M. Slade joined the Head-quarters and service troops of the regiment at Basawal from England in December, 1878, and served with them during the remainder of the campaign. Was present at the action of Futtehabad. (Mentioned in despatches.)

Captain the Hon. J. P. Napier joined the Head-quarters and service troops of the regiment at Daka from the Depôt at Rawal Pindi 24 Nov., 1878, and served with them during the remainder of the campaign. Was present at the fording of the Kabul River on the night of the 31st March, 1879.

Bt. Major J. P. Brabazon served throughout both the first and second campaigns; first with the detached squadron of the regiment in the Kuram Valley F.F., and afterwards as Officiating Brigade Major and Staff Officer of Cavalry Brigade of the Division, being present at the assault and capture of the Peiwar Kotal, and taking part in the operations in the Khost Valley, including the action of Matun. In the second campaign was Brigade Major of Cavalry in the Kabul and Kabul-Kandahar Field Forces. Was present at the action of Charasiab, and the operations around Kabul and defence of Sherpur in Dec., 1879. Accompanied the force under Sir F. Roberts from Kabul to the relief of Kandahar, and was present at the reconnaissance of the 31st Aug., 1880, and the battle of Kandahar. (Mentioned five times in despatches; Brevet of Major.)

Lieuts. E. T. Rose, the Earl of Airlie, C. Sandes, and H. T. Allsopp, Captain S. Murphy (*A.P.D.*), *and Vet. Surg. W. Appleton* served with the regiment throughout the campaign—Lieut. Sandes as Adjutant. Were present at the assault of Ali Musjid and the action of Futtehabad.

Lieut. R. T. Dalton (*retired*) joined the detached squadron of the regiment in the Kuram Valley in January, 1879, and served with it till March, 1879.

Lieut. W. E. Phillips accompanied a detachment of remounts for the 9th Lancers to Kabul in March, 1880, having served at the regimental depôt during the first campaign.

Lieut. R. B. W. Fisher served throughout both campaigns: first with the detached squadron of the regiment in the Kuram Valley F.F., and subsequently, till the conclusion of the first campaign, with the Head-quarters in the Peshawar Valley F.F. Was present at the assault and capture of the Peiwar Kotal, the operations in the Khost Valley, including the action of Matun, and the action of Futtehabad. In the second campaign served as Transport Officer in the Kabul F.F., and took part in the operations round Kabul and the defence of Sherpur in Dec., 1879. Accompanied the force under Sir F. Roberts from Kabul to the relief of Kandahar, and was present at the battle of Kandahar. (Twice mentioned in despatches.)

Lieut. P. F. Durham served throughout the campaign, first with the detached squadron of the regiment in the Kuram Valley F.F., and subsequently with the Head-quarters in the Peshawar Valley F.F. Was present at the assault and capture of the Peiwar Kotal, the operations in the Khost Valley, including the action of Matun, and the action of Futtehabad.

Lieut. R. H. F. W. Wilson served with the regiment throughout the first campaign, being present at the taking of Ali Musjid and the action of Futtehabad. Served throughout the second campaign as Transport Officer in the Kabul and Kabul-Kandahar Field Forces, being present at the operations around Kabul and the defence of Sherpur in Dec., 1879, taking part in the march from Kabul to the relief of Kandahar, and being present at the battle of Kandahar. (Twice mentioned in despatches.)

Lieut. C. S. Greenwood served with the regiment during the campaign. Was present at the taking of Ali Musjid, and the fording of the Kabul River on the night of the 31st March, 1879.

Lieut. C. M. Grenfell joined the Head-quarters and service troops of the regiment 15 March, 1879, and served with them during the remainder of the campaign. Was present at the fording of the Kabul River on the night of the 31st March, 1879.

Lieut. H. F. Harford. (Drowned. See Biographical Division.)

Lieut. the Hon. G. L. Bryan served with the regiment throughout the campaign. Was present at the taking of Ali Musjid and the action of Futtehabad, in which he acted as Orderly Officer to Brigadier-General C. Gough. (Mentioned in despatches.)

Riding-Master H. McGee joined the Head-quarters and service troops of the regiment in Feb., 1879, and served with them during the remainder of the campaign. Was present at the action of Futtehabad.

Quartermaster W. King served with the regiment throughout the campaign. Was present at the taking of Ali Musjid.

15TH (THE KING'S) HUSSARS.

THE 15th Hussars, under the command of Colonel Swindley, left Mirat in October, 1878, to join the army in Southern Afghanistan. Moving by rail to Multan, the regiment marched from that station along the left bank of the Indus to Mithankote, where, the river being crossed, the Marri country was entered. After passing through Dera Bughti, the southern debouchure of the Bolan Pass was reached early in December, 1878.

Intense cold was experienced at the summit of the Pass, and the troop horses suffered much from the effects of the climate and the scarcity of fodder. After a short halt at Quetta, the regiment was pushed on to the foot of the Khojak Pass, where one squadron was sent forward under Major Luck to join the advanced Cavalry commanded by Brigadier-General Palliser. This squadron, when covering the advance of the left column in the forward movement on Kandahar, was actively engaged with the enemy's Cavalry on the 4th Jan., 1879, at Takht-i-pul. The enemy, about 400 in number, were surprised by the squadron and completely defeated, leaving 26 dead on the field, and losing altogether about 100 in killed, wounded, and prisoners. For his services on this occasion Major Luck, who was in command of the Cavalry, was appointed a Companion of the Bath. On the same day another squadron of the regiment under Captain Langtry was engaged in the Ghlo Pass.

Kandahar fell without further opposition on the 8th Jan., 1879; and a few days afterwards the 15th Hussars accompanied General Stewart's force to Kalat-i-Ghilzai. After a fortnight's halt there, it received orders to return to Kandahar, and shortly afterwards was sent back to the Pishin Valley to form part of the force under General Biddulph destined to open out the new route to India through Yargistan. Beyond an affair in which only the advance guard was engaged, the column met with no opposition, and the regiment returned to its quarters at Mirat in May, 1879, after an absence of seven months.

In April, 1880, the 15th Hussars was again placed under orders of readiness for active service; and on the defeat of the British troops at Maiwand, was ordered to join the army in Afghanistan under General Phayre.

Starting in August under the command of Lt.-Colonel Luck, C.B., the regiment reached Quetta in ten days, having proceeded by rail as far as the foot of the Bolan Pass. The heat being intense at that time of year, both men and horses suffered greatly, and the loss in both was excessive.

Arrived at Quetta, the regiment, in common with the rest of General Phayre's Division, was delayed in its further advance; and by the time that the forward movement was at length made, it was found the army under General Roberts had succeeded in rendering the necessity for further hostile operations unnecessary.

After a short halt at Kandahar, the regiment was ordered back to India, where it arrived in the month of October, 1880.

SERVICES IN AFGHANISTAN OF OFFICERS OF THE 15TH (KING'S) HUSSARS.

Colonel J. C. Swindley (*h.p.*) commanded the regiment in the Quetta and Kandahar Field Forces in the first campaign, taking part in the advance on and occupation of Kandahar and Kolat-i-Ghilzai.

Lt.-Colonel G. Luck, C.B., served with the regiment in the Quetta and Kandahar Field Forces in the first campaign, taking part in the advance on and occupation of Kandahar and Kalat-i-Ghilzai. Commanded the Advanced Cavalry of Brigadier-General Palliser's Force at the action of Takht-i-pul. (Slightly wounded; C.B.) Commanded the regiment, in General Phayre's Division, in the second campaign, taking part in the second advance on Kandahar. (Twice mentioned in despatches.)

Lt.-Colonel H. Langtry served with the regiment in the Quetta and Kandahar Field Forces in the first campaign, taking part in the advance on and occupation of Kandahar and Kalat-i-Ghilzai. Commanded a detached squadron of the regiment in the affair in the Ghlo Pass. Served with the regiment in General Phayre's Division in the second campaign, taking part in the second advance on Kandahar.

Major W. White, Captain G. D. F. Sulivan, and *Lieuts. J. H. Sewell, M. Allfrey*, and *H. L. Daly* served with the regiment in the Quetta and Kandahar Field Forces in the first campaign, taking part in the advance on and occupation of Kandahar and Kalat-i-Ghilzai; also, with the exception of Lieut. Daly, who was employed as a Commissariat Officer, served with the regiment in General Phayre's Division in the second campaign, taking part in the second advance on Kandahar.

Major F. H. Beck, Lieuts. W. J. Burke, C. E. Browne, J. R. P. Gordon, H. E. S. Pocklington, T. O. W. C. de Crespigny, and *Vet.-Surg. C. Gillard*, served with the regiment in General Phayre's Division in the second campaign.

Major H. Hall, Captain A. G. Holland, and *Lieut. the Hon. R. Leigh* served with the regiment in the Quetta and Kandahar Field Forces in the first campaign, taking part in the advance on and occupation of Kandahar and Kalat-i-Ghilzai, and being present at the action of Takht-i-pul—Lieut. Leigh as Orderly Officer to Brigadier-General Palliser. Also served with the regiment in General Phayre's Division in the second campaign. (Mentioned in despatches.)

Captain A. Smirke served with the regiment in the Quetta and Kandahar Field Forces in the first campaign, taking part in the advance on and occupation of Kandahar and Kalat-i-Ghilzai, and being present at the affair in the Ghlo Pass.

Captain A. T. Middleton (*6th Dn. Gds.*), *Lieut. A. W. D. Campbell* (*Bengal Staff Corps*), and *Major R. Sheehy* (*A.P.D.*) served with the regiment in the Quetta and Kandahar Field Forces in the first campaign, taking part in the advance on and occupation of Kandahar and Kalat-i-Ghilzai.

Capt. C. F. J. Douglas served during the second campaign, first as Brigade Major, Cavalry Brigade, Reserve Division, at Peshawar, and afterwards with the regiment as Adjutant, in General Phayre's Division.

Lieut. the Hon. A. Manners served with the regiment in the Quetta and Kandahar Field Forces in the first campaign, taking part in the advance on and occupation of Kandahar and Kalat-i-Ghilzai, and being present at the affair in the Ghlo Pass. Also served with the regiment in General Phayre's Division in the second campaign, taking part in the second advance on Kandahar.

ROYAL ARTILLERY.

D BATTERY, A BRIGADE, R.H.A.

ON the 15th Oct., 1878, Battery D/A, R.H.A., under the command of Major P. E. Hill, marched from Mirat, where it was then stationed, for Peshawar. On arrival at Rawal Pindi, however, directions were received for it to proceed to Campbellpur, and there await further orders. Detailed to the newly-constituted 2nd Division Peshawar Valley F.F., the battery quitted that station on the 18th Nov. for Naushahra, and from thence subsequently continued its march to Peshawar and Jamrud, where the Head-quarters of the Division were eventually located.

On the 19th Dec., 1878, Major Hill marched with two guns of the battery, mounted on elephants, from Jamrud, to take part in the first Bazar Valley expedition; but it being found, on arriving at the heights of Shagai, that the country was not accessible for elephants, the two guns remained encamped there until the return of the infantry of the Expeditionary Force, when they accompanied it back to camp at Jamrud. The left division of the battery was subsequently employed in the second Bazar Valley expedition, marching from Jamrud on the 24th Jan., and returning on the 4th Feb., 1879.

At the latter end of March, 1879, the battery was moved up to Basawal, where it remained until after the conclusion of the first campaign. On the 5th June it commenced its return march to India, and on the 9th idem recrossed the frontier, and moved into quarters at Peshawar.

Receiving orders on the 14th Dec., 1879, to march to the Khyber to reinforce General Bright's Division, D/A, R.H.A., now under the command of Brevet Lieut.-Colonel Sidney Parry, left Peshawar on the following day, and made its way to Jalalabad, remaining halted ten days, *en route*, at Landi Kotal, and leaving two guns at Basawal.

On the 13th Jan., 1880, in consequence of a reported attempt by a hostile body of Mohmands to cross the Kabul River at Ali Boghan, two guns were suddenly ordered out under an escort of two squadrons of the Carabiniers to prevent this movement, and effectually succeeded in doing so. When the order to turn out was received, an inspection of "stripped harness and saddlery" was being made by the commanding officer, notwithstanding which, the division, under the command of Lieut. A. Hewat, was harnessed and in action at Ali Boghan, nine miles distant from the camp, within fifty-eight minutes. After twenty-two rounds had been fired by the guns at various ranges, the Mohmands dispersed.

On the 29th Jan., 1880, the battery marched back to Basawal, and continued to do duty along the Khyber line of communications till its return to India on the 4th April, 1880.

E BATTERY, A BRIGADE, R.H.A.

In January, 1880, Battery E/A, R.H.A., under the command of Major W. W. Murdoch, was moved up from Mian Mir, whither it had proceeded twelve months before from Umballa, to Peshawar, and for a period of ten months served as a unit of the Peshawar District Force, which was commanded successively by Major-General Ross and Brigadier-General Hankin.

On the District Force being reduced to a peace footing in the autumn of the year, the battery quitted Peshawar, and proceeding to Mirat, went into quarters.

F BATTERY, A BRIGADE, R.H.A.

On the massing of the troops on the frontier in the autumn of 1878, Battery F/A, R.H.A., under the command of Major W. Seviling, was ordered up from Campbellpur, where it was at the time stationed, to Kohat, and from thence to Thal, to form part of the force under the command of General Roberts.

Taking part in the advance of the Division into Afghanistan, the battery was engaged, on the 28th Nov., 1878, in the skirmish of that date with the enemy. In the assault and capture of the Peiwar Kotal on the 2nd Dec., four guns were told off to support the turning movement commanded by the General in person, two guns remaining temporarily in camp, and subsequently being prominently engaged in the direct attack on the enemy's position conducted by Brigadier-General Cobbe. For the next few months the battery, broken up into divisions, did duty at Fort Kuram, Hazar Pir, and Thal, eventually reuniting and proceeding to Ali Khel, where it remained with the advanced troops on the Kuram line till the succeeding autumn.

On the renewal of hostilities in September, 1879, F/A, R.H.A., now under the command of Major J. C. Smyth-Wyndham, made its way over the difficult Shutargardan Pass without casualty or mishap, and took part with the newly-organized Kuram Division, Kabul Field Force, in the advance on and occupation of Kabul. During the action of Charasiab, on the 6th Oct., the battery was in reserve.

On the 1st Nov. two guns of the battery left Kabul with the force under Brigadier-General Macpherson, which proceeded to Kata Sang to meet the advanced portion of General Bright's Division from the Khyber.

On the 1st Dec. two guns of the battery left Kabul for India, forming part of the escort of the ex-Amir, who, since the 27th September, had been a prisoner in the British camp.

Four guns of the battery accompanied the column under Brigadier-General Macpherson, which was despatched from Kabul on the 8th Dec., 1879, to force a gathering of the enemy towards Maidan, and were left on that day with the Cavalry of the force, at Killa Affshar. On the 10th they were engaged in an attempt to cut off the enemy's retreat, but were precluded by the physical difficulties of the country from getting into action. The following day the Cavalry and Artillery, now under the command of Brigadier-General Massey, made their way across country to await the arrival of Brigadier-General Macpherson's force on the Ghazni road, and in doing so, came into disastrous conflict with overwhelming numbers of the enemy at Killa Kazi. The battery, after getting three times into action, was at length ordered by Sir F. Roberts, who had arrived on the scene and assumed command, to retire before the oncoming hordes, whose advance the charges of the Cavalry failed to check. After they had moved back a short distance, the guns were completely stopped in their further retirement by a deep watercourse, and it became necessary to spike and abandon them. In this engagement, a gallant young officer of the Battery, Lieut. E. Hardy, and one man, were killed; seven horses were also killed, and two wounded. Later in the day, after the defeat of the enemy by Brigadier-General Macpherson's force, the guns were recovered by a party of men under Col. MacGregor, R.A., Deputy Quartermaster-General.

On the 14th Dec., four guns of the battery, under Captain Pipon, were brought into action near the south-west corner of the Sherpur cantonments in covering the advance of Brigadier-General Baker's force in support of a detachment holding the conical hill after the assault of the Asmai Heights, and contributed to rendering the enemy's position untenable. While this event was in progress, the two other guns were despatched with a small force of Cavalry under Brigadier-General Gough to disperse a body of the enemy who were reassembled on the Siah Sang.

After the withdrawal of the troops within the lines of Sherpur, the battery took part during the siege in the defence of the cantonment, and was engaged in the repulse of the enemy's attack on the 23rd Dec.

On the 20th April, 1880, two guns of the battery accompanied the force under Brigadier-General Jenkins, which marched on that day towards Charasiab, and on the 25th idem performed excellent service in the defeat of the enemy near Childukhtean.

Quitting Kabul on the 11th May, 1880, the battery commenced its laborious return-march to India. After recrossing the frontier, it made its way back to its old station, Campbellpur.

I BATTERY, A BRIGADE, R.H.A.

Throughout the campaign of 1878-1879, Battery I/A, R.H.A., under the command of Major Æ. de V. Tupper, formed part of the Reserve Division, Peshawar Valley Field Force, and did duty at Rawal Pindi and Peshawar.

On the renewal of hostilities in September, 1879, the battery, at the time stationed at Peshawar under the command of Major M. W. Ommanney, was detailed to the Khyber Division, and for a period of eight months served at various posts on the Northern line, extending from Jamrud to Gandamak.

As a unit of the moveable column under Brigadier-General C. Gough, I/A, R.H.A., took part in the advance of that force, in November, 1879, to effect a junction with the Kabul troops. Subsequently, throughout the winter, it formed part of the garrison of Gandamak.

On the 3rd April, 1880, four guns of the battery accompanied the moveable column under the command of Brigadier-General Arbuthnot from Safed Sang on the expedition against the Wazir Kugianis, and on the 11th idem two guns took part in the advance of the same column into the Hissarak Valley.

In June, 1880, I/A, R.H.A., returned to Peshawar, and for a time formed part of the District Force under the command of Brigadier-General Hankin. On this force being reduced to a peace footing, the battery proceeded to Sialkot, and went into quarters.

A BATTERY, B BRIGADE, R.H.A.

On the 29th Oct., 1878, Battery A/B, R.H..A, under the command of Brevet Colonel D. McFarlane, left Mian Mir for Multan, and after waiting for a short time at that station, and subsequently at Jacobabad, for the assembling of the Division under the command of General Stewart, continued its advance on the 1st Dec. across the Put Desert to Dadar, the travelling being very heavy for draught cattle, and great difficulty being experienced in obtaining water. Marching to Quetta through the Bolan Pass, and suffering great loss in baggage animals through the dearth of supplies, the battery entered Afghanistan, and on the 30th Dec. crossed the Khogak Pass. The Right and Centre divisions left Chaman on the following day, and joined the advanced Cavalry of the Right Column, under Brigadier-General Kennedy, and of the Left Column, under Brigadier-General Palliser. On the 4th Jan., 1879, the Right Column, entering the Mel Valley, encountered large parties of the enemy's cavalry, who retreated on fire being opened upon them from the guns of the Centre division. Late in the afternoon the Left Column touched these parties, and fire was opened upon them by the guns of the Right division. Darkness shortly afterwards set in, and during the night the enemy retired.

The battery arrived at Kandahar with Divisional Head-quarters, on the 8th Jan., 1879, and on the 14th idem took part in the advance to Kalat-i-Ghilzai, where it remained, on short rations, from the 21st Jan. till the 6th Feb., the mortality amongst the horses and camels being very great through want of food and inadequate covering; on the latter date it commenced its return march to Kandahar, which was reached on the 28th Feb.

In April, 1879, Major H. de. G. Warter arrived at Kandahar, and took over the command of the battery from Captain R. G. S. Marshall, on whom it had devolved *vice* Colonel McFarlane, invalided.

On the 1st June, 1879, the battery moved from camp into huts, and on the 19th July into the cholera camp. At this time it suffered severely from cholera, no less than fifteen men succumbing to that disease between the 14th July and the 3rd August.

Ordered into the Pishin Valley, the battery quitted camp on the 4th Aug., and proceeding to Arombi Karez, remained there from the 13th Aug. till the 29th Sept. On that date it commenced its return march to Kandahar, where it arrived on the 6th Oct. For the next six months it did duty in cantonments.

As a unit of the Ghazni Field Force, A/B., R.H.A., marched from Kandahar for Kabul on the 30th March, 1880. In the battle of Ahmad Khel on the 19th April it was prominently engaged, and rendered important service. Fire was opened by the battery at 1,600 yards, but the enemy advancing rapidly, this range was decreased until case shot was used, and immediately afterwards, shrapnell reversed. The Ghazis charging almost to the muzzles of the guns, and the Infantry on the left falling back, the battery was retired some 90 yards, when the front attack of the enemy having failed, the fire was divided between parties on the left, and parties of Cavalry on the extreme right. On this day one officer and one man were wounded. At the action of Arzu on the 23rd April, A/B., R.H.A. was engaged in shelling the villages; and in the subsequent pursuit of the enemy, one horse of the Right half-battery was wounded.

After remaining in the Logar and Chardeh Valleys until the 4th Aug., 1880, the battery encamped on the Siah Sang. On the 7th Aug. it marched from Kabul for India by way of the Khyber Pass, and on the 26th idem arrived at Jamrud, having been one year and nine months across the frontier. It subsequently proceeded to Umballa, and on the 2nd Dec., 1880, entered cantonments.

During the period of its service in the war, the battery lost 32 non-commissioned officers, and also 35 horses, from disease.

D BATTERY, B BRIGADE, R.H.A.

As a unit of the 2nd or Reserve Division of the Kandahar Field Force, Battery D/B, R.H.A., under the command of Major F. W. Ward, served throughout the earlier months of 1880 at Karachi, whither it had proceeded at the latter end of January from Bombay.

On it being decided by Government to reinforce the garrison of Kandahar, the battery was ordered to the front, and moved by successive divisions to Sibi, and subsequently, through the Bolan Pass, to Quetta. In the meantime news had been received of the reverse sustained by General Burrows' brigade at Maiwand, and of the siege of Kandahar; and orders were given for the immediate formation of a relieving column under the command of General Phayre. Detailed to this force, the battery eventually took part in its advance to Kandahar, where it arrived three weeks after the relief of the garrison by General Roberts.

With the remainder of General Phayre's Brigade, the battery marched to Dahila, in the Argandab Valley, on the 7th Oct., where it remained until orders were received to move again into Kandahar. Entering the city on the 1st Nov., 1880, it did not again leave it until the final evacuation in June, 1881.

E BATTERY, B BRIGADE, R.H.A.

Battery E/B., R.H.A., consisting of 7 officers, 164 men, 200 horses, and 6 guns (9-prs. M.L.), left Kirki on the 16th Jan., 1880, and proceeded by march route to Bombay, where it embarked for Karachi. On disembarking it was conveyed by rail to Nari, where it was halted for nearly six weeks awaiting transport.

On leaving Nari, the battery marched through the Bolan Pass to Quetta, which it reached on the 25th March; after halting there a couple of days, it proceeded on to Kandahar, where it eventually arrived on the 5th April, 1880.

As a unit of Brigadier-General Burrows' flying column, the battery marched from Kandahar on the 4th July for Girishk. In the encounter with the Wali Shere Ali Khan's mutinied troops on the 14th July, it succeeded in getting four times into action, contributing materially to the defeat of the enemy. The 6-pounder smooth-bore guns which were recaptured on this day were formed into a battery under the command of Captain J. R. Slade, and manned by men of the 66th Regt., assisted by a few gunners of E/B., R.H.A.

In the Cavalry reconnaissance of the 23rd July, two of E/B.'s guns were again engaged.

On the 27th July, on the bloody field of Maiwand, and subsequently throughout the retreat, the battery played a brilliant and conspicuous part. On that disastrous day its losses amounted to no less than 2 officers (Major Blackwood and Lieut. Osborne), and 19 non-commissioned officers and men killed, 2 officers (Lieuts. Fowell and Maclaine), and 14 non-commissioned wounded, and 63 horses left dead on the field. Only one officer escaped unwounded—Captain J. R. Slade, who brought the battery out of action, and commanded it through the retreat of all that was left of General Burrows' force, which it covered, to Kandahar, bringing in as many of the wounded and exhausted as could be carried on the guns and carriages. It was during this fearful retreat that Lieut. Hector Maclaine was taken prisoner while endeavouring to procure water for the wounded from one of the neighbouring villages. 46 horses of the battery succumbed to the sufferings and hardships, and 111 natives of the battery establishment were killed or died before the walls of Kandahar were reached.

During the siege of Kandahar the guns of E/B., R.H.A., were mounted on the ramparts, three on the Herat face, and one on the Idgah gate, under Captain Slade. In the battle of Kandahar on the 1st

Sept., 1880, the battery was attached to the Cavalry Brigade under Brigadier-General Hugh Gough, and took part in the crowning defeat of the enemy, covering the advance of the Left Infantry Brigade under Brigadier-General Baker.

On the 8th Oct., 1880, E/B., R.H.A. left Kandahar for India, and on the 1st Nov. reached Jacobabad, where it remained till the 3rd Dec., taking part in the Viceroy's durbar. On this day it was inspected by H.E. the Viceroy, who complimented it in high terms for its conduct during the campaign.

On the 3rd Dec. the battery proceeded by rail to Karachi, and there embarked for Bombay. On arrival it was publicly complimented by their Excellencies the Commander-in-Chief and the Governor, and a public dinner was given to the non-commissioned officers and men.

The battery left Bombay by route march on the 17th Dec., 1880, and on the 27th idem reached Kirki, there to be stationed. For its services in Afghanistan it received the special thanks of the Viceroy and the Commander-in-Chief in general orders, and the following officers, non-commissioned officers, and men, were decorated: Captain Slade, with a Companionship of the Bath; Sergeant Mullane and Gunner Collis, with the Victoria Cross; Sergeant-Major Paton, Quartermaster-Sergeant Munroe, Sergeant Burridge, Corporal Thorogood, Bombardier Payne, Gunner Tighe, Driver Bishop, and Trumpeter Jones, with the medal for distinguished conduct in the field.

H BATTERY, C BRIGADE, R.H.A.

On the 21st Oct., 1878, Battery H/C., R.H.A., under the command of Major C. E. Nairne, marched from Sialkot, Punjab, for Campbellpur, where it remained halted till the 4th Dec., when it proceeded to Naushahra to join the 2nd Division Peshawar Valley F.F., under the command of General Maude.

After doing duty at Taru, Peshawar, and Jamrud till the 11th April, 1879, the battery crossed the frontier and moved up to Basawal, where it remained till the 8th May. On that date it was ordered back to Peshawar, and from thence to Naushahra and Sialkot, where it arrived on the 9th June, 1879.

I BATTERY, C BRIGADE, R.H.A.

Battery I/C, R.H.A., under the command of Major G. R. Manderson, formed part of the advance guard of the 1st Division Peshawar Valley Field Force, which marched from Jamrud to enter the Khyber Pass on the 21st Nov., 1878.

Four guns of the battery opened fire on nearing Ali Musjid, but were taken out of action on the arrival of a field battery and a 40-pounder Armstrong battery, which formed part of the main column of the force. Later in the day, when a general advance on Ali Musjid was made, Major Manderson was directed to take the battery down to the Khyber stream, and assist in covering the attack of the Infantry on the Fort. For this purpose four guns were brought into action on the left bank of the stream, and two guns, under Lieut. Walsh, on the right bank, all at about 1,000 yards distance from the Fort. The four guns remained in action until the ammunition in their limbers (the ammunition waggons had unfortunately not been permitted to accompany the advance guard) was expended, when they were withdrawn. The casualties on this day were one rank and file and two horses killed, and five rank and file wounded. On the 23rd Nov., the battery accompanied the force which advanced to Daka and subsequently to Jalalabad, where it remained in camp throughout the succeeding winter months.

In February, 1879, Major Manderson was promoted, and Major the Hon Alex. Stewart succeeded to the command of the battery.

On the 31st March I/C, R.H.A., advanced with the Cavalry Brigade towards Gandamak, and on the 2nd April took part in the action of Futtehabad, contributing to Brigadier-General C. Gough's crushing defeat of the enemy.

After the signing of the treaty of peace at Gandamak, the battery was amongst the first of the units of the Division to march back to India. It suffered severely, *en route*, from the epidemic of cholera which was raging on the Northern line, losing one officer and thirteen men in five days.

Early in September, 1879, I/C, R.H.A., received orders for England; but these orders were countermanded immediately after the news of the massacre of the Kabul Embassy reached India, and the battery was directed to join the Division under the command of Sir F. Roberts in the Kuram Valley. Not having supplemented its deficiencies in men, horses, and stores, however, after returning from the first campaign, its advance was delayed; but on receipt of the news of the investment of Sherpur, it was ordered to proceed by forced marches to Peshawar, of the garrison of which station, on arrival, it formed part. As troops arrived from the South, it was again ordered forward, and reached Daka on the 1st Jan., 1880.

On the 15th Jan. the battery, forming part of the small mixed force under Col. Boisragon, the Cavalry and Horse Artillery under the immediate command of Lt.-Col. the Hon. Alex. Stewart, was engaged in the encounter with the Khan of Lalpura and his followers, who had crossed the Kabul River and occupied the Gara Heights at the Western mouth of the Khyber Pass. The battery shelled the heights, and enabled the Infantry to make a direct attack and carry them, the enemy dispersing, utterly routed, towards Kam Daka.

It now being decided to reduce the force of Artillery in Afghanistan, the battery was ordered to India, and recrossed the frontier on the 14th Feb., 1880.

H BATTERY, 1st BRIGADE, R.A.

In the autumn of 1878, Battery H/1, R.A., under the command of Major F. A. Pritchard, was ordered up from Secunderabad to Multan, and throughout the first campaign, and during part of the second, remained stationed there as a unit of the Reserve Division of the Army employed in the Southern theatre of operations.

In the autumn of 1880 the battery, under the command of Major C. Crosthwaite, took part in the advance of General Phayre's Division to Kandahar, where it arrived at the latter end of September.

With the remainder of General Phayre's Division, the battery marched to Dahila, in the Argandab Valley, on the 7th Oct., and remained there until orders were received to move again into Kandahar. On the final evacuation of the city in June, 1881, the battery returned to India.

I BATTERY, 1st BRIGADE, R.A.

When, in 1878, the despatch of troops from India to the Mediterranean was determined on, I/1, R.A., was one of the batteries selected for transportation; but the threatening aspect of the Kabul question caused the authorities to decide on keeping the force in Sind intact, and the battery was soon under orders to join the Afghan expeditionary force.

As a unit of General Biddulph's Division, Battery I/1, R.A., under the command of Major H. C. Lewes, marched to Kandahar *viâ* the Khojak Pass, arriving at its destination, after encountering many obstacles and experiencing much hardship and privation, on the 9th Jan., 1879. On the 16th idem it marched with General Biddulph's Division towards the Halmand, and after proceeding up the Argandab Valley, and eventually halting within a few miles of Girishk in the immediate neighbourhood of the spot which was afterwards the battle-field of Maiwand, returned with the rest of the force to Kandahar.

Conformably with a scheme formulated by Government for the reduction of the number of troops in Afghanistan before the hot weather should set in, the battery now received orders to return to India. Quitting Kandahar on the 20th Feb., it retraced its steps by way of the Khojak Pass to Quetta, where it arrived on the 9th March; on the 11th it continued its march, and after travelling by rail from Sukkur to Karachi, eventually made its way to Kirki, where it marched into quarters on the 22nd April, 1879.

C BATTERY, 2nd BRIGADE, R.A.

At the latter end of January, 1880, Battery C/2, R.A., under the command of Major P. H. Greig, then stationed at Haidarabad, was placed under orders to join the force under General Phayre which was being formed for the purpose of relieving the Bengal troops in the Southern theatre of operations.

In the spring of the year the battery arrived at Kandahar, from whence, shortly afterwards, two of the guns proceeded to Kalat-i-Ghilzai, to reinforce the garrison of that place.

On the 28th July, 1880, two guns of the battery, under the command of Captain Law, accompanied the small mixed force under Brigadier-General Brooke which sallied out from Kandahar to cover the last few miles of the retreat of the scattered remnants of Brigadier-General Burrows' Brigade from Maiwand, and were instrumental in rendering signal aid. Subsequently withdrawing, on the same day, with the rest of the troops within the walls of Kandahar, the battery took part in the defence throughout the ensuing siege, one gun being posted at the North-East bastion, one at the Bar Durani Gate, one at the Kabul Gate, and one at the Topkhana Gate. On the 16th Aug., 1880, the battery was employed in covering the advance of the columns on the ill-starred sortie to Deh Khwaja, after previously shelling the village.

On the 24th Aug. the two guns C/2, R.A., on detachment at Kalat-i-Ghilzai, joined, with the rest of the garrison of that place, the force under Sir F. Roberts advancing from Kabul to the relief of Kandahar, and after the arrival of the Division at its destination on the 31st idem, rejoined the battery.

At the battle of Kandahar on the 1st Sept., 1880, the battery was detached from Brigadier-General Burrows' command, and throughout the day took part in the operations of the 1st Brigade Kabul-Kandahar Field Force, under Brigadier-General Macpherson, covering the advance of the Infantry, and shelling the village of Gandi Mullah Sahibdad. On this day 5 officers and 135 men of the battery were under arms, and the casualties were, 2 men wounded, and 1 horse killed.

On the division being broken up, and the forces in Southern Afghanistan reorganized, the battery was ordered back to India, and eventually made its way to Ahmadnagar.

D BATTERY, 2ND BRIGADE, R.A.

Detailed, early in November, 1878, to the Multan Division of the army destined for the invasion of Southern Afghanistan, Battery D/2, R.A., under the command of Major E. Stavely, was moved up to Sukkur, and marching by way of the Bolan Pass to Quetta, advanced by the Gwaja route to Kandahar, eventually arriving at its destination; after enduring the hardships and privations and surmounting the obstacles encountered by the other units of General Stewart's Division, on the 9th Jan., 1879.

On the 15th Jan. the battery took part in the advance of General Stewart's Column on Kalat-i-Ghilzai, and remained for some days encamped at Zaldak, returning, with the rest of the force, at the latter end of February, to Kandahar.

For a period of eight months Battery C/2, R.A., formed part of the garrison of Kandahar; at the expiration of that period it was ordered back to India, and returning by way of Quetta and the Bolan Pass, eventually made its way to Kirki.

F BATTERY, 2ND BRIGADE, R.A.

As a unit of the 2nd or Reserve Division of the Kandahar Field Force, Battery F/2, R.A., under the command of Major J. R. J. Dewar, served throughout the first six months of 1880 at Haidarabad, whither it had proceeded in January, 1880, from Kirki.

On it being decided by Government to reinforce the garrison of Kandahar, the battery was ordered to the front, and proceeded to Sibi, and subsequently, through the Bolan Pass, to Quetta. In the meantime news had been received of the reverse sustained by General Burrows' Brigade at Maiwand, and of the siege of Kandahar, and orders were issued for the immediate formation of a relieving column under the command of General Phayre. Detailed to this force, the battery eventually took part in its advance to Kandahar, where it arrived three weeks after the relief of the garrison by General Roberts.

With the remainder of General Phayre's Brigade, the battery marched into the Argandab Valley on the 7th Oct., and remained there till orders were received to move again into Kandahar. On the final evacuation of that city in June, 1881, the battery returned to India.

C BATTERY, 3RD BRIGADE, R.A.

On the 5th Oct., 1878, in view of the impending outbreak of hostilities with Afghanistan, Battery C/3, R.A., under the command of Major H. C. Magenis, left its station, Jalandhar, for the front, and after a march of some 450 miles joined General Maude's Division of the Army of Invasion, then in course of concentration at Peshawar.

From the 22nd Dec., 1878, till the 25th March, 1879, the battery was stationed at Jamrud, after which it moved up through the Khyber Pass to Daka, where it remained till the conclusion of the first campaign. At the latter end of April it took part in the affair with the Mohmands at Kam

Daka, materially assisting in rescuing 150 men of the Mhairwara Battalion, under Captain O'M. Creagh, from a most perilous position.

On the 3rd June, 1879, the battery commenced its return march to India, suffering *en route*, and at Peshawar, from a severe outbreak of cholera, which carried off 23 men out of a total of 110 then present in a period of six weeks.

On the renewal of hostilities in September, 1879, C/3, R.A., was one of the first batteries sent across the frontier. Marching again through the Khyber Pass, it was now broken up into divisions, two guns being left at Basawal, two advancing to Jalalabad, and two to Gandamak. On General Bright's arrival at Gandamak with a battery of Horse Artillery, the two guns at that advanced post rejoined the division at Jalalabad.

During the winter months the battery took part in many minor expeditions which, though necessitating a good deal of severe marching, invariably resulted in the enemy coming to terms without offering armed resistance.

In March, 1880, the two guns at Basawal moved up to Jalalabad and rejoined the others. The following month the battery, leaving one division behind under the command of Lieut. Granet, advanced to Safed Sang. On the 15th May these two guns were relieved by a division under Lieut. Robinson, which remained at Jalalabad till the evacuation. During the hot weather several expeditions were sent out from Jalalabad, in all of which C/2, R.A., took part.

On the evacuation of the advanced posts on the Northern line in August, 1880, the battery marched down to India, and after halting at Campbellpur till the middle of August, proceeded to Agra, and eventually returned to England.

E BATTERY, 3RD BRIGADE, R.A.

Throughout the Afghan campaign of 1878-1879, Battery E/3, R.A., under the command of Major T. M. Hazlerigg, formed part of the 1st Division, Peshawar Valley Field Force.

Brigaded with the 2nd Infantry Brigade, the battery advanced with the Division from Jamrud on the 21st Nov., 1878, and took part in the direct attack, on that day, on Ali Musjid. Reaching the Shagai ridge about noon, the battery took up a position on the heights from which it went into action, the fire of four of the guns being directed on the Fort, and that of the other two on the works on the hill to the enemy's right. Though the wind was strong, the battery managed to make fair practice. During the day it fired 98 rounds of shrapnel, and 48 rounds of common shell; its only casualty was 1 officer's horse killed by a round shot.

On the advance of the main body of the division on the 23rd Nov., E/3, R.A., was left with the 4th Infantry Brigade in charge of the camp at Ali Musjid. It was subsequently moved up, in divisions, through the Pass, and during the remainder of the first campaign did duty at various posts extending to Gandamak and including Daka and Jalalabad. On the recall of the troops after the conclusion of peace, it was one of the first batteries to commence the toilsome return march to India, eventually making its way to Campbellpur after suffering severely from the excessive heat of the season and the pestilential climate of the country traversed.

On the renewal of hostilities in the Autumn of 1879, E/3, R.A., was ordered up from Campbellpur to Kohat, and throughout the ensuing campaign served in divisions at that station, at Thal, and at various outposts, as a unit of the Kuram Division. Shortly after the withdrawal of the troops to India, the battery was ordered home, and proceeded to Woolwich.

G BATTERY, 3RD BRIGADE, R.A.

On the 17th Oct., 1878, Battery G/3, R.A., under the command of Major Sidney Parry, then stationed at Rawal Pindi, was placed under orders for active service. Supplementing its deficiencies in horses —no less than 49 of which had recently succumbed, in the space of nine days, to the deadly Ludiana fever—it marched on the 30th Oct. to join the Kuram Division of the Army of Invasion, under General Roberts, and arrived at its destination on the 8th Nov. Leaving three guns at Kohat, the other half-battery, with Major Parry in command, marched on the 16th Nov. to Thal, and taking part in the advance of the 2nd Brigade of the Division into hostile territory, crossed the Kuram River on the 23rd.

On the 2nd Dec., 1878, the half-battery, as a unit of Brigadier-General Cobbe's command, was engaged in the front attack on the Peiwar Kotal, rendering distinguished service in the brilliant capture of the apparently impregnable range of heights so tenaciously held by the enemy. For its conduct on this occasion it was warmly thanked in orders.

After the retreat of the Afghan army, the battery was left to form part of the garrison of the Peiwar Kotal, and having built huts for officers and men, remained on the hill during the severe winter succeeding early spring. In April, 1879, it was relieved, having previously been reinforced earlier in that month by the three guns from Kohat. The whole battery now proceeded to Ali Khel, the most advanced post of the Division; there it remained until the Peace of Gandamak brought the first campaign to a close, when it returned to the Kuram Valley.

Conformably with the forward concentration of the troops under Sir Frederick Roberts' command on the renewal of hostilities in the autumn of 1879, the battery commenced its march from Kuram, where it had remained in camp throughout the summer, on the 25th Sept. After making its way over the difficult Surkai Kotal, Shutargardan, and Shinkai Kotal, it reached Kushi on the 1st Oct., and joining Divisional Head-quarters, took part in the advance on Kabul. At the action of Charasiab on the 6th Oct., three guns, accompanied by Major Parry, in command, were engaged, the other three guns, under Lieut. H. V. Cowan, being left in reserve in camp. After the defeat of the enemy, the Division marched to Kabul, and in November the battery, together with the rest of the troops, took up its quarters in the Sherpur cantonments.

On the 3rd Nov., 1879, Major Sidney Parry proceeded to India on appointment to the Horse Artillery, and the command of the battery devolved on Captain R. Purdy, who continued to hold it until relieved by Major W. R. Craster on the 3rd Dec., 1879.

At the latter end of November, two guns, under Lieut. H. V. Cowan, proceeded into the Maidan Valley with the reconnaissance under Brigadier-General Baker, returning on the 2nd Dec.

During the operations round Kabul in the month of December, 1879, the battery was prominently engaged, taking part, on the 13th and 14th respectively, in the assaults of the Takht-i-Shah and the Asmai Heights. With the rest of the force it was retired, on the 14th, within the lines of Sherpur, and took part in the defence of the cantonments throughout the siege. On the 23rd it was engaged in the repulse of the enemy's attack, and in the counter-attack, four guns being ordered out through the Behmaru Gorge to shell a village lying to the North-East of the cantonments, and working considerable execution.

On the 31st July the battery was ordered to Killa Kazi to fire a salute in honour of the Amir Abdul Rahman, and returned to Kabul on the 4th Aug., 1880. The next day it commenced its return march to India, and arrived at Peshawar, under the command of Captain H. T. Curling, on the 25th idem.

C BATTERY, 4TH BRIGADE, R.A.

On the impending outbreak of hostilities with Afghanistan in the autumn of 1878, Battery C/4, R.A., under the command of Major J. C. Auchinleck, then stationed at Mirat, was ordered to Rawal Pindi, where for the next few months it did duty as a portion of the Reserve Division of the Kuram Valley Field Force.

In March, 1879, the battery was moved up to the frontier and into hostile territory, leaving three guns, *en route*, at Kohat. On the 12th May the advanced half-battery, accompanied by Major Auchinleck in command, arrived at Kuram, where it remained throughout the remainder of the first campaign.

As a unit of the Kuram Division, C/4, R.A., served through the second campaign from the date of the renewal of hostilities till the final evacuation of the Valley. By the latter end of September, 1879, one half-battery had been pushed on to the advanced post of Ali Khel, the other remaining temporarily at Kuram. On the 14th Oct. the former was engaged at Ali Khel in the repulse of the determined attack made by the Mangals on that post, contributing materially to their defeat.

Broken up into divisions, the battery served for the remainder of the campaign at various posts extending from Kuram to Ali Khel, taking part from time to time in the various expeditions conducted into the surrounding country, and receiving a full share of the work which fell to the lot of the Division.

On the evacuation of the Kuram Valley, C/4, R.A., recrossed the frontier, and making its way back to Rawal Pindi, eventually proceeded to Lahore.

RECORDS OF SERVICE.

D BATTERY, 4TH BRIGADE, R.A.

When stationed at Rawal Pindi, in December, 1879, Battery D/4, R.A., under the command of Major J. F. Free, received orders to proceed to Peshawar.

Leaving two guns behind, the remainder of the battery quitted Rawal Pindi on the 16th Dec., and for a period of five months after arriving at its destination served as a portion of the Peshawar District Force, under the command, successively, of Major-General Ross and Brigadier-General Hankin.

In the middle of May, 1880, the four guns returned to Rawal Pindi, where they were rejoined by the division which had remained behind.

E BATTERY, 4TH BRIGADE, R.A.

At the latter end of September, 1878, Battery E/4, R.A., under the command of Major T. C. Martelli, then stationed at Multan, received orders to proceed to Quetta to form part of the Division assembling there under the command of General Biddulph; and after an extremely severe march through the deep hot sands of the Dera Bughti country, and subsequently through the Bolan Pass, it arrived at its destination in the second week of November.

Taking part in the advance, by the Khojak route, on Kandahar, the battery, with the main body of the Division, entered Kandahar on the 8th Jan., 1879.

The day after the arrival of the battery at Kandahar, it had to deplore the loss of a promising young officer, Lieut. H. V. Willis, who fell by the hand of a fanatic while watching some craftsmen who were at work in one of the bazaars; and again, on the 6th Feb., it suffered a loss of two men from a similar murderous attack.

On the departure of General Biddulph's column for the Halmand, the E/4, R.A., remained behind to form part of the garrison of Kandahar, taking up its quarters in the citadel.

Conformably with a scheme shortly afterwards formulated by Government for the reduction of the forces in Southern Afghanistan before the hot weather should set in, the battery received orders to return to India. Leaving Kandahar on the 15th Feb., 1879, it retraced its steps through the Khojak and Bolan Passes, and eventually made its way to Jalandhar.

G BATTERY, 4TH BRIGADE, R.A.

On the 4th Nov., 1878, Battery G/4, R.A., under the command of Major Sir J. W. Campbell, left Miam Mir for Multan, and from thence proceeded by way of Sukkur to Quetta, where it arrived, after a toilsome march, on the 26th Dec. Escorted by a company of the 59th Foot, it now took part in the advance on Kandahar of Sir D. Stewart's Division of the Army of Invasion, making its way through the Gwaja Pass, and reaching its destination on the 9th Jan., 1879.

On the 14th Jan., 1879, G/4 R.A., quitted Kandahar, with the force under Sir D. Stewart, for the advance on Kalat-i-Ghilzai, which was entered on the 22nd. On the return of the main body of the force, the battery was left with Brigadier-General Hughes' Brigade to garrison that post, and remained in the fort till the 22nd Feb., when it marched back to Candahar. During this interval it was mainly employed in foraging, supplies having to be gathered in from villages lying many miles distant. Many natives of the battery establishment died from cold, and several horses were lost through the insufficiency and bad quality of the forage.

On arriving again at Kandahar on the 2nd March, G/4 was stationed with the rest of the force in the large camp which was formed near the city, and remained there until early in May, when it moved into quarters consisting of the mud huts occupied by the British Army in 1840-42. During the next four months, for which it remained stationary, it lost through disease its Sergeant-Major, its Quartermaster-Sergeant, and two men, the latter succumbing to a violent outbreak of cholera in July and August.

On the 2nd Sept., 1879, G/4, R.A., marched with the Cavalry Brigade to Chaman, *en route* for India; but was recalled by telegram to Kandahar on the receipt of the news of the outbreak at Kabul. Immediately after its return, two guns of the battery were moved forward to Kalat-i-Ghilzai, and remained at that post until the other two divisions of the battery arrived there in April, 1880.

As a unit of the 2nd Brigade of the Ghazni Field Force, G/4, R.A., took part in the advance of the Division from Kandahar on the 31st March, 1880, being rejoined, *en route*, by the two guns which had been performing garrison duty at Kalat-i-Ghilzai. At the battle of Ahmad Khel, on the 19th April, the battery did great execution by the fire of case and inverted shrapnel from a position in front of the rest of the troops at the time of the Ghazi rush, and afterwards, distributed in divisions on the flanks, assisting in preventing the turning movement attempted by the enemy. After the victory, the force marched on to Ghazni. At the affair at Arzu the battery was at first in reserve; but as the enemy held out, it was ordered up with other reinforcements, and, besides for some time shelling the villages, was able to bring a most effective fire to bear from various positions on masses of the enemy in the open.

Taking part in the forward movement of the force into the Logar Valley, the battery remained there, and in the surrounding districts, for the next three months. During that period there was no action in which Artillery was engaged, but there were two or three night alarms, and shots were fired into camp.

On the 2nd Aug., 1880, G/4, R.A., arrived in Kabul, and shortly afterwards took part in the laborious return-march of the force under Sir Donald Stewart to India. On the 2nd Sept. it arrived at Peshawar, and after remaining there till the 2nd of April, 1881, proceeded to Mirat.

L BATTERY, 5TH BRIGADE, R.A.

At the latter end of December, 1879, Battery L/5, R.A., under the command of Major W. R. C. Brough, was ordered up from Mian Mir, where it was then stationed, to join the Khyber Reserve Division.

On arriving at the frontier the battery was broken up into divisions, and throughout the remainder of the campaign served at various posts, extending as far as Daka, in different sections of the newly constituted Khyber Line Force.

In May and June, 1880, divisions of the battery accompanied the forces under Brigadier-Generals Gib and Doran on the expeditions to Mazina and Kama, shortly after the successful conclusion of which the battery was reunited at Pesh Bolak: there it remained doing duty till the commencement of the evacuation of Northern Afghanistan in August, 1880, when it marched back to India, and eventually proceeded to Multan.

No. 1 BATTERY, 8TH BRIGADE, R.A.

This battery, under the command of Major J. Haughton, marched from Rawal Pindi for the Kuram Valley on the 2nd Oct., 1879, and on the 13th idem joined Brigadier-General J. A. Tytler's expeditionary force at Kohat. This force was intended to punish the Zaimusht tribe for their depredations in British territory, and for the recent murder of Lieut. Kinloch, B.S.C.; but on the receipt of intelligence of fighting in the Hariab Valley, the Column pushed on to Kuram, and 1/8, R.A., was sent to join Brigadier-General Gordon's force at Ali Khel, where it arrived on the 28th Oct., 1879.

After the evacuation of the Hariab Valley on the 8th Nov., the battery marched with General Gordon's force over the Peiwar Kotal and up the Chakmani Valley to punish a refractory tribe. No resistance was offered, and a fine was inflicted.

1/8, R.A., now returned to Kuram, and shortly afterwards took part with General Tytler's force in the deferred Zaimusht expedition, entering the hostile territory at Bulesh Khel on the 8th Dec., 1879. The battery was first engaged with the enemy at Tarah on the 10th Dec., and then again on the 13th and 14th in the final advance on the Zaimusht stronghold of Zawa, which was stormed on the latter date. The services it rendered on these occasions were warmly acknowledged in an order addressed by the Brigadier-General to the troops.

From the 26th Jan. until the 31st March, 1880, 1/8, R.A., was stationed at Thal, after which it moved up the Valley to Kuram, Shalozan, and Peiwar Kotal, where it remained until the close of the war.

No. 6 BATTERY, 8TH BRIGADE, R.A.

In September, 1879, 6/8, R.A., under the command of Major T. Graham, received orders to proceed from Lucknow, where it was then stationed, to Peshawar, to be equipped with the 7-pounder muzzle-loading jointed gun, and converted into a mountain battery. On its arrival at Peshawar in December, it was further directed, in consequence of the news which had been received of the disturbances at Kabul, to hurry on the equipment, and proceed with all speed to the capital to join Sir F. Roberts' force. The equipment of mules and native drivers having been with some difficulty completed, it left Peshawar on the 16th March, and reached Kabul on the 2nd April, 1880.

On the 16th April four guns proceeded with the force under General Ross, which was despatched to meet and facilitate the advance of the Ghazni Field Force, and took part in the encounters with the enemy on the 24th, 25th, and 26th April at Zaidabad. On the 24th April the two guns which had been left at Kabul, under the command of Lieut. A. F. Liddell, were detailed to accompany a force sent out to assist Col. Jenkins, who was hard pressed by the enemy at Charasiab, but arrived too late to take part in the action.

The Ghazni Force joined the force under General Ross on the 27th April, and the latter returned towards Kabul, a detachment, accompanied by two guns, 6/8, R.A., proceeding on the 29th to burn the fort of Abdul Gafur.

The force under General Ross reached Kabul on the 2nd May. On the 8th of the same month four guns, 6/8, R.A., were detailed to accompany the column under General Baker, which marched into the Logar Valley, and returned through the Maidan Valley to Kabul on the 29th.

Selected to accompany the force under Sir F. Roberts on its memorable march to the relief of Kandahar, 6/8, R.A., was attached throughout to the 1st Infantry Brigade, under the command of General Macpherson, and at the battle of Kandahar on the 1st Sept., took a prominent part with it in the crowning defeat of the enemy.

The battery remained at Candahar until the final evacuation of that place by the British troops in the Spring of 1881, when it returned to India.

Nos. 13 AND 16 BATTERIES, 8TH BRIGADE, AND No. 8 BATTERY, 11TH BRIGADE, R.A.

The Royal Artillery Siege Train of the Kandahar Field Force was organized at Sukkur, Sind, during November and December, 1878, and consisted at first of the following Staff and batteries, viz.: Colonel E. J. Bruce, R.A., Commanding; Major W. H. Noble, R.A., Staff Officer; Captain R. A. Lanning, R.A., Adjutant; Battery 13/8, R.A., under the command of Major E. S. Burnett; Battery 16/8, R.A., under the command of Major J. H. Blackley; Battery 8/11, R.A., under the command of Major H. H. Murray. The train was organized in three divisions, the 1st consisting of four 25-pounder R.M.L. guns of 18 cwt.; the 2nd of four 40-pounder R.M.L. guns of 34 cwt.; and the 3rd of four 6·3-inch R.M.L. Howitzers of 18 cwt. Each division included also a proportion of ammunition wagons, store carts, baggage animals, &c.

The train commenced its march forward on the 16th Dec., 1878, but shortly after the fall of Kandahar it was halted. The head-quarter Staff (Major Noble excepted), and the garrison batteries, were then directed to return to India, and the several divisions of the Train, each under a subaltern officer with two non-commissioned officers and ten picked gunners, the whole under Major Noble, were ordered to continue their march.

The Train crossed the Kutchi desert, viâ Shikarpur, Jacobabad, Barshori, and Bagh, to Dadar, at the mouth of the Bolan Pass. From thence it marched to Quetta, viâ Kirta, Mach, and Darwaza.

The Siege Train was parked at Quetta in Royal Artillery charge until July, 1879, when it was broken up and the material handed over to the Ordnance Department.

No. 11 BATTERY, 9TH BRIGADE, R.A.

Throughout the Afghan Campaign of 1878-1879, Battery 11/9, R.A., under the command of Major J. R. Dyce, served with the army operating on the Khyber Line.

Attached to the advance guard of the 3rd Infantry Brigade, 1st Division, Peshawar Valley Field Force, the battery took part in the advance of the Division on the 21st Nov., 1878, and was engaged in the direct attack, on that day, on Ali Musjid. Moving up a mountain path, on the right of the main road, to the Shagai Heights, the battery halted, and about 3 p.m. pushed forward to a rocky ridge, 1,400 yards distant from the Fort, to cover the Infantry advance. Against this position, on the right flank, the enemy made a demonstration, opening a musketry fire at 800 yards, and gradually shortening it to 450 yards, from the cliffs. From this fire, which was eventually effectually silenced by a division of the battery, five gunners were wounded.

After the flight of the enemy and the capture of Ali Musjid, 11/9, R.A., took part in the advance of the 1st Division to Landi Kotal; from thence it was ordered back, on the 29th Nov., to the Shagai Heights, and subsequently became an integral part of the 2nd Division, under General Maude's command. In the first of the Bazar Valley expeditions, in December, 1878, two divisions of the battery were employed with the column operating from Ali Musjid, the remaining division, under the command of Lieut. O. S. Smyth, performing effective service with Brigadier-General Tytler's column, operating from Daka. Again, in the second expedition against the Zaka Khel Afrides, at the latter end of January and the beginning of February, 1879, the whole battery took part, one division accompanying the Jamrud column, another division, the Ali Musjid column, and the remaining division, the Basawal column.

At the latter end of March, two guns accompanied the force under Brigadier-General Tytler, which marched from Basawal and inflicted punishment for recent misdemeanours on the inhabitants of the Deh Sarak villages beyond Pesh Bolak; and from the 19th till the 23rd April, two guns were employed in the operations in the neighbourhood of Kam Daka.

In May, 1879, the three divisions of the battery, which had recently been separated, were reunited at Landi Kotal, and eventually remained to form part of the force holding that post after the conclusion of the first campaign, and the evacuation of the advanced posts on the Northern line.

Throughout the campaign of 1879-1880, 11/9, R.A., again discharged a heavy share of arduous and important work. Serving as a unit of the Khyber from the date of the renewal of hostilities till August, 1880, the battery took part in almost all of the numerous expeditions which were conducted by the various sections of that Division into the wide extent of territory embraced in its operations,—including the Lughman Valley expedition, the expedition against the Wazir Kugianias, and the operations in the Hissarak Valley in April, 1880, and was employed, either in separate divisions or collectively, at nearly every post on the northern line extending to Jagdalak.

At the beginning of August, 1880, 11/9, R.A., was ordered up to Kabul. Selected to accompany the force under Sir F. Roberts in its memorable march, during that month, to the relief of Kandahar, the battery was attached to the 3rd Infantry Brigade, under the command of Brigadier-General MacGregor. In the reconnaissance of the 31st August, two guns accompanied Brigadier-General Gough's force, and were brought into action, the other four, with the rest of the 3rd Brigade being placed under arms to cover the retirement; and in the crowning defeat of the enemy at the battle of Kandahar, on the following day, the whole battery was engaged.

After remaining a short time at Kandahar, and subsequently taking part, during the last months of 1880, in the expedition which was conducted into the Marri country, the battery returned to India, eventually making its way to Jutogh.

No. 12 BATTERY, 9TH BRIGADE, R.A.

In March, 1880, Battery 12/9, R.A., under the command of Major H. L. Gwyn, was ordered to proceed from Karachi, whither it had recently arrived from Attock, to Kabul.

The battery reached its destination early in April, 1880, and for the next four months did duty with the 1st Brigade, 2nd Division, of the Field Force, to which it was attached.

On the evacuation of Kabul by the British troops in August, 1880, Battery 12/9, R.A., returned to India, commencing its march on the 5th, and recrossing the frontier on the 24th of that month.

No. 13 BATTERY, 9TH BRIGADE, R.A.

On the 19th Nov., 1878, Battery 13/9, R.A., equipped with three 40-pounder Armstrong guns, marched from Peshawar, under command of Major C. W. Wilson, to join the force under Sir Sam. Browne at Jamrud. Engaged in the front attack on Ali Musjid on the 21st, the battery came into action from a position on the Shagai Heights at a range of 2,850 yards, and after discharging six rounds, completely silenced the enemy's artillery fire from the Fort. The guns continued in action till dusk, and again opened fire at daybreak the following morning, when Ali Musjid was found to have been evacuated during the night. The captured artillery (25 guns) with all the ammunition, were removed under the superintendence of Major Wilson, with some assistance from Major Hazlerigg's battery; and in performing this duty the officers and men were frequently fired upon by the Afridis, the officers on one occasion using their revolvers in defence.

The heavy battery, 13/9, R.A., remained in position on the Shagai ridge after the departure of the main body of the Division, and was reinforced by Major Hazlerigg's battery and various details of Cavalry and Infantry, the whole being commanded by Major Wilson, R.A. Incessant attacks by day and night were made on the camp by Afridis till the end of the eighth day, when Brigadier-General Appleyard arriving with the 81st Foot and Major Dyce's battery, 13/9, R.A., returned to Jamrud, and the captured guns were taken into Peshawar.

On the 9th March, 1879, the battery marched to Ali Musjid, and subsequently to Jalalabad, from whence it advanced with the rest of the Division to Gandamak: there it remained till the conclusion of the campaign, when it returned through the Khyber Pass to India.

The outbreak of cholera amongst the troops on the Northern line fell heavily on the battery, the last victim being Captain W. P. Graves, who throughout the whole of the operations had been conspicuous for his zeal and gallantry.

No. 14 BATTERY, 9TH BRIGADE, R.A.

On the 17th March, 1880, Battery 14/9, R.A., under the command of Major G. A. Crawford, having been ordered up for service from Firozpur, crossed the frontier, and proceeded to Quetta, where it remained in garrison until it was detailed to the force under General Phayre's command destined for the relief of Kandahar.

Forming part of this brigade, one division of the battery, with 25-pounder guns, accompanied by Major Crawford in command, and another division, under Captain E. Buckle, marched to Kandahar, arriving some time after the relief of the beleaguered garrison by the force under Sir F. Roberts from Kabul.

At Kandahar, 14/9, R.A., was re-equipped, as a heavy battery, taking over 40-pounder guns.

With the exception of three weeks spent with the remainder of General Phayre's force in the Argandab Valley, the battery remained at Kandahar until the final evacuation of that city by the British troops in June, 1881, when it returned to India.

No. 5 BATTERY, 11TH BRIGADE.

On the 25th Sept., 1878, Battery 5/11, R.A., equipped with three 40-pounder guns and three 8-inch mortars, under the command of Major C. Collingwood, left Morar, where it was then stationed, for Multan, having received orders only the previous day to proceed on active service. Detailed to General Stewart's Division of the Army of Invasion, the battery quitted Multan on the 10th and 11th Nov., and, proceeding by rail to Sukkur, commenced its laborious march by way of Dadar and the Bolan Pass to Quetta, and eventually to Kandahar. After suffering great hardship and privation, it eventually arrived at its destination on the 13th Jan., 1879, with its elephants and draught-oxen sadly diminished in number from the combined effects of semi-starvation and over-work.

At the latter end of July, 1879, 5/11, R.A., was ordered back to Quetta, where it arrived about the middle of August, and remained, forming part of the garrison, until the following February. In June and July it lost five non-commissioned officers and men from a severe epidemic of cholera which had broken out in Kandahar, and now many more were placed on the sick-list from the effects of the excessive heat endured during the march back, the temperature in the day-time having averaged 110° to 120° in the men's tents.

Ordered a second time to Kandahar, 5/11, R.A., equipped with two 40-pounder guns and two 6·3-inch Howitzers, under the command of Captain G. M. B. Hornsby, left Quetta on the 9th Feb., 1880, and reached its destination at the latter end of the same month. Arrived at Kandahar, it exchanged equipments with Battery 6/11, R.A., taking over four 40-pounder B.L. guns, and two 8-inch mortars, and retaining them till the conclusion of the campaign.

Immediately after the receipt of the news of the disaster at Maiwand, the battery was moved into the citadel, two guns occupying the North-West angle, and one gun the South-East angle of the city, the remaining gun the South-West angle of the citadel, and the mortars being used as occasion required; and later on one gun being withdrawn from the North-West angle to the South-West angle of the city.

During the siege the guns were daily employed in keeping down the enemy's fire from Picquet Hill and other places, and the mortars performed useful service in shelling the surrounding villages and molesting parties of the enemy who attempted to throw up earth-works and establish batteries. Lieut. Bell-Irving had the honour of firing the first shot at Ayub Khan's force, on its arrival before Kandahar about six days after the battle of Maiwand, from his gun at the N.-W. angle of the city, and succeeded so effectually, though from a range of considerably over 4,000 yards, in harassing him, as to cause him to abandon his idea of encamping near Kandahar, and to retire to the neighbourhood of Kokoran. On the morning of the 16th Aug. the battery was employed in shelling the village of Deh Khwaja, and in covering the advance of the infantry during the disastrous sortie.

At the battle of Kandahar on the 1st Sept., 1880, the four 40-pounders took up a position at the base of the Picquet Hill at 8.30 a.m., being a portion of the force told off for the direct feint attack, and immediately went into action, opening fire on the enemy's guns in position on the Baba Wali Kotal. The battery was in action for nearly four hours, during which it expended 161 rounds, and materially assisted in silencing the enemy's fire.

On the 16th Oct., 1880, 5/11, R.A., left Kandahar for India, and reached Multan at the beginning of September. The high compliment was paid the battery of being selected to escort to India the guns, thirty in number, captured from Ayub Khan.

No. 6 BATTERY, 11TH BRIGADE, R.A.

As a unit of General Stewort's Division of the Army of Invasion, Battery 6/11, R.A., equipped with four 40-pounder B.L. guns and two 8-inch mortars, under the command of Major J. R. Tillard, arrived at Quetta on the 1st Jan., 1879, after an extremely laborious journey from Gwalior, from whence it had started on the 18th Oct., 1878. Halting for three days, it resumed its march on the 4th Jan., and on the 17th idem reached Kandahar, having previously undergone a highly satisfactory inspection at Deh-i-Haji.

On the departure of Generals Stewart and Biddulph's forces for Kalat-i-Ghilzai and Girishk, the battery took up its quarters in the citadel, and remained as part of the garrison of Kandahar until after the conclusion of the first campaign.

On the sudden concentration of the troops under General Stewart's command early in September, 1879, in consequence of the massacre of the British Embassy at Kabul, Battery 6/11, R.A., returned to Kandahar from Abdul Rahman, whither it had marched a few days previously. On the 23rd of the same month two guns accompanied Brigadier-General Hughes' Brigade in its advance on Kalat-i-Ghilzai, and, taking part in the reoccupation of that post, remained there till the return of the troops to Kandahar in the first week in November, when it rejoined the rest of the battery.

Selected, in March, 1880, to form part of the newly-constituted Ghazni Field Force, the battery was directed to exchange equipments with 5/11, R.A., and on the 30th of that month quitted Kandahar on the march towards Kabul. At the action of Ahmad Khel on the 19th April, 6/11, R.A., performed distinguished service, some well-directed shells from the two 40-pounders checking, at a critical juncture, the forward movement of the enemy's horsemen round the British left flank. During the affair at Arzu on the 23rd idem, the battery remained in camp, the protection of which was left by the General to Major Tillard.

On the 28th April, 6/11, R.A., was detached from the Ghazni Force to that under General Ross at Shekabad, with which it entered Kabul on the 2nd May. There it remained until the final evacuation of the capital by the British troops in August, 1880, when it commenced its return-march by the Khyber route to India. After suffering severely from the unhealthy climate of the country traversed, the battery recrossed the frontier on the 13th Sept., and made its way to Lucknow.

For movements of 8/11, R.A., see 13 and 16/8, R.A.

No. 10 BATTERY, 11TH BRIGADE, R.A.

In March, 1880, Battery 10/11, R.A., under the command of Major C. D. A. Straker, was ordered up from Delhi to Peshawar, and from thence to Kabul, where it arrived on the 5th April, and remained for a period of five weeks.

On the 10th May, 1880, the battery commenced its return march to India, and on the 27th idem arrived at Peshawar, where it remained doing duty as a portion of the District Force under the command of Brigadier-General Hankin until the conclusion of the campaign.

NO. 11 BATTERY, 11TH BRIGADE, R.A.

At the beginning of October, 1878, Battery 11/11, R.A., under the command of Major N. H. Harris, was warned for active service in Afghanistan, and marched from Jutogh where it was stationed, on the 7th of the same month, crossing the Indus at Mithankot, and proceeding towards Kandahar by the Dera Bughti route, through the Bolan Pass and by Quetta, overtaking General Biddulph's Column at Killa Abdula in the Pishin Valley, crossing the Khwaja range, and marching on to Kandahar, where it arrived, with the other units of the force, on the 8th Jan., 1879.

From Kandahar two divisions of the battery accompanied General Stewart to Kalat-i-Ghilzai, the remaining division being attached to the force under General Biddulph which marched to Girishk. Of the two former, one marched back by the Argandab Valley, and the other by the Arghesan Valley, on the return of the columns to Kandahar at the latter end of February, 1879.

During the summer of 1879 the battery was quartered at Kokaran, a few miles distant from Kandahar, on the Herat road. At this post it lost a promising young officer in the death, from typhoid fever, of Lieut. S. E. L. Lendrum, R.A.

At the latter end of August, 1879, arrangements were made for the return of the Kandahar force to India; but early in September, in consequence of the massacre of the British Embassy at Kabul, orders were received to stand fast. At the end of the same month the right half-battery formed part of the brigade under Brigadier-General Hughes which advanced on and reoccupied Kalat-i-Ghilzai. On the night of the 23rd Oct. two guns of the battery accompanied the force which was ordered out from Tazi, where the brigade was encamped, to disperse a hostile gathering of Ghilzais, under the leadership of Sahib Jan, and the following morning took part in the defeat of the enemy at Shah Jui. Early in November, head-quarters and four guns of the battery, with the rest of Brigadier-General Hughes' force, returned to Kandahar, where they were quartered throughout the succeeding winter, the remaining two guns being left behind with a small detachment at Kalat-i-Ghilzai.

At the end of March, 1880, 11/11, R.A., accompanied the force under Sir Donald Stewart in its advance from Kandahar towards Kabul, and was present both at the battle of Ahmad Khel on the 19th April, and the attach on the Arzu villages on the 23rd. Subsequently advancing with the other units of the force into the Logar Valley, the battery remained in that district till the succeeding July, when it proceeded to Kabul: there it remained till the evacuation of that city by the British troops in August, when it commenced its return march by the Khyber route to India, and arrived at Peshawar on the 9th Sept., 1880.

SERVICES IN AFGHANISTAN OF OFFICERS OF THE ROYAL ARTILLERY.

Lieut.-General Sir M. A. S. Biddulph, K.C.B. (For services see "Staff.")
Major-General J. E. Michell, C.B. (For services see "Staff.")
Major-General Sir C. G. Arbuthnot, K.C.B. (For services see "Staff.")
Brigadier-General C. R. O. Evans. (For services see "Staff.")
Colonel W. J. Williams, C.B. (For services see "Staff.")
Major-General W. French, C.B. (*retired*). (For services see "Staff.")
Colonel H. M. G. Purvis. (For services see "Staff.")
Colonel A. C. Johnson, C.B. (For services see "Staff.")
Colonel C. B. Le Mesurier. (For services see "Staff.")
Colonel W. Stirling, C.B., R.A., commanded F/A, R.H.A., in the Kuram Valley F.F., and was in command of the Horse Artillery of the Division, during the first campaign, being present at the assault and capture of the Peiwar Kotal. (Mentioned in despatches; C.B.)

Lieut.-Colonel E. P. Hill commanded D/A, R.H.A., throughout the period of its service in the first campaign.

Lieut.-Colonel C. W. Wilson commanded 13/9, R.A., throughout the period of its service in the war, being present at the capture of Ali Musjid. (Mentioned in despatches; Brevet of Lieut.-Colonel.)

Lieut.-Colonel N. H. Harris commanded 11/11, R.A., throughout the period of its service in the war, being present at the action of Shah-Jui, the battle of Ahmad Khel, and the attack on the Arzu villages. (Mentioned in despatches.)

Lieut.-Colonel Sir J. W. Campbell, Bt., commanded G/4, R.A., throughout the period of its service in the war, with the exception of three months in the winter of 1879-1880, during which the battery was at Kandahar. Was present at the battle of Ahmad Khel and the attack on the Arzu villages. (Mentioned in despatches; Brevet of Lieut.-Colonel.)

Lieut.-Colonel Æ. de V. Tupper commanded I/A, R.H.A., throughout the first campaign.

Lieut.-Colonel C. Collingwood commanded 5/11, R.A., from the commencement of the war till Oct., 1879.

Lieut.-Colonel G. A. Crawford commanded 14/9, R.A., throughout the period of its service in the war. (Mentioned in despatches.)

Lieut.-Colonel E. Staveley commanded D/2, R.A., throughout the period of its service in the war.

Major J. R. Dyce commanded 11/9, R.A., throughout the first campaign, being present at the capture of Ali Musjid and the affairs at Deh Sarak and Kam Daka. (Mentioned in despatches.) (Died at Landi Kotal of cholera, contracted while on field service, 14 July, 1879.)

Major E. S. Burnett commanded 13/8, R.A., throughout the period of its service in the war.

Major H. C. Lewes commanded I/1, R.A., throughout the period of its service in the war.

Bt. Lieut.-Colonel J. Haughton commanded 1/8, R.A., throughout the period of its service in the war, being present at the capture of Zawa. (Mentioned in despatches; Brevet of Lieut.-Colonel.)

Major W. H. Noble. (For services see "Staff.")

Bt. Lieut.-Colonel C. A. Gorham. (For services see "Staff.")

Lieut.-Colonel J. C. Smyth-Windham (*retired*) commanded F/A., R.H.A., throughout the second campaign, being present at the action of Charasiab, and the operations round Kabul in December, 1879, including the action of Killa Kazi. (Twice mentioned in despatches.)

Bt. Lieut.-Colonel the Hon. A. Stewart commanded I/C, R.H.A., from Feb., 1879, till the conclusion of the first, and throughout the period of its service in the second campaign, being present at the action of Futtehabad, and the affair at Kam Daka. (Mentioned in despatches; Brevet of Lieut.-Colonel.)

Major W. W. Murdoch commanded E/A, R.H.A., throughout the period it was employed in the war.

Bt. Lieut.-Colonel J. C. Auchinleck commanded C/4, R.A., throughout the period it was employed in the war, being present at the action of Ali Khel. (Mentioned in despatches; Brevet of Lieut.-Colonel.)

Major J. H. Blackley commanded 16/8, R.A., throughout the period of its service in the war.

Bt. Lieut.-Colonel S. Parry commanded G/3, R.A., throughout the first and during the second campaign till 3rd Nov., 1879, on appointment to R.H.A., and subsequently commanded D/A, R.H.A., throughout the period it was employed in the second campaign. Commanded the Artillery of Brigadier-General Cobbe's force at the assault and capture of the Peiwar Kotal, and the Artillery of the right attack at the action of Charasiab, and at the affair at Ali Boghan. (Twice mentioned in despatches; Brevet of Lieut.-Colonel.)

Bt. Lieut.-Colonel H. C. Magenis commanded C/3, R.A., throughout the first campaign, and in the second campaign till May, 1880. (Mentioned in despatches.)

Major P. F'G. Gallwey. (For services see "Staff.")

Major T. C. Martelli commanded E/4, R.A., throughout the period of its service in the war.

Major J. C. D'U. Murray served in the first campaign.

Major H. L. Gwyn commanded 12/9, R.A., throughout the period of its service in the war.

Bt. Lieut.-Colonel T. M. Hazlerigg commanded E/3, R.A., throughout both campaigns, being present at the capture of Ali Musjid. (Mentioned in despatches; Brevet of Lieut.-Colonel.)

Major G. W. C. Rothe. (For services see "Staff").

Major C. S. Harvey served with F/A, R.H.A., in the first campaign, being present at the assault and capture of the Peiwar Kotal. (Mentioned in despatches.)

Major C. Crosthwaite commanded H/1, R.A., throughout the second campaign.

Major J. M. Murray served with D/A, R.H.A., from March, 1879, till the conclusion of the first campaign.

Major J. M. Douglas served with I/A, R.H.A., throughout the first campaign, and commanded 11/9, R.A., throughout the second, including the march from Kabul to the relief of Kandahar, the reconnaissance of the 31st Aug., 1880, and the battle of Kandahar. (Mentioned in despatches.) (Died at Jutogh from the effects of illness contracted while on service in the field.)

RECORDS OF SERVICE.

Major J. L. Bell served with G/3, R.A., throughout the first campaign.

Major J. Younger served with H/C, R.H.A., throughout the period it was employed in the war.

Major G. M. B. Hornsby served with 5/11, R.A., as Captain, from the outbreak of the war till Dec., 1879, and commanded the battery from that date till the conclusion of hostilities, including the siege of Kandahar, the sortie to Deh Khwaja, and the battle of Kandahar. Marched with the battery to India in charge of the corpse of Brigadier-General Brooke, and of the Artillery captured from Ayub Khan. (Mentioned in despatches.)

Major J. W. Inge. (For services see "Staff.")

Major F. Galloway served in the first campaign. (Brevet of Major.)

Capt. J. A. Kelso. (Killed in action. See Biographical Division.)

Major R. McStewart. (For services see "Staff.")

Major J. F. Brough served with I/1, R.A, throughout the period it was employed in the war.

Capt. E. D. Shafto. (Deceased. See Biographical Division.)

Major A. Campbell served with A/B, R.H.A., from May, 1880, till the conclusion of the campaign.

Major A. H. J. Des Barres served in the first campaign

Bt. Major J. R. Slade, C.B., served first with D/A, R.H.A., from Jan. till March, 1879, taking part in the first Bazar Valley expedition; subsequently as Adjutant R.A., 1st Division Peshawar Valley F.F.; and eventually with E/B, R.H.A., throughout the period it was employed in the war, commanding the battery after the decease of Major Blackwood, and being present at the action of Girishk (in which he acted as Orderly Officer to Brigadier-General Burrows), the battle of Maiwand, the defence of Kandahar, and the battle of Kandahar. (Three times mentioned in despatches; Brevet Major, C.B.)

Bt. Major J. C. Robinson served with 6/8, R.A., throughout the period of its service in the war, taking part in the advance from Kabul to the relief of Kandahar, and being in command of the battery at the battle of Kandahar. (Mentioned in despatches.)

Bt. Major H. Pipon served with F/A, R.H.A., during the first and part of the second campaign, taking part in the advance on and occupation of Kandahar, and being present at the operations round Kabul and defence of Sherpur in Dec., 1879. Subsequently served as Adjutant, R.A., 1st Division Kabul F.F., and Kabul-Kandahar F.F., taking part, in that capacity, in the advance from Kabul to the relief of Kandahar, and being present at the battle of Kandahar. (Three times mentioned in despatches; Brevet of Major.)

Capt. J. Keith served with G/4, R.A., from the commencement of the war till Jan., 1879, when he was appointed Adjutant, R.A., Kandahar F.F.

Capt. R. A. Lanning. (For services see "Staff.")

Captain J. C. Robson. (Deceased. For services see "Staff.")

Capt. E. Wighton served with 16/8, R.A., throughout the period it was employed in the war.

Capt. G. T. Carré served with 1/8, R.A., throughout the period it was employed in the war, being present at the assault of Zawa. (Mentioned in despatches.)

Capt. C. E. Beadnell served with D/B, R.H.A., throughout the period it was employed in the war.

Capt. G. C. Bayly served with 13/8, R.A., throughout the period it was employed in the war.

Capt. H. Roberts served with 11/11, R.A., as 2nd in command, throughout the period it was employed in the war, being present at the battle of Ahmad Khel and the action of Arzu.

Capt. H. F. Smyth served during the first campaign in the Kuram Valley F.F., and subsequently in command of a Hazara battery in the 1st Division, Peshawar Valley F.F. Subsequently served with I/A, R.H.A., throughout the second campaign.

Bt. Major F. L. Graves served with 6/11, R.A., throughout the period it was employed in the war, commanding the battery during the return-march from Kabul to India. Took part in the advance from Kandahar to Kabul, and was present at the battle of Ahmad Khel. (Wounded by a fanatic; mentioned in despatches; Brevet of Major).

Bt. Major H. R. L. Morgan commanded No. 1 Mountain Battery, P.F.F., from 15 Dec., 1878, till 20 March, 1881, being present at the operations in the Khost district, including the action of Matun, commanding the Artillery in the actions with the Ghilzais, near the Shutargardan in Oct., 1879; the operations of General Baker's Brigade near Maidan in Nov., 1879; the operations of General Macpherson's Brigade, near Kabul, 10, 11, 12, 13, and 14 Dec., 1879; being present throughout the defence of Sherpur; and at the repulse and pursuit of the enemy, 23 Dec., 1879; and accompanying the expedition to Hissarak in April, 1880. (Several times mentioned in despatches; Brevet of Major.)

Bt. Major R. Corbett served with E/3, R.A., throughout the first and during part of the second campaign, being present at the capture of Ali Musjid; subsequently served with A/B., R.H.A., from March till May, 1880, being present at the battle of Ahmad Khel, in which he was dangerously wounded. (Mentioned in despatches; Brevet of Major.)

Capt. A. J. Pearson. (For services see "Staff.")

Capt. W. Taylor served with H/1, R.A., throughout the first, and during part of the second campaign.

Bt. Major R. Wace commanded No. 2 Bombay Mountain Battery from Dec., 1878, till Feb., 1881, being present at the action of Baghao. (Twice mentioned in despatches; Brevet of Major.)

Capt. W. Law. (For services see "Staff.")

Capt. C. H. Hamilton. (For services see "Staff.")

Capt. R. H. W. Plunkett served with C/4, R.A., throughout the second campaign.

Capt. B. F. Domvile served with L/5, R.A., in the second campaign, being present at the operations in the Mazina Valley. (Mentioned in despatches.)

Capt. C. B. Wickham. (For services see "Staff.")

Capt. E. Blaksley. (For services see "Staff.")

Capt. A. A. Newman served with 10/11, R.A., throughout the period of its service in the war.

Bt. Major A. Broadfoot served with 11/9, R.A., in the first campaign, being present at the capture of Ali Musjid, and taking part in both the expeditions into the Bazar Valley, in the first of which he commanded the battery. Left Jamrud to purchase mules for Government, 21 Feb., 1879. Was in temporary command of No. 2 Derajat Mountain Battery at commencement of second campaign. Appointed to command of the Gatling Battery 16 Sept., 1879, and was present with it at the action of Charasiab and on the Shah Darwaza, 8 and 9 Oct., 1879. Left Kabul 3 Nov., 1879, to take over command of No. 4 Hazara Mountain Battery, and commanded it till the conclusion of the campaign, taking part in numerous minor expeditions, and being present at the actions near Zaidabad, 25 and 26 April, 1880. (Twice mentioned in despatches; Brevet of Major.)

Bt. Lieut.-Colonel G. T. Pretyman. (For services see "Staff.")

Capt. P. K. L. Beaver served with G/4, R.A., from Jan., 1879, till March, 1880.

Capt. N. Powlett served with C/3, R.A., throughout the period it was employed in the war.

Capt. W. P. Graves served with 13/9, R.A., throughout the period it was employed in the war, being present at the capture of Ali Musjid. (Since deceased.)

Capt. A. Radford served with D/2, R.A., throughout the period it was employed in the war.

Capt. S. G. Smyth served with D/4, R.A., throughout the period it was employed in the war.

Capt. A. B. Stopford. (For services see "Staff.")

Capt. H. A. Rigg served with E/3, R.A., during the latter part of the second campaign.

Capt. A. E. Duthy served with 11/9, R.A., in both campaigns, taking part in numerous minor operations, accompanying the force under Sir F. Roberts from Kabul to the relief of Kandahar, and being present at the battle of Candahar. (Mentioned in despatches.)

Capt. C. M. H. Downing served with E/4, R.A., throughout the period it was employed in the war.

Capt. E. Walsh served with I/C, R.H.A., from the commencement of the war till promoted Captain in Feb., 1879, being present at the assault and capture of Ali Musjid.

Capt. W. W. Smith served with D/A, R.H.A., from the commencement of the war till February, 1879.

Capt. W. Aitken served with No. 3 Mountain Battery from the commencement of the war till promoted Captain shortly after the return of the reconnaissance to the Halmand.

Capt. C. H. Atchison served with F/A, R.H.A., in the first campaign, being present at the assault and capture of the Peiwar Kotal. (Mentioned in despatches.)

Capt. W. Riddell served with F/A, R.H.A., in the first campaign, being present at the assault and capture of the Peiwar Kotal.

Capt. F. H. G. Cruickshank. (For services see "Staff.")

Capt. W. W. M. Smith served with 13/8, R.A., throughout the period it was employed in the war.

Capt. F. A. Yorke served with H/C, R.H.A., during the earlier part of the first campaign.

Bt. Major W. G. Knox served during the first campaign with 13/9, R.A., and took part, as Orderly Officer to Col. Williams, C.B., Commdg. the Artillery 1st Division Peshawar Valley F.F., in the capture of Ali Musjid. Was subsequently appointed Adjutant of Artillery to the 1st Division, which appointment he held till promotion to Captain in Jan., 1879, removed him from Afghanistan to Zululand. (Mentioned in despatches.)

Capt. E. Buckle served in the first campaign with E/3, R.A., being present at the capture of Ali Musjid. In Jan., 1879, was transferred to 14/9, R.A., on promotion to Captain, and served with that battery throughout the period it was employed in the war. (Mentioned in despatches.)

Capt. F. C. Clarke served with C/4, R.A., in the first campaign. (Died at Kohat, 6 June, 1879.)

Capt. E. A. Johnson. (For services see "Staff.")

Capt. G. R. Hadaway. (For services see "Staff.")

Capt. P. Hussey served with C/4, R.A., during the first campaign.

Capt. H. T. Curling, commanded G/3, R.A., during the return of the battery to India at the end of the second campaign.

Capt. R. Purdy served with I/C, R.H.A., till June, 1879, being present at the capture of Ali Musjid and the action of Futtehabad. Joined G/3, R.A., at Kabul, and held temporary command of the battery from 3 Nov. till 3 Dec., 1879. Was present at the affairs round Kabul in Dec., 1879, including the assaults of the Takht-i-Shah and the Asmai Heights, and the action of the 23rd. (Mentioned in despatches.)

Capt. D. McK. D. Waterfield. (For services see "Staff.")

Bt. Major H. T. Lugard served as Lieutenant with 11/11, R.A., throughout the first and during part of the second campaign, being present at the action of Shah-Jui. Served as Captain with G/4, R.A., in the second campaign, being present at the battle of Ahmad Khel and the action of Arzu. Subsequently, from June to Oct., 1880, served as Adjutant, R.A., Kuram Valley Force. (Mentioned in despatches; Brevet of Major.)

Capt. J. Leach served with D/A, R.H.A., throughout the first campaign.

Capt. W. M. Campbell served with No. 2 Mountain Battery, P.F.F., in the second campaign. Was attached to No. 1 Mountain Battery during the operations round Kabul from 10th to 14th Dec., 1879. Commanded the Artillery in the S. W. Bastion throughout the defence of Sherpur. Was subsequently employed on special remount and recruiting duty for the Mountain batteries in Afghanistan. (Mentioned in despatches.)

Capt. C. H. H. Mayne served with A/B, R.H.A., from the commencement of the war till Dec., 1879, being present at the affair in the Mel Valley. (Mentioned in despatches.)

Capt. C. M. Western served with A/B, R.H.A., from the commencement of the war till Feb., 1879.

Capt. the Hon. W. C. Rowley. (For services see "Staff.")

Capt. W. L. Davidson served with 12/9, R.A., throughout the period of its service in the war.

Capt. C. C. Lindsay served with No 4 Mountain Battery, P.F.F., throughout the first campaign. (Mentioned in despatches.)

Capt. R. H. S. Baker served with I/A, R.H.A., throughout the first, and during the earlier part of the second campaign, and subsequently with 10/11, R.A., till the conclusion of the war.

Capt. R. G. W. Hepburne served with I/C, R.H.A., throughout the first campaign, being present at the capture of Ali Musjid, and the action of Futtehabad.

Capt. H. T. H. Repton served with 8/11, R.A., throughout the period it was employed in the war, and with G/4, R.A., during the latter part of the second campaign.

Capt. G. D. Fanshawe served with C/3, R.A., throughout the first campaign.

Capt. H. N. Jervois served with No. 1 Mountain Battery, P.F.F., throughout both campaigns, being present at the assault and capture of the Peiwar Kotal (in command of the battery after the death of Capt. Kelso), the affair in the Sapari Pass, and the action of Matun, commanding a division of the battery in the Kuram Valley in the second campaign, and taking part in the Zaimusht expedition. (Mentioned in despatches.)

Capt. E. F. Wodehouse served with 13/9, R.A., throughout the first campaign, being present at the capture of Ali Musjid, and with I/C, R.H.A., throughout the period it was employed in the second campaign, being present at the action on the Gara Heights near Kam Daka. (Mentioned in despatches.)

Capt. E. C. Trollope served with H/C, R.H.A., throughout the period it was employed in the war.

Capt. G. G. Monck-Mason served with D/A, R.H.A., from the commencement of the war till Jan., 1879.

Capt. F. J. W. Eustace. (For services see "Staff.")

Capt. E. B. Coke. (For services see "Staff.")

Capt. C. J. Long served with I/A, R.H.A., throughout the period it was employed in the war.

Capt. J. J. Swinton. (For services see "Staff.")

Capt. N. P. Fowell served with E/B, R.H.A., in the second campaign, being present at the action of Girishk, the battle of Maiwand, in which he was dangerously wounded, and the defence of Kandahar. (Mentioned in despatches.)

Capt. H. W. Brackenburg served in the Kuram Valley during the first campaign, and with F/A, R.H.A., during the second.

Capt. R. W. P. Robertson served with No. 2 Bombay Mountain Battery in both campaigns, being present at the action of Baghao. (Mentioned in despatches.)

Capt. H. V. Hunt served with H/C, R.H.A., throughout the period of its service in the war.

Capt. D. C. Dean-Pitt. (For services see "Staff.")

Capt. R. A. C. King served with No. 3 Mountain Battery, P.F.F., during the latter part of the time it was employed in the war, taking part in the operations in the Pishin Valley.

Capt. G. R. Challenor served with D/2, R.A., throughout the first campaign.

Capt. E. C. Wace served with No. 4 Mountain Battery throughout the period it was employed in the war, being in temporary command of it from the 18th July to the 23rd Sept., 1879, and from the 29th Oct. to the 7th Nov., 1879, and taking part in the operations in the Lughman Valley. (Mentioned in despatches.)

Capt. F. W. Campbell served with I/A, R.H.A., during the latter part of the second campaign.

Capt. E. M. Baker served with 6/8, R.A., from the Spring of 1880, till the conclusion of the war, taking part in the advance from Kabul to the relief of Kandahar, and being present at the battle of Kandahar.

Capt. W. S. Walford served with C/4, R.A., throughout the first campaign.

Capt. M. W. Saunders served with I/A, R.H.A., during the early part of the first and throughout the second campaign.

Capt. W. H. Suart served with D/B, R.H.A., throughout the period it was employed in the war.

Capt. E. M. Flint served with E/A, R.H.A., throughout the period it was employed in the war.

Capt. P. F. P. Hamilton served with A/B, R.H.A., throughout both campaigns, being present at the affair in the Mel Valley, the battle of Ahmad Khel, and the action of Arzu. (Mentioned in despatches.)

Lieut. H. Maclaine. (Deceased. See Biographical Division.)

Capt. H. P. Willoughby. (For services see "Staff.")

Capt. J. D. Kirwan served with D/B, R.H.A., throughout the period it was employed in the war.

Capt. J. H. Wodehouse served with F/A, R.H.A., throughout the second campaign, being present at the action of Charasiab, and the operations round Kabul in December, 1879. (Mentioned in despatches.)

Capt. F. Beaufort served with A/B, R.H.A., from Feb., 1880, till the return of the battery to India at the latter end of the second campaign, being present at the battle of Ahmad Khel and the action of Arzu.

Capt. J. W. Murray. (For services see "Staff.")

Capt. A. F. Liddell served with 6/8, R.A., in the advance to Kabul, and remained with the battery, taking part, in the operations in which it was employed, till appointed to the Horse Artillery in May, 1880. (Twice mentioned in despatches.)

Capt. A. Mansel served with D/4, R.A., throughout the period it was employed in the war.

Capt. A. H. Hewat served with D/A, R.H.A., throughout the period it was employed in the second campaign, being present in command of the two guns, at the affair at Ali Boghan. (Mentioned in despatches.)

Capt. H. G. Weir served with D/A, R.H.A., from Feb., 1879, till the conclusion of the first campaign.

Capt. H. J. Lyster served with No. 3 Mountain Battery, P.F.F., in the first campaign, taking part in the reconnaisance to the Halmand and the return to India by the Thal-Chotiali route. Served with No. 2 Mountain Battery in the second campaign, taking part in the advance from Kabul to the relief of Kandahar, and the battle of Kandahar.

Lieut. F. M. Goold-Adams served in the first campaign with 13/9, R.A., and throughout the second campaign with A/B, R.H.A., being present at the battle of Ahmad Khel and the action of Arzu.

Lieut. P. Saltmarshe served with 5/11, R.A., from the commencement of the war till April, 1879, and from that date till Aug., 1879, as Commissary of Ordnance at Kandahar.

Lieut. J. W. Hawkins served with D/A, R.H.A., from April, 1879, till the conclusion of the first campaign, and throughout the period the battery was employed in the second campaign.

Lieut. F. M. Bland served with H/1, R.A., in the first camgaign.

Lieut. E. H. Pickwoad served with D/2, R.A., throughout the period it was employed in the war.

Lieut. A. D. Addison served during the first campaign with 8/11, R.A., and during the second campaign, from Oct., 1879, till June, 1880, with 11/11, R.A., being present at the battle of Ahmad Khel and the action of Arzu.

Lieut. O. S. Smyth served with 11/9, R.A., throughout the first and during the second campaign, being present at the capture of Ali Musjid, and taking part in the expedition into the Bazar Valley, and numerous minor operations. (Mentioned in despatches.)

Lieut. A. H. C. Phillpotts served with D/B, R.H.A., throughout the period it was employed in the war.

Lieut. E. Vaughan-Hughes served with F/A, R.H.A., in the second campaign, being present at the operations round Kabul in December, 1879.

Lieut. T. S. Lett served with C/3, R.A., throughout the period of its service in the war. (Since deceased.)

Lieut. E. Gunner served with G/3, R.A., throughout both campaigns, being present at the action of Charasiab, and the operations round Kabul in December, 1879, including the assaults of the Takht-i-Shah and the Asmai Heights, and the action of the 23rd.

Lieut. E. Hardy. (Killed in action. See Biographical Division.)

Lieut. G. W. R. Howard-Vyse served with I/1, R.A., throughout the period it was employed in the war.

RECORDS OF SERVICE.

Lieut. I. D. Wright. (Killed in action. See Biographical Division.)

Lieut. H. R. Ross. (Deceased. See Biographical Division.)

Lieut. J. C. Shirres served with No. 1 Mountain Battery, P.F.F., throughout both campaigns, being present at the assault and capture of the Peiwar Kotal, the forcing of the Sapari Pass, the action of Matun, the repulse of the enemy at the Shutargardan, in Oct., 1879, the operations round Kabul and defence of Sherpur, Dec., 1879, and the operations in Hissarak, April, 1880. (Mentioned in despatches.)

Lieut. H. V. Cowan served with G/3, R.A., from the commencement of the war till the 1st Aug., 1879, being present at the assault and capture of the Peiwar Kotal. Was Acting Adjutant, R.A., Kuram Force, from 1st Aug. till end of Sep., 1879, when he rejoined G/3, R.A., and served with it till May, 1880, being present at the action of Charasiab and in the operations round Kabul in Dec., 1879, including the assault of the Asmai Heights. From May till Sept., 1880, served as Orderly Officer, and subsequently as Aide-de-Camp to Major-General Hills.

Lieut. S. D. Rainsford served with E/3, R.A., throughout both campaigns, being present at the capture of Ali Musjid.

Lieut. F. L. Cunliffe served with I/1, R.A., throughout the period it was employed in the war.

Lieut. J. W. M. Newton served in the second campaign, being present at the assault of Zawa. (Mentioned in despatches.)

Lieut. C. M. Haggard served with G/3, R.A., throughout the first and during the second campaign till appointed to R.H.A., 3rd. Nov., 1879, being present at the assault and capture of the Peiwar Kotal, and the action of Charasiab.

Lieut. E. G. Osborne. (Killed in action. See Biographical Division.)

Lieut. T. H. J. Woodrow served with 13/8, R.A., throughout the period it was employed in the war, commanding the guns in the advance of the Siege Train to Quetta.

Lieut. D. E. Dewar served with 6/8, R.A., in the advance from Peshawar to Kabul, from whence he was shortly afterwards invalided.

Lieut. A. C. Bailward served with No. 1 Mountain Battery, P.F.F., from 5 May till July, 1879, taking part in various reconnaissances. While *en route* to rejoin that battery in Oct., 1879, was present at the repulse of the enemy's attack on the camp at Ali Khel. During defence of Sherpur had charge of some heavy and other guns mounted on the defences. Left Kabul 5 Jan., 1880, to return to England on sick leave.

Lieut. A. Keene served with No. 2 Bombay Mountain Battery throughout the period it was employed in the war. (Mentioned in despatches.)

Lieut. W. A. Plant served with E/B., R.H.A., in the second campaign. Was Adjutant, R.A., Southern Afghanistan F.F., from March, 1880, until invalided the same year. Commanded gun at S.E. Bastion during siege of Kandahar and sortie to Deh Khwaja. (Mentioned in despatches.)

Lieut. E. A. Smith served with No 2 Mountain Battery, P.F.F., throughout both campaigns, taking part in the operations in the Khost Valley, including the action of Matun, the operations round Kabul and defence of Sherpur, Dec., 1879, the advance from Kabul to the relief of Kandahar, and the battle of Kandahar. (Mentioned in despatches.)

Lieut. E. C. F. Holland. (For services see "Staff.")

Lieut. G. S. Jones. (For services see "Staff.")

Lieut. C. V. B. Kuper served with 8/11, R.A., throughout the period it was employed in the war.

Lieut. C. A. Montanaro. (Died of wounds received in action. See Biographical Division.)

Lieut. T. F. T. Fowle served with 5/11, R.A., throughout both campaigns, with the exception of four weeks in July, 1880, during which period he acted as Commissary of Ordnance with the force under Brigadier-General Burrows in the expedition to Girishk. Was present at the battle of Maiwand (during which he was attached for duty with the Wali's smooth-bore guns), throughout the defence of Kandahar, and at the battle of Kandahar. (Mentioned in despatches.)

Lieut. B. Duff served with the Ordnance Field Park, Kandahar F.F., in the second campaign.

Lieut. S. M. Rogers served with 11/11, R.A., throughout the period it was employed in the war, being present at the battle of Ahmad Khel and the action of Arzu.

Lieut. R. Wynyard served with H/1, R.A., in the first campaign.

Lieut. E. W. Fleming served with 13/9, R.A., throughout the period it was employed in the war.

Lieut. A. Bell-Irving served throughout both campaigns with 5/11, R.A., and the Horse Artillery, being present throughout the defence of Kandahar, and at the battle of Kandahar. (Mentioned in despatches.)

Lieut. T. V. W. Phillips served with 1/8, R.A., till early in 1880, when he was invalided to England.

Lieut. R. E. Boothby served with C/4, R.A., from the latter end of the first campaign till the conclusion of the second.

Lieut. R. A. Bannatine. (For services see "Staff.")

Lieut. Sir G. V. Thomas, Bt., served with G/4, R.A., from the commencement of the war till Nov., 1879, when he was invalided to India from Kandahar.

Lieut. J. W. Dunlop served with 1/8, R.A., in the second campaign, being present at the assault of Zawa. Was Acting Adjutant to the Artillery of the Kuram Force from Nov., 1879, till June, 1880. Rejoined his battery, L/5, R.A., at Pesh Bolak in July, 1880, and served with it till the conclusion of the campaign.

Lieut. G. F. A. Norton served with 16/8, R.A., throughout the period it was employed in the war.

Lieut. R. L. Haines served with C/4, R.A., throughout the period it was employed in the war.

Lieut. W. S. Churchward served with 13/9, R.A., throughout the period of its service in the war, being present at the capture of Ali Musjid. Subsequently served with 6/11, R.A., taking part in the advance from Kandahar to Kabul, and being present at the battle of Ahmad Khel. (Mentioned in despatches.)

Lieut. C. E. Walker served with 11/9, R.A., in both campaigns, being present at the capture of Ali Musjid, and taking part in numerous expeditions and minor operations. (Mentioned in despatches.)

Lieut. P. L. Williams served with E/4, R.A., throughout the period it was employed in the war.

Lieut. W. A. Smith served with No. 2 Bombay Mountain Battery in the second campaign.

Lieut. R. E. L. Dacres. (Deceased. See Biographical Division.)

Lieut. E. A. Lambart served with G/4, R.A., throughout the period it was employed in the war, being in command of the two guns of the battery at Kalat-i-Ghilzai from Nov., 1879, till April, 1880, and being present at the battle of Ahmad Khel and the action of Arzu.

Lieut. F. B. Elmslie. (For services see "Staff.")

Lieut. N. B. Inglefield served with I/1, R.A., throughout the period it was employed in the war.

Lieut. H. S. Hudson served with H/1, R.A., during part of the time it was employed in the war.

Lieut. F. R. Thackeray served with No. 1 Mountain Battery, P.F.F., in the second campaign, being present throughout the operations in Hissarak in April, 1880, and commanding a division of the battery in the expeditions to Besud and Kama.

Lieut. C. A. Anderson served with 13/9, R.A., throughout the first campaign, being present at the capture of Ali Musjid. Served with the Hazara Mountain Battery throughout the second campaign, commanding two guns during the fighting about Jagdalak in Dec., 1879, and in the Lughman Valley expedition. (Three times mentioned in despatches.)

Lieut. A. E. Hay served with 6/11, R.A., from the commencement of the war till the Spring of 1880, being present at the battle of Ahmad Khel. Subsequently served with 6/8, R.A., till the conclusion of the war, taking part in the advance to the relief of Kandahar, and being present at the battle of Kandahar.

Lieut. F. G. Stone served with 5/11, R.A., from the outbreak of the war till Oct., 1879.

Lieut. J. R. K. L. Heyland served with F/2, R.A., throughout the period it was employed in the war.

Lieut. S. E. L. Lendrum. (Deceased. See Biographical Division.)

Lieut. L. C. M. Blacker served with 6/11, R.A., throughout the first and during the early part of the second campaign.

Lieut. G. G. Simpson served with L/5, R.A., throughout the period it was employed in the war.

Lieut. H. M. Sandbach served with No. 4 Mountain Battery, P.F.F., from the 1st May, 1879, till the conclusion of the war, being present at the action of Shekabad. (Mentioned in despatches.)

Lieut. W. C. Pollard (S.C.) served with E/4, R.A., throughout the period it was employed in the war.

Lieut. J. J. Porteous served with L/5, R.A., throughout the period it was employed in the war.

Lieut. H. V. Willis. (Assassinated. See Biographical Division.)

Lieut. H. G. Pelly served with H/1, R.A., during the latter part of the first, and throughout the second campaign.

Lieut. J. S. Minter served with No. 2 Bombay Mountain Battery in the second campaign, being present at the affair at Baghao. Was Station Staff Officer at Chaman from 22 July till 27 Aug., 1880. Commanded two guns with the column co-operating in the Marri expedition.

Lieut. C. P. Triscott served with No. 2 Mountain Battery in the second campaign, taking part in the advance from Kabul to the relief of Kandahar.

Lieut. R. T. Roberts served with 1/8, R.A., from May, 1880, till the conclusion of the campaign.

Lieut. F. E. Allsopp served during the war from April, 1879, till May, 1880, part of the time with No. 2 Mountain Battery, and part of the time as Adjutant, R.A., Kabul F.F., being present at the action of Charasiab, and taking part in the operations round Kabul and the defence of Sherpur in Dec., 1879. (Mentioned in despatches.)

Lieut. J. W. B. Meade served with 11/11, R.A., from Jan., 1880, till the return of the battery to India, being present at the battle of Ahmad Khel and the action of Arzu.

Lieut. E. W. Briscoe served with E/4, R.A., during the latter part of the period it was employed in the war.

Lieut. H. M. Slater served with G/4, R.A., from Nov., 1879, till the return of the battery to India, being present at the battle of Ahmad Khel and action of Arzu.

Lieut. H. J. Baly served with C/2, R.A., during the early part of the time it was employed in the war.

Lieut. C. T. Robinson served with C/3, R.A., throughout the period it was employed in the war.

Lieut. E. B. Anderson served with 16/8, R.A., throughout the period it was employed in the war.

Lieut. W. J. A. Beatson served with D/4, R.A., throughout the period it was employed in the war.

Lieut. W. J. Honner served with No. 1 Mountain Battery, P.F.F., from June, 1880, until the conclusion of the war.

Lieut. C. C. Townsend served with 12/9, R.A., in the 2nd Division Kabul F.F. till invalided.

Lieut. W. H. S. Earle crossed the frontier 1st Oct., 1879, and was present at the affair at Ali Khel on the 14th idem. Served with G/3, R.A., from the 1st Nov., 1879, till the conclusion of the campaign, being present in the operations round Kabul in Dec., 1879, including the assault of the Takht-i-Shah and the action of the 23rd.

Lieut. H. A. Carleton served with 6/11, R.A., throughout the first campaign, and with H/1, R.A., in the second, taking part successively in the advance of each battery to Kandahar.

Lieut. F. B. Jackson served with 1/8, R.A., throughout the period it was employed in the war, being present at the assault of Zawa.

Lieut. E. H. S. Calder served with 14/9, R.A., and with No. 2 Bombay Mountain Battery in the second campaign.

Lieut. E. A. Fanshawe served with C/4, R.A., throughout the period it was employed in the war.

Lieut. C. E. Callwell served with the Peshawar Heavy Battery in the second campaign, and brought a convoy of the captured guus from Kabul to India.

Lieut. W. St. P. Bunbury served with D/2, R.A., throughout the period it was employed in the war, and subsequently with F/2, R.A., in the advance to the relief of Kandahar.

Lieut. F. H. J. Birch served with D/4, R.A., throughout the period it was employed in the war. (Mentioned in despatches.)

Lieut. H. H. Rogers served with 1/8, R.A., from the beginning of 1880 till the conclusion of the war.

Lieut. C. B. Watkins served with G/4, R.A., throughout the period it was employed in the war, being present at the battle of Ahmad Khel and the action of Arzu.

Lieut. E. J. Granet served with C/3, R.A., throughout the second campaign.

Lieut. G. V. Kemball served with E/3, R.A., in the second campaign.

Lieut. H. K. Jackson served with D/2, R.A., in the second campaign.

Lieut. H. A. Inglis served with 6/8, R.A., throughout the period of its service in the war, being present at the affairs at Zaidabad, taking part in the advance from Kabul to the relief of Kandahar, and being present at the battle of Kandahar.

Lieut. G. B. Smith served with C/2, R.A., throughout the period it was employed in the war, taking part in the defence of Kandahar, and being present at the battle of Kandahar. (Mentioned in despatches.)

Lieut. N. S. Ogilvie served with 14/9, R.A., throughout the period it was employed in the war.

Lieut. H. L. Gardiner, served with C/2, R.A., throughout the period it was employed in the war, taking part in the defence of Kandahar, and being present at the battle of Kandahar. (Mentioned in despatches.)

Lieut. F. E. Cowper-Smith served with 11/9, R.A., in the second campaign. (Died at Safed Sang, 26 July, 1880, from illness contracted while on field service.)

Lieut. H. E. F. Goold-Adams served with 10/11, R.A., during the earlier part of the time it was employed in the war.

Lieut. G. L. W. Grierson served with F/2, R.A., throughout the period it was employed in the war.

Lieut. C. G. Neish served with 12/9, R.A., throughout the period it was employed in the war.

Lieut. A. M. C. Dale served with 1/8, R.A., from May, 1880, till the conclusion of the war.

Lieut. G. S. Mellish served with 12/9, R.A., during the latter part of the time it was employed in the war.

LATE BENGAL.

Lieut.-General (local) Sir F. S. Roberts, Bt., G.C.B., C.I.E., V.C. (For services see "Staff.")
Major-General Sir J. Hills, K.C.B., V.C. (For services see "Staff.")
Major-General A. H. Lindsay, C.B. (retired). (For services see "Staff.")

Colonel E. J. Bruce. (For services see "Staff.")

Bt. Colonel T. P. Smith. (For services see "Staff")

Lieut.-Colonel G. R. Manderson, C.B., commanded I/C, R.H.A., from the commencement of the war till Feb., 1879, being present at the assault and capture of Ali Musjid. (Mentioned in despatches; C.B.)

Lieut-Colonel D. MacFarlan commanded A/B, R.H.A., from the commencement of the war till the 27th Feb., 1879.

Colonel F. V. Eyre (retired). (For services see "Staff.")

Lieut.-Colonel C. E. Nairne commanded H/C, R.H.A., throughout the period it was employed in the war.

Bt. Lieut.-Colonel W. R. Craster commanded G/3 R.A., from the 3rd Dec., 1879, in the second campaign, being present in the operations round Kabul in Dec., 1879, including the storming of the Takht-i-Shah and the Asmai Heights, and the action of the 23rd. (Mentioned in despatches; Brevet of Lieut.-Colonel.)

Bt. Lieut.-Colonel H. de G. Warter commanded A/B, R.H.A., from April, 1879, till the return of the battery to India at the latter end of the second campaign, being present at the battle of Ahmed Khel and the action of Arzu. (Mentioned in despatches; Brevet of Lieut.-Colonel.)

Major F. W. Ward commanded D/B, R.H.A., throughout the period of its service in the war. (Mentioned in despatches.)

Major G. F. Blackwood. (Killed in action. See Biographical Division.)

Major M. W. Ommanney commanded I/A, R.H.A., throughout the second campaign.

Bt. Lieut.-Colonel J. A. Tillard commanded 6/11, R.A., from the commencement of the war till appointed to the Horse Artillery in Aug., 1880, taking part in the advance from Kandahar to Kabul, being present at the battle of Ahmad Khel, and commanding the camp during the action of Arzu. Accompanied Sir F. Roberts' force from Kabul to the relief of Kandahar, and on arrival took over the command of E/B, R.H.A., which battery he commanded at the battle of Kandahar. (Three times mentioned in despatches; Brevet of Lieut.-Colonel.)

Major H. H. Murray commanded 8/11, R.A., throughout the period of its service in the war.

Major J. H. Alexander commanded C/B, R.A., from May, 1880, to the conclusion of the campaign.

Major S. Cargill. (For services see "Staff.")

Major J. Charles commanded No. 3 Mountain Battery, P.F.F., throughout the period of its service in the war.

Bt. Colonel E. F. Chapman, C.B., A.D.C. (For services see "Staff.")

Bt. Lieut.-Colonel T. Graham commanded 6/8, R.A., throughout the period of its service in the war, taking part in the advance from Kabul to the relief of Kandahar, but being debarred by severe illness from being present at the battle of Kandahar. Commanded the R.A. with Genl. Ross's force from the 16th to the 27th April, 1880, and with Genl. Baker's force from the 8th to the 29th May, 1880. (Mentioned in despatches; Brevet of Lieut.-Colonel.)

Bt. Lieut.-Colonel C. Cowie. (For services see "Staff.")

Major J. R. J. Dewar commanded F/2, R.A., throughout the period of its service in the war. (Mentioned in despatches.)

Major J. F. Free commanded D/4, R.A., throughout the period of its service in the war.

Major J. A. S. Colquhoun. (For services see "Staff.")

Major S. E. Pemberton. (For services see "Staff.")

Major R. W. Smith served with I/C, R.H.A., throughout the period it was employed in the war, being present at the assault and capture of Ali Musjid, and the action on the Gara Heights near Kam Daka. (Mentioned in despatches.)

Bt. Major R. G. S. Marshall served with A/B, R.H.A., from Oct., 1878, till Dec., 1879, being present at the affair in the Mel Valley. (Mentioned in despatches; Brevet of Major.)

Capt. H. S. Higginson served with G/4, R.A., during the latter part of the second campaign.

Bt. Major E. J. de Lautour commanded No. 4 Mountain Battery, P.F.F., from the commencement of the war till June, 1879, being present in the flank march at the taking of Ali Musjid, and being specially employed in the reconnaissances in the Mohmand and Lughman countries. (Mentioned in despatches; Brevet of Major.)

Capt. A. D. Wintle. (For services see "Staff.")

Capt. A. D. Anderson. (For services see "Staff.")

Capt. F. P. W. Freeman served with D/A, R.H.A., throughout the period it was employed in the second campaign.

Bt. Lieut.-Colonel G. Swinley commanded No. 2 Mountain Battery, P.F.F., throughout both campaigns, being present in the operations in the Khost Valley, including the action of Matun, the action of Charasiab, the operations round Kabul, and defence of Sherpur, Dec., 1879, the march from Kabul to the relief of Kandahar, and the battle of Kandahar. (Six times mentioned in despatches; Brevet of Major and of Lieut.-Colonel.)

LATE MADRAS.

Colonel A. H. Dawson. (For services see "Staff.")
Colonel A. R. Gloag. (For services see "Staff.")
Bt. Colonel B. L. Gordon, C.B. (For services see "Staff.")
Bt. Colonel H. McLeod. (For services see "Staff.")
Major H. F. Pritchard commanded H/1, R.A., during the first campaign.
Lieut.-Colonel H. S. Visct. Guillamore (*retired*), commanded H/1, R.A., during the latter part of the first campaign.
Major C. D. A. Straker commanded 10/11, R.A., throughout the period of its service in the war.
Major W. R. C. Brough commanded L/5, R.A., throughout the period it was employed in the war, being present at the operations in the Mazina Valley. (Mentioned in despatches.)

LATE BOMBAY.

Major P. H. Greig commanded C/2, R.A., throughout the period it was employed in the war, taking part in the defence of Kandahar, and being present at the battle of Kandahar. (Twice mentioned in despatches.)
Bt. Lt.-Colonel F. J. Caldecott. (For services see "Staff.")

ROYAL ENGINEERS.

BENGAL, MADRAS, AND BOMBAY SAPPERS AND MINERS.

Major B. Blood served as Field Engineer and commanded the Bengal Sappers and Miners in the Khyber Line Force from Jan., 1880, till the return of the troops to India.

Bt. Lt.-Colonel W. North commanded the Bengal Sappers and Miners throughout the first campaign, being present at the assault and capture of Ali Musjid, the forcing of the Khyber Pass, and various subsequent minor operations. Served throughout the second campaign, first as Adjutant Bengal Sappers and Miners with Khyber Line Force, then as commanding R.E. with Genl. C. Gough's brigade during the fighting at Jagdalak and advance to relief of Kabul in Dec., 1879, finally in command of Bengal Sappers in 2nd Division, Kabul F.F., until the conclusion of the campaign, acting as commanding R.E. with Sir J. Ross's force in operations about Wardak and Shekabad in April, 1880. (Mentioned in despatches; Brevet of Major and of Lt.-Colonel.)

Bt. Major L. F. Brown commanded No. 10 Company Bengal Sappers and Miners in both campaigns, taking part in the advance on Kandahar and the Halmand, and the advance from Kandahar to Kabul, being present at the battle of Ahmad Khel, and eventually returning to India by the Khyber route. (Mentioned in despatches; Brevet of Major.)

Capt. W. W. B. Whiteford commanded Nos. 2 and 5 Companies Bombay Sappers and Miners, being the Engineer force of the Reserve Division in the Bolan, from Jan. till Nov., 1879; employed on Kandahar State Railway, Nov., 1879, till July, 1880; as Adjutant R.E. 2nd Division S. Afghanistan F.F., July till Oct., 1880, accompanying General Phayre to Kandahar; and on Kandahar State Railway from Oct., 1880. (Mentioned in despatches, and recommended for a Brevet Majority.)

Capt. C. C. Rawson commanded K Company Madras Sappers and Miners during the first campaign, in the 2nd Division Peshawar Valley F.F. till the 18th March, 1879, and in the 1st Division Peshawar Valley F.F. till the return of the troops to India, being employed on various sections of the Khyber line, and at various posts extending from Landi Kotal to Gandamak. Was present with the reserve in camp during the action of Futtehabad.

Capt. A. R. F. Dorward commanded C Company Madras Sappers and Miners in the Khyber Division during the second campaign, being employed at Landi Kotal, Ali Boghan, and other posts on the line in constructing protective works, roads, bridges, &c. Took part with General Doran's Column in the operations in the neighbourhood of Kam Daka in Jan., 1880.

Capt. H. Dove commanded 3rd Company Bengal Sappers and Miners throughout the war, being employed during the first campaign on various sections of the Khyber line extending to Gandamak, and during the second campaign on sections extending to Kabul. Was present at the skirmishing at Jagdalak Kotal and the defence of that post in Dec., 1879. Accompanied General Ross's expedition to Zaidabad in April, 1880, and was variously employed in the Bala Hissar, Kabul, till the retirement in Aug., 1880.

Capt. P. Haslett commanded 4th Company Bengal Sappers and Miners, to which was attached a Field Telegraph Train, in General Stewart's Division, throughout the war, being employed on various duties on nearly every section of the routes followed by that force. Took part, during the first campaign, in the advance on Kandahar and Kalat-i-Ghilzai, and was present at the action of Takht-i-pul. During the second campaign proceeded on duty a second time to Kalat-i-Ghilzai; marched with Sir D. Stewart's force from Kandahar to Kabul, being present at the battle of Ahmad Khel, and returned, in Aug., 1880, by the Khyber route to India. (Mentioned in despatches.)

Lieut. M. Martin served with 4th Company Bengal Sappers and Miners, in the force under Sir Donald Stewart's command during the second campaign, taking part in the advance from Kandahar to Kabul, being present at the battle of Kandahar, and eventually returning to India by the Khyber route.

Lieut. C. B. Henderson served with I Company Madras Sappers and Miners, in the Khyber Division, during the second campaign, being employed in constructing a bridge over the Kabul River, improving the defences of Fort Sale, cutting a pathway over the Siah Koh range, &c. Took part in the Lughman Valley expedition in Jan., 1880.

Lieut. L. Langley served with C Company Madras Sappers and Miners, in the Khyber Division, during the second campaign, being employed at Landi Kotal, Ali Boghan, and other posts on the line in constructing protective works, roads, &c.

Lieut. S. H. Exham served as Adjutant, Bengal Sappers and Miners, on the Khyber line, throughout the first campaign.

Lieut. E. Glennie served throughout the first campaign in the 1st Division Peshawar Valley F.F., with the Bengal Sappers and Miners, being present at the assault and capture of Ali Musjid. Served from May, 1880, till the conclusion of the war as Asst. Field Engineer with the force under Sir F. Roberts, taking part in the advance from Kabul to the relief of Kandahar, and being present at the battle of Kandahar. (Mentioned in despatches.)

Lieut. H. P. Leach commanded No. 8 Company Bengal Sappers and Miners, in the Peshawar Valley F.F. during the first campaign, and in the Kuram Valley force throughout the second campaign, taking part in the Bazar Valley expedition, and being present at the action of Deh Sarak and the assault of Zawa. (Mentioned in despatches.)

Lieut. E. S. Hill commanded No. 5 Company Bengal Sappers and Miners, in General Biddulph's Column, during the first campaign, taking part in the advance on Kandahar and to the Halmand, and the return to India by the Thal-Chotiali route. Commanded the same Company in the Khyber and Kabul Field Forces during the second campaign, taking part in the advance of Brigadier-General C. Gough's brigade to Kabul.

Lieut. J. C. L. Campbell commanded No. 2 Company Bengal Sappers and Miners, and acted as Asst. Field Engineer throughout both the campaigns in Northern Afghanistan, being present at the assault and capture of Ali Musjid, and the fighting about Jagdalak in Dec., 1879, including the repulse of the attack on the Jagdalak Kotal Fort.

Lieut. G. H. W. O'Sullivan served in command of No. 2 Company Bombay Sappers and Miners, and as Asst. Field Engineer from the commencement of the war till Aug., 1880, being employed in road-making from Sibi up the Nari Valley from Dec., 1879, till June, 1880. Was subsequently invalided to Quetta with typhoid fever, but rejoined his company in Sept., and served with it at Kandahar till the 27th Nov., 1880.

Lieut. R. E. Hamilton served with the Madras Sappers and Miners in the first campaign in the 2nd Division Peshawar Valley F.F. till the 18th March, 1879, and in the 1st Division Peshawar Valley F.F. till the return of the troops to India, being employed on various sections of the Khyber line, and at various posts, extending from Landi Kotal to Gandamak. Was present with the reserve in camp during the action of Futtehabad.

Lieut. J. B. Sharpe commanded a company of Bengal Sappers and Miners from the commencement of the war till Sept., 1879, taking part in the advance of General Biddulph's division on Kandahar and to the Halmand, and being variously employed on the lines of communication, and in building quarters in the Kandahar district.

Lieut. T. Digby served with I Company Madras Sappers and Miners in the Khyber Division during the second campaign, being employed in constructing a bridge over the Kabul River, improving the defences of Fort Sale, cutting a pathway over the Siah Koh range, &c. Took part in the Lughman Valley expedition in Jan., 1880.

Lieut. M. C. Barton commanded No. 9 Company Bengal Sappers and Miners, in General Stewart's Division during the first campaign, taking part in the advance on Kandahar and Kalat-i-Ghilzai, and being present at the action of Takht-i-pul.

Lieut. C. H. Darling commanded the A Company Madras Sappers and Miners, in the Khyber Force, during the second campaign, was employed as Asst. Field Engineer on various sections of the line extending to Jalalabad, and accompanied the Flying Column in the expedition into the Lughman Valley, the expedition against the Wazir Kugianis, and the expedition into the Hissarak Valley. (Twice thanked in orders.)

Lieut. P. T. Buston served during both campaigns with the 7th Company Bengal Sappers and Miners, in the Kuram and Kabul Field Forces, commanding the Company after the death of Lieut. Nugent at Kabul. Was present in the operations round Kabul and the defence of Sherpur in Dec., 1879. (Mentioned in despatches.)

Lieut. J. D. Fullerton served as Acting Adjutant Bombay Sappers and Miners from Oct., 1879, till May, 1880, with the Southern Afghanistan F.F. in the Bolan and Hurnai Passes.

Lieut. E. C. Spilsbury crossed frontier Aug., 1880, and advanced with General Phayre's Division on Kandahar. Commanded No. 5 Company Bombay Sappers and Miners employed on road-making at Chappar Rift from Sept., 1880, till Feb., 1881, and subsequently No. 4 Company between Spin Tangi, Kuch, and Quetta.

Lieut. G. T. Jones served as Asst. Field Engineer under General Phayre, and with No. 2 Company Bombay Sappers and Miners from Dec., 1878, till March, 1880, in the Bolan Pass, Nari Valley, &c. Served in the same capacity under General Primrose from March till Oct., 1880, and was at first employed in fortifying the posts of Dabrai, Gatai, and Mel Karez. Was present throughout the defence of Kandahar, during which he was constantly under fire with the working parties, his horse being on one occasion mortally wounded. Commanded No 2 Company Sappers in the sortie to Dehkwaja, and at the battle of Kandahar. (Mentioned in despatches; twice thanked in orders; recommended for the Victoria Cross.)

Lieut. W. D. Conner commanded B Company Madras Sappers and Miners in the 2nd Division Peshawar Valley F.F. during the first campaign, being employed on various sections of the line extending to Torkhama, and accompanying the first expedition into the Bazar Valley.

Lieut. R. V. Phillpotts served during both campaigns with No. 8 Company Bengal Sappers and Miners: in the first with the Peshawar Valley Field Force, accompanying the second expedition into the Bazar Valley; in the second, with the Kuram Field Force.

Lieut. W. D. Lindley served during the first campaign with E Company Madras Sappers and Miners in the 2nd Division Peshawar Valley F.F., being employed on various sections of the line extending to Basawal. During the second campaign served with A Company in the Khyber Force, on sections of the line extending to Jalalabad, accompanying the Flying Column in the expedition into the Lughman Valley, the expedition against the Wazir Kugianis, and the expedition into the Hissarak Valley.

Lieut. E. H. Bethell served in command of No. 5 Company Bombay Sappers and Miners and as Asst. Field Engineer with the Reserve Division Kandahar F.F., in the Bolan Pass, the Pishin Valley, and the Hurnai Valley, from March, 1879, till June, 1880.

Lieut. F. W. T. Attree served during the first campaign with B Company Madras Sappers and Miners in the 2nd Division Peshawar Valley F.F., being employed on various sections of the line extending to Torkhama.

Lieut. the Hon. M. G. Talbot served during the second campaign with No. 3 Company Bengal Sappers and Miners in the Khyber Column, being present at the fighting at Jagdalak in Dec., 1879. In April, 1880, was temporarily attached to the Survey Dept., Kabul F.F. Subsequently, as Orderly Officer to General Ross, accompanied Sir F. Roberts' force in its advance from Kabul to the relief of Kandahar, and was present at the battle of Kandahar. (Mentioned in despatches.)

Lieut. W. F. H. Stafford served in command of No. 6 Company Bengal Sappers and Miners with the 1st Division Peshawar Valley F.F. from 1st Jan., 1879, till the conclusion of the first campaign, accompanying the expeditions to Maidanak and the Lughman Valley. During the second campaign took part in the advance of General C. Gough's Brigade to Kata Sang, was present at Pezwan during the December disturbances, and accompanied the Hissarak Valley expedition in April, 1880. Was employed throughout in laying field telegraphs, road-making, and fortifying posts on the line of communications.

Lieut. R. A. Wahab served during the first campaign with B Company Madras Sappers and Miners in the 2nd Division Peshawar Valley F.F., being employed on various sections of the line extending to Torkhama. During the second campaign served with A Company in the Khyber Force, on sections of the line extending to Jalalabad, accompanying the Flying Column in the expedition into the Lughman Valley, the expedition against the Wazir Kugianis, and the expedition into the Hissarak Valley.

Lieut. W. A. E. St. Clair commanded No. 4 Company Bombay Sappers and Miners at Kandahar and on the line of communications during the latter part of the second campaign.

Lieut. C. Maxwell served with No. 5 Company Bengal Sappers and Miners during both campaigns: in the first, with General Biddulph's Division, taking part in the advance on Kandahar and to the Halmand; in the second, with the Khyber and Kabul Field Forces, taking part in Brigadier-General C. Gough's advance to Kabul.

Lieut. W. Coles served in command of No. 4 Company Bombay Sappers and Miners, and as Asst. Field Engineer, from the commencement of the war till Sept., 1880, and in command of No. 3 Company from Nov., 1880, till the evacuation of Kandahar. Was employed in road-making in the Nari Valley till March, 1880. Advanced with General Phayre's force on Kandahar, and assisted in blocking the Gwaja Pass and blowing up Abu Said's fort. Accompanied Brigadier-General Wilkinson's force to Maiwand in Jan., 1881.

Lieut. G. E. Shute served with C Company Madras Sappers and Miners in the Khyber Division during the second campaign; being employed in constructing protective works, roads, bridges, &c., at Landi Kotal, Ali Boghan, and other posts on the line. Took part with Brigadier-General Doran's Column in the affair at Kam Daka.

Lieut. H. J. W. Jerome served with No. 4 Company Bengal Sappers and Miners during both campaigns with the force under Sir D. Stewart's command, taking part in the advance on Kandahar and Kalat-i-Ghilzai, the advance from Kandahar to Kabul, and the return to India by the Khyber route, and being present at the affair at Takht-i-pul and the battle of Ahmad Khel.

Lieut. A. C. McDonnell served during the first campaign with E Company Madras Sappers and Miners in the 2nd Division Peshawar Valley F.F., being employed on various sections of the line extending to Basawal.

Lieut. A. H. Mason served during the first campaign with 2nd Company Bengal Sappers and Miners in the 1st Division Peshawar Valley F.F. between Chardeh and Ali Boghan, and afterwards at Gandamak, till the conclusion of peace; subsequently served in the Khyber Brigade at Landi Kotal till invalided home in Nov., 1879.

Lieut. A. R. Ancrum served during the first campaign with No. 6 Company Bengal Sappers and Miners, in the 1st Division Peshawar Valley F.F., being employed principally on telegraph work on sections of the Khyber line extending to Gandamak. (Died of typhoid fever at Peshawar, 7th June, 1879.)

Lieut. C. B. Mayne served with No. 3 Company Bengal Sappers and Miners during both campaigns: in the first, with the 1st Division Peshawar Valley F.F.; subsequently with the Khyber Brigade at Landi Kotal, and at Peshawar; eventually, from Jan., 1880, with the 1st Division Kabul F.F.

Lieut. M. J. Slater served with Nos. 3 and 4 Companies Bombay Sappers and Miners, and as Asst. Field Engineer, throughout the war, being employed the greater part of the time in the Nari Valley, and subsequently at Kandahar. Was attacked by robbers while engaged in road-making over the Chappar Mountain, and had his horse shot under him.

Lieut. A. H. Randolph served with No. 3 Company Bengal Sappers and Miners during both campaigns: in the first, with the 1st Division Peshawar Valley F.F.; subsequently with the Khyber Brigade at Landi Kotal; eventually, from Jan., 1880, with the 1st Division Kabul F.F.

Lieut. L. C. Jackson served with No. 2 Company Bengal Sappers and Miners, in the 1st Division Peshawar Valley F.F., during the first campaign.

Lieut. F. B. Longe served with No. 2 Company Bengal Sappers and Miners in the Kuram Valley F.F., during the first campaign, and with the Kabul Field Force, part of the time attached to the Survey Dept., during the second campaign, being present at the operations round Kabul and defence of Sherpur in Dec., 1879. Took part in the advance from Kabul to the relief of Kandahar, and was present as Orderly Officer to General Ross at the battle of Kandahar. (Twice mentioned in despatches.)

Lieut. G. H. B. Gordon served during both campaigns with No. 2 Company Bengal Sappers and Miners, and as Asst. Field Engineer in the Divisions operating on the Khyber line.

Lieut. E. C. Stanton served during both campaigns with No. 6 Company Bengal Sappers and Miners, and as Asst. Field Engineer, in the Divisions operating on the Khyber line; being present at the taking of Ali Musjid.

LATE BENGAL.

Lt.-Colonel E. T. Thackeray, V.C., C.B., commanded the Bengal Sappers and Miners with the Khyber Line Force during the second campaign till Jan., 1880. Was present at the affair near Jagdalak on the 17th Dec., 1879, and on the 24th Dec., while in command of a small mixed force at Jagdalak Kotal, repulsed a determined attack made on that post by 3,000 Ghilzais, inflicting a heavy loss on the enemy, and being so severely wounded as to necessitate his immediate return to India. (Mentioned in despatches.)

LATE MADRAS.

Bt. Lt.-Colonel Ross Thompson served as Field Engineer and commanded the Q.O. Madras Sappers and Miners in the second campaign. Accompanied the Lughman Valley Expedition in Jan. 1880, and in Feb. reconnoitred an alternative route from Jalalabad to Jagdalak through the Valley and the Adrak-Badrak country. Was present at the operations in the Hissarak country in April, 1880, including the destruction of the forts and the affairs of the 12th and 14th. Accompanied the second Lughman expedition, and was present at the destruction of the forts and the affair of the 11th June when recrossing the Kabul River. (Brevet of Lt.-Colonel.)

Bt. Lt.-Colonel C. A. Sim served as Field Engineer and commanded the Q.O. Madras Sappers and Miners in the first campaign, performing duty on various sections of the Khyber line and at various posts extending from Jamrud to Gandamak. Accompanied the first expedition into the Bazar Valley, and was present at the destruction of the forts and minor operations. (Mentioned in despatches; Brevet of Lt.-Colonel.)

LATE BOMBAY.

Bt. Colonel John Hills, C.B., commanded the Bombay Sappers and Miners from Nov., 1879, till March, 1880; was Commanding R.E., Southern Afghanistan F.F., from March, 1880, till 23 May, 1881, being present at Kandahar throughout the siege, and at the battle of Kandahar; and was Commanding R.E., Quetta Division, from May, 1881. (Mentioned in despatches; C.B.)

For services of the under-mentioned officers, see "Staff":—

Bt. Lt.-Colonel G. E. L. S. Sandford, Majors E. N. Peters, S. W. Jenner, E. Harvey, A. Hill, W. A. J. Wallace, and *M. W. Rogers, Captain G. F. O. Boughey, Bt. Majors E. M. Larmine,* and *T. H. Holdich, Captain W. H. Haydon, Bt. Major W. S. S. Bisset, Captains J. L. Macpherson* and *J. T. Wright, Bt. Major W. G. Nicholson, Captains R. R. Pulford* and *M. C. Brackenbury, Bt. Lt.-Colonel R. G. Woodthorpe, Captain S. L. Jacob, Bt. Major C. F. Call, Captains C. H. M. Kensington, R. F. Moore, G. Henry, C. H. Bagot, G. W. Bartram, C. F. Fuller, H. A. Yorke, H. O. Selby, F. T. N. Spratt, W. W. Robinson, W. Peacocke, R. T. Orpen, G. R. R. Savage, J. W. Thurburn, C. Hoskyns,* and *F. Beauclerk, Lieuts. St. G. C. Gore, R. H. Brown, D. A. Scott, F. B. G. D'Aguilar, W. T. Shone, W. H. White, J. M. T. Badgley, H. W. Duperier, H. L. Wells, B. Scott, S. Grant, W. H. Chippendall, A. C. Bruce, J. H. C. Harrison, T. P. Cather, H. W. Smith, W. G. Bowyer, C. L. Young, J. C. Addison, G. Davidson, E. Blunt, J. Burn-Murdoch, R. C. Maxwell, A. C. Foley, J. Neville, R. Jennings, G. H. Sim, J. C. Campbell, H. Finnis, J. A. Ferrier, A. L. Mein, S. A. E. Hickson, G. C. P. Onslow, E. A. Waller, A. H. Kenney, E. S. E. Childers, J. G. Day, G. M. Porter, G. K. Scott-Moncrieff, F. Peel, H. E. S. Abbott,* and *H. H. Barnet, Royal Engineers; Major-General F. R. Maunsell, C.B., Bt. Colonel D. Limond, C.B., Major-General W. Hichens, C.B.* (Retired), *Bt. Colonel Æ. Perkins, C.B., A.D.C., Lt.-Colonel C. N. Judge* (Retired), *Bt. Lt.-Colonels G. S. Hills, W. B. Holmes, H. F. Blair,* and *O. B. C. St. John, C.S.I., Bt. Colonel James Browne, C.S.I., Bt.-Lt.-Colonel B. Lovett, C.S.I., Majors W. J. Heaviside, R. P. Tickell, M. A. Alves,* and *C. Strahan, Royal (late Bengal) Engineers); Colonel R. H. Sankey, C.B., Lt.-Colonel J. G. Lindsay,* and *Major S. C. Clarke, Royal (late Madras) Engineers;* and *General Sir M. K. Kennedy, K.C.S.I., Bt. Colonel J. Bonus, Major T. F. Dowden, Bt. Lt.-Colonel A. Le Mesurier, Major K. A. Jopp, Bt. Lt.-Colonel W. M. Campbell,* and *Majors M. J. Macartney* and *E. O'D. Twemlow, Royal (late Bombay) Engineers.*

For services of the under-mentioned officers, see Biographical Division:—

Bt. Lt.-Colonel E. P. Leach, V.C., Capt. R. C. Hart, V.C., Lieuts. T. R. Henn, A. E. Dobson, C. Nugent, J. T. Rice, and *B. Poulter, Royal Engineers; Captain J. Dundas, V.C., Royal (late Bengal) Engineers;* and *Captain G. M. Cruickshank, Royal (late Bombay) Engineers.*

INFANTRY.

1st BATTALION 5th (NORTHUMBERLAND) FUSILIERS. (NOW 1st BATTALION NORTHUMBERLAND FUSILIERS.)

N the 8th Oct., 1878, the 1st Battn. 5th Fusiliers, then stationed in the hills at Chakrata, was warned by telegraph for service in Afghanistan, and on the 18th of that month the regiment—800 strong, and in fine condition—began its march to the front, under the command of Lt.-Colonel T. Rowland.

Detailed to Brigadier-General Doran's Brigade of the 2nd Division Peshawar Valley F.F., the 5th Fusiliers joined divisional head-quarters at Jamrud on the 13th Dec., and for the next three months was employed on convoy duty up the Khyber Pass, and in various expeditions.

At the latter end of Dec., 1878, 350 men of the regiment, under Major J. Creagh, took part with the Ali Musjid Column in the first of the Bazar Valley expeditions, and were employed in the work of destroying the villages and towers of the hostile Zaka Khels. During the return march the duty of clearing the heights between which the Column threaded its way devolved on the rear-guard, under Major Creagh, and was effectually performed, considerable loss being inflicted on the enemy.

Previously to the departure of the expedition, a midnight attack made by a body of these tribesmen on the Signal Station on the Sarkai Hill was repulsed by a picquet of the 5th, under Lieut. Frend.

On the 1st Jan., 1879, the Khyber Pass being reported closed, a column of the 5th Fusiliers and Mhairwara Battalion, under Lt.-Colonel Harkness, was sent to clear it for the passage of a convoy. Having secured the neighbouring heights, the convoy was safely passed up.

In the second expedition into the Bazar Valley, at the latter end of January, 1879, the regiment again took part, 300 men under Major Creagh being detailed to Brigadier-General Blyth's column. The force remained in the district ten days, and was engaged in daily skirmishes with the tribes.

On the 21st March the 5th Fusiliers advanced from Jamrud up the Khyber Pass, and went into camp at Basawal on the 23rd. The same evening three companies of the regiment under Major H. H. Taylor formed part of the punitory force under Brigadier-General Tytler which marched to Deh Sarak, and defeated a body of 3,000 Mohmands, with heavy loss, on the following day.

During the early days of April, two privates of the regiment were stabbed by Afghans while on duty. In both cases their assailants suffered the penalty of death. On the 7th of that month, Lieut. A. C. Godwin died at Peshawar, whither he had been sent back sick; and on the 10th, Lieut. J. G. Ogle, another promising young officer, succumbed to fever in camp at Basawal. About this time, cholera, an epidemic which was not finally shaken off till the latter end of August, broke out in the ranks, and together with fever, dysentery, and sun-stroke, claimed no less than seventy victims.

On the 22nd April Captain W. C. Ormond marched with his company from Daka to Kam Daka to the assistance of a party of the Mhairwara Battalion under Captain O'M. Creagh beset by a body of some 2,000 Mohmands, and assisted in dispersing the enemy. In this affair two sergeants of the regiment were wounded.

After peace had been concluded, the battalion commenced its return march from Basawal, and on the 8th June emerged from the Khyber after a slight skirmish with a band of marauders on the Mackeson road. After recrossing the Indus, the regiment was sent to encamp on the hills above Abbottabad.

On the renewal of hostilities in the autumn of 1879, the 5th Fusiliers was again warned for active service. Two companies under Major Creagh proceeded to Kohat, and the Head-quarters marched from Abbottabad on the 14th Nov. After encamping a month at Hassan Abdal, the regiment reached Peshawar by double marches on the 20th Dec. On the 24th idem, one company marched for Landi Kotal, followed by another company on the 29th, and two more, under Major Taylor, on the 8th Jan., 1880. In the meantime the two companies under Major Creagh had rejoined Head-quarters from Kohat.

A detachment of the 5th formed part of the escort of the Afghan General, Daud Shah, from Landi Kotal, and a company of the regiment, under Lieut. Clark, took charge of him in the Fort of Peshawar.

On the 15th Jan., 1880, 200 men of the regiment, under Major Taylor, moved out from Landi Kotal with the force under Brigadier-General Doran which, in co-operation with a column from Daka, attacked some 3,000 Mohmands who had crossed the Kabul River and taken up positions threatening the Khyber route. The enemy were attacked in most difficult country, driven from ridge to ridge, and dispersed. In this encounter one man of the 5th was wounded. The Head-quarters of the regiment at the same time sent 200 men under Major Newbolt with a flying column under Colonel Hearne, M.N.I., from Peshawar, to operate on the left flank of the enemy near Fort Michin; but this force did not succeed in getting into action.

On the 21st Jan. Head-quarters marched for Landi Kotal, arriving on the 23rd; one company, under Lieut. Lambart, reached Daka Fort on the 25th idem; and two other companies, under Major Newbolt, arrived at Basawal on the 4th Feb. On the 13th April the regiment advanced to Pesh Bolak, and there remained till the 5th May, when, marching to Jalalabad, it encamped outside Fort Sale on the 7th. During the following night, news was suddenly received of a raid having been made from the Lughman Valley on Commissariat cattle collected at the west side of the city, and the regiment, under command of Colonel Rowland, at once turned out in pursuit. Coming up with the raiders in the neighbourhood of the Darwuta Pass, the Fusiliers succeeded in inflicting considerable loss on their rear-guard, and subsequently occupied the Pass. After being out sixteen hours, the regiment returned with the loss of one man killed.

During the second and third week in May, parties of the regiment were successively moved forward until 250 men had arrived at Gandamak under Major Newbolt. Two companies also garrisoned the Fort at Jalalabad.

On the 18th May, Head-quarters and 200 men of the 5th Fusiliers, with other details, crossed over the Kabul River into the Besud district, and forming part of the force commanded by Brigadier-General Doran, were engaged in the defeat of the Safis near the village of Beninga on the following day. Twenty-five of the enemy shut themselves up in a tower, and resisted to the last. Several of them made a sortie, but were met hand to hand by Col. Rowland, Capt. Kilgour, Colour-Sergt. Wood, and Private Openshaw, and were killed; and five who still remained alive were subsequently despatched, after a desperate encounter in the fort itself, by Capt. Kilgour and Colour-Sergt. Wood, who had charged in to close the conflict. In this affair Col. Rowland and three men of the regiment were wounded. On the 21st and 22nd May the regiment was employed in destroying forts in the district, and enforcing other punitory measures; and on the 22nd and two succeeding days the brigade recrossed the river.

On the 2nd June Head-quarters and three companies marched to Girdi Kas to join a force which was being concentrated for an expedition into the Kama district, and on the 5th a party of the regiment under Lt.-Colonel Harkness crossed the river with other details under the command of Brigadier-General Doran, and was employed in destroying the towers and fortified villages of the hostile inhabitants. After sufficient punishment had been inflicted, the column recrossed the river, and the regiment returned to Jalalabad.

The 23rd June saw the 5th Fusiliers again called upon for an expedition against the village of Daulatzai in the Shinwari country south of Jalalabad. The expeditionary force experienced great distress from the extreme heat on the burning plain that had to be crossed, one private of the regiment succumbing from exhaustion. The column was away twenty-four hours, the greater portion of the time under arms.

On the 11th Aug., 1880, the battalion commenced its return-march to India, and on the 19th idem passed out of the Khyber. Its loss during the second campaign was, one man killed by the enemy, twelve who died from illness, and fifty or sixty who were invalided to India.

After being concentrated at Mirat, the regiment finally sailed from Bombay on the 8th Nov., and on the 10th Dec., 1880, landed in England, after an Indian service of fourteen years.

RECORDS OF SERVICE.

SERVICES IN AFGHANISTAN OF OFFICERS OF THE 1st BATTN. 5TH (NORTHUMBERLAND) FUSILIERS (NOW 1st BATTN. NORTHUMBERLAND FUSILIERS).

Colonel T. Rowland, C.B., commanded the regiment throughout the period of its service in the war, taking part in the operations in the Besud and Kama districts, and the expedition to Daulatzai. Commanded a column in the pursuit of raiders at the Darunta Pass. (Mentioned in despatches; C.B.)

Lt.-Colonel J. G. Harkness, Majors J. R. Newbolt and *A. R. W. Thistlethwaite, Captain G. Hart Dyke, Brevet Major H. Kilgour,* and *Captains S. Boxwell* and *A. Chancellor,* and *Qr.-Mr. F. Drake* served with the regiment throughout the period it was employed in the war; *Lt.-Colonel Harkness* commanding the column sent to clear the Khyber Pass, 1 Jan., 1879, taking part in the operations in the Besud district, and commanding the detachment of the regiment in the operations in the Kama district; *Major Newbolt* commanding the three companies detached to Safed Sang from May, 1880, till the conclusion of hostilities; *Major Thistlethwaite* doing duty throughout as Acting Paymaster, but taking part, in command of his company, in the second Bazar Valley expedition, the operations in the Besud and Kama districts, and the expedition to Daulatzai; *Captain Hart Dyke* taking part in both the Bazar Valley expeditions, and being present at the action of Kam Daka; *Major Kilgour* taking part in both the Bazar Valley expeditions (in the second of which he did duty as Assistant Transport Officer), and being present at the action of Deh Sarak, the affair at the Darunta Pass, and the operations in the Besud district (for his distinguished gallantry on the 19th May, 1880, being mentioned in despatches and receiving the Brevet of Major); *Captain Boxwell* taking part in both the Bazar Valley expeditions, being present at the affair at the Darunta Pass and the operations in the Besud district, and accompanying the expeditions to Kama and Daulatzai (serving as Adjutant from 19 May, 1880); and *Captain Chancellor* taking part in the first Bazar Valley expedition, and being present at the action of Deh Sarak and the affair at the Darunta Pass.

Lt.-Colonel J. Creagh (retired), Lt.-Colonel H. H. Taylor (retired), and *Major W. C. Ormond (retired)* served throughout both campaigns; *Lt.-Colonel Creagh* commanding the detachments of the 5th Fusiliers which took part in the Bazar Valley expeditions, accompanying, in command of signallers, the Zaimusht expedition under Brigadier-General Tytler, and being employed as Assistant Quartermaster-General to General Bright from Jan., 1880, till the conclusion of the war; *Lt.-Colonel Taylor* taking part in both the Bazar Valley expeditions, commanding detached companies of the regiment at the actions of Deh Sarak and Kam Daka, and being employed as Brigade Transport Officer, Khyber Line Force, from Feb., 1880, till the conclusion of the war; and *Major Ormond* commanding the detachment of the regiment at the action of Kam Daka, being present at the affair at the Darunta Pass and the operations in the Besud district, and being employed as Provost Marshal, Khyber Line Force, at Landi Kotal, from January till April, 1880.

Captain H. S. Williams served with the regiment in the first campaign, being present at the action of Deh Sarah. (Since deceased.)

Captain E. Le M. Trafford served as Adjutant with the regiment in both campaigns, until promotion into the 2nd Battalion, 1 May, 1880, taking part in the second Bazar Valley expedition.

Captain H. R. Gall served as Orderly Officer to Brigadier-General Doran throughout the first campaign, and with the 5th Fusiliers in the second campaign, taking part in the first Bazar Valley expedition, being present at the action of Kam Daka.

Captain M. W. Biddulph. (For services see "Staff.")

Lieuts. P. F. Lambart, G. M. Harding, A. E. Whitaker, and *W. H. Sitwell* served with the regiment in the second campaign; *Lieut. Lambart* being present at the affair in the Darunta Pass and the operations in the Besud district; and *Lieut. Whitaker* being present at the affair in the Darunta Pass.

Lieuts. H. E. Buchanan, R. K. Kays, J. W. Malet, G. Frend, and *H. L. Clark* served with the regiment in both campaigns; *Lieut. Buchanan* taking part in both the Bazar Valley expeditions and being present at the affair at the Darunta Pass; *Lieut. Kays* being present at the operations in the Besud and Kama districts, and taking part in the expedition to Daulatzai: *Lieut. Malet* taking part in both the Bazar Valley expeditions, being present at the actions of Deh Sarak and Kam Daka and the affair at the Darunta Pass, and acting as Orderly Officer to Brigadier-General Gib from January till

April, 1880; *Lieut. Frend* commanding the picquet at the repulse of the Afridi attack on the Sarkai Hill, acting as Provost Marshal of the 2nd Brigade, 2nd Division, Peshawar Valley F.F. at Basawal during the first campaign, and as regimental Transport Officer during the second, and proceeded to Kabul in the Spring of 1880 in charge of transport animals; and *Lieut. Clark* taking part in the second Bazar Valley expedition.

Lieuts. H. B. Thornhill (*M.S.C.*) and *T. Y. Whittingdale* served with the regiment in the first campaign; *Lieut. Thornhill* taking part in both the Bazar Valley expeditions; and *Lieut. Whittingdale* in the second.

Lieut. A. L. Pennington served with the regiment in the first campaign, and with the 39th B.N.I. in the second, taking part in the first Bazar Valley expedition, being present at the action of Kam Daka, and being attached to the Quartermaster-General's Dept. for surveying camps.

Lieut. J. G. Ogle served with the regiment in the first campaign, being present at the action of Deh Sarak. (Died in camp at Basawal, 10 April, 1879.)

Lieut. A. C. Godwin served with the regiment in the first campaign. (Invalided to Peshawar, where he died, 7 April, 1879.)

Captain W. F. Longbourne, A.P.D., served with the regiment in the first campaign, taking part in both the Bazar Valley expeditions, and acting as Provost Marshal, 2nd Division Peshawar Valley F.F., from 7 Feb. till 6 June, 1879.

2ND BATTN. 7TH (ROYAL FUSILIERS) (NOW 2ND BATTN. ROYAL FUSILIERS [CITY OF LONDON REGT.]).

IN the early days of January, 1880, the 2/7th Fusiliers was broken up in half-battalions, Head-quarters and four companies, under the command of Lt.-Colonel Daubeny, being stationed at Bombay, and the remaining four companies, under the command of Major Kerr, at Ahmadnagar. Orders having been received for the regiment to hold itself in readiness to proceed on active service into Afghanistan, the detachment at Ahmadnagar rejoined Head-quarters on the 29th, and the regiment, thus reunited, embarked at Bombay on the 6th February for Karachi, as one of the two British battalions selected to form part of the Bombay Brigade under General Phayre's command, at the time destined to relieve the Bengal troops in the Southern theatre of operations. From Karachi the regiment proceeded to Sibi, and there, and at Nari Ford, it was detained for some five weeks. Continuing its forward movement on the 22nd March, it arrived at Quetta on the 3rd April, and again marching on the 14th, eventually reached its destination, Kandahar, on the 26th idem.

For the next few months after arriving at Kandahar the 2/7th Fusiliers remained, with the rest of the troops under General Primrose's command, in cantonments, small parties occasionally varying the ordinary routine duties by taking part in the reconnaissances which were conducted into the surrounding country.

On the 28th July, on the news of the disaster sustained by our arms at Maiwand reaching Kandahar, 70 rifles of the 2/7th, under Lieut. Rodick, formed part of the force under Br.-Genl. Brooke which sallied out to the relief of the survivors of Br.-Genl. Burrows' ill-fated brigade. Later in the day, on the arrival of General Burrows at the city walls, one company of the regiment under the command of Captain Adderley, marched out to Abasabad, and performed useful service in holding the eastern outskirts of the village till the last stragglers had made their way into Kandahar.

During the siege of Kandahar the 2/7th was quartered in the citadel, and was employed on the South and East faces of the defence. Major Moore (Paymaster) was given the command of the marksmen who were told off to the bastions, and rendered excellent service. On the 31st July two companies of the regiment formed part of the force which was sent out to disperse a hostile gathering in the village of Khairabad, and succeeded in killing thirty of the enemy. Covering parties to protect the men employed on the defensive works were from time to time furnished by the regiment; and while in command of one of these, on the 6th August, Lieut. de Trafford was wounded. On the 12th a few rifles of the regiment, while engaged on this duty, rendered a good account of themselves in rushing the garden of Mir Dil Khan, on the Herat road, killing several of the enemy in carrying it.

In the ill-starred sortie to Deh Khwaja on the 16th August, four companies of the 2/7th—two in the 1st attacking column, one in the 2nd, and one in the 3rd—were engaged, Lt.-Colonel Dauben being in command of the 1st Column. In spite of the obstinate resistance offered to them, and the stupendous numbers to which they were opposed, the two first columns succeeded in forcing their way through the village and back again to its Southern entrance, the companies of the battalion prominently contributing by their steadiness under the galling fire to which they were subjected, to the successful performance of this feat. Lieut. Wood, leading his men in a most forward manner, was mortally wounded, and Lieut. Marsh, his brother officer, while helping him into a dhoolie, was shot through the heart. Besides these officers, 22 men of the battalion were killed in the engagement, and two officers (Major Vandaleur and Captain Connolly) and 28 men wounded. Major Vandaleur died, ten days afterwards, from the effects of his wound. For the gallantry he displayed on this day in assisting Lieut. Chase, Staff Corps, in carrying one of the wounded men into Kandahar, Private Ashford was subsequently decorated with the Victoria Cross.

Brigadier-General Brooke having been killed in action on the 16th August, Lt.-Colonel Daubeny was selected to take over the command of the 2nd Infantry Brigade, and the command of the regiment devolved on Major Beauchamp.

In the crowning defeat of the enemy at the battle of Kandahar on the 1st September, after the relief of the beleaguered garrison by the force under Sir Frederick Roberts, 13 officers and 376 men of the 2/7th Fusiliers were under arms, 2 officers and 132 men being on duty in the Citadel and City.

On the 18th April, 1881, the battalion quitted Kandahar for India, and on the 20th May arrived at Bellary, Madras. Its total casualties during the period of its service in Afghanistan were 69 officers, non-commissioned officers, and men.

SERVICES IN AFGHANISTAN OF OFFICERS OF THE 2ND BATTN. 7TH (ROYAL FUSILIERS) (NOW 2ND BATTN. ROYAL FUSILIERS [CITY OF LONDON REGT.]).

Lt.-Colonel A. G. Daubeny. (Deceased. See Biographical Division.)

Lt.-Colonel H. Kerr took part with the battalion in its advance to Sibi, from whence he was invalided on the 23rd Feb., 1880. (Died in England 11th Dec., 1881.)

Lt.-Colonel W. B. Colvin. (For services see "Staff.")

Major T. B. Vandaleur joined the battalion in Afghanistan with a draft in May, 1880, and served with it until mortally wounded in the sortie to Deh Khwaja. (Died at Kandahar 26th Aug., 1880.)

Lt.-Colonel F. Beauchamp (1st Battn.) served with the battalion throughout, being in command from the 17th Aug. till the 26th Sept., 1880. Was present at the sortie to Deh Khwaja, took part in the defence of Kandahar, and commanded the battalion at the battle of Kandahar. (Mentioned in despatches.)

Major F. C. Keyser joined the battalion with a draft on the 30th March, 1880, and served in Afghanistan till the conclusion of the war, most of the time as Superintendent of Army Signalling to the Kandahar Field Force, and subsequently in the same capacity to the Army in Southern Afghanistan. Was engaged with the force under Br.-Genl. Brooke in covering the retreat of the remnants of Burrows' brigade from Maiwand, took part in the defence of Kandahar, and was present at the battle of Kandahar. (Twice mentioned in despatches.)

Major W. W. Chard and *Lieuts. C. D. M. Gall, H. Porter, G. C. Herbert, and G. W. Z. Moss* served with the battalion throughout, taking part in the defence of Kandahar and the sortie to Deh Khwaja, and being present at the battle of Kandahar.

Major T. Groube (1st Battn.), *Captain R. B. Manning*, and *Qr.-Mr. H. Clowes* served with the battalion throughout, taking part in the defence of Kandahar.

Captain W. Connolly served with the battalion throughout, taking part in the defence of Kandahar, and the sortie to Deh Khwaja, in which he was wounded.

Captain E. W. Adderley joined the battalion with a draft on the 30th March, 1880, and served with it till the conclusion of the war. Was engaged with the force under Br.-Genl. Brooke in covering the retreat of the remnants of Burrows' brigade from Maiwand, took part in the defence of Kandahar and the sortie to Deh Khwaja, and was present at the battle of Kandahar. (Mentioned in despatches; Brevet of Major.)

Captain R. B. P. Rodick (1st Battn.) served with the battalion throughout, being engaged with the force under Br.-Genl. Brooke in covering the retreat of the remnants of Burrows' brigade from Maiwand, taking part in the defence of Kandahar, and being present at the battle of Kandahar. (Mentioned in despatches.)

Captain G. F. Thunder, and *Lieuts. H. H. Drummond-Wolff, E. M. Barttelot*, and *W. L. Forbes* served with the battalion throughout, taking part in the defence of Kandahar, and being present at the battle of Kandahar. Lieut. Forbes acted as Orderly Officer to Col. Daubeny after the latter was appointed to the command of a brigade.

Lieut. A. H. Daunt served with the 1st Bombay Grenadiers (to which regiment he was attached as a probationer) in the Reserve Division under General Phayre from December, 1878, till September, 1879, when he was invalided. Rejoined 2/7th Fusiliers in Kandahar in February, 1881, and served with the battalion in Afghanistan during the rest of the time it remained there.

Lieut. H. J. H. Dive accompanied a draft for the battalion in its advance into Baluchistan. Was drowned 1st May, 1880, while bathing in the neighbourhood of the Bolan Pass.

Lieut. M. L. Shipley. (For services see "Staff.")

Lieut. G. C. de Trafford served with the battalion throughout, taking part in the defence of Kandahar. Was wounded while in command of a covering-party on the 6th August, 1880.

Lieut. F. P. F. Wood. (Killed in action. See Biographical Division.)

Lieut. E. S. Marsh. (Killed in action. See Biographical Division.)

Major F. G. F. Moore (A. P. D.) served with the battalion throughout, taking part in the defence of Kandahar, during which he commanded the sharp-shooters. (Mentioned in despatches.)

2ND BATTN. 8TH (THE KING'S) REGT. (NOW 2ND BATTN. THE KING'S [LIVERPOOL REGT.]).

ON the 15th Oct., 1878, having received orders to proceed to the frontier to form part of the force under General Roberts, which, in view of the impending invasion of Afghanistan was then in course of concentration, the 2nd Battn., "The King's," marched from Rawal Pindi to Thal, detaching, *en route*, two companies under the command of Captain A. Lewis, which remained at Kohat to form part of the garrison of that station.

Detailed to the 1st Infantry Brigade of the Kuram Valley Field Force, Head-quarters and the service companies of the battalion crossed the frontier, with the rest of the Division, on the 21st Nov., 1878, and advanced up the valley to Muhammad Azim's fort. In the reconnaissance which was conducted towards the Peiwar Kotal on the 28th, the regiment was actively engaged in skirmishing up the hills towards the mouth of the Pass.

Left in camp with the other units of Brigadier-General Cobbe's command on the night of the 1st Dec., 1878, when the main body of the Division, under General Roberts, marched on its flanking movement for the Spin Gawi Kotal, the battalion took part, on the following day, in the direct attack on and capture of the enemy's position on the Peiwar Kotal. At daybreak, one company, under the command of Captain Dawson, Acting Field Officer, was told off as an escort to the artillery of the brigade, and remained with the guns in the successive positions from which they delivered their effective fire till 2 p.m., the remainder of the regiment being extended to the right and slightly in advance. About noon Brigadier-General Cobbe was wounded, and Col. Barry Drew succeeded to the command of the brigade, that of the regiment devolving on Major Tanner. Gradually advancing from ridge to ridge, the companies made their way over precipitous and broken ground to the crest of a hill from which the final attack was delivered and the Afghan batteries silenced. Shortly afterwards the Kotal itself was gained, and the camp, from which the enemy had precipitately fled a few moments before, occupied.

After the defeat of the enemy on the 2nd Dec., the 2/8th established itself in winter quarters, the main body of the regiment occupying the valley close to where the Afghan camp had been pitched, and detached companies holding the hills which commanded both sides of the Pass. Here it was destined to remain for many months. In the early part of January, 1879, night attacks by the Mangals and Jagis were constantly threatened, and the troops were more than once under arms. With the exception of detachments which, during the succeeding months, were distributed along the line of communications at Kuram and Hazar Pir, the battalion continued in its quarters at the Peiwar Kotal, with the rest of the advanced troops of the Division, till after the conclusion of the first campaign.

On the renewal of hostilities in the autumn of 1879, the 2nd Battn. 8th, The King's, again formed part of the Division operating on the Kuram line. At the time of the occurrence of the massacre of the

British Envoy and Escort at Kabul, the Head-quarters and six companies were still holding the advanced position of the Peiwar Kotal, and here they were shortly afterwards joined by the detachment which during the first campaign had been in garrison at Kohat and Thal. During the ensuing operations of the Army of Invasion, the regiment was employed, in the main, in étappen duty; but though no opportunities for distinguishing itself in the field again arose, it had its full share of the privations and hardships which fell to the lot of the Division to which it was attached, and performed a considerable amount of hard and not unimportant work. On the 14th Oct., 1879, a large body of Mangals and Jagis attacked the post of Ali Khel, and the 2/8th was employed in their repulse and in the vigorous counter-attack which resulted in their defeat. A small detachment—40 rifles—took part, in the following December, in the expedition conducted into Zaimusht territory under Brigadier-General Tytler. In May, 1880, 100 rifles of the regiment formed part of the force under Major Beddy, 29th B.N.I., which proceeded from Kuram to Mandoria to act under Brigadier-General Newdigate in repelling a threatened attack by Waziris on Bannu; and again, during the same month, another detachment accompanied the expeditionary force which was despatched from Peiwar to Karmanna to capture the Malik Nanak Shamu Khel, and destroyed his stronghold.

On the evacuation of the Kuram Valley in October, 1880, after suffering somewhat severely during the preceding summer-months from sickness, the 2nd Battn., The King's, returned to India, having been serving continuously in Afghanistan for nearly two years.

SERVICES IN AFGHANISTAN OF OFFICERS OF THE 2ND BATTN. 8TH (THE KING'S) REGT. (NOW 2ND BATTN. THE KING'S [LIVERPOOL REGT.].)

Colonel F. B. Drew, C.B. (*exchanged to 1st Battn. West Yorkshire*), commanded the battalion in Afghanistan from the time of the breaking out of hostilities till he succeeded, 2nd Dec., 1878, to the command of the 1st Bde. Kuram F.F., *vice* Br.-Genl. Cobbe, wounded. Commanded the Infantry portion of the Khost Valley expeditionary force. Was present at the reconnaissance of the 28th Nov., 1878, the assault and capture of the Peiwar Kotal, and the action of Matun. Reassumed command of the battalion 14th March, 1879, and remained in command of it till the conclusion of the first campaign. (Three times mentioned in despatches; C.B.)

Colonel G. C. E. Grogan commanded the battalion during the second campaign from Nov., 1879, till the 9th Aug., 1880, when he succeeded to the command of the Lower Kuram Brigade, *vice* Br.-Genl. Newdigate, invalided. (Mentioned in despatches.)

Colonel E. Tanner, C.B. (*1st Battn.*), served with the battalion throughout the first and during the second campaign, commanding it from the 2nd Dec., 1879 (*vice* Col. Drew, who succeeded to the command of the 1st Bde. Kuram F.F.) till the 14th March, 1879. Was present at the reconnaissance of the 28th Nov., 1879, and the assault and capture of the Peiwar Kotal. Commanded at Fort Kuram from the end of Nov., 1879, till the 12th Jan., 1880. Left Peiwar 29th April, 1880, for England, to take over the command of the 1st Battn. (Mentioned in despatches; C.B.)

Lt.-Colonel G. H. Cochrane served with the battalion throughout the first campaign, being present at the skirmish of the 28th Nov., 1878, and the assault and capture of the Peiwar Kotal. (Mentioned in despatches.)

Major W. Bannatyne and Lieut. V. A. M. Fowler served with the battalion during the second campaign.

Lt.-Colonel J. Dawson (*retired*) served with the battalion throughout both campaigns, being present at the skirmish of the 28th Nov., 1878, and the assault and capture of the Peiwar Kotal. (Mentioned in despatches.)

Lt.-Colonel E. Jervis (*retired*) served with the battalion throughout both campaigns, being present at the skirmish of the 28th Nov., 1878, the assault and capture of the Peiwar Kotal, and the affair at Ali Khel in Oct., 1879. (Mentioned in despatches; Brevet of Major.)

Major B. F. Handy marched with the battalion in October, 1878, as far as Kohat, where he was left, sick. On his way to join Head-quarters at the Peiwar Kotal in 1879 was again invalided, and proceeded home.

Major N. Short marched with the battalion in October, 1878, as far as Kohat, where he was left, sick. Rejoined Head-quarters in the Spring of 1879, and served with the battalion till the conclusion of the war.

Captain T. B. Humfrey joined the battalion (having exchanged from the 1st Battn.) with a draft from England in the Spring of 1880, and served with it till the conclusion of the war.

Captains S. N. Roberts, J. M. Taylor, and *W. L. Brereton,* and *Lieuts. L. S. Mellor, O'D. C. Grattan, L. C. Dundas,* and *J. B. Edwards* served with the battalion throughout both campaigns, being present at the skirmish of the 28th Nov., 1878, and the assault and capture of the Peiwar Kotal.

Lt.-Colonel A. Lewis (retired) served throughout both campaigns, being left in command of the two companies at Kohat on the advance of the battalion into hostile territory in 1878, and rejoining Head-quarters in the summer of 1879.

Captain A. H. Cope joined Head-quarters on promotion from 1st Battn. during the autumn of 1879, and served with the battalion till the conclusion of the war.

Captain A. A. Ruck and *Lieut. P. Schletter* served with the battalion during both campaigns.

Captain G. V. Turner served with the battalion throughout both campaigns, being present at the skirmish of the 28th Nov., 1878, and the assault and capture of the Peiwar Kotal, during which he acted as Orderly Officer to Brigadier-General Thelwall, and commanding the half-company which took part in the Zaimusht expedition under Br.-Genl. Tytler in December, 1879.

Capt. F. J. Whalley served with the battalion throughout the first campaign, being present at the skirmish of the 28th Nov., 1878, and the assault and capture of the Peiwar Kotal. During the second campaign served as a Transport Officer in the Kuram Valley.

Lieut. A. C. G. Banning (1st Battn.) served with the battalion throughout the first campaign, being present at the skirmish of the 28th Nov., 1878, and the assault and capture of the Peiwar Kotal.

Lieut. E. L. Maisey served throughout both campaigns, during the first as Aide-de-Camp to Br.-Genl. Cobbe. Was present at the skirmish of the 28th Nov., 1878, and the assault and capture of the Peiwar Kotal. (Mentioned in despatches.)

Lieut. C. G. Robertson served throughout both campaigns, during the first with the Head-quarters of the battalion, being present at the skirmish of the 28th Nov., 1878, and the assault and capture of the Peiwar Kotal; during the second as Transport Officer with the Kabul and Kabul-Kandahar Field Forces, being present at the action of Charasiab, the occupation of Kabul, and the defence of Sherpur, and taking part in the advance of the force under Sir F. Roberts to the relief of Kandahar, and the battle of Kandahar. (Twice mentioned in despatches.)

Lieut. H. G. Evans served with the battalion throughout both campaigns, being present at the skirmish of the 28th Nov., 1878, the assault and capture of the Peiwar Kotal, and the affair at Ali Khel in October, 1879.

Qr.-Mr. P. Spencer served with the battalion during both campaigns, being present at the assault and capture of the Peiwar Kotal.

2ND BATTN. 9TH (EAST NORFOLK) REGT. (NOW 2ND BATTN. NORFOLK REGT.)

ON returning in the spring of 1878 from the Jowaki campaign, the 2nd Battalion 9th Regt. was quartered at Peshawar. In the latter days of September of the same year the mission under Sir Neville Chamberlain assembled at that station with the view of proceeding to Kabul, and a force consisting of the 2/9th and some Native Infantry regiments was despatched to Burj Hari Singh, on the Jamrud road, to support it on its advance into the Khyber. It was anticipated that the mission would be refused a passage beyond Ali Musjid, as the commandant of that fort had sent word to Sir N. Chamberlain that such was his intention, and it was confidently expected that, in the event of this threat being carried out, the force at Burj Hari Singh would be ordered up to carry the place by assault, a course which was not, however, adopted in the sequel by Government. The force ultimately returned to Peshawar, and the 2/9th being a portion of the garrison of that place, was held in reserve during the campaign then commencing. The pass becoming closed for the passage of convoys soon after the action of Ali Musjid and the advance of Sir Sam. Browne's Division to Daka, two companies of the regiment, under Major Ridsdale, were sent out to Jamrud to reinforce the garrison of that post, and while there were employed on convoy duty between that fort and Ali Musjid, in which they had repeatedly to beat off attacks of the enemy. The officers and men of these companies received the war medal and batta.

On the conclusion of the first campaign in May, 1879, the 2/9th was moved from Peshawar to Naushahra, and remained quartered there till after the massacre of the Kabul Embassy. The order for the battalion to hold itself in readiness to proceed on active service reached Naushahra on the 11th Sept., 1879, and on the 17th it marched for Peshawar, and was detailed to the 1st Brigade of the Khyber Column. Difficulties of transport prevented the assembly of the column *en masse* before penetrating the Pass. The 2/9th was one of the first regiments equipped, and reached Jamrud before any other corps in the Division. Here, however, cholera broke out in the ranks, and carried off five men in a few hours. The regiment was therefore diverted off the main road and kept in quarantine for a week, at the expiration of which it resumed its march. During the interval, however, the Guide Corps had passed it, and penetrating the Pass, which it found undefended, arrived on the 28th Sept. at Daka, where the battalion joined it on the 1st Oct. The regiment took part in the advance of Brigadier-General Gough's Brigade through Basawal, Barikab, and Jalalabad to Gandamak, and eventually to Kata Sang, where it joined hands with the force under Brigadier-General Macpherson, advancing from Kabul. In retracing its steps on the following day, the regiment, with the other units of the brigade, threaded the narrow and tortuous defile of Jagdalak, the scene of severe fighting in the retreat of the English army under Genl. Elphinstone in 1841. Shortly after its return, on the probability arising of Gandamak becoming the winter quarters of the brigade, the battalion was employed, with the rest of the troops, in building huts on the new site selected for the cantonment.

On the 3rd Dec., 1879, 100 rank and file of the regiment formed part of the escort of the ex-Amir Yakub Khan on the latter passing through Gandamak to Safed Sang; and on the night of the 4th a guard of forty rank and file, under Lt. Borton, was mounted over his person.

In the second week in December the battalion formed part of the brigade under Brigadier-General C. Gough, which set out from Gandamak on its trying march to the relief of General Roberts' force at Sherpur. One wing reached Jagdalak, twenty-four miles distant, on the evening of the 14th, and passed the night in hourly expectation of being attacked, the other wing, in the rear division, arriving, after meeting with some slight opposition, on the evening of the following day. On the night of the 16th, the fires of the enemy lit up the surrounding country, and shots fell into camp; but morning dawned without the force being actually attacked. Detachments, including parties of the 2/9th, were sent out to bring in convoys of stores on the succeeding days—the duty, involving some severe fighting, giving opportunities to Major Roberts and Lts. Straghan, Lombe, and Mayne to distinguish themselves. On the 24th Dec., 1879, the day succeeding the attack of the enemy on, and their repulse from, Sherpur, the brigade reached its destination, and became an integral part of General Roberts' force.

When quarters were taken up in the Bala Hissar on the 9th Jan., 1880, the 9th Regt. occupied the Royal Square, and for three months the men were employed in working parties, levelling the greater portion of the enceinte, and opening out roads and communications. In the beginning of April the battalion moved out of the Bala Hissar, and encamped on the Siah Sang heights, and was there joined by a strong draft of nearly 300 men brought up by Major Morgan, who had proceeded down country in February for the purpose. The brigade, now forming part of the Division under Genl. Ross, marched on the 16th April into the Maidan country, and thence to Shekabad, where it was engaged in several skirmishes with the Wardak tribe; and after coming into communication with Genl. Stewart's force advancing from Ghazni, returned to Siah Sang. In June the brigade again moved out into the Koh Daman country, where it remained for nearly a month. Colonel Daunt was at this time appointed to the command of the 2nd Brigade, 2nd Division, and the command of the regiment devolved on Major Morgan.

On the evacuation of Kabul, and the return of the troops under General Stewart to India, the 2/9th was the last regiment to march out of the gates of Sherpur.

As the battalion in its advance on Kabul had occupied the post of honour as one of the leading corps of the leading brigade, so, now, on the retirement of the force, it formed part of the rear-guard for the whole army. On the 7th Sept., 1880, the regiment reached Jamrud, after a severe and harassing march, notwithstanding which it mustered an effective strength on parade of 550 bayonets, exclusive of two companies which had preceded Head-quarters in charge of a sick convoy from Kabul.

SERVICES IN AFGHANISTAN OF OFFICERS OF THE 2ND BATTN. 9TH REGT. (NOW 2ND BATTN. NORFOLK REGT.)

Bt. Colonel W. Daunt, C.B., commanded the battalion in both campaigns till the 11th July, 1880, taking part in the advance to Kabul in December, 1879. Commanded, with rank of Brigadier-General, the 3rd Brigade of General Hills' Division from 12th July, 1880, till 4th Sept., 1880. (Twice mentioned in despatches; C.B.)

Lt.-Colonel C. J. C. Roberts served with the battalion during the war, taking part in the advance to Kabul in December, 1879. Was prevented by ill-health from taking command on Col. Daunt being appointed to a Brigade, and was subsequently invalided to India. (Twice mentioned in despatches.)

Major A. B. Morgan served with the battalion throughout both campaigns, taking part in the advance to Kabul in December, 1879. Commanded the battalion from the 12th July, 1880, till the date of its return to India.

Lt.-Colonel W. H. E. Ridsdale (retired) commanded, during the first campaign, the detachment of the battalion which operated in the Khyber. Served with the battalion throughout the second campaign, taking part in the advance to Kabul.

Major C. M. Stockley served throughout both campaigns: first, as Brigade Major to the 1st Brigade, 1st Division, in Southern Afghanistan, from 28th Nov., 1878, till March, 1880, and afterwards with the battalion in Northern Afghanistan. (Mentioned in despatches; Brevet of Major.)

Captain G. S. Burton served with the battalion during the war, taking part in the advance to Kabul in December, 1879. Subsequently served as Brigade Major to the 1st Brigade, 3rd Division, Northern Afghanistan Field Force, and in the same capacity to the Khyber Brigade at Landi Kotal.

Captain T. Farley served with the battalion during the war. Was ordered home from Gandamak for duty at the Depôt.

Captain J. W. M. Cotton and *Lieuts. H. J. Shuckburgh, W. G. Straghan, O. Mayne, J. L. Govan* (1st Battn.), and *B. W. Morton* served with the battalion during the war—*Lieut. Shuckburgh* as Adjutant, and *Lieut. Straghan* part of the time as Acting Adjutant—taking part in the advance to Kabul in December, 1879.

Lieut. F. A. Currie. (For services see "Staff.")

Lieut. G. M. Griffin served with the battalion during the war, taking part in the advance to Kabul in December, 1879. Had charge of the Regimental Transport till June, 1880, when he was invalided to India.

Lieut. L. H. Phillips served during the first campaign with the detachment in the Khyber, and during the second campaign, till October, 1879, with the head-quarters. Invalided to England from Jalalabad.

Lieuts. E. W. Cunliffe and *A. S. Vesey* served during the first campaign with the detachment in the Khyber.

Lieut. R. H. F. Lombe served with the battalion during the war, taking part in the advance to Kabul in December, 1879. (Twice mentioned in despatches for steadiness and coolness in handling his men.)

Lieut. J. Thompson served with the battalion nearly the whole time it was across the frontier.

Lieut. G. E. Bunbury joined head-quarters at Kabul with a draft from England in April, 1880, and served with the battalion during the remainder of the campaign.

Lieut. A. C. Becher served with the battalion during the war, taking part in the advance to Kabul in December, 1879. Served as Orderly Officer to Brigadier-General C. Gough from 1st June to 7th Sept., 1880.

Lieut. G. S. Ommanney served with the battalion during the war, taking part in the advance to Kabul in December, 1879. (Mentioned in despatches.)

Lieut. F. J. D. Lugard served with the battalion during the war from the date of its crossing the frontier till August, 1880, when he was invalided to England.

Lieut. C. E. Borton served with the battalion during the war, taking part in the advance on Kabul in December, 1879. Served as Orderly Officer to Brigadier-General W. Daunt from 23 July till 4 Sept., 1880.

Quartermaster A. Reeves served with the battalion during the war from the date of its crossing the frontier till April, 1880, taking part in the advance to Kabul in December, 1879.

2ND BATTN. 11TH (NORTH DEVONSHIRE) REGT. (NOW 2ND BATTN. DEVONSHIRE REGT.)

ON the news reaching India of the advance of Ayub Khan from Herat, the Government decided to reinforce the garrison of Kandahar. For this purpose the 2nd Battn. 11th Regiment, under the command of Lt.-Colonel Corrie, was ordered to move by rail, on the 23rd July, 1880, by successive companies, from Karachi and Haidarabab to Sibi; and from thence through the Bolan Pass the men were transported in country bullock-carts to Dozan.

The original plan was, for the whole battalion to assemble at Quetta, before proceeding to Kandahar; but on the march, the news arrived of the disaster at Maiwand, and the contemplated formation of a division under General Phayre, in consequence of which the companies, on reaching Quetta, were hurried on to Gulistan Karez, a small fort in the Pishin Valley, one march from the Khojak, and close to the entrance of the Gwaja and Rogani Passes. At this place the whole battalion had assembled by the 22nd Aug., 1880.

The difficulty of concentration in consequence of the strain on the Commissariat and Transport Departments was the ostensible reason for the delay of General Phayre's Division; and this ultimately prevented the 11th Regiment from reaching Kandahar until the 18th Sept., three weeks after the relief of the garrison by General Roberts.

On the 20th of that month the battalion moved to Khan-i-Girdab in the Argandab Valley, eighteen miles from Kandahar. On the 4th Oct. two companies were detached to Dahila, sixteen miles further up the valley, to which place the whole brigade, with the exception of Head-quarters and four companies of the 11th Regt., moved on the 7th. There it remained until orders were received to move again into Kandahar. Entering the city on the 1st November, it did not again leave it until the final evacuation in June, 1881.

The 11th was the first regiment of European soldiers that had ever marched through Sind and the Bolan during the hottest season of the year. Notwithstanding the precautions taken, numerous cases of heat-apoplexy, and many deaths occurred. The battalion was composed principally of young soldiers, who, when stationed at Poona during the previous year, had suffered considerably from fever, the effects of which many had not shaken off, but who, nevertheless, on hearing the news of the investment of Kandahar, were eager to push on to its relief. The natural difficulties of a march through such a country at such a time of the year—the thermometer at several of the halting-places marking 111° and 112° at 9 o'clock in the morning—were overcome by the physical endurance of the men; but orders, counter-orders, and counter-marches, bad water at the camping grounds, half rations, quarter rations, and always bad rations, between Quetta and Kandahar, together with the lack of change of clothing for picquet and night duties in a trying climate, laid the seeds of diarrhœa and dysentery, and eventually cost the regiment —which left Karachi, on the 23rd July, 715 strong—in deaths, 2 officers and 136 men, and left Head-quarters on the 1st Jan., 1881, with only 215 men available for duty.

The following officers served with the 2nd Battn. 11th Regt. in the war, taking part in the advance to Kandahar:—

Colonel W. T. Corrie (in Command) (mentioned in despatches); *Lt.-Colonels W. A. Smyth*, and *J. W. Green (1st Battn.)*; *Majors E. L. Street* and *F. F. Gibbons* (invalided from Kandahar); *Captains W. H. Marriott, R. S. I. O'Brien, D. T. Kinder* (invalided from Gulistan Karez), *J. H. Yule*, and *R. E. Kelsall*; *Lieuts. C. W. Park, T. A. H. Davies, E. T. Stanley* (invalided from Kandahar), *A. Phayre (Probationer Staff Corps), C. P. W. Pirie, R. H. Light*, and *E. J. Ellicombe* (invalided from Kandahar) and *Quartermaster G. Evans*.

For services of *Capt. J. W. Andrews* and *S. K. Harris*, see "Staff."

For services of *Lieut. W. H. Bishop* and *Capt. A. A. D. Weigall* (*A.P.D.*) see Biographical Division.

1st BATTN. 12TH (EAST SUFFOLK) REGT. (NOW 1st BATTN. SUFFOLK REGT.)

ON the 4th April, 1879, the battalion received orders to hold itself in readiness to join the 3rd Brigade, 2nd Division, Peshawar Valley Field Force, under command of Lieut.-General Maude, and on the 12th idem marched from Naushahra. On the 14th it crossed the frontier into Afghanistan, and on the 16th arrived at Landi Kotal, its destination.

On the 21st of the same month two companies marched with a small column under command of Lieut.-Colonel F. B. Norman, 24th B.N.I., to operate against the Mohmand tribe, who had crossed the Kabul River into territory in our occupation.

Next day (22nd April) three more companies were despatched to the Fort of Daka under command of Lieut.-Colonel C. J. C. Sillery, in view to reinforce a small party of Native Infantry holding the village of Kam Daka. With these three companies of the battalion were sent two mountain guns.

Whilst *en route* to Daka, Lieut.-Colonel Sillery received an order to detach immediately the two guns with 100 men of the battalion as escort to Kam Daka, to the relief of the Native Infantry, hard pressed in that village. This was done, and the guns, supported by the company of the battalion, came into action, and assisted in rescuing 150 men of the Mhairwara Battalion, under Captain O'M. Creagh, from a most perilous position. This done, the Senior Officer on the spot, Major Dyce, R.A., ordered a retreat on Daka, and directed the movement to be covered by the company of the 1st Battalion 12th Regiment. This service, owing to the rugged nature of the ground, and the persistence with which the retirement was pressed by large numbers of an enemy well acquainted with every bye-path and cattle track, was very difficult, but was successfully carried out; not, however, without the loss of a sergeant and a private killed, and two privates severely, and three slightly, wounded.

After the signing of the treaty of Gandamak the battalion was one of the two British regiments selected to remain in military occupation of the Khyber line, and to be stationed at Landi Kotal. Cholera broke out in its most virulent form amongst our troops retiring from the advanced posts, and claimed many victims from the battalion,—two officers (Captain R. B. Reed and Surgeon-Major J. Wallace, M.D.), and thirty-two non-commissioned officers and men succumbing to this disease within a few weeks.

In September, 1879, the massacre of the British Embassy at Kabul caused preparations to be hurried forward for the second invasion of Afghanistan. On the 29th of that month the Fort of Daka was re-occupied without opposition, two companies of the battalion forming part of the advanced guard which was pushed forward to take possession. In the middle of December three companies were sent to Jalalabad, and by the 21st idem the battalion was concentrated there, except two companies which had been left to garrison the post of Basawal.

During January, 1880, the Head-quarter wing was engaged in a skirmish with the Mohmand tribe at Ali Boghan.

On the 28th January Head-quarters and four companies crossed the Kabul River with other troops of all arms detailed to occupy the Lughman Valley. This occupation was not contested, and continued till the 16th March, when the valley was evacuated, and the battalion once more concentrated at Gandamak.

In the beginning of April the battalion formed part of an expedition sent to enforce payment of a fine levied on the Wazir Kugianis.

At the end of April, in consequence of the large number of men of the battalion in hospital, and the debilitated state of a large number of the remainder, orders were issued for a medical inspection by a Board of Officers. This resulted in the battalion being directed to return to India on relief by the 5th Fusiliers. On arrival of a portion of the relieving corps at Gandamak, the battalion marched, on the 15th May, for India.

On arrival at Jalalabad the battalion was detained, owing to disturbances in the Besud district. A wing under command of Lieut.-Colonel Sillery was here detached to form part of a column sent to operate against the enemy, whilst the Head-quarter wing resumed its march towards India. On the 19th May a sharp action was fought at Beninga against greatly superior numbers, which resulted in the complete defeat of the enemy with very heavy loss. The wing 1st Battalion 12th Regiment had one man severely wounded on this occasion, and four others slightly. Private Longworth greatly distinguished himself in the action.

Head-quarters recrossed the frontier on 26th May and arrived at Peshawar on 27th, the detached wing rejoining shortly afterwards.

During the service of the battalion in Afghanistan—a period of about 13 months—its losses were heavy. Two officers and 71 non-commissioned officers and men died in Afghanistan; one officer (Captain Mayer) and 18 men in India; nearly all from the results of active service. In addition to this, 260 non-commissioned officers and men were invalided to India.

The excellent service rendered by the battalion during the campaign was acknowledged by its Brigade and Divisional Generals, and by the General Officer Commanding in Afghanistan.

In recognition of the services of the 1st Battalion Her Majesty was pleased to command that the word "Afghanistan, 1878-80" should be added to the honourable distinctions already borne on the colours of the regiment.

SERVICES IN AFGHANISTAN OF OFFICERS OF THE 1ST BATTN. 12TH (EAST SUFFOLK) REGT. (NOW 1ST BATTN. SUFFOLK REGT.)

Colonel G. F. Walker commanded the battalion during the war. Commanded the brigade which occupied the Lughman Valley, the troops engaged in the affair at Ali Boghan, and eventually the 3rd Brigade of General Phayre's Division, taking part in the advance from Quetta to Kandahar in the autumn of 1880. (Mentioned in despatches.)

Colonel C. J. C. Sillery (*2nd Battn.*) served with the battalion throughout the campaign, taking part in the expedition against the Wazir Kugianis, and commanding the detached wing in the operations in the Besud district, including the action of Beninga. (Mentioned in despatches.)

Lt.-Colonel W. T. Baker served with the battalion throughout the campaign. (Mentioned in despatches.)

Bt. Lt.-Colonel H. P. Pearson. (For services see "Staff.")

Major H. M. Lowry served with the battalion throughout the campaign, taking part in the occupation of the Lughman Valley, the expedition against the Wazir Kugianis, and the operations in the Besud district, including the action of Beninga.

Major H. L. W. Phillips served with the battalion throughout the campaign, commanding the detachment at the affair at Kam Daka, and taking part in the expedition against the Wazir Kugianis, and the operations in the Besud district, including the action of Beninga. (Mentioned in despatches.)

Major C. F. Morris served with the battalion from November, 1879, till the conclusion of the campaign, taking part in the operations in the Besud district, including the action of Beninga.

Captain H. Magee served with the battalion until July, 1879, when he was invalided. (Subsequently died from the effects of exposure during the campaign.)

Captain R. O'S. Brooke (*A.P.D.*) served with the battalion from April till October, 1879. (Mentioned in despatches.)

Captain J. C. R. Glasgow served with the battalion from March, 1880, till the conclusion of the campaign.

Captain O. Williams and Lieut. F. W. Scudamore and W. Giles served with the battalion throughout the campaign, being present at the affair at Ali Boghan, and taking part in the occupation of the Lughman Valley and the expedition against the Wazir Kugianis.

Captain C. R. Townley served with the battalion, as Adjutant, throughout the campaign, being present at the affair at Ali Boghan.

Captain A. S. Hext and Lieut. J. G. Smith (*Probationer Staff Corps*) served with the battalion from the latter end of 1879 till the conclusion of the campaign, being present at the affair at Ali Boghan, and taking part in the occupation of the Lughman Valley, and the expedition against the Wazir Kugianis.

Lieut. C. D. Cave served with the battalion throughout the campaign, taking part in the expedition against the Wazir Kugianis, and the operations in the Besud district, including the action of Beninga.

Captain G. Shields (*h.p.; A.P.D.*) served with the battalion until promoted on half-pay in May, 1879.

Lieut. J. B. M'Donell served with the battalion till the latter end of 1879, being subsequently appointed to the charge of signalling Khyber Line F.F.

Lieut. R. C. Onslow (*Bengal Staff Corps*). (For services see 10th Bengal Lancers.)

Lieut. G. F. C. Mackenzie served with the battalion from November, 1879, till the conclusion of the campaign, taking part in the expedition against the Wazir Kugianis, and the operations in the Besud district, including the action of Beninga.

Lieut. A. J. R. Hutchinson (*Bengal Staff Corps*) served with the battalion throughout the campaign, being present at the affair of Kam Daka. (Mentioned in despatches.)

Lieut. W. F. Perceval served with the battalion till the latter part of 1879, when he was invalided. (Subsequently died from the effects of exposure during the campaign.)

Lieut. J. M. Carpendale (*Bengal Staff Corps*) served with the battalion till the spring of 1880, being present at the affair at Ali Boghan, and taking part in the occupation of the Lughman Valley.

Lieut. F. P. Hutchinson served with the battalion throughout the campaign, being present at the affair at Ali Boghan, and taking part in the occupation of the Lughman Valley.

Lieut. A. M. Brabazon served with the battalion throughout the campaign.

Lieut. E. J. Medley and Quartermaster W. Cox served with the battalion throughout the campaign, taking part in the expedition against the Wazir Kugianis.

Lieut. F. Graham served with the battalion throughout the campaign, taking part in the occupation of the Lughman Valley, the expedition against the Wazir Kugianis, and the operations in the Besud district, including the action of Beninga.

Lieut. A. F. Poulton (2nd Battn.) served with the battalion from December, 1879, till the conclusion of the campaign.

Lieut. E. A. Kemble served with the battalion from March till May, 1880, when he was invalided.

2ND BATTN. 14TH (P.W.O.) REGT. (NOW 2ND BATT. P.W.O. [WEST YORKSHIRE] REGT.)

ON the 17th December, 1879, the 2nd Battn. 14th P.W.O. Regt., then stationed at Lucknow, received orders to proceed to Peshawar to form part of the Reserve Division of the force operating in Northern Afghanistan. By the middle of January, 1880, the concentration of the troops forming the Division had advanced sufficiently to warrant the adoption on the Khyber line of new étappen duty, and the Battalion, detailed to the 2nd Brigade of General Ross's force, under the command of Brigadier-General Hill, proceeded from Peshawar to Jamrud. There it remained till the beginning of April, when it was moved up the Pass to Landi Kotal, and subsequently marched through the Khurd Khyber to Pesh Bolak—the most distant post in the enemy's country in which it was destined to do duty.

In May, 1880, the 2/14th formed part of the moveable column, under the command of Brigadier-General Gib, which marched from Pesh Bolak on the 18th of that month to disperse the hostile gathering of the enemy under Ghulam Ahmad, and on the 20th was engaged in the action of Mazina. In an order subsequently issued by the Brigadier-General congratulating the troops employed in the expedition on the successful termination of their labours, the following passage occurs:—

"The 2/14th Regt., although composed chiefly of young soldiers, behaved with great steadiness, coolness, and gallantry, and were kept well in hand by their commanding officer, Colonel Warren, assisted by his Company officers.

"The action was well calculated to produce wild firing, but there was none, and the per-centage of rounds fired was marvellously low for a long day's fighting. Captain Noyes, 2/14 Regt., behaved with great gallantry in storming a sungah, in which he got wounded, and the Brigadier-General will have much pleasure in bringing his name to the notice of the Major-General Commanding."

On the 1st June, 1880, a mixed force, including four Companies of the battalion, the whole under Colonel Warren, 2/14th, marched for Girdi Khas, to join the column under Brigadier-General Doran proceeding from Jalalabad to operate in the Kama district. On the 4th June two companies under Colonel Warren crossed the Kabul River, two companies remaining as escort to the guns of Battery L/5, R.A., which accompanied the expedition. After destroying the towers of certain hostile tribesmen in the neighbourhood of Sunga Serai, the column recrossed the river, and the detachments under Colonel Warren returned to Pesh Bolak.

On the 12th August the battalion commenced its return march to India, and crossing the frontier on the 19th August, proceeded to Naushahra, where it moved into quarters. Its casualties during the period of its service in Afghanistan were, 1 officer, and 29 non-commissioned officers and men.

SERVICES IN AFGHANISTAN OF OFFICERS OF THE 2ND BATTN. 14TH (P.W.O.) REGT. (NOW 2ND BATTN. P.W.O. [WEST YORKSHIRE REGT.])

Colonel D. S. Warren, C.B., commanded the battalion throughout the period of its service in Afghanistan. Was in command at Pesh Bolak from April till August, 1880, and commanded the Headquarters and five companies of the battalion at the action of Mazina, 20th May, 1880, and the Pesh Bolak force despatched to co-operate with Brigadier-General Doran in the Kama expedition, June, 1880. (Mentioned in despatches.)

RECORDS OF SERVICE.

Colonel W. Young (retired), Captain V. R. Rae, Lieut. R. J. Roberts, Major W. Franklin (A.P.D.), and Quartermaster J. Bayley served with the battalion throughout the period it was employed in the war. *Captain S. J. Butler (1st Battn.)*, till he was invalided to India through illness contracted in the field.

Major H. A. Burton joined the battalion at Pesh Bolak on promotion in May, 1880, and served with it during the remainder of the time it was employed in Afghanistan. Commanded four companies in the Kama expedition.

Captain F. W. Harrington served with the battalion throughout the period it was employed in the war, being present at the action of Mazina.

Major H. McL. Hutchinson. (For services see "Staff.")

Lt.-Colonel W. W. Haywood (retired) served as Brigade Major with the Quetta Field Force from 9th Nov., 1878, till 14th April, 1879, taking part in the advance on and occupation of Kandahar, and the opening up of the Thal-Chotiali route to India. (Thanked in orders.) Subsequently served with the battalion throughout the period it was employed in Afghanistan, being present at the action of Mazina, and taking part in the Kama expedition.

Major D. A. Ogden (h. p.), and Lieuts. W. R. C. Baird and A. J. H. Murray served with the battalion during the war until invalided through illness contracted in the field. Took part in the Kama expedition.

Captain A. W. Noyes served during the war, first as Brigade Transport Officer to the Khyber Force, and subsequently with the battalion, taking part in the action of Mazina, in which he was wounded. (Mentioned in despatches for conspicuous and gallant conduct in leading a charge during the action. Was eventually invalided to India.)

Capt. C. A. Morris served with the battalion throughout the period it was employed in the war, being present at the action of Mazina, and taking part in the Kama expedition.

Capt. A. Ruttledge (1st Battn.). (For services see "Staff.")

Capt. C. S. Gordon served with the battalion during the war, being present at the action of Mazina, and taking part in the expedition to Kama. Was Provost Marshal to the Pesh Bolak force from 12th July, 1880, till the conclusion of the campaign.

Capt. J. W. Thruston served with the 27th P.N.I. from 2nd Dec., 1878, till invalided in June, 1879, and with the same regiment throughout the second campaign, taking part in the action of Deh Sarak, in which he commanded the detachment engaged; and the destruction of the Ghilzai villages in Dec., 1879. (Mentioned in despatches.)

Lieuts. R. L. Geaves and H. Walker (1st Battn.) served with the battalion during the war until invalided through illness contracted in the field. Were present at the action of Mazina, and took part in the Kama expedition.

Lieut. E. E. S. Schuyler served as Assistant Superintendent of Transport, Kuram Field Force, from 31st March till 18th June, 1879, and subsequently with the battalion till invalided to India through illness contracted in the field.

Lieut. F. W. Kitchener served as Assistant Superintendent of Transport, Kuram Field Force, from 10th April till 23rd Sept., 1879; as Brigade Transport Officer to the Kabul Field Force from 24th Sept., 1879, till 20th Jan., 1880; and as Equipment Transport Officer to the Kabul Field Force from 21st Jan. till 18th May, 1880. Accompanied Sir Frederick Roberts across the Shutargardan, and was present at the actions of Charasiab, Karez Mir, and Chardeh Valley, and took part in the defence of Sherpur. Rejoined the battalion at Pesh Bolak on the 27th May, 1880, when he was appointed Adjutant, and served with the Head-quarters till the conclusion of the campaign, taking part in the Kama expedition. (Mentioned in despatches.)

Lieut. A. W. St. George served with the battalion till invalided from Jamrud.

Lieut. C. M. Lester served with the battalion during the war, being present at the action of Mazina, and taking part in the Kama expedition. Was Regimental Transport Officer from the 10th Feb. till the 20th June, 1880, and held the appointment of Provost Marshal at Landi Kotal from 13th April till 2nd May, 1880.

Lieut. G. W. Mitchell (1st Battn.) served with the battalion during the war. Proceeded in charge of a transport convoy to Kabul, 7th March, 1880.

Lieut. C. P. Barchard. (For services see "Staff.")

Lieut. H. G. Vialls served with the battalion during the war, being present at the action of Mazina. Was appointed Regimental Transport Officer, 21st June, 1880, and served in that capacity till the conclusion of the campaign.

2ND BATTN. 15TH (YORKSHIRE EAST RIDING) REGT. (NOW 2ND BATTN. EAST YORKSHIRE REGT.)

THE 2nd Battalion 15th Regt. formed part of the Reserve Division Southern Afghanistan Field Force, which, during the early part of March, 1880, was concentrated at Karachi, Sind.

After the receipt of the news of the disaster at Maiwand, the Head-quarters and eight companies left Karachi on the 4th August, 1880, for Sibi; and marching through the Bolan Pass in detachments—with inadequate transport, with insufficient water, and in burning heat—arrived at Quetta on the 20th of the month. Notwithstanding the great hardships they endured, the men worked with admirable spirit. The trying nature of the march is attested by the fact that some 100 of them—chiefly young soldiers who had been recently sent out—were placed *hors de combat* by sunstroke and heat-apoplexy before reaching the Afghan frontier.

The battalion advanced with the Division under Major-General Sir R. Phayre, C.B., which marched through the Khojak Pass, and eventually arrived at Kandahar too late to take part in the battle of the 1st September, 1880.

The Division was shortly afterwards broken up, and the battalion returned to India in the month of December of the same year.

The following officers served with the 2nd Battn. 15th Regt. in the war, taking part in the advance to Kandahar:—

Lt.-Colonel R. L. Dashwood (in command) (mentioned in despatches); *Major H. B. Le Mottée; Captains G. H. Johnston, G. C. K. P. Roupell, W. H. Rushbrooke,* and *T. G. Shortland* (left in command of one company at Gulistan Karez); *Lieuts. W. W. Ward* (1st Battn.), *C. F. Garnett, P. Low, E. Hanstock* (appointed Provost Marshal to the 2nd Division, Southern Afghanistan F.F., in September, 1880), *L. L. Steele* (as Adjutant), *G. H. M. Conran, B. M. Hamilton* (appointed Brigade Transport Officer 3rd Brigade 2nd Division Kandahar F.F.), *W. B. Piers* (*Probationer Staff Corps*), *W. T. Davies* (*Probationer Staff Corps*), *R. W. Sherard* (*Probationer Staff Corps*), *H. F. E. Hodges* (*Probationer Staff Corps*), *C. H. W. Maunsell, J. R. F. Sladen, Captain W. L. Barr* (A.P.D.), and *Qr.-Mr. C. J. Knott.*

For services of *Lt.-Colonel H. J. Hallowes, Bt. Lt.-Colonel C. J. Burnett, Major H. L. Dundas, Captain A. Bowles, Lieut. F. G. Pogson, Lieut. A. Foster,* and *Lieut. H. St. L. Wood,* see "Staff."

1ST BATTN. 17TH (LEICESTERSHIRE) REGT. (NOW 1ST BATTN. LEICESTERSHIRE REGT.)

THE 1st Battn. 17th Regt., when quartered in the Murree Hills, Punjab, received telegraphic orders on the 23rd Sept., 1878, to proceed to Kohat for active service in Afghanistan, but a few days later its destination was altered to Peshawar, for the same object.

Having moved down to the plains as soon as carriage could be procured, the battalion left Rawal Pindi on the 11th Oct., 1878, under the command of Bt. Lieut.-Colonel W. D. Tompson, Colonel A. H. Cobbe having been appointed a Brigadier-General in the Kuram Valley Force.

Detailed to the 2nd Brigade, 1st Division, Peshawar Field Force, under the command of Brigadier-General J. A. Tytler, C.B., V.C., the battalion, having stored its colours in the Peshawar arsenal, crossed the border on the 19th Nov., 1878; and during the 21st and 22nd, whilst the main body of the Division was engaged in the direct attack on Ali Musjid, was employed, with the other units of the brigade to which it belonged, in the arduous duty of turning the enemy's flank over the Rotas heights.

The Khyber Pass having been entered, the regiment advanced with the brigade to Daka, at which post it remained encamped for a period of four weeks.

As a unit of the Daka column, the 1/17th took part, in December, 1878, in the first Bazar Valley expedition under General Maude. In the operations which were conducted both on the 21st and 22nd of the month, it was hotly engaged, losing two men killed and one wounded, and inflicting severe losses on the enemy. On the 24th Dec., 1878, the battalion proceeded to Basawal. There it remained till the end of March, 1879, keeping up communications with the Divisional Head-quarters at Jalalabad, and the 2nd Division in the Khyber Pass as far as Jamrud, its duties principally consisting in escorting treasure, road-making, and intrenching its camp and that of the brigade, and in taking part, from time to time, in retaliatory raids.

On the 26th Dec., 1878, a detachment under Bt. Major C. McPherson was sent to increase the garrison at Daka.

Taking part with the Basawal column in the second Bazar Valley expedition, the battalion was employed from the 25th Jan. to the 4th Feb., 1879, in the renewed operations which were conducted against the Zaka Khel Afridis. On the return of the brigade to Basawal, the detachment from Daka rejoined regimental Head-quarters.

On the 9th Feby., 1879, Captain Lonsdale's company was sent on detachment to Barikab, to hold that post, and later on, to Ali Boghan. On the 19th idem a company under Lieut. Webb proceeded to Girdi Khas, on the Kabul River, on similar duty.

From the 18th to the 21st March, Head-quarters and four companies were employed as part of the expeditionary force under Br.-Genl. Tytler, which proceeded into the Maidanak district to exact retribution for recent attacks made by the Shinwaris upon surveying parties, and assisted in destroying several of their towers and villages. In consequence of an attack subsequently made by the tribesmen on a camel guard,—an attack which was brilliantly repelled by a small party of the regiment, with a few Sepoys of the 27th P.N.I., under the command of Lieut. R. J. G. Creed, 1/17th—operations were renewed by General Tytler's force on the 24th March, on which day 250 men of the regiment, under Lt.-Colonel Utterson, were engaged in the successful action of Deh Sarak. On the 26th, the 2nd Brigade marched to Barikab, where regimental Head-quarters were joined by the Girdi Khas detachment as well as by that under the command of Lt.-Col. Utterson. On the following day the regiment marched into Jalalabad, when Captain Lonsdale's company also rejoined.

The 1/17th was employed in intrenching the camp and in assisting to erect Fort Sale at Jalalabad until midnight, 31st March, when the Left half-battalion, made up to 400 men, under Bt. Major C. M'Pherson, marched to Futtehabad with a force under Brigadier-General C. Gough, C.B., V.C. On the 2nd April, 1879, three companies of the Left half-battalion were engaged, under the command of Captain Brind, in the action of Futtehabad. In this engagement the regiment lost a gallant young officer—Lieut. Wiseman, who was killed in capturing a standard—and five rank and file killed and wounded.

On the night of the 2nd April the rest of the battalion arrived from Jalalabad; and on the 13th the brigade marched to Safed Sang, where it was for some weeks employed in intrenching the position and road-making towards Kabul.

On the 28th April three companies of the 1/17th under Lt.-Col. Utterson, joined a covering party four miles beyond Safed Sang, and two days afterwards assisted in burying the bleached bones of the remnant of the 44th Regiment, who were slaughtered whilst making their last stand during the disastrous retreat from Kabul in 1842.

When the Amir Yakub Khan entered Gandamak to sign the treaty of peace, he was received by a guard of honour from the regiment.

Safed Sang was evacuated on the 7th June, 1879, and after a very trying march, and many casualties from heat-cholera and typhoid fever, the battalion reached Landi Kotal. At this post it remained as part of the newly constituted Khyber Brigade, till the 14th August, when it finally left Afghanistan for Peshawar.

In tendering his thanks to the brigade in a farewell order, Brigadier-General Tytler adverted in warm terms to the services which had been rendered by the 1/17. The battalion, he observed, had been under his command from the first operations, and had shared with him the fatigues and privations of the flank march to Kata Kushtia, both operations in the Bazar Valley, and repeated expeditions, including the forced march to Maidanak, and the highly successful operations against the Shinwaris at Deh Sarak. The excellent conduct of the regiment on all these occasions, as well as during the monotony of uneventful camp life, had earned for it his lasting admiration, and, he believed, that of the whole Khyber Army; and he begged to tender his best thanks to Lieut.-Colonel Tompson, the officers, N.-C. officers, and men of this gallant corps, for their services while under his command.

Lieut.-General Sir Sam. Browne, reported, on the 13th Octr., 1879, as follows :—

"H.M. 17th Regt. has been one of the most useful in the Division. Its good discipline, and the heartiness with which it entered into any work it had to do, reflects the greatest credit on Lt.-Colonel W. D. Tompson, who commanded it to my entire satisfaction, and on Lieut. (now Captain) F. G. Anderson, the Adjutant, whose services are specially mentioned by his Commanding Officer."

SERVICES IN AFGHANISTAN OF OFFICERS OF THE 1ST BATTN. 17TH (LEICESTERSHIRE) REGT. (NOW 1ST BATTN. LEICESTERSHIRE REGT.)

Brigadier-General A. H. Cobbe, C.B., h.p. (For services see "Staff.")

Colonel W. D. Tompson, C.B., commanded the battalion throughout the period of its service in the war, being present at the taking of Ali Masjid, the operations at Chinar in Dec., 1878, both the Bazar Valley expeditions, and the operations at Maidanak in March, 1879. (Mentioned in despatches; C.B.)

Colonel A. H. Utterson, Lt.-Colonel C. M'Pherson, Major W. Lonsdale, Bt. Major C. F. W. Moir, Captains C. W. Vulliamy, E. A. H. Webb, J. G. Anderson (as Adjutant), G. J. Buller, C. W. Boddam, and *R. J. G. Creed, Lieuts. M. R. Hyslop, W. S. Stewart-Saville,* and *G. J. Younghusband, Captain G. H. Turner, A.P.D.,* and *Quartermaster John Fuller* served with the regiment throughout the period it was employed in the war, being present at the taking of Ali Musjid. *Colonel Utterson* also took part in the second Bazar Valley expedition, and commanded the detachment at the action of Deh Sarak (mentioned in despatches); *Lt.-Colonel M'Pherson* also took part in the second Bazar Valley expedition, and was in command of the camp at Futtehabad during the action of the 2nd April, 1879 (mentioned in despatches); *Major Lonsdale* also took part in the operations at Chinar, and both the Bazar Valley expeditions (mentioned in despatches); *Major Moir* in the operations at Chinar, and the second Bazar Valley expedition, and in the second campaign served as a Transport Officer with the Kuram Valley F.F. (mentioned in despatches; brevet of Major); *Captain Vulliamy,* in the operations at Chinar, both the Bazar Valley expeditions, and the operations at Maidanak; *Capt. Webb,* in the second Bazar Valley expedition; *Capt. Anderson,* in the operations at Chinar, and the second Bazar Valley expedition; *Capt. Buller,* in the operations at Chinar, and the actions of Deh Sarak and Futtehabad; *Capt. Boddam,* in the operations at Chinar; *Capt. Creed,* in the operations at Chinar, both the Bazar Valley expeditions, and the action of Deh Sarak; acted as Orderly Officer to Brigadier-General Tytler from 1 June, 1879 (mentioned in despatches, and received the Royal Humane Society's medal for saving, while fully accoutred, the life of a private who was drowning in the Kabul River, on the 7th Feb., 1879); *Lieut. Hyslop,* in the operations at Chinar and the first Bazar Valley expedition; *Lieut. Stewart-Savile,* in the second Bazar Valley expedition, and the actions of Deh Sarak and Futtehabad; and *Lieut. Younghusband,* in the operations at Chinar and the second Bazar Valley expedition, and the action, and subsequently attached to the Guides Infantry, served with that regiment from 28th May, 1880, till the conclusion of the second campaign.

Major F. S. S. Brind joined the battalion 21 Dec., 1878, and served with it till the conclusion of the campaign, being present, in command of the three companies which were engaged, at the action of Futtehabad. (Mentioned in despatches; Brevet of Major).

Captain J. H. C. Michel joined the battalion 25 Jan., 1879, and served with it till the conclusion of the campaign, being present at the operations at Maidanak and the action of Deh Sarak.

Capt. T. F. H. de Burgh served with the battalion during the war.

Capt. W. W. Clarke joined the battalion 26 March, 1879, and served with it till the conclusion of the campaign, being present at the action of Futtehabad.

Lieut. E. Allfrey joined the battalion 1 Feb., 1879, and was present with it at the operations at Maidanak. (Died at Safed Sang, 13 May, 1879, from the effects of illness contracted in the field.)

Lieut. A. W. McKinstry served in the second campaign with the 5th Punjab Infantry, taking part in the advance on Kabul, and being present at the action of Charasiab.

Lieut. E. H. Griffith joined the battalion 6 Dec., 1878, and served with it till the conclusion of the campaign, being present at the operations at Chinar, and taking part in the second Bazar Valley expedition.

For services of *Bt. Lieut.-Colonel J. O. Travers* and *Lieut. F. W. Reader,* see "Staff"; and of *Capt. J. H. Gamble* (deceased), *Lieut. N. C. Wiseman* (deceased), and *Lieut. E. H. Watson* (deceased), see Biographical Division.

1st BATTN. 18th (ROYAL IRISH) REGT. (NOW 1st BATTN. ROYAL IRISH REGT.)

IN December, 1879, the 1st Battalion Royal Irish, then stationed at Firozpur, received orders to proceed on Kabul scale to Peshawar. The regiment marched on the 4th Jany., 1880, and arriving at its destination on the 25th idem, was posted to the Reserve Division of the force operating on the Khyber line.

On the Reserve Division being broken up in March, 1880, the Royal Irish was detailed to garrison Peshawar, where it remained till it received orders, in the ensuing month, to proceed on service into Northern Afghanistan.

The battalion arrived at Landi Kotal on the 2nd May, 1880, and was posted to the 1st Section Khyber Line Force. Shortly afterwards, one company was detached to Daka, but in the month of June it was withdrawn, and rejoined Head-quarters, the post being considered too unhealthy for prolonged occupation by European troops.

The regiment remained at Landi Kotal during the whole summer, performing convoy and other duties. On the return of the troops from Kabul, it was detailed to form part of the newly constituted Khyber Brigade, and, with the other units of that force, was employed for several months in holding the country from Jamrud to Landi Khana, the only part of Northern Afghanistan retained by the British after the evacuation of Kabul.

It being considered advisable, during this period, that British troops should be quartered at Ali Musjid, in consequence of the tribes in the neighbourhood constantly harassing convoys, &c., one company of the regiment was detailed to that post.

On the final evacuation of the Khyber, on the 18th March, 1881, the Royal Irish returned to India. During the period of its service in the war, the battalion suffered heavily from the unhealthy nature of the climate in which it was employed, losing from disease over sixty-two non-commissioned officers and men, including Quartermaster Richard Barrett, who had been twenty-six years in the regiment.

The undermentioned officers served with the 1st Battn. 18th Royal Irish, in the war, and have received the medal :—

Colonel M. J. R. MacGregor (in command); *Majors R. I. Adamson, H. Shaw, V.C.* (also served as Station Staff Officer at Landi Kotal from May till August, 1880, and for a time as Brigade Major, 1st Section Khyber Line Force); *Lt.-Colonel St. G. A. Smith* (retired), *Majors A. J. A. Jackson* (also served as Brigade Transport Officer, Reserve Division, from 26 Feb. till 30 April, 1880, proceeding, in the interval, in charge of a convoy, from Peshawar to Jalalabad; and as Treasury Officer from 6 June till 31 Dec., 1880), *J. G. Butts* (retired), *F. S. Bolton* (retired), *Captains W. W. Lawrence, J. W. Graves, S. Phillips, J. H. A. Spyer* (2nd Battn.), *P. A. Morshead* (was appointed to the Transport Service in June, 1880), *H. S. Lye* (2nd Battn.) (mentioned in despatches), *C. E. Le Quesne* (2nd Battn.), *Lieuts. H. M. Hatchell* (also served as Orderly Officer to Brigadier-General W. Roberts from January till July, 1880), *Hon. M. H. H. M'Donnell, N. A. Francis, R. M. Maxwell, A. I. Wilson, D. M. Thompson, B. J. C. Doran,* and *Quartermaster R. Barrett* (died at Landi Kotal, October, 1880).

For services of *Lieuts. S. S. Parkyn* and *P. B. Lindsell*, see "Staff."

1st BATTN. 25th KING'S OWN BORDERERS. (NOW 1st BATT. KING'S OWN BORDERERS.)

AFTER suffering severely from a cholera epidemic at Faizabad during the months of August and September, 1878, in which sixty-nine men died in a few days, the 1st Battalion King's Own Borderers, ascertaining that its next move was likely to be to Dum Dum, while regiment after regiment was being hurried to the frontier for the invasion of Afghanistan, made known to H.E. the Commander-in-Chief through Major Terry, who was in temporary command, its wish not to be passed over for active service. On the 18th Oct. a telegram ordering it to the front was received; and three days afterwards, on the evening of the 21st, it left its quarters and proceeded in service order to Jhelum, at which station it arrived, under command of Col. Ruddell, on the 25th. As soon as transport could be obtained it marched to Rawal Pindi, where it remained from the 1st to the 19th Nov., when a further forward movement was made to Haji Shah. Here it was posted to the 1st (Brigadier-General Blyth's) Brigade, 2nd Division, Peshawar Valley Field Force.

On the 4th Dec., 1878, the 1/25th crossed the Indus, and after remaining for a short time at Naushahra, proceeded by half-battalions to Jamrud. The battalion was there inspected, on the first day of the new year, by General Maude, who expressed himself satisfied with its general appearance, and with the good conduct of the men since joining his Division.

In January, 1879, four companies of the regiment took part in the second Bazar Valley expedition, being detailed to the Jamrud column of General Maude's command. During the night of the 26th of that month the casualties of the battalion, from the fire of the enemy on the picquets, were one man killed and two wounded. At daybreak on the 27th 300 men under Col. Ruddell were sent by the Lieutenant-General to scour the Chinar Hill, and succeeded in inflicting a loss on the enemy of eight men killed. In the operations of the force under Col. Thompson, 6th B.N.I., which was detached on the 29th to blow up the towers at Halwai, one man of the battalion was wounded. The objects of the expedition being accomplished, the troops returned, in the early days of February, to the line of communications; and shortly afterwards the regiment was ordered to Landi Kotal, where it remained performing escort and other duties, till the peace of Gandamak brought the first campaign to a close.

In the third week of December, 1879, the King's Own Borderers—under Major Ramsay, who had assumed command owing to the failure of health of Col. Ruddell—having been again ordered to the front, proceeded in half-battalions from Peshawar, where it was then stationed, viâ Jamrud to Landi Kotal, and formed part of the 3rd Brigade, 2nd Division Kabul Field Force, under the command of Brigadier-General Doran. A depôt had been formed and left at Peshawar under the command of Captain Ross; and during the month two companies, under Captain McCausland, were moved to Basawal, a third company, under Lieut. Dandridge, to Jalalabad, and another company, under Captain Dixon, to Daka.

In January, 1880, 200 bayonets of the regiment, under Major Ramsay, took part with the column under the personal command of Brigadier-General Doran, in the expedition against the Mohmands of Kam Daka; two companies, under Captain H. Dixon, forming part of Col. Boisragon's column co-operating from Daka. Upwards of 5,000 of the enemy were defeated on the heights above Kam Daka by the column last named, with heavy loss; on the 15th large numbers of them being cut up on the plain below by a portion of Brigadier-General Doran's column, including the details of the 1/25th, which, after traversing eighteen miles of difficult mountainous country, and capturing a position, had been pushed on for the purpose of intercepting them. After burning the villages of Kam Daka and Raina, the columns returned. For his services during the operations Captain Dixon was mentioned in despatches.

A welcome accession of strength to the battalion, in the form of a draft of 110 non-commissioned officers and men, under the command of Captain Carleton, reached Landi Kotal on the 15th Jan., 1880.

On the 20th Jan. Head-quarters and four companies marched for Jalalabad, which was reached on the 23rd.; A company was left at Daka, and C and E companies at Basawal. A few days afterwards F, G, and H companies, under Captain Carleton, proceeded to Darunta to join the force engaged in making a road over the range of mountains separating the Lughman Valley from the Jalalabad plain.

On the 26th Jan. Major Terry, who had been employed in the Kuram Valley in the Transport Department, rejoined, and took over the command of the battalion.

A, C, and E companies marched into Jalalabad on the 27th Jan., and the same day Head-quarters, together with B and D companies, proceeded to join the Lughman expeditionary force under the command of Major-General Bright, C.B., at Darunta. During the operations which ensued in the valley various companies of the battalion took part in the occupation of Fateh, Muhammad Khan and Azmat Allah Khan's forts, and subsequently in the reconnaissance to Adrak Badrak, conducted by Col. Boisragon.

On the 26th Feb., 1880, a combined force consisting of G company, 1/25, and other details, under the command of Major Ramsay, marched to Durgai. This party, after making a road to the head of the Valley, received orders to proceed to Pezwan, from whence, shortly afterwards, it was ordered to Jagdalak to form part of the garrison of that post, to the command of which Major Ramsay had been appointed. G company remained at Jagdalak till the end of the campaign.

On the 13th March, 1880, Head-quarters returned to Jalalabad, F and H companies, under Captain Carleton, remaining in the Lughman district till the 16th, when the Valley was finally evacuated.

A few days afterwards alterations occurred in the constitution of the divisions and the distribution of commands, the 1/25th appearing as a unit of the 3rd Section Khyber Line Force, commanded by Brigadier-General Hill.

In the first days of April, 1880, the battalion took part with the Jalalabad Moveable Column, commanded by Brigadier-General Doran, in the expedition despatched against the Wazir Kugianis, a co-operating force advancing at the same time from Rozabad. On the objects of the expedition being accomplished, and the troops returning to their stations, 1/25th and 12th Regiments changed columns, the former marching to Safed Sang.

On the 9th April A, D, and E companies, under the command of Captain Dixon, left Safed Sang for Jagdalak Kotal, and two days afterwards Head-quarters marched to Pezwan. Both Head-quarters and the companies under Captain Dixon remained at these posts, respectively, till the final retirement in August. The battalion took all convoy guard duties up to the last; and in June and July the men thus employed were exposed to a temperature which ranged up to 115° in the shade.

On the 19th June, 1880, a very sudden attack was made on a convoy near Jagdalak Kotal. Fire was opened at close quarters, four sepoys of the 31st P.N.I. were cut down, and the whole party was thrown into momentary confusion. Sergt. Hamilton, 1/25th, who was proceeding at the time to Jagdalak, rallied the guard, and by crowning a commanding point overawed the enemy, and gave time for assistance to be brought. His conduct on this occasion was recognized by the grant of a distinguished service medal. On the 4th July a combined force from the garrison of Pezwan, under Major Terry, took part in the expedition which, in consequence of a repetition of similar attacks, was ordered into the Hissarak Valley to destroy the fortified Ghilzai villages of Nargashai, Arab Khel, and Jokan. In the smart skirmish which ensued on the 5th, a sergeant of the battalion was wounded. Captain Curtis was in command of the advance-guard, and for the services he rendered was mentioned in despatches.

On the 12th August, 1880, the battalion commenced its return march to India, and on the 28th idem arrived at Peshawar, where it moved into quarters.

SERVICES IN AFGHANISTAN OF OFFICERS OF THE 1ST BATTN. 25TH (KING'S OWN BORDERERS). (NOW 1ST BATTN. KING'S OWN BORDERERS.)

Colonel J. A. Ruddell (h. p.) commanded the battalion in the first campaign, taking part in the second Bazar Valley expedition. (Mentioned in despatches.)

Major F. S. Terry (h. p.) served with the 27th P.N.I., as Wing Commander, at the assault and capture of Ali Musjid, and afterwards with his own regiment till the conclusion of the first campaign, taking part in the second Bazar Valley expedition, under General Maude, to whose staff he was attached as Orderly Officer. In the second campaign served, first as General Transport Officer to the Kuram Field Force, and was in charge of the transport of the Zaimusht expedition; subsequently (from 26 Jan., 1880, till the final retirement in August, 1880) in command of the battalion, and of the post of Pezwan, taking part in the Lughman Valley expedition, the expedition against the Wazir Kugianis, and the expedition into the Hissarak Valley in July, 1880. (Mentioned in despatches.)

Lt.-Colonel N. C. Ramsay served with the battalion throughout, commanding it from the date of the renewal of hostilities in the autumn of 1879 till the 25th Jan., 1880. Took park in the Bazar Valley expedition, the expedition against the Mohmands of Kam Daka (in Brigadier-General Doran's column), and the Lughman Valley expedition.

Major J. T. L. Carwithen, Captain A. G. S. Beadnell, and Lieut. L. Gordon served with the battalion in the first campaign—Lieut. Beadnell as Adjutant,—taking part in the Bazar Valley expedition.

Major F. E. Carleton served with the battalion in the second campaign, taking part in the Lughman Valley expedition, the expedition against the Wazir Kugianis, and the expedition into the Hissarak Valley. (Medal.)

Major H. J. Harvey served with the battalion in the first campaign, taking part in the Bazar Valley expedition. Commanded a mixed force in a very exposed position in the Khyber, at Landi Khana.

Major W. G. Thomas (2nd Battn.). (For services see "Staff.")

Major J. L. Ross served with the battalion throughout, taking part in the expedition against the Mohmands of Kam Daka, the expedition against the Wazir Kugianis, and the expedition into the Hissarak Valley. (Mentioned in despatches.)

Captain F. H. T. Curtis served with the battalion in the second campaign, taking part in the expedition against the Wazir Kugianis, and the expedition into the Hissarak Valley, in which he commanded the advance guard. Proceeded to Kabul in May, 1880, in charge of details for various regiments. (Mentioned in despatches.)

Major F. E. Lloyd (retired) served with the battalion in the first campaign, taking part in the Bazar Valley expedition. Subsequently served as Brigade Major, 2nd Brigade, 3rd Division. In the second campaign served as Field Engineer, Kuram Valley Force.

Captain J. R. M'Causland served with the battalion throughout, taking part in the expedition against the Mohmands of Kam Daka, in which he commanded the detachment of the regiment forming part of Brigadier-General Boisragon's column.

Captains J. H. H. S. D. Hogarth, A. Leith-Hay Mackay, and Lieut. J. B. Thompson served with the battalion in the first campaign.

Captain A. H. Hope and Lieut. C. L. Woolcombe served with the battalion throughout, taking part in the expedition against the Mohmands of Kam Daka (in Brigadier-General Doran's column), the Lughman Valley expedition, and the expedition against the Wazir Kugianis. Lieut. Woolcombe held, for a time, the appointment of Station Staff Officer at Pezwan.

Captain H. G. Dixon served throughout both campaigns: in the first, as Orderly Officer to Brigadier-General Blyth, taking part, in that capacity, in the Bazar Valley expedition; in the second, with the battalion, taking part in the expedition against the Mohmands of Kam Daka (in which he commanded 200 men of the regiment, in Brigadier-General Boisragon's column, at the action of the 15th Jan., 1880), the Lughman Valley expedition, and the expedition against the Wazir Kugianis. (Mentioned in despatches.)

Captain C. C. W. Dandridge served with the battalion in the first campaign, taking part in the Bazar Valley expedition. In the second campaign served with the 2nd Division Kabul Field Force as Brigade Major and Deputy Assistant Quartermaster-General to the 2nd Brigade.

Captain C. T. Becker served with the battalion throughout—in the second campaign as Acting Adjutant—taking part in the expedition against the Mohmands of Kam Daka (in Brigadier-General Doran's column), the expedition against the Wazir Kugianis, and the expedition into the Hissarak Valley.

Lieuts. F. A. C. Claughton, J. M. Fleming, and H. V. Cox served with the battalion in the second campaign, taking part in the Lughman Valley expedition.

Lieuts. G. N. Mayne and R. H. B. Taylor served with the battalion in the second campaign, taking part in the expedition against the Wazir Kugianis, and the expedition into the Hissarak Valley. Lieut. Taylor proceeded to Kabul in May, 1880, with details for various regiments.

Lieut. J. M. A. Retallick, Staff Corps. (For services see 45th B.N.I.)

Lieut. L. J. E. Bradshaw, Staff Corps. (For services see 24th P.N.I.)

Lieut. C. D. Gibbon served with the battalion in the first campaign, taking part in the Bazar Valley expedition. (Since deceased.)

Lieut. J. H. E. Reid, Staff Corps. (For services see 3rd Bombay Cavalry.)

Lieut. F. M. Turner served with the battalion throughout, taking part in the Bazar Valley expedition, the Lughman Valley expedition, and the expedition against the Wazir Kugianis. (Mentioned in despatches.)

Lieut. J. Hope served with the battalion throughout, taking part in the Bazar Valley expedition, the expedition against the Mohmands of Kam Daka (in Brigadier-General Boisragon's column), the Lughman Valley expedition, and the expedition against the Wazir Kugianis.

Lieut. D. J. O. Taylor, Staff Corps, served with the battalion in both campaigns.

Lieut. C. J. Corfield served with the battalion in the second campaign, taking part in the expedition against the Wazir Kugianis.

Lieut. J. W. C. Hutchinson served with the battalion throughout, taking part in the Lughman Valley expedition, and the expedition against the Wazir Kugianis.

Lieuts. C. T. P. Keene and G. de W. Verner served with the battalion in the second campaign, taking part in the expedition against the Mohmands of Kam Daka (in Brigadier-General Doran's column), the Lughman Valley expedition, and the expedition against the Wazir Kugianis. Lieut. Verner also took part in the Lughman Valley expedition.

2nd Lieut. E. D. Los. (Deceased. See Biographical Division.)

2nd Lieut. H. Spoor. (Deceased. See Biographical Division.)

Lieut. C. J. E. M'Arthur served with the battalion in the second campaign.

Lieut. J. C. Drummond served with the battalion in the first campaign. (Since deceased.)

Major G. Pumfrett, A.P.D., served with the battalion in the first campaign.

Quartermaster J. Swiney served with the battalion throughout, taking part in the Bazar Valley expedition, and the expedition against the Wazir Kugianis.

51ST REGT. (KING'S OWN LIGHT INFANTRY). (NOW 1ST BATTN. KING'S OWN LIGHT INFANTRY [SOUTH YORKSHIRE REGT.]).

ON the 21st Nov., 1878, the 51st K.O.L.I., as a unit of the 4th Brigade, 1st Division, Peshawar Valley F.F., advanced into the Khyber Pass, and the same day was engaged in the front attack on Ali Musjid. Marching from Jamrud, whither it had recently made its way from Subathu, the regiment, under the command of Colonel Madden, came within range of the enemy's guns about 1.30 p.m., and two hours later went into action, six companies occupying various advanced positions on the surrounding heights, and remaining engaged till darkness closed in. The casualties of the regiment during the day were, one man killed and two wounded. At 7 a.m. the following morning, three companies, under Lt.-Colonel Ball Acton, conformably with orders received the previous night, crossed the river to support the projected assault of the 3rd Brigade on a ridge to the enemy's right, and made their way to where the 81st Regt. was awaiting the order to attack. It was then discovered that the fort had been abandoned in the night, and Lt.-Colonel Acton's companies shortly afterwards entered it. In the meantime two companies of the regiment under Lieuts. Seppings and Bennett, took possession of the enemy's camp by the river, capturing some twenty prisoners, two guns, and a quantity of ammunition.

The regiment remained at Ali Musjid on the further advance of the main body of the Division. From the 24th to the 29th Nov. there was constant firing into the camp at night by the Afridis, considerable numbers of whom assembled on the adjacent ridges. On the night of the 25th Nov. a daring attempt was made by some two or three hundred of these tribesmen to rush a small picquet, consisting of one sergeant and fifteen rank and file, under Lieut. Johnson, placed on a hill to the left of the Khyber stream. The attack was gallantly repulsed, the enemy being very roughly handled. Of the picquet, Sergt. Binge was severely, and four men were slightly, wounded. In consequence of the unsettled state of the tribes, the regiment was constantly on duty, for some time getting only one night's rest out of four or five.

On the 19th Dec., 1878, three companies under Lt.-Colonel Acton left Ali Musjid on the first expedition into the Bazar Valley, and during the succeeding fortnight were engaged with the rest of General Maude's force in destroying the villages and towers of the hostile Zaka Khel. While leading the column during its retirement from the Valley on the 22nd Dec., the companies were engaged in some sharp skirmishing with the enemy on the surrounding heights. In the second expedition into the Bazar Valley at the latter end of January, 1879, the regiment was again represented, 200 men under Major Burnaby marching from Ali Musjid on the 25th of that month, and after being engaged in the various operations of the expeditionary force, returning on the 4th Feb. In the meantime shots continued to be fired at night into the camp at Ali Musjid, severely wounding, on the 19th Dec., two sentries.

On the 8th March, 1879, the 51st K.O.L.I. was transferred to the 3rd Brigade, 1st Division, and on the 17th idem marched towards Jalalabad, where it arrived on the 24th. Three companies under Lt.-Col. Acton took part, *en route*, in an expedition sent out from Basawal to Maidanak on the night of the 19th to punish a section of the Shinwari tribe who had attacked a Survey party under Capt. Leach, R.E.; and on the 1st April a company under Captain Kenneth accompanied the ill-fated expedition into the Lughman Valley in which the greater part of a squadron of the 10th Hussars was swept away in the Kabul river and drowned.

After being encamped a month at Jalalabad, the regiment advanced to Safed Sang, where it arrived on the 27th April, and remained till after the conclusion of peace. On the 8th May it formed part of the guard of honour which received H.H. Yakub Khan.

Commencing its return march towards India on the 5th June, 1879, the 51st L.I., after recrossing the frontier, made its way to Cherat. The excessive fatigue and hardship endured on the march resulted in many casualties, no less than thirty-five deaths occurring in the month of June, and nine more in July.

In his report on the services of officers of the 1st Division Peshawar Valley F.F., the Lieut.-General commanding referred to the 51st as " a regiment excellent in its discipline, and excellent in the soldier-like spirit it has shown throughout."

On the renewal of hostilities in the autumn of 1879 the 51st K.O.L.I. was again ordered up for active service, and as a unit of Brigadier-General Arbuthnot's Brigade of Major-General Bright's Division, marched to Jalalabad, where it arrived on the 23rd Oct., 1879.

Four companies of the regiment escorted the ex-Amir Yakub Khan from that city to Basawal, starting on the 4th and returning on the 8th Dec., 1879.

In the middle of December the regiment advanced to Safed Sang. On the 17th of that month, in response to a request for reinforcements from Brigadier-General C. Gough, who was then at Jagdalak, three companies under Lt.-Col. Ball Acton marched for Pezwan. Finding, on arrival, that Col. Norman, commanding at that post, was also *en route* to open communications with the advanced brigade, and had bivouacked five miles farther on the road, Col. Acton detached twenty-five men to the Pezwan Kotal, and the following morning continued his advance. After marching four miles, he came upon the enemy assembled in considerable force, and turning up a nullah to their right, drove them from the position they had taken up. Communications were then opened with Col. Norman's force, and subsequently with that of General Gough, after which the Pezwan party returned. On the 28th one company of the regiment quitted Pezwan for Jagdalak, and was replaced by another company. The following day a mixed force under Col. Acton, including two companies of the 51st, also marched for Jagdalak, and when within sight of its destination again came into contact with and dispersed a large body of the enemy. In this encounter one man of the regiment was wounded.

In the middle of January, 1880, Head-quarters of the regiment marched from Safed Sang to Pezwan, where they were rejoined by one of the companies from Jagdalak, and shortly afterwards received a welcome addition in the shape of a draft of 215 men who had recently arrived from England. During this month the regiment was placed, by a redistribution, in the 1st Brigade, 2nd Division, Kabul F.F., and on that force being broken up in March, became a unit of the Gandamak moveable column.

On the 22nd March Lieut. Thurlow was shot by a band of robbers while riding with his brother officer, Lieut. Reid, between Jagdalak and the Kotal. For the gallantry he displayed on this occasion Lieut. Reid was recommended for the distinction of the Victoria Cross. A few days afterwards a convoy under the command of Lieut. Pollock, while proceeding to Jagdalak Kotal, was attacked by a large body of marauders. The party was immediately reinforced by the company under command of Capt. Nugent, with Lieut. Reid, and the enemy were dispersed with considerable loss, eleven camels which had been driven off by them being recovered. On the 9th April the companies at Jagdalak rejoined Head-quarters.

In the second week in April the regiment took part with the moveable column in the expedition into the Hissarak Valley, and was engaged in several sharp skirmishes with the enemy. On the night of the 12th Sergeant McCarthy, a gallant and popular soldier, was shot while turning out his picquet; and in the course of the various operations which were conducted, six men of the regiment were wounded. Shortly after the return of the expeditionary force the regiment was moved up to Jagdalak.

On the 31st May, 1880, the 51st K.O.L.I. marched with the moveable column to Safed Sang, *en route* for the Lughman Valley, and for several days took part in carrying out the retributive measures with which that district was visited. On the 11th June part of the rear-guard, commanded by Major Burnaby, while recrossing the Kabul river, was hotly fired on, Major Burnaby receiving a contusion of the face by a spent bullet. The hard work and exposure to which the column was subjected were excessive, and during the return march to Safed Sang many men fell out from the ranks from exhaustion. On the 4th July Head-quarters and four companies assembled at Pezwan, another company arriving next day after a slight skirmish *en route*.

The last expedition in which the regiment took part was one led by Col. Ball Acton against the Ghilzai villages of Nargusai, Arab Khel, and Jokan, which were destroyed in the first week in July as punishment for various raids committed by the tribes on convoys, &c.

On the 9th Aug., 1880, the 51st K.O.L.I. commenced its return march to India, and after arriving at Peshawar on the 23rd idem, proceeded to Lawrencepur, and eventually to Bareilly.

The casualties of the regiment during the second campaign were, two officers and men killed, fourteen wounded, and 151 invalided, of whom twenty-two died.

SERVICES IN AFGHANISTAN OF OFFICERS OF THE 51ST REGT. (KING'S OWN LIGHT INFANTRY.) (NOW 1ST BATTN. KING'S OWN LIGHT INFANTRY [SOUTH YORKSHIRE REGT.].)

Colonel S. A. Madden, C.B., commanded the regiment throughout the first campaign, taking part in the capture of Ali Musjid. (Mentioned in despatches; C.B.)

Colonel C. B. Acton, C.B., served with the regiment throughout both campaigns, commanding it throughout the second. Took part in the capture of Ali Musjid, the first Bazar Valley expedition, the fighting at Jagdalak in Dec., 1879, the Hissarak expedition in April, 1880, the Lughman Valley expedition in June, 1880, and the destruction of the Ghilzai villages in July, 1880. (Mentioned in despatches; C.B.)

Lt.-Colonel E. B. Burnaby, Major J. V. Nugent, Captains T. J. Seppings, C. C. Smyth, and *J. G. Sparke* and *Lieut. H. A. W. Johnson* served with the regiment throughout both campaigns: *Lt.-Colonel Burnaby* taking part in the capture of Ali Musjid, the second Bazar Valley expedition, the expedition to Hissarak, the Lughman Valley expedition, and the destruction of the Ghilzai villages (mentioned in despatches, Brevet of Lt.-Colonel); *Major Nugent* taking part in the capture of Ali Musjid, the first Bazar Valley expedition, the fighting at Jagdalak in Dec., 1879, the Hissarak expedition, the Lughman Valley expedition, and the destruction of the Ghilzai villages (mentioned in despatches, Brevet of Major); *Capt. Seppings* taking part in the capture of Ali Musjid and the Hissarak expedition; *Capt. Smyth* taking part in the capture of Ali Musjid and the fighting at Jagdalak in Dec., 1879 (mentioned in despatches); and *Capt. Sparke* and *Lieut. Johnson* taking part in the capture of Ali Musjid, the second Bazar Valley expedition, the Hissarak expedition, the Lughman Valley expedition, and the destruction of the Ghilzai villages (mentioned in despatches).

Majors R. C. Græme and *A. S. Carter (retired), Capt. E. L. Burnett, Lieuts. G. E. Lloyd, F. A. C. Kreyer (S.C.),* and *Major E. Roberts (A.P.D.)* served with the regiment in the first campaign: Major Græme taking part in the capture of Ali Musjid and the first and second Bazar Valley expeditions (mentioned in despatches); *Major Carter* taking part in the first Bazar Valley expedition; *Capt. Burnett* and *Lieut. Lloyd* taking part in the capture of Ali Musjid and the first Bazar Valley expedition; and *Major Roberts* taking part in the capture of Ali Musjid.

Capts. G. F. White and *G. H. Denshire,* and *Lieuts. F. Corbett, H. Earle, P. W. A. A. Milton, C. G. R. Thackwell, W. B. Butler,* and *J. S. Cave-Browne-Cave* served with the regiment in the first and throughout the second campaign: *Capt. Denshire* and *Lieut. Cave-Browne-Cave* taking part in the fighting at Jagdalak in Dec., 1879, the Hissarak expedition, the Lughman Valley expedition, and the destruction of the Ghilzai villages; *Lieut. Milton* taking part in the fighting at Jagdalak in Dec., 1879, the Lughman Valley expeditions in April and June, 1879, the Hissarak expedition, and the destruction of the Ghilzai villages, in which he acted as Orderly Officer (mentioned in despatches); *Lieut. Corbett* taking part in the Hissarak expedition, the Lughman Valley expedition, and the destruction of the Ghilzai villages (mentioned in despatches); *Lieut. Earle* taking part in the Hissarak expedition; *Lieut. Thackwell* taking part in the Hissarak expedition and Lughman Valley expedition; and *Lieut. Butler* taking part in the fighting at Jagdalak.

Captain B. H. Barrington Kennett served with the regiment in both campaigns, taking part in the second Bazar Valley expedition, the Lughman Valley expedition (in command of the detachment of the 51st L.I.) in April, 1879 (in which the squadron of the 10th Hussars was swept away in the Kabul River and drowned), and the Hissarak expedition. (Mentioned in despatches.)

Captain J. O'B. Drury, A.P.D., served with the regiment throughout the first campaign, taking part in the capture of Ali Musjid and the first Bazar Valley expedition.

Lieut. B. E. Spragge and *Captain T. M. Murray (Quartermaster)* served with the regiment throughout the first and during part of the second campaign; *Lieut. Spragge* taking part in the capture of Ali Musjid, the second Bazar Valley expedition, and the Hissarak expedition (mentioned in despatches); and *Capt. Murray* taking part in the capture of Ali Musjid.

Lieuts. J. E. Preston, C. H. L. Baskerville, H. A. S. Reid, H. A. Merewether, J. Strachey, and *A. R. Power* served with the regiment in the second campaign: *Lieuts. Baskerville, Reid,* and *Power* taking part in the expedition to Hissarak (mentioned in despatches); and *Lieut. Merewether* taking part in the expedition to Hissarak, the Lughman Valley expedition, and the destruction of the Ghilzai villages.

For services of *Major A. S. Wynne,* see "Staff;" and of *Lieut. F. G. Pollock,* see 8th Bengal Cavalry.

59TH (2ND NOTTINGHAMSHIRE) REGT. (NOW 2ND BATTN. EAST LANCASHIRE REGT.)

ON the breaking out of hostilities with Afghanistan, the 59th Regiment, then quartered at Dagshai, was placed under immediate orders for the front. It proceeded under command of Col. Lacy to Multam, where, forming part of Genl. Sir D. Stewart's Division, it remained till the 8th Nov., 1878. Col. Lacy being at this time appointed to a brigade command in Genl. Biddulph's Division, Lieut.-Col. Lawson assumed command of the regiment.

Continuing its forward movement by rail to Rohri, and crossing the Indus at Sukkur after a halt of a few days, the 59th marched to Jacobabad, arriving on the 25th Nov. On the 3rd Dec., one company, under command of Captain Lawlor, marched for Quetta, escorting the Engineer Field Park, two other companies performing similar duty with the guns of Batteries G/4 and D/2, R.A. Head-quarters and four more companies followed on the 7th Dec., 1879, the remaining company, under command of Captain Gordon, being left at Jacobabad for the purpose of escorting the Siege Train, which marched on the 13th idem.

Head-quarters arrived at Quetta on the 24th Dec., and taking part, on the 27th, in the advance on Kandahar of Brigadier-General Hughes' Brigade, were present at the capture and occupation of that city on the 8th Jan., 1879.

On the 14th Jan. Head-quarters and four companies, under command of Lieut.-Col. Lawson, marched with the Division for Kalat-i-Ghilzai, and remained there for three months. On the return of the regimental Head-quarters to Kandahar, Col. Lacy reassumed command, his brigade being now broken up.

The 59th Regiment formed part of the garrison of Kandahar until the evacuation of that city was commenced in August, 1879, when the left half-battalion, under command of Lt.-Col. Frampton, proceeded to the Pishin Valley. On the 8th Sept., the Right half-battalion with Head-quarters, commanded by Col. Lacy, also quitted the city. They had not proceeded farther than Abdul Rahman, however, before the news of the massacre of the Kabul Embassy gave rise to their immediate recall to Kandahar. On the 23rd Sept., 1879, they started again for Kalat-i-Ghilzai, forming part of the flying column engaged in the operations threatening Ghazni, which terminated in the action of Shah-Jui on the 24th Oct., 1879. In this encounter with the enemy, two companies were engaged, Head-quarters and two companies occupying the Fort of Kalat-i-Ghilzai. On the return of the column from Shah-Jui, Head-quarters and two companies accompanied it to Kandahar, two companies being detailed to remarn as part of the garrison of Kalat-i-Ghilzai. After the arrival of Head-quarters at Kandahar, the regiment occupied the citadel and cantonments for a period of some five months.

As a constituent part of General Sir D. Stewart's Division, the 59th took part in the advance from Kandahar—which was commenced on the 31st March, 1880—to Ghazni and Kabul. At Kalat-i-Ghilzai, which was reached on the 8th April, 1880, the two companies which had remained at that place forming part of the garrison, were incorporated in the Division, which continued its march. On the 19th April, the regiment took an active part in the battle of Ahmad Khel, and was again engaged with the enemy at Arzu on the 23rd of the same month.

Marching from Ghazni on the 25th April, 1880, the Division entered the Wardak Valley, where communications were opened with the force under command of General Ross, which had been detached from Kabul to meet it. Shortly afterwards, the Ghazni Field Force was absorbed into the Kabul command.

On the 29th April, 1880, the 59th Regiment, as part of the force detailed to watch the movements of Muhammad Jan, marched from Zaidabad for the Logar Valley. Two companies, under command of Capt. Stoyte, were employed in constructing a road for the passage of the guns over the Yambroak Pass, the Head-quarters and remaining companies accompanying the main body of the Division, at this time under command of Brigadier-General Hughes, to its destination by a different route which was impracticable for artillery.

As part of General Hills' Division, the regiment remained in and about the Logar Valley from the 3rd May till the end of July, when it proceeded to Kabul, and remained there encamped until the final evacuation of the city. It then returned to India, arriving at Peshawar on the 4th Sept., 1880.

The losses sustained by the 59th Regiment by death, from first to last during the war, were, two officers, and sixty-one non-commissioned officers and men.

RECORDS OF SERVICE.

SERVICES IN AFGHANISTAN OF OFFICERS OF THE 59TH (2ND NOTTINGHAMSHIRE) REGT. (NOW 2ND BATTN. EAST LANCASHIRE REGT.)

Colonel Richard Lacy (*retired*) commanded a brigade of General Biddulph's Division during the operations in the Pishin Valley and the subsequent advance on and capture of Kandahar. Continued in command in the advance to Girishk and operations on the Halmand. On the return of the Division to Kandahar assumed command of the 59th Regiment, and continued in command during the occupation of Kandahar by Sir D. Stewart. Was in command of the Right half-battalion (forming part of Brigadier-General Hughes' Brigade) during the occupation of Kalat-i-Ghilzai (Oct., 1879). Commanded the regiment on the march of Sir D. Stewart's Division from Kandahar to Kabul, and continued in command till the final withdrawal of the troops from Kabul. Commanded the regiment at the battle of Ahmad Khel and the action of Arzu. (Mentioned in despatches.)

Lieut.-Colonel J. Lawson assumed command of the regiment at Multan, and remained in command during the advance on and capture of Kandahar. Commanded the Right half-battalion during the march on and capture of Kalat-i-Ghilzai (January, 1879). Served with the Right half-battalion during the subsequent occupation of Kalat-i-Ghilzai in Oct., 1879. Was in command of two companies of the regiment (forming part of the Brigade of Brigadier-General Hughes) in the advance to Shah-Jui. Served with the regiment during the march from Kandahar to Kabul. Invalided to England from Kabul. Present at the battle of Ahmad Khel, in which he was severely wounded. (Brevet of Lieut.-Colonel.)

Bt. Major L. A. Powys. (Deceased. See Biographical Division.)

Lieut.-Colonel W. J. Frampton joined the regiment from the Depôt, and assumed command of the Left half-battalion at Kandahar 10 Feb., 1879. On evacuation of Kandahar in Aug., 1879, commanded the Left half-battalion on the march to the Pishin Valley. Returned with it to Kandahar on the concentration of the Division consequent on the news of the massacre of the Kabul Embassy. Served with the regiment during the march from Kandahar to Kabul, and up till the final withdrawal of the troops from Kabul. Was present at the battle of Ahmad Khel and action of Arzu. (Brevet of Lieut.-Colonel.)

Major H. H. Griffiths served with the regiment throughout both campaigns, and performed the duties of field officer from 19 April, 1880, till the final withdrawal of the troops from Kabul. Present at the battle of Ahmad Khel and action of Arzu, acting as Major of the Left half-battalion in the latter engagement.

Major E. Gunter joined the regiment with a draft from the Depôt in Jan., 1880, and served throughout the second campaign. Completed his staff course on the staff of Brigadier-General Hughes, during the march from Kandahar to Kabul. Present at the battle of Ahmad Khel.

Captain D. T. Chisholm. (Deceased. See Biographical Division.)

Major E. H. Sartorius, V.C. (See Biographical Division.)

Captain R. Elias resigned his appointment of Brigade Major at Sialkot on the outbreak of hostilities, and joining the regiment at Multan, served with it throughout both campaigns. Commanded the detachment of the regiment forming part of the garrison of Kalat-i-Ghilzai from Nov., 1879, to April, 1880. Served with the regiment during the march to Kabul, and till the final withdrawal of the troops from Kabul. Present at the battle of Ahmad Khel and action of Arzu.

Captain J. L. J. Gordon (1st Battn. Royal Canadians) served with the regiment in both campaigns. Was in command of the company escorting the siege train from Jacobabad to Kandahar. Proceeded to India on conclusion of first campaign. Returned to Kandahar in Feb., 1880, in charge of drafts for various regiments, accomplishing the march from Quetta in eight days. Marched with the Head-quarters to Kabul. Commanded the company forming the personal escort to Major-General Hills during the withdrawal of the troops from Kabul. Present at the battle of Ahmad Khel and action of Arzu. (Received the thanks of General Hills.)

Captain W. P. Lawlor served with the regiment throughout both campaigns. Was in command of the company escorting the Engineer Field Park from Jacobabad to Kandahar. Present at the battle of Ahmad Khel and action of Arzu.

Captain J. Stoyte joined the regiment from the Depôt on the 30th March, 1880. Served with it during the march from Kandahar to Kabul. Commanded the company forming the personal escort of Sir D. Stewart during the evacuation of Kabul and the withdrawal of the troops. Present at the battle of Ahmad Khel and action of Arzu.

Captain R. E. Buchanan (*retired*) served with the regiment till arrival at Quetta. Proceeded from Quetta to India in charge of a sick convoy. Rejoined the regiment at Kandahar in March, 1880, and served with it during the remainder of the campaign. Present at the battle of Ahmad Khel and action of Arzu.

Captain C. V. S. Downes. (For services see "Staff.")

Captain B. W. Lucas served with the regiment throughout. Performed the duties of Baggage Master to the Brigade during the march from Kandahar to Kabul. Present at the battle of Ahmad Khel and action of Arzu.

Lieut. W. Fulton (*retired*) joined the regiment from the Depôt in Jan., 1880, and served with it to the end of the campaign. Present at the battle of Ahmad Khel and action of Arzu. (Medal with clasp.)

Lieut. J. F. Irwin served throughout both campaigns. Was Orderly Officer to Brigadier-General Hughes from Nov., 1878, till 3rd Jan., 1880. Was sent in command of a small force of all arms to attack Muhammad Jan on the 23rd Oct., 1879, and was present at the action of Shah Jui on the following day. Rejoined the regiment 3rd Jan., 1880, and was present with it at battle of Ahmad Khel and action of Arzu. Served as Baggage Master to 2nd Brigade from June to August, 1880. (Mentioned in despatches.)

Lieut. M. W. Battye served throughout both campaigns. Was present with the regiment at the battle of Ahmad Khel and action of Arzu. During the operations in the Logar Valley officiated as Deputy Assistant Commissary-General to the 2nd Brigade.

Lieut. P. H. N. Lake served with the regiment during the advance on and occupation of Kandahar, and was subsequently employed as Assistant Field Engineer. Invalided to India Sept., 1880.

Lieut. A. G. Leonard served with the regiment throughout, acting, during a portion of the time, as Regimental Transport Officer. Was present at the battle of Ahmad Khel and the action of Arzu.

Major R. J. Watson (*1st Batt. Worcestershire Regt.*) served with the regiment, as Adjutant, during both campaigns. Invalided to India August, 1879. Rejoined the regiment at Kandahar on the 3rd March, 1880, and was present at the battle of Ahmad Khel (wounded) and action of Arzu. Officiated as Brigade Major to the 2nd Brigade, 3rd Divis., N. Afghanistan Field Force on march from Kabul to India. (Mentioned in despatches; promoted to a Captaincy in the 29th Regt. with Brevet of Major.)

Lieut. H. A. B. Boulderson (*Probationer Madras Staff Corps*) served with the regiment in both campaigns. Present at the battle of Ahmad Khel and action of Arzu. Appointed a Probationer for the Staff Corps, and joining the 25th B.N.I. at Kabul, accompanied it to Kandahar with Sir F. Roberts' force, and was present at the battle of Kandahar.

Lieut. C. F. H. Medhurst served with the regiment during the early part of the first campaign, taking part in the advance on and occupation of Kandahar. Was subsequently invalided to England.

Lieut. M. C. White joined the regiment at Kandahar, on appointment, in March, 1879, and served with it till the end of the campaign. Was present at the battle of Ahmad Khel and action of Arzu.

Lieut. H. M. Twyman joined the regiment at Kandahar, on appointment, in March, 1879, and served with it till the end of the campaign. Was present at the battle of Ahmad Khel and action of Arzu. (Mentioned in despatches for conspicuous gallantry at the battle of Ahmad Khel.)

Lieut. P. B. McAdam joined the regiment at Kandahar, on appointment, in January, 1880, and served with it to the end of the campaign. Present at the battle of Ahmad Khel and action of Arzu.

Bt. Major W. G. Small, A.P.D., served with the regiment in both campaigns. Took part in the advance on and occupation of Kandahar and Kalat-i-Ghilzai, and in the operations in the Logar Valley. Was present at the battle of Ahmad Khel and action of Arzu. Accompanied the force under Sir F. Roberts from Kabul to the relief of Kandahar, and was present, in charge of the field treasure chest, at the battle of Kandahar. (Mentioned in despatches; Brevet of Major.)

Quartermaster Rowland served with the regiment throughout both campaigns, including the occupation of Kandahar and advance on and capture of Kalat-i-Ghilzai. Was present at the battle of Ahmad Khel and action of Arzu.

2ND BATTN. 60TH (KING'S ROYAL RIFLE CORPS). (NOW 2ND BATTN. KING'S ROYAL RIFLE CORPS.)

ON the 23rd Sept., 1878, the 2nd Battalion 60th Rifles, at that time quartered at Mirat, India, received orders by telegram to hold itself in readiness to proceed on active service. Three companies on detachment at Fategarh having rejoined Head-quarters on the 6th Oct., the regiment, under the command of Major Ashburnham, left Mirat on the 18th Oct. for Multan, to join the 1st Brigade of the Reserve Division, South Afghanistan Field Force.

On the 14th Nov. the battalion left Multan by rail for Sukkur, where H Company, under Captain Farmer, was detached as personal escort to Lt.-General Stewart, and thence proceeded by route march to Jacobabad; from this place G Company, under Captain Forster, marched independently as escort to A/B, R.H.A., E Company, under Captain Trotman, as escort to 5/11, R.A., and F Company, under Captain Charley, as escort to I/1, R.A. The Head-quarters and the remaining four companies followed on the 4th Dec., and after a most trying march across the Kach Desert and through the Bolan Pass, arrived at Quetta on the 23rd idem. Gulistan Karez in the Pishin Valley was reached on the 29th, and the following day the Division, under Lt.-General Stewart, left for Kandahar, crossing the Khwajah Amran range by the Gwaja Pass. At Kushab, G Company, which had accompanied Col. Kennedy's column through the Khojak Pass, and had skirmished with the Afghan cavalry in the advance, rejoined Head-quarters; and on the 8th Jan., 1879, the battalion took part in the triumphal march of the troops through Kandahar, which had surrendered on the previous day.

On the 15th Jan. the 2/60th (including D and E companies, which had recently rejoined), forming part of the 1st Brigade under Brigadier-General Barter, left Kandahar for Kalat-i-Ghilzai, Lt.-General Stewart with the 2nd Brigade having marched the previous day. At Jaldak, which was reached on the 21st, it was heard that Kalat-i-Ghilzai, distant fifteen miles, had been entered by the 2nd Brigade without opposition; and on the 3rd Feb. the return march was commenced. On Kandahar being reached, Lt.-Col. Collins took command of the battalion, which, shortly afterwards, established itself for the summer in the mud barracks which had been constructed by the British troops during the former occupation in 1839.

The summer of 1879 was passed in comparative rest, though murderous attacks by fanatics on individual soldiers were of common occurrence. In the month of July a severe epidemic of cholera broke out; and the battalion, which, together with the remainder of the troops, suffered severely, was split up into detachments, and encamped at different spots in the vicinity of the city.

On the 17th Sept., 1879, when the regiment was on the point of marching with the 1st Brigade as rear-guard to the troops returning to India, orders were suddenly received, in consequence of the massacre of the Kabul Embassy, to hold fast and reoccupy the cantonments. Shortly after this, G Company, under Captain Chalmer, relieved H Company as escort to Lieut.-General Stewart. With the exception of occasional attacks by Ghazis, the winter passed without any eventful occurrences.

At the latter end of March, 1880, the 2/60th, forming part of the Ghazni Field Force, took part in General Stewart's advance to Kabul. At the battle of Ahmad Khel on the 19th April, G Company, under Lieut. Davidson, escorting the Lieut.-General, was hotly engaged, the rest of the battalion arriving in time to take part in the final repulse of the enemy. On the 23rd April the 2/60th was engaged in the action of Arzu, and inflicted heavy losses on the enemy. The march was then continued into the Logar Valley, where Brigadier-General Hughes took command of the troops, G Company accompanying General Stewart to Kabul. The battalion remained encamped in the Valley till the 17th June, when it marched to Charasiab. On the 28th July it proceeded to Indiki, where the whole Division was concentrated; and subsequently moving up to Kabul, encamped outside the Bala Hissar.

In the month of August, 1880, the 2/60th took part, as a unit of the 3rd Brigade, under Brigadier-General McGregor, in the memorable march of the Division under Sir Frederick Roberts to the relief of Kandahar. On the night of the 31st Aug., immediately after the arrival of the troops at the southern capital, the regiment was employed, and for a time was under a heavy fire, in the reconnaisance in force under Brigadier-General Gough; and in the crowning defeat of the enemy at the battle of Kandahar on the following day, it was again engaged.

Leaving, shortly afterwards, for India, the battalion reached Quetta on the 19th Sept., and Sibi on the 7th Oct., 1880, having marched a distance of over 2,000 miles during the campaigns. The following day Lt.-Col. Collins died of dysentery, and Major Byron took command.

On the 11th Oct., 1880, the battalion left Sibi with the expeditionary force sent under the command of Br.-General McGregor against the tribe of Marris. After surmounting enormous difficulties of transport and supplies, and some slight opposition from the natives in the passes, Kahan, the capital, was reached on the 6th Nov., and the Marri chiefs made their submission. The force then continued its march towards India; and the battalion reached Mirat on the 24th Nov., 1880, after an absence of over two years on active service.

On the 10th Jan., 1881, the 2/60th, under the command of Lt.-Col. Algar, left Bombay for Natal, South Africa, for service against the Boers of the Transvaal.

SERVICES IN AFGHANISTAN OF OFFICERS OF THE 2ND BATTN. 60TH (KING'S ROYAL RIFLE CORPS). (NOW 2ND BATTN. KING'S ROYAL RIFLE CORPS.)

Lieut.-Colonel J. J. Collins. (Deceased. See Biographical Division.)

Lieut.-Colonel C. Ashburnham, C.B., served with the battalion in the war from Oct., 1878, till June, 1880, commanding it in the advance on and occupation of Kandahar and Kalat-i-Ghilzai, and being present at the battle of Ahmad Khel, the surrender of Ghazni, and the action of Arzu. (C.B.)

Lieut.-Colonel W. G. Byron served with the battalion in the war from Oct., 1878, till Nov., 1880. Took part in the advance on and occupation of Kandahar and Kalat-i-Ghilzai. Was present at the battle of Ahmad Khel, the surrender of Ghazni, and the action of Arzu. Marched with Sir F. Roberts' force from Kabul to the relief of Kandahar, and was present at the battle of Kandahar. (Mentioned in despatches; Brevet of Lieut.-Colonel.) Commanded the battalion in the Marri expedition under Brigadier-General Macgregor. (Mentioned in despatches.)

Lieut.-Colonel J. Charley (4th Battn.), *Major C. L. C. de Robeck* (retired), *Captains W. Foster* (3rd Battn.), and *H. S. H. Riddell* (retired), and *Lieut. D. C. W. Lysons* served with the battalion in the war from Oct., 1878, till Feb., 1880; from Oct., 1878, till Feb., 1879; from Oct., 1878, till Feb., 1879, and from Oct., 1878, till Oct., 1879, respectively, taking part in the advance on and occupation of Kandahar and Kalat-i-Ghilzai.

Major J. G. Crosbie served with the battalion in the war from June to Sept., 1880, taking part in the march of Sir F. Roberts' force from Kabul to the relief of Kandahar, and being present at the battle of Kandahar.

Major G. H. Trotman (4th Battn.) served with the battalion in the war from Oct., 1878, till July, 1880, taking part in the advance on and occupation of Kandahar and Kalat-i-Ghilzai, and being present at the battle of Ahmad Khel, the surrender of Ghazni, and the action of Arzu.

Major G. L. McL. Farmer served with the battalion in the war from Oct., 1878, till Nov., 1879. Commanded the escort to Sir Donald Stewart, and took part in the advance on and occupation of Kandahar, and Kalat-i-Ghilzai. Served in the Marri expedition. (Mentioned in despatches).

Captain E. W. H. Crofton. (Deceased. See Biographical Division.)

Major R. Chalmer. (For services see "Staff.")

Major W. Tilden served with the battalion in the Marri expedition.

Brevet Major J. N. Blackwood-Price, Captain H. T. Marsham, Lieuts. Lord F. Fitzgerald, and *H. C. Leigh* served with the battalion from Oct., 1878, till Nov., 1880. Took part in the advance on and occupation of Kandahar and Kalat-i-Ghilzai. Were present at the battle of Ahmad Khel, the surrender of Ghazni, and the action of Arzu. Marched with Sir F. Roberts' force from Kabul to the relief of Kandahar, and were present at the battle of Kandahar. (For their services Major Blackwood-Price and Captain Marsham were mentioned in despatches, and the former received Brevet of Major.) Served in the Marri expedition under Brigadier-General MacGregor.

Captain T. S. Clarke served with the battalion in Afghanistan from Feb. to Dec., 1879.

Captain C. Hope, Captain T. P. Lloyd (A.P.D.), and *Qr.-Mr. W. Holmes* served with the battalion in the war from Oct., 1878, till Sept., 1880, from Oct., 1878, till Nov., 1880, and from Oct., 1878, till Oct., 1880, respectively. Took part in the advance on and occupation of Kandahar and Kalat-i-Ghilzai. Were present at the battle of Ahmad Khel, the surrender of Ghazni, and the action of Arzu. Marched with Sir F. Roberts' force from Kabul to the relief of Kandahar, and were present at the battle of Kandahar. (For his services Captain Hope was mentioned in despatches.)

Captain W. S. Anderson (3rd Battn.) and *Lieuts. R. C. D. Wilson, H. R. Lovett, R. E. W. Copland-Crawford*, and *R. G. H. Couper* served with the battalion from Dec., 1879, till Nov., 1880, from Feb.,

1879, till Nov., 1880; from Feb., 1879, till Nov., 1880, and from March, 1879, till Nov., 1880, respectively. Were present at the battle of Ahmad Khel, the surrender of Ghazni, and the action of Arzu. Marched with Sir F. Roberts' force from Kabul to the relief of Kandahar, and were present at the battle of Kandahar. (Served in the Marri expedition under Brigadier-General MacGregor.)

Lieut B. T. G. Montgomery. (For services see "Staff.")

Lieut. E. A. Sandford served with the battalion in the war from March till October, 1879.

Lieut. G. S. Baynes served in the war from Oct., 1878, till Nov., 1879, taking part with the battalion in the advance on and occupation of Kandahar and Kalat-i-Ghilzai. Served as Assistant Field Engineer in the Kandahar Field Force from Feb. to Aug., 1879.

Lieut. A. Davidson served in the war from Oct., 1878, till Nov., 1880. Took part with the battalion in the advance on and occupation of Kandahar and Kalat-i-Ghilzai. Commanded the escort of Sir Donald Stewart from Kandahar to Kabul, and was present at the battle of Ahmad Khel, the surrender of Ghazni, and the action of Arzu. Served as Aide-de-Camp to Sir Donald Stewart at Kabul. Marched with Sir F. Roberts' force from Kabul to the relief of Kandahar as extra Aide-de-Camp to Major-General Ross, and was present at the battle of Kandahar. (Twice mentioned in despatches.) Served in the Marri expedition under Brigadier-General MacGregor.

Lieut. H. D. Banks served with the battalion in the war from Oct., 1878, till Aug., 1880, taking part in the advance on and occupation of Kandahar and Kalat-i-Ghilzai, and being present at the battle of Ahmad Khel, the surrender of Ghazni, and the action of Arzu. Served in the Marri expedition under Brigadier-General MacGregor.

Lieut. R. E. Golightly served in the war from Oct., 1878, till Nov., 1880, as Orderly Officer to Brigadier-General Fane, from Oct., 1878, till Feb., 1879, and subsequently with the battalion till the conclusion of hostilities. Took part in the advance on and occupation of Kandahar and Kalat-i-Ghilzai. Was present at the battle of Ahmad Khel, the surrender of Ghazni, and the action of Arzu. Marched with Sir F. Roberts' force from Kabul to the relief of Kandahar, and was present at the battle of Kandahar. Served in the Marri expedition as Superintendent of Field Telegraphs.

Lieut. E. J. Montagu-Stuart-Wortley. (For services see "Staff.")

Lieut. Lord G. G. G. Tewkesbury and *F. A. Fortescue* served with the battalion in the war from Dec., 1879, till Oct., 1880, and from April till Oct, 1880, respectively. Were present at the battle of Ahmad Khel, the surrender of Ghazni, and the action of Arzu. Marched with Sir F. Roberts' force from Kabul to the relief of Kandahar, and were present at the battle of Kandahar.

63RD (WEST SUFFOLK) REGT. (NOW 1ST BATTN. MANCHESTER REGT.)

THE 63rd (West Suffolk) Regiment received orders to proceed on active service to Southern Afghanistan on the 29th July, 1880, two days after the disastrous action at Maiwand. The first detachment, consisting of the Head-quarters and two companies, under command of Lieutenant-Colonel W. L. Auchinleck, left Umballa on the 12th Aug., and the remainder of the regiment moved by detachments of two companies each, on the 13th, 14th, and 15th, reaching Quetta on the 24th, 25th, 26th, and 27th Aug., respectively,

The first detachment (two companies), under Captain H. R. Cook, left Quetta on the 25th Aug., followed by two companies under Lieutenant and Adjutant H. S. Smith on the 26th, to join Major-General Phayre's force, then concentrating at Chaman, where they arrived on the 30th and 31st, and joined the 2nd Brigade, Kandahar Field Force.

On the 31st Aug. they advanced with the force to Mel Karez, where they arrived on the 2nd Sept., when the news was received of General Roberts' successful action at Kandahar on the 1st September. The half-battalion arrived at Kandahar on the 20th of the same month with the 2nd Brigade.

The Head-quarters and four companies were detained at Quetta to escort a convoy until the 29th Aug., when they marched to Killa Abdula, and remained there from the 2nd Sept. till the 6th Oct., on which date the march was resumed to Kandahar.

The 63rd remained quartered in the cantonments at Kandahar until the evacuation took place on the 22nd April, 1881, when the regiment was employed to watch the line of communications in the Pishin Valley, leaving detachments at Killa Abdula and Gulistan Karez, Head-quarters and four companies being quartered at Quetta.

The under-mentioned officers served with the 63rd Regiment in the war, and are entitled to the medal:—

Lieut.-Colonel W. L. Auchinleck (in command), *Major C. O. James* (invalided home 15th Nov., 1880, and died on his arrival at Southampton, 3 Feb., 1881); *Captains W. L. Gronow* (ordered to join Depôt in India 15 Nov., 1880), *H. R. Cook* (commanded the half-battalion which accompanied Major-General Phayre advancing to the relief to Kandahar), and *H. Chevers; Lieuts. A. G. B. Stubbs, H. S. Smith* (as Adjutant, and commanded the two companies which proceeded to join Major-General Phayre's advanced force), *W. B. Graham, F. W. Thomas, L. H. Reid, W. C. R. Lang, F. B. Mein, T. P. B. Ternan, W. J. R. Wickham* (appointed Assistant Road Commandant 26th Jan., 1881), *E. W. Codrington,* and *D. J. T. O'Brien,* and *Quartermaster D. White* (invalided to India 4 April, 1881).

For services of *Lieut.-Colonel N. X. Gwynne* and *Major R. W. Studdy,* see "Staff;" and of *Brevet Major H. F. Jackson,* see "67th Regt."

66TH (BERKSHIRE) REGT. (NOW 2ND BATTN. PRINCESS CHARLOTTE OF WALES' [BERKSHIRE] REGT.)

IN December, 1878, the 66th Regiment moved from Bombay, where it was then stationed, to Karachi, and during the year 1879 remained in Sind. Selected, early in 1880, as one of the two British battalions which were to form part of the Bombay Brigade under General Phayre's command at the time destined to relieve the Bengal troops in the southern theatre of operations, the regiment, under the command of Lt.-Colonel Galbraith, quitted Karachi on the 10th February, and making its way through Quetta to Kandahar, reached its destination on the 25th March. At Nari Bank, *en route,* one company, under the command of Captain McMath, with his subaltern, Lieut. Lynch, was detached for the purpose of taking on to Chaman, as a present from Government to the Wali Shere Ali Khan, the battery of smooth-bore guns which were subsequently turned against our troops by the mutineers at Girishk, and which, being there recaptured, played a not unimportant part a fortnight afterwards on the field of Maiwand. After delivering the battery to the Wali's representative at Chaman, Captain McMath's company marched on to Kandahar, and there rejoined Head-quarters.

In the month of April two companies of the 66th, under the command of Captain Mackinnon, were detached from Head-quarters to form part of the garrison of Kalat-i-Ghilzai, and did not return to Kandahar till the end of August. At night, on the 1st May, a small party, under the command of Lieut. O'Donel, was told off from this detachment to accompany, on signalling duty, the force under Colonel Tanner, which proceeded to Kaj Baz to exact retribution from the inhabitants of the district for recent attacks on convoys. On the following day the enemy assembled in considerable force on the Shahbolan hill, and were dispersed by Colonel Tanner's force with heavy loss.

For the next few months after arriving at Kandahar the 66th Regiment remained, with the rest of the troops under General Primrose's command, in cantonments, small parties occasionally varying the ordinary routine duties by taking part in the reconnaissances which were conducted into the surrounding country.

Detailed to the brigade under Brigadier-General Burrows which marched from Kandahar on the 5th July to support the army of the Wali Shere Ali Khan, the Head-quarters and six companies took part in the advance of that force to the Halmand. In the action with the Wali's mutinied troops in the neighbourhood of Girishk on the 14th of the month, Head-quarters and five companies were engaged, one company remaining on the left bank of the river to guard the camp. After the defeat and flight of the enemy, Captain McMath's company appropriately performed the duty of dragging into camp the recaptured smooth-bore guns, which, four months before, had been delivered by it into the hands of the Wali's representative. On this day four men of the regiment were wounded, one mortally.

On the 27th July occurred the disastrous encounter with Ayub Khan's army at Maiwand, the bloody field on which the 66th won for itself imperishable renown. On that day 15 officers and 364 non-commissioned officers and men held the right of the fighting line, 4 officers and 63 n.-c. officers and men formed the baggage-guard in the rear, and 1 officer and 42 n.-c. officers and men manned the smooth-bore battery in the centre. It was not until after four consecutive hours' fighting, when the Native Infantry on the left broke and retreated, that the companies commenced to retire in detached groups, which never lost their discipline or cohesion. The greater number of the officers and men, fighting hand to hand with the Ghazis, made their way across the watercourse in the rear of the line to a walled enclosure, where, surrounded by the whole Afghan army, they formed round the colours, determined to defend them to the last. An account of how valiantly they bore themselves at this juncture is contained in the official letter bearing date 1st October, 1880, addressed to the Adjutant-General in India by General Primrose, who justly observes that "history does not afford any grander or finer instance of gallantry and devotion to Queen and country than that displayed by the 66th Regiment on the 27th July, 1880." In this letter the manner in which the officers of the regiment met their deaths is thus recounted :—" Lieutenant-Colonel James Galbraith was last seen on the nullah bank, kneeling on one knee, with a colour in his hand, officers and men rallying round him; and on this spot his body was found. Here, too, fell Captain William Hamilton McMath, a gallant soldier, and one who would, had his life been spared, have risen to distinction in Her Majesty's service. Close by, 2nd Lieutenant Harry James Outram Barr was shot dead over one of the colours. Captains Ernest Stephen Garratt and Francis James Cullen were both killed on the field in front of the nullah, up to the last moment commanding their companies and giving their orders with as much coolness as if on an ordinary regimental parade. Captain Walter Roberts was mortally wounded in the garden, where the last stand was made; and here, also, fell Lieutenant Maurice Edward Rayner, Lieutenant Richard Trevor Chute, 2nd Lieutenant Walter Rice Olivey, and 2nd Lieutenant Arthur Honywood. The two latter officers were seen holding up the colours, the pole of one of which was shattered to pieces, as rallying points; and Lieutenant Honywood was shot down while holding a colour high above his head, shouting, " Men, what shall we do to save this?" Sergeant-Major Alexander Cuppage was shot dead outside the garden while carrying a colour; and many other non-commissioned officers and men laid down their lives in the attempt to save the colours of their regiment on that day. With the gallant band who made this last grand effort fought and died Major George Frederick Blackwood, Royal Horse Artillery; Lieutenant Thomas Rice Henn, Royal Engineers; and Lieutenant Charles William Hinde, 1st Bombay Grenadiers, Native Infantry, with some of his men. The men of the 66th on baggage guard, under the command of Captain J. Quarry, did excellent service during the retreat. The party told off to man the smooth-bore battery under Lieutenant G. De la M. Faunce worked their guns steadily and well during the fight." Of the 20 officers and 469 men who went into action, 10 officers and 275 men were killed, and 2 officers and 30 men wounded. On the 28th the last remnants of the regiment reached Kandahar, after participating with the other survivors of the ill-fated brigade in the retreat, carried on for over forty miles, almost without water and without food.

During the siege of Kandahar, all that were left of the 66th were quartered in the Barrack Square, and were employed on working parties, often under fire, and by night guarded the Idgah, Topkhana, and Bar Durani gates. Seven more deaths occurred in the ranks at this time from sickness.

On the 24th August, the two companies of the regiment, under the command of Captain Mackinnon, at Kalat-i-Ghilzai, joined, with the rest of the garrison at that place, the force under Sir Frederick Roberts advancing from Kabul to the relief of Kandahar; and after the arrival of the division at its destination on the 31st, rejoined the Head-quarters in the citadel. In the crowning defeat of the enemy at the battle of Kandahar on the following day, eleven officers and 229 non-commissioned officers and men were under arms, two officers and 146 n.-c. officers and men being on duty in the citadel and city.

On the 1st October, the 66th Regt., under the command of Lt.-Colonel Hogge, marched from Kandahar for India, and after short halts at Quetta and Karachi reached Bombay on the 28th November. It was then sent up to the small hill-station of Khandalla on the Western Ghats, which it quitted on the 19th January, 1881, to embark for England.

SERVICES IN AFGHANISTAN OF OFFICERS OF THE 66TH [BERKSHIRE] REGT. (NOW 2ND BATTN. PRINCESS CHARLOTTE OF WALES' [BERKSHIRE] REGT.)

Lt.-Colonel J. Galbraith. (Killed in action. See Biographical Division.)

Colonel S. G. C. Hogge resigned the appointment of Commandant Deolali Depôt to assume command of the regiment in succession to Lt.-Colonel Galbraith, killed at Maiwand. Arrived at Kandahar 22 Sept., 1880, and on that date took over the command from Major Oliver.

Major C. V. Oliver. (Deceased. See Biographical Division.)

Lt.-Colonel J. T. Ready served with the regiment throughout, taking part in the action of Girishk, the battle of Maiwand (in which he commanded the baggage-guard of the brigade), and the defence of Kandahar, during which he had charge of the Herat Gate from the 17th Aug., 1880, till the arrival of the relieving force.

Captain E. S. Garratt. (Killed in action. See Biographical Division.)

Major G. W. M. Hall. (For services see "Staff.")

Major J. Quarry served with the regiment throughout, taking part in the action of Girishk (in which he commanded the baggage-guard of the 66th), the defence of Kandahar, and the sortie to Deh Khwaja, and being present at the battle of Kandahar. (Twice mentioned in despatches; Brevet of Major.)

Captain T. Harris served with the regiment during the war. Acted as Deputy Assistant Quartermaster-General to Brigadier-General Burrows' Brigade, and was present at the action of Girishk, and the battle of Maiwand, in which he was wounded, and the defence of Kandahar. (Mentioned in despatches.)

Captain W. H. McMath. (Killed in action. See Biographical Division.)

Captain W. A. D. Mackinnon served with the regiment throughout. Commanded the detachment at Kalat-i-Ghilzai from April till the latter end of August, 1880, when he marched down with the relieving force under Sir Frederick Roberts to Kandahar, and was present at the reconnaissance of the 31st August and the battle of Kandahar.

Captain F. J. Cullen. (Killed in action. See Biographical Division.)

Captain W. Roberts. (Killed in action. See Biographical Division.)

Captain W. J. de la P. Beresford-Peirse officiated as Deputy Assistant Quartermaster-General on the lines of communication from February to May, 1880, and subsequently took part with the regiment in the action of Girishk, the battle of Maiwand, the defence of Kandahar, and the battle of Kandahar. In September, 1880, acted as Baggage Master to the brigade under Brigadier-General Daubeny which proceeded to the field of Maiwand for the purpose of burying the dead. (Mentioned in despatches.)

Lieut. M. E. Rayner. (Killed in action. See Biographical Division.)

Captain F. McC. Bruce served with the regiment throughout. Was with the detachment at Kalat-i-Ghilzai from April till the latter end of August, 1880, when he marched down with the relieving force under Sir Frederick Roberts to Kandahar, and was present at the reconnaissance of the 31st August and the battle of Kandahar.

Captain St. G. J. Rathbone. (For services see "Staff.")

Lieut. G. de la M. Faunce served with the regiment throughout, taking part in the action of Ghirishk, the battle of Maiwand (in which he was in charge of the party of men of the 66th told off to work the smooth-bore battery), the defence of Kandahar, and at the battle of Kandahar. (Mentioned in despatches.)

Lieut. J. W. H. Fitzgerald served with the regiment throughout. Was with the detachment at Kalat-i-Ghilzai from April till the latter end of August, when he marched down with the relieving force under Sir Frederick Roberts to Kandahar, and was present at the reconnaissance of the 31st August and the battle of Kandahar.

Lieut. R. T. Chute. (Killed in action. See Biographical Division.)

Lieut. M. L. O'Donel served with the regiment throughout. Was with the detachment at Kalat-i-Ghilzai from April till the latter end of August, 1880, and took part in the storming of the Shahbolan hill at Kaj Baz on the 2nd May. Marched down from Kalat-i-Ghilzai to Kandahar with the relieving force under Sir Frederick Roberts, and was present at the reconnaissance of the 31st August and the battle of Kandahar. (Mentioned in despatches.)

Lieut. C. M. Edwards served with the regiment during the war, taking part in the defence of Kandahar, and being present at the battle of Kandahar.

Lieut. H. Lynch served with the regiment throughout, taking part in the action of Girishk and the battle of Maiwand, in which he was severely wounded, and being present in Kandahar during the siege. (Mentioned in despatches.)

Lieut. W. A. E. Lonergan served with the regiment throughout, taking part in the action of Girishk, the battle of Maiwand, and the siege of Kandahar.

Lieut. G. L. Melliss (Probationer Staff Corps) served with the regiment throughout. In the advance to the Halmand acted as Regimental Transport Officer, and was present at the action of Girishk and the battle of Maiwand. After arrival of regiment at Kandahar, acted as Officiating Quartermaster, and was present during the defence and at the battle of Kandahar.

2nd Lieut. A. Honywood. (Killed in action. See Biographical Division.)

Lieut. R. E. T. Bray served with the regiment throughout, taking part in the action of Girishk, the battle of Maiwand, and the defence of Kandahar, and being present at the battle of Kandahar.

2nd Lieut. W. R. Olivey. (Killed in action. See Biographical Division.)

2nd Lieut. H. J. O. Barr. (Killed in action. See Biographical Division.)

Lieut. F. W. McT. Bunny proceeded to Sibi *en route* to join the regiment at Kandahar, but was from thence invalided, with sunstroke, to India.

Lieut. A. M. Caulfield served with the regiment, in the ranks, throughout, being present at the action of Girishk, the battle of Maiwand, in which he was wounded, and the defence of Kandahar. (Received, in addition to the medal for the campaign, a distinguished service medal, and was subsequently promoted to commissioned rank.)

Quartermaster Jones took part in the advance of the regiment to Nari Bank, from whence he was invalided to England.

Quartermaster Hollyer served with the regiment during the war, taking part in the defence of Kandahar, and being present at the battle of Kandahar.

2ND BATTN. 67TH REGT. (NOW 2ND BATTN. HAMPSHIRE REGT.)

ON the 11th December, 1878, the 67th Regt., then stationed at Bangalore, received orders to proceed to Afghanistan with all possible despatch. Leaving, by rail, on the 14th, it reached Jhelum, the then terminus of the line, distant 2,700 miles, on the 28th Dec., 1878; and moving to Lawrencepur on the 29th Jan., 1879, remained there, forming part of the army of reserve, for some seven weeks. While quartered at this station it suffered the loss of a promising young officer in the death, from enteric fever, on the 27th Feb., of Lieut. H. Crowe.

Detailed to the Kuram Valley Field Force, the regiment left Lawrencepur on the 19th March, 1879, and passing through Kohat, arrived at Thal on the 5th April. Crossing the frontier on the 8th idem, it now marched to Fort Kuram, which was reached on the 12th; and continuing its forward movement past the Peiwar Kotal, arrived at Bian Khel on the 18th of the month. Here a permanent camp was laid out, in which the regiment remained, actively employed in road-making, escort duties, and occasional reconnaissances, till the end of July, when, in consequence of the unhealthiness of the camp and the casualties suffered from enteric fever, Head-quarters and four companies were removed to Gandah Wandi, the remaining four companies being encamped on high ground in the neighbourhood.

On the 29th September, 1879, after the receipt of news of the massacre of the Kabul Embassy, the 67th Regt., forming part of the 1st (Macpherson's) Brigade of General Roberts' advancing Division, left Ali Khel *en route* for Kabul. In the Hazardarakht defile, near Karatiga, on the same day, a determined attack was made on and repulsed by the regimental rear-guard, which suffered a loss of two men wounded. Kushi was reached on the 1st Oct., on which day the force was joined by the Amir Yakub Khan.

Forming the rear-guard of the Division, the regiment marched to Charasiab on the 6th Oct., 1879, and both throughout the march and after arriving at the camping ground was subjected to a heavy fire from large numbers of the enemy who covered the surrounding hills. The 67th took no actual part in the battle of Charasiab, the brigade of which it formed part being detained in rear to guard the ammunition, baggage, and treasure of the division—one company only, under Major Seton, being detached to escort artillery. On the morning of the 8th, an advance was made upon Beni Hissar, and a wing of the regiment, under Major Kingsley, was detached to co-operate with Brigadier-General Baker's Brigade in the advance along the hills to the left of the pass leading to Kabul.

On Genl. Roberts making a formal entry into the Bala Hissar on the 12th October, 1879, the 67th led the Escort. Immediately after the General's proclamation was read, the regiment encamped in the Durbar Garden, the charge of the State prisoners being handed over to it.

In consequence of the explosions which occurred in the arsenal on the 16th October, 1879, from the effects of which the regiment miraculously escaped, the Bala Hissar had to be hastily quitted, and a was formed on the Siah Sang heights. There the regiment remained till the 1st November, when it was detailed to form part of the force under Brigadier-General Macpherson which proceeded to Seh Baba to open up communications with the brigade advancing from Gandamak. Shortly afterwards, on the 8th, a portion of regiment took part in the advance of Macpherson's brigade to Sirobi, on the right bank of the Kabul River, and on the 10th a company under Capt. A. J. Poole, with Lieut. P. Carnegy, which was out foraging, was attacked by Safis in overwhelming strength near the village of Doaba. The little force made a gallant resistance, and in spite of the vast numbers of the enemy, managed to hold them in check, inflicting heavy losses on them, till the camels were safely withdrawn and relief arrived from the main body of the column. The casualties suffered in this highly creditable little affair were, three men killed, and Capt. Poole and four men wounded. On the 20th the regiment returned to Sherpur.

On the 8th December, 1879, Head-quarters and six companies formed part of the brigade under Brigadier-General Macpherson which was suddenly despatched into the Koh Daman Valley to prevent a junction being effected between the forces under Mir Butcha and Muhammad Jan, and returned, after severe fighting, on the 11th. Both in the engagement at Mir Karez on the 10th, in which the enemy were signally defeated, and in the action in the Chardeh-Valley with the section of Muhammad Jan's army to which the Brigade was opposed on the 11th, when the Horse Artillery guns, lost earlier in the day by the Cavalry Brigade, were retaken, the 67th took a prominent part. In the meantime, on the afternoon of the 11th, a portion of one of the remaining companies left at Sherpur, under Capt. Jarvis with Lieut. Shaw, was ordered up to the Bala Hissar Hill to reinforce a picquet, and in the ascent was exposed to a heavy fire from the Takht-i-Shah. During the succeeding night the picquet, under command of Capt. Jarvis, three times repulsed determined attacks of the enemy, inflicting heavy loss on them.

The 67th took part in the severe fighting which now ensued around Kabul. On the 12th Dec., 1879, two companies under Lieuts. Carnegy and Fagan, with the picquet under Capt. Jarvis, took part in Col. Money's prolonged assault of Takht-i-Shah, the remainder of the regiment acting with the rest of Macpherson's Brigade, in reserve. On the following day two companies under Capts. Potter and Blundell were engaged with the reconnoitring force which exacted retribution for murders of Cavalry Patrols committed by the villagers resident in the neighbourhood of Deh-i-Mozung. On the night of the 13th the regiment bivouacked on the Bala Hissar heights, and on the following day was again heavily engaged. Three companies under Major Baker were despatched from the Sher-Dawaza to reinforce the left attack of Brigadier-General Baker's brigade on the Southern slope of the Azmai Heights. Two other companies checked the enemy's advance from Deh Mozang, and later in the afternoon, when Brigadier-General Macpherson's brigade was ordered to retire on Sherpur, the two remaining companies of the regiment, under Capt. Blundell, together with two companies of the 72nd Highlanders and two of the 5th Goorkhas, the whole under command of Lieut.-Col. Knowles, 67th, formed the rear-guard of the brigade, and was subjected to a heavy fire from the enemy, whilst returning through the Kabul Gorge.

After the severe fighting on the 14th Dec., 1879, the regiment with the rest of the Kabul Field Force, was concentrated in Sherpur, where for nine days the army was surrounded by the enemy under Muhammad Jan. The 67th took part in the several attacks on the surrounding Killas during the siege, and was entrusted with the defence of the South-East portion of the Sherpur Cantonment. On the morning of the 23rd Dec., 1879, the final attack was made by the Afghans on that part of the Cantonment held by the 67th and 28th P.N.I. Later in the afternoon, when the enemy was beaten off, the regiment formed part of the force that issued from Sherpur and drove them over the Siah Sang ridge into Kabul, two companies occupying Ibraim Khan Killa as an advance post to facilitate the march of the retrieving force under Brigadier-General C. Gough. On the 27th Dec., the regiment proceeded with the force under Brigadier-General Baker into Kohistan, and after destroying the forts of Mir Butcha, returned on the 31st idem. From that date till the 28th May, 1880, Head-quarters remained stationary at Kabul.

In a brigade order issued by Brigadier-General Macpherson on the occasion of the transfer of the 67th Regt. from the 1st to the 2nd Division of the Field Force, which took place in the month of March, 1880, the following passage occurs:—

"The manner in which the regiment performed the arduous and somewhat onerous duty of protecting the immense string of transport animals (during the advance from Ali Khel) reflected the highest credit on the training of the officers and men. It was a matter of pride and satisfaction to the Br.-Genl. to have with the assistance of the 67th Regt. executed this convoy duty without the loss of a single convoy or baggage animal by the hands of the enemy.

"The admirable shooting of the marksmen in clearing the hills of bodies of the enemy who were threatening an attack on the 7th Oct., at Charasiab, was duly brought to the notice of the Lieut.-Genl. Commdg. the Force.

"In the difficult march over the Bala Hissar on the night of the 8th Oct., the steadiness and silence preserved in the ranks exhibited a confidence that was most praiseworthy.

"During the expedition to Kata Sang and Sirobi, and the crossing of the Kabul River, an attack was made on a forage escort, and the defence made by Capt. Poole with his Company against what seemed overwhelming odds, is an incident of which the Regt. may feel justly proud. Br.-Genl. Macpherson trusts that the skill and gallant conduct displayed on that occasion will meet with due recognition.

"On the 10th Dec., when the Kohistan tribes were brought to action at Mir Karez, the dash and eagerness of the 67th to close produced the happiest results, by gaining a formidable position strongly held, with small loss—a result entirely attributable to the quickness with which they handled the enemy.

"The rapidity of the flank march on the 11th Dec., testifies to the remarkable condition and marching power of the Regt. The exertions of the Force on that day were well rewarded by its having the satisfaction of driving the Afghan leader, Muhammad Jan, and his hosts, from every position in the plain of Chardeh, and nothing more tended to this success than the steady volley firing of the 67th.

"When the Force was directed to withdraw from the heights of the Bala Hissar on the 14th, their bearing during that delicate operation exhibited the best qualities of the soldier; for this, their conduct throughout the siege, and invaluable service rendered at all times, Br.-Genl. Macpherson offers his warmest thanks to Col. Knowles and all ranks of the 67th."

On the 25th April, 1880, three companies of the 67th, under Major Kingsley, were detailed to form part of the reserve force under Genl. Baker which was despatched to the Sang-i-Nawishta Pass to support Col. Jenkins and Genl. Macpherson, operating in the Logar Valley, in the neighbourhood of Chil-dukhtean.

The Head-quarters of the 67th remained stationary at Kabul till the 28th May, 1880, when orders were issued for the departure of the regiment, with the 45th Sikhs, to Jagdalak, to relieve Brigadier-General Arbuthnot's Flying Column. The regiment remained at this post till the 11th June, 1880, when it left for Kabul.

The remainder of the campaign, in so far as the 67th Regt. was concerned, was uneventful. The march to Jagdalak and back resulted in an outbreak of fever which weakened the regiment for some time, and was the cause of its not being selected as one of the corps which participated in the march to the relief of Kandahar. The regiment quitted the Bala Hissar on the 12th August, 1880, and after an exhausting march recrossed the frontier on the 1st September. A slight outbreak of cholera occurring in the Punjab, delayed the return of the regiment to Bangalore, which was eventually reached on the 6th November, 1880.

SERVICES IN AFGHANISTAN OF OFFICERS OF THE 67TH REGT. (NOW 2ND BATTN. HAMPSHIRE REGT.)

Colonel C. B. Knowles, *C.B.*, commanded the regiment in both campaigns. Was present at Charasiab and the operations preceding the occupation of Kabul, and took part in the expedition to Sirobi (including the affair at Doaba), the operations in the Koh Daman Valley (including the action of Mir Karez and the defeat of Mir Butcha), the action in the Chardeh Valley, 11th Dec., 1870, the operations round Kabul 12th to 14th Dec. (including the action on the Asmai heights), the defence of Sherpur, and the expedition to Kohistan. Was in temporary command of the 1st Brigade, 2nd Division. (Twice mentioned in despatches; C.B.)

Lieut.-Colonel W. H. Bell Kingsley and Major M. C. Seton served with the regiment in both campaigns. Were present at the affair at Karatiga (in which Lieut.-Colonel Kingsley commanded the rear-guard), and at Charasiab and the operations preceding the occupation of Kabul. Took part in the expedition to Sirobi, the defence of Sherpur, and the expedition to Kohistan. For his services Lieut.-Colonel Kingsley was twice mentioned in despatches, and received the Brevet of Lieut.-Colonel. Major Seton held for a time the appointment of Provost Marshal of the Kabul Field Force, and subsequently served on the staff of Brigadier-General Baker.

Lieut.-Colonel G. M. Cardew (*h.p.*) served with the regiment in both campaigns. Was present at Charasiab and the operations preceding the occupation of Kabul.

Major G. Baker, Lieuts. P. M. Carnegy, E. L. Hight, and H. H. F. Fagan, and Captain E. Pierson (*Quartermaster*) served with the regiment in both campaigns. Were present at Charasiab and the operations preceding the occupation of Kabul, and took part in the expedition to Sirobi, the operations in the Koh Daman Valley (including the action of Mir Karez and the defeat of Mir Butcha), the action in the Chardeh Valley, the operations round Kabul 12th to 14th Dec., 1879 (including the action on the Asmai heights), the defence of Sherpur, and the expedition to Kohistan. Major Baker held for a time the appointment of Brigade Major to 1st Brigade, 2nd Division, and for his services was mentioned in despatches, and received the Brevet of Major. For his gallantry at the affair at Doaba, at which Major Baker and Lieut. Fagan were also present, Lieut. Carnegy, who commanded the foraging party after Captain Poole was wounded, was brought favourably to the notice of the Commander-in-Chief.

Major A. J. Poole served with the regiment in both campaigns. Was present at Charasiab and the operations preceding the occupation of Kabul, and took part in the expedition to Sirobi, in which he commanded the foraging party engaged at Doaba, where he was severely wounded, and for the gallantry he displayed was brought to the notice of the Commander-in-Chief. (Mentioned in despatches; Brevet of Major.)

Major J. E. Blundell, Captain D. M. Potter, and Lieuts. H. W. Smith and E. F. Sullivan served with the regiment in the second campaign. Took part in the operations in the Koh Daman Valley, including the action of Mir Karez and the defeat of Mir Butcha, the action in the Chardeh Valley, the operations round Kabul 12th to 14th Dec., 1879 (including the action on the Asmai heights), the defence of Sherpur, and the expedition to Kohistan. Major Blundell also took part in the expedition to Sirobi, and for his services was mentioned in despatches.

Brevet Major R. E. C. Jarvis served with the regiment in both campaigns. Was present at Charasiab and the operations preceding the occupation of Kabul. Took part in the expedition to Sirobi, the operations round Kabul 11th to 14th Dec., 1879 (including the repulses of the enemy in their night attack, on the 11th; on the picquet on the Sher Darwaza, of which he was in command), and the defence of Sherpur. Was appointed Brigade Major, 1st Infantry Brigade, 21st Dec., 1879, and serving in that capacity till the conclusion of the war, was present at the second action of Charasiab, took part in the march of the force under Sir F. Roberts from Kabul to the relief of Kandahar, and was present at the battle of Kandahar. (Four times mentioned in despatches; Brevet of Major.)

Captain J. S. White served with the regiment in both campaigns. Was present with the rear-guard when attacked at Karatiga, and at Charasiab and the operations preceding the occupation of Kabul. Took part in the expedition to Sirobi, including the affair at Doaba.

Captain F. B. Garfit served with the regiment in the first and in part of the second campaign. Had charge of the Field Treasure chest, Kuram Valley, from Sept., 1879, till Feb., 1880.

Captain J. H. F. H. Connellan served with the regiment in both campaigns. Was present at Charasiab, where he acted as Orderly Officer to Brigadier-General Macpherson, and the operations preceding the occupation of Kabul. Took part in the expedition to Sirobi, the operations in the Koh Daman Valley (including the action of Mir Karez and the defeat of Mir Butcha), and the defence of Sherpur.

Captain R. F. Atkinson and *Lieut. A. C. M. Gompertz* served with the regiment in both campaigns. Were present at Charasiab and the operations preceding the occupation of Kabul, and took part in the expedition to Sirobi (including the affair at Doaba), the defence of Sherpur, and the expedition to Kohistan.

Captains H. A. Tapp and *W. E. Briggs, Lieuts. R. P. Macdonald, A. M. Lloyd, M. E. O'Donoghue, and S. C. Gough* served with the regiment during the latter part of the second campaign.

Captains W. W. Dunlop (retired) and *R. G. Wardlaw Ramsay* (2nd Battalion Highland Light Infantry), and *Lieut. H. E. F. Ramsden* (Madras Staff Corps) served with the regiment in the first campaign.

Lieut. E. H. Le Marchant served with the regiment in the first and in part of the second campaign.

Lieut. M. A. Tuite served with the regiment in both campaigns. Took part in the expedition to Sirobi, the operations round Kabul 11th to 14th Dec., 1879, and the defence of Sherpur.

Lieut. D. G. W. Shaw served with the regiment in the second campaign. Took part in the operations round Kabul from 11th to 14th Dec., 1879 (including the repulses of the enemy in their night attack, on the 11th, on the picquet on the Sher Darwaza), the defence of Sherpur, and the expedition to Kohistan.

Captain G. W. Smith, A.P.D., served with the regiment in both campaigns. Had charge of the Field Treasure Chest, Kuram Valley, April and May, 1879. Was present at Charasiab and the operations preceding the occupation of Kabul, and took part in the defence of Sherpur, where he commanded a detached post.

Brevet Major H. F. Jackson (1st Battalion Manchester regiment) served as Adjutant of the 67th Regiment in both campaigns. Was present at Charasiab and the operations preceding the occupation of Kabul, and took part in the expedition to Sirobi (including the affair at Doaba), the operations round Kabul from 11th to 14th Dec., 1879, the defence of Sherpur, and the expedition to Kohistan. (Mentioned in despatches; Brevet of Major.)

70TH (SURREY) REGT. (NOW 2ND BATTN. EAST SURREY REGT.)

AT the latter end of September, 1878, the 70th Regt., then stationed at Multan, received orders to proceed to Quetta to form part of the Division which was there assembling under the command of General Biddulph, in view of the impending invasion of Afghanistan. Halting for a time at Rajanpur to complete its provision-column, the regiment, under the command of Colonel Piggott, made its way through the deep sands and over the waterless tracts of the Dera Bughti country to the southern débouchure of the Bolan Pass. Having experienced all the depressing influences of a hot season at Multan, which had enforced a constant confinement to barracks, and being suddenly set on the march at a time of year and in a country subject to great sun heat, the 70th suffered considerably from exposure caused by tedious escort and rear-guard duties, and before it arrived at Dadar no less than 100 rank and file had become unfit to march.

Quetta was at length reached on the 9th Nov., 1878, and here the regiment remained encamped till the 21st, on which day the forward movemt of the Division was commenced. At Haiklezai, where a halt was made from the 27th Nov. till the 8th Dec., Colonel Piggott held temporary command of the main body of the column, General Biddulph being absent on one of the reconnaissances which were conducted into the surrounding country. At this time the organization of the Division was rendered more complete by the arrival of the brigadiers, the 70th Regt. being detailed to the 1st (General Lacy's) Brigade.

With the other units of the brigade, the regiment arrived at the foot of the southern slope of the Khoja Amran range on the 12th Dec., 1878, and during the remainder of the month was employed in road-making and improving the water supply. On the 1st Jan., 1879, the advance was continued, and on the 8th idem the 70th took part in the triumphal march through Kandahar, which had surrendered on the previous day.

Leaving two companies on garrison duty at Kandahar, Head-quarters and the remainder of the regiment took part, in the third week in January, in the advance of General Biddulph's Division to the Halmand, and throughout the succeeding month were employed in holding various posts on the line traversed by the expeditionary force.

At the latter end of February, 1879, the intention of Government to reduce the number of troops in Southern Afghanistan before the hot weather might set in, was announced, and it became known that the 70th was one of the battalions selected to return to India. In conformity with this decision, General Biddulph's Division at once returned to Kandahar, and a reconstitution of the forces took place. In the meantime the two companies of the 70th, which had been left behind on the departure of the Division to the Halmand, had been sent down to Chaman on escort duty, and eventually marched by way of Dadar to India.

Detailed now to the 3rd Brigade of the newly constituted force which was destined to open up the Thal-Chotiali route to India, Head-quarters and six companies of the 70th quitted Kandahar early in March, and after making their way over some 1,200 miles of new territory, crossed the Indus and the Chenab, and eventually arrived at Subathu at the latter end of April, 1879.

Though the regiment suffered severely from exposure during the earlier period of its service in Afghanistan, the condition of the men at the conclusion of the return-march to India was most satisfactory, few cases of sickness, and none of serious illness, being present.

The under-mentioned officers served with the regiment during the period it was employed in the war, and have received the medal:—

Colonel H. de R. Piggott (in command), *Lt.-Colonel J. R. Collins, Majors L. Hornby* and *J. J. C. Miller, Captains W. J. Tibbs, F. H. Maturin, F. F. Roupell, T. A. Freeman, R. B. Burnaby, W. A. G. Smith* and *F. R. P. Kane, Lieuts. H. W. Pearse, A. E. Couper, H. Ringwood, H. R. W. Lumsden, R. L. C. Birch, F. G. Delamain, E. H. Rodwell, G. A. Carruthers, J. G. Hunter, H. F. K. Waldron, H. L. Smith, R. D. C. Davies, M. G. Bolton, R. D. Wynyard,* and *J. Nagle* (also served on General Biddulph's staff as Provost Marshal from 25th Dec., 1878, till 17th March, 1879), and *Captain R. S. Riddell, A.P.D.*

72ND HIGHLANDERS. (NOW 1st BATTN. SEAFORTH HIGHLANDERS.)

THE 72nd Highlanders was one of the first of the battalions which were ordered to the front in view of the impending outbreak of hostilities with Afghanistan in the Autumn of 1878. Marching on the 18th Oct. of that year from Sialkot, where it was then stationed, the regiment arrived at Kohat on the 8th Nov.; and on the 17th idem the right wing, under command of Lt.-Colonel F. Brownlow, marched for Thal, and as a unit of the Kuram Valley Field Force, crossed the frontier.

In the assault of the Peiwar Kotal on the 2nd Dec., 1878, after having taken part in the previous reconnaissance, the 72nd Highlanders was prominently engaged, capturing, in the first turning movement, carried out under General Roberts' immediate command, stockade after stockade in brilliant succession, and continuing to render distinguished service in the front line both on the Peiwar ridge and in the second turning movement. During the following week a portion of the regiment took part in the reconnaissance to the Shutargardan Pass.

The right wing of the 72nd formed part of the force under General Roberts which marched from Ali Khel on the 12th Dec. for Fort Kuram, and which, in the early morning of the 14th, was attacked by Mangals in the Sapiri defile. In the protracted rear-guard fight which took place on that day, four non-commissioned officers and men of the regiment worthily acquitted themselves, in defending Captain F. Goad, Assistant Superintendent of Transport, who was mortally wounded, from his assailants; keeping vast numbers of the enemy at bay till relief arrived. For the gallantry he displayed on this occasion Sergt. W. Greer subsequently received commissioned rank.

Early in January, 1879, the Left wing of the regiment, under Lt.-Colonel Clarke, which had, in the meantime, remained at Kohat, took part with the expeditionary force under General Roberts in the occupation of the Khost valley, and the operations in the surrounding district, including the action of Matun on the 7th of the month. On this occasion it was employed in defending the front and left flank of the camp, and afterwards in carrying the villages on the right and rear. On the return of the expeditionary force to Divisional Head-quarters, the regiment went into camp for the winter, subsequently removing, in April, to Ali Khel, where it remained quartered with the rest of the advanced troops on the Kuram line for a period of five months.

When the massacre of the British Embassy at Kabul resulted in the advance of our troops on the capital, the 72nd Highlanders, under the command of Lt.-Colonel Clarke, formed part of the 2nd (Brigadier-General Baker's) Brigade of the newly-constituted Kuram Division, Kabul Field Force. On the 13th Sept., 1879, Ali Khel was quitted for the Shutargardan. The camp of the 72nd was fired into on the night of the 19th Sept.; and three days afterwards a small detachment was engaged in a fruitless pursuit of a body of the enemy who had attacked the garrison of a block-house on the Surkai Kotal. On the 4th Oct. some parties of the regiment, under Major Stockwell, covering the crossing of the troops over the Logar River at Zaidabad, drove off, at the point of the bayonet, bodies of the tribesmen who assembled to dispute the advance. Charasiab was reached on the evening of the 5th, and in the decisive defeat of the enemy which ensued at that place on the next day, the 72nd, employed as one of the two leading battalions in General Baker's outflanking movement, performed distinguished service. One company, under Captain Brooke-Hunt, was directed to crown the heights in front of the peak which formed the extreme advanced point on the right of the enemy's position; while the rest of the regiment, under Lt.-Colonel Clarke, led the main attack on the "Red Ridge," extending from the peak towards the enemy's centre. After two hours' severe fighting, both points were successfully carried, the enemy, in spite of the desperate resistance they offered, being driven back to a second ridge some 600 yards distant. In the final assault on the advanced peak on the enemy's right, the conspicuous gallantry displayed by Pte. MacMahon caused him to be recommended for the Victoria Cross. The new position taken up by the enemy was shortly afterwards carried in a series of rushes, as was a third ridge on which they took their final stand. The casualties of the Regiment in this engagement were 1 officer (Lieut. Fergusson) wounded, and 37 men killed and wounded. On the 8th Oct. two companies took part in Genl. Baker's pursuit of the enemy; and on the 10th Kabul was entered.

The force now established itself in winter quarters, and with the exception of 300 men of the 72nd being detached to Butkhak at the latter end of November to assure the safety of convoys proceeding by the Lataband route, nothing of importance, in so far as the regiment was concerned, occurred till the second week in December, when the uprising of the country under the leadership of Muhammad Jan resulted in severe fighting round Kabul. On the 11th Dec, 1879, 200 men of the 72nd who were sent to hold the Deh-Mozang gorge succeeded in barring the enemy's approach through it, and during the succeeding night a picquet on the Bala Hissar hill, including details of the regiment, three times repulsed determined attacks on the position held by it. The following day a detachment took part in Col. Money's assault of the Takht-i-Shah, on which occasion three non-commissioned officers of the regiment—Colour-Sergt. Macdonald, and Sergts. Cox and McIlveen—greatly distinguished themselves. In the second attack on the Takht-i-Shah, on the 13th, Colour-Sergt. John Yule, of the 72nd, who was the first man who reached the summit, captured two standards. On the 14th, 194 rifles of the regiment, under Lt.-Colonel Brownlow, C.B., took part in General Baker's force in the seizure of the conical hill and the storming of the Asmai heights, Lt.-Colonel Clarke leading the successful attack on the former position, and remaining on it in command during its retention, and Lt.-Colonel Brownlow leading the subsequent stubbornly-contested assault on Asmai. The forward gallantry of Lance-Corporal Sellar in the attack earned for him the Victoria Cross. When, later in the day, the little force on the conical hill was overwhelmed by the enemy Captain Spens of the 72nd sacrificed his life in an heroic personal attempt to stem their advance; and during the retirement of General Baker's troops down the eastern face of Asmai, under a heavy fire, the example set by Lt.-Colonel Brownlow and Major Stockwell of the regiment caused both those officers to be mentioned in warm terms in despatches. On the evening of the 14th, the 72nd retired, with the rest of the force, within cantonments. During the period embraced by the four days' fighting and the subsequent defence of Sherpur—from the 11th to the 23rd December, 1879—the casualties of the regiment amounted to—2 officers (Capt. Spens and Lieut. Gaisford) killed, 3 officers (Lieuts. Ferguson, Sunderland, and Egerton) wounded, and between 40 and 50 non-commissioned officers and men killed and wounded.

In the month of May, 1880, the 72nd Highlanders formed part of the column under Sir F. Roberts which proceeded into the Logar and Maidan districts, and eventually returned to Kabul without having met with opposition.

Selected to form part of the force under Sir F. Roberts destined for the relief of Kandahar in August, 1880, the 72nd Highlanders, as a unit of the 2nd Brigade under the command of Brigadier-General Baker, participated in the memorable march from Kabul to the Southern capital. During the reconnaissance which took place after the arrival of the force on the 31st August, the regiment was in reserve; but in the crowning defeat of the enemy at the battle of Kandahar on the following day, it was one of the two leading battalions of the 2nd Brigade. In forcing its way through the tenaciously-held lanes and walled enclosures which lay in the line of attack, the regiment suffered an irreparable loss in the death of its gallant and beloved colonel (Col. Brownlow, C.B.), Capt. St. John Frome being also killed, Captain Murray and Lieut. Monro severely wounded, and over 30 non-commissioned officers and men killed or wounded. The names of three non-commissioned officers—Colour-Sergts. Jacob and Lauder, and Lance-Corp. Gordon—who displayed conspicuous gallantry during the engagement, were brought to notice in the General's despatch.

The 72nd Highlanders left Kandahar on the 15th Sept., 1880, and marching *viâ* Quetta and the Bolan Pass, arrived on the 9th Oct. at Sibi, from whence it proceeded by wings, after a few days' halt, to Mian Mir, to take part in the review held before the Viceroy.

The casualties of the regiment during the two years it was on active service were—4 officers, and 37 men killed or died from wounds, 1 officer and 44 men died from disease, 5 officers and 77 men wounded —three of the former twice.

SERVICES IN AFGHANISTAN OF OFFICERS OF THE 72ND HIGHLANDERS (NOW 1ST BATTN. SEAFORTH HIGHLANDERS).

Lt.-Colonel F. Brownlow C.B. (Killed in action. See Biographical Division.)
Bt. Lt.-Colonel W. H. J. Clarke. (Deceased. See Biographical Nivision.)
Lt.-Colonel C. M. Stockwell, C.B., served with the regiment throughout both campaigns. Besides being engaged in numerous minor operations, took part in the Khost Valley expedition, and was present at the action of Matun; commanded the rear-guard of the Division at Zaidabad during the night attack of the 4th Oct., 1879; was present at the action of Charasiab, and in the operations round Kabul in December, 1879 (twice mentioned in despatches); accompanied Sir F. Roberts' force in the march to the relief of Kandahar, and commanded the regiment at the battle of Kandahar after the death of Col. Brownlow, and brought it out of action. (Mentioned in despatches; C.B.)

Lt.-Colonel C. W. R. Guinness, Major R. Garnett, and Lieut. W. Greer served with the regiment throughout both campaigns. Besides being engaged in numerous minor operations, took part in the assault and capture of the Peiwar Kotal, the repulse of the enemy's attack on the rear-guard at Zaidabad, the action of Charasiab, and the operations round Kabul in December, 1879; accompanied Sir F. Roberts' force in the march to the relief of Kandahar, and were present at the battle of Kandahar. *Lt.-Colonel Guinness*, during part of the time, was Brigade Major to Brigadier-General Macpherson. For his services he was three times mentioned in despatches, and was awarded the Brevet of Lt.-Colonel. *Major Garnett* and *Lieut. Greer* were also mentioned in despatches, and were awarded, respectively, the Brevet of Major and commissioned rank.

Major W. F. Kelsey and *Lieuts. F. P. L. White* (Bengal Staff Corps) and *J. G. Downing* (Madras Staff Corps) served with the regiment from the commencement of the war till June, 1879, taking part in the Khost Valley expedition, and being present at the action of Matun.

Lt.-Colonel J. M. Tingcombe (retired) served with the regiment in the first phase of the second campaign, and was present at the action of Charasiab.

Captain St. J. T. Frome. (Killed in action. See Biographical Division.)

Major T. S. Gildea and *Captain J. W. Hughes-Hallett* served with the regiment from the commencement of the war till August and July, 1879, respectively, and were present at the assault and capture of the Peiwar Kotal. (Mentioned in despatches.)

Major T. A. A. Barstow. (For services see "Staff.")

Captain N. J. Spens. (Killed in action. See Biographical Division.)

Captain R. H. Brooke-Hunt, Brevet Major C. H. Fergusson, and *Lieut. G. W. B. Swiney* served with the regiment, respectively, from March, 1879, till January, 1880; from March, 1879, till January, 1880, and from November, 1878, till January, 1880; and, besides taking part in minor affairs, were present at the action of Charasiab, and the operations round Kabul in December, 1879. *Captain Brooke-Hunt* and *Major Fergusson* were mentioned in despatches. *Major Fergusson* was wounded both at Charasiab and in the operations round Kabul—in the latter, severely, and for his services was awarded the Brevet of Major.

Captain J. V. Lendrum served in the war from December, 1879, till the conclusion of hostilities. Took part in the relief of the Sherpur cantonments, and serving with the regiment, accompanied Sir F. Roberts' force in the march to the relief of Kandahar, and was present at the battle of Kandahar.

Captains C. Roberts and *H. P. Gore-Langton* (3rd Battn. Prince Albert's Somersetshire L.I.), and *Lieut. H. G. Lang* served with the regiment, respectively, from May, 1880, April, 1880, and March, 1880, till the conclusion of the war, accompanying Sir F. Roberts' force in the march to the relief of Kandahar, and being present at the battle of Kandahar.

Brevet Major M. N. G. Kane served in the war from March, 1879, till the conclusion of hostilities, part of the time as Orderly Officer, and also as Brigade Major and Deputy Assistant Quartermaster-General to Brigadier-General Baker. Was present at the action of Charasiab, and in the operations round Kabul in December, 1879. Accompanied Sir F. Roberts' force in the march to the relief of Kandahar, and was present at the battle of Kandahar. (Three times mentioned in despatches; Brevet of Major.)

Brevet Major R. H. Murray and *Lieut S. C. H. Monro* served with the regiment throughout both campaigns, *Major Murray* till April, 1880, as Adjutant, and *Lieut. Monro* part of the time as Regimental Transport Officer, and from April, 1880, as Adjutant. Besides being engaged in numerous minor operations, were present at the assault and capture of the Peiwar Kotal, the action of Charasiab, and the operations round Kabul in December, 1879. Accompanied Sir F. Roberts' force in the march to the relief of Kandahar, and were present at the battle of Kandahar. Both were severely wounded at the battle of Kandahar, and *Lieut Monro* was also wounded in the assault of the Peiwar Kotal. (Twice mentioned in despatches.)

Lieut. the Hon. R. C. Drummond served with the regiment in both campaigns. Was present at the assault and capture of the Peiwar Kotal. Accompanied Sir F. Roberts' force in the march to the relief of Kandahar, and was present at the battle of Kandahar. (Mentioned in despatches.)

Lieut. R. L. Milne served with the regiment throughout both campaigns, part of the time as Acting Adjutant. Besides being engaged in numerous minor affairs, took part in the Khost Valley expedition, and was present at the action of Matun, the repulse of the enemy in the rear-guard attack at Zaidabad, the action of Charasiab, and the operations round Kabul in December, 1879. Accompanied Sir F. Roberts' force in the march to the relief of Kandahar (during the latter part of it as Regimental Transport Officer), and was present at the battle of Kandahar. (Twice mentioned in despatches.)

Lieut. J. A. Campbell served with the regiment in the war from February till December, 1879, and was present at the action of Charasiab.

Lieut. C. H. Gaisford. (Killed in action. See Biographical Division.)

Lieuts. H. C. F. Macdonald and *E. E. Robertson* served with the regiment in the war from January, 1879, till the conclusion of hostilities. Besides being engaged in numerous minor affairs, took part in the Khost Valley expedition, the action of Charasiab, and the operations round Kabul in December, 1879. Accompanied Sir F. Roberts' force in the march to the relief of Kandahar, and were present at the battle of Kandahar.

Lieuts. L. Sunderland and *A. L. Campbell* served with the regiment in the war from March, 1879, till the conclusion of hostilities. Were present at the action of Charasiab, and in the operations round Kabul in December, 1879. Accompanied Sir F. Roberts' force in the march to the relief of Kandahar, and were present at the battle of Kandahar.

Lieut. G. G. A. Egerton served with the regiment in the war from November, 1879, till the conclusion of hostilities. Was present in the operations round Kabul in December, 1879, in which he was dangerously wounded. Accompanied Sir F. Roberts' force in the march from Kabul to the relief of Kandahar, and was present at the battle of Kandahar. (Mentioned in despatches.)

Captain J. Walsh (Quartermaster) served in the war from August, 1879, till the conclusion of hostilities, from December, 1879, as Provost Marshal, Kabul and Kabul-Kandahar F.F. Was present at the action of Charasiab as Acting Orderly Officer, and in the operations round Kabul and defence of Sherpur in December, 1879. Accompanied Sir F. Roberts' force in the march from Kabul to the relief of Kandahar, and was present at the battle of Kandahar. (Twice mentioned in despatches.)

78TH HIGHLANDERS (ROSS-SHIRE BUFFS). [NOW 2ND BATTN. SEAFORTH HIGHLANDERS (ROSS-SHIRE BUFFS).]

THE 78th Highlanders, under the command of Lt.-Colonel A. E. Warren, left Poona on the 9th August, 1880, as part of the reinforcement furnished to the Army in Afghanistan by the Bombay Presidency, on the news of the battle of Maiwand reaching India.

The regiment was sent by sea to Karachi, where it was detained for ten days, till Major-General Phayre, C.B., telegraphed orders for it to move on Quetta.

Starting on the 24th August, the regiment was sent on to Sibi in four detachments, the Head-quarters and two companies leaving on the 24th, two companies on the 25th, two on the 26th idem, and two on the 1st of September. These two last had been detained as a garrison for Karachi and Haidarabad (Sind), on the occasion of the anticipated outbreak of Pathans in Sind at that time.

From Sibi the various detachments of the regiment proceeded *viâ* the Bolan Pass to Quetta by forced marches. At Sibi four companies had been ordered to march to Kalat to the assistance of the Khan, who expected a rising of the Kakar Pathans; but this order was cancelled by telegraph four or five days later, before the leading detachment had turned off the Quetta road in the direction of Kalat.

The seven days' march to Quetta, owing to the great heat of the weather and want of transport, was of a very arduous description. At Quetta the regiment was halted, the news of General Sir Frederick Roberts' victory on the 1st September being received the evening that the Head-quarters of the regiment marched in.

During the stay of the 78th in Quetta, considerable sickness prevailed amongst the troops in garrison, and 104 men of the 752 that had been in Karachi were invalided.

On the 3rd November the Head-quarters and four companies, under command of Lt.-Colonel Warren, marched for Kandahar, the other four companies remaining in Quetta till the 23rd November, when, being relieved by the 61st Regiment, they also moved forward and eventually rejoined the first half-battalion. The Head-quarters reached their destination on the 15th Nov., 1880, and were posted to the 2nd Infantry Brigade, being quartered in the old cantonments till the evacuation took place.

The Brigade of which the 78th Highlanders formed part quitted Kandahar on the 20th April, 1881. The regiment arrived at Sibi on the 13th May, whence it proceeded by rail to Bengal.

The following Officers crossed the frontier before the 20th September, 1880, and have received the medal:—

Colonel A. E. Warren (Commanding); *Major T. Mackenzie; Lt.-Colonel W. C. Smith; Major A. Murray; Captains G. W. R. M. Waugh, D. Stewart, W. W. Sandeman, W. B. MacDougall;*

Lieutenants *P. S. Harvey, Kenneth R. Mackenzie, W. de B. Hatton, D. Craige-Halkett, H. S. Barlow, H. Davidson, R. Graham-Campbell* (Adjutant), *G. R. V. Hume, Geo. Mackintosh, R. A. Fraser, A. C. Christopher, F. B. Lund, D. C. F. Macintyre,* and Captain *Parr Campbell* (Quartermaster).

For services of Brevet Major H. G. Grant, see "Staff."

81ST REGT. (NOW 2ND BATTN. LOYAL NORTH LANCASHIRE REGT.)

EARLY in October, 1878, the 81st Regiment, then stationed at Peshawar, was warned for active service, and subsequently formed part of the 3rd Brigade, 1st Division, Peshawar Valley Field Force, under the command of Brigadier-General Appleyard.

On the 19th Nov. the regiment left with the brigade for Jamrud, where a halt was made on the following day. On the morning of the 21st the brigade crossed the Afghan frontier, and took part in the attack on Ali Musjid.

The Right half-battalion, 250 strong, under the command of Captain Faircloth, formed part of the advance guard, and a portion of the regiment was the first unit of the force which was engaged with the enemy.

The Left half-battalion, which headed the main body of the force half a mile in rear of the advance guard, arrived at the Shagai Heights, opposite Ali Musjid, about 11.20 a.m., having met with no opposition. Shortly after this the attack was commenced by the Artillery, during which the Left half-battalion was inactive. About 2.30 p.m., under orders from Sir S. Browne, Lieut. Morrice went with H Company to clear a slope to the right, supposed to be occupied by the enemy. The remainder of the half-battalion, consisting of three companies, then advanced down a ravine to the right, and subsequently crossed the Khyber stream, continuing their progress on the other side, up a series of ravines, till they arrived on a ridge on the British left and in front of the two redoubts protecting the right of Ali Musjid. During the progress to this point, E Company, under Lieut. Wheler, was detached to escort Major Dyce's Mule Battery, and A Company, under Lieut. Walpole, joined the half-battalion. The three companies A, F, and G were advancing under a heavy fire of musketry and artillery in support of the 27th N.I. to the attack of the redoubts, when the halt sounded, and they received orders to bivouac for the night on the ridge. The following morning they advanced by way of the redoubts to Ali Musjid, which was found to be abandoned.

The Right half-battalion, under Captain Faircloth, proceeded also to the Shagai Heights without opposition, when some of the enemy's cavalry appearing in sight, the leading company (Lieut. Walpole's) was ordered to skirmish. It did not rejoin the right half-battalion, but came up with the other in the afternoon. The remaining companies were employed in protecting the right flank until about 3.30 p.m., when, being relieved by the 51st K.O.L.I., they proceeded up the valley in search of the regiment, continuing to advance until they reached Battery I/C, R.H.A., which was in action. Shortly after this the Assistant Quartermaster-General ordered them to advance in support of the 14th Sikhs' attacks on the advanced outpost to the right of the enemies' position. Captain Wynne's company was sent forward, the remaining two companies being kept in support by Captain Faircloth. In this order they crossed the river under a heavy fire of musketry and round shot, fortunately without loss. They reached the ridge on which the 14th and 27th N.I. Regiments were engaged, but were met by about 200 men of those battalions retiring. Captain Faircloth was then informed that orders for the retirement had been given, and that none of the 81st were in that direction; so he made his way back to his old position near the Horse Artillery battery, and bivouacked for the night. On the 22nd orders were received by him to rejoin the Left half-battalion. After this was done, the Right half-battalion was directed to cut off some of the enemy who were driving off their cattle to the British left; but the latter had too good a start, and after some firing at long ranges, and a most fatiguing détour, the companies rejoined the Head-quarters at Ali Musjid. The whole regiment bivouacked in the valley under the Fort on the 22nd, and on the following day marched to Kata Kushtia, a distance of about four miles, where it bivouacked on the nights of the 23rd and 24th. On the 25th an advance was made to Landi Kotal, where the regiment encamped, and received orders to remain.

On the 28th Nov., 1878, in consequence of a supposed attempt to recapture Ali Musjid, C, D, and

F Companies, under command of Major Jackson, were suddenly ordered to return to the Fort. The remainder of the battalion followed the next day, and was encamped on the Shagai Heights from that date till the 26th Dec., when it was moved down to the Ali Musjid Valley.

On the 30th Nov. the regiment, with two mountain guns, was employed in an attempt to surround some Afridis who had attacked and turned back a convoy proceeding from Jamrud the previous day, and in clearing the road. Seven companies, together with the guns, under the command of Col. Chichester, proceeded for some distance along the Jamrud road, and at Mackeson's bridge turned to the right into the hills, where they took up several positions. The enemy, however, being well acquainted with the ground, did not allow them to approach within range on this side; but a party that had been detached under Major Prinsep, XIth Bengal Lancers, to which A Company, under Lieut. Walpole, was attached, succeeded in exchanging shots with them, and detained them long enough to enable the guns to open fire. The principal object of the reconnaissance having been effected, the force was ordered to withdraw. In the retirement occasional opportunities of firing at long range, of which the troops took advantage, presented themselves.

On the 9th January, 1879, the 81st Regiment, having invalided over 200 men to Peshawar, and being reported sickly, was ordered into that station *en route* to Naushahra. The regiment arrived at Peshawar on the 10th Jan., 1879: there its destination was changed to Rawal Pindi, for which station the march was commenced on the 16th Jan., and concluded on the 24th idem.

SERVICES IN AFGHANISTAN OF OFFICERS OF THE 81ST REGT. (NOW 2ND BATTN. LOYAL NORTH LANCASHIRE REGT.)

The undermentioned officers served with the regiment throughout, being present at the taking of Ali Musjid:—

Colonel R. B. Chichester, C.B. (*late 81st Regt.*) (in command, C.B.); *Lt.-Colonels H. J. Faircloth* (*retired*) (in command of the right half-battalion; mentioned in despatches; Brevet of Major), and *W. H. N. Jackson* (*retired*); *Captains H. Walpole, H. C. B. Farrant, B. A. Satterthwaite, C. E. Sawyer* (as Orderly Officer to Brigadier-General Appleyard), and *F. H. Wheler; Lieuts. H. Crosbie, P. Palmes*, and *F. R. Borrow; Major C. H. Hignett* (*A.P.D.*); and *Quartermaster M. Hanlon*.

Colonel C. J. Skerry (*retired*) took part in the advance of the regiment to Jamrud, from whence he was invalided.

Major W. H. Warren was invalided at Peshawar, and remained in command of the regimental depôt at that station during the war.

Major G. A. Wilson served with the regiment in the war from the commencement of hostilities till the 18th Dec., 1878, and *Majors M. S. Wynne* (*retired*) and *T. E. Lindoe* (*h.p.*) till the 1st Jan., 1879; being present at the taking of Ali Musjid.

Major W. C. Mathews and *Captain S. Jackson* served with the regiment in the war from the 3rd Dec., 1878, till the 19th Jan., 1879, *Captain F. Ryley* and *Lieuts. A. C. H. Thomas* and *J. H. Young* (*Probationer Staff Corps*) from the 30th Dec., 1878, till the 9th Jan., 1879, and *Lieut. J. Davidson* from the 12th Dec., 1878, till the 9th Jan., 1879.

Captain W. S. Morrice served with the regiment in the war from the commencement of hostilities till the 22nd Dec., 1879, and was present at the taking of Ali Musjid. (Since deceased.)

Lieut P. R. S. Churchward served with the regiment in the war from the commencement of hostilities till the 27th Dec., 1878, and was present at the taking of Ali Musjid. Subsequently served as Transport Officer with the Kuram Valley Field Force from the 24th Oct., 1879, till the 24th May, 1880, and in the same capacity with the Khyber Field Force from the 25th May, 1880, till the 23rd Aug., 1880.

For the services of *Colonel W. B. Browne* (*h.p.*), *Lt.-Colonel H. T. Jones* (*h.p.*), and *Captain E. C. Morris*, see "Staff."

85TH (KING'S LIGHT INFANTRY). (NOW 2ND BATTN. KING'S LIGHT INFANTRY [SHROPSHIRE REGT.])

IN October, 1878, in view of the impending outbreak of hostilities with Afghanistan, the 85th L.I. was ordered to proceed from Lucknow on service, but on arrival at Multan was halted there, there being no further need of reinforcements.

The massacre of the Kabul Embassy in the autumn of 1879, resulting in a renewal of hostile operations, the regiment left Multan for the Kuram Valley on the 23rd September, and arrived at Kohat on the 15th October. Posted to the Brigade under the command of Brigadier-General Tytler, it entered Afghanistan, and proceeded to Kuram, detachments being sent on, at intervals, to Ali Khel and Balesh Khel.

Portions of the regiment were now employed in the various minor operations of the Kuram Valley Field Force, assisting in dispersing tribal gatherings, enforcing payment of fines, and the like.

In December, 1879, the 85th L.I. formed part of the expeditionary force under Brigadier-General Tytler which proceeded into Zaimusht territory to inflict punishment on the tribesmen of that district. Wings of the regiment were engaged, respectively, in the various operations of both the Right and Left columns, including the attack on the ridge to the north and east of the village of Bagh, on the 13th of the month, and the assault and destruction of Zawa, on the 14th.

After returning from the Zaimusht expedition at the latter end of December, 1879, the 85th L.I. was stationed at Thal, Shalozan, and the Peiwar Kotal. During the succeeding summer and autumn it was employed on the line of communications, and in January, 1881, it returned to India.

SERVICES IN AFGHANISTAN OF OFFICERS OF THE 85TH (KING'S LIGHT INFANTRY). (NOW 2ND BATTN. KING'S LIGHT INFANTRY [SHROPSHIRE REGIMENT.])

Lt.-Colonel E. M. Beadon commanded the regiment during the war from the 9th May, 1880, till the conclusion of hostilities.

Lt.-Colonel W. Galbraith served throughout the first campaign as Assistant Adjutant-General, Kuram Valley Field Force, in which capacity he was present at the assault and capture of the Peiwar Kotal, and took part in the operations in the Hariab and Khost Valleys. In the second campaign served, first as Assistant Adjutant-General, Kuram Division, Kabul Field Force, and besides being engaged in numerous minor operations, was present at the action of Charasiab and the occupation of Kabul. Took part with the Kuram Force in the Zaimusht expedition, and subsequently commanded the regiment from the 17th Dec., 1879, till the 8th May, 1880. (Four times mentioned in despatches; Brevet of Lt.-Colonel.)

Major G. W. Smith. (For services see "Staff.")

Major the Hon. C. Dutton. (For services see "Staff.")

Major D. A. Grant served with the regiment throughout, commanding it from the time it crossed the frontier till the 16th Dec., 1879. Took part, in command of the regiment, in the Zaimusht expedition, and was present at the assault and destruction of Zawa. (Mentioned in despatches; Brevet of Major.)

Captains the Hon. E. A. H. à Court, E. H. G. Ravenhill, F. W. Robinson, and *E. H. Ives,* and *Lieuts. C. H. Collette, J. Spens, A. H. J. Doyle, R. H. Fowler, C. T. Dawkins,* and *H. R. Browne* served with the regiment throughout, taking part in the Zaimusht expedition, and being present at the assault and destruction of Zawa. For their services Captain à Court and Lieut. Collette were mentioned in despatches.

Captain F. Longford and *Lieuts. I. W. T. S. Smythe, P. Bulman,* and *C. G. H. Sitwell* served with the regiment throughout, taking part in the Zaimusht expedition.

Lieut. E. Burrell. (For services see "Staff.")

Lieut. W. B. Capper served with the regiment in the war till April, 1880, when he was appointed Aide-de-camp to General Watson, in which capacity he served till the conclusion of hostilities. Took part in the Zaimusht expedition, and was present at the assault and destruction of Zawa.

Lieut. H. V. Wilbraham served with the regiment throughout, *Lieuts. C. E. Mardell* and *R. N. R. Reade* from May, 1880, till the conclusion of the campaign.

92ND (GORDON) HIGHLANDERS. (NOW 2ND BATTN. GORDON HIGHLANDERS.)

WHEN orders were received for the 92nd Highlanders to proceed on active service, the Headquarters were stationed at Sitapur, Oudh, and the Left wing was at Benares. Making its way by rail to Jhelum, the regiment marched on the 30th Dec., 1878, for Kohat, which was reached on the 25th Jan., 1879. Here it remained till the 26th March, when it proceeded (strength—31 officers, 787 non-commissioned officers and men) to Ali Khel, joining there the Advance Division of the Kuram Valley Field Force under General Roberts.

It was not until five and a half months afterwards, in view of the second outbreak of hostilities, that the 92nd Highlanders received orders to advance on the Shutargardan. On the 24th Sept., 1879, the march was commenced up the Hazar-darakht defile (strength—16 officers, 686 non-commissioned officers and men), Captain McCallum's company being left in the Fort at Karatiga to assist in keeping open the communications until General Roberts might have passed. On the 28th the General and his staff were attacked in the neighbourhood of Karatiga, and part of Captain McCullum's company, under Lieut. Grant, assisted in driving off the enemy. On this occasion Colour-Sergeant Macdonold greatly distinguished himself, and subsequently received, in recognition of his gallantry, commissioned rank.

Detailed to the 1st (Brigadier-General Macpherson's) Brigade, Kuram Division Kabul Field Force, then concentrating at Kushi, the 92nd Highlanders, with the rest of the advancing troops, left that post on the 2nd October, 1879, and reached Charasiab on the evening of the 5th idem. During the night orders were received for a wing of the regiment to parade at 7 a.m. next day, and proceed as a covering party to a regiment of Native Infantry, which was to improve the road through the Sang-i-Nawishta. While carrying out this duty the party was fired upon by the Afghans, who, being concealed in the neighbouring gardens and orchards, had hitherto escaped notice. In the action which now became general Major White commanded the right attack, the wing of the 92nd forming part of the little force of all arms placed at his disposal by General Baker. This wing captured in rapid succession three precipitous hills, strongly held by the enemy, which commanded the entrance to the Sang-i-Nawishta defile, a detachment of two companies, under Captain Oxley, at the same time rendering important service in co-operating in the main (left) attack. For his distinguished gallantry in this action—in which the casualties of the regiment were 3 killed and six wounded—Major White subsequently received the Victoria Cross. On the 7th Oct., 1879, the 92nd bivouacked at Beni Hissar, and on the following day took part in General Baker's pursuit of the enemy in the direction of Baber's Tomb. On the 10th the Division entered Kabul, and established itself in winter quarters.

The 92nd Highlanders formed part of the Brigade under General Baker which proceeded on the 21st Nov., 1879, to Maidan, on the Ghazni road, and returned to Kabul, after some fighting, on the 1st Dec. On the 9th of that month the regiment again left the capital with the force under General Baker's command which proceeded into the Maidan district to co-operate with General Macpherson's Brigade in intercepting a large body of the enemy known to be advancing on Kabul. The march on the 10th was exceedingly trying, and throughout the night the rear-guard (80 men, under Captain McCullum) had to remain in a narrow gorge, where the cold was intense and the men suffered much. On the morning of the 11th the enemy appeared in considerable force, and attacked the rear-guard as it was leaving camp, wounding two men. Though the fighting continued until Maidan was reached, all the baggage was safely brought in. On nearing the camping ground at Argandi, large bodies of the enemy appeared crowning a ridge which commanded the road to Kabul; and it became necessary, before the camp could be pitched, to dislodge them. This duty was rapidly and effectually carried out by a portion of the regiment under Major White, ably led by Lieut. Scott Napier. All that night the outlying picquets were constantly engaged. On the morning of the 12th the regiment marched with the rest of the Brigade for Kabul, large bodies of the enemy being in sight on all sides, and some of the hills having to be cleared by artillery fire. Sherpur was reached about 5 p.m. Early next morning the 92nd proceeded with a force of all arms under General Baker to storm the Takht-i-Shah, a spur of which, running down to Beni Hissar, was strongly held by the enemy. Four companies under the command of Major White, supported by the Guides Infantry (Colonel Jenkins, C.B., being in command of the assaulting column) were sent to clear the ridge, the 92nd leading. In spite of the stubborn resistance offered, and the great strength of the enemy, the ridge was at length carried, the 92nd losing, however, in the attack, two gallant lives it could ill afford, those of Lieut. Forbes and Colour-Sergt. Drummond. For the gallantry he displayed on this occasion, Lieut. Dick-Cunyngham subsequently received the Victoria Cross. The ridge cleared, the regiment moved forward to the conical hill, nearly every foot of the way being stubbornly contested. The next day (the 14th) two companies under Captain Gordon and Lieut. Gilpin-Brown took part in the assault of the Asmai Heights, in which Captain Gordon was very severely wounded. By their gallant behaviour in the assault, Sergt. McLaren and Corp. McKay earned the "distinguished conduct" medal. The casualties of the regiment, on the 13th, were, 1 officer and 3 non-commissioned officers and men killed, and 19 wounded; on the 14th, 1 officer and 4 men wounded.

Throughout the investment of Sherpur the 92nd proceeded every night to the gorge leading through the Behmaru ridge, being told off as a portion of the reserve. In the repulse of the enemy on the 23rd December, the regiment lost one man killed and five wounded.

On 20th April, 1880, a wing of the 92nd marched for Childukhtean, about three miles beyond Charasiab, as a constituent part of the force under the command of Col. Jenkins, C.B., which was ordered out to keep in check the tribesmen of the Logar district. On the morning of the 25th, at daybreak, the camp was surrounded and attacked by the enemy in great force. An unequal fight was maintained till 1 p.m., when, heliographic communication having been opened with Kabul, reinforcements under General Macpherson, including the Head-quarters of the 92nd, under Col. Parker, arrived on the scene, and a general advance was ordered. The enemy were now dispersed with heavy loss. In this engagement the 92nd lost one killed and five wounded. The wing under Col. Parker left Sherpur about 9 a.m., marched fifteen miles out, fought for one and a half hours, and returned to Sherpur the same night, arriving there at 8 p.m., having covered over thirty miles of ground in eleven hours.

The 92nd Highlanders, under the command of Col. Parker, was one of the regiments selected to form part of the force under Sir Frederick Roberts which, in the month of August, 1880, performed its memorable march from Kabul to the relief of Kandahar. In the crowning defeat of the enemy at the battle of Kandahar on the 1st Sept., the day succeeding the arrival of the Division at the Southern capital, the regiment, as one of the two leading battalions in the right attack, played a conspicuous part, being engaged in the successive captures of the villages of Gandi Mullah Sahibdad, and Pir Paimal, and finally carrying at the point of the bayonet the entrenched position on which the enemy had taken up their last stand. The casualties on this day numbered 14 non-commissioned officers and men killed, 2 officers and 70 non-commissioned officers and men wounded. In the engagement Captain Menzies' life was saved by Privates Dennis and Roddick, who received the "distinguished conduct" medal for their gallantry, as did also Lance-Corpl. McIntosh, Corpl. McGilevray, and Privates Gray and Grieve.

On the night of the 1st Sept., 1880, the 92nd Highlanders bivouacked in Ayub Khan's camp, returning to cantonments next day. On the 28th of the month the regiment left Kandahar and proceeded to Mian Mir.

SERVICES IN AFGHANISTAN OF OFFICERS OF THE 92ND (GORDON) HIGHLANDERS. (NOW 2ND BATTN. GORDON HIGHLANDERS.)

Colonel G. H. Parker, C.B. (h.p.), commanded the regiment throughout. Was present at the action of Charasiab and subsequent pursuit of the enemy and the occupation of Kabul. Took part in the operations around Kabul, and defence of Sherpur, in December, 1879, including the action of the 23rd Dec., and was present at the action of Childukhtean. Accompanied the force under Sir F. Roberts from Kabul to Kandahar, and was present at the reconnaissance of the 31st Aug., 1880, and the battle of Kandahar. (Three times mentioned in despatches; C.B.)

Lt.-Colonel G. S. White, C.B., V.C. (For services see Biographical Division.)

Lt.-Colonel J. C. Hay served with the regiment in the second campaign. Was present at the action of Charasiab and subsequent pursuit, and at the occupation of Kabul. (Mentioned in despatches.)

Major G. K. McCallum served with the regiment in the second campaign. Commanded the company which was on detachment at Karatiga when Sir F. Roberts and staff were attacked on the 27th Sept., 1879. Was present at the action of Charasiab and subsequent pursuit of the enemy, and the occupation of Kabul. Took part in the expedition to Maidan in November, 1879, and the operations around Kabul and defence of Sherpur in December, including the action of the 23rd Dec. (Mentioned in despatches.)

Bt.-Major L. C. Singleton. (Killed in action. See Biographical Division.)

Major H. F. Cotton served with the regiment in the second campaign. Was present at the action of Charasiab, and the occupation of Kabul. (Mentioned in despatches.)

Major R. B. McEwen (h.p.) served with the regiment in the advance over the Shutargardan. Was appointed Provost Marshal to the Kabul Field Force on its formation, and continued to serve in that capacity till the 15th Nov., 1879. Was present at the action of Charasiab and the occupation of Kabul. (Brevet of Major.)

Major P. F. Robertson served with the regiment in the second campaign. Was present at the action of Childukhtean. Accompanied the force under Sir F. Roberts from Kabul to Kandahar, and was present at the battle of Kandahar. (Mentioned in despatches.)

Bt.-Major A. D. McGregor served during the war in the Kuram, Kabul, and Kabul-Kandahar Field Forces. Was, part of the time, Orderly Officer to Brigadier-General Macpherson, in which capacity he took part in the expedition to open up communications with the Khyber Field Force. Was present at the action of Doaba, 10th Nov., 1879, took part in the operations around Kabul and defence of Sherpur in December, 1879, including the actions of Karez Mir and Chardeh, 10th and 11th Dec., and the action of the 23rd Dec., and was also present at the action at Childukhtean. Was subsequently Deputy Assistant Quartermaster-General to Brigadier-General Macpherson, and in that capacity accompanied the force under Sir F. Roberts from Kabul to Kandahar, and was present at the reconnaisance of the 31st Aug., 1880, and the battle of Kandahar. (Four times mentioned in despatches; Brevet of Major.)

Captain R. F. Darvall served with the regiment in the second campaign. Was present at the occupation of Kabul and the action of Childukhtean. Accompanied the force under Sir F. Roberts from Kabul to Kandahar, and was present at the reconnaissance of the 31st August, 1880, and the battle of Kandahar. (Mentioned in despatches.)

Captain R. H. Oxley served with the regiment in the second campaign. Was in command of two companies at the action of Charasiab and in the subsequent pursuit of the enemy, and took part in the occupation of Kabul. (Mentioned in despatches.)

Bt. Major D. F. Gordon served with the regiment during the second campaign. Was present at the action of Charasiab and subsequent pursuit of the enemy, and the occupation of Kabul. Took part in the operations around Kabul and defence of Sherpur in December, 1879, including the assault and capture of the Takht-i-Shah and the assault of the Asmai Heights, in which he was shot through the chest and left leg. (Mentioned in despatches; Brevet of Major.)

Bt. Major the Hon. J. S. Napier served during the war in the Peshawar, Kabul, and Kabul-Kandahar Field Forces. Commanded two companies of Bengal N.I. at the action of Ali Musjid. Took part with the 92nd Highlanders in the expedition to Maidan, and the operations around Kabul and defence of Sherpur in December, 1879, including the assault and capture of the Takht-i-Shah, and was present at the action of Childukhtean. Accompanied the force under Sir F. Roberts from Kabul to Kandahar, and was present at the reconnaissance of the 31st Aug., 1880, and the battle of Kandahar. (Three times mentioned in despatches; Brevet of Major.)

Bt. Major C. W. H. Douglas served with the regiment during the war as Adjutant in both campaigns. Was present at the action of Charasiab and subsequent pursuit of the enemy, and the occupation of Kabul. Took part in the expedition to Maidan, and the operations around and defence of Sherpur Kabul in December, 1879, including the assault and capture of the Takht-i-Shah and the action of the 23rd Dec. Was present at the action of Childukhtean. Accompanied the force under Sir F. Roberts from Kabul to Kandahar, and was present at the reconnaissance of the 31st Aug., 1880, and the battle of Kandahar, in which his horse was shot. (Twice mentioned in despatches; Brevet of Major.)

Captain S. A. Menzies served with the regiment in both campaigns. Was present at the action of Charasiab and subsequent pursuit of the enemy, and the occupation of Kabul. Took part in the operations around Kabul and defence of Sherpur in December, 1879, including the action of the 23rd Dec. Was present at the action of Childukhtean. Accompanied the force under Sir F. Roberts from Kabul to Kandahar, and was present at the reconnaissance of the 31st Aug., 1880, and the battle of Kandahar, in which he was severely wounded.

Captain H. Bayly served with the regiment in both campaigns. Was present at the action of

Charasiab and subsequent pursuit of the enemy, and the occupation of Kabul. Took part in the operations around Kabul in December, 1879, including the assault and capture of the Takht-i-Shah and the action of the 23rd Dec. Was present at the action of Childukhtean. Accompanied the force under Sir F. Roberts from Kabul to Kandahar, and was present at the reconnaissance of the 31st Aug., 1880, and the battle of Kandahar.

Captain W. H. Dick-Cunyngham, V.C. (For services see Biographical Division.)

Lieut. St. J. Forbes. (Killed in action. See Biographical Division.)

Lieut. I. S. M. Hamilton served with the regiment and as Orderly Officer on the Staff of Brigadier-General Massy, during the second campaign. Was present at the action of Charasiab and subsequent pursuit of the enemy, and the final occupation of Kabul. (Mentioned in despatches.)

Lieut. E. Gilpin-Brown served with the regiment in the second campaign. Was present at the action of Charasiab and subsequent pursuit of the enemy, and the final occupation of Kabul. Took part in the expedition to Maidan, and the operations around Kabul and defence of Sherpur in December, 1879, including the assault and capture of the Takht-i-Shah and the assault of the Asmai Heights.

Lieuts. E. C. Bethune and W. C. Boyd served with the regiment in the second campaign and were present at the operations round Kabul and defence of Sherpur in December, 1879, including the action of the 23rd Dec.

Lieut. F. F. Ramsay served with the regiment throughout. Was present at the action of Charasiab and subsequent pursuit of the enemy, and the occupation of Kabul. Took part in the expedition to Maidan, and the operations round Kabul and defence of Sherpur in December, 1879, including the assault and capture of the Takht-i-Shah and the action of the 23rd Dec. Was present at the action of Childukhtean. Accompanied the force under Sir F. Roberts from Kabul to Kandahar, and was present at the reconnaissance of the 31st Aug., 1880, and the battle of Kandahar. (Mentioned in despatches for gallant behaviour at Childukhtean.)

Lieuts. R. A. Grant and H. A. Macdonald served with the regiment throughout. Were present at the affair at Karatiga on the 27th Sept., 1879, the action of Charasiab and subsequent pursuit of the enemy, and the occupation of Kabul. Took part in the expedition to Maidan, and the operations around Kabul and defence of Sherpur in December, 1879, including the assault and capture of the Takht-i-Shah and the action of the 23rd Dec. Were present at the action of Childukhtean. Accompanied the force under Sir F. Roberts from Kabul to Kandahar, and were present at the reconnaissance on the 31st Aug., 1880, and the battle of Kandahar. In recognition of his gallant conduct at Karatiga, Lieut.—then Colour-Sergt.—Macdonald, received his commission. (Mentioned in despatches.)

Lieuts. A. D. Fraser, Forbes Macbean, and H. Wright served with the regiment throughout. Were present at the action of Charasiab and subsequent pursuit of the enemy, and the final occupation of Kabul. Took part in the expedition to Maidan, and the operations around Kabul and defence of Sherpur in December, 1879, including the assault and capture of the Takht-i-Shah and the action of the 23rd Dec. Were present at the action of Childukhtean. Accompanied the force under Sir F. Roberts from Kabul to Kandahar, and were present at the reconnaissance of the 31st Aug., 1880, and the battle of Kandahar. During June and July, 1879, Lieut. Fraser was Orderly Officer to Br.-Genl. Forbes at Ali Khel.

Lieut. D. W. Stewart served with the regiment in the second campaign. Was present at the action of Childukhtean. Accompanied the force under Sir F. Roberts from Kabul to Kandahar, and was present at the reconnaissance of the 31st Aug., 1880, and the battle of Kandahar, in which he was severely wounded.

Lieut. G. Staunton served with the regiment in the second campaign. Accompanied the force under Sir F. Roberts from Kabul to Kandahar, and was present at the reconnaissance of the 31st Aug., 1880, and the battle of Kandahar.

Captain J. Bignell (Quartermaster) served with the regiment in the first campaign. Returned to India from Ali Khel in 1879.

4TH BATTN. RIFLE BRIGADE.

IN November, 1878, the 4th Battn. Rifle Brigade, commanded by Colonel H. R. L. Newdigate, was quartered at Peshawar. About the 15th of that month orders were received for it to form part of the 1st (Brigadier-General Macpherson's) Brigade of the 1st Division Peshawar Valley Field Force, then assembling at that station under the command of Lt.-Genl. Sir Sam. Browne, K.C.S.I., C.B., V.C.

Taking part in the operations resulting in the capture of Ali Musjid, the battalion was employed, on the 21st and 22nd November, 1878, in the flanking movements of the 1st Brigade over the precipitous Rhotas Heights in reverse of the Fort, and after the retreat of the Afghan forces participated in the forward movement of the Division to Daka, and subsequently to Jalalabad.

In January, 1879, the Head-quarters and major part of the battalion proceeded from Jalalabad to Basawal to join the force under the command of Brigadier-General Tytler, which was about to march from that post into the Bazar Valley in the second expedition against the Zaka Khel Afridis. After taking part in the various operations which ensued, including the reconnaisance and skirmish of the 28th January near Halwai, they returned with the other units of the column, and rejoined Divisional Head-quarters on the 7th February. On that day all the available men of the battalion left at Jalalabad under the command of Captain St. Paul, took part in an expedition across the Kabul River into the Kunar Valley against a force of Mohmands, who dispersed after a few shots had been fired.

A portion of the 2nd Battalion Rifle Brigade formed part of the expeditionary force under the command of Brigadier-General Jenkins which crossed the Lughman River on the 22nd February, 1879, and after penetrating a distance of thirty miles into new country, returned to Jalalabad on the 25th idem. Again, on the 31st March, 300 men of the battalion accompanied the force under the command of Brigadier-General Macpherson in the second Lughman Valley expedition, crossing the Siah Koh range, in a forced march of twenty-six hours' duration, covering in that time some thirty-five miles of most difficult country, and eventually returning to Jalalabad on the 4th April.

The battalion advanced with the remainder of the Brigade to Safed Sang, where it remained till after the signing of the treaty of Gandamak. Quitting that post for Murree on the 3rd June, 1879, it crossed the frontier on the 13th, and arrived at the foot of the hills near Abbottabad on the 30th idem. During the return-march cholera broke out in the ranks, and together with heat apoplexy, claimed no less than seventy-six lives in the space of three weeks.

SERVICES IN AFGHANISTAN OF OFFICERS OF THE 4TH BATTN. RIFLE BRIGADE.

Colonel H. R. L. Newdigate, C.B., (*h.p.*) commanded the battalion throughout the first campaign. Was present at the taking of Ali Musjid, and took part in the Bazar and Lughman Valley expeditions. In the second campaign commanded the Lower Kuram Brigade (command extending from Kohat to Bulesh Khel) from April till August, 1880, when he was invalided to India. (Mentioned in despatches; C.B.)

Colonel C. B. Dashwood (*retired*) served with the battalion as Senior Major from the commencement of the war till January, 1879. Was present at the taking of Ali Musjid.

Lt.-Colonel H. Wood, joined the battalion on the 10th April, 1879, and served with it till the conclusion of the campaign.

Major FitzRoy Stephen served with the battalion as Junior Major from the commencement of the war till April, 1879. Was present at the taking of Ali Musjid, took part in the Bazar Valley expedition, and commanded a detachment of the battalion in the first Lughman Valley expedition.

Lt.-Colonel H. J. T. Walpole (*retired*) served with the battalion throughout the campaign. Was present at the taking of Ali Musjid, and took part in the Bazar Valley expedition.

Major H. S. Brownrigg. (For services see "Staff.")

Major W. H. M. Fitzherbert served with the battalion throughout the campaign. Was present at the taking of Ali Musjid, and took part in the Bazar Valley and first Lughman Valley expeditions.

Capt. T. A. Maberley (*retired*) served with the battalion from the commencement of the war till April, 1879. Was present at the taking of Ali Musjid, and took part in the Bazar Valley expedition.

Major C. H. St. Paul served with the battalion throughout the campaign. Was present at the taking of Ali Musjid. Commanded a detachment of the battalion in the expedition into the Kunar Valley, and took part in the second Lughman Valley expedition.

Captain J. J. Preston. (Deceased. See Biographical Division.)

Captains F. Howard, H. F. Forbes (*1st Battn.*)*, and H. A. Cholmondeley, and Lieuts. A. R. Pemberton and W. P. St. G. Mildmay* served with the battalion throughout the campaign—*Captain Cholmondeley* as Adjutant, and *Lieut. Pemberton* as Transport Officer. Were present at the taking of Ali Musjid, and took part in the Bazar and Lughman Valley expedition.

Captain P. G. Hill (retired) served with the battalion from January, 1879, till the conclusion of the campaign, taking part in the Kunar Valley expedition.

Captain F. C. Howard (2nd Battn.) served with the battalion from the commencement of the war till April, 1879, being present at the taking of Ali Musjid.

Captain W. W. Hammond (2nd Battn.) and *Lieuts. G. S. P. Hornby* and *G. F. Leslie* served with the battalion throughout the campaign. Were present at the taking of Ali Musjid, and took part in the Kunar and Lughman Valley expeditions.

Bt. Major J. D. Mansel. (For services see "Staff.")

Lieut. Lord Ossulton served with the battalion from January, 1879, till the conclusion of the campaign, taking part in the Lughman Valley expedition. (Since deceased. See Biographical Division.)

Captain A. H. W. Harvey (3rd Battn.) served with the battalion from January, 1879, till the conclusion of the campaign. Took part in the Bazar and Lughman Valley expeditions.

Lieuts. A. E. H. Colville and the Hon. W. Coke served with the battalion from April, 1879, till the conclusion of the campaign.

Lieut. J. Sherston. (For services see "Staff.")

Lieut. C. à. Court (3rd Battn.) served with the battalion from the commencement of the war till December, 1878, when he was invalided. Was present at the taking of Ali Musjid.

Lieut. H. F. M. Wilson served with the battalion throughout the campaign. Was present at the taking of Ali Musjid, and took part in the Kunar Valley expedition.

Major J. J. Bailey (A.P.D.) and Quartermaster J. Lamb served with the battalion throughout the campaign, being present at the taking of Ali Musjid.

ARMY MEDICAL DEPARTMENT.

URGEON W. B. ALLIN, *M.B.*, served with the 8th Hussars, in the Khyber Division, during the second campaign.

Surgeon-Major A. Anderson was in medical charge of a battery of Horse Artillery in the Kandahar F. F. during the second campaign.

Surgeon-Major Geo. Andrew, M.B., served during the first campaign with the Peshawar Valley F.F., and during the second campaign with the Khyber Division and Khyber Line Force.

Surgeon-Major M. Anthony, M.D., served with the Khyber Line Force, and Khyber Brigade, in medical charge of the 1st Battn. 18th Regt., during the second campaign.

Surgeon-Major G. Ashton, M.B.

Surgeon-Major C. A. Atkins was in medical charge of the 72nd Highlanders throughout the second campaign, being present at the night attack on the rear-guard at Zaidabad, the action of Charasiab (horse shot), the operations around Kabul and defence of Sherpur in Dec., 1879, including the Deh Mozang gorge, the assault and capture of the Asmai Heights (mentioned in despatches), and the final repulse of the enemy, taking part in the advance from Kabul to the relief of Kandahar, and being present at the battle of Kandahar. (Mentioned in despatches.)

Surgeon-Major G. Atkinson, M.B. (Deceased. See Biographical Division.)

Surgeon-Major A. G. Bartley, M.D., served during the second campaign with the N. Afghanistan F.F.

Surgeon J. M. Beamish, M.D., served during the first campaign in medical charge of the 1st Division Siege Train, Kandahar F.F., at Dadar and in the Bolan Pass.

Surgeon-Major J. F. Beattie, M.D.

Surgeon-Major T. Bennett.

Surgeon-Major W. F. Bennett, M.D., served during the second campaign with the Kabul and Kabul-Kandahar Field Forces, taking part in the advance from Kabul to the relief of Kandahar, and being present at the battle of Kandahar.

Surgeon-Major R. H. Bolton. (Deceased. See Biographical Division.)

Hon. Brigade Surgeon J. Bonnyman, M.D. (retired), served with the Kandahar F.F. during the second campaign.

Surgeon I. Boulger served with the 85th L.I., in the Kuram F.F., during the second campaign.

Surgeon-Major J. Bourke (retired) served with the Kabul F.F. during the second campaign, was in charge of the new Ambulance Corps during the advance on and occupation of Kabul by Sir F. Roberts, and at the action of Charasiab. (Mentioned in despatches.)

Surgeon-Major W. C. Boyd served with the Kabul F.F. during the second campaign, being present at the operations round Kabul and defence of Sherpur in Dec., 1879.

Surgeon-Major R. M. Bradford.

Surgeon W. H. Briggs served with the N. Afghanistan F.F. during the second campaign.

Surgeon John Brodie, M.B., served in the first campaign with the 67th Regt. during a severe epidemic of typhoid fever in the Kuram Valley in 1879; in the second campaign took part in the advance of the Kuram Division Kabul F.F. on Kabul, and was present at the action of Charasiab; was in medical charge of the 67th Regt. during the operations round Kabul and defence of Sherpur in Dec., 1879; accompanied the advance from Kabul to the relief of Kandahar (in charge of a section of the Field Hospital), and was present at the battle of Kandahar. (Thanked by Col. Parker and the officers and men of the 92nd Highlanders for aid rendered to the wounded under fire.)

Surgeon-Major John Fitz G. Brodie served during the first campaign, first in medical charge of D/2, R.A., taking part in the advance on and occupation of Kandahar, and afterwards, from 16 Feb., 1879, till the return of the battery to India, in medical charge of I/1, R.A.

Surgeon A. W. Browne served with the N. Afghanistan F.F. during the second campaign.

Surgeon-Major R. F. Buchanan served with the Kuram Valley F.F. during the first campaign.

Surgeon W. A. Burgess served with the Kandahar F.F. during the first campaign.

Surgeon-Major W. F. Burnett served with the Khyber Line Force, in medical charge of the 1st Battn. 25th K.O.Bs., during the second campaign.

Surgeon J. T. Carey, M.B., served with the Kuram Valley F.F. during the first campaign, being present at the assault and capture of the Peiwar Kotal. (Mentioned in despatches.)

Surgeon A. W. Carleton, M.B., accompanied Sir D. Stewart's Division in the advance from Kandahar on Ghazni and into the Logar Valley, being present at the battle of Ahmad Khel and the action of Arzu.

Brigade Surgeon R. W. Carter served with General Phayre's Division in S. Afghanistan, in medical charge of the 63rd Regt., during the second campaign.

Surgeon S. H. Carter, M.B., arrived at Kandahar, 2 March, 1879, in medical charge of drafts for the 2/60th and 70th Foot, and remained there till 29 March, 1880; accompanied Sir D. Stewart's Division in the advance from Kandahar on Ghazni, and was present at the battle of Ahmad Khel and the action of Arzu; was with General Hill's force in the Logar valley during the operations in May, June, and July, 1880; and eventually returned to India by the Khyber route on the evacuation of Kabul.

Brigade Surgeon W. Cattell was in medical charge of the 10th Hussars throughout the first campaign, being present at the taking of Ali Musjid and action of Futtehabad.

Surgeon H. Charlesworth served with the 1st Battn. 5th Fusiliers, on the Khyber Line, during both campaigns.

Surgeon-Major M. Cogan served in Southern Afghanistan with General Phayre's Division during the second campaign, organizing the Principal Base European Hospital at Kandahar. (Mentioned in reports, and thanked by Governor-General in Council.)

Surgeon P. Connolly.

Surgeon-Major H. Cornish. (Killed in action. See Biographical Division.)

Surgeon H. Cotton served with the N. Afghanistan F.F. during the second campaign.

Hon. Brigade Surgeon W. Creagh (retired).

Surgeon-Major W. Creyk, M.B., served with the N. Afghanistan F.F., in medical charge of I/A, R.H.A., during the second campaign.

Surgeon-Major J. d'Altera during the first campaign organized a Depôt Hospital at Multan for European troops at the front in Southern Afghanistan; and during the second campaign, served with the Kuram F.F.

Surgeon-Major G. S. Davie, M.D., served with the Peshawar Valley F.F. during the first campaign. (Mentioned in despatches.)

Surgeon-Major F. A. Davy, M.D., served with the Khyber Line Force during the second campaign.

Surgeon-Major R. W. Davies was in medical charge of the Carabineers from Oct., 1879, till Sept., 1880, taking part in the affair at Ali Boghan, 13 Jan., 1880, and the expeditions into the Lughman Valley and against the Wazir Kugianis, under General Bright.

Surgeon P. J. Dempsey, M.D., served with the S. Afghanistan F.F. during the second campaign.

Surgeon W. Donovan served during the second campaign with the 3rd Brigade, Kuram Division Kabul F.F., and subsequently with the Kuram Force, till the withdrawal of the troops to India, taking part, in medical charge of the 85th L.I., in the Zaimusht expedition, and being present at the storming and destruction of Zawa.

Surgeon J. C. Dorman, M.B., served during the first campaign with the Quetta Division, and during the second campaign, with the Kuram F.F., being present at the fighting at Ali Khel and the Shutargardan.

Surgeon-Major W. E. Dudley served with General Phayre's Division in Southern Afghanistan during the second campaign, in medical charge of the 78th Highlanders.

Surgeon-Major R. C. Eaton served in medical charge of the 1st Battn. Royal Irish, in the 1st Section Khyber Line Force, during the second campaign.

RECORDS OF SERVICE.

Surgeon-Major J. D. Edge, M.D., served with the Kandahar F.F. during the second campaign.

Brigade Surgeon J. Ekin, M.B., served during the second campaign with the Kabul and Kabul-Kandahar Field Forces, taking part in the advance from Kabul to the relief of Kandahar, and being present at the battle of Kandahar. (Mentioned in despatches.)

Surgeon I. B. Emerson.

Surgeon-Major E. J. H. Evatt, M.D., served throughout the first campaign with the 1st Division Peshawar Valley F.F., being present, in charge of the advanced section of the Field Hospital, at the taking of Ali Musjid and the forcing of the Khyber Pass; establishing a Field Hospital at Daka; accompanying, as Senior Medical Officer with General Tytler's Column, the expedition into the Bazar Valley; advancing with the Division to Gandamak; and eventually taking part, in charge of a Field Hospital, in the return-march of the troops to India in June, 1879. (Mentioned in despatches for "indefatigable care of the wounded," and thanked in Orders.) In the second campaign had charge of a Field Hospital with General C. Gough's Brigade, and took part in the advance to the relief of Sherpur; established the Bala Hissar General Hospital; accompanied General Ross's force towards Ghazni; and eventually returned to India on the evacuation of Kabul.

Brigade Surgeon J. G. Faught served with the N. Afghanistan F.F. during the second campaign.

Surgeon E. H. Fenn served in the second campaign in charge of 6/8, R.A., being present at the affairs at Zaidabad, 25 and 26 April, 1880, taking part in the advance from Kabul to the relief of Kandahar, and being present at the battle of Kandahar. (Mentioned in despatches.)

Surgeon-Major A. J. Ferguson served during the second campaign with the Khyber Line Force, being present at the operations in the Mazina Valley. (Mentioned in despatches.)

Surgeon-Major J. Ferguson served with the Khyber Line Reserve during the second campaign.

Surgeon.Major R. P. Ferguson served during the first campaign with the 2nd Division Peshawar Valley F.F.

Surgeon-Major N. Ffolliott.

Surgeon-Major W. Ffolliott served throughout the first campaign with the 2nd Division Peshawar Valley F.F., being in charge of the Divisional Field Hospital at Landi Kotal. In the second campaign advanced to Kabul with the 9th Lancers, and remained there, in charge of the Ambulance Corps, till Dec., 1879, when he returned to India in charge of a convoy of sick and wounded.

Surgeon John Findlay, M.B., served during the second campaign with the Kandahar F.F., being in Kandahar throughout the siege. As Assistant to Surgeon-Major Waghorn, treated the wounded who were brought in from the fields of Maiwand and Deh Khwaja, and was present at the battle of Kandahar.

Surgeon-Major J. E. Fishbourne served throughout the first campaign with the Peshawar Valley F.F., first in charge of the 2nd Division Field Hospital at Jamrud, and afterwards of the 1st Division Field Hospital at Jalalabad. Served with the 4th Battn. Rifle Brigade, and had charge of the Field Hospital of the Bannu Column Mahsud Waziri Expeditionary Force, during the advance into Waziristan in May, 1881.

Surgeon J. W. H. Flanagan served with the Kandahar F.F. during the second campaign.

Surgeon-Major Joseph Fleming, M.D., served in medical charge of the 67th Regt. from Dec., 1878, till Sept., 1879, and subsequently in charge of the 2nd Battn. 8th Regt., and all the troops at the Peiwar Kotal, till 28 Dec., 1879, when he was ordered to India. Subsequently proceeded to Kabul, and from April to July, 1880, served there in charge of a section of the Field Hospital, and as Brigade Surgeon, 1st Brigade, 2nd Division, N.A.F.F. In July, 1880, returned to India in charge of the Divisional Field Hospital, and of all the sick and wounded from Kabul and of the Ghazni F.F., prior to the evacuation.

Surgeon-Major S. Flood (retired).

Surgeon-Major E. Footner, M.B., served with the Kandahar F.F. in medical charge of the 70th Regt., during the first campaign.

Surgeon-Major P. T. Frazer served during the first campaign with the 1st Division Peshawar Valley F.F., being present at the forcing of the Khyber Pass.

Surgeon T. J. Gallwey, M.D.

Surgeon-Major A. G. Gaye served with the Southern Afghanistan F.F., under General Phayre, in 1880.

Deputy Surgeon-General J. Gibbons, C.B. (For services see "Staff.")

Surgeon-Major G. J. Gibson, M.D., served in medical charge of the 2nd Battn. 8th Regt., throughout the first campaign, being present at the assault and capture of the Peiwar Kotal. (Mentioned in despatches.)

Surgeon-Major H. C. Gillespie, M.D.

Surgeon-Major B. T. Giraud, M.D., served in medical charge of the 2nd Battn. 7th Fusiliers throughout the period of its service in the war, being present at the defence of Kandahar, the sortie to Deh Khwaja, and the battle of Kandahar. (Mentioned in despatches.)

Surgeon J. A. Gormley, M.D., served with the 6th Dragoon Guards, in the Khyber Division, during the second campaign.

Surgeon-Major H. R. Greene.

Surgeon J. J. Greene, M.B.

Surgeon-Major J. Greig, M.B. (retired.)

Surgeon-Major G. C. Gribbon, M.B., served during the first campaign in medical charge of the 1st Battalion 25th King's Own Borderers, with the Peshawar Valley F.F., taking part in the Bazar Valley expedition.

Surgeon W. L. Gubbins, M.B., served with the 2nd Division Peshawar Valley F.F., throughout the first campaign, in medical charge of the Divisional Staff, and during part of the time in medical charge of the 1/5th Fusiliers, taking part, with the battalion, in the first of the Bazar Valley expeditions. In the second campaign served in charge of a detachment of the 5th Fusiliers, with the Kuram F.F. from Nov., 1879, till Jan., 1880, when he was transferred to the Khyber Line Force, and held medical charge of the Head-quarters Staff till invalided to England, in June 1880, from illness contracted in the field. Took part in the affair at Kam Daka, Jan., 1880, and the Hissarak expedition, April, 1880. In addition to his other appointment, held the post of Secretary to the Principal Medical Officer, and was also Sanitary Officer to the Khyber Line Force.

Brigade-Surgeon A. Guthrie M.D. (For services see Staff.)

Surgeon-Major A. R. Hall served with the S. Afghanistan F.F. during the second campaign.

Deputy Surgeon-General J. A. Hanbury, M.B., C.B. (For services see "Staff.")

Surgeon-Major W. M. Harman, M.B., served with the Kuram F.F. during the second campaign.

Surgeon-Major C. H. Harvey, M.D., served with the Kandahar F.F. during the second campaign, being present in Kandahar throughout the siege. (Mentioned in despatches.)

Deputy Surgeon-General H. B. Hassard, C.B. (For services see "Staff.")

Surgeon A. E. Hayes.

Deputy Surgeon-General J. Hendley, C.B. (For services see "Staff.")

Surgeon-Major W. G. R. Hinds, M.D., served with the 1st Division Kandahar F.F. from Feb. till Nov., 1880, being present at Kandahar throughout the siege. Was in medical charge, first of the 66th Regt., and afterwards of No. 1 Field Hospital.

Surgeon R. D. Hodson served with the Kandahar F.F. during the second campaign.

Surgeon-Major E. Hopkins.

Surgeon-Major F. Howard, M.D., served with the Peshawar Valley F.F. during the first campaign.

Surgeon John Hoysted served during the second campaign, from 19 Dec., 1879, till 26 May, 1880, with the Division operating on the Khyber line, being present, with Col. Boisragon's Column, at the defeat of the Mohmands at Kam Daka in Jan., 1880, and taking part in the Lughman Valley and Hissarak expeditions under General Bright. Was in temporary medical charge of the 1/25th, K.O.Bs., and subsequently in medical charge of C/3, R.A., and I/A, R.H.A., returning with the latter to India.

Surgeon-Major T. N. Hoysted served with the Kuram Valley F.F. during the first campaign, being present at the assault and capture of the Peiwar Kotal.

Surgeon G. A. Hughes, M.B., served with the Royal Artillery in the second campaign.

Surgeon-Major J. H. Hunter.

Surgeon-Major R. Jackson served in medical charge of the 2nd Battn. 8th Regt. at Peiwar Kotal during the year 1880. Was the senior Medical Officer present, and had charge of the Depôt Field Hospital.

Surgeon-Major T. W. Jackson, M.B., served with the Kandahar F.F. during the second campaign.

Surgeon-Major H. Jagoe, M.B., served with the Kandahar F.F. during the second campaign.

Surgeon-Major J. H. Jeffcoat served with the Peshawar Valley F.F., in medical charge of the 10th Hussars, during the first campaign.

Surgeon P. G. Jevers served with the 1st and 2nd Divisions Peshawar Valley F.F. from Dec., 1878, till the conclusion of the first campaign, taking part in medical charge of 11/9, R.A., in the advance through the Khyber and the first Bazar Valley expedition. During the second campaign, served from Jan. till July, 1880, with the Kuram F.F., in medical charge of the 4th Battn. Rifle Brigade.

Surgeon P. H. Johnston, M.D., served with the Kuram F.F. during the second campaign. Was attached to No. 1 Mountain Battery in the Zaimusht expedition, and was present at the storming and capture of Zawa.

Hon. Brigade-Surgeon M. G. Jones (retired) served with the Peshawar Valley F.F. during the first campaign, accompanying the retirement from Gandamak on the conclusion of hostilities. (Mentioned in despatches.)

Surgeon A. C. Keith, M.B. (Deceased. See Biographical Division.)

Surgeon-Major R. Keith, M.D.

Surgeon E. W. Kelsall served with the Kandahar F.F. during the second campaign, being present in Kandahar throughout the siege. (Mentioned in despatches.)

Surgeon-Major H. Kelsall. (Deceased. See Biographical Division.)

Surgeon W. W. Kenny, M.B., served with the Khyber Line Force during the second campaign, being attached for duty to the 2nd Battn. 14th Regt.

Surgeon H. C. Kirkpatrick, M.D., served with the N. Afghanistan F.F. during the second campaign.

Surgeon-Major M. Knox.

Surgeon-Major J. Langdon.

Surgeon G. T. Langridge served during the first campaign in medical charge of the detached squadron 9th Lancers in the Kuram Valley, subsequently accompanying it, during the second campaign, in the advance on Kabul, and being present at the affair at Jagi Thana, the action of Charasiab, the skirmishes on the 7th and 8th Oct., 1879, and the cavalry pursuit on the 9th. Was afterwards attached to the 92nd Highlanders, and took part in the operations round Kabul and defence of Sherpur in Dec., 1879, and the expeditions into the Maidan district.

Surgeon W. J. Le Grand, M.D.

Surgeon-Major R. Lewer, M.D., served in medical charge of the 9th Lancers, on the Khyber line, during the first campaign, from 13 March, to 7 June, 1879, and during the second campaign from 11 Oct., 1879, and as Sanitary Officer to the Kabul F.F. from 11 Nov., 1879, till the conclusion of hostilities, being present at the operations round Kabul and the defence of Sherpur in Dec., 1879. (Brought to special notice for good service.) As Acting Brigade Surgeon of the Cavalry Brigade, took part in the advance from Kabul to the relief of Kandahar, and was present at the battle of Kandahar. (Mentioned in despatches.)

Surgeon-Major A. Long served with the S. Afghanistan F.F. during the second campaign.

Surgeon-Major E. L. Low, M.B., served uninterruptedly during both campaigns, from 21 Nov., 1878, till 23 Jan., 1880, in medical charge of F/A, R.H.A., taking part in the assault and capture of the Peiwar Kotal, the advance over the Shutargardan Pass, the action of Charasiab, the action of Killa Kazi (in which four guns of the Battery had to be temporarily abandoned), the recovery of the four guns (being the only officer of the Battery present), and the subsequent operations round Kabul and defence of Sherpur in Dec., 1879.

Surgeon-Major F. Lyons, M.D., served with the S. Afghanistan F.F. during the second campaign.

Surgeon-Major J. J. McCarthy, M.D.

Surgeon J. A. McCracken, M.D., crossed the frontier with the 25th K.O.Bs., 16 Dec., 1879, and served during the war till the return of the troops to India: first in charge of Field Hospital of No. 2 Flying Column, Khyber Line Force, and afterwards as Chief Sanitary Officer on the Divisional Headquarters Staff of General Bright. Was also Secretary to the Principal Medical Officer of the Khyber Line Force.

Surgeon-Major G. W. McNalty, M.D., served during the first campaign with the Peshawar Valley F.F., and during the second campaign with the Kabul and Kabul-Kandahar Field Forces, being present at the affair at Zaidabad, taking part in the advance from Kabul to the relief of Kandahar, and being present at the battle of Kandahar. (Mentioned in despatches.)

Surgeon J. McNamara, M.D., served during the second campaign, from 10 Feb. till 11 Nov., 1880, in medical charge of C/2, R.A., being present in Kandahar throughout the siege, and taking part in the reconnaissance of 31 Aug., 188. Accompanied, in medical charge, the force under Brigadier-General Brooke which went out, 28 July, 1880, to cover the retreat of the remnants of Brigadier-General Burrows' Brigade from Maiwand. (Mentioned in despatches.)

Surgeon J. G. McNeece served with the Kandahar F.F. during the second campaign.

Surgeon P. J. McQuaid, M.D., served during the second campaign with Sir. F. Roberts' Division, taking part in the advance on and occupation of Kabul, and being present at the action of Charasiab and the affairs round Kabul and defence of Sherpur in Dec., 1879, including the actions of Karez Mir and Killa Affshar.

Surgeon-Major W. McWatters served with the Khyber Line Force, in medical charge of the 1st Battn. 17th Regt. during the second campaign.

Brigade-Surgeon W. G. N. Manley, V.C., served with the Kandahar F.F. during the first campaign. (Mentioned in despatches.)

Surgeon-Major E. C. Markey served during the first campaign with Sir D. Stewart's Division, taking part in the advance on and occupation of Kandahar, and being present at the action of Takht-i-pul. Served during the second campaign with the Kabul and Kabul-Kandahar Field Forces, taking part in the advance from Kabul to the relief of Kandahar and being present at the battle of Kandahar. Subsequently accompanied the Marri Expeditionary force. (Twice mentioned in despatches.)

Brigade Surgeon C. Martin was in medical charge of the Kuram Valley and Ali Khel Hospitals during the first campaign. (Mentioned in despatches.)

Surgeon-Major J. Martin served with the 1st Division Peshawar Valley F.F., in medical charge of the 81st Regt., during the first campaign, being present at the bombardment and capture of Ali Musjid. (Wounded.)

Brigade Surgeon R. W. Meadows, M.B., served during the second campaign with the Kandahar, Ghazni, and Kabul Field Forces, taking part in the advance from Kandahar on Ghazni and into the Logar Valley, and the retirement from Kabul by the Khyber route to India, and being present at the battle of Ahmed Khel and the action of Arzu. (Mentioned in despatches.)

Hon. Deputy Surgeon-General J. Meane (retired) served with the Kuram Valley F.F. throughout the first campaign, in medical charge of the 72nd Highlanders, being present at the assault and capture of the Peiwar Kotal, the advance to Ali Khel, and the march through the Sapari defile. Was in charge of the Divisional Base Hospital at Kuram and the Peiwar Kotal; and was Senior Medical Officer British Forces throughout the campaign.

Surgeon-Major A. Minto, M.B.

Surgeon O. F. Molloy.

Surgeon-Major J. H. Moore served during both campaigns with the force under Sir D. Stewart, taking part in the original advance on and occupation of Kandahar and Kalat-i-Ghilzai, the advance from Kandahar on Ghazni and into the Logar Valley, and the retirement from Kabul by the Khyber route to India, and being present at the battle of Ahmad Khel and the action of Arzu. (Mentioned in despatches.)

Surgeon J. J. La V. Morris, M.D., served in the first campaign with the Kuram Valley F.F., and in the second, with the Kabul F.F. Was present at the action of Charasiab, the occupation of Kabul, and the operations round Kabul and defence of Sherpur in Dec., 1879. Accompanied General Baker's Brigade into Kohistan in Jan., 1880, in charge of Field Hospital. Was in medical charge of the 92nd Highlanders at the second action of Charasiab. (Twice mentioned in despatches.)

Surgeon-Major H. S. Muir, M.D., served in S. Afghanistan during both campaigns, in medical charge of 11/11, R.A., taking part in the advance on and occupation of Kandahar and Kalat-i-Ghilzai, and the second occupation of Kalat-i-Ghilzai, and being present at the action of Shahjui. (Mentioned in despatches.)

Surgeon-Major R. Murphy.

Surgeon-Major T. Murtagh served with the S. Afghanistan F.F. during the second campaign.

Surgeon-Major W. Nash, M.D., served with the 72nd Highlanders throughout the first campaign, being present at the assault and capture of the Peiwar Kotal, the reconnaissance to the Shutargardan, and the passage of the Sapari Pass. Was latterly in charge of the Divisional Field Hospital at Ali Khel. (Mentioned in Orders.)

Brigade Surgeon N. Norris served in medical charge of the 1st Battn. 5th Fusiliers throughout the period the regiment was employed in the second campaign.

Surgeon-Major H. J. O'Brien, M.B.

Surgeon-Major T. O'Farrell, M.D., served with the Kandahar F.F. during the second campaign.

Surgeon-Major W. O'Halloran served in Southern Afghanistan during the latter part of the second campaign.

Deputy Surgeon-General J. O'Nial, C.B. (For services see "Staff.")

Surgeon-Major J. J. O'Reilly served in Southern Afghanistan during the latter part of the second campaign.

Surgeon-Major E. O'Sullivan served with the 6th Dragoon Guards, in the Khyber Division, during the second campaign.

Hon. Brigade Surgeon T. Oughton.

Surgeon-Major O. Owen.

Surgeon-Major T. W. Patterson served with the Kuram F.F. during the second campaign.

Surgeon J. Pedlow, M.D., served with the Khyber Line Force during the second campaign, being in charge of Field Hospitals at Basawal and Pesh Bolak. Was present at the action of Mazina, in medical charge of a wing of the 8th R.I. Hussars.

Surgeon-Major J. H. Porter. (Deceased. See Biographical Division.)

Surgeon C. K. Powell, M.D.

Surgeon-Major A. F. Preston, M.B., served during the second campaign in medical charge of the 66th Regt., taking part in its advance to Kandahar, and subsequently, with General Burrows' Brigade, to the Halmand. Was present at the action of Girishk, and the battle of Maiwand, in which he was severely wounded while attending a disabled man in the front line of fire. Was in Kandahar throughout the siege. (Mentioned in despatches.)

Surgeon-Major W. S. M. Price served with the Peshawar Valley F.F. during the first campaign, being present at the operations in the Bazar Valley, and the affair at Deh Sarak.

Surgeon R. H. Quill, M.B.

Hon. Brigade Surgeon M. Quinlan (retired).

Surgeon W. J. R. Rainsford served with the Khyber F.F. during the second campaign.

Surgeon-Major T. Ramsay served with the Division under Sir F. Roberts during the second campaign, taking part in the advance on and occupation of Kabul, and being present at the action of Charasiab and subsequent operations.

Surgeon-Major W. B. Ramsbotham, M.D., served in medical charge of the 1st Battn. 17th Regt. during the first campaign, being present at the taking of Ali Musjid.

Surgeon-Major A. H. Ratigan served with the 1st Battn. 17th Regt. in the Peshawar Valley F.F. during the first campaign.

Brigade Surgeon J. B. C. Reade served with Sir D. Stewart's Division during the first campaign, taking part in the advance on and occupation of Kandahar. (Mentioned in despatches.)

Surgeon-Major J. Reddick served with the Kandahar F.F. during the second campaign.

Surgeon H. J. Robbins served with the Kuram F.F. during the second campaign.

Surgeon-Major John Robinson proceeded on field service in medical charge of the 59th Foot in Nov., 1878, and served in Southern Afghanistan with that regiment, and in medical charge of the Brigade Staff, and subsequently of the Staff of the Kandahar F.F., till the conclusion of the first campaign.

Surgeon E. A. Roche served with the S. Afghanistan F.F. during the second campaign.

Surgeon-Major E. A. H. Roe served with the Kandahar F.F. during the second campaign.

Brigade Surgeon S. B. Roe, M.B., C.B., served with the Kabul and Kabul-Kandahar Field Forces throughout the second campaign, being present at the action of Ali Khel, taking part in the advance from Kabul to the relief of Kandahar, and being present at the battle of Kandahar. (Twice mentioned in despatches.)

Surgeon J. G. Rogers, M.B., served from the outbreak of the war till Feb., 1880, with Sir D. Stewart's Division, in medical charge first of I/1, R.A., and afterwards of D/2, R.A., taking part in the advance on and occupation of Kandahar, and returning with the latter battery to India. On the occurrence of the disaster at Maiwand, again volunteered for service, and proceeded in medical charge of the 78th Highlanders with General Phayre's Brigade, to Kandahar, returning with the regiment to India in Feb., 1881.

Surgeon-Major H. C. Rose, M.D.

Surgeon-Major T. Rudd, M.D., served with the Khyber Line Force during the second campaign.

Surgeon G. M. Russell, M.B., served with the N. Afghanistan F.F. during the second campaign.

Surgeon-Major W. F. Ruttledge served in medical charge of C/3, R.A., with the Peshawar Valley F.F. throughout the period it was employed in the first campaign and early part of the second, being present at the relief of the village of Kam Daka in April, 1879, and taking part in the advance of Brigadier-General C. Gough's Brigade to Gandamak. Was subsequently in medical charge of European and Native Field Hospital, and Superintendent of Sick Transport at Jalalabad. Proceeded to Kabul Feb., 1880, to take charge of sick transport of both divisions of the Field Force and of F/A, R.H.A.; and on the departure of that battery, superintended the transport of all the sick from Kabul to Gandamak, and equipped with transport both the Kabul-Kandahar F.F. and the force returning to India by the Khyber route. Returned in medical charge of the 2nd Battn. 9th Regt. to Gandamak, and from thence to Peshawar in charge of a section of the Field Hospital.

Surgeon-Major M. J. Ryon.

Surgeon-Major George Shaw served with the Khyber F.F. during the second campaign.

Surgeon W. B. Slaughter served in S. Afghanistan during the second campaign.

Surgeon-General A. Smith, M.D., C.B. (For services see "Staff.")

Surgeon-Major J. F. Supple served with the 51st L.I. in N. Afghanistan during the second campaign.

Surgeon R. G. Thomsett served during the first campaign, part of the time in medical charge of the Divisional Field Hospital at Thal. Accompanied the force under General Roberts into the Khost district, and was present at the action of Matun.

Surgeon-Major D. A. S. Thorburn, M.D., served in medical charge of the 2nd Battn. 14th Regt., with the Khyber Line Force, during the second campaign, being present at the operations in the Mazina Valley.

Brigade Surgeon A. M. Tippetts. (For services see "Staff.")

Surgeon F. W. Trevor, M.B., served with the Kandahar F.F. during both campaigns.

Surgeon C. P. Turner was appointed, on the outbreak of the war, to the medical charge of the Head-quarters Staff of the 1st Division Peshawar Valley F.F. Was present at the bombardment and capture of Ali Musjid, and accompanied the troops sent against the Shinwari villages. During March and April, 1879, was in temporary medical charge of the 4th Battn. Rifle Brigade, and accompanied the regiment in the demonstration from Jalalabad into the Lughman Valley. (Received the thanks of H.E., the Commander-in-Chief, for "zeal and devotion displayed in the discharge of most trying duties.")

Surgeon-Major F. A. Turton, M.D., served with the Kandahar F.F. during the first campaign.

Surgeon-Major W. Veneur served with the 15th Hussars in the Kandahar F.F. during the first campaign.

Surgeon-Major Henry Waghorn was in medical charge of No. 1 Field Hospital, Kandahar F.F., from Feb. till Sept., 1880, being present in Kandahar throughout the siege, treating all the wounded who were brought in from the fields of Maiwand and Deh Khwaja, and having charge of a dressing station at the battle of Kandahar.

Surgeon J. Wallace, M.D. (Deceased. See Biographical Division.)

Surgeon-Major T. Walsh served with the Khyber and Kabul Field Forces during the second campaign, taking part in the advance of Brigadier-General C. Gough's Brigade to the relief of Sherpur. (Mentioned in despatches.)

Surgeon L. B. Ward served with the first Division Peshawar Valley F.F. during the first campaign, being present at the capture of Ali Musjid. (Mentioned in despatches.)

Surgeon-Major J. Warren.

Surgeon-Major C. W. Watling arrived at Kandahar 16 Oct., 1879, and served throughout the remainder of the campaign in medical charge of the 59th Regt., taking part in the advance on Ghazni to Kabul, and being present (in action) at the battle of Ahmad Khel and the action of Arzu. Returned by the Khyber route, on the evacuation of Kabul, to India, having charge of a section of the Field Hospital, and acting as Medical Store-keeper, in addition to discharging his regimental duties.

Surgeon B. W. Wellings served with the Southern Afghanistan F.F. during the second campaign.

Surgeon-Major H. B. White served with the Division under Sir F. Roberts during both campaigns; first in medical charge of a section of the Field Hospital at Ali Khel; afterwards in medical charge of G/3, R.A., in the Kuram Valley, subsequently accompanying the battery in the advance on and occupation of Kabul, being present at the action of Charasiab, and the operations round Kabul and defence of Sherpur in Dec., 1879, including the storming of the Tahkt-i-Shah and the Asmai Heights; and eventually, in medical charge of the 2nd Battn. 9th Regt., accompanying the battalion in the advance towards Ghazni, and being present with it at the affair at Zaidabad.

Surgeon-Major S. G. White, M.D., served with the N. Afghanistan F.F. during the second campaign.

Hon. Brigade Surgeon W. S. Whylock, M.D., served with the force under Sir D. Stewart during both campaigns, taking part in the advance on and occupation of Kandahar, the advance from Kandahar on Ghazni and into the Logar Valley, and the retirement from Kabul by the Khyber route to India, and being present at the battle of Ahmad Khel and the action of Arzu. (Mentioned in despatches.)

Surgeon J. F. Williamson, M.B., served with the force under Sir F. Roberts throughout the second campaign, taking part in the advance on and occupation of Kabul, and the advance from Kabul to the relief of Kandahar, and being present at the action of Charasiab, the operations round Kabul and defence of Sherpur in Dec., 1879, and the battle of Kandahar. (Mentioned in despatches.)

Surgeon J. G. Williamson served in S. Afghanistan during the second campaign.

Surgeon-Major James Wilson, M.B., served with the Khyber Line Force during the second campaign. Took part in the Hissarak expedition. (Mentioned in despatches.)

Surgeon-Major W. D. Wilson, M.D., served during the first campaign in medical charge of the Siege Train in Sind, and during the second campaign with the Kuram F.F., in medical charge of the troops at Peiwar Kotal.

Surgeon-Major W. T. Wilson, M.D., served in S. Afghanistan during the second campaign.

Surgeon-Major T. Wood, M.D., served with the Peshawar Valley F.F. during the first campaign, being in medical charge of the 4th Battn. Rifle Brigade.

Surgeon-Major J. H. Wright. (Deceased. See Biographical Division.)

Surgeon-Major Thomas Wright served during the second campaign with the Kuram F.F., being in medical charge of the European Base Hospital from 26 Nov., 1879, till it was broken up on 1 Nov., 1880.

Surgeon F. S. Young served with the 59th Regt. in the Kandahar F.F. during the first campaign.

H.M. INDIAN NATIVE REGIMENTS.

1st REGT. BENGAL CAVALRY.

AT the commencement of the Afghan war the 1st Bengal Cavalry, then stationed at Sialkot, was told off for the reserve.

On the 14th Nov., 1878, a party consisting of 4 non-commissioned officers and 30 Sowars, under command of Jemadar Kurrum Khan, was sent for escort duty to Jhelum, from whence it proceeded in charge of a large convoy of ammunition to Jamrud, and was employed through the whole of the first campaign in the Transport Department, in the Khyber.

Telegraphic orders for the regiment to hold itself in readiness to proceed on active service were received on the 26th Feb., 1879; and four days afterwards it marched from Sialkot to Kohat, where it arrived on the 27th March.

On the 3rd July the Left wing, under the command of Major A. R. Chapman, marched to Thal, the Right wing, under the command of Lieut. A. M. Renny, following on the 19th idem.

The regiment now took up the outposts of Surazain, Gandiur, Chapri, Mandori, Alizai, and Shinak, and was chiefly employed in escorting the mails and convoys, and keeping clear the line of communication between Thal and Kuram on the one side, and Thal and Hangu on the other.

Shortly after the renewal of hostilities in the autumn of 1879, a squadron, of which Lieut. Gartside-Tipping subsequently assumed command, was ordered up to Bulesh Khel to relieve the 14th Bengal Lancers.

On the 18th Sept., 1879, a party consisting of 25 rank and file of the regiment, under the command of Jemadar Mustapha Khan, proceeded to Kuram to do duty with the Transport Department. This party subsequently accompanied Sir F. Roberts' avenging army over the Shutargardan to Kabul, and remained there until the city was finally evacuated, when it rejoined Head-quarters.

As a unit of the Zaimusht expeditionary force, a troop of the regiment under Major Glascock, with Lieut. Renny, left Bulesh Khel on the 8th Dec., 1879, and after taking part in the retaliatory operations which were conducted in the district visited, rejoined Head-quarters at Thal on the 16th idem.

During the previous year the amount of hardship and exposure endured by the regiment had been considerable.

At the beginning of 1880, the effects of the hardship and exposure to which both the men and horses had been subjected became painfully apparent, and the regiment was ordered to move down to Togh to form a standing camp: there it remained until the 13th April, when it returned, under the command of Col. Jenkins, to Thal. A few days afterwards detachments took up the outposts of Kapinga, Manduri, and Ahmad-i-Shana; and on the 23rd April a party of 40 sabres, under the command of Lieut. Cazalet, relieved a party of the 18th Bengal Cavalry at Chupri. At the same time Major Campbell took command of the detachment at Manduri, and Head-quarters marched back to Kohat.

During the night of the 1st May, 1880, a sharp attack was made by a body of Waziris on the Chupri outposts, and was effectively repelled, with the loss of one Sowar of the regiment, by the detachment holding them. The parties holding Chupri and Manduri being relieved by the 18th Bengal Cavalry, marched on the 1st June to Thal, and after a few days took up the outposts from Thal to Hangu.

About the beginning of Sept., 1880, Head-quarters were sent from Kohat to Hangu, to deal with the raiders who were expected to be on the look-out for loot on the return of the Kuram Field Force to India: there they remained until the 2nd Nov., when all the detachments having rejoined, the regiment moved on to Kohat, and eventually, on the 27th Dec., marched for Cawnpore.

The losses sustained by the 1st Bengal Cavalry during the period the regiment was employed in the war were, 2 British and 4 Native officers, 8 non-commissioned officers, 3 trumpeters, 48 Sowars, and 60 camp followers; also 134 horses and 89 ponies.

The undermentioned officers of the 1st Regt. Bengal Cavalry served in the war:—

Colonel R. Jenkins rejoined the regiment 3 April, 1880, from furlough on medical certificate in England, and commanded it until appointed to the command of the Lower Kuram Brigade. (Died at Rawal Pindi 9 Sep., 1880, of illness contracted while on field service.)

Major A. R. Chapman served with the regiment throughout, commanding it till 3 April, 1880, and again from the date of the appointment of Col. Jenkins to the command of the Lower Kuram Brigade, till the conclusion of the war.

Major T. B. M. Glascock, and *Lieuts. G. B. Renny* (Adjutant), *A. M. Renny* (Attached), and *W. H. Cazalet* (Attached) served with the regiment throughout; *Lieut. G. G. Dawes*, till invalided at Kohat, where he died on the 7th June, 1879; and *Major C. W. Campbell* (Attached) till invalided home.

Lieut. R. F. Gartside-Tipping served first as Assistant Road Commandant, Kuram Valley F.F., and afterwards with the regiment, till invalided home.

For services of *Bt. Major F. C. Burton*, see "Staff."

3RD REGT. BENGAL CAVALRY.

ON the renewal of hostilities in Afghanistan in the autumn of 1879, the 3rd Bengal Cavalry, under the command of Lt.-Colonel Mackenzie, was stationed at Peshawar, whither it had recently been moved from Lucknow. Detailed to Brigadier-General Arbuthnot's Brigade of Major-General Bright's Division, the regiment advanced at the latter end of September, 1879, by successive wings, through the Khyber Pass, and during the succeeding winter was employed in holding various posts extending from Jamrud to Gandamak, keeping open the line of communications, escorting convoys, and taking part in the numerous reconnaissances and expeditions which were conducted into a wide extent of surrounding territory.

On the 26th Dec., 1879, one troop of the regiment formed part of the force under Lt.-Col. Fryer, 6th Dragoon Guards, which was sent out from Jalalabad to obtain information concerning an attack which had been made by a body of Shinwaris two days previously on a post near Ali Boghan; and again on the 29th a mixed force under Lt.-Colonel Mackenzie, which included a troop of the 3rd Bengal Cavalry, marched from Jalalabad to Barikab, where it was joined by a squadron of the regiment and other details, and proceeded to visit a cluster of villages some ten miles distant, which were supposed to be sheltering a number of the tribesmen who had been engaged in the attack. Shortly after daybreak on the 30th, the villages of Banda, Kuddi, and Roghani were reached, and surrounded, and ten hostages were carried back by the expeditionary force to Barikab.

A party consisting of seventy-five sabres of the regiment and a like detachment of the 6th Dragoon Guards, under the command of Major Cracroft, proceeded from Jalalabad on the 3rd Jan., 1880, on a reconnaissance into the country contiguous to the Lughman Valley. On the 13th idem a hundred sabres of the regiment formed part of a force under Colonel Walker, 12th Foot, which was sent to reinforce Ali Boghan, and assisted in dispersing a large gathering of Mohmands, who had attacked the post on the previous day, and were still threatening it.

Ordered from Gandamak to Kabul on relief by the 17th Bengal Cavalry, the regiment marched for the capital, and arrived at its destination on the 17th Feb., 1880.

As part of the column under General Ross which left Kabul in the middle of April, 1880, to effect a junction with the Ghazni Field Force, and returned on the 2nd May, the 3rd Bengal Calvary was engaged in the various operations which were conducted in the Logar and Maidan districts. On the 20th April one squadron accompanied the brigade under Brigadier-General C. Gough which destroyed the towers of the refractory chief, Bahadur Khan. On the 25th idem, at the action of Shekabad, one troop of the regiment was engaged in the direct attack on the enemy's position to the north-west of the camp, and a half troop in the attack delivered on his left.

In the middle of June, 1880, the 3rd Bengal Cavalry left Sherpur with Brigadier-General C. Gough's Brigade for Pughman, and for the next six weeks, until the force was recalled to Kabul in view of the evacuation, took part with it in its various operations in the Koh-Daman and surrounding districts. On the 20th June a squadron of the regiment, with other details, under Lt.-Colonel Mackenzie, were sent to support a force under Colonel Norman on the Ghazni road, and drove a body of the enemy from a position it had taken up on the Kotal-i-Takht.

As a portion of the Cavalry Brigade of the Kabul-Kandahar F.F., the 3rd Bengal Cavalry took part in the memorable march from Kabul to the relief of Kandahar. On the 31st Aug., 1880, the regiment had the honour of being selected, with the 15th Sikhs and two Horse Artillery guns, for the reconnaissance of the enemy's position; and advancing two miles beyond the position where the remainder of General Gough's force was halted, drew the enemy's fire upon itself from the strongly entrenched Pir Paimal village, and then fell back, "admirably handled"—to quote the words of Sir F. Roberts' depatch—"by its Commandant, Lt.-Colonel Mackenzie." In the crowning defeat of the enemy on the following day, the regiment was again engaged, taking part in the pursuit, which was continued till the evening, and pushing beyond the line of Ayub's retreat towards Kakrez. In this engagement the casualties of the regiment were 1 officer and 1 man wounded, the latter mortally; 2 horses killed, and 1 wounded.

After taking part with Brigadier-General Baker's force, in the operations which were conducted against the Achakzai tribe, the regiment marched down to Sibi, from whence it eventually proceeded to Mian Mir.

The undermentioned officers of the 3rd Regt. Bengal Cavalry served in the war:—

Lt.-Colonel A. R. D. Mackenzie commanded the regiment throughout the campaign. Commanded a mixed force which captured the Shinwari villages in Dec., 1879. Took part in the march from Kabul to the relief of Kandahar, the reconnaissance of 31 Aug., 1880, the battle of Kandahar, and the operations against the Achakzais. (Mentioned in despatches.)

Lt.-Colonel B. Cracroft and *Major G. W. Willock* served with the regiment throughout the campaign, taking part in the action of Shekabad, the march from Kabul to the relief of Kandahar, the reconnaissance of 31 Aug., 1880, and the battle of Kandahar. Both were twice mentioned in despatches. *Lt.-Colonel Cracroft* also took part in the capture of the Shinwari villages. *Major Willock* was wounded at the battle of Kandahar.

Captains G. T. Morris and *C. H. V. Garbett* served with the regiment throughout the campaign, taking part in the march from Kabul to the relief of Kandahar, the reconnaissance of 31 Aug., 1880, the battle of Kandahar, and the operations against the Achakzais. *Captain Garbett* also took part in the capture of the Shinwari villages. Both were mentioned in despatches.

Bt.-Major G. H. Elliott served during the first and early part of the second campaign on the Khyber line with the Transport Dept., and subsequently, till the conclusion of the war, with the regiment, taking part in the march from Kabul to the relief of Kandahar, the reconnaissance of 31st Aug., 1880, and the battle of Kandahar. (Mentioned in despatches; Brevet of Major.)

Captain H. N. Webb served with the regiment during the campaign, taking part in the advance from Kabul to the relief of Kandahar, the reconnaissance of 31 Aug., 1880, the battle of Kandahar, and the operations against the Achakzais.

4TH REGT. BENGAL CAVALRY.

THE 4th Bengal Cavalry was employed during the latter part of the second campaign on the Khyber line of communications.

From the 15th March, 1880, till immediately prior to the evacuation of the capital, the regiment furnished detachments at all the posts between Safed Sang and Kabul, viz.: Pezwan, Jagdalak, Seh Baba, Lataband, and Butkhak.

A squadron of the regiment, under Captain Harenc and Lieut. Delamain, formed part of the Safed Sang Moveable Column commanded by Brigadier-General Arbuthnot.

A portion of the regiment, with the head-quarters, accompanied Brigadier-General Arbuthnot's Column in its expedition to Wazir Kila and Hissarak, in April, 1880.

On the evacuation of Kabul and the advanced posts on the Khyber line, the regiment returned to India.

The undermentioned officers served with the 4th Regt. Bengal Cavalry during the period it was employed in the war:—

Lt.-Colonels M. M. Prendergast (in command) and *F. P. W. Freeman*, *Majors D. Adamson* and *C. E. Harenc*, *Captains H. C. Lamb* and *A. de V. Alexander*, and *Lieuts. E. H. H. Montresor* and *F. G. Delamain*.

For services of *Colonel G. C. Hankin*, see "Staff."

5TH REGT. BENGAL CAVALRY.

EARLY in 1880 the 5th Regt. Bengal Cavalry proceeded on field service from Nowgong, and joined the Reserve Division at Peshawar.

Till the middle of March, 1880, the regiment performed garrison duty at Jamrud and Ali Musjid.

On the Reserve Division being broken up, two squadrons of the 5th Bengal Cavalry were moved forward to Basawal, the remaining squadron, broken up into small detachments, strengthening the garrisons of various posts en route, the regiment now appearing as a unit of the 1st Section Khyber Line Force, under the command of Brigadier-General Gib.

In May, 1880, one squadron of the 5th Bengal Cavalry, under Major Shakespear, formed part of the force under Brigadier-General Gib which marched from Pesh Bolak on the 18th of that month to disperse the hostile gathering of the enemy under Ghulam Ahmad, and on the 20th was engaged in the action of Mazina.

The regiment remained serving in the Khyber till the final evacuation of the Pass in March, 1881, when it returned to India, eventually proceeding to Sitapur.

The undermentioned officers served with the 5th Regt. Bengal Cavalry during the period it was employed in the war:—

Majors H. A. Shakespear (in command) (mentioned in despatches) and *R. B. Graham*, *Captains J. P. D. Vanrenen* and *M. Armstrong*, and *Lieut. G. L. Garstin* (since transferred to 9th Bengal Cavalry).

Lt.-Colonel W. Musgrave commanded a detachment 15th Bengal Cavalry at Dera Ghazi Khan from May till Oct., 1879, and commanded the Vitakri F.F. from 18 Oct., 1879, till it was broken up.

Lieut. W. W. Lean served with the 12th Bengal Cavalry throughout the period it was employed in the war, being present at the capture of the Peiwar Kotal, the action of Charasiab, and the operations round Kabul and defence of Sherpur in Dec., 1879. Was transferred to the 5th Bengal Cavalry as Adjutant in April, 1880, and served with it in the Khyber till it returned to India.

Lieut. W. F. C. C. Plowden served with the 2nd Sikhs in both campaigns, till invalided from Kabul in Aug., 1880. Was present at the battle of Ahmad Khel and the action of Arzu.

8TH REGT. BENGAL CAVALRY.

ON the 27th Sep., 1878, the 8th Bengal Cavalry left Multan on field service in Southern Afghanistan as a unit of the force under Lt.-General Sir D. Stewart, forming part of the Cavalry Brigade under Brigadier-General Fane, and proceeding by the Dera Bughti route and Bolan Pass, reached Quetta on the 31st Dec., 1878.

The Head-quarters wing took part in the advance on and occupation of Kandahar and Kalat-i-

Ghilzai, and formed part of the moveable column, under Col. B. Ryall, which proceeded into the Arghazan Valley, and defeated a small body of the enemy who attacked the British camp on the 10th Feb., 1879.

The Left wing remained a few days at Quetta; but on the 11th Jan., 1879, a full squadron, under Major Chapman, was detailed for service with the Pishin moveable column. To join and co-operate with this force, the squadron made a continuous march, during the two succeeding days, to Gulistan, from thence to Arumbi, in an expedition against the Atchakzais, and from thence on to Kila Abdula, covering a distance of 64 miles without a regular halt. In Feb., 1879, it furnished an escort to Sir R. Sandeman to Kandahar. This squadron subsequently formed a portion of the 1st (Major Keen's) Column of the Thal-Chotiali F.F., which opened up the new route, eastward, to India, and left Kushdil Khan on the 11th March. On the 16th idem a few men of the squadron, under Ressaldar Muhammad Ali Khan, surrounded and stormed a steep hill on which a body of Kakar Pathans had taken up a strong position, and captured 52 armed men; on the 21st the squadron assisted in repelling a rear-guard attack; and at the action of Baghao, which lasted from 2.30 p.m. till dusk, and in which from 400 to 500 of the enemy were killed, it was again engaged. On this occasion Major Chapman and Lieut. Pollock were present, and the latter had his charger wounded. The head-quarters of the regiment formed a portion of Brigadier-General Nuttall's column of the same force, which followed the route traversed by Major Keen's column. On the 30th April the regiment arrived at Multan.

Having again received orders to proceed on field service, the 8th Bengal Cavalry left Multan on the 5th, 6th, and 7th Aug., 1880, for Sibi. A few days after arriving there, a squadron under Captain Aberigh-Mackay was ordered on to Quetta, from whence it was moved on to the line of communications in the Pishin Valley. In the meantime the remainder of the regiment, under command of Lt.-Colonel Chapman, was also ordered up to Quetta, whither it proceeded by forced marches, covering the route from Pir Chauki to its destination, in the intense heat of August, in three days. At Quetta the regiment was attached to Brigadier-General Walker's Brigade, and shortly afterwards marched to Kila Abdula, where it was rejoined by the detached squadron. A troop of the regiment, under Lieut. Story, took part in an expedition on the 11th Sept., 1880, against the Atchakzais, and again in the same month the regiment was employed in a second expedition, under command of Lt.-Colonel Chapman, against a section of the same tribe, in the Arumbi Valley. Shortly afterwards the regiment returned to Quetta, and from thence returned, under orders for India, to Sibi, furnishing an escort to Sir F. Roberts through the Bolan Pass. After remaining some three months, however, at Sibi, the regiment was ordered to return direct to Kandahar. After reaching Kokaran, it joined the Cavalry Brigade under Brigadier-General Wilkinson, and remained in the neighbourhood of Kandahar until the final evacuation of that city by the British forces.

The undermentioned officers of the 8th Regt. Bengal Cavalry served in the war:—

Major-General B. W. Ryall (retired) commanded the regiment throughout the first campaign : in the advance on and occupation of Kandahar and Kalat-i-Ghilzai, and the return to India by the Thal-Chotiali route. Commanded a moveable column in the Arghazan Valley, and repulsed an attack made by the enemy on the British camp 10 Feb., 1879.

Lt.-Colonel H. Chapman commanded a wing of the regiment throughout the first campaign : in the advance to Kandahar, the opening up of the Thal-Chotiali route, the action of Baghao (charger wounded), and minor affairs. Mentioned in despatches (Brevet of Lt.-Colonel). Commanded the regiment throughout the period it was employed in the second campaign. Commanded a mixed force in an expedition against the Atchakzais in the Arumbi Valley.

Majors A. F. Lindsay and *J. A. McNeale*, and *Capt. J. F. D. Fordyce* served with the regiment throughout the first campaign ; Capt. Fordyce, as Adjutant, taking part in the advance on and occupation of Kandahar and Kalat-i-Ghilzai, and the return to India by the Thal-Chotiali route. *Major Lindsay* also served with the regiment in the second campaign, from Nov., 1880.

Captain J. L. Aberigh-Mackay commanded a detached squadron of the regiment in the Pishin Valley during the second campaign, from Aug. till Sept., 1880, when ordered to return to Multan to take command of the regimental depôt. Served with a detachment at Sibi in Feb. and March, 1881.

Lieuts. J. de C. D. Meade and *J. H. Parsons* served with the regiment in the second campaign, taking part in the expedition against the Atchakzais and the advance to Kandahar.

Lieut. G. H. Lumsden. (Assassinated. See Biographical Division.)

Lieut. R. Story, King's Royal Rifle Corps, served with the 8th Bengal Cavalry during the second campaign, taking part in both the expeditions against the Atchakzais. Was invalided to England from Sibi in Nov., 1880.

Lieut. F. G. Pollock, South Yorkshire Regt., served with the 8th Bengal Cavalry throughout the first campaign, taking part in the advance to Kandahar, the opening up of the Thal-Chotiali route, the action of Baghao, and minor affairs. In the second campaign served, first with the 51st K.O.L.I., taking part in the Hissarak expedition, the Lughman Valley expedition (June, 1880), and the destruction of the Ghilzai villages (July, 1880), and afterwards, from Dec., 1880, with the 8th Bengal Cavalry, taking part in the advance to Kandahar.

10TH (DUKE OF CAMBRIDGE'S OWN) REGT. BENGAL CAVALRY (LANCERS).

IN Oct., 1878, the 10th Bengal D.C.O. Lancers marched from Umballa, and in March, 1879, entered the Khyber, where it was chiefly employed, during the first phase of the war, in holding the Pass from Jamrud to Basawal, and after the signing of the treaty of Gandamak formed part of the rear-guard of the force retiring from Jalalabad. During the campaign small parties were frequently engaged with the enemy, in keeping open the line of communications, and in reconnaissances.

In April, 1879, the Daka garrison, under command of Major Barnes, 10th Bengal Lancers, of which the head-quarters of the regiment formed a part, was seriously threatened by a formidable force of Mohmands, who crossed the Kabul River. The enemy was met by a party of Infantry from the garrison under Captain O'M. Creagh, who, being greatly overmatched, took up a defensive position, and was quickly surrounded. Reinforcements of all arms were sent from the fort; and a part of the 10th Bengal Lancers, under Captain Strong of the regiment, made a brilliant charge which drove the enemy into the river, and materially assisted in enabling Captain Creagh's force to retire.

The regiment remained in the Khyber on the retirement of the main body of the forces, suffering great privation from the inadequacy of the supply of forage and water, and performing much hard work with convoys.

On the renewal of hostilities in the autumn of 1879, the regiment formed part of Brigadier-General C. Gough's brigade, and under the command of Major W. H. Macnaghten, accompanied it as far as Jagdalak. It was the first corps of the army to pass through this celebrated defile since 1842, and from the 15th to the 31st Dec., 1879, was engaged on many occasions, both mounted and dismounted, with the Ghilzais under Asmatallah Khan. The regiment subsequently furnished a squadron under Captain Barrow, giving detachments at the posts Seh Baba, Lataband, and Butkhak.

The severe work performed by the regiment, and the bad fare on which it had subsisted during the period of its service in Afghanistan, and more particularly in the Khyber, throughout the most trying months of the year, now began to tell so severely on the horses, that in February, 1880, it was considered necessary to order it back to India to recruit.

The undermentioned officers of the 10th (Duke of Cambridge's Own) Bengal Cavalry (Lancers) served in the war :—

Brigadier-General Sir C. H. Palliser, K.C.B. (For services see "Staff.")

Lt.-Colonel O. Barnes commanded the regiment during the first campaign, and for some time commanded at Fort Daka. Invalided to England.

Major A. England (retired) served with General Maude's Division in the first campaign. Commanded the regiment in the second campaign during the advance up the Jalalabad Valley, and was present at the fighting at Jagdalak.

Bt. Lt.-Colonel D. M. Strong served with the regiment in the first campaign. Commanded the force sent to the relief of Captain Creagh's position at Daka. Served under Brigadier-General C. Gough in the second campaign, being present at the fighting at Jagdalak. (Mentioned in despatches and Victoria Cross order; Brevets of Major and Lt.-Colonel.)

Bt. Major S. D. Barrow served with the regiment throughout the period it was employed in the war. Was Staff Officer at Daka for two months, and during the affair at Kam Daka. Was present at the fighting at Jagdalak. (Twice mentioned in despatches.) Served from 1st April to 4th June, 1880, as Assistant Road Commandant, Khyber Line, and from 8th June to 25th Aug., 1880, as Aide-de-Camp to General Hills, Commanding 3rd Division N.A.F.F. Was present as Orderly Officer to Brigadier-General Palliser, at the Cavalry action of Patkao Shana, in which he was severely wounded in both arms by sword-cuts, and had his horse wounded by a gunshot. (Mentioned in despatches, and brought to notice of Government by H. E. the Commander-in-Chief; Brevet of Major.)

Captain L. A. C. Cook served as Assistant Superintendent of Transport, Kandahar F.F., from 19 Nov., 1878, till 20 May, 1879. Under orders from Q.M.G. Dept., surveyed and reported on the route subsequently known as "Phayre's route" from Jacobabad to Dadar. Served with the 5th Bengal Cavalry on the Khyber line from May, 1880, till its abandonment.

Lieut. E. J. F. Wood served from Oct., 1878, till March, 1879, with the 19th Bengal Lancers, taking part in the advance on and occupation of Kandahar and Kalat-i-Ghilzai; and from May, 1879, till Feb., 1880, with the 10th Bengal Lancers, as Adjutant. Was present at Jagdalak, as Station Staff Officer, during the fighting in Dec., 1879. (Mentioned in despatches.)

Lieut. C. E. Pollock served with the regiment in both campaigns, being present at the relief of Captain Creagh's position at Kam Daka (in which his horse was wounded), and taking part in the advance up the Jalalabad Valley. Invalided to England.

Lieut. F. H. R. Drummond. (For services see 11th Bengal Lancers.)

Lieut. A. Burlton-Bennet. (Deceased. See Biographical Division.)

Lieut. C. G. L. Fagan served with the 14th Bengal Lancers in the Khyber Pass during the second campaign.

Lieut. R. C. Onslow served during the first campaign with the 1st Battn. 12th Foot; subsequently from July, 1879, with the 10th Bengal Lancers, being present at the fighting at Jagdalak; eventually, from Aug. till Oct., 1880, as Assistant Road Commandant in the Kuram Valley.

11TH (PRINCE OF WALES'S OWN) REGT. BENGAL CAVALRY (LANCERS).

IN November, 1878, orders were received for the 11th Bengal Lancers, then stationed at Naushahra, to be held in readiness for active service. The regiment marched for Peshawar 17th of that month, and on the 20th joined the Cavalry Brigade of the Peshawar Valley F.F. at Jamrud. Next day it took part in the advance up the Khyber Pass, and was present at the capture of Ali Musjid.

It was the fortune of the 11th to be left on the line of communications through the Khyber Pass, while the other two regiments of the Cavalry Brigade advanced to Jalalabad with the main body of the Division. A period of heavy escort and convoy duties ensued, enlivened at first by night demonstrations made by hostile bodies of the hill-men, and by the escorts of convoys having occasionally to fight their way through portions of the Pass; and occasional expeditions had to be made across the hills in pursuit of casual bands of marauders.

Towards the end of December the regiment moved to Daka, and took charge of the communications thence to Jalalabad, to which place it followed the rest of the force early in January, 1879. While Sir Sam. Browne's head-quarters remained at Jalalabad, the line of communication from Daka was occupied alternately by the 11th and the Guide Cavalry. During this period various expeditions and reconnaissances were made from Jalalabad, in several of which detachments of the regiment took part. Detachments were also present with Brigadier-General Tytler's two expeditions against the Shinwaris, on the first occasion under Lieut. E. E. Money, who commanded the Cavalry with the expedition, and on the second under Lieut. H. H. R. Heath. Ninety lances of the regiment were present under the latter officer at the action of Deh Sarak.

During the winter months the regiment lost a few men from pneumonia.

When the advance to Gandamak took place, a wing of the regiment remained at Jalalabad under Brevet Major A. H. Prinsep (who also commanded the troops at that place); the head-quarter wing under Major R. E. Boyle (Commandant) accompanying the Cavalry Brigade with the head-quarters of the Field Force. The line of communication from Jalalabad to Gandamak was at the same time occupied by detachments of the regiment.

This disposition lasted until the Field Force returned to India after the conclusion of the treaty of Gandamak. The regiment reached its old quarters at Naushahra on the 17th June, 1879, having suffered slightly from cholera during the march.

The undermentioned officers of the 11th (Prince of Wales's Own) Bengal Cavalry (Lancers) served in the war:—

Lt.-Colonel R. E. Boyle commanded the regiment (with two interruptions) throughout the campaign.

Lt.-Colonel A. H. Prinsep served with the regiment throughout the campaign, commanding it on two occasions during the temporary absence of the Commandant. Commanded at Jalalabad from the latter end of April, 1879, till the regiment returned to India.

Captain S. A. Swinley. (Deceased. See Biographical Division.)

Major W. I. Bax and *Lieut. S. B. Beatson* served with the regiment throughout the campaign; *Capt. E. E. Money*, from Feb., 1879, till the conclusion of the operations; *Lieut. H. H. R. Heath*, with one brief intermission of absence on duty, throughout the campaign; *Lieut. H. Burne*, from the outbreak of hostilities till Jan., 1879.

Lieut. F. H. R. Drummond served with the 10th Bengal Lancers during the first campaign, and as Orderly Officer to Brigadier-General C. Gough during the second campaign, taking part, in Dec., 1879, in the advance to the relief of Sherpur. (Mentioned in despatches.)

12TH REGT. BENGAL CAVALRY.

THE 12th Bengal Cavalry, under the command of (now) Col. Sir Hugh Gough, K.C.B., V.C., marched on the 26th Sept., 1878, from Jhelum for Kohat, where it arrived on the 12th Oct.; and making its way to Togh, two marches further on, remained encamped there till the 19th Nov.

As a unit of the Kuram Valley F.F., the regiment crossed the frontier at Thal on the 21st Nov., and headed the advance of the force up the Kuram Valley. On the 26th Nov. it accompanied General Roberts in the reconnaisance in which the Kabul troops, in the cantonment of Habib Kila, were first seen. The regiment, in two wings, covered the advance of the two parallel columns which moved up from Kuram to Habib Kila in the advance of the 28th Nov.; twenty men alone, under Lieut. Lynch, going on from Habib Kila as personal escort to General Roberts, and taking part in the collision with the enemy on that day.

The regiment was present at the storming and capture of the Peiwar Kotal on the 2nd Dec.; one squadron, sent forward under Capt. Green and Capt. Moore, behaving with great steadiness under a very galling fire. This squadron was later in the day taken over the Kotal by Col. Gough, and pursued the Kabul troops for some distance the other side; but darkness put an early stop to the pursuit.

Continual reconnaissances and severe work over most difficult country, in intense frost and cold, occupied the regiment till the 26th Dec., when the head-quarters moved back to Bulesh Khel, furnishing nine detached posts about the country, and leaving one squadron, 100 strong, under Capt. Green and Lieut Lean, at Zabardast Kila: this squadron endured great hardships; the constant work of patrolling between Ali Khel and the Peiwar Kotal, the snow and scarcity of forage, its isolation, and an ever-impending attack by the Mangals, all rendering its situation most difficult and precarious.

During the month of January, 1879, Col. H. Gough, C.B., V.C., accompanied the expedition to Khost in command of the Cavalry.

On the 16th March, 1879, the whole regiment was again collected at Kuram; 8 British officers and 473 native ranks being present.

The regiment remained in camp at Kuram without any active employment, except a successful raid into the Mukhbil country by a squadron under Capt. Green and Lieut. Lynch on the 16th April to recover stolen horses, until the 21st May, when it marched to take part in the great parade of the whole force at Ali Khel on the Queen's birthday.

On the 5th June the regiment marched as an escort to General Roberts in a reconnaissance through the Chakmani Valley, the Mukhbil country, and up the Lujjia defile; and on the 18th June marched to Shalozan, where a standing camp for the summer was formed.

On the 14th July a squadron of the regiment, under Capt. Broome and Lieut. Lynch, left Shalozan to escort Major Cavagnari and his party to the top of the Shutargardan on their way to Kabul, returning after completion of this duty on the 22nd July.

News of the massacre of the Embassy at Kabul having been received on the 7th Sept, 1879, the regiment, leaving all surplus baggage stored at Kuram, marched on the 16th to Habib Kila, on the 19th to Zabardast Kila, and on the 24th Sept. crossed the Shutargardan; and having joined Brigadier-General Baker with his advanced force on the Shinkai Kotal, pushed on to Kushi and occupied it without opposition. The next few days were occupied in making reconnaissances about the Logar Valley in the neighbourhood of Kushi. The command of the regiment had devolved upon Major Green from the date of leaving Kuram, Col. Gough having taken up his duties as Brigadier-General in charge of communications.

As a unit of the Cavalry Brigade, the 12th Bengal Cavalry took part in the advance of the troops under Sir F. Roberts to Charasiab, which was reached on the 5th Oct. That evening, a troop of the regiment, under Lieut. Lean, reconnoitred the road over the hills into the Chardeh Valley, returning by the Tudiki road.

On the morning of the 6th Oct., a squadron of the regiment under Lieut. Lean returned to Safed Sang to assist Brigadier-General Macpherson's Brigade, which was coming on with the baggage, encountering fire from the Ghilzais nearly all the way. Lieut. Lynch, with twenty men, was sent at daybreak to reconnoitre the road through the Sang-i-Nawishta Defile towards Kabul, but found it strongly held by the enemy, who were swarming over all the hill-tops. This party remained throughout the day with the right attack, the action which ensued being commenced about 7 a.m. by the enemy opening fire with his artillery from the heights above the defile. The remainder of the regiment was held in reserve.

Early on the morning of the 7th Oct. the advance on Kabul was continued, and during that and the three succeeding days and nights the 12th Bengal Cavalry had its full share of the heavy and important work which fell to the lot of the Cavalry Brigade in connection with the capture of the capital.

On the 17th Oct. the regiment moved into the Sherpur cantonment from a camp it had occupied near the Bala Hissar; but on the 30th, in consequence of a loss of six horses which it sustained from Ludiana disease, it moved out again to a fresh camp, $1\frac{1}{4}$ mile to the South-East. Throughout the month it was actively employed in making reconnaisances along the Turkistan road and into the Chardeh Valley.

Quitting its camp on the 1st Nov., the 12th Bengal Cavalry marched to Butkhak, and there joined a force under Brigadier-General Macpherson which had been despatched to effect a junction with Brigadier-General Charles Gough's force, advancing from Jagdalak. On the 2nd and 3rd exploring expeditions were made, with each of which a portion of the regiment was sent. On the latter date, Surgeon C. W. Calthrop joined the head-quarters with two native officers and a party of recruits from the depôt, having come over the Shutargardan with the last convoy before the road was closed. This party had been engaged with the Mangals at the attack made by the latter on Ali Khel, and had done good service. On the 6th Nov., the Kabul and Khyber forces joined hands at Kata Sang.

The 12th Bengal Cavalry now took part in the operations of Brigadier-General Macpherson's force in the neighbourhood of Naghlu, on the left bank of the Kabul River. On the 10th Nov. it was the first regiment to arrive on the scene of an attack which was being made by the Safis of Tagao on a party of the 67th Foot, under Capt. Poole, and by its opportune appearance assisted in causing the enemy to take to flight. On the 13th Nov. the Brigade made its way back to Butkhak, where the regiment remained, together with a company of the 67th Foot, for the rest of that month.

On the 1st Dec. the head-quarters and two squadrons of the regiment marched in charge of the Ex-Amir Yakub Khan for Jagdalak, and on the 7th again left Butkhak, in charge of other political prisoners, for the same destination, returning on the 11th idem.

The fighting round Kabul having begun on the 10 Dec., the 12th Bengal Cavalry moved on the 11th of that month into the space between the two forts at Butkhak, throwing up an earthwork round front and flanks in case of an attack. No attack, however, took place; and at 8 o'clock in the evening of the 14th Dec., a summons to return to Sherpur having been received, the regiment, together with the company of the 67th Foot, marched from Butkhak, and reached the Cantonment in safety about 3 a.m. on the 15th. The rear squadron of the regiment on this march, having lost the touch in the darkness, got near the wall of the city, and encountered a sharp fire thence; no damage resulting, however, except the loss of some baggage.

From the 15th to the 21st Dec. the regiment shared the work with the rest of the Cavalry Brigade, some portion of it going out every day to patrol and reconnoitre, and the whole of the men remaining out all night—five troops lying in the trenches on the Behmaru Ridge, and 36 men, under Lieut. Wilton, having charge of a bastion on the south wall of the cantonment.

At 2 a.m. on the 22nd Dec. the regiment left Sherpur with orders from Sir F. Roberts to work its way out to Butkhak through the enemy's position, and effect a junction there with the Lataband garrison under Col. Hudson. Issuing from the cantonment in single file through an aperture made in the sand-bag barricades of the eastern gate, the regiment moved on under the guidance of Ressaidar Bahawaldin Khan, 11th Bengal Lancers, a resident of the place, towards the foot of the Siah Sang range.

The noise caused by the leading horses breaking the ice in crossing a large drain some 500 yards from the wall of Sherpur, attracted the notice of the enemy; who, however, thinking it was one of the usual patrols, contented themselves with firing a few random shots in the direction from whence the sound proceeded.

Losing one horse drowned in this drain, the regiment moved on some 400 yards further in the same order to the bank of the Kabul River. The river was swollen from the recent fall of snow, and the further bank was steep; the ascent of it, too, was made worse as each horse in succession carried up more water, which immediately froze; in consequence of this, the weakest horses, especially in the rear squadron, numbed by the freezing water, failed to struggle up to the top, and rolled back upon their riders into the river; and some ten men, who had lost their horses altogether, were sent back on foot to Sherpur, which, under cover of the darkness, they reached safely.

After $1\frac{1}{2}$ hour spent in extricating the rear of the regiment from the river, during which time the two leading squadrons were halted, fortunately without making a sound, close to a village occupied by the enemy, the regiment crossed the Siah Sang range and pushed on at a trot to the Logar Bridge.

Finding the bridge not held by the enemy, and still intact, the regiment crossed and approached Butkhak, but was attacked by a force which issued thence in great numbers, and which kept up such a fire that the squadrons, hampered by the broken ground, intersected by ravines, were compelled to make a wider détour, keeping at a trot, and as far as possible out of the fire of the enemy, who were advancing in skirmishing order, so as to gain the Lataband side of Butkhak: for day having now broken, all possibility of returning to Sherpur was cut off.

Having gained the Lataband side, parties of the regiment were dismounted with carbines, in succession, as the retirement went on, and by their fire caused the enemy to retreat upon Butkhak.

Having fortunately found the Lataband road open, the regiment reached Lataband without further molestation, and joined the garrison there (whose orders to march to Butkhak had not previously arrived), and Brigadier-General Charles Gough's brigade, which arrived from Jagdalak during the afternoon. The loss of the regiment this day was 3 men killed and 4 wounded, one of whom subsequently died. The officers with the regiment were Major Green, Lieut. Lynch, Lieut. Wilson, and Dr. Calthrop.

On the 23rd Dec. the Lataband garrison, with the 12th B.C. and Gen. C. Gough's brigade marched viâ Butkhak (now found to be abandoned), to a spot near the Logar Bridge, which was still found standing, though barricaded, and there bivouacked for the night. On this day the final attack upon Sherpur had taken place; and having been completely repulsed, the enemy had all dispersed by the evening, leaving the country between Kabul and the Logar River quite clear. On the 24th, therefore, the troops under General C. Gough had only to march unopposed, but in a heavy snowstorm, into the cantonment.

On the 26th Dec., 1879, the 12th Bengal Cavalry, together with 100 men of the 9th Foot, marched from Sherpur Cantonment to Butkhak, and took possession of the two forts there.

Having received orders to proceed to Jalalabad, the regiment marched on the 2nd Jan., 1880, from Butkhak, in charge of General Daud Shah, now a prisoner, and in company with Sir Michael Kennedy and his party; and arrived at its destination on the 7th.

After a stay of twelve days at Jalalabad, orders having been received to return to India, the regiment marched on the 19th Jan., and arrived at Peshawar on the 25th; and having halted there two days, marched to Naushahra, and eventually to Jhelum, where it arrived on the 27th April, 1880, after an absence of nineteen months.

The undermentioned officers of the 12th Regt. Bengal Cavalry served in the war:—

Colonel Sir Hugh Gough, K.C.B., V.C. (For services see "Staff.")

Lt.-Colonel H. A. McNair and *Major M. J. Moore* (*retired*) served with the regiment from the commencement of the war until invalided home on the 3rd May and 2nd April, 1879, respectively, were present at the capture of the Peiwar Kotal.

Bt. Lt.-Colonel J. H. Greene and *Captains W. B. Wilson* and *J. B. Lynch* served with the regiment throughout the period it was employed in the war, the former commanding it during the second campaign, from Sept., 1879, till its return to India, and all being present at the capture of the Peiwar Kotal, the actions of Charasiab and Kabul, and the operations at and round Sherpur in Dec., 1879. *Lt.-Colonel Greene* was mentioned, for his services, in despatches, and received the Brevet of Lt.-Colonel; *Capt. Wilson* held, throughout, the appointment of Adjutant; and *Capt. Lynch*, besides being present at the engagements mentioned, took part in the passage of General Roberts' force through the Mangior Defile.

Major A. P. Broome served with the Transport Dept. in the first campaign, and subsequently, from 2 May, 1879, till invalided 16 Nov., 1879, with the regiment, being present at the actions of Charasiab and Kabul. (Mentioned in despatches.)

Lieut. W. W. Lean. (For services see 5th Bengal Cavalry.)

Lieut. G. Ulick Browne joined the regiment at Butkhak 19 Nov., 1879, and served with it till its return to India, being present at the operations at and around Sherpur in Dec., 1879.

Lieut. H. Goad joined the regiment at Butkhak 1 Jan., 1880, and served with it till its return to India. Had previously been present, attached to the 10th Bengal Lancers, at the affairs at Jagdalak, 24 and 29 Dec., 1879.

13TH REGT. BENGAL CAVALRY (LANCERS).

THROUGHOUT the first campaign the 13th Bengal Lancers formed part of the 2nd Division Peshawar Valley F.F., under the command of General Maude, and served at Jamrud and in the Khyber Pass.

In the third week in December, 1878, one troop of the regiment, under Major Nacnaghten, formed part of the force under General Maude which proceeded on the first expedition into the Bazar Valley, and on the 21st was entrusted with the destruction of the village of Halwai, a duty it most efficiently performed.

From the 24th Jan. till the 4th Feb., 1879, 145 men of the regiment under Lt.-Colonel Low took part with the Jamrud Column in the second expedition into the Bazar Valley. On the 27th Jan. they were engaged, with other Cavalry details under the command of Lt.-Col. Low, in cutting off the retreat of the Afridis from the China hill, and on the 29th in reconnoitring towards the Sasobai Pass, when they again came into contact with the enemy. On this occasion Lieut. A. R. Murray of the regiment behaved with great gallantry in going to the assistance of a Sowar whose horse was killed.

On the 24th March, 1879, a detachment of the regiment under Major Thompson formed part of the force under Brigadier-General Tytler which defeated the Mohmands with heavy loss at Deh Sarak.

On the 8th June, 1879, the regiment returned to India, and made its way back to Rawal Pindi.

On the renewal of hostilities in the autumn of 1879 the 13th Bengal Cavalry was again ordered on service, and making its way to Kohat, where it arrived on the 28th Sept., proceeded from thence to join the force under Brigadier-General Gordon in the Kuram Valley.

The regiment, broken up into detachments and constantly employed in patrolling the country, escorting convoys, and similar duty, remained in and about the Kuram Valley during the whole of the second campaign.

From the 8th till the 21st Dec., 1879, a squadron of the regiment took part with the expeditionary force under Brigadier-General Tytler in the operations which were conducted in the Zaimusht country. On the 10th it formed part of a force of all arms under Lt.-Col. Low, 13th Bengal Lancers, which encountered and dispersed the enemy at the villages of Kandoh and Katak Meyla, and on the 14th it was present at the capture of Zawa.

On the evacuation of the Kuram Valley in October, 1880, the regiment returned to India.

The undermentioned officers of the 13th Regt. Bengal Cavalry (Lancers) served in the war :—

Lt.-Colonel R. C. Low, C.B., commanded the regiment throughout the first and earlier part of the second campaigns, taking part in the second Bazar Valley and Zaimusht expeditions. Subsequently served as Chief Director of Transport with the Kabul and Kabul-Kandahar Field Forces, taking part in the advance from Kabul to the relief of Kandahar, and the battle of Kandahar. (Twice mentioned in despatches. C.B.)

Major W. H. Macnaghten served with the regiment in the first campaign, till 27 May, 1879, taking part, in command of the troop which was engaged, in the first Bazar Valley expedition. In the second campaign served in command of the 10th Bengal Lancers in the advance to Jagdalak, and was present at the fighting in the neighbourhood of that post in Dec., 1879. (Twice mentioned in despatches.)

Bt. Lt.-Colonel C. R. Pennington served with the regiment throughout the period it was employed in the war, commanding it in the second campaign from Jan., 1879. Took part in the first Bazar Valley and Zaimusht expeditions. (Mentioned in despatches; Brevet of Lt.-Colonel.)

Majors H. E. Ryves and *D. H. Thompson* served with the regiment from Jan., 1879, till the end of the first and throughout the second campaign. Major Thompson took part in the first Bazar Valley expedition, and commanded the detachment engaged in the action of Deh Sarak. For his services he was mentioned in despatches, and received the Brevet of Major.

Captain G. W. Deane served with the regiment throughout the first campaign.

Lieut. F. S. Gwatkin served with the regiment throughout the period it was employed in the war.

Lieut. J. H. Balfour served with the regiment throughout the second campaign.

Lieuts. A. R. Murray and *G. H. Lumsden*. (Deceased. See Biographical Division.)

14TH REGT. BENGAL CAVALRY (LANCERS).

ON the outbreak of the war with Afghanistan, the 14th Bengal Lancers was stationed at Peshawar, where, on the 6th January, 1879, it received orders to march, with as little delay as possible, to Kohat, to join the Kuram Field Force, under General Roberts. On arriving at Kohat the Right wing, under Major Mitford, was pushed on to Thal. The duties here, principally connected with the communications, were very harassing, and brought the men of the wing into frequent collision with the marauding hill-tribes of the neighbourhood, particularly during the occupation of the Khost Valley.

In the beginning of April, the Left wing arrived at Thal from Kohat, and the regiment, thus reunited, marched to Kuram, which was reached on the 13th of that month. A squadron under Captain Eardley-Wilmot was detached to the post of Bulesh Khel, where one of the officers—Lieut. C. J. S. Whittall—died of cholera; and all, whether at Kuram or Bulesh Khel, suffered severely from fever and dysenteric and scorbutic affections.

On the 23rd of Sept., 1879, the 14th Bengal Lancers marched on foot over the Peiwar Kotal pass, the horses being laden with five days' provisions for themselves and their riders, as no supplies were procurable between Kuram and Kushi—five long and fatiguing marches over the two difficult passes of Peiwar Kotal and Shutargardan. On the 30th idem the regiment had a slight skirmish, resulting in the capture of a hostile village, and on the 6th Oct. it was engaged in the action of Charasiab—partly on the right attack, under Major Mitford and Captain Neville, partly on the right rear, under Captain Eardley-Wilmot. On the 8th Oct. the 14th Bengal Lancers was actively engaged in the Cavalry pursuit, resulting in the complete dispersal of the Kabul army, and the capture of seventy-two pieces of artillery.

When the Kohistan and Ghazni troops marched on Kabul in December, 1879, the regiment took a prominent part in all the engagements which ensued, particularly in that of the 11th Dec., when a small party under Captain Neville and Lieut. Forbes greatly distinguished themselves in the defence of the guns, repeatedly charging large masses of the enemy's infantry. Lieut. Forbes was first wounded, and afterwards killed. Captain Neville's charger was wounded.

From this day until the final defeat of the Afghans on the 23rd Dec. the regiment was almost incessantly under arms—in the open plain, mounted, by day, and on the walls and Behmaru Ridge, on foot, by night. A party consisting of a non-commissioned officer and three men performed the very dangerous service of opening communication with Brigadier-General C. Gough's force, being let down over the walls by night.

On the 5th Jan., 1880, the regiment marched out of Sherpur on its way back to India, and re-crossed the Frontier on the 26th of the same month, at Jamrud.

The undermentioned officers of the 14th Regt. Bengal Cavalry (Lancers) served in the war:—

Colonel T. G. Ross, C.B., commanded the regiment during the second campaign, being present at the operations round Kabul and defence of Sherpur in Dec., 1879. (Mentioned in despatches; C.B.) (Since deceased.)

Lt.-Colonels R. C. W. Milford and *R. Eardley-Wilmot, Bt. Major J. P. C. Neville*, and *Lieut. P. R. Bairnsfather* served with the regiment throughout the period it was employed in the war, taking part in the advance on and occupation of Kabul, the action of Charasiab, and the operations round Kabul and the defence of Sherpur in Dec., 1879, and were all mentioned in despatches. *Lt.-Colonel Mitford* commanded the regiment in the first campaign, and for his services received the Brevet of Lt.-Colonel; *Lt.-Colonel Eardley-Wilmot* was present at the bombardment and capture of Ali Musjid, in addition to the engagements enumerated above, and also received the Brevet of Lt.-Colonel, and *Major Neville* the Brevet of Major. *Lieut. Bairnsfather* held the appointment of Adjutant throughout.

Captain C. S. Morrison. (Deceased. See Biographical Division.)

Lieut. G. W. Younghusband served with the 2nd Punjab Cavalry throughout both campaigns, being present at the action of Shahjui, the battle of Ahmad Khel, and the action of Arzu.

Lieut. W. G. Yate served with the 25th P.N.I., in Sir Donald Stewart's Division, during both campaigns.

Lieut. C. J. S. Whittall served with the regiment during the first campaign. (Died of cholera at Bulesh Khel, 20 June, 1879.)

Lieut O. E. S. Forbes, 3rd Hussars (Attached), served with the regiment during both campaigns, till killed in action at Kabul, 12 Dec., 1879.

15TH REGT. BENGAL CAVALRY.

EARLY in February, 1879, the 15th Bengal Cavalry proceeded from Multan, where the regiment was then stationed, to Dera Ghazi Khan, to form part of a column about to be formed under the command of Lt.-Colonel Guy Prendergast, 15th Bengal Cavalry, which was destined to march into Baluchistan to act as a support to the force under Major-General Biddulph marching eastwards from Pishin.

Two and a half squadrons marched from Dera Ghazi Khan with this column, which bore the designation of the Dera Ghazi Column, Thal-Chotiali Field Force—on the 24th Feb., 1879, and making their way through the Chachar Pass, and subsequently through the Han Pass, arrived on the 3rd April at Chotiali, where a junction was effected with the leading column (Major Keen's) of Major-General Biddulph's force. On the 5th April part of the Dera Ghazi Column, including one and a half squadron 15th Bengal Cavalry, accompanied by the column under Major Keen, set out on its return march to the Vitakri Valley; and on the 9th April took up its position on a camping-ground near Nahar-Ki-Kot, which it had previously occupied during the advance. Here, by the 12th, it was joined by the other units of General Biddulph's force, and by the squadron of the regiment which had been left at Chotiali to await the arrival of Brigadier-General Nuttall's column. On the 14th, the greater portion of the assembled troops departed for India, the Dera Ghazi Column, strengthened by the 1st Punjab Infantry and other details, remaining behind, and being reconstituted as the Vitakri Field Force, under the command of Brigadier-General Nuttall. As a portion of this force, the command of which, on the departure of General Nuttall for Jacobabad on the 17th May, reverted to Lt.-Colonel Prendergast, the squadrons 15th Bengal Cavalry continued to serve until the final evacuation of the position.

In the beginning of October, 1879, in consequence of a severe outbreak of scurvy which visited the troops at Vitakri, orders were issued for all men suffering from that disease to be sent down to Dera Ghazi Khan, under the command of Col. Prendergast, instructions being at the same time given for a detachment 15th Bengal Cavalry which had been left at that station, under Lt.-Col. W. Musgrave, and the Head-quarters and wing 30th Madras N.I., which were stationed at Rajanpur, under Col. Georges, to proceed to Vitakri to reinforce the garrison there. These instructions were carried out by the 18th, the command of the Vitakri force devolving, on that date, on Col. Georges.

In December, 1879, the Vitakri F.F. returned through the Chachar Pass to Dera Ghazi Khan, where it was broken up, the 15th Bengal Cavalry returning to Multan.

The undermentioned officers of the 15th Regt. Bengal Cavalry served in the war:—

Colonel G. A. Prendergast commanded the Dera Ghazi Column, Thal-Chotiali F.F., from the date of its formation in Feb., 1879, till it was merged in the Vitakri F.F. in April, 1879; and the Vitakri F.F. from May till Oct., 1879. Commanded the regiment throughout the period it was employed in the war.

Lt.-Colonel W. Musgrave, 5th Bengal Cavalry. (For services see 5th Bengal Cavalry.)

Lt.-Colonel E. D. H. Vibart served with the detachment of the regiment at Dera Ghazi Khan from Feb. till Oct., 1879, commanding it from Feb. till June. Accompanied the detachment to Vitakri in Oct., 1879, and served with the Vitakri F.F. till it was broken up.

Major R. Atkins and *Captain F. R. Ditmas* served with the regiment in the Dera Ghazi Column and Vitakri F.F. throughout the period it was employed in the war.

Captain S. D. Turnbull. (For services see "Staff.")

Lieut. F. P. L. White joined the detachment at Dera Ghazi Khan in June, 1879, and served with the regiment at that station and at Vitakri during the remainder of the period it was employed in the war.

17TH REGT. BENGAL CAVALRY.

THROUGHOUT the first campaign the 17th Bengal Cavalry formed part of the garrison of Peshawar.

From the latter end of September, 1879, till the middle of March, 1880, the regiment was employed on the Khyber line of communications, broken up into detachments, forming portions of the brigades and columns commanded by Brigadier-Generals Arbuthnot and Doran, and occupying posts extending from Jamrud to Gandamak.

In the third week in January, 1880, 50 sabres of the 17th Bengal Cavalry took part, with Col. Boisragon's column, in the operations which were conducted against the hostile Mohmands in the neighbourhood of Kam Daka, being present at the assault of the Gara heights on the 15th of that month.

From the 27th Jan. till the 5th March, 1880, one squadron 17th Bengal Cavalry formed part of the expeditionary force under Col. Walker, 12th Foot, accompanied by General Bright, operating in the Lughman Valley.

In the middle of March, 1880, the 17th Bengal Cavalry was ordered on to Kabul, and on the 24th of that month arrived at its destination.

On the 8th May, 1880, the regiment accompanied the force under Sir F. Roberts into the Logar Valley. Two squadrons returned to Kabul with the General on the 29th idem, the other squadron remaining in the Maidan and Kohistan districts with Brigadier-General Baker for another ten days. On the return of the column to Kabul on the 8th June, the regiment encamped on the plain between the Western foot of the Behmaru hills and the lake.

The regiment remained at Kabul till the 16th July, 1880, when it returned to the line of communications. On the evacuation of the capital in August, 1880, it was ordered back to India, and on the 30th of that month re-crossed the frontier.

The undermentioned officers served with the 17th Regt. Bengal Cavalry during the period it was employed in the war:—

Lt.-Colonel T. J. Watson (in command during the first phase of the campaign), *Major E. G. Newnham* (commanded the squadron employed in the Lughman Valley expedition, and the regiment in the advance to Kabul), *Captains B. H. S. Gower* and *E. W. Chalmers*, and *Lieuts. A. W. D. Campbell* (served also throughout the first campaign with Sir D. Stewart's Division, taking part in the advance on and occupation of Kandahar and Kalat-i-Ghilzai) and *F. H. Probyn*.

Captain R. F. Trotter was attached during the first campaign to the 27th P.N.I., and in command of the skirmishers of the Left advance, was present at the bombardment and capture of Ali Musjid, being the first officer on the heights before the Fort.

For services of *Lt.-Colonel M. H. Heathcote, C.B.*, and *Lieut. G. F. Willes*, see "Staff."

18TH REGT. BENGAL CAVALRY.

IN September, 1879, the 18th Bengal Cavalry, under the command of Major T. R. Davidson, was ordered up for service from Umballa to Peshawar, where it arrived on the 1st Oct.: from thence it proceeded to Thal, detaching, en route, one squadron, under the command of Major Marsh, at Kohat, the two remaining squadrons crossing the frontier and making their way to Bulesh Khel.

Forming part of the Kuram Division under the command of General Watson, the regiment was now employed in holding the line of communications from Thal to Bulesh Khel, whither Major Marsh's squadron marched from Kohat in January, 1880.

In December, 1879, a troop of the regiment under Major Wheeler took part in the Zaimusht expedition under Brigadier-General Tytler, and was present at the storming and capture of Zawa.

In May, 1880, a detachment of the regiment under the command of Captain Richardson, while reconnoitring in the neighbourhood of Thal, encountered a large body of Kabul Khel Waziris and Khostwals, and after a smart skirmish, defeated and dispersed them. The effect of this spirited little affair, for which a Brevet Majority was afterwards conferred on Captain Richardson, became immediately apparent in the cessation of the raids of the tribesmen across the frontier.

The 18th Bengal Cavalry remained in the Kuram Valley and on the frontier until the withdrawal of the forces, and continued to do duty at Thal until it was detailed to the 2nd Division of the Waziri Expeditionary Force, under the command of General J. J. Gordon, C.B., in the operations of which, during the months of March and April, 1881, it took part.

During the period of its service at Thal and in the Kuram Valley the 18th Bengal Cavalry lost no less than 180 horses and 80 ponies from the "sura," a sickness common to the frontier, the effect of bad fodder and over-work.

On the return of the Waziri Expeditionary Force, the regiment made its way back to Naushahra, where it arrived at the end of May, 1881, and went into quarters.

The undermentioned officers of the 18th Regt. Bengal Cavalry served in the war:—

Major T. R. Davidson commanded the regiment throughout, with the exception of an interval between June and Oct., 1880, during which he was invalided.

Majors H. C. Marsh and *R. Wheeler, Bt.-Major G. L. R. Richardson,* and *Lieuts. W. H. F. McMullen, G. A. Money,* and *J. E. Nixon* served with the regiment throughout: *Major Marsh* commanding it from June till Oct., 1880, during the absence of Major Davidson on sick leave, and being engaged in several small skirmishes with marauders in the Kuram Valley, who attempted to drive off horses out for grass; *Major Wheeler* commanding the detachment which took part in the Zaimusht expedition, and being present at the storming of Zawa; *Major Richardson* commanding the reconnoitring party which cut up the force of tribesmen near Thal in May, 1880 (Brevet of Major); *Lieut. Money* holding the appointment of Adjutant throughout; and *Lieut. Nixon* acting as Aide-de-Camp to Brigadier-General Tytler in the Zaimusht expedition, and being present at the storming of Zawa.

19TH REGT. BENGAL CAVALRY (LANCERS).

ON the 24th Sept., 1878, the 19th Bengal Lancers, then stationed at Mian Mir, received telegraphic orders to march at once and join General Sir D. Stewart's Division of the Army of Invasion, then assembling at Multan. On the 26th Sept. it commenced its march, and after being halted for a month at Rajanpur, on the right bank of the Indus, proceeded by the Dera Bughti route to Dadar, at the mouth of the Bolan Pass. From this point it accomplished the march to Kandahar, a distance of 260 miles, through a country containing but few supplies and almost destitute of forage, in fifteen days, where it joined the Division. Three days afterwards it formed part of the advance guard in the advance on and occupation of Kalat-i-Ghilzai. From here a squadron was detached, together with a squadron 15th Hussars, 3 mountain guns, and 2 companies Infantry, the whole under command of Major (then Captain) Biscoe, to reconnoitre the Argandab Valley and send in supplies, which was accomplished successfully. The whole force then returned to Kandahar, where the regiment remained cantoned from March, 1879, till March, 1880.

On the 29th March, 1880, the regiment marched with Sir D. Stewart's Column towards Ghazni, and was present at the battle of Ahmad Khel, in which action it lost 5 men killed, and 1 European officer dangerously, 2 European officers slightly, and 52 Natives variously wounded; also at the action of Arzu, outside Ghazni. It then proceeded with the Division under Sir J. Hills, V.C., K.C.B., into the Logar Valley, and was present at the cavalry action of Patkao Shana, where it lost 2 men killed and 15 wounded.

On the 15th July it marched into Kabul, and on the 7th August was ordered to return to India, where it arrived on the 26th August.

For its services, the European officers have received 4 Brevets, and the Native Ranks 17 decorations of the "Order of Valour."

The undermentioned officers of the 19th Regt. Bengal Cavalry (Lancers) served in the war:—

Colonel W. Fane, C.B. (retired). (For services see "Staff.")

Colonel P. S. Yorke was appointed to the command of the regiment, *vice* Col. Fane, and joined at Kandahar in Dec., 1879. Commanded the regiment till its return to India, being present at the actions of Ahmad Khel, Arzu, and Patkao Shana.

Lt.-Colonel A. G. Owen officiated in command of the regiment during the first advance on and occupation of Kandahar and Kalat-i-Ghilzai. In Feb., 1880, was invalided to England. (Brevet of Lt.-Colonel.)

Bt. Lt.-Colonel W. Biscoe served with the regiment during the first advance on and occupation of Kandahar and Kalat-i-Ghilzai. Commanded a column of all arms sent out from Kalat-i-Ghilzai to reconnoitre and collect revenue in the Argandab Valley. In Nov., 1879, was appointed Political Officer at Kalat-i-Ghilzai, and received thanks of Government for surprise and attack of Kajbaz Hill, occupied by the enemy. Rejoined the regiment in Kabul, 19 July, 1880. (Brevet of Lt.-Colonel.)

Bt. Major G. M. Abbott, and *Lieuts. H. S. Massy* and *S. D. Gordon* served with regiment throughout, being present at the actions of Ahmad Khel, Arzu, and Patkao Shana. *Major Abbott* was twice mentioned in despatches, and received for his services the Brevet of Major. *Lieut. Gordon* was also mentioned in despatches.

Bt. Major E. Bruce served with regiment throughout, being present at the actions of Ahmad Khel and Arzu. (Mentioned in despatches; Brevet of Major.)

Captain E. A. Young served with regiment, as Adjutant, till the 19th April, 1879, when he was dangerously wounded at the battle of Ahmad Khel, receiving eleven sabre-cuts and a gunshot-wound, and having his horse shot under him.

1st REGT. BENGAL NATIVE INFANTRY.

DURING both the first and second campaigns the 1st Regt. Bengal N.I. served at the base of operations at Peshawar and at all the Doaba outposts, furnishing escorts for treasure and stores to Jamrud, and sending out small detachments for the protection of the valley.

A portion of the regiment took part with the Flying Column in the operations against the Mohmands in January, 1880.

A portion of the regiment moved as escort of treasure from Peshawar to Gandamak in March, 1880.

The undermentioned officers served with the 1st Regt. Bengal N.I. during the war:—

Lt.-Colonel L. H. P. de Hochepied-Larpent (in command), *Majors G. Atkins* and *G. R. Grylls*, *Captain T. J. Bailey* (took part, in command of the detachment employed in the operations against the Mohmands in Jan., 1880), and *Lieuts. C. H. Morris* (served as Baggage-Master to the forces returning by the Khyber route in Aug., 1880) and *F. Hawkins* took part in the operations against the Mohmands in Jan., 1880.

For services of *Captain W. More-Molyneux* and *Lieut. G. H. More-Molyneux*, see "Staff."

2nd (QUEEN'S OWN) REGT. BENGAL NATIVE (LIGHT) INFANTRY.

AS a portion of the Kuram Reserve, the 2nd Regt. N.L.I. served during the first campaign at Kohat, Edwardosabad, and Thal.

On the renewal of hostilities in the autumn of 1879 the regiment proceeded to Peshawar, and from thence was moved up to Ali Musjid to join Brigadier-General Doran's Brigade of the Khyber Force; shortly after its arrival, however, it was found by a medical board to be suffering so deplorably from sickness as to be unfit for further active service, and it was accordingly ordered back to India.

The undermentioned officers served with the 2nd Regt. N.L.I. during the period it was employed in the war:—

Colonel T. N. Baker (Offg. in command), *Major J. A. D. Gordon*, *Captains B. Channer* and *C. W. Monypenny*, *Major A. Harden*, and *Lieut. S. C. F. Peile*.

5th REGT. BENGAL NATIVE (LIGHT) INFANTRY.

IN November, 1879, the 5th Regt. N.L.I. proceeded on service from Bhaugulpur, where it was then stationed, to Thal, and joined the 2nd Brigade Kuram Field Force, under the command of Brigadier-General Tytler.

On relief by the 13th N.I. in March, 1880, the regiment crossed the frontier and moved up to Balesh Khel.

For the next six months the 5th N.L.I., broken up into detachments, continued to serve at various posts in the Kuram Valley, and on the frontier, 50 men of the regiment forming part of the garrison of Chapri when that post was attacked by a large body of Waziris on the 1st May, 1880.

On the evacuation of the Kuram Valley in November, 1880, the regiment returned to India, and eventually proceeding to Jhansi, went into quarters.

The undermentioned officers served with the 5th Regt. Bengal N.L.I. during the period it was employed in the war:—

Colonel E. Venour (in command), *Lt.-Colonel H. A. Lewes, Major A. T. Davis* (also served as Station Staff Officer at Thal), and *Lieuts. H. Read, H. G. Ryland,* and *G. P. Hatch, Wiltshire Regt.* (attached).

Lieut. A. Adye, 5th Regt. Infantry, Hyderabad Contingent, served with the Transport Corps, 2nd Division Peshawar Valley F.F., throughout the first campaign, and with the 5th N.L.I. from the renewal of hostilities till May, 1880.

Captain C. H. Stoddart. (For services see "Staff.")

6TH (QUEEN'S OWN) REGT. BENGAL NATIVE (LIGHT) INFANTRY.

IN October, 1878, the 6th Regt. Bengal L.I., then quartered at Lucknow under the command of Colonel G. H. Thompson, was suddenly ordered to Cawnpore for duty: at that station it was warned for service, and on the 18th Oct. proceeded by rail to Lahore, from whence it was ordered to make its way by double marches to Peshawar; rail, however, was obtained three marches out from Lahore as far as Jhelum, and after several detentions the regiment reached its destination on the 19th Nov., 1878, as part of the 4th Brigade, 1st Division Peshawar Valley F.F., under the command of General Sir Sam. Browne.

On the 21st Nov., Head-quarters and five companies were engaged with the 3rd and 4th Brigades in the direct attack on Ali Musjid, the remaining three companies, under Captain Birch, forming the rear-guard of the Division.

Shortly afterwards, the regiment was transferred from the 1st to the 2nd Division Peshawar Valley F.F., under General Maude. It remained at Ali Musjid, and had occasional brushes with the enemy, until the 2nd Jan., 1879, when it marched to garrison Landi Kotal, in the Khyber Pass.

On the 25th Feb., 1879, Head-quarters and 300 men, under Colonel Thompson, proceeded from Landi Kotal over the Bori Kandao Pass to join the force under General Maude which was moving out on the second expedition into the Bazar Valley. Whilst in the Bazar Valley, the force was daily engaged in skirmishes with the enemy. The Head-quarters and 300 men returned to Landi Kotal on the 6th March, and remained there till the 20th idem, on which date the regiment was ordered back to Ali Musjid.

In June, 1879, when the 2nd Division Peshawar Valley F.F. was broken up, the regiment was ordered to Peshawar, where it arrived on the 11th of July, 1879, having been detained en route by an outbreak of cholera.

For various periods during the second campaign, detachments of the regiment held Fort Jamrud.

The undermentioned officers served with the 5th Regt. N.L.I. throughout, taking part in the capture of Ali Musjid, and the second expedition into the Bazar Valley:—

Major-General G. H. Thompson, retired (in command. Commanded a column in the second Bazar Valley expedition, and for his services was mentioned in despatches), *Major W. Atkins* (commanded the regiment in the second Bazar Valley expedition, and for his services was mentioned in despatches), *Captain W. J. A. Birch* (mentioned in despatches), and *Lieuts. C. H. Westmorland* (as Adjutant) and *C. R. Tate* (since transferred to 16th Bengal Cavalry).

Lt.-Colonel R. H. Inglis and *Captain L. M. Boileau* also served with the regiment during the war.

8TH REGT. BENGAL NATIVE INFANTRY.

IN August, 1879, the 8th Regt. Bengal N.I. was ordered up from Rawal Pindi to Peshawar, and from thence to Ali Musjid, where it arrived on the 26th of that month, having crossed the frontier on the previous day.

On receipt of the news of the massacre at Kabul, the regiment was directed to take part in the forward movement on the Khyber line, which was immediately ordered; but in consequence of the excessive sickness from which it was suffering—a result attributable to the unhealthiness of its quarters, and the incessant and harassing picquet and convoy duties which had fallen to its lot since its arrival in the Pass—the order to march was countermanded, and as a unit of the 3rd Brigade of the 2nd Division, under the command of Brigadier-General Doran, it remained for a month or two longer at Ali Musjid.

A detachment of 150 of all ranks, under the command of Captain Webb, marched to Daka on the 21st Dec., 1879, and on the 15th Jan., 1880, performed distinguished service in the defeat of the Mohmands at Kam Daka. General Bright, telegraphing to Brigadier-General Doran, expressed his appreciation of "the spirited and gallant manner in which the detachments 8th N.I. and 21st P.N.I., under Captains Webb and Young, respectively, carried the enemy's strong position on the Gara Heights." In this affair Jemadar Bahadur Khan of the regiment was killed at the head of his company.

On the 25th Jan., 1880, the Head-quarters of the regiment marched to Jalalabad, and from thence advanced to Safed Sang, where they arrived on the 1st Feb., and were taken on to the strength of the garrison, forming part of the 1st Brigade, 2nd Division, under the command of Brigadier-General Arbuthnot. On the following day detachments of the regiment, under Captain Fishe, marched to Pezwan.

On the 3rd April, 1880, Lt.-Colonel Smith, 8th N.I., was appointed Commandant at Safed Sang.

Forming part of the No. 1 Moveable Column, Head-quarters marched from Safed Sang on the 12th April, 1880, for Hissarak, and were engaged in the operations which were subsequently conducted in that district by Brigadier-General Arbuthnot. The casualties of the regiment on this occasion were, 1 Sepoy killed and 1 wounded.

At the latter end of June, 1880, Head-quarters marched to Wazir Bagh, and a detachment of 273 men under Lieut. Mansel furnished Rozabad and Fort Battye, and proceeding to Safed Sang and Pezwan, formed part of the Moveable Column Camp under General Bright, returning to Jalalabad on the 12th Aug. On that day the Head-quarters of the regiment left Wazir Bagh for Jalalabad Fort, and during the night guarded the gates of Jalalabad city.

On the 23rd Aug., 1880, the regiment commenced its return-march to India, and arriving at Burj Hari Singh on the 31st idem, made its way from thence to Rawal Pindi.

The undermentioned officers of the 8th Regt. Bengal Native Infantry served in the war:—

Major-General G. A. Williams (retired), joined and took over command of the regiment at Ali Musjid, from whence, shortly afterwards, he was invalided, and handed over the command to Lt.-Colonel Smith.

Lt.-Colonel R. Smith commanded the regiment—except during a brief interval at Ali Musjid—from the date of its departure from Rawal Pindi till 12 July, 1880, where he was invalided to England. Was appointed Commandant at Safed Sang, 3 April, 1880. Was present at the attack of the Mohmands on the rafts, between Jalalabad and Daka.

Major C. J. Walter joined the regiment at Ali Musjid, where he acted as Station Staff Officer during Nov. and Dec., 1879. Invalided to England 3 Jan., 1880.

Captain Arthur Fishe joined the regiment at Safed Sang, and served with it till its return to India, commanding it from 7th July, 1880. Was present at the attack on the rafts on the Kabul River.

Major E. H. Webb joined the regiment 1 Oct., 1879, at Ali Musjid, and served with it till invalided to England from Jalalabad. Commanded the detachment at the storming of the Gara Heights, and took part in the Hissarak expedition.

Lieut. G. D. C. Gastrell served with the regiment throughout, taking part in the Hissarak expedition.

Lieut. W. G. Mansel served with the regiment throughout, commanding the detachment with the Flying Column Camp in July and Aug., 1880.

Lieut. W. S. Hewett served with the 19th P.N.I. throughout both campaigns, taking part in the advance on and occupation of Kandahar, the advance to the Halmand, the second advance to Kandahar, the advance on Ghazni and to Kabul (during which he acted as Assistant to the officer in charge of Army Signallers), and the return march by the Khyber route to India, and being present at the battle of Ahmad Khel and the action of Arzu.

Lt.-Colonel H. de Brett, 18th *N.I.* (*attached*), joined the regiment at Jalalabad, and commanded it during the return-march to India.

Lieut. C. du P. Richardson-Griffiths, Bedfordshire Regt. (*attached*), served with the regiment at Ali Musjid.

Lieut. W. J. Newell (*attached*), joined the regiment at Safed Sang, and served with it till its return to India.

9TH REGT. BENGAL NATIVE INFANTRY.

IN January, 1880, the 9th Regt. Bengal N.I. proceeded on field service from Mian Mir, and joined the Reserve Division at Peshawar.

Till the middle of March, 1880, the regiment performed garrison duty at Jamrud and Ali Musjid.

On the Reserve Division being broken up, the Head-quarters were moved up to Jalalabad, detachments strengthening the garrisons of Fort Battye and Ali Boghan, the regiment now appearing as a unit of the 2nd Section Khyber Line Force, under the command of Brigadier-General Doran.

In the early days of April, 1880, a wing of the 9th N.I. took part with the Jalalabad Moveable Column in the operations which were conducted against the Wazir Kugianis.

In the early days of June, 1880, a detachment of the 9th N.I. took part with the expeditionary force under Brigadier-General Doran in the operations which were conducted across the Kabul River in the district of Kama.

On the evacuation of Kabul in August, 1880, the regiment returned to India, and proceeded to Jhansi.

The undermentioned officers served with the 9th Regt. Bengal Native Infantry during the period it was employed in the war:—

Colonel T. E. Webster (in command), *Majors F. F. J. Toke* and *R. A. Price, Captain H. A. Wodehouse,* and *Lieuts. A. T. Weller* and *C. W. Ravenshaw.*

11TH REGT. BENGAL NATIVE INFANTRY.

THE 11th Native Infantry marched from Rawal Pindi on the 1st Jan., 1879, to join the Reserve of the Kuram Field Force at Kohat. On the 31st March it crossed the frontier and made its way over the Peiwar Kotal to Bian Khel, where it remained till June, 1879. On the peace of Gandamak being concluded, the regiment was ordered down the Valley to the line of communications hitherto held by the Contingents of the Native Princes.

Until September, 1879, the regiment formed part of the garrison of Bulesh Khel, which consisted of the 14th Bengal Lancers, 3 Mountain guns, and the 11th and 21st Native Infantry, the whole under command of Lt.-Col. Harris, 11th N.I.

On the murder of Sir Louis Cavagnari, the 11th N.I. was hurried up to join the force under Sir F. Roberts at Ali Khel, and was eventually left to garrison that post on the British advance on Kabul. On the 14th October the post of Ali Khel was attacked in force by the tribes, who were repulsed with loss, the 11th N.I. having only two men wounded. In November the regiment took part in the Chakmani expedition, and then returned again to Bulesh Khel, where, with two companies of the 8th King's and two 9-pounder guns, it formed, in December, the base of the Zaimusht expedition under Brigadier-General Tytler.

From January to May, 1880, the regiment held the line of communications between Bulesh Khel and Thal. On the 10th June it marched for India, having lost by death during the war 2 field officers and 160 non-commissioned officers and men.

The undermentioned officers of the 11th Regt. Bengal Native Infantry served in the war:—

Colonel P. H. F. Harris commanded the regiment throughout. Commanded the Bian Khel garrison during May, 1879, and the Bulesh Khel garrison after the peace of Gandamak. Was present at the repulse of the enemy's attack on Ali Khel, 14 Oct., 1879. (Mentioned in despatches.)

Major H. G. Becher. (Deceased. See Biographical Division.)

Major C. M. Bushby was invalided home shortly after the regiment proceeded on service, and died in England in February, 1879.

Major A. J. Stead served with the regiment until Feb., 1880, when he was sent down to Oude to recruit for it. Commanded the Left wing at Thal during June and July, 1879. Was present at the repulse of the enemy's attack on Ali Khel.

Major E. P. Ommanney served with the regiment throughout, and was left in command of three companies at Kohat during July and Aug., 1880, after the return to India. Was present at the repulse of the enemy's attack on Ali Khel.

Captain V. A. Schalch served with the regiment, as Adjutant, throughout, and also acted at various times as Staff Officer to the Commandant of the posts of Ali Khel, Bian Khel, and Bulesh Khel. Was present at the repulse of the enemy's attack on Ali Khel.

Lieut. A. P. Williamson. (For services see 5th Punjab Cavalry.)

12TH (THE KELAT-I-GHILZIE) REGT. BENGAL NATIVE INFANTRY.

ON the 2nd Oct., 1878, the 12th Kelat-i-Ghilzie Regt. arrived by rail at Multan, where it remained until it received orders to take part, as a unit of the 2nd Brigade of Sir Donald Stewart's Division of the Army of Invasion, in the advance on Kandahar. On the 21st Nov. it arrived at Mithankot.

The 1st detachment of the regiment, under the command of Captain A. G. Hartshorne, who was relieved by Captain A. Oldham at Lehri, left Mithankot in charge of a convoy of 1,000 camels, with Commissariat supplies, on the 25th Nov., 1878, and rejoined regimental Head-quarters at Quetta on the 23rd Dec., 1878.

The 2nd detachment, under the command of Lt.-Colonel W. Macdonald, left Mithankot on the 27th Nov., 1878, in charge of another convoy of camels with Commissariat stores, and rejoined regimental Head-quarters on the 11th Dec., 1878, at Lehri.

The Head-quarters and Left wing, under Captain H. S. Anderson, left Mithankot on the 29th Nov., 1878, and on the 11th Dec. arrived at Lehri: here Lt.-Colonel Macdonald took over the command, and the regiment, continuing its advance, arrived on the 23rd Dec. at Quetta, where it was joined by Captain Oldham's detachment.

Leaving behind a detachment of no less than 125 sick, the regiment marched out of Quetta with Brigadier-General Hughes' Brigade on the 27th Dec., 1878, and arrived at Kandahar on the 9th Jan., 1879.

On the 15th Jan. the Head-quarters and Right wing of the regiment marched with the other units of the brigade on Kalat-i-Ghilzai, where it arrived on the 22nd idem, and remained until the return of Brigadier-General Hughes' force to Kandahar, which was reached on the 2nd March.

In consequence of the excessive amount of sickness prevailing in the ranks, the Head-quarters and Right wing of the regiment now received orders to return to India, whither the Left wing, under Captain Oldham, acting as an escort to E/4, R.A., and the sick of the 2nd Division, had already preceded them. The Head-quarters and Left wing accordingly quitted Kandahar on the 15th March, and eventually made their way to Agra, where they arrived on the 19th April, 1879.

The undermentioned officers served with the regiment throughout, taking part in the advance on Kandahar and Kalat-i-Ghilzai:—

Colonel W. Macdonald (in command), *Major H. S. Anderson, Captain A. F. Barrow* (as Adjutant), and *Lieut. J. W. E. Angelo.*

Majors A. Oldham and *A. G. Hartshorne* also served with the regiment throughout, taking part in the advance to Kandahar, where they remained with the Right half-battalion, Captain Oldham commanding it, during the absence of Head-quarters and the Left half-battalion at Kalat-i-Ghilzai.

Lieut. G. A. Collins served with the 13th N.I. in the Kuram Division, as Adjutant, during the second campaign, till invalided in Jan., 1880, taking part in the Zaimusht expedition.

13TH REGT. BENGAL NATIVE INFANTRY.

ON the outbreak of the Afghan war, the 13th Regt. Bengal N.I., which had recently returned to India from the expedition to Cyprus and Malta, was suffering severely from Cyprus fever, and was not amongst the corps ordered to the front; but on the renewal of hostilities in the autumn of 1879, it was one of the first warned for service, and was immediately afterwards directed to proceed to Peshawar to join the Khyber Division—an order which, however, was subsequently countermanded, its destination being changed to Thal.

Making its way from Agra under the command of Colonel Watson, the regiment arrived at Thal on the 3rd Oct., 1879, with a strength of but 423 of all ranks, it having been found necessary to leave many in hospital en route. Its numbers were supplemented, however, shortly afterwards by the arrival of a detachment of 174 men, under Captain Bingham, from Fattehgarh.

On the 6th Oct. Colonel Watson, who had assumed command of the station as senior officer, made a rapid march from Thal into the Zaimusht country, with all the troops available, with the intention of surprising a strong body of the tribesmen who were reported to be at the time in the neighbourhood, threatening the outposts; but though some twenty miles of country were covered by Colonel Watson's force, it did not succeed in sighting the enemy.

During October and November the regiment remained at Thal furnishing strong patrols and guards for the camp which had been formed there, and outposts along the line of communications up the Kuram Valley.

On the 28th Oct., a strong detachment under Lt.-Colonel G. B. Stevens, with Captain W. M. Meacham, took part, with other troops, in a night surprise of a body of the Kabul Khel Waziris.

On the 30th Nov. the Head-quarters and as many men as were found to be fit for service marched for Bulesh Khel, escorting 1,500 transport animals for Brigadier-General Tytler's column, which had assembled at that post in view of the long-projected Zaimusht expedition. The regiment reached its destination on the 2nd Dec., and as a unit of the expeditionary force, took part in the advance into Zaimusht territory on the 8th idem, and was engaged in the various operations which were conducted by General Tytler during the succeeding ten days, including the storming and capture of Zawa.

On the 19th Dec. the regiment was directed to proceed with all speed to Thal, as an attack on the garrison of that place was hourly expected. It arrived on the following day; but its services not being required, it was ordered to push on to Kuram to relieve the 11th Regt. N.I., and reached its destination on Christmas eve.

Employed with garrison work and outpost duty, the regiment remained at Kuram till the end of February, 1880, when it marched down to occupy the posts of Chapri, Mandoria, and Alizai, the whole being under the command of Captain Bingham, who had his Head-quarters at Mandori.

In February, 1881, the regiment was moved down to Kohat, where it remained till the end of March: at the latter end of that month it was ordered to Bareilly, where it arrived on the 6th April, and went into quarters.

The undermentioned officers of the 13th Regt. Bengal Native Infantry served in the war:—

Colonel J. T. Watson commanded the regiment till 8 Dec., 1879, when he was invalided to England. Commanded at Thal from 2 Oct. till 30 Nov., 1879.

Colonel W. Playfair served with the regiment from 9 Nov. till 25 Dec., 1879, commanding it throughout the Zaimusht expedition.

Bt. Lt.-Colonel G. B. Stevens, Captain W. M. Meacham, and *Lieut. E. H. Molesworth* served with the regiment from 10 Nov., 1879, till the date of its return to India. *Lt.-Colonel Stevens* commanded the detachment of the regiment engaged in the surprise of the Kabul Khel Waziris, commanded the Chapri outposts from 24 till 30 Nov., 1879, and took part in the Zaimusht expedition; and commanded the party of the regiment engaged in the storming and capture of Zawa (mentioned in despatches; Brevet of Lt.-Colonel). *Captain Meacham* took part at the surprise of the Kabul Khel Waziris and the Zaimusht expedition; was present at the storming and capture of Zawa, and acted as Station Staff Officer first at Chapri and afterwards at Thal. *Lieut. Molesworth* officiated as Adjutant, and performed the duties of regimental Transport Officer throughout.

Captain E. H. Bingham served, first as Transport officer with the Quetta F.F., from 8 Oct., 1878, till invalided 28 Feb., 1879, having charge of all transport arrangements at Quetta; afterwards with the regiment, from 9 Sept., 1879, till 16 May, 1880, performing the duties of Station Staff Officer at Thal during Oct. and Nov., 1879, taking part in the Zaimusht expedition, and commanding the Mandoria, Chapri, and Alizai outposts during March and April, 1880.

Lieut. G. A. Collins. (For services see 12th N.I.)

Lieut. W. J. Fairbrother served during the first campaign with the Mhairwara Battalion in the Khyber Column, taking part in the first Bazar Valley expedition, and commanding a detachment at the action of Kam Daka, and during the second campaign with the 29th P.N.I. in the Kuram Valley, taking part in the Chakmani and Zaimusht expeditions, and being present at the storming and capture of Zawa.

Colonel N. Barton, 25th P.N.I. *(attached).* (For services see 25th P.N.I.)

Lieut. A. G. McCarthy, 39th B.N.I. *(attached).* (For services see 39th B.N.I.)

14TH (THE FEROZEPORE) REGT. BENGAL NATIVE INFANTRY.

EARLY in October, 1878, the 14th Regt. N.I., then stationed at Peshawar, was warned for active service, and subsequently formed part of the 3rd Brigade 1st Division Peshawar Valley Field Force, under the command of Brigadier-General Appleyard.

On the 19th Nov. the 14th Sikhs left with the brigade for Jamrud, and on the morning of the 21st crossed the frontier and took part in the attack on Ali Musjid.

One half-battalion, 250 strong, led the advance guard of the column, the remainder of the regiment following with the main body of the force. On the enemy's cavalry being sighted, the half-battalion crowned the heights to the right and left, and shortly afterwards 100 men under Captain Maclean were sent down to intercept the retreat of the enemy's advance piquet. On the artillery opening fire from the Shagai heights, two companies of the regiment were ordered to skirmish up a ridge which lay between the British position and the Fort, and having cleared it, they lay down under cover. About 2 p.m., when the attack on the enemy's right was ordered, and the brigade moved forward, the detachment under Captain Maclean, which had been sent down from the heights to cut off the retreat of the piquet, was ordered to skirmish up the steep slope in advance, and soon became hotly engaged. While the men were still fighting their way upwards, the order to retire was sounded; but the ridge which had been crowned was held during the night. During the engagement, the casualties of the regiment were, 8 men killed, and Lieut. Maclean and 16 men wounded. Shortly after daylight it was discovered that the enemy had abandoned the fort a few hours previously, and fled.

The 14th Sikhs took part in the advance of the main body of the Division on the 23rd Nov. to Kata Kushtia, and from thence to Landi Khana, where it remained on the return of the 3rd Brigade to Ali Musjid; within a few weeks, however, the regiment was found to be suffering so severely from sickness that it became necessary for it to return to Peshawar, where it arrived in the middle of December, 1878.

The undermentioned officers served with the 14th Regt. Bengal N.I. during the period it was employed in the war, being present at the taking of Ali Musjid:—

Colonel L. H. Williams (in command), *Lt.-Colonel W. Campbell, Lt.-Colonel R. A. Wauchope* (also served as Brigade Major, 3rd Brigade, 1st Division, Peshawar Valley F.F., from 16 Dec., 1878, till the conclusion of the campaign; mentioned in despatches; Brevet of Lt.-Colonel), *Major James Cook* (also served with 27th N.I. from 27 Nov. till 29 Dec., 1878, taking part in the first expedition to the Bazar Valley; mentioned in despatches; Brevet of Major), *Captain J. G. Maclean* (till 23 Dec., 1878), *Captain C. J. Jamieson,* and *Lieut. J. W. Hogge.*

Major L. Macdonald served with the 27th P.N.I. from 21 Dec., 1878, till the conclusion of the first campaign, and with the same regiment throughout the second campaign, being present at the action of Ali Boghan, and taking part in numerous minor expeditions. (Mentioned in despatches.)

Lieut. H. H. Ozzard served with the 1st Goorkhas throughout the first campaign.

15TH BENGAL NATIVE INFANTRY (LOODIANAH SIKHS).

THE Loodianah Sikhs were at Sialkot when warned for service in September, 1878. All officers and men on leave were ordered to join at once, and on the 28th the regiment marched for Multan, where it arrived on the 24th Oct., and joined the 1st Brigade of Sir Donald Stewart's Division of the Army of Invasion. Colonel Barter had been appointed to command the brigade, with rank of Brigadier-General, and Major Hennessy succeeded to the command of the regiment, with Captain D. W. Inglis as 2nd in command: both these officers obtained their promotion to Lt.-Colonel and Major, respectively, shortly afterwards, and Lieuts. H. A. Abbott and N. K. Stewart to Captain, by regular promotion.

After proceeding by rail to Sukkur, the regiment was separated into half-battalions, the Right half-battalion, under the command of Captain Inglis, proceeding to Kandahar and Kalat-i-Ghilzai with the Brigade, and the remainder of the regiment, under the command of Major Hennessy, escorting a large convoy to Kandahar, where it was rejoined by the Right half-battalion in February, 1879. The regiment was placed in garrison in the Citadel, an important post it held until March, 1880, its admirable discipline and conduct (a thoroughly Sikh corps in the midst of a fierce fanatical Mussulman population) being the theme of general remark, and gaining repeated commendation from the authorities.

On the 29th March, 1880, the regiment marched out of Kandahar with the column consisting of 11/11, R.A., the 1st Punjab Cavalry, and the 1st Brigade, the whole under Brigadier-General Barter, and traversing the valley of the Khushk-i-Nakhud, joined the Kandahar force *en route* for Kabul on the 15th April at Karez-i-Oba. On the 19th it was present at the battle of Ahmad Khel, and on the 23rd, at the action of Arzu, near Ghazni; and subsequently proceeding with the Brigade into the Logar Valley, it was engaged in the various operations which were conducted in that and the neighbouring districts during the succeeding months, including the passage of the Tungi Wardak defile, and the repulse of the enemy's attack on Brigadier-General Barter's camp on the night of the 12th May, 1880, at Jabar Kila.

Detailed, with the 1st Brigade, to form part of the Kabul-Kandahar Field Force, the regiment took part, in the month of August, 1880, in the memorable march to the relief of the Southern capital. On the 31st it was present, as the only infantry regiment employed, in the reconnaissance of Ayub Khan's position, when its steady repulse of the rush of a large body of Ghazis, some 6,000 or 7,000 in number, obtained special mention in the despatches; and on the following day, in the crowning defeat of the enemy at the battle of Kandahar, it was again engaged.

In October, 1880, the regiment returned to India, marching with the force under Brigadier-General MacGregor which reopened the Hurnai route to Sibi.

The undermentioned officers of the 15th Bengal Native Infantry (Loodianah Sikhs) served in the war:—

Colonel R. Barter, C.B. (For services see "Staff.")

Lt.-Colonel G. R. Hennessy commanded the regiment throughout both campaigns: in the advance to and occupation of Kandahar, the advance from Kandahar on Ghazni and to Kabul, the march from Kabul to the relief of Kandahar, and the return to Sibi by the Hurnai route; and at the battle of Ahmad Khel, the action of Arzu, the operations in the Logar Valley, the reconnaissance of 31 Aug., 1880, and the battle of Kandahar. (Twice mentioned in despatches.)

Major D. W. Inglis, Captain H. A. Abbott, and *Lieut. R. C. Hadow* served with the regiment throughout both campaigns, taking part in the advance to and occupation of Kandahar, the advance from Kandahar on Ghazni and to Kabul, the march from Kabul to the relief of Kandahar, and the return to Sibi by the Hurnai route, and being present at the battle of Ahmad Khel, the action of Arzu, the operations in the Logar Valley, the reconnaissance of 31 Aug., 1880, and the battle of Kandahar. *Major Inglis* also commanded the Right half-battalion in the advance on and occupation of Kalat-i-Ghilzai, and for his services was mentioned in despatches, as also was *Capt. Abbott.*

Major R. E. S. Smyth served with the regiment in both campaigns, and during part of the second was in charge of the Field Treasure Chest of the Kandahar Force. Took part in the advance to and occupation of Kandahar, the advance from Kandahar on Ghazni and to Kabul, the march from Kabul to the relief of Kandahar, and the return to Sibi by the Hurnai route, and was present at the battle of Ahmad Khel, the action of Arzu, the operations in the Logar Valley, and the battle of Kandahar.

Captain F. A. Remmington served with the regiment in the first campaign till invalided to England, taking part in the advance on and occupation of Kandahar and Kalat-i-Ghilzai.

Lieuts. Tudor Lay, H. S. Fitzgerald (Durham L.I.) (attached), and *G. Adye (1st Cavalry, Hyderabad Contingent) (attached)*, served with the regiment in the second campaign, taking part in the march from Kabul to the relief of Kandahar, and the return to the Sibi by the Hurnai route, and being present at the reconnaissance of 31 Aug., 1880, and the battle of Kandahar.

Lieut. E. D. J. O'Brien, South Lancashire Regt. (attached), served in the second campaign, first with the 1st Punjab Cavalry, being present at the action of Patkao Shana (mentioned in reports), and afterwards with the 15th Sikhs, taking part in the march from Kabul to the relief of Kandahar, and the return to Sibi by the Hurnai route, and being present at the reconnaissance of 31 Aug., 1880, and the battle of Kandahar.

Lieut. C. C. Hodgkinson, 11th Bombay N.I. (attached), served in both campaigns, first with the 59th Foot, taking part in the advance to Kandahar and the advance from Kandahar on Ghazni and to Kabul, and being present at the battle of Ahmad Khel and the action of Arzu; and afterwards with the 15th Sikhs, taking part in the march from Kabul to the relief of Kandahar, and being present at the reconnaissance of 31 Aug., 1880, and the battle of Kandahar.

16TH (THE LUCKNOW) REGT. BENGAL NATIVE INFANTRY.

AT the latter end of December, 1879, about three months after the opening of the second campaign, the 16th Lucknow Regt. N.I. received directions to hold itself in readiness for active service; and on the 8th Feb., 1880, it marched from Jhansi under orders to join the Reserve Division then being formed at Peshawar. Arriving at its destination on the 7th March, it was posted to the 1st Brigade of the Division.

On the 15th March, 1880, the regiment marched to Ali Musjid, leaving two companies under the command of Major A. F. Taylor as a garrison for Fort Jamrud.

On the 27th March, 1880, in consequence of the reorganization of the Northern divisions, the 16th N.I. became a unit of the 1st Section Khyber Line Force.

From the date of its arrival till the final evacuation of the Pass in March, 1881, the regiment continued to serve in the Khyber, garrisoning Ali Musjid and Jamrud, and the small intervening forts. On the 21st March, 1881, it recrossed the frontier.

The undermentioned officers served with the 16th Lucknow Regt. N.I. during the period it was employed in the war:—

Colonel R. S. Moseley (in command; also commanded the post of Ali Musjid from 16 March, 1880, till final evacuation), *Lt.-Colonel W. G. Cubitt, V.C., 43rd Bengal L.I.* (held charge of the Fort of Ali Musjid till 21 May, 1880), *Major A. B. Clare* (acted as Camp Quartermaster at the post of Ali Musjid from 27 July till 26 Sept., 1880), *Major J. T. Whish* (acted as Provost-Marshal at the post of Ali Musjid from 16 March till 26 May, 1880, and commanded at Fort Jamrud from 27 May till 15 Sept., 1880), *Major A. F. Taylor* (commanded at Fort Jamrud from 16 March till 25 May, 1880, and acted as Camp Quartermaster at the post of Ali Musjid from 26 May till 26 July, 1880), *Lieut. A. Montanaro* (served as Adjutant throughout, and acted as Station Staff Officer at Ali Musjid from 16 March, 1880, until final evacuation), and *Lieut. A. D. Enriquez* (also served in the first campaign as Transport Officer and Staff Officer of the Transport Train in the Bolan Pass. [Mentioned in reports.] From 27 Sept., 1880, till final evacuation, acted as Camp Quartermaster in the Khyber).

19TH REGT. (PUNJAB) BENGAL NATIVE INFANTRY.

THIS regiment was stationed at Multan in the autumn of 1878, when orders were received by it to hold itself in readiness for active service. On the 29th Sept., 1878, it marched for Quetta, proceeding by Dera Ghazi Khan, Rajanpur, and the Dera Bughti route, and reaching its destination on the 4th Nov.

RECORDS OF SERVICE.

As a unit of General Biddulph's Division of the Army of Invasion, the 19th P.N.I. took part, in January, 1879, in the advance on and occupation of Kandahar. At the latter end of that month it accompanied the same force in its advance to the Halmand, returning to Kandahar on the 4th March.

In the beginning of February, 1879, the 19th P.N.I. was sent back to garrison Quetta, and remained there for a period of ten months. During the autumn, a detachment of 250 men, under the command of Lt.-Colonel Bergman, accompanied the Agent to the Governor-General into the Marri country to open up the route for the new line of railway from Sibi to the Pishin Valley, and was employed on this duty upwards of five months.

On the 19th Feb., 1880, the 19th P.N.I. marched out of Quetta to join the force being formed at Kandahar for the advance on Ghazni, and on arriving there was attached to the Cavalry Brigade under Brigadier-General Palliser. Taking part in the advance of the Field Force from Kandahar on the 29th March, the regiment was prominently engaged, on the 19th April, at the battle of Ahmad Khel, one company, under Lieut. Marshall, forming part of the escort of the two advanced batteries of Artillery, three companies, under Major Waller, which had been held temporarily in reserve, reinforcing the left of the Infantry line at the critical moment when the Ghazis swept down upon it, and the remaining half-battalion forming up to the right, and contributing materially by its fire to the final rout of the enemy. In the action of Arzu, on the 23rd April, the regiment was again engaged.

The 19th P.N.I. took part with the Field Force in its continued advance, and remained with it in and about the Logar Valley till the 6th Aug., when it marched into Kabul, and was broken up.

On the 10th Aug., 1880, the regiment commenced its return march by the Khyber route to India, convoying sick, and ordnance stores. On the 28th idem it reached Peshawar, and was directed to proceed into cantonments at Sialkot, where it arrived on the 25th Sept., 1880.

During the period of nearly two years, throughout which it was absent on active service, the regiment suffered much from the heavy nature of the work it was called upon to perform, and the rigours of the climate to which it was subjected, losing, in the course of the two campaigns, upwards of 126 men from disease.

The undermentioned officers of the 19th Regt. (Punjab) Bengal Native Infantry served in the war :—

Major-General E. B. Clay (*retired*) commanded the regiment throughout the first campaign : in the advance on and occupation of Kandahar, and the advance to the Halmand.

Lt.-Colonel A. Copland, C.B., served with the regiment throughout both campaigns, commanding it throughout the second. Took part in the advance on and occupation of Kandahar, and the advance to the Halmand ; and commanded the regiment in the second advance to Kandahar, the advance on Ghazni, and to Kabul, and the return march to India, and at the battle of Ahmad Khel and the action of Arzu. (Mentioned in despatches ; C.B.)

Lt.-Colonel C. H. Bergman, Bt. Lt.-Colonel J. E. Waller, Captain D. E. Gouldsbury, and *Lieuts. H. T. Faithfull* and *W. S. Marshall* served with the regiment throughout both campaigns, taking part in the advance on and occupation of Kandahar, the advance to the Halmand, the second advance to Kandahar, the advance on Ghazni and to Kabul, and the return march by the Khyber route to India, and being present at the battle of Ahmad Khel and the action of Arzu. *Lt.-Colonel Bergman* commanded the detachment which accompanied the Agent to the Governor-General into the Marri country, and opened up the route for the railway between Sibi and Pishin. *Bt. Lt.-Colonel Waller* was mentioned in despatches for his services at Ahmad Khel, and received the Brevet of Lt.-Colonel.

20TH REGT. (PUNJAB) BENGAL NATIVE INFANTRY.

IN September, 1878, the 20th Regt. P.N.I., then stationed at Peshawar, was warned for active service, and subsequently formed part of the 1st Division Peshawar Valley Field Force.

As a unit of the 1st Infantry Brigade, the regiment was engaged on the 21st and 22nd Nov. in the difficult flanking operations which were conducted by Brigadier-General Macpherson over the precipitous Rhotas heights in reverse of Ali Musjid, and which contributed to effecting the abandonment of the Fort and the retreat of the Afghan forces. On the former day a small force detached under Major Gordon, 20th P.N.I., from Turbai, came across a party of the enemy, and with a few men under Captain Meiklejohn, 20th P.N.I., effected the capture of 50 of their number.

Accompanying the subsequent advance of the 1st Division through the Khyber, the 20th P.N.I. took part, successively, in the occupation of Daka and Jalalabad, where it remained serving from the 20th Dec., 1878, till after the signing of the treaty of Gandamak. On the 11th June, 1879, it commenced its return march to India, and on the 17th idem recrossed the frontier.

During the period the 20th P.N.I. was employed in the first campaign, detachments of the regiment, besides performing minor duties, took part in the expedition beyond Ali Bogham in support of the force under Brigadier-General Jenkins, which was engaged in the destruction of the village of Shirgirh, 11th Jan., 1879; the expedition to relieve Mayar in Kama, 7th Feb., 1879; and the expedition to Katz, across the Kabul River, in pursuit of Azmatallah Khan, Ghilzai, 31st March to 2nd April, 1879.

On the renewal of hostilities in the autumn of 1879, the 20th P.N.I. was again ordered on service, and throughout the second campaign, from the middle of September, 1879, till October, 1880, was employed at various posts in the Kuram Valley and on the frontier as a unit of the columns commanded by Generals Tytler, Gordon, and Watson.

On the 31st Oct., 1879, a detachment of the regiment formed part of a flying column under Col. Rogers, 20th P.N.I., which made a demonstration against 3,000 hostile Lasherzais, near Bulesh Khel, and dispersed them.

From the 8th till the 21st Dec., 1879, the regiment took part with the expeditionary force under General Tytler in the operations which were conducted in the Zaimusht country, a detachment being engaged with the party under Col. Rogers, 20th P.N.I., in the destruction of the Watazai villages on the 8th Dec., a detachment, with other details under Col. Rogers, being left to defend the camp of the expeditionary force on the 13th Dec., and a detachment being engaged on the following day in action of Zawa.

On the evacuation of the Kuram Valley the regiment was withdrawn to Thal, and from thence eventually made its way to Jalandhar.

The undermentioned officers served with the 20th Regt. P.N.I. during the period it was employed in the war:—

Colonel R. G. Rogers, *C.B.* (in command throughout both campaigns, with the exception of an interval during the second, in which he commanded the Rawal Pindi Brigade), *Lt.-Colonel W. H. Gordon* (throughout both campaigns, and in command during part of second), *Lt.-Colonel J. Bartleman* (from 1 Feb., 1879, till conclusion of first campaign, and also during second campaign), *Major W. H. Meiklejohn* (throughout both campaigns), *Major G. M. D. Hill* (throughout both campaigns), *Captain L. B. Irwin* (from outbreak of war till Jan., 1879, and from 17 May, 1879, till conclusion of first campaign, and also during part of second campaign), and *Lieut. W. O. Harris* (throughout both campaigns). *Colonel Rogers* was mentioned in despatches for the operations in the Lughman Valley and in the Zaimusht country, and for his services received a Companionship of the Bath; *Lt.-Colonel Gordon* was mentioned in despatches for Ali Musjid and the Zaimusht operations; and *Lt.-Colonel Bartleman* and *Major Meiklejohn* were mentioned in despatches for the Zaimusht operations.

21ST REGT. (PUNJAB) BENGAL NATIVE INFANTRY.

THE 21st P.N.I. was quartered at Rawal Pindi when it received orders, on the 8th Oct., 1878, to proceed to Thal, to form part of the force assembling there under the command of General Roberts for the impending invasion of Afghanistan; and marching on the 16th idem by way of Kohat, eventually reached its destination on the 13th Nov., 1878.

On the 7th Dec. the regiment proceeded with General Roberts to Hazar Pir, and remained garrisoning that post till the 2nd Jan., 1879, when it marched with the expeditionary force under General Roberts for Khost, and took part in the operations which were conducted in that district during the succeeding fortnight. At the action of Matun on the 7th, the Left wing took and burned two villages, and captured 82 prisoners, the Right wing at the same time taking and burning three villages, and losing 1 man, killed. During the night of the 8th the regiment assisted in repelling an attack which was made by the enemy on the camp. On the 10th the Left wing accompanied General Roberts on a raid, the Right wing remaining and garrisoning Matun.

The regiment left Matun on the 27th Jan. for Hazar Pir, where it arrived on the 31st idem, and remained till the 5th March; it then proceeded to Shinak to repair the road, a duty on which it remained engaged till the 27th of that month, on which date it marched for Kuram, arriving on the 1st April. On the 8th the regiment advanced to Ali Khel, and from thence, on the conclusion of peace, proceeded to Bulesh Khel, where it remained throughout the succeeding summer. While the regiment was at Bulesh Khel, the regiment lost 1 Subadar and 1 Sepoy, killed by the Massugais, while wood-cutting.

On the 25th Sept., 1879, the 21st P.N.I. was relieved by the 20th P.N.I., and marched for the Shutargardan, where it arrived on the 30th, the rear-guard having been attacked by and having beaten off the enemy in the Hazardarakht defile *en route*. Remaining to form part of the garrison, the regiment took a prominent part in the action of the 2nd Oct., when the enemy's attack on the Shutargardan was repulsed with the infliction of heavy loss; and again on the 14th it was engaged in the action of the Surkai Kotal, when the enemy received another severe lesson, being beaten off and dispersed with great slaughter. During the 18th and 19th Oct. the Shutargardan was besieged, some 15,000 of the enemy surrounding it, and keeping up a heavy but comparatively ineffective fire, till they retired on receipt of intelligence of the arrival of Brigadier-General Hugh Gough's force at Kushi. On the evacuation of the Shutargardan on the 21st Oct. the regiment marched to Kushi, but on arriving there received orders to return to Ali Khel owing to the disturbed state of the country surrounding that post, and retracing its steps, arrived at its destination on the 29th.

The 21st P.N.I. remained at Ali Khel with the force under Brigadier-General Gordon till the withdrawal from that post; it was then told off to garrison Habib Killa, and continued there from the 9th Nov., 1879, till the 18th April, 1880, suffering much from the excessive severity of the climate.

After remaining in the Kuram Valley till the conclusion of the war, the regiment marched to Peshawar.

The undermentioned officers of the 21st Regt. (Punjab) Bengal Native Infantry served in the war:—

Colonel. J. B. Thelwall, C.B. (*retired*). (For services see "Staff.")

Bt. Lt.-Colonel F. W. Collis officiated in command of the regiment throughout, taking part in the Khost Valley expedition, and being present at the action of Matun, the defence of the Shutargardan, and the action of the Surkai Kotal. (Mentioned in despatches; Brevet of Lt.-Colonel, and permanent command of the regiment.)

Major J. G. T. Carruthers served with the regiment throughout, taking part in the Khost Valley expedition, and being present at the action of Matun and the defence of the Shutargardan.

Captain G. H. C. Dyce served with the regiment throughout, taking part in the Khost Valley expedition, and being present at the action of Matun, the defence of the Shutargardan, and the action of the Surkai Kotal. (Mentioned in despatches for gallant conduct.)

Lieut. H. H. Sweetenham served with the regiment, as Adjutant, throughout the first campaign, and till Jan., 1880, during the second. (Since deceased.)

Lieut. W. H. Young served with the regiment in both campaigns.

Lieut. W. C. Faithfull served with the 20th P.N.I. throughout both campaigns, taking part with that regiment in the capture of Ali Musjid, the Zaimusht expedition, and numerous minor operations.

Lieut. C. M. Fitzgerald, Commissariat Dept., served with the regiment in the first campaign, and with the Commissariat Dept. in the second. Was present at the assault and capture of the Peiwar Kotal and the action of Matun. Held for three months the Commissariat charge of Pezwan, Jagdalak, and Seh Baba. Was present with Col. Jenkins' force at the second action of Charasiab. Proceeded in Commissariat charge of 2nd Brigade 2nd Division N.A.F.F. to Koh-i-Daman, and of the Cavalry Brigade, Kabul-Kandahar F.F., in the march to the relief of Kandahar, and was present at the battle of Kandahar.

Lieut. P. M. Carpendale served with the regiment in the second campaign from May till Oct., 1880.

22ND REGT. (PUNJAB) BENGAL NATIVE INFANTRY.

THROUGHOUT the first campaign the 22nd Regt. Punjab N.I. formed part of the garrison of Peshawar.

On the renewal of hostilities in the autumn of 1879 the regiment formed part of the 2nd Brigade Khyber Division, under the command of Brigadier-General Arbuthnot.

Participating in the forward movement of the troops on the Khyber line in December, 1879, in view of the advance of Brigadier-General C. Gough's Brigade to the relief of Sherpur, the 22nd P.N.I. was moved rapidly forward by wings, the Head-quarters arriving by the end of that month at Safed Sang, detachments being furnished *en route* at Daka, Basawal, Barikab, Fort Battye, and Rozabad, and three companies being sent forward to reinforce Pezwan. The regiment suffered at this time very severely from the unhealthy nature of the climate and the exposure to which it was subjected, losing on the 21st Jan., 1880, its Commandant, Colonel J. J. O'Brien, amongst many others.

At the latter end of March the Head-quarters 22nd P.N.I. moved to Seh Baba, where the whole regiment, with the exception of the Jagdalak detachment, was shortly afterwards concentrated.

On the evacuation of the advanced posts on the Khyber line in August, 1880, the regiment returned to India, and proceeding to Mian Mir, went into quarters.

The undermentioned officers served with the 22nd Regt. Puujab Native Infantry during the period it was employed in the war:—

Colonel J. J. O'Brien (Deceased. See Biographical Division), *Colonel B. T. Stafford* (in command from 21 Jan., 1880), *Major C. H. Bridges, Captains J. G. Hare* (died of pneumonia at Safed Sang, 3 Jan., 1880), *A. S. M'Rae* and *R. Gordon,* and *Lieuts. R. H. Rattray* and *F. E. C. H. Gordon-Cumming, Cheshire Regt.* (attached).

Lieut. J. Lamb served with the Mhairwara Battalion in the first campaign till 22 March, 1879, and with the 24th P.N.I. throughout the second campaign, taking part in the fighting at Jagdalak in Dec., 1879, the march from Kabul to the relief of Kandahar, and the battle of Kandahar. (Mentioned in despatches.)

23RD REGT. (PUNJAB) BENGAL NATIVE INFANTRY (PIONEERS).

AS a unit of the Kuram Valley F.F., the 23rd Punjab Pioneers crossed the frontier at Thal on the 20th Nov., 1878, and took part in the advance into Afghanistan.

On the 28th Nov., 1878, the regiment took part in the reconnaissance in force which was conducted to the foot of the Peiwar Kotal, and on the 2nd Dec. was present at the assault and capture of that position, being prominently engaged in both the first and second turning movements which were carried out under General Roberts' immediate command. On that day the regiment had to deplore the loss of a gallant officer in the death of Major A. D. Anderson, who fell while leading his men in the front fighting line under a murderous fire from the enemy.

In the second week in December, 1878, the 23rd Pioneers, after advancing with the rest of the Division to Ali Khel, marched from that post to Fort Kuram with the Brigade under General Roberts which was attacked by the Mangal hordes in the Mangior defile. On the return of the Brigade it was left, with other details, at Kuriah; and during the following month it took part in the operations in the Khost Valley.

The regiment was employed on the Thal and Kuram road from Feb. till April, 1879, after which it returned to Ali Khel; from thence, on the 1st June, it marched to Shalozan, whence a wing was detached to the Shank Gorge, and was there employed till the beginning of Sept., 1879, in felling timber, quarrying stone, &c., while the wing at Ali Khel was engaged in road-making, lime-burning, and the like, on the site of the proposed cantonment.

On the receipt of news of the Kabul massacre, the 23rd Pioneers was pushed forward to seize and hold the Shutargardan Pass, and subsequently took part in the advance of Sir F. Roberts' Division on Kabul. Early on the morning of the 6th Oct. a working party of the 23rd was sent forward, with supports, to the entrance of the Sang-i-Nawishta defile, where the fire of the enemy was first drawn. In the action (of Charasiab) which was fought later in the day, two companies, under Captain Paterson, were engaged in the right attack under Major White, 92nd Highlanders, and the remainder of the regiment in General Baker's left flanking movement, and assisted in carrying in brilliant succession ridge after ridge of the heights upon which the enemy took up his position. For their forward gallantry in the capture of the enemy's guns by Captain Paterson's detachment, Jemadar Beer Singh and two Sepoys subsequently received the Order of Merit. The enemy defeated and dispersed, the regiment took part in the continued advance of the Division, and was engaged, during the two succeeding days, in the operations which resulted in the fall of Kabul.

In November, 1879, the left wing of the 23rd Pioneers was detached to Lataband. In December the Right wing garrisoned Sherpur during the investment of that place, and was afterwards employed in blowing down the various fortified enclosures round the British cantonments. The left wing rejoined Head-quarters on the 24th December, 1879, and the whole regiment was subsequently employed in making roads and opening up the country round Sherpur.

In April, 1880, the 23rd Pioneers formed part of the Column under General Ross, which proceeded into the Wardak country to co-operate with the force under Sir Donald Stewart advancing from Kandahar, and was engaged in the various operations which were conducted during the succeeding months, including the actions near Zaidabad on the 25th and 26th April.

As a unit of the 1st Brigade Kabul-Kandahar F.F., the regiment took part, in August, 1880, in the advance to the relief of Kandahar. During the march the regiment was constantly employed in constructing camps, improving roads, and other important work, and after the arrival of the Division at its destination it was engaged, on the 1st Sept., 1880, in the defeat of Ayub Khan and the capture of his guns before Kandahar.

The 23rd Pioneers was one of the first battalions which quitted Kandahar for India, and after an absence of a little more than two years on service, arrived at its cantonments at Mian Mir, Punjab, on the 2nd Oct., 1880.

The undermentioned officers of the 23rd (Punjab) Bengal Native Infantry (Pioneers) served in the war :—

Major-General A. A. Currie, C.B. (*retired*), commanded the regiment throughout the first, and during the earlier part of the second campaign: at the assault and capture of the Peiwar Kotal, the passage of the Mangior defile, the action of Charasiab, and the subsequent operations resulting in the fall of Kabul. (Mentioned in despatches; C.B.)

Lt.-Colonel H. Collett, C.B., served throughout the first campaign as Assistant Quartermaster-General with the Kuram Valley F.F., and during the second campaign, first as Assistant Quartermaster-General with the 1st Division Kabul F.F., and afterwards in command of the regiment. Besides being present at numerous minor affairs, took part in the assault and capture of the Peiwar Kotal, the operations at Shekabad, the march from Kabul to the relief of Kandahar, and the battle of Kandahar. (Four times mentioned in despatches; C.B.)

Major A. D. Anderson. (Killed in action. See Biographical Division.)

Bt. Major H. Paterson served with the regiment—with the exception of two brief intervals during which he was detached to the Depôt to equip and bring up recruits—throughout both campaigns, taking part in the assault and capture of the Peiwar Kotal, the Passage of the Mangior defile, the action of Charasiab and subsequent operations resulting in the fall of Kabul, the actions near Zaidabad, 25 and 26 April, 1880, the march from Kabul to the relief of Kandahar, and the battle of Kandahar. (Mentioned in despatches; Brevet of Major.)

Bt. Major S. V. Gordon served with the regiment throughout the second campaign, taking part in the action of Charasiab, and subsequent operations resulting in the fall of Kabul, the actions near Zaidabad, 25 and 26 April, 1880, the march from Kabul to the relief of Kandahar, and the battle of Kandahar, and commanding the wing of Lataband during the investment of Sherpur. (Twice mentioned in despatches; Brevet of Major.)

Captain J. F. J. Miller served with the regiment in the Kuram Valley from April till Aug., 1879, when he reverted to the Dept. Public Works.

Captain V. G. L. Eyre, and *Lieuts. D. Chesney* and *A. E. Jones* served with the regiment throughout both campaigns, taking part in the assault and capture of the Peiwar Kotal, the passage of the Mangior defile, the action of Charasiab and subsequent operations resulting in the fall of Kabul, the defence of Sherpur, the actions near Zaidabad, 25 and 26 April, 1880, the advance from Kabul to the relief of Kandahar, and the battle of Kandahar. *Lieut. Chesney* was wounded at the battle of Kandahar, and for his services at the action of Charasiab was mentioned in despatches.

Lieut. W. H. Jameson served with the 29th P.N.I. in the first campaign, from 23 Dec., 1878, and throughout the second campaign, taking part in the Zaimusht expedition and action of Zawa.

24TH REGT. (PUNJAB) BENGAL NATIVE INFANTRY.

IN October, 1878, the 24th Regt. P.N.I., then stationed at Jhansi, was warned for active service, and proceeding to Peshawar, formed part of General Maude's Division of the Army of Invasion.

In January, 1879, 356 men of the regiment took part with the Jamrud Column in the operations which were conducted by General Maude in the second expedition into the Bazar Valley. While engaged with a detached force in blowing up the towers of Halwai on the 28th, a sepoy of the regiment was wounded. On the 31st some men of the regiment forming part of the rear-guard of a convoy particularly distinguished themselves in following Lieut. Hart, R.E. (on whom the Victoria Cross was subsequently conferred for his gallantry), to the assistance of a wounded sowar under a heavy cross fire.

A few weeks after the return of the Bazar Valley expeditionary force to the line of communications, one wing of the regiment was moved forward to Landi Kotal, the other wing remaining at Jamrud. There they were employed, respectively, on garrison and escort duty till after the signing of the treaty of Gandamak.

During the interval between the first and second campaigns, the 24th P.N.I. continued to serve in the Pass as a unit of the Khyber Brigade.

Shortly after the renewal of hostilities in the autumn of 1879, the regiment, taking part in the forward concentration of the troops on the Khyber line, advanced by wings to Daka, Jalalabad, and Gandamak, where Head-quarters arrived at the latter end of October. On the 3rd Nov. six companies marched from that post with the Moveable Column under Brigadier-General C. Gough for Kata Sang, where a junction was effected with the Kabul Field Force.

In the first week in December, 1879, the regiment returned from Gandamak to Jalalabad, in view of General Bright's then projected expedition into the Lughman Valley; but during the succeeding week it was moved back again, owing to reinforcements being required to enable Brigadier-General C. Gough's Column to march for Kabul. On the 16th the regiment arrived at Pezwan, and the following day moved out, under Col. Norman, to co-operate with a force under Major Macnaghten, 10th Bengal Lancers, from Jagdalak against some bodies of Ghilzais, who were dispersed. On the 18th Col. Norman, co-operating with another force from Jagdalak commanded by Major Rowcroft, 4th Goorkhas, dispersed a renewed gathering of the Ghilzais, and the following day marched into Jagdalak in command of a mixed force including the regiment, again encountering and defeating the enemy en route. On the departure of Gough's brigade for Kabul on the 21st Dec., the 24th P.N.I., with other details under the command of Col. Norman, remained at Jagdalak, one company of the regiment being detached to Jagdalak Kotal, and subsequently taking part, on the 23rd, in the repulse of a determined attack made on that post by a large body of the enemy. On the 24th Col. Norman, who had on that day effected a junction with a force advancing from Pezwan, had another brush with the enemy while returning, and again on the 29th sallied out from his camp at Jagdalak, and in co-operation with a force under Col. Ball Acton, 51st L.I., defeated with heavy loss 2,000 Ghilzais under Azmatallah Khan. The following day the 27th P.N.I. occupied Seh Baba and Lataband, and remained holding those advanced posts, keeping open the communications with the capital, for a period of ten weeks. On the 19th March, 1880, the regiment advanced to Kabul, and encamped on the Siah Sang heights.

In the middle of April, 1880, the 27th P.N.I. accompanied the force under General Ross which marched from Kabul to effect a junction with the Ghazni Field Force, and at the action of Shekabad, on the 25th of that month, was hotly engaged, three companies forming part of Major Combe's force in the right attack, and a wing reinforcing Major Rowcroft's Column.

On the 14th June, 1880, the 24th P.N.I. left Sherpur with Brigadier-General C. Gough's Brigade for Pughman, and for the next six weeks, until the force was recalled to Kabul in view of the evacuation, took part with it in its various operations in the Koh Daman and surrounding districts. On the 20th June, six companies of the regiment formed part of a force under Col. Norman which engaged and defeated the enemy on the Ghazni road.

Forming part of Macpherson's brigade of the Kabul-Kandahar Field Force, the 27th P.N.I. took part, in August, 1880, in the advance to the relief of the southern capital, and on the 1st Sept. was engaged in the crowning defeat of the enemy at the battle of Kandahar. In this engagement lost 1 man killed, and 1 non-commissioned officer and 10 men wounded.

On the reconstitution of the forces in Southern Afghanistan the 27th P.N.I. commenced its return march to India, eventually proceeding to Multan, where it arrived after an absence of over two years on active service.

The undermentioned officers of the 24th Regt. (Punjab) Bengal Native Infantry served in the war:—

Colonel F. B. Norman, C.B., commanded the regiment throughout the period it was employed in the war, with the exception of an interval in March and April, 1879, taking part in the Bazar Valley expedition, the fighting round Jagdalak in Dec., 1879 (in command of a force of all arms), the march from Kabul to the relief of Kandahar, and the battle of Kandahar. (Three times mentioned in despatches; Brevet of Lt.-Colonel, C.B.)

Bt. Lt.-Colonel E. Stedman and *Lieut. J. G. Ramsay* served with the regiment throughout the period it was employed in the war, taking part in the Bazar Valley expedition, the fighting round Jagdalak in Dec., 1879, the action of Shekabad, the march from Kabul to the relief of Kandahar, and the battle of Kandahar. For his services *Lt.-Colonel Stedman* was twice mentioned in despatches, and received the Brevet of Lt.-Colonel.

Captain P. H. Wallerstein served with the regiment in the first campaign from Jan. till June, 1879, and throughout the second campaign, taking part in the fighting round Jagdalak in Dec., 1879, the action of Shekabad (in which he commanded the three companies in the right attack), the march from Kabul to the relief of Kandahar, and the battle of Kandahar.

Captain J. J. Money-Simons served with the Transport Dept. at Multan throughout the first campaign, and with the regiment throughout the second, taking part in the fighting round Jagdalak, the action of Shekabad, the march from Kabul to the relief of Kandahar, and the battle of Kandahar. (Mentioned in despatches.)

Lieut. H. R. Marrett, Commisst. Dept., served with the regiment during the first campaign, and with the Commisst. Dept., Kabul F.F., during the second campaign.

Lieut. J. J. E. Bradshaw served with the 25th K.O.Bs. throughout the first campaign, taking part in the Bazar Valley expedition, and with the 24th P.N.I. throughout the second campaign, taking part in the fighting round Jagdalak in Dec., 1879, the action of Shekabad, the march from Kabul to the relief of Kandahar, and the battle of Kandahar. (Twice mentioned in despatches.)

Lt.-Colonel W. A. Franks, Bengal Infantry, served with the regiment from Jan. till May, 1879.

25TH REGT. (PUNJAB) BENGAL NATIVE INFANTRY.

ON the 6th Nov., 1878, the 25th Regt. P.N.I., having received orders for service, proceeded by rail from Khanpur, where it was then stationed, to Multan, and marching by the Dera Bughti route and Bolan Pass to Quetta, crossed the frontier, and eventually joined a portion of the advanced troops of Sir Donald Stewart's Division at Gulistan Karez.

As a unit of the Column under Brigadier-General Palliser proceeding by the Ghwaja route, the 25th P.N.I. took part, in January, 1879, in the advance of the Division on Kandahar. The regiment was present, on the 4th of that month, at the action of Takht-i-pul, and on the 8th idem in the triumphal march of the troops through the streets of the Southern capital.

On the 15th Jan., 1879, the 25th P.N.I., forming part of Brigadier-General Barter's Brigade, accompanied Sir Donald Stewart's advance on Kalat-i-Ghilzai. From Jaldak it was detached with other details to reconnoitre the Argandab Valley, and send in supplies; a duty which was successfully accomplished. In the beginning of March it returned with the other portions of the force to Kandahar, and there remained cantoned throughout the succeeding summer. At the latter end of March the regiment received a welcome accession in the shape of a strong draft from India.

Early in September, 1879, the 25th P.N.I. was directed to return to India. It had only proceeded as far as Chaman, however, when, in consequence of the receipt of news of the Kabul massacre, it was ordered back again, and marching by wings, arrived at Kandahar at the latter end of the same month.

On the 29th March, 1880, Head-quarters and seven companies 25th P.N.I. marched out from Kandahar with Brigadier-General Barter's Brigade to take part in the advance of the Bengal Division on Ghazni, a detached company, forming part of the personal escort of Sir D. Stewart, following on the 31st idem. On the 19th April the regiment was engaged in the battle of Ahmad Khel, and on the 23rd, in the action of Arzu; and subsequently proceeding with the Brigade into the Logar Valley, it was employed in the various operations which were conducted in that and the neighbouring districts during the succeeding three months, including the passage of the Tungi Wardak defile, and the repulse of the enemy's attack on Brigadier-General Barter's camp during the night of the 12th May, 1880, at Jabar Kila.

Detailed to the 3rd Brigade of the Kabul-Kandahar Field Force, the 25th P.N.I. took part, in the month of August, 1880, in the memorable march to the relief of the Southern capital, and on the 1st Sept., the day after the arrival of the Division at its destination, was engaged in the defeat of Ayub Khan's army at the battle of Kandahar.

In October, 1880, the regiment returned to India, marching with the force under Brigadier-General MacGregor which re-opened the Hurnai route to Sibi.

The undermentioned officers of the 25th Regt. (Punjab) Bengal Native Infantry served in the war:—

Colonel J. W. Hoggan, C.B., commanded the regiment throughout both campaigns : in the advance on Kandahar and Kalat-i-Ghilzai, the advance from Kandahar on Ghazni and to Kabul, and the march from Kabul to the relief of Kandahar, and at the action of Takht-i-pul, the battle of Ahmad Khel, the action of Arzu, and the battle of Kandahar. (Three times mentioned in despatches ; C.B.)

Colonel N. Barton served with the regiment throughout the first campaign, taking part in the advance on Kandahar and Kalat-i-Ghilzai, and being present at the action of Takht-i-pul. Commanded the 13th N.I. in the Kuram Division from 1 March, 1880, till it arrived at Rawal Pindi, 31 March, 1881. (Mentioned in despatches.)

Major J. N. Steel and *Lieuts. G. H. B. Coats* and *C. H. H. Beley* served with the regiment throughout both campaigns, taking part in the advance on Kandahar and Kalat-i-Ghilzai, the advance on Ghazni and to Kabul, and the march from Kabul to the relief of Kandahar, and being present at the action of Takht-i-pul, the battle of Ahmad Khel, the action of Arzu, and the battle of Kandahar. For his services *Lieut. Beley* was mentioned in despatches.

Bt. Major W. V. Ellis served throughout both campaigns, taking part with the regiment in the advance on Kandahar and Kalat-i-Ghilzai, and the action of Takht-i-pul; as Provost Marshal to the Field Force, in the advance on Ghazni and to Kabul, the battle of Ahmad Khel, and the action of Arzu; and with the regiment, in the march from Kabul to the relief of Kandahar, and the battle of Kandahar. (Twice mentioned in despatches ; Brevet of Major.)

Lieut. P. E. Anderson (Deceased. See Biographical Division.)

26TH REGT. (PUNJAB) BENGAL NATIVE INFANTRY.

ON the 27th Sept., 1878, the 26th Punjab Infantry proceeded by rail from Mian Mir to Multan, under orders to march to Quetta on field service; and quitting Multan on the 1st Oct., the third day after its arrival, made its way by the Dera Bughti route and the Bolan Pass to its destination, where it arrived on the 5th Nov.

As a unit of Brigadier-General Nuttall's Brigade of Major-General Biddulph's Division of the Army of Invasion, the regiment took part in the advance into Afghanistan, leaving Quetta on the 22nd Nov., 1878, and marching into Kandahar on the 10th Jan., 1879. During the passage of the Khojak Pass by General Biddulph's Division, two companies of the 26th, under the command of Lieut. Ryland, who was in charge of the Pass, furnished numerous escorts to signallers and covering parties for working detachments; and later, on the Division quitting Chaman, two companies of the regiment under the command of Major A. B. Hepburn were left to garrison that post.

The regiment remained at Kandahar, forming part of the garrison, till the 17th Feb., 1879, when, conformably with the scheme formulated by Government to reduce the number of troops at the Southern theatre of operations before the hot weather should set in, it received orders to return to India, and acting as escort to a battery of Artillery and the Native General Hospital, made its way back by the Khojak Pass, suffering great hardships and privations *en route.*

The undermentioned officers served with the 27th Regt. P.N.I. throughout the period it was employed in the war:—

Colonel M. G. Smith (retired) (in command), *Lt.-Colonel A. Tulloch, Major A. B. Hepburn, Captains C. J. R. Fulford, L. Denning,* and *S. H. P. Graves,* and *Lieuts. H. A. Ravenshaw* and *H. G. Ryland.*

27TH REGT. (PUNJAB) BENGAL NATIVE INFANTRY.

IN October, 1878, the 27th Regt. P.N.I., then stationed at Naushahra, was warned for active service, and subsequently formed part of the 3rd Brigade, 1st Division, Peshawar Valley Field Force, under the command of Brigadier-General Appleyard.

On the 19th Nov., 1878, the regiment marched with the brigade from Peshawar to Jamrud, and on the morning of the 21st idem crossed the frontier and took part in the front attack on Ali Musjid. By the time that it was decided, as darkness closed in on that day, to postpone the assault, and the order was given to cease firing, the 27th P.N.I. had pushed forward to the support of the 14th Sikhs on to the steep slope leading to the peak which formed the right flank of the Afghan position, and the leading companies were hotly engaged with the enemy in their successive lines of entrenchments. At this juncture the regiment suffered severely, losing Major Birch, Lieut. Fitzgerald, and 4 men killed, and 6 men wounded. At daybreak on the following morning it was found that the Fort had been abandoned during the night, a result to which the attack of the 3rd Brigade had materially contributed.

The 27th P.N.I. took part in the advance of the 1st Division to Daka. On the return of Brigadier-General Appleyard from Land Khana to Ali Musjid, the regiment was transferred to Brigadier-General Tytler's brigade, and continued to serve with it till the conclusion of the first campaign.

In the third week in December, 1878, three companies of the regiment, under Major James Cook, took part with Brigadier-General Tytler's column in the first expedition into the Bazar Valley. During the advance through the Tubbai Pass on the 22nd, the companies were employed in crowning the surrounding heights, and were again and again hotly engaged with the enemy.

In January, 1879, 104 men of the regiment took part with Brigadier-General Tytler's column in the second expedition into the Bazar Valley, and on the 28th of that month, in the reconnaissance of the Bokhar Pass, came into warm conflict with the enemy.

From the 18th to the 21st March, 1879, a portion of the regiment took part in Brigadier-General Tytler's operations against the Shinwaris in the Maidanak district, and assisted in destroying several of their towers and villages; and again on the 24th March, a portion of the regiment was engaged in the successful action of Deh Sarak.

On the 31st March Head-quarters and 210 men of the regiment formed part of the force under Brigadier-General C. Gough which marched from Jalalabad towards Gandamak, and on the 2nd April were engaged in the front line at the action of Futtehabad.

On the 8th June, 1879, the regiment, forming part of the rear brigade of the troops returning to India, left Gandamak, and after remaining halted a few days at Landi Kotal, continued its march, and recrossed the frontier on the 27th idem.

On the renewal of hostilities in the autumn of 1879, the 27th P.N.I. was again ordered on service, and from September, 1879, till the latter end of March, 1880, served at various posts on the Khyber line, the head-quarters arriving at Daka in October, and at Jalalabad in December, 1879.

On the 26th Dec., 1879, 100 men of the regiment formed part of a force under Lt.-Colonel Fryer, 6th Dragoon Guards, which was sent out from Jalalabad to obtain information concerning an attack which had been made by a body of Shinwaris two days previously on a post near Ali Boghan; and again on the 29th idem 70 men of the regiment marched from Barikab with a force under Lt.-Colonel Mackenzie which visited and destroyed the Ghilzai villages of Banda, Kuddi, and Boghani.

On the 13th Jan., 1880, a portion of the regiment formed part of the force under Colonel Walker, 12th Foot, which was sent to reinforce Ali Boghan, and assisted in dispersing a large body of Mohmands who were threatening that post.

From the 28th Jan. till the 16th March, 1880, Head-quarters and four companies of the regiment were employed with the expeditionary force under General Bright which crossed the Kabul River and occupied the Lughman Valley.

Shortly after the return of the Lughman expeditionary force the 27th P.N.I. was ordered on to Kabul, and arrived at its destination on the 26th March. On the 17th May one wing, escorting a large convoy of camels, returned to Lataband, and thither, on the 26th July, it was followed by the remainder of the regiment.

On the retirement from Kabul and the advanced posts on the Khyber line in August, 1880, the 27th P.N.I. marched to Landi Kotal, and there continued to serve, as a portion of the Khyber Brigade, till the final evacuation of the Pass in March, 1881.

The undermentioned officers served with the 27th Regt. P.N.I. during the period it was employed in the war:—

Lt.-Colonel C. J. Hughes (throughout both campaigns, in command), *Major H. H. Birch* (killed in action: see Biographical Division), *Captain R. A. Swetenham* (from Dec., 1878, till Feb., 1879, and from March, 1879, till conclusion of first campaign, and throughout second campaign), *Major C. W. Babington* (from 31 Dec., 1878, till conclusion of first campaign), *Lieut. T. O. Fitzgerald* (killed in action: see Biographical Division), *Lieut. G. A. Williams* (throughout first campaign), and *Lieut. S. W. T. Roberts* (deceased: see Biographical Division). *Lt.-Colonel Hughes* was mentioned in despatches for his services in the action of Futtehabad, and *Lieut. Williams* for his services in the first Bazar Valley expedition.

Lieut. A. E. P. Burn served with the Mhairwara Battalion throughout the first campaign, taking part in both the Bazar Valley expeditions, and with the 27th P.N.I. throughout the second campaign.

Lieut. A. Wallace was attached to the 13th N.I. in the Kuram Valley from 2 Oct. till Dec., 1879, and to the 5th N.L.I. from Dec., 1879, till Nov., 1880, also in the Kuram Valley.

28TH REGT. (PUNJAB) BENGAL NATIVE INFANTRY.

WHEN stationed at Moradabad in the autumn of 1878, the 28th Regt. P.N.I. received orders to proceed to Thal to join the force assembling there under the command of General Roberts. The regiment had not the good fortune to take part in the original advance of the Field Force into hostile territory, but joined Divisional Head-quarters in the Kuram Valley in the month of December.

On the 2nd Jan., 1879, the 28th P.N.I. marched with the expeditionary force under General Roberts from Hazar Pir for Khost, and took part in the operations which were conducted in that district during the succeeding fortnight. At the action of Matun on the 7th Jan. the regiment was engaged in support of the cavalry, and performed effective service in the repulse of the enemy to the north-west of the camp. In the last week in January the regiment returned with the other units of the expeditionary force to Hazar Pir, and on the 4th Feb. proceeded with General Roberts to Habib Killa, from whence it was shortly afterwards ordered up to Peiwar Kotal in relief of the 2nd Punjab Infantry. From Peiwar Kotal the regiment was subsequently moved to Ali Khel, and from that advanced post to Kuram, where it remained serving throughout the summer months after the treaty of Gandamak had brought the first campaign to a close.

On the renewal of hostilities in the autumn of 1879 the 28th P.N.I. was again detailed for service with the Division under Sir F. Roberts. Moving from Ali Khel with Divisional Head-quarters on the 27th Sept. to the Shutargardan, the regiment was engaged, during the afternoon of that day, in the skirmish with the enemy at Jagi Thana, subsequently occupying the heights on the southern side of the Hazardarakht defile—to which the Mangals and Ghilzais had tenaciously clung—during the passage of the entire column.

The 28th P.N.I. took no actual part in the action of Charasiab, the brigade (Macpherson's) of which it formed part being detained in rear to guard the ammunition, treasure, and baggage of the division. On the 8th Oct. the regiment proceeded with Brigadier-General Macpherson to co-operate with Brigadier-General Baker's Brigade in the advance along the hills to the left of the Pass leading to Kabul, and on the 12th it accompanied General Roberts in his formal entry into the Bala Hissar.

The 28th P.N.I. marched from Kabul on the 1st Nov. with the force under Brigadier-General Macpherson which proceeded to open up communications with the advanced brigade of General Bright's Division. While at Sirobi, on the 10th of that month, a detachment of 80 rifles formed part of the reinforcement which proceeded to the aid of a company of the 67th Foot hotly engaged with a large body of Safis at Doaba. On the departure of Brigadier-General Macpherson's force for Sherpur from Butkhak, the 28th P.N.I. was left to occupy Lataband, and with other details under Colonel Hudson's command continued to hold that important post in the face of hostile combinations throughout the disturbed period which ensued. On the 16th Dec. a force of 1,000 Safis threatened Col. Hudson's camp, and were attacked and dispersed with heavy loss. On the 22nd idem the post was relieved by Brigadier-General C. Gough's brigade, with which the regiment, together with the remainder of Col. Hudson's command, advanced to Sherpur, arriving on the 24th.

The next seven months, in so far as the 28th P.N.I. was concerned, were comparatively uneventful, the regiment remaining throughout that period at Kabul, with the exception of an interval during which one wing again occupied Lataband. On the evacuation of the capital in August, 1880, the regiment commenced its return march to India, and in the middle of September, 1880, arrived at Peshawar.

The undermentioned officers of the 28th (Punjab) Bengal Native Infantry served in the war:—

Colonel J. Hudson, C.B., commanded the regiment throughout the period it was employed in the war, and the force at Lataband in Dec., 1879. Took part in the action of Matun, the advance on and occupation of Kabul, the affair at Jagi Thana, and the advance to the relief of Sherpur. Defeated with heavy loss a force of 1,000 Safis at Lataband, 16 Dec., 1879. (Three times mentioned in despatches; C.B.)

Major G. S. Hills served with the regiment in both campaigns, till invalided. Took part in the action of Matun, the affair at Jagi Thana, and the operations round Kabul (in which he commanded a force of time-expired men and various detachments) and defence of Sherpur in Dec., 1879. (Mentioned in despatches.)

Major H. S. Marshall served with the regiment from 26 March, 1879, till its return to India, taking part in the affair at Jagi Thana, the affair at Doaba (in which he commanded the detachment engaged), and the action of Lataband. (Mentioned in despatches.)

Major A. Landon. (For services see "Staff.")

Captain F. A. S. D'Acosta de St. Laurent served with the regiment from 10 April, 1879, till its return to India, taking part in the affair at Jagi Thana and the action of Lataband.

Captain A. R. Porter served with the regiment in the first campaign from 31 Jan., 1879.

Lieuts. C. J. Dennys and *A. A. Lane* served with the regiment throughout the period it was employed in the war, taking part in the action of Matun, the affair at Jagi Thana, and the action of Lataband. *Lieut. Lane* also took part in the affair at Doaba, and for his services was mentioned in despatches.

Lieut. H. F. Lyons-Montgomery served throughout both campaigns, first with the regiment, and afterwards with the Commissariat Dept., Kabul and Kabul-Kandahar Field Forces. Took part in the operations in Khost, the action of Charasiab, the operations round Kabul and defence of Sherpur in Dec., 1879, the action of Zaidabad, the march from Kabul to the relief of Kandahar, and the battle of Kandahar. (Mentioned in despatches.)

29TH REGT. (PUNJAB) BENGAL NATIVE INFANTRY.

IN September, 1878, the 29th Regt. P.N.I., then stationed at Talagang, received orders for service, and proceeded to Thal to join the Division there assembling under the command of General Roberts.

Taking part in the advance of the Field Force into Afghanistan on the 21st Nov., the regiment was smartly engaged in the reconnaissance in force on the 28th. While leading his company against the front of the Afghan position on the Peiwar range, Captain Reid was severely wounded, and during the day the additional casualties were, 1 Sepoy killed and 5 wounded.

In the assault and capture of the Peiwar Kotal on the 2nd Dec., 1878, the 29th P.N.I., as one of the battalions employed in the flanking operations carried out under General Roberts' personal command, was prominently engaged: first acting in support of the Highlanders and Goorkhas in carrying the stockades; then, led by the General in person along the crest of the Peiwar towards the pass leading over its centre, coming into hot conflict with immense numbers of the enemy, and maintaining the action till after reinforcements on both sides arrived; and finally, when the second turning movement was ordered, holding the hill overlooking the Spin Gawi road, and protecting the field hospital which had been established there.

The 29th P.N.I. remained encamped at Peiwar till the third week in December, when it joined Divisional Head-quarters at Kuram. On the 24th of that month a Sepoy of the regiment was hanged for having, during the night of the 1st Dec., when the British force was advancing to the attack of the Peiwar Kotal, treacherously fired off his rifle with the intention of giving the alarm to the enemy. Sentences of imprisonment for desertion were also awarded by Courts-martial to several other men of the 29th, and were affirmed. At the same time General Roberts published an order sympathizing with "this gallant and distinguished regiment" on account of the disgrace brought upon it by those offenders. Its conduct in all the operations, he observed, had been excellent, and in the action of the 2nd Dec. it had fought splendidly.

On the 26th Dec., 1878, the regiment marched from Kuram for Thal, and separated in wings and broken up in detachments, it continued to serve at that station, at Hazir Pir, and at other posts in the Kuram Valley and about the frontier, till the conclusion of the first campaign.

Shortly after renewal of hostilities in the autumn of 1879, one wing of the 29th P.N.I. was moved forward to Ali Khel, and on the 14th Oct. took part in the repulse of the attack on that post made by the Jagis and Mangals.

On the 26th Oct., 1879, a large convoy left Ali Khel for Kabul under the command of Col. Gordon, 29th P.N.I., who returned to the Kuram Valley early in the following month.

In the second week in November, 1879, on the evacuation of Ali Khel, a portion of the regiment took part in the Chakmani expedition to enforce the payment of a fine. The object of the expedition was successfully accomplished, and the force reached Bulesh Khel on the 24th of that month.

From the 8th till the 23rd of December, 1879, Head-quarters and four companies of the 29th P.N.I., under the command of Col. Gordon, took part with the expeditionary force under Brigadier-General Tytler in the operations which were conducted in the Zaimusht country. On the 8th a detachment was employed with other details, under Col. Gordon, in the destruction of the Watazai villages, and in the actions of Bagh and Zawa; on the 13th and 14th, the four companies (which formed part of the Right Column, commanded by Col. Gordon), were prominently engaged, capturing, on the former day, two most important positions, and repulsing the enemy's attack, in a close hand-to-hand conflict, with heavy loss. For the gallantry he displayed on this occasion Jemadar Fusl Ahmad was subsequently awarded the Order of Merit.

On the return of the Zaimusht expeditionary force, the regiment was ordered to Shalozan, and continued to serve in and about the Kuram Valley till its evacuation by British forces.

The undermentioned officers of the 29th Regt. (Punjab) Bengal Native Infantry served in the war :—

Colonel J. J. H. Gordon, C.B., commanded the regiment throughout both campaigns. Took part in the reconnaissance of 28 Nov., 1878, the assault and capture of the Peiwar Kotal, and the Zaimusht expedition, including the action of Zawa, in which he commanded a column of the Expeditionary force. (Twice mentioned in despatches ; C.B.)

Majors E. Beddy and *C. E. D. Branson* served with the regiment in the second campaign. *Major Branson* was present at the actions of Ali Khel and Zawa, and for his services was mentioned in despatches.

Lt.-Colonel G. N. Channer, V.C., served with the regiment in the first campaign till 1 Jan., 1879, taking part in the reconnaissance of 28 Nov., 1878, and the assault and capture of the Peiwar Kotal. (Mentioned in despatches; Brevet of Lt.-Colonel.)

Captain F. R. C. Voyle served with the regiment throughout the first campaign, taking part in the reconnaissance of 28 Nov., and the assault and capture of Peiwar Kotal.

Bt. Major A. J. F. Reid served with the regiment in the first campaign till disabled, taking part in the reconnaissance of 28 Nov., 1878, in which he received a severe and dangerous wound in the loins while leading his company against the enemy's position. Served with the regiment during the second campaign, taking part in the action of Zawa. Subsequently, from Jan., 1881, till the evacuation of Kandahar, served with the S. Afghanistan F.F. (Mentioned in despatches; Brevet of Major.)

Lieuts. R. W. Macleod and *H. P. Picot* served with the regiment in both campaigns, taking part in the reconnaissance of 28 Nov., 1878, the assault and capture of the Peiwar Kotal, and the actions of Ali Khel and Zawa. Both officers were mentioned, for their services, in despatches.

Major R. H. F. Rennick (attached) crossed the frontier with the regiment 21 Nov., 1878, and after arrival at Kuram Fort was appointed Staff Officer to the garrison. On 27 Dec., 1878, was appointed Political Officer of the Hariab, and served in that capacity till 30th June, 1879. Proceeded to Ali Khel, thirteen miles in advance of the British outposts, 29 Dec., 1878, and with an escort of 25 men remained there, in the midst of a hostile and fanatical population, throughout the winter. Broke up the hostile combination of Jagis and Mangals, threatening the Peiwar garrison, in Jan., 1879. Opened up and conducted the negotiations with the Ghilzai chief, Padshah Khan, which materially contributed to the acceptance by the Amir of the terms of the treaty of Gandamak.

30TH REGT. (PUNJAB) BENGAL NATIVE INFANTRY.

ON the 25th Sept., 1879, the 30th Regt. P.N.I. marched from Firozpur for service in Afghanistan, and on the 20th Oct. reached Landi Kotal, in the Khyber: there it remained till the 16th Dec., when it was moved forward to occupy the posts of Daka and Basawal, the Head-quarters, under Colonel Boisragon, holding the former, and 200 men, under Lt.-Colonel Campbell, proceeding to the latter, each officer commanding, respectively, the post occupied by him.

On the 15th Jan., 1880, the 30th P.N.I. formed part of the column under Col. Boisragon which was sent to attack the Mohmands who had crossed the Kabul River and occupied the Gara Heights in great force. The enemy were driven back with heavy loss, and pursued to Kam Daka, where they recrossed the river. While employed on this expedition, the regiment camped out four days without tents.

On the 22nd Jan., 1880, the 30th P.N.I. marched from Daka and Basawal to join the column in course of formation at Jalalabad for service in the Lughman Valley, and subsequently advancing with the expeditionary force, took part in the various operations which were conducted in that district till the 16th March, when it returned to Jalalabad.

On the 18th March, 1880, the regiment proceeded to Lataband, and remained there till the evacuation of the advanced posts on the Khyber line. On the 10th Aug., 1880, it commenced its return march to India, and on the 29th idem recrossed the frontier.

The undermentioned officers of the 30th (Punjab) Bengal Native Infantry served in the war:—

Major-General T. W. R. Boisragon, C.B. (retired), commanded the regiment during the campaign till 4 March, 1880. Commanded the Daka Column in the operations against the Mohmands in Jan., 1880, including the storming of the Gara heights. (Mentioned in despatches; received the thanks of the Commander-in-Chief; C.B.)

Lt.-Colonel R. D. Campbell served with the regiment throughout the period it was employed in the war, commanding it from the 4th March, 1880; also commanded the posts of Basawal and Lataband.

Major H. W. Webster, Captains W. G. C. Halkett and *G. F. Young*, and *Lieut. F. G. L. Mainwaring* served with the regiment throughout the period it was employed in the war, being present at the storming of the Gara Heights, in which *Major Webster* commanded the advanced line of skirmishers. *Lieut. Mainwaring* also served during the first campaign with the Transport Dept. in the Khyber.

Lieut. F. C. Maisey. (For services see "Staff.")

Lieut. F. S. St. Quintin, Leicestershire Regt. (attached), served with the regiment during the campaign from May, 1880, till its return to India.

31ST REGT. (PUNJAB) BENGAL NATIVE INFANTRY.

IN the middle of September, 1879, the 31st Regt. P.N.I. quitted Rawal Pindi for service in Afghanistan, and on the 2nd Oct. arrived at Landi Khana. Throughout the remainder of the campaign it served at various posts on the Khyber line extending to Jagdalak, in the columns commanded by Brigadier-Generals Doran, Arbuthnot, and Sale Hill.

On the 26th March, 1880, 150 men of the regiment under Lieut. Angelo halted at Fort Battye while *en route* for a more advanced station. During the night the post was attacked in a most determined manner by large numbers of Shinwaris and Kugianis. The attack was brilliantly repulsed by the little garrison after a sharp hand-to-hand encounter, in which Lieut. Angelo and three men of the regiment were killed, and several others wounded.

From the 4th till the 6th April, 1880, the regiment took part in the operations which were conducted against the Wazir Kugianis by the force under Brigadier-General Arbuthnot, and, shortly afterwards, in the operations which were conducted in the Hissarak Valley, on several occasions being engaged in sharp skirmishes with the enemy.

On the 31st May the 31st P.N.I. marched with the moveable column under Brigadier-General Arbuthnot from Jagdalak, *en route* for the Lughman Valley. During the operations which were carried out in that district in the early days of June the regiment occupied the camp on the right bank of the Kabul River.

A detachment of the regiment, consisting of 94 rifles, accompanied the force under Colonel Ball Acton, 51st L.I., which marched from Pezwan in the last week in July, 1880, and destroyed the Ghilzai villages of Nargusai, Arab Khel, and Jokan, as punishment for various raids which had been made by the tribes on convoys.

On the evacuation of Kabul and the advanced posts on the Khyber line, the regiment returned to Peshawar.

The undermentioned officers served in the 31st Regt. (Punjab) Bengal Native Infantry during the period it was employed in the war:—

Bt. Lt.-Colonel F. Tweddell (in command), *Major E. W. Smyth, Captains A. C. G. Lydiard* and *B. C. Graves*, and *Lieuts. M. I. Gibbs* and *J. L. O'Bryen*.

For services of *Colonel H. M. Wemyss*, C.B., see "Staff," and of *Lieut. F. C. C. Angelo* (killed in action) see Biographical Division.

32ND REGT. (PUNJAB) BENGAL NATIVE INFANTRY (PIONEERS)

ON the outbreak of the Afghan war the 32nd Regt. P.N.I. was at Quetta, where it had been engaged since January, 1878, in constructing the defences of the Fort, and had suffered much from the malarious climate.

As the Pioneer battalion of General Biddulph's Division of the Army of Invasion, the regiment took part in the advance of that force on the 20th Nov., 1878, and on the 12th Dec. reached the Khojak Kotal, where it was for some time employed—in severe cold, and with scanty field kit—in improving the road. At the latter end of December the services of the regiment were lent to the 1st Division, and for several days it was actively engaged in the construction of the road over the Gwaja Pass. It eventually took part in the advance by that route on Kandahar, and on the 2nd Jan., 1879, formed the rear-guard, and protected the baggage at the action of Takht-i-pul. On the 8th the regiment arrived with the rest of the troops at the southern capital. For the good work it had done during the past month it received the cordial acknowledgments of the Lieut.-General.

On the 16th Jan. the 32nd P.N.I. marched with General Biddulph's Division for the Halmand and Girishk, and from the 2nd till the 22nd Feb. was engaged in road-making and bridging the river. On the latter date the Division commenced its return march for Kandahar, where it arrived on the 2nd March, and was broken up.

As a unit of the 2nd Column of the Thal-Chotiali F.F., the regiment took part in the return march by the new route to India, first, however, assisting in subduing the Kakar Pathans, a tribe which had continually threatened Quetta. Though no enemy was encountered by the column during its march to the frontier, the regiment was pretty constantly engaged in overcoming the physical obstacles presented by the country traversed, on several occasions working at night. On the 25th April it reached Mithankot, and eventually made its way to Jhelum, where it arrived on the 19th May, 1879.

During the first campaign the regiment lost by death, 1 British and 2 native officers, and 96 rank and file, the mortality being mainly attributable to pneumonia.

Detailed during the second campaign to serve as the Pioneer battalion of the Reserve Division at Peshawar, the 32nd P.N.I. left Jhelum on the 9th Jan., 1880, but on arriving at its destination in February, it was ordered on to Landi Kotal, where it joined the Khyber Line Force. In April, 1880, it was moved on to Pesh Bolak, leaving detachments *en route*

The 32nd P.N.I. formed part of the moveable column under Brigadier-General Gib which marched into the Mazina Valley on the 18th May, 1880, to disperse the gathering under Ghulam Ahmad, and on the 26th was engaged at the action of Mazina. The regiment was mentioned in warm terms for the manner in which it fought as well as worked. Its casualties in the action were 3 men wounded.

From the 28th May till the 8th June the 32nd P.N.I. was absent on the Kama expedition, taking part in the various operations which were conducted within that period on the north side of the Kabul River. After the return of the expeditionary force the regiment remained serving on the Khyber line till the evacuation in August, when it marched back to India, and went into quarters at Rawal Pindi.

The undermentioned officers of the 32nd Regt. (Punjab) Bengal Native Infantry (Pioneers) served in the war:—

Lt.-Colonel H. Fellowes (Deceased. See Biographical Division).

Major C. E. Bates served with the regiment during the first campaign till invalided at Quetta.

Bt. Lt.-Colonel A. C. W. Crookshank served with the regiment throughout the period it was employed in the war, officiating in command of it from the date of the death of Lt.-Colonel Fellowes (5 May, 1879), and taking part in the advance on and occupation of Kandahar, the action of Takht-i-pul, the advance to the Halmand, the return march to India by the Thal-Chotiali route, the action of Mazina, and the operations in Kama. (Mentioned in despatches; Brevet of Lt.-Colonel.)

Captain A. P. Samuells (Deceased. See Biographical Division).

Major T. Nicholls served with the regiment from Dec., 1878, *Captain H. C. Halkett* and *Lieut. C. Hogge* throughout the period it was employed in the war. Took part in the advance on and occupation of Kandahar, the action of Takht-i-pul, the advance to the Halmand, the return-march to India by the Thal-Chotiali route, the action of Mazina, and the operations in Kama.

Major E. C. S. Jackson served with the Depôt at Quetta till invalided 28 Feb., 1879.

Lieut C. B. Porter served with the regiment in the first campaign till invalided in April, 1879.

Lieut. W. H. Allen, Cheshire Regt. (attached), and *Lieut. E. De Brath, the Buffs (attached)*, served with the regiment in the second campaign, being present at the action of Mazina, and taking part in the operations in Kama.

39TH REGT. BENGAL NATIVE INFANTRY.

THE 39th Regt. N.I. left Mirat by rail on the 13th Nov., 1878, for Multan, where it arrived on the 15th idem; it was shortly afterwards, however, sent back to Lawrencepur, and remained at that station from the 13th Jan. till the 18th March, 1879. On that date it was ordered to proceed to Ali Musjid; and arriving at its destination on the 28th idem, was taken on the strength of the 2nd Division Peshawar Valley F.F., under the command of General Maude.

After the signing of the Gandamak treaty, the regiment remained at Ali Musjid, as a unit of the Khyber Brigade.

On the renewal of hostilities in the autumn of 1879, the 39th N.I. formed part of the 3rd Brigade Jalalabad F.F.—a designation afterwards changed to the 2nd (Khyber) Division Kabul F.F. The hard work performed during the previous months, however, and the unhealthiness of the district in which it had served, shortly afterwards resulted in an amount of sickness so excessive as to necessitate the regiment being ordered back to India—its sick-list showing at one time the appalling total of 480 cases of fever, and a daily average, during the last four months of the year, of 452·88; the deaths in the same period amounting to 75.

On the 1st Nov., 1879, the 39th N.I. left Ali Musjid for Naushahra, where it arrived on the 8th idem. After recovering in health from the change of climate, the regiment furnished, for a period of six months, the Doaba outposts.

The undermentioned officers of the 39th Regt. Bengal Native Infantry took part in the war:—

Colonel G. W. Fraser commanded the 3rd Infantry Brigade, 2nd Division, Peshawar Valley F.F., from 18 April till 3 June, 1879, and the Khyber Brigade from 8 July till 9 Sept., 1879. Commanded the regiment at Ali Musjid from 3 June till 6 July, 1879, and also from 27 Sept. till 1 Nov., 1879.

Major F. Gellie served with the regiment during the period it was employed in the war as Offg. Commandant and Offg. 2nd in command, from 24 Aug. till 2 Nov., 1879.

Major H. O. Cumberlege served with the regiment in both campaigns, commanding it for a time during the interval between them. Was also Station Staff Officer at Ali Musjid.

Captain A. T. Banon. (For services see "Staff.")

Captain R. G. Handcock served with the regiment, as Adjutant, from March till Nov., 1879, in both campaigns.

Lieut. C. W. Harris served with the regiment in the second campaign, and afterwards with the 17th N.I. at Kandahar.

Lieut. A. L. Pennington. (For services see 5th Fusiliers.)

41ST REGT. BENGAL NATIVE INFANTRY.

THE 41st Regt. N.I. proceeded on field service from Morar, Gwalior, on the 5th Jan., 1880, and joined the Reserve Division at Peshawar.

Till the middle of March, 1880, the regiment garrisoned Fort Jamrud.

On the Reserve Division being broken up, the 41st N.I. was moved forward to Landi Kotal, and joined the Khyber Line Force. During the succeeding months it supplied detachments for Ali Musjid and Landi Khana.

The regiment remained serving in the Khyber till the final evacuation of the Pass in March, 1881, when it returned to India.

The undermentioned officers of the 41st Regt. Bengal Native Infantry served in the war:—

Colonel H. S. Obbard commanded the regiment and commanded at Landi Kotal, till 11 June, 1880, when he vacated his appointment on obtaining Colonel's allowance.

Lt.-Colonel H. S. Tucker, C.B. (For services see "Staff.")

Major V. W. Tregear served with the regiment throughout the period it was employed in the war, first as 2nd in command, and afterwards from 11 June, 1880, as Officiating Commandant. Served also as Provost Marshal to the 3rd Brigade Reserve Division.

Captains H. M. Rose and *B. Wemyss*, and *Lieut. G. H. Watson* served with the regiment throughout the period it was employed in the war. Captain Rose commanded the detachment at Ali Musjid, and Captain Wemyss the detachment at Landi Khana. The latter also served as Provost Marshal to the Khyber Brigade.

Lieut. C. F. Vyse served as Officiating Deputy Assistant Commissary-General with the Kuram Valley F.F. from Oct., 1879, till invalided in Feb., 1880. Rejoined the regiment in the Khyber 23 June, 1880, but again had to return to India five days afterwards in consequence of a stroke of heat apoplexy.

45TH REGT. BENGAL NATIVE INFANTRY (RATTRAY'S SIKHS).

THE 45th Sikhs was stationed at Alipore, Calcutta, when in October, 1878, it received orders to proceed to Peshawar on service. On arriving at its destination it joined the 4th Brigade Khyber Field Force, and till the evacuation of Kabul in August, 1880, served with the armies operating in Northern Afghanistan.

During the earlier portion of the first campaign the regiment held Jamrud, keeping open the communications with Ali Musjid, and for some weeks performing very heavy escort and convoy duties, being frequently engaged in skirmishes with the enemy.

In December, 1878, the 45th Sikhs advanced to Daka, where it remained till March, 1879. At the latter end of that month it moved forward to Jalalabad, and joined the 2nd Brigade, 1st Division, under the command of Brigadier-General Tytler. During this interval 114 men of the regiment, under Lieut. McRea, took part in the 1st Bazar Valley expedition, and Head-quarters and three companies, under Lt.-Colonel Armstrong, took part in the second Bazar Valley expedition.

On the 2nd April, 1879, three companies of the regiment, under Major Woodruffe, were engaged in the action of Futtehabad.

In May, 1879, on the return of the troops from the advanced posts to India, the regiment formed part of the rear-guard brigade, which marched from Gandamak to Jalalabad under Brigadier-General Tytler, and from Jalalabad to Landi Kotal under Lt.-Colonel Armstrong, 45th Sikhs. Landi Kotal was reached on the 24th June, 1879, and at that post the regimen tremained, serving as a unit of the Khyber Brigade, throughout the interval between the first and second campaigns.

On the renewal of hostilities in the autumn of 1879, the 45th Sikhs formed part of the 2nd Brigade Khyber Division, under the command of Brigadier-General Arbuthnot.

Participating in the forward movement of the troops on the Khyber line, in view of the advance of Brigadier-General C. Gough's Brigade to the relief of Sherpur, the 45th Sikhs marched from Jalalabad and

Gandamak, where it had been serving in half-battalions, to Jagdalak, and took part in the fighting with the forces under Azmatallah Khan, which occurred in the neighbourhood of that post in December, 1879. The regiment afterwards held during the severe winter the posts of Jagdalak and Seh Baba until March, 1880, when it received orders to join Sir F. Roberts' Head-quarters at Sherpur.

On the 25th April, 1880, the regiment marched out from Sherpur with the force under Brigadier-General sent to the relief of Colonel Jenkins, and took part in the second action of Charasiab, two companies remaining behind to guard the Sang-i-Nawishta defile.

In May, 1880, the 45th Sikhs and 67th Foot, under the command of Lt.-Colonel Armstrong, marched from Kabul to Jagdalak, to hold in check Azmatallah Khan, who was at the time threatening the line of communications. After successfully performing its mission, the force returned to Kabul on the 16th June.

The regiment remained at Kabul till the final evacuation of that city in August, 1880, when it took part in the return march of the troops to Peshawar, as a unit of the Rear-guard Brigade.

The undermentioned officers of the 45th Regt. Bengal Native Infantry (Rattray's Sikhs) served in the war :—

Lt.-Colonel F. M. Armstrong, C.B., commanded the regiment throughout both campaigns: in the second Bazar Valley expedition, the engagement with Azmatallah Khan at Jagdalak, and the action of Charasiab. (Mentioned in despatches; C.B.)

Lt.-Colonel C. L. Woodruffe, and *Lieuts. H. N. McRae* and *H. R. L. Holmes* served with the regiment throughout both campaigns: *Lt.-Colonel Woodruffe* commanding the wing engaged at the action of Futtehabad and taking part in the action of Charasiab (mentioned in despatches; Brevet of Lt.-Colonel); *Lieut. McRae* taking part in both the Bazar Valley expeditions (in command of the detachment engaged, in the first), the engagement at Jagdalak, and the action of Charasiab (mentioned in despatches); and *Lieut. Holmes* taking part in the second Bazar expedition (in which he was severely wounded while in command of a company covering the retirement), the action of Futtehabad (in which he was struck by a spent ball), the engagement at Jagdalak, and the action of Charasiab (mentioned in despatches).

Captain R. J. Waller served with the regiment in both campaigns, taking part in the action of Futtehabad, the engagement at Jagdalak, and the action of Charasiab.

Lieut. R. C. S. McCausland served with the regiment in the first campaign, till invalided. Took part in the first Bazar Valley expedition.

Lieut. F. M. Barclay. (Died of wounds. See Biographical Division.)

Lieut. J. M. A. Retallick served with the 25th K.O.Bs. in the first campaign, taking part in the second Bazar Valley expedition. Joined the 45th Sikhs at Jalalabad in Dec., 1879, and served with the regiment till the conclusion of the campaign, taking part in the engagement at Jagdalak and the action of Charasiab.

1st GOORKHA REGT. (LIGHT INFANTRY).

UNDER the command of Colonel J. S. Rawlins, the 1st Goorkhas L.I. moved from Dhurmsala, Lahore Division, in September, 1878, to form part of the force under Sir Donald Stewart assembled at Multan. Arrived there on the 9th Nov., the regiment railed to Sukkur, trans Indus, where it was employed till the 25th Dec. in guarding the Siege Train, and loading and storing supplies and munitions of war.

During the month of December the 1st Goorkhas moved in several detachments towards Kandahar, the Head-quarters, under Col. Sale Hill (Colonel Rawlins having been invalided), marching on the 26th in charge of the Quetta Field Park and a large ordnance convoy, the other detachments preceding it, escorting sections of the Siege Train and Treasure. The regiment finally assembled at Kandahar on the 13th Feb., 1879, forming part of the brigade under Brigadier-General Nuttall, and furnishing the rear and out-look picquets to the force, as well as numerous detachments as escorts, convoys, and foraging parties in the Kalat-i-Ghilzai direction and Argandab Valley. The work performed by the regiment up to and during this period was of the most arduous and harassing description, the difficulties encountered, especially in crossing the Khoja Mountains, being enhanced by the inclemency of the weather and heavy snow-falls.

On the 26th Feb., 1879, the regiment left Kandahar, forming part of the force detailed to return to

India by the Thal-Chotiali route under Major-General Biddulph, and was attached to No. 2 Column. During the march the 1st Goorkhas almost invariably furnished the vanguard, a duty which entailed very harassing work, all heights having to be crowned, and the country reconnoitred. At Nahar-ki-kot the force was broken up; and on the 11th April the regiment marched to India viâ the Chachar Pass, and finally reached its station, Dhurmsala, on 8th May, 1879.

In compliance with telegraphic orders, the 1st Goorkhas L.I., under the command of Colonel Sale Hill, again marched on service from Dhurmsala on the 26th Dec., 1879, and on the 22nd Jan., 1880, arrived at Fort Jamrud, where it was posted to 2nd Brigade Reserve Division, Lt.-Colonel Story now assuming command *vice* Colonel Sale Hill, who was appointed a Brigadier-General in the Field.

The regiment was employed during the months of February and March in guarding the Khyber Pass and furnishing escorts and convoys, one company, under Lieut. Kempster, being detached at the latter end of March to escort Mr. Scott while surveying to the North-East of the Kabul River and the country adjacent to the Sumshai Pass and the Shiliman Range.

On the Reserve Division being broken up, the 1st Goorkhas L.I. was attached to the No. 1 Moveable Column at Safed Sang, and took part with it in the Kuggia and Hissarak expeditions, and the operations in the Lughman Valley.

Subsequently to these operations, from the 16th June till the breaking up of the Khyber Line Force on the 10th Aug., 1880, the regiment was employed in keeping the line of communication, and stationed at Jagdalak Kotal and Seh Baba, was constantly engaged in patrolling, and crowning the heights for, and guarding convoys. These duties were effectively performed; and during the whole period, the safety of the road was thoroughly secured.

On the 11th Aug., 1880, the regiment commenced its return march to India, and after re-crossing the frontier, eventually made its way back to Dhurmsala, where it arrived on the 26th Sept., 1880.

The undermentioned officers of the 1st Goorkha Regt. (Light Infantry) served in the war:—

Major-General J. S. Rawlins (*retired*), commanded the regiment in its advance to Sukkur, where he was invalided.

Colonel R. Sale Hill, C.B., commanded the regiment throughout the first campaign, and the No. 2 Column Thal-Chotiali F.F. during the return march to India. In the second campaign commanded, first the 2nd Brigade Reserve Division, and subsequently the 3rd Section Khyber Line Force and the No. 1 Moveable Column from the dates of their formation till they were respectively broken up. (Mentioned in despatches; C.B.)

Lt.-Colonel P. Story served with the regiment throughout the period it was employed in the war, during the first campaign, as 2nd in command, and during the second campaign, in command, taking part in the Kuggia and Hissarak expeditions.

Major G. Young joined the regiment in N. Afghanistan from sick leave in April, 1880, and officiated as 2nd in command till the conclusion of the campaign.

Major C. St. J. B. Barnett, and *Lieuts. J. P. W. Spankie* (*3rd Goorkha Regt.*) and *G. H. Robinson* served with the regiment throughout the period it was employed in the war, taking part in the Kuggia, Hissarak, and Lughman Valley expeditions.

Captain G. F. Churchill, and *Lieuts. R. C. Temple* and *H. H. Ozzard* (*14th B.N.I.*) served with the regiment throughout the first campaign.

Lieut. F. J. Kempster, Royal Canadians (*attached*), served with the regiment throughout the period it was employed in the second campaign, taking part in Kuggia, Hissarak, and Lughman Valley expeditions. Acted as Orderly Officer to Brigadier-General Sale Hill from 19 Jan. till 25 Feb., 1880.

Lieut. E. W. F. Martin, Border Regt. (*attached*), served with the regiment throughout the period it was employed in the second campaign, taking part in the Kuggia and Hissarak expeditions.

2ND (P.W.O.) GOORKHA REGT.

IMMEDIATELY on the return to India of the Malta and Cyprus expeditionary force, the 2nd Goorkhas, which formed a portion of it, was ordered on service to Afghanistan, and making its way to Ali Musjid, arrived there in December, 1878, within a fortnight of the capture of the fort by the British.

In the third week in December, 1878, 500 men of the regiment, under Col. Macintyre, took part with Brigadier-General Doran's column in the operations which were conducted by General Maude in the first expedition into the Bazar Valley. During the return march on the 22nd of that month, one Goorkha was mortally wounded.

From the 25th Jan. till the 4th Feb., 1879, 312 men of the regiment under Col. Macintyre took part with Brigadier-General Appleyard's column in the second expedition into the Bazar Valley. In a rear-guard attack which was ably repelled by a detachment under Major Battye on the 26th, two Goorkhas were wounded, and in a skirmish with the enemy during the retirement from Halwai on the 28th, after the destruction of the towers, one Goorkha was killed and one wounded.

In March, 1879, the 2nd Goorkhas was moved forward through the Khyber Pass to Basawal. On the 24th of that month 50 men of the regiment under Captain Becher formed part of the force under Brigadier-General Tytler which defeated the Mohmands with heavy loss at Deh Sarak, a second detachment arriving on the field later in the day.

The regiment remained at Basawal, with a detachment of two companies at Barikab, till after the signing of the treaty of Gandamak, when it marched back to India, recrossing the frontier on the 9th June, 1879, and returning to Dehra Dun.

On the renewal of hostilities in the autumn of 1879, the 2nd Goorkhas was again ordered on service, and as a unit of Brigadier-General C. Gough's Brigade advanced through the Khyber Pass to Daka, Jalalabad, and Gandamak, where Head-quarters arrived at the latter end of October. During November, and again in the early days of December, the regiment was employed on outpost duty, separate wings occupying Pezwan and Jagdalak Fort, and furnishing Jagdalak Kotal with a detachment of 40 rifles. On the 19th of that month 187 men of the regiment, under Captain Becher, formed part of the force under Col. Norman, 24th P.N.I., which defeated with heavy loss a large body of Ghilzais. On that day the regiment was reunited at Jagdalak; and on the 21st idem it marched with Brigadier-General C. Gough's brigade for Sherpur, where it arrived on the 24th Dec., 1878, and remained till the evacuation of Kabul in August, 1879.

On the 25th April, 1879, 104 men of the 2nd Goorkhas, under Captain Hill, accompanied Brigadier-General Macpherson's column into the Chardeh plain in support of Col. Jenkins' force, which was engaged in the neighbourhood of Charasiab. In the action which ensued, the detachment, leading, with the 92nd Highlanders, the other units of the column, performed highly distinguished service in the right attack, capturing the enemy's principal standard, and subsequently rushing the orchards in which the Afghans took up their second position.

Forming part of Macpherson's Brigade of the Kabul-Kandahar Field Force, the 2nd Goorkhas took part, in the month of August, 1880, in the advance to the relief of the Southern capital. In the crowning defeat of the enemy at the battle of Kandahar on the 1st Sept. the regiment, as one of the two leading battalions of the 1st Brigade, played a conspicuous part, being engaged in the successive captures of the villages of Gandi Mullah Sahibdad and Pir Paimal, and finally assisting in carrying the entrenched position on which the enemy made their final stand. The casualties of the regiment on this day were, 8 men killed, and Lt.-Colonel Battye and 21 men wounded.

On the reconstitution of the forces in Southern Afghanistan, the regiment marched for India, and eventually returned to its old quarters at Dehra Dun.

The undermentioned officers of the 2nd (P.W.O,) Goorkha Regt. served in the war :—

Major-General D. Macintyre, V.C. (retired), commanded the regiment during the first campaign till invalided in May, 1879, taking part in both the Bazar Valley expeditions. (Mentioned in despatches.)

Lt.-Colonel A. Battye, C.B., served with the regiment throughout both campaigns, commanding it from May, 1879, during the first, and throughout the second campaign, taking part in the first Bazar Valley expedition, the fighting at Jagdalak, the advance to the relief of Sherpur, the march from Kabul to the relief of Kandahar, and the battle of Kandahar, in which he was wounded. (Three times mentioned in despatches; Brevet of Lt.-Colonel; C.B.)

Major H. P. P. Nash, Bt. Lt.-Colonel S. E. Becher, Captain W. P. Newall, and *Lieut. H. S. Wheatley* served with the regiment throughout both campaigns, taking part in the operations in the Bazar Valley, the fighting at Jagdalak, the advance to the relief of Sherpur, the march from Kabul to the relief of Kandahar, and the battle of Kandahar. *Lt.-Colonel Becher* was also present, in command of a detachment, at the action of Deh Sarak. For his services he was three times mentioned in despatches, and received the Brevet of Lt.-Colonel.

Bt. Major W. Hill and *Lieut. E. Travers* served with the regiment throughout the second campaign, taking part in the fighting at Jagdalak, the advance to the relief of Sherpur, the march from Kabul to the relief of Kandahar, and the battle of Kandahar. *Bt. Major Hill* was also present, in command of a detachment, at the second action of Charasiab. For his services he was mentioned in despatches, and received the Brevet of Major. *Lieut. Travers* was also mentioned in despatches.

3RD GOORKHA REGT. (KEMAOON BATTALION.)

ON the 12th Oct., 1878, the 3rd Goorkha Regt. marched from Almora to Bareilly, and proceeding thence to Mithankot, made its way by the Dera Bughti route to Dadar. The marches through the deep, hot sands, and over the waterless tracts of the desert were long and tedious, at times extending to 28 and 30 miles in length. Arrived at its destination, the regiment joined Sir Donald Stewart's Division of the Army of Invasion, and was posted to the 2nd Infantry Brigade under Brigadier-General Hughes, with which it continued to serve throughout the ensuing campaign.

The 3rd Goorkhas marched by wings through the Bolan Pass to Quetta, Kandahar, and Kalat-i-Ghilzai, the Head-quarters and Left wing escorting 5/11, R.A., from Quetta to Kandahar, and the Right wing performing like duty with 6/11, R.A., from Dadar. The draught cattle becoming unfitted for work, the Goorkhas, associated with detachments of the 59th Foot and 60th Rifles, supplied the deficiency with manual labour, dragging the heavy artillery through water and shingle and over rock and sand. The work was of the most severe description, one march of 22 miles occupying 20 hours in accomplishing it.

The Head-quarters and Left wing of the regiment returned from Kalat-i-Ghilzai by way of the Arghazan Valley to Kandahar in the depth of winter, arriving at its destination, after suffering great privations from exposure to the snow and from difficulties of transport and supplies, on the 22nd Feb., 1879. On that day the Right wing, in its turn, commenced the return journey, and on the 2nd March, 1879, rejoined regimental Head-quarters.

From the dates of its return, the 3rd Goorkhas formed part of the garrison of Kandahar, the men constantly working on fatigue and escort duty. In June the regiment suffered from an epidemic of fever, and in July, from an epidemic of cholera, in consequence of which six companies moved into the cholera camp, with good result. The total number of deaths in the regiment from this disease amounted to 42, 7 camp followers also succumbing.

On the 1st Aug., 1879, the Head-quarters and Right wing, as escort to 5/11, R.A., left Kandahar for Quetta, where they arrived on the 16th idem, the heat during the march having ranged up to 115° in tents. On the 3rd Sept. the left wing also quitted the Southern capital for the same destination, but had only proceeded three marches when it received orders, in consequence of the Kabul massacre, to return, which it did with all speed. On the 23rd Sept. it marched with Brigadier-General Hughes' Brigade for Kalat-i-Ghilzai and Shah Jui; and at the action fought at that place on the 24th Oct. formed a portion of the reserve. On the 26th idem it commenced its return march for Kandahar. In the meantime the Head-quarters and Right wing had been delayed at Quetta for want of carriage ; but the difficulty being at length surmounted, it commenced its march, and forming an escort for treasure, arrived at Kandahar on the 21st Nov., 1879.

The regiment remained at Kandahar till 31st March, 1880, on which date it marched, as a unit of Sir Donald Stewart's Division, for Ghazni. On the 19th April it was engaged at the battle of Ahmad Khel, forming the extreme left of the line of Infantry, and rendering signal service by forming up into rallying squares at the critical moment when the Ghazi rush swept back the Cavalry on the skirmishers. In the official despatch bearing date 28 May, 1880, the following passage occurs : "Sir Donald Stewart refers to the resolute firmness with which the key of the position was held by the 2nd Sikhs and 3rd Goorkhas under Brigadier-General Hughes' direction, when the right of the line was pushed back." Ghazni was entered on the 20th April, and two days afterwards the regiment was present at the bombardment of the Arzu villages.

Taking part in the advance of the Division into the Logar Valley, where the command of it was made over to General Hills, the 3rd Goorkhas continued with it in that district throughout the succeeding summer.

On the evacuation of Kabul in August, 1880, the regiment took part in the trying return march of Sir Donald Stewart's force by the Khyber route to India, recrossing the frontier on the 9th Sept., 1880, and eventually making its way to Lahore in time to take part in the Viceroy's durbar.

On the departure of Sir Donald Stewart's Division from Kandahar, the 3rd Goorkhas furnished a body of signallers, which, under the command of Captain E. B. Bishop, was constantly on duty from the date of its formation till the date of the arrival of the regiment at Peshawar.

The undermentioned officers of the third Goorkha (Kemaoon) Regt. served in the war :

Major-General A. Paterson (retired), commanded the regiment in the first campaign, and till the 7th Oct., 1879.

Colonel H. H. Lyster, C.B., V.C., served with the regiment throughout the period it was employed in the war, commanding it during the second campaign, from 8th Oct., 1879. Commanded the regiment at the battle of Ahmad Khel and the action of Arzu. (Mentioned in despatches; C.B.)

Majors G. C. Gregory and *R. E. K. Money*, and *Lieut. C. Pulley*, served with the regiment throughout the period it was employed in the war, the latter as Adjutant, being present at the battle of Ahmad Khel and the action of Arzu. *Major Money* commanded the detached wing which escorted 6/11, R.A., through the Bolan Pass to Kandahar.

Major L. Smith. (Deceased. See Biographical Division.)

Bt. Major E. B. Bishop served throughout both campaigns: in the first as Superintendent of Army Signalling with the advanced Cavalry, and as Orderly Officer to Brigadier-General Palliser, taking part in the advance on Kandahar and to the Halmand, and being present as Signalling Officer at the action of Takht-i-pul; and in the second campaign, with the 3rd Goorkhas, and as Signalling Officer to Brigadier-General Hughes, taking part in the advance on Ghazni and to Kabul, and the return march to India by the Khyber route, and being present at the battle of Ahmad Khel and the action of Arzu. (Mentioned in despatches; Brevet of Major.)

Lieut A. F. G. Browne served with the regiment in the first campaign, and till invalided from Quetta, 28 Oct., 1879.

Lieut. J. L. O'Bryen, 31st. P.N.I., served with the regiment in the first campaign, and till transferred to the 31st P.N.I. in Dec., 1879.

Lieut. J. A. S. Thomson, Leinster Regt. (attached), joined the regiment at Kandahar 27 March, 1880, and served with it till the conclusion of the campaign, being present at the battle of Ahmad Khel and the action of Arzu.

Lieut. G. H. Loch, Wiltshire Regt. (attached), joined the regiment in the Logar Valley 24 June, 1880, and served with it till the conclusion of the campaign. Acted as Orderly Officer to Brigadier-General Hughes from 5 to 23 Aug., 1880.

4TH GOORKHA REGT.

IN September, 1878, the 4th Goorkha Regt. received orders to hold itself in readiness to proceed on active service, and on the 2nd Oct. marched from Bukloh for Peshawar, under the command of Lt.-Colonel P. J. Turton.

As a unit of the 1st Brigade 1st Division Peshawar Valley F.F., the regiment was engaged, on the 21st and 22nd Nov., in the difficult flanking operations which were conducted by Brigadier-General Macpherson over the precipitous Rhotas heights in reverse of Ali Musjid, and which contributed to effecting the abandonment of the Fort and the retreat of the Afghan forces. Accompanying the subsequent advance of the Division through the Khyber, the 4th Goorkhas took part, successively, in the occupation of Daka, Jalalabad, and Gandamak.

In January, 1879, 200 picked men of the regiment under Major Rowcroft, forming a portion of Brigadier-General Tytler's Column, marched from Basawal on the second expedition into the Bazar Valley, and the 28th of that month, in the reconnaissance of the Bokhar Pass, were hotly engaged, the enemy contesting every hill-top for a distance of nearly five miles.

On the 31st March, 1879, 300 picked men of the 4th Goorkhas, under Major Rowcroft, took part in Brigadier-General Macpherson's expedition to the Lughman Valley, in pursuit of Azmatallah Khan, accomplishing a forced march of 26 hours' duration, in which 35 miles of most difficult country, including the almost inaccessible range of the Siah Koh, were covered.

The campaign concluded, the regiment commenced its return march to India from Gandamak on the 2nd June, and eventually reached Bukloh on the 13th July, having been detained four days in cholera camp at Jhelum. Though, in common with the other regiments of the Division, its sufferings during the march were intense, it was fortunate in losing no more than 11 fighting men and a like number of camp followers from the fell disease which claimed so many victims.

On the renewal of hostilities in the autumn of 1879, the 4th Goorkhas was again ordered to the front, and marching from Bukloh on the 25th Sept., under the command of Lt.-Colonel Rowcroft, reached Gandamak, after a week's detention at Jalalabad, on the 15th Nov.

As a unit of Brigadier-General Charles Gough's brigade, the regiment marched from Gandamak on the 14th Dec. to Jagdalak, and in the fighting which ensued in the neighbourhood of that post—notably in the affairs of the 17th and 18th Dec.—took a prominent part. Continuing with the Brigade in its advance to the relief of Sherpur, the regiment arrived with it at its destination on the 24th Dec. On the 1st Jan., 1879, it moved into the Bala Hissar, which was occupied by Brigadier-General C. Gough's brigade till the end of March.

In the middle of April, 1880, the 4th Goorkhas accompanied the force under General Ross which moved out from Kabul to co-operate with the division under Sir Donald Stewart advancing from Ghazni, and took part in the operations which were conducted by it in the Maidan and neighbouring districts. In the action of Shekabad, on the 25th April, one wing of the regiment was engaged with the column of all arms, under the command of Lt.-Colonel Rowcroft, which defeated the enemy on the hills above Zaidabad, driving them, with heavy loss, from their numerous strong positions; while the remaining four companies, under Major Mainwaring, were occupied on the extreme left, watching a large force which was threatening a flank attack. For the steadiness and intelligence the men displayed in this action, the regiment received warm commendation in the General's despatch.

In the middle of June, 1880, the 4th Goorkhas left Sherpur with Brigadier-General C. Gough's brigade for Pughman, and for the next six weeks, until the force was recalled to Sherpur in view of the evacuation of Kabul, took part with it in its various operations in the Koh Daman and surrounding districts. On the 28th June, four companies under Colonel Rowcroft, were engaged in the affair of Sofian, against Mir Butcha's levies, the result of a reconnaissance on the road towards Istalif.

As a portion of the 3rd Brigade of the Kabul-Kandahar F.F., the 4th Goorkhas took part, in August, 1880, in the memorable march to the relief of Kandahar. On the 31st Aug. the regiment occupied the centre of the position taken up by MacGregor's brigade in the village of Absabad when the Cavalry reconnaissance drew the enemy forward, and assisted in checking their advance by a well-directed fire; and after maintaining its position throughout the succeeding night, the regiment was engaged, on the 1st Sept., in the battle of Kandahar, a half-company under Jemadar Ramu Thappa, which was sent up by Col. Rowcroft to clear a hill on the arrival of the Brigade near Ayub's camp, particularly distinguishing itself, shooting or bayoneting every Ghazi of forty-six who remained to defend the height.

On the 8th Sept. the 4th Goorkhas marched with MacGregor's Brigade towards Quetta, and on the 16th idem formed part of a column of all arms which was detached at Killa Abdula, under the command of Col. Rowcroft, to restore order and collect supplies in the Panizai country. The column rejoined the brigade on the 27th Sept. at Kach, and the regiment subsequently took part with the latter in its expedition through the Marri country, eventually arriving at Rajanpur on the 16th Nov. From Rajanpur the regiment proceeded by rail to Umritsur, and from thence by route march to its own station, Bukloh, which it reached on the 9th Dec., 1880, after an absence of more than two years on service.

The undermentioned officers of the 4th Goorkha Regt. served in the war:—

Colonel J. P. Turton commanded the regiment during the first campaign till invalided, 31 May, 1879. Took part in the capture of Ali Musjid and the forcing of the Khyber Pass. (Mentioned in despatches.)

Lt.-Colonel F. F. Rowcroft, Commandant 44th Bengal L.I., served with the regiment throughout both campaigns, commanding it from the 1st June, 1879. Took part in the capture of Ali Musjid and forcing of the Khyber Pass, the second Bazar Valley expedition, the pursuit of Armatallah Khan, the advance to the relief of Sherpur, the fighting at Jagdalak, the action of Shekabad (in which he commanded a column), the march from Kabul to the relief of Kandahar, the reconnaissance of 31 Aug., 1880, the battle of Kandahar (wounded), and the operations against the Marris. (Three times mentioned in despatches.)

Major J. Hay served with the regiment throughout the first campaign, and during the second campaign from Feb. till May, 1880. Took part in the capture of Ali Musjid and forcing of the Khyber Pass, and the action of Shekabad. (Mentioned in despatches.)

Major E. P. Mainwaring rejoined the regiment from sick leave in Jan., 1879, and served with it during the remainder of the first and throughout the second campaign, taking part in the advance to the relief of Sherpur, the fighting at Jagdalak, the action of Shekabad, the march from Kabul to the relief of Kandahar, the battle of Kandahar, and the operations against the Marris. (Twice mentioned in despatches; Brevet of Major.)

Major G. W. Rogers served throughout both campaigns; in the first as Orderly Officer to Brigadier-General Tytler, and in the second with the regiment. Took part in the capture of Ali Musjid and forcing of the Khyber Pass, the second Bazar Valley expedition, the action of Deh Sarak, the fighting at Jagdalak, the advance to the relief of Sherpur, the action of Shekabad, the march from Kabul to the relief of Kandahar, the battle of Kandahar, the reconnaissance of 31 Aug., 1880, and the operations against the Marris. (Mentioned in despatches; Brevet of Major.)

Captain C. A. Mercer and *Lieut. H. J. Bolton* served with the regiment throughout both campaigns, taking part in the capture of Ali Musjid and the forcing of the Khyber Pass, the second Bazar Valley expedition, the advance to the relief of Sherpur, the fighting at Jagdalak, the action of Shekabad, the march from Kabul to the relief of Kandahar, the reconnaissance of 31 Aug., 1880, the battle of Kandahar, and the operations against the Marris. *Lieut. Bolton* also took part in the pursuit of Azmatallah Khan. (Both mentioned in despatches.)

Bt. Major N. R. Stewart. (For services see "Staff.")

Lieut. C. G. Adye, West Yorkshire Regt. (*attached*), served with the regiment during the first campaign, taking part in the capture of Ali Musjid and the forcing of the Khyber Pass.

5TH GOORKHA REGT. (HAZARA GOORKHA BATTALION).

THIS regiment was warned for active service on the 24th Sept., 1878, and on the 2nd Oct. marched from Abbottabad, where it was then stationed, *via* Kohat for Thal, arriving there on the 23rd Oct., and joining the Kuram F.F., under the command of General Roberts.

As a unit of the 2nd Brigade, commanded by Brigadier-General Thelwall, the 5th Goorkhas crossed the frontier into Afghanistan on the 22nd Nov., 1878. In the assault of the Peiwar Kotal, on the 2nd Dec., after taking part in the previous reconnaissance, the regiment was prominently engaged throughout the day, leading the advance in both the first and second turning movements carried out under General Roberts' personal command, and capturing in brilliant style the first of the enemy's stockades. On the 7th Dec. the 5th Goorkhas took part in the reconnaissance of the Shutargardan, returning to Ali Khel, whither the Division had advanced from the Peiwar Kotal, on the 11th. The following day the regiment accompanied the force under General Roberts which marched from Ali Khel for Fort Kuram, and on the 13th formed the rear-guard of the column which was attacked by hordes of Mangals in the Sapari defile. For nearly five hours it was engaged, over most difficult ground, with a bold and active enemy, thoroughly acquainted with the locality; but so successfully was its duty performed, that not a single baggage-animal or load was lost. "It is, therefore," writes General Roberts in his despatch, "my pleasure and my duty to bring the gallant conduct of this fine regiment to special notice." In this engagement Captain Powell, of the regiment, was mortally wounded, 3 Goorkha Sepoys were killed, and 11 wounded, 1 mortally.

The 5th Goorkhas passed the remainder of the winter in the Kuram Valley. In January, 1879, 200 men under Captain Cook accompanied General Roberts to Khost. On the 1st April the regiment proceeded again to Ali Khel, and joined the 2nd Brigade under Brigadier-General Cobbe; and from that advanced post, at the latter end of July, 1879, it marched to the Shutargardan as part of the escort of Sir P. L. N. Cavagnari.

Immediately after the receipt of news of the Kabul massacre, on the 8th Sept., the 5th Goorkhas marched from Ali Khel to Karatiga, and from there led the advance of the troops to Kushi, where the 2nd Brigade, under Brigadier-General Baker—of which the regiment became a unit—was formed. Taking part in the advance on Kabul of the newly-constituted Division under Sir F. Roberts' command on the 1st Oct., the regiment was employed during the crossing of the Logar River at Zaidabad on the 4th, in driving off the tribesmen who disputed the advance, and in the action of Charasiab, on the 6th, was again engaged, taking a prominent part both in the assault of the "Red Ridge" and the position on which the enemy made their final stand. On the 8th Oct. the regiment marched to the Shahr Darwaza hill, and remained there till the 12th, when it was brought down to occupy the upper portion of the Bala Hissar. Four days afterwards occurred the terrific explosion in the Amir's arsenal, causing the death of 1 native officer, 5 non-commissioned officers, and 6 rank and file. The regiment fell in, in good order, and took up a position half a mile from the fort. From the 17th Oct. till the middle of December, the men were employed at the Sherpur cantonment in building barracks, storing grain, and making preparations generally for the winter.

On the 8th Dec. the 5th Goorkhas, attached to a force under the command of Brigadier-General Macpherson, marched to the Surkh Kotal, and was engaged both in the defeat of the enemy at Karez Mir, on the 10th Dec., and again in the Chardeh Valley, on the following day. In the former action, Major Fitz-Hugh and 1 man were wounded; and in the latter, 1 man was killed and 2 wounded. On the 12th and 13th the regiment performed brilliant service in the assaults of the Takht-i-Shah, suffering a loss, on the first day, of 3 men killed, and Major Cook, V.C., and 6 men wounded, the former mortally.

On the 14th, after retaining possession during the previous night of the position gained, the regiment retired with the rest of the force within the lines of Sherpur, losing on this day 1 native officer and 2 men killed, and 2 men wounded. During the siege of Sherpur parties of the 5th Goorkhas took part in some of the sorties from the cantonment; and on the 23rd Dec. the regiment was engaged in the repulse of the enemy's attack.

In the 2nd week in May, 1880, the 5th Goorkhas marched from Sherpur with the force under Brigadier-General Baker into the Logar and Wardak Valleys, eventually returning to cantonments on the 15th June.

As a unit of the 2nd Brigade Kabul-Kandahar Field Force, the regiment took part, in the month of August, 1880, in the march to the relief of Kandahar, and on the 1st Sept. was engaged in the defeat of Ayub Khan's army.

On the 15th Sept., 1880, the 5th Goorkhas marched from Kandahar for Sibi, where it arrived on the 8th Oct. It there joined the force under Brigadier-General MacGregor, and marched with it in its expedition through the Marri country to Rajanpur, from whence it eventually made its way to Abbottabad, arriving on the 7th Dec., 1880, after an absence of over two years and two months on service.

The undermentioned officers of the 5th Goorkha Regt. (Hazara Goorkha Battalion) served in the war:—

Lt.-Colonel A. Fitz-Hugh, C.B., commanded the regiment throughout both campaigns: in the assault of the Peiwar Kotal, the affair in the Sapari defile, the actions of Charasiab, Surkh Kotal (wounded), Chardeh, and subsequent operations round Kabul and defence of Sherpur in Dec., 1879, the advance from Kabul to the relief of Kandahar, the battle of Kandahar, and the operations against the Marris. (Five times mentioned in despatches; Brevet of Lt.-Colonel; C.B.)

Lt.-Colonel J. Sym commanded the regiment during the intervals between the first and second campaigns, and served with it, as 2nd in command, throughout the second, taking part in the action of Charasiab, the operations round Kabul and defence of Sherpur in Dec., 1879, the march from Kabul to the relief of Kandahar, the battle of Kandahar, and the operations against the Marris. (Twice mentioned in despatches; Brevet of Lt.-Colonel.)

Major J. Cook, V.C. (Mortally wounded in action. See Biographical Division.)

Major E. Molloy served from 21 Oct., 1878, till 29 Oct., 1879, as Interpreter to the Lieutenant-General Commanding the Kandahar F.F.; from the 30th Oct., 1879, till the 20th Jan., 1880, as Political Officer at Kalat-i-Ghilzai; and from Feb., 1880, till the conclusion of the war, with the 5th Goorkhas. Took part in the original advance on and occupation of Kandahar and Kalat-i-Ghilzai, the second occupation of Kalat-i-Ghilzai, the advance from Kabul to the relief of Kandahar, the battle of Kandahar, and the operations against the Marris. (Mentioned in despatches; Brevet of Major.)

Captain C. F. Powell. (Mortally wounded in action. See Biographical Division.)

Lieuts. A. R. Martin, C. C. Chevenix-Trench, and *C. C. St. E. Lucas* served with the regiment throughout the war, taking part in the assault of the Peiwar Kotal, the affair in the Sapari defile, the action of Charasiab, the operations round Kabul and defence of Sherpur in Dec., 1879, the march from Kabul to the relief of Kandahar, the battle of Kandahar, and the operations against the Marris. For his services the former was three times mentioned in despatches, and the two latter twice.

Lieut. W. R. Yeilding served during the first campaign with the 1st Sikh Infantry, in the 1st Division Peshawar Valley F.F., taking part in the occupation of Jalalabad and the Khyber; and during the second campaign from Jan., 1880, with the 5th Goorkhas, taking part in the advance from Kabul to the relief of Kandahar, the battle of Kandahar, and the operations against the Marris.

Lieut. A. A. Barrett served with the 3rd Sikh Infantry throughout the second campaign, taking part in the defence of the Shutargardan, including the actions of 2 Oct. and 14 Oct., 1879, the operations round Kabul and defence of Sherpur in Dec., 1879, the advance from Kabul to the relief of Kandahar, the battle of Kandahar, and the operations against the Marris.

1ST REGT. PUNJAB CAVALRY.

IN October, 1878, the 1st Punjab Cavalry was warned for service, and made its way from Dera Ghazi Khan by the Dera Bughti route and Bolan Pass to Quetta. As a unit of General Biddulph's Division of the Army of Invasion, the regiment shortly afterwards entered Afghanistan, and for several weeks was actively employed in the reconnaissances which were conducted over a large area of the Pishin district.

Forming part of the Left column of the troops under Brigadier-General Palliser's command, the regiment, furnishing detachments for posts on the line of communications, accompanied the advance by the Ghwaja route on Kandahar, and on the 4th Jan., 1879, was engaged in the action of Takht-i-pul, one detachment, under Captain Atkinson, taking part in the rout of the Afghan Cavalry to the north of the Ghlo Kotal, and another detachment, under Captain Hervey, coming into contact with the enemy later in the day. Captain Atkinson, by the opportune aid he rendered in cutting down an Afghan who was aiming a carbine at close quarters at Captain Abadie, 9th Lancers, probably saved that officer's life. For their forward gallantry in the action 1 Jemadar and 3 Sowars were recommended in despatches for the Order of Merit. The casualties of the regiment were, 3 Sowars wounded, 1 horse killed, and 1 wounded.

The 1st Punjab Cavalry took part in the march through Kandahar on the 8th Jan., 1879, and taking up its quarters in the citadel on the departure of the Columns for Kalat-i-Ghilzai and Girishk, remained serving at the Southern capital throughout the succeeding spring and summer.

On the 21st. Jan., 1879, a few sabres of the regiment forming part of the garrison of Chaman moved out from that post with other details under Major Tulloch, 26th N.I., against a band of marauders. The expedition was highly successful, Nashkar Khan, a notorious robber, and ten of his followers, being slain.

On the 27th March, 1879, 30 sabres of the regiment formed part of the force under Major Humfrey, Jacob's Rifles, which defeated with heavy loss over 2,000 Barechi Pathans at Syud But, in Shorawak.

On the 10th April the regiment formed part of a small force under Brigadier-General Palliser which advanced into the Khakrez district to collect revenue. The objects of the expedition were successfully accomplished, and the force returned te Kandahar on the 2nd May.

In the beginning of September, 1879, the 1st Punjab Cavalry was ordered back to India; while still *en route* for Quetta, however, it received directions, in consequence of the receipt of news of the Kabul massacre, to return with all speed to Kandahar, where it arrived early in October.

As a unit of Brigadier-General Barter's brigade, the 1st Punjab Cavalry marched out of Kandahar on the 29th March, 1880, to take part in the advance of the Bengal Division on Ghazni, and both in the battle of Ahmad Khel, on the 19th April, and the action of Arzu, on the 23rd idem, was prominently engaged. In the former engagement (in which two squadrons, detached from General Barter's brigade, fought under General Palliser's command) the casualties of the regiment were, 1 Havildar and 18 rank and file wounded, 32 horses wounded, and 5 missing; and in the latter, 1 Sowar killed and 7 wounded, and 5 horses wounded. Subsequently taking part in the continued advance of the Field Force into the Logar Valley, the 1st Punjab Cavalry was employed in the various operations which were conducted in that and the neighbouring districts till the 6th Aug., when the Division marched into Kabul, and was broken up. On the 1st July, 1880, a portion of the regiment was engaged with Brigadier-General Palliser's force in the Cavalry affair of Patkao Shana, and rendered a most creditable account of itself. For his forward gallantry in this action, Major Atkinson was subsequently recommended for the Victoria Cross.

On the evacuation of Kabul in Aug., 1880, the regiment marched by the Khyber route to India, eventually returning to Dera Ismail Khan.

The undermentioned officers of the 1st Regt. Punjab Cavalry served in the war:—

Lt.-Colonel C. S. Maclean, C.B., commanded the regiment throughout the period it was employed in the war, taking part in the action of Takht-i-pul, the battle of Ahmad Khel, and the actions of Arzu and Patkao Shana. Also held the appointment of Political Officer with the Cavalry Brigade 2nd Division Kandahar F.F. in the first campaign. (Three times mentioned in despatches; C.B.)

Bt. Lt.-Colonel G. C. Bird served with the regiment throughout the first campaign and during part of the second. Was employed on escort duty from Oct., 1878, till March, 1879. Accompanied the Ghazni F.F. as Brigade Major, Cavalry Brigade, and was present in that capacity at the battle of Ahmad Khel and the actions of Arzu and Patkoa Shana. (Twice mentioned in despatches; Brevet of Lt.-Colonel.)

Lt.-Colonel J. R. B. Atkinson, Captain H. de la M. Hervey, and *Bt. Major D. S. Cuninghame* served with the regiment throughout the period it was employed in the war, taking part in the action of Takht-i-pul, the battle of Ahmad Khel, and the action of Arzu. *Lt.-Colonel Atkinson* and *Major Cuninghame* also took part in the action of Patkao Shana. For their services all three were mentioned in despatches: *Lt.-Colonel Atkinson* three times, receiving the Brevet of Lt.-Colonel, and being recommended for the Victoria Cross; *Major Cuninghame* twice, receiving the Brevet of Major.

Captain A. M. Muir served with the regiment throughout the first campaign and during part of the second, being present at the action of Takht-i-pul, and as Interpreter and Aide-de-Camp to Sir D. Stewart during the second, taking part in the battle of Ahmad Khel, and the action of Arzu. (Mentioned in despatches.)

Lieut. W. F. Hennell. (Deceased. See Biographical Division.)

Lieut. H. A. Deane served with the regiment during the second campaign, taking part in the battle of Ahmad Khel and the action of Arzu. (Mentioned in despatches.)

2ND REGT. PUNJAB CAVALRY.

ON the 24th Sept., 1878, orders were received for the 2nd Punjab Cavalry to hold itself in readiness to proceed on active service, and on the 5th Oct. it commenced its march, *viâ* the Dera Bughti route and Bolan Pass, to Quetta, where it arrived on the 27th idem. During the three weeks it remained at that station, the regiment suffered severely from fever and dysentery.

Leaving 68 sick at Quetta, the 2nd Punjab Cavalry advanced on the 21st Nov. with the troops under General Biddulph on Pishin, 100 sabres under Major Clifford having marched the previous day. After arriving at Pishin, the regiment was actively employed in reconnoitring, three squadrons, under Capt. Campbell, taking part in the examination of the surrounding district conducted by Col. Moore, A.Q.M.G., and various parties penetrating into the Gwaja, Rogani, and Khojak Passes. On the 26th the regiment advanced to Spin Baldak.

As a unit of the portion of the Cavalry Brigade under Brigadier-General Palliser which was commanded by Col. Kennedy, 2nd Punjab Cavalry, and led the advance of General Stewart's force by the Gwaja route, the regiment marched from Spin Baldak on the 2nd Jan., 1879, leaving detachments *en route*, and on the 4th was engaged, under Major Lance, in the affair of Takht-i-pul, in which the enemy were caused by Col. Kennedy's force to abandon a position they had taken up before the Ghlo Kotal, and were forced through the Pass to be dealt with by the Left column advancing under Brigadier Palliser's personal command. On the 8th Jan. the regiment took part in the triumphal march of the troops through Kandahar, which fell without further opposition.

As a portion of the advance guard of General Biddulph's Division in the march to Girishk, the 2nd Punjab Cavalry left Kandahar on the 16th Jan., 1879, and crossed the Halmand on the 31st idem. For the seven weeks during which the force was absent from Kandahar, the regiment was constantly employed with the Cavalry Brigade in foraging and reconnoitring duties. On the 26th Feb., during the return-march, 80 sabres under Capt. Broome were sent out from the camp at Ata Karez to assist a force under Col. Macolmson which had been attacked at Khushk-i-Nakhud, but arrived on the scene after the enemy had been dispersed. On the 3rd March, 1879, the regiment arrived at Kokaran, and went into camp.

The 2nd Punjab Cavalry remained in camp till the 30th Aug., 1879, when, in compliance with orders received, it marched for India. On reaching Chaman, however, it was directed, in consequence of the Kabul massacre, to return with all speed to Kandahar, where it arrived on the 13th Sept.

On the 22nd Sept. the regiment marched out of Kandahar with the force under Brigadier-General Hughes, and on the 30th took part in the second occupation of Kalat-i-Ghilzai. Four days afterwards Head-quarters and 200 sabres under Major Lance (89 sabres, under Capt. Campbell, remaining with other details at Kalat-i-Ghilzai) accompanied the advance of the Brigadier-General to Tazi, on the Ghazni road, and in the action of Shahjui, on the 24th Oct., played a prominent part. At the beginning of the engagement one squadron under Capt. Broome, in Col. Kennedy's force, seized a mound from which the first shot was fired, and with the other squadron of the regiment, under Major Lance, hung upon the flank of the enemy, and inflicted some loss upon them, as they retired to the ruins in which they ultimately took up their position. During the attack of the main body of Col. Kennedy's force which followed, Major Lance's squadron escorted the Artillery, Captain Broome's being posted some distance to the left to cut off fugitives; and on the latter the enemy, driven out from the ruins, bore down in two heavy columns. Captain Broome, seeing the distance he was from support, retired his squadron, thus enabling Major Lance to attack the charging enemy in flank and check their onslaught, Captain Broome, in turn, throwing himself upon them. A *mêlée* ensued, in which Sahib Jan, their leader, was killed, and the remainder dispersed. In this action Captain Broome, who had his horse shot under him, and 26 native officers and men were wounded, Duffadar Abdul Rahim—a gallant soldier who had distinguished himself in the action of Khushk-i-Nakhud—mortally. 4 horses also were killed, and 12 wounded.

Leaving 100 sabres under Captain Campbell, with Lieut. Younghusband, as part of the garrison of Kalat-i-Ghilzai, the remainder of the regiment, with the main body of Brigadier-General Hughes' force, returned to Kandahar on the 8th Nov., and rejoining the Cavalry Brigade, remained there throughout the ensuing winter and early spring.

Attached again to Brigadier-General Hughes' Brigade, the 2nd Punjab Cavalry took part, on the 31st March, 1880, in the advance of Sir Donald Stewart's Division on Ghazni from Kandahar, the detachment under Capt. Campbell rejoining Head-quarters on the arrival of the force at Kalat-i-Ghilzai. At the battle of Ahmad Khel on the 19th April, one squadron of the regiment, under Captain Campbell, acted as escort to Battery A/B, R.H.A., which commenced the action, the remaining two squadrons being posted to the right, and being engaged in the difficult task of keeping off the crowds of horse and foot that threatened the flanks of the Battery. After the repulse of the enemy's main attack on General Hughes' Infantry, the regiment took part, for a distance of three miles, in the Cavalry pursuit. The squadron escorting A/B, R.H.A., had, in the meantime, been closely pressed by large masses of the attacking force, and had acquitted itself with a steadiness and spirit which called forth the admiration of the officers of the Battery. In this engagement Captain Broome, Lieut. Stewart, and 20 non-commissioned officers and men were wounded, and 5 horses were killed, 21 wounded, and 2 lost. At the attack on the village of Arzu, on the 23rd, the regiment, early in the day, took up a position 800 yards in front of the village of Shalez, a dismounted squadron under Lieuts. Younghusband and Batten being employed in keeping down the fire of the enemy's sharp-shooters.

The 2nd Punjab Cavalry took part with the Field Force in its continued advance, and remained with it in and about the Logar Valley until the 6th Aug., 1880, when it marched into Kabul, and was broken up. On the 1st July 147 sabres of the regiment, under Col. Kennedy, were engaged with the Cavalry Brigade at the action of Patkao Shana, Captain Bishop greatly distinguishing himself by charging single-handed into a group of three of the enemy, who fought desperately, but were eventually killed.

On the 10th Aug., 1880, the Head-quarters and Left wing of the regiment commenced their return march, by the Khyber route, to India, the Right wing following on the next day. At Burj Harri Singh the regiment was reunited, and proceeding to Peshawar, marched down the frontier, and arrived at Dera Ghazi Khan, its destination, on the 4th Oct., 1880.

The undermentioned officers of the 2nd Regt. Punjab Cavalry served in the war:—

Colonel T. G. Kennedy, C.B., Commandant Punjab Frontier Force, served throughout both campaigns. Commanded the Right Advance Column in the advance on Kandahar, and at the action of Takht-i-pul. Commanded the troops engaged at the action of Shahjui, and the regiment at the battle of Ahmad Khel, the second part of the action of Arzu (commanded the Cavalry Brigade in the first part of the action), and the action of Patkao Shana. (Three times mentioned in despatches; C.B.)

Bt. Lt.-Colonel F. Lance served with the regiment from the 14th Dec., 1878, till the conclusion of the second campaign, commanding it at the actions of Takht-i-pul, Shahjui, and the first part of the action of Arzu, and being present at the battle of Ahmad Khel. (Mentioned in despatches; Brevet of Lt.-Colonel.)

Bt. Lt.-Colonel J. H. Broome served with the regiment throughout both campaigns, commanding a squadron at the actions of Takht-i-pul, and Shahjui (in which he was severely wounded, and had his horse shot under him), the battle of Ahmad Khel (in which he was again wounded, and had his horse disabled), and the actions of Arzu and Patkao Shana. (Mentioned in despatches; Brevet of Lt.-Colonel.)

Bt. Lt.-Colonel R. C. R. Clifford served throughout both campaigns. Commanded the line of communications from Quetta to Kandahar from 1 Jan., 1879, till end of March, 1880. Accompanied the Ghazni F.F. to Kabul as Assistant Political Officer, and held the appointment till the evacuation of Kabul, when he rejoined the regiment, and returned with it by the Khyber route to India. Was present at the battle of Ahmad Khel. (Mentioned in despatches; Brevet of Lt.-Colonel.)

Major J. R. Campbell served with the regiment from the commencement of the war till 28 April, 1880, on which date he was invalided to England. Was present at the battle of Ahmad Khel and the action of Arzu. (Mentioned in despatches.)

Bt. Major L. T. Bishop served throughout both campaigns. Was present, with the regiment, at the action of Takht-i-pul, and as Deputy Assistant Quartermaster-General, Ghazni F.F., at the battle of Ahmad Khel and the action of Patkao Shana. (Twice mentioned in despatches; Brevet of Major.)

Lieut. C. J. L. Stewart served with the regiment in both campaigns, being present at the action of Takht-i-pul, and the battle of Ahmad Khel, in which he was severely wounded.

Lieut. A. C. Batten served with the regiment from March, 1879, till 15 May, 1880, and with the 9th Lancers from that date till the conclusion of the war, taking part in the action of Shahjui, the battle of Ahmad Khel (mentioned in despatches), the action of Arzu, the march from Kabul to the relief of Kandahar, and the battle of Kandahar.

3RD REGT. PUNJAB CAVALRY.

IN the spring of 1880 the 3rd Punjab Cavalry was ordered on service, and quitting Edwardesabad, where it was then stationed, for Kabul, arrived at its destination in the beginning of April, 1880.

As part of the column under General Ross which left Kabul in the middle of April to effect a junction with the Ghazni Field Force, and returned on the 2nd May, two squadrons of the regiment were engaged in the operations which were conducted, during that interval, in the Logar and Maidan districts.

As part of the force under Brigadier-General Macpherson which proceeded from Sherpur to the support of Brigadier-General Jenkins, in the Chardeh plain, one troop of the regiment was engaged in the second action of Charasiab.

During May, June, and July, 1880, Head-quarters and two squadrons 3rd Punjab Cavalry were engaged in the operations conducted by General Roberts and Brigadier-Generals Baker and C. Gough, in the Logar, Maidan, and Pughman districts.

As a portion of the Cavalry Brigade of the Kabul-Kandahar Field Force, the 3rd Punjab Cavalry accompanied, in August, 1880, the advance from Kabul to the relief of the southern capital, and on the 1st Sept. was engaged in the defeat of Ayub Khan's army at the battle of Kandahar, taking part in the pursuit, which was continued till the evening, and pushed beyond the line of the enemy's retreat towards Khakrez. In this engagement the casualties of the regiment were, 1 British officer (Lieut. L. S. H. Baker), 2 non-commissioned officers, 4 rank and file wounded, 3 horses killed, and 9 wounded.

After taking part with the expeditionary force under Brigadier-General Macgregor in the operations which were conducted against the Marris, the regiment returned to India, and proceeded to Kohat.

The undermentioned officers of the 3rd Regt. Punjab Cavalry served in the war:—

Lt.-Colonel A. Vivian commanded the regiment throughout the period it was employed in the war, taking part in the march from Kabul to the relief of Kandahar, the battle of Kandahar, and the operations against the Marris. (Mentioned in despatches.)

Majors W. C. Anderson and *J. D. Macpherson*, *Captain C. C. Egerton* and *Lieut. L. S. Hyde Baker* served with the regiment throughout the period it was employed in the war, taking part in the march from Kabul to the relief of Kandahar, the battle of Kandahar, and the operations against the Marris. All were mentioned, for their services, in despatches. *Major Anderson* also served during the first campaign as Deputy Adjutant and Quartermaster-General, Punjab Chiefs' Contingent. *Lieut. Baker* also commanded the detachment engaged in the second action of Charasiab, and was wounded at the battle of Kandahar.

Bt. Major J. Davidson. (For services see "Staff.")

Lieut. W. Lambert served throughout the second campaign, first with the Transport Dept., 1st Division Kabul F.F., taking part in the advance on and occupation of Kabul, the action of Charasiab, and the operations round Kabul and defence of Sherpur in Dec., 1879; afterwards, with the 3rd Punjab Cavalry, taking part in the march from Kabul to the relief of Kandahar, the battle of Kandahar, and the operations against the Marris. (Mentioned in despatches.)

Lieut. J. B. De la P. Beresford served with the 9th Lancers during the first campaign, and with the 3rd Punjab Cavalry during the second, taking part in the march from Kabul to the relief of Kandahar, the battle of Kandahar, and the operations against the Marris.

5TH REGT. PUNJAB CAVALRY.

A WING and Head-quarters of the 5th Punjab Cavalry marched from Kohat for Thal on the 10th Oct., 1878, to join the force under General Roberts destined to operate in the Kuram Valley, then in course of formation.

On the 4th Dec. one troop crossed the frontier, and advanced to Hazar Pir, forming part of a small Column detailed to keep open the communication with Kuram. The remainder of the wing marched for the same destination on the 29th Dec., and joining the expeditionary force then about to enter the Khost Valley, took part with it in the operations which were conducted in that district during the succeeding three weeks. At the action of Matun on the 7th Jan., 1879, one troop, dismounted, carried a hill occupied in force by the Mangals, and another troop, charging a large retiring body of the enemy, inflicted severe loss upon them.

After returning, on the 2nd Feb., 1879, the wing proceeded to Fort Kuram, arriving on the 11th idem.

During the visit of H. E. the Commander-in-Chief to the Kuram Valley, a troop of the regiment formed a portion of his escort.

On the 21st May, 1879, the wing 5th Punjab Cavalry marched to Ali Khel, and after taking part in the Queen's birthday review, returned to Kuram. From thence, on the 31st May, it marched for Thal, furnishing posts along the line of communications, and arriving at its destination on the 5th June.

On the renewal of hostilities in the autumn of 1879, the 5th Punjab Cavalry again formed part of the force under Sir F. Roberts' command. The Left wing marched from Kohat on the 12th Sept., and the Right wing and Head-quarters on the 17th Sept., the latter overtaking the former on the 27th idem at Ali Khel, from whence the regiment accompanied the General, on the following day, to Kushi. The march of the Right wing, including the passage of the Peiwar and Shutargardan, which was accomplished in eleven days without a single sore back, was favourably noticed in reports. The column when on the march from Ali Khel was attacked at Karatiga by a body of Mangals, and in the skirmish which ensued Captain Vousden's horse was shot under him.

Taking part in the advance from Kushi on Kandahar, the regiment was engaged, as Divisional Cavalry, on the 6th Oct., in the action of Charasiab, participating in the right attack, and at the close of the engagement pursuing the enemy up to the Sang-i-Nawishta defile. On the 8th Oct. it proceeded with the Cavalry Brigade to the Chardeh Valley, and the following day took part in the pursuit of the enemy to Argandi, overtaking and cutting up several small parties.

The 5th Punjab Cavalry encamped in the Sherpur cantonment on the 10th Oct., and remained there till the 17th idem, guarding the captured guns, and searching the surrounding villages for arms.

Forming part of the force under Brigadier-General Hugh Gough sent to relieve the garrison of the Shutargardan, the regiment marched for Kushi on the 17th Oct. From thence one squadron made its way back to Kabul with a convoy, the two remaining squadrons returning with the relieving force, after it had accomplished its mission, by a longer route through the Logar Valley.

The regiment took up its quarters in the Shah Bagh, outside cantonments, on the 10th Nov., and proceeded to hut itself. During the succeeding three weeks two squadrons marched with Brigadier-General Baker's force towards Argandi, and one squadron, forming part of Yakub Ali's escort, accompanied him as far as Butkhak.

On the 9th Dec. Head-quarters and five troops of the regiment accompanied the force under Brigadier-General Baker on its flank march on Maidan, and were engaged in the harassing rear-guard fight which took place on the 11th. The following day one troop was left at Deh-i-Mozang with Brigadier-General Macpherson's Brigade, and did not rejoin Head-quarters till the evening of the 13th. On that day five troops were engaged with the enemy at Beni Hissar and on the Siah Sang plateau. On the 14th, previous to the retirement within the cantonment, the regiment, broken up into detachments, was again engaged. Captain Vousden on this day winning his Victoria Cross by a brilliantly delivered charge into a large body of the enemy.

From the 14th to the 23rd Dec. the 5th Punjab Cavalry, with the rest of the Division, remained in Sherpur, furnishing a picquet nightly on the East Behmaru Hill, and daily sending out patrols. On the latter date the regiment acted against the right flank of the Afghan force attacking the N.E. corner of the cantonment, and cut up detached bodies of the enemy, advancing, later, on to the Siah Sang plateau, and on the following day being engaged with Brigadier-General H. Gough's force in the pursuit of the enemy to Charasiab.

The 5th Punjab Cavalry remained at Sherpur till the 21st Feb., 1880. On that date the regiment commenced its return march to India, and on the 6th March, 1880, arrived at Peshawar.

The undermentioned officers of the 5th Regt. Punjab Cavalry served in the war:—

Lt.-Colonel Ben. Williams was present, as Aide-de-Camp to Sir Sam. Browne, at the capture of Ali Musjid and the forcing of the Khyber Pass. Commanded the post of Hazar Pir from 4 Dec., 1878, till 1 Jan., 1879. Commanded the Head-quarter wing 5th P.C. from 2 Jan., 1879, till the end of the first campaign, taking part in the Khost Valley expedition and the action of Matun; and commanded the regiment during the second campaign from 27 Oct., 1879, taking part in the operations round Kabul and defence of Sherpur in Dec., 1879. (Twice mentioned in despatches; Brevet of Lt.-Colonel.)

Bt. Lt.-Colonel F. Hammond served with the regiment throughout the period it was employed in the war, commanding it, during the second campaign, till the 27th Oct., 1879. Took part in the Khost Valley expedition, the action of Matun, the skirmish at Karatiga (in command of the regiment), the action of Charasiab (in command of the Cavalry of the right attack) and the Cavalry pursuit, and the operations round Kabul and defence of Sherpur in Dec., 1879, including the Cavalry pursuit 24 Dec. (Twice mentioned in despatches; Brevet of Lt.-Colonel.)

Bt. Lt.-Colonel J. C. Stewart, and *Lieuts. C. F. Gambier* and *G. Pycroft, 25th K.O.Bs. (attached) (deceased)*, served with the regiment throughout the period it was employed in the war, taking part in the Khost Valley expedition, the action of Matun, the skirmish at Karatiga, the action of Charasiab and Cavalry pursuit, and the operations round Kabul and defence of Sherpur in Dec., 1879, including the Cavalry pursuit of 24 Dec. *Lt.-Colonel Stewart* commanded an independent troop at the action of Matun, and in a charge inflicted severe loss on the enemy. For his services he was twice mentioned in despatches, and received the Brevet of Lt.-Colonel. *Lieut. Gambier* was severely wounded in the action of 23 Dec., and for his services was mentioned in despatches. *Lieut. Pycroft* died at Edwardesabad 28 Aug., 1880, from the effects of illness contracted in the field.

Major F. S. Carr served as Deputy Assistant Quartermaster-General, Kuram Valley F.F., throughout the first campaign, taking part in the assault and capture of the Peiwar Kotal, the Khost Valley expedition, and the action of Matun. Served with the regiment throughout the period it was employed in the second campaign, taking part in the skirmish at Karatiga, the action of Charasiab and Cavalry pursuit, and the operations round Kabul and defence of Sherpur in Dec., 1879, including the Cavalry pursuit of 24 Dec., 1879. (Three times mentioned in despatches; Brevet of Major.)

Bt. Major W. J. Vousden, V.C. (For services see Biographical Division.)

Captain J. B. Watts served with the regiment from the outbreak of the second campaign till the middle of Oct., 1879, taking part in the skirmish at Karatiga, and the action of Charasiab and Cavalry pursuit. (Mentioned in despatches.)

Lieut. A. P. Williamson served with the 11th N.I. in the Kuram Valley throughout the period that regiment was employed in the war.

QUEEN'S OWN CORPS OF GUIDES.

ON the 12th Sept., 1878, 100 sabres of the Guide Cavalry and 50 rifles of the Guide Infantry, under command of Lt.-Colonel F. H. Jenkins, accompanied by Major G. Stewart and Capt. Wigram Battye, marched from Mardan as escort to the Kabul Mission (Sir Neville Chamberlain) which, being refused a passage through the Khyber Pass on the 25th Sept., returned.

The Corps of Guides marched from Mardan, on the 3rd Oct., 1878, and from the 8th Oct. until the advance on Ali Musjid on the 20th Nov. was encamped at Jamrud at the mouth of the Khyber Pass, and was employed in reconnoitring the mountains about the Pass.

On the 20th Nov. the Infantry of the Corps formed part of the advance guard of the 2nd Brigade under Brigadier-General Tytler, which was ordered to march round the Rhotas Mountains and intercept the enemy's line of retreat from Ali Musjid up the Khyber Pass at Kata Kushtia. The Guide Cavalry accompanied the front attack under Sir Sam. Browne on the 21st Nov. About 4 p.m. on the 21st Nov., the Guide Infantry and 1st Sikhs, under Lt.-Col. F. H. Jenkins, reached the heights above Kata Kushtia, and were mainly instrumental in causing the evacuation of Ali Musjid during the night of the 21st Nov. They captured 280 prisoners and 256 Enfield rifles, besides accoutrements of sorts, and 25 horses and mules.

After the capture of Ali Musjid the Corps of Guides accompanied the 1st Division to Daka, from whence it marched, with the 3rd Brigade 1st Division, on the 17th Dec., towards Jalalabad.

Fifty sabres of the Guide Cavalry and 250 rifles of the Guide Infantry formed part of a force sent into the Kama District, under Brigadier-General F. H. Jenkins, on the 11th Jan., 1879, to capture some Syads who were causing mischief and inciting Mohmand robbers to plunder the country. The Kabul and Kunar rivers and their branches had to be forded, an arduous undertaking at that season of the year, owing to the rapidity of the current and the icy coldness of the water. The object of the expedition was successfully effected.

On the 21st Feb., 1879, 70 sabres Guide Cavalry and 250 rifles Guide Infantry formed part of an expeditionary force sent into the Lughman Valley under Brigadier-General F. H. Jenkins. The object of the expedition was political, and was successfully attained.

The Guide Cavalry under Major Wigram Battye (Major Stewart being detached on special duty) accompanied by Lt. W. R. P. Hamilton and Surgeon J. Lewtas, marched with the Cavalry Brigade under Brigadier-General C. Gough on the 31st March, 1879, to Futtehabad.

On the 1st April, 200 rifles Guide Infantry under Capt. F. D. Battye, accompanied by Lt. H. W. Hughes, formed part of a column under command of Major R. B. Campbell, ordered on special duty into the Lughman Valley, returning to Jalalabad the next day.

The Guide Cavalry were hotly engaged in the action fought by Brig.-Genl. C. Gough against the Kugianis near Futtehabad on the 2nd April, 1879, and lost 4 killed (including their commanding officer Major Wigram Battye and one native officer) and 28 wounded (3 of whom since died). 7 horses were also killed and 37 wounded. 5 men received 3rd Class and a native officer received 2nd Class Order of Merit for gallantry on this occasion.

On the 12th April, 1879, the Head-quarters of the Corps, with the Cavalry and 320 rifles of the Infantry under Lt.-Col. F. H. Jenkins, accompanied by Major Stewart, Captains Hammond and Battye, Lt. Hamilton and Surgeon A. H. Kelley, marched with the Head-quarters of the 1st Division to Gandamak. The remainder of the Corps, under Major Campbell, with Lieuts. Cooke, Collis, and Hughes, and Surgeon J. Lewtas, remained at Jalalabad.

The Corps commenced its return march to India on the 6th June, 1879, the Guide Cavalry forming part of the rear-guard of the Army, under Brigadier-General Tytler.

The Guide Infantry arrived at Mardan on the 20th June, and the Cavalry on the 23rd June.

On the 26th June, 1879, 25 Cavalry and 52 Infantry, and 1 Hospital Assistant of the Corps, under command of Lt. W. R. P. Hamilton, marched from Mardan as escort to the Kabul Embassy (Sir P. L. N. Cavagnari). Of this escort, 1 Sepoy died at Kabul of sickness, the remainder (with the exception of 4 Cavalry and 4 Infantry) fell in defence of the Residency on the 3rd Sept., 1879. Of the 8 men who survived, 3 alone escaped from the massacre, the remaining 5 happening to be away on duty at the time.

On the 21st Sept., 1879, the Corps of Guides marched from Mardan, under orders to the Khyber Pass, and being attached to Brigadier-General C. Gough's Brigade, reached Gandamak on the 23rd Oct., 1879.

The Corps formed part of the flying column under Brigadier-General C. Gough, which proceeded on the 2nd Nov. to open communications with General Roberts' Division, and met Brigadier-General Macpherson's Brigade advancing from Kabul at Kata Sang on the 6th idem.

On the 7th Nov. Brigadier-General Gough returned to Gandamak, leaving the Guides to hold the posts on the road, the whole of the posts being under the command of Lt.-Col. Jenkins. The Head-quarters of the Corps, with the Left wing of the Infantry, 54 sabres of the Cavalry, and other details, occupied Jagdalak Kotal until nearly the end of November, when they advanced to Jagdalak, leaving a detachment of Infantry at the Kotal. The Right wing and 103 sabres of the Cavalry occupied Pezwan, under command of Major Campbell.

On the 8th Dec. the Left wing and Cavalry from Pezwan joined the Head-quarters at Jagdalak, and the next day the Corps marched towards Kabul, where it arrived on the night of 11 Dec., having made a forced march of 36 miles (from Seh Baba) that day.

On the 13th Dec. the Guide Infantry, under Col. F. H. Jenkins, formed part of a force under Brigadier-General Baker employed in taking the heights of Takht-i-Shah, and acted in support of the 92nd Highlanders.

In the meantime the Guide Cavalry under Lt.-Col. G. Stewart were engaged (with the 9th Lancers) with a large body of the enemy near the Siah Sang ridge. They made two charges, and lost 3 killed and 18 wounded, also 10 horses killed and 16 wounded. One Sowar obtained the 3rd Class Order of Merit.

On the 14th Dec. the Guide Infantry were again attached to Brigadier-General Baker's Brigade, and were engaged in storming the Asmai heights. The advance column, consisting of 72nd Highlanders, 92nd Highlanders, detachment, and Guide Infantry, were under Col. F. H. Jenkins. The Guide Infantry were under command of Lt.-Col. Campbell, and lost 13 killed (including 1 native officer) and 29 wounded (including Capt. Battye and 1 native officer). Of the wounded, the native officer and 2 men subsequently died. 12 men received 3rd Class Order of Merit.

From the 15th to the 23rd Dec., 1879, the Corps was employed in the defence of Sherpur.

On the morning of the 23rd Dec., in the repulse of the enemy's attack on the Cantonment, the Guides lost 2 men killed and 2 wounded (including a native officer, who afterwards died).

On the 26th Dec. the Corps marched with Brigadier-General Baker's Brigade to the Koh-i-Daman, and returned to Sherpur on the 31st, after destroying the forts and vineyards belonging to Mir Butcha.

The Corps passed the winter in Sherpur in tents, being the only Regiment unprovided with quarters.

On the 20th April, 1880, the Corps marched out of Sherpur to the Logar Valley, as part of a force under command of Col. F. H. Jenkins, and returned to Sherpur on the evening of 25 April, after the fight at Charasiab, in which the Corps lost 3 killed and 23 wounded (of whom 2 subsequently died); also 9 horses killed, and 23 wounded. Two men and a Hospital Assistant received the 3rd Class Order of Merit.

On the 11th August Kabul was evacuated and the return march to India commenced, the Corps of Guides forming the rear-guard. The Corps reached Mardan on 6 Sept., 1880.

The undermentioned officers of the Queen's Own Corps of Guides served in the war:—

Col. F. H. Jenkins, C.B., A.D.C. to the Queen, commanded the escort to the Kabul Mission, which was refused a passage through the Khyber Pass in Sept., 1878. Commanded the Corps of Guides throughout both campaigns, except from 16 Dec., 1878, to 23 March, 1879, when he commanded the 3rd Brigade, 1st Division Peshawar F.F., with the rank of Brigadier-General. At the storming of Asmai commanded the attacking column. Commanded a section of the Sherpur defences during its investment from 15 to 23 Dec., 1879. Commanded a force of Cavalry and Infantry in the Logar Valley from 20 to 25 April, 1880, including the action at Charasiab, 25 April, 1880. (Four times mentioned in despatches; C.B.; appointed A.D.C. to the Queen, with rank of Colonel.)

Lt.-Colonel R. B. Campbell served with the Guide Infantry throughout both campaigns, taking part in the capture of Ali Musjid, the assaults of the Takht-i-Shah and Asmai heights (when he commanded the regiment), the defence of Sherpur, and the action of Charasiab (in command of the Corps). Commanded the Corps from 16 Dec., 1878, to 23 March, 1879. (Three times mentioned in despatches; Brevet of Lt.-Colonel.)

Lt.-Colonel G. Stewart accompanied the escort to the Kabul Mission in Sept., 1878. Commanded the Guide Cavalry throughout both campaigns, except from 16 Dec., 1878, to 23rd March, 1879, when he officiated as 2nd in command of the Corps. Commanded the Guide Cavalry at capture of Ali Musjid, Siah Sang, and Charasiab. (Three times mentioned in despatches; Brevet of Lt.-Colonel.) Was sent home on medical certificate, July, 1880.

Major Wigram Battye. (Killed in action. See Biographical Division.)

Major R. C. Hutchinson served with the Guide Cavalry throughout both campaigns, taking part in the capture of Ali Musjid, the action at Siah Sang, the defence of Sherpur, and the action of Charasiab. Was on remount duty in India when the action at Futtehabad was fought. Obtained his Majority 9 Dec., 1879, and succeeded to the Offg. Command of the Guide Cavalry on the 22nd July, 1880, consequent on Lt.-Col. Stewart's departure on sick leave.

Major A. G. Hammond, V.C. For services see Biographical Division.

Capt. F. D. Battye served as Adjutant of the Corps throughout both campaigns, and was present with the Infantry at the capture of Ali Musjid and the assaults of the Takht-i-Shah and Asmai heights, in the latter of which he was wounded. Was sent to India on recruiting duty in Jan., 1880. Rejoined at Kabul in March, and was present at the action of Charasiab. (Three times mentioned in despatches.)

Lieut. M. C. Cooke-Collis served throughout both campaigns. Was present with the Infantry at the capture of Ali Musjid, the defence of Sherpur, and the action of Charasiab. (Mentioned in despatches.)

Lieut. W. R. P. Hamilton, V.C. (Killed in action. See Biographical Division.)

Lieut. H. W. Hughes served with the Corps throughout both campaigns: with the Infantry in the first campaign, taking part in the capture of Ali Musjid; and with the Cavalry in the second campaign, taking part in the action at the Siah Sang, the defence of Sherpur, and the action of Charasiab. (Mentioned in despatches.)

Lieut. R. B. Adams joined Head-quarters at Jagdalak in Nov., 1880, and marched with the corps to Kabul, was present with the Infantry in all the subsequent operations, including the assaults of the Takht-i-Shah, and Asmai heights, the defence of Sherpur, and the action of Charasiab. Succeeded to Offg.-Adjutancy of the Corps, 22 July, 1880. (Mentioned in despatches.)

1st REGT. SIKH INFANTRY.

ON the 3rd Oct., 1878, in compliance with telegraphic orders, the 1st Regt. Sikh Infantry, under the command of Major A. G. Ross, marched from Kohat to Peshawar, in view of a proposed attack on Ali Musjid.

From the 7th Oct. till the 20th Nov. the regiment was encamped at Jamrud, with the force under Lt.-Colonel Jenkins, Guides, watching the Khyber Pass. On the 9th Nov. it was placed on the strength of the 2nd (Brigadier-General Tytler's) Brigade, Peshawar Valley F.F.

Taking part, on the 20th and 21st Nov., in the flank march of the 2nd Brigade viâ Lashura and

Sapri, the 1st Sikh Infantry, with the Corps of Guides, arrived on the hills above Kata Kushtia, in the Khyber, on the 21st, in time to open fire on the Afghan Cavalry retreating from Ali Musjid, and on the 22nd was present at the surrender of a portion of the Afghan Infantry.

The regiment reached Daka with the 1st Division on the 25th Nov., and was in garrison in the Fort till the 12th Dec. On the 13th idem it marched to Basawal; and after being attached for a few days to Brigadier-General Macpherson's Brigade, was brought on to the strength of the 3rd Brigade under Brigadier-General Jenkins, afterwards commanded by Brigadier-General Appleyard.

On the 20th Dec. the 1st Sikh Infantry, with the other units of the 1st Division, arrived at Jalalabad, and remained there till after the signing of the treaty of Gandamak. On the 11th June, 1879, it commenced its return march to India, and recrossing the frontier on the 18th idem, made its way back to Kohat, where it arrived on the 21st.

During the period the 1st Sikh Infantry was employed in the first campaign, detachments of the regiment, besides performing many minor duties, took part in the expedition into the Mir Jan Khel hills near Daka, 9 and 10 Dec., 1878; the expedition to relieve Mayar in Kama, 7 Feb., 1879; the expedition into Lughman territory, 22 to 25 Feb., 1879; and the expedition to Katz, across the Kabul River, in pursuit of Azmatallah Khan Ghilzai, 31 March to 2 April, 1879.

In the second campaign the 1st Sikh Infantry, under the command of Lt.-Colonel Rice, was employed on reconnoitring and escort duty in the Zaimusht country, during Brigadier-General Tytler's expedition into that territory in December, 1879.

The undermentioned officers of the 1st Regt. Sikh Infantry served in the war:—

Lt.-Colonel H. C. P. Rice commanded the regiment throughout the period of its service in the second campaign.

Bt. Lt.-Colonel A. G. Ross and *Lieut. J. A. H. Pollock* served with the regiment throughout the period it was employed in the war, *Lt.-Colonel Ross* commanding it throughout the first campaign, and for his services being mentioned in despatches, and receiving the Brevet of Lt.-Colonel.

Majors C. C. Brownlow and *T. F. Bruce* (6th Punjab Infantry), *Captain F. R. Begbie*, and *Lieut. A. C. Bunny* served with the regiment in the first campaign. Major Brownlow, from 13 Jan., 1879, till the return to India; *Major Bruce*, from the commencement of the war till 31 March, 1879; *Captain Begbie*, from the commencement of the war till 13 Jan., 1879; and *Lieut. Bunny*, from 14 Feb., 1879, till the return to India.

2ND REGT. SIKH INFANTRY.

WHEN stationed at Dera Ghazi in the autumn of 1878, the 2nd Regt. Sikh Infantry received orders, on the 8th Oct., to proceed on field service, and making its way, under the command of Lt.-Colonel Boswell, by the Dera Bughti route and Bolan Pass to Quetta, formed part of the garrison of that place till March, 1879. In that month it advanced to Khushdil Khan, and joining the Pishin Moveable Column, remained employed in and about the Valley on convoy and garrison duty for a period of eleven months.

On the 9th Feb., 1880, the 2nd Sikhs marched for Kandahar, and on the 31st March took part, as a unit of Brigadier-General Hughes' Brigade, in the advance of Sir Donald Stewart's Division on Ghazni. At the battle of Ahmad Khel, on the 19th April, the regiment was prominently engaged, holding the centre of the line formed by the 2nd Brigade at the critical moment when the Ghazis rushed down upon it, and pouring a destructive fire into the oncoming hordes. That the 2nd Sikh Infantry rendered a good account of itself is attested by the fact that no fewer than 296 dead bodies of the enemy were counted on the ground more immediately swept by the fire of its Sniders. In the action of Arzu, on the 23rd April, the regiment was again engaged.

The 2nd Sikhs took part with the Field Force in its continued advance, and remained in and about the Logar Valley until ordered into Kabul on the 26th July. From that date until the evacuation of the capital, the regiment garrisoned the Bala Hissar.

Detailed to the 2nd Brigade Kabul-Kandahar Field Force, under the command of Brigadier-General Baker, the 2nd Sikh Infantry took part, in August, 1880, in the memorable march to the relief of Kandahar. During the reconnaissance which took place after the arrival of the force at its destination on the 31st Aug., the regiment was in reserve; but in the crushing defeat of the enemy at the battle of Kandahar on the following day, it was one of the two leading battalions of the 2nd Brigade, and performed distinguished service, clearing the tenaciously-held gardens and walled enclosures which lay in the line of attack in a manner which is warmly testified to by the General in his despatch. The casualties of the regiment on this day were, 3 Sepoys killed, and 1 British Officer and 23 Sepoys wounded, the former very severely. 2 native officers, 1 non-commissioned officer, and 4 Sepoys, who were mentioned by name in despatches, were subsequently admitted to the Order of Merit for conspicuous gallantry during the action.

From the 21st till the 24th Sept., 1880, the regiment took part in the operations of Brigadier-General Baker's brigade against the Achakzais, and from the 10th Oct. till the 4th Dec., 1880, in the operations of Brigadier-General MacGregor's force in the operations against the Marris, after which it returned to Dera Ghazi Khan, and went into cantonments.

The regiment was absent on service two years, two months, and two days, during which period its casualties were as follows:—Killed in action: 2 non-commissioned officers, and 6 Sepoys; died from disease: 2 native officers, 18 non-commissioned officers, and 143 Sepoys; wounded: 2 havildars, 29 Sepoys, and 2 camp followers; discharged as invalids: 4 native officers, 20 non-commissioned officers, and 18 Sepoys; granted leave on medical certificate: 6 British officers, 2 native officers, 140 non-commissioned officers and Sepoys.

The undermentioned officers of the 2nd Regt. Sikh Infantry served in the war:—

Major-General R. D'O. C. Bracken (Retired), accompanied the regiment to Kandahar, from whence he shortly afterwards returned to India and retired from the service.

Lt.-Colonel J. J. Boswell, C.B., commanded the regiment throughout the period it was employed in the war: at the battle of Ahmad Khel, the action of Arzu, in the march from Kabul to the relief of Kandahar, at the battle of Kandahar, the operations against the Achakzais, and the operations against the Marris. (Twice mentioned in despatches; C.B.)

Bt. Lt.-Colonel H. M. Pratt served throughout both campaigns: throughout the first, and during the second, till Aug., 1880, with the 5th Punjab Infantry, commanding that regiment from the 5th Oct., 1879, till the 25th April, 1880, and during the remainder of the second campaign, with the 2nd Sikhs, as second in command. Took part in the assault of the Peiwar Kotal and previous reconnaissance of 28 Nov., 1878, the action of Charasiab (in command of the 5th P.I.), the operations round Kabul and defence of Sherpur in Dec., 1879 (in command of the 5th P.I.), the march from Kabul to the relief of Kandahar, the battle of Kandahar, and the operations against the Achakzais and Marris. (Twice mentioned in despatches; Brevet of Lt.-Colonel.)

Major J. B. Slater served with the regiment in the second campaign, taking part in the actions of Ahmed Khel and Arzu, the march from Kabul to the relief of Kandahar, and the battle of Kandahar, in which he was severely wounded. (Mentioned in despatches.)

Bt. Lt.-Colonel F. E. Hastings served with the regiment throughout the period it was employed in the war, taking part in the battle of Ahmad Khel, the action of Arzu, the march from Kabul to the relief of Kandahar, the battle of Kandahar, and the operations against the Achakzais and Marris. (Mentioned in despatches; Brevet of Lt.-Colonel.)

Captain W. O. Thompson served with the regiment throughout the period it was employed in the first campaign. Was invalided from the Pishin Valley.

Lieuts. C. G. M. Fasken and *F. C. Dunlop* served with the regiment throughout the second campaign, taking part in the battle of Ahmad Khel, the action of Arzu, the march from Kabul to the relief of Kandahar, the battle of Kandahar, and the operations against the Achakzais and Marris.

3RD REGT. SIKH INFANTRY.

THE 3rd Regt. Sikh Infantry was stationed at Edwardesabad on the N. W. Frontier of the Punjab when the massacre at Kabul of the English mission took place.

Receiving orders by telegram to join the force assembling under command of Sir F. Roberts, the regiment left its station on the 11th Sept., 1879, and proceeding by double marches viâ Thal, Kuram, and Ali Khel, reached the Shutargardan on the 25th Sept., leaving a company under Jemadar Sher Mahomed at the Karatiga post at the head of the Hazardarakht defile.

On the 27th September this company was engaged with the enemy who had assembled to dispute the passage of the troops accompanying the Lieut.-General and his Head-quarters.

RECORDS OF SERVICE.

On the 28th Sept., Sir F. Roberts proceeded to Kushi, leaving the 3rd Sikhs with the 21st P.N.I. and No. 1 Mountain Battery, the whole under command of Lt.-Colonel G. Noel Money, 3rd Sikhs, to garrison the Shutargardan, and keep open his communications with the Kuram Valley.

A detachment under a British officer from the Shutargardan occupied a block-house on the Surkai Kotal above Karatiga.

On the 2nd Oct. a large body of the enemy threatening the Shutargardan was attacked and defeated with heavy loss. On the 14th they assembled in still larger numbers, and were again attacked; and after a heavy engagement were totally routed and pursued for two miles, but did not wholly disperse, taking up a position on the Spegah road, about five miles distant. Here they received daily large accessions to their numbers, till their total strength amounted to 17,000 men.

On the night of the 15th Oct. the garrison was withdrawn from the Surkai Kotal. On the 16th the Shutargardan was completely invested by the enemy, who, on the morning of the 18th, commenced a determined attack on the position. The following day a force under command of Brigadier-General Hugh Gough arrived at Kushi from Kabul, and established heliographic communication with Colonel Money, who at once resumed the offensive. The enemy, disheartened by the failure of their attacks and the near approach of reinforcements, broke and dispersed.

On the 20th October General Gough reached the Shutargardan, the heights being held and the road protected by the 3rd Sikhs and 21st P.N.I.

On the 21st Oct. the regiment proceeded with two guns to destroy some Ghilzai villages whose inhabitants had plundered several convoys and joined in the recent attacks.

The Shutargardan was abandoned on the 30th Oct., and the regiment marched to Kabul viâ the Logar Valley, arriving on the 4th Nov. Here it was attached to the 2nd Brigade, under command of Brigadier-General Baker, and remained under his command until the end of the war.

The 3rd Sikhs accompanied the force under General Baker which marched into the Maidan Valley on the 21st Nov., and after collecting supplies and punishing refractory villages, returned to Kabul on the 1st Dec.

On 8th Dec. the regiment, temporarily attached to a force under the command of Brigadier-General Macpherson, marched to the head of the Chardeh Valley, and was engaged both in the defeat of the enemy at the Surkh Kotal, on the 10th Dec., and again in the Chardeh Valley on the 11th Dec., when the guns taken by them earlier in the day from General Massey were recaptured,

The 3rd Sikh Infantry took part in the attack and capture of the Takht-i-Shah hill on 12th and 13th Dec., and was again engaged on 14th before the retirement within the cantonment.

During the siege of Sherpur by the enemy from the 14th to 23rd Dec., the regiment was engaged in four sorties, in all of which the desired object was attained.

On the 31st Dec. the regiment was detached to Lataband, returning to Kabul on the 21st Jan., 1880.

In May, 1880, the 3rd Sikh Infantry accompanied the force under Sir F. Roberts which marched into the Logar, Wardak, and Maidan Valleys, and returned to Kabul on the 12th June. During this expedition the regiment was detached with the 2nd Ghoorkhas, a squadron of Cavalry, and some guns, under Colonel Money, to surprise and destroy the forts of Padshah Khan, Chief of the Southern Ghilzais. No resistance was experienced, and the forts were completely destroyed.

As a unit of Brigadier-General Baker's Brigade, the 3rd Sikhs took part, in the month of August, 1880, in the march of the force under Sir F. Roberts from Kabul to the relief of Kandahar, and on the 1st Sept. was engaged in the crushing defeat of Ayub Khan's army. In this engagement the regiment captured three guns, and was the first battalion to penetrate the enemy's camp.

On the 15th Sept., 1880, the 3rd Sikhs commenced its return march to India. Arriving at Sibi on the 10th Oct., it was there detailed to the force under General Macgregor which was sent to act against the refractory Marri tribe; and marching through the Marri country, eventually arrived with the expeditionary column at Dera Ghazi Khan on the 17th Nov., 1880.

The undermentioned officers of the 3rd Regt. Sikh Infantry served in the war :—

Lt.-Colonel G. Noel Money, C.B., commanded the regiment throughout the campaign and in the Marri expedition, the force holding the Shutargardan in Oct., 1879, and the attacking force in the assault of the Takht-i-Shah hill, 12 and 13 Dec., 1879. Attacked and defeated the enemy at the Shutargardan, 2, 14, and 20 Oct., and took part in the actions of Surkh Kotal and Chardeh, the defence of Sherpur, the march from Kabul to the relief of Kandahar, and the battle of Kandahar. (Repeatedly mentioned in despatches; received the thanks of the Viceroy and Commander-in-Chief in India by telegram for defence of Shutargardan; C.B.)

Bt. Lt.-Colonel C. J. Griffiths, Major W. B. Aislabie, and *Lieuts. W. Cook* and *W. D. Gordon*

served with the regiment throughout the campaign; *Lt.-Colonel Griffiths* commanding the attack on the heights above the Shutargardan, 2 Oct. (slightly wounded), and 14 Oct., and taking part in the defence of the Shutargardan, the actions of Surkh Kotal, Chardeh (in which he commanded the rear-guard repulse of the enemy), Takht-i-Shah (13 Dec.), and the engagement on 14 Dec., the defence of Sherpur, the march from Kabul to the relief of Kandahar, and the battle of Kandahar (three times mentioned in despatches; Brevet of Lt.-Colonel); *Major Aislabie* taking part in the defence of the Shutargardan, the actions of 2 Oct. (in which he succeeded to the command of the attack, on Major Griffiths being wounded), and 14 Oct., 1879, Surkh Kotal, Chardeh, Takht-i-Shah (13 Dec.), and engagement on 14 Dec., the defence of Sherpur, the march from Kabul to the relief of Kandahar, and the battle of Kandahar (three times mentioned in despatches); *Lieut. Cook* (who had previously served with the Khyber F.F. throughout the first campaign, and was present at the capture of Ali Musjid and the forcing of the Sissobai Pass) taking part in the defence of the Shutargardan, the actions of 2 Oct. and 14 Oct., 1879, Surkh Kotal, Chardeh (in which he was severely wounded), the defence of Sherpur, the march from Kabul to the relief of Kandahar, the battle of Kandahar, and the Marri expedition (mentioned in despatches; brought prominently to notice for distinguished gallantry on 14 Oct., 1879); and *Lieut. Gordon* taking part in the defence of the Shutargardan, the actions of 2 and 14 Oct., 1879, Surkh Kotal, Chardeh, and engagement of 14 Dec., 1879, the defence of Sherpur, the battle of Kandahar, and the Marri expedition.

Major W. C. Ramsden served with the regiment from Jan., 1880, till the conclusion of the campaign, taking part in the march from Kabul to the relief of Kandahar, the battle of Kandahar, and the Marri expedition.

Lieut. C. H. M. Smith served in the Survey Dept. with the Kuram Valley F.F. throughout the first campaign, being present at the assault and capture of the Peiwar Kotal. Served during the second campaign as Deputy Assistant Quartermaster-General with Sir F. Roberts' Division, taking part in the advance on and occupation of Kabul, and being present at the action of Charasiab. Served with the regiment during the defence of Sherpur. (Three times mentioned in despatches.)

Lieut. E. J. N. Fasken served with the regiment from the commencement of the campaign till invalided to England in April, 1880, taking part in the defence of the Shutargardan, the actions of 2 Oct. and 14 Oct., 1879, Surkh Kotal, and Chardeh, the assault of the Takht-i-Shah, 12 Dec. (in which, while commanding the detachment of the 3rd Sikhs which was engaged, he was severely wounded), and the defence of Sherpur.

Lieut. A. A. Barrett. (For services see 5th Goorkhas.)

Captains J. N. S. Kirkwood, 6th Regt. Hyderabad Contingent (Attached), and *Bt. Major A. J. T. Welchman, 7th Bengal Cavalry (Attached)*, served with the regiment from 20 Jan. till 29 June, 1880, the former in command of the Mounted Infantry of the regiment.

1st REGT. PUNJAB INFANTRY.

ON the outbreak of the war the 1st Punjab Infantry was stationed at Quetta, Baluchistan. Forming part of the Division under General Biddulph's command, the regiment crossed the frontier on the 20th Nov., 1878, and marched towards the Pishin Valley in Southern Afghanistan.

During the night of the 9th Jan., 1879, 35 men of the regiment, under Subadar Fyztulub, were attacked while on convoy duty at Kila Abdula by some 300 Atchakzais, whom they defeated with great slaughter. Four of the enemy's dead were found almost on the bayonets of the men. For the judgment of his arrangements and the coolness he displayed, Subadar Fyztulub received, as a special reward, the 1st Class Order of Merit.

On the 12th Jan., 1879, the regiment took part with the other units of the Pishin Moveable Column under Major Keen, 1st P.I., in a night surprise of the hostile Kakarzais in the Arambi Valley. The expedition was successful; and after a number of villages had been destroyed, the regiment returned to Kila Abdula, where it arrived at 5.30 p.m. on the 13th, having marched a distance of 32 miles.

As a unit of the No. 1 Column, Thal-Chotiali F.F., under the command of Major Keen, the 1st Punjab Infantry took part, in the Spring of 1879, in the opening up the new route, eastwards, to India. On the 21st March, the rear-guard of the column, under Captain Lorne Campbell, 1st P.I., was attacked in a difficult pass by some 200 tribesmen, who were driven off with loss, 1 man of the regiment being killed. On the 24th idem the column arrived at Baghao; and about two hours afterwards the videttes which were posted galloped into camp with information of the approach of a tribal army of Zhoband Bori Pathans, some 3,000 strong, which was bearing down upon the position in line, and was also covering the hills to the right. Four companies of the 1st Punjab Infantry were left to protect the camp, and the remainder of the regiment, under Major Higginson, marched out to meet the advance, a party under Major Vallings being thrown into skirmishing order in front of the artillery. After the guns had fired a few rounds, the enemy's line was seen to widen out at both ends. To meet this new distribution, the party under Major Vallings at once moved to the left, while two companies under Major Higginson and Captain Campbell were sent to attempt to crown the heights to the right. The hills were extremely precipitous and difficult to ascend; but the two companies, using hands and feet with the utmost determination, and at times mounting one another's shoulders, succeeded, under a heavy fire from the enemy and undeterred by rolling masses of rock, in scaling and clearing them. In the meantime the party under Major Vallings, having stopped a rush to the left, followed the now retreating enemy into the gorge out of which they had issued prior to the attack. On this day the regiment lost 2 killed and 5 wounded. The gallant conduct displayed during the action by Majors Higginson and Vallings, Captain Campbell, and Lieut. Pears, was brought to the favourable notice of the Major-General in despatches; and for the excellent services they rendered, Subadar-Major Pyabb Sirdar Bahadur, 1 Jemadar, 1 non-commissioned officer, and 2 Sepoys of the regiment were admitted to the 1st Class Order of Merit.

The next day the march was continued, and on the 21st May, 1879, the regiment eventually arrived at Dera Ismail Khan, after an absence from India of more than two years.

The undermentioned officers of the 1st Punjab Infantry served in the war:—

Lt.-Colonel F. J. Keen, C.B., commanded the regiment in the first campaign. Commanded the Pishin Moveable Column from 1 Jan. till 3 March, 1879, and the No. 1 Column Thal-Chotiali F.F. from the date of its formation till it was broken up. Effected the night surprise of the Arambi villages, and defeated the enemy at the action of Baghao. (Mentioned in despatches, and thanked in orders; Brevet of Lt.-Colonel; C.B.)

Majors T. Higginson and *A. Vallings*, *Captain L. R. H. D. Campbell*, and *Lieut. T. C. Pears* served with the regiment throughout the period it was employed in the war, taking part in the night surprise of the Arambi villages, and the action of Baghao. All were mentioned in despatches. *Captain Campbell* was also thanked in orders by Sir D. Stewart for "energy displayed in keeping open the line of communications through the Khojak Pass during very severe weather," and commanded the rear-guard which repulsed the enemy's attack 21 March, 1879. *Lieut. Pears* acted as Staff Officer to the No. 1 Column, Thal-Chotiali F.F., and during the second campaign accompanied Mr. Lepel Griffin, as 3rd Political Assistant, on his special mission to Kabul in Feb., 1880.

Major H. Howell served with the regiment during the campaign.

Lieut. C. B. Brownlow served with the regiment from 22 Nov. till 31 Dec., 1878; with the 2/60th Rifles, (attached), from 1 Jan. till 31 July, 1879, accompanying the battalion in the advance to Kandahar and Kalat-i-Ghilzai; and with the 3rd Goorkhas (attached), from 1 Aug. till 18 Oct., 1879, accompanying them in the second advance on Kalat-i-Ghilzai.

Captain H. Showers. (Assassinated. See Biographical Division.)

2ND REGT. PUNJAB INFANTRY.

THE 2nd Regt. Punjab Infantry, under the command of Lt.-Colonel H. Tyndall, formed part of the 1st Brigade of the Division under General Roberts which crossed the Kuram into Afghanistan on the 21st Nov., 1878.

On the 28th Nov., 1878, the regiment was present at the affair at the foot of the Peiwar.

On the night of the 1st Dec., 1878, the regiment formed part of the right flank attack on the Peiwar heights under the immediate command of General Roberts, and was engaged with the enemy during the greater part of the following day. Whilst General Roberts was carrying out the second turning movement, the regiment was left to hold the ridge which had been gained by our troops, and repulsed several attacks of the enemy, bivouacking on the same ground during the night.

Throughout the winter of 1878-1879 the 2nd Punjab Infantry was under canvas on the Peiwar heights, employed on fatigue, picquet, and escort duties of the most arduous description. Hard work, combined with exposure to snow and excessive cold, produced great sickness and mortality amongst the native ranks, the want of warm clothing, which was not issued until towards the close of the winter season, being keenly felt.

Subsequently the regiment was ordered down to Habib Killa in the Kuram Valley, being relieved by the 28th N.I., and on April, 1879, on the recommendation of a medical committee, was ordered back to India.

The undermentioned officers of the 2nd Regt. Punjab Infantry served in the war:—

Lt.-Colonel H. Tyndall, C.B., commanded the regiment throughout the period it was employed in the war, being present at the action of the Peiwar Kotal. (Mentioned in despatches; C.B.)

Majors E. C. Codrington and *A. H. Turner, Captains A. D. Strettell* and *J. M. D. Lewes*, and *Lieut. R. R. N. Sturt* served with the regiment throughout the period it was employed in the war, being present at the action of the Peiwar Kotal. *Major Turner* afterwards served from April till July, 1879, in the Transport Dept. of the Kuram Force, and during the advance on Kabul in Oct., 1879, as Political Officer to the Ghilzai tribes on the route from Ali Khel to Kushi; was present at the actions on the Shutargardan, and subsequently marched with the Shutargardan force to Kabul; proceeded to India in Dec., 1879, in political charge of the ex-Amir Yakab Khan, and returning to Kabul, served there as Political Officer till the final evacuation, accompanying, in the meantime, the force under Brigadier-General Macpherson into the Logar Valley on the 25th April, 1879, and being present at the second action of Charasiab. (Twice mentioned in despatches.) *Captain Strettell* was appointed Station Staff Officer at Habib Killa on the regiment being ordered down from the Peiwar heights, and continued to hold the appointment after the regiment returned to India.

Lieut. B. M. Allen rejoined the regiment at Habib Killa from the regimental depôt, and served with it during the remainder of the time it was employed in the war.

4TH REGT. PUNJAB INFANTRY.

ON the 1st Oct., 1879, the 4th Regt. Punjab Infantry was suddenly ordered to proceed from Edwardesabad, where it was then stationed, to Thal, with a view to forming part of a force destined to punish the Zaimusht tribes for their numerous depredations.

The regiment marched on the 5th Oct., and on the 7th idem arrived at Thal, from whence it was summoned on the 19th to proceed by forced marches and without tents to Ali Khel, 85 miles distant; continuing its advance, it arrived at its destination on the 23rd, having escorted a convoy of several hundreds of baggage animals from the Peiwar Kotal on the last march.

On the 28th Oct. the regiment marched to Karatiga, escorting another heavy convoy, and returned to Ali Khel on the 31st idem.

With the rest of the troops at Ali Khel, the 4th Punjab Infantry marched on the 8th Nov., 1879, on an expedition into the Chakmani Valley, to coerce and fine for misdemeanour the various tribes and nomads. This duty performed, the regiment returned to Kuram, arriving on the 15th.

Marching on the 8th Dec., 1879, with the expeditionary force under Brigadier-General Tytler, the 4th Punjab Infantry took part, during the succeeding fortnight, in the operations which were conducted by the column in the Zaimusht territory, and at the action of Zawa on the 14th formed the leading portion of the advanced guard of General Tytler's Column, under the command of Lt.-Colonel Close, which forced the Pass, and destroyed the villages. The enemy at one time occupied a very formidable position, and their fire being accurate and well sustained, the regiment suffered some loss, Lieut. and Adjutant T. J. O'D. Renny falling mortally wounded early in the engagement. Seeing that a front attack would be attended with great loss, Col. Close despatched part of the regiment under Major Hawes to turn the enemy's flank. The movement was highly successful: the regiment fired a volley and charged with great impetuosity, causing the enemy to vacate the position with considerable loss, and enabling the rest of the force to advance without further molestation.

On the 23rd Dec., 1879, the expeditionary force returned to Thal, from whence the regiment made its way back to Edwardesabad, arriving on the 29th idem.

The undermentioned officers of the 4th Regt. Punjab Infantry served in the war:—

Colonel H. P. Close commanded the regiment throughout the period it was employed in the war, taking part in the Zaimusht expediton, and being present, in command of the advanced guard of General Tytler's column, at the action of Zawa. (Mentioned in despatches.)

Majors A. J. D. Hawes and *A. McC. Bruce*, and *Lieuts. O. C. Radford, A. Daniell,* and *G. W. C. Bruce* served with the regiment throughout the period it was employed in the war, taking part in the

Zaimusht expedition, and being present at the action of Zawa. For his services *Major Hawes* was mentioned in despatches.

Bt. Major A. Gaselee. (For services see "Staff.")

Lieut. T. J. O'D. Renny. (Killed in action. For services see Biographical Division.)

5TH REGT. PUNJAB INFANTRY.

ON the 8th October, 1878, the 5th Regt. Punjab Infantry received orders to proceed by forced marches to Thal; and leaving Kohat, where it was then stationed, on the 10th idem, reached its destination three days afterwards, being the first battalion of what afterwards became the Kuram Valley F.F. to arrive on the border.

Taking part in the advance of the Division into hostile territory on the 21st Nov., 1878, the regiment, as the leading corps of the force, was smartly engaged in the reconnaissance in force of the enemy's position on the 28th Nov., Subadar-Major Aziz Khan, Bahadur, being killed, and 4 Sepoys wounded.

On the 2nd Dec., 1878, the 5th Punjab Infantry formed part of the force which was engaged in the assault and capture of the Peiwar Kotal, first being employed in the direct advance under Brigadier-General Cobbe, and subsequently, after being moved by General Roberts to the extreme right, forming the leading battalion in the second movement of the day, which caused the enemy to vacate their almost impregnable position. Its casualties in the action were, 4 men wounded. The enemy defeated and dispersed, the regiment took part in the advance to Ali Khel, and afterwards, on the 13th Dec., returned to Kuram.

Selected to escort the 19 captured guns, together with the sick and wounded, back to Kohat, the regiment commenced its march on the 24th Dec., and reached that station on the 4th Jan., 1879. On the 6th March it proceeded to rejoin Divisional Head-quarters, escorting treasure; and from that date, till September, 1879, was employed on various duties in the Kuram Valley.

On the 7th Sept., 1879, conformably with the orders which were issued for a renewed invasion, the 5th Punjab Infantry, as a unit of the advanced guard of Sir F. Roberts's force, under Brigadier-General Baker, marched forward to the Shutagardan and Kushi. On the 6th Oct., 1879, the regiment took part in the action of Charasiab, one wing, under the command of Captain C. M. Hall, being the more prominently engaged. Its casualties in this engagement were, 4 men killed, and Captain C. Young and 4 men wounded. That evening it bivouacked on the heights, and during the two following days took part in the advance on and occupation of Kabul.

From the 14th Oct. till the 4th Nov. the regiment was absent from Kabul with the force under Brigadier-General Hugh Gough which proceeded to the Shutargardan to relieve the British troops which had been surrounded and attacked by the enemy. Shortly after this duty was accomplished, it formed part of the force under Brigadier-General Baker, which marched from Kabul on the 21st Nov. into the Maidan district to forage and to survey the country, and returned on the 1st Dec., after destroying a number of walled villages. On the 9th Dec. it again proceeded with Brigadier-General Baker up the Logar and into the Maidan Valley; and acting as a portion of the rear-guard during the retirement which was necessitated by a combination of the tribes threatening Kabul, took part in a considerable amount of desultory fighting which ensued. On the 11th Dec., the casualties of the regiment numbered, 1 man killed and 5 wounded, and on the 12th—the day on which General Baker's Brigade returned to Sherpur —1 man wounded.

In the operations round Kabul on the 13th and 14th Dec., the 5th Punjab Infantry took a prominent part, a detachment under Major Pratt, on the 13th, seizing one of the strongly-fortified villages on the Ben-i-Shahr road, and keeping open the communications with Brigadier-General Baker, and on the following day a wing under Captain Hall being engaged in the assault of the Asmai heights, and 100 rifles of the regiment, in conjunction with the 72nd Highlanders and Guides, holding for a time the small conical hill where, later in the day, they were overwhelmed by the enemy. On the 13th the casualties of the regiment were, 4 men wounded, and on the 14th, 1 man killed and 14 wounded. Withdrawing, on the latter date, with the rest of the Division, within the lines of Sherpur, the regiment took part in the defence of the cantonment throughout the siege, and on the 23rd Dec. was engaged in the repulse of the enemy's attack.

On the 27th Dec. the 5th Punjab Infantry marched out with the force under Brigadier-General Baker towards the Koh-i-Daman, and returned on the 31st, after destroying Mir Butcha's fort. The snow lay thick on the ground, the cold was intense, and the work severe. From the beginning of 1880 till the month of May in the same year the regiment was cantoned in Sherpur, but constantly employed on convoy and various fatigue duties. In the second week in May, it accompanied the force under Sir F. Roberts through the Logar Valley, returning *viâ* Maidan and Argandi to Kabul on the 1st June.

On the 6th Aug., 1880, the 5th Punjab Infantry was specially paraded before the Lieut.-General, who, after presenting Orders of Merit to the Native officers and men who had gained that reward, was pleased to express his approbation of the behaviour of the regiment, both in the field and in quarters, during the past two years while serving under his command. On the same day, the regiment moved into the Bala Hissar to garrison it, and took over the picquets on the Sher Darwaza heights. On the evacuation of Kabul, the 5th P.I. picquets were the last to hold these heights above the city, and also to quit the Bala Hissar, the keys of which were handed over by the Officer Commanding to the Amir's representative.

The 5th Punjab Infantry marched from Kabul on the 11th Aug., and returning to the Punjab *viâ* the Khyber Pass, reached Kohat, its station, on the 10th Sept., 1880, after being exactly twenty-three months on service. During that period the Head-quarters accomplished 124 marches, covering a distance of 1,349 miles. The total casualties of the regiment during the war were—118 officers, non-commissioned officers, and men killed or died from disease, and 40 wounded.

The under-mentioned officers of the 5th Regt. Punjab Infantry served in the war:—

Lt.-Colonel J. W. McQueen, C.B., commanded the regiment from the date of its taking the field till 5 Oct., 1879, and again from 26 April, 1880, till the date of its return to India. Commanded the advance guard at the reconnaissance of 28 Nov., 1878, and the second turning movement at the assault of the Peiwar Kotal. (Twice mentioned in despatches; Brevet of Lt.-Colonel; C.B.)

Bt. Lt.-Colonel H. M. Pratt. (For services see 2nd Sikh Infantry.)

Major C. McK. Hall and *Lieuts. R. F. Jameson* and *J. P. Sparling* served with the regiment throughout the period it was employed in the war, taking part in the reconnaissance of 28 Nov., 1878, the assault and capture of the Peiwar Kotal, the action of Charasiab, and the operations round Kabul and defence of Sherpur in Dec., 1879. *Major Hall* was in detached command of a wing of the regiment at the action of Charasiab, and of the wing which was engaged at the storming of the Asmai heights, and for his services was twice mentioned in despatches.

Captain G. Gaisford served with the regiment in the Kuram Valley from March till Aug., 1879, when he was transferred to the command of the Khyber Jezailchi Corps, an appointment he continued to hold till the conclusion of the campaign. Was present at the action of Kam Daka. (Mentioned in despatches.)

Lieut. J. E. Mein joined the regiment at Kabul in Dec., 1879, and served with it till the conclusion of the campaign, taking part in all the operations round Kabul in which it was engaged, and in the defence of Sherpur.

Major C. Young served with the regiment in the Kuram Valley in 1878, and took part with it in the advance on and occupation of Kabul, being present at the action of Charasiab, in which he was wounded. (Mentioned in despatches.)

Lieut. C. W. Young, 17th B. N. I. (Attached), served with the regiment in the Kuram Valley from March till July, 1879.

Lieuts. E. W. St. G. Welchman, 1st Infantry, Hyderabad Contingent (Attached), and *C. J. Orr, 3rd Infantry, Hyderabad Contingent (Attached)*, joined the regiment at Kabul in Jan., 1880, and served with it, respectively, till Sept. and July, 1880.

CENTRAL INDIA HORSE.

A WING each of the 1st and 2nd Regiments Central India Horse, numbering 8 European Officers and 522 Native Officers, Non-commissioned Officers, and men, under the command of Lt.-Colonel C. Martin, crossed the frontier at Jamrud into Afghanistan on the 3rd Feb., 1880, and for the next six months were employed on the Khyber line of communications, with head-quarters at Jalalabad.

On the 18th May the head-quarters, consisting of 79 sabres, crossed the Kabul river, then much swollen, and in flood from the melted snow from the hills, the men swimming their horses across. The following day the Regiment was engaged under the orders of Brigadier-General Doran against a large body of Pathans who had entered the Besud Valley under the leadership of Mullah Khalil. The Pathans, who greatly outnumbered the British force, fled to the refuge of their hills at the first shot, the

Central India Horse killing some 25, with a loss of 1 Native Officer and 2 men severely wounded, 1 horse killed and 4 wounded. On the 21st the regiment was employed in punishing the principal men who had encouraged the invasion of the valley, by destroying their forts; and on the 23rd the regiment returned to Jalalabad, the men again swimming their horses across the Kabul river, 1 syce and 1 horse being drowned in the operation.

A gathering under the leadership of the same Mullah Khalil and Moghul Khan of Goshta having threatened the neighbouring valley of Káma, a force under Brigadier-General Doran, including 181 sabres of the Central India Horse, again crossed the Kabul river lower down. The expedition met with no opposition, the gathering having dispersed. After destroying the fort of a refractory Khan, the force returned to Jalalabad, the men of the Central India Horse swimming their horses for the fourth time across the Kabul river—which, as before, was in high flood, the current running seven miles an hour, and the water icy cold—with loss of 1 sowar, drowned.

The Central India Horse had now been engaged for some months in harassing patrol and escort duties, and in pursuing bands of marauders under the Mullah Fakir, and was preparing to return to India, when orders were suddenly received to join the force being held ready at Kabul under Sir F. Roberts to relieve Kanhahar. Gathering with all speed its scattered detachments, the regiment started on its journey of 128 miles, and by forced marches at the rate of 23 miles a day, with baggage, accomplished the distance and joined Sir F. Roberts on his first march out of Kabul on the 9th August. Taking part, during the three weeks succeeding, in the memorable march to Kandahar, the regiment—which started 476 sabres strong and mustered 449 of all ranks on the 1st Sept.—took part in the crushing defeat of Ayub Khan. In the pursuit, Lieutenant Chamberlain and 5 men were wounded, and 2 horses were killed.

The regiment shortly afterwards returned to its cantonments, having been in the field exactly one year. During that period it lost 18 men from disease and the effects of excessive fatigue.

The under-mentioned officers of the Central India Horse served in the war:—

Lt.-Colonel C. Martin, C.B., commanded the Central India Horse throughout the period it was employed in the war: in the expeditions to Besud and Kama, the march from Kabul to the relief of Kanhahar, and the battle of Kandahar. (Twice mentioned in despatches; C.B.)

Lt.-Colonel H. M. Buller, Major J. Colledge, and *Lieuts. A. Masters* and *H. E. Ravenshaw* served with the Central India Horse throughout the period it was employed in the war, taking part in the expeditions to Besud and Kama, the march from Kabul to the relief of Kandahar, and the battle of Kandahar. *Lt.-Colonel Buller, Major Colledge,* and *Lieut. Masters* were mentioned, for their services, in despatches, the former receiving the Brevet of Lt.-Colonel. *Lieut. Ravenshaw*, who had also taken part in the first campaign as a Transport Officer in Southern Afghanistan, died at Lahore on the 13th Oct., 1880, from the effects of privation and exposure endured during the war.

Lieut. A. G. A. Durand served with the Mhairwarra Battalion, as Adjutant, throughout the first campaign, taking part in both the Bazar Valley expeditions.

Lieut. G. K. Daly served with the Guide Cavalry from Nov., 1879, till 28 July, 1880, when he joined the Central India Horse, and served with it till the conclusion of the war. Took part in the operations in the Koh-i-Daman, the second action of Charasiab, the march from Kabul to the relief of Kandahar, and the battle of Kandahar. (Mentioned in despatches.)

For services of *Bt. Lt.-Colonel M. G. Gerard, Major A. H. S. Neill,* and *Lieuts. G. E. Money* and *N. F. F. Chamberlain,* see "Staff."

BHOPAUL BATTALION.

THE Bhopaul Battalion volunteered for active service at the commencement of the first campaign in 1878, and in November of that year proceeded by rail to Jhelum, and marched thence towards Peshawar. When the regiment quitted Sehore, and for nine months previously, the only officers with it were Colonel H. Forbes, the Commandant, and Captain G. R. Peart, 2nd in Command; on the march, Lieut. E. S. Masters joined the corps as Adjutant, and Lieut. W. J. Orr as Wing Officer.

On arrival at Agra the regiment exchanged its muzzle-loading rifles for the breech-loading Snider. This entailed every spare moment on the march from Jhelum being devoted to teaching the use of the new weapon.

On arrival at Naushahra the Left wing, under command of Captain Peart, was detached to garrison Hoti Mardan, while the Right wing remained at Naushahra. This allowed time for perfecting the men in the use of the new arm, and putting them through a short course of target practice.

In March, 1879, the Right wing moved up the Khyber as far as Lundi Kotal, and shortly afterwards the Left wing was moved to Ali Musjid, and until the signing of the Treaty of Gandamak shared in the daily duties of those camps.

On the conclusion of peace, the regiment returned to Sehore, arriving in June, 1879.

The under-mentioned officers of the Bhopaul Battalion served in the War:—

Major-General Hamilton Forbes (*Retired*), commanded the regiment in its advance to Lundi Kotal, and subsequently till the conclusion of the campaign, the 2nd Brigade Kuram Valley F.F.

Major G. R. Peart marched with the regiment from Sehore, and commanded the Left wing when detached at Hoti Mardan and Ali Musjid.

Lieut. E. S. Masters joined the regiment as Offg. Adjt. on the march from Sehore, and served with the Head-quarters till the conclusion of the campaign.

Lieut. W. J. Orr joined the regiment as Offg. Wing Officer on the march from Sehore, and served with the Left wing till the conclusion of the campaign.

MHAIRWARRA BATTALION.

IN October, 1878, the Mhairwarra Battalion volunteered for service in Afghanistan, and on the 26th of that month marched from Ajmir, where it was then stationed, for Jamrud, the local duties of the men proceeding on service being performed by their pensioned relations. The regiment reached its destination on the 30th Nov., 1878, and throughout the first campaign served as a unit of the 2nd Division Peshawar Valley F.F.

As a portion of the Ali Musjid Column, Head-quarters and 400 men of the regiment, under the command of Major F. W. Boileau, took part in the operations which were conducted in the Bazar Valley in December, 1879; and in the second expedition led by General Maude into the same district in January, 1879, Head-quarters and 320 men of the battalion were again engaged.

At the latter end of March, 1879, the regiment was moved forward to Daka, arriving on the 29th of that month.

On the 21st April two companies of the regiment, under Captain O'Moore Creagh, marched to Kam Daka, where they were surrounded and attacked on the following day by a large body of the enemy. The little force made a very gallant defence, holding the position it had taken up until reinforcements arrived. In this affair the battalion lost 4 men killed and 12 wounded. For the gallantry he displayed on the occasion, Captain Creagh subsequently received the Victoria Cross.

On the 7th of June the Mhairwarra battalion commenced its return march from Daka to India, and reaching Peshawar on the 11th idem, proceeded from thence to Ajmir, where it arrived on the 3rd of July, 1879.

The under-mentioned officers of the Mhairwarra Battalion served in the war:—

Lieut.-Col. F. W. Boileau commanded the Mhairwarra Battalion throughout the period of its service in the war, taking part in both the Bazar Valley expeditions. (Brevet of Lieut.-Colonel.)

Lieut. J. A. Bell served with the Mhairwarra Battalion throughout the period it was employed in the war.

For services of *Major O'M. Creagh, V.C.*, see Biographical Division; of *Lieut. A. G. A. Durand*, see C.I. Horse; of *Lieut. A. E. P. Burn*, see 27th P.N.I.; of *Lieut. W. J. Fairbrother*, see 13th B.N.I.; and of *Lieut. J. Lamb*, see 22nd P.N.I.

1ST REGIMENT MADRAS LIGHT CAVALRY.

THE 1st Regiment Madras Light Infantry, under the command of Lieut.-Colonel E. M. Cherry, left Secunderabad on the 19th of April, 1880, under orders for Kandahar, and proceeding by way of Bombay and Karachi, reached Jacobabad on the 5th of May.

A squadron of the 2nd Madras Light Cavalry, under Capt. W. B. Warner, with Lieut. R. G. Jones, joined the 1st Light Cavalry on the 11th of May, 1880, in order to bring the regiment up to its full strength.

On the 22nd of July the regiment was railed from Jacobabad to Sibi, with orders to proceed to Kandahar direct, and commenced its march the same evening. It was supplied with unbroken pack-bullocks for transport; but though six men were told off to each animal to load it, it was found next to impossible to accomplish this feat, and of the 350 bullocks which were supplied, only 80 arrived at the end of the first march.

The regiment arrived at Quetta on the 3rd of August, 1880; and detaching one squadron, under Captain Warner, which ultimately formed part of the advanced Cavalry Brigade of General Phayre's force, continued its advance to Kushdil Khan, where it arrived on the 7th of August. While *en route*, a letter was received from the Officer Commanding at Kushdil Khan hastening the regiment forward, as he was in expectation of his small garrison being overwhelmed by the hill tribes. Nothing, however, came of the projected attack; the tribes, hearing of the arrival of the reinforcement, not venturing nearer than a neighbouring village, which they looted during the night.

The 1st Light Cavalry remained at Kushdil Khan from the 7th Aug. till the 18th Oct., 1880, during which period rumours were constantly heard of a projected attack. On the 25th Aug. a squadron proceeded to Kila Abdulla, to join Sir R. Phayre's force. At this post the officer commanding it, Captain Hope, was invalided. The squadron under Captain Warner, after returning from Kandahar, was stationed at Gulistan, where he also had to appear before a medical board, and leave for England. The command of this squadron devolved on Lieut. Jones, who subsequently proceeded with it to Shorawak to collect supplies, where it remained till the end of March, 1881.

The Head-quarters received orders on the 16th Oct., 1880, to return from Kushdil Khan to Quetta, and from thence down the Bolan Pass to Muskoff, Sibi, Thulli, &c. From these posts the regiment furnished small detachments for the Marri country.

The Head-quarters reached Thulli on the 6th Jan., and remained there till the 27th April, 1881, when the regiment was relieved by the Sind Horse, and continuing its march, eventually made its way to Bangalore, where it arrived on the 15th May, 1881, after an absence of one year and twenty-five days on service.

The under-mentioned officers served with the 1st Regiment Madras Light Cavalry during the period it was employed in the war:—

Lt.-Colonel E. M. Cherry (in command), *Lt.-Colonel A. D. Parsons* (invalided from Jacobabad, July, 1880), *Major H. R. Hope* (invalided from Kila Abdulla, Aug., 1880), *Captain A. W. H. Hornsby, Lieuts. A. P. Westlake* and *G. S. Kerrich, Major W. B. Warner* and *Lieut. R. G. Jones, 2nd Light Cavalry (Attached).*

Lieut. E. E. W. Lawford served during the second campaign, from Oct., 1879, till the conclusion of the war, first as Transport Officer on line of communications between Quetta and Kandahar, then as Offg. General Transport Officer at Kandahar, then as Brigade T. O. with General Burrows's Brigade, being present at the action of Girishk, the Cavalry skirmish at Khushk-i-Nakhud, and the battle of Maiwand. Was in Kandahar throughout the Siege, and remained there as Paymaster, Transport Train, till end of Oct., 1880. Joined the 1st Light Cavalry at Sibi, and served with it till its return from service.

1st REGIMENT MADRAS NATIVE INFANTRY.

AS a unit of the Kuram Reserve Division, the 1st Regt. Madras N.I. garrisoned Kohat from the 8th Nov., 1879, the date of its arrival at that station, till the close of the year: it was then ordered to Peshawar, and from thence proceeded by double marches to Landi Kotal, where it arrived on the evening of the 14th Jan., 1880.

On the 15th Jan., Head-quarters and 300 rank and file joined the force, under Brigadier-General Doran, proceeding to Kam Daka to attack the Mohmands, and after taking part in the operations which were conducted in the neighbourhood of that post, returned to Landi Kotal on the 18th and 19th idem.

On the 21st Jan., 1880, the regiment was moved forward to Daka, where it remained till the 22nd March. On that date it was ordered on to Jalalabad, whither it advanced, leaving detachments *en route* at Barikab, Girdikas, Lachipur, and Ali Bogan. Barikab and Ali Boghan were subsequently abandoned, the garrisons proceeding to Chardeh.

On the 30th April, 1880, Captain Quin, commanding at Barikab, made a most successful capture. Hearing that a convoy had been looted, he went out with one British officer (Lieut. Pink, of the 2nd "Queen's"), the Native Political Assistant, and eight men of the Central India Horse, recovered the plunder, and brought in over 50 of the raiders as prisoners. They were all armed, but gave up their arms when ordered to do so, apparently imagining that a large force was in close proximity.

From the 15th to the 24th May, 1880, 100 rank and file of the regiment formed part of the expeditionary force, under Brigadier-General Doran, operating in the Besud Valley.

The regiment remained at Jalalabad till the 22nd Aug., 1880, when it commenced its return march to India.

The under-mentioned officers of the 1st Regt. Madras Native Infantry served in the war :—

Colonel F. Dawson, C.B., 11*th Madras N.I.*, commanded the regiment till invalided shortly before the conclusion of the campaign, taking part in the operations at Kam Daka and in the Besud Valley. (Mentioned in despatches ; C.B.)

Lt.-Colonel H. S. Robinson served with the 15th Regt. Madras N.I., in the Khyber, during the period it was employed in the war.

Lt.-Colonel G. Tyndall served with the regiment throughout the period it was employed in the war, commanding it after the return of Col. Dawson to India, and taking part in the operations at Kam Daka and in the Besud Valley.

Major E. Shaw served during the second campaign, first with the 15th Regt. Madras N.I. in the Khyber, and afterwards with the 1st Regt. Madras N.I.

Major F. Hope Mathias, 38*th Madras N.I.,* and *Lieuts. H. D. Keary* and *A. H. Clark-Kennedy* served with the regiment throughout the period it was employed in the war, the latter as Adjutant, taking part in the operations at Kam Daka.

Captain E. Quin served with the regiment throughout the period it was employed in the war. While commanding at Barikab, effected the capture of a band of armed marauders who had crossed the Kabul River and looted a convoy. (Commanded by General Bright and Brigadier-General Doran.)

Captain G. C. Fenwick and *Lieut. J. W. Parker, North Staffordshire Regt. (Attached),* served with the regiment throughout the period it was employed in the war, taking part in the operations in the Besud Valley.

Lieut J. H. Jones, East Surrey Regt. (attached), served with the regiment during the period it was employed in the war.

4TH REGT. MADRAS NATIVE INFANTRY.

IN September, 1879, the 4th Regt. Madras N.I. proceeded on field service from Bangalore, and joined the Reserve Division at Peshawar.

During December, 1879, and the earlier part of January, 1880, the regiment performed garrison duty at Ali Musjid. During the latter month it was moved forward to Lundi Kotal, and shortly afterwards advanced with Brigadier-General Doran's Brigade to Jalalabad, furnishing various posts *en route.*

From the 15th to the 18th Jan., 1880, a portion of the regiment was engaged with Brigadier-General Doran's column in the operations which were conducted against the hostile Mohmands in the neighbourhood of Kam Daka, terminating in the destruction of Raina, across the Kabul River.

In the last week in March, 1880, two companies of the regiment formed part of a column under Lieut.-Colonel Hodding, 4th Madras N.I., which was sent from Jalalabad to Lachipur to support Azim Khan against Moghul Khan of Goshta, and two more companies formed part of another column under Brigadier-General Doran which proceeded to the same destination with the object of reinforcing the former. Moghul Khan taking to flight, the united columns returned to Jalalabad.

During the night of the 26th March, 1880, the garrison of Fort Battye, consisting of 100 men of the 4th Madras N.I., and a few other details, the whole under Major Blenkinsop, 4th M.N.I., repelled with great gallantry a most determined attack made by a large combined force of Shinwaris and Kugianis, inflicting considerable loss upon them.

In the first week in April, 1880, a portion of the 4th Madras N.I. formed part of the expeditionary force under Brigadier-General Doran which conducted operations against the Wazir Kugianis in the first week in April, 1880.

In the third week in May, 1880, a portion of the 4th Madras N.I. crossed the Kabul River with the expeditionary force under Brigadier-General Doran, and took part in the operations which were conducted against the Safis and men of the Kunar Valley in the Besud district, including the action of Beninga.

In the first week in June, 1880, a portion of the 4th Madras N.I. took part with the expeditionary force under Brigadier-General Doran in the operations which were conducted across the Kabul River in the district of Kama.

The regiment remained serving on the Khyber line till the evacuation of Kandahar in August, 1880, when it marched back to India and returned to Bangalore.

The under-mentioned officers served with the regiment during the period it was employed in the war, being present at the action of Kam Daka:—
Lt.-Colonel G. C. Hodding (in command). (Mentioned in despatches.)
Major J. H. M. Barnett. (Mentioned in despatches.)
Lieut. D. D. Passy (was also present at the operations in Kama) and *Lieut. H. Eardley-Wilmot, 3rd Madras Cavalry* (attached).
Major J. Godson. (Deceased. See Biographical Division.)
Major E. G. Blenkinsop commanded at Fort Battye when it was attacked during the night of the 26th March, 1880.
Captain J. E. Porteous served with the regiment as regimental Transport Officer during the period it was employed in the war, being present at the action of Kam Daka, the operations against the Wazir Kugianis, the operations in Besud, and the action of Beninga (in which he commanded the detachment engaged), and the operations in Kama (during which he acted as Orderly Officer to Brigadier-General Doran). (Mentioned in despatches.)

15TH REGT. MADRAS NATIVE INFANTRY.

IN September, 1879, the 15th Regt. Madras N.I. proceeded on field service from Bangalore, and in November joined the Reserve Division at Peshawar.

Till the middle of March, 1880, the regiment performed garrison duty at Peshawar and Jamrud.

In the third week in January, 1880, a portion of the regiment formed part of a small flying column under the command of Col. Hearn, 15th Madras N.I., which was sent out from Peshawar to operate, near Fort Michin, on the left flank of a large body of Mohmands who had crossed the Kabul River, and were about to be attacked in the neighbourhood of Daka by co-operating columns under Brigadier-General Doran and Col. Boisragon.

On the Reserve Division being broken up, the Head-quarters 15th Madras N.I. moved forward to Daka, detachments being furnished for Barikab and Haft Chah. The regiment now appeared as a unit of the 1st Section Khyber Line Force, under the command of Brigadier-General Gib.

In the early days of June, 1880, a detachment of the 15th Madras N.I. took part with the expeditionary force under Brigadier-General Doran in the operations which were conducted across the Kabul River in the district of Kama.

The regiment remained serving on the Khyber line till the evacuation of Kabul in August, 1880, when it marched back to India, and returned to Bangalore.

The under-mentioned officers served with the 15th Regt. Madras N.I. during the period it was employed in the war:—
Colonel G. Hearn (in command; also commanded a flying column sent out from Peshawar in January, 1880, to operate against the Mohmands), *Lieut.-Colonel A. T. Cox, Majors L. B. Bance, A. S. Grove, C. R. Broadstreet,* and *W. P. O. Boulderson,* and *Lieuts. E. R. J. Presgrave* and *E. S. Hastings, 25th Madras N.I.*

21ST REGT. MADRAS NATIVE INFANTRY.

ON the 11th Feb., 1879, orders were received at Multan for a wing of the 21st Regt. Madras N.I., which had recently arrived at that station from Bellary, to proceed to Dera Ghazi Khan, to form part of a column—subsequently designated the Dera Ghazi Column, Thal-Chotiali F.F.—under the command of Lt.-Colonel Guy Prendergast, 15th Bengal Cavalry. Conformably with these orders the Left wing of the regiment, under Major F. Beckford Middleton, marched from Multan on the 13th Feb., and crossing the Cheneband Indus, arrived at its destination on the 16th idem.

On the 24th Feb., 1879, the Left wing marched with the Column from Dera Ghazi Khan, and taking part in its successive advances through the Chachar and Han Passes, arrived on the 3rd April at Chotiali, where a junction was effected with the leading column (Major Keen's) of Major-General Biddulph's force, advancing eastwards from Pishin. On the 5th April, part of the Dera Ghazi Column, including the wing of the 21st, accompanied by the column under Major Keen, set out on its return march to the Vitakri Valley; and on the 9th April the Dera Ghazi Column occupied its old camping-ground near Nahar-Ki-Kot, where, by the 12th, the whole of General Biddulph's force arrived. On the 14th the greater portion of the assembled troops departed for India, the Dera Ghazi Column, strengthened by the 1st Punjab Infantry, remaining behind, and being reconstituted as the Vitakri Field Force, under the command of Brigadier-General Nuttall. As a portion of this force, the command of which subsequently reverted to Lieut.-Colonel Prendergast, and eventually devolved on Colonel Georges, 30th Madras N.I., the Left wing of the 21st N.I. continued to serve until the final evacuation of the position in December, 1879, when it made its way back through the Chachar Pass to Dera Ghazi Khan, and eventually to Trichinopoly.

During the latter part of its service, the regiment, in common with the other troops at Vitakri, suffered much from the severe outbreak of scurvy which visited the Force in the autumn of 1879.

The under-mentioned officers served with the wing 21st Regt. Madras N.I. in the Dera Ghazi Column Thal Chotiali F.F. and the Vitakri F.F., throughout the period it was employed in the war:—

Major T. B. Middleton (in command), *Major W. Stainforth* (acted as Transport Officer of the Vitakri F.F. from 15 April till 31 Oct., 1879), and *Lieut. M. H. S. Grover* (as Adjutant).

30TH REGT. MADRAS NATIVE INFANTRY.

AT the end of November, 1878, when stationed at French Rocks, near Mysore, the 30th Regt. Madras N.I. received orders to proceed on service to Afghanistan; and quitting its station on the 5th Dec., made its way to Multan, where it arrived on the 28th idem.

On the 2nd Jan., 1879, the Head-quarters and Right wing, under the command of Colonel Georges, left for Mithankot, and were encamped there from the 7th till the 10th Feb.: on that date they proceeded to Rajanpur, and for the next eight months were employed in supplying a line of Frontier outposts, and sending convoys with supplies to the more advanced posts.

On the 6th Oct., 1879, the Head-quarters and Right wing were ordered up to the standing camp at Vitakri.

In the meantime the Left wing, which had been left behind at Multan under the command of Major St. John, received telegraphic orders on the 27th Jan., 1879, to proceed by forced marches to Dera Ghazi Khan, where it arrived on the 31st idem.

Detailed to the Dera Ghazi Column of the Thal-Chotiali F.F., under the command of Lt.-Colonel Guy Prendergast, the Left wing took part in the advance of that force at the latter end of Feb., 1880, through the Chachar and Han passes to Chotiali, where a junction was effected with the brigade under Brigadier-General Nuttall's command marching eastwards from Pishin. The wing remained at Chotiali three days after General Nuttall's brigade continued its march from that place, and then, following it, joined the remainder of General Biddulph's Division concentrated at Nahar-Ki-Kot. After a brief halt at that post, Colonel Prendergast's column was ordered on to Vitakri, where it formed a standing camp. Here the Left wing remained till shortly after the arrival of the Head-quarters and Right wing, at the latter end of October, 1879, when it was sent down to Dera Ghazi Khan, the remainder of the regiment following on the 9th Jan., 1880.

While at Dera Ghazi Khan, the regiment supplied all the Infantry outposts along the frontier, the work entailed being continuous and severe.

On the 22nd Nov., 1880, the 30th Madras N.I. marched from Dera Ghazi Khan to Multan, from whence it was railed to Trichinopoly.

From the date of its arrival at Multan in Dec., 1878, till the date of its return to Trichinopoly in Nov., 1880, the regiment formed part of the Reserve Force under the command of Sir Donald Stewart.

The under-mentioned officers of the 30th Regt. Madras N.I. served in the war:—

Colonel T. C. Georges commanded the regiment throughout the period of its service in the war, and the Vitakri F.F. during the latter part of the second campaign.

Major F. C. St. John commanded the Left wing throughout the period the regiment was employed in the war, taking part in the opening up from the eastward of the Thal-Chotiali route. (Received the thanks of Govt.)

Major F. S. Fitzpatrick served with the regiment during the war, being detached to Thal to escort Artillery, &c.

Lieut. R. H. C. Tufnell served with the Head-quarters throughout the period the regiment was employed in the war.

Lieuts. T. W. J. M. Georges and *J. M. Clements*, Erinpoorah Irregular Force (Attached), served with the Left wing throughout the period the regiment was employed in the war, taking part in the opening up, from the eastward, of the Thal-Chotiali route. *Lieut. Georges* acted for a time as Staff Officer to the Vitakri F.F.

2ND REGT. BOMBAY LIGHT CAVALRY.

DURING the spring and early summer of 1880, the 2nd Bombay Light Cavalry served at Jacobabad, Quetta, and Sibi, in the Reserve Division Kandahar Field Force.

On the forward concentration of the troops in August, 1880, in consequence of the news of the disaster at Maiwand, the regiment was moved up to Kila Abdulla, and as a unit of General Phayre's relieving force took part in the advance to Kandahar.

The regiment remained serving in the neighbourhood of Kandahar and on the line of communications till after the evacuation of that city by the British Forces.

The under-mentioned officers served with the 2nd Regt. Bombay Light Cavalry during the period it was employed in the war:—

Lieut.-Colonel A. W. Macnaghten, Majors W. H. J. Stopford and *J. Fagan, Captain W. H. D. Jones,* and *Lieut. A. Pringle.*

3RD (QUEEN'S OWN) REGT. BOMBAY LIGHT CAVALRY.

IN February, 1880, the 3rd (Queen's Own) Regt. Bombay Light Cavalry left Disa and Rajkot, and marched by squadrons to Kandahar, a distance of over 800 miles, the great desert from Disa to Rohri on the Indus *viâ* Umerkot being crossed *en route*. The 2nd Squadron was kept two months on outpost duty in the Kurnai Pass; but the whole regiment concentrated at Kandahar on the 1st June.

Forming part of the Cavalry Brigade with General Burrows's force, 300 sabres of the regiment marched out of Kandahar on the 4th July, 1880, for Girishk, and on the 14th idem took part in the action on the Halmand, the pursuit of the Wali's mutineers, and the capture of his six smooth-bore guns, charging down and taking possession of the latter after they had been silenced by the Horse Artillery.

From the 14th to the 26th July, the regiment was employed in constant reconnoitring duty, and on the 23rd July went out with the R.H.A. and drove back a strong reconnoitring party of the enemy's cavalry.

On the 27th July, 1880, the 3rd Bombay Cavalry was engaged in the battle of Maiwand. Broken up in detachments, and kept standing under a murderous fire for four hours, without a vestige of cover, the regiment underwent as severe an ordeal as any to which Cavalry can be subjected; but the men remained perfectly steady in line, although shells and round shot were raking through their ranks. When the Ghazi rush took place, and the guns and Infantry fell back, they formed up, and charged to the best of their power, sweeping along the rear of the retreating Infantry and cutting up the Ghazis, who were close upon and hacking down the Sepoys. The 1st Bombay Grenadiers subsequently acknowledged publicly the great assistance rendered them by the 3rd Cavalry at this critical juncture. The regiment covered the retirement of the four Horse Artillery guns from the field, keeping in perfect order during the trying night march, and was the last portion of the Brigade to cross the Argandab River; Lieut. Geoghegan, who had remained behind at Hussa-Madat with 40 sabres to bring up stragglers, being far in rear of all. For this officer the regiment waited at the ford across the Argandab, and eventually marched into the Kandahar Citadel at 3 p.m. on the 28th July, having mounted at Khushk-i-Nakhud at 5 a.m. on the 27th, and having been thirty-four hours in the saddle without food. Its casualties in the battle were, 1 officer and 20 non-commissioned officers and men killed, and 2 officers and 19 non-commissioned officers and men wounded. 58 horses were also killed, and 42 wounded.

From the 29th July to the 30th August the 3rd Bombay Cavalry was employed daily, during the defence of Kandahar, in reconnoitring duty, and nightly, in guarding a portion of the walls against attack.

On the 16th Aug., 1880, 100 sabres of the regiment and 2 officers took part in the sortie and storming of Deh Khwaja. This detachment made two most successful charges, driving back and cutting up 80 to 100 of the enemy, suffering a loss of 5 men killed and 12 wounded, and 13 horses killed and 12 wounded.

At the battle of Kandahar, on the 1st Sept., 1880, the 3rd Bombay Cavalry was employed nearly all day in watching large numbers of Ghazis collected on the low hills in front of the Baba Wali Kotal, and guarding the right flank of the force which made a feint of delivering a direct attack on their position on the Pass. Crossing the Kotal in the afternoon, the regiment took part in the pursuit of Ayub's broken army for 15 miles up the valley of the Argandab, getting amongst the fugitives, and sabring a considerable number. Its casualties during the pursuit were, 1 native officer and 1 man killed; 1 horse was also killed, and 2 wounded.

On the 3rd Sept., 1880, the 3rd Bombay Cavalry marched from Kandahar, and occupied the road posts extending to Kushdil Khan, in the Pishin Valley, and was engaged throughout the succeeding severe winter in escorting the daily mails both ways, and in giving escorts to officers and others passing to and fro. The Head-quarters were in Kandahar till the 15th Nov., 1880, when they marched down to the mouth of the Bolan, escorting a sick convoy, and encamped at Kushdali till the regiment was concentrated there in April, 1880, in which month it proceeded to India.

The 3rd Bombay Cavalry lost by death during the campaign, either killed in action, or died from wounds or disease, 1 European officer, 53 Natives of all ranks, and 171 horses.

The under-mentioned officers of the 3rd Queen's Own Regt. Bombay Light Cavalry served in the war:—

Major A. P. Currie commanded the regiment throughout the period of its service in the war: at the action of Girishk, the battle of Maiwand, the defence of Kandahar, and the battle of Kandahar. (Mentioned in despatches.)

Major J. F. Willoughby served with the regiment during the war, being in Kandahar throughout the defence, and present at the battle of Kandahar.

Captain M. Mayne and *Lieut. T. P. Geoghegan* served with the regiment throughout the period it was employed in the war, being present at the action of Girishk, the battle of Maiwand, the defence of Kandahar, the sortie to Deh Khwaja, and the battle of Kandahar. *Captain Mayne* was twice hit at the battle of Maiwand, first with a spent ball in the chest, and afterwards with a piece of shell, which grazed his shoulder. While reconnoitring during the siege, his horse was wounded under him. At the sortie to Deh Khwaja he commanded the detachment of the regiment which was engaged, and for his services on that occasion, as also for the services he rendered during the siege, was mentioned in despatches. *Lieut. Geoghegan* had two horses shot under him, one at Maiwand, and one at Deh Khwaja. For his services he was mentioned in despatches.

Lieut. J. Monteith served during the second campaign as Orderly Officer to Brigadier-General Nuttall, being present at the action of Girishk, the battle of Maiwand, the defence of Kandahar, the sortie to Deh Khwaja, and the battle of Kandahar. (Three times mentioned in despatches.)

Lieut. W. C. Owen. (Killed in action. See Biographical Division.)

Lieut. J. H. E. Reid, King's Own Borderers (Attached), served with the regiment during the campaign, being present at the action of Girishk and the battle of Maiwand, in which he was wounded, and being in Kandahar throughour the siege. (Mentioned in despatches.)

POONA HORSE.

ON the 17th Jan., 1880, the Poona Horse, then stationed at Sirur in the Bombay Presidency, received orders to hold itself in readiness for service in Southern Afghanistan. At that time about half the regiment was serving under the Civil authorities in the Poona, Sholapur, and Sattara Districts: these parties were ordered to rejoin Head-quarters at Sirur immediately; and on the 28th of the month the regiment marched for Bombay, where it arrived on the 5th Feb., 1880.

From Bombay the Poona Horse proceeded in four detachments to Sibi; the first two leaving on the 7th Feb., under Major Hogg and Lieut. Minchin respectively; the 3rd, on the 13th, under Major Stevenson, and the Head-quarters, under Lieut.-Colonel La Touche, with Captain Erskine, Lieut. and Adjutant Anderson, and Surgeon Stewart, on the 15th.

The regiment concentrated at Sibi on the 27th Feb., and remained there till the 13th March, when a wing, under Major Stevenson, commenced its march to Quetta. On the 22nd March, a party of 30 sabres, under a Native Officer, was detached as escort to Major-General Primrose, who was proceeding to Kandahar to take the command of the Field Force; and on the following day, the Head-quarters started for Quetta, a small party being left behind to escort Brigadier-General Brooke to Kandahar. Head-quarters arrived on the 10th April at Quetta, from whence, a few days previously, a squadron under Major Erskine, who had advanced with Major Stevenson's Wing, had marched to Kushdil Khan.

On the 20th April the regiment resumed its march to Kandahar, leaving detachments at the six posts on the line from Chamon. Major Stevenson, who had been left behind at Quetta on the departure of Head-quarters, died there on the 26th April from pleuro-pneumonia; Lieut.-Col. H. Phillipps, of the 2nd Bombay Light Cavalry, being appointed to succeed him.

Kandahar was reached on the 1st May, and on the 27th, Lieut.-Colonel Phillipps arrived to take up his appointment, Major Hogg on the following day being appointed Brigade-Major to the Cavalry Brigade under Brigadier-General Nuttall.

On the departure of Brigadier-General Burrows's Brigade for the Halmand at the end of June, the Poona Horse, on account of its numerical weakness (only some 180 men of all ranks being with Head-quarters) remained for garrison duty in Kandahar. When the news of the disaster of Maiwand came in, a party of 50 men, under Captain Anderson, proceeded with Brigadier-General Brooke's force to Sinjiri to cover the retreat of the stragglers, and "inflicted"—to quote the words of the Brigadier's despatch—"considerable loss on the enemy by two well-executed charges." For their conduct on this occasion, seven men were recommended for, and obtained the Order of Merit. Another party of 30 men, under a Native officer, was sent to Mundi Hissar to bring in the post stationed there, and pass on orders for the posts of Abdul Rahman to Gatai to fall back on Chaman.

During the siege of Kandahar the Poona Horse (total strength 220 of all ranks) was employed every day on covering and working parties. The regiment also took part in the affair at Khairabad, and the sortie to Deh Khwaja. At the sortie, in which 100 of all ranks were engaged, 1 Native officer was killed, and Surgeon Stewart and 5 men were wounded. 9 horses were also killed, and 16 (of which 3 were afterwards destroyed) wounded. Two men of the regiment, who were orderlies to General Brooke, were for their gallantry on this occasion decorated with the Order of Merit.

On the advance guard of General Roberts's force being signalled at Robat on the 27th Aug., a party of 50 sabres proceeded as an escort to Lieut.-Colonel St. John, the Resident, to communicate with Brigadier-General Hugh Gough, who commanded the Cavalry Brigade and advance guard of the Kabul Kandahar Force.

At the battle of the 1st September the regiment was out with the Bombay Cavalry Brigade, under Brigadier-General Nuttall, and when the enemy were retreating, was detached to prevent stragglers escaping through the Kotal-i-Murcha Pass.

The parties of the regiment who had concentrated at Chaman on the withdrawal of the posts from the line of communications were during the investment of Kandahar employed under Major Westmacott, Road Commandant, in keeping open the Khojak Pass. Later on they were joined by the troop under Major Erskine from Kushdil Khan, and formed part of Major-General Phayre's advance force for the relief of Kandahar.

On the 8th Sept., 1880, Head-quarters and 200 sabres marched as part of Brigadier-General Daubeny's Brigade to Maiwand, for the purpose of searching for arms and prisoners and burying the dead. After a three days' halt at that place, the Brigade marched back to Kokaran, at which place Major Erskine with some 180 men rejoined. On the breaking up of this Brigade the regiment was transferred to the Cavalry Brigade under Brigadier-General Wilkinson, and on the 16th Oct., moved with that force into a new camping-ground at Kohak; Lieut.-Col. Phillipps being at the same time detached with one squadron to Kandahar. The Head-quarters and remainder of the regiment followed on the 3rd Nov., and remained in quarters till the 20th Jan., 1881, when it was ordered to proceed with a force of all arms under command of Brigadier-General Wilkinson to Maiwand. On the 12th Feb. the regiment, with the other units of this force returned to Kandahar, and remained there till the final evacuation, when it made its way back to India.

The under-mentioned officers of the Poona Horse served in the war:—

Colonel C. D'U. La Touche commanded the regiment throughout the period of its service in the war: during the siege of Kandahar, at the sortie to Deh Khwaja, and at the battle of Kandahar. Commanded the force engaged in the sortie to Khairabad. (Mentioned in despatches.)

Lieut.-Colonel H. Phillipps served with the Head-quarters of the regiment from 27 May, 1880, till the return to India, taking part in the defence of Kandahar, the sortie to Khairabad, and the battle of Kandahar.

Major G. C. Hogg served with the Head-quarters during the advance to Kandahar. Was appointed, 1 May, 1880, Brigade-Major to the Cavalry Brigade, and in that capacity took part in the advance to the Halmand, the action of Girishk, the battle of Maiwand, the defence of Kandahar, and the sorties to Khairabad, and Deh Khwaja, in which his horse was shot. (Three times mentioned in despatches.)

Major C. M. Erskine commanded the squadrons of the regiment which formed part of General Phayre's force marching to the relief of Kandahar. (Mentioned in despatches.)

Captain J. W. Anderson served, first with the Head-quarters of the regiment, commanding the party sent out in General Brooke's force to cover the retreat of the stragglers from Maiwand, and taking part in the defence of Kandahar, and the sorties of Khairabad and Deh Khwaja. Served as Brigade-Major Bombay Calvalry Brigade at the battle of Kandahar. (Mentioned in despatches.)

Captain H. P. Young. (For services see "Staff.")

Lieut. H. D. M. Minchin served with the Head-quarters throughout the period the regiment was employed in the war, taking part in the defence of Kandahar, the sorties to Khairabad, and Deh Khwaja, in which his horse was shot, and the battle of Kandahar.

2ND REGIMENT SIND HORSE.

A SQUADRON of the 2nd Regiment Sind Horse, under the command of Captain C. A. de N Lucas, took part, as escort to Sir R. Sandeman, the Governor-General's Agent for Baluchistan, in the advance on and occupation of Kandahar in 1878-1879, It ultimately returned by the Thal-Chotiali route to India, and was present on the 24th March, 1879, at the action of Baghao.

The regiment proceeded on active service from Jacobabad in February, 1880. The 1st Squadron, under Captain Lucas, made its way to Thal-Chotiali, and the 2nd Squadron (which was joined on the 21st April by Captain James, who took over the command,) under Lieut. Abbott, to Hurnai, where they assisted in protecting the line of communications. A troop of the remaining squadron, under Lieut. Monteith, went up the Hurnai route as escort to Sir R. Sandeman; and the Head-quarters, with the remaining troop, went to Quetta, and protected the line of communications from there to Kila Abdulla.

On receipt of the news of the battle of Maiwand in August, 1880, the regimental Head-quarters were ordered to Seggi. By the 26th Aug. the 2nd Sind Horse was concentrated at Kila Abdulla, and the same day made a forced march of 60 miles to Akhta Khan, to protect the water-supply. The Regiment returned to Gatai on the 30th, and marched with the Cavalry Brigade of General Phayre's Division, under Brigadier-General Wilkinson, to the relief of Kandahar. When within 25 miles of its destination, news was received by General Phayre's force, on the 3rd Sept., of the defeat of Ayub Khan's army by General Roberts.

RECORDS OF SERVICE.

The 2nd Sind Horse remained with the Cavalry Brigade in the vicinity of Kandahar till the 25th Sept., when the Head-quarters and two squadrons joined the 1st Infantry Brigade at Khana Girdal and Dahila, in the Argandab Valley, the 1st Squadron accompanying the Cavalry Brigade to Kokaran. On the 9th Nov., the Head-quarters rejoined the Cavalry Brigade, with which the regiment remained till the 24th Feb., 1881, when it took up the line of communications to Kila Abdulla, furnishing Mundi Hissar, Abdul Rahman, Mel Karez, Dubrai, Gatai, Chaman, and Kila Abdulla.

After the evacuation of Kandahar, the regiment returned to Quetta.

The under-mentioned officers of the 2nd Regt. Sind Horse served in the war:—

Major M. M. Carpendale commanded the regiment throughout the period it was employed in the second campaign. (Mentioned in despatches.)

Captain C. A. de N. Lucas commanded the 1st Squadron in both campaigns, taking part in the original advance on and occupation of Kandahar, and the opening up of the Thal-Chotiali route to India, and being present at the action of Baghao. (Mentioned in despatches.)

Captain M. James served with the regiment during the period it was employed in the war from 21st April, 1880. (Mentioned in despatches.)

Captain W. Loch served as Political Officer with the Cavalry Brigade during the advance to Kandahar, and afterwards in charge of the Pishin district. (Mentioned in despatches.)

Captains F. Abbott and *D. G. Mackenzie* served with the regiment throughout the period it was employed in the second campaign.

Lieut. J. Monteith. (For services see 3rd Bombay Cavalry.)

Lieut. E. V. P. Monteith served as Adjutant 3rd Sind Horse throughout both campaigns, being present at the action of Girishk, the affair of the 23rd July, 1880 (in which he commanded the troop of his regiment which was engaged), the battle of Maiwand, the defence of Kandahar, the sortie to Khairabad, and the battle of Kandahar. (Twice mentioned in despatches.)

3RD REGIMENT SIND HORSE.

IN September, 1878, the 3rd Sind Horse then stationed at Jacobabad, was warned for service, and in December made its way through the Bolan Pass to Quetta, and subsequently across the Afghan frontier into the Pishin district.

In January, 1880, the regiment accompanied the advance of General Biddulph's division on Kandahar, 30 sabres forming part of the right column of Brigadier-General Palliser's force proceeding by the Ghwaja route, and the remainder of the regiment following the Khojak route, 40 sabres being detached at Fort Chaman for garrison duty. On the 4th Jan. the detachment proceeding by the Ghwaja route was engaged in the action of Takht-i-pul, and on the 8th idem the regiment took part in the march through the streets of Kandahar.

As a portion of the Cavalry Brigade under Brigadier-General Palliser, the 3rd Sind Horse took part, in the middle of January, 1879, in the advance of General Biddulph's division to the Halmand, and besides being constantly employed on reconnoitring duty, conducted the ferrying operations of the force after its arrival at its destination. On the return march the regiment formed part of the rear-guard of the Brigade commanded by Col. Malcolmson, 3rd Sind Horse, which defeated the enemy with heavy loss at Khushk-i-Nakhud on the 26th Feb., 1880. In this engagement the casualties of the regiment were, Major Reynolds (who fell while gallantly leading the pursuit) and 4 men killed, Colonel Malcolmson and 23 men wounded; 3 horses were also killed, and 25 wounded.

On the 21st Jan., 1879, the detachment of the regiment at Chaman moved out from that post with other details under Major Tulloch, 26th N.I., against a band of marauders. The expedition was highly successful, Nashkar Khan, a notorious robber, and ten of his followers being slain.

On the 7th March, 1879, the 3rd Sind Horse left Kandahar with General Biddulph, and on the 15th idem arrived at Chaman. Joining there the Pishin Moveable Column, the regiment remained employed on convoy and garrison duty in and about the Pishin Valley for a period of twelve months.

In March, 1880, the head-quarters of the regiment returned to Kandahar, one squadron remaining at Khushdil Khan, one troop at Chaman, with detachments at Mundi Hissar and Abdul Rahman.

From the 30th March till the 5th April, 1880, a detachment of the regiment was employed with the force under Lieut.-Colonel Durand, 10th N.I., on the expedition from Hurnai to the Chapar rift, which resulted in the recovery of the body of Captain Showers, 1st P.I., who had been murdered by Kakar Pathans.

On the 17th April a troop of the regiment reconnoitred from Kandahar to Dubrai, to open up communications with that post after the massacre of its garrison, which included two sowars of the 3rd Sind Horse, and on the same day a detachment marched from Khushdil Khan with the same object.

On the 27th April a detachment of the regiment was engaged with other details in the destruction of Abu Said's Fort.

In the beginning of May, 1880, one squadron of the regiment proceeded from Kandahar to Kalat-i-Ghilzai, and subsequently remained, forming part of the garrison of that place till the arrival in August of the force under Sir F. Roberts marching from Kabul to the relief of Kandahar.

Forming part of the Cavalry Brigade of Brigadier-General Burrows's force, Head-quarters and 207 sabres of the 3rd Sind Horse marched out of Kandahar on the 4th July for the Halmand, 50 sabres subsequently arriving as a reinforcement after the brigade had reached Kushk-i-Nakhud. On the 14th July the regiment performed distinguished service in the action of Girishk; on the 23rd, it assisted in driving back a strong reconnoitring party of the enemy's cavalry; and on the 27th it was engaged in the disastrous battle of Maiwand. On this day the casualties of the regiment were, 14 men killed and 5 wounded, 40 horses killed and 9 wounded.

After arriving with the remnants of the brigade at Kandahar, the 3rd Sind Horse was employed throughout the siege in reconnoitring duty and in guarding the walls.

On the 16th Aug., 1880, 100 sabres of the regiment took part in the sortie to Deh Khwaja. Its casualties on this day were, 6 men killed, and Colonel Malcolmson and 2 men wounded, and 15 horses killed and 7 wounded.

On the 1st Sept., 1880, the 3rd Sind Horse was engaged with the Cavalry Brigade under Brigadier-General Nuttall in the defeat of Ayub Khan's army at the battle of Kandahar, taking part in the pursuit which was carried on for fifteen miles up the Valley of the Argandab.

After taking part with Brigadier-General Daubeny's Brigade in the expedition to the field of Maiwand, and being employed for a time on the Kandahar communications, the regiment returned to India, making its way back to Jacobabad.

The under-mentioned officers of the 3rd Regt. Sind Horse served in the war:—

Colonel J. H. P. Malcolmson, C.B., commanded the regiment throughout both campaigns. In command of a force of Cavalry and Infantry, defeated 1,500 Alizais at the action of Kushk-i-Nakhud. Took part in the action of Girishk, the battle of Maiwand, the defence of Kandahar, the sortie to Deh Khwaja, and the battle of Kandahar. (Four times mentioned in despatches.)

Major W. Reynolds. (Killed in action. See Biographical Division.)

Major J. E. Gordon served with the regiment in the first campaign till invalided, 3 May, 1879, and again during the second campaign, taking part in the actions of Shah Jui and Girishk, the battle of Maiwand, and the defence and battle of Kandahar. (Mentioned in despatches.)

Captain P. J. Maitland served in the first campaign, first with the regiment, from 27 Dec., taking part in the action of Kushk-i-Nakhud and afterwards with the Survey Dept., mapping the country round Kandahar. In the second campaign served as Deputy Assistant Quartermaster-General, 3rd Division Kabul F.F. (Mentioned in despatches.)

Captain H. C. Hogg served with the regiment throughout the first campaign, taking part in the action of Khushk-i-Nakhud. (Mentioned in despatches.)

Captain E. D. N. Smith and *Lieut. A. N. Monteith* served with the regiment throughout both campaigns, taking part in the actions of Khushk-i-Nakhud (in which Capt. Smith's charger was wounded) and Girishk, the battle of Maiwand, the defence of Kandahar, the sortie to Deh Khwaja, and the battle of Kandahar. Both were mentioned, for their services, in despatches, *Captain Smith* twice.

Captain E. V. P. Monteith. (For services see 2nd Sind Horse.)

1st REGT. BOMBAY NATIVE INFANTRY (GRENADIERS).

THE 1st Regt. Bombay Grenadiers was stationed at Ahmedabad when, in November, 1878, it was ordered to hold itself in readiness for service in Afghanistan. In December it embarked for Bombay, and on the 16th of that month arrived at Sukkur.

Till June, 1879, the Bombay Grenadiers furnished numerous escorts on the line of communications from Jacobabad to Quetta, and small posts at each intervening stage. In February, 1879, Head-quarters left Jacobabad and crossed the frontier, escorting the Siege Train, and for the next twelve months were employed in the Bolan Pass in making roads and escorting stores. On the expiration of that period the regiment marched for Kandahar, escorting the Siege Train from Quetta, and on arriving at its destination was quartered in the Citadel.

As a unit of the Infantry Brigade, the 1st Grenadiers, 646 strong, took part in the advance of General Burrows's force in July, 1880, for the Halmand, and during the action of Girishk, on the 14th of that month, assisted in guarding the camp. At the battle of Maiwand, on the 27th, 476 of all ranks held the left of the fighting line, 170 being on baggage and rear-guard duty. On this disastrous day the losses sustained by the regiment were of appalling magnitude. Of the 7 British officers present, 2 were killed, and 2 wounded; of the 15 native officers, 8 were killed, and 4 wounded; and of the 624 men, 347 were killed, and 55 wounded. The remainder underwent the indescribable horrors of retreat, straggling into Kandahar, on the 28th, by twos and threes.

All that was left of the regiment assisted in the defence of Kandahar from 28th July till the 31st Aug.; and on the 1st Sept. two companies were mustered to take part in the defeat of Ayub Khan's army.

The 1st Grenadiers left Kandahar on the 8th Oct., 1880, for India, and eventually arrived at Bombay on the 3rd Dec.

The under-mentioned officers of the 1st Regt. Bombay Native Infantry (Grenadiers) served in the war:—

Colonel C. T. Heathcote, C.B. (For services see 19th Bombay N.I.)

Colonel H. S. Anderson commanded the regiment throughout the period it was employed in the war, except during an interval between Nov., 1879, and April, 1880, when he was invalided to England. Commanded the regiment at the battle of Maiwand, when he was severely wounded by a shell. Was present in Kandahar throughout the siege. (Mentioned in despatches.)

Lieut.-Colonel C. M. Griffith joined the regiment in the Bolan Pass in Oct., 1879, and served with it throughout the remainder of the campaign, being present at the battle of Maiwand, the defence of Kandahar, and the battle of Kandahar, in which he commanded the companies under arms. (Mentioned in despatches.)

Major W. R. Trevelyan joined the regiment in May, 1879, and served with it in the Bolan Pass till invalided to England in Feb., 1880.

Captain J. Grant served with the regiment throughout the period it was employed in the war, being present at the battle of Maiwand, in which he was severely wounded. Was in Kandahar throughout the siege. (Mentioned in despatches.)

Lieut. C. W. Hinde served with the regiment, as Adjutant, till killed in action at the battle of Maiwand, 27 July, 1880.

Lieut. W. C. Aslett served with the regiment throughout the period it was employed in the war, being present at the battle of Maiwand, in Kandahar throughout the siege, and at the battle of Kandahar. At the battle of Maiwand a bullet struck his helmet, turning it completely round, and another smashing in his sword-guard, killed a man at his side.

For the services of *Lieuts. C. G. Whitby* and *F. Whittuck*, deceased, see Biographical Division.

4TH REGT. BOMBAY NATIVE INFANTRY (RIFLE CORPS).

THE 4th Bombay Rifles left Karachi for field service on the 8th Feb., 1880, and during the ensuing hot weather was distributed in detachments along the Bolan Pass, Head-quarters being in garrison at Quetta.

Early in July, 1880, the regiment was ordered on to Kandahar, and arrived shortly before the news was received of the disaster sustained by General Burrows's Brigade at Maiwand. Throughout the ensuing siege it was detailed to guard the Herat and Kabul faces of the city, and daily furnished working and covering parties which were employed outside the walls.

At the battle of Kandahar, on the 1st Sept., 1880, the regiment formed a portion of and led in skirmishing order the advance of the Bombay Brigade, which was employed in keeping the enemy in check at the Baba Wali Kotal. For the good service it rendered on this occasion, it was mentioned by Sir F. Roberts in his despatch. The following morning it proceeded to Mazra, and took over the charge of Ayub Khan's standing camp from Brigadier-General Macpherson's Brigade, occupying it, and forming an outpost to the remainder of the force at Kandahar till the 8th Sept.

On the 9th Sept., 1880, the 4th Bombay Rifles accompanied the brigade under Brigadier-General Daubeny which was despatched from Kandahar to Maiwand on the 9th Sept., 1880, for the purpose of searching the villages *en route* for prisoners and arms, and burying the remains of those who fell at the battle of the 27th July, 1880, and during the retreat.

On the 29th Oct., 1880, the 4th Bombay Rifles left Kandahar for Kach and Chappar on the Hurnai route, and has since been employed in holding those outposts.

The regiment had no casualties in action; but many men died, and many more returned invalided to India, from the effects of the climate and constant exposure.

A company of the 26th Regt. Bombay N.I. was attached to the regiment from the date of its proceeding on service until November, 1880, and was present throughout the defence of Kandahar, during which it had one man wounded.

The under-mentioned officers of the 4th Regt. Bombay Native Infantry (Rifle Corps) served in the war:—

Colonel W. Bannerman commanded the regiment throughout the period it was employed in the war, being present at the battle of Kandahar.

Lieut.-Colonel G. B. Crispin. (Deceased. See Biographical Division.)

Major W. S. Seton served with the regiment from 7 April, 1880, during the remainder of the period it was employed in the war, being present at the battle of Kandahar.

Major F. F. Comyn served with the regiment till invalided to England 23 Feb., 1880; rejoined 24 March, 1881.

Major W. Marshall. (For services see 19th Regt. N.I.)

Major S. Carter. (For services see 27th Regt. N.I.)

Lieuts. D. C. W. Harrison and *A. W. L. Bayly* served with the regiment throughout the period it was employed in the war, the former as Adjutant, being present at the battle of Kandahar. *Lieut. Bayly* acted as Station Staff Officer at Quetta from 4 April till 3 July, 1880.

Lieut. D. F. A. R. Ancketill, Lothian Regt. (Attached), joined the regiment at Kandahar 30 Sept., 1880.

5TH REGT. BOMBAY NATIVE (LIGHT) INFANTRY.

DURING the spring and summer of 1880 the 5th Regt. Bombay L.I. served in wings and detached companies at Thal-Chotiali, Sibi, and Hurnai, and was employed in protecting the Nari Valley railway line.

On the forward concentration of the troops in August, 1880, in consequence of the news of the disaster at Maiwand, the regiment was moved up to Kila Abdulla, and as a unit of Brigadier-General Brown's Brigade of Major-General Phayre's relieving force, took part in the advance to Kandahar.

The regiment remained serving in the neighbourhood of Kandahar and on the line of communications till after the evacuation of that city by the British forces.

The under-mentioned officers served with the 5th Regt. Bombay L.I. during the period it was employed in the war.—

Colonel F. Roome (also served in command of the Thal-Chotiali Force during 1880), *Colonel R. A. C. Hunt* (commanded the regiment in the advance to Kandahar; mentioned in despatches), *Majors A. Poole* and *R. Hennell, Captain P. C. Heath* (deceased; also served as Brigade-Major 2nd Division Kandahar F.F.), and *Lieuts. C. O. Nicholetts* and *J. C. Francis*.

8TH REGT. BOMBAY NATIVE INFANTRY.

AS a unit of Brigadier-General James's Brigade of Major-General Phayre's Division, the 8th Regt. Bombay N.I. took part, in August and September, 1880, in the advance to the relief of the beleaguered garrison of Kandahar.

The regiment remained serving in the neighbourhood of Kandahar and on the line of communications till after the evacuation of that city by the British Forces.

The under-mentioned officers served with the 8th Regt. Bombay N.I. during the period it was employed in the war:—

Colonel S. Fellows (in command; mentioned in despatches), *Major H. S. Tandy*, *Captain F. W. V. Leckie*, and *Lieuts. A. L. D. Fordyce* and *J. R. Sandwith*.

Major H. C. Morse served with the 9th Regt. Bombay N.I. in the second campaign till 14 Nov., 1880. Was slightly wounded, 6 Aug., 1880, in one of the skirmishes in the Khojak Pass.

9TH REGT. BOMBAY NATIVE INFANTRY.

THE 9th Regt. N.I., under the command of Major V. Birch, left Bombay on the 4th Feb., 1880, and arrived on the 7th idem at Karachi, where it remained as part of the Reserve Division of the Kandahar F.F. until the 11th July. During this interval the Left half-battalion, under the command of Major Morse, was pushed forward by detachments, which were engaged in making roads in the Chappar Mountains near Quetta, and in holding posts in the Bolan Pass, and on the line of rail.

On the 11th July, 1880, Head-quarters and the other half-battalion, under the command of Lieut.-Colonel Sibthorpe, who had rejoined from furlough, followed, and joined the Left half-battalion at Quetta on the 25th. The march was a most trying one, owing to the excessive heat. On the 27th July the regiment, with two mountain guns, marched to Gulistan Karez, a small fort in the Pishin Valley, and arrived on the 29th. In the expectation that this post would be attacked, three days were spent in strengthening and improving the defences. About 10 p.m. on the 31st July, 300 men of the 9th, and two guns, marched for the Khojak Pass, twenty miles distant, and arrived at 8 o'clock the next morning. The crest was found to be occupied by the enemy, who had been emboldened by the news of the reverse sustained by the British arms at Maiwand to assemble in the Pass, with a view to intercepting the reinforcements under General Phayre on their march to Kandahar, and had since dawn detained a party of the Poona Horse, firing on both sides having been smartly kept up. After a slight skirmish, in which the two mountain guns took an active part, the Pass was cleared, and the detachment 9th N.I. encamped. During the night the enemy returned, and fired into the camp—a proceeding which recurred during several succeeding nights, with constant skirmishing going on by day. On the 4th Aug., 1880, 30 men of the regiment, under Lieut. Preston, stormed a height held by some 100 of the enemy, who had stopped a convoy proceeding towards Kila Abdulla, and drove them out of a breastwork they occupied. On the 5th Aug., 50 men of the 9th and the two guns, acting in concert with a similar detachment from Chaman, moved out, and after a sharp skirmish with another body of the enemy, drove them out from their defensive works. After this no further annoyance was suffered, and convoys moved through the Pass without molestation. The remainder of the month was spent in throwing up earthworks and forming an entrenched camp, the force being augmented for this purpose with two companies of the 10th N.I. and two companies of Sappers.

On the 27th Aug., 1880, Major Birch, with a detachment of 157 men, marched for Chaman, and pushed on to Gatai, a post which, in common with all the other posts between Chaman and Kandahar, had been abandoned after the disaster at Maiwand; and four days afterwards, the Head-quarters left the Khojak, and arrived at the same place. On the 2nd Sept. Majors Birch and Morse marched with detachments to Mahomed Aman. Lieut. Godfray, with the Gulistan and Bolan detachments, rejoined Head-quarters on the 4th; and on the 10th, Major Birch, with his detachment, did the same. On the 12th a detachment under Major Birch returned to Chaman; and on the 18th, the Head-quarters, leaving behind a detachment under Major Morse, marched for Kandahar, where they arrived on the 20th Sept., 1880.

Majors Birch and Morse, with their detachments, subsequently rejoined Head-quarters, and the regiment remained at Kandahar until its final evacuation.

The under-mentioned officers of the 9th Bombay Native Infantry served in the war:—

Lieut.-Colonel L. H. Sibthorpe commanded the regiment throughout the period it was employed in the war, being present, in command of the field detachment, at the re-occupation of, and skirmishing in, the Khojak Pass.

Major V. Birch served with the regiment in the campaign till invalided, 2 Nov., 1880, being present at the skirmishing in the Khojak Pass.

Major H. C. Morse. (For services see 8th Bombay N.I.)

Major C. H. Coles served with the 10th Bombay N.I. in S. Afghanistan during the second campaign till 1 Nov., 1880, when he rejoined the 9th Bombay N.I., and served with it during the remainder of the time it was employed in the war.

Capt. A. W. Proudfoot served with the regiment in the campaign till 1 Feb., 1881. Was Staff Officer to the field detachment which reoccupied the Khojak Pass, and was present at the skirmishing.

Lieut. H. Godfray served with the regiment throughout, commanding the detachment at Gulistan in Aug., 1880. Was Staff Officer in Killa Abdula.

Lieut. R. W. Preston served with the regiment throughout, being present at the skirmishing in the Khojak Pass, and commanding the party which carried a position held by the enemy on the 4th Aug., 1880.

10TH REGT. BOMBAY NATIVE (LIGHT) INFANTRY.

DURING the spring and summer of 1880 the 10th Regt. Bombay L.I., broken up into detachments, served at Quetta, Gwal, Abdul Rahman, &c., as a portion of the Reserve Division Kandahar Field Force.

At the latter end of March, 1880, a detachment of the regiment, under Lieut.-Colonel Durand, took part in the successful expedition to the Chapar Pass for the recovery of the remains of Captain Showers.

At the latter end of April, 1880, a wing of the regiment took part with the flying column under Major-General Phayre in the reconnaissance of the Panizai and Sarangzai Pathan districts.

On the forward concentration of the troops in August, 1880, the regiment was moved to Kila Abdulla, and as a unit of Brigadier-General James's Brigade of Major-General Phayre's relieving force, took part in the advance to Kandahar.

The regiment remained serving in the neighbourhood of Kandahar and on the line of communications till after the evacuation of that city by the British forces.

The undermentioned officers served with the 10th Regt. Bombay L.I. during the period it was employed in the war:—

Colonel H. H. James (Commandant), *Lt.-Colonel A. Durand*, *Major C. E. Blowers* (commanded the regiment in the advance to Kandahar; mentioned in despatches), *Captains B. G. Humfrey* and *L. A. T. M'Cudden*, and *Lieut. W. S. Widdicombe.*

Lieut. J. Ashby served with the 16th Bombay N.I. till 17 June, 1880, when he was invalided to England.

16TH REGT. BOMBAY NATIVE INFANTRY.

THE 16th Regt. Bombay N.I. left Malegaon on field service on the 9th Jan., 1880, and reaching Sibi on the 30th idem, continued its advance to Quetta, where it arrived on the 23rd Feb.

After the murder of Capt. Showers, Commandant Belooch Guides, on the Chapar-Quetta road, the Right wing 16th N.I., under the command of Lieut.-Colonel Iredell, with Capt. Watson, was sent out on the 28th March, 1880, to co-operate with a column from Dargai in exacting retribution for the crime. With this column a junction was effected on the 3rd April; and the village of Amadun was occupied. The objects of the expedition were successfully carried out, Captain Showers's body being recovered and brought back, and a force of Kahars being driven from a strong position taken up by them near the Kujlak defile.

A force consisting of two guns No. 2 Mountain Battery, 400 rifles 10th Bombay L.I., and 400 rifles 16th Bombay N.I., having assembled at Amadun, marched, under the command of Lieut.-Colonel Iredell, with Captain Watson and Lieuts. Seymour and Ashby, and accompanied by General Phayre, through the Kowas Valley and back through the Chapar Valley to Kach.

On the 6th April the Head-quarters and Left wing 16th N.I. marched to Gwal, and subsequently to Kach, where they arrived on the 2nd June, and were rejoined by the Right wing. The regiment was now employed in opening up a new road between Quetta and Kach.

On the 18th July the Right wing, under Lieut.-Colonel Iredell, was sent to Chaman to garrison that post, and remained there from the 23rd July till the 31st Aug., when it was sent on with the advanced force of the division under General Phayre marching to the relief of Kandahar.

The Head-quarters and Left wing of the regiment, under Colonel Pierce, with Lieut.-Colonel Davis and Lieut. Seymour, were attacked on the 16th Aug., 1880, while encamped at Kach in the open, by a body of over 2,000 Kakar Pathans. After over three hours' hard fighting, the enemy were driven off with considerable loss. The strength of the 16th N.I. present was 314 of all ranks, besides whom there were 150 sick, of various regiments, also encamped in the open. On the 19th Aug. a party, including 200 rifles 16th N.I. under Lieut. Seymour, attacked and burned the villages of Kach and Amadun.

The Right wing 16th N.I., under Lieut.-Col. Iredell, rejoined Head-quarters at Kach on the 18th Nov., and the regiment marched to Quat Mundai in the Marri country, where it formed part of the Quat Mundai F.F., under the command of Colonel Pierce, from 1 Dec., 1880, till 8 March, 1881, and was employed in opening out roads in the Marri country.

On the 8th March, 1881, the regiment arrived at Sibi, and remained garrisoning that post and the posts in the Bolan extending to Koita till the 22nd May, 1881, when it returned to India to be quartered at Poona.

The under-mentioned officers of the 16th Regt. Bombay Native Infantry served in the war:—

Colonel T. W. W. Pierce commanded the regiment throughout, and at the action of Kach. Commanded the Quat Mundai F.F. from 1 Dec. till 8 March, 1881, when it was broken up. Commanded at Sibi from 9 March till 4 May, 1881. (Mentioned in Orders, and received commendation of Govt. of Bombay and Governor-General in Council.)

Lieut.-Colonel F. S. Iredell served with the regiment throughout. Commanded the Gwal F.F. from 6 April till 18 May, 1880, and the Chaman garrison from 23 July till 26 Aug., when he was sent in command of General Phayre's advanced force to the relief of Kandahar. Commanded the Argandab F.F. from 1 till 17 Sept., 1880. (Mentioned in despatches.)

Lieut.-Colonel A. H. Davis served with the regiment from 11 Jan. till 25 Aug., 1880, being present at the action of Kach.

Lieut.-Colonel W. G. Trevor rejoined the regiment at Kach, 28 Oct., and served with it till it returned to India.

Captains J. R. Watson and *J. T. Carruthers* served with the regiment till invalided, 28 July, 1880. *Captain Carruthers* acted as Station Staff Officer at Quetta from 4 March till 4 April, 1880.

Lieut. H. W. Seymour served with the regiment throughout, except during an interval between 6 May and 31 July, when he officiated as Aide-de-Camp to General Phayre. Was present at the action of Kach, in which he was slightly wounded. Was Station Staff Officer at Sibi from 8 March till 20 May, 1881.

Lieut. J. W. Gordon joined the Right wing of the regiment at Chaman, 31 Aug., 1880, and took part in the advance of General Phayre's force to the relief of Kandahar. Was Staff Officer of the Argandab F.F. from 10 till 21 Sept., 1880, and of the Quat Mundai F.F. from 1 Dec., 1880, till 6 Feb., 1881, when he was sent into Sibi sick, and invalided to England.

Lieut. P. H. Saulez joined the regiment at Kach, 14 Sept., 1880, and served with it till it returned to India.

19TH REGT. BOMBAY NATIVE INFANTRY.

ON the 12th Dec., 1878, the 19th Regt. Bombay N.I. left Karachi, where it was then stationed, for Sukkur, with orders to join the Reserve Brigade about to assemble there under the command of Major-General Phayre. It arrived at its destination on the 14th idem, and proceeding thence to Jacobabad, was employed from the 16th Dec., 1878, till the 26th Feb., 1879, in making a military road from that station to Dadar, a distance of 109 miles.

On the 27th Feb., 1879, the regiment left Dadar and proceeded up the Bolan Pass, making *en route* a new roadway extending to Darwaza, a distance of 63 miles, passable for heavy guns and the like. This important piece of work was completed in the month of September, and was subsequently reported on by Sir R. Temple, who, in an exhaustive minute, eulogizes it as "a signal example of what may be accomplished by a small body of troops with their trained followers," and refers in favourable terms to the endurance and willingness of the men employed upon it.

The 19th N.I. arrived at Dozan, in the Bolan Pass, on the 11th April, 1879, and the Head-quarters remained there till the 28th Jan., 1880.

In June, 1879, the regiment suffered severely from an outbreak of cholera, about fifty of the Sepoys succumbing to this disease.

In Septemper, 1879, Major R. Le P. Trench, with a detachment of 105 rank and file, was sent into the Kakar Pathan and Marri country as an escort to Sir R. Sandeman. This party remained in and about the assigned districts till January, 1880, and accompanied Sir R. Temple on his tour made through them in November, 1879.

On the 30th Jan., 1880, the regiment proceeded from Dozan to relieve the Bengal troops in the Pishin Valley and at Chaman, and was shortly afterwards ordered on from thence to Kandahar, where Head-quarters arrived on the 30th March, 1880. From that date till the 3rd Sept., 1880, the regiment formed part of the Kandahar garrison, under the command of General Primrose.

On the 16th April, 1880, occurred the massacre of Major Waudby, 19th N.I., Road Commandant, with a small party, at Dubrai, on the Chaman road. The heroic nature of the defence of this post has stamped it as one of the most brilliant episodes of the campaign. The party, which consisted of Major Waudby, 2 Sepoys of the regiment, 1 Duffadar and 2 Sowars of the 3rd Sind Horse, and some servants, succeeded in holding at bay for upwards of two hours, before being finally overwhelmed, 300 of the enemy, 18 of whose dead bodies were subsequently found in the immediate proximity of the mud building in which the final stand was made. On the receipt of news of the attack on Dubrai, a small force, of which two companies of the regiment under Lieut. Phillipps formed part, were sent out from Kandahar to conduct retributive measures. No resistance was offered; the headmen were taken prisoners; and two forts and villages were destroyed.

When news of the disaster of Maiwand was received, the 19th Regt., which had moved into and occupied the Kandahar Citadel on the departure of Brigadier-General Burrows's Brigade, was told off to defend the Southern or Shikapur face of the city, on which it was considered likely the enemy would deliver their attack. From the 28th July till the 16th Aug. daily covering and working parties were furnished by the regiment for clearing the ground and demolishing cover outside the walls. In one of these, which on the 12th Aug. had to retire under a heavy fire, a Havildar and private of the regiment displayed great gallantry in assisting Lieuts. Waller and Jones, R.E., in bringing a wounded man into cover within the walls, and for their conduct were recommended by Brigadier-General Brooke for the Order of Merit.

In the sortie to Deh Khwaja on the 16th Aug., 250 rank and file of the 19th Bomhay N.I., under Colonel C. T. Heathcote, who also commanded the column (the 3rd) of which they formed part, were hotly engaged. In this engagement Major R. Le P. Trench and Lieut. F. C. Stayner fell while gallantly leading their men against overwhelming numbers, and 50 Native officers and rank and file of the regiment were also killed or wounded.

No more fighting took place till the arrival at Kandahar of the relieving division under Sir F. Roberts, when, on the 1st Sept., at the battle of Kandahar, the 19th Regt. formed part of the brigade under the command of Brigadier-General Burrows which threatened the Baba Wali Kotal while the main body of the army attacked the right flank of Ayub Khan's position.

Meantime, on the 26th June, 1880, Major Jacob was ordered to occupy the line of outposts between Kandahar and Chaman; and starting with 210 rank and file, he posted detachments at Mundi Hissar,

Abdul Rahman, Mel Karez, Dubrai, and Gatai, making his head-quarters at Mel Karez. On the 28th July, 1880, after the receipt at Kandahar of news of the Maiwand disaster, he was directed to concentrate with all speed his detachments on Chaman. Retiring from Mel Karez to Gatai, and again from Gatai to Chaman, he was heavily pressed upon by large bodies of the enemy, upon whom, however, he succeeded in inflicting considerable loss. For "the soldierlike manner in which he executed the difficult duty entrusted to him," Major Jacob received the high commendation of the Major-General Commanding, and of the Commander-in-Chief of the Bombay Army. His detachments, during the siege of Kandahar, performed excellent work in keeping open the Khojak Pass, and in escorting through it convoys, which were frequently attacked. They did not rejoin regimental Head-quarters till October, 1880, when the 19th Bombay N.I. marched out of Afghanistan.

On the 3rd Sept., 1880, the 19th Bombay N.I. was sent out from Kandahar to open up communications with General Phayre's Division, advancing from Chaman. After this duty was performed, the regiment was broken up into detachments on the line of communications between Kandahar and Chaman, and were employed in keeping the various posts supplied with fodder for the large numbers of Transport animals passing to and fro.

On the 23rd Oct., 1880, the 19th Bombay N.I. was ordered down to Sibi, where the Head-quarters remained, detachments being sent forward to occupy posts for some distance on the Bolan and Hurnai routes. In March, 1881, the regiment returned to India, proceeding by way of Karachi to Maligaan in Khandiesh.

The under-mentioned officers of the 19th Regt. Bombay Native Infantry served in the war :—

Major-General W. Creagh (Retired) commanded the regiment during the period it was employed in the war till Dec., 1880. Held temporary command of the Bombay Reserve Brigade in the Bolan Pass from 31 July till 27 Nov., 1879. (Mentioned in despatches.)

Colonel C. T. Heathcote, C.B., commanded the 1st Grenadiers from Nov., 1879, till April, 1880, in the Bolan Pass and advance to Kandahar, and the 19th Regt. from May, 1880, till the end of the war: throughout the siege, and at the battle of Kandahar, commanded the Shikapur face of the city walls during the siege. Commanded a column in the sortie to Deh Khwaja, and all three columns during the retirement, after the death of General Brooke. (Twice mentioned in despatches; C.B.)

Lieut.-Colonel W. Jacob served with the regiment during the war from April, 1880. Commanded the line of outposts between Kandahar and Chaman, and conducted the operations resulting in their successful withdrawal at the end of July, 1880. (Highly commended by Commander-in-Chief and Govt. of Bombay.) Was subsequently in command of the outposts in the Murree Hills.

Majors S. J. Waudby and *R. Le P. Trench*. (Killed in action. See Biographical Division.)

Major R. Westmacott. (For services see "Staff.")

Major W. Marshall, 25th Bombay L.I., served in the second campaign till Aug., 1880, with the 4th Bombay Rifles. Joined the 19th Regt. at Kandahar, and served with it till the conclusion of the war, being present throughout the siege and at the battle of Kandahar.

Lieut. F. Stevenson served with the regiment, as Adjutant, till Jan., 1880, when he was appointed Orderly Officer to Brigadier-General Hughes. Accompanied the Ghazni F.F. to Kabul, and was present at the battle of Ahmad Khel and the action of Arzu. Took part in the march from Kabul to the relief of Kandahar, and entering the city with an advanced party, served for two days, attached to the 25th P.N.I., on the walls. Was present, as Adjutant of the 19th Regt., at the battle of Kandahar. (Mentioned in despatches.)

Lieut. G. E. Walter served with the regiment in the war till invalided to England from Dozan in Oct., 1879.

Lieut. F. C. Stayner. (Killed in action. See Biographical Division.)

Lieut. C. R. Phillipps served with the regiment from Nov., 1879, till the conclusion of the war. Commanded the two companies sent to punish the villages implicated in the massacre of Major Waudby and party. Commanded several covering parties during the siege of Kandahar, and was present at the battle of Kandahar.

Lieut. H. Melvill, 26th Bombay N.I., served with the regiment from Nov., 1879, till invalided in Nov., 1880, being present throughout the siege and at the battle of Kandahar.

Mr. Boteler, Supt. of Telegraphs, was attached as a subaltern to the regiment after the death of Lieut. Stayner on the 16th Aug., 1880. Acted as Asst. Field Engineer to the Force during the siege, and was present at the battle of Kandahar. (Mentioned in despatches.)

Lieut. G. D. Giles, 1st Sind Horse, served with the regiment during the war till transferred to the 1st Sind Horse in Nov., 1879.

23RD REGT. BOMBAY NATIVE (LIGHT) INFANTRY.

ON the 10th March, 1880, the 23rd Regt. Bombay N.L.I.—strength, 621 of all ranks—under the command of Colonel J. Harpur, left Ahmadnagar to join the Reserve Division ordered to concentrate in Sind, and on the 17th March arrived at Sukkur.

The Right half-battalion, under command of Major Gatacre, with Lieut. Tobin, crossed the frontier on the 2nd April, and occupied the posts on the Sibi-Hurnai route as far as Spin-Tangi.

The Head-quarters and Left half-battalion, under command of Colonel Harpur, proceeded to Jacobabad on the 5th April, and on the 5th May arrived in Sibi. After remaining for three weeks under canvas on an open sandy plain, with the thermometer frequently registering 120° Fahrenheit, the half battalion relieved the 1st Baluchis, and went into the Sibi outpost lines vacated by them. During the whole period the Head-quarters were stationed in Sibi, from the 5th May till the 21st Aug., 1880, the regiment was broken up into small detachments, on outpost, and was continually employed, during the hottest season of the year, in the harassing and trying duties of convoy and escort guards. Several deaths occurred from heat-apoplexy, including that of Dr. Simpson, the Medical Officer of the regiment.

Major Gatacre, with two companies of his half-battalion, was ordered, on the 1st June, 1880, to the Sangan Valley for the protection of Government Transport Animals which had been sent there to graze; and Lieut. Tobin, with the remaining two companies, was left to guard the posts and line of communications between Spin-Tangi and Sibi. Owing to Major Gatacre's exertions, a quantity of commissariat stores, and some troop-horses, which had been plundered by the Marris, were recovered.

On the 4th August, 1880, a small party of the regiment, under Lieut. Tobin, attacked and dispersed a band of Pathans and Marris at Sinari, killing ten of them, who had assembled to waylay and plunder a convoy coming from Hurnai. Lieut. Tobin, in a personal encounter with a Pathan, received a severe sword-cut on the left arm, and had his horse wounded, but killed his adversary.

The Right half-battalion, under Major Gatacre, rejoined Head-quarters on the 8th Aug. Lieut. Tobin having received orders to withdraw his outposts and return to Sibi, proceeded to do so. He was attacked *en route* by the Marris, and lost 6 men killed and 5 wounded. His men, in addition to escorting a large convoy of stores and treasure, had to protect a gang of 1,500 panic-stricken railway labourers, by whom they were greatly hampered and impeded in their movements. Lieut. Tobin, for his excellent services on this occasion, received the commendations of the Government of India, and was also thanked by his Excellency the Commander-in-Chief, Bombay, and the Major-General Commanding the Lines of Communication.

The regiment left Sibi on the 21st Aug., 1880, and proceeded by night marches through the Bolan Pass to Quetta, from whence it continued its advance on the 31st idem, with a convoy of 300 carts laden with food supplies urgently required at the front. The drivers had deserted, and could not at the time be replaced, so 300 men of the 23rd undertook the work of driving the carts, and after incessant labour—draught cattle being weak and ill-conditioned and scarcely able to draw their loads—brought the convoy safely to its destination, and deservedly merited the approbation of the Brigade and Divisional authorities, which was conveyed to them, for their services.

On the 6th Sept., 1880, the 23rd Bombay N.I., reached Killa-Abdula, and taking part, as a unit of the 3rd Brigade, in the advance of General Phayre's Division, arrived on the 23rd idem at Kandahar. There it remained till the 22nd Oct., when it was told off for duty on the line of communications, and furnished the outposts of Abdul Rahman, Mel Karez, Dubrai, and Gatai: two companies to each.

On the withdrawal of the British Army from Kandahar, the regiment commenced its return-march to India, accompanying the last brigade of General Hume's force to Quetta, and eventually making its way to Ahmedabad, where it arrived on the 28th May, 1881.

The under-mentioned officers of the 23rd Regiment Bombay Native (Light) Infantry served in the war:—

Colonel J. Harpur commanded the regiment throughout the period it was employed in the war, and the troops at Sibi from 6th May till 21st Aug., 1880.

Colonel M. R. Bruce (Retired) crossed the frontier with the regiment, 6 May, 1880, but shortly afterwards returned to India, and retired from the service.

Major J. Gatacre served with the regiment throughout. Recovered a quantity of looted property from the Marris in the Sangan Valley, and destroyed their village. Commanded the fort of Gulistan from 5 to 10 Sept. 1880, and the posts of Gatai and Dubrai from 25 Oct., 1880, till 26 April, 1881.

Major F. T. Ebden served with the regiment till invalided to England in Sept., 1880.

Captain E. C. Kellie served with the regiment throughout. Was Staff Officer at Sibi from 25 May till 21 Aug., 1880, and at Abdul Rahman from 23 Oct., 1880, till 24 April, 1881.

Lieut. W. St. J. Richardson served with the regiment till May, 1880, and subsequently with the 1st Belooch N.I. till invalided to England.

Lieut. R. I. Scallon served with the 2nd Belooch N.I. from Nov. 1879, till Sept., 1880, being present at the affairs of Khan Khel and Kaj-baj, near Khalat-i-Ghilzai, and the battle of Kandahar, and accompanying Brigadier-General Daubeny's expedition to Maiwand. Rejoined 23rd N.L.I. in Sept., 1880.

Lieut. F. J. Tobin served with the regiment till Aug., 1880. Commanded the detachment engaged in the skirmish of the 4th Aug., 1880, in which he was severely wounded in a personal encounter with one of the enemy. Commanded the detachments of 23rd N.L.I. and Cavalry, on withdrawal of outposts to Sibi in Aug., 1880, and repulsed an attack of a large body of Marris *en route*. (Received the commendation of Government, and the thanks of H.E. the Commander-in-Chief, Bombay.)

24TH REGT. BOMBAY NATIVE INFANTRY.

THE 24th Regt. Bombay N.I., while at Mehidpur and Agar, received orders in February, 1880, to proceed on active service, and left for Haidarabad by wings, arriving there on the 18th and 20th March, respectively.

After remaining in the Reserve for three months, the regiment was ordered to the front, and crossing the Sibi frontier on the 14th July, 1880, marched *via* the Bolan Pass, to Quetta, where it arrived on the 28th idem, just before the receipt of news of the Maiwand disaster.

The heat of the weather during the march through the Bolan was so excessive, that although the regiment left Nari Bank at 10 p.m., on a march of only ten miles, no less than thirty native officers and men were incapacitated before it was concluded. One man died on the spot, a Havildar died during the course of the day, and 2 native officers and about 22 men had to be invalided from Quetta, as totally unfit for further service.

The 24th N.I. remained at Quetta till the 25th of Aug., providing the outposts of Ghazaband and Dina Karez. During this period a company, under the command of Major C. P. Newport, was despatched to Kach to bring in a sick convoy from that post, and arriving there on the day after it had been attacked, took part in the burning of the villages of Kach and Amadure. Taking place as it did immediately after the attack, in which the tribes had lost heavily, this reprisal completely checked all further rising amongst the Kakar Pathans in that part of the country.

On the 25th Aug. the 24th N.I. was ordered to the Khojak Pass, where it arrived on the 31st. It remained in defence of that post during the march of Sir F. Roberts's Brigade from Kabul to the relief of Kandahar and the subsequent defeat of Ayub Khan, and till after the force had passed over on its return to India.

At 10 p.m. on the 19th Sept., sudden orders were received to march to Kach and join General MacGregor's force, with imperative instructions to reach that destination by the 24th. At the moment of receiving the order, there was not a draught animal with the regiment; and it was 12 midnight on the 29th, before the transport arrived: mostly camels, many without even a rope to hold them by. The regiment commenced, however, to pack, and the rear-guard left by 7 a.m. The whole march to Kach was, owing to the disgraceful state of the transport, most fatiguing; kit, tents, and hospital stores were abandoned all along the road, the rear-guard, on two occasions, carrying the boxes of ammunition themselves, when the half-starved animals dropped down in a dying state under their loads. On reaching Kach it was found that General MacGregor's force had not arrived, and the regiment remained there, with only three tents, for two days. It was then ordered to proceed to Durgai, two marches on, and was there eventually joined by the remainder of the brigade. Two companies were left behind, under a native officer in command of the Durgai post, and the remainder of the regiment proceeded to Sharagh, where two more companies, under the command of Major Newport, were detached. The Head-quarters and Left wing then proceeded to Hurnai, arriving on the 2nd. It was nearly two months before the tents and kit left at the Khojak and Kila Abdulla were recovered, and the end of November arrived before any extra warm clothing was issued to the regiment. The result of such severe marching, and so much exposure to the inclement weather, and want of warm clothes, was a heavy mortality among the men, and a large percentage of sick. While at Quetta the regiment provided escorts to accompany the Political Officers in hunting up troublesome bands of robbers, and received praise and thanks for the way in which both native officers and men behaved.

On the withdrawal of the British troops, the regiment returned to India, and went into quarters at Ahmadabad.

The under-mentioned officers of the 24th Regt. Bombay Native Infantry served in the war :—

Colonel J. H. Henderson commanded the regiment in its advance to Quetta. Was appointed to the command of the line of communications, with the rank of Brigadier-General, 16 Aug., 1880, during the absence of General Phayre at Kandahar. On return of General Phayre, was appointed to the command of the Pishin Moveable Column, from which he was transferred, 19 Jan., 1881, to that of the 1st Brigade S. Afghanistan F.F. at Kandahar.

Lieut.-Colonel R. M. Chambers served with the regiment throughout the period it was employed in the war, commanding it from 14 Aug., 1880. Commanded at the Khojak Pass from 25 Aug. till 20 Sept., 1880, and subsequently at the Hurnai post.

Major C. P. Newport served with the regiment throughout, as 2nd in command. Commanded the force which attacked and burned the villages of Kach and Amadun, receiving the thanks of the Political Officer for valuable assistance rendered. Commanded the post of Sharagh on withdrawal of Head-quarters.

Captain W. J. Morse served with the regiment throughout, having charge of the regimental transport. Officiated as Adjutant from 14 Aug., 1880.

Captain W. H. Lyster served with the regiment till appointed Brigade-Major to the Brigadier-General Commanding the Line of Communications, 16 Aug., 1880, and remained at Quetta in that capacity until invalided, 1 Nov., 1880.

Lieut. A. A. Pearson served with the regiment, as Adjutant, till invalided to England 15 Feb., 1881. Acted as Staff Officer during the time the regiment was in Quetta, and also during the occupation of the Khojak Pass.

27TH REGT. BOMBAY NATIVE INFANTRY (1ST BELOOCH LIGHT INFANTRY.)

IN October, 1878, the 1st Belooch L.I. left Haidarabad on active service, and proceeded to the frontier, where a portion of the regiment, under Major Hogg, was employed, during the first campaign, in the Bughti Hills and at Sibi.

On the 6th April, 1880, the Head-quarters crossed the frontier and marched by the Hurnai route to Sharagh, arriving on the 11th May. Detachments of the regiment were stationed at Nassik, Kost, Durgai, N. Chapar, and Kach, the strongest, consisting of 150 men under Lieut. Mackenzie, being at Durgai. These posts were furnished to assist in keeping open the communications with Sibi and Quetta, and to protect the Sappers who were constructing the road for the railway. In June the detachment from Sibi, under the command of Lieut. Richardson, 23rd N.I. (Attached), rejoined Head-quarters.

On the 9th Aug. 1880, conformably with the forward concentration which was ordered in consequence of the disaster at Maiwand, the Head-quarters marched from Sharagh, and on the 17th idem arrived at Killa Abdula. A detachment, 150 strong, was posted at Khushdil Khan, and a company at Azad Khan. On the 25th Aug. the regiment moved on to Chaman, and the following day, forming part of a flying column, marched to Murgai Chaman and Actai Khan to collect supplies and blow up Abu Said's Fort, on completion of which duty it proceeded to Gatai, and there joined Brigadier-General T. Brown's Brigade. As a unit of that force it subsequently made its way to Kandahar, marching into cantonments on the 20th Sept.

From the 1st to the 25th Oct. the regiment was employed in collecting supplies in the neighbourhood of Zungrabad; and on the 2nd Nov. again marched out of Kandahar, for the same purpose, to Khana Girdab and Dahila, remaining absent till the 19th idem. On the 20th Jan., 1881, it marched with Brigadier-General Wilkinson's column for Maiwand, and on the 12th Feb. returned to the neighbourhood of Kandahar. On the 25th April the regiment was completely washed out of its quarters by a terrific storm which broke over and flooded the village in which it was encamped, the water rising to a height of three feet, and causing many houses to fall.

The 27th N.L.I. marched from Kandahar for India on the 20th April, and arrived at Haidarabad on the 18th May, 1881.

During the whole of the first campaign, and whilst on the Hurnai route in 1880, the regiment was constantly employed on escort duty between Jacobabad, Sibi, Quetta, Kandahar, Thal-Chotiali, and Vitakri. For its physique and military bearing, it received a warm encomium from Sir R. Temple; and for its steadiness and good conduct, and the readiness of the men to turn out on every occasion when their services were required, it was highly praised by Generals Phayre and Hume, under whom it served.

The under-mentioned officers of the 27th Regt. Bombay Native Infantry (1st Belooch Light Infantry) served in the war:—

Colonel T. Bell served during the first campaign with Jacob's Rifles, first at Quetta, and afterwards, during May and June, in detached command at Kalat. Commanded the 1st Belooch Regt. throughout the period it was employed in the war. Commanded the "Flying Column," a force of all arms, in the advance to Murgai Chaman. (Mentioned in despatches.)

Major A. Hogg, *Captain T. H. Mackenzie*, and *Lieut. A. C. Yate* served with the regiment throughout the period it was employed in the war: *Major Hogg* commanding at Sibi from Dec., 1878, till May, 1880; *Captain Mackenzie* commanding for a time at Durgai, and acting as Staff Officer to the Murgai Chaman Flying Column; and *Lieut. Yate* acting as Adjutant from 7 April till 9 Oct., 1880.

Major S. Carter served with the 4th Regt. Bombay N.I. in S. Afghanistan from Feb., 1881, till its return to India.

Captain J. Grant, *Lieut. A. L. Sinclair*, and *Lieut. C. E. Peirse*, 1st W.I. Regt. (*Attached*), served with the regiment, respectively, from Oct., 1880, Nov., 1880, and Nov., 1880, the latter acting for a time as Orderly Officer to Brigadier-General Henderson.

28TH REGT. BOMBAY NATIVE INFANTRY.

THE 28th Bombay N.I., with one company of the 20th Bombay N.I. attached for service, left Surat for the front on the 22nd Jan., 1880. Strength: 7 European officers, 15 Native officers, 720 rank and file.

The regiment marched up the Bolan Pass in five detachments, and was finally distributed as follows: Head-quarters at Chaman, 15th March; three companies under Lieut.-Colonel Newport, at Khushdil-Khan; two companies under Major Singleton at Kila Abdulla; one company under Lieut. Fox at Gulistan Karez.

On the 26th April a force consisting of 100 Sepoys 28th N.I., 2 guns No. 2 Mountain Battery, and 40 sabres Poona Horse, left Chaman, under Major Singleton, to co-operate with the Wali of Kandahar in bringing to submission a Native Chief of the Fort of Abu Said, 30 miles from Chaman. The Fort surrendered on the 27th without firing a shot.

In July, the country beginning to be much disturbed, the regiment was ordered to march on Kandahar by detachments.

The detachments under Colonel Newport and Major Singleton reached their destination on the morning of the 25th and 26th July respectively, and the Head-quarters arrived simultaneously with the routed troops from Maiwand, on the morning of the 28th July. The regimental rear-guard was attacked while marching in outside the walls; but the Pathans were driven off, with the loss of 3 killed and 7 prisoners.

On the 31st of July three companies of the regiment under the command of Lieut.-Colonel Newport and Lieut. Reilly, were ordered out to clear the village of Khairabad, near the N.E. bastion. The village was cleared, with the loss of 1 Sepoy killed and 2 wounded.

On the 16th Aug. four companies of the regiment, under the command of Lieut.-Colonel Nimmo, Lieut.-Colonel Newport, and Lieut. Reilly, with Dr. Keith in medical charge, took part in a sortie to Deh Khwaja. The attacking line under Colonels Nimmo and Newport forced its way through the village, and débouched on the other side. Casualties: Lieut.-Colonel Nimmo twice wounded, once dangerously; Lieut.-Colonel Newport and 30 rank and file killed, and 20 wounded.

Throughout the defence of Kandahar the regiment was engaged in almost all the skirmishes around the walls, and contributed its full share to all covering and working parties.

On the 1st Sept. four companies, under the command of Major Singleton and Lieut. Chase, took part in the battle of Kandahar, forming a portion of the escort to General Gough's Cavalry Brigade and to E/B, R.H.A. The remainder of the regiment remained with the Bombay Brigade, under Lieut.-General Primrose and Brigadier-General Burrows.

On the 2nd Sept. the 4th (Rifles) N.I. and 28th N.I. marched to Mazra, and took charge of Sirdar Ayub Khan's captured camp and stores.

The regiment returned to Kandahar on the 8th Sept. On the 12th Oct. it marched to Chaman, and was located there, and in detachments at Khushdil Khan and Kila Abdulla.

During the winter of 1880-1881, the Head-quarter companies at Chaman were almost daily engaged on the Khojak Pass in passing over convoys of carts and beasts preparatory to the evacuation of Kandahar. On most occasions the weather was very severe, and the work of keeping the Pass open most trying to the Sepoys.

General Hume, C.B., Commanding in Southern Afghanistan, expressed his thanks to the Commanding Officer for the excellent work done by the regiment.

The regiment left these posts for India on the 1st May, and arrived at Karachi on the 23rd May, 1881.

The under-mentioned officers of the 28th Regt. Bombay Native Infantry served during the war:—

Colonel J. R. Nimmo commanded the regiment till 5 Oct., 1880, when compelled to proceed to England on medical certificate, in consequence of wounds received at the sortie to Deh Khwaja. Was present throughout the siege of Kandahar, and commanded the portion of the regiment engaged in the sortie to Deh Khwaja, in which he was twice severely wounded. (Mentioned in despatches.)

Lieut.-Colonel W. H. Newport. (Killed in action. See Biographical Division.)

Lieut.-Colonel F. C. Singleton served with the regiment throughout, commanding it at the battle of Kandahar, and from 18 Oct., 1880. Was in detached command of the Killa Abdula post until ordered to Kandahar. Commanded a detachment of the regiment forming part of the force under General Brooke which marched out from Kandahar to cover the retreat of the fugitives from Maiwand. Subsequently commanded the posts of Chaman and Killa Abdula, and regulated the traffic across the Khojak during the evacuation. (Twice mentioned in despatches.)

Major J. Ketchen joined the regiment in Dec., 1880, and was in detached command of the Kila Abdulla post from date of arrival till all the troops of the Kandahar Force had passed through after the evacuation.

Lieut. E. A. Barclay. (For services see "Staff.")

Lieut. R. E. D. Reilly served with the regiment throughout, as Adjutant: twice acting as Staff Officer at Chaman; taking part in the defence of Kandahar, the attack on Khairabad, the sortie to Deh Khwaja, and the battle of Kandahar; and commanding for a time the post of Kila Abdulla.

Lieut. W. St. L. Chase, V.C. (For services see Biographical Division.)

Lieut. W. E. K. Fox, Royal Irish Regt. (*Attached*), served with the regiment throughout, taking part in the defence of Kandahar, the sortie to Deh Khwaja, and the battle of Kandahar, and being on different occasions in command of the posts of Gulistan and Gatai.

Lieut. P. H. J. Aplin, East Yorkshire Regt. (*Attached*), took part in the advance of General Phayre's force to the relief of Kandahar, and joined the regiment in Sept., 1880. Marched with the Head-quarters to Chaman, and subsequently commanded the South Khojak post and the post of Kila Abdulla.

29TH (2ND BELOOCH) REGT. BOMBAY NATIVE INFANTRY.

THE 2nd Belooch Regt. was stationed at Dera Ghazi Khan and Rajanpur, when, on the 24th Sept., 1878, it received orders to proceed to Quetta to form part of General Biddulph's Division of the Army of Invasion. The Head-quarters marched from Dera Ghazi Khan on the 2nd Oct., and picking up the Left wing at Rajanpur, proceeded to Quetta *viâ* the Dera Bughti route and Bolan Pass, arriving on the 2nd Nov., 1878.

The regiment crossed the Afghan frontier on the 21st Nov., 1878, as a portion of the advance guard of General Biddulph's Division, and was employed during the remainder of the month in making roads across the Khojak and Gwaja passes. On the 3rd Jan., 1879, it joined Brigadier-General Palliser's advance Cavalry Brigade at Hussi Ahmed, and the following day was engaged in the action of Takht-i-pul, subsequently continuing in the advance, and taking part in the entry of Sir Donald Stewart's force into Kandahar on the 8th.

The 2nd Beloochis accompanied General Biddulph's Division in its advance to Girishk in January, 1879; and a portion of the regiment was engaged in the action of Khushk-i-Nakhud, when the attack on Colonel Malcolmson's rear-guard was repulsed. It returned with the Division as far as Kokaran, and subsequently formed part of the garrison of that place under Brigadier-General Palliser from March till the beginning of September, 1879, when it was ordered back to India. The regiment had only proceeded as far as Chaman, however, when, on the 6th Sept., 1879, in consequence of the receipt of news of the Kabul massacre, it was directed to return with all speed to Kandahar, where it arrived on the 8th.

As a unit of Brigadier-General Hughes's Force, the 29th N.I. took part in the re-occupation of Kalat-i-Ghilzai in September, 1879, and on the 24th Oct. a portion of the regiment was engaged in the action of Shah Jui.

From October, 1879, until relieved by the Kabul-Kandahar F.F. in August, 1880, the regiment formed part of the garrison of Kalat-i-Ghilzai, under the command of Colonel Tanner. Joining Sir F. Roberts's Force, it accompanied it in the remainder of its march to the relief of Kandahar, and on the 1st Sept., 1880, took part, attached to Brigadier-General Baker's Brigade, in the crushing defeat of Ayub Khan's army.

From the 9th till the 23rd Sept., the 2nd Belooch Regt. was absent with Brigadier-General Daubeny's Brigade on its expedition to the field of Maiwand. On the latter date the regiment returned to Kokaran, from whence it was ordered down to garrison Chaman and Kila Abdulla.

On the 20th Oct., 1880, the regiment marched to Sibi, and after forming the reserve of Brigadier-General MacGregor's force till December, marched into the Marri country, and was engaged in quelling the rising of the hostile tribes. In January, 1881, it returned to Sibi, and from that month till the middle of March, 1881, was employed as a portion of the Pishin Moveable Column, after which it returned to India.

The under-mentioned officers of the 29th (2nd Belooch) Regt. Bombay Native Infantry served in the war :—

Lieut.-Colonel G. Nicholetts. (Deceased. See Biographical Division.)

Colonel O. V. Tanner, C.B., served with the regiment as 2nd in command from the outbreak of the war till 1 June, 1879, when he returned to India to take up his appointment of A.A.G., Northern Division, and commanded the regiment from Oct., 1879, till appointed Brigadier-General Commanding the Pishin Column, 19 Jan., 1881. Commanded a reconnoitring party of Cavalry, Infantry, and Sappers during the advance to the Halmand, and a detachment of the regiment at the action of Khushk-i-Nakhud. (Mentioned in despatches; Brevet of Colonel.) Commanded the garrison of Kalat-i-Ghilzai from 12 Oct., 1879, till it was relieved by the Kabul-Kandahar F.F., and commanded portions of the garrison at the actions of Kaj Baj, 1 May, 1880, and Sir-i-Asp, 1 July, 1880. Took part in the advance to the relief of Kandahar, and commanded the regiment at the battle of Kandahar. (Mentioned in despatches; C.B.)

Lieut.-Colonel J. Galloway served with the regiment throughout the period it was employed in the war, commanding it from 19 July till 12 Oct., 1879, and being present at the action of Takht-i-pul and the relief and battle of Kandahar.

Major G. C. Sartorius and *Capt. W. A. Broome* served with the regiment, the latter as Adjutant, from the outbreak of the war till Sept., 1879, *Captain Broome* being also present at the action of Takht-i-pul.

Major G. F. Bryant served with the regiment from May, 1879, till March, 1881, being present at the relief and battle of Kandahar.

Lieut. H. E. W. Beville served with the regiment throughout the period it was employed in the war, from Sept., 1879, as Adjutant. Was present at the action of Takht-i-pul and the relief and battle of Kandahar.

Lieut. R. C. G. Mayne served with the regiment from Jan., 1879, till Dec., 1880, being present at the relief and battle of Kandahar.

Lieut. J. F. M. Campbell, 70th Regt. (Attached). (Deceased. See Biographical Division.)

30TH REGT. BOMBAY NATIVE INFANTRY (JACOB'S RIFLES).

IN September, 1878, the Right wing of Jacob's Rifles, under Major Humfrey, with Lieut. Baugh, left Jacobabad, where the regiment was then stationed, for Quetta, as Political Agent's escort to Mikran Coast: the wing was halted at Quetta, and was the first reinforcement sent to the garrison from India.

In October, 1878, the Head-quarter wing of the regiment, under Colonel Mainwaring, also left Jacobabad for Quetta, where it arrived during the first week in November, 1878, and with the Right wing formed part of the 1st Brigade of General Biddulph's Division of the Army of Invasion.

At the latter end of Nov., 1878, the Right wing, under Major Humfrey, proceeded to Kalat.

During the winter of 1878 the Head-quarters and Left wing occupied tents inside the Fort of Quetta, Col. Mainwaring, as senior officer, commanding the station. Besides heavy guard duties, the regiment supplied numerous escorts to Pishin and Kandahar, the Bolan Pass, and the Mustung Valley.

On the 27th March, 1879, 180 men of the Kalat detachment, together with 30 sabres 1st Punjab Cavalry, the whole under Major Humfrey, totally defeated with severe loss over 2,000 Barechi Pathans at Syud But in Shorawak.

During the summer of 1879 the companies at Quetta suffered from cholera; and during the succeeding autumn the wings exchanged quarters, by a company at a time.

The Left wing returned from Kalat to Quetta in April, 1880, and under Major Iredell and Lieut. Salmon, marched for Kandahar. After the massacre of Major Waudby and his party at Dubrai, this wing left some 150 men in detachments at Gatai, Dubrai, and Mel Karez, on the road between Chaman and Kandahar. On the 23rd April the Head-quarters and Right wing left Quetta, and on the 5th May reached Kandahar, after which the regiment occupied quarters in the Garkha village, and was posted to the 2nd Brigade. In June, 1880, one company, with a troop 3rd Bombay Light Cavalry, escorted a surveying party to Maiwand and back. Towards the end of that month the regiment was placed under orders to relieve the Baluchis at Kalat-i-Ghilzai, the 19th N.I. sending a wing to relieve the detachments on the Kandahar-Chaman road.

On the 5th July the regiment, having been transferred to the 1st Brigade, proceeded with Brigadier-General Burrows's force to Girishk, and on the 14th three Companies, under Captain Harrison and Lieut. Salmon, took part in the skirmish resulting in the capture of the Wali's guns from the mutineers. On the 27th July, 1880, the regiment was engaged in the battle of Maiwand. Forming, on that disastrous day, the centre of the Infantry line, it advanced across the nullah, the Right wing, for about half an hour subsequently, lying down on the open stony plain to avoid the enemy's Artillery fire, and the Left wing, under Major Iredell, forming, for a brief interval, a reserve. About this time Captain H. F. Smith was struck by a shell and killed. Immediately afterwards Lieut. Cole and two companies of the Left wing were sent to the left flank of the 1st Grenadiers, Major Iredell, with the other two companies, forming up on the left of the Right wing. Even at this state of the engagement thirst began to be felt, the day being unusually hot, and the men, owing to want of carriage, having been obliged to carry their greatcoats. The six companies forming the centre of the line now advanced up to and lay down beside the Horse Artillery guns, where they—and more especially the two companies to the left, which were wholly destitute of cover—began to suffer considerably, the enemy's fire being directed chiefly towards the battery. When the action had lasted over four hours, and swarms of the enemy emerging within 500 yards of the British position, from a nullah, attacked the left flank of the line, the two detached companies 30th N.I.—which had lost their Commanding Officer, Lieut. Cole, killed, and two Native officers out of three wounded, and had otherwise suffered severely—fell back; and the Horse Artillery guns and 1st Grenadiers were compelled to retire. Their left flank and rear being thus laid open to the enemy, the six companies 30th N.I. fell back on the 66th, who in turn moved towards the garden enclosures on the other side of the nullah they had originally crossed, the greater portion of the two Native Infantry regiments making for the same cover. Lieut. Justice fell mortally wounded at this time, and died while Lieut. Rayner, 66th, and Captain Harrison, 30th N.I., were attempting to carry him away. Though short of ammunition, the troops made a stand at the garden enclosures until they were ordered by the General to retire. Here Major Iredell was dangerously wounded. After a night of terrible suffering, the remnants of the regiment reached Kandahar on the 28th July, and went into the citadel. Its strength before going into action was, of the Native ranks, about 600: of these, some 400 were in the fighting line, the remainder, being either sick, or protecting the baggage, under Lieut. Salmon. Over 200 of the Native ranks perished, and about 30 wounded reached Kandahar. Of 6 European officers in the fighting line, 3 were killed, and 1 was dangerously wounded.

The 30th N.I. took part in the defence of Kandahar throughout the siege, having charge of the Bar Durani Gate front. On the 16th Aug. Lieuts. Salmon and Adye, 83rd Foot, who were both attached to the regiment, highly distinguished themselves by affording assistance to officers and men wounded at Deh Khwaja. During the battle of Kandahar, on the 1st Sept., the regiment formed part of the city reserve, which Col. Mainwaring commanded. The following day a company under Captain Harrison brought the guns captured from Ayub Khan over the Baba Wali Pass, and on the 16th Oct. the regiment finally left Kandahar as escort to the same as far as Quetta, from whence it returned to Jacobabad on the 8th Nov., 1880.

During the two campaigns the 30th N.I. lost by death over 300 of the Native ranks.

The under-mentioned officers of the 30th Regt. Bombay Native Infantry (Jacob's Rifles) served in the war :—

Colonel W. G. Mainwaring, C.I.E., commanded the regiment throughout both campaigns, being present at the battle of Maiwand and the defence of Kandahar. Commanded at Quetta from Nov., 1878, till April, 1880. Commanded the City reserve at the battle of Kandahar. (Three times mentioned in despatches.)

Colonel T. Bell, 1st Belooch Regt. (For services see 1st Belooch Regt.)

Colonel W. T. Mills (Retired) served with the regiment at Quetta and Kalat from the spring till the autumn of 1879.

Lieut.-Colonel F. T. Humfrey commanded the Kalat detachment from Nov., 1878, till Dec., 1879, when he proceeded to Quetta, and from thence on medical certificate to Europe. Rejoined the regiment at Kandahar 6 Sept., 1880, and returned with it to India. In command of a detachment 30th N.I. and 30 sabres 1st Punjab Cavalry, defeated over 2,000 Barechi Pathans at the action of Syud But. (Mentioned in despatches; Brevet of Lieut.-Colonel.)

Major J. S. Iredell, 20th Bombay N.I., rejoined the regiment at Quetta in Jan., 1880, and commanded the Left wing in the advance to Kandahar. Was present at the battle of Maiwand, in which he was dangerously wounded, and throughout the siege of Kandahar. (Mentioned in despatches.)

Bt.-Major W. C. Harrison rejoined the regiment at Quetta in Dec., 1878. As Provost-Marshal to the force, accompanied Sir D. Stewart's first advance on and occupation of Kandahar and Kalat-i-Ghilzai. Served at Quetta and Kalat in 1878, 1879, and 1880. Reached Kandahar 15 May, 1880, in charge of a draft for the regiment, and took part in the advance to Girishk, commanding the three companies engaged in the skirmish of 14 July, 1880, and taking part in the battle of Maiwand, the defence of Kandahar, and the battle of Kandahar. (Mentioned in despatches; Brevet of Major.)

Captain C. F. Baugh proceeded in Sept., 1878, with the regiment to Quetta, and acted as Station Staff Officer till he died in August, 1879.

Lieut. M. B. Salmon, 2nd W.I. Regt., joined the regiment in April, 1880, and served with it till the conclusion of the campaign. Proceeded with the Left wing to Kandahar. Commanded detachments on the Kandahar-Chaman road. Accompanied the regiment to Girishk, and took part in the skirmish of the 14th July, 1880, the battle of Maiwand (in command of the baggage-guards), and the defence of Kandahar. Distinguished himself in rescuing wounded men coming in from the sortie to Deh Khwaja. (Recommended for Victoria Cross.)

Lieuts. W. N. Justice and D. Cole. (Killed in action. See Biographical Division.)

INDIAN MEDICAL DEPARTMENT.

BENGAL.

SURGEON-MAJOR *J. E. T. AITCHISON, M.D.*, served during the first campaign as Botanist with the Kuram F.F.. Was present with the 29th N.I., at the reconnaissance of 28 Nov., 1878, and the assault and capture of the Peiwar Kotal.

Surgeon-General F. F. Allen, M.D., Q.H.P., C.B. (Retired). (For services see "Staff.")

Surgeon-Major S. C. Amesbury, M.D., served as Senior M.O. on the Khyber line throughout the first campaign, taking part in the capture of Ali Musjid and the advance to Gandamak. Erected, with coolie labour, the Amesbury Frontier Flour Mills. In the second campaign organized the field hospitals at Gandamak, and served as Staff Surgeon and Sanitary Officer at Safed Sang, where he was in charge of the field hospitals N.I. (Thanked in orders.)

Surgeon John Anderson served in the war from 20 Oct., 1879, to 17 Aug., 1880, holding medical charge, successively, of the Native Field Hospital and Coolie Corps, Gandamak, till 31 Dec., 1879; the garrisons of Jagdalak and Seh Baba, till 31 March, 1880; the 17th Bengal Cavalry and details of native troops at Kabul till 30 June, 1880; and a sick convoy returning from Kabul, 15 July, 1880.

Surgeon J. Armstrong officiated in medical charge of the 17th N.I. with the force under Major-General Hume from 17 Nov., 1880, till 6 May, 1881.

Surgeon A. Barclay, M.B., served with the Peshawar Valley F.F. from the outbreak of the war till 16 June, 1879, being present at the capture of Ali Musjid.

Surgeon T. E. L. Bate served with the Khyber Line Force in the second campaign.

Surgeon C. H. Beatson served with the 1st Division Peshawar Valley F.F. in the first campaign.

Surgeon-Major H. W. Bellew, C.S.I. (For services see "Staff.")

Surgeon S. F. Bigger served in medical charge of the 13th N.I. from 3 Oct., 1879, till Jan., 1881, taking part in the Zaimusht expedition, and being present at the capture of Zawa.

Surgeon J. Blood served with the field hospital, Sir D. Stewart's Division, from the outbreak of the war till June, 1879, taking part in the advance on and occupation of Kandahar, and returning to India by the Thal-Chotiali route.

Surgeon-Major H. M. B. Boyd served in medical charge of the 14th N.I. during the first campaign, being present at the assault and capture of Ali Musjid.

Surgeon E. S. Brander, M.B., served in medical charge of the 41st N.I. at Jamrud and Landi Kotal, from 1 Feb., 1879, till invalided at the end of May, 1879. While at Jamrud was in charge of the garrison.

Surgeon S. Brereton served during the first campaign with the 1st Division Kandahar F.F. (Since deceased.)

Surgeon-Major James Browne, M.D., was in medical charge of the Native Base Hospital, Kabul F.F., Peshawar, from 3 Feb. till 30 Sept., 1880. Rejoined his regiment, the 41st N.I., at Landi Kotal, 15 Nov., 1880, and served with it till 28 Dec., 1880.

Surgeon S. H. Browne, M.D., served with Sir D. Stewart's Division from the outbreak of the war till 1 Aug., 1879, and subsequently with the Khyber Line Force.

Surgeon W. H. Cadge was in medical charge Left wing 25th N.I. and Native Base Hospital, Kandahar F.F., from 1 Nov., 1878, till 22 March, 1879; of cholera and rest hospitals and detachments at Fort Jamrud, 10 April till 28 July, 1879; and subsequently of 17th N.I. on S. Afghanistan line of communications.

Surgeon-Major W. S. Caldwell (*Retired*) served in medical charge of the 27th P.N.I. during the first campaign, taking part with the attacking force in the assault and capture of Ali Musjid.

Surgeon-Major C. W. Calthrop joined the 12th Bengal Cavalry 3 Nov., 1879, at Sherpur, having taken an active part in the action of Ali Khel *en route*. Served with the regiment throughout the remainder of the period it was employed in the war, taking part in the operations round Kabul and defence of Sherpur in Dec., 1879.

Surgeon-Major G. C. Chesnaye served throughout the first campaign in medical charge 4th Goorkhas, and as Senior M.O. 1st Brigade 1st Division Peshawar Valley F.F. (Thanked in orders for services during campaign and throughout cholera epidemic.) Served throughout the second campaign: first, in medical charge 4th Goorkhas and of Brigadier-General C. Gough's Brigade, taking part in the advance to Sherpur, and being present at the affairs at Jagdalak and Jagdalak Kotal; next, as P.M.O. in the Bala Hissar; afterwards, as P.M.O. of the force under Major-General Ross acting towards Ghazni, being present at the action of Zaidabad and the destruction of Abdul Gafur's fort; subsequently, as P.M.O. of Brigadier-General C. Gough's force in Koh Daman; eventually as Brigade Surgeon 3rd Brigade Kabul-Kandahar F.F., taking part in the march to the relief of Kandahar, being present at the reconnaissance of 31 Aug., 1880, and battle of Kandahar, and having supervision of all wounded of the Indian Forces present (mentioned in despatches); and, finally, as P.M.O. of the force under Brigadier-General MacGregor, in the operations against the Marris.

Surgeon W. Coates, M.D., was attached to the Divisional Field Hospital, Peshawar Valley F.F., throughout the first campaign, being present at the capture of Ali Musjid. During the second campaign was in charge of the Native Field Hospital 1st Division Kabul F.F. from 6 Oct., 1879, till 17 April, 1880; being present at the action of Charasiab, the operations round Kabul, and the defence of Sherpur. From 18 April till Dec., 1880, was in medical charge 5th Goorkhas, taking part in the march from Kabul to the relief of Kandahar, the battle of Kandahar, and the operations against the Marris.

Surgeon D. W. D. Comins served in the second campaign, first with the Khyber F.F., and afterwards at Sherpur.

Surgeon-Major H. D. S. Compigné, M.D., served during the second campaign, as Medical Officer Deoli Irregular Force with the Kuram Division under General Watson.

Surgeon G. A. Cones served during the first campaign in medical charge of the General Field Hospital, Daka, and of the 24th P.N.I., with General Maude's Division, and during the second campaign, in medical charge of the 31st N.I., the 17th B.C., the 22nd N.I., and the General Field Hospital at Seh Baba, with General Bright's Division.

Surgeon-Major F. G. Constant, M.D., served in medical charge of the 12th B.C., with the Kuram Valley F.F., from the outbreak of the war till 16 Sept., 1879.

Surgeon-Major H. Cookson (*Retired*) served in medical charge of the Native Base Hospital, Kuram F.F., during the first campaign.

Surgeon J. L. Corbett, M.D., served during the first campaign with the Bhopaul Battn. in General Maude's Division, and during the second campaign with the 29th N.I. in the Kuram Force, taking part in the Zaimusht expedition, and being present at the capture of Zawa.

Surgeon-Major C. P. Costello served in medical charge of the Native Base Hospital, Kuram F.F., throughout the first campaign (thanked in orders), and in medical charge of the 1st Goorkha L.I. with the Khyber Division, during the second campaign, from Dec., 1879, till Aug., 1880, taking part as Senior M.O. with the Flying Column in the Lughman Valley expedition.

Surgeon E. Cretin, M.B., served with 31st N.I. in the Khyber Line Force during the second campaign, being present at the action of Kam Daka, and taking part in the Lughman Valley, Wazir Kugiani, and Hissarak expeditions.

Surgeon James Crofts, M.D., served with the forces in the Kuram Valley during both campaigns, being present, with the 11th N.I. at the repulse of the enemy's attack on Ali Khel.

Surgeon A. M. Crofts served with the 26th N.I. in Sir D. Stewart's Division during the first campaign, taking part in the advance on and occupation of Kandahar; with the 4th Battn. Rifle Brigade on its return march from the Khyber, June-July, 1879; in medical charge 10th Bengal Lancers and cholera and rest hospitals at Jamrud July to Sept., 1879; and in medical charge of the 10th Bengal Lancers throughout the period it was employed in the second campaign, being present at the fighting at Jagdalak in Dec., 1879.

Surgeon-Major R. W. Cunningham, M.D., served in medical charge of the 15th N.I. throughout both campaigns, taking part in the advance on and occupation of Kandahar, the advance on Ghazni and into the Logar Valley, and the march from Kabul to the relief of Kandahar, and being present at the battle of Ahmad Khel, the action of Arzu, the operations in the Logar Valley, the reconnaissance of 31 Aug., 1880, and the battle of Kandahar. (Mentioned in despatches; thanked in orders.)

Brigade-Surgeon G. V. Currie was in medical charge of the 10th Bengal Lancers, and senior M.O. at Daka during the first campaign, being present at the action of Kam Daka.

Deputy Surgeon-General A. J. Dale, M.B. (For services see "Staff.")

Surgeon G. R. Daphtary, M.D., served during the second campaign as M.O. 3rd N.I. in the Reserve Division Kandahar F.F.

Surgeon C. A. Daubeny served with the Khyber Line Force during the second campaign. (Died in hospital at Peshawar.)

Surgeon L. R. Dawson, M.D., served during the first campaign at Ali Musjid and Jamrud till invalided.

Surgeon-Major L. F. Dickson, M.D., served in medical charge of the 13th N.I. with the Kuram Force in the 2nd campaign.

Surgeon B. Doyle served in medical charge of the garrisons of Fort Battye, Rozabad, and of No. 4 Mountain Battery during the second campaign.

Surgeon J. Duke served throughout the second campaign, first as M.O. 5th Goorkhas and Derajat Mountain Battery, being present at the occupation of the Shutargardan and action of Charasiab; subsequently as M.O. Derajat Mountain Battery, being present at the rear-guard fights at Maidan and Argandi, 11 and 12 Dec., 1879, the assaults of the Takht-i-Shah and Asmai heights (mentioned in despatches as having been conspicuous for unremitting attention to the wounded under a heavy fire), and the defence of Sherpur; afterwards as M.O. 3rd Punjab Cavalry, being present at the action of Zaidabad, taking part in the march from Kabul to the relief of Kandahar: being present at the battle of Kandahar and the operations against the Marris. Served for a time on the Staff of General Roberts. Opened a dispensary at Ali Khel 13 May, 1879, and for several months attended many of the inhabitants of the Hariab Valley in their own homes.

Surgeon-Major O. T. Duke, M.B., served during the first campaign on the Kandahar line of communications. Was present as Political Officer and volunteer at the action of Syud But (mentioned in despatches), and Chapar Mountain, 2 April, 1880, as Assistant Political Officer with Sir R. Sandeman.

Surgeon E. H. Dumbleton served with the Kuram Valley F.F. in the first campaign. (Died at Ali Khel, 5 Oct., 1879.)

Surgeon A. Duncan, M.D., served in medical charge of 23rd Punjab Pioneers in the first and during part of the second campaign. Was severely wounded at the action of Charasiab. (Mentioned in despatches.)

Surgeon-Major W. Duncan, M.B., served with the Kuram Valley F.F. throughout the first campaign, holding successively the following charges and appointments: General Hospital, Head-quarters and Divisional Staff Sanitary Officer, Camp Followers' Hospital, 7th Co. Sappers and Miners, 28th N.I., 14th B.L., General Hospital, and Cholera Hospital at Kuram.

Surgeon-Major W. Eddowes served in medical charge of the 2nd Goorkhas during the second campaign.

Surgeon G. A. Emerson served throughout both campaigns, first with the 3rd Goorkhas, accompanying the regiment to Kandahar and Kalat-i-Ghilzai; subsequently on the Kandahar line of communications; afterwards in the Native Field Hospital at Kandahar; and finally with the 2nd Punjab Cavalry, being present at the battle of Ahmad Khel and the action of Arzu.

Brigade-Surgeon A. Eteson, M.D., served in medical charge of the Sappers and Miners at Jalalabad, with the 1st Division Peshawar Valley F.F., during the first campaingn.

Surgeon-Major George Farrell served in medical charge of the 5th Goorkhas, throughout the first and during the second campaign, being present at the assault and capture of the Peiwar Kotal (mentioned in despatches; thanked in orders), the passage of the Mangior defile, the action of Charasiab, and the operations round Kabul and defence of Sherpur in Dec., 1879 (again mentioned in despatches).

Surgeon J. E. C. Ferris served during the second campaign with the 1st Bengal Cavalry in the Kuram F.F.

Surgeon-Major W. Finden served on the Staff of Sir D. Stewart during the advance on and occupation of Kandahar, 1878-1879; was in medical charge of the 2nd Goorkhas during the occupation of Kabul; accompanied the Kabul-Kandahar F.F. in the march to the relief of Kandahar, and was present at the battle of Kandahar. (Mentioned in despatches.)

Surgeon-Major J. M. C. N. Fleming, M.D., served in medical charge of the Base Hospital, Kuram Valley F.F., during the first campaign.

Surgeon J. C. Fullerton served in S. Afghanistan from the outbreak of the war till March, 1880, taking part, as M.O., with the 1st Punjab Cavalry, in the advance on and occupation of Kandahar, and being present at the action of Takht-i-pul, in attendance on the wounded on the field.

Surgeon-Major W. M. Galloway served in medical charge of the 45th N.I. from Oct., 1878, till July, 1879, being present at the capture of Ali Musjid, and taking part in the advance to Jalalabad. (Died at Rawal Pindi, 22 July, 1879.)

Surgeon W. Gillies served with the 5th Bengal Cavalry in the Khyber Line Force during the second campaign.

Surgeon H. A. C. Gray. (Deceased. See Biographical Division.)

Surgeon-Major G. Griffith served in medical charge of the 18th B.C. during the second campaign, taking part in the Zaimusht expedition.

Surgeon G. S. Griffiths served throughout the first campaign with the 1st P.I., returning to India by the Thal-Chotiali route, and being present at the action of Baghao. Served in the second campaign as M.O. of the Base Hospital, Kuram F.F., and took part in the Zaimusht expedition.

Surgeon W. E. Griffiths served with the 21st N.I. throughout both campaigns, being present at the action of Matun and the defence of the Shutargardan.

Surgeon J. S. Gunn, M.B., served with the 4th Bengal Cavalry in the Khyber Line Force during the second campaign. (Deceased.)

Surgeon P. de H. Haig served during the first campaign as M.O. Field and Base Hospitals, Peshawar.

Surgeon N. J. Halpin, M.D., served with the 1st Division Peshawar Valley F.F. during the first campaign.

Surgeon H. Hamilton, M.D., served throughout the second campaign, first officiating in medical charge of the 12th B.C., and afterwards of the 23rd Pioneers, taking part in the advance on and occupation of Kabul, and the march from Kabul to the relief of Kandahar, and being present at the action of Charasiab, and subsequent pursuit, the operations round Kabul and defence of Sherpur in Dec., 1879, and the battle of Kandahar. (Mentioned in despatches.)

Surgeon G. C. Hancock, M.B., served in medical charge of the 5th Punjab Cavalry throughout both campaigns, being present at the actions of Matan and Charasiab, and the operations round Kabul and defence of Sherpur in Dec., 1879.

Surgeon G. F. A. Harris served with the 16th N.I. in the Khyber Reserve and Khyber Line Force throughout the period it was employed in the war.

Surgeon A. Hemsted served with the Peshawar Valley F.F. and Reserve Division during the first campaign till invalided.

Surgeon-Major A. P. Holmes, M.D., served with the 1st Sikhs throughout the period the regiment was employed in the war, being present at the taking of Ali Musjid, the operations in the Zaimusht country, and in minor expeditions.

Surgeon C. B. Hunter served throughout the second campaign, holding medical charge of Native Field Hospital, Landi Kotal; of reconnoitring party to Pesh Bolak; of garrison of Fort Jamrud; and of half-battalion 12th Foot; doing duty, European Field Hospital, Landi Kotal, and Royal Irish Regt., Landi Kotal; and holding medical charge of Cholera Hospital, Ali Musjid.

Brigade-Surgeon R. F. Hutchinson, M.D., was in medical charge of the Base Hospital for Natives, Peshawar, from 16 Nov., 1878, till 17 Dec., 1879.

Surgeon D. M. Jack served with Sir Donald Stewart's Division during the second campaign.

Surgeon-Major W. Jackson served in medical charge of the 2nd Punjab Infantry throughout the first campaign, being present at the assault and capture of the Peiwar Kotal.

Surgeon-Major J. W. Johnston, M.D., served in medical charge of the 3rd Goorkhas throughout both campaigns. Performed a successful operation on the favourite wife of the Amir Abdul Rahman at Kandahar in Dec., 1879. Was appointed Botanist and Geologist to the Ghazni F.F., and was present at the battle of Ahmad Khel and the action of Arzu.

Surgeon-Major W. N. Keefer served throughout both campaigns in medical charge of the 20th N.I., and during the second, in medical charge of the General Hospital for Native troops, Kuram and Thal. Was present at the storming and capture of Ali Musjid and of Zawa.

Surgeon-Major D. F. Keegan, M.D., served with the Central India Horse during the second campaign, being present at the action of Besud, taking part in the march from Kabul to the relief of Kandahar, and being present at the battle of Kandahar.

Surgeon A. H. Kelly. (Killed in the massacre of the Kabul Embassy. See Biographical Division.)

Surgeon J. Lewtas, M.B., served during both campaigns, attached to the Corps of Guides and the 29th N.I. Was present, with the former, at the taking of Ali Musjid, the action of Futtehabad, the operations round Kabul and defence of Sherpur in Dec., 1879, and the second action of Charasiab, and took part, with the latter, in both the Bazar Valley expeditions. (Twice mentioned in despatches.)

Surgeon-Major H. J. Linton served with the 24th N.I. throughout both campaigns, taking part in the Bazar Valley expedition and the march from Kabul to the relief of Kandahar, and being present at the fighting at Jagdalak in Dec., 1879, and the battle of Kandahar. (Mentioned in despatches.)

Surgeon S. Little, M.D., served with the 4th Bengal Cavalry in the second campaign, taking part in the Wazir Kugiani and Hissarak expeditions.

Surgeon C. J. McCartie, M.D., served with the 2nd Punjab Cavalry from 22 Nov., 1878, till 26 March, 1880, taking part in the advance on and occupation of Kandahar and Girishk, and the second occupation of Kalat-i-Ghilzai, and being present at the actions of Takht-i-pul and Shahjui. Was wounded near Kandahar by a bullet through the shoulder. (Brought to notice of the Commander-in-Chief.)

Surgeon D. J. Macdonald served with the Khyber Reserve and Khyber Line Force during the second campaign.

Surgeon D. P. MacDonald, M.D., served in the first campaign with the Field Hospital 1st Division Peshawar Valley F.F., and in medical charge of the Cholera Hospital at Jalalabad during the return of the troops from Gandamak in May and June, 1879, and during the second campaign with the 17th Bengal Lancers in the Khyber Line Force.

Surgeon H. K. McKay served in medical charge of the 32nd Pioneers during the first campaign, taking part in the advance on and occupation of Kandahar, the advance to the Halmand, and the return to India by the Thal-Chotiali route.

Surgeon-Major C. J. McKenna served in the first campaign with the 39th N.I., and as Senior Medical and Sanitary Officer at Ali Musjid, 2nd Division Peshawar Valley F.F., till 18 June, 1879. (Thanked in orders.)

Surgeon A. W. Mackenzie, M.B., served at Base Hospital for Native troops, Peshawar, from Nov., 1878, till Feb., 1879, and in medical charge of 3rd Punjab Cavalry during March and April, 1880, and of No. 2 Mountain Battery from April till conclusion of the war, being present at the second action of Charasiab, taking part in the march from Kabul to the relief of Kandahar, and being present at the battle of Kandahar and the operations against the Achakzais.

Surgeon-Major S. Mackertich served with the 5th Punjab Infantry in the Kuram Valley in 1878.

Surgeon R. Macrae, M.B., from Dec., 1878, till April, 1879, was in medical charge of the station at Thal, where he organized a hospital for the Commissariat, Transport, and Camp Followers of the Kuram Valley F.F. From April, 1879, till the conclusion of the first campaign, and throughout the second, was in medical charge of the 2nd Goorkhas, taking part in the return march through the Khyber in June, 1879, and being present at the fighting at Jagdalak, and the operations in the Koh Daman, &c. Acted for a time as Sanitary Officer to the 2nd Division Kabul F.F. (Thanked in orders.)

Surgeon H. Mallins, M.B., was attached to the Bengal Sappers and Miners from outbreak of war till 2 March, 1879, and from that date till invalided to Europe served with the 27th P.N.I. Was present at the attack on Ali Musjid and the action of Futtehabad. (Thanked in orders.)

Surgeon-Major D. N. Martin, M.D., served in medical charge of the 30th P.N.I. in the Khyber Line Force during the second campaign.

Surgeon W. A. Mawson served with No. 4 Mountain Battery during the first campaign, being present at the bombardment and capture of Ali Musjid, and minor affairs, and with the 14th Bengal Lancers throughout the period the regiment was employed in the second campaign, being present at the action of Charasiab and the operations round Kabul and defence of Sherpur in Dec., 1879.

Surgeon T. Molony, M.D., served with the 3rd Sikhs from Sept., 1879, till invalided to England in July, 1880, being present at the defence of the Shutargardan (including the actions of 2 and 14 Oct., 1879), and the operations round Kabul and defence of Sherpur in Dec., 1879.

Surgeon James Moran, M.D., served throughout the first campaign, first in medical charge of the 14th N.I., and subsequently of the 6th N.I., with the Peshawar Valley F.F.

Surgeon J. Mullane, M.D., served throughout both campaigns, first with the 19th P.N.I., taking part in the advance on and occupation of Kandahar and the advance to the Halmand, afterwards in medical charge of the Native Base Hospital, Quetta, and finally with the 25th P.N.I., taking part in the advance on Ghazni and the march from Kabul to the relief of Kandahar, and being present at the battle of Ahmad Khel, the action of Arzu, and the battle of Kandahar.

Surgeon W. R. Murphy served with the 25th P.N.I. throughout the first campaign, taking part in the advance on Kandahar and Kalat-i-Ghilzai, and being present at the action of Takht-i-pul, and with the 19th Bengal Cavalry in the second campaign, taking part in the advance on Ghazni and to Kabul, and being present at the battle of Ahmad Khel and the actions of Arzu and Patkao Shana. (Mentioned in despatches.)

Surgeon C. H. Murray served with the Khyber Reserve and Khyber Line Force under General Bright in the second campaign. (Died in hospital at Peshawar.)

Surgeon J. A. Nelis, M.B., served with the 2nd Sikhs throughout the war, taking part in the advance on Ghazni and the march from Kabul to the relief of Kandahar, and being present at the battle of Ahmad Khel, the action of Arzu, the battle of Kandahar, and the operations against the Achakzais and Marris.

Surgeon-Major J. H. Newman, M.D., served in medical charge of the Mhairwarra Battalion, with the 2nd Division Peshawar Valley F.F. during the first campaign.

Surgeon G. M. Nixon, M.B., served as M.O. 5th N.I. and Surgeon to the Lower Kuram Brigade in the second campaign.

Surgeon P. F. O'Connor served with the 1st P.C. throughout both campaigns, taking part in the advance on and occupation of Kandahar, and the advance on Ghazni, and being present at the battle of Ahmad Khel, and the actions of Arzu and Patkao Shana. (Mentioned in despatches.)

Surgeon M. O'Dwyer, M.B., served with the Bengal Sappers and Miners, the Coolie Corps, at the cholera camps, and with the 39th N.I. in the Khyber Brigade from May till Sept., 1879.

Surgeon-Major C. F. Oldham served with the 1st Goorkhas in S. Afghanistan during the first campaign, taking part in the return march by the Thal-Chotiali route.

Surgeon C. W. Owen, C.I.E., served in medical charge of the Head-quarters Staff of Sir F. Roberts from 26 Sept., 1879, till 6 Aug., 1880, and in medical charge of the Head-quarters Staff of Sir D. Stewart, as also in medical charge of the 45th N.I. from 6 Aug., 1880, till the dissolution of the N. Afghanistan F.F. Took part in the advance on and occupation of Kabul, and was present at the actions of Charasiab, Chardeh, 11 Dec., 1879 (wounded), and Siah Sang, 13 Dec., 1879, and the defence of Sherpur. Established the Charitable Dispensary in Kabul City. (Twice mentioned in despatches; thanked by Government; C.I.E.)

Surgeon W. Owen, M.D., served in the Kandahar F.F. during the first campaign.

Surgeon E. Palmer, M.D., served with the 3rd Bengal Cavalry throughout the second campaign, taking part in the march from Kabul to the relief of Kandahar, and being present at the battle of Kandahar.

Surgeon-Major A. McM. Paterson was attached to the Base and Field Hospital, Kuram, from the end of the first campaign till 6 Nov., 1879, and during the second campaign was employed on staff and regimental duty with the Khyber Reserve and Khyber Line Force.

Surgeon-Major R. Power served with the 11th Bengal Lancers throughout the first campaign, being present at the capture of Ali Musjid.

Surgeon-Major C. E. Raddock served with the 31st N.I. throughout the second campaign. Superintended the Field Hospital at Landi Kotal, and was Senior M.O. 3rd Brigade 2nd Division Khyber Force.

Surgeon A. S. Reid, M.B., served in medical charge of the 8th N.I., and of the Field Hospital at Safed Sang throughout the second campaign.

Surgeon G. S. Robertson served in medical charge of the Transport in the Khyber, Khurd Khyber, and at Sherpur during the second campaign.

Surgeon E. L. Robinson (Retired).

Surgeon T. Robinson, M.B., served with the 4th Punjab Infantry in the Kuram Force during the second campaign.

Surgeon-Major W. A. C. Roe served with the 21st N.I. in the Kuram Valley from 19 April, 1879, till 10 July, 1880.

Surgeon-Major E. Sanders served with the 2nd Sikhs in S. Afghanistan during the early part of the first campaign, and with the 20th N.I. in the Kuram Valley during the latter part of the second campaign.

Surgeon-Major A. B. Seaman served with the 2nd N.I. in the Khyber Force during 1879.

Surgeon W. A. Simmonds served in medical charge of Swinley's Mountain Battery at Thal till Dec., 1878, and of the 5th P.I. from 15 Dec., 1878, till the return of the regiment to Peshawar in Sept., 1880, being present at the action of Charasiab, and the operations round Kabul and defence of Sherpur in Dec., 1879. Acted as Superintendent of Field Telegraphy to Brigadier-General H. Gough on the retirement from the Shutargardan.

Surgeon J. C. C. Smith served with the 27th N.I. during the second campaign. Was in medical charge of the Transport Corps Hospital at Kabul, and on duty in the Field Hospital on the return of the troops by the Khyber route to India.

Surgeon-Major F. A. Smyth served with the 27th N.I. in the Khyber Brigade under Brigadier-General C. Gough

Surgeon W. B. Smyth, M.D. (Assassinated. See Biographical Division.)

Surgeon A. E. R. Stephens served with the 19th N.I. from Dec., 1878, till Aug., 1880, taking part in the advance on and occupation of Kandahar, and the advance on Ghazni and to Kabul, and being present at the battle of Ahmad Khel and the action of Arzu.

Surgeon R. N. Stoker served in the Native Field Hospital at Ali Musjid, and afterwards with the Mhairwarra Battalion, during the first campaign.

Surgeon-Major A. B. Strahan served with No. 1 Mountain Battery in the second campaign, being present at the operations round Kabul and the defence of Sherpur in Dec., 1879, and the operations in the Hissarak Valley.

Surgeon T. H. Sweeny was employed on general duty with the 1st Division Kabul F.F. in the second campaign, being present at the operations round Kabul and the defence of Sherpur in Dec., 1879.

Surgeon-Major E. O. Tandy served with the 8th Bengal Cavalry throughout the first campaign, taking part in the advance on and occupation of Kandahar and Kalat-i-Ghilzai, and the return march to India by the Thal-Chotiali route. Accompanied the Head-quarters to Sibi in Aug., 1880, when he was invalided to England.

Surgeon-Major E. Taylor served in medical charge of the 23rd Pioneers throughout the first campaign, being present at the assault and capture of the Peiwar Kotal.

Surgeon-Major George Thomson, M.B., served in medical charge of the 1st Punjab Cavalry, and of the Native Base Hospital at Quetta during the first campaign.

Surgeon-General S. C. Townsend, C.B. (For services see "Staff.")

Surgeon F. J. Twohy, M.D., served in medical charge of the 12th N.I. throughout the first campaign, taking part in the advance on and occupation of Kandahar and Kalat-i-Ghilzai.

Surgeon-Major S. T. Veale, M.D., served in medical charge of the 19th P.N.I. throughout both campaigns, taking part in the advance on and occupation of Kandahar, and the advance on Ghazni and to Kabul, and being present at the battle of Ahmad Khel and the action of Arzu.

Surgeon J. E. Walsh, M.D. (Deceased. See Biographical Division.)

Surgeon G. Watson, M.D. (Deceased. See Biographical Division.)

Brigadier-Surgeon G. A. Watson served in medical charge of the 19th Bengal Lancers throughout the first campaign, taking part in the advance on and occupation of Kandahar and Kalat-i-Ghilzai. Was Senior M.O. of Brigadier-General Hughes's force on the return march to Kandahar.

Surgeon P. A. Weir, M.B., served in medical charge of the 41st N.I., with the N. Afghanistan F.F. from 20 June till 31 Oct., 1880.

Surgeon A. H. Williams, M.B., was in medical charge of the 9th N.I., with the Khyber Line Force, during the second campaign.

Surgeon F. W. Wright, M.B., served with the 19th Bengal Lancers during the advance on and occupation of Kandahar, and afterwards in the Native Base Hospital, Kandahar F.F., during the first campaign. From Aug., 1879, till Aug., 1880, served in medical charge of the 45th Sikhs, being present at the fighting at Jagdalak in Dec., 1879. From Aug., 1880, till the conclusion of the war, served in medical charge of the 3rd Sikhs, taking part in the advance from Kabul to the relief of Kandahar, and being present at the battle of Kandahar and the operations against the Marris.

Surgeon-Major Robert Temple Wright, M.D., served in medical charge of the 8th Bengal Cavalry during the second campaign, taking part in the march to Kandahar, and being present at the operations against the Achakzais. Was P.M.O. at Sibi, Sanitary Officer of Brigadier-General Henderson's Brigade, and Staff Officer and Secretary to Deputy Surgeon-General Simpson, P.M.O. Southern Afghanistan F.F.

MADRAS.

SURGEON R. M. ALLEN served with the 4th M.N.I. in the Khyber Line Force during the second campaign.

Surgeon-Major H. M. D. Archdall served during both campaigns, first with the Sind Reserve, and afterwards with the Vitakri F.F.

Surgeon H. Armstrong served in medical charge of the 1st Light Cavalry, with the S. Afghanistan F.F. during the second campaign.

Surgeon L. Beech served in medical charge of the 1st M.N.I. from 13 Jan. till 19 May, 1880, being present at the actions of Kam Daka and Besud.

Surgeon C. H. Bennett, M.D., was employed from 14 Nov. till 19 Dec., 1879, in bringing back a convoy of sick from Vitakri to Dera Ghazi Khan.

Surgeon H. St. Clair Carruthers served in the Divisional Field Hospital at Jalalabad during the second campaign.

Surgeon J. S. Dill, M.D., served in medical charge of the 4th M.N.I., with the Khyber Reserve and Khyber Line Force, from 12 Nov., 1879, till 2 Sept., 1880.

Surgeon S. L. Dobie served in medical charge of the 1st Light Cavalry, with the S. Afghanistan F.F., during the second campaign.

Surgeon D. Elcun served with various detachments in S. Afghanistan, including Kandahar, during the second campaign.

Surgeon J. Hunter, M.B., served in the Field Hospital Khyber Line Force, at Landi Kotal, from 20 June till 14 Sept., 1880.

Surgeon-Major J. P. McDermott served in medical charge of the 36th M.N.I., with the Rawal Pindi Division, and of the 15th M.N.I., with the Khyber Line Force, during the second campaign.

Surgeon-Major C. E. McVittie was in medical charge of the 3rd Cavalry, H.C., and Senior Medical officer at Sibi in 1880.

Surgeon J. J. Moran, M.D., served with the Khyber Line Force from 25 Nov., 1879, till 1 Aug., 1880, with the 22nd P.N.I. and various charges of European details, also in charge of the Native Field Hospital, Safed Sang.

Surgeon-Major J. North was employed on general duty with the Kandahar F.F. in 1880.

Surgeon T. H. Pope, M.B., was employed on Regimental and Staff duty with the Dera Ghazi Column, Thal-Chotiali F.F., and with the Vitakri F.F., during both campaigns.

Surgeon F. C. Reeves was employed on general duty with the S. Afghanistan F.F. during 1880 and 1881.

Surgeon S. C. Sarkies did duty with the Kabul Native Field Hospital under Surgeon-Major Farrell, and was subsequently in officiating medical charge of the 29th P.N.I. at Kuram from July till Oct., 1880, during the second campaign.

Surgeon C. Sibthorpe served in medical charge of the Queen's Own Sappers and Miners throughout the first campaign.

Surgeon A. J. Sturmer accompanied the 36th M.N.I. to Rawal Pindi, Nov., 1878, till Jan., 1879, and from thence proceeded with the 11th B.N.I. to Ali Khel, 1 Jan. till 14 June, 1879.

Surgeon W. H. Thornhill, M.D., served with the Khyber Line Force in various charges during the second campaign, from 22 Dec., 1879, till 4th Sept., 1880.

Surgeon W. H. Thornhill, M.D., served with the Khyber Division during the second campaign from 22 Dec., 1879, till 4 Sept., 1880, being in medical charge of the General Field Hospital at Jagdalak, of the Native Field Hospital at Jalalabad, of the troops and followers at Darunta, in the Lughman Valley expedition, and other charges.

Surgeon H. G. L. Wortabet, M.B., served in the second campaign.

BOMBAY.

SURGEON *A. F. ADAMS* served in medical charge of the Native Base Hospital at Quetta during the second campaign. (Deceased.)

Surgeon H. Adey served with the 27th Bombay N.I. throughout both campaigns.

Surgeon-Major James Arnott, M.D., joined the 19th Bombay N.I. at Dozan in Nov., 1879, and served with it till its return to India. Was P.M.O. of the Reserve Division while in the Bolan Pass. From 4 July, 1880, and throughout the siege of Kandahar, was Staff Surgeon in charge of the Head-quarters Staff, and Sanitary Officer in the Citadel. Was present, in charge of Col. Heathcote's column, at the sortie to Deh Khwaja, and in charge of the 4th and 19th Bombay N.I., at the battle of Kandahar. (Twice mentioned in despatches.)

Surgeon W. A. Barren served with the 4th Bombay Rifles in the 1st Division Kandahar F.F. during the second campaign, being present throughout the siege and at the battle of Kandahar.

Surgeon-Major A. Barry, M.D., served in medical charge of the 2nd Bombay Light Cavalry during the second campaign, taking part in the advance to the relief of Kandahar.

Surgeon M. L. Bartholemeusz, M.B., served with the 2nd Sind Horse during the second campaign, taking part in the advance to the relief of Kandahar.

Surgeon-Major R. H. Batty served with the 4th Bombay Rifles in the 1st Division Kandahar F.F. during the second campaign, being present throughout the siege and at the battle of Kandahar.

Deputy Surgeon-General L. S. Bruce. (For services see "Staff.")

Surgeon F. Burness was employed on general duty with the 2nd Division Kandahar F.F. during the second campaign.

Surgeon G. E. E. Burroughs served with the 3rd Sind Horse throughout the first campaign, being present at the action of Khushk-i-Nakhud. Officiated in medical charge of the 3rd Bombay Light Cavalry during its march from Disa to Kandahar, and then rejoining the 3rd Sind Horse, served with that regiment till the conclusion of the war, being present at the action of Girishk (during which he acted as Orderly Officer to Brigadier-General Nuttall), the battle of Maiwand, the defence of Kandahar, the sortie to Deh Khwaja, and the battle of Kandahar. (Mentioned in despatches; thanked in orders.)

Surgeon-Major E. P. Burrowes served with the 15th Bombay N.I. in the 2nd Division Kandahar F.F. during the second campaign.

Surgeon A. R. Campbell, M.D., served during 1880 in medical charge of the Sibi-Quetta Railway Staff.

Surgeon W. P. Carson was employed on general duty and officiated in medical charge of the 5th Bombay N.L.I. with the 2nd Division Kandahar F.F. during the second campaign.

Brigade Surgeon W. E. Cates served in medical charge of the 19th Bombay N.I. throughout the period it was employed in the first campaign and till Oct., 1879, when he was invalided to England from Dozan.

Surgeon O. H. Channer was employed on general duty with the 2nd Division Kandahar F.F. during the second campaign.

Surgeon J. W. Clarkson served with the 23rd N.I. in the 2nd Division Kandahar F.F. during the second campaign.

Surgeon-Major P. W. Cockell served with the 3rd Bombay, N.L.I. in the 2nd Division Kandahar F.F. during the second campaign.

Surgeon P. J. Damanier was employed on general duty with the 2nd Division Kandahar F.F. during the second campaign.

Surgeon A. H. C. Dane, M.D., served in medical charge of the 1st Bombay Grenadiers throughout the period the regiment was employed in the war, being present at the action of Girishk, the battle of

Maiwand, the defence of Kandahar, the sortie to Deh Khwaja, and (in charge of Brigadier-General Daubeny's Column) at the battle of Kandahar. (Mentioned in despatches.)

Surgeon-Major J. Davidson, M.B., was employed on general duty with the 2nd Division Kandahar F.F. during the second campaign.

Surgeon J. H. Earle was employed on general duty with the 1st Division Kandahar F.F. during the second campaign. Accompanied Brigadier-General Burrows's brigade to the Halmand, and was present at the action of Girishk, the battle of Maiwand (in charge of the Native Field Hospital), the defence of Kandahar, and the battle of Kandahar.

Surgeon J. B. Eaton, M.B., served from Jan. till Aug., 1880, in medical charge of the 16th Bombay N.I.; from Aug. till Oct., 1880, in medical charge of the 5th Bombay N.L.I.; and from Oct., 1880, in medical charge of the Bombay Sappers and Miners, holding the appointment of Staff Surgeon and Sanitary Officer at Kandahar, and subsequently at Quetta. While *en route* from Chappar to Kach was attacked by a body of the enemy, and had his horse shot under him.

Surgeon A. S. Faulkner served during the second campaign in medical charge of the Sibi-Quetta Railway Staff, till invalided in 1880.

Surgeon-Major S. B. Halliday served in medical charge of the 13th Bombay N.I., with the S. Afghanistan F.F. during the second campaign.

Surgeon W. K. Hatch, M.B., served with the 29th Bombay N.I. in S. Afghanistan during the second campaign.

Surgeon-Major J. A. Howell served in medical charge of the 24th Bombay N.I. throughout the period the regiment was employed in the war.

Surgeon F. Jones served with the 10th Bombay N.L.I. in the 2nd Division Kandahar F.F. during the second campaign.

Surgeon-Major J. F. Keith, M.D., served in medical charge of the 28th Bombay N.I. throughout the period it was employed in the war, being present at the defence of Kandahar, the sortie to Deh Khwaja, during which he was continuously engaged under fire in attending the wounded of all detachments and the battle of Kandahar, throughout which he was in charge of a detachment of Royal Fusiliers and Battery E/B, R.H.A., besides the regiment. Was present on several occasions with covering parties outside the walls of Kandahar.

Surgeon K. R. Kirtikar served from Dec., 1878, till April, 1879, in medical charge of the 19th Bombay N.I. and 1st Sind Horse, successively, in the Reserve Division; from April till July, 1879, in medical charge of the Sangsilla and Sibi outposts, successively; and from 26 July, 1879, till the conclusion of the war, in medical charge of the 30th Bombay N.I., holding, during part of the time, in addition, temporary charge of the Native Base Hospital at Quetta, and acting also as Civil Surgeon. Was present with the 30th Bombay N.I. at the battle of Maiwand and the defence and battle of Kandahar. (Appointed Civil Surgeon, Tanna, in recognition of gallant behaviour at Maiwand.)

Surgeon J. C. Lucas served in officiating medical charge of the Sappers and Miners from the beginning of 1880 till after the battle of Kandahar, when he was compelled to proceed to India on sick leave. Returned to Afghanistan in Feb., 1881, and served in medical charge of the 23rd Bombay N.L.I. till its return to India.

Surgeon F. F. Mac Cartie was employed on general duty with the 2nd Division Kandahar F.F. during the second campagn.

Surgeon J. McCloghry served with the 1st Sind Horse in the 2nd Division Kandahar F.F. during the second campaign.

Surgeon R. Manser served in medical charge of the Native Base Hospital at Kandahar during the second campaign, being present throughout the siege.

Surgeon H. D. Masani served in medical charge of the Depôt Hospital at Sibi during the second campaign.

Surgeon C. Monks was employed on general duty with the 2nd Division Kandahar F.F. during the second campaign.

Surgeon-Major E. Morton served in medical charge of the 29th Bombay N.I. during both campaigns. (Deceased.)

Surgeon H. P. Roberts (*Retired*), served in medical charge of the 9th Bombay N.I. during the second campaign till 19 Nov. 1880, being present at the skirmishes in the Khojak Pass.

Surgeon-Major C. G. H. Ross (*Retired*), served in medical charge of the 4th Bombay Rifles till invalided to England 27 Feb., 1880.

Surgeon-Major J. B. Simpson, M.B., served in medical charge of the 23rd Bombay N.L.I., during the second campaign. (Died at Sibi, of heat apoplexy, 13 Aug., 1880.)

Surgeon A. R. Stewart served in medical charge of the Poona Horse during the period the regiment was employed in the war, being present at the defence of Kandahar, the sorties to Khairabad and Deh Khwaja, in the latter of which he was twice wounded, and the battle of Kandahar.

Surgeon A. W. F. Street served with the 30th Bombay N.I. at Quetta and Kalat from Nov., 1878, till Oct., 1879; with the 3rd Sind Horse in the Pishin Valley and at Kandahar from Oct., 1879, till May, 1880; and with the 3rd Bombay Light Cavalry from May, 1880, till March, 1881, being present at the action of Girishk, the affair of the 23rd July, 1880, the battle of Maiwand, the defence of Kandahar, and the battle of Kandahar and subsequent pursuit.

Surgeon-Major R. C. Thorp, M.D., served in medical charge of the 5th Bombay N.L.I. in the 1st Division Kandahar F.F. during the second campaign.

Surgeon E. Tully was employed on general duty with the 1st Division Kandahar F.F. during the second campaign. Was in medical charge of the Civil Dispensary at Kandahar, being present throughout the siege.

Surgeon T. E. Worgan was employed on general duty with the 1st Division Kandahar F.F. during the second campaign, being present at the defence of Kandahar and the sortie to Deh Khwaja.

CHISWICK PRESS:—C. WHITTINGHAM AND CO., TOOKS COURT, CHANCERY LANE.

THE AFGHAN CAMPAIGNS OF 1878-1880.

THE AFGHAN CAMPAIGNS,

OF 1878—1880,

BY

SYDNEY H. SHADBOLT,

OF THE INNER TEMPLE, BARRISTER-AT-LAW;

Joint Author of "The South African Campaign of 1879."

Dedicated, by permission, to

LIEUT.-GENERAL SIR F. S. ROBERTS, BART., G.C.B., C.I.E., V.C., R.A.

COMMANDER-IN-CHIEF OF THE MADRAS ARMY.

COMPRISING HISTORICAL AND BIOGRAPHICAL DIVISIONS, AND CONTAINING A RAPID SKETCH OF THE WAR, MAPS ILLUSTRATING THE OPERATIONS AND THE MOVEMENTS OF THE FORCES, ONE HUNDRED AND FORTY PERMANENT PHOTOGRAPHS OF OFFICERS WHO LOST THEIR LIVES IN THE CAMPAIGNS AND OF RECIPIENTS OF THE VICTORIA CROSS, WITH MEMOIRS PREPARED FROM MATERIALS FURNISHED BY THEIR RELATIONS AND SURVIVING COMRADES, SUMMARIES OF THE MOVEMENTS IN THE FIELD OF THE VARIOUS REGIMENTS WHICH WERE ENGAGED, AND SEPARATE RECORDS OF THE SERVICES OF EVERY BRITISH OFFICER WHO WAS EMPLOYED IN THE WAR.

Biographical Division.

Τεθνάμεναι γὰρ καλὸν ἐπὶ προμάχοισι πεσόντα
ἄνδρ' ἀγαθόν, περὶ ᾗ πατρίδι μαρνάμενον.
TYRTÆUS, *Gnom. eleg.* iv., 1, 2.

CONTENTS OF BIOGRAPHICAL DIVISION.

	PLATES.	PAGES.
PORTRAITS AND BIOGRAPHICAL NOTICES OF OFFICERS WHO LOST THEIR LIVES IN THE WAR	I.—XIX	1—255
PORTRAITS AND RECORDS OF SERVICE OF RECIPIENTS OF THE VICTORIA CROSS	XX.	259—269

ERRATA.

Plate II. and p. 16, *for* " Beeke," *read* " Becke " throughout.

P. 108, l. 27 . . *for* " of his 44 men, 8 to 10 were wounded," *read* " of his 44 men, the survivors, from 8 to 10, were wounded."

P. 190 . . . . *for* " Edmund " Walker Samuells, *read* " Edward " Walker Samuells throughout.

LIEUT. P. E. ANDERSON, Staff Corps,
25th (Punjab) Bengal N.I.

MAJOR A. D. ANDERSON, Staff Corps,
23rd (Punjab) Bengal N.I. (Pioneers.)

SURGEON-MAJOR G. ATKINSON, M.B.,
Army Medical Department.

LIEUT. F. C. C. ANGELO,
Probationer Staff Corps.

LIEUT. F. M. BARCLAY, Staff Corps,
45th Bengal N.I. (Rattray's Sikhs).

LIEUT. H. J. O. BARR,
66th (Berkshire) Regt.

CAPTAIN W. B. BARKER,
10th (P.W.O. Royal) Hussars.

Reproduced by permanent photo-process by the London Stereoscopic Company.

Major H. G. Becher, Staff Corps,
11th Bengal N.I.

Major Wigram Battye, Staff Corps,
Queen's Own Corps of Guides.

Major H. H. Birch, Staff Corps,
27th (Punjab) Bengal N.I.

Captain John Beeke,
21st Bombay N.I. (Marine Battalion).

Lieut. W. H. Bishop,
2nd Battn. 11th (North Devonshire) Regt.

Major G. F. Blackwood,
Royal Horse Artillery.

Surgeon-Major R. H. Bolton,
Army Medical Department.

LIEUT.-COLONEL F. BROWNLOW, C.B.,
72nd (Duke of Albany's Own Highlanders).

BRIG.-GENERAL H. T. BROOKE,
Kandahar Field Force.

LT. A. BURLTON-BENNET, Staff Corps,
10th (Duke of Cambridge's Own)
Bengal Cavalry (Lancers).

CAPTAIN S. G. BUTSON,
9th (Queen's Royal) Lancers.

LIEUT. J. F. M. CAMPBELL, Staff Corps,
Attached 2nd Baluch Regt.

MAJOR SIR P. L. N. CAVAGNARI,
K.C.B., C.S.I.,
Minister and Plenipotentiary at Kabul.

CAPTAIN C. A. CARTHEW, Staff Corps,
Offg. D.A.Q.M.G., Khyber Brigade.

Reproduced by permanent photo-process by the London Stereoscopic Company.

LIEUT. R. T. CHUTE,
66th (Berkshire) Regt.

CAPTAIN D. T. CHISHOLM,
59th (2nd Nottinghamshire) Regt.

BT. LIEUT.-COLONEL W. H. J. CLARKE,
72nd (Duke of Albany's Own Highlanders).

LIEUT.-COLONEL R. S. CLELAND,
9th (Queen's Royal) Lancers.

LIEUT. DUNCAN COLE, Staff Corps,
Jacob's Rifles.

BT. MAJOR JOHN COOK, V.C., Staff Corps,
5th Goorkha Regt.

LIEUT.-COLONEL J. J. COLLINS,
2nd Battn. 60th (King's Royal Rifle Corps).

Reproduced by permanent photo-process by the London Stereoscopic Company.

LIEUT.-COL. G. B. CRISPIN, Staff Corps,
4th Bombay N.I. (Rifles).

SURGEON MAJOR H. CORNISH, F.R.C.S.,
Army Medical Department.

CAPTAIN G. M. CRUICKSHANK,
Royal (late Bombay) Engineers.

CAPTAIN E. W. H. CROFTON,
4th Batt. 60th (King's Royal Rifle Corps).

CAPTAIN F. J. CULLEN,
66th (Berkshire) Regt.

LIEUT.-COLONEL A. G. DAUBENY,
2nd Battn. 7th (Royal Fusiliers).

LIEUT. R. E. L. DACRES,
Royal Artillery.

LIEUT. A. E. DOBSON,
Royal Engineers.

LIEUT. G. G. DAWES, Staff Corps,
1st Bengal Cavalry.

LIEUT.-COL. H. FELLOWES, Staff Corps,
32nd (Punjab) Bengal N.I. (Pioneers).

CAPTAIN J. DUNDAS, V.C.,
Royal Engineers.

LIEUT. T. O. FITZGERALD, Staff Corps,
27th (Punjab) Bengal N.I.

CAPTAIN ST. J. T. FROME,
72nd (Duke of Albany's Own Highlanders).

LIEUT. ST. J. W. FORBES,
92nd (Gordon Highlanders).

Reproduced by permanent photo-process by the London Stereoscopic Company.

LIEUT.-COLONEL JAMES GALBRAITH,
66th (Berkshire) Regt.

LIEUT. C. H. GAISFORD,
72nd (Duke of Albany's Own Highlanders).

CAPTAIN J. H. GAMBLE,
1st Battn. 17th (Leicestershire) Regt.

CAPTAIN E. S. GARRATT,
66th (Berkshire) Regt.

CAPTAIN F. T. GOAD, Staff Corps,
5th Infy. Regt., Haidarabad Contingent.

The Rev. G. M. GORDON, M.A.,
Church Missionary Society.

MAJOR J. GODSON, Staff Corps,
4th Madras N.I.

Reproduced by permanent photo-process by the London Stereoscopic Company.

LIEUT. W. R. P. HAMILTON, V.C.,
Staff Corps, Queen's Own Corps of Guides.

SURGEON H. A. C. GRAY, M.B., C.M.,
Bengal Medical Department.

LIEUT. EDWARD HARDY,
Royal Horse Artillery.

CAPTAIN G. J. HARE, Staff Corps,
22nd (Punjab) Bengal N.I.

SUB-LIEUT. F. H. HARFORD,
10th (P. W. O. Royal) Hussars.

CAPTAIN P. C. HEATH, Staff Corps,
Brigade Major, Kandahar Field Force.

LIEUT. C. J. R. HEARSEY,
9th (Queen's Royal) Lancers.

LIEUT. W. F. HENNELL, Staff Corps,
1st Punjab Cavalry.

LIEUT. T. RICE HENN,
Royal Engineers.

2nd LIEUT. A. HONYWOOD,
66th (Berkshire) Regt.

W. JENKYNS, M.A., C.S.I.,
Bengal Civil Service,
Secretary to the British Embassy at Kabul.

LIEUT. W. N. JUSTICE,
Probationer, Staff Corps.

SURGEON-MAJOR H. KELSALL,
Army Medical Department.

SURGEON A. H. KELLY,
Bengal Medical Department.

Lieut. F. G. Kinloch, Staff Corps,
5th Bengal Cavalry.

Captain J. A. Kelso,
Royal Artillery.

Lieut. S. E. L. Lendrum,
Royal Artillery.

2nd Lieut. E. D. Los,
1st Battn. 25th (King's Own Borderers).

Lieut. G. H. Lumsden,
Probationer, Staff Corps.

Captain W. H. McMath,
66th (Berkshire) Regt.

Lieut. H. Maclaine,
Royal Horse Artillery.

Lieut. C. A. Montanaro,
Royal Artillery.

2nd Lieut. E. S. Marsh,
2nd Battn. 7th (Royal Fusiliers).

Captain C. S. Morrison,
14th Bengal Cavalry (Lancers)

Lieut. A. R. Murray, Staff Corps,
11th (P.W.O.) Bengal Cavalry (Lancers).

Bt. Lieut.-Colonel W. H. Newport,
Staff Corps, 28th Bombay N.I.

Lieut. C. Nugent,
Royal Engineers.

Lieut.-Col. Nicholetts, Staff Corps,
Commandant 2nd Baluch Regt.

MAJOR C. V. OLIVER,
66th (Berkshire) Regt.

COLONEL J. J. O'BRYEN, Staff Corps,
Commandant 22nd (Punjab) Bengal N.I.

LIEUT. E. G. OSBORNE,
Royal Horse Artillery.

2nd LIEUT. W. R. OLIVEY,
66th (Berkshire) Regt.

LIEUT. LORD OSSULTON,
4th Battn. Rifle Brigade.

CAPTAIN E. W. PERRY,
40th (2nd Somersetshire) Regt.

LIEUT. W. C. OWEN, Staff Corps,
3rd Bombay Cavalry (Queen's Own).

LIEUT. BROWNLOW POULTER,
Royal Engineers.

OFFG. DEP. SURG.-GENL. J. H. PORTER,
Army Medical Department.

CAPTAIN C. F. POWELL, Staff Corps,
5th Goorkha Regt.

BREVET-MAJOR L. A. POWYS,
59th (2nd Nottinghamshire) Regt.

CAPTAIN J. J. PRESTON,
4th Battn. Rifle Brigade.

CAPTAIN R. B. REED,
1st Battn. 12th (East Suffolk) Regt.

LIEUT. M. E. RAYNER,
66th (Berkshire) Regt.

Major W. Reynolds, Staff Corps,
3rd Regt. Sind Horse.

Lieut. T. J. O'D. Renny, Staff Corps,
Adjutant, 4th Punjab Infantry.

Lieut. J. T. Rice,
Royal Engineers.

2nd Lieut. W. P. Ricardo,
9th (Queen's Royal) Lancers.

Lieut. S. W. T. Roberts,
Probationer, Staff Corps.

Lieut. H. R. Ross,
Royal Artillery.

Captain W. Roberts,
66th (Berkshire) Regt.

CAPTAIN E. W. SAMUELLS,
Bengal Staff Corps,
Dep. Superintendent of Revenue Surveys.

CAPTAIN A. P. SAMUELLS,
32nd Bengal N.I. (Punjab Pioneers).

CAPTAIN E. D. SHAFTO,
Royal Artillery.

CAPTAIN T. A'B. SARGENT,
78th Highlanders (Ross-shire Buffs).

BT.-LIEUT.-COLONEL A. M. SHEWELL,
Staff Corps, Offg. Dep.-Com.-Gen. 1st Cl.

BT. MAJOR L. C. SINGLETON,
92nd (Gordon Highlanders).

CAPTAIN H. F. SHOWERS, Staff Corps,
1st Punjab Infantry.

Major L. Smith, Staff Corps.
3rd Goorkha Regt.

Captain H. F. Smith, Staff Corps,
Jacob's Rifles.

Surgeon W. B. Smyth,
A.B., M.B., L.R.C.S.I.,
Bengal Medical Department.

Captain N. J. Spens,
72nd (Duke of Albany's Own Highlanders).

Lieut. H. H. S. Spoor,
1st Battn. 25th (King's Own Borderers).

Bt. Lieut.-Col. R. G. T. Stevenson,
Poona Horse.

Lieut. F. C. Stayner, Staff Corps,
19th Bombay N.I.

Reproduced by permanent photograph by the London Stereoscopic Company.

CAPTAIN S. A. SWINLEY,
11th (P.W.O.) Bengal Cavalry (Lancers).

CAPTAIN E. STRATON,
2nd Battn. 22nd Regt. (The Cheshire).

2ND LIEUT. B. S. THURLOW,
51st (King's Own Light Infantry).

MAJOR R. J. LE POER TRENCH,
19th Bombay N.I.

BR.-GENERAL J. A. TYTLER, C.B., V.C.,
Bengal Staff Corps.

SURGEON-MAJOR J. WALLACE,
M.A., M.D., M.R.C.S.,
Army Medical Department.

LIEUT. E. P. VENTRIS,
3rd Regt. (The Buffs).

2nd LIEUT. E. H. WATSON,
1st Battn. 17th (Leicestershire) Regt.

SURGEON J. E. WALSH, M.D.,
Bengal Medical Department.

MAJOR S. J. WAULDY, Staff Corps,
19th Bombay N.I.

SURGEON G. WATSON, M.B.,
Bengal Medical Department.

CAPTAIN A. A. D. WEIGALL,
Army Pay Department.

LIEUT. F. WHITTUCK, Staff Corps,
1st Bombay N.I. (Grenadiers).

LIEUT. C. G. WHITTY,
Probationer, Staff Corps.

CAPTAIN F. H. WINTERBOTHAM,
Madras Infantry.

LIEUT. H. V. WILLIS,
Royal Artillery.

LIEUT. N. C. WISEMAN,
1st Battn. 17th (Leicestershire) Regt.

2ND LIEUT. F. P. F. WOOD,
7th (Royal Fusiliers).

LIEUT. I. D. WRIGHT,
Royal Artillery.

LIEUT. G. M. YALDWIN,
2nd Batt. 6th (Roy. 1st Warwicksh.) Regt.

SURGEON-MAJOR J. H. WRIGHT,
M.R.C.S., and L.S.A. Lond.,
Army Medical Department.

RECIPIENTS OF THE VICTORIA CROSS FOR SERVICES IN THE CAMPAIGNS.

Bt. Maj. O'M. Creagh, V.C., Staff Corps,
Mhairwarra Battalion.

Lt. W. St. L. Chase, V.C., Staff Corps,
28th Bombay N.I.

Captain W. H. Dick Cunyngham, V.C.,
The Gordon Highlanders.

Maj. A. G. Hammond, V.C., Staff Corps,
Queen's Own Corps of Guides.

Captain R. C. Hart, V.C.,
Royal Engineers.

Major E. H. Sartorius, V.C.,
The East Lancashire Regt.

Bt. Lieut.-Col. E. P. Leach, V.C.,
Royal Engineers.

MAJOR A. D. ANDERSON, STAFF CORPS,

23RD (PUNJAB) BENGAL N.I. (PIONEERS).

WITH the news telegraphed to India of the assault and capture of the Peiwar Kotal on the morning of the 2nd December, 1878, came the melancholy tidings of the death of a distinguished officer of the 23rd Punjab Pioneers—Major A. D. Anderson—who had fallen whilst gallantly leading a handful of skirmishers against one of the advanced positions of the enemy.

Alexander Dunlop Anderson, the subject of this memoir, was the third son of Dr. A. Dunlop Anderson, some time Surgeon in H.M. 49th Regiment, and for forty years Physician in Glasgow. He was born on the 3rd February, 1841, in the city with which his father's name had already long been identified. Having received the rudiments of his education at a private school at Edinburgh, he was from thence transferred to Cheltenham College. In June, 1858, he passed his examination at Addiscombe. Entering the service as Ensign in September of the same year, he was temporarily attached to the 1st Battalion, 10th Regiment. In February, 1859, he was transferred to the 1st Battalion, 19th Regiment, then in India; and joining that corps shortly afterwards in Bengal, did duty with it for a period of three years and a half. In the meantime (July, 1859), he had been promoted Lieutenant. In June, 1862, he was appointed Interpreter to the regiment, and acted in that capacity, and subsequently as Station Interpreter at Mian Mir, till the following August. On the reorganization of the Indian army, he was posted, in September, 1862, to the 41st Bengal Infantry, to the adjutancy and quarter-mastership of which regiment he was, within a short period, successively promoted. In October, 1865, some little time after having passed the Interpreter's examination, he was transferred as Adjutant to the 23rd Punjab Pioneers, with which corps he served almost continuously till the day of his death.

Lieutenant Anderson accompanied the 23rd Pioneers to Abyssinia in 1868, and served with them in that country from the outbreak to the cessation of hostilities. For his conduct at the action of Arogee on the 10th April, 1868, he was singled out for special commendation in Sir R. Napier's despatch; and on the 13th April, 1869, he was present at the capture of Magdala.

Promoted Captain in September, 1870, and being at the time in Europe, on furlough, he vacated, in accordance with regulations, his appointment of Adjutant of the 23rd Pioneers. On his return to India in November, 1870, he was attached for duty to the 4th N.I., then at Allahabad, but at his own request was almost immediately retransferred to the 23rd Pioneers, of which regiment he was appointed, at the end of February, 1871, Officiating Adjutant. About the middle of March he was ordered to take over the duties of Wing Commander, *vice* Major Taylor, then on furlough, an appointment in which he was confirmed on its becoming permanently vacant in June, 1872. In the meantime (September, 1871), he had been offered the appointment of Commandant of the Bhutan Coolie Corps, but his services, unfortunately, could not be spared from his regiment, and he was reluctantly obliged to decline the post.

Having passed with high credit, in the first days of June, 1874, in Military Law, and obtained a certificate of proficiency in Fortification at the Garrison Course of Instruction held at Rawal Pindi, Captain Anderson again availed himself of eighteen months' furlough to Europe. While in England, he obtained an extra first-class certificate at Hythe, and completed a course of instruction in Reconnaissance and Field Works at the School of Military Engineering at Chatham. On the expiration of his furlough he rejoined the 23rd Pioneers at Jhelum. After taking part with the regiment in the Imperial Assemblage at Delhi at the latter end of 1876, he accompanied it, in the spring of the following year, to Simla. In September, 1878, he was promoted to the rank of Major, having already, from the month of March of that year, officiated as second in command, *vice* Major Collett, appointed to the Quarter-Master-General's Department.

On the massing of the troops on the frontier in the last days of September, 1878, preparatory to the invasion of Afghanistan, the 23rd Pioneers, which were detailed to General Roberts' Division, left Simla for the trans-Indus. Crossing the frontier at Thal with the regiment on the 21st November, Major Anderson accompanied it to Kuram, and was present with it at the reconnaissance in force at the foot of the Peiwar Kotal on the 28th November. It was on the morning of the 2nd December, 1878, while leading a party of skirmishers against one of the positions on the heights held by the enemy, that he lost his life, being struck with a shot whilst well in advance of his little band of followers. So hot was the fire of the enemy at the spot where he fell, that two of the four men who were with him at the moment of his death were also killed, and the remaining two were compelled, in retiring, to leave the bodies of their companions in the enemy's hands.

Major Anderson's remains, which were recovered on the following day, lie buried in the same grave with those of Captain Kelso, R.A., on a spur of the Peiwar range, overlooking the Hariab Valley. The love borne him by the men of the regiment was amply testified by the large concourse that assembled at his funeral to pay their last tribute of respect to his memory, as well as by the beautiful tablet which has been erected by his brother officers in the Cathedral of Glasgow.

LIEUT. P. E. ANDERSON, STAFF CORPS,

25TH (PUNJAB) BENGAL N.I.

THE subject of this memoir was the eldest son of the late Reverend Philip Anderson, a Chaplain in the Honourable East India Company's service, who for many years officiated at Kolaba in the Bombay Presidency, a memorial window erected to whose memory in his church records the estimation in which he was held by his congregation.

Philip Edward Anderson entered the service through Sandhurst; proceeded to India in 1867 at the age of nineteen years, and joined H.M. 96th Regiment, then in garrison at Barrackpur. From this corps he was transferred to H.M. 109th Regiment a few months later at Multan, from whence he subsequently proceeded to enter the Military College at Rurki. On the completion of his studies, after passing successfully in the native languages, he joined the Bengal Staff Corps, and was appointed to the regiment with which he served till the day of his death.

When war was declared against the Amir of Afghanistan in the autumn of 1878, Lieutenant Anderson's regiment was stationed at Umballa, in the Punjab. At extremely short notice it proceeded by rail to Multan, and joined a portion of the force under Sir Donald Stewart directed upon Kandahar. The 25th Punjab Infantry was one of the most advanced regiments of the force, and, in consequence, suffered to a considerable extent from the hardships inseparable from a long march over roadless deserts in a most trying climate. Almost immediately after arriving at Kandahar, the regiment proceeded towards Kalat-i-Ghilzai; and it was the fearful exposure and fatigue, combined with the intense cold endured during this expedition and the return march in the depths of winter, which laid the seeds of the disease (phthisis) to which the subject of this notice eventually succumbed at Kandahar, on the 6th August, 1879, after a most painful illness courageously borne.

Lieutenant Anderson was a talented and energetic young officer, and his loss is most deeply felt, not only by his regiment, but by the many friends he left behind both in India and England. He married in 1875; and owing to his untimely death his widow has been left dependent for her support on the small pension granted to the relict of a subaltern officer.

LIEUT. F. C. C. ANGELO,

PROBATIONER STAFF CORPS.

FREDERICK CANNING CORTLANDT ANGELO was the only son of Lieutenant Frederick Cortlandt Angelo, 16th Grenadiers, Bengal Army, and Superintendent Ganges Canal, Public Works Department, who was killed in the defence of the entrenchments at Cawnpore in June, 1857. He was born in Calcutta, three months after his father's death, on the 21st September 1857, and was educated at Dr. Thompson's Collegiate School, St. Heliers, Jersey. At the age of seventeen years he entered Sandhurst as Indian Cadet; and passing out from the College after the usual course, was gazetted, in February, 1874, to the 40th Foot. He joined that regiment in Calcutta, and remained with it until the autumn of 1879, when he applied for the Staff Corps, —having in the meantime (February 1877) obtained his lieutenancy.

Posted to the 31st P.N.I., then on service in Afghanistan, he joined the headquarters at Landi Kotal, and took part with the regiment in the Lughman Valley expedition, and the various operations in which it was subsequently engaged. In March, 1880, the 31st P.N.I. was moved to Safed Sang. Shortly after the headquarters left Jalalabad, Angelo, who had been left behind with various details, was ordered up to Fort Battye in charge of a detachment of 150 men. Reaching the Fort on the evening of the 25th March, the little force proved the means of saving it from falling into the hands of the vast numbers of the enemy who beset it during the ensuing night. In the ably conducted defence of the post, the subject of this notice met his death.

Though Lieutenant Angelo's life was too brief to admit of its including many brilliant achievements, this, at least, may be said of him: that in an hour of sore need he acquitted himself as was to be expected of one of his race and name. Descended from a family of soldiers in both the paternal and maternal lines, he found a soldier's grave amongst the same rugged hills where the remains of one of his uncles, thirty-six years previously, were carried to their last resting-place.

SURGEON-MAJOR GEORGE ATKINSON, M.B.,

ARMY MEDICAL DEPARTMENT.

THE subject of this notice, who died near Kabul on the 25th April, 1880, shortly after the battle of Ahmed Khel, was the second son of the late George Guy Atkinson, Esq., J.P., of Ashley Park, Nenagh, Co. Tipperary. He was born at Ashley Park on the 11th October, 1840, and received his education at Ranelah, Athlone, Mr. Weir's Collegiate School at Parsonstown, and Trinity College, Dublin, whither he proceeded in 1859. He graduated in 1863, and entered the Army a year later. After his Netley training, he was ordered to India, where he was posted to the 54th Regiment. He was subsequently transferred to the 1st Battalion 19th Regiment, with which he served in the Hazara campaign of 1868, including the expedition against the tribes in the Black Mountain, receiving the medal and clasp.

In 1873 he returned to Ireland on furlough, on the expiration of which he served at Portsmouth and Aldershot till 1876, when he was again sent out to India. In the meantime (April, 1876) he had been promoted to the rank of Surgeon-Major.

Dr. Atkinson was stationed in the Bengal Presidency when the Afghan war broke out in 1878. Immediately prior to the commencement of hostilities he proceeded in medical charge of G/4 R.A.—which had been detailed to General Stewart's Division—*via* Multan to Rurki; and crossing the Indus with the battery, accompanied it to Quetta. He then took part in the advance to Kandahar, and the subsequent operations in which the battery was engaged, sharing its perils and hardships, and coping successfully with the heavy work which the latter threw upon his hands. At the battle of Ahmed Khel on the 19th April, 1880, in which G/4 played an important part, Dr. Atkinson, according to the testimony of his commanding officer, "had hard work during the action." The nights were at this time excessively cold, and the exposure now began to tell upon him. In the course of the march to Ghazni he was seized with pleuromonia, to an attack of which he fell a victim at Hafazai, within a week from the day of the battle.

Dr. Atkinson was a devoted officer, distinguished for his strong sense of duty, and for an amiable disposition which endeared him to all with whom he came in contact. His memory is perpetuated by a marble tablet in Nenagh Church, erected by his bereaved mother and brother, who deeply mourn their irreparable loss.

LIEUT. F. M. BARCLAY, STAFF CORPS,

45TH BENGAL N.I. (RATTRAY'S SIKHS).

FRANK MILES BARCLAY, who lost his life in the first of the recent Afghan campaigns, was the sixth son of Surgeon-General Charles Barclay, Madras Army (retired). He was born in 1855, at Quilon, in Southern India. Although quite young in the service—having only entered the army in February, 1875—he had already, at the time of his death, given great promise of a bright future. He began his career in the 19th (Princess of Wales' Own) Regiment; and was present with the Corps when it received its colours from Her Royal Highness at Sheffield in 1875. Soon afterwards he was ordered out to India, and eventually passed into the Bengal Staff Corps.

Lieutenant Barclay was engaged in qualifying himself for the Political Department when the Afghan War broke out; and his regiment—Rattray's Sikhs—was amongst those ordered to the front. This famous corps did excellent service throughout the war, and Barclay was constantly engaged in unconspicuous, but none the less arduous and dangerous work in and about the Khyber Pass, including the second Bazar expedition.

On the 17th March, 1879, while he was in command of an escort attached to a surveying party under Captain Leach, R. E., a sudden attack was made upon them by a section of the Shinwari tribe. Captain Leach was slightly wounded, and Lieutenant Barclay received a gun-shot through the right shoulder, which penetrated to the lung. With the help of Captain Leach (who, for his gallantry in assisting his disabled comrade, afterwards received from Her Majesty the Victoria Cross), he was removed to Landi Kotal, where he died on the 31st March. In him the army lost a young soldier of high promise, and the Bengal Staff Corps a most accomplished officer.

CAPTAIN W. B. BARKER,

10TH (P.W.O. ROYAL) HUSSARS.

ILLIAM BROMBY BARKER was born at Mansfield on the 24th May, 1835, and received his education at the school in his native town. He entered the army as a trooper in the 16th Lancers at the age of seventeen years; and his genius for the service is attested by the fact that, after passing rapidly through the various non-commissioned grades, he obtained, in November, 1867, commissioned rank. In June, 1867, he was appointed Adjutant of the Regiment, in which capacity he served for a period of nearly ten years. He became Lieutenant in March, 1871; and in July, 1877, obtained his troop. In this interval, nine out of the twenty-five years of his service were passed in India.

Captain Barker now exchanged into the 10th Hussars; and in March, 1878, joined that regiment in India. On the concentration of the forces in view of the impending invasion of Afghanistan, he proceeded as second in command with the squadron of the regiment which, under Captain Bulkeley, was ordered to Kohat. Taking part in the advance into the enemy's country of General Roberts' division, to which the squadron had been detailed, he was present at the capture of the Peiwar Kotal; and for his conduct in the action at Matun on the 7th January, 1879, in the Khost Valley expedition, he was singled out for special commendation in Brigadier-General Hugh Gough's despatch to the A.Q.M.G. of the Force. In February, 1879, he was ordered to Rawal Pindi to take command of the Depôt. About the same date the detached squadron was directed to rejoin the head-quarters of the regiment, then at Jalalabad.

During the short time Captain Barker remained in charge of the Depôt, he suffered severely from the effects of recent exposure to the sun. He nevertheless proceeded by double marches on receiving orders, at the latter end of May, to rejoin the regiment. Just before reaching Daka Fort he was laid completely prostrate with sun-stroke, from the effects of which—according to his own testimony—he could not have recovered had it not been for the tender nursing he received at the hands of Lieut. Hearsey, of the 9th Lancers, a gallant young officer who subsequently fell in action at Kabul. His health continued fairly good from this time till the beginning of October, when he was ordered to Jhelum to fit saddles to the transport animals. The prolonged exposure to the sun which this duty entailed soon told upon him, and he began rapidly to lose strength; on the 4th November he was taken suddenly worse, and seven days afterwards, on the 11th, he died.

In a letter, covering a complimentary document from H.R.H. the Duke of Cambridge, penned after an inspection of the 16th Lancers, received by Captain Barker in the month of March, 1872, from General (then Colonel) Wilkinson, the latter writes:—" I cannot send you this without assuring you how thoroughly I appreciate your invaluable help; your untiring and unremitting exertions to support the credit and efficiency of the Regiment; and it is to this, in a very great measure, that I attribute the satisfactory state of things at the last autumn inspection, General Barton's report upon which has called forth the remarks of H.R.H." If evidence of the survival of this zeal to the last sad chapter of Captain Barker's life be needed, it is to be found in an eulogium bestowed upon him by Brigadier-General Sir Hugh Gough, written at Kabul, and bearing date 5th March, 1880, in which the able manner in which he performed his duties during the campaign is warmly dwelt upon.

Captain Barker married, in February, 1878, Bertha, third daughter of Mr. George Brothers, of Canterbury, who survives him.

2ND LIEUT. H. J. O. BARR.

66TH (BERKSHIRE) REGIMENT.

ARRY JAMES OUTRAM BARR, who, "At Maiwand about 4 p.m. on the 27th July, 1880, fell dead across the colour he was then carrying"—according to evidence adduced at the subsequently holden court-martial—was not the first of his family who forfeited his life in the Queen's service in Afghanistan—his maternal grandfather having been Colonel Keith, Deputy Adjutant-General of the Bombay Army, who died in that country whilst serving as Adjutant-General with the forces under Lord Keane in 1839.

The youngest son of Lieutenant-General Barr of the Bombay Staff Corps, he was born in Brighton on the 7th January, 1861. His education was begun under Dr. H. Barker, LL.D., at the Gymnasium School at Old Aberdeen, where he remained for a period of nearly seven years. From thence he was transferred to Weston-super-Mare, to read with Mr. Hoppel, M.A., for the Indian Civil Service; but showing a decided preference for the army, he was sent for one term to Captain Massie's to be prepared for the Sandhurst examination. In February, 1879, at the age of seventeen years, he was presented by Lord Cranbrook with an honorary East Indian cadetship, and entered Sandhurst; and in November of the same year he passed out eighteenth in order of merit, with honours, having obtained certificates in Fortification and Drill.

Gazetted to the 66th Regiment in January, 1880, he left England for India two months afterwards; and reaching Karachi by way of Bombay, immediately received orders to join the head-quarters of the Regiment, then at Kandahar. He proceeded thither with a detachment under Major Vandaleur of the 7th Fusiliers, arriving at his destination at the latter end of May.

To a mere lad, "fresh and blooming from England," as he described himself in a letter to his father, thrown suddenly into the whirl and excitement of actual campaigning at the very outset of his career, the life he had embarked upon presented many novel features. The physical features of the country, the customs of an alien race, even the necessity for taking precautions against danger on emerging from camp, were matter for perpetual wonder and reflection; whilst the ever-recurring rumours and counter rumours of the prospect of fighting kindled his hopes and fired his imagination. That he became popular with his brother-officers from the hour of his arrival amongst them, the numerous letters written by them to members of his family after his death amply testify.

On the 4th July, 1880, Barr accompanied the Regiment in the brigade which, under General Burrows, left Kandahar for Girishk with the object of encountering Ayub Khan. The march—which, in consequence of the excessive heat, had to be conducted at night—was a severe one: "stumbling, fumbling, slipping along; digging the Colour-shaft deep into the earth"—thus young Barr describes his own part in the performance.

Girishk was reached on the 11th; and three days afterwards—on the morning of the 14th—Barr received his baptism of fire in the successful encounter which took place with the Wali's mutinied troops. On this occasion he availed himself of an opportunity which presented itself for rendering valuable service. To the left of the second position taken up by the enemy was a garden, from behind the walls of which a harassing fire was being kept up upon his company. Captain Quarry, of the 66th, was ordered to advance with twenty men to take the garden; but on the way he was delayed by having to ford a stream with muddy bottom, in which his men floundered up to their armpits. Barr was now ordered to advance to his assistance, and succeeded, with Lieutenant Faunce, in reaching the further bank. Getting about twenty-five men together, they were enabled to take the wall with a rush, shooting down in their advance every individual of the band which held it.

After the action the Brigade returned to Khushk-i-Nakhud, en route for Kandahar. In the disastrous encounter with the enemy which ensued on the 27th, Barr lost his life, in the manner already recorded, with the three hundred officers and men of his regiment who fell, having been seen by the late Major C. V. Oliver, a few minutes before his death, "marching along as calmly and steadily as if on parade."

MAJOR WIGRAM BATTYE, STAFF CORPS,

QUEEN'S OWN CORPS OF GUIDES.

THE Service has sustained the loss of one of its brightest ornaments, and the Government of India the services of a most distinguished and gallant soldier." Such were the words used by the Commander-in-Chief in his report on the action at Futtehabad in announcing the death of the subject of this memoir.

Wigram Battye was the eighth son of George Wynyard Battye, Esq., of the Bengal Civil Service, and brother of Lieutenant Quintin Battye, who, belonging to the same regiment as himself, was mortally wounded when leading his men against the mutineers at Delhi, on the 9th June, 1857. He was born in Kensington, London, on the 13th May, 1842, and was educated at Mount Radford House, Exeter, under the Rev. C. R. Roper; Corse Vicarage, Gloucestershire, under the Rev. C. H. Malpas; Clapham, under Mr. Long; Hampstead, under the Rev. W. H. Perkins; and Keir House, Wimbledon, under Mr. Murray. Passing the examination for an Indian cadetship in December, 1858, he was gazetted to an ensigncy in the 6th Europeans, and joined that regiment in March of the following year. Six months afterwards he obtained his lieutenancy. He was attached for duty to the 3rd Goorkhas from May, 1861, to May, 1863, when he was selected by the Viceroy to fill a vacancy in the Corps of Guides, then stationed at Mardan, one of the salient points of the north-west frontier of India. His subsequent career was passed with that corps, and in it he officiated successively as Wing-Officer, Adjutant, and Commandant of Cavalry.

Wigram Battye was with the Guides when, in 1863, the Umbeyla war broke out, and distinguished himself greatly in the subsequent operations in which the corps took part. Whilst leading his men to repulse one of the desperate night attacks made by the enemy, he was shot through the body. The wound was a most severe one, and for a long time a fatal result was feared. A good constitution, however, enabled him to pull through, but he was compelled to visit Europe to endeavour to complete the cure. Though, in course of time, the wound healed, he never shook off its effects. Whenever he took violent exercise, these made themselves painfully apparent.

Major Battye rejoined the Corps of Guides in 1865, and between that period, and his return to Europe on furlough in 1870, took part in the many expeditions, some of greater, some of less importance, undertaken against the wild tribes on the frontier. In all these he was to the front. In 1866 he accompanied the expedition to the Sundkhar Valley. In 1869 he acted as orderly officer to General Keyes in the Miranzar expedition, and for his services received the thanks of that officer. His daring, and his appreciation of their soldierly qualities, had gained for him the confidence of the stalwart frontier soldiers who served under him; and it is no exaggeration to say that he had become their hero, their Paladin, and that they would have followed him anywhere. Hence, whenever the expeditions, too numerous to detail, were despatched to the front, he was invariably selected to accompany them.

In 1870, Major Battye revisited Europe on furlough. On the breaking out of the Franco-German War in July of that year, he hastened to join the army led by the Crown Prince, and accompanied it as a non-combatant throughout, till the capitulation of Paris. For the services he rendered to the sick and wounded during the hostilities, he received the German war-medal in steel, with the non-combatant ribbon.

At the close of 1871 Wigram Battye returned to India, and once again rejoined his regiment. During the years that followed, until the breaking out of the Afghan War, he was constantly engaged on the frontier. He accompanied the detachment of Guide Infantry which formed part of a flying column despatched into Jowaki-Afridi territory in the last days of August, 1877. When, three months later, the Infantry of the corps were employed in another punitory expedition, he, being in command of the Cavalry, remained at Mardan commanding the station, and led a detachment in the surprise of the Utman Khel village of Sapiri, for his services on which occasion he received the thanks of the Secretary of State, and of the Government of India. He was present with the corps, under Major R. B. Campbell, in the surprise of the Ranizai village of Skhakat, on the 13th March, 1878, and of the Utman Khel villages, under Lieut.-Colonel F. H. Jenkins, on the 20th and 21st of the same month.

In October, 1878, Wigram Battye was selected to accompany Sir Neville Chamberlain in his mission to Kabul, and commanded the escort at the interview between the Master of the Amir's Horse and Sir Louis Cavagnari. He was present with the Infantry of the corps at the capture of Ali Musjid on the 21st November, and in the subsequent advance of Sir Sam Browne's force to Daka and Jalalabad; and he commanded a detachment of Guide Cavalry under Br.-General Tytler, C.B., V.C., in his operations in the Kama Valley, for his services on which occasion he was mentioned in the Brigadier's despatch.

On the 31st March, 1879, the Guide Cavalry, under Major Wigram Battye, marched with the Cavalry Brigade under Brigadier-General C. Gough, C.B., V.C., from Jalalabad to Futtehabad. It was at this place, on the 2nd April, that Battye was slain, leading his gallant men in an attack on the Kugiani Afghans, an attack which had virtually succeeded the moment he fell dead. The incident was thus described by an eye-witness:—

"Charging at the head of his men, Wigram Battye received a severe wound in the side from a rifle bullet. His men begged him to stop and have it attended to, but he refused, and continued to ride on, the blood pouring from his body. In traversing, a few seconds later, a deep *nullah* commanded by the enemy, and which it was necessary to cross to reach them, he was pierced in the heart by another bullet. His life at once passed away, but the Guides took a terrible vengeance."

In a despatch written by Sir Sam. Browne on the occasion of Major Wigram Battye's death, the following passage occurs:—

"Of Major Wigram Battye it is very bitter for me to speak. The Viceroy is aware of the noble end of this gallant officer, and it is some consolation to me in mourning over his loss to feel that he died, as he would have wished, at the head of his gallant Guides. Endowed both mentally and physically far beyond the average, it is no flattery to say that Wigram Battye united in his person all the best qualities which it should be the wish of every officer to emulate. Throughout his brief but distinguished career, he conducted himself in his private capacity as a high-minded English gentleman, and in his public, as an able and chivalrous soldier; and, it seems fitting, that to such a life the death of a hero should have been accorded."

The death of Major Wigram Battye called forth from the men he had so long commanded an unprecedented outburst of grief, which continued to find expression long after his body was carried to the grave.

"There is a very sacred spot at Jalalabad," wrote a correspondent to the "Pioneer," "where rest the remains of Wigram Battye, a hero whose praises fill every mouth. I lately overtook a Sepoy of the Guides proceeding to the grave to water the flowers with which the affection of his devoted comrades and soldiers has embellished it. 'The whole regiment,' said he, in his simple Punjab language, 'weep for Battye: the regiment would have died to a man rather than harm should befall Battye.'"

Subsequently, by the unanimous desire alike of officers and men of the Corps of Guides, the body of Wigram Battye was conveyed to Mardan, that it might rest in the place where he had been known and appreciated for so many years. A tablet to his memory and to that of his brother Quintin has been placed by the officers of his regiment in the crypt of St. Paul's.

MAJOR H. G. BECHER, STAFF CORPS,

11TH BENGAL N.I.

HE details of the services of the subject of this notice, which have been received up to the time of going to press, though somewhat meagre in character, are sufficient to denote that his career was a not undistinguished one.

As a volunteer civilian, Henry George Becher served in the Indian Mutiny, in 1857, and was decorated by Government with the medal.

After obtaining a commission, he took part, in 1860, in the Sikkim expedition, raising and commanding the Coolie Corps, and having sole charge of the transport.

His next term of active service was in the Bhutan campaign of 1864-1865, throughout which he served with the 11th Regiment Bengal Native Infantry, and for which he received the medal with clasp.

In 1868 he took part, as an officer attached to the transport train, in the Abyssinian expedition, for which he received a third medal.

His active career was brought to a close in the Afghan war. Taking part with his regiment, the 11th B. N. I., in its advance to Kohat, he performed garrison duty with it for a time at that station, and then accompanied it over the Peiwar Kotal to Bian Khel, subsequently returning with it down the Kuram Valley to the line of communications. On the renewal of hostilities in the autumn of 1879, he proceeded with the regiment to Ali Khel. A few days after that post was reached, however, his health so completely broke down as to necessitate his being invalided to England; but the change came too late, and he eventually died in this country on the 26th October, 1880.

The deceased officer's commissions bear date as follows:—

Ensign	6th January, 1859.
Lieutenant	12th December, 1859.
Captain	6th January, 1871.
Major	6th January, 1879.

CAPTAIN JOHN BEEKE,

21ST BOMBAY N.I. (MARINE BATTALION).

HE subject of this notice, who died of cholera at Jhelum, Punjab, on the 27th October, 1879, was the second son of John Beeke, Esquire, of Northampton. He was born on the 24th July, 1842; was educated at Addiscombe; and entered the army in 1860. In February, 1867, he was appointed to the Bombay Marine Battalion. He served through the Abyssinian War of 1867-'68, with especial credit, and received from Colonel Merewether, at its termination, both an official and a demi-official acknowledgment of his good services. In 1878 he accompanied the expedition to Malta and Cyprus, and distinguished himself by the zeal and energy with which he carried through the duties allotted to him. Shortly after the renewal of hostilities in Afghanistan, in the autumn of 1879, he was sent on special service to the Punjab. At the time of his death he was engaged at Jhelum in superintending the transport of ponies to the front; and it was when he had almost brought this duty to a successful conclusion that he was attacked with cholera, and died in a few hours.

In Colonel Carnegie's Battalion order of the 29th October, 1879, the following passage occurs:—" In Captain Beeke the battalion has lost one of its oldest and best tried officers, who, by his friendly disposition, untiring zeal, and devotion to his duties, endeared himself to all ranks, and proved himself a most valuable servant to Government." And on the 5th November, 1879, a copy of the following intimation was published:—" The Commander-in-Chief has received with much regret the intelligence of the sudden death, while engaged on special service, of Captain Beeke, Wing Commander 21st Regiment Native Infantry (Marines), who was an officer of marked ability and professional knowledge."

At the instance of the officers and men of the 21st, by whom the deceased was greatly beloved, a memorial fund was raised; and, in order to promote the efficiency of the Regiment, in which he took a heartfelt interest, and to perpetuate his name therein, the money was invested for the purpose of establishing two prizes to be shot for annually, to be called the " Beeke Prizes."

Captain Beeke married, in 1870, Rosina Elizabeth, only daughter of Archibald Low, Esquire, of Porchester, Hants.

MAJOR H. H. BIRCH, STAFF CORPS,

27TH (PUNJAB) BENGAL N.I.

HENRY HOLWELL BIRCH was the first of the long roll of British officers who rendered up their lives in their country's service in the war with which these volumes deal. He was the youngest son of Lieut.-Colonel F. W. Birch, who was himself killed in the Indian Mutiny of 1857 whilst in command of the 41st Royal Infantry at Sitapur, Oudh. Born in India on the 2nd September, 1837, he was sent at an early age to England for his education. After some thirteen years he returned to the country of his birth, serving as officer on board an India merchantman until 1857. In that year, while he was on leave and staying with his father at Sitapur, the Mutiny broke out, and he, with some relatives and friends, had to fly to Lucknow, where he formed one of the illustrious garrison throughout the defence of the Residency. He subsequently served with the field force at the Alum Bagh in 1857-58, and was present at the capture of Lucknow in 1858. For the services he rendered on these occasions he received a medal and two clasps, and obtained a direct commission in Her Majesty's army.

In 1860 Major Birch was posted to the 19th, now the 27th, Punjab Infantry, and in the following year served with that corps in China, obtaining the medal. He was present with his regiment in 1866 with the force in Eusofzai under Brigadier-General Doran, C.B., and again with the force sent out to Lushai under Brigadier-General C. Brownlow in 1871-72, and for his services on this occasion he received a third medal. He rose steadily in his regiment through the various grades, and in 1875 was appointed second in command.

During the Jowaki campaign of 1877-78, the 27th Punjab Native Infantry was again ordered out for service; and in consequence of the temporary appointment of the Commandant to the Brigade Staff, the command of the regiment devolved upon Major Birch.

It was as Acting Commandant of his corps that he took part, on the outbreak of hostilities with Afghanistan in the autumn of 1878, in the advance of Brigadier-General Appleyard's brigade into the Khyber Pass, and in the direct attack on

Ali Musjid on the 21st November. By the time that it was reluctantly decided, as darkness closed in on that day, to postpone the assault, and the order was given to cease firing, the 27th Punjab Native Infantry had pushed forward to the support of the 14th Sikhs on to the steep slope leading to the peak which formed the right flank of the Afghan position, and the leading companies were actively engaged with the enemy in their successive lines of entrenchment. Whilst a steady musketry fire was being poured upon them, and the enemy's artillery was simultaneously enfilading them, Captain Maclean, of the 14th Sikhs, who was badly wounded, finding his men in extreme peril, shouted for help. To this appeal Major Birch responded with eager alacrity, and it was while gallantly leading his companies forward that he fell shot through the heart. How his body was recovered by his gallant Adjutant, Lieut. Fitzgerald, who rendered up his life in defending it, is written elsewhere. On the morning after the attack it was found untouched by the enemy, and was conveyed to Peshawar, where it was buried, with full military honours, on the 24th November.

Major Birch's commissions bear date as follows:

Ensign	4th August, 1858.
Lieutenant	26th April, 1860.
Captain	4th August, 1870.
Major	4th August, 1878.

LIEUTENANT W. H. BISHOP,

2ND BATTALION, 11TH (NORTH DEVONSHIRE) REGIMENT.

THE subject of this notice, who died at Kandahar, of dysentery, on the 23rd November, 1880, was the elder son of William Louis Mosheim Bishop, Captain 46th Bengal Native Infantry, who was killed on the 9th July, 1857, by the mutineers of the 9th Bengal Cavalry and the 46th Bengal Native Infantry at Sialkot, Punjab, where he was officiating as Brigade Major to the troops—his wife (born Emma Rebecca Usborne), and his two children, who were with him at the time, making their escape into the fort at the station.

William Henry Bishop was born on the 28th June, 1855, and received his early education at a school at Blackheath. When about sixteen years of age, he went to study with a private tutor at Bonn, on the Rhine, and from thence proceeded to Queen Elizabeth's Grammar School, Cranbrook, Kent. Evincing some taste for farming, he entered, in January, 1873, the Agricultural College at Cirencester; but receiving, in the month of December of the same year, a Queen's Indian Cadetship in recognition of his father's services, he decided to embark on a military career. In January, 1874, he passed his examination, and on the 17th April, 1874, was gazetted to a Sub-Lieutenancy in the 1st Battalion, 11th Foot. Being desirous to see foreign service, he exchanged a few months afterwards into the 2nd Battalion of the regiment, then stationed in the Bombay Presidency, and sailed to join Head-quarters in October, 1874. He obtained his Lieutenancy in September, 1876, and in the course of his Indian service held the appointment of Interpreter to the regiment, and for two successive years was employed on the Famine Staff.

On the regiment being ordered into Afghanistan in July, 1880, Lieutenant Bishop took part with it in its advance into the enemy's country. His term of active service, eagerly looked forward to, was destined, alas! to be of short duration. The hardships he endured in the disastrous march through the Bolan Pass in the burning summer heat completely sapped his health, and within a month of his reaching Kandahar he succumbed—to the heartfelt regret of the regiment—to the fatal disease which had already claimed as victims so many of his gallant countrymen.

MAJOR G. F. BLACKWOOD,

ROYAL HORSE ARTILLERY.

ON the 27th of July, 1880, the memorable death of Major George Frederick Blackwood, on the field of Maiwand, added yet another honoured name to the already long roll of gallant Scotch officers who had fallen in the war with which these volumes deal.

The subject of this memoir was the second son of the late Major William Blackwood, of the Bengal Army, and a grandson of the founder of the eminent publishing house of that name. Born at Moradabad, India, in the year 1838, he was educated at the Edinburgh Academy, under Dr. Harvey, now its Rector, who speaks very warmly of his former pupil, and characterizes his translations from the Latin as having been marked by a spirit and fidelity beyond those of any of his class-fellows. He subsequently studied under the late Captain Orr, at the Military Academy in Lothian Road, Edinburgh, and from thence passed to Addiscombe, where, in due course, he made choice of the Artillery branch of the Bengal Service. Gazetted to a Lieutenancy in December, 1857—a time when a chapter of stirring events was being unfolded in the East—Blackwood was at once sent out to India, and had not long to wait before being engaged in the stern work of actual campaigning. Immediately after arriving at Bombay, he was hurried up to the seat of war, and served in the suppression of the Mutiny with the Rohilkhand Moveable Column, under the command of Lieutenant-Colonel Wilkinson, 42nd Royal Highlanders. In this force he was entrusted with the command of two guns. The services he rendered during the operations gained for him, at their conclusion, a Divisional Adjutancy of Artillery, the duties of which he discharged from 1859 to 1862 at Bareilly and Gwalior. From November, 1862, to December, 1863, he acted as Adjutant of the 22nd Brigade, R.A., and afterwards as Adjutant of the 19th Brigade, until September, 1864, when he was appointed to A/C, R.H.A.—now known as A/B, R.H.A.—one of the first troops of the old Bengal Horse Artillery which was ordered home after the amalgamation. In February, 1867, he received promotion.

In the autumn of 1871, Captain Blackwood had the honour of being specially selected by Lord Napier of Magdala, from a large number of officers whose claims were submitted, to command the Artillery in the Lushai expedition, under Brigadier-General Bourchier, C.B., and in the month of November he was again in the field. In the course of the operations which ensued, he was present at the attacks on Tipai Mukh, Kungnung, and Taikuni; and by the ability he displayed, not only in action, but on the march, amply justified Lord Napier's selection. In General Bourchier's despatch of the 29th March, 1872, the following passage occurs:—"Captain Blackwood and officers R.A. nobly sustained the reputation of the corps. The word 'difficulty' was unknown to them." A report drawn up by Blackwood on the Artillery in the campaign contained many valuable suggestions as to the nature of the gun most suitable for such service, and on the management of artillery and the equipment of elephants in mountain, jungle, and morass campaigning; and was printed and published by the Government of India. For his services in the expedition, the subject of this notice was rewarded, in September, 1872, with a Brevet-Majority.

During the absence of Lieutenant-Colonel Hills, C.B., in England, Major Blackwood temporarily commanded a battery of the Royal Horse Artillery. Promoted to a Regimental Majority in 1876, he exchanged into G/3, R.A., and subsequently brought this battery to such a state of efficiency as to call forth expressions of approbation from the highest military authorities in India. In February, 1878, the Duke of Cambridge was pleased to remark that the battery was "in a very high state of efficiency: Major Blackwood highly commended."

In the summer of 1878, failing health rendered it necessary for Major Blackwood to return to England on sick leave; and, to his deep regret, he was prevented, on the outbreak of hostilities with Afghanistan in the autumn of that year, from taking part in the first campaign. He had, however, the gratification of hearing that, notwithstanding the ranks of the horses of G/3, R.A., having been almost decimated with the frightful scourge known as the Ludiana disease, the battery had been selected for service with the fighting column under General Roberts in the Kuram Valley.

Returning to India, the subject of this memoir was appointed to the command of E/B, Royal Horse Artillery. In January, 1880, he proceeded with the battery on active service to Kandahar; and in the operations of General Burrows' brigade in the month of July, commanded it both in the encounter with the Wali's mutinous troops, and on the bloody field on which it won imperishable renown. In the action first alluded to, on the 14th of the month, E/B, R.H.A., performed distinguished service; and General Primrose reports that "the remarkable energy with which the battery was brought up to the front reflects the highest credit on Major G. F. Blackwood." Blackwood himself, in the last letter, alas! that he was destined ever to write, gives a graphic account of this smart little affair:—"I got into action four times, and did a fair amount of execution," he observes modestly with reference to his own share in the proceedings. A short quotation, too, from a letter written home by a corporal of the battery, will not, perhaps, be here out of place. "One shell," remarks the writer, "dropped close to the Major, but he stood his ground and gave his words of command the same as if we were on the field of drill, without shot or shell flying about;" and then adds—in simple language, but with an honest enthusiasm which Blackwood's nature was well calculated to inspire —"There is not a man in the whole Battery but what would go through fire and water for a Commander like the Major."

At the disastrous battle of Maiwand, on the 27th of the month, Major Blackwood was the senior Artillery officer present with General Burrows' force. While directing the movements of the battery in the centre of the fighting line, he was struck, some little time after he had been in action, with a bullet through the thigh; and giving over the command of his guns to Captain Slade, he retired for a few minutes from the front to have his wound dressed. It is characteristic of the man, and of a piece with other instances of his indomitable pluck, that, finding he could not receive, without leaving the field, the attention he urgently needed, he preferred to return to rejoin his battery; and he was actually with his guns when the order to limber up and retire was given. The evidence relating to the next stage of the disaster is conflicting and uncertain; but it is clear that, sore spent with his wound, and unable to mount, Blackwood managed to make his way on foot with the remnant of the 66th Regiment, the Bombay Sappers, and others, to the garden in the right rear of the line of battle, where the last desperate stand was made. Before reaching this garden his wound broke out afresh; and it is pleasant to relate that a young officer of the 66th (Lieutenant Pearce), affording one of the many instances of self-abnegation which were not wanting on that sad day, stopped to assist him in binding it up. The manner in which the devoted little band in the enclosure fought on till only eleven of them were left, is recorded, on evidence received from a Colonel of Artillery of Ayub Khan's Army, in the letter bearing date 1st October, 1880, written to the Adjutant-General in India by General Primrose, who goes on to tell how the eleven remaining charged out of the garden and died with their faces to the foe, fighting to the death. "Such was the nature of their charge and the grandeur of their bearing," adds the General, "that, although the whole of the Ghazis were assembled around them, not one dared approach to cut them down. Thus standing in the open, back to back, firing steadily and truly, every shot telling, surrounded by thousands, these eleven officers and men died." It was in this charge—as has been now clearly ascertained from the subsequent examination of the ground, from the positions in which the bodies were found, and from other corroborative evidence—that the gallant and lamented Major Blackwood fell, bringing to a close, not unworthily, a career of the finest promise and a life which he deemed it a high honour to render up in the service of his Queen and country, and in sustaining untarnished the honour of the British arms.

We may fitly close this brief notice with two extracts from private letters, which may be taken to represent the estimation in which the deceased officer was held throughout the service. "Blackwood's death," wrote General Sir James Hills, "weighs also most heavily on his brother officers and friends—not one of whom but deeply regrets his loss, not only as a personal one, but also as a public one to the regiment and the army, for no better officer ever entered the Service"—a tribute to the memory of Major Blackwood which is supplemented by one who enjoyed his friendship for upwards of twenty years—Major Anthony Murray, R.A.—in these words :—"We loved and admired him for his genuine and unselfish character. Whatever he undertook, he entered into with his whole heart; and whatever he did, he did well. In him the Service has lost a thorough soldier, and our regiment one of its brightest ornaments. Had he lived he must have risen to high distinction."

SURGEON-MAJOR R. H. BOLTON,

ARMY MEDICAL DEPARTMENT.

ROBERT HENRY BOLTON, who died at Kandahar on the 27th February, 1880, was the second son of Robert C. Bolton, Esq., of Doneraile, County Cork. He was born on the 1st October, 1839, and after receiving his education at the Royal College of Surgeons, and the King and Queen's College of Physicians, Ireland, served for a period in the Royal Elthorne (Middlesex) Militia. In September, 1863, he entered the Army Medical Department as Assistant Surgeon, and was shortly afterwards detailed for service in the Madras Presidency. After doing duty for two years at various stations in India, he was despatched to Burmah, and there completed three years more of his service. Returning to England at the beginning of 1869, he was posted for duty a few months later, to the 3rd Dragoon Guards. He served with that regiment for three years, at the expiration of which period, on rumours of the proposed unification system taking effect, he became anxious to return to India. With this object in view, he exchanged into the 2nd Battalion 23rd (Royal Welsh) Fusiliers. Almost immediately afterwards the Ashanti War broke out, and the regiment was ordered to the Gold Coast. Accompanying it in medical charge of the left wing, he served with it through the whole of the second phase of the war, and received the medal with clasp for Coomassie.

On the departure of the 23rd Fusiliers to Gibraltar, Surgeon-Major Bolton reverted to the Staff. In January, 1878, he was again ordered out to India, being detailed for duty to the Bombay Presidency. On the second outbreak of hostilities in Afghanistan in September, 1879, whilst in charge of the Station Hospital at Nimach, Rajputana, he was transferred, with nine other medical officers, to the Bengal Presidency, and received orders to proceed immediately to Kandahar. The great hardship and exposure which he underwent in the march through the Bolan Pass and on to his destination, pursued in the depth of winter and in the face of innumerable delays and difficulties which presented themselves, proved too much for a constitution which had been previously weakened by ague and dysentery; and shortly after his arrival—on the 27th February, 1880, at the age of forty years—he died from the effects of the rupture of an abscess in the liver.

BRIGADIER-GENERAL H. F. BROOKE,

COMMDG. 2ND INFANTRY BRIGADE, KANDAHAR FIELD FORCE.

ENRY FRANCIS BROOKE, who was killed in the sortie from Kandahar on the 16th August, 1880, while endeavouring to save the life of Captain Cruickshank, R.E., who was mortally wounded, was the eldest son of George and Lady Arabella Brooke, of Ashbrooke, Co. Fermanagh. He was born on the 3rd August, 1836. At the age of eighteen years he was gazetted, in June, 1854, to an ensigncy in the 48th Foot; and landing with that regiment in the Crimea on the 21st of April, 1855, served with it in the siege and fall of Sebastopol, earning the medal with clasp and the Turkish medal. Throughout the campaign of 1860 in China, he acted as Aide-de-Camp to Sir Robert Napier, being present in that capacity at the action of Tangku, the assault of the Taku Forts—in which he was severely wounded,—and the final advance on and surrender of Pekin. For his services on these occasions, for which he was several times mentioned in despatches, he received the brevet of Major and the medal with two clasps.

In addition to the post of Aide-de-Camp to Sir Robert Napier in China, General Brooke held, in the course of his distinguished career, the following staff appointments:—Bde.-Major, Bengal, from 14th April, 1863, to 3rd Jan., 1865; Assist. Adjt.-Gen., from 3rd Jan., 1865, to 23rd April, 1866, and again from 31st July, 1872, to 18th Jan., 1876; Deputy Adjt.-Gen., Bengal, 19th Jan., 1876, to 15th Nov., 1877; Adjt.-Gen. (local Br.-Gen.), Bombay, 23rd Nov., 1877, to 28th March, 1880; Br.-Gen., Commanding 2nd Infantry Brigade, Kandahar, 28th March, 1880, till the day of his death. It will thus be seen that, in order to assume command of a brigade on active service, he gave up temporarily the better paid and more comfortable, though responsible position, of Adjutant-General of the Bombay Army.

General Brooke arrived at Kandahar about the 23rd April, 1880, and at once assumed the command of the garrison, which, up to the date of his arrival, had been held—in addition to the chief command of the forces in Southern Aghanistan—by General Primrose. For the benefit of those who enjoyed his friendship or acquaintance it will be unnecessary to mention that his first thought was to make a thorough and complete inspection of the limits of his command, and of the troops placed at his disposal; but it is probably not generally known that he considered it his imperative duty to place on record his sense of the very imperfect condition of the fortifications, and to point out the obvious necessity for some defensive works being at once thrown up. These representations were re-submitted, on his arrival shortly afterwards, by General Burrows. Economy being, however, necessary, it was considered by the authorities inadvisable to incur the considerable charges which would be entailed by placing the defences of the city in a satisfactory state.

General Brooke's next care was to make himself acquainted with the surrounding country; and many were the excursions carried out by him over road, by-path, hill-pass, and river, to a distance of fifteen miles in every direction. Accompanied sometimes by a small party of officers, sometimes merely by an escort of a couple of sowars, one a qualified interpreter, the active Brigadier would start at daybreak, and after remaining for an hour or two in some village or orchard to converse with the natives, would return to barracks late in the day. In this manner he had made himself thoroughly acquainted with the environs of the city—a most necessary knowledge in a country so deficient in road-communication as Kandahar. It was due also to General Brooke's representations that a system of cavalry patrols and reconnaissances was initiated, which, though not furnished to the extent which he deemed advisable, was productive of good, and increased the general stock of knowledge.

Thus affairs went on till the approach of Ayub Khan's army began to arouse the turbulent spirits among the population, and disturbances began. General Brooke and Major Adam were fired upon on the 16th July in the Morcha Pass by a party among the rocks above them; and though the hill was surrounded by cavalry till nightfall, and a party of infantry was scrambling over it all the day, no trace of the would-be assassins was found. Fortunately their shots only killed one of the sowar's horses.

Thus far General Brooke in quiet times; but it was when the news of Maiwand was brought in, and dangers and difficulties arose, that his cool head, clear understanding, and soldierly insight made his influence more important. It was in compliance with his request, personally made and strongly urged, that the small detachment of all arms was sent out under his command to cover the last few miles of the retreat. Though the relief it was able to render was restricted by the orders it received not to proceed beyond the village of Kokaran, there can be little doubt that several lives were saved through its instrumentality, the large bodies of the country people, who had collected on either side of the route, dispersing rapidly on its approach.

On General Brooke's return to the city at about 2 p.m., after an absence of some seven hours, it was discovered that the orders for the withdrawal of the outlying corps, which it had been found necessary to issue, had been misunderstood. Instead of having packed up everything, and brought it into the central enclosure, preparatory to the retirement to the city, most of the troops in the cantonments had withdrawn at once, leaving their baggage and camp equipage in their quarters, where it had been looted by the villagers. Portions of it were subsequently recovered by detachments sent out for the purpose. By nightfall all the troops were withdrawn into the city, in an orderly manner, under General Brooke's directions.

In the train of important subsequent events—including the elaborate and now eagerly pushed forward defence of the city, the house-to-house visitation, and search for arms in the disaffected quarters, and the ultimate extra-mural ejection of the Pathans—the energy and perseverance of General Brooke were conspicuous. Always good-humoured, smiling, and cheerful, he was just the man to restore the drooping spirits of troops smarting under such a defeat as that of Maiwand; and his youth, and powerful frame, rendered him apparently impervious to fatigue.

Thus he continued to set a brilliant example until the fatal 16th of August. The sortie of that day, to the village of Deh Khwaja, was undertaken in opposition both to his own advice and to that of General Burrows; and had, indeed, been planned for the previous week, but abandoned in deference to their opinion. Other counsel, however, prevailed; and when, on being sent for on the evening of the 15th, General Brooke was told that the operation was to be carried out, and that he was to have the command, his mouth was, as he himself said, closed. He was so emphatic in expressing his disapproval of the project to some private friends, that the opinion gained ground with some of them that he felt a presentiment that the morrow would be fatal to him, and desired thus to place on record his opinion of the unwisdom of the movement. His phrase was: "It will either be a walk over, or a very serious business. In the former case, it will be useless as a demonstration; in the latter, it must entail heavy loss." Whether the idea as to his presentiment of his own fate be correct or not, there can be no question as to the soundness of his estimate of the value of the sortie.

After the two attacking columns had forced their way under a heavy fire through the southern portion of the village, General Brooke, in the face of remonstrances, returned almost alone to render assistance to Captain Cruickshank, R.E., and a party who were gallantly endeavouring to escort that officer, then dangerously wounded, to the walls. Running the gauntlet of the village, attended by his mounted trumpeter (Mr. Glynn, of Battery C/2, R.A., who remained with him till he fell, and miraculously reached Kandahar unwounded), and assisted by a sergeant of the 7th Fusiliers, he succeeded in reaching Captain Cruickshank, and began to carry him towards the Kabul gate. It was in this enterprise that he lost his life.

The night of the 16th of August was a sad one in Kandahar. Each regiment had its own loss—especially in officers—to deplore; but it is not too much to say that in no case was the regret more wide-spread and deep than that which was evinced for the death of the gallant Brigadier.

Sprung from a family of soldiers, the subject of this memoir was possessed, in a marked degree, of the qualifications for success in the profession whose interests he held so deeply at heart. Of sound and excellent judgment; of rare humanity; a devoted friend; contemptuous of his own personal safety, yet holding it a sacred charge never to risk the safety of the constituents of his command without due reason, he would surely, had he been spared, have fulfilled the high promise of his brief but distinguished career. It was otherwise ordered; but it is some consolation to his relations and friends to feel that his death was not unworthy of himself.

After skilfully conducting, in the face of overwhelming difficulty, the operation which had been entrusted to his hands, he deliberately sacrificed his life in the vain attempt to save that of his friend.

LIEUT.-COLONEL FRANCIS BROWNLOW, C.B.,

72ND (DUKE OF ALBANY'S OWN HIGHLANDERS).

HE subject of this memoir, whose name will long remain identified with that of the distinguished regiment whose fame, during a lifetime, he did much to sustain, and whose honour he held jealously at heart, was the eldest son of William Brownlow, Esq. (eldest son of the Rev. Francis and Lady Catherine Brownlow, daughter of the 8th Earl of Meath), by his marriage with Charlotte (daughter of William Browne, Esq. of Brownes Hill, Carlow, and Lady Charlotte, daughter of the Earl of Mayo). He was born on the 19th July, 1836, and was educated at Harrow. Entering the 72nd Highlanders as Ensign by purchase on the 8th September, 1854, he had not long to wait before undergoing the stern experience of active service. He embarked with the regiment, a month after joining head-quarters, for the Crimea; and serving with it throughout its various operations in the war, was present in the expedition to Kertch, at the siege and fall of Sebastopol, and at the attack of the 18th June. In the last days of July, 1856, he returned with the regiment to England; and had barely attained his twentieth year before he bore on his breast the Crimean and Turkish medals, with the clasp for Sebastopol.

His term of home-service was of short duration. In September, 1857, the 72nd was ordered out to India, and Brownlow proceeded with it to earn a second medal by participating in the serious work which was to fall to its lot. He was present in the Mutiny at the siege and capture of Kotah; was with the leading column of assault on the 30th March, 1858; and subsequently served throughout the operations in Central India, being present in the pursuit of the rebel forces under Tantia Topee and Rao Sahib in 1868-59. In August, 1862, he obtained his company.

After returning with the 72nd to England, and continuing with it during its tour of home service, he again accompanied it to India, embarking with it from Ireland in February, 1871. In the meantime (May, 1870) he had obtained his Majority; and in August, 1877, he succeeded to the command of the regiment.

Colonel Brownlow was still in command of the 72nd, when, in view of the impending invasion of Afghanistan, it received orders, in the autumn of 1878, to join the Kuram Valley Field Force. Taking part with it in the advance into the enemy's country, he commanded it throughout the operations which were brought to a close by the signing of the treaty of Gandamak. For the brilliant manner in which he led his men in the assault of the Peiwar Kotal on the 2nd December, 1878, he was mentioned in eulogistic terms in Sir Frederick Roberts' despatch, and subsequently received the Companionship of the Bath.

After the conclusion of peace, Colonel Brownlow proceeded, in July, 1879, on leave to England. He had scarcely arrived in this country, however, when he was recalled to the theatre of the recent operations by the renewal of hostilities. Hurrying out with all speed, he succeeded in reaching Kabul on the 3rd December, in time to command the 72nd throughout the critical series of events with which the year closed. In the storming of the Asmai Heights on the 14th December, he led the advance; and for the brilliant example he set his men was spoken of in terms of warm admiration by Colonel Jenkins, the officer in command of the advance. On the withdrawal within the Sherpur cantonments, one of the five sections into which the defences were divided was entrusted by the General to his charge.

Colonel Brownlow continued in command of the regiment for the remainder of the time it remained in Kabul, and during the memorable march to Kandahar. It was in the battle with Ayub Khan's army on the 1st September, 1880, whilst gallantly leading the regiment through the lanes and walled enclosures in the stubbornly contested advance of Baker's brigade, that he met his death.

It is not too much to say that the loss of their beloved Colonel was regarded in the light of a personal bereavement by every officer and man of the gallant regiment which he had so often led to victory.

"In his death," wrote Sir Frederick Roberts in his despatch of the 26th December, "the Army has experienced a great loss. He had on many occasions highly distinguished himself as a leader,—at the Peiwar Kotal, during the operations around Kabul at the latter end of 1879, and notably on the 14th December, when he won the admiration of the whole force by his brilliant conduct in the attack and capture of the Asmai heights,"—words which have been supplemented in an earnest tribute paid by the General to Colonel Brownlow's memory in a farewell address delivered by him to the 72nd and 92nd Highlanders on the occasion of his departure for India, and which found an echo in the hearts of all to whom the deceased officer was known.

Colonel Brownlow married, in 1878, Effie Constance, daughter of the late Colonel Robert Tytler, 38th Bengal Infantry, by whom he leaves issue a son.

LIEUT. A. BURLTON-BENNET, STAFF CORPS,

10TH (DUKE OF CAMBRIDGE'S OWN) BENGAL CAVALRY (LANCERS).

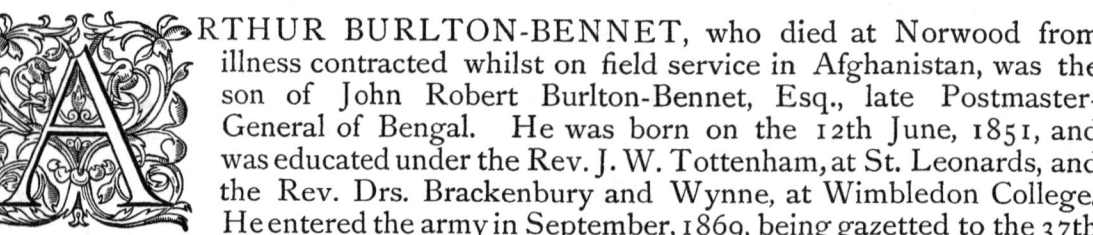RTHUR BURLTON-BENNET, who died at Norwood from illness contracted whilst on field service in Afghanistan, was the son of John Robert Burlton-Bennet, Esq., late Postmaster-General of Bengal. He was born on the 12th June, 1851, and was educated under the Rev. J. W. Tottenham, at St. Leonards, and the Rev. Drs. Brackenbury and Wynne, at Wimbledon College. He entered the army in September, 1869, being gazetted to the 37th Foot. Proving himself an efficient and accomplished young officer, he was offered, after a brief term of service, the Adjutancy of the regiment; but having decided to embark on an Indian career, was unwilling to accept the appointment. After applying himself diligently to a course of study, he passed the higher standard examination in native languages, and was posted to the 30th Native Infantry. He was shortly afterwards, however, transferred to the 10th Bengal Lancers, with which regiment he served till immediately prior to his death.

After being admitted to the Staff Corps, and passing successfully through a course of garrison instruction, Burlton-Bennet held various Staff appointments. Shortly before his death, he was selected to fill the post of Adjutant of the regiment.

On the outbreak of hostilities with Afghanistan he proceeded with the regiment into the Khyber, and participated in the arduous duties which fell to its lot in the Pass. The hard work he performed, and the constant exposure he underwent, laid the seeds of the disease to which he eventually succumbed. Shortly after the signing of the treaty of Gandamak, it was found necessary to invalid him to England; but the change failed to restore his shattered health, and barely two months after he reached his destination, he died, on the 23rd October, 1879, at his father's house at Norwood.

Arthur Burlton-Bennet's loss is deeply regretted, not only by his brother officers but a wide circle of friends. His love of sport of every description was intense, and his presence will be more especially missed by his companions in the hunting-field. On the news of his death being received in India his commanding officer made feeling allusion to the fact that the regiment had lost a valued friend; and H.R.H. the Duke of Cambridge, who was pleased to say he had made his acquaintance while in Malta, wrote expressing the regret he felt at the sad occurrence which had deprived the service of so smart and promising an officer.

CAPTAIN S. G. BUTSON,

9TH (QUEEN'S ROYAL) LANCERS.

STRANGE GOULD BUTSON, who was killed at Siah Sang, in the neighbourhood of Kabul, on the 13th December, 1879, while charging the enemy at the head of a squadron of the 9th Lancers, was the elder son of the Very Rev. C. H. Gould Butson, M.A., J.P., Vicar of Clonfert, and Dean of Kilmacduagh, St. Brendon's, Clonfert, Eyre Court, Ireland, by his marriage with Helena Eyre, only daughter of the Rev. Edward Eyre Maunsell, M.A., Vicar of Galway; and was a grandson, in the paternal line, of the late Venerable J. Strange Butson, M.A., J.P., Archdeacon of Clonfert.

The subject of this notice was born in the year 1851, and was educated by Mr. Walter Wrenn, London, and by him prepared for the Royal Military College, Sandhurst. He was gazetted, in July, 1870, to a cornetcy in the 9th Lancers; and after a term of some three years of home service, embarked with that regiment for India. In October, 1871, he was promoted Lieutenant, and in February, 1878, obtained his troop.

Captain Butson was serving with the regiment at Sialkot, Punjab, in the autumn of 1878, when, in view of the impending hostilities with Afghanistan, it was ordered up into the neighbourhood of Peshawar. He accompanied the first expedition to the Bazar Valley, under Major-General Maude, as a volunteer, in December, 1878; and subsequently served with the detached squadron of the 9th Lancers under Captain Apperley in the Kuram Valley, from the 17th March to the 27th September, 1879. Shortly after the renewal of hostilities he was appointed Aide-de-Camp to Brigadier-General Massy, and took part in the advance on Kabul, the actions of Jaji Thana, Charasiab, Kabul (8th and 9th October), and the operations in the second week in December. For his services during the march he was most favourably mentioned in despatches. It was in the action of Siah Sang, on the 13th of December, while leading a squadron on the summit of a hill up which he had just charged against large numbers of the enemy, that he fell, pierced to the heart by an Afghan bullet.

In a letter written by Brigadier-General Dunham Massy, the following words occur:—" He (Captain Butson) has died a soldier's death, and is deeply lamented by his brother officers and by all who came in contact with him. By his death the Service has been deprived of a most gallant and promising officer, and one who, had he been spared, would have proved a brilliant ornament to his profession."

Captain Butson's remains were buried, with military honours, on the evening of the 13th December, in the little cemetery at Sherpur, where those of so many of his fellow countrymen have found a last resting-place.

LIEUT. J. F. M. CAMPBELL, STAFF CORPS,

ATTACHED 2ND BALUCH REGIMENT.

JOHN FREDERICK MELFORT CAMPBELL was the eldest son of the late Captain Patrick Campbell, R.N., of the family of Melfort, Argyleshire, by his marriage with Gertrude, only daughter of the late Captain Joseph Barnes, R.A. He was born on the 12th December, 1856, and was educated at the Royal Naval School, New Cross. From this establishment he passed, in the midsummer examination of 1875, tenth out of a hundred and thirty-five candidates for direct commission in the Line; and being shortly afterwards gazetted to the 70th Foot, joined that regiment at Peshawar.

While serving in the Punjab, young Campbell passed with distinction through the Garrison Class at Sialkot, the preliminary examination in Native Languages, and, in due course, the final examination for the Staff Corps. There is something touching, judged in the light of after events, in a passage penned by him in reference to this period of his career, in a letter written a few days before his death to his mother. "My mind," he writes, "is at rest, now that I have finished that examination. Hitherto my life has been one long preparation for these examinations, and I am becoming rather tired of them."

In October, 1878, he accompanied the 2nd Baluch Regiment, with which he was then serving as a probationer, from Dera Ghazi Khan to Quetta, where the regiment joined the force under General Biddulph, which, in view of the impending invasion of Afghanistan, was then in course of concentration. He proceeded with the regiment in its advance, two months afterwards, into the enemy's country, and was present with it, in Palliser's Brigade, at the action at Takht-i-pul, and with Sir Donald Stewart's force in the subsequent advance on and occupation of Kandahar.

In the last days of January, 1879, he took part in the advance of General Biddulph's Division to Girishk, and on its return performed garrison duty at Kokaran. It was while marching from this post to Chaman, in the month of August, that he began to feel the effects of the hardship and exposure which, in common with his brother officers, he had undergone. Immediately after arriving at Chaman he was seized with cholera, and a few hours afterwards, on the morning of the 19th August—exactly a month from the date on which his Colonel (Nicholetts), towards whom he entertained a strong attachment, had fallen a victim to the same disease—he died, deeply regretted by his brother officers, with whom the gentleness of his ways and the unassuming manliness of his character had made him a general favourite.

CAPTAIN C. A. CARTHEW, STAFF CORPS,

16TH BENGAL CAVALRY,

OFFG. DEPY. ASST. QR.-MR.-GENL., KHYBER BRIGADE.

CHARLES ALFRED CARTHEW was the second son of General Morden Carthew, C.B., of H.M. Indian Army, Madras. He was born on the 3rd September, 1841, and was educated at a private school and at Cheltenham College. In April, 1861, he entered the army as Ensign in the 33rd Regiment, having obtained a direct commission by purchase; became Lieutenant, also by purchase, in April, 1865; and in February, 1866, entered the Bengal Staff Corps.

Posted to the 16th Bengal Cavalry, Carthew served as 1st squadron subaltern in that regiment during the campaign in the Black Mountain, Hazara, in 1868, and obtained the Frontier medal with clasp. In 1871, having suffered from repeated attacks of Indian fever, he was sent home on medical certificate; and although during the whole of his visit to England he continued in a low state of health, he was so anxious to improve his professional knowledge and fit himself for higher employment, that he obtained permission to attend a course of Military Surveying and Field Engineering, and took a Chatham 1st class certificate in those subjects. He also went through a course of instruction in Army Signalling and Telegraphy, for which he obtained a certificate as Instructor. In April, 1873, after completing his twelve years' service, he was promoted Captain.

After his return to India he officiated from time to time in the Quartermaster-General's Department. In May, 1876, he was appointed Officiating Quartermaster-General of the Allahabad Division for three months, on the expiration of which period he was sent to the Presidency till April, 1877. In October, 1878, he was appointed, again, in the same position, to the Umballa Division under General Hughes, and retained the post till September, 1879, when, at the beginning of the second Afghan campaign, he was appointed to the staff of Brigadier-General Arbuthnot as Deputy Assistant Quartermaster-General.

Captain Carthew was returned as slightly wounded when crossing troops over the Kabul River on the 9th June, 1880, under fire of the enemy, on the return from the Lughman Valley expedition. The zeal and energy and soldierlike qualities he displayed commended him to the favourable notice of those he served under. Brigadier-General Arbuthnot, on being relieved of the command of his Brigade, wrote on the 17th June, 1880, as follows:—"I wish to bring to the notice of the Lieutenant-General Commanding the Khyber Line Force, Captain C. A. Carthew, 16th Bengal Cavalry, the Deputy Assistant Quartermaster-General, as an officer of untiring zeal, with a good knowledge of the working of his department. I would also recommend him to the favourable consideration of the Lieutenant-General Commanding." And Major-General Bright, writing on the same date, heartily concurred in the terms of the Brigadier's favourable report.

On the return of the army from Kabul to India, Captain Carthew was directed to superintend the passage of the troops over the Indus at Attock; and the able way in which he organized and carried out all the arrangements, received the marked approval of the Commander-in-Chief in India, and of Brigadier-General Hankin, commanding the Peshawar District. Between the 20th of August and the 21st of September, 1880, he passed over the ferry at Attock no less than 20,496 soldiers and followers, 13,345 animals, 762 carts and 80 guns and waggons, without a single accident or mishap of any kind; and not a bale of goods was reported lost, although the Indus was in a state of heavy flood, the current running about seven miles an hour. But the constant exposure to the sun day after day during the most trying time of the year, acting on a constitution already enfeebled by the fatigues of the campaign, was more than he could bear; and when his heavy work of the passage of the troops was done—but not till then—he was once more and for the last time laid low with the deadly Peshawar fever, and died at Landi Kotal on the 12th October, 1880, in the thirty-ninth year of his age, within a few months of the time when he would have obtained his majority.

It is some poor consolation to his friends to know that Captain Carthew's exertions were appreciated by the Commander-in-Chief and the Government of India. On the 29th of October, 1880, the Quartermaster-General of the Army wrote to the Military Secretary to the Government, expressing his Excellency's satisfaction with the arrangements made in this work of the passage of the troops over the Indus; and his regret that by the death of Captain Carthew the Army and the Government of India were deprived of a most valuable public servant; and on the 9th November, 1880, the Military Secretary to the Government of India wrote to the Quartermaster-General of the Army concurring, on behalf of the Government, with Sir Frederick Haines' verdict. The practical result of this marked approbation of Captain Carthew's exertions and services was, that he was gazetted permanently to the Quartermaster-General's Department just one day before he died. Had he been spared he would, in all human probability, have risen to distinction. The fact of his having to retrace his steps and return to the pestilential climate of Landi Kotal to take up his appointment, gave the finishing blow, and extinguished the last spark of hope of his ever leaving Afghanistan.

Captain Carthew's remains were buried at Peshawar. His wife and three daughters survive him.

MAJOR SIR P. L. N. CAVAGNARI, K.C.B., C.S.I., B.S.C.,

MINISTER AND PLENIPOTENTIARY AT THE COURT OF KABUL.

F the many brilliant and promising careers cut short in the course of the operations with which these volumes deal, it may safely be affirmed that there was none more brilliant or full of promise than that of the widely-lamented subject of this memoir, who, still young in years but full of honours, rendered up his life in his country's service in the burning Residency at Kabul on the 3rd of September, 1879.

Pierre Louis Napoleon Cavagnari, the eldest son of Major the Count Adolphe Cavagnari, by his marriage with Caroline, third daughter of Hugh Lyons Montgomery, Esq., of Laurenstown House, Co. Down, Ireland, was born at Stenay, Department of the Meuse, on the 4th July, 1841. The Count Cavagnari, belonging to an ancient and noble family of Parma, served with the French forces under the first Empire, and subsequently became Private Secretary to Prince Lucien Buonaparte. His son, though born in France, was brought up from an early age in England, and received the whole of his education in the country of his adoption. After five years' study at Christ's Hospital, London, he passed into the East India Company's Service as a direct cadet, entering on a career which, from its outset, was an eventful one. No sooner had he set foot in India than he became engaged in the stern work of actual warfare. He joined the 1st Bengal Fusiliers (now the Royal Munster Fusiliers), in April, 1858, as Ensign; and serving with that regiment through the Oudh Campaign of 1858-59, was present at the capture of five guns from the Nasirabad Brigade at Shahelatganj, earning the mutiny medal. In March, 1860, he obtained his Lieutenancy. He was appointed, in 1861, to the Bengal Staff Corps, and the same year (the twentieth of his age) was gazetted Assistant-Commissioner in the Punjab, a post he continued to hold, and the duties of which he discharged with signal ability, for a period of five years. In 1866 he was given the political charge of the Kohat district, where he remained, incessantly active, until 1877, finding, in the tenure of the appointment, wide scope for his peculiar abilities, and steadily acquiring a reputation amongst his contemporaries for the skill and address with which he acquitted himself in dealing with the subtleties of frontier diplomacy. During this period of his career, besides being constantly employed in minor affairs, he acted as Chief Political Officer with the Kohat forces under General Keyes in the Bazoti expedition, and was present at the surprise and destruction of the village of Gara on the 27th February, 1869; again served, in the same capacity, in the Waziri expedition of April, 1869, and again in the blockade of the Kohat Pass Afridis in 1875-77. In the course of these operations his marked ability brought him prominently to the front, and his name was constantly on the public tongue. Up and down the frontier, from year to year, he added achievement to achievement, till his restless energy became a by-word amongst the turbulent hill-tribes, who were made by him to feel, in some instances for the first time, that their mountain fastnesses were powerless to shelter them from retribution due for their misdemeanours. For the services he rendered, he received, on several occasions, the thanks of the Secretary of State for India, the Governor-General and Council, and the Punjab Government; and on the 1st of January, 1877, on the Imperial title being proclaimed at Delhi, he was appointed a Companion of the Order of the Star of India.

In May, 1877, Major (then Captain) Cavagnari was transferred from Kohat to Peshawar; and in the Jowaki expedition of that year he was again to the fore. The Sapiri expedition of February, 1878, was, with the consent of Government, arranged and carried out by him, its object being the capture of the principal and leader of the band of robbers who, in December, 1875, had attacked and killed several native workmen near the English fort of Abazai, a raid known as the Swat Canal outrage. With this purpose in view, Cavagnari procured fifty men of the Corps of Guides, made a rapid night march, and surprised the object of his search in a mosque in Sapiri, capturing both him and his son. This feat, which was accomplished fifteen months after the perpetration of the crime which was its motive cause, has been spoken of as one of the most dashing little affairs on the frontier. Major Cavagnari immediately afterwards undertook, too, the Skhakat expedition of February, 1878, and the Utman Khel expedition of March of the same year, adding, in the conduct of them, fresh honours to the long roll already acquired by him.

Chosen to accompany Sir Neville Chamberlain on his mission to Shere Ali in September, 1878, Major Cavagnari was sent into the Khyber Pass with a small escort to ascertain the intention of the Amir relative to the reception of the embassy. The advance of the mission was stopped; and had it not been for the peculiar tact displayed by the avant courier at the interview which took place between him and the governor of Ali Musjid (Faiz Muhammad Khan), it is probable that the lives of himself and the escort who accompanied him would have been sacrificed, the governor of the fort remarking that, had the leader of the party been any other than Cavagnari, he would have fired on it.

It is an open secret that, after the rejection of the mission, a course of proceeding in reference to what had happened, fraught with great issue, originated with Major Cavagnari and was actually accepted by Government—a course which, had it been found possible to carry it into effect, might even have averted the war with which these volumes deal. The proposition was, that taking immediate action with regard to the insult offered to the Indian Government in the rejection of its ambassador, the little force at the time stationed at Jamrud should make a dash on Ali Musjid and surprise and capture it. On the eve of the attempt, however, intelligence that the garrison of the fort had been largely augmented, and that further reinforcements were then *en route* from Daka, was received. The proposed course was consequently abandoned.

On the outbreak of actual hostilities in November, 1878, Major Cavagnari accompanied the force under Sir Sam. Browne, as Chief Political Officer, into Afghanistan; and by his unrivalled knowledge of the character of the hill tribes who commanded the passes on the northern line, by the sagacity he displayed in the delicate and difficult dealings he had with them in his political capacity, and by the rapidity and dash with which he acted when the employment of force proved necessary, more than sustained his high reputation both as a soldier and a diplomatist. It was Cavagnari who, on the 22nd November, 1878, after the defeat and flight of the enemy at Ali Musjid, rode on, accompanied by a handful of Guide Cavalry, to Daka, a post beyond the northern débouchure of the Khyber Pass; and who, on the arrival of the advance guard of the column two days afterwards, had turned his time to such good account, that he was ready to tender to the General the submission of the powerful Khan of Lalpura, and to proffer the services of the head men of the villages in the Khurd Khyber: again, on the 1st December, availing himself of inter-tribal hostility as a means for inflicting punishment on the Zaka Khels, a section of the Afridi clan who had been harassing convoys and raiding on the line of communications, the unresting "Political" led a body of armed Kuki Khels, supported by mountain guns, against them, and, taking them by surprise, burned their villages, broke up their hostile combination, and was back at his post within twenty-four hours from the time of his quitting it; and when, after the death of Shere Ali, the recognition of Yakub Khan as his successor was ultimately decided on, it was Cavagnari who successfully conducted the negotiations which resulted in the treaty of Gandamak. "Although there are certain names not mentioned amongst those who are most conspicuous in the field and in council," observed the Secretary of State for India (Viscount Cranbrook) in motioning, in the House of Lords, a vote of thanks to the Army, "still I think your lordships would not feel justified in passing them over, and among them is the name of that distinguished person who negotiated the treaty with the Amir, Major Cavagnari. Before the affairs in Afghanistan, his name was not much known in England, but now it is well known for the intelligence and sagacity which enabled him to bring about the treaty of peace which in less skilful hands might have failed." In recognition of his eminent services, the subject of this allusion was subsequently created a Knight Commander of the Order of the Bath.

Selected at the close of the operations to proceed to Kabul as Envoy and Minister Plenipotentiary of the British Government to the Court of His Highness the Amir Yakub Khan, Major Cavagnari, accompanied by a small escort, made his way to the capital, reaching his destination on the 24th July, 1879. As is related elsewhere, the mission was received on its arrival with every outward manifestation of respect, although, as early as the 6th of August, signs of hostility towards it on the part of a section of the army and the people were not wanting. On that day, large bodies of turbulent soldiery, who had returned to Kabul on the previous evening from Herat, paraded the streets of the city, and manifested their dissatisfaction by beating drums to gather the people together, and abusing the Ambassador by name. A native officer of an Indian Cavalry Regiment, Ressaldar-Major Nakshband Khan, who happened at the time to be spending his furlough at one of the suburbs of Kabul, his native village, hastened to warn the Envoy of the coming storm. "Keep up your heart," the latter is reported to have responded: "dogs that bark don't bite." With earnest iteration the Ressaldar-Major urged that the danger was real and imminent. Cavagnari's reply was characteristic of the man, and of a piece with other instances of his notorious disregard of personal danger when the dignity of the Government he represented was to be upheld. "They can only kill the three or four of us here," he said quietly, "and our death will be avenged."

As time went on, the relations subsisting between the Embassy and the Amir appear to have become somewhat strained, and indications of the menacing attitude of the people to have multiplied. Notwithstanding this, no cause for immediate alarm seems to have been felt at the Residency; and even up to the last, the Viceroy of India was able to telegraph to the home Government: "All well at the Kabul Embassy." That this confidence was misplaced, the sequel disastrously proved. On the 3rd of September occurred the revolt which brought the labours of the mission, and with them the life of the subject of this memoir, to a sudden and tragical close—an episode which, from the stubborn character of the defence of the Residency against overwhelming numbers, and the heroic bravery displayed by the little band comprising the Embassy, has made a page in history which the British nation will be slow to forget. It was not until after repeated onslaughts had been made upon the building by the infuriated rabble of soldiery and townspeople that Sir Louis received his first wound, a contusion of the forehead from a half-spent rifle-ball. Concerning what immediately followed, such evidence as exists is vague and conflicting; but it would appear that, when the Residency was fired, the subject of this memoir was conveyed to another part of the building, and tended by Dr. Kelly. The last act of the drama is more clearly written. After a portion of the wall of the bath-room in which the last stand was made had been knocked away, and the assailants swarmed in hordes through the breach, Sir Louis was rendered senseless by a sword-cut from behind which clove his head, and was immediately afterwards crushed to death by portions of the burning wall and roof of the building falling in upon him. Thus was cut short the brilliant career of a soldier and diplomatist who, by his wisdom, his gallantry, his chivalry, and his humanity, had won not only the admiration but also the affection of his countrymen, and whose death has been aptly referred to as a distinct step backwards in the work of frontier progress and pacification. Endowed with an instinctive delicacy of apprehension; possessed, to an extraordinary degree, of the power of gauging relative magnitudes, and ever ready, in council, to forego a temporary advantage to secure a permanent gain; having the gift of tongues; profound in his knowledge of native character, and therefore readily able to deal with natives; holding his own life as naught where the interest or dignity of the country he represented was at stake, Sir Louis Cavagnari was a public servant who had made himself indispensable, at a critical juncture, to the Government of India, and it is not too much to say that his loss can be regarded as nothing less than a national calamity.

The news of the massacre at Kabul, which produced in England a thrill of consternation comparable only to that which followed the announcement of the disaster sustained by our arms at Isandhlwana, was telegraphed to Lady Cavagnari by the Viceroy, Lord Lytton, who, interpreting the emotion of the country, brought his message to a conclusion with the words: "Every British heart in India feels for you."

Her Majesty the Queen, telegraphing from Balmoral, expressed her sympathy with the bereaved lady in her great sorrow, referring to the death of Sir Louis as "a loss to the nation at large;" and again, in an autograph letter, condoled with her in her great affliction. In a paragraph in the "Gazette of India," the Government hastened to express its keen sense of the loss which the empire had sustained by the tragic and premature death of so able a public servant. The Chancellor of the Exchequer (Sir Stafford Northcote), the first member of the Ministry to publicly comment on the deplorable news, spoke of the Envoy in these terms: "It is impossible that England can fully appreciate the very serious loss we have sustained by the death of one so eminent, so worthy of our gratitude, as that distinguished man Sir Louis Cavagnari." Many more public utterances, denoting a feeling widespread as it was deep, were made on the same melancholy theme; and with a quotation from one of them—a speech of Lord Lytton's, delivered at Calcutta—as interpreting the feeling of all, we may fitly close this brief memoir. "The high abilities of Sir Louis Cavagnari," observed the Viceroy, "were known to all by the valuable results of their successful exertion in the service and for the interests of India; and by all, I believe, they were ungrudgingly acknowledged. For rarely has any man, in attaining so rapidly to public eminence, provoked so little private jealousy or personal animosity on the part of his less successful contemporaries. But to me, his immediate chief, throughout a period of much difficulty and anxiety, special opportunities were given to appreciate, not only the steadfast courage, the foresight and sagacity, the rare fertility of resource which marked his public service, but also the nobility, gentleness, and modesty, the manly unselfishness and endearing charm of his personal character. By the premature death of Sir Louis Cavagnari, India has suffered an irreparable national loss."

CAPTAIN D. T. CHISHOLM,

59TH (2ND NOTTINGHAMSHIRE) REGIMENT.

THE subject of this notice was the fourth son of the late Rev. Charles Chisholm, J. P., Rector of Southchurch, Essex, Rural Dean, Chaplain to the Duke of York; was grandson of the Rev. Cooke Tylden Pattenson, of Storden Park, Kent, Rector of Ulsted and Frinsted, in the same county; and was a cousin of the Chisholm of Erchless Castle, Inverness.

Duncan Tylden Chisholm was born on the 14th June, 1832. After serving for a time in the East Kent Militia, he was gazetted, in April, 1861, to an ensigncy by purchase in the 3rd West India Regiment, and did duty with that corps for a period of four years in the West Indies and on the West Coast of Africa, being promoted Lieutenant in October, 1864.

In January, 1865, he exchanged into the 59th Foot, in which regiment he remained till the day of his death. He served with it in the suppression of the Fenian riots of 1866-1867, and in Ceylon and the East Indies from 1867 to 1878. From February, 1870, to May, 1871, he acted as Paymaster to the Karachi Depôt.

Accompanying the regiment on active service into Afghanistan in the autumn of 1878 as Paymaster, he took part with it in the advance on Kandahar, and in the subsequent advance on and occupation of Kalat-i-Ghilzai. In July, 1879, while at Kandahar, he was stricken down with typhoid fever, to which disease he fell a victim, after a few days' illness, on the 30th of the month, sincerely regretted by all who knew him. He was buried in the old cemetery of the city, where a handsome tombstone erected to his memory by his brother officers, marks his grave.

Captain Chisholm was twice married. He leaves a widow (Mary, daughter of Mr. John Gordon Lillie, of Aberdeen) and two sons to mourn his loss.

LIEUTENANT R. T. CHUTE,

66TH (BERKSHIRE) REGIMENT.

RICHARD TREVOR CHUTE, who was killed in action at Maiwand on the 27th July, 1880, was the youngest son of the late Richard Chute, Esq., D.L., of Chute Hall, Co. Kerry, and the Honourable Mrs. Chute, daughter of the late Lord Ventry; and was a nephew of General Sir Trevor Chute, K.C.B. He was born in Kerry on the 17th September, 1856, was educated at Wimbledon School, and in 1875 joined the Cavan Militia, from which, in October, 1877, he received his commission as 2nd Lieutenant in the 66th Regiment. He embarked, shortly afterwards, for India to join the Headquarters, and after serving for a period at Kolaba, Haidarabad, and Karachi, he received, in June 1879, his lieutenancy. He was subsequently appointed Acting Quartermaster to the regiment, in which capacity he served till the day of his death.

On the 66th being ordered to the front, in February, 1880, Chute proceeded with it in its march through the Bolan, and shared with it at Kandahar the duties which fell to its lot. He took part, in the first week of July, in the advance of Burrows' Brigade to the Halmand, and during the action in the neighbourhood of Girishk on the 14th of the month his company was one of those detailed to guard the camp on the left bank of the river. In the disastrous battle of Maiwand on the 27th, he fell fighting gallantly against the overwhelming numbers of the enemy, being one of the little band who sold their lives so dearly in the garden where the last desperate stand was made.

BREV. LIEUT.-COLONEL W. H. J. CLARKE,

72ND (DUKE OF ALBANY'S OWN HIGHLANDERS).

ILLIAM HENRY JAMES CLARKE, who died at Allahabad on the 7th April, 1880, from illness contracted on service in the field, was the son of the late Colonel W. H. H. J. Clarke, 53rd Regiment. He was born on the 14th July, 1833. After preliminary education, he entered the Royal Military College, Sandhurst, and having completed the usual course of study in that institution, was gazetted, in August, 1851, to an ensigncy in the 53rd Foot, then stationed at Mhow. He served with that regiment until 1860, and was present with it in the Indian Mutiny at the actions of Chutra, Gopalganj, Khodaganj, and the entry into Fatehgarh; the storming and capture of Mianganj, the siege and capture of Lucknow, the affair of Kursi, the passage of the Gogra, at Faizabad, on the 25th November, 1858, the action of Tulsipur, and several minor affairs. For his services on these occasions he was mentioned in despatches and received the medal with clasp. In 1860 he obtained his company, and in the following year exchanged into the 72nd Highlanders, with which distinguished corps he served continuously till immediately prior to his death.

The regiment was ordered home in 1866, and was quartered at various stations in Great Britain and Ireland for some five years, at the expiration of which it again returned to India. Eighteen months afterwards (June, 1872) Captain Clarke succeeded to a Majority consequent on the promotion of Colonel Page to the Brigade Staff, and in 1877, in due course, became senior Major of the regiment, obtaining also the rank of Brevet Lieut.-Colonel in November, 1878.

In October, 1878, the 72nd Highlanders was one of the first regiments ordered to the front in view of the impending hostilities with Afghanistan. On arriving at Kohat from Sialkot, at which place the 72nd had been for some time quartered, the right wing of the regiment was detailed for the advance of General Roberts' Division into the enemy's country, while the left wing, under Colonel Clarke, remained temporarily at Kohat. In January, 1879, the subject of this notice proceeded in command of his half battalion to take part in the Khost Valley Expedition, and was present at the capture of Matun. For the soldierly qualities he displayed, and for his capability for command in the field, he gained for himself the respect of all ranks, as well as the approbation of the General Officer Commanding. The left wing rejoined the head-quarters at Peiwar about the end of March, and shortly afterwards the regiment proceeded to Ali Khel, where it remained until after the conclusion of the peace of Gandamak. On the renewal of hostilities in the autumn of 1879 in consequence of the massacre of the Embassy, Colonel Clarke, on whom the command of the regiment had devolved in the absence on furlough of Colonel Brownlow, advanced with Sir Frederick Roberts' force over the Shutargardan towards Kabul. At the battle of Charasiab, on the 6th October, during which his horse was shot under him, he displayed great coolness and personal gallantry. He was subsequently present with the regiment at the occupation of Kabul and the Bala Hissar, throughout the investment of Sherpur, and in the attack on the Asmai heights.

About the middle of December, 1879, Colonel Clarke's health, undermined by the vicissitudes and hardships of field service, began to fail, and later in the month he was seized with a sharp attack of pneumonia, followed by other severe and dangerous symptoms. It was therefore deemed absolutely necessary to invalid him to India with a view to his ultimately proceeding to England, as the only means of obtaining his restoration to health—a hope, unfortunately, never to be realized. Under great difficulties he reached Bengal, but while proceeding down country towards Bombay by easy stages, he fell into so precarious a condition at Allahabad that he was obliged to remain there, and shortly afterwards died at that place, on the 7th April, 1880.

By the death of Lieut.-Colonel Clarke the army lost a most distinguished and gallant soldier, and one who, had he been spared, would have doubtless added to the high reputation he had so justly earned throughout the service, especially among those with whom he was more intimately associated. His interest in his regiment was always of the greatest, and was only equalled by his anxiety and jealousy for its honour and good name, to uphold which none strove harder than he.

Lieut.-Colonel Clarke married, in 1868, Laura, daughter of the late Herbert Taylor Lewis, Esq., 40th Regiment, and granddaughter of the late Sir E. Lacon, Bart., M.P. for Great Yarmouth.

LIEUT.-COLONEL R. S. CLELAND,

9TH (QUEEN'S ROYAL) LANCERS.

ROBERT STEWART CLELAND was the third son of the late Samuel Cleland, Esq., of Stormont Castle, in the County of Down, and grandson of the Rev. John Cleland, Precentor in the Cathedral of Armagh and Rector of Killevey. He was born on the 24th June, 1840, and was educated at Eton and Harrow, subsequently being prepared for examination at Sandhurst by the Rev. A. Morrison, of Wotton Bassett. Gazetted in July, 1857, to a cornetcy in the 7th Dragoon Guards, he embarked, a few months later, for India. After the suppression of the Mutiny, he returned to England in charge of time-expired men; and exchanging into the 9th Lancers within a few months from the date of his arrival, remained in that regiment, serving in successive grades and in various parts of the world, till the day of his death.

Colonel Cleland was in command of the 9th Lancers at Sialkot in the autumn of 1878, when, in view of the impending outbreak of hostilities with Afghanistan the regiment was ordered to Taru, to form part of the 2nd (Reserve) Division of the Peshawar Valley Field Force. On the forward concentration of the northern force, the regiment was moved into the Khyber, and there shared the duties connected with guarding the communications which devolved upon the troops under General Maude's command. About the time of the signing of the treaty of peace at Gandamak Colonel Cleland fell ill, and was invalided to Murree, from whence, shortly afterwards, he proceeded to the Chini Hills.

On the renewel of hostilities in the autumn of 1879 the 9th Lancers, then at Sialkot, were ordered to the front, to form part of the Kabul Field Force under Sir Frederick Roberts. Colonel Cleland, though still suffering, hastened up with all speed to resume his command. From the effects of making two long marches daily, his pony fell lame. After proceeding twenty-eight miles on foot in one day, and fifteen the next morning, he reached Simla, and eventually rejoined the regiment at Jhelum.

The 9th Lancers arrived at Kabul in the first days of November, 1878, and a month afterwards took part in the critical events which marked the close of the year. At the action of Killa Kazi on the 11th December, while gallantly leading the cavalry charge against overwhelming numbers of the enemy during the retirement, Colonel Cleland was dangerously wounded. Becoming unconscious, he was placed in a dhoolie, which was subsequently abandoned by its bearers, with the guns, in a watercourse; he was, however, saved from the approaching enemy by the gallantry of Serjeant-Major Young of the regiment, who, finding that he did not reply when spoken to, dismounted, and dragged him out of the litter into the water, the contact with which revived him. The sergeant offered him his horse, which Colonel Cleland refused. A few moments afterwards he managed to seize the bridle of an animal galloping past with empty saddle, and was assisted to mount. Ordering Young to collect and lead the scattered men who were by this time coming up, and taking a sergeant (Finn) to accompany him, he started for Sherpur, eight miles distant. His elbow-joint had been shattered by a sword-cut, and a bullet with which he had been struck was still in his side. That he managed to reach the cantonments over such country as lay before him, speaks of itself for his heroic courage and endurance.

During the time Colonel Cleland remained at Kabul, he was most kindly and carefully tended. When he was able to be moved he was taken by easy stages in a dhoolie to Jamrud, accompanied by his devoted friend Captain Stewart Mackenzie, 9th Lancers, who asked and obtained the necessary permission from Sir F. Roberts. It was found necessary, however, to halt for some little time at Fort Battye and at Gandamak on the journey down, in consequence of alarming attacks of dysentery coming on. From Jamrud, where the road for wheel traffic commences, he was driven to Rawal Pindi, in Sir F. Maude's carriage, reaching that officer's house on the night of the 7th April, in an apparently almost dying condition. After a fortnight's rest and tender nursing, he became, however, sufficiently recovered to bear the journey to Sir F. Maude's cottage at Murree, the nearest hill station. Here he improved rapidly till the 15th June, when erysipelas appeared in his wounded arm. From this time he gradually sank, and eventually died, tenderly nursed to the last by Lady Maude, on the 7th August.

In a Divisional Order bearing date 12th August, 1880, Sir Frederick Maude wrote with reference to the death of Colonel Cleland (whom—to use his own words—he mourned as a brother) as follows: "Not only have the ever-glorious 9th Lancers lost a gallant soldier worthy of being at the head of such a distinguished regiment, but the Army and country an officer whose sole aim was to do his duty." And in a Field Force Order, issued by Sir Frederick Roberts on the same melancholy occasion, the following words occur: "By the death of Lieut.-Colonel Cleland, Sir F. Roberts, in common with a large number of officers and soldiers, has lost a valued friend, whilst Her Majesty's Army has been deprived of the services of a most promising and gallant officer."

Much beloved by his men, to whose welfare and comfort he was devoted, and in each and all of whom he took a strong personal interest, Colonel Cleland will long be mourned in the ranks of the 9th Lancers, not only as a just and appreciative commanding officer, but also as a warm-hearted and sympathetic friend.

LIEUT. DUNCAN COLE, STAFF CORPS,

JACOB'S RIFLES.

THE subject of this memoir, who was born on the 8th May, 1859, was the second son of Charles D. Cole, Esq., Retired Paymaster of the late Indian Navy, and some time Consul and Agent for the Government of India at Jiddah, Red Sea; and was descended in the maternal line from the late Rear-Admiral William Holt. He was educated at the Royal Naval School, New Cross, and from thence proceeded, in July, 1876, to Sandhurst. At the expiration of the usual course at the College, he passed out with a first-class certificate, and was gazetted to the 83rd Foot. Proceeding to join that regiment, then in Bombay, he was informed, on arriving in India, that several appointments on probation had been made to the Bombay and Madras Staff Corps direct from Sandhurst; and was almost immediately attached for duty to the 1st Grenadiers. On passing the examination in native languages—which he did several months before the expiration of the allotted time, and for his success was highly complimented by the President of the Committee—he was temporarily attached to H.M. 15th Regiment. A few months afterwards he was again transferred to the 14th Bombay Infantry, with which regiment he proceeded to Aden. Almost immediately after arriving at that station, however, he was yet once again transferred—this time to fill a vacancy in Jacob's Rifles, then on field service in Afghanistan. He joined that regiment—his connection with which, alas! was destined to be brief—at Kandahar in the month of May, 1880, and accompanied it to Girishk in the following July. In the fatal encounter with the enemy at Maiwand on the 27th of that month, he commanded two companies of the left wing of the regiment under Major Iredell, which, early in the engagement, were sent to cover the left flank of the Grenadiers. It was at the moment before the two companies under his command—after working over ground absolutely denuded of cover, and being exposed, after four hours' continuous fighting, to the fierce rush of the encircling hordes of the enemy—were driven in, that Lieutenant Cole fell, killed by a round shot, at the same time that two of the native officers out of the three with him were wounded.

Duncan Cole was not the first of his race who has fought in his country's service, his father having been present in the Chinese War in 1839-42, and the Burmese War in 1852; and four of his uncles in the maternal line having individually or collectively fought in the Crimean War and the Indian Mutiny, in addition to both the wars last named.

LIEUT.-COLONEL J. J. COLLINS,

2ND BATTALION, 60TH (KING'S ROYAL RIFLE CORPS).

JAMES JOSEPH COLLINS, who died of dysentery at Nari Bank, near Sibi, on the 8th October, 1880, was the fourth son of William Collins, of Knaresborough, Yorkshire, Esquire, and was born at Knaresborough, February 3rd, 1837. He was gazetted Ensign, by purchase, to the 60th Royal Rifles, August 25th, 1854, at the early age of seventeen years, and was posted to the 2nd Battalion, in which he obtained his Lieutenancy, 23rd March, 1855. He shortly afterwards joined the Head-Quarters at the Cape, remaining there until the close of 1857, when he returned to England on private affairs. Soon after his arrival in this country, he found himself posted to the 4th Battalion of the regiment, on its formation; and in this battalion he obtained his company, by purchase, 19th July, 1859. He accompanied it to North America in 1861, and returned to England with it on the completion of its tour of Foreign Service in Canada and New Brunswick. He was gazetted Brevet-Major, 5th July, 1872, and promoted, May 24th, 1873, to a Majority in the 3rd Battalion, which had recently returned from India. On the 21st August, 1878, he was appointed, as Lieutenant-Colonel, to the command of the 2nd (his original) Battalion, then serving in India, which he proceeded to join, reaching India too late to accompany it in its march to Afghanistan, where it had in the meantime, been ordered. Immediately on landing he hastened up country, and in February, 1879, took over, at Kandahar, the command of this fine battalion, which he found in splendid order and in a most efficient state, and which he commanded with pride during the campaign of 1879-1880.

Colonel Collins remained at Kandahar during the occupation of that city by Sir Donald Stewart's army, and accompanied it, in the spring of 1880, in its advance on Ghazni and Kabul, taking part in the actions fought at Ahmed Khel, on the 11th, and at Arzu on the 23rd April, and was favourably mentioned in despatches for his services on these occasions.

After a short stay at Kabul, the 2nd Battalion of the 60th was one of the three European Regiments selected to accompany Sir Frederick Roberts in his now historical march to the relief of Kandahar, and was attached to the 3rd Brigade

(Macgregor's), which formed the reserve at the Battle of Kandahar, where Ayub Khan's army was totally routed. For his services Colonel Collins was again mentioned in despatches.

The battalion was now ordered to return to India with Macgregor's Brigade, by way of the Marri country; and a few days after leaving Quetta, while marching through the Bolan Pass, Colonel Collins, for the first time in a service of upwards of twenty-six years, found himself, on the 2nd October, placed on the sick list with what at first appeared to be a slight attack of dysentery. The fatigues and hardships of the campaign, assisted by the bad water supplied on the line of march, had undermined his constitution. He suffered so severely from the heat and the shaking of the dhooli in which he accompanied his battalion through the Bolan Pass, that he sank quite suddenly and unexpectedly at Nari Bank, near Sibi, on the 8th October, after an illness of six days, to the regret and consternation of his battalion, officers and men, by whom no commanding officer was ever more beloved and respected.

On the day following his decease, he was followed by his battalion to the grave, and buried at Sibi with military honours. Subsequently his remains were, at the urgent wish of his widow and relations, exhumed and conveyed to England, where they found a last resting-place in the churchyard of Leatherhead, Surrey, on the 3rd February, 1881, by a curious coincidence the forty-fourth anniversary of his birth.

The following extract from a notice, headed "In memoriam," that appeared in the "Celer et Audax Gazette," of the 3rd Battalion, 60th Rifles, shows how highly Colonel Collins was esteemed in the regiment:—

"We regret greatly having to record the death of Lieut.-Colonel Collins, from dysentery at Sibi, Beloochistan, on the 8th October. . . . . . Most of us knew him well, and deeply shall we mourn his loss. He was a good soldier, and a kind-hearted, steady friend; ever ready to give advice to those who sought it, and always striving to promote the well-being and comfort of his brother officers and of the men under his command. And now on his way home after months of toil and hardship and victory, has a fell disease carried off one with whom we have lived on terms of intimacy for twenty-six years, without ever hearing from his lips one unkind word. We cannot better perpetuate his memory than by striving to follow his example."

Lieut.-Colonel Collins married, in 1874, Constance Edith Emma Utterton, the youngest daughter of the late Bishop of Guildford, who, with three young daughters, survives him.

BT. MAJOR JOHN COOK, V.C., STAFF CORPS,

5TH GOORKHA REGT. (HAZARA GOORKHA BATTALION).

"HER MAJESTY has lost the services of an officer who would, had he been spared, have risen to the highest honours of his profession." Such are the words used by Sir Frederick Roberts in his Divisional Order of December, 1879, in announcing the death of the subject of this memoir.

John Cook was born at Edinburgh in August, 1843, and was the second son of Alexander Shank Cook, a well-known Scottish Advocate and Sheriff; and grandson of George Cook, D.D., who was for many years leader of the moderate party in the Church of Scotland. He received his early education at the Edinburgh Academy, and subsequently proceeded to Addiscombe, where he was among the last of the cadets who studied there, and who entered the college under the old nomination system. The boy's future profession was decided at a very early age, his father having received a nomination to Addiscombe for him when he was only eleven years old.

At the age of seventeen years he went to India, and soon after his arrival was posted to the 3rd Sikhs, with which regiment he went through the Umbeyla campaign. He was mentioned in despatches for his distinguished conduct during the operations, and was specially thanked by his Colonel for his gallantry in leading a very effectual bayonet charge. In 1868 he took part in the Hazara expedition. For these services he received the India medal with two clasps.

After ten years' service he took the furlough to which he was entitled, and spent a year at home, returning to India in 1871. In 1872 he was promoted to the rank of Captain, and in 1873 was transferred to the 5th Goorkhas as Wing Commander. In 1877 he took another year's furlough, returning to India in 1878. When the Afghan War broke out, the 5th Goorkhas joined the Kuram Field Force under General Roberts, and during the whole war followed the fortunes of that distinguished commander. At the battle of the Peiwar Kotal on the 2nd December, 1878, this regiment had the honour of leading the attack, and it was on this occasion that Captain Cook won his Victoria Cross. After the first stockade of the enemy had been brilliantly carried, he "charged out of the entrenchment"—

to quote the record of the incident given in the number of the "London Gazette" which announces the bestowal of the decoration—"with such impetuosity that the enemy broke and fled. Perceiving at the close of the *mêlée* the danger of Major Galbraith, Assistant Adjutant-General, Kuram Field Force, who was in personal conflict with an Afghan soldier, Captain Cook distracted his attention to himself, and aiming a sword-cut which the Durani avoided, sprang upon him and grasping his throat, grappled with him. They both fell to the ground. The Durani, a most powerful man, still endeavouring to use his rifle, seized Captain Cook's arm in his teeth, until the struggle was ended by the man being shot through the head." A fortnight afterwards he again distinguished himself by the gallantry he displayed whilst in command of a wing of the 5th Goorkhas in the Sapiri Defile on the 13th December. For nearly five hours the regiment maintained a rear-guard fight over most difficult ground with a bold and active enemy thoroughly acquainted with the locality; and though the two officers with him—Captains Goad and Powell—were mortally wounded, he succeeded, with Major Fitz Hugh, in beating off the Mangals and in bringing the convoy safely into camp.

When the Kabul insurrection broke out in the autumn of 1879, the 5th Goorkhas were among the troops who accompanied General Roberts in his march to the scene of the massacre. At the battle of Charasiab on the 6th October, Captain Cook, in command of two companies of the regiment, again on two occasions performed signal service—firstly, while forming part of the reinforcement of the flanking company of the attacking columns operating on the enemy's centre; and secondly in the assault on the main ridge. A sketch of him at the head of his gallant little men in the act of carrying one of the heights appeared in the "Graphic" of the 6th December, 1879.

While quartered in the Bala Hissar the 5th Goorkhas lost many men by the exploding of the powder magazine. In a letter describing the occurrence, Captain Cook referred to it as being the most appalling sight he had ever witnessed, and spoke highly of the gallantry of our soldiers in entering the burning building and rescuing their injured comrades. Shortly afterwards he had the pleasure of meeting his younger brother, Lieutenant Walter Cook, 3rd Sikhs, when that officer's regiment entered Kabul after its spirited defence of the Shutargardan Pass; and the two, as may be imagined, keenly appreciated each other's society during the short time that elapsed before the beginning of the stern work with which the year drew to a close. On the 11th of December, detachments of the 5th Goorkhas and 3rd Sikhs were fighting shoulder to shoulder, and more than once the brothers were side by side. On that day Walter Cook received a ball in the chest which came within an inch of touching his lungs; and barely twenty-four hours afterwards, John received his death wound.

The following is an extract from a letter of a brother officer of Major Cook's (the latter, it should be mentioned, had received brevet promotion in recognition of his services a few weeks before his death) written to Major Cook's sister, and giving the particulars of the manner in which he fell:—

"On the 12th of this month our regiment was ordered by General Macpherson to storm a high conical hill about three miles from this city, on which the enemy was strongly posted, and we were supported by three companies of John's old regiment, the 3rd Sikhs Infantry. John led the advance with two companies of our regiment, and we soon came under the enemy's fire, which occasioned a few casualties among the men. We got about half-way up the hill, but the enemy's fire became so galling that it was found impossible with our small numbers to get on any farther, and it was determined that we should take shelter under some rocks and wait for reinforcements from cantonments. Whilst lying under these rocks, your brother observed large bodies of the enemy coming up a spur to help those already on the top of the conical hill, and he went back about fifty yards to inform Colonel Money, of the 3rd Sikhs, who was in command of us, of what he had seen. No one could show the smallest part of his body from behind the rocks without having several bullets fired at him; and in going back to Colonel Money a heavy fire was kept up on John, but he escaped untouched. In returning, however, he had to run the same gauntlet, and just as he reached the rock under which we were lying, a bullet struck him, passing through the bone of the left leg just below the knee."

Major Cook received immediate surgical attendance on the field, but nearly twenty-four hours elapsed before he could be conveyed into shelter. For two days his wound did well, but mortification then set in, and on the 19th of the month (December, 1879) he died.

In Major Cook the Punjab Frontier Force lost one of its representative men, and the Indian Army an officer it could ill spare. His name—to quote one of his brother officers—was synonymous with all that is true and brave and chivalrous. He was modest to a degree. In a letter written to one of his sisters after the battle of the Peiwar, in which he tells of his having been recommended for the Victoria Cross, he adds, with characteristic generosity, "I think the dead deserve it most." Such was the disposition which endeared him to a wide circle of relatives and friends who watched with interest and admiration his progress in the profession he had adopted, and who, while mourning his loss, will never cease to be proud of his memory. It is some consolation to them to feel that, in the words of Sir Frederick Roberts, "he ended a noble career in a manner worthy even of his great name for bravery."

SURGEON-MAJOR HENRY CORNISH, F.R.C.S.,

ARMY MEDICAL DEPARTMENT.

HENRY CORNISH, an officer who, after performing most valuable service in the Afghan War, was mortally wounded at Majuba Hill, Transvaal, on the 27th February, 1881, was the second son of Charles Henry Cornish, F.R.C.S.E. He was born on the 4th June, 1844, at Taunton, and was educated at King William's College, Isle of Man. After attending as a pupil at the Taunton and Somerset Hospital, and passing through the curriculum of the University and Surgical Schools at Edinburgh, and Netley, he was appointed, in 1866, Assistant-Surgeon to Her Majesty's Forces, and was sent almost immediately afterwards to Mauritius, in consequence of an outbreak of malarious fever in the island. In 1868 he proceeded to the Cape in charge of invalids; and after reaching his destination was detailed to, and did duty with, the force engaged in quelling the Kaffir outbreak on the Orange River.

In 1872 he returned to England, and was appointed Assistant-Surgeon to the 10th Royal Hussars, then stationed at Colchester. On the embarkation of the regiment for India in 1873, he accompanied it; and was with it at Delhi at the time of H.R.H. the Prince of Wales' grand review of the army. In October, 1878, he was gazetted Surgeon-Major.

He accompanied the 10th Hussars in its advance into Afghanistan after the outbreak of hostilities with that country in the autumn of 1878; and was with the two squadrons of the regiment in the disastrous fording of the Kabul River, when forty-seven troopers and one officer were drowned. It is affirmed that he owed his own safety on this occasion mainly to the experience he had acquired in former days whilst serving in Africa.

In June, 1879, he took part in the return of the 10th Hussars and the 4th Battalion Rifle Brigade through the Khyber Pass, to India, "which," to quote words used in General Orders by the Commander-in-Chief, "with cholera on the line of March, excessive heat, entire absence of shade, and a scarcity of water.... must be considered one of the most trying operations of the war." For the services he rendered on this occasion he was specially commended; and in a Regimental

Order bearing date the 15th July, 1879, Colonel Newdigate, Commanding 4th Battalion Rifle Brigade, says: "The Officer Commanding cannot allow Surgeon-Major Cornish to leave the battalion without expressing the thanks of all belonging to it, for the unremitting attention, and care, by him of the sick, during the late very trying march."

He continued with the 10th Hussars till near Christmas, 1880, when, having been nearly eight years in India, he decided to avail himself of permission to return to England. Just after he had completed his arrangements for the voyage, however, he received on the 30th December a telegram from Colonel Luck, 15th Hussars, intimating that the regiment was ordered to the Cape, and expressing a hope that Cornish would accompany it. The latter, ever ready where active service was concerned, instantly wired back, "Delighted to go with you."

On the 2nd June, 1881, he embarked at Bombay with the 15th in the "Euphrates," and landing in February at Durban, marched to the camp at Mount Prospect. He was there attached to the 92nd (Gordon Highlanders), and subsequently accompanied that distinguished regiment in Sir George Colley's ill-fated occupation of the Majuba Mountain. It was in the retreat, whilst, assisted by the Piper of the 92nd, he was in the act of carrying a wounded man of the regiment, whose bearer had fled, that he was mortally wounded, "fearlessly," as the Surgeon-General reports, "doing his duty."

He was removed to O'Neil's Farm, where he died on the 1st March, 1881, and was buried in the cemetery at Mount Prospect, in which the remains of Sir George Colley and Commander Romilly have also found a last resting-place. Thus after nearly sixteen years of foreign service, closed the career of a gallant officer, beloved by all who knew him.

LIEUT.-COLONEL G. B. CRISPIN, STAFF CORPS,

4TH BOMBAY N.I. (RIFLES).

GEORGE BELL CRISPIN, who died at sea from illness contracted whilst on field service in Afghanistan, was the son of the late General Crispin of the Bombay Army, and nephew of the late Captain William Crispin, R.N., A.D.C. He entered the service in the year 1852. Serving with the 4th Bombay Rifles in the Persian Campaign of 1856-57, he was present at the landing at Hallelah Bay and surrender of Bushire (for which he received the medal with clasp) and was subsequently employed for some time as Postmaster to the Forces. At the close of the Persian Campaign he proceeded to the Punjab, and served on the North-Western Frontier for many years with the 2nd, 3rd, and 5th Cavalry Regiments. During this period, when doing duty at Bhawalpur, where he was the only European officer, he succeeded in suppressing the mutiny that broke out at Ahmadpur, thirty-two miles distant; the troops under his command consisting of two companies of the 4th Sikhs, and a troop of the 2nd Punjab Cavalry. For the services he rendered on this occasion he received the thanks of Colonel Minchin, the Political Agent of Bhawalpur. Together with most of the troops, he suffered severely from fever contracted on the expedition. He subsequently returned to the Bombay Presidency, and after doing duty with the 28th and 13th Regiments, was appointed Wing-Officer of his own corps, the 4th Rifles. He commanded two companies of the regiment in the suppression of the riots in Bombay, and was thanked for his services on that occasion by General Gell, commanding the division.

Colonel Crispin left Karachi with the 4th Bombay Rifles as second in command on its receiving orders to proceed, in February, 1880, on field service to Afghanistan. He remained in command of two companies on detachment in the Bolan for nearly four months, being the only European officer during that time stationed in the Pass. At the expiration of that period he proceeded by forced marches to Quetta, from thence convoying ammunition and treasure to Kandahar, where he arrived safely only the day before the investment of the city commenced. After serving with the regiment throughout the siege, he took part with it in the victory gained by Sir Frederick Roberts over Ayub Khan's army on the 1st September.

From the hard work and exposure he underwent previous to and during the siege, his health now became greatly impaired. Though he continued for a time to set a bright example by his untiring zeal, he was, at last, having become completely prostrated, compelled to proceed to Europe on medical certificate. The change of scene and climate came, unfortunately, too late to repair his wasted strength, and he died at sea during the voyage home, between Aden and Suez, on the 24th October, 1880.

Colonel Crispin leaves a wife and three children to bitterly mourn his loss, and many relations and sincere friends, by whom his memory will always be held in the highest esteem.

CAPTAIN E. W. H. CROFTON,

4TH BATTALION, 60TH (KING'S ROYAL RIFLE CORPS).

EDWARD WALTER HOME CROFTON, who died of cholera at Landi Kotal, Afghanistan, on the 19th October, 1879, was the only son of the late Colonel E. W. Crofton, C.B., and Frances Amelia, daughter of John Home, Esq., his wife, now one of the residents of Hampton Court Palace. He was born on the 12th May, 1842, and was educated at Woolwich. Gazetted, in June, 1861, to an ensigncy in the 2nd Battalion, 60th Rifles, he served for a time at the Depôt at Winchester. In May, 1865, he became Lieutenant by purchase, and two years afterwards embarked with the battalion for India. On his arrival in Bengal (November, 1867) he was placed by the late Brigadier-General Buchanan, R.A., in command of the company of local Infantry at Fort William—an appointment which he held, and the important duties of which he carried out to the General's satisfaction, till he was invalided home in the summer of 1869. Throughout the drill season of 1867 and 1868 he acted as Orderly Officer on all brigade field days, and at all inspections, and acquitted himself, according to the testimony of the General, with zeal and ability. For some time, too, during this period of his Indian service, he performed the duties of Assistant Musketry Instructor in the battalion in a manner which evoked the commendation of his Colonel.

After spending some months in England, Crofton again embarked for India to join his regiment. Proceeding with drafts under Colonel Forde, R.A., to Bombay in H.M.S. "Crocodile" and "Malabar," he acted during the voyage out as Adjutant of the Troops, and for the assistance he rendered was favourably recommended. Rejoining his regiment in the Punjab, he became its Musketry Instructor in January, 1871, and during a three years' incumbency of that appointment, "contributed greatly," in the words of his Commanding Officer, "to the very fair position the battalion held."

In July, 1873, he was promoted to a company in the 4th Battalion, which he joined in England a few months afterwards. During the period of its home service, he held the appointment of Deputy Assistant Adjutant and Quartermaster-General in the Western District, and during his tenure of the office the ability he displayed again caused him to be singled out for commendation. He returned with the battalion to India in the autumn of 1876, and after serving for two years at Agra, was appointed, by the Governor-General, Adjutant of the newly-raised Agra and Masuri Volunteer Corps, a post he was eminently qualified to fulfil. At this time he was in possession of a first-class Hythe certificate (Musketry), had been through a four months' course (at the School of Military Engineering, Chatham) of Reconnaissance and Field Works, Engineering, and Pontooning, had passed the Lower Standard examination in Hindi and Persian, and had been acting Staff-Officer at the Landaur Depôt.

Captain Crofton had long been eagerly desirous of seeing active service. On the second outbreak of hostilities in Afghanistan in the autumn of 1879, he volunteered for the front, and was appointed extra Aide-de-Camp to General Bright, whom he joined at Peshawar, and subsequently accompanied to Landi Kotal. His term of service was destined to be, alas! of but short duration. On the 18th October he was seized with cholera, to which fell disease he succumbed on the following day, to the deep regret of all who knew him.

Captain Crofton's memory is perpetuated by a monument erected over his grave in the little cemetery at Landi Kotal by his brother-officers as a token of the esteem and love in which they held him; and further testimony of his worth is given by General Bright, who laments that in him he had lost a most distinguished Staff-Officer, and one who had endeared himself to all by his unselfishness and great consideration for others.

Sprung from a family of soldiers, he was not the first of his race and name who distinguished himself in Her Majesty's service. His father, Colonel Crofton, C.B., R.A., besides serving in the first Carlist War (for which he received the Order of the First Class for San Ternado), commanded the Osmanli Horse Artillery at Scutari in 1855, and was appointed Brigadier-General in the China War of 1860, and Colonel on the Staff at Malta, where he died; and his grandfather, Captain Crofton, served as Brigade-Major to Sir Colin Halkett, and was slain in June, 1815, at Waterloo.

CAPTAIN G. M. CRUICKSHANK,

ROYAL (LATE BOMBAY) ENGINEERS.

GEORGE MACDONALD CRUICKSHANK was the third son of the late Major James John Farquharson Cruickshank, Bombay Engineers. He was educated at Wimbledon School, and obtained his commission from Addiscombe at the age of sixteen years, following in the footsteps of his two elder brothers, who had both joined the corps previously. Shortly after his arrival in India, he was employed in the Public Works Department, and remained so till he was ordered to join the Field Force at Kandahar in 1880.

Captain Cruickshank was appointed to take charge of the Sappers detailed to General Brooke's attacking columns for the ill-fated sortie from that city on the 16th August, 1880, and in this capacity the duty devolved on him of forcing, one after another, the gateways in the houses of the village of Deh Khwaja, being all the time exposed to a plunging fire from the roofs of the adjoining houses. Finally, in breaking into one courtyard, he was severely wounded and became unconscious. Immediately on hearing of his fall, General Brooke, who had by this time worked his way through the village to its northern outskirts, made a gallant effort to save him. He succeeded in getting him into a dhoolie, and conveying him some fifty yards beyond the village walls. At this point the dhoolie-bearers appear to have fled. "Then General Brooke"—thus runs the touching report given by one of Cruickshank's friends—"would not leave him, and they died side by side."

The following extract is taken from a letter written by Colonel Hills, C.B., R.E., from Kandahar, bearing date 10th October, 1880:—

"Poor Cruickshank well deserved the Victoria Cross over and over again, and would, had he survived, certainly have been recommended for it. His pluck, readiness of resource, and quiet energy, won him many friends, and had he been spared, his services would have been rewarded, for he came splendidly to the front on every occasion.

"Quiet, but invariably in the very front of everything, wherever any dangerous work was to be done, one found him there, keeping the men at their work by his thorough pluck and coolness. No man was better known or more respected than he was.

"When we heard he had been left behind, all the Wing Engineers went out to try and get his body in, but he was too far away from the walls, and too close to the village to get there. On the first opportunity we went out, and buried him under a green tree near where he fell, service being read over him and General Brooke and others by the Rev. Mr. Cane, who was a personal friend of his. No one respected him more than I did." .

Captain Cruickshank married Sophie, daughter of Major Reynolds, Bombay Staff Corps, who predeceased him. He leaves issue four children.

CAPTAIN F. J. CULLEN,

66TH (BERKSHIRE) REGIMENT.

RANCIS JAMES CULLEN, who was killed in action at Maiwand on the 27th July, 1880, was the fourth son of the late Francis Nesbitt Cullen, Esq., J.P., of Corry, County Leitrim, and grandson of the late Colonel James Cullen, of Shreeny House, in the same county.

Born at Corry on the 7th September, 1844, he was educated in Dublin at Dunbar's Academy, from whence he passed direct into the Royal Military College, Sandhurst, in September, 1863. Passing out in February, 1865, he obtained a free commission for the ability he displayed at the previous examination, and was gazetted in the same month to an Ensigncy in the 1st West India Regiment. He shortly afterwards joined that corps at Kingston, Jamaica, where he served under the late Governor Eyre in the rebellion which broke out immediately after his arrival.

In 1867 he accompanied his regiment to Africa, where he served for two years in Senegambia. In the autumn of 1869 he obtained his Lieutenancy without purchase, and was posted to the 66th Foot. He joined that gallant corps some months afterwards in Bombay, and continued to serve with it, with one interval of furlough, till the day of his death. In October, 1879, he obtained his company.

Captain Cullen accompanied the regiment on its being ordered up to Kandahar in February, 1880, and shared with it the duties which fell to its lot after arriving at its destination. In the first week in July he took part in the advance of Burrows' Brigade to the Halmand, and commanded the company of his regiment, which, acting as the General's rear-guard, crossed the river in the neighbourhood of Girishk on the 14th of the month to observe the movements of the Wali's mutinied troops. A fortnight afterwards, in the disastrous encounter with the enemy at Maiwand, he fell fighting gallantly at the head of his company, in the field in front of the Nullah, close to the spot where Colonel Galbraith and his brother officers, McMath, Garratt, and Barr, rendered up their lives. "Your son," wrote the late Major C. V. Oliver, (a gallant officer of the 66th, who survived that fatal day, and subsequently commanded the scanty remnant of the regiment at General Roberts' defeat of Ayub

Khan's army on the 1st September) to Captain Cullen's bereaved mother, "was seen to fall . . . . . doing his duty as a gentleman and a soldier. I was standing by his company for some time only a little while before he fell, and nothing could have been cooler or better than his behaviour. Amongst the many friends I lost on that day there are few I regret so much."

The brief record of the manner in which Captain Cullen faced his death reads as an echo of the anticipations formed after the first tidings of the disaster reached them by the many friends to whom, during his life, he had endeared himself.

LIEUTENANT R. E. L. DACRES,

ROYAL ARTILLERY.

RICHARD EDMUND LYONS DACRES, who died of typhoid fever at Landi Kotal, Afghanistan, on the 13th May, 1879, was the fourth son of Admiral Sir Sydney Colpory Dacres, G.C.B., Visitor and Governor of Greenwich Hospital, and nephew of General Sir Richard Dacres, G.C.B., Constable of the Tower. He was born at Haslar Hospital, Gosport, on the 18th February, 1856, and was educated at Cheltenham College, from whence he proceeded to Woolwich. Quitting the Academy after the usual course, he was gazetted, in August, 1875, to a Lieutenancy in the Royal Artillery.

In January, 1877, Dacres was ordered out to India. Posted to 6/11, R.A., he joined that battery at Rawal Pindi, and did duty with it until it was ordered down country, when he was transferred, at his own request, to Battery 11/9, R.A., which took its place.

On the outbreak of the Afghan War in the autumn of 1878, he accompanied the Battery in its advance, in the 1st Division Kyber Field Force, into the enemy's country. Taken ill with typhoid fever, on the march to Ali Musjid, he had to be sent back to Peshawar, and to suffer the keen disappointment of not being present at the attack and capture of the Fort; but partially recovering, he rejoined his battery, and subsequently took part with it in the Bazar Valley expedition in the last days of January and the beginning of February, 1879, in the affair at Deh Sarak on the 25th March, and in the operations against the Mohmands at Kam Daka on the 22nd and 23rd April, gaining credit throughout for the ability he displayed as an officer, and particularly distinguishing himself in his management of the two guns of which he was in command in the operations last named. It was after a toilsome march back to Landi Kotal on the return of the expedition against the Mohmands, that he was a second time attacked with typhoid fever, to the effects of which he succumbed after an illness of twelve days' duration, in the twenty-fourth year of his age, universally mourned by his comrades, whose admiration he had gained by his conduct both in the field and in camp, and whose affection he had won by his sociability and the friendliness of his disposition.

LIEUT.-COLONEL A. G. DAUBENY,

2ND BATTALION, 7TH (ROYAL FUSILIERS).

ALFRED GOODLAD DAUBENY, second son of the late Rev. Andrew Alfred Daubeny, of Redland Lodge, near Bristol, and of Frances Elizabeth, his wife, daughter of Richard Goodlad, Esq., was born on the 28th May, 1834, and was educated at Cheltenham and Sandhurst. He entered the Army in November, 1852, being gazetted to an ensigncy in the 90th Light Infantry. Two years afterwards he proceeded with that regiment to the Crimea, and there served with it from the 5th December, 1854, till the termination of hostilities, having been present, in the interim, at the capture of the Quarries, the siege and fall of Sebastopol, and the attack on the Redan on the 18th June, and having formed one of the storming party on the 8th September. For his services on these occasions he received the medal with clasp, and the Turkish medal.

On the reduction of the Army he was temporarily placed on half-pay; but in 1857 was brought into the 7th Royal Fusiliers, with which regiment he served in successive grades, at Gibraltar, in Canada, England, Ireland, and India.

In September, 1879, he obtained the command of the 2nd Battalion, and in February, 1880, proceeded with it in its advance to Kandahar. Here he commanded it through the siege till the 16th August, the date of the ill-starred sortie to Deh Khwaja, in which he greatly distinguished himself by his gallant behaviour in leading the charge across an open space near the north end of the village. This space (about 150 yards across) was surrounded on all sides by houses and walls held in force by the enemy, the fire from which was terrific. For his conduct on this occasion he was specially mentioned in General Primrose's despatch, as also for his behaviour throughout the siege.

General Brooke having fallen in the sortie, Colonel Daubeny was selected by General Primrose for the command (temporary) of the brigade thus rendered vacant. He subsequently received orders to proceed in his new capacity to the field of Maiwand to bury the dead, recover lost guns and rifles, and draw up a report on the subject of the field and the battle. For his services on this occasion, and more especially for the masterly nature of the treatise he prepared in fulfilment of the last-named of the duties apportioned to him, he received the thanks of Government.

It was about the time these acknowledgments reached him that Colonel Daubeny was seized with small-pox, and a few days afterwards, on the 21st November, 1880—to the heartfelt grief of every officer and man of his regiment, to the command of which he had reverted on his return from Maiwand—fell a victim to the virulent complaint to which so many of his countrymen in Afghanistan had already succumbed.

Colonel (then Major) Daubeny married, at Poona, in October, 1875, Emma Mackenzie, daughter of A. Rogers, Esq., of the Bombay Civil Service, by whom he had two daughters who survive him.

The deceased officer's commissions bear date as follows:—

Ensign by purchase	23rd November, 1852.
Lieutenant „	8th September, 1854.
Captain	30th November, 1855.
Major by purchase	23rd June, 1867.
Lieut.-Colonel	25th September, 1878.

LIEUTENANT G. G. DAWES, STAFF CORPS,

1st BENGAL CAVALRY.

GEORGE GRAHAM DAWES was the eldest son of the late Colonel Michael Dawes, of the Bengal Artillery, by his marriage with Louisa, daughter of the Rev. John Burdett, Rector of Banagher, King's County, Ireland. He was born at Meerut, Bengal, on the 17th May, 1846, and remained in India till in his ninth year, when he was taken to England. After receiving some preliminary education at Brighton, he proceeded to the Blackheath Proprietary School, then under the management of the Rev. J. Matheson, and entering eagerly into both work and play, won the approbation of his masters by the steadiness with which he pursued his studies, and the affection and admiration of his young contemporaries by his cheery disposition and by his prowess in the cricket-field, the play-ground, and as a member of the Volunteer Corps. It was his father's wish that he should adopt the Indian Civil Service for his career, and with the object of doing so, he underwent, on leaving Blackheath, a course of private tuition; the sedentary life which close study necessitated soon, however, began to tell severely on his health, and he was unsuccessful at the examination for which he eventually went up. He then determined to enter the Army; and competing, in May, 1868, at the examination for direct commissions, succeeded in taking first place in the list of candidates, easily distancing all competitors. While awaiting his commission, he turned the time at his disposal to profitable account, occupying himself with the study of Oriental languages. In December, 1868, he was gazetted to the 4th (Light) Hussars, then serving at Mirat, whither he shortly afterwards proceeded to join head-quarters. Finding, on arrival at his destination, an examination in languages being held, he sent in his name as a competitor, and taking excellent marks, passed the lower standard within a fortnight of his setting foot in India. In December, 1869, he passed the higher standard examination, and received the appointment of Interpreter to the regiment.

After doing duty for a twelvemonth as a probationer, the subject of this notice entered the Bengal Staff Corps. In November, 1872, he was gazetted to the

1st Cavalry, then stationed at Cawnpore, and was selected shortly afterwards to fill the post of Officiating Adjutant to the regiment—an appointment which he held, and the duties of which he continued to discharge with zeal and ability, for a period of three years.

Falling ill in the autumn of 1876, he applied for and obtained his two years' furlough, and proceeded to England. The period passed rapidly and pleasantly in foreign travel. Although, at its expiration, Dawes cannot be said to have been completely restored to health, he nevertheless abstained from applying for an extension of his leave: rumours of war, and of his regiment being ordered to the front, had reached him; and hurrying out, he rejoined the head-quarters at Sialkot in November, 1878, when his appointment to the Adjutancy was at once confirmed.

In March, 1879, the 1st Bengal Cavalry was ordered to Kohat to form part of the Reserve Division of the Kuram Valley Field Force. A few months after it had been in garrison at this post, cholera broke out in its ranks; and to this virulent disease—at midnight, on the 7th June, 1879—the subject of this notice fell a victim.

Most loving and unselfish in his family circle, generous and true in his friendship, witty, humorous, and with a spontaneous gaiety of disposition that age could never have dulled, George Graham Dawes was ever a welcome companion and guest. His cheery presence will long be missed in the places which knew it. Of the many who had the privilege of claiming friendship with him, it may truly be said that there is not one who does not mourn his untimely death.

LIEUTENANT A. E. DOBSON,

ROYAL ENGINEERS.

ALFRED EDMUND DOBSON, who died at Safed Sang, Afghanistan, on the 20th July, 1881, was the eldest surviving son of the late Rev. William Dobson, M.A., for fifteen years Principal of the Cheltenham College. He was born on the 14th July, 1849, at Cheltenham, and was educated at the College, entering it in 1857 at the age of eight years, and remaining in it till 1865. During the greater portion of the interval he studied under the Rev. T. A. Southwood, the head of the Military Department, from whom he received the highest testimonials for conduct, diligence, and proficiency. In 1865 he entered Woolwich, his name appearing fourth in the list of successful candidates at the midsummer examination; and passing out of the Academy after the usual course, he succeeded in again taking fourth place. Gazetted to the Royal Engineers, he did duty for two years at Chatham, and then proceeded to India. After serving for a twelvemonth at Bangalore, he was employed for nearly six years on Public Works in the Wainad District, and during the period approved himself a zealous and accomplished officer, winning praise for the able manner in which he performed much important work. He was subsequently sent to Burmah, from whence, after a few months, he was recalled for service with the Field Force in Afghanistan.

Proceeding in command of the I Company Madras Queen's Own Sappers and Miners, which had been detailed to the 2nd Division Kabul Field Force, Dobson reached Jalalabad in November, 1879. "During the march up," writes one of his brother officers, "he was the life of the party, never sparing himself, always ready and cheerful." He took part with his company, in December, in the expedition to Barikot, and in January, 1880, in the expedition to the Lughman Valley, and rendered important service in the construction of a bridge over the Kabul River, the improvement of the defences of Fort Sale, and the construction of a road over the southern barrier of the Daronta Gorge. A month afterwards he commanded his company in the reconnoitering expedition along the right bank of the Kabul River, penetrating into unknown country, and mapping a portion of the new route to the capital. These duties, and others of a like nature which were subsequently allotted to him in his capacity of Assistant Field Engineer, necessitated constant exposure and great hardship, and eventually began to tell upon his health. In March he was sent to Lachipur, and a few weeks afterwards to Safed Sang. While stationed at this post his health completely broke down, and on the 20th July, 1880, he succumbed to the deadly malarial fever, to which so many of his countrymen fell victims.

Lieutenant Dobson's remains, followed to the grave by the Generals both of the Division and the Brigade with their respective staffs and all the other officers at the post, were buried with military honours in the cemetery, and a headstone, subsequently erected to his memory by the Sappers of his company, by whom he was greatly beloved, marks the place where he rests. Among the many expressions of sorrow and of regard called forth by his death, feeling allusion is made in a Division Order issued by General Bright on the occasion, to the loss the Service had sustained in him, "a loss which," to quote the words of Major Ross Thompson, R.E., under whom he had long served, "is felt not only by his brother officers, but by every one who knew his good and kind and manly character."

The deceased married, in October, 1871, Florence Henrietta, fourth daughter of William Barnett, Esq., formerly M.P. for Maidstone. He leaves a widow and three children.

CAPTAIN JAMES DUNDAS, V.C.,

ROYAL ENGINEERS.

HE following notice, with the exception of a few trifling alterations, was penned by Captain W. Broadfoot, R.E., one of Captain Dundas's oldest friends, and appeared in the "Royal Engineer Journal" of the 2nd February, 1880. The writer has so ably recorded the various incidents of Captain Dundas's life, that the Editor of this work takes the liberty of transcribing the memoir *in extenso*.

James Dundas was the eldest son of the late George Dundas, one of the Judges of the Court of Session in Scotland, and of Elizabeth his wife, eldest daughter of the late Colin Mackenzie, Esq., of Portmore, Peebleshire. He was born on the 12th September, 1842, and was educated at the Edinburgh Academy, Trinity College Glen Almond, and Addiscombe College, from which he was appointed Lieutenant in the Royal (late Bengal) Engineers in June, 1860.

After passing through the usual course of study at Chatham, he sailed for India in March, 1862. On arrival he was posted to the Head-quarters of the Sappers and Miners at Rurki, and after a short service there was transferred to the Public Works Department in Bengal. His talent and sound judgment being recognized he was, after a short service, promoted to the grade of Executive Engineer and entrusted with the charge of one of the most responsible divisions in that Presidency.

In 1865 he accompanied the expedition to Bhutan under General Tombs C.B., V.C., and so distinguished himself as to be recommended by that officer for the Victoria Cross. The official report of the circumstances is as follows:—

"A party of the enemy, from 180 to 200 in number had barricaded themselves in the block-house, which they continued to defend after the rest of the position had been carried, and the main body was in retreat. The block-house, which was loopholed, was the key of the enemy's position. Seeing no officer of the storming-party near him, and being anxious that the place should be taken immediately, as any protracted resistance might have caused the main body of the Bhoteas to rally, the British forces having been fighting in a broiling sun, on very steep and difficult ground for upwards of three hours, the General ordered these two officers (Major Trevor and Lieutenant Dundas) to show the way into the block-house. They had to climb up a wall which was fourteen feet high, and then to enter a house, occupied by some 200 desperate men, head foremost through an opening not more than two feet wide, between the top of the wall and the roof of the block-house."

Major-General Tombs states that on desiring the Sikh soldiers to swarm up the wall, none of them responded to the call until these two officers had shown them the way, when they followed with the greatest alacrity. Both officers were wounded.

After the termination of the Bhutan expedition, Lieutenant Dundas rejoined the Public Works Department. He returned to England on leave in 1870, and again in 1877, rejoining his appointment in India early in 1878.

During the summer of that year he saved the life of a native under circumstances which showed that in addition to the high chivalrous courage which won for him the V.C., he possessed that calm and cool determination which is perhaps the highest form of human courage.

A house in the Simla bazaar was on fire, and the roof had partly fallen in and buried a native, to such an extent that he could not get out and would infallibly have been burnt to death or suffocated. Captain Dundas, who was passing, made an attempt to rescue the man, but was driven out of the place by the falling rubbish and by the smoke. He called for a volunteer from the crowd to help him, when a gallant officer of the Royal Artillery responded, and again he attempted the rescue, and this time his efforts were successful. He received some severe burns about the hands.

Captain Dundas was for a number of years associated with General Sir Alexander Taylor, K.C.B., R.E., in charge of one of the principal branches of the Public Works Department; the estimation in which his services were held is shown by the following passages which occur in a letter written by that distinguished officer shortly after Captain Dundas's death :—

"James Dundas having been my personal assistant from 1871 to 1879, there is probably no one better entitled than I am to say, from experimental knowledge, that in him the Corps has lost one of its 'very best.'

"A man of high abilities, well cultivated—a modest, high-minded English gentleman, brave, gentle, and courteous, I do not know that he ever gave offence to any one; far less do I believe that he had an enemy. To me he was an invaluable professional assistant; and I owe much to his varied and accurate engineering knowledge, to his trustworthy and universal popularity. But he was much more to me than a highly talented assistant, he was a greatly valued and respected personal friend.

"In the spring of 1879, he was specially selected for transfer to the Secretariat of the Government of India in the Public Works Department, but service in the field was more acceptable to his chivalrous disposition, and after a short tour of duty at Head-quarters of Government he found his way to the front last summer, on the fresh outbreak of war in Afghanistan."

When General Roberts advanced on Kabul in the autumn of 1879, he selected Dundas to accompany the Field Force as Commanding Royal Engineer, believing that Colonel Perkins had left Kuram; but the latter subsequently rejoined the Division. The manner in which the Engineers carried out the duty of providing shelter for the troops after the retirement into the Sherpur cantonments at the close of the year received the warm acknowledgments of the General. "No body of officers," he writes in his Division Order issued on the subject, "could have worked more zealously, or with better results."

On the afternoon of the 23rd December, Captain Dundas, with Lieutenant Nugent, was ordered to join General Macpherson's force to aid in the destruction of the line of forts held by the enemy on the south side of the British position at Sherpur. It was while carrying out this duty, through a fatally premature mine explosion which has been attributed to the use of a home-made quick-match in lieu of one of the fuzes which had been sent out and were found to be worthless, that he lost his life. His body was recovered by his comrades on the same day, and at their hands received a soldier's burial.

James Dundas succeeded, in 1877, to the estate of Ochtertyre, in Perthshire, on the death of his uncle, the Right Hon. Sir David Dundas.

LIEUT.-COL. HALFORD FELLOWES, STAFF CORPS,

32ND (PUNJAB) BENGAL N.I. (PIONEERS).

THE subject of this notice was born at the Leigh, Bradford, Wilts, on the 16th October, 1833, and was the youngest son of the late Rear-Admiral Sir Thomas Fellowes, K.C.B. He entered the Indian Army in 1851 as Ensign in the 31st Regiment (now 2nd Queen's Own) Light Infantry, with which he served through the Santal campaign of 1855-56. During the Mutiny in 1857, and in the subsequent operations in 1858-59 in the Saugor district and Central India (for which he received the medal with clasp), he served as Adjutant of the regiment, which was one of the very few Bengal corps that remained faithful throughout. He was Brigade-Major at Allahabad and Umballa from 1865 to 1867, and during the Abyssinian campaign of the latter year (for his services in which he was mentioned in despatches and received a second medal) he served as Brigade-Major under Sir Donald Stewart. From 1871 to 1877 he was second in command of the 23rd Pioneers, on the expiration of which period he was transferred to the 32nd Pioneers, and succeeded to the command of the regiment in November, 1878.

The 32nd Pioneers had been stationed at Quetta, Baluchistan, for ten months before the Afghan War broke out, and had suffered greatly from the unhealthy climate. In the month of November, 1878, the regiment was detailed to General Stewart's division of the army of invasion, and subsequently took part in General Biddulph's advance from Kandahar to Girishk, losing many of its number from dysentery during the month it stayed there. On the return march it formed part of the Thal-Chotiali Field Force, which succeeded in opening up the new route. It was in the course of the return journey that Colonel Fellowes was seized with the disease which proved fatal to him. The marches were very long, the heat was excessive, and there was often either an absence of water, or the water obtained was so bad as only to accelerate the disease. On the 6th April, 1879, at the urgent request of the surgeon of the regiment, General Biddulph allowed him to be left behind under a strong guard, in the hope that moving by easy stages might save his life; but it was not to be. At noon on the 9th of April, at a place called Kala

Chupri, in the Hun Pass, he quietly passed away, and the next day his body was carried on to Legari Barkhan, where the force had halted, and was buried the same evening with full military honours, every officer from the General downwards following it to the grave. Six commanding officers bore the pall—a Union Jack—and the service was read by Major Crookshank, 32nd Pioneers, amidst the tears of many of the men of the regiment, by whom their Colonel was greatly respected and beloved. A roughly carved cross was placed at the head of the grave, which was protected with large stones and planted with willows.

In his General Order of the 10th April, 1879, General Biddulph wrote that "He had not been closely connected with the regiment for five months without learning to appreciate the zeal, ability, and tact with which Lieut.-Colonel Fellowes discharged the onerous duties which from time to time devolved upon him; and he desired to place on record the high opinion he had formed of the gallant officer. By Colonel Fellowes' death, the 32nd Pioneers had sustained a deplorable loss, and General Biddulph in sympathizing with the corps, and his friends, recorded with deep regret that Her Majesty's Indian Army had been deprived of a good and faithful soldier, while he was to all appearance in the full vigour and usefulness of life;" and Major Crookshank, in his Regimental Order of the same date, paid the following tribute to his memory:—"Colonel Fellowes' high character, both professionally as a soldier, and socially as a Christian and a friend, soon secured for him the love and esteem of the officers of the regiment, who will long mourn the loss of a kind, self-denying, and sympathizing commanding officer and comrade."

LIEUT. T. O. FITZGERALD, STAFF CORPS,

27TH (PUNJAB) BENGAL N.I.

DESCENDED from a family whose name has from time immemorial been associated with the Army Service, a son of the late and brother of the present Knight of Glin, Thomas Otho Fitzgerald, the subject of this memoir, is not the first of his gallant race who has laid down his life at his country's call.

He was born at Glin Castle, co. Limerick, on the 23rd February, 1849, and after receiving his education at Kingstown School, entered Sandhurst. His course at the college was a notable one : not only did he display, as a smart under-officer, a special aptitude for his profession, and win a more than local reputation by his prowess in all kinds of athletic sports, but by his largeness of heart and the never-failing geniality of his ways he endeared himself to his contemporaries to an extent to which few before or after him have succeeded in doing; and it is not too much to say that there are few regimental ante-rooms in which his death is not mourned as that of a brother.

Quitting Sandhurst in 1869, he was gazetted, in the month of November of that year, to the 19th Foot; and in October, 1871, obtained his Lieutenancy. In due course he entered the Bengal Staff Corps, and was posted to the 27th Punjab Infantry, with which regiment he served continuously till the day of his death. For the Jowaki campaign of 1877-78, in which he took part throughout, he received the medal.

On the outbreak of hostilities with Afghanistan in the autumn of 1878, the 27th Punjab Native Infantry formed part of the 3rd Infantry Brigade, under Brigadier-General Appleyard's command, of the Khyber Field Force; and taking part with the regiment in the advance of the Division into the Khyber Pass, Fitzgerald was present in the direct attack on Ali Masjid, on the 21st November. As darkness was closing in on that day, some one hundred men of the 14th Sikhs under Captain Maclean, supported by seven companies of the Punjabis under Major Birch, were fighting their way up the steep slope, above which impended the Afghan left flank position, against the stone breastworks so obstinately held by the enemy—their advance enfiladed by a heavy artillery fire. A few moments before the order to retire was sounded, Captain Maclean had rushed forward with a handful of his men into a position in which he found himself in urgent need of support; and Major Birch, gallantly responding to his call for assistance, fell shot dead as he advanced to succour him, his companies being at the same time swept back by the hail of lead with which they were met from the breastworks. Fitzgerald's opportunity had now come; and with reference to one of his soldierly instincts it is superfluous to say that he availed himself of it.

The Afghan fire can only be described as murderous; but he would not have it that his chief's body should be left to the mercy of the enemy. Rushing forward with his gallant orderly, he succeeded in reaching and raising it. At this moment a bullet struck him in the wrist. With the characteristic remark, "Oh, that's nothing!" he lifted Major Birch's body in his arms, and carried it to a more sheltered spot. Laying it down, he was in the act of tying a handkerchief round his wounded arm when a second bullet struck him, passing through his chest, and killing him instantaneously. The Afghan fire was no more to be faced, and the bodies had to be left where they lay; on the morning of the morrow, however, they were recovered, both of them having been left untouched by the enemy. They were conveyed, by the General's orders, to Peshawar; and on the 24th November, 1879, were buried in the cemetery at that station with full military honours.

LIEUTENANT ST. J. W. FORBES,

92ND (GORDON HIGHLANDERS).

ST. JOHN WILLIAM FORBES was the third son of Lieut.-Colonel John Forbes and Lucy Georgina his wife, youngest daughter of Thomas Whitmore, Esq., of Apsley, Shropshire. He was born at Malvern Link on the 20th January, 1856, and was educated at Eton, where his father and mother resided. Passing direct from the college, he was gazetted in November, 1873, to the 72nd Highlanders; but a few weeks afterwards was transferred to the 92nd, which he joined at Multan early in 1874. During the brief span of his career in that distinguished regiment, he filled every appointment that a subaltern can hold—that of Adjutant, Quartermaster, Instructor of Musketry, and Interpreter. He went through the garrison course at Sialkot, and was in the first class; and while at home on leave in 1877 he obtained a first-class extra certificate at Hythe. In order that he might act as Adjutant to the detached wing of the 92nd at Benares, he returned to India before the expiration of his leave, and receiving the appointment, retained it till the regiment was reunited in December, 1878, in view of its departure on active service into Afghanistan. With reference to one of Forbes's enthusiastic temperament, with a love for his profession that was little less than a passion, it is superfluous to say that he threw himself heart and soul into the new sphere of activity which now presented itself. He took part in the advance of the regiment in the spring of 1879 to Ali Khel, where it joined the Advance Division of the Kuram Field Force. For two months he acted as Orderly Officer to Brigadier, now Major-General, Hamilton Forbes, and won the approbation of that distinguished officer by the zeal and energy with which he performed his new duties; and subsequently he acted for a short time in the same capacity to General Macpherson. During the battle of Charasiab, on the 6th October, in which the 92nd performed gallant service, the duties of the post of Acting Quartermaster which he held necessitated his remaining in camp; but he was present at the occupation of Kabul, and in the expedition to Maidan in November. It was during the operations of General Roberts' force which marked the close of the year, at the moment of crowning the summit of the Takht-i-Shah at the head of his breathless company on the 13th December, that he rendered up his life in a heroic personal attempt to save the body of his Colour-Sergeant (gallant James Drummond, who had fallen at his side) from mutilation. To the 92nd General Baker had given the post of honour on that day, viz., to lead the attack. The four companies of the regiment—two in advance, two in support—swept over half a mile of swamp at the double, under a heavy fire from the Beni Hissar spur. Barely waiting a moment at the base of the Takht-i-Shah to take breath, they commenced ascending the heights, the men straining every nerve to gain the crest before the enemy could collect in numbers to resist them. "Your son," writes one of Forbes's brother officers to Colonel Forbes, "was at this time leading his company in the most gallant manner, his company being then on the right. Before reaching the top we had lost our compact formation, as, owing to the extreme steepness of the ascent, many men were quite out of breath; and a few of the most active only, headed by your son, led the advance. On reaching the spur, without a moment's hesitation, your son, accompanied only by his Colour-Sergeant, with some eight or ten men behind, with the most determined bravery charged up the ridge where one of the enemy's standards was waving. Before he had gone far, Colour-Sergeant Drummond, a most gallant and splendid non-commissioned officer, fell shot through the body; and immediately several of the enemy, who had until this moment remained concealed, rushed down upon your son, who stood to defend his Colour-Sergeant, and give up his life in his defence. He was overpowered by numbers, not, however, before he had killed the first man who attacked him, and still fought bravely until he fell shot through the head." So runs the brief record. We have to turn elsewhere to ascertain how the gallant writer of the letter, with a few men of his company, himself avenged the death of his comrade, bayonetting or shooting down every man of the band of ten who had not fled.

The body of St. John Forbes was recovered, and buried on the morning of the 15th December, 1879, in the little cemetery within cantonments. "His character,"—to quote the words of a distinguished officer under whom he served—"does not end with his life, but remains an influence on the side of right and goodness, quickened into warmer life, in the hearts of all who valued him, by his gallant and noble death."

CAPTAIN ST. J. T. FROME,

72ND (DUKE OF ALBANY'S OWN HIGHLANDERS).

ST. JOHN THOMAS FROME, who was killed at the battle of Kandahar on the 1st September, 1880, was descended from the old Dorsetshire family of that name, and was the only son of General Frome, Colonel Commandant Royal Engineers, and Jane, his wife, daughter of the late Colonel Alexander Light, 25th King's Own Borderers.

He obtained his first commission in the 72nd as Ensign, by purchase, in 1861; became Lieutenant, also by purchase, in April, 1864; and obtained his company in April, 1872.

Captain Frome served with his regiment through the whole of the two Afghan campaigns. At the assault of the Peiwar Kotal he commanded the leading company of the 72nd, which was sent in advance to support the 5th Goorkhas, and for his services on this occasion was favourably mentioned in despatches. He was with the force at Ali Khel during the winter of 1878-79; in the subsequent advance upon Kabul; at the battle of Charasiab (for his conduct in which action he was again recommended); at the capture of Kabul; the occupation and defence of the Sherpur cantonments; in the memorable march from Kabul to Kandahar; and at the battle of the 1st September, in which he fell at the head of his company, when clearing the fortified enclosures covering Ayub Khan's position.

Sir Frederick Roberts, in his Field Force Order issued after the battle of Kandahar, speaks of Captain Frome as "a gallant and distinguished soldier"; and in his address to the 72nd and 92nd Highlanders, delivered on leaving for India, after paying a just tribute to the memory of Colonel Brownlow, late commanding the 72nd, he adds: "With him fell an equally gallant spirit, Captain Frome." Similar testimony is borne by his brother officers, by whom his loss as "a proved friend and true soldier" is sincerely regretted; and one of high rank, under whom he served during the Afghan campaign, thus writes of him:—"He was an excellent officer, and the coolness and gallantry with which he always led his company into action was the admiration of all who were ever with him under fire."

LIEUTENANT C. H. GAISFORD,

72ND (DUKE OF ALBANY'S OWN HIGHLANDERS).

CECIL HENRY GAISFORD, who fell in action before Kabul on the 14th December, 1879, was the eldest son of Lieut.-Colonel Gaisford, of The Grove, Dunboyne, late of the 72nd Highlanders. He was born at Galway on the 20th September, 1856, and was educated at Eton. Entering the army in September, 1876, he proceeded, twelve months afterwards, to India; and on the 30th November, 1877, joined, at Sialkot, the head-quarters of the 72nd Highlanders, his father's old regiment, to which he had been gazetted.

On the eve of the outbreak of the Afghan War, in the autumn of 1878, Gaisford was on detachment at Ranikhet in command of a company, his Captain having left for England. The responsible duty of marching his men and followers a distance of 500 miles to overtake the regiment, then en route for the front, consequently fell to him. He accomplished this in two months; and, joining the right wing, served with it in the whole of its subsequent operations till the day of his death. He was one of those who took part in the successful and gallant assault of the Peiwar Kotal on the 2nd December, 1878, which was carried in spite of the desperate resistance of the enemy; a few days afterwards he took part, with 250 of the 72nd, in General Roberts' reconnaissance to the Shutargardan; and on the 15th December he was present at the repulse of the Mangals in the Sapiri defile. During the spring and autumn of 1879 he acted as Adjutant to his regiment, and as Brigade Major at Ali Khel. On the renewal of hostilities, in September, 1879, he was again at the Shutargardan, in General Baker's Brigade; and at the battle of Charasiab, on the 6th October, was with the two companies of the 72nd when they so splendidly carried the Red Ridge, the enemy's right centre.

On the 14th December, 1879, Gaisford commanded one of the companies of his regiment, which, under Colonel Brownlow, stormed the Asmai heights. The operations on this occasion have been variously described, but all accounts agree that the capture of the highest peak by the 72nd and Guides was "splendid." Of this there can be no doubt, for it was in full view of Sherpur. It was in the evening of the same day, on the orderly retirement from the hill which had been so bravely won, that Gaisford received his death-wound. The awful suddenness of the shock could not, however, quell the gallantry of his spirit. Indicating his sword, he called on his comrades to take care of it, "because it was his father's."

"He died like a soldier, full of courage," wrote Colonel Brownlow, his Commanding Officer, in a letter to Colonel Gaisford. "I never saw anyone more cool or self-possessed under very trying circumstances. He was a most promising officer, and you already know I thought very highly of him. During the whole of the day and during the retirement, accomplished under the heavy fire of the enemy, he was hardly a moment out of my sight, and he could not have behaved better than he did"—testimony of his worth joined in by Major Stockwell, who wrote: "Under fire he was as brave as the best." It will perhaps not be out of place here to add that before he was eighteen years of age he had gained the Royal Humane Society's medal for gallantry in saving life, and that in his own home circle he was lovable and beloved, having ever a bright smile and a kindly word for all. The peasantry in the neighbourhood appreciated his rectitude so fully that his decision used invariably to be accepted as final in the adjustment of the little differences they were in the habit of referring to him.

Lieutenant Gaisford was buried with military honours in the cemetery near Sherpur, at the extreme west end of the Bemaru heights, where his comrades have placed a marble slab over his grave.

LIEUT.-COLONEL JAMES GALBRAITH,

66TH (BERKSHIRE) REGIMENT.

HE subject of this memoir was the fifth son of Samuel Galbraith, Esq., of Clanabogan, in the County of Tyrone, Ireland, and of Susannah Jane, his wife, daughter of the Rev. Robert Handcock, D.D., of Dublin and of Lacken, Co. Roscommon, and granddaughter of William Handcock, Esq., for many years M.P. for Athlone. In Burkes' "Landed Gentry" the Galbraiths of Clanabogan are stated to have been of Scotch descent, and to have settled in Ulster in the reign of Charles I.

Educated at home, James Galbraith passed his examination at Sandhurst for a commission in the Army, and was gazetted in December, 1851, to an Ensigncy, by purchase, in the 66th Regiment, with which gallant corps to the last his life was identified. He proceeded, on appointment, to the Depôt, then stationed in Guernsey; and after serving there for some eighteen months embarked for Canada to join the Head-quarters. While in that country he was promoted (June, 1854) to a Lieutenancy. The regiment was ordered home in the autumn of the same year, and a few months after its arrival in England was sent to Gibraltar. In the spring of 1855 Galbraith was sent home to the Depôt (which had been transferred to Leeds), to act as Paymaster and Quartermaster. In February, 1856, he obtained his company, by purchase.

Captain Galbraith sailed for the East Indies in the year 1857, with two companies of the regiment, under command of Major Benson, in H.M.S. "Gloriana," and joined the Head-quarters at Cannanor, where the 66th was stationed for over four years. For some part of this period he commanded a detachment at Calicut. Returning to England with the regiment for its term of home service, he did duty with it at Devonport, Aldershot, Guernsey, Jersey, the Curragh, and Dublin, and obtained while stationed in Ireland (August, 1869) his Majority.

On the regiment being ordered a second time to India, in 1870, Major Galbraith commanded a wing, during the voyage out, in one of Her Majesty's troopships; and three companies while stationed at Haidarabad, Sind. He subsequently commanded the regiment at Belgaum during parts of the years 1874 and 1875, and again at Haidarabad from the spring of 1879 till he succeeded to the permanent command at Karachi, in November, 1879. In the interval (October, 1877) he obtained his Brevet Lieutenant-Colonelcy.

In February, 1880, the 66th was ordered to Kandahar, and arrived there under his command on the 25th March, 1880, four days before the departure of the Bengal troops for Kabul under command of Sir Donald Stewart. Colonel Galbraith commanded the regiment on the 14th July, when the mutineers of the Wali's army were defeated near Girishk and his guns retaken. It was on the 27th July, 1880, on the fatal field of Maiwand, that he fell, fighting manfully against the overwhelming numbers of Ayub Khan's followers. "He was last seen," writes General Primrose in his despatch, "on the nullah bank, kneeling on one knee, with a colour in his hand, officers and men rallying round him." When the battle-field was revisited by the force under command of Brigadier-General Daubeny, in September, his body, and that of his old friend Captain McMath, were found together, with those of many of their gallant comrades.

Colonel Galbraith was a gallant soldier and a true friend. His even temper and calm judgment peculiarly fitted him for command; and those who served under him will ever respect and honour his memory.

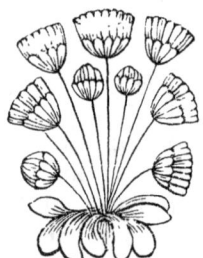

CAPTAIN J. H. GAMBLE,

1ST BATTALION 17TH (LEICESTERSHIRE) REGIMENT.

JOHN HENRY GAMBLE, who died at Landi Kotal, Afghanistan, on the 14th July, 1879, from illness contracted while on field service, was the eldest son of Clarke Gamble, Esq., Q.C., of Pinehurst, Toronto. He was educated at Upper Canada College and Cheltenham College, England, where he remained a student until July, 1860, when he proceeded to Sandhurst. Passing out of the Royal Military College after the usual course, he was gazetted, in July, 1862, to an Ensigncy in the 1st Battalion 17th Foot, which he shortly afterwards joined in Quebec, where it was then stationed. After returning with the battalion to England in 1864, he was promoted, in September, 1865, to a Lieutenancy, and subsequently served with the 2nd Battalion of the regiment in Jamaica, Canada, England, and Ireland. On the 2nd Battalion being ordered to India in the spring of 1877, he remained for duty at the Depôt, but in the autumn rejoined Headquarters at Mhow; almost immediately afterwards, however (November, 1877), he was gazetted to a company in the 1st Battalion, then in cantonment at Murree, and immediately rejoined his old friends at that station.

On the outbreak of hostilities with Afghanistan in the autumn of 1878, Captain Gamble took part, in command of his company, in the advance of the battalion into the enemy's country and in the operations which ensued; was present with it in the flank march over Rhotas heights in reverse of Ali Musjid, 20th to 22nd November, 1878; the affairs at Chinar, 9th and 10th December; the first and second Bazar Valley expeditions; and the affairs at Maidanah, 18th to 21st March, 1879. After the signing of the treaty of peace at Gandamak, the battalion retraced its steps from the advanced position of Safed Sang, where it was at the time stationed, to Landi Kotal, where it arrived, with its ranks sadly thinned by disease, after a most trying march. The situation of the camp was very unhealthy, the heat intense, and the water supply bad and difficult of access. Cholera and fever broke out among the troops; and day after day the number of victims increased, till it was found necessary to shift the camp. The new position was found to be a little cooler. "After the heat we have had," wrote Captain Gamble in one of his letters, "92° feels delicious." During the march he had been greatly weakened by an attack of dysentery. In the last letter he wrote (bearing date 4th July, 1879), he spoke cheerfully of his condition; but four days afterwards, on the 9th, a renewed attack completely prostrated him. Worn out with fatigue and anxiety, he now sank rapidly, and on the 14th of the month passed away peacefully, amid the deep regrets of his brother officers and the men of the regiment, by all of whom he was greatly beloved.

Captain Gamble was a man of singular sweetness and gentleness of disposition, who attracted towards him all who knew him, and bound them to him by such tender cords that he never lost a friend or made an enemy. We may fittingly close this brief notice with extracts from two regimental orders issued on the occasion of his death, which will serve to show the esteem in which he was held by the Commanding Officers under whom he served. In the first, which bears date Landi Kotal, 15th July, 1879, these words occur:—"He (Captain Gamble) was a most able officer, zealous and conscientious in the performance of his duties, and a good friend to all, in whatever position they might be. In the death of Captain Gamble the 17th Regiment loses an officer whom it will be hard to replace, and the Commanding Officer feels sure that every man in the regiment joins in mourning the loss sustained." The second Order, publishing a memorandum received from Colonel (Brigadier-General) Cobbe, bearing date 2nd August, 1879, is as follows:—"It is with feelings of the deepest sorrow that Colonel (Brigadier-General) Cobbe has heard of the death of Captain Gamble, of the 1st Battalion, at Landi Kotal. Although this officer has only served for some few months under Colonel Cobbe's immediate command, the period was quite sufficient to enable him to form a most high estimate of his character and capabilities, and to appreciate his value as a most useful and excellent officer, and for whom he had contracted a strong personal friendship. Colonel Cobbe requests the officer commanding the battalion to allow this memorandum to be published in Regimental Orders, as a record of his personal feelings, as well as his sympathy with the officers and soldiers of the 1st Battalion 17th Regiment, at the sad loss sustained by them all in the death of Captain Gamble."

CAPTAIN E. S. GARRATT,

66TH (BERKSHIRE) REGIMENT.

ERNEST STEPHEN GARRATT was the eldest son of the Reverend Samuel Garratt, Honorary Canon of Norwich, and Vicar of St. Margaret's, Ipswich, and Lœtitia Sarah Bathsua, his wife, daughter of the Reverend Bowater James Vernon, who was Senior Chaplain to the Forces in St. Helena at the time of the death of the Emperor Napoleon I., when the 66th Regiment happened to be stationed in the island.

The subject of this memoir was born on the 28th September, 1845, and was educated at Marlborough, and under private tutors at Geneva and elsewhere. In 1865, when nineteen years old, he obtained a direct commission as Ensign in the 66th Regiment, then lately returned from India. In July, 1867, he became Lieutenant; and during the five years the regiment was on home service, was quartered at Aldershot, the Channel Islands, Plymouth, and the Curragh. He embarked with the regiment in the spring of 1870, on its again being ordered to India, and obtained his company while on the voyage out.

General Barclay, formerly Lieutenant-Colonel of the 66th, giving the opinion he formed of him during the period of his Indian service, writes: "I first made his acquaintance at Belgaum in 1875; he was then in command of a detachment at the fort, and I was much struck, on inspecting his company, with the thoughtful manner in which all arrangements for the comfort of his men were carried out. No care or even expense was spared. His company, from his Colour-Sergeant to the youngest soldier, would have done anything for him." And a brother officer, who lived on terms of great intimacy with him, writes: "One thing which always struck me about him was his great kindness of heart. I never remember to have heard him speak a harsh or unkind word of anybody, and if a disparaging word was said of anyone in his presence, he would always put in a kind word for the subject of the remarks." It is perhaps worthy of mention, too, that during this period of his service he nursed his brother officer, Captain McMath, through a long and dangerous illness—the result of an encounter with a wounded panther—and was instrumental, as his patient was wont to affirm, in saving his life.

After serving for some years at various stations in Bombay, he returned on leave to England, married, and rejoined the regiment at Ahmadnagar; and after another voyage home, where he held for eighteen months an appointment at the Depôt, at Reading, was once more ordered to India in the autumn of 1879, three months before the departure of the 66th from Karachi to Kandahar.

While at Kandahar he was very much occupied with experiments in telegraphy. "He was a first-rate electrician," writes Lieutenant Hamilton, of the 2nd Queen's, Aide-de-Camp to General Primrose, to whose quarters Garratt was in the habit of resorting to test his telephones; and the General himself says: "I have always heard him spoken of in high terms by those who knew him; and I was particularly struck with the amount of intelligence he always displayed. He was considered a very good officer, and scientific in his pursuits, which made itself prominent by his knowledge and practice of telegraphy and the telephone."

"We are all like brothers," is one of his own expressions in a letter written at this period to his wife respecting the officers in the regiment, between whom and himself there evidently existed a very strong feeling of friendship—the more pleasant to think of, since "in their deaths they were not divided." Before this letter closed, the action with the Wali's troops, near Girishk, had taken place. After describing the pursuit and capture of the guns, he continues: "Then, as the enemy still held the valley to which they had retreated, we were ordered to clear it; and in this three of our men were wounded badly. One or two shots came so close to me that my horse shied"—he was senior Captain on active service, and doing Field Officer's duty—"and nearly threw me, as I was acting galloper between the General and the Regiment."

A fortnight afterwards, on the 27th July, 1880, the battle of Maiwand was fought. "When they were surrounded at the end," writes one of the officers of the 66th, in a private letter, "he turned the rear-rank of his company about to fire to the rear as well as to the front." His death took place when the regiment was retiring to the garden where the last stand was made. One of the men of his company gives the following particulars:—"I saw Captain Garratt fall. I stopped to see if I could render him any assistance. I then noticed that he had a bullet wound between the temple and the jaw bone, and that his eyes were closed. I raised his arm and found that he was dead." And General Primrose, making reference to him and his brother officer, Captain Cullen, in his letter to the Adjutant-General, published in the "Gazette" of the 31st December, 1880, tells how they "were both killed on the field in front of the nullah, up to the last moment commanding their companies and giving their orders with as much coolness as if on ordinary regimental parade."

A large pile of stones marks the place where the Afghans themselves buried those whom they found dead on the field. There his body lies with the rest of those with whom he fell. The burial-place of the 66th was left undisturbed by either friend or foe.

CAPTAIN F. T. GOAD, STAFF CORPS,

5TH INFANTRY REGIMENT, HAIDARABAD CONTINGENT.

REDERICK THEOPHILUS GOAD, who received his death-wound in the Mangior Pass, Kuram Valley, on the 13th December, 1878, was the second son of Major Samuel Boileau Goad, 3rd Bengal Cavalry, and of his wife Emma Gordon, daughter of John Leith Davidson, Esq. He was born on the 25th August; 1842, at Simla, and after receiving his education in England was gazetted, on the 12th March, 1861, to H.M. 72nd Highlanders. Joining that regiment in Bengal, he did duty with it at various stations in the Presidency until it was ordered home, when, being anxious to prolong his Indian service, he exchanged into the 45th Foot. He subsequently accompanied that corps to Abyssinia, and, serving with it throughout the campaign, was present at the storming and capture of Magdala, for which he received the medal and clasp, and was also highly commended by Lord Napier for the zealous and most useful service rendered by him in the Transport Department, in which he had been specially selected to serve at a time when Transport officers were much needed.

In 1865 he passed second out of seventy-two in the competitive examination for the Bengal Staff Corps, Two years afterwards he returned to England, and while in this country underwent a course of training at the School of Musketry at Hythe, where he came out with an extra first-class certificate, also winning, as the best shot in the right wing, a handsome silver cup. He was in the Haidarabad Contingent when he obtained his company in August, 1873, and was second in command of the 5th Infantry Regiment in the contingent when he volunteered for the Transport service at the opening of the Afghan War.

Captain Goad was at once detailed for service to the Kuram Valley Field Force, in connection with which he rendered, according to the testimony of the General, most valuable aid in the difficult task of organizing the Transport trains. It was in the march of the brigade of troops under Sir Frederick Roberts from Ali Khel to Fort Kuram in December, 1878, while in charge of the long baggage train which was treacherously attacked by a horde of Mangals, that he received his mortal wound. The incident is thus related by the "Standard" correspondent :—

"Captain Goad was marching along at the head of a long string of camels, which were attended by five soldiers of the 72nd Highlanders, besides their own drivers. Suddenly there came round the rock, close to the road in the defile, a band of some one hundred Mangals. The Highlanders mistrusted them and wanted to fire, but they put up their hands and signalled they were friendly, whereupon Captain Goad told the soldiers to lower their rifles. The Mangals came within thirty yards. They saw an immense number of camels and a quantity of baggage defended by only half-a-dozen men. The temptation was too great for them. With extraordinary rapidity they unslung their guns from their backs and commenced to fire. Captain Goad was the first to fall. He was hit by a ball delivered from a long bell-mounted gun. The ball went through his sword and penetrated both thighs a little above the knee. The charge in the blunderbuss must have been enormous. Four Highlanders stood round him where he lay, the fifth ran back to tell the 5th Goorkhas to come on. These four men stood shoulder to shoulder and again and again repulsed the shrieking Mangals, who could not stand the terrible fire of the breechloaders.

"Even poor Goad lying on the ground with his legs shattered gave the Mangals three shots from his revolver, at the same time encouraging the men to stand firm. At last the 5th Goorkhas came up, but not before the four brave fellows had shot away every round of their seventy cartridges. Even on his death-bed Goad remembered with gratitude the generous bravery of the four soldiers who stood round him and defied a Mangal to touch him."

On the following day, the 14th, Captain Goad's left leg was amputated. The hope that the operation might save his life proved, however, futile; he rapidly sank, and died a few hours afterwards. His remains were buried close to the Kuram Fort, being followed to the grave by a large number of officers, including the General and his staff.

The following is an extract from Sir Frederick Roberts' despatch of the 18th December, 1878:—

"It was about this time that Captain Goad, who had been most active in keeping order in the baggage train, received the wound from the effects of which, I deeply regret to say, he subsequently died. I desire to record the high value which I had placed on the services of this officer.

"Belonging to the 5th Infantry of the Haidarabad Contingent, Captain Goad volunteered for active service, and owing to his experience of Transport work, and to his natural ability, he had already rendered most valuable aid in the difficult task of organizing the transport trains. I much deplore his death, both personally, and on account of the loss which the public service has sustained."

A thorough soldier, ready to undergo any fatigue or hardship, self-sacrificing to a degree, Captain Goad was greatly beloved by all who knew him. His love of sport was little less than a passion, and much to his amusement caused him to be alluded to in the Indian journals on more than one occasion as "The Nimrod of the Deccan." He was a good linguist, speaking Hindustani in several dialects with ease and fluency.

The deceased officer married, in July, 1877, Katherine, daughter of the late Robinson Elsdale, Esq., of Moulton, Lincolnshire, and it was during the enforced absence of his wife, sent home with fever, that he volunteered for the campaign. He leaves one son, an infant two months old at the time of his death.

MAJOR JOHN GODSON, MADRAS STAFF CORPS,

4TH MADRAS NATIVE INFANTRY.

HE subject of this notice, who died on the 25th December, 1880, from illness contracted while on service in Afghanistan, was born in London on the 11th December, 1834. Passing, after due preparation, the examination for an Indian cadetship, he entered the service in his twenty-first year. Gazetted to an Ensigncy in the 52nd Regiment N.I. in July, 1855, he immediately proceeded to India, and joined that regiment at the latter end of the September following. Twelve months afterwards he obtained his Lieutenancy. He performed regimental duty, at various stations, from September, 1855, till January, 1863, at the expiration of which interval he was given the charge of pensioners and payments at Vizagapatam and Vizianagarum—an appointment he continued to hold for upwards of ten years. During this period he entered the Madras Staff Corps, and was promoted (July, 1867) to the rank of Captain.

Reverting to regimental duty in August, 1873, Captain Godson was attached for some time to the 12th Madras N.I. In July, 1875, he obtained his Majority, and was transferred to the 4th Madras N.I., with which regiment—holding successively the appointments of Officiating Wing Commander, Wing Commander, Officiating Second in Command and Wing Commander, and Second in Command and Wing Commander—he served continuously till the day of his death.

On the formation of the Madras Brigade for field service, after the renewal of hostilities with Afghanistan in the autumn of 1879, Major Godson accompanied his regiment, which was detailed to the Khyber Line Force, to Peshawar, and advancing with it into the Pass, shared with it at Ali Musjid, and eventually at Jalalabad and Safed Sang, the various duties which fell to its lot. Commanding a detachment of 100 rank and file, he took part in the expedition under Colonel Hodding, 4th Madras N.I., which proceeded on the 26th March, 1880, from Jalalabad to Lachipur to support the British nominee for the government of the district against a threatened attack, and returned on the 31st idem. In April, 1880, he was given the command of Fort Battye, and retained the appointment for a period of six weeks. He also took part in the operations in Kamah in the early days of June, commanding the detachment of the regiment which was engaged.

During the term of service of the 4th Madras N.I. in Northern Afghanistan, Major Godson's duties were frequently of a trying nature, entailing protracted exposure to the vicissitudes of the climate and considerable privation; and towards the latter end of the war his health began to fail him. After the conclusion of hostilities and the evacuation of the northern line, the regiment was moved down country to Bangalore. This station Major Godson reached only to die. In the forty-sixth year of his age, on Christmas Day, the 25th December, 1880, he fell a victim to the rigours of the recent campaign, deeply regretted not only by his brother officers and the men of his regiment, amongst whom he left a high reputation for every manly quality, but also by a wide circle of private friends who held him dear.

THE REV. G. M. GORDON, M.A.,

CHURCH MISSIONARY SOCIETY.

GEORGE MAXWELL GORDON, second and youngest son of the late Captain J. E. Gordon, R.N., M.P. for Dundalk, of Hadlow Park, Tonbridge, and of Barbara, youngest daughter of the late Samuel Smith, Esq., M.P., of Woodhall Park, Herts, was born in 1838. After receiving a private education, he graduated at Trinity College, Cambridge. He was then ordained. After holding two curacies, he offered his services to the Church Missionary Society in 1866, and remained a missionary at his own cost for a period of fifteen years, until his death. The following particulars of his missionary work have been supplied by the Editorial Secretary of the Society for this notice.

In 1867 Mr. Gordon went to Madras to join the Itinerant Mission which had been started by the late Rev. D. Fenn among the villages surrounding that city, and living in tents, travelled continually from place to place. His health breaking down, he took a voyage to Australia to recruit it. Returning to India, he resumed his itinerations in Madras. Subsequently, when in this country, he was offered, and declined, an Australian bishopric.

In 1871, travelling through Persia *en route* to India, on missionary work, he proceeded to the Punjab, and joining the Rev. T. V. French, now Bishop of Lahore, assisted him in establishing the Divinity College at Lahore, where he continued to work till 1874. He then set up an Itinerant Mission in connection with that College on the banks of the Jhelum, with Pind Dadan Khan as centre. His zeal and self-denial in the years that followed are described by General Maclagan in a contribution to the "Church Missionary Intelligencer" for October, 1880.

In 1876 he visited Dera Ghazi Khan, on the Indus, and established, at his own expense, a mission among the Baluch tribes within the British frontier.

Meanwhile, the Afghan War broke out, and Mr. Gordon volunteered to act as Chaplain to the force under General Sir Michael Biddulph, K.C.B. He proceeded with it to Quetta, and thence to Kandahar, in the winter of 1878-79. Returning to the Punjab, he resumed charge of the Church Missionary Society's stations at Pind Dadan Khan and Dera Ghazi Khan. Then he accompanied Bishop French to Quetta, and again joined the Forces as Chaplain at Kandahar, where he did good work among the soldiers in the citadel, and was most constant in his attention to the sick and wounded in hospital. He fell in the disastrous sortie on the 16th August, 1880. The event is thus described by an eye-witness, his fellow Chaplain, the Rev. A. G. Cane:—

"On that morning he was in the hospital, seeing the wounded as they were brought in. About 7 a.m. he left the hospital, and went to the Kabul Gate. There he heard that a number of wounded lay in a ziaret, some 400 yards from the walls. He was incorrectly informed that no one would venture out to bring them in, since four officers had already gone out there. Mr. Gordon, accompanied by Major Adam, at once set out with a dhoolie and bearers for the ziaret; they were under a most galling fire from both flanks, and as Mr. Gordon stood in the doorway of the little hut, a bullet from the village of Kairabad pierced his arm and entered his side, and the dhoolie which he took out brought him in. He suffered considerably in the morning, but about 3.30 passed away quietly, as if in sleep. He was buried the same evening along with several officers and men in a little cemetery within the city walls, and now rests, as he would have wished, beside those to whom he had faithfully ministered and amongst whom he fell."

SURGEON H. A. C. GRAY, M.B., C.M.,

BENGAL MEDICAL DEPARTMENT.

HENRY ALFRED CHATHAM GRAY, who died of cholera on the 4th July, 1879, at Peshawar, on the return march of troops from Afghanistan, was the eldest son of Honorary Surgeon Daniel Henry Gray, of the Madras Medical Establishment, and was born at Mercara, in Coorg, on the 23rd October, 1849. After receiving private tuition from his father, he entered Bishop Corrie's Grammar School in Madras, and subsequently, in 1866, matriculated at the University. A few months afterwards he obtained a Government Scholarship in the Madras Medical College, where—having abandoned, under the circumstance, his intention of continuing his University course—he commenced his studies in October 1867. In the following year he passed his Preliminary Scientific examinations, and two years later, the first examination for M.B. and C.M. Having, however, a predilection for the higher branches of medical science, he resolved to prosecute and complete his studies in an English university, with the view of obtaining a commission in the Indian Medical Service; and proceeding to England in May, 1871, in medical charge of a passenger ship, was enrolled shortly after his arrival as a medical student in the Edinburgh University. Here he distinguished himself by obtaining first-class honours in medical subjects; and in August, 1873, took his degree. During his collegiate career he devoted his leisure hours to the study of science and general literature, and published a poem which has been favourably reviewed by the Press in Scotland and Madras. After leaving the University, he officiated for a time, for friends, at Scarborough, Melrose, and other places.

In August, 1874, he obtained a commission in the Indian Medical Service, passing sixth in the list of successful candidates; and in October proceeded to Netley. In February, 1875, he was found qualified, and in the following May arrived at Calcutta, where he was employed in the Presidency General Hospital, and with the 25th Bengal Native Infantry. He was ordered to assume medical charge of the 18th Bengal Native Infantry at Agra in October, and a month afterwards marched with the regiment to Baxar Dewar. Summoned to England on urgent private affairs in the spring of 1876, he took six months' leave, at the expiration of which period he returned to Bengal, and was ordered to proceed in medical charge of convicts to Port Blair. On completion of this duty he went back, in December, 1876, to Calcutta.

The Madras Presidency being threatened at this time with a severe famine, Gray volunteered his services. On arriving in Madras in April, 1877, he was appointed Sanitary Medical Officer of the Chingleput district; his duties, which included the inspection of the villages and the direction of the medical and sanitary arrangements of the relief camps, involving much travelling and a considerable amount of exposure and hardship. He was subsequently ordered to the Karnul districts, and while there contracted malarial fever. His services in the famine campaign ranged over a period of eighteen months.

In October, 1878, in view of the impending Afghan War, he was recalled to Bengal, and was detailed for service to Sir Sam. Browne's Division. In the course of the campaign he had charge of the Native Field Hospital at Ali Musjid, and did valuable work at Dakka, Jalalabad, Safed Sang, and Gandamak, receiving the commendation of the principal medical officers under whom he served for his energy and for his attention to the sick under his care. It was on the return march of the troops to Bengal, at Peshawar, that he was seized with cholera; and his strength having been exhausted by his recent severe work, he succumbed almost immediately to the disease.

The Commander-in-Chief, in placing on record his appreciation of the valuable services rendered to the Army by the Medical Department mentions the subject of this memoir by name.

Mr. Gray was a frequent contributor to the " Indian Medical Gazette " and other scientific journals. By his untimely death the Madras Medical College lost one of its ablest and most distinguished students.

LIEUT. W. R. P. HAMILTON, V.C., STAFF CORPS,

QUEEN'S OWN CORPS OF GUIDES.

E had a brilliant career before him; he understood well the business in which he was engaged, and he was not afraid of the consequences which his duty entailed upon him." Such were the words used by Viscount Cranbrook, Secretary of State for India, with reference to the subject of this memoir in announcing to the House of Lords the disaster which had overtaken the Kabul Embassy.

Walter Richard Pollock Hamilton was the fourth son of Alexander Hamilton, Esquire, J.P., of Inistioge, Ireland, and Emma his wife, daughter of the late Right Hon. Sir Frederick Pollock, Bart., for twenty-two years Lord Chief Baron of Her Majesty's Court of Exchequer; and was great grandson of the Right Rev. Hugh Hamilton, D.D., Lord Bishop of Ossory. He was born on the 18th August, 1856, and was educated at Eagle House, Wimbledon, and Felsted School, Essex. In January, 1874, he obtained twenty-first place in the open examination for the Army, and was gazetted to the 70th Regiment. After serving for a few months at the Depôt, he embarked for India in October, 1874, and on arriving, joined the Head-quarters at Rawal Pindi.

On obtaining his Lieutenancy, Hamilton was offered, and accepted, a commission in the Corps of Guides. Within three months of joining that distinguished regiment, he passed the higher standard examination in languages, and was detailed to the Cavalry. Throughout the Jowaki-Afridi expedition of 1877-8 under General Keyes, he served as Aide-de-Camp to the commanding officer; and on the 14th March, 1878, was present at the operations against the Ranizai village of Skhakat.

In October, 1878, in view of the impending hostilities with Afghanistan, the Corps of Guides was moved to Jamrud at the mouth of the Khyber, and for a period of six weeks was employed in reconnoitering the mountains about the Pass. In the first of the two campaigns which followed, Hamilton participated throughout with the cavalry of the corps in the heavy work which fell to its lot. He was present in the front attack at the capture of Ali Musjid. In March, 1879, he commanded a troop on escort duty with a surveying party under Lieutenant Leach, R.E., which succeeded in beating off an attack of the Shinwari tribe. Taking part, in the last days of March, 1879, in the advance of General C. Gough's Brigade to Futtehabad, he was present at the engagement in that place—in which his dear and gallant friend Wigram Battye met his death—on the 2nd April; and his heroic bravery on the occasion won for him the Victoria Cross. The record which appears against his name in the "London Gazette" announcing Her Majesty's intention to bestow the decoration runs as follows :—" For conspicuous gallantry during the action . . . . in leading on the Guide Cavalry in a charge against very superior numbers of the enemy, and particularly at a critical moment when his Commanding Officer (Major Wigram Battye) fell, Lieutenant Hamilton, then the only officer left with the regiment, assumed command and cheered on his men to avenge Major Battye's death. In this charge Lieutenant Hamilton, seeing Sowar Dowlut Ram down, and attacked by three of the enemy whilst entangled with his horse (which had been killed), rushed to the rescue, and followed by a few of his men, cut down all three, and saved the life of Sowar Dowlut Ram." A few days after the action he marched with the Head-quarters of the corps to Gandamak, and was one of the officers who subsequently escorted Yakub Khan into the British Camp.

When it was determined to send an Embassy to Kabul, and Sir Louis Cavagnari was selected to act as Minister and Plenipotentiary, he chose Lieutenant Hamilton to accompany him as Political Assistant, as well as to command his escort of seventy-five men of the Corps of Guides. As is related elsewhere, the entire Embassy and escort, with the exception of one or two members of the latter, were foully massacred after a six weeks' residence in the capital, on the 3rd September, 1879. That portion of the official account of the tragedy which refers to the subject of this memoir states, "that at his final charge to silence a gun, which he did silence, Lieutenant Hamilton fell where he said he would fall, killing on his way to inevitable death three men with his pistol and two with his sword." Thus ended the brief career of as gallant a young officer as ever held Her Majesty's commission, regretted with a deep regret—which found expression in the words of his Sovereign, of Cabinet Ministers, and of the heads of the British and Indian Armies—as a loss to the service and the country.

We close this notice with some lines—dealing with a subject which, by a strange fatality, was on the eve of recurrence—penned by Walter Hamilton late in August, and posted by him eight days before the massacre of the Embassy took place :—

THE VILLAGE BÉHMARU: SCENE OF THE OUTBREAK OF THE KABUL DISASTER, 1841.

REVISITED, AUGUST, 1879.

    Though all is changed, yet remnants of the past
      Point to the scenes of bloodshed, and alas!
    Of murder foul; and ruined houses cast
      Their mournful shadow o'er the graves of grass
    Of England's soldiery, who faced a lot
      That few, thank heaven! before or since have shared;
    Slain by the hand of treachery, and not
      In open combat, where the foe ne'er dared

To show themselves. The fatal, honest trust
   Placed in an enemy who loved a lie,
And knew not honour, was a trust that cost
   The lives of those that gave it. Yet to die
Game to the last, as they did, well upheld
   Their English name. E'en now their former foe
Frankly avers the British arms were quelled
   By numbers only, and the cruel snow.
'Tis forty years since British soldiers turn'd
   To look their last on this now peaceful scene,
Whose lingering gaze spoke volumes as it yearn'd
   For vengeance due to treachery so mean.
And vengeance true did Pollock, Sale, and Nott
   Deal with a timely and unerring hand,
As they with victory effaced the blot
   Which just had dimmed the annals of our land.
And now while standing here, where side by side
   Fell many fighting with a fruitless bent,
Regret were uppermost, were't not for pride
   Which gives no place for weaker sentiment.
And Pride might well be foremost if one thought
   That though fair Fortune smiled not for a while,
How England's fame shone brighter as she fought,
   And wrench'd lost laurels from their funeral pile,
And rose at last from out misfortune's tide
Supreme—for God and right were on her side.

LIEUTENANT EDWARD HARDY,

ROYAL HORSE ARTILLERY.

HE subject of this memoir, who was killed in the action in the Chardeh Valley, near Kabul, on the 11th December, 1879, was the youngest son of the Rev. Charles Hardy, Vicar of Hayling Island, Hampshire. He was born on the 25th July, 1853; was educated at Blundell's School, Tiverton; and after a short preparation with Mr. Frost of South Kensington, passed into the Royal Military Academy, Woolwich, as Cadet, in January, 1872. He received his commission as Lieutenant in October, 1873. In 1874 he joined Battery G/3 Royal Artillery, then serving in India. During a severe epidemic of cholera which subsequently occurred, Hardy, as senior subaltern, was commanding the battery, owing to the illness of his senior officer. Writing of his conduct at this trying time, Captain Rooke says: "He threw all his heart into attending to the amusements and welfare of his men. We were camped out during the rainy season, and if he had been an officer of long standing in the service, he could not possibly have carried out the work better than he did." He returned to England on sick leave in 1876, and early in 1877 was appointed to the Depôt at Sheffield. Subsequently he was appointed to Battery H/6 Royal Artillery: and in October, 1878, went again to India, and was stationed at Lucknow. In the following spring, having volunteered for active service, he was appointed to Battery F/A, Royal Horse Artillery, then with the force under General Sir F. Roberts in Afghanistan. Accompanying the battery over the difficult Shutargardan Pass on the second outbreak of hostilities, he was present with it in October, 1879, at the occupation of Kabul.

On the 11th December, as subaltern to Major Smith Windham, Hardy was ordered out with four guns of the battery, escorted by two squadrons 9th Lancers and one squadron 14th Bengal Lancers, the whole under General Massy, to join General Macpherson on the Ghazni road; the object being for the two brigades to make a combined attack upon the Kohistanis who were reported to be assembling in force. Before, however, this movement could be effected, the enemy attacked the small force in overwhelming numbers, and owing to the swampy nature of the ground the guns got into difficulties. In spite of two desperate charges made by the cavalry, the enemy pressed on with great determination, and finally closed upon the guns, which were now abandoned and fell into their hands. Hardy was killed on the last gun, which was some distance behind the others, and on the limber of which lay a wounded officer of the 14th Bengal Lancers, who had been made over to his charge, and whom he refused to desert. This officer—Lieutenant Forbes—twice wounded before, had again been hit after he had been placed on the gun, and was now perfectly helpless. Hardy was last seen standing over him, surrounded by the enemy and using his revolver. The revolver was found, some days afterwards, near the spot, with three barrels still undischarged, and with the steel extracting-rod completely severed by a sword-cut; showing that the enemy had closed upon him, as he nobly stood his ground to defend his wounded comrade.

Under the heading "Martyrs to Duty," mention is made of Lieutenant Hardy's death in Major Mitford's book, "To Kabul with the Cavalry Brigade." After describing incidents of the action, the writer continues as follows : "Shortly afterwards, the guns took a wrong turning, and some delay occurred, during which the enemy swarmed down in overwhelming numbers. The drivers cut the traces, and one of the men called to Hardy to gallop away with them, but the gallant young fellow said, 'No! I won't desert my guns; besides, I can't leave that youngster' (alluding to Forbes). So they both met their deaths."

Lieutenant Hardy was buried with military honours in the Bemaru cemetery on the 31st December, and a wooden cross, erected by his brother officers, marks his grave.

His Commanding Officer, writing to announce his death, expresses "The great sympathy of the battery and deep regret at the loss they had sustained : also their admiration of one who died after fighting his guns very manfully under most trying circumstances."

The deceased officer married, in February, 1878, Emma Lennard, only daughter of Henry Downes, Esq., of Tiverton, Devon, who survives him.

SUB-LIEUTENANT F. H. HARFORD,

10TH (P.W.O. ROYAL) HUSSARS.

FRANCIS HARVEY HARFORD, who was drowned in the Kabul River on the night of the 31st March, 1879, was the second son of William Henry Harford, Esq., D.L., J.P., of Barley Wood, Somersetshire, and Old Down, Gloucestershire, and was godson and nephew in the maternal line of the late Lieut.-Colonel Harvey Tower, of the Coldstream Guards.

The subject of this notice was born in March, 1858, and having passed his early years at Laurence Weston, entered Winchester in 1871. Leaving the college in December, 1873, he proceeded to Bonn to study under Dr. Perry for Sandhurst, having been destined from his earliest youth for the Army. In 1876, before he had attained eighteen years of age, he succeeded in passing with credit the entrance examination for Sandhurst, obtaining full marks for German, in which language he was proficient. Addicted to all manly pursuits, he approved himself while at the college a keen sportsman and an accomplished hand at polo, for which game he retained his fondness to the last, being engaged in a match at Jalalabad only a few hours before his death.

Passing out from Sandhurst in 1877 in the first class, he was gazetted to the 16th Foot, then serving in Ireland. It was but for a short time, however, that he did duty with his first regiment; H.R.H. the Prince of Wales conferring on him an appointment to the 10th Hussars, then serving in India, he was transferred to that corps in October, 1877.

He left England in the following December, and joined the Head-quarters at Rawal Pindi. On the outbreak of the Afghan War in the autumn of 1878, he accompanied the regiment into the Khyber, and was present with it, on the 21st November, at the taking of Ali Musjid.

During the events which immediately succeeded, the 10th Hussars were stationed at Jalalabad. It was in the neighbourhood of this post, in the accident which consigned in the space of a few moments forty-six men of the regiment to one common grave, that Harford met his death. Forming one of the ill-fated squadron which was told off to accompany the force directed to co-operate with General

Macpherson's column in the second Lughman Valley expedition, he was swept away with the rest of the squadron, during the night of the 31st March, 1879, in the disastrous fording of the Kabul River at Kala-i-Sak, and was one of those found missing when the roll was called after the accident. On the 4th April his body was found lying untouched, and was buried with military honours on the evening of the same day, the General and all the officers in garrison following it to its last resting-place.

Few young soldiers have gone to an early grave more deeply regretted than the gallant but ill-fated subject of this brief memoir. His life was one of the finest promise, and there are none who knew him who could doubt that that promise would have been fulfilled to the utmost had he lived.

LIEUTENANT C. J. R. HEARSEY,

9TH (QUEEN'S ROYAL) LANCERS.

CHARLES JOHN RUMBALL HEARSEY, who was killed in action in the neighbourhood of Kabul on the 11th December, 1879, was the eldest son of the late Sir John Bennet Hearsey, K.C.B., by his marriage with Emma, daughter of Charles Rumball, Esq. He was born at Sialkot in the Punjab on the 7th February, 1856, and was educated at Boulogne, under the Rev. J. Bewsher, and at Ockbrook, Derbyshire, under the Rev. Joseph Jackson Shawe. In 1875 he entered the Army with an Indian Cadetship, and shortly afterwards joined the 9th Lancers, then serving in Bengal.

Immediately prior to the outbreak of hostilities with Afghanistan in the autumn of 1878, Hearsay proceeded with his regiment to Taru, on its being ordered up into the neighbourhood of Peshawar to form part of the Reserve Division. He subsequently accompanied the head-quarters and two squadrons which, under Colonel Cleland, were moved into the Khyber in the spring of 1879, on the forward concentration of the Northern Division of the Army of Invasion, sharing, at various stations in the Pass, the duties which fell to their lot, and returning with them into British territory after the signing of the treaty of peace at Gandamak. On the second outbreak of hostilities, in September, 1879, he served in the regiment in the force under Sir Frederick Roberts, taking part in the advance of the 2nd Division on Kabul, and being present at the operations in the second week in December. In the action of Killa Kazi on the 11th December, while gallantly charging with his troop against overwhelming numbers of the enemy, in the desperate effort made by the Lancers to save the surrounded guns, he fell shot through the heart. His body was subsequently recovered, and with that of his brother officer Ricardo, was buried with military honours in the cemetery at Sherpur.

The cool self-possession with which young Hearsey rode to almost certain death is of itself evidence of the fact that he was not wanting in one at least of the soldierly qualities which distinguished his late gallant father.

CAPTAIN P. C. HEATH, STAFF CORPS,

BRIGADE MAJOR, KANDAHAR FIELD FORCE.

PERCY CHARLES HEATH, who was killed in action on the 27th July, 1880, at Maiwand, was the third son of Major-General Heath, of the Bombay Army. He was born on the 11th April, 1847, and was educated at Sydney College, Bath, from whence he proceeded to Sandhurst. Passing out of the college after the usual course, he was gazetted to the 45th Sherwood Foresters, and proceeded to India, where the head-quarters were then stationed. He served with his regiment throughout the Abyssinian campaign of 1868-69, being present at the storming and capture of Magdala, and obtaining the medal. On the termination of the war he returned to India as Aide-de-Camp to Major-General Sir George Malcolm, commanding the Mhow Division. In July, 1869, he entered the Bombay Staff Corps, and was appointed Adjutant of the 17th Native Infantry. In June, 1874, he was transferred to the Adjutancy of the 5th Native Light Infantry. He subsequently served in the Quartermaster-General's department of the Bombay Army, and on the formation of the Bombay column for service in Southern Afghanistan, he was appointed Brigade-Major to the 1st Infantry Brigade under the command of Brigadier-General Burrows. This brigade formed part of the Girishk Column which was sent out to co-operate with the Wali's army on the Halmand against Ayub Khan, who was advancing from Herat. At the time the force left Kandahar, Captain Heath was prevented by a severe attack of illness from accompanying his brigade, but taking advantage of the despatch of a convoy of commissariat stores, he rejoined it at Khushk-i-Nakhud on the 18th July. Towards the close of the action at Maiwand, and shortly before the Native Infantry broke, he was with Brigadier-General Burrows on the left of the line, when a rifle bullet struck him in the head, and he fell dead from his horse.

LIEUTENANT THOMAS RICE HENN,

ROYAL ENGINEERS.

THE subject of this memoir, who perished on the field of Maiwand, Afghanistan, on the 27th July, 1880, was the third son of Thomas Rice Henn, of Paradise Hill, in the County of Clare, Esquire, J.P. and D.L., one of Her Majesty's Counsel and Recorder of Galway, by Jane Isabella, his wife, daughter of the Right Honourable Francis Blackburne, Lord Chancellor of Ireland.

He was born on the 2nd November, 1849, in Dublin, and was educated at Windermere College, and the Royal Military Academy, Woolwich, into which he passed at the early age of seventeen years—without any special preparation, and having attended the examination solely in order that he might understand its character and be prepared for it on a subsequent occasion—second in the list of successful candidates. He obtained his commission in the Royal Engineers in July, 1869, and after serving for a period at Chatham, was ordered out to India. On arrival, he was posted to the Bombay Sappers and Miners, and passing through successive grades, serving at various stations, and winning approbation from all with whom he was associated by the zeal and ability he displayed in the discharge of his duties, he continued in that corps till the day of his death.

For some little time prior to the outbreak of the Afghan War, Henn had been stationed at Kirki, where he held the appointment of Officiating Quartermaster of the Corps. In January, 1879, he took part, in command of No. 2 Company, in the advance into Baluchistan of the detachment which was ordered up to form part of the Reserve Division of the Kandahar Field Force, and for several months was employed in the Bolan Pass on the road-constructing and other duties upon which it was engaged. He subsequently proceeded in command of his company to Kandahar, where, shortly after his arrival, he was selected to fill the staff appointment of Brigade Major of Engineers. It will perhaps be not out of place here to record the high estimation in which his talents and energy were held by Major-General Phayre, C.B., who recommended him in his despatches, and was at one time anxious to make him an Assistant Political Officer, and who, in his Field Force Order of the 22nd October, 1880, has paid a deserved tribute to his memory. In the first days of July, 1880, he took part in the advance of Burrows' Brigade to the

Halmand, and in the disastrous encounter with the enemy at Maiwand on the 27th of the month, he rendered up his life in an act of heroism which his country will be slow to forget. As regards his conduct on that fatal day, some interesting details have been given in a letter addressed to Sir Michael Roberts Westropp, Chief Justice of Bombay, by Lieut.-Colonel Hills, C.B., R.E., late Commanding Engineer at Kandahar, who writes as follows :—

"When I was appointed Commanding Engineer, I at once requested that he and his company of Sappers might be sent up to the front. On the move forward of the Brigade to Girishk, he and forty-four men and non-commissioned officers accompanied the force, and did excellent service during the long and trying marches. On the battle-field of Maiwand he and his Sappers were posted alongside the battery of Horse Artillery, and I am glad to say that they were the last of all the troops to leave the line of battle. Captain Slade, commanding the Horse Artillery (Major Blackwood having been severely wounded), told Henn he was going to limber up, and when he started off, he says, Henn made his men stand up and fire a volley into the crowd of Ghazis and regular troops pouring down upon them, and then gave the order to retire quietly and steadily. He had been wounded in the arm some time before this, but remained with his men to the last. He followed the line of retreat of the 66th towards the wall of the first garden, across the large nullah, and in a small water-channel in that garden he and the remains of his men took their stand with some men of the 66th and Grenadiers, and here he fell, using a rifle to the last: as far as I can ascertain, he was finally shot through the head and suffered little. Around this place were found, lightly buried, Henn and 14 Sappers, 23 men of the Grenadiers, and 46 men of the 66th: the mound in front was found strewn with horses of the mullahs and cavalry of the enemy, proving that our poor fellows had died hard and gallantly."

Lieut.-Colonel Hills then states that of his 44 men 8 to 10 were wounded, "so that his men under his noble example did their duty grandly." Again—"Their steadiness and admirable conduct is greatly attributable to his example and teaching. All I can add is, that he was a general favourite and greatly esteemed for his talents, and had he been fortunate enough to have survived, would have thoroughly earned his Brevet on the attainment of his Captaincy. In him I have lost a warm coadjutor and friend, and our Service an excellent soldier: one of the men of the 66th brought in his sword, which had been presented to him by his uncle. He had served under me for seven years, and no one could more thoroughly appreciate his sterling qualities and cheerfulness under trying circumstances."

Lieut.-General Primrose, in his despatch of the 1st October, 1880, giving details of the battle, states, on the authority of a Colonel of Artillery of Ayub Khan's army who was present at the time, that a party, estimated by the latter to consist of 100 officers and men, made a most determined stand in the garden. "They were surrounded by the whole Afghan army, and fought on until only 11 men were left, inflicting enormous loss upon the enemy. These 11 charged out of the garden and died with their faces to the foe, fighting to the death. Such was the nature of their charge and the grandeur of their bearing, that although the whole of the Ghazis were assembled around them, not one dared approach to cut them down. Thus standing in the open, back to back, firing steadily and truly, every shot telling, surrounded by thousands, these 11 officers and men died; and it was not until the last man had been shot down, that the Ghazis dared advance upon them."

From an examination of the ground, from corroborative evidence, and from the position in which the bodies were found, it has now been clearly ascertained that this last stand was made by a party made up of the 66th Regiment, the Bombay Grenadiers, and the Sappers; and that the achievement of the eleven was the achievement of Henn, Hinde (of the Grenadiers), and Blackwood of the Horse Artillery (who had been carried, earlier in the action, a wounded man, to the ground on which he died), together with eight soldiers of the gallant 66th, whose officers, ten in number, had all fallen previously, as is minutely described in General Primrose's despatch, striving to save the colours of their regiment.

It only remains to be added, that Lieut.-General Sir Garnet J. Wolseley, K.C.B., who has examined such existing evidence as bears upon the disastrous battle of Maiwand, has stamped a distinguished soldier's approbation upon the conduct of the lamented subject of this memoir, and in a letter written to Lieutenant Henn's father, with a soldier's sympathy for the dead and for the living, has pronounced an eulogium upon him which may well remain graven upon the hearts of his family. "No hero," writes Sir Garnet, "ever died more nobly than he died; and I only wish it were possible for the country, for which he died, to properly evince its gratitude to his memory. I did not have the advantage of knowing him; but I envy the noble manner of his death. If I had ten sons, I should be indeed proud if all ten fell as he fell." And again he writes: "Had your son lived, he would, I presume, have been decorated by the Queen as one of her bravest soldiers." That, had he lived, he would have upheld the military fame of his gallant countrymen, and the honour of the profession which his life adorned and which he loved so well, his friends may rest assured, and in the assurance find consolation.

LIEUT. W. F. HENNELL, STAFF CORPS,

1st PUNJAB CAVALRY.

WILLIAM FREDERIC HENNELL, who fell a victim to cholera on the 21st July, 1879, at Kandahar, during the occupation of that city by our troops, was the youngest son of Colonel Samuel Hennell, formerly Resident in the Persian Gulf, and of Anne Inman Orton, his wife. He was born at Bushire in October, 1850. His parents soon afterwards returning to England, his early years were spent at Springfield, in the village of Charlton Rings, Gloucestershire. He was educated at Cheltenham College; and after passing through Sandhurst, received, in February, 1870, his commission in the 36th Regiment, then serving at Rawal Pindi, and afterwards at Mian Mir in the Punjab. Early in 1874 he entered the Bengal Staff Corps, and was at first appointed Officiating Wing Subaltern in the 23rd Pioneers, joining that regiment at Jhelum.

Having served his probationary year, he entered the Punjab Frontier Force, and was appointed Officiating Squadron Subaltern of the 1st Punjab Cavalry, stationed at Rajanpur, on the frontier. His regiment was one of the first ordered on active service in the Afghan War, and formed part of General Stewart's Division of the Army of Invasion.

During the greater part of the march to Kandahar Hennell filled the post of Acting Adjutant; and to the efficiency with which he performed the duties of his office, Major Maclean, who commanded the regiment, has testified in the very highest terms. After being present at the action of Takht-i-pul, he entered Kandahar with the regiment on the 9th January, 1879, and remained there till he succumbed to cholera, on the 21st July. He was universally beloved in the camp, and in his death everyone felt he had lost a personal friend.

2ND LIEUTENANT ARTHUR HONYWOOD,

66TH (BERKSHIRE) REGIMENT.

THE subject of this notice, who was killed in his twentieth year at the battle of Maiwand on the 27th July, 1880, while defending the Queen's colour of his regiment, was the fourth son of the late Sir Courtenay Honywood, and Anne Maria, his wife, second daughter of the late W. Paynter, Esq., of Richmond, and of Belgrave Square, London.

Arthur Honywood was born in the year 1860 at Evington Place, Ashford, and received his education in Hertfordshire. Proceeding to Sandhurst, he passed out of the college after the usual course, and was gazetted, in August, 1879, to a second Lieutenancy in the 66th Regiment. He embarked shortly afterwards for India, and joined the Head-quarters at Karachi, in time—to his infinite satisfaction—to take part with the regiment in its march to Kandahar. His term of service was destined, alas! to be of short duration. In the first days of July, 1880, he accompanied the 66th in its advance in Burrows' Brigade to the Halmand, and was present, on the 14th of the month, at the dispersing of the Wali Shere Ali Khan's mutinied troops in the neighbourhood of Girishk. At the battle of Maiwand, on the 27th, he was struck with a bullet early in the engagement. "I met him," writes one of his brother officers in reference to the last sad act of the drama of that day, "in one of the gardens, wounded through the leg." It is known that he reached the garden where the last desperate stand was made—that spot which has become sacred to the memory of the little band of heroes who, in their determination to sell their lives dearly, watered it so copiously with their blood. The sequel—in so far as the subject of this notice is concerned—is supplied in General Primrose's despatch: "Lieutenant Honywood was shot down whilst holding a colour high above his head, shouting, 'Men, what shall we do to save this?'"

WILLIAM JENKYNS, M.A., C.I.E., BENGAL C. S.,

SECRETARY TO THE BRITISH EMBASSY AT KABUL.

THE subject of this memoir, who rendered up his life in the last desperate charge from the gates of the burning Residency at Kabul on the evening of the 3rd of September, 1879, was the eldest son of his father, a gentleman bearing the same name, and occupying the office of Inspector of Buildings in the city of Aberdeen. Born on the 23rd August, 1847, he was educated partly at the Aberdeen Grammar School, and from thence proceeded, in 1864, to the University, gaining, by open competition, the Udny Duff Bursary. In 1867, during the third session, he capped his first success by carrying off the £10 prize for the best essay on a given subject; and in 1868 he graduated. With reference to his career as a student, which was throughout a notable one, we cannot do better than quote some passages from the interesting inaugural address delivered by Professor Geddes, from his Chair at the University, to one of the Arts classes, at the opening of the winter session of 1879. "In the year 1864," observed the Professor, in the course of his remarks, "I first became acquainted with William Jenkyns. He stood 4th in the Bursary List of that year, and I was therefore prepared to find in him a good scholar. I early became sensible that he was that, and much more, an earnest student, one that loved duty for its own sake, rejoiced in it, and devoted himself to it. His personal appearance was prepossessing . . . . and there was a light in the eye giving evidence of a fine spirit dwelling within—*mens pulchra*, to change the common quotation, *in corpore pulchro*. His course at College was one of great distinction. In every class of the curriculum he was a 'prizeman,' except in Natural Philosophy, where he was 1st O.M.; in that of Logic he stood second, and similarly in all the other classes. He studied for the Indian Civil Service, and came out 4th in the list of successful candidates at the examination—an ordeal far more difficult then than now,—having to contend, still a stripling, with men twenty-one or twenty-two years old, that being the age in those days up to which competition was allowed. The position he even then attained was so notable that I referred to it in a published address, now exactly ten years ago, at the opening of the session, in the following words:—'Another fact which I recall with the utmost pleasure on this occasion is the circumstance that one of our most promising classics only the other day, in 1868, in the month of his graduation at Aberdeen, came in 4th in the Indian Civil Service competition. To stand as high as 4th in that ordeal, while still what we call a 'Magistrand,' and wearing the scarlet gown, is, in my judgment, a feat equal to standing 1st with the usual addition of two years' special training, customary after the Magistrand year. You all know his name—no less amiable he was than accomplished—William Jenkyns.'"

After passing into the Indian Civil Service, the subject of this memoir spent two years in London, training for the work of the Judicial Department; and that he turned the time at his disposal to good account is attested by the fact that he took, during this period, no less than three of the money prizes offered for competition by the authorities. On the 7th October, 1870, he left Aberdeen for Bombay, embarking on the new phase of his career which was rapidly to bring him to the front in the ranks of Indian civilians. His first station was Multan, where he acted as Assistant Commissioner. In 1872 he was sent to Dera Ismail Khan, where, in addition to other work, he discharged the duties of Inspector of Schools. His next station was Mianwali. In the course of his service in the trans-Indus, he set himself to acquire the languages of the frontier—Pushto, the Afghan language, and Baluchi, the Baluch language. In both of these he passed distinguished examinations, and received handsome rewards; and it is perhaps worthy of record that he was the only British officer who, at the time, had succeeded in accomplishing this linguistic feat. He next set himself to the acquisition of Persian, and subsequently passed with high honour an examination in that language at Calcutta, receiving a prize of £200. In Arabic, too, he was prepared to pass a similar examination, but the exigencies of the public service prevented him from getting leave of absence from his post to attend for it. The fact of his having passed all these linguistic tests now brought him prominently into notice; and when Sir Lewis Pelly was despatched, in 1876, to Peshawar, as the British representative at the conference with the Amir of Afghanistan, Jenkyns received the appointment of Interpreter and Secretary to the Embassy.

After the dissolution of the conference, the subject of this memoir was selected to fill the post of Political Agent in Ladak, a distant province of the Kashmir Government, bordering upon Yarkund. He subsequently held various other appointments, including the Assistant-Commissionership of Peshawar. That in the tenure of one and all of these offices he discharged his duties with zeal and ability, is evidenced not only by the fact of his steady progress, but by the testimony of those under whom he worked and with whom he served.

On the outbreak of the Afghan War in the autumn of 1878, William Jenkyns was appointed a political officer with Sir Sam. Browne's Division of the Army of Invasion, and served with the force on the Northern line through the whole of the first campaign. In the negotiations which were consummated by the treaty of peace at Gandamak, he rendered material aid; and it is a pleasant picture which has been drawn of the delight expressed by his gallant and revered chief, Cavagnari, as the latter slung the precious document over the back of his able coadjutor, and despatched him at daybreak on his now historical journey to Simla and back. For thirteen hours Jenkyns remained continuously in the saddle, covering in that space of time, in the month of May, the 120 miles of broken ground which lies between

Gandamak and Peshawar, hurrying on to Simla, obtaining the Viceroy's ratification of the treaty, returning to Peshawar, taking again to the saddle, and eventually riding in to Gandamak on the third day after he had started on his errand. For this feat and for his services prior to it, a Companionship of the Order of the Indian Empire—a decoration which, alas! was destined never to reach him—was conferred upon him by Government.

During the wintering of the troops at Jalalabad, the subject of this notice occupied himself with collecting information specially with a view to revenue administration in the event of the district being annexed. For the mass of data he gathered together and subsequently published, he received the formal thanks of the Government of India. In sending a copy of his book to Professor Geddes, of Aberdeen University, with a letter from which most of the incidents detailed above have been gathered, he makes allusion to the little volume in a characteristic sentence. "It is nothing," he writes, "in itself, and can have no interest for you; but I send it merely to show I have been working"—and further on, adds:—"and that my thoughts are still of King's College."

On the despatch of the British Embassy under Sir Louis Cavagnari to the Court of Kabul, Mr. Jenkyns was "specially selected, in recognition of his proved merits and abilities,"—to quote the words of Government—to fill the post of First Assistant Political Officer. Incessantly active, he found time to address, after the arrival of the Embassy at its destination, a series of interesting letters to the "Pioneer" newspaper, descriptive of the capital in its physical, social, and political aspects, and presenting a vivid picture of the every-day life of the Embassy itself—the paying of ceremonial visits, the attendance at the parade-ground for public sports, the rides in the neighbourhood of the city, and the like. So matters went on, comparatively quietly, till the fatal 3rd of September—that day on which, in violation of almost the only law which Afghans profess to hold sacred, was re-enacted, after an interval of thirty-eight years, the ghastly tragedy which has stamped the name of its perpetrators in letters of blood on the page of history to be held up to everlasting execration. Of the little band who, after many hours' continuous fighting, sallied out, sword in hand, from the gates of the burning Residency, William Jenkyns was the last officer seen alive. In the thirty-second year of his age, in the hour when his manhood was fulfilling the splendid promise of his youth, he fell at his post, dying as a hero dies. Though destined, like many a hero, to be short-lived, he discharged during the brief span of his career, with a rare ability, multifarious and varied duties, and he has left behind him a name which his countrymen will not willingly let die.

LIEUTENANT W. N. JUSTICE,

PROBATIONER, STAFF CORPS.

WILLIAM NAPIER JUSTICE, who was killed in action at Maiwand on the 27th July, 1880, while serving with Jacob's Rifles as a probationer for the Bombay Staff Corps, was the eldest and only son of Lieut.-Colonel H. A. Justice, of the Madras Staff Corps, and of Isabella Caroline, his wife, daughter of Dr. Thomas Oxby, of the Bengal Medical Service. He was born at Singapore on the 6th January, 1858, and was educated at Cheltenham College. Gazetted, in September, 1876, to a Lieutenancy in the second Battalion 17th Foot, he embarked with that regiment a fortnight afterwards for Bombay, and proceeded with it to Mhow. After passing the necessary examinations, he was attached to the 21st Bombay Native Infantry (Marine Battalion) as a probationer for the Staff Corps.

In August, 1879, Lieutenant Justice was transferred to Jacob's Rifles, and in the month of October joined the Head-quarters at Quetta, Baluchistan. Appointed shortly afterwards to the Quartermastership of the regiment, and performing the duties of the post in a manner which called forth warm acknowledgment from his commanding officer, he accompanied the Rifles to Kandahar, and in July, 1880, took part with them in the advance of Burrows' Brigade to the Halmand. It is perhaps worthy of record that on the 23rd of the month he despatched from Khushk-i-Nakhud a letter to a friend in Bombay, showing a peculiarly correct appreciation of the position of affairs as they then were, and giving evidence of a power of observation which, had he been spared, would have stood him in good stead in his profession. His career, however, was destined to be cut short at its outset. In the disastrous encounter with the enemy at Maiwand, at the moment when he was attempting to rally his men at the most critical juncture of the battle, he fell mortally wounded, and a few moments afterwards expired in the arms of his brother officers, Captain Harrison and Lieutenant Rayner, of the 66th, as they were attempting to carry him into a less exposed position.

SURGEON A. C. KEITH, M.B.,

ARMY MEDICAL DEPARTMENT.

ALEXANDER CROMBIE KEITH was born on the 11th December, 1849, and was the youngest son of the late William Keith, Esq., M.D., of Aberdeen, and Burnette, his wife, daughter of James Silver, Esq., of Netherley, Kincardineshire. Educated at the Gymnasium, Old Aberdeen, and the Aberdeen University, where he took his degree, he entered the Army Medical Department in February, 1877, and went out to India the following year.

Till proceeding into Afghanistan on active service, Dr. Keith was stationed at Attock, where for some time he performed the duties of Civil Surgeon, and during an outbreak of cholera organized a camp hospital, for which he received the commendation of the authorities.

On the second outbreak of hostilities with Afghanistan in the autumn of 1879, he was detailed for service to Sir Frederick Roberts's Division of the Army of Invasion, and accompanying it in its advance, was present at the battle of Charasiab, the occupation of Kabul, and the defence of the Sherpur cantonments. Shortly after the reassertion of British supremacy in the capital, however, his career was brought to an untimely close. A chill caught by him during a reconnaissance was followed by an attack of pneumonia, which ended fatally on the 13th January, 1880.

Dr. Keith's kindly disposition, and his devotion to the sick committed to his charge, made him a general favourite, and caused his death to be deeply and widely regretted. He was a keen and excellent sportsman, and his genial companionship will long be missed by the friends with whom he was wont to make excursions with gun or rifle against the game of the country.

SURGEON A. H. KELLY,

BENGAL MEDICAL DEPARTMENT.

AMBROSE HAMILTON KELLY, who was killed in the defence of the British Residency at Kabul on the 3rd September, 1879, was the eldest son of William Russell Kelly, of Dublin, Solicitor. He was born on the 30th September, 1845, and was educated at the Rathmines School, then under the management of the Rev. Roger North. His studies in Medicine and Surgery were pursued at Dr. Steevens' Hospital, Dublin, where he was a resident pupil for two sessions, and obtained the highest prize awarded by the Governors. His diploma as Licentiate in Surgery from the Royal College of Surgeons, Ireland, is dated 26th January, 1869; and in the month of March following he obtained the diploma of the King and Queen's College of Physicians. On the 1st October, 1869, he gained his commission as Surgeon in the Bengal Medical Service, and proceeding to Calcutta in the spring of the following year, settled down to the uneventful life of ordinary professional routine in an Indian cantonment till the despatch of the Lushai punitory expedition gave him an opportunity for seeing active service and earning a medal and clasp. In the interval between the date of his arrival in Bengal and the winter of 1871-72, he did duty at the Presidency General Hospital (from the 7th June to 4th August, 1870), was attached to the 13th Bengal Cavalry and the 2nd Central India Horse (from the 4th August, 1870, to the 29th May, 1871), held medical charge of the Bengal Sappers and Miners (from 29th May to the 7th August, 1871), and officiated with the 3rd Bengal Native Infantry (from the 7th August to the 18th October, 1871). On the date last quoted he was placed in medical charge of the 22nd Punjab Infantry, and proceeding with that regiment into Lushai territory, was present with it throughout in the various operations of the Cachar Column.

On the return of the Expeditionary Force in the spring of 1872, Dr. Kelly was transferred for duty to the 1st Punjab Infantry, in the medical charge of which regiment he officiated for some twelve months. On the expiration of that period, the credit he had gained and the skill he had exhibited on various occasions secured him the coveted post of Surgeon to the Guides—a corps in which his eminent predecessors Bellew and Courtenay had performed distinguished service before him. From March 1873, till the time of his death, he was intimately associated not only with this famous regiment, but also, in his capacity of Civil Surgeon of Hoti-Mardan, with the entire Eusufzai district; and the peculiar facilities he enjoyed of intercourse with the inhabitants gave him considerable influence and gained him much respect amongst them. We next find him taking part in the expedition against the Afridis under General Keyes—for which he obtained a second clasp—in the winter of 1877-78, and in March, 1878, present at the surprise of the Ranizai village of Skhakat and the attack on the Utman Khel villages. The outbreak of the Afghan War once more called the Guides to the front; and from the memorable 21st September, 1878, till the signing of the peace of Gandamak and the close of the first campaign, Dr. Kelly was present with his regiment, adding to his high reputation by the success with which he coped with the heavy work which fell to his hand. There are many officers and men of the late Peshawar Valley Field Force who, amongst other reminiscences, will not soon forget the humanity and self-abnegation with which he devoted his abilities to the care of the sick and wounded Afghans and Kugianis at Gandamak.

On it being decided by Government to despatch a mission to the Court of Kabul, Dr. Kelly was selected to fill the post of Medical Officer to the Embassy, and in that capacity accompanied Sir Louis Cavagnari to the capital, in the month of July, 1879. Besides finding time, during his short residence in Kabul, to write home a series of deeply interesting letters—some of which have been made familiar to the public by their insertion in the columns of the "Times" newspaper—Dr. Kelly opened a dispensary in the city, which was daily thronged with applicants anxious to secure the skill of the "Feringhi" for their various ailments, which was freely bestowed on all. On the ill-fated 3rd of September, 1879, he met his untimely and tragical death, fighting manfully in the defence of the Residency with his gallant comrades in arms.

The subject of this memoir, Ambrose Kelly, was a man remarkable alike for his spirit of adventure and his high social gifts. Tall in stature, powerful in physique, a keen sportsman, something of a naturalist, and possessed of a great knowledge of horticulture, he was eminently qualified for the career he had chosen. It seems fitting that one whose life had been spent as his had, should have been found ministering to the last to the needs of the afflicted. Cut off in his prime, and, like his predecessor Lord in the first Afghan War, an ornament to his profession, his loss is deeply felt, not only by his brother officers, but by the Bengal Medical Service in general.

In Sandford Church, Dublin, a very handsome and interesting memorial of Dr. Kelly has been erected. It consists of a richly engraved mural brass tablet, and of a pair of stained-glass figure windows—the former, a tribute of the love and esteem of his brother officers, and the latter of the affection of his family.

SURGEON-MAJOR HENRY KELSALL,

ARMY MEDICAL DEPARTMENT.

THE name of Kelsall is not unknown in Her Majesty's Service, the father of the subject of this memoir having been a Surgeon in the Navy, and no less than three of his uncles—including Colonel Joseph Kelsall, who formerly commanded the 70th Regiment—having served with distinction in the Army.

Henry Kelsall, who was an only son, was born at Plymouth on the 28th March, 1834, and received his education at Orchard Hill, Northam, Frankfort-on-the-Maine, and University College, London. After subsequently pursuing, for a time, the study of Medicine at Guy's Hospital, and with Dr. Grouse in Suffolk, he entered the Army in September, 1855.

Gazetted to a troop of Royal Horse Artillery, then under orders for the Crimea, he was about to proceed to the seat of war, when his departure was arrested by the arrival in England of the news of the conclusion of peace. He continued to serve with this troop until appointed Assistant Surgeon to the 20th Foot, with which regiment he remained during the whole of its last term of Indian service, sharing the heavy and important work which fell to its lot. In the Mutiny campaign he was present at the affairs of Chanda, Umipur, and Sultanpur, under General Sir T. H. Franks, the taking of the Fort of Dauraha, and the siege and final capture of Lucknow; in the subsequent operations in Oudh, at the affairs of Mianganj, MorarMow, the Fort of Simri, Birah, and Baxa Ghat; and in the later campaign, under Lord Clyde, at the affairs of Chardu, the Fort of Masjidia, and Banki. For his services he was honourably mentioned in General Evelyn's despatches, and received the medal with clasp for Lucknow.

On the return of the 20th Regiment to England Kelsall was appointed, at his own request, to the Staff, in order that he might have leisure to prepare for his promotion to the rank of Surgeon, which he obtained in March, 1870. He was soon afterwards gazetted to the 2nd Battalion 1st Royal Scots, and remained in medical charge of that regiment until recent regulations abolished all such appointments.

Promoted Surgeon-Major in November, 1872, he did duty for a time at the

General Hospital, Devonport, and as Principal Medical Officer at Pembroke Dock.

On the outbreak of the Afghan War, Surgeon-Major Kelsall applied to serve in India, and was sent to take charge of Battery I/C, Royal Horse Artillery, which he joined on the 28th of March, 1879, direct from England, and continued with until the return march from Afghanistan. The strain of severe duties and the amount of exposure he underwent in a trying climate, proved, however, too much for a constitution already impaired by long residence in India and a recent severe illness, and on the 6th June, 1879, he fell a victim to an attack of pleurisy at Daka. His heroic fortitude and the disinterestedness he displayed throughout this illness in bestowing his entire attention on those around him, were of a piece with the broad humanity of his life: to the last all his care and thought were for others. Thus, not unworthily, ended the career of an officer whose professional attainments frequently gained for him recognition from those under whom he served both in quarters and in the field.

Surgeon-Major Kelsall's accomplishments were not few. He spoke several modern languages with fluency, possessed a considerable knowledge of drawing and of music, was an excellent horseman, and proficient in most field sports; these attributes, added to his more sterling qualities, gained for him the respect and esteem of all with whom he was associated in the different appointments he held.

The deceased married, in 1862, Annie, daughter of Mr. John Milne, of Montrose, who, with one son, survives him.

CAPTAIN J. A. KELSO,

ROYAL ARTILLERY.

JOHN ANDREW KELSO, who was killed at the Peiwar Kotal on the 2nd December, 1878, was the only son of the late John Kelso, Esq., of the Indian Civil Service, a gentleman who for many years had charge of the Government Revenue Survey in the Province of Assam.

The subject of this memoir was born on the 22nd February, 1839. After passing the earlier portion of his life with his parents in India, he proceeded to England, and studied for several years at King's College, London, from whence he entered Woolwich. Passing out from the Academy after the usual course, he was gazetted, in November, 1860, to the Royal Artillery, and, joining his battery in India shortly afterwards, did duty with it at various stations in the Bengal and Madras Presidencies for a period of seven years.

In March, 1868, Kelso was posted Subaltern to No. 2 Light Field Horse Battery, Haidarabad Contingent, and continued to serve with it until April, 1873, when he received his promotion and reverted to the regular service. After a twelve-months' interval, he was appointed Commandant of No. 2 Light Field Horse Battery, Punjab Frontier Force, which in January, 1877, was converted into No. 1 Mountain Battery, mules being substituted for horses. With this he served throughout the Jowaki campaign of 1877-78, obtaining the medal with clasp, and receiving honourable mention in Brigadier-General Keyes' despatches for the zeal and activity he displayed during the operations. Shortly after the conclusion of hostilities a severe attack of fever necessitated his proceeding on sick leave to the hill station of Murree.

In October, 1878, the battery was ordered up to Jamrud in view of the impending outbreak of war with Afghanistan, being detailed to Sir Sam. Browne's Division of the Army of Invasion, and Captain Kelso at once rejoined and resumed command of it. General Roberts, however, applying for its services, it was sent, a month later, to join the Kuram Force at Kohat, and proceeding from thence to Thal, took part in the subsequent advance of the division into the enemy's country. It was during the assault of the Peiwar Kotal on the 2nd December, in the hour of victory, that Captain Kelso met a soldier's death, being shot through the head at the moment when—to quote the words of an eye-witness—he had "moved up the steep slope with incredible rapidity, and, wheeling to the right, formed up on the left of the Highlanders, and opened fire."

Captain Kelso was an officer of high repute in the service, and the sorrow caused by his death was both deep and wide-spread.

After referring in his despatch to the assistance rendered by the battery in the advance, and to the determined manner in which the guns were fought, General Roberts, coupling the name of the deceased with that of the late Major Anderson of the 23rd Punjab Pioneers, wrote as follows :—" The death of these officers is mourned by the whole force, for both were well known as brave and excellent soldiers ;" and in a private letter, after expressing his great admiration for Captain Kelso's very soldierly qualities, the General added : " Few men could have done what he did with his battery in so short a time, and I considered myself extremely fortunate in having him with my column."

Captain Kelso married, in January, 1867, at Trichinopoly, Marion, third daughter of the late W. H. Ranking, M.D., F.R.C.P.L., of Norwich. He leaves a widow, with one son and three daughters.

LIEUT. F. G. KINLOCH, STAFF CORPS,

5TH BENGAL CAVALRY.

FRANCIS GARDEN KINLOCH, who was killed in the Kuram Valley, Afghanistan, on the 29th September, 1879, was the third son of Colonel Grant Kinloch, of Logie, Forfarshire, and Agnes Garden, his wife (of Troup and Glenlyon). He was born in the year 1852, and was educated at Brighton College, and under the Rev. E. A. Claydon, at Blackheath. In 1872 he was appointed to the Highland Light Infantry Militia, with which he served as Musketry Instructor after receiving an extra first-class certificate at Hythe.

Gazetted to a lieutenancy in the Gordon Highlanders in February, 1874, he joined that regiment at Multan, and did duty with it at various stations in the Bengal Presidency. After acquiring, and passing in, the necessary Oriental languages, he was admitted to the Bengal Staff Corps. In 1877 he joined the 5th Bengal Cavalry, and in the following year was appointed Adjutant of the regiment.

Shortly after the outbreak of hostilities with Afghanistan young Kinloch volunteered for active service, "in any capacity so that he might go to the front." His application was supported by his Commanding Officer. "I have much pleasure," wrote Colonel Charles Gough, "in recommending him as an intelligent and active young officer, who would work hard and do well whatever he may be put to." Scarcely was the requisite permission gained, however, before an attack of fever laid him prostrate, and necessitated his being sent on sick leave to Simla. Shortly aftewards the massacre of the British Embassy took place, and an immediate advance on Kabul by the Kuram and Khyber armies was ordered. Though scarcely convalescent, Kinloch again volunteered "for the front," and was ordered to join the 12th Bengal Cavalry, then with General Roberts at the Shutargardan. Starting immediately, he proceeded by way of Kohat to Thal. Having joined Dr. Bellew, he accompanied him into the Kuram Valley, *en route* for Kabul. On the morning of the 29th September, 1879, finding that his baggage bullocks had not kept up, he turned back a short distance to hurry them on, when some forty men of the Orakzai tribe, who were lying in ambush behind some rocks near the road, fired a fatal volley, which, according to the testimony of his Sowar orderly, who escaped, killed him instantaneously. His body was recovered the same afternoon, and was buried next day in the cemetery at Thal—every officer and soldier in the garrison following it to its last resting-place. His sword and revolver, which were carried off by the enemy, were recovered some months afterwards by Brigadier-General Tytler's avenging column, and restored to his family.

Lieutenant Frank Kinloch's untimely and tragical end was deeply regretted by the officers of the different corps in which he had served, and by all others who had known him. The estimation in which he was held is attested by many warm expressions of regard which occur in letters written after his death to members of his family. "He was as promising a young soldier as ever I saw," wrote Sir Charles Brownlow, K.C.B., who had made his acquaintance while commanding at Rawal Pindi. "I often said he would be heard of if he saw any service." In a letter written by Major Shakspeare, his Commanding Officer, the verdict is concurred in in the following words :—" The regiment will feel his loss the more as time rolls on. The service has lost a good officer, and the 5th Bengal Cavalry a good Adjutant. I shall find it hard to replace him."

LIEUTENANT S. E. L. LENDRUM,

ROYAL ARTILLERY.

THE subject of the following brief memoir, who died of typhoid fever at Kokaran, near Kandahar, on the 30th April, 1879, aged twenty-three years, was the youngest son of the late James Lendrum, D.L., of Magheracross, Co. Fermanagh, and of Anne, his wife, daughter of the late Samuel Vesey, D.L., of Derrabard, Co. Tyrone.

Samuel Edward Latham Lendrum was born on the 10th September, 1855, and received his early education at Portora Royal School, in his native county. In September, 1873, he entered the Royal Military Academy, Woolwich, and after undergoing the ordinary course of three years, was gazetted to Battery 4/5 Royal Artillery. His commission bears date September 2, 1876. His home service, chiefly at Woolwich, extended over about eighteen months In the autumn of 1877 he embarked with his battery for India, and proceeded with it to Morar (Gwalior), where it was stationed for upwards of a year.

On the outbreak of hostilities in Afghanistan, Lieutenant Lendrum's battery was not among those selected for active service; he succeeded, however, in effecting a transfer to Mountain Battery 11/11, which formed a portion of Sir Donald Stewart's command. Joining his new battery at Simla, he accompanied the division in its laborious march through the Bolan Pass and across the Khoja range, reaching Kandahar on the 8th January, 1879. After a brief stay here, he took part with the battery in General Stewart's advance to Kalat-i-Ghilzai, from whence, with two guns, accompanied by 100 sabres of 15th Lancers and 50 Goorkhas, he was despatched for the purpose of collecting grain stored by the Amir. He was absent with this party just a month, having advanced up the Arghesan Valley as far as Maruf, when, their object being accomplished, they received orders to return to Kandahar. Here Lieutenant Lendrum remained till the middle of April, when he was seized with the fever which ultimately proved fatal to him. On the symptoms becoming serious, he was removed to the neighbouring village of Kokaran, and here, after thirteen days' illness, he died, tended to the last with extreme kindness by Surgeon-Major H. Skey Muir, M.D., as well as by two gunners, who had volunteered to nurse him.

Lieutenant Lendrum's ardent devotion to his profession, and the high opinions expressed of him by his Commanding Officers, had seemed to give earnest of a bright career. He was possessed of a gallant spirit that had never failed him, and was of a nature the most open, frank, and generous. These were his salient qualities, and they had gained for him, to an unusual degree, the warm affection of all among whom he was thrown. On his leaving Morar for active service the gunners of his old battery presented him with a mark of their regard; and over his last resting-place within the citadel of Kandahar a marble slab has been erected "by his brother officers in token of their esteem."

2ᴺᴰ LIEUTENANT E. D. LOS,

1ST BATTALION, 25TH (KING'S OWN BORDERERS).

ERNEST DANIEL LOS was the eldest son of Peter Roland Los, Esq., of the Hague, formerly for many years Consul for the Netherlands at Sunderland, and of Harriett, his wife, eldest daughter of the late Thomas Gray, Esq., of Balbirnie, near Montrose, N.B. He was born at Sunderland on the 6th January, 1860, and after receiving his earlier education abroad, was transferred, in compliance with his wish to enter the Army, to the United Services College, Westward Ho, North Devon, where for two years he had the advantage of studying under the head-mastership of Mr. Carmell Price. Energetic alike at work and at play, he won the hearts both of his masters and his young contemporaries by the manliness of his character and the geniality of his ways, and in course of time became prefect of the college. At midsummer, 1878, he entered Sandhurst, his name appearing thirteenth in the list of 160 candidates. Passing out from the college after the usual course, he succeeded in obtaining eighth place and taking honours. In August, 1879, he was gazetted to the 1st Battalion, 25th King's Own Borderers, then stationed in the Punjab on its return from active service in Afghanistan; and embarking for India a month afterwards, he joined the Head-quarters at Peshawar.

In December, 1879, in consequence of the serious events which were happening at Kabul, the regiment was a second time ordered to the front, and proceeded to Landi Kotal in half battalions. Taking part in the advance, Los was present, under Captain Dixon, with Colonel Boisragon's column, which, co-operating with General Doran's brigade, dispersed the Mohmands at Kam Daka on the 15th January, 1880, wresting the Gara heights from a force ten times its number. "He commanded the left flank of the front line of skirmishers," writes his senior officer, "and showed great courage in the bold way in which he climbed the hillside under a dropping fire." He subsequently took part with the regimental head-quarters in the Lughman Valley expedition, holding successively the appointments of Head Quartermaster and Transport officer, and the command of a company. In the tenure of these offices he showed, according to the testimony of his Commanding Officer, "an aptitude for and love of soldiering." In the first days of April he took part in the operations against the Wazir Kugianis; and in the middle of the month marched with the head-quarters to Pezwan. At this post he was seized with enteric fever, to which he succumbed on the 31st May, only a few hours before his friend and brother officer Lieutenant Herbert Spoor fell a victim to the same fatal disease.

Lieutenant Los's remains rest in the little cemetery at Pezwan. A headstone, erected by his brother-officers in token of the love and esteem they bore him, marks his grave.

LIEUTENANT G. H. LUMSDEN,

PROBATIONER, BENGAL STAFF CORPS.

GORDON HUGH LUMSDEN, who was assassinated in the Kuram Valley, on the night of the 19th February, 1880, was the younger son of Captain J. T. Lumsden, who was killed during the Mutiny, while with Lord Clyde's force advancing to the relief of the Residency, Lucknow; was a grandson of the late Henry Lumsden, Esq., of Auchindoir, Aberdeenshire; and a cousin of Sir Peter Lumsden, K.C.B., C.S.I., late Adjutant-General of the Army in India.

The subject of this notice was born on the 2nd February, 1857, and was educated at the College School, Taunton, under the Rev. W. Tuckwell, M.A. Being desirous to enter the Indian Civil Service, he commenced preparation for the examination at the age of sixteen years, with Mr. Scoones of London; but his health twice failing him while studying, necessitated a change of plan. Obtaining an Indian cadetship in consideration of his father's services, he entered the Army, and was gazetted to a Lieutenancy in Her Majesty's 43rd Light Infantry, then serving in India. After doing duty with that regiment for a twelve-month at Bellary, Madras, he proceeded in June, 1877, to Bangalore for the course of Garrison Instruction, and obtained a first-class certificate. Posted, in May, 1878, to the 8th Bengal Cavalry as a probationer for the Staff Corps, he subsequently served with that regiment throughout the Afghan Campaign of 1878-1879, accompanying the head-quarter wing to Kandahar and Kalat-i-Ghilzai, and being present with it in the expedition into the Arghæsan Valley, and in the defeat of the body of the enemy which attacked the British camp on the 10th February, 1879. On the return of the 8th Cavalry to Multan after the close of the campaign, he proceeded to Calcutta for the study of the oriental languages, and after a few months' preparation succeeded in passing with credit the Higher Standard examination.

In January, 1880, Lumsden was posted to the 13th Bengal Lancers, and full of eagerness and hope at the prospects of a continuation of active service, joined that regiment in the Kuram Valley. His expectations, alas! were destined never to be fulfilled. On the night of the 19th February, he retired, after mess, to his tent, and the next morning was found by his servant lying dead at the foot of his bed, covered with dagger-wounds, the attitude of his body denoting that a struggle with his assassinator had taken place. A man who subsequently came into the camp stated that he had met, many miles distant in the Mangal country, a professional thief, who boasted that for two nights he had prowled about the camp marking the positions of the tents, and that on the third, after lying hidden in a nullah till after midnight, he had crept up to and entered the one which appeared to be easiest of access; that while in the act of retracing his steps after collecting a number of articles, he had knocked something down; that the sahib who was sleeping within, awakened by the noise, had jumped up and seized his sword; and that he had sprung upon him and stabbed him till he died.

Thus, at its very outset, was cut short a career full of promise—a life which, notwithstanding the shortness of its duration, had given evidence of a development sufficient to satisfy the wide circle of friends who held it dear.

LIEUTENANT HECTOR MACLAINE,

ROYAL HORSE ARTILLERY.

THE subject of this memoir, whose quite recently murdered body was found in the camp of Ayoub Khan near Kandahar, by the victorious troops of General Sir Frederick Roberts on the 1st September, 1880, was the eldest son of William Osborne Maclaine, Esq., J.P., D.L., of Kyneton, Gloucestershire, and his wife Anna, only surviving child of the late John Thurburn, Esq., J.P., of Murtle, Aberdeenshire; was grandson of Colonel Hector Maclaine, who served with distinction in the Peninsular War; and was a grand-nephew of Major John Maclaine, who fell at Waterloo; of Captain Murdoch Maclaine, the only British officer killed at Maida; and of General Sir Archibald Maclaine, K.C.B., who was knighted for his defence of Matagorda,

Hector Maclaine was born on the 24th November, 1851, at Murtle, and was educated by private tutors at home until January, 1865, when he went to Eton. In January, 1870, he entered the Royal Military Academy at Woolwich. His commission in the Royal Artillery bears date 6th January, 1872. After serving for a time with the 5th Brigade at home, he proceeded, in October, 1873, to India, and joining Battery B/18, served with it at Haidarabad and Karachi. In 1874 he returned home with the battery (which after its arrival in England was transformed into I/2) and did duty with it at Woolwich, Preston, Coventry, and Athlone, until July, 1878, when he was appointed to the Horse Artillery. Two months afterwards he proceeded to India in charge of drafts for E/B, R.H.A., which battery he joined at Mhow, and subsequently proceeded with it to Kirki.

In December, 1879, owing to the Artillery losses sustained by our Army in the neighbourhood of Kabul, orders were received from Simla for a Lieutenant from a Horse Artillery Battery in the Bombay Presidency to be sent to the front. Maclaine at once volunteered to go, and on Christmas-day was despatched to the Khyber Pass to join Battery I/C, with which he subsequently served at Daka until it returned to India, when he left it to rejoin his old Battery (E/B) which had left Kirkee in February, 1880, for active service at Kandahar. Overtaking it a little way beyond Sibi, where it was delayed for want of transport, he marched with it through the Bolan Pass to Kandahar, which was reached on the 10th April, 1880.

In June, 1880, Maclaine, having been laid up for five weeks with fever, was sent in charge of invalids and convalescents to Baba Wali, and while there received notice that E/B was ordered out to join General Burrows' force in support of the Wali Shere Ali. Though no serious fighting was at this time expected, he left Baba Wali in the highest spirits at the prospect of any active service, and rejoined the battery. In the pursuit of the Wali's mutinous troops in the neighbourhood of Girishk, on the 14th July, E/B took an active part, and Maclaine, being allowed to choose his own ground for his guns, did considerable execution with them at comparatively close range. After the action the camp was moved to Kushk-i-nakhud. On the 23rd July there was a slight skirmish with about 500 of the enemy's horsemen, and Lieutenant Maclaine with Colonel Malcolmson was sent to look out for another body of the enemy reported near. In the disastrous action at Maiwand on the 27th of the month Maclaine was the first to get into action, going forward with his two guns to the left front and opening fire. The splendid behaviour of the battery while working the guns under fire for more than three hours, and the tremendous execution done, are testified to by the survivors, and received the highest praise in the despatches. When the native infantry broke, and the cavalry failed to charge, the swarms of Ghazis made a final and determined rush for the guns, and those of Lieutenant Maclaine being slightly in advance of the others, were unfortunately surrounded and taken before he was able to extricate them. From one account it would appear that it was impossible to retire the two guns, the limbers having gone back for more ammunition; and that after firing one last round Maclaine and his gunners had to fight their way out to rejoin Captain Slade and the other four guns of the Battery. Lieutenant Maclaine was slightly wounded in the hand. He assisted Captain Slade in the retreat, the other officers of the Battery being killed or wounded, and was in charge of the advance guns all through the terrible night of the 27th, the horrors and sufferings of which are now so well known. Many officers have testified to his noble and unselfish conduct and care for the wounded who crowded the guns. Early on the morning of the 28th, having been almost without food, water, or rest for nearly thirty hours, he and a non-commissioned officer left the road at the village of Sangiri in search of water for the wounded, who were suffering tortures of thirst. Lieutenant Maclaine was taken prisoner, though how is not exactly known: he never came back; and no trace of the non-commissioned officer has ever been found. It would appear that he must have been overpowered by numbers. Some natives say he went into a house, in search of some vessel in which to carry water to those sinking on the road, and that there he was hemmed in and taken. In the list of casualties he was returned as killed or missing; and the Royal Artillery Regimental List for the month of August was published without his name, his place in his Battery being filled up. Some time after Ayub Khan's army had surrounded Kandahar, it became known, however, that a British officer was a prisoner in his camp, and this prisoner was subsequently discovered to be Lieutenant Maclaine. Efforts were made for his recovery, but without success. Sir F. Roberts, hearing of his captivity, wrote from Kalat-i-Ghilzai to Ayub Khan, demanding his release. Native spies had reported the unfortunate prisoner to be ill of fever some time before this. When General Roberts and his troops had completed their march from Kabul to the relief of Kandahar, the former again endeavoured to obtain the release of Lieutenant Maclaine, but with no result. On the 1st September, in the hour of the crowning victory over the enemy, and with his triumphant brother officers and fellow-soldiers near at hand, he was murdered by his fanatic guard, and his dead body, yet warm, was found outside his little tent near that of Ayub Khan, by the 92nd Highlanders. Some Sepoy prisoners escaped alive; and it is probable that if Lieutenant Maclaine, who was a strong, athletic man, had not been weak from illness, he too might have effected his escape. Three healed wounds were found on his chest, inflicted by Ghazis who had attacked him in his captivity. In his tent was found a small scrap of paper, on which were a few pencilled words in the form of a diary, as follows :—

"July 28th. Kushk-i-nakud.
   „ 29th. Sangiri.
   „ 30th. Given to Cavalry, Sher Ahmed Khan—Imprisoned in Kokaran.
August 4th. Sirdar Noor Mohamed Khan arrived, and I got better treatment in his bungalow.
   „ 6th. Was handed over to Ayoub Khan in camp at Kokaran; well treated.
   „ 7th. Marched to near Kandahar Karez.
   „ 8th. Some shells from city in camp.
   „ 9th. Ayoub Khan moved camp N.W. of old Kandahar hill. City I believe surrounded by troops, but mostly Ghazis. Fighting near city most days.
   „ 14th. Loss of British cavalry and horses.
   „ 15th. Post captured. Two shells burst, well ranged, but wide of camp."

This is all the record of his captivity which exists. He was buried with military honours in Kandahar, together with the three officers who fell in the engagement, and between two of his own gunners.

Lieutenant Maclaine's cruel fate excited a most profound sensation among the troops. When the news of his most pathetic death reached England it created very wide-spread sympathy, and expressions of sorrow reached his family from the Queen, the Duke of Cambridge, and all the officers under whom he had served.

The following was entered in the Orders of his old Battery, I/2, R.A. :—

"It is with deep regret that Major Ward has read the announcement of the murder of Lieutenant Maclaine... By those who knew him he will be remembered as an officer of singularly soldierlike qualities, winning the regard and esteem of all with whom he was associated. All ranks of his old Battery have now to deplore his untimely end; and in paying their tribute of respect to his memory, the Battery would also express their sympathy and condolence with his bereaved relatives. Of the late Lieutenant Maclaine it may be truly said 'he died at the post of duty.'" And Major Ward adds: "Words would fail to express the sorrow felt by his old comrades on hearing the sad intelligence of his cruel fate. By all the men who ever served under him he was greatly beloved. His name will long be held in affectionate remembrance by the Battery in which the earlier years of his military life were spent." Similar testimony of his worth, and of the profound sorrow caused by his untimely fate, is given by Sir Frederick Roberts, in his despatch; by Colonel the Honourable A. Stewart, R.H.A., in a communication addressed to the "Times" newspaper, who says: "He was not only a good energetic officer and soldier, but an active, dashing, powerful, and enterprising man. I had frequent opportunities of seeing and admiring his great energy, his love of soldiering, and excellent military qualities;" by Colonel Hastings, R.A., under whom he had formerly served in India, who writes: "He is most deeply regretted by every one of us who knew him, old and young: all who have served with him confirm the opinion I formed of him—a thorough good soldier and a perfect English gentleman;" and by Major Slade, R.H.A., in a letter in which the assistance he rendered in the hour of defeat is warmly dwelt upon.

It only remains to be added, that beloved and respected as Hector Maclaine was in the Service, he was no less beloved and respected in civilian circles, and that, as an expression of their admiration for his qualities and their sympathy with his parents, the friends and neighbours of his family in Gloucestershire have erected a very handsome window in Thornbury parish church to his memory.

CAPTAIN W. H. M^CMATH,

66TH (BERKSHIRE) REGIMENT.

WILLIAM HAMILTON McMATH was the second son of Hamilton McMath, Esq., of Thornford, Co. Monaghan, Ireland, and of Mary his wife, eldest daughter of James Parker, Esq., of Mount Kearney, Co. Down. He was born on the 4th February, 1845. After some early training in the Grammar School, Dundalk,—where he was elected Captain by his companions, and won twice running the silver medal, the highest prize awarded,—he was removed to King William's College, Isle of Man, where, in 1861, he studied under the Rev. Gilmour Harvey and Dr. Dixon, the then Head Masters. He subsequently underwent a short special preparation for Sandhurst under Mr. De Burgh, of Dublin; and after passing through the usual course at the College was gazetted, in August, 1865, to an Ensigncy in the 66th Foot.

Joining the regiment at Davenport, he proceeded with it in January, 1867, to Aldershot, and subsequently to Jersey and Guernsey. In August, 1868, he purchased his Lieutenancy, and in October of the same year obtained a first-class certificate, extra, at the School of Musketry at Hythe.

After serving for twelve months at the Curragh and Dublin, he embarked with the 66th, in 1870, for India. While in Bengal he was temporarily attached to the 25th Native Light Infantry. On his leaving that corps to rejoin the 66th, a Regimental Order was issued by the Commandant, making warm allusion to the satisfactory manner in which he had performed his duties, and expressing regret for the loss of so promising an officer.

While stationed at Haidarabad in the Spring of 1871, and subsequently while at Belgaum in the years 1874 and 1875, McMath, with whom sport was little less than a passion, found many opportunities for enjoying his favourite pastime. On one occasion, while pursuing the larger game of the country in the district last named, severe injuries were inflicted on him by a wounded panther. He fortunately succeeded in killing the beast after it closed with him, and, holding his lacerated flesh together, managed, with the aid of his native attendants, who kept pouring water on his head, to walk a distance of six miles to his quarters. There he was tenderly nursed by his brother-officer and bosom friend, Captain Ernest Garratt, to whose care, as he was wont to assert, he owed his life. His constitution was excellent, and so thoroughly did he recover his strength that he was able to take part, in January, 1876, in the long march of the 66th, to Poona, a distance of 220 miles.

After holding for a time the Adjutancy of the Regiment, he obtained, in April, 1877, his company. Early in 1878 he availed himself of leave of absence, and visited England. He returned to India the same year, and rejoined the Head-quarters of the regiment at Kolaba. In March, 1879, he was appointed Officiating Adjutant in the camp of Deolali, through which all troops proceeding from and to England had to pass; and in November of the same year he was again at Poona, temporarily doing duty as Brigade Major.

On the 31st January, 1880, he received, to his great satisfaction, orders to rejoin the regiment for service in Afghanistan. He reached the Head-quarters at Nari Bank, and was there detached, with Lieutenant Lynch and his company, for the purpose of taking up to Kandahar a present of a battery of artillery from the Government to the Wali, Shere Ali Khan. In a letter describing this performance, he writes: "We had hard work taking the guns up the Bolan, also through the Gazaband and Khojak Passes. The latter operation took me two days, having had to encamp the first night on the top of the Khoja Amran Mountains, and taking the battery down the mountain was tough work. I, however, did not lose a single man, camel, bullock, or thing, and handed the battery over complete to the Afghans." This was at Chaman. The day the guns were handed over he received a telegram from Sir Donald Stewart, thanking him for bringing the battery forward with so little delay.

After reaching Kandahar he received the appointment of Commandant of the body guard of the General (his former chief, General Primrose), and had quarters in his garden. In the first days of July he took part in the advance of Burrows' Brigade to the Halmand, and acted as Brigade Major to the Field Force during the action on the 14th with the Wali's mutinied troops at Girishk. In a letter describing the operations of that day, he writes: "I was fourteen hours in the saddle on the 14th without having had a meal, and on the night of the 15th the whole of our force fell back upon this place, a march across a desert of twenty-five miles without a drop of water. Left the Halmand at 6 p.m., and did not arrive till 8 a.m., another fourteen hours in the saddle."

At the battle of Maiwand, on the 27th, McMath was seen steadying his company, to the command of which he had reverted, and was heard quietly to remark: "That's right, men; go on giving them volleys like that!" The company was the third from the right of the fighting line. Shortly after it was forced to retire, Captain McMath was struck by a round shot, which frightfully shattered his shoulder. His faithful servant, Haider Beg—a soldier who eventually escaped into Kandahar—ministered to his wants with water until ordered by him to quit the field and save his own life. The end was not far distant. Within a few minutes from the time of his receiving his first wound a bullet pierced his heart, immediately putting an end to his sufferings. Thus fell one of the best of men and most genial of comrades: "one who"—to quote from General Primrose's letter to the Adjutant-General, published in the "London Gazette" of the 31st

December, 1880—"had his life been spared, would have risen to distinction in Her Majesty's Service."

It is moving to record that Captain McMath's little dog "Nellie"—a pet of the regiment—which had followed her master into action, was subsequently found by the burying party lying dead at his side.

2ND LIEUTENANT E. S. MARSH,

2ND BATTALION, 7TH (ROYAL FUSILIERS).

EVERARD SWAINE MARSH, second son of the Rev. William Marsh, Vicar of Wethersfield, near Braintree, Essex, was born on the 8th June, 1858. He was educated at Wellington College, and when he left, in 1875, was a member of the cricket eleven, and the football twenty. From thence he proceeded to Blackheath, for private tuition under Professor Wollfram. After serving one training in the year 1878 with the West Essex Militia, he entered Sandhurst, and after the usual course, passed out from the college at the final examination second in priority, receiving a prize for Military Topography and Reconnaissance. Gazetted to a second Lieutenancy in the 7th Fusiliers in January, 1879, he joined the regiment at Bombay in the following March, and served with it in that Presidency for a period of two years.

In February, 1880, the battalion was ordered into Afghanistan on active service, and the subject of this notice took part with it in its march to Kandahar. In the month of July he accompanied the relieving force which was sent out to cover the retreat of the remnant of General Burrows' Brigade after the disaster at Maiwand, and with twenty of his men succeeded in taking no less than nine of the Ghazis prisoners, besides killing others. His services on this occasion, for which he was publicly praised by General Brooke, formed a fitting prelude to the act of heroism with which, three weeks afterwards, he closed his brief career.

In the fatal sortie to Deh Khwaja on the 16th August, he rendered up his life in the vain attempt to save that of his wounded brother-officer, Lieutenant Wood. His Colonel, in a letter to his parents, gives the following account of the manner in which he met his death:—" It was at the close of the action at Deh Khwaja that he was killed. He had passed through the thick of the fight, and was returning on Kandahar, when he was told that the dhoolie-bearers had left Lieutenant Wood, who was mortally wounded, to the mercy of the enemy. He at once got some men together and led them to the rescue, but in attempting to lift the dhoolie he was shot dead. It was a gallant act, and he died a soldier's death."

LIEUTENANT C. A. MONTANARO,

ROYAL ARTILLERY.

CHARLES ALFRED MONTANARO, who died on the 20th December, 1879, from the effects of a wound received in action before Kabul on the previous day, was the eldest son of Alfred Montanaro, Esq., late Commissary, Ordnance Department, of Great Grimsby, Lincoln, and formerly of Clifton, Somersetshire, by his marriage with Caroline Eliza, daughter of Captain J. Birch, 73rd Regiment, late of Crosby Lodge, Cumberland. He was born on the 20th June, 1855, and was educated at the Southampton College. Passing direct into Woolwich at his first attempt in February, 1872, he remained at the Academy for the usual course, his terms tallying with those of the late ill-fated Prince Imperial. In August, 1874, he obtained his commission, being gazetted to Battery 5/4 Royal Artillery, with which he did duty for eighteen months at Gosport.

Embarking with the battery in January, 1876, for India, he served with it at Allahabad and Morar until the beginning of 1878, when he joined the Punjab Frontier Force, being appointed to No. 2 Derajat Mountain Battery (Major Swinley's) at Abbottabad.

On the breaking out of hostilities with Afghanistan in the autumn of 1878, Montanaro took part in the advance of the battery which was detailed to the Kuram Valley Field Force, into the enemy's country, and was subsequently present with it in the operations in the Khost Valley, and at the action of Matun. On the renewal of hostilities in the autumn of 1879, the battery again formed a portion of the force under Sir Frederick Roberts, and did excellent service in the long train of events embodied in the second campaign. Accompanying it in the advance on Kabul, Montanaro was present at the battle of Charasiab on the 6th October, 1879, and at the subsequent occupation of Kabul and defence of Sherpur. On the 14th December, 1879, in the operations round Kabul, he distinguished himself by the gallant and determined manner in which he fought his guns on the conical hill till the enemy closed upon them, and by the material assistance he then rendered in bringing them out of action. How he stood to them to the last is recorded in the General's despatch of the 23rd December, 1879, which twice mentions his name. Five days afterwards, on the morning of the 19th, the battery was ordered outside cantonments with a small brigade to shell the enemy out of a village lying to the south-east of Sherpur. Scarcely had the guns gone into action in the open, when a heavy fire was poured upon them by the enemy from the front and flank. At the first discharge young Montanaro received his death-wound, a bullet fired at about 800 yards' distance striking him in the side, traversing his chest, and lodging in his spine. He fell immediately and heavily, as if dead, but when being lifted up gave the order, "Run the gun back." Carried at once into the Native Field Hospital, he received every care which the medical skill and devoted attention of Dr. Duke, the Surgeon of the battery, could bestow. His case, however, was, from the first, hopeless; he never rallied, and died quietly in the evening of the following day. As his first thought, when he was stricken down, was for his guns, so his last thought was for the home circle he loved. A few hours before he passed away, even as the death stupor was stealing on him, he dictated to Major Swinley, who was watching over him, a letter to his father. "I did not like to telegraph to you, for fear it should be too great a shock to you all"—so runs one of the essentially characteristic sentences.

In a letter testifying to the blank left by Lieutenant Montanaro's death, his commanding officer deplores the loss to himself, of a friend, and to the service, of a clever and most promising officer; and Sir Frederick Roberts, making reference to the sad event in his despatch of the 23rd December, 1879, recalls his mention of "this promising young officer's gallantry in standing to his guns to the last on the 14th December." That the estimate formed of him, and thus expressed, is not exaggerated, letters received from many unexpected sources after his death bear ample witness.

The subject of this notice was the inventor of a time-fuze that has been favourably reported on, and also of a saddle for carrying Pioneers' tools, which has been for some time in use, and in connection with which his name is perpetuated, it being entered in the equipment table as "Montanaro's Pattern."

CAPTAIN C. S. MORRISON,

14TH BENGAL CAVALRY (LANCERS).

CLAUDE STEUART MORRISON was the youngest son of the late James Colquhoun Morrison, Esquire, of Palermo, Sicily. He was born at Helensburgh, Dumbartonshire, on the 25th September, 1844, and was educated at the Glasgow Academy, the Forest School, Walthamstow, and Addiscombe. Entering the Indian Army in June, 1861, he did duty for two years with the 1st Battalion, 20th Foot; and after passing his examination in Hindustani was attached for a few months to the 6th Punjab Infantry and the 28th Bengal Native Infantry, respectively. In October, 1864, he was posted to the 3rd Goorkhas, and served with that regiment in the Right Column Dwar Field Force, as Officiating Quartermaster, through the whole of the Bhutan campaign of 1864-1866, being severely wounded in the temple at the outset. He received the Frontier medal, with clasp for Bhutan; and Brigadier-General Tytler testified, in his memorandum of the 31st of March, 1865, to the gallantry he displayed on all occasions of contact with the enemy. In the course of the campaign he held the appointment of Detachment Staff Officer to the camp in advance of Baxar.

On peace being concluded, Morrison proceeded for duty with a wing of his regiment to Bareilly; but his health—which had been undermined by fever contracted during his recent field service—giving way, he was sent home to Europe on eighteen months' leave. After returning to India, he continued for about a year to do duty with his old corps. He was then (August, 1869) appointed to the 14th Bengal Lancers, in which regiment—holding successively the appointments of 3rd and 2nd Squadron Officer, Adjutant, and Squadron Commander—he remained till the day of his death.

In March, 1870, he was promoted to the rank of Captain; and a few weeks afterwards was selected to form one of the deputation sent to Karauli. During a three months' residence at that place, he won golden opinions at head-quarters by the tact and judgment he displayed. "I do not think," wrote the Governor-General's Agent for the States of Rajputana, in recommending him for political employment, "that a better man could be selected;" and the Governor-General in Council was also pleased to signify his approbation of the manner in which his recent duties had been performed.

After doing duty with his regiment for a time subsequently to his rejoining it, he went through the short course of garrison instruction at Rawal Pindi, being specially mentioned for Fortification, Surveying, and Military Law; and three years later succeeded in passing for Army Staff employment. Almost immediately afterwards he again found his way to the front on active service, receiving the appointment of Provost-Marshal to the Force under Brigadier-General Ross in the Jowaki campaign of 1877-1878. "For most zealously carrying out the duties entrusted to him," he was favourably brought to notice in the General's despatch.

Accompanying the Right Wing of his regiment in January, 1879, to Thal, Captain Morrison did duty with it on the frontier during the first of the two Afghan campaigns, frequently crossing into the enemies' territory in pursuit of parties of freebooters, and earning the war medal. After the signing of the treaty of peace at Gandamak he remained with the regiment in spite of ill-health during the trying hot weather which ensued; and on the renewal of hostilities in the autumn of 1879, took part in the advance of the force under Sir Frederick Roberts across the Shutargardan. He was present at the battle of Charasiab (for which a clasp has been granted) on the 6th October, and at the subsequent entry into Kabul: there he remained till the end of November, when, yielding reluctantly to the repeated solicitations of the medical officers, he consented to seek rest, and accompanied the first sick-convoy to Peshawar. He arrived in India in so debilitated a state as to necessitate his being at once sent home on twelve months' leave; but the change came too late to save his life, and he died at the residence of his brother within a few months of reaching this country.

Captain Morrison's death is most deeply and deservedly regretted by all in the regiment. He was a most energetic, painstaking, and thorough officer, ever ready to take an extra turn of duty, or to do anything in his power to help or please his companions.

LIEUT. A. R. MURRAY, STAFF CORPS,

11TH (P.W.O.) BENGAL CAVALRY (LANCERS).

ARCHIBALD ROSS MURRAY was the eldest son of Brigadier-General J. I. Murray, C.B., who in the Mutiny raised that distinguished regiment the 14th Bengal Lancers, late "Murray's Jât Horse." Having obtained a Queen's Indian cadetship in recognition of his father's services, he joined the Depôt of the 44th Regiment in 1874. Shortly afterwards he was transferred to the 9th Foot, and accompanied that regiment to India, remaining with it till 1877, when he was attached to the 13th Bengal Lancers as a Staff Corps probationer.

On the outbreak of the Afghan War, Murray accompanied his regiment to Jamrud and into the Khyber Pass, where it formed part of the Second Division of the Peshawar Valley Field Force. He took part, in December, 1879, with the detachment engaged in the Bazar Afridi expedition under Sir Frederick Maude, and for the gallantry he displayed was mentioned in the General's despatch. During the next six months he continued with the regiment at various posts from the Khyber to Jalalabad, and in the month of June, 1879, shared with it the severe return march to India. Shortly afterwards he was permanently transferred to the 11th P.W.O. Bengal Lancers. He did not, however, live to join that corps. On the 18th July, 1879, his bright and promising career was cut short by cholera, to which disease he succumbed, after a few hours' illness, at Tret Punjab, at the early age of twenty-four years.

In a letter expressing his regard for the subject of this memoir, General Maude writes as follows :—"I had professionally a high opinion of him. I had intended, had his regiment not been sent to the front, to have made him my orderly officer, so as to give him an opportunity of seeing more service." And Colonel Low, of the 13th Bengal Lancers, in referring to his death, says : "When he left us we all felt it to be a regimental misfortune. A finer fellow or more promising officer I never saw."

A handsome memorial has been erected in the Church at Rawal Pindi "In affectionate remembrance" of him by his brother officers of H.M. 9th Foot and 13th Bengal Lancers.

BT. LIEUT.-COL. W. H. NEWPORT, STAFF CORPS,

28TH BOMBAY N.I.

WILLIAM HENRY NEWPORT, second son of the late Major Christopher Newport of the Bombay Army, was born at Bombay on the 23rd February, 1837, and was educated at Cheltenham and Addiscombe. Entering the Bombay Army in December, 1855, he was gazetted to the 3rd Europeans, and subsequently served with that regiment through the Indian Mutiny. He was present at the siege and capture of Ratgarh, the action of Baroda, where he carried the Queen's colours, the relief of Saugor, the capture of Garakota, the forcing of the Madenpur Pass, the siege and storming of Jhansi, the battle of Betwa, and the storming of Lohari, where he was severely wounded. At the assault of Jhansi he assisted in carrying out, under heavy fire, a wounded officer, after the order to retire had been given. For this act of gallantry, as also for leading stormers at the assault of Lohari, he was mentioned in despatches. He also took part in the actions at Kunch, Muttra, and Galauli; in the capture of Kalpi, and in the battle and subsequent capture of Gwalior. For these services he received the medal with clasp, and brevet rank on his promotion in 1867.

After the Mutiny, Lieutenant Newport joined the Staff Corps, and was posted for duty to the 18th Bombay Native Infantry. He served with a detachment of that regiment against the Waghirs in Kathiawar in 1865-66, and in Abyssinia in 1867. It was in that year that he was promoted to the rank of Captain and Brevet-Major. After this he served for a short time with the 25th, the 28th, and the 16th Native Infantry. From 1874 to 1876 he officiated as Fort Adjutant at Asurgarh, at the expiration of which period he returned as Wing Officer to the 28th Native Infantry. In the meantime (December, 1875) he had obtained his Majority. In 1877 he became second in command of the regiment, and received his Brevet Lieutenant-Colonelcy.

Lieut.-Colonel Newport returned to England on leave in June, 1878, but was recalled in October, 1879, to join his regiment on its being ordered up for service in Afghanistan. Engaged on varied duty during the spring of 1880, he marched with his regiment to reinforce the garrison of Kandahar on the 16th July of that year, and on the morning of the 16th of August sallied forth to take his part in the sortie which ended so disastrously. The history of that ill-fated attempt to capture the village of Deh Khwaja is well known; suffice it to say, that Lieut.-Colonel Newport led the detachment of the 28th who were with him, together with a company of the 7th Fusiliers, in the most gallant manner into the village. They reached an open space surrounded by walls, whence a deadly fire was at once opened upon them; and finding themselves hemmed in on every side, and cut off from all chance of reinforcements, a retreat was ordered. It was not until the last of this gallant little band were leaving that fatal spot, that Lieut.-Colonel Newport was observed standing, resting on his sword. On being questioned by Captain Adderley of the Fusiliers as to why he did not come on, he pointed to a bullet-wound in his left breast, and ordered him to take the men out of the village as fast as he could. He was carried a short distance by some of his own men, assisted by one or two of their comrades of the Fusiliers, but died in their arms, his body being afterwards recovered and buried with those of the other officers and men who fell at the same time.

As a soldier, Lieut.-Colonel Newport won the esteem and goodwill of all who became associated with him; whilst in private life he endeared himself to a large circle of relatives and friends, by his affectionate solicitude for the one, and the ever-ready hand of friendship he extended to the other.

An extract from a letter of his Commanding Officer, Colonel Nimmo (who was also severely wounded in this ill-fated engagement), may fitly close this short summary of an honourable career: "He won the admiration of all by his gallantry and bravery; and often when lying on my back unable to move, the men used to come and speak to me of him, recounting how splendidly he had behaved, and what confidence they had in him."

Lieut.-Colonel Newport married in November, 1868, Caroline Tunno, youngest daughter of the late Stanley Clarke, Esq., of Charlton Kings, Cheltenham, by whom he had issue four daughters.

LIEUT.-COL. GILBERT NICHOLETTS, STAFF CORPS,

COMMANDANT 2ND BALUCH REGIMENT.

HE subject of this memoir, who died at Kokaran, near Kandahar, of cholera, on the 18th July, 1879, was the eldest son of John Nicholetts, Esq., of South Petherton, Somerset. He was born on the 13th July, 1826; and after receiving an education at Rugby, entered the Indian Army in July, 1848, obtaining a Lieutenancy in 1st Bombay Fusiliers. After serving with that regiment for a period of six years, he was transferred, in 1854, as Adjutant, to the 1st Baluchis.

On the Persian War breaking out in 1856, Gilbert Nicholetts accompanied the late General John Jacob to the Persian Gulf; and serving with the 1st Sind Horse, was present at the attack on and capture of the Mohamra Forts. For his services he received the Persian medal and clasp. When peace was proclaimed, he rejoined the 1st Baluchis, which regiment had been despatched to the Punjab and Northwest Provinces, on the outbreak of the Mutiny. In the campaign that followed in 1857-58, he was with the regiment throughout in the conspicuous part it played. While serving against the Fatehgarh rebels, he was present at the action at Gangri on the 14th December, 1857, and took part in the advance on and occupation of the enemy's position at Kasganj. Subsequently, while serving against the Rohilkhand rebels, he was present at the action at Anupshahr, the skirmish at Dinapur, the destruction of the enemy's boats, and at many minor affairs on the banks of the Ganges. In the campaign in 1858 he participated in the attack on the enemy's fortified position at Rampur Kussia, succeeding to the temporary command of the regiment on his Colonel (Farquhar) being disabled, and retaining it through the remainder of the campaign. He was present at the surrender and occupation of the Fort of Amethi, and subsequently with Lord Clyde's column at the occupation of Sankarpur, the action with Beni Madho at Dhundia Keria, and with a movable column detached after the action to drive the enemy across the Gumti. He then rejoined the force with the Commander-in-Chief at Lucknow, and served throughout the operations across the Gogra, including the advance on and occupation of Baraitch, the action with the Nana's force at Brigidia, and occupation of the Fort, the capture of the Masjidia Fort, the defeat of the Nana's force at Banki, and the final expulsion of the rebels across the Rapti, on the 31st December, 1858, earning a second medal.

In 1866 Captain Nicholetts (who had, in the meantime, received his promotion) was specially selected by the Commander-in-Chief of Bombay to command the 2nd Baluchis; and when, in October, 1877, the regiment was ordered up to the frontier, the high state of discipline and efficiency in which it left Karachi, was sufficient to show that Sir Robert Napier's confidence had not been misplaced.

In October, 1878, Colonel Nicholetts proceeded, in command of the regiment, from Dera Ghazi Khan to Quetta, to join the force under General Biddulph which was in course of concentration, in view of the impending hostilities with Afghanistan. He took part with the regiment in the advance into the enemy's country in November, and was present at the action at Takht-i-pul and the subsequent entry into Kandahar on the 8th January, 1879; and afterwards, between January and July, in the expeditions to Girishk, Har Kalabist, and the Khakrez Valley.

His distinguished career was now drawing to a close. In the second week of July, while in command of the regiment at Kokaran, he was seized with cholera, to the ravages of which disease he succumbed on the 18th of the month.

Lieutenant-Colonel Nicholetts was a thorough soldier, distinguished for the great love he bore his profession. Though he was strict in maintaining discipline in the regiment which he had raised to such a high state of efficiency, his genial manner and kindness of heart rendered him deservedly beloved by all ranks. By his untimely death the Indian Army sustained a heavy loss.

LIEUTENANT CHARLES NUGENT,

ROYAL ENGINEERS.

THE subject of this memoir, who lost his life through the premature explosion of a mine during the operations in the vicinity of Kabul on the 23rd December, 1879, was the eldest son of General C. L. Nugent, by his marriage with Charlotte Marcia, fifth daughter of the late Major-General Pitt, K.H., Commanding the Forces in New Zealand. He was born at Auckland, New Zealand, on the 19th February, 1850, and was educated at St. Andrew's, Scotland, under Mr. Thomas Hodge, and Dublin, under Mr. H. Basset. He entered the Royal Military Academy in 1869, and passing out twenty-first in priority after the usual course, was gazetted, in August, 1871, to the Royal Engineers.

After serving for three years in England, he proceeded, in September, 1874, to India. On his arrival, he was posted to the Bengal Sappers and Miners, and did duty for four years at Rurki and Rawal Pindi.

On the concentration of the troops on the frontier in the autumn of 1878, in view of the impending hostilities with Afghanistan, Lieutenant Nugent proceeded in command of the No. 7 Company of the Sappers and Miners to join the Kuram Valley Field Force, and taking part in the advance into the enemy's country, rendered important service on the road over the Shutargardan Pass, and in other localities. On the renewal of hostilities in the autumn of 1879, he took part, in command of his company, in the advance of the force under Sir Frederick Roberts, on Kabul, and was present at the battle of Charasiab on the 6th October, and the subsequent entry into that city. During the occupation of Sherpur, he was employed on the works for the defence of the cantonment, in the construction of which he and his brother officers won golden opinions, by the zeal and ability they displayed; and was also previously engaged in the hazardous duty of destroying the large quantity of powder lying loose about the Bala Hissar. On the 23rd December he was directed to join General Macpherson's force with his company, to aid in the destruction of the line of forts held by the enemy to the southward of the cantonment. In performing this duty he entered, in company with Captain Dundas, V.C., Royal Engineers, a fort immediately under the Siah Sang, and before he emerged from it two violent mine explosions took place. On search being made immediately afterwards, his lifeless remains, together with those of Captain Dundas, were discovered by his comrades. Death had apparently been instantaneous, the bodies having been thrown by the explosion—the premature nature of which has been attributed to the too rapid consumption of a home-made quick-match—completely across the enclosure of the fort.

Lieutenant Nugent was buried with Captain Dundas on the 25th December, in the Sherpur cemetery. In a Division Order issued by Sir Frederick Roberts on the day of the funeral, the following words occur:—"Both Captain Dundas and Lieutenant Nugent had gained the esteem and admiration of all by their manly, modest, and courteous bearing. By their death the Corps of Royal Engineers has lost two most valuable officers, and the Kabul Field Force two gallant and much lamented comrades."

COLONEL J. J. O'BRYEN, STAFF CORPS,

COMMANDANT 22ND (PUNJAB) BENGAL N.I.

AMES JOSEPH O'BRYEN was the sixth surviving son of Terence O'Bryen, Esquire, of Glancolumbkill, County Clare, Ireland, a lineal descendant of the ancient royal line of Thomond —the last of whom, Murrough O'Brien, on surrendering his kingdom or principality to King Henry VIII. in 1543, obtained for himself and his heirs permission to change the *i* in the family name into *y*.

In November, 1843, the subject of this notice obtained an Ensigncy in the 16th Native Infantry (Grenadiers) in the Honourable East India Company's Service. Taking part in the Sutlej campaign of 1845-46, he was present at the battles of Mudki, Firozshah, and Sobraon, in the latter of which he was wounded. The gallantry he displayed in action won for him the commendation of his Commanding Officer, Brigadier Maclaren, who was himself mortally wounded in the campaign. For his services he received the medal and two clasps.

Posted to the Adjutancy of the regiment in 1852, O'Bryen continued to hold the appointment till the disbanding of the Grenadiers in the Mutiny of 1857. For the next six years he did duty in different parts of India, being for a time barrack-master of Moradabad and Almorah, and also officiating second in command of the newly-raised 16th, or Lucknow Regiment. He was admitted to the Staff Corps on its formation; and in 1863 obtained his Majority. In 1864 he became permanent second in command of the 22nd Punjab Infantry, in which capacity he served in the Lushai expedition of 1872, receiving the medal and clasp. In 1874 he obtained command of his regiment as well as his Colonelcy, and three years afterwards served with it during the Jowaki campaign of 1877, the clasp for the same being awarded to him.

In December, 1879, Colonel O'Bryen marched with his regiment into Afghanistan on its being ordered up from the Peshawar district to form part of the 2nd Division of the Kabul Field Force. It was but for a little time, however, that he was able to share with it in the Khyber the duties which fell to its lot. His long service of thirty-six years and upwards had some time since begun to tell on his constitution; but though advised by his medical officer to take a few months' leave and recruit his health, he steadily refused to desert his post at so critical a time. His condition rapidly grew worse; and five weeks after crossing the frontier he succumbed to the effects of exposure and hardship, dying at Safed Sang on the 21st of January, 1880, in the 57th year of his age. By his death, the Service lost a most efficient, active, and zealous officer, conspicuous alike for his gallantry and his great goodness of heart.

Colonel O'Bryen married, in 1851, Louisa, daughter of R. Barnes, Esquire, of Purneah, Bengal, and leaves a large family.

MAJOR C. V. OLIVER,

66TH (BERKSHIRE) REGIMENT.

CHARLES VALENTINE OLIVER was the second son of John Dudley Oliver, Esquire, of Cherrymount, County Wicklow, Ireland, who was the head of a younger branch of the Olivers, of Castle Oliver, County Limerick, a family well known in Ireland for many generations.

The subject of this memoir was born on the 9th March, 1836, and was one of five brothers who entered the Army within a short time of each other. He was gazetted to the 66th Regiment, as Ensign, in 1854, and passed his whole service in that distinguished corps in various parts of the world, including India, Gibraltar, the Channel Islands, Great Britain, and Ireland. Although never purchased over, his promotion was slow, and he only obtained his regimental majority a short time before his death.

Major Oliver was one of the officers sent out to Jamaica in 1866 to serve on the court-martial which tried two officers accused of acts of cruelty in putting down the negro rebellion in that island, and which honourably acquitted them. After his return to England, he served with the regiment at Aldershot, Jersey, Guernsey, the Curragh, and Dublin; and in 1870 proceeded with the head-quarters a second time to India. When the regiment was stationed at Karachi, he was for a considerable time in charge of the Sanitarium of Ghizri.

Major Oliver marched with the regiment to Kandahar in February, 1880, and was present at the action on the Halmand, near Girishk, on the 14th July. At the battle of Maiwand, on the 27th, he was one of the three officers present with the colours who came out unhurt. It is said that he and General Burrows were the two last to leave the field, and they were so hard pressed that he was obliged, in self-defence, to shoot with a rifle two or three of the Afghan cavalry who attacked them on the open plain. It will perhaps not be out of place here to remark on the pain and distress he was subjected to through his name being confused with that of another officer, and being quoted in several of the English journals in a list published by them of the survivors of the battle who were the first to reach Kandahar, thus making it appear that he had ridden on ahead of his men. The officer alluded to was another of the same name belonging to a different service. The fact is, that telegraphic communication had been severed some hours before Major Oliver with the scanty remnant of his regiment reached the city walls. He arrived in a state of great exhaustion from which he never quite recovered.

Although Major Oliver suffered much from weakness during the siege, he nevertheless commanded all that was left of the 66th at the battle of Kandahar on the 1st September. After the defeat of Ayub Khan's army, he continued in a low state of health, and he subsequently fell an easy victim to the disease—small-pox—which eventually carried him off on the 10th October, 1880. His death was thus alluded to in the "Kandahar News:"—"All our readers will receive with feelings of deep sorrow and regret the sad news of the death of Major C. V. Oliver, 66th Regiment, which occurred yesterday morning in the citadel, from small-pox. After bringing back the remnants of his regiment from the fatal and terrible field of Maiwand, and the still more terrible retreat on Kandahar, and passing safely through the perils of the siege, he was on the eve of marching to India, en route to England with his regiment, when the fell disease struck him down, and in little more than a week our Queen and country had to deplore the loss of a faithful servant, and the 66th Regiment, the Kandahar Field Force, and the whole Army, a fine soldier, brave officer, good companion, and staunch friend. Requiescat in pace."

2ND LIEUTENANT W. R. OLIVEY,

66TH (BERKSHIRE) REGIMENT.

HE subject of this notice, who was killed at Maiwand on the 27th July, 1880, while carrying the Queen's colour of his regiment, was the second son of Lieut.-Colonel W. R. Olivey, Chief Paymaster, Army Pay Department (for nearly twenty years Paymaster of the 1st Battalion, 12th Regiment) and Elizabeth, his wife, only daughter of the late R. Goodfellow, Esq., of Falmouth, Cornwall.

Walter Rice Olivey was born at Sydney, New South Wales, on the 19th March, 1860. After receiving a preliminary education, he was prepared for Sandhurst at the Grammar School at Bury, in Lancashire, by the Rev. E. H. Gulliver, the then head-master, and went direct from that establishment to the College. Passing out in December, 1879, fifteenth in the honour list, and taking the prize for Military Topography, he was gazetted, a month afterwards, to the 66th Regiment, and on the 11th March, 1880, left Portsmouth for India, to join headquarters.

Olivey reached Kandahar in time to take part with the regiment in the advance of Burrows' Brigade to the Halmand in the first days of July, and was present on the 14th of that month at the dispersing of the mutinied troops of the Wali Shere Ali Khan in the neighbourhood of Girishk. At the battle of Maiwand, on the 27th, he forfeited his young life with the 300 officers and men of the regiment who fell. Early on that day he was severely wounded, but would not relinquish the colour he was carrying, though urged to do so. "I was speaking to him after he was wounded," writes one of his brother officers. "His helmet was off and a handkerchief was tied round his head." He was last seen in the garden where the final desperate stand was made, encouraging the men around him, and holding his colour aloft as a rallying point.

LIEUTENANT E. G. OSBORNE,

ROYAL HORSE ARTILLERY.

EDMUND GEORGE OSBORNE, who was killed in action at Maiwand on the 27th July, 1880, was the fourth son of Robert Osborne, Esq., of Laurence Weston, Henbury, Gloucestershire, and Emily Theresa, eldest daughter of Admiral Charles Warde, K.H., of Squerryes Court, Westerham, Kent. He was born on the 10th December, 1853, and was educated at Sydney College, Bath. In the spring of 1872 he competed for admission into the Royal Military Academy at Woolwich, and succeeded, out of a large number of candidates, in taking second place. Passing out of the Academy at Midsummer, 1873, he was gazetted to a Lieutenancy in the Royal Artillery, and shortly afterwards proceeded to Bengal in one of the garrison batteries. A few weeks after arriving in India he exchanged into Field Battery F/4 Royal Artillery, then stationed at Saugor. He was subsequently appointed District Adjutant of Artillery at Jabalpur, and retained the post till the autumn of 1878.

On the concentration of the troops on the frontier, in view of the impending invasion of Afghanistan, Osborne received the appointment of Adjutant of the Royal Artillery Kuram Valley Field Force, and subsequently served in his new capacity through the whole of the first campaign. For his conduct in the assault and capture of the Peiwar Kotal he was honourably mentioned in General Roberts' despatch of the 2nd December, 1878; and Colonel Lindsay, commanding the artillery of the force, reported that he had "received valuable assistance from Lieutenant E. G. Osborne, R.A., his Adjutant, and that this officer was most useful, in aiding the officers of No. 1 Mountain Battery, especially after Captain Kelso was killed." He subsequently took part in the Khost Valley expedition, and in nearly all the minor affairs in which the force was engaged.

On the conclusion of the first Afghan campaign, Lieutenant Osborne returned to England on leave. In less than a week after his arrival at home, however, the news of the Kabul massacre and of the renewal of hostilities reached him, and he at once hurried out with all speed to India. On arriving in Bombay, he was ordered to rejoin his battery at Saugor, but very shortly afterwards was again sent to the front for service with Sir Frederick Roberts' Division. On his way up country, the intelligence reached him of his transfer to Battery E/B, Royal Horse Artillery, then on its march to the front to form part of the South Afghanistan Field Force. Joining the battery *en route*, he accompanied it to Kandahar. He subsequently took part in the advance of Burrows' Brigade, in the first week in July, 1880, to the Halmand, and did excellent service with his guns in the encounter with the Wali's mutinied troops in the neighbourhood of Girishk. In the disastrous battle of Maiwand, on the 27th of the month, he remained unhurt till he was ordered to limber up his guns and retire. Few of his men were left at this time to carry out the order; and at once dismounting, he went to their assistance. It was in the performance of this act that he was shot dead, rendering up his life at his post with a heroism which has contributed in securing the verdict that on that ill-fated day " the conduct of the Artillery was beyond praise."

" I would bear testimony," writes Major A. H. Murray, R.A., " to his (Lieutenant Osborne's) high spirit and love of his profession. I am also aware that the late Major Blackwood had the highest opinion of him as an energetic and reliable young officer. Whenever there was tough work to do, young Osborne was to the front, and doing it well. He was a keen sportsman and brilliant polo player—altogether as fine a specimen of the British subaltern as I have met in twenty-four years' service."

LIEUT. W. C. OWEN, STAFF CORPS,

3RD BOMBAY CAVALRY (QUEEN'S OWN).

WILLIAM CHARLES OWEN was the only son of William Louis Owen, Esq., of the Bengal Police; was grandson of the late Major Arthur Owen, of the 26th Bengal Native Infantry, Honourable East India Company's Service; and great-nephew of the late General Sir John Hearsay. He was born the 11th of June, 1848, and received his education under Mr. Berridge, at the Collegiate School, St. John's Wood, and under Mr. Ogle, at St. Clere, Sevenoaks. From the school last named he passed into Sandhurst in February, 1871; and obtaining while at the college the first prize for drawing, and a prize for gymnastics, passed out in the first class.

In December, 1871, he was gazetted to a sub-lieutenancy in the 3rd King's Own Hussars, and joined that regiment at Ahmadnagar in November, 1872. While serving with the head-quarters at Mhow, he went through a course of garrison instruction. In May, 1878, he was appointed a probationer for the Bombay Staff Corps, and subsequently passed the final examination for that branch of the service —his papers being pronounced "first-rate."

Posted to the 3rd Queen's Own Bombay Light Cavalry, Owen did duty with it at various stations in the Presidency till February, 1880, when it was ordered up from Disa for service in the Afghan War. Accompanying it to Kandahar, he subsequently took part with it, in the first days of July, in the advance of Burrows' Brigade to the Halmand, and in the successful encounter, on the 14th, with the Wali's mutinied troops in the neighbourhood of Girishk. In the disastrous battle of Maiwand on the 27th, after being kept standing, with the rest of the regiment, under a murderous fire for four hours without a vestige of cover, he is said to have been shot while charging through the horde of Ghazis who were swarming on the rear of the then retreating Infantry.

This promising young officer met his death in the courageous discharge of his duty; and his name will not soon be forgotten in his regiment. " A more genuine and honest fellow "—to quote the words of one of his brother officers, written after his death—"never breathed." He leaves a widow and an infant son.

LIEUT. EDMUND PALMER, STAFF CORPS,

BENGAL COMMISSARIAT DEPARTMENT.

HE subject of this memoir was the eldest son of Lieutenant-Colonel Edmund Palmer, R.A., and great-grandson of John Palmer, Esq., M.P. for the City of Bath, and Comptroller-General of the Post Office. He was born at St. Helena, on the 10th February, 1851, and after receiving a private education, was prepared by Mr. Thompson, of St. Heliers, Jersey, for Sandhurst. He entered the Royal Military College in 1868, and passing out after the usual course, obtained a commission, by purchase, in November 1870, in the 1st Battalion the Buffs, which regiment he joined a few months afterwards at Sitapur. During his service in Bengal he acted for a short period as Interpreter to the Battalion, and only relinquished the post in order to enter the Staff Corps. Of his proficiency as a regimental officer, the late Colonel Cox, of the Buffs, on more than one occasion, expressed his appreciation.

In January, 1875, Lieutenant Palmer succeeded in passing the Higher Standard examination; and subsequently served as Wing Subaltern with the 41st Bengal Native Infantry, until he was appointed, in 1877, to the Commissariat Department of the Indian Staff Corps. After doing duty for a time at various stations in Bengal, he was selected, in February, 1879, to serve on the Commissariat Staff of the Khyber Field Force, and remained actively employed on the line of communications till the day of his death. During this period the zeal and intelligence with which he performed the harassing duties which fell to his lot, earned for him the character of a "hard-working man;" and his genial and cheerful disposition endeared him to his comrades, and helped to relieve the tedium of duty in the isolated forts on the line of communication. He was mortally wounded, on the evening of the 14th April, 1880, in the Hissarak expedition, while acting as galloper to Colonel Ball-Acton, commanding the force, and died on the morning of the 15th. On the following day he was buried with military honours at Pezwan.

Lieutenant Palmer leaves a widow (daughter of Dr. S. C. Amesbury, of the Bengal Army, Surgeon-Major Bengal Sappers and Miners, and Station Staff-Surgeon and Civil-Surgeon, Rurki) and an infant daughter.

LIEUTENANT EDMUND PALMER, STAFF CORPS.

The deceased officer was sprung from a family which has rendered the country good service. His grandfather, Captain Edmund Palmer, of H.M.S. "Hebrus," obtained a Companionship of the Bath and the gold medal for the capture of the French frigate, "L'Etoile," the last tricolour hauled down in the old war; his grandmother was niece of the great Earl of St. Vincent; and his maternal grandfather, Lieutenant-Colonel Ross, was dangerously wounded at the battle of Vittoria.

CAPTAIN E. W. PERRY,

40TH (2ND SOMERSETSHIRE) REGIMENT.

ERNEST WENMAN PERRY, who died of cholera at Quetta, Baluchistan, on the 19th of June, 1879, was the fourth son of James Bracey Perry, Esq., of Ley Hall, Handsworth, Staffordshire, and Marianne, his wife, daughter of William Wenman, Esq., of Gosbrooke, Staffordshire. He was born on the 2nd August, 1846, and was educated at Leamington. In May, 1870, he was gazetted to an Ensigncy in the 2nd West India Regiment, and in June, 1871, purchased his Lieutenancy. Exchanging shortly afterwards into the 40th Foot, he accompanied that regiment, in October, 1872, to India, and served with it for a period of six years at various stations in Bengal.

On the outbreak of hostilities with Afghanistan in the autumn of 1878, Captain Perry volunteered for active service in any capacity, and after some delay was sent to the front on Transport Service. Detailed for duty to General Stewart's Division of the Army of Invasion, he served through the whole of the first campaign on the Kandahar line of communication and at the base, sharing the arduous and important work which fell to the lot of the department to which he was attached, and approving himself an officer of energy and resource in overcoming the innumerable difficulties incident to his appointment. The exposure and hardship which he underwent in the course of the operations eventually proved, however, too much for him, and within a few weeks of the signing of the treaty of Gandamak, he fell a victim to the disease to whose ravages so many of his fellow-countrymen subsequently succumbed.

OFFICIATING DEP. SURG.-GEN. J. H. PORTER,

ARMY MEDICAL DEPARTMENT.

JOSHUA HENRY PORTER, who died in the Sherpur cantonment near Kabul, on the 9th of January, 1880, while serving as Principal Medical Officer of the Force under the command of General Sir F. Roberts, was the eldest son of the late Joshua Porter, Esq., High Sheriff of Dublin, and was born on the 24th May, 1831. He received his early education under the tuition of the Rev. Thomas Flynn, of Dublin, and went afterwards to the Diocesan School of Elphin, on Mr. Flynn becoming head master of that institution. His bright, happy disposition as a boy made him a general favourite with his masters and schoolfellows. At an early age he exhibited a special taste for mechanical pursuits, and in after life his aptness in this direction proved to be of much service to him in his surgical practice. He expressed a desire to become a surgeon while still very young, and when, on leaving school, he was apprenticed to his uncle, the late W. H. Porter—then the eminent Professor of Surgery in the Royal College of Surgeons of Ireland—he devoted himself to the study of Surgery and Medicine with the same steadiness of purpose and zeal that distinguished him subsequently throughout his professional career. The records of the Meath Hospital and County of Dublin Infirmary show that while a student there he gained the junior Surgical prize in the session of 1849-50, the prize in Clinical Surgery in 1850, and the senior Surgical prize in the session of 1850-51. Dr. Samuel Gordon, President of the College of Physicians, and Vice-President of the British Medical Association in Ireland, when commenting publicly in Dublin on the death of Mr. Porter, referred to this part of his life in the following terms:—" To some of us he was known in his student days as the most intelligent and painstaking clinical clerk of his time, and at the same time the most genial companion. His watchful care over the patients entrusted to his charge, and the sense of responsibility which he felt, augured well for the further development of industry, observation, and conscientiousness, when he came to be a qualified surgeon; and these three qualities he combined in a higher degree than perhaps is often met with."

In 1852 Mr. Porter became a Licentiate of the Royal College of Surgeons of

Ireland, and in June, 1853, he was gazetted Assistant-Surgeon in the 97th Regiment. In May, 1854, this regiment embarked for foreign service, and towards the end of the following month landed in the Piræus. Shortly afterwards, in July, the regiment was visited by an appalling outbreak of cholera, which taxed the energies of the regimental medical staff to the utmost. The conscientious and unselfish attention which Mr. Porter devoted to the discharge of his trying duties on this occasion, established his reputation among all ranks in the corps as a thoroughly good and reliable surgeon. In November of the same year, the 97th Regiment left Greece and proceeded to the Crimea, where it remained actively engaged in the siege operations until the fall of Sebastopol. In 1857 Mr. Porter proceeded with his regiment to India, and took part in numerous engagements with the Sepoy mutineers, including the siege and capture of Lucknow, and the storming of the Kaisèr Bagh. He was also engaged in the subsequent military operations in Bundlecund in 1859. The value of the services rendered by him during the nineteen years he passed in the 97th Regiment, and the feelings of esteem and affectionate regard which existed towards him in the minds of his comrades of all grades, cannot be better shown than by quoting from a farewell letter written to him by Major Annesley, the officer commanding the 97th, at the time he was leaving the regiment to take up another appointment:—

"As you will soon be leaving us," says the writer, "I hope you will allow me to bear testimony not only to your very high character as an officer and a gentleman, but to the invaluable services you have rendered the 97th Regiment as medical officer during the nineteen years you have served in it. I saw you join, and I now see you leave; and the very great regret I feel at losing you as a companion and medical adviser is shared by every officer and soldier in the regiment.

"I have had opportunities of witnessing and admiring the skill, energy, and unremitting attention you have always shown in the performance of your duties, and at times under very trying circumstances. During the fearful epidemic of cholera in the Piræus, where we lost so many men, during the terrible winter of 1854, in the Crimea, and later, when the 97th formed the assaulting and ladder party at the storming of the Redan, and you were in sole charge of the many wounded on that occasion; again in India during the Mutiny, when the regiment suffered from cholera, small-pox, and sunstroke;—on all these occasions your services were deserving of the highest praise. Under fire you have proved yourself a gallant soldier; in the hospital, a most careful, kind-hearted, and eminently skilful surgeon and physician.

"During your stay in the 97th Regiment you succeeded in gaining the confidence, respect, and esteem of every man in it."

It would not be easy to conceive a tribute to meritorious service of which an army medical officer might be more justly proud than of this.

The appointment which Mr. Porter entered upon after leaving the 97th Regiment, and for which he was selected solely from the professional reputation and high character he had already won in the service, was the Assistant Professorship of Military Surgery in the Army Medical School at Netley. In this new position he displayed all the superior qualities which had been anticipated. As an operating surgeon he proved himself to possess judgment, resolution, and skill. In his province of supervising and instructing the young surgeons who were about to enter the public service, while maintaining regularity and strict discipline, he was never wanting in kind consideration and tact. His industry and professional zeal formed a good example to all with whom he was associated. During the time he was holding the appointment, notwithstanding the numerous demands on his time, he found opportunities of publishing several surgical essays and reports of much practical value, more particularly a work which is now in its second edition, the "Surgeon's Pocket-book," specially adapted for the use of medical officers in the military medical service. This work had originally gained one of the prizes offered by the Empress of Germany, on the occasion of the Vienna World-Exhibition, for the "best handbook on surgical appliances and operations for the battlefield." During the same period, too, in April, 1876, the Alexander Memorial prize of £50 and a gold medal were awarded to Mr. Porter for the best essay on a particular surgical subject. This prize had been open to competition by all the executive medical officers of the Army. Mr. Porter also, during this period, took an active interest in the ambulance work of the Society of St. John of Jerusalem, in England, of which he was an Honorary Associate.

In January, 1879, Surgeon-Major Porter left England for active service in India, and was shortly afterwards posted to the charge of one of the field hospitals of Sir Sam. Browne's Division of the Army operating in Afghanistan. He accompanied the Division to Jalalabad, and afterwards moved to the front at Gandamak. When the troops were about to quit the last-named position, he was selected to accompany an officer of the Quartermaster-General's Department, and join in organizing the camping and hospital arrangements for the return of the troops through the Khyber Passes to India. He received great praise for the energy and judgment with which he accomplished this important duty under the trying circumstances of the intense heat and many difficult conditions which prevailed at the time. His Excellency Sir Frederick Haines, the Commander-in-Chief, by General Order, dated, Simla, 14th October, 1879, announced that "while grateful to all for the zeal and devotion displayed in the discharge of most trying duties, the Commander-in-Chief is more especially so to Surgeons-Major J. H. Porter and J. A. Hanbury, of the British Medical Service, for their able and efficient arrangements;" and in a subsequent paragraph conveyed the special thanks of the Viceroy and Governor-General in Council to these two medical officers. Surgeon-Major Porter remained a short time at Peshawar, where he superintended the hospital arrangements for the reception and treatment of the officers and men who had fallen sick during the return march to India, and was then appointed to officiate as Deputy Surgeon-General of the Allahabad Division.

On the resumption of hostilities which followed the massacre of the Staff of the British Embassy at Kabul, Mr. Porter was suddenly ordered to leave Allahabad and join the head-quarters of General Roberts at Ali Khel. On reaching his destination he was ordered to take charge of the Divisional Field Hospital, but on the first march of the force, on September the 27th, an attack was made upon it near Jaji Thana by some of the hill-tribes, and in this encounter Dr. Townsend, the Principal Medical Officer of the Division, was wounded in the face and compelled to retire from the field. This casualty left Surgeon-Major Porter senior medical officer, and from that date until his fatal illness, including the time when the Division fought its way over the Shutargardan Pass to the city of Kabul, up to the last assault of the enemy on the Sherpur cantonments, he discharged the duties of his new office. Here, again, although the period of his service with the Division was relatively brief, Surgeon-Major Porter acquired the confidence and regard of officers and men of all ranks in the force. The Divisional Order which was issued by Sir Frederick Roberts at the time of his decease runs as follows:—"The Lieutenant-General announces with deep regret the death of Officiating Deputy Surgeon-General J. H. Porter, Principal Medical Officer of the Division. Dr. Porter served in the Crimea, Indian Mutiny, and the late Afghan campaigns with distinction, and had gained experience from them which has been invaluable in the important office he has lately held. By his death Her Majesty's Service is deprived of an officer of great merit. The Lieutenant-General in company with the officers and men of the force, loses a friend whose professional skill was always at the service of the sick and suffering, and whose kindness of disposition had endeared him to all." And the then Minister for War, Colonel Stanley, in moving the Army Estimates for the year 1880 in the House of Commons, paid a striking tribute to his memory. "The medical service, and the medical world in general," he said, "have suffered a great loss by the death of Deputy Surgeon-General Porter at Sherpur. He died in the discharge of his duty as truly as if he had laid down his life on the field of battle. He leaves behind him a reputation to which his friends will look with satisfaction and a memory dear to all those who knew him.'" The illness to which Mr. Porter succumbed was a severe attack of pneumonia, a malady which was prevalent at the time in the cantonment.

Surgeon-Major Porter occupied a position in the estimation and regard of his professional brethren no less distinguished than that which he held among his military companions and friends of the combatant ranks. Professor Maclean of Netley, who was intimately acquainted with his personal character as well as with his work as a surgeon, thus publicly spoke of him: "I have in my life known few men more worthy of being loved and respected. As a surgeon he was cautious, patient, painstaking; he laid surgical hands rashly on no man; but, when his mind was made up to act, his hand executed with rare skill what his mind had conceived. He was eminently a successful surgeon. No woman had a more tender heart: he was a loyal colleague, and a much trusted friend."

This memoir cannot perhaps be more fitly closed than by quoting the words uttered by one on the first occasion which offered itself of publicly testifying to the admirable qualities which had distinguished his friend—of one who was ably assisted by Surgeon-Major Porter for five years in discharging the duties of the chair of Military Surgery at the Army Medical School at Netley, namely, Surgeon-General Thomas Longmore, C.B., to whom the editor of this work is indebted for the particulars already given. "The soundness of his judgment in surgical diagnosis," observed the professor in reference to his late colleague, "the dexterity he had acquired as an operator, his zeal for the professional reputation of his department, his indefatigable industry and devotion to duty, his warm-hearted and amiable disposition, formed a combination of qualities which made not only myself, but others who were well acquainted with him, look forward to his filling the highest posts in his department with distinguished credit; and though all too brief, his career in Afghanistan, particularly that part of it when he was directing the medical affairs of the Kabul Field Force, as testified by the honourable tribute paid to it by the General Commanding and by the regrets of his comrades, sufficiently proved that these anticipations had been well grounded. The death of Surgeon-Major Porter was an irreparable calamity to his personal friends, and a grievous loss to the branch of the profession of which he had already become a conspicuous ornament."

Surgeon-Major Porter held the Crimean medal with clasp for Sebastopol, the fifth class of the Medjidié, and Turkish medal; and the Indian Mutiny medal with clasp for Lucknow. He also received the German steel war medal and the bronze cross of the French National Aid Society for service with the British ambulance during the Franco-German War of 1871.

The grave of Surgeon-Major Porter in the British cemetery near Sherpur has been protected by a massive stone, which bears not only an inscription in English, but also an appropriate one in Persian. The latter was added by his thoughtful and loving comrades in the hope of insuring to the ground hallowed by so many affectionate memories due respect in the future, after it had passed from their guardianship into the hands of others, strangers in race and religion. His brother-officers and friends have also placed a handsome marble monument to his memory in the chapel of the Royal Victoria Hospital at Netley. This monument bears upon it a medallion-portrait in profile of the deceased officer.

LIEUTENANT BROWNLOW POULTER,

ROYAL ENGINEERS.

HE subject of this notice, who died at Peshawar on the 22nd June, 1879, from the effects of illness contracted in the field, was the eldest son of Brownlow Poulter, Esq., of Lee Park, Blackheath, and Charlotte Laura, his wife, daughter of the Rev. John Drake, Rector of Stourton, Wilts. He was born on the 18th July, 1852, and received his education at Winchester College. Having entered the Royal Military Academy, Woolwich, in the autumn of 1869, he passed out after the usual course, and in February, 1872, obtained his commission in the Royal Engineers.

For some eighteen months he did duty at Chatham, at the expiration of which period (October, 1874) he was ordered out to India. After serving for two years at Bangalore he was sent to Tanjore, being selected for special duty in connection with the water supply of that place. There he remained, employed on Public Works, till December, 1878, when he was called upon for service with the Field Force in Afghanistan.

Accompanying the K Company Queen's Own Sappers and Miners to Jamrud, and from thence on to Landi Kotal, the subject of this notice did not spare himself—as is shown in the sad sequel—in the fresh sphere of activity which now presented itself.

In the month of March, 1879, the Company was transferred from the 1st to the 2nd Division of the Peshawar Valley Field Force, and moved forward to Jalalabad. During General Gough's action at Futtehabad, it was left in camp in reserve; but on the 4th April it formed part of the force taken out by the General towards Lakhi, and performed important service in blowing up the villages of the Khans who had not given in their submission. It was subsequently moved on to Gandamak, where it remained till the signing of the treaty of peace. During this period Lieutenant Poulter was detached in command of a party to reconstruct Fort Rosabad—a duty he performed with marked ability. A short time after he rejoined divisional headquarters, he took part in the return march of the troops to India. The heavy nature of his recent duties, however, carried out in a pestiferous climate, now began to tell upon him, and he reached Peshawar only to die. On the 22nd June, 1879, in the twenty-seventh year of his age, he fell a victim to enteric fever, honoured by his men and loved by his comrades, to whom he set a bright example by the courage and endurance with which he had met the hardships of the march, and by the resignation with which he eventually succumbed to them.

CAPTAIN C. F. POWELL, STAFF CORPS,

5TH GOORKHA REGIMENT.

CHARLES FOLLIETT POWELL was the youngest son of the late Captain Scott Powell, of the 23rd Royal Welsh Fusiliers, and nephew of Major Charles Powell, 49th Regiment, who was killed in the Crimea. He was born in the year 1844, and was educated at the Rev. W. Hodgson's school, at Streatham. After the death of his eldest brother, who had just been gazetted to the 19th Foot, he determined to enter the Army; and, having been prepared by private tuition, was eventually gazetted to the 96th Regiment, which he joined at Shorncliffe in March, 1864, shortly before it left England for the Cape. He served for four years in British Kaffraria; and after a year's leave home, rejoined his regiment in India, where it had, in the meantime, proceeded. While stationed at Dum Dum, he qualified for the Indian Service, and joined the Bengal Staff Corps. He was subsequently attached to the 1st and 2nd Regiments Punjab Infantry, and lastly, to the 5th Goorkhas, for which gallant corps he conceived a deep affection, and with which he served till the day of his death.

Captain Powell worked hard at the details of his profession, and was a thorough soldier. He was also a genial, and high-spirited lover of society, and entered with zeal into everything that might be going on. His short snatches of holiday were spent with the gun, and every autumn he would seek sport in Kashmir. Full of life and incident, were the letters he sent home, which did not omit to describe his failures in sport as graphically as his successes.

The only active service in which Captain Powell was engaged was the Afghan War. Taking part with his regiment, in the autumn of 1878, in the advance of the force under General Roberts into the enemy's country, he was present, on the 2nd December, in the assault and capture of the Peiwar Kotal, in which the 5th Goorkhas played so brilliant a part. Of this affair he sent an accurate account, not wanting in some humorous incidents, to his brother, Dr. Douglas Powell; but the letter was preceded, alas! by the intelligence of his own death.

In the return march of the brigade under General Roberts from Ali Khel to Fort Kuram, Captain Powell was with the baggage guard of the Goorkhas, which, for five hours, on the 13th December, 1878, repelled the attacks of the Mangal hordes in the Sapiri defile. He was there mortally wounded; and five days afterwards, on the 18th of the month, died.

"He was hit, poor fellow, in an unfortunate rear-guard affair, under my command, whilst discharging his duty most gallantly and well." The distinguished officer and dear friend of Captain Powell who wrote these words, Major Cook, V.C., did not long survive the subject of them. Similar testimony is given in the General's despatch, wherein allusion is made to Captain Powell as having been "most forward and gallant in the fight."

BREVET-MAJOR L. A. POWYS,

59TH (2ND NOTTINGHAMSHIRE) REGIMENT.

LITTLETON ALBERT POWYS, who died of cholera at Kandahar on the 6th August, 1879, was the eldest son of the Rev. Littleton Charles Powys, sometime Fellow of Corpus Christi, Cambridge, and for thirty years Rector of Stalbridge, Dorsetshire.

The subject of this notice was born on the 27th July, 1840, and was educated at the Sherborne Grammar School. In October, 1858, he was gazetted to an Ensigncy in the 83rd Foot, and proceeding shortly afterwards to Bombay, joined the head-quarters of the regiment in that presidency. He served with the 83rd at various stations in India, and subsequently in England and Ireland for a period of eight years, being promoted in the interval Lieutenant, in December, 1860, and Captain, in February, 1866.

On obtaining his company, Powys exchanged into the 59th Foot, then in Ireland. On the regiment completing its tour of home service, he embarked with it for Colombo, and did duty with it in Ceylon, and in India. An enthusiastic sportsman, he made many expeditions against the larger game of the country. While elephant hunting in the summer of 1868 in the neighbourhood of Trincomali, he narrowly escaped being killed, and with the last bullet in his pouch succeeded in saving the life of one of his brother officers.

In 1877 Captain Powys returned home on sick leave, but on the first rumour of the impending war with Afghanistan reaching him, he again hurried out to India. Rejoining his regiment at Dagshai, he accompanied it, in the autumn of 1878, in its forward movement to Multan, and proceeding with it at the close of the year through the Bolan, shared the arduous artillery-escort duties which fell to its lot in the Pass. He subsequently took part with the regiment, in Sir Donald Stewart's Division, in the advance on and capture of Kandahar.

During the occupation of Kandahar, Major Powys took an active part in making provision for the health and comfort, and forwarding the efficiency of his regiment, objects which he always had greatly at heart. From January to February, 1879, he commanded the Left half battalion, and in the last days of July he received the command of a cholera camp. The amount of labour which fell to his lot at this period was considerable. At the end of one long day spent in making arrangements for the comfort of his charges, he was himself stricken down with the disease with which he was attempting to cope. After the first seizure he rallied, but again losing strength, died on the 6th August.

A mural tablet in Stalbridge Church records the estimation in which Major Powys was held by his friends at home, and a monument in the cemetery at Kandahar, erected by the regiment, testifies to the regard entertained for him by his brethren in arms. "Genial, generous, gentle, and kind"—to quote the words of the little Journal published at Kandahar—"the heart and soul of his regiment, his loss will be felt not more by his brother officers than by the non-commissioned officers and men, whose welfare and happiness were equally his own."

CAPTAIN J. J. PRESTON,

4TH BATTALION, RIFLE BRIGADE.

JENICO JOHN PRESTON, who died at Safed Sung, Afghanistan, on the 1st May, 1879, was the eldest son of the Hon. Thomas Preston, of Silverstream, Co. Meath, Ireland, and of Margaret, his wife, daughter of John Hamilton, Esquire, of Sundrum, Ayr. He was born at Gormanston Castle, the residence of Viscount Gormanston, his grandfather, on the 11th February, 1846, and was educated at Dr. Newman's school at Edgbaston. Entering Sandhurst, he passed out from the college, after the usual course, first in the list at the final examination in December, 1865, and was gazetted, a month afterwards, to the 8th Foot. He did not, however, join that regiment, being transferred almost immediately to the 4th Battalion Rifle Brigade.

Proceeding to Canada, where the regiment was then stationed, he served with it in that country till its return home in September, 1867, and then continued to do duty with it in England and Ireland for the six years which elapsed before it was again ordered abroad. During that period he began to acquire—by devoting himself assiduously to the study of his profession, for which he had, from the first, conceived a strong affection—the high reputation for thoroughness for which he became pre-eminently distinguished. After taking a first-class certificate at Hythe, he officiated for two years as Musketry Instructor to his battalion, and subsequently, in 1870, received the appointment of Adjutant—a post he retained, and the duties of which he discharged with signal ability, till July, 1878, when he obtained his company.

In October, 1873, Preston proceeded with his regiment to India, and served with it at Umballa for two years. When, in 1875, General Ross took command of the force ordered to Perak, he was selected by that distinguished officer to serve as his Aide-de-Camp; and when, in the operations which ensued, Major Hawkins, Brigade-Major to the Force, was killed, Preston was appointed to take his place. The Perak expeditionary force was recalled in April, 1876; and he returned to his regiment at Umballa, decorated with the medal with clasp.

On obtaining his company in July, 1878, Captain Preston was posted to the Depôt at home, and was looking forward to some relaxation after his hard work. The outbreak of hostilities with Afghanistan, and the fact of his regiment being ordered to the front, caused him, however, instantly to abandon his intention of returning to England.

Accompanying the Battalion in its advance in Sir Sam. Browne's Division into the Khyber, he took part with it, on the 21st November, 1878, in the flank movement on Ali Musjid, in the subsequent advance to Jalalabad, in the Bazar Valley expedition under Brigadier-General Tytler in January, 1879, and in the pursuit of Azmatallah Khan in the month of April. In the expedition last named, an accident befell him which, in all probability, sowed the seeds of the illness to which he eventually succumbed. In fording the Surkab River at night, he was closely pressed upon by the man immediately following him; and losing his footing in the swift current, he was completely immersed. The baggage not being at hand, and no change of clothes procurable, he was nearly frozen in the extreme cold of the early morning, and was afterwards subjected to the violent alternation of excessive heat during the long and wearisome march which followed. The night of the 1st April he passed—still in the same clothes—in an open shed, and again on the following day took part in a trying march back to camp. From this time he was never quite himself, appearing to feel the heat very much—a most unusual thing for him, and a sure sign, with regard to one of his strong constitution and regular habits, that something was wrong. When on the 12th April the Brigade marched from Jalalabad, *en route* for Safed Sang, he was very unwell, though it is superfluous to say that while moving to the front no word of complaint passed his lips. On the 19th of the month matters became so bad, however, as to necessitate his being placed upon the sick list; and four or five days afterwards he was prostrated with a fever of malignant type. Dr. Wood, of the regiment, was unremitting in the care and attention he bestowed upon him, and he had the advantage of being nursed by his intimate friend Captain Howard, who was indefatigable in his devotion, and also by Captain Fitz-Herbert, another brother officer; indeed, all in camp vied in their endeavours to contribute any comfort or little luxury. His case, however, was hopeless. He died on the morning of the 1st May, and was buried next day in the corner of the cemetery at Safed Sang nearest to Kabul, where a monument surrounded by a wall of masonry, erected by his comrades to his memory, marks his grave.

Captain Preston was an officer who will not soon be forgotten in the regiment of whose honour he was as jealous as he was of his own good name; and to associate his memory in a fitting way with an object dear to him in life, his brother officers have subscribed to a fund to be invested in some institution devoted to the welfare of soldiers and their families. "It is needless to tell," wrote Colonel Newdigate, on the occasion of Captain Preston's death, "how universally he was loved in the Battalion, as it was impossible for anyone to know him without loving him and admiring his fine character. There was not a better soldier in the Army."

LIEUTENANT M. E. RAYNER,

66TH (BERKSHIRE) REGIMENT.

MAURICE EDWARD RAYNER, who was killed at Maiwand on the 27th July, 1880, was the second son of the late Lloyd Rayner, a Liverpool merchant. He was born at Liverpool on the 16th September, 1857, and was consequently in his twenty-third year at the time of his death. Educated at the Rev. O. C. Waterfield's school at East Sheen, Surrey, and subsequently at Harrow School, he left the latter at Christmas, 1874, to compete in the December open examination of that year for first Army appointments. He passed 65th in order of merit out of 329 candidates, of whom the first 152 were alone successful, and in 1875 received the offer of a direct commission in the 66th Regiment, then stationed at Belgaum, Bombay. Gazetted to a Sub-Lieutenancy on the 3rd February, 1875, he sailed from Southampton to join the Head-quarters of the 66th in the following March. In May, 1877, he obtained his Lieutenancy; and in the course of his Indian service he held for a time the post of Interpreter to the regiment, and subsequently that of Adjutant till the day of his death.

Lieutenant Rayner accompanied the regiment to Kandahar in February, 1880, and took part with it, in July, in the advance to the Halmand. At the battle of Maiwand, on the 27th of the month, he was last seen alive, but badly wounded, hard by the garden enclosure where the last desperate stand round the colours of the 66th was made. There his body was subsequently found, and was buried with those of his gallant comrades.

Lieutenant Rayner was a keen sportsman, and had shown considerable prowess in the cricket-field. A promising young officer, devoted to his profession, his example may serve to show that a military career may be auspiciously commenced without interest and without purchase.

CAPTAIN R. B. REED,

1ST BATTALION, 12TH (EAST SUFFOLK) REGIMENT.

ROBERT BAYNES REED was the second son of Baynes Roach Reed, M.D., by his marriage with Emma, daughter of the late St. Paul Pane, Vicar of Tetbury, Gloucestershire. He was born on the 23rd November, 1837, and was educated at Cheltenham College, Gloucester Grammar School, and Marlborough College. After serving two trainings in the North Gloucester Militia, he entered the Army, being gazetted, in May, 1859, to an Ensigncy in the 2nd Battalion, 12th Foot. After doing duty in this country for a period of five years, and obtaining, in July, 1872, his Lieutenancy, he accompanied the regiment, in 1864, to India. In June, 1867, he received the appointment of Instructor of Musketry to the battalion, the duties of which post he discharged in a highly creditable manner till September, 1873, when he was selected to fill the office of Deputy Assistant Adjutant-General for Musketry, at Umballa. In the meantime (November, 1872), he had obtained his company.

Captain Reed continued to hold his staff appointment till 1879. Early in June of that year he effected an exchange from the 2nd into the 1st Battalion of the regiment, then on active service in Afghanistan, and obtaining permission to join head-quarters, hurried up with all speed to Landi Kotal, where they were at the time stationed, and reached that post on the 18th of the month. His term of active service, long eagerly looked forward to, was destined, alas! to be of short duration. The journey through the Khyber had been a trying one. Although in apparently good health on his arrival, he was shortly afterwards attacked with cholera, and in a few hours the gallant 12th had lost an officer and a friend who was loved and respected by every member of the regiment, even to the mothers and little children in barracks. In his last hours he was tended with all care by Dr. Wallace, the honoured surgeon of the battalion, who, succumbing a fortnight afterwards to the same fatal disease which carried off his patient, now rests in a grave by his side.

In a regimental after-order bearing date 24th June, 1879, the following words occur:—" Through his (Captain Reed's) death the Service has lost a most valuable officer. By those who have known him so well his many good qualities will be ever remembered.

"Lieut.-Colonel Walker feels that he speaks with the voice of the regiment in saying that its officers and men have lost in Captain Reed the kindest and most genial, warm-hearted friend."

LIEUT. T. J. O'D. RENNY, STAFF CORPS,

ADJUTANT, 4TH PUNJAB INFANTRY.

THOMAS JOHN O'DWYER RENNY, who died at Chinarak on the 15th December, 1879, from the effects of a wound received the day previous at the attack on Zawa, in the expedition under General Tytler against the Zaimusht tribe, was the third son of the late Colonel Robert Renny, C.B., Bengal Staff Corps, Adjutant-General Oudh Division, and of Caroline Franklin, his wife. He was born at Masuri, in the Himalayas, on the 15th August, 1846. After receiving the rudiments of his education at the Rev. Mr. Maddock's school at Masuri, and subsequently at the Manor House, another school in the same hill-station, he was sent home at the close of 1861, and was for some time at Merchiston Castle School, near Edinburgh. From Edinburgh he proceeded to Riga, and was for a time engaged in mercantile pursuits, but these proving distasteful to him, he studied for the Army, and succeeded in due course in passing the examination for direct commission. His appointment, however, was temporarily delayed in order to enable him to return to Bengal with Colonel Renny—at the time home on furlough—who had expressed a wish that his son might be posted to some regiment serving in India. Owing to the sad loss young Renny sustained in the death of his father within a few months of his arrival in India, the purchase of his commission devolved on his revered uncle, Mr. Thomas Renny, of Riga, and in April, 1868, he was appointed as Ensign to the 36th Foot. With that regiment he served for some four years, being promoted to his Lieutenancy in October, 1871.

Having devoted himself to the study of native languages, Lieutenant Renny succeeded in passing the test examination for the Bengal Staff Corps, and in January, 1872, was posted to the 4th Punjab Infantry. Taking part in the frontier affairs in which the regiment was from time to time engaged, he saw a good deal of active service, and was more than once mentioned in despatches. In November, 1877, he was appointed to the Adjutancy of his regiment, a post which he continued to hold till the day of his death.

Lieutenant Renny accompanied the 4th Punjab Infantry in its advance, in October, 1879, into Afghanistan, and subsequently took part with it in the punitory

LIEUTENANT T. J. O'D. RENNY, STAFF CORPS.

expedition under Brigadier-General Tytler, despatched against the Zaimusht tribes. It was while engaged with a large number of the enemy on the 8th December, in the forcing of the Zawa Pass, that he received his death-wound. Though he was at once carefully tended, he never recovered consciousness, and expired shortly afterwards. By the forethought of his brother officers his body was not suffered to remain in hostile territory, but was sent down to Kohat, and there buried.

In a letter received from the late Sir G. P. Colley, Private Secretary to the Viceroy, the following words occur :—" From my old connection with the Punjab Frontier Force, I know how highly Lieutenant Renny was valued in the force. The Viceroy was much distressed to hear of the loss of so valuable an officer." This tribute to the memory of the deceased is supplemented by the words of the Commandant of his regiment : " None," he writes, " was better or braver than this much-loved officer."

MAJOR WILLIAM REYNOLDS, STAFF CORPS,

3RD REGIMENT SIND HORSE.

THE subject of this notice, who was killed in action at Khushk-i-Nakhud, South Afghanistan, on the 26th February, 1879, was the eldest son of Major William Reynolds, of the Bombay Invalid Department, and grandson of William Reynolds, Esquire, of Milford House, Hants. He was born on the 31st October, 1841, and entered the Indian Army in January, 1859. The outset of his career was eventful. Gazetted to an Ensigncy in the 1st Bombay Grenadiers, he served with that regiment, a few months after joining it, in the expedition against the Waghirs in Okamandle and Kathiawar, and was present at the combined attack on their position on the Barda Hills on the 18th December, 1859. He was subsequently attached for a short time to the 19th Native Infantry, but in June, 1863, was transferred to the 3rd Sind Horse, with which regiment he served continuously till the day of his death.

After doing duty for some years on the frontier, he accompanied the regiment in 1867 to Abyssinia, and serving with it throughout the campaign, was present at the operations against Magdala, and received the medal. He subsequently returned with the regiment to India. In January, 1871, he was promoted to the rank of Captain, and in January, 1879, to that of Major.

On the breaking out of hostilities with Afghanistan in the autumn of 1878, the 3rd Sind Horse, which was stationed at Mustang and Dadar, was detailed to General Biddulph's Division of the Army of Invasion, and in December formed part of the garrison of Quetta. Taking part with the Division in the advance on and occupation of Kandahar, it participated, in the month of February, in the forward movement of the Brigade under General Biddulph to Girishk. On the withdrawal of the 2nd Division of the Column from that place on the 26th of the month, a small force composed of detachments of the 3rd Sind Horse and 29th Bombay Infantry, under Colonel Malcolmson, was detailed to act as a rear-guard. Reaching the village of Khushk-i-Nakhud about mid-day, the little force encamped, but was shortly afterwards threatened by a large body of the enemy. When the latter had advanced to within a few hundred yards, a heavy fire was opened by them, and

Major Reynolds, who was commanding the squadron of the Sind Horse, was struck with a bullet in the side. Colonel Malcolmson, unaware of what had happened, now ordered him to make a movement in preparation for charging the enemy, who were rapidly approaching ground favourable for the operations of cavalry; but being shortly afterwards informed of the wound he had received, directed him to give over the command of the squadron to another officer. This, however, Major Reynolds refrained from doing, and a few minutes afterwards took part in the effective charge which was delivered on the Afghan left centre. When, after ten minutes' fierce hand-to-hand fighting, the enemy broke, and the cavalry were ordered in pursuit, Major Reynolds, gallantly dashing forward with his squadron, sabred one of a group of Afghans who had gathered together and were making a last desperate stand. A moment afterwards his horse stumbled and threw him heavily; and before he could rise he was set upon and slain.

Major Reynolds's body was carried by his comrades to Kandahar, and buried in the Sirdar's garden. A headstone, erected to his memory by his family, marks his grave, and a mural tablet set up in Milford Church by his widow bears record of his heroic end; a mural tablet, too, has been erected to his memory in the Bombay Cathedral by Colonel Malcolmson and the officers of the 3rd Regiment Sind Horse. The regret which was universally felt for the loss of so highly esteemed and promising an officer, and the admiration for the manner in which he met his death, found expression—besides being testified to in many private letters—in the despatches both of Sir Donald Stewart and Colonel Malcolmson.

2ND LIEUTENANT W. P. RICARDO,

9TH (QUEEN'S ROYAL) LANCERS.

WILLIAM PERCY RICARDO, who fell in action in the neighbourhood of Kabul on the 11th December, 1879, was the only son of Frederick Ricardo, Esq., of Onslow Gardens, London. He was born on the 22nd April, 1857, and was educated at Edgbaston, under Dr., now Cardinal Newman. After three years' training in the Wilts Militia, he was gazetted, on the 13th March, 1878, to the 9th Lancers, and sailed for India in September of that year to join the Head-quarters of the regiment, then stationed at Sialkot, in the Punjab. By the time he reached Bengal, the 9th Lancers had been ordered up to Taru to form part of the Reserve Division of the Peshawar Valley Field Force, in view of the impending hostilities with Afghanistan. After serving for a few weeks with the Head-quarters, he proceeded with the detached squadron under Captain Apperley in January, 1879, to join the Kuram Valley Force, and subsequently took part with it, on the second outbreak of hostilities, in the advance on Kabul. He was present at the actions of Jaji Thana, Charasiab (in which he commanded, with marked ability, the main portion of the squadron), Kabul (8th and 9th October), and the operations outside cantonments in the second week in December. It was at the action of Killa Kazi on the 11th of that month, when gallantly charging the enemy with a troop of his regiment, that he lost his life.

Lieutenant Ricardo was buried on the evening of the same day in the little cemetery of Sherpur, where the remains of his brother officers Captain Butson and Lieutenant Hearsey have also found a last resting-place. Though cut short at its very outset, his career was yet not too brief to give evidence of his marked aptitude for the profession on which he had centred his affections and his hopes.

LIEUTENANT J. T. RICE,

ROYAL ENGINEERS.

JAMES THOMAS RICE was the youngest son of Colonel James George Allerton Rice, Honourable East India Company's Service, and was born at Calcutta in March, 1852. His educational career was a promising one. Early in 1865 he entered Cheltenham College, and gradually rose in the school till, at the age of sixteen years, he became prefect. Leaving Cheltenham in June, 1869, head of the Modern Department, and with the silver medal for Mathematics, he passed into Woolwich eighth in the list of successful candidates. On quitting the Academy he obtained the prize for Military History, and took sixth place in the list of cadets obtaining commissions in the Royal Engineers; and was gazetted to his Lieutenancy in December, 1871.

After passing through the usual course at Chatham, Lieutenant Rice embarked, in September, 1874, for India, and on arrival was posted to the Head-quarters Bengal Sappers and Miners at Rurki. Transferred in the course of a few months to the Public Works Department, and appointed to the 3rd Circle Military Works, Mirat Division, he became in a very short time Assistant Engineer, 1st Grade.

On the breaking out of the Afghan War in the autumn of 1878, Lieutenant Rice had the satisfaction of being selected to fill the important post of Assistant Field Engineer to the Khyber Line Force, and was at once ordered to the front. The ample promise of valuable service of which his brief career had given evidence was destined, however, never to be fulfilled. While journeying to Thal he caught a severe cold, and shortly after arriving at that post was prostrated with typhoid fever of so malignant a nature that from the first little hope was entertained of his recovery. He was removed as expeditiously as possible to Kohat, where, never rallying, he died at the house of his brother, Lieut.-Colonel Harry Rice, on the 23rd December, 1879.

LIEUTENANT S. W. T. ROBERTS,

PROBATIONER, BENGAL STAFF CORPS.

STEPHEN WILLIAM THORNHILL ROBERTS, who died from the effects of cholera on the 16th June, 1879, in the hospital at Landi Kotal, Afghanistan, was the fifth son of the late Arthur Austin Roberts, C.B., C.S.I., of the Bengal Civil Service, and of Elizabeth his wife, daughter of the late Colonel William Henville Wood, of the Honourable East India Company's Bengal Army. He was born on the 25th August, 1854, at Naini Tal, India, and was educated at Harrow, subsequently receiving private tuition for the Army. In April, 1873, he was appointed Sub-Lieutenant in the Royal Lancashire Artillery Militia, in which he served two trainings. He was gazetted to a Lieutenancy in the 39th Foot, in February, 1875, and joining that regiment in Bengal, served with it for a period of two years. Being desirous to enter the Staff Corps, he was posted on probation, in June 1877, to the 4th Bengal Native Infantry, from which regiment he was transferred, in August of the same year, after passing the lower standard examination in Native Languages, to the 27th Punjab Infantry, then quartered at Naushahra. He subsequently served with that regiment throughout the Jowaki-Afridi campaign, approving himself, according to the testimony of his Colonel, a zealous and accomplished young officer.

On the return of the 27th Punjab Native Infantry to Naushahra, Lieutenant Roberts obtained leave to proceed to Rawal Pindi to pass in Garrison Drill; but hearing that a force was to be sent to Afghanistan, and that part of his regiment had been ordered up to the Khyber, he begged for permission to join it. After some delay and difficulty, his request was granted; but, to his disappointment, he did not arrive in the Pass till two days after the capture of Ali Musjid.

From this time to the day of his death he was actively employed. He took part in the memorable action of Futtehabad on the 2nd April, 1879, and in the expedition to the Bazar Valley, in which the troops suffered severely from cold and exposure. Colonel Hughes, who took over the command of the regiment shortly after the capture of Ali Musjid, expressing his appreciation of Lieutenant Roberts' services at this period, writes as follows: "He was a good officer, and never happier than when there was a chance of seeing service. He took great interest in the organization of the regimental transport, of which he took charge as Quartermaster, and he was of the greatest assistance to me in that capacity. His good temper and cheerfulness endeared him to all." General Tytler also commended the manner in which, when on detached service, he had performed his duty. It is some evidence, too, of his ability, that, during the excitement of the war, and in the midst of much engrossing work, he succeeded in passing one of the examinations requisite for entrance into the Staff Corps.

On the return march of the troops to India, Roberts suffered much from the effects of sunstroke and fever—consequences of exposure undergone during the great heat of the season. On reaching Daka, he was ordered to proceed by easy stages to Murree to recruit his strength; but on the way he was seized with cholera, which, acting on an enfeebled state of health, ended fatally the third day after his admission to the hospital at Landi Kotal. He was buried with military honours, and was followed to the grave by all at the station. His brother officers have expressed a desire to erect a monument to his memory; but owing to the uncertainty of retaining Landi Kotal as a military post, this has not yet been done.

Sir James Bourne, late Colonel of the Royal Artillery Militia, writing with reference to the subject of this notice, pays the following tribute to his memory: "We have lost a most earnest and accomplished young officer, and one who, had he been spared, would have continued an ornament to his profession. We were all glad to see him promoted to more active service, but have now to mourn that his career has been so suddenly brought to an end, even at the post of honour."

CAPTAIN WALTER ROBERTS,

66TH (BERKSHIRE) REGIMENT.

THE subject of this notice, was the third son of Major-General Howland Roberts, Honourable East India Company's Service. He was born at Haidarabad in the Deccan on the 9th March, 1846; was educated at Cheltenham College; and passed through the Royal Military College at Sandhurst. In February, 1865, he was gazetted to an Ensigncy without purchase in the 3rd West India Regiment, and obtained his Lieutenancy by purchase in December of the same year. He served on the West Coast of Africa till June, 1866, and in the West Indies till his regiment was disbanded in April, 1870. In September, 1871, he exchanged from half-pay into the 66th Regiment, then stationed at Karachi, Sind; and joining that corps two months afterwards, served with it for a period of three years. In September, 1874, he was appointed Staff Officer at Mount Abu Sanitarium, where he remained for his term of two years. On rejoining Head-quarters in November, 1876, he was appointed to act as Adjutant of the regiment—an appointment which he held until he obtained his company on the 14th November, 1879, and continued to hold subsequently during the march of the 66th to Kandahar in the spring of 1880.

At the engagement with the mutinous troops of the Wali Shere Ali Khan near Ghirish on the 14th July, 1880, Captain Roberts commanded his company on the right flank of the line. At the battle of Maiwand, on the 27th of the same month, he was mortally wounded while making a desperate stand with his men against overwhelming numbers. He was led out of the garden in which he had been hit, and taken to the rear, but shortly afterwards died from the effects of his wound and exhaustion from long exposure, without sustenance or relief, to the rays of a burning sun. His body was brought into Kandahar and buried on the night of the 28th in the palace garden.

Captain Roberts' memory will ever be held dear by those with whom he served. He was a thorough soldier, and a man beloved by all who knew him.

The deceased married, in July 1867, Julia Mary, daughter of the late Captain P. H. Delamere, of the 21st Fusiliers and 3rd West India Regiment.

LIEUTENANT H. R. ROSS,

ROYAL ARTILLERY.

HUGH ROSE ROSS was the second son of George W. H. Ross, of Cromarty, N. B., Colonel of the Highland Rifle Militia, and Adelaide Lucy, his wife, third daughter of Duncan Davidson, of Tulloch, Lord Lieutenant of Ross-shire. He was born at Cromarty House on the 31st May, 1854, and was educated at the Rev. J. C. Jenkins' school at Brussels, aferwards studying with the Rev. Dr. Frost, LL.D., Kensington, and in 1872 passing into the Royal Military Academy, Woolwich. In October, 1873, he was gazetted to a Lieutenancy in the Royal Artillery, and did duty for a twelvemonth at Woolwich and Aldershot. In September, 1874, he was posted to Battery F/5, Field Artillery, which he joined, a month afterwards, at Sitapur, India.

For the next four years Lieutenant Ross served with the Battery in Bengal. That the manner in which he performed the duties allotted to him won the approbation of his Commanding Officer, is attested by the warm expressions of acknowledgment addressed to him by the latter on his being transferred to a new sphere of activity. "May you go on as well as you have done since I have had the pleasure of knowing you," is one amongst many kindly phrases used in a letter written to him on that occasion.

On the breaking out of hostilities with Afghanistan in the autumn of 1878, Ross volunteered for active service, and had the honour—of which he was justly proud—of being the first Artillery subaltern selected to fill a vacancy in one of the batteries ordered to the front. His promising career was destined, however, to be cut short at its very outset. When at Quetta on the march to Kandahar, he was attacked with dysentery, but refrained from reporting his illness, lest he might be left behind. Taking part in the further advance of the Battery, he continued to perform his duties with the utmost cheerfulness; at length, however, he became completely prostrated, and eventually died in camp in the Pishin Valley on the 12th January, 1879.

In a letter written by the Deputy Adjutant-General of Artillery in India, expressing his sorrow for the loss the regiment had sustained by the death of so promising an officer, the following passage occurs: "He was a good soldier, and a very fine young fellow. I took great interest in him." And an officer who was with him when he died, paying a well-merited tribute to his memory, writes: "He was universally loved, and will be very deeply regretted by us all."

CAPTAIN A. P. SAMUELLS,

32ND BENGAL N.I. (PUNJAB PIONEERS).

ALEXANDER PRINGLE SAMUELLS, the younger of two brothers who lost their lives in connection with the Afghan War, was the third son of the late Edward Alexander Samuells, Esq., C.B., of the Bengal Civil Service. He was born at Muzaffarpur, India, on the 8th August, 1843, and was educated at Loretto, Musselburgh, N.B., and Wimbledon. In 1860 he entered the Indian Army as an Ensign on the general list of Infantry, and was attached to the 7th Royal Fusiliers through the Umbeyla (N. W. Frontier) campaign of 1863-4, being present at all the operations in which that regiment took part. After hostilities were concluded, he was appointed to the 32nd Punjab Pioneers, with which corps he served continuously until his death. Alexander Samuells took part in the Bhutan campaign of 1864-65, and subsequently assisted in the construction of the Ranikhet road and in the Bengal Famine Relief Works of 1874. In 1877 he accompanied the 32nd to Quetta, Baluchistan, as Wing Commander, having been appointed successively Wing Officer, Quartermaster, and Adjutant; and took part in all the military works on which the regiment was engaged, both on the Quetta fortifications and in the Bolan Pass. He subsequently served with the regiment throughout the campaign in South Afghanistan, being present—during part of the time as second in command—in the advance over the Khojak Pass, the occupation of Kandahar, the reconnaissance to Girishk on the Halmand, and the expedition against the Kakur tribes in the Thal-Chotiali country. On the conclusion of hostilities he was appointed permanently second in command, in succession to Colonel Fellowes, who died on the return march.

Captain Samuells' health had suffered much during this campaign; and in the hot weather which succeeded, he became seriously ill with dysentery and fever. Notwithstanding his debilitated state, he accompanied the regiment to the Khyber Pass and Jalalabad Valley on the renewal of hostilities in the autumn of 1879, and remained with it—taking his share in all the trying work which fell to its lot in the second campaign—until July, 1880, when his health completely broke down. He was then invalided, but too late. The return through the Pass was more than he was equal to, and on arrival at Rawal Pindi he died of hospital abscess.

Captain Alexander Samuells had received the Indian war medal with clasps for Umbeyla and Bhutan, and was entitled to the Afghanistan medal. At a course of garrison instruction he had been specially mentioned for proficiency in Military Law; and he had successfully passed the examinations qualifying for service on the Staff. Throughout his career he bore the reputation of an officer possessing sound judgment and great *esprit de corps*. His loss was deeply felt by all ranks of the 32nd, both British and Native; for in life he had been distinguished for the sympathetic interest he took in all regimental matters and in every individual member of the corps, from his British comrades to the youngest Sepoy.

Captain Samuells married, in 1874, Georgina Margaret, eldest daughter of the late George Paterson, Esq., of Castle Huntly, Perthshire, N.B. A memorial has been erected over his tomb by the officers of his regiment and the Sepoys of his company.

CAPT. E. W. SAMUELLS, BENGAL STAFF CORPS,

DEPUTY SUPERINTENDENT OF REVENUE SURVEYS.

EDMUND WALKER SAMUELLS, was the second son of the late Edward Alexander Samuells, Esq., C.B., of the Bengal Civil Service. He had served in the Survey Department from the year 1863; and in the autumn of 1878, in view of the impending outbreak of war with Afghanistan, was ordered up from the Deccan to join Sir Sam. Browne's Division of the Army of Invasion. Taking part in the advance into the Khyber Pass, he was present, in his capacity as one of the Survey officers, at the attack and capture of Ali Musjid, on the 21st November, 1878, and subsequently proceeded as far as Basawal, with the view of procuring all the geographical information possible of the country traversed by our Army. The exertions he made to this end, however, brought on an attack of typhoid fever, which, acting on a constitution weakened by much exposure and hard work during several years previously, ended fatally. When the Force marched to Jalalabad, he was sent back on the 15th December, 1878, prostrated in health, from Basawal to the Base. The fatigue and hardships of the journey, however, caused a relapse; and arriving at Peshawar at 2 p.m. on the 20th of the month in a dying state, he expired in the 2nd Division Base Hospital at 10 p.m. on the same day, at the early age of thirty-six years. The surgeon (Ryan) who had charge of him on the journey down, writes: "He bore it all with the fortitude of a true soldier; and not a murmur ever escaped his lips."

The worth of this officer cannot be better attested than by a quotation from the official report of the services he rendered at the close of his career, made by his immediate superior on the spot: "At the taking of Ali Musjid," writes Major H. C. B. Tanner, "Captain Samuells was much exposed to the enemy's fire, but he carried on his plane-tabling under the cannon of the enemy as coolly as if he were in no danger. Unfortunately he has written no report of his proceedings, but he told me that one round shot actually passed beneath his plane-table, and that, in the Shaghai heights, he and his party had many narrow escapes. His plane-table section of the far-famed Khyber Pass will remain a record of Survey operations done in a most creditable manner under very adverse circumstances. Throughout the action he was under a hot artillery fire delivered frem twenty-four guns, and it is to be for ever regretted that he should only escape the dangers of that day to fall a victim to typhoid fever a few weeks later."

The following additional testimony to his worth and character will be found in the report submitted to the Indian Government by the Deputy Surveyor-General of India:—" During the course of Captain Samuells' service, he has been engaged in many varied and important duties, in all of which he so acquitted himself that he has acquired a high character for intelligence, energy, and perseverance. By the death of Captain Samuells the Revenue Branch of the Survey Department of India has lost one of its most valued officers."

CAPTAIN T. A'B. SARGENT,

78TH HIGHLANDERS (ROSS-SHIRE BUFFS).

THOMAS A'BECKET SARGENT, who died at Kandahar, of typhoid fever, on the 21st January, 1881, was the elder son of Thomas Sargent, Esq., of Porchester Terrace, Paddington, formerly Secretary to the Board of Inland Revenue, by his wife, Mary Jane, daughter of William Becket Turner, Esq., of Wantage, Berks, and of Penleigh House, near Westbury, Wilts. He was born at Paddington on the 30th October, 1845, and received his education chiefly at Eton, where he remained five years. His school career was a bright and happy one. Scarcely anyone could have been a more general favourite than he among his young contemporaries; and while quite a little library of presentation volumes received by him on quitting the college gives evidence of his popularity, numerous pieces of plate bear witness to a prowess on the river, and in athletic sports generally, for which he early became famed.

On leaving Eton at Christmas, 1864, at the age of nineteen years, he read with Mr. Arnold, of Surbiton, with a view to entering the Army; and passing the examination for direct commission shortly afterwards, was gazetted in November, 1865, to an Ensigncy in the 78th Highlanders. After doing duty for two years and a half at the Depôt at Stirling and Aberdeen, and purchasing, in the meantime, his Lieutenancy, he joined the head-quarters in Canada, and remained there till the regiment returned home in 1872—a period of three years and a half. He was subsequently detached, in April, 1873, and stationed at the Brigade Depôt at Fort George. In March, 1877, he obtained his company.

After serving at Fort George about two years, he obtained, on the recommendation of the Commandant, the Staff appointment of Aide-de-Camp to the General of the Northern District of England, a post which he held more than five years, resigning it only upon being ordered to rejoin his regiment in Afghanistan, in August, 1880. In the pestilential climate of Kandahar, he was cut off in the prime of his manhood, within the short space of five months from the date of his departure from England.

As in his school days, so also in after life, he made many friends. "He was a true and valued friend to me," wrote one of the Generals under whom he had served, on receiving the news of his death; and the other, in expressing his grief for the loss of so promising an officer, paid an equally warm tribute to his memory. The following words, written by an officer of the 78th Highlanders, are taken from one of the many letters testifying to his worth, received by his family after his death, and will serve to indicate the estimation in which he was held in his regiment. "He was a fine fellow," observes the writer, "every inch a soldier. It is sad to see anyone cut off so young, but doubly so, when he had such a career before him as he doubtless had. He will leave many in his profession to mourn him, for in his short, and as far as it went successful career, he made a host of friends. All ranks, from the highest to the lowest, who knew and appreciated his worth, will mourn his untimely end; and none more so than his old comrades of the 78th."

Captain Sargent's brother officers, in taken of their regard, have erected a monument over his grave; and one of the Generals to whom he acted as Aide-de-Camp, has also put up, in his own parish church, a cenotaph to his memory. It is some consolation to his family to learn how sincerely he was beloved by those with whom he was most intimately associated in his profession.

CAPTAIN E. D. SHAFTO,

ROYAL ARTILLERY.

EDWARD DUNCOMBE SHAFTO, who was killed on the 16th October, 1879, by the explosion of the magazine in the Bala Hissar, Kabul, was a member of an old County of Durham family, the Shaftos of Whitworth Park, being the eldest son of the Rev. A. Duncombe Shafto, Rector of Brancepeth, Durham, by his wife Dorothea Ann, second daughter of G. H. Wilkinson, Esq., of Haspeley Park, Durham. He was born at Houghton le Spring in the same county on the 14th June, 1843, and was educated, before entering Woolwich, at the Rev. E. Pound's school at Malton, and at Carshalton. In April, 1861, he was gazetted to the 9th Brigade Royal Artillery. After doing duty for a short time at Dover, he was appointed Aide-de-Camp to General Ormsby, Royal Artillery, and continued to hold the appointment until, in 1866, he was selected to fill the post of Aide-de-Camp to General Sir A. Borton, then commanding a brigade at the Curragh. In July, 1870, he quitted Ireland for India, accompanying Sir Arthur Barton to Bangalore, on the latter being ordered out to take up his appointment of General of the Mysore Army. On the expiration of his Chief's command in 1875, he returned to England, and in 1876 passed with such credit through the long course at Shoeburyness that he was offered the post of Instructor; on his declining this he was offered and accepted the Adjutancy of the 16th Brigade of Royal Artillery at the Mount, Madras; and on that brigade being absorbed into another in England, he was appointed District Adjutant.

On the outbreak of the Afghan War, volunteers were called for from the Artillery; and eagerly responding, Shafto was one of the first whose services were accepted. After doing duty in the Kuram Valley during the first campaign, he was appointed, on the renewal of hostilities, Ordnance Officer to the Force under General Roberts advancing on Kabul. It was on the fourth day after the Division reached its destination that the magazine explosion in which he met his untimely end occurred.

By the unassuming manliness of his ways and the sweetness of his temper, Captain Shafto had made many friends, and the news of his death caused deep sorrow to a wide circle. " His bright intelligent face won my heart the first time I saw him, and I never expect to replace him," wrote Sir Frederick Roberts; and Colonel Gloag, Royal Artillery, in a regimental order, refers to him as having been "an officer who was good, talented, and brave, and also a devoted servant of his Queen and Country,"—a verdict which will be concurred in by all to whom the deceased was known.

Captain Shafto's acquaintance with a soldier's work in all its details was thorough, and contributed largely to his high reputation. Besides being an ardent sportsman, and a deadly hand with gun or rifle, he was devotedly fond of travelling, and contrived during his annual privilege-leave to visit Japan, Java, and Kashmir. As master of the Bangalore foxhounds, no man could have given greater satisfaction or have been more popular.

BT. LIEUT.-COL. A. M. SHEWELL, STAFF CORPS,

OFFG. DEPY. COMMISSARY-GENERAL, 1st CLASS.

ARTHUR MARK SHEWELL was one of four brothers, sons of the late Edward Warner Shewell, of the Royal Crescent, Cheltenham, who joined the Honourable East India Company's Service between the years 1840 and 1856, and of whom three have since died in the service. The subject of this notice, the younger of the four, entered the army as ensign in December, 1856, and was posted to the 2nd Bombay European Light Infantry, now Her Majesty's 106th Regiment. He was promoted to a Lieutenancy in September, 1857 ; and in July, 1863, was appointed to the Staff Corps.

"One who knew him well," writing to the "Standard" newspaper after Shewell's death, records the following characteristic incident in his career at this period :—" In the year 1864 there was a fearful outbreak of cholera in B/18 Royal Artillery, at Baroda, where young Shewell was then Commissariat Officer. Not only did he voluntarily give his untiring aid day and night in nursing the sick, but every morning he was to be seen mounted on his pony with a large basket slung on his arm, which was filled with delicacies for the sick women and children who, being convalescents, were encamped two or three miles off. These delicacies were not provided by Government, but supplied by his own generosity and that of a few friends. Perhaps it needed more moral courage for a young officer thus burdened to ride through the camp than it would to face the enemy ; but whenever a kindness or an unselfish action was to be done, Arthur Shewell was the man to do it."

On the war with Abyssinia being declared in 1867, Lieutenant Shewell volunteered for employment in his capacity of an officer of the Commissariat Department, which he had a short time before joined. His services were accepted, and were subsequently so highly appreciated by Lord Napier that, although only that of a subaltern, his name was specially mentioned in his Lordship's final despatch ; and the same gazette which announced his promotion to the rank of Captain, contained an intimation of Her Majesty having conferred on him a brevet-majority.

On the breaking out of the Afghan War in 1878, Lieut.-Colonel Shewell (who had been, in the interim, again promoted) had important duties assigned to him, being placed in charge of the line of communications between Sukkur and Quetta—an appointment which entailed not only heavy responsibility, but excessive exposure in the most trying part of the year to the intense heat of the plains at the debouchure of the Bolan. Whilst he was employed on this duty, cholera broke out at Eri-Na-Dur. To the quiet steadfastness and self-abnegation with which he set himself to cope with this virulent disease, a letter written by his commanding officer to one of the daily journals bears ample witness. After quoting at length from a graphic record of his work which appeared in a paper entitled "A Transport Service for Asiatic Warfare," read at the United Service Institution in June, 1880, General Howard Vyse concludes his communication with these words :—" I saw Lieut.-Colonel Shewell after his return to Karachi during the summer of 1879, but with his innate modesty, he would say but little about his heroism. He did, however, admit that it was 'trying' when he had to bury seventeen poor natives during the twenty-four hours."

On the outbreak of the second campaign, Lieut.-Colonel Shewell, who was promoted Officiating Deputy Commissary-General for the occasion, was specially selected by Sir Richard Temple to assume entire charge of the commissariat arrangements of the Kandahar Field Force. That he performed the onerous duties incident to his appointment to the entire satisfaction of the whole Division, is evidenced by a most complimentary order on the subject issued by Sir Donald Stewart on his departure for Kabul.

The manner in which Arthur Shewell met his death is of a piece with the broad humanity of his life. On the morning of the 16th August, 1880, the day of the fatal sortie to Deh Khwaja, hearing that a wounded man was lying helpless outside the Kabul gate, he volunteered to take a dhoolie for him. In helping him into it, he himself received a wound from the effects of which he died a fortnight afterwards, on the 2nd September, 1880.

CAPTAIN H. F. SHOWERS, STAFF CORPS,

1ST PUNJAB INFANTRY.

OWE FREDERICK SHOWERS, who was murdered by a body of Kakar Pathans on the 14th March, 1880, while riding on duty between Chapari and Quetta, was the bearer of a name, and a worthy descendant of ancestors well known in India for every soldierly quality, and whose services for four generations stand recorded in monumental tablets in the old Cathedral of Calcutta, and memorial tombs on some of India's most noted battle-fields. He was the eldest son of the late Major-General Sir George Showers, who commanded a brigade at the siege of Delhi, and nephew of Lieut.-General C. L. Showers. Educated at Wellington College, he proceeded to India in 1861, and was gazetted to the 104th Fusiliers, of which regiment he soon became Adjutant. On promotion to Captain, he entered the Staff Corps and was posted to the Central India Horse, and afterwards transferred, in 1872, to the 1st Punjab Infantry. In 1877 he was appointed Garrison Instructor in the Umballa Division, but threw up the post in order to join his regiment proceeding on service into Afghanistan on the breaking out of the war in 1878. He was present in the action fought by the Thal-Chotiali Column under Major Keen in forcing and opening that route, and was mentioned in the despatches. His conduct in the field and special acquirements brought him into notice. He was first appointed by Sir Donald Stewart to the Intelligence Department; and subsequently was employed by Sir Robert Sandeman, Governor-General's Agent in Baluchistan, in defining the boundaries of the Pishin district, and acquitted himself of his duties with signal ability and zeal. Attended by but a handful of men, Captain Showers was in the habit of traversing unknown routes in disturbed tracts, and returned with plans full of valuable information, on more than one occasion. He at length fell a victim through treachery, within a few weeks of his being appointed, in recognition of his services, to the command of the Baluch Corps of Guides.

"No more gallant officer fell during the war." The sentence occurs in a letter written with reference to Captain Showers by Sir R. Sandeman—who had many opportunities of observing the cool steadfastness with which his subordinate was wont to carry out the work to which he set his hand. It expresses nothing more than what might have been expected of one of the deceased officer's name and race.

The Editor of this work is indebted to the "Times" Kandahar correspondent for the greater portion of this notice.

BREVET MAJOR L. C. SINGLETON,

92ND (GORDON HIGHLANDERS).

THE subject of this memoir, though not one of those whose name is included in the death-roll of the Afghan War, was an officer who performed such distinguished service in the operations with which these volumes deal, and lost his life so soon after the close of the war, that some brief notes on his career will not be found out of place in this division of the work.

Loftus Corbet Singleton was the fourth son of Henry Corbet Singleton, Esq., J.P., D.L., of Aclare, Co. Meath, Ireland, and Jane Percival, his wife, daughter of Lieutenant-General William Loftus, and was one of five brothers who entered the Service within a short period of one another. He was born on the 2nd August, 1842, and after receiving his education at Cheltenham College, was gazetted, in March, 1861, to an Ensigncy in the 18th Royal Irish Regiment; he was shortly afterwards, however, transferred to the 92nd Highlanders, in which distinguished corps—serving in successive grades, and holding at intervals various appointments—he remained till the day of his death.

Joining the regiment in India, he returned with it, about three months afterwards, to England, and did duty with it in Great Britain till it was again ordered abroad. In the interval, (July, 1864), he purchased his Lieutenancy. In January, 1868, he embarked with the head-quarters for India, and served in Bengal for a period of three years. In September, 1869, he obtained his company by purchase, and during the term of his Indian service he held for a time the appointment of Musketry Instructor to the regiment.

Captain Singleton returned to England early in 1871, and shortly afterwards was selected to fill the important post of Adjutant of the Galloway Rifle Volunteers. During his tenure of this appointment—the duties of which he discharged with signal ability for a period of five years—he won a popularity such as it is accorded to few to earn, touching evidence of which is afforded in the letters of sympathy, addressed to his widow by each corps separately, on the occasion of his death.

In November, 1877, Singleton rejoined his regiment in India, and a twelve-month afterwards accompanied it in its advance to the frontier, in view of the recent outbreak of war with Afghanistan, subsequently proceeding with it to Ali Khel, where it joined the Advance Division of the Kuram Valley Field Force. Taking part with it, on the renewal of hostilities in the autumn of 1879, in the advance on Kabul, he served through the whole of the second campaign, leading the men of his company repeatedly into action, and receiving honourable mention on more than one occasion in report or despatch. He was present, on the 6th October, at the battle of Charasiab, in which the 92nd performed gallant service, and at the subsequent occupation of Kabul, and taking part in the train of important events with which the year closed, was present in General Baker's action on the 11th December, at the storming of the Takht-i-Shah on the 13th, and in the covering of the retirement from the Asmai Heights on the 14th idem. During the defence of Sherpur he was always to be seen at the head of his men, and at the action of Childukhtean, on the 25th April, 1880, the conspicuous gallantry he displayed in leading on the right of the fighting line obtained for him special commendation in despatches. Participating in the memorable march of Sir Frederick Roberts' force from Kabul to Kandahar, he was again present at the crowning defeat of the enemy on the 1st September, 1880. For his services during the operations he received the Brevet of Major.

Ordered to South Africa immediately after the outbreak of war with the Transvaal Boers, the 92nd Highlanders disembarked at Durban early in 1881. Accompanying the regiment to Mount Prospect, Major Singleton subsequently took part with it in Sir George Colley's ill-starred occupation of the Majuba Mountain on the night of the 26th February. It was at the moment when, shortly after dawn on the 27th, the enemy swept over the ridge of the mountain plateau in overwhelming numbers, and shot down or captured the few who were left to defend it, that he received his death-wound, being struck by rifle bullets twice during the engagement. He lingered on for two months, but rapidly sinking after undergoing amputation of a limb, eventually died on the 1st of May, and at the hands of his comrades received a soldier's sepulture.

"Most reliable in the field; possessed of excellent judgment." Such are the attributes of the deceased referred to in a private letter written by Sir Frederick Roberts, who, paying an earnest tribute to his memory, justly says that "by his death Her Majesty has lost a true and gallant soldier."

Major Singleton married, in 1872, Emmeline Theodora, only surviving daughter of Thomas de Moleyns, Esq., Q.C. He leaves a widow and two children, a son and daughter.

CAPTAIN H. F. SMITH, STAFF CORPS,

JACOB'S RIFLES.

HUGH FREDERICK SMITH, who was killed in action at Maiwand on the 27th July, 1880, was the younger son of Hugh W. Smith, Esq., M.A., of Westbourne Park, London, and of Julia Frances, his wife, and was a nephew of the late Captain C. F. Smith, 71st Highlanders, who was killed in action in the Umbeyla campaign of 1863.

The subject of this notice was born on the 28th June, 1846. Educated at Tonbridge School, where he early became a favourite with his young contemporaries, his devotion to all kinds of athletic exercises, in which he excelled, contributing not a little to his popularity, he proceeded to Sandhurst in February, 1865, and passing out of the college after the usual course, was gazetted, in June, 1866, to the 88th Foot. In the following year he joined that regiment in India, and remained with it until, in 1870, it returned to England, when he entered the Bombay Staff Corps. In the meantime (May, 1870) he had obtained his Lieutenancy. Posted now to Jacob's Rifles, he joined the Head-quarters at Jacobabad, and holding successively and with credit the various appointments tenable by a subaltern, continued in that regiment till the day of his death. In the course of his service he returned to England, in 1877, for a term of sick leave; and it is characteristic of him that during the brief period he remained at home, he undertook a four months' course of Engineering at Chatham, in addition to taking, after the usual course, an extra first-class Hythe certificate. Returning to India, he became Captain in June, 1878, and, notwithstanding his promotion, continued to retain to the last, in consequence of the dearth of junior officers of sufficient experience, the post of Adjutant of the regiment.

Taking part in the autumn of 1878 in the advance of the head-quarter wing of the regiment to Quetta in view of the impending hostilities with Afghanistan, Captain Smith shared with it throughout the first campaign the various garrison and escort duties which fell to its lot, holding for a brief period the post of Station Staff-Officer, and proceeding in the month of March, 1879, in charge of drafts for different corps to Kandahar. Accompanying the head-quarters and right wing of the regiment from Quetta in the advance into hostile territory in April, 1880, he proceeded a second time to Kandahar, and subsequently took part in the forward movement of Burrows' Brigade to the Halmand. In the disastrous encounter with the enemy at Maiwand on the 27th July, 1880, he fell early in the engagement, being killed by the bursting of a shell shortly after crossing the nullah with his regiment in support of the Horse Artillery.

Of the many sympathetic letters written with reference to the late Captain Hugh Smith to his family, one and all testify to his signal worth and to the high estimation in which he was held. By his death the Staff Corps lost an officer of great promise, and a blank was created in the regiment which will not soon be filled up.

MAJOR LIONEL SMITH, STAFF CORPS,

3RD GOORKHA REGIMENT.

THE subject of this memoir, who died at Kalat-i-Ghilzai on the 25th January, 1879, was the youngest son of E. J. Smith, Esq., of the Bengal Civil Service, and was born at Weymouth on the 5th May, 1838. After receiving his earlier education principally at private schools both abroad and at home, he entered the Army, being gazetted in July, 1856, to an Ensigncy in the 96th Foot. Within a few months of his obtaining his commission he elected to join the Honourable East India Company's Service, and was posted, in December, 1856, to the 36th Regiment Light Infantry. During the Indian Mutiny campaign he was engaged as a volunteer when the rebels were repulsed from the guns at Jalandhar on the night of the 7th June, 1857, and five days afterwards was promoted to the rank of Lieutenant. In October and November, 1858, he served with the Thamaon Battalion in Oudh. On the 30th July, 1862, he was appointed to Her Majesty's 104th Fusiliers, and in November, 1863, obtained his company in that regiment. He entered the Staff Corps in May, 1866; and again doing duty with the Thamaon Battalion in 1869, served in General Horsford's Brigade against the Mutineers on the Nipal frontier, and was present at the action of Sakla Ghât on the 9th February. In December, 1876, he was promoted to his Majority.

Major Lionel Smith was serving with the 3rd Goorkhas at the time of the breaking out of the Afghan War in the autumn of 1878. Sharing with the regiment the heavy duties which fell to its lot in the first campaign, he took part with it in Brigadier-General Hughes' Brigade of Sir Donald Stewart's Division, in the advance on and occupation of Kandahar, and in the subsequent advance on Kalat-i-Ghilzai. The unhealthy nature of the climate and the severity of recent work now began to tell upon him; he was taken ill with dysentery on the march, and eventually fell a victim to the complaint within a few hours of the column reaching its destination.

Major Lionel Smith had received during his service an extra certificate at the Royal Military College, a medal for the Indian Mutiny, and a first-class extra Hythe certificate.

SURGEON W. B. SMYTH, A.B., M.B., L.R.C.S.I.,

BENGAL MEDICAL DEPARTMENT,

ILLIAM BEATTY SMYTH, who was killed at Chapari, Afghanistan, on the 20th June, 1879, was the third son of William Smyth, banker, Strabane, Ireland. He received his early education at Raphoe Royal School and Dungannon Royal School, from whence, obtaining an exhibition, he proceeded to Trinity College, Dublin. During his University course he threw himself heart and soul into his work; and that he approved himself a scholar of no mean calibre, the many honours he reaped—including the silver medal *Hist. Scient., Polit., et Litt. Angl.*—bear ample witness.

Quitting the University in 1876, he underwent a short course of preparation for the Indian Medical Service; and passing the examination in January, 1877, entered the Army the same year. After spending a few months at Calcutta, during which he passed the examination in Native Languages, he was posted to the 8th Regiment Bengal Native Infantry, then serving at Agra.

On the breaking out of the Afghan War in the autumn of 1878, Dr. Smyth proceeded to the front in medical charge of No. 7 Company Bengal Sappers and Miners, which was detailed for service to General Roberts' Division of the Army of Invasion; and taking part in the advance into hostile territory, was present at the assault and capture of the Peiwar Kotal. In the course of his association with the Kuram Field Force, he was attached for duty to more than one of the regiments which formed part of the Division, and took a full share of the heavy work which fell to the lot of the Medical Department in the winter of 1878 and the spring of 1879. While at the Peiwar cantonments, he was ordered to Thal to take charge of a cholera camp; but on reaching his destination, he found that the camp had been broken up. Making his way back, he halted on the evening of the 25th June, 1879, at Chapari, pitching his tent away from the guard. During the night some thieves pulled down the loose stone wall of a surrounding enclosure without disturbing anyone; and one man entering the tent, seized and made off with the pillow on which Dr. Smyth was sleeping. Instantly starting in pursuit, but unhappily omitting to carry his revolver, Dr. Smyth came up with the thief, and threw him. In a moment he was surrounded and set upon by the whole band, and was so severely wounded that he died immediately. The crime was traced to the Watazai section of the Zaimusht race; but as the assassins could not be discovered, retributive justice was meted out by firing three large villages of the tribe to which they belonged.

Brave even to rashness, as the character of his tragic death gives evidence; carrying out, utterly regardless of consequences to himself, what he deemed to be his duty, Dr. Smyth was one of those officers of whom the profession has just occasion to feel proud. His nature was genial and kindly, and his death not only leaves a blank in his family that can never be filled, but is deeply mourned by all to whom he was known.

CAPTAIN N. J. SPENS,

72ND (DUKE OF ALBANY'S OWN HIGHLANDERS).

NATHANIEL JAMES SPENS, who was killed in action at Kabul on the 14th December, 1879, was the third and last surviving son of the late Nathaniel Spens, of Craigsanquhar, Fife, and of Janet Law Guild, his wife. He was born on the 3rd March, 1845, and was educated at Edinburgh and Woolwich. Entering the Army in June, 1864, he was gazetted to an Ensigncy in the 72nd Highlanders, then on its tour of home service, and at once joining his regiment, served with it at various stations in Great Britain and Ireland, obtaining his Lieutenancy by purchase in June, 1868.

In February, 1871, he accompanied the 72nd on its departure from Ireland for India, and continued serving with it in Bengal till, in November, 1878, it was ordered to the front in view of the impending hostilities with Afghanistan. In the meantime (March, 1878), he had been promoted Captain.

Captain Spens' company formed part of the left wing of the 72nd, which, under Lieut.-Colonel Clarke, remained in garrison at Kohat till the close of the year, and subsequently, in January, 1879, took part in General Roberts' occupation of the Khost district. In the action of Matun, on the 7th of the month, the 72nd defended the front and left flank of the camp, and subsequently, with the other units of Colonel Barry Drew's little force, carried the Mangal villages on the right and rear.

In April, 1879, the left wing, having joined the head-quarters, proceeded with the division to Ali Khel, and remained there till the massacre of the British Embassy necessitated an immediate advance on Kabul. At the battle of Charasiab, on the 6th October, the company commanded by Spens was one of the leading ones which took part in the attack on the Red Ridge, so obstinately held and so brilliantly carried; and which supported Chesney's company of the 23rd Pioneers in carrying the second ridge on which the enemy took up his position.

In the storming of the Asmai heights on the 14th December, in the operations round Kabul, Captain Spens was in command of the sixty-four men of the 72nd, who, with the Guides Infantry, under Lieut.-Colonel Clarke, successfully assaulted and for a time held the little conical hill to the right of the main attack. It was while endeavouring to prevent this position from being retaken, in a heroic personal attempt to stem the advance of the overwhelming numbers of the enemy, that he sacrificed his life. The incident is thus related by one of his brother officers. After telling how the Afghans, reassembled and reinforced, had rushed up the side of the hill, and that a charge was ordered to be made by the Sepoys, the writer continues as follows:—" Spens volunteered to lead, which he did in splendid style. Heading a good way in front, he dashed at the leading files of the enemy, cut down the front man, and was immediately cut down himself by the enemy as they surged forward." His body was recovered, and was buried by his brother officers in the cemetery at Sherpur, the pipers of the regiment striking up " Lochaber no more "— his favourite air—as it was lowered into the grave.

" Spens behaved most gallantly," wrote Sir Frederick Roberts, in a letter expressing a wish that it might have been possible to secure for the representatives of the deceased officer the Victoria Cross. The reflection that he was one who could not fail to acquit himself worthily when his opportunity might come, and that his death was therefore, under the circumstances, a necessity, is some poor consolation to his comrades in arms, by whom his memory will ever be held dear.

LIEUTENANT H. H. S. SPOOR,

1ST BATTALION 25TH (KING'S OWN BORDERERS).

HE subject of this memoir, who died at Pezwan, Afghanistan, on the 1st of June, 1880, was a descendant of the Spoor family, of Trebartha, Cornwall, being the only son and heir, also last surviving child, of the late Nicholas Appleby Spoor, Esq., of Whitburn, Durham, and Warkworth, Northumberland, formerly a Captain in the 6th Royals, and latterly of the 25th King's Own Borderers, and of Dora Anna, his wife, second daughter of the late John Oliver, Esq., formerly of Newcastle-on-Tyne, and grand-daughter (maternally) of Henry Shadforth, Esq., of Over Dimsdale Hall, near Yarn, Yorkshire.

Herbert Henry Shadforth Spoor was born at Fulwood, Preston, Lancashire (where the depôt of the 25th was at the time of his birth stationed) on the 22nd of April, 1857, and was educated chiefly at the Proprietary School and the College, Cheltenham. Receiving a Queen's cadetship, he entered the Royal Military College at Sandhurst in February, 1877; and passing out after the usual course, was gazetted, in May, 1878, to the 8th (the King's) Regiment. Being anxious, however, to serve in his father's old corps, he was transferred to the " Borderers," and joined the 2nd Battalion at Plymouth on the 6th of July of the same year. In September, 1879, he embarked for India, and early in November joined the 1st Battalion of the regiment at Peshawar. Accompanying the head-quarters a month afterwards in the second advance into Afghanistan, he was sent in advance in command of the baggage-guard to Jalalabad. He subsequently took part with the regiment in the Lughman Valley expedition, and after returning to Jalalabad was sent in command of a company to assist in guarding the Daronta ford of the Kabul river. Finally he went on to Gandamak, Safed Sang, and Pezwan, where in April he was appointed General Transport Officer to the station. At this time he was suffering from tropical dysentery, brought on by exposure and fatigue. In May he was employed on a survey of the fortifications of Pezwan. Being in a weak state from his former illness, he was unable to withstand the effects of the intense heat, and was seized with an attack of enteric fever, to which he rapidly succumbed, having cheerfully and bravely performed the duties allotted to him to the last.

Herbert Spoor's remains rest in the little cemetery at Pezwan, where they were buried with military honours by his brother officers and the men of the regiment, by whom he was sincerely lamented.

LIEUT. F. C. STAYNER, STAFF CORPS,

19TH BOMBAY N.I.

RANCIS CHARLES STAYNER, who fell in the disastrous sortie from Kandahar on the 16th August, 1880, was the second son of James Stayner, Esq., of Ilminster, Somerset. He was born on the 27th July, 1854; and after receiving tuition from the Rev. Edward Girdleston at Weston-super-Mare, passed on to Harrow, and from thence, in 1873, to Trinity College, Cambridge, with the intention of qualifying for the legal profession. During his academical course he evinced more than ordinary ability; and his amiable disposition rendered him a universal favourite amongst his schoolfellows and contemporaries at college.

In 1876 he relinquished his intention of embracing a legal career, and commenced, in London, a course of preparation for the Sandhurst examination. Succeeding in taking a place among the successful candidates, he entered the Royal Military College in February, 1876, and passing out after the usual course, was gazetted to a Sub-Lieutenancy in the 5th Fusiliers, then serving in Bengal. In February, 1877, he embarked for India to join the head-quarters; on arriving at Bombay, however, he was posted to the 15th Native Infantry as a probationer for the Staff Corps, and proceeded to join that regiment at Ahmadnagar.

After being attached for musketry instruction for a few months in the summer of 1878 to the 2nd Queen's, at Poona, Stayner was finally posted as Sub-Lieutenant to the 19th Bombay Native Infantry, then forming part of General Primrose's reserve force, and quartered at Karachi, at which station he arrived, in company with the General, in the month of December. During the year 1879 he took his share in the heavy work which fell to the lot of the regiment in its employment on the Public Works, in Baluchistan; and notwithstanding the exacting nature of his duties, succeeded in passing a highly creditable examination in the higher standard of Hindustani.

In March, 1880, Lieutenant Stayner took part with the regiment, as Adjutant, in its advance to Kandahar, and remained with the head-quarters in cantonments, and subsequently in the citadel, till the 16th August. In the attack upon the village of Deh Khwaja on that fatal day, he commanded the portion of his regiment which formed part of No. 3 Column under the command of Colonel Heathcote, and was ordered by him to assault the northern side of the position. Whilst gallantly performing this duty he was killed by a matchlock ball, death being instantaneous. His body was carried back to the citadel, and was interred the same evening with those of four other officers in separate graves in a corner of the new garden cemetery, the burial service being read by the Rev. A. Cane.

Colonel Heathcote, of the 19th Bombay Natal Infantry refers in the warmest terms to Lieutenant Stayner's zeal and bravery; while his brother officers have lost no opportunity of placing on record their deep appreciation of his noble, kindly and generous nature.

BREV. LIEUT.-COL. R. G. T. STEVENSON,

POONA HORSE.

RODERICK GEORGE THOMAS STEVENSON, who died at Quetta on the 24th April, 1880, was the fourth son of Brigadier-General Thomas Stevenson, who served for forty years in the Bombay Artillery. He was born at Poona on the 6th April, 1836, and was educated at Cheltenham College. Receiving a direct Bombay Cavalry cadetship, he was appointed Cornet in the 2nd Light Cavalry on arriving in India in August, 1855, and two years afterwards (November, 1857) obtained his Lieutenancy. During the six years succeeding the date of his arrival in India, he did duty with his regiment in Rujputana and Central India; and accompanying it on service in the Indian Mutiny, was present at the action of Nimbhaira, the siege of Nimach, the capture of Kotah, and with the force under Sir J. Michell, K.C.B., in Central India, receiving the Mutiny medal with clasps for Central India. In March, 1862, Stevenson proceeded on sick certificate to England, where he remained till March, 1865, obtaining promotion, in the interval, to the rank of Captain. On returning to India he was attached to the 3rd Bombay Light Cavalry, and did duty with a squadron at Kaladgi, where he also held the office of Station Staff Officer, until April, 1866, when he was appointed to command the 2nd Squadron of the regiment.

In February, 1867, Captain Stevenson exchanged into the Poona Horse, with which corps he served at Sirur, and on the frontier of Upper Sind, until June, 1871, when he was appointed to officiate as 2nd in command of the 3rd (Queen's Own) Light Cavalry, then serving at Nimach. He commanded that regiment for nine months, at the expiration of which (April, 1872) he took leave to England. Returning to India in April, 1874, after having, in the interval, obtained his Majority, he rejoined the Poona Horse at Sirur. In the following year he proceeded to command a detached squadron in Khandesh, where he remained until the withdrawal of the squadron in 1878. In 1876 he succeeded to the appointment of permanent second in command of the regiment.

Major Stevenson took part with the Poona Horse in January, 1880, in its forward movement into Baluchistan, *en route* for Kandahar. Proceeding in command of two squadrons to Quetta, he reached that station in the last days of March, and was looking forward eagerly to the stirring times which seemed imminent. His anticipations of further active service were, however, unhappily destined never to be fulfilled. A few days before the regiment quitted Quetta for Kandahar, he was attacked with pleuro-pneumonia, to which complaint, after a short illness, he succumbed on the 24th April, within ten days of his receiving his Brevet Lieutenant-Colonelcy.

Lieutenant-Colonel Stevenson was a thorough soldier, and was highly esteemed by both officers and men, European and Native, of the regiment, who sincerely regretted his death. He married, in 1865, Rosalie Maitland, daughter of Thomas Mackenzie, C.B., Indian Medical Department. His father, Lieutenant-Colonel Thomas Stevenson, died at Sukkur in Upper Sind, in the year 1849, while commanding the Horse Artillery Brigade, Sind Field Force.

CAPTAIN EDWARD STRATON,

2ND BATTALION, 22ND REGIMENT (THE CHESHIRE).

HE subject of this memoir, who was killed at the battle of Kandahar on the 1st September, 1880, was the fifth son of the late John Warde Straton. After passing the examination for direct commissions in the line, he was gazetted on the 25th June, 1861, to an Ensigncy in the 2nd Battalion, 22nd (Cheshire) Regiment, and soon afterwards joined that corps at Malta. He obtained a Lieutenancy, by purchase, on the 23rd June, 1863. In 1865, he embarked with the regiment at Malta for Mauritius, where it was stationed till 1867, when it returned to England.

Lieutenant Straton was appointed Adjutant of the Battalion on the 20th April, 1868, and held that appointment till the 23rd April, 1872. He obtained a second-class Musketry certificate on the 1st October, 1868. On the 14th May, 1872, he was gazetted a Captain without purchase, under the new regulations. In August of the same year he obtained a certificate of proficiency in Military Gymnastics, and was employed upon the Staff of the Northern Corps d'Armée in the autumn manœuvres.

In the autumn of 1873, Captain Straton accompanied his regiment to India, and was quartered at Hazarabagh. From thence the battalion was removed to Ranikhet, of which station Captain Straton was appointed Station Staff Officer on the 31st November, 1876, and held that appointment till the 31st December, 1877. He had previously acted as Staff Officer to Major-General Payn whilst at Hazarabagh, and subsequently to Major-General M. A. S. Biddulph, at Ranikhet.

During the time he was at Ranikhet, he studied heliography, and gained that knowledge of the work which proved so useful later on; and on the 22nd February, 1878, he obtained a certificate as a qualified Instructor in Army Signalling. In 1878 the regiment was ordered to Allahabad, and Captain Straton was appointed Transport Officer of that station 10th October, 1878.

On the outbreak of the Afghan War, Captain Straton applied to be employed in the Army Signalling Department, but was not ordered to the front till April, 1879, when he joined the Kuram Field Force as Superintendent of Army Signalling in succession to Captain Barstow, 72nd Highlanders. After the massacre of the Kabul Embassy, Captain Straton was attached to Sir F. Roberts' Field Force, and accompanying it throughout its advance, was present at Charasiab, and during the operations ending in the occupation of Kabul; also at the affair at Dulia on the 10th November, 1879; during the investment of Sherpur by the Afghans in December, 1879, and also at Ali Boghan, near Jalalabad, on 12th January, 1880.

In connection with the actions above referred to, Captain Straton was mentioned in the despatches both of Brigadier-General Baker and Sir Frederick Roberts. The former makes allusion to the signalling arrangements as having been " of great service during the day's operations;" and the latter writes as follows :—" I wish especially to bring to notice the valuable aid I have received from Captain E. Straton, 22nd Foot, Superintendent of Army Signalling. In a country like Afghanistan, signalling by heliograph and flags is of the greatest assistance; the able and intelligent manner in which Captain Straton has carried on his work has helped materially to the success of the operations." In submitting, too, an abridged list of those whose services had been more particularly marked and valuable, Sir F. Roberts a second time mentions Captain Straton's name, and again in his despatch of the 23rd January, 1880, writes :—" I cannot overrate the value of the work done by the Army Signallers with this force, and I consider that the success which has attended their efforts is mainly due to the energy and intelligence of Captain E. Straton, 22nd Regiment, Superintendent of Army Signalling."

Major A. Wynne, 51st Regiment, thus refers to the affair of Ali Boghan, on the 12th January, 1880, in a paper read at the United Service Institution on 13th March, 1880 :—

" But perhaps one of the most prominent services rendered as yet by the heliograph, was during Captain Straton's visit to Jalalabad in January last. On the 12th of that month, when at one of the signal stations of Ali Boghan, he found out that the Mohmands had crossed the Kabul river; this intelligence he at once flashed off to Jalalabad, and that night a brigade started to intercept the enemy. During the following day communication was successfully maintained between General Bright's Head-quarters at Jalalabad, the brigade sent out, and a detachment crowning the heights. At 1.15 p.m. on the 13th, Captain Straton saw about 1,500 men of the enemy retiring across the river at such a point that, if they had succeeded in crossing, the brigade would have been cut off from Jalalabad and the detachment from its main body. But intimation was at once signalled to all concerned, and by 3 p.m. a couple of guns sent out from Jalalabad were shelling the enemy with such good effect that they beat a hasty retreat."

Then followed the monotonous life in cantonments, broken only by short expeditions into the neighbouring country, until the end of July, when orders arrived for Sir F. Roberts to march to Kandahar. Captain Straton was attached to the Kabul-Kandahar Field Force, and again was successful in demonstrating the usefulness of the heliograph.

It was at the battle of Kandahar on 1st September, 1880, when the victory was almost won, and Captain Straton was on his way to the Baba Wali Kotal to announce the success to Sir F. Roberts by heliograph, that he met his death. The following are the words used by the General with reference to the event in his despatch describing the march and the battle :—

" Shortly before the final advance, Major-General Ross, wishing to inform me by heliograph that he had succeeded in turning the enemy's position, directed Captain Straton, 22nd Foot, Superintendent of Army Signalling, to proceed with a company of the 24th Punjab Native Infantry to the Baba Wali Kotal. This gallant officer had only gone a short distance when a Ghazi, springing out of a ravine close to him, shot him dead. In Captain Straton, Her Majesty's Service has lost a most accomplished, intelligent officer, under whose management Army Signalling, as applied to field service, reached a pitch of perfection probably never before attained. His energy knew no difficulties, and his enthusiasm was beyond praise. He had won the highest opinions from all with whom his duties had brought him in contact, and his death was very deeply felt throughout the whole force."

The value of the work done by the Army Signallers is thus referred to by Colonel Chapman, Chief of the Staff of the Kabul-Kandahar Field Force, in a paper read at the United Service Institution, 9th March, 1881 :—

"It may here be noticed that the great perfection to which the practice of Army Signalling had been brought, made the heliograph a very important aid in the communication of intelligence. Under the direction of the late Captain Straton, Superintendent of Army Signalling at Kabul, the trained signallers of the force were constantly employed, and by the judicious use of the heliograph on many occasions, the troops, both cavalry and infantry, were spared fatigue, the several brigades being constantly in communication by signal. . . . . . . Later on, it will be seen how much depended on the working of the heliograph between Kandahar and the camp in the Tarnak Valley, on the 27th August; but the benefits conferred on the Kabul Field Force by its staff of army signallers under their gallant leader, cannot be forgotten."

The following extract, taken from the "Army and Navy Gazette" of the 11th September, 1880, may fitly close this notice :—". . . He (Captain Straton) fell in the performance of his duties almost in the moment of victory. His loss will be deeply deplored, not only by the officers and men of his regiment, but by a very large number of friends throughout the service. A man of indomitable courage and untiring energy, he was passionately fond of his profession, and singularly zealous in the performance of his duties. First in every manly exercise, kind-hearted, and courteous, he was a noble specimen of an officer and a gentleman."

CAPTAIN S. A. SWINLEY,

11TH (P.W.O.) BENGAL CAVALRY (LANCERS).

SILAS ADAIR SWINLEY, who died of typhoid fever at Safed Sang, Afghanistan, on the 24th May, 1879, was the second son of the late Major-General G. H. Swinley, Royal (late Bengal) Artillery. He was born at Agra, North West Provinces, India, on the 11th July, 1843. Obtaining a direct commission in April, 1861, he was placed on the General List of cavalry officers of the Bengal Establishment, and at once embarked for India.

Landing at Calcutta in May, 1861, Swinley proceeded to Mirat, and in June, 1861, was appointed to do duty with the 8th Hussars, with which regiment he remained till the 9th November, 1862; he was then posted to the 3rd Bengal Cavalry, and served with that corps in successive grades for a period of eight years. In the month of December, 1870, he met with an accident while on parade, falling from his horse and injuring himself so severely as to necessitate his taking furlough to England for two years on medical certificate. On his return to India in 1873, he received the appointment of Station Staff Officer at Nowgong, Bundelkhand; and officiating at intervals as cantonment Magistrate and first-class Political Agent at that station, retained that post till December, 1876. He was then despatched on special duty to Madras, and for several months did valuable and important work in connection with the famine which raged over that presidency in 1876 and 1877.

In November, 1877, Captain Swinley was appointed 3rd Squadron Commander to the 11th (Prince of Wales' Own) Bengal Lancers. On the outbreak of hostilities with Afghanistan in the autumn of 1878, he took part in the month of November, in the advance of Sir Sam. Browne's Division into the Khyber Pass, being present at the capture of Ali Musjid, and subsequently sharing with his regiment, during the succeeding winter and early spring, the heavy convoy and escort duties which fell to its lot. It was while he was on detached duty, commanding a post between Jalalabad and Gandamak, that he was attacked with the fever which subsequently proved fatal to him. It is characteristic of him that he sent no intimation of his illness to regimental head-quarters, but continued in a spirit of self-devotion to do duty for days after he should have applied to be relieved. When he rode into Gandamak with the daily escort, his health was completely broken; and a few days afterwards, on the 24th May, 1879, he died, deeply regretted by the many friends to whom his sterling qualities had endeared him.

Captain Swinley's commissions bear date as follows :—

Cornet, General List Cavalry	20th April, 1861.
Lieutenant	24th September, 1863.
Brevet-Captain	20th April, 1873.
Captain	4th September, 1873.

2ᴺᴰ LIEUTENANT B. S. THURLOW,

51ST (KING'S OWN LIGHT INFANTRY).

BENJAMIN SMITH THURLOW was a member of the Suffolk family of that name, being the third son of the late George John Thurlow, Esq. He was born on the 23rd July, 1858, and was educated at King Edward the Sixth's Grammar School, Birmingham, and Mr. Kippin's Military College, Woolwich. Competing at the examination for entrance into Sandhurst in December, 1877, he succeeded in taking a place among the successful candidates, and, passing out of the college with honours after the usual course, was gazetted, in May, 1878, to the 58th Foot. Being desirous, however, to join a regiment serving in India, he was transferred, almost immediately, to the 51st King's Own Light Infantry, and was attached for a few months to the 101st Light Infantry, then quartered in Guernsey, to await the trooping season in the autumn.

In November, 1878, Thurlow embarked for India, and on arriving, proceeded to join his regiment at Ali Musjid, in the Khyber Pass, where, at the time, it was stationed. Subsequently taking part with it in the forward movement to Jalalabad and Gandamak, he shared the convoy and escort duties upon which it was employed, and eventually returned with it, after the signing of the treaty of peace, to India.

Lieutenant Thurlow accompanied the regiment in its second advance into Afghanistan on the renewal of hostilities in the autumn of 1879, and, in the spring of 1880, was doing duty with a detachment in the neighbourhood of Jagdalak. On the afternoon of the 22nd March, he started with his brother-officer, Lieutenant Reid, to ride over to that post, which was about a couple of miles distant. After the two had proceeded a few hundred yards along the bottom of a gorge, Reid heard three or four musket-shots fired almost simultaneously from the hills on each side of the road. The horses started forward at a gallop, and Thurlow, who was a few yards in front, was seen by Reid to fall heavily to the ground. Directly the latter could rein in his horse, he turned, and perceived an Afghan running towards Thurlow's apparently inanimate body for the purpose of robbing it. Putting spurs to his horse, Reid dashed at full speed towards the thief, who raised his rifle and fired point blank at his heart. At this critical juncture the horse shied suddenly on one side, and by so doing almost miraculously saved the life of its rider, whose coat-sleeve—so near was he to the muzzle of the gun when the shot was fired—was burnt away above the elbow. Closing with the Afghan, Reid now succeeded in bringing his revolver to bear on him, and blew out his brains; but no sooner was this done than some thirty of the band rushed upon him. He succeeded, however, in escaping, and making his way to Jagdalak, from whence parties were subsequently despatched to the spot where the affray had taken place. There Lieutenant Thurlow's body was found, and was interred on the following day with military honours.

The untimely and tragical end of the subject of this notice called forth many expressions of sympathy from unexpected sources. Though the term of his service with the regiment was of short duration, it was nevertheless not too brief to admit of his winning the esteem and affection of his comrades.

MAJOR R. J. LE POER TRENCH,

19TH BOMBAY NATIVE INFANTRY.

RICHARD JOHN LE POER TRENCH, the youngest son of the late Rev. John le Poer Trench, of Temple Michael, in the parish of Longford, Ireland, was born at Temple Michael Glebe, his father's rectory, in the year 1843. He was educated at King William's College, Isle of Man, and Cheltenham, from whence he passed the examination for a direct appointment—given to him by Mr. Bailly, one of the then East India directors—in the Indian Army. Gazetted to an Ensigncy in the 24th Bombay Infantry in September, 1859, he served with that regiment for some three years, at the end of which he proceeded home on sick-leave. On his return to India he applied himself to the study of the native languages. Having passed the Higher Standard examination, he was appointed Quartermaster to the 19th Bombay Infantry, with which regiment he subsequently served continuously till the day of his death—a period of some thirteen years.

Major Trench was at home on leave in the summer of 1878, but returned to India in time to rejoin his regiment before it received orders, after the outbreak of hostilities with Afghanistan, to hold itself in readiness to form part of the Reserve Division, then in course of concentration on the frontier. During the last eventful year of his service, while employed with his regiment in the formidable work of constructing a military road through the hitherto almost impassable Bolan defile, he was "most conspicuous," to quote the words of General Creagh, "for the energy he displayed, and for his fertility of resource in overcoming difficulties in the work, never tiring, and always encouraging his men at their laborious and unaccustomed employment by his own ready and cheerful example."

In September, 1879, Trench was sent in command of an escort to Sir R. Sandeman into the Kakar Pathan and Marri country. This party remained in and about the assigned districts till January, 1880, accompanying Sir R. Temple in his tour made in the neighbourhood in November, 1879. Most of the marches performed were made through exceedingly difficult country; and Trench's name was more than once mentioned in the Bombay journals for the combination of skill and patience which he displayed in taking trains with camels over passes hitherto regarded as inaccessible to such beasts of burden.

Major Trench rejoined the Head-quarters of the 19th Bombay Infantry at Kandahar, having marched his escort party there on completion of its duty, and taken up detachments of infantry and of artillery *en route*. After sharing with the regiment during the siege the various duties which fell to its lot, he took part with it, on the 16th August, 1880, in the fatal sortie to Deh Khwaja, commanding the two companies which formed part of Colonel Daubeny's column. When they had advanced up to the village, Trench was ordered to take his men and some of the Fusiliers into an enclosed field on the right, and drive back the enemy, who were here showing in force and endeavouring to break through to help those inside. This work he performed—according to the testimony of eye-witnesses—splendidly, all who saw him being loud in their praise of the way in which he handled his men, and the very complete manner in which he drove back the enemy, giving them volley after volley until they turned and fled to cover. After this he was moved into the village. When the retreat was sounded, he was standing in a ditch with some eighty of his men, who were working terrible havoc amongst the enemy with their fire. He is reported to have leapt up with the exclamation, "Retreat? this is no time for retreat!"—his last words; for a few moments afterwards a bullet fired from a house-top struck him in the back of the head, killing him instantaneously. "Thus died," wrote Colonel Heathcote, in reference to his fall, "as gallant an officer as ever held Her Majesty's commission." His body was brought in by his men; and in the evening of the same day received at the hands of his comrades a soldier's sepulture.

It will perhaps not be out of place to conclude this brief notice with the following extract from a letter written with reference to Major Trench by Major-General William Creagh, one who was some time his commanding officer:—

"He was a perfect type of a fine open-hearted Irishman. As an officer he could not be surpassed in anything that constitutes a good soldier, full of zeal and devotion to his profession, as daring as a lion. His death was a severe loss, not only to his own regiment, but to the Army."

BRIGADIER-GENERAL J. A. TYTLER, C.B., V.C.,

BENGAL STAFF CORPS.

JOHN ADAM TYTLER, who died at Thal, Punjab, on the 14th February, 1880, was the third son of John Tytler, Surgeon, Honourable East India Company's Service, his mother being a daughter of W. Gillies, Esq., of London. He was born at Monghyr, Bengal, on the 29th October, 1825, and was sent home, when five years of age, to the care of his mother's sisters, under whose charge he remained until the arrival of his parents in England in 1835. The family resided for a year in London, and then proceeded to Jersey, where John Tytler attended a day school in the vicinity of St. Heliers, kept by a Mr. de Joux. In March, 1837, Mr. Tytler died; and in the autumn of 1838 his widow—having in view the education of her family, and desiring to be near her relations—took up her residence in Edinburgh. There John Tytler attended the Academy, and in course of time bore off several prizes. On attaining his seventeenth year, he was transferred to a school at Lisle, where, remaining for a twelvemonth, he completed his education. In 1843 he received an Infantry commission in the Company's Service from his father's old friend Sir Jeremiah Bryant, and in the autumn of that year proceeded to India. The various incidents of his subsequent career are so amply and ably set forth in an obituary notice which appeared in the columns of the "Times" newspaper on the 23rd February, 1880, that, with these brief premises, the Editor of this work takes the liberty of transcribing the memoir as it was given. After making allusion to the deceased officer as "one of the best and bravest of the rising Generals of the Army in India—the bearer of a name honoured alike in that country and in this," the writer continues as follows:—

"In December, 1844, John Adam Tytler entered the Indian Army, in the ranks of which several of his relations were then serving; he was posted to the 66th Native Infantry, and first saw active service on the Peshawar frontier, under Sir Colin Campbell, in 1851. In the Indian Mutiny he was unfortunate enough to be detained in the Kumaun hills, and so was present at none of the great sieges of that campaign; but in February, 1858, at the action of Churpura, his men, being somewhat staggered by the heavy fire of grape with which they were received on approaching the enemy's position, showed signs of wavering. Lieutenant Tytler, seeing that personal example was all that was necessary to rally them, put spurs to his horse, and, dashing on ahead, alone attacked the rebel gunners; for a few seconds he was personally engaged in a hand-to-hand fight, and before his men reached him had been dangerously wounded in three places. He recovered, however, sufficiently to take part in the closing scenes of the suppression of the Mutiny, and to receive the Victoria Cross for his indomitable valour at the action of Churpura. In the Umbeyla expedition of 1863 Captain Tytler, V.C., commanded his regiment, the 4th Goorkhas, with marked credit, and was prominently noticed in despatches. Four years later, in the Hazara expedition, under Sir Alfred Wilde, we find him again leading the same gallant regiment—one of the model corps in the Bengal Army—and once more his name is honourably mentioned in orders. In 1872 he served through the Lushai expedition, and for his eminent services was nominated a Companion of the Bath. On the outbreak of the Afghan War, it was inevitable that Colonel Tytler's services would secure for him a brigade command, and it was equally certain that his great experience in hill warfare would prove of equal value to himself and the Government he had served so well. After the fall of Ali Musjid, at which he commanded one of the flanking brigades, he was intrusted with the onerous task of maintaining communications between Sir Samuel Browne's force and Peshawar. Here he acted with rare skill and sagacity; twice he led his brigade into the Afridi hills in order to chastize certain sections of that turbulent clan who were harassing convoys in the neighbourhood of the Khyber. Later on he defeated the Shinwaris in a sharp engagement. After the Treaty of Gandamak General Tytler was placed in command of the troops between Landi Kotal and the old frontier; but ill-health compelled him to resign his brigade before the outbreak of last September. Immediately on learning of the massacre of the Embassy, though still suffering from the effects of the previous campaign, the gallant General placed his sword at the disposal of the Viceroy. He was a man who could not be permitted to rust in idleness when mountain warfare was on the *tapis*, and the Commander-in-Chief evinced a wise determination when he nominated General Tytler to the command of the troops destined to act against the hostile Zaimushts. These operations were conducted with consummate skill. A resolute stand was made by the enemy, and in the frontal attack we lost a brave young officer in Lieutenant and Adjutant Renney. The General's plans were not to be denied, and while the main body held the enemy in check in front, a strong force under the personal guidance of the Brigadier swept the Zaimushts from their rocky fastnesses, which they hitherto had deemed impregnable. Never physically a strong man, the exposure and hardship of the two winter campaigns must naturally have told on a frame enfeebled by dangerous wounds; and just as he was about to reap the rewards of a distinguished career, pneumonia—that fell disease on the Punjab Frontier—has claimed him as its last and most valued victim. Modest and unassuming, as all brave men are, few who did not know General Tytler would recognize in him a man who had won the Victoria Cross for an act which onlookers deemed a ride to certain death; still less would they consider him one capable of converting raw Goorkha levies into one of the smartest regiments in the Indian Army. A long record of hard service has been closed by a death no less honourable than if won on the battle-field. He will be mourned, not merely by the few who knew and loved him well, but by the many who admired his daring gallantry, his earnest perseverance, and the patience with which he bore what most men would have deemed official neglect; for though General Tytler commanded his regiment on three separate campaigns and earned the warmest praises of all the Generals under whom he served, he never received Brevet promotion for his distinguished services in the field. Even his brilliant conduct in the late Afghan War was unrewarded by riband or professional advancement. His death deprives the Queen of the services of one of the best and bravest men who have ever worn her Cross, and the Indian Army of a General whose place it will not be easy to fill. He was an officer of the old school, and one of its best and most valued representatives."

LIEUTENANT E. P. VENTRIS,

3RD REGIMENT (THE BUFFS.)

EDWARD PEYTON VENTRIS, who died at Bagh, Baluchistan, on the 14th April, 1879, was the eldest son of the Rev. Edward Favell Ventris, Rector of Church Aston, Shropshire, by his marriage with Rose, daughter of Mr. Thomas Fisher, of St. Osyth, Essex. He was born at Colchester on the 28th July, 1856, and was educated at Newport Salop Grammar School, under the Rev. Dr. Charles Waring Saxton and Mr. Thomas Collins, and subsequently at Spring Grove, under Mr. Wyatt. After passing a creditable examination for direct appointments, he obtained a commission in the Buffs, and was gazetted 2nd Lieutenant in February, 1874.

Leaving England for India in the following September, Ventris joined his regiment at Calcutta. Here he remained till the 27th September, 1875, when he proceeded to Lucknow for garrison instruction. Before he had completed his course, however, an order came for all officers to rejoin Head-quarters, in view of the departure of the Buffs, in the then impending expedition to Perak; and embarking with the regiment in November, 1865, he served with it in the Malay Peninsula throughout the operations of the force. The expedition terminating in the middle of March in the following year, he landed at Calcutta on the 27th of that month, and at once proceeded with his regiment to Cawnpore. Having contracted a slight fever after his return to India, he was compelled to have recourse to the hills for a few months, at the expiration of which, his health being recruited by the colder climate, he returned to complete his garrison course at Lucknow, from which he had been so unexpectedly called away. The regiment eventually removed from Cawnpore to Meerut.

On the outbreak of hostilities with Afghanistan, Lieutenant Ventris, eager to make his way to the theatre of war, volunteered for active service "in any capacity," and being a very good and promising officer, was appointed, on the recommendation of Colonel Morley, to the Transport Service of the South Afghanistan Field Force. Proceeding on the 1st February, 1879, to Lahore, he received orders to go on to Sukkur, and became finally located at Haji-ka-Shehar, where he became the assistant of Lieutenant-Colonel Cherry in the Transport Train. Here his arduous duties, carried out in a trying climate, and with only bad water to be had, brought on an illness from which he died.

Colonel Cherry, in writing of the subject of this brief notice, says:—"Ventris was always the same—amiable and gentlemanly, and ever anxious to do his duty;" and General Phayre, in recording his death, speaks of the energy and perseverance with which he performed the difficult duties assigned to him.

A tomb, surrounded by an iron railing, erected by the officers of the Transport Train and Staff, marks the spot where Lieutenant Ventris was buried.

SURGEON-MAJOR JOHN WALLACE,
M.A., M.D., M.R.C.S.,

ARMY MEDICAL DEPARTMENT.

HE subject of this memoir was the fourth son of Mr. Wallace, Chapel of Leggat, Auchterless, Aberdeenshire. He received his education in Scotland, and was a distinguished student both at the Universities of Aberdeen and Edinburgh. At the former he obtained the degree of M.A. in 1859; and at the latter that of M.D. in 1862, in which year he also became a member of the Royal College of Surgeons, England. Taking first place among the candidates for commissions for the Army Medical School in March, 1864, he left Netley at the close of the session, and did duty for a brief period on the Staff. He was then appointed to the 12th Regiment, and proceeded almost immediately afterwards to New Zealand. Serving with the regiment in the Maori War of 1864-1866, for which he obtained the medal, he was present at the attack and capture of the fortified pass of Otapawa, and several minor affairs. After three years spent in New Zealand, he returned with the regiment to England, and continued with it throughout the period of its home service.

His unostentatious self-devotion to duty, his wide sympathies, and his unfailing patience, had early brought him into cordial relationship alike with the officers and men of the regiment—relationship which his after association with the corps only served still further to strengthen and augment. In the autumn of 1875, when the battalion was stationed at Kinsale, typhoid fever of a most virulent type broke out in the ranks; and Dr. Wallace, who was at the time away on leave of absence, was at once telegraphed for. In reference to the services which he then rendered, a letter, couched in warm terms of admiration, was addressed by the Officer Commanding to the Assistant Adjutant-General of the District: "During the long and anxious time which followed the outbreak," wrote Colonel Foster, "it may be said that Surgeon Wallace almost lived in the Hospital; day and night was he to be found in attendance on the sick, taking only a snatch of rest now and then, and that very frequently by the bedside of a sufferer; in fact, his indefatigable exertions and untiring devotion to the patients were truly laudable." His services upon that occasion were brought under the notice of H.R.H. the Commander-in-Chief, and received his highest approval.

Dr. Wallace accompanied the regiment to India on the expiration of its term of home service, and was doing duty with it, when, on the outbreak of hostilities with Afghanistan, it marched from Naushahra, and joined the Peshawar Valley Field Force. In the previous autumn he had been much weakened by fever, then prevalent; and he now entered on the harassing duties of the campaign before his health was fully re-established. In the pestiferous climate of the country through which the Northern Division of the Army pursued its route, work soon fell to his hand which severely taxed even his unflagging energy. Worn out while in charge of the Field Hospital at Landi Kotal with the ceaseless exertion and anxiety entailed by his endeavours to cope with the fearful amount of sickness which was decimating the ranks at that post during the evacuation of the Northern line, he fell a victim on the 16th July, 1879, at the early age of thirty-nine years, to the terrible disease—cholera—which he had done so much to alleviate in others.

We may aptly conclude this brief notice of one who fittingly closed his useful life at the post of duty, by quoting at length from the official Orders issued on the occasion of his death. In a Regimental Order bearing date 16th July, 1879, the following tribute is paid to his memory; "In a period of thirteen years and upward that Dr. Wallace served with the regiment, he endeared himself to everyone, by the care and kind attention he bestowed so willingly on all. Lieut.-Colonel Walker, the officers, non-commissioned officers, men, women, and children, have by Dr. Wallace's death lost a most true, valued, and kind-hearted friend; and the Commanding Officer is well aware he cannot do sufficient justice to the many good and sterling qualities of the deceased: he can truly say, a less selfish man never lived, and he firmly believes that Dr. Wallace's deep sense of duty and devotion to the sick men of the battalion have been the cause of his most lamented death." And in a Brigade Order of the 17th idem, the last chapter of the deceased officer's career is thus epitomized:—" In charge of the Field Hospital at Landi Kotal, during a most trying and arduous time, he devoted himself to his duties with an energy which was ceaseless and untiring, and with a skill and kindness which will be remembered with gratitude by many a British soldier in this garrison. Thinking always of others, he took no heed of himself, but working on through sickness, as he had done in health, he laid himself open to the attacks of the disease which has stricken him down, and has robbed his profession and his regiment of an honour to both."

SURGEON J. E. WALSH, M.D.,

BENGAL MEDICAL DEPARTMENT.

JOHN EDWARD WALSH, who died of cholera at Kandahar on the 24th July, 1879, was the eldest son of J. R. Walsh, Esq., of Martinstown House, Co. Limerick. He was born on the 2nd of May, 1855, and received the rudiments of his education at home. When sufficiently prepared, he was sent to the Abbey Grammar School, Tipperary, one of Erasmus Smith's foundations, where he studied under the head-mastership of the late Mr. T. Matthews, M.A., of St. John's, Cambridge. Entering the Queen's College, Cork, in October, 1873, he took a first literary scholarship on Matriculation, and shortly afterwards a first prize in English composition. His career at Cork was one of high promise: in addition to bearing off numerous prizes, he obtained a Medical scholarship and several exhibitions. He took his degrees in Medicine and Surgery at the Queen's University, Dublin, in October, 1877; and in the following February was a successful candidate in London for an appointment in the Indian Medical Service.

In October, 1878, Walsh was ordered out to India. After being stationed for a time at Mirat he was sent to Mian Mir, where he was attached to one of the native regiments. His next move was to Multan. There he passed the lower standard examination in Hindustani; and there, too, he was subsequently appointed to take medical charge of the relieving force under the command of Colonel Bedford, Royal Engineers, then *en route* for Quetta and Kandahar. In view of the rough and difficult nature of the country, subsequently traversed by the troops after crossing the Indus, the fact that only one man was lost out of the 700 of which, including camp followers, the force was composed, speaks of itself for the efficiency of the medical care bestowed on it during the march. In recognition of the Surgeon's successful and zealous attention, the officer commanding made allusion to him, in the handsomest and most complimentary terms, in his report to the General.

Dr. Walsh had been barely two months in Kandahar, when, cholera breaking out among the camp followers, he was placed in charge of one of the wards of the hospital for patients suffering from that fatal disease. An enthusiast in his profession, he laboured with unceasing and devoted zeal, never sparing himself in his efforts to alleviate pain or soothe the last moments of a sufferer. For a time he continued cheerfully to cope with the ever-increasing work; but at length, utterly worn out, he fell at his post, a victim to the disease whose ravages he had been for weeks successfully combating. He died like a true soldier, in the performance of his duties, passing away after a few hours of great suffering, in his twenty-fourth year, in the springtime of his life, full of hope, of future promise, of intellectual and physical energy. His naturally spontaneous and affectionate disposition had endeared him to the whole garrison, and his death was mourned with a depth of feeling which, in view of the brief term of his service, was as remarkable as it was affecting.

It is some consolation to Dr. Walsh's family to know that he was watched over during his last hours by some of his comrades with a chivalrous devotion which no brother's care could exceed. His remains repose in the burial-ground outside Kandahar, where those of hundreds of his countrymen found a last resting-place forty years previously. A marble slab, erected by his brother medical officers to his memory, marks his grave.

2ᴺᴰ LIEUTENANT E. H. WATSON,

1ST BATTALION, 17TH (LEICESTERSHIRE) REGIMENT.

EDWARD HERBERT WATSON, who died on the 4th July, 1879, at Murree, Punjab, from illness contracted while on field service in Afghanistan, was the eldest son of Lieutenant-General E. D. Watson, of the Bengal Infantry, by his marriage with Adelaide, daughter of the late Venerable Archdeacon Barnes, Rector of Sowton, Devonshire.

The subject of this notice was born on the 13th December, 1858, and was educated at Haileybury, from whence, shortly after attaining his eighteenth year, he passed direct into the Royal Military College, Sandhurst. He there received a certificate of merit for Military Law, and honourable mention for exemplary conduct.

Gazetted, in May, 1878, to the 17th Foot, young Watson did duty for a few months at the Depôt, and at the close of the year embarked for India to join the 1st Battalion of the regiment, then on active service in Afghanistan. On the 25th January, 1879, he reached Basawal, where the Head-quarters were at the time stationed, and from that date till the signing of the treaty of peace, shared with the regiment, in the neighbourhood of that post, the various escort and other duties which fell to its lot. From the 18th to the 21st March he was present with the Head-quarters at Maidanak, subsequently proceeding with the battalion to Jalalabad and Safed Sang, and accompanying it, on its retracing its steps, to Landi Kotal. The trying nature of the march, the intense heat, and the pestiferous climate of the country traversed now began to tell upon him, and while at the post last named, he was seized with the deadly malarial fever to which so many of his countrymen fell victims. In the hope that a more bracing atmosphere might restore him to health, he was moved down, by easy stages, to Murree; but the change came too late, and he died shortly after reaching his destination.

Though no opportunity presented itself to the subject of this notice, during the short term of his service, for distinguishing himself in action, his career was not too brief to admit of his winning the esteem and affection of his comrades. He had endeared himself—according to the testimony of his Commanding Officer—to all around him, and his early death was deeply lamented in the regiment.

SURGEON GEORGE WATSON, M.B.,

BENGAL MEDICAL DEPARTMENT.

HE subject of this notice was the eldest son of Mr. Edward Watson, farmer, Crawfordjohn Farm, Lanarkshire, Scotland. He was born on the 4th September, 1844, and received his earlier education at the Crawfordjohn Parish School, under the late Mr. Robb. At the age of fifteen he entered the University of Edinburgh to study Medicine; and passing in the greater number of his subjects with honours before obtaining his majority, took the degree of M.B. in the year 1866, at the age of twenty-one years. Shortly afterwards he received the appointment of House Surgeon to the Dumfries and Galloway Royal Infirmary, which responsible position he held for seventeen months, availing himself during its tenure of the daily opportunities which presented themselves for improving his professional attainments and acquiring a practical knowledge of the surgical art. Taking, in the year 1868, the degree of L.R.C.S., Edinburgh, he continued to practise in various parts until 1872, when he passed for the Indian Medical Service, his name appearing ninth in the list of successful candidates. He received his commission in March, 1872; and after passing through the usual course at Netley, embarked in the autumn for India.

On arriving at his destination, Watson did duty for a month at the General Hospital, and was subsequently posted successively to the 33rd Bengal Native Infantry, the 8th Bengal Cavalry, and the 14th Bengal Lancers. In January, 1876, he was permanently appointed to the 13th Bengal Lancers.

In the autumn of 1878 Dr. Watson volunteered for active service in Afghanistan, and was attached for duty to the Artillery of Sir Sam. Browne's Division of the Army of Invasion. Accompanying the Division into the Khyber, he was present, on the 21st November, at the attack and capture of Ali Musjid. In January, 1879, he took part with a detachment of his own regiment, which he had in the meantime rejoined, in the Bazar Afridi expedition under Sir F. Maude; and continuing with the regiment, subsequently did duty with it on the Northern Line at various posts extending to Jalalabad, eventually participating with it in the trying return march to India in June, 1879.

On the renewal of hostilities in the autumn, Watson proceeded with the 13th Bengal Lancers by forced marches to the Kuram Valley; and in the month of December, accompanied the portion of his regiment which took part in the expedi- against the Zaimushts, returning eventually to Kuram. In the course of his subsequent duties, which were performed in the unhealthy climate of the valley, he suffered repeatedly from attacks of fever, till at length, in July, 1880, a move to higher ground was deemed necessary for the re-establishment of his health, and he left for the Peiwar Kotal. The change came, however, too late: a few days after he arrived at his destination his fever took an enteric form, and on the 25th of the month he expired.

In addition to performing his regimental duties, Dr. Watson had been for some time in medical charge of the Head-quarter Staff. During the brief term of his service he had become universally beloved and esteemed.

The deceased officer was buried, with military honours, in the cemetery at Fort Kuram.

MAJOR S. J. WAUDBY, STAFF CORPS,

19TH BOMBAY NATIVE INFANTRY.

SIDNEY JAMES WAUDBY, who was killed at Dubrai, Southern Afghanistan, on the 16th of April, 1880, was the son of the Rev. W. R. P. Waudby, Rector of Stoke Albany, Market Harborough. He was born in 1840 at Kentish Town; and was educated at Marlborough College and Rossall. In 1858, having obtained a commission in the Company's Service, he proceeded to India, and was attached at first for a few months to the 72nd Highlanders, then stationed at Mhow. He was afterwards gazetted as Ensign to the 19th Bombay Infantry, with which corps he served uninterruptedly until the day of his death—a period of over twenty-one years.

In 1860 Waudby accompanied a field force sent to coerce some turbulent Bhils who had risen in rebellion near the Narbada, and contracted, when on that service, a very dangerous illness, from the pestilential nature of the jungles of the country in which the force was operating. In 1866 he was appointed to the Adjutancy of the regiment, a position he continued to hold until he was promoted to the rank of Major in 1878. The next eighteen years of his life, with the exception of two intervals in which he visited England, were passed in the uneventful duties of an Indian cantonment, varied, however, year by year, by expeditions against the large game of the country—tigers, bison, and bears, of which a great number fell to his rifle. Besides being a keen sportsman, he was a most daring rider, and almost always succeeded—no matter how large the field was—in taking the first spear in all the hunts he attended.

In November, 1878, Major Waudby accompanied his regiment as second in command on field service to Southern Afghanistan; but being in the Reserve Brigade, did not, during the first part of the war, get beyond the head of the Bolan Pass. For several months he was actively and continuously employed with his regiment on escort and other duties, but more especially in assisting in the construction of the military road, 165 miles in length, from Jacobabad to within a short distance of Quetta, the existence of which is mainly due to the exertions of the 19th Bombay Infantry. For his services on this work he was mentioned in the highest terms in General Orders by General Phayre, and Sir Richard Temple, Governor of Bombay.

In December, 1879, Major Waudby succeeded to the temporary command of the regiment, and marched with it to Kandahar. On a permanent commanding officer being appointed, in April, 1880, he—not caring for the quiet life of a peaceful cantonment, as Kandahar then was—applied for, and at once obtained the post of Road Commandant between Kandahar and Quetta, just then become vacant: a position of much responsibility in that wild, lawless country, and one that required constant moving about, together with great tact and vigilance. He at once started on his first inspection of the line; and on his return reached Dubrai—a small commissariat post about fifty miles distant from Kandahar—on the 16th April. On his arrival here, he was informed that an attack was to be made on the post that night by a large body of Kakur Pathans—a very formidable race. He had no one with him on whom he could rely except his small escort, consisting of two privates of his own regiment and three men of the Sind Horse—the guard belonging to the post being composed of some local Pathans lately engaged for the purpose, but who could not be trusted on an emergency, and who were, in consequence, more a source of danger than of help.

Major Waudby immediately proceeded to make the post—which consisted of a small enclosure surrounded by a wall some four feet high—as defensible as possible by means of grain bags and whatever material was near at hand, blocking up the one gateless entrance. At about 11 p.m. the enemy, over 300 in number, suddenly came on and commenced the attack. The native local guard all fled on their first appearance, one man, however, being cut down by a Sind Horseman just as he was in the act of joining them. After a time the assailants by mere force of numbers drove the defenders out of the large area of the courtyard into their redoubt, the top of the Commissariat buildings, which consisted of a single line of low sheds flanking the enclosure on the south side. These were built after the Afghan fashion, with domed roofs. Six of these small domes rose above the level of the façade; and from behind these Major Waudby's party held their attackers at bay for two or three hours. At length the numbers of the gallant little band grew smaller, and the enemy, having succeeded in effecting a lodgment upon the roof, drove them down again to the enclosure. Here they now took refuge inside one of the buildings, and here the last desperate struggle took place. Time after time the enemy charged the narrow gateway of the stronghold, but without success; for barring the approach stood Major Waudby, armed with his shot gun, and making terrible havoc with any who came near him. Eleven corpses were subsequently found at this spot lying close to one another, every one disfigured with shot-wounds—the charges at that close range flying almost like a bullet between the eyes. But at length the place became no longer tenable. The enemy had succeeded in breaking a hole through the roof, and a plunging fire upon the little party was now commenced. Major Waudby had been wounded in the foot already from above; the ammunition of his men was totally exhausted; and on both sides of them the buildings were blazing fiercely. The last rush was now made—not, alas! with any hope of escape on the part of the defenders, but with the fierce determination to sell their lives as dearly as possible. The struggle did not last long. What sword-cuts or bayonet-thrusts were interchanged can never be known; but just outside the little building which had been held so bravely was found the body of Major Waudby, and on each side of it, recognizable solely by the fragments of their uniform, lay those of the two brave soldiers of the 19th. In this gallant and memorable defence, the assaulting Afghans lost over thirty in killed and wounded, and were taught, not for the first time, that English officers and native soldiers know how to fight and how to die.

The following is an extract from a letter written to Major Waudby's father by General Brooke, commanding the Brigade of which the 19th Regiment formed a part, and who arrived at Dubrai the very morning after the occurrence above narrated took place:—" Before this time the telegraph has informed you of the death of your son, with an account of his splendid conduct; but being one of those who first visited the scene of his gallant fight, I cannot resist writing a few lines to assure you how deeply impressed I and every man both British and native in the force which I commanded, and indeed in the whole Army in Southern Afghanistan, have been by the grand example he has set us all—for no more noble instance of the sacrifice of self to the demands of duty has ever come to my knowledge than that displayed by your son, who accepted almost certain death rather than flinch from what he held to be his duty. Your son was warned early in the afternoon of the certainty and gravity of the impending attack, and asked by some of the native soldiers and servants who were with him to retire on the next post, which he could easily have done. I fully understand the fine spirit that induced him to refuse to listen to the suggestion, and, hopeless as he well knew the defence must be, to decide to lose his life rather than to throw even a shadow of discredit on the courage and spirit of Englishmen in the East. Had I, as a senior officer, been in the vicinity at the time, and learnt the exact situation, and the impossibility of reinforcing the garrison, I should have held myself bound to order the evacuation of the post; but this he—acting for himself—could not and would not do; and I honour him for his decision. He seems to have done all an educated and good soldier could have done to improve the defences, and to have made the best possible use of the means at his disposal; and appears to have held the overwhelming numbers at bay for a considerable time. It is clear that before he was overpowered and killed he and his two Sepoys had killed fifteen and wounded eighteen of the enemy. We actually found thirteen dead bodies of the attacking party on the ground; and the enemy acknowledged to having carried off two dead bodies and eighteen wounded. We have lost an admirable officer; but the sacrifice has not been in vain, as he has set an example which cannot be forgotten, and has by his gallantry stimulated the ardour of all our troops in a most remarkable manner. Major Trench (an officer of the 19th Bombay Infantry, who subsequently fell fighting in the sortie from Kandahar) will tell you of the real sorrow evinced by his regiment, and the anxiety of all, notably the natives, to commemorate his memory in a fitting manner. Nothing can compensate his family—his widow and his children—for their loss; but I trust their sorrow will be alleviated in some degree by learning how universally he was respected and liked in his life, and admired in his death."

Some months afterwards, the 19th Regiment, on their return march from Kandahar, had the melancholy satisfaction of performing the last sad rites of a soldier's funeral over the grave of their lamented comrade. It was then observed that other graves in the vicinity had been dug up and violated, even those of Muhamadans—co-religionists of the people of the country—not having escaped.

Major Waudby's alone was left uninjured and intact. On the villagers being asked the reason for such a distinction having been made, they replied, "An Afghan always respects the brave; and no braver man ever lived than the Englishman who lies buried there."

Major Waudby married, in 1875, Mary Alice, daughter of the late Edward Attwood, Esquire, and has left issue two sons.

CAPTAIN A. A. D. WEIGALL,

ARMY PAY DEPARTMENT.

THE subject of this notice was the youngest son of the late Rev. E. Weigall, Incumbent of Buxton, Derbyshire, and Rural Dean, and was a brother of the late Captain Stewart Weigall, of the 77th Regiment.

Arthur Archibald Denne Weigall was born in France on the 21st September, 1844, and received his early education at the Macclesfield Grammar School, whence he proceeded to Rossall School. From there he passed for direct commission in 1864, taking fifth place in the list of successful candidates. Gazetted in July, 1864, to an Ensigncy by purchase in the 76th Regiment, he did duty for a few months at the Depôt at Belfast, and then embarked, in 1865, for India, to join the Head-quarters in the Madras Presidency. In June, 1867, he purchased his Lieutenancy. In the course of his Indian service he passed the examination for the Staff Corps; but being reluctant to sever himself from his old regiment, abstained from availing himself of his success. After serving at various stations in the Madras Presidency, he proceeded with the regiment to Burmah. He had not been long in that country, however, before he became a martyr to so acute a form of rheumatism as to necessitate his being invalided home for eighteen months. On the expiration of his leave in 1869 he returned, restored to health, to his regiment in India, and remained with it till it came home in 1876. He at this time held—and for some time previously had held—the post of Adjutant.

On obtaining his company in October, 1876, and having passed the Hythe Musketry course with a first-class certificate, Captain Weigall exchanged into the 57th Foot, and proceeded to join the Head-quarters of the regiment in Ceylon. Thence he accompanied the 57th to Natal; and serving with the regiment in the Zulu War, was present at the relief of Ekowe and in all the subsequent operations, including the battle of Ginghilovo. At the engagement last named he was struck by a spent ball; but though his arm was contused he did not return his name in the list of wounded. He continued to serve with the regiment in South Africa till it was ordered home in 1879, when he accompanied it to Ireland.

A few months after returning from South Africa, Captain Weigall, seeing no prospect of promotion, joined the Army Pay Department, and was posted to the 2nd Battalion, 11th Regiment, then on active service in South Afghanistan. He at once embarked for India, and in due course made his way to Sibi. The effects of the African climate, from which—though he had never been off duty during the whole of the campaign in Zululand—he suffered when in Dublin, rendered the long and trying march through the Bolan Pass, to join the Head-quarters of the regiment, a task of exaggerated magnitude, and he arrived at Quetta completely exhausted. Though he became sufficiently restored to health to enable him to take part in the forward movement of the regiment into Afghanistan, he never completely recovered; and reaching Kandahar only to die, eventually succumbed on the 22nd December, 1880, in the thirty-seventh year of his age. He left behind him an enviable memory: to know him was to love him, as the universal sympathy manifested at his death fully testifies—officers and men feeling that a brave and thorough soldier and a true friend had passed away from them.

Captain Weigall married, in September, 1876, Alice Henrietta Leveson, second daughter of Surgeon-General Cowen, A.M.D. (retired). He leaves a widow and two children—the youngest, a boy born only five weeks before his death—to mourn his loss.

LIEUTENANT C. G. WHITBY,

PROBATIONER, BOMBAY STAFF CORPS.

CLEMENT GEORGE WHITBY was the eldest son of Dr. Whitby, of Leamington, and was born at Ottery St. Mary, in 1854. He was educated at Wellington College, where he obtained an open classical scholarship, and at Keble College, Oxford, from whence, after passing his moderations, he entered the Army on the 16th February, 1874, as a Sub-Lieutenant in H.M.'s 17th Foot, which his grandfather (one of the Whitbys of Creswell Hall, Staffordshire) had at one time commanded. He immediately proceeded to join his regiment at Peshawar, where it was then quartered. After serving with it for nearly two years, he became a Probationer for the Staff Corps, and joined the 4th Bombay Native Infantry, at Satara. When the Afghan war broke out, Whitby was at once attached to Jacob's Rifles, then quartered at Quetta, and with this regiment he served for some time, being for many months on detachment at Kalat. He was subsequently attached, during the constructing of the road through the Bolan Pass, to the 1st Grenadiers, and assisted in that undertaking till it was completed.

Lieutenant Whitby was well known throughout India by his many contributions to various journals, his chief writings being the "Jottings of a Subaltern," in the "Times of India." He was the originator of the "Kandahar News" (the little journal now so well known throughout both India and England), of which he continued editor until he marched with General Burrows' Force, for the disastrous enterprise in which he lost his life.

In the action near Girishk on the 14th July, 1880, he took no part, being left to guard the camp; but on the fatal 27th July, at Maiwand, he was given command of the baggage guard, which during the engagement twice repulsed the enemy's attack. His horse being still fresh when the retreat was ordered, he managed to struggle on as far as the last village, ten miles from Kandahar, where, within sight of the walls of the city, he was shot through the head by one of the villagers who came swarming out to attack the exhausted remnant of the brigade.

Lieutenant Whitby had passed in the Higher Standard examination in Hindustani, and the Final examination for the Staff Corps, to which he would have been gazetted in a short time, had he survived.

LIEUTENANT FRANK WHITTUCK, STAFF CORPS,

1st BOMBAY N.I. (GRENADIERS).

THE subject of this notice, who died at Kandahar on the 5th September, 1880, was the fifth son of Captain Whittuck, late of Her Majesty's 82nd Regiment, of Ellsbridge House, Keynsham, Somersetshire, by his marriage with Frances Matilda, eldest daughter of the late Lieut.-Colonel Slater, 82nd Regiment.

He was born on the 16th July, 1856, and was educated at the Hermitage, Lansdown, and Sydney College, Bath, eventually passing into the Royal Military College, Sandhurst. In January, 1876, he was gazetted to the 1st Battalion, 17th Regiment (Leicestershire), then in India; but as a probationer for the Staff Corps he at once joined the 12th Bombay Native Infantry at Dharwar. After doing duty for a period with this regiment, he was attached for a short time to the 20th Native Infantry at Baroda, from whence he was ordered to Mhow, to do duty for six months with Her Majesty's 17th Foot. He then rejoined the 12th Native Infantry at Rajkot, and was finally posted to the 1st Bombay Grenadiers, then employed in constructing the military road through the Bolan Pass. After a long and toilsome journey undertaken in the coldest season of the year, he came up with his regiment, and afterwards proceeded with it to Kandahar.

Taking part with the Grenadiers, in the first days of July, 1880, in the advance of Burrows' Brigade to the Halmand, and in the return march to Khushk-i-Nakhud, Lieutenant Whittuck was present with them at the battle of Maiwand, on the 27th of the month, being one of the three officers of the regiment who escaped untouched on that disastrous day. The trials and privations endured through the terrible retreat in which for thirty hours the troops were without food or water, and the subsequent very heavy duties which devolved upon the garrison (at the time sadly reduced in numbers), during the siege, must have been too much for this young officer's strength. Towards the end of August he was attacked with dysentery whilst on duty on the ramparts, from the effects of which—owing to his constitution being much weakened by previous attacks of fever—he never recovered. The last letter his family received from him was penned just one week before the battle of the 27th July; its writer was full of hope and spirits, and apparently without the least idea of the enemy's proximity in such formidable strength.

Lieutenant Whittuck was an officer devoted to his profession. During the short period of his service he was an earnest student of native languages, several examinations in which he passed very creditably. He was also much attached to sport of every kind, and being a good rider and a light weight, he not infrequently rode successfully at race meetings. Of an essentially honourable nature, he endeared himself to all who knew him by his pleasing manners and amiable, unselfish disposition.

LIEUTENANT H. V. WILLIS,

ROYAL ARTILLERY.

HERBERT VALIANT WILLIS, who was assassinated at Kandahar on the 10th January, 1879, was the eldest son of William Valiant Willis, and Eliza Frances, his wife. Born at Waterloo, in the County of Lancashire, on January 18th, 1856, he passed his early days at Arley, in Staffordshire. He was educated at St. Nicholas College, Lancing, Sussex, till he attained the age of seventeen years, when he was placed under the care of Dr. Frost, of Kensington Square, London, to be prepared for the Royal Military Academy, into which he passed, after nine months' study, in February, 1875. Whilst at Woolwich, he distinguished himself in drawing and horsemanship, and ultimately passed out from the Academy tenth in priority for the Artillery. After attending the gunnery course at Shoeburyness, he was gazetted to E/4 Royal Artillery, then in India, and proceeding out in the "Malabar" troopship in October, 1877, joined his battery at Allahabad, where it had halted on its march to Multan. During the following hot season he was sent in charge of invalids to Dalhousie, where he remained until war was declared with Afghanistan.

Lieutenant Willis was enthusiastically fond of his profession, and from the first earnestly studied it. On the outbreak of war he immediately applied for, and obtained permission to rejoin his battery, which had been ordered to the front, and overtook it on the banks of the Indus. From the time of his leaving Dalhousie until the day after the entry of the troops into Kandahar (being the day before he received his death-wound) he kept a most interesting record of the arduous march of the battery through the Bolan Pass, in the form of a diary, contriving to send it home with great regularity. The chief part of this account, which was published in a local newspaper, was eagerly looked for and read, and created much interest in the neighbourhood of the writer's home. He possessed a singularly humane and gentle disposition, and was beloved by all with whom he associated. In his letters written during the campaign, he repeatedly mentions with pain the sufferings of the camp-followers and of the animals. On one occasion, having been sent back during the night to bring up some waggons which had stuck in an almost impassable part of the route, he came upon about a dozen natives, who had dropped behind, unable to walk farther. On his return he picked them all up, putting them, where there was room, on the waggons and horses, giving them restoratives, and bringing them all safely into camp. But for his timely aid they would all have perished during the night. To his subordinates he endeared himself by his consideration for them, and his cheerfulness in sharing their hard work; and he would frequently dismount and walk in order that some tired man might rest.

The day after the entry of the troops into Kandahar, Willis obtained leave to go into the city, attended by an escort of men and accompanied by Lieutenant Williams, R.A., of the same battery. With his usual thought for those under him, he gave the men leave to go about the town to make purchases, telling them to be careful, and not to separate. He and Lieutenant Williams then dismounted, holding their horses, and taking the precaution to stand back to back. Whilst they were watching some shoemakers at work in one of the bazaars, a fanatic, creeping stealthily up, suddenly pushed between them, and stabbed Lieutenant Willis in the chest. A short struggle ensued, but the fanatic escaped, and after slightly wounding several other victims, was cut down by a non-commissioned officer of the 2nd Punjab Cavalry, aided by Captain Harvey of the 1st Punjab Cavalry, who was himself wounded in the hand. Lieutenant Willis fell down fainting, the knife having penetrated some way into the right lung. Carried to the camp, he received unremitting attention, and for a time hopes were entertained of his recovery; during the third night, however, the wound broke out afresh, and then all hope was over. He was tenderly cared for and watched by his brother officers, the battery doctor, and the chaplain to the forces, the Rev. G. M. Gordon, who, in a letter announcing his death to his mother, stated that he felt it a privilege to have been with him in his last hours, and added that his manly simplicity, and his cheerful endurance of the hardships of the recent trying march, had endeared him to all around him. The major of his battery, Major T. C. Martelli, wrote in the same tone of affectionate regard towards him, as also did many other of his brother officers. He was buried in a quiet and shaded spot in the midst of the Fort garden, within the walls of Kandahar, chosen by General Biddulph, who, with his Staff and the greater part of the troops, attended his funeral. His early death under such melancholy circumstances cast a gloom over the camp, and called forth an expression of deep commiseration and sympathy with his bereaved family, which was most touching, and will always be remembered by them with great gratitude.

Lieutenant Willis died on the 15th January, 1879, within three days of his twenty-third birthday.

CAPTAIN F. H. WINTERBOTHAM,

MADRAS INFANTRY.

RANCIS HESKINS WINTERBOTHAM, a member of the old Gloucestershire family of that name, was the fifth son of the late John B. Winterbotham, solicitor, of Cheltenham, by his marriage with Mary Prowse, daughter of Mr. James Batten, of Plymouth, and was a cousin of the late Mr. Henry Winterbotham, M.P. for Stroud, whose premature death soon after his appointment as Under Secretary of State for the Home Department was the cause of much regret.

The subject of this memoir was born on the 19th November, 1838, and was educated at Cheltenham College, where he had the advantage of studying under the head-mastership of the late Rev. William Dobson. He continued as a pupil at the College till 1857, and subsequently matriculated at the London University.

Obtaining a commission in the then East India Company's Army, Winterbotham was sent out, in the spring of 1859, to the Madras Presidency; on arrival he was posted to the 40th Native Infantry, and subsequently did duty with that regiment at Bangalore, at Singapore, and at Cannanor in Malabar. In 1867 he was granted two years' sick-leave to England, and paid this country what proved to be his first and last visit during a term of twenty years' foreign service.

He returned to India in 1869, and having passed with credit the requisite Examinations in Surveying and Military Engineering, was permanently posted to the Queen's Own Sappers and Miners.

On the outbreak of the Indian famine of 1876-77, Captain Winterbotham proceeded on special duty—waiving his claim to the well-earned furlough to which he was entitled—to Bellary, and was employed in the relief camps for a period of several months, rendering valuable and important service.

While engaged on detachment with a portion of his company in a series of experiments in night signalling, shortly after returning to Bangalore on the conclusion of the famine campaign, he received the message, "Sappers ordered on foreign service. Destination unknown. Return immediately." It proved to be a summons for departure on the expedition to Malta, of which so much was afterwards heard.

The opportunity of seeing active service seemed at last to have arrived; but, much to Captain Winterbotham's disappointment, his company was not one of those which were ultimately sent to the Mediterranean. The prospect of war, however, kept him in India; and in December, 1878, he had the satisfaction of receiving orders to proceed in command of his company to join Sir Sam. Browne's Division of the Army of Invasion in Afghanistan. He accomplished more than 2,000 miles of the journey from Bangalore most satisfactorily, and wrote home from Jhelum in good health and spirits; but during the forward march from that station the cold and exposure he underwent brought on a violent attack of pneumonia, and on arriving at Peshawar in the first week of January, 1879, he had at once to go into hospital. There, under the watchful care of Dr. Molloy, A.M.D., aided by the kind attentions of Major and Mrs. Pearson, he was slowly recovering, when dysentery supervened, and he died on the 14th February.

Captain Winterbotham had considerable skill as a draftsman, as the plans and charts prepared by him on various occasions show; his power of organization, too, was great, as also was the faculty he possessed of attaching to himself the men under his command, and few deaths have been more keenly felt at Bangalore than his. An eye-witness relates that many swarthy faces were moist with tears when the announcement that he had fallen a victim to the rigours of the war was made to the men on parade. His career, like those of many of his gallant brethren in arms, was cut short just when the long-awaited chance of earning distinction seemed at hand. The "Madras Mail," in concluding a notice of his death, truly says:—"In the deceased the Madras Army has lost a man of the highest integrity, and a thoroughly efficient and painstaking officer"—a verdict which has had the unanimous concurrence of all those amongst whom he worked, and by whom he was known.

The portrait is from a photograph of the deceased taken before he left England, no recent likeness having been sent by him from India.

LIEUTENANT N. C. WISEMAN,

1st BATTALION, 17th (LEICESTERSHIRE) REGIMENT.

NO accurate account of the antecedents of this young officer has, up to the present, been obtained. The Army Lists show that he purchased an Ensigncy in the 17th Regiment in June, 1868, became Lieutenant in October, 1871, and was holding the appointment of Interpreter at the time of his death.

Lieutenant Wiseman accompanied his regiment into Afghanistan on the outbreak of war in the autumn of 1878, and served in the flank march over the Rhotas heights in reverse of Ali Musjid from the 20th to the 22nd November; was present at the affairs at Chinar on the 9th and 10th December; took part in both the first and the second Bazar Valley expeditions; and was also present at the affairs at Maidanak (18th to 21st March, 1879), and Deh Sarak (24th March, 1879), and at the action of Futtehabad on the 2nd April, 1879, in which he was killed while capturing one of the enemy's standards in a most gallant and determined manner.

The deceased, had he lived, would have been entitled to the medal with clasp.

2ND LIEUTENANT F. P. F. WOOD,

7TH (ROYAL FUSILIERS).

FREDERIC PHILIP FORSTER WOOD was the elder son of the Rev. Frederic Wood, M.A., Rector of Erwarton with Woolverstone, Suffolk, by his marriage with Emily, second daughter of the late John Pratt, Esq., J.P., of Adderstone, Northumberland. He was born on the 13th March, 1857, and was educated at Rossall, and Bury St. Edmund's Grammar School, from whence he proceeded to the Royal Military College, Sandhurst. Passing out after the usual course, he was gazetted, in January, 1878, to a second-lieutenancy in the 33rd Foot, but was temporarily attached to the 76th Regiment at Aldershot. In September, 1878, he exchanged into the 2nd Battalion, 7th Royal Fusiliers, and sailed for Bombay on the 13th December of that year to join the regiment at Kolaba.

In February, 1880, Wood embarked with his battalion in H.M.S. *Crocodile*, for Karashi, on its being ordered to the front, and subsequently took part in its march from Sibi to Kandahar through the deep hot sands and the Bolan and Khojack Passes. His diary, written with the utmost regularity up to the night before he fell, is full of very interesting details of the advance, the daily routine in Kandahar, and the preparations for the defence of the city against the advance of Ayoub Khan's army. He appears to have thrown himself heart and soul into fulfilling the new duties which devolved upon him, and to have early won the love and esteem of all with whom he came in contact.

On the morning of the 16th August, in the disastrous sortie to Deh Khwaja, Lieutenant Wood commanded the support of the leading party (the company under Captain Chard, brother of Major Chard, V.C., R.E., of Rorke's Drift fame) in the attack. To the conspicuous gallantry with which he bore himself on this occasion, the united testimony of his Colonel, his brother officers, and his men, bears vivid witness. Colonel Daubeny, in a letter to Wood's father, relates how his son " was shot when leaving an enclosure that he had stormed and cleared at the point of the bayonet;" Major Keyser, of how "he won the admiration of every man under his command," a statement corroborated by one of the men of his company in simple language noted down by Captain Chard : " Mr. Wood, he did lead us well, Sir !"

When he had received no less than five gunshot wounds, and his life-blood was ebbing fast, his brother officer, Lieutenant Marsh, got him into a dhoolie, and in doing so rendered up his own life. The end was by this time near. "As I helped him into the litter," writes Surgeon-Major Byng Giraud, of the Medical Department, in a letter to the Rev. Mr. Wood, "he flung his arms round my neck, and said, 'God bless you, old fellow. Tell my father that I have done my duty.' I sent him off the field in charge of a soldier who was wounded in the arm, but by the time he reached the Kabul gate, he had only strength to point to a ring on his finger, to Dr. Kelsall, but was unable to say what he wanted done with it. He died immediately after this."

A transcript of the following particulars penned by the writer last named in the letter already quoted from, may fitly close this brief notice:—"A Fusilier who was with him told me that just before he was wounded, your son and a party of some ten of the Fusiliers had stormed into a walled enclosure full of Afghans, and that he had slain five or six with his own sword, and when I came up it was still wet with their blood. Your son fought and died as became an English soldier."

LIEUTENANT I. D. WRIGHT,

ROYAL ARTILLERY.

THE subject of this memoir, who was killed in action at Jagdalak on the 29th December, 1879, was the eldest son of C. Ichabod Wright, Esq. (Lieutenant-Colonel, late commanding the Robin Hood Rifle Volunteers, and M.P. for Nottingham in 1868-69), of Mapperley, and Stapleford Hall, Notts, and Watcombe Park, Torquay, was a grandson of the late I. C. Wright, Esq., the translator of Homer and Dante, and a great-grandson of the first Lord Denman.

Ichabod Denman Wright was born on the 4th April, 1853, and received his education at the Rev. E. Burney's Academy, Gosport. Entering the Royal Military Academy at Woolwich in July, 1871, he passed out after the usual course, and was gazetted, in April, 1873, to the Royal Artillery. For some two years he was quartered at Aden, at the expiration of which period he proceeded to India, and served there until the end of 1878, when he was sent home on sick-leave. In September, 1879, he was offered a transfer into a battery stationed in England; but preferring to return to India, he was allowed to do so, and was sent out in command of drafts on the 30th of that month. After taking these to Peshawar, he was to have rejoined his own battery at Mhow; but being most anxious to see active service, he obtained permission to take the next detachment towards the front.

Lieutenant Wright was shortly afterwards attached to Battery 11/9 Royal Artillery, which he joined at Gandamak on the 26th December, 1879, his Christmas-day having been spent in a twenty-one mile march, through heavy sand, in pouring rain, and without food. The Battery, under the command of Major J. M. Douglas, R.A., was at the time *en route* from Landi Kotal to Jagdalak. On the 29th of the month, about 4 p.m., whilst on the last march (from Pezwan), a rapid firing was heard in advance, and the enemy was found in force on a mountain to the right of the road, engaged with a party sent out to reconnoitre from Jagdalak. The battery wheeled to the right, proceeding a short distance up a nullah, and then ascended a hill to the left. Just as the summit was reached, Lieutenant Wright, who was standing at the side of Major Douglas taking directions as to the disposition of the guns, was struck by a musket-shot, the ball passing through his body and lodging in the base of his spine. He fell back with the exclamation, "I have got it"; and instantly losing consciousness, expired a few minutes afterwards. His body was conveyed by his comrades into Jagdalak, and was buried, just outside the ramparts, the same evening, the Officer Commanding the Battery officiating by the light of a lantern at the impressive ceremony over the grave.

Of a singularly bright and happy disposition, accustomed to treat the little worries and discomforts of life with a whimsical gaiety which rarely failed to communicate itself to those about him, Lieutenant Wright was one whose company was always welcome. "I liked him very much," wrote his Commanding Officer after a three days' acquaintance with him, "he was so cheerful and zealous;" a view of his character which is supported by Surgeon-Major Oughton of the Battery, in a letter in which occurs this passage:—"He had a singular faculty of ingratiating himself with his comrades in a very short time. On the night of the 27th December, with the snow lying a foot deep outside, he contributed not a little to the general joviality of the season by playing songs and fantasias on the violin, on which instrument he was an accomplished performer."

Lieutenant Wright possessed, in addition, more sterling qualities; and his death has been justly described by Major Douglas as "a loss to the Battery and to the regiment at large."

SURGEON-MAJOR J. H. WRIGHT, M.R.C.S. AND L.S.A. LOND.,

ARMY MEDICAL DEPARTMENT.

JOHN HARRINGTON WRIGHT, who died at Attock, British India, on the 21st June, 1879, was the only son of the late John Wright, M.D., of Story's Gate, Westminster; was stepson of the late William Edmunds, Esq., M.R.C.S., J.P., Surgeon Superintendent of Robben Island, Cape of Good Hope; and was a grandson of the late Thomas Wright, M.A., formerly Rector of Whitechapel, his maternal grandfather being the late J. Harrington, Esquire, who served on the Army Hospital Staff through the whole of the Peninsular campaigns.

The subject of this memoir was born at Story's Gate on the 31st May 1841, and subsequently accompanied his mother and stepfather to the Cape Colony, where he spent his earlier years, receiving his education at the Grahamstown College. Passing through the medical curriculum at King's College Hospital, London, he became a Member of the Royal College of Surgeons in April, 1865, and a Licentiate of the Society of Apothecaries in December of the same year. In March, 1866, he entered the Army as a Staff Assistant Surgeon, was promoted Surgeon in March, 1873, and in March, 1878, attained the rank of Surgeon-Major.

Almost the whole of his life in the Service was spent abroad. After quitting Netley, he was first attached, in October, 1866, to the Royal Engineers, at Aldershot. In July, 1867, he sailed for the Cape of Good Hope; and from the time of his arrival until he again returned to England in May, 1871, was constantly on the move, visiting in the interim St. Helena, Mauritius, Singapore, Hong Kong, and Japan, and being in medical charge successively, of no less than ten different corps or regiments. For a short time after his return home he was attached to the 19th Hussars. In August, 1871, he was transferred for duty to the 17th Brigade Royal Artillery, and remained with it until the autumn of 1873. In October of that year he embarked for India, attached to the 4th Battalion Rifle Brigade, with which distinguished corps he continued, with the exception of a brief interval in 1879, until the day of his death.

Mr. Wright took part with the regiment in the Jowaki expedition of 1877-1878, and for his services therein was recommended for the Medal and Clasp.

After five years' service in the hottest parts of India, he was under sailing orders to return to England in November, 1878; but the Afghan War having been determined upon, the exigencies of the Service necessitated his abandoning his intention. Taking part with his regiment in its advance, in Sir Sam. Browne's Division, into the enemy's country, he was present with it at the capture of Ali Musjid on the 21st November, 1878, in the subsequent operations in the Khyber, and in the march to Jalalabad. In January, 1879, he was detached from the Rifle Brigade and placed in medical charge of the Field Hospital of the 2nd Division Peshawar Valley Field Force, the duties in connection with which were harassing and incessant.

The heavy work of the campaign, following on his five years' previous service in India, now began to tell heavily upon him, and frequent breaks of continuity in his diary of 1879, together with casual remarks which occur in it, indicate that although he was bravely doing his work, he was quite unfit for it, and only managed to struggle on from a high sense of duty. His condition gradually became worse and worse, till at length, utterly worn out, he succumbed at Attock to an attack of heat apoplexy, which his enfeebled constitution was unable to throw off.

In a letter written from Peshawar in the month of August, 1879, Dr. A. C. Keith—a promising young officer of the Medical Department who himself subsequently fell a victim to the rigours of the war—gives the following characteristic details of the closing chapter of the late Surgeon-Major Wright's career:—" I urged him," he writes, after describing how he found him at Attock utterly prostrated in strength, but still continuing to discharge his duty, "to leave the tent in which he was staying (the weather being very hot and close at that time), and stay with me at my bungalow till the regiment crossed the river; but his well-known and excessive zeal prevented his doing what was absolutely necessary for his own health, and to all my propositions he replied that the regiment was too sick to leave in the hands of a junior officer," and that "by crossing the river he would be too far from the regiment to carry on his work.

"In the Medical Department his loss is sincerely regretted by all. In the regiment to which he belonged the men have lost their best friend, and the officers a brother of whom all were proud."

The verdict contained in the last paragraph is concurred in by all who had the privilege of being on terms of intimacy with the deceased officer, and has been expressed in equally warm terms by another writer—Colonel Newdigate, late Commanding the Battalion.

LIEUTENANT G. M. YALDWYN,

2ND BATTALION 6TH (ROYAL 1ST WARWICKSHIRE) REGIMENT.

ILBERT MOORCROFT YALDWYN was the youngest son of the late General Yaldwyn, H.M.'s Indian Army, of Blackdown, Sussex. He was born at Bellary, in India, on the 31st of May, 1854, and was educated at Wellington College. Entering the Army in October, 1873 he was gazetted to a Lieutenancy in the 2nd Battalion 6th Foot, and did duty with the regiment in this country till the conclusion of its term of home service. During this period he went through the course at the School of Musketry at Hythe, and obtained a double first certificate.

In October, 1878, he sailed with his regiment for India, and shortly after arriving there volunteered for active service in Afghanistan, into which country he was subsequently sent on transport duty.

Stationed at various posts on the Khyber line, he shared throughout the first campaign in the heavy and important duties which fell to the lot of the branch of the Service to which he had been detailed, meeting the incessant calls made upon him, and the innumerable difficulties with which he was beset, with a readiness of resource remarkable in one so young. The wear and tear of the work, coupled with constant exposure under violent alternations of temperature, at length, however, proved—as it did to so many of his gallant comrades—too much for him, and while stationed at Gandamak he was attacked with typhoid fever. After some weeks' illness, he became convalescent, and had reached Peshawar on his way to the hills for change of air, when he was seized with cholera, to which fatal disease he succumbed in a few hours, on the 12th June, 1879.

A handsome brass tablet has been erected in Lurgashall Church, Sussex, to Lieutenant Yaldwyn's memory, by his brother officers, as a token of the affection and esteem in which they held him.

THE VICTORIA CROSS.

GAZETTED PARTICULARS OF THE ACTS OF VALOUR FOR WHICH THE RECIPIENTS OF THE VICTORIA CROSS WERE RECOMMENDED, WITH OTHER RECORDS OF SERVICE.

THE REV. J. W. ADAMS,* BENGAL ECCLESIASTICAL ESTABLISHMENT, LATE CHAPLAIN TO THE KABUL FIELD FORCE.—*London Gazette, 26th August,* 1881 :—" During the action of Killa Kazi, on the 11th December, 1879, some men of the 9th Lancers having fallen, with their horses, into a wide and deep 'nullah' or ditch, and the enemy being close upon them, the Rev. J. W. Adams rushed into the water (which filled the ditch), dragged the horses from off the men upon whom they were lying, and extricated them, he being at the time under a heavy fire, and up to his waist in water.

"At this time the Afghans were pressing on very rapidly, the leading men getting within a few yards of Mr. Adams, who, having let go his horse in order to render more effectual assistance, had eventually to escape on foot."

Mr. Adams, V.C., was ordained in 1863 by the Bishop of Winchester, and proceeded to India in 1868, being appointed Military Chaplain at Peshawar. He subsequently served in the same capacity at Lord Napier's Camp of Exercise at Hassan Abdal, in the Punjab, where he also had charge of the General Hospital for Europeans—at Kashmir, at Mirat, and at the Army Head-quarters Camp formed at Delhi in 1875, when the Prince of Wales visited India. In 1878 he accompanied the Kuram Valley Field Force into Afghanistan, and served under General Roberts' command throughout the war. He has been repeatedly mentioned in despatches, and several times thanked for the brave and noble work done by him during the cholera epidemics at Peshawar and elsewhere.

LIEUTENANT WILLIAM ST. LUCIEN CHASE, BOMBAY STAFF CORPS, AND PRIVATE JAMES ASHFORD,* THE ROYAL FUSILIERS.—*London Gazette, 7th October,* 1881 :—" For conspicuous gallantry on the occasion of the sortie from Kandahar, on the 16th August, 1880, against the village of Deh Khwaja, in having rescued, and carried for a distance of over 200 yards, under the fire of the enemy, a wounded soldier, Private Massey, of the Royal Fusiliers, who had taken shelter in a block-house. Several times they were compelled to rest, but they persevered in bringing him into a place of safety.

"Private Ashford rendered Lieutenant Chase every assistance, and remained with him throughout."

Lieutenant W. St. L. Chase, V.C., entered the Army in 1875, being gazetted, in the month of September of that year, to Her Majesty's 15th Foot. After doing duty with the Head-quarters of his regiment in India for a period of two years, and passing, with distinction, the necessary examinations, he was admitted to the Bombay Staff Corps, and did duty, successively, at Poona, Ahmadabad, Baroda, and Surat. Serving with the 28th Bombay Native Infantry in the Afghan War, he accompanied the Head-quarters of the regiment—a constituent of the Kandahar Field Force—in January, 1880, to Chaman, from whence he was subsequently detached, after the massacre of Major Waudby and his party at Dubrai, in May, 1880, to the command of the post of Gatai. He was present with the 28th Native Infantry throughout the defence of Kandahar, taking part with the four companies in the ill-starred sortie to Deh Khwaja, in reference to which the appalling casualty-roll of the regiment included Lieut.-Colonel Newport and thirty rank and file killed, and Lieut.-Colonel Nimmo (commanding) and twenty rank and file wounded. "Many gallant deeds," wrote the late Lieut.-Colonel A. G. Daubeny, 7th Fusiliers, in giving a vivid account of the affair in a private letter, "were done on that day. Thus, while holding our ground to cover the retreat of stragglers or wounded, an officer (Lieutenant Chase) was suddenly seen coming towards us from the block-house with a wounded soldier on his back, and attended by a Fusilier. The enemy had also seen him, and turned their fire on him. A few yards, and he is down, and all thought he was done for. Not so; he only wanted breath; and, jumping up, he brought his man in amid a shower of bullets, and the cheers of our men." The Rev. A. G. Cane, late Chaplain to the Force, writing on the same event, observes: "I soon had my attention directed to a man leaving one of the Ziarets with another on his back. He was then, I suppose, about 400 yards off, and running as fast as possible towards the walls. There was a fearfully heavy fire directed on him from the villages (Kairabad and Deh Khwaja) on both sides. After running for about a hundred yards I saw both fall and lie flat on the ground, the bullets all the time striking the ground, and raising the dust where they struck all round them. I, of course, was under the impression that they had been hit. Soon, however, I noticed Mr. Chase get up again, and again take the man on his back for another stage of about the same distance, and again lie down for rest. Again he got up and carried his burden for a third stage, and again lay down. By this time he had got close to the walls. Only those who saw the terrific fire that was brought to bear on those two coming in can realize how marvellous was their escape untouched. At the time they came in they were almost the only object on which the enemy were directing their fire, as the rest of the fugitives had already reached shelter." For this feat, the subject of these allusions was subsequently decorated with the Victoria Cross.

After the regiment left Kandahar, Lieutenant Chase was given the command of the Killa Abdulla Post, and continued in the tenure of the appointment until relieved in the month of November. In January, 1881, he was again sent to command the post of Jatai on the line of communications, and remained there until all the troops of the Kandahar Evacuating Force had passed through it en route to India.

GUNNER JAMES COLLIS,* ROYAL HORSE ARTILLERY.—*London Gazette, 17th May,* 1881:—"For conspicuous bravery during the retreat from Maiwand to Kandahar, on the 28th July, 1880, when the officer commanding the battery was endeavouring to bring on a limber, with wounded men, under a cross fire, in running forward and drawing the enemy's fire on himself, thus taking off their attention from the limber."

BREVET-MAJOR O'MOORE CREAGH, BOMBAY STAFF CORPS.—*London Gazette*, 18*th November*, 1879 :—"On the 21st April, Captain Creagh was detached from Daka with two companies of his battalion to protect the village of Kam Daka on the Kabul River against a threatened incursion of the Mohmands, and reached that place the same night. On the following morning the detachment, 150 men, was attacked by the Mohmands in overwhelming numbers, about 1,500; and the inhabitants of Kam Daka, having themselves taken part with the enemy, Captain Creagh found himself under the necessity of retiring from the village. He took up a position in a cemetery not far off, which he made as defensible as circumstances would admit of, and this position he held against all the efforts of the enemy, repeatedly repulsing them with the bayonet until three o'clock in the afternoon, when he was relieved by a detachment sent for the purpose from Daka. The enemy were then finally repulsed, and being charged by a troop of the 10th Bengal Lancers, under the command of Captain D. M. Strong, were routed and broken, and great numbers of them driven into the river.

" The Commander-in-Chief in India has expressed his opinion that but for the coolness, determination, and gallantry of the highest order, and the admirable conduct which Captain Creagh displayed on this occasion, the detachment under his command would, in all probability, have been cut off and destroyed."

Major Creagh, V.C., was gazetted to an Ensigncy in the 95th Regiment on the 2nd October, 1866, and after serving at the Depôt at Pembroke Dock till January, 1869, embarked for India, and joined the service companies of his regiment at Mhow. In June, 1870, he entered the Bombay Staff Corps, and was promoted Lieutenant. After serving for a few weeks with the Marine Battalion and 25th Bombay Light Infantry, he was appointed Officiating Adjutant of the Deoli Irregular Force, and Station Staff Officer at Deoli. In June, 1871, he was selected to fill the post of Adjutant of the Mhairwara Battalion, then being reorganized on its transfer from the Civil to the Military establishment. Of this corps he was appointed, in 1878, while still holding the post of Adjutant, Officiating Commandant; and in the month of October in the same year he was promoted Captain in the Bombay Staff Corps.

When the Mhairwara Battalion volunteered for service in Afghanistan on the outbreak of hostilities, Major—then Lieutenant—Creagh, was the only European officer present with it, and commanded it throughout its subsequent march from Ajmir, Rajputana, to Hassan Abdal, Punjab. Prior to this occasion the corps had not, since its establishment in 1822, moved more than thirty miles from its head-quarters.

As second in command, Major Creagh took part in the subsequent operations of the battalion in Afghanistan, serving in the Peshawar Valley Force, at Ali Musjid till March, 1879, when the regiment was ordered to garrison Daka Fort. During this interval Major Creagh surveyed the route through Bourg to the Bazar Valley, and took part in the first expedition into that district. On the 20th April he was sent with a detachment of his regiment to Kam Daka, and for the services he there rendered, as already described, the Victoria Cross has been conferred upon him by his Sovereign. "I consider the cool determination of Captain Creagh to do his duty," wrote Lieutenant-General Mande with reference to this affair, " his self-possession, and the gallant example he set to his little band, were most conspicuous;" and in the report of Major Barnes, Commanding at Daka Fort, the following words occur: "*In this miserable position, fully commanded by the surrounding hills, he (Captain Creagh) made a noble defence, and deserves the greatest praise I can afford him.*" On the signing of the peace of Gandamak the subject of these allusions returned with the Mhairwara Battalion to Ajmir. For his services in the campaign he was awarded, in addition to the Victoria Cross, a Brevet-Majority.

On the renewal of hostilities in the autumn of 1879, Major Creagh volunteered for service, and was ordered to Ali Khel with Brigadier-General Gordon. After arriving there, he was appointed Deputy Assistant Quartermaster-General to the Kuram Force, and subsequently Quartermaster-General. He served in Kuram from September, 1879, to November, 1880, and was senior officer of his department with the force. He was present at the repulse of the attack on Ali Khel on the 14th October, and served in the Zaimusht expedition. On peace being concluded, he rejoined the Mhairwara Battalion.

CAPTAIN WILLIAM HENRY DICK CUNYNGHAM, THE GORDON HIGHLANDERS.—*London Gazette, 18th October,* 1881:—"For the conspicuous gallantry and coolness displayed by him on the 13th December, 1879, at the attack on the Sherpur pass, in Afghanistan, in having exposed himself to the full fire of the enemy, and by his example and encouragement rallied the men who, having been beaten back, were, at the moment, wavering at the top of the hill."

Captain W. H. Dick Cunyngham, V.C., is the youngest son of the late Sir William Hamner Dick Cunyngham, Baronet, of Prestonfield, and Lambrughton, N.B. He was born on the 16th June, 1851, and was educated at Trinity College, Glenalmond, N.B., and the Royal Military College, Sandhurst. Gazetted to an Ensigncy in the 92nd Highlanders in February, 1872, he was successively promoted Lieutenant, in February, 1873, and Captain, in October, 1881. His services with the 92nd include a term of eight years (January, 1873, to January, 1881) spent in India, during which period he held the appointment of Adjutant of a wing of the regiment from January, 1877, to April, 1878. Eventually, in October, 1880, he was selected to fill the regimental Adjutancy—a post he continues to hold at the present time.

Captain Dick Cunyngham served over a wide extent of territory and in various capacities, through the whole of the Afghan War. Detailed, in the first instance, to the Transport Department of the Quetta Field Force, he took part in the advance of Sir Donald Stewart's Division on Kandahar. In the subsequent forward movement on Kalat-i-Ghilzai he was attached to the Head-quarters Staff; and on the return of General Biddulph's Column by the Thal-Chotiali route to India, he accompanied it in the capacity of Transport Officer. Rejoining his regiment, which had, in the meantime, been sent to the front on the Kuram line, he served with it in nearly the whole of its diverse operations in the second campaign, from the renewal to the cessation of hostilities. Besides taking part in numerous minor affairs, he was present at the action with the hill tribes at Ali Khel on the 14th October, 1879, in the expedition to Maidan in November, and in the operations in the neighbourhood of Kabul from the 8th to the 23rd December, including the assault of the Takht-i-Shah (for the valour he displayed on which occasion the Victoria Cross was subsequently conferred on him), and the action of the 23rd of the month. "After the fall of the officer and colour-sergeant," writes Sir Frederick Roberts with reference to the deaths of Lieutenant

St. John Forbes and Colour-Sergeant James Drummond, in describing in his despatch, bearing date 23rd January, 1880, the brilliant manner in which the commanding position held by the enemy on the 13th December was carried by the 92nd Highlanders, "there was a momentary waver, when Lieutenant W. H. Dick Cunyngham rushed forward and gallantly exposing himself to the full fire poured upon this point, rallied the men by his example and cheering words, and calling upon those near to follow him, charged into the middle of the enemy." As Adjutant of a wing of the 92nd, the subject of this allusion was present, on the 25th April, 1880, at the action at Childukhtean (for his services on which occasion he was mentioned in despatches); and after participating with the regiment in the memorable march of General Roberts' column to the relief of Kandahar, he took part in the reconnaissance of the 31st August, and the final crushing defeat of the enemy on the 1st September, for his services on which occasion he was again mentioned in despatches.

On the conclusion of the Afghan War, Captain Dick Cunyngham accompanied the 92nd to South Africa, and served with it in the Transvaal campaign of 1881. In addition to the Victoria Cross, he has received the Afghan medal with two clasps, and the Kabul-Kandahar bronze star.

MAJOR ARTHUR GEORGE HAMMOND, BENGAL STAFF CORPS.—*London Gazette, 18th October, 1881* :—"For conspicuous coolness and gallantry at the action on the Asmai Heights, near Kabul, on the 14th December, 1879, in defending the top of the hill with a rifle and fixed bayonet, against large numbers of the enemy, whilst the 72nd Highlanders and Guides were retiring; and again, on the retreat down the hill, in stopping to assist in carrying away a wounded Sepoy, the enemy being not sixty yards off, firing heavily all the time."

Major A. G. Hammond, V.C., entered Addiscombe College in February, 1861, and on the 7th June of the same year obtained his commission, gaining second place in the examination, and taking four prizes. He landed at Calcutta on the 31st December, 1861, and was attached to Her Majesty's 82nd Regiment, then quartered at Delhi. On the 17th October, 1862, he joined the 12th (Kalat-i-Ghilzai) Native Infantry, and having passed the P. H. examination in Hindustani, was posted, in September, 1863, to the Corps of Guides, which regiment he joined on the 17th of that month at Mardan. The Guides formed part of the army which was then being assembled for the Umbeyla campaign; and Lieutenant Hammond was placed in command of the detachment of the corps which was left to hold the fort at Mardan. In May, 1864, he was appointed Quartermaster of the Regiment; in November, 1865, Wing Commander; in June, 1867, he was admitted to the Bengal Staff Corps; and in April, 1875, he passed in Military Surveying and Field Engineering at the Rurki College by "the Higher Standard, with great credit."

Major—then Captain—Hammond served with his regiment as Wing Commander through the whole of the Jowaki campaign of 1877-78, including the capture of Payah and Jammu, and the forcing of the Naru-Kula Pass, receiving the medal and clasp. For the "gallant actions" he performed, and for the "zeal and energy" he displayed in the campaign, he was twice mentioned in Brigadier-General Keyes' despatch of the 15th August, 1878. He was with his regiment, too, in the operations against the Ranizai village of Skhakat on the 14th March, 1878, and also in the attack on the Utman Khel villages on the 21st idem.

Major Hammond served with the Guide Infantry through the whole of the

Afghan War. Besides taking part in numerous minor affairs, he was present at the capture of Ali Musjid, the operations round Kabul in December, 1879, including the storming of the Takht-i-Shah on the 13th, and the Asmai Heights on the 14th of the month, the march into Koh-i-Daman, and the second action at Charasiab on the 25th April, 1880. With reference to his conduct on the 14th December, 1879, for which Her Majesty the Queen conferred on him the Victoria Cross, Sir Frederick Roberts, describing the events of that day in his despatch bearing date 23rd January, 1880, uses the following words:—"*Another officer who greatly distinguished himself on this occasion was Captain A. G. Hammond, Queen's Own Corps of Guides. He had been very forward during the storming of the Asmai Heights, and now, when the enemy were crowding up the western slopes, he remained with a few men on the ridge until the Afghans were within thirty yards of them. During the retirement, one of the men of the Guides was shot. Captain Hammond stopped and assisted in carrying him away, though the enemy were at the time close by, and firing heavily.*"

Major Hammond's commissions are dated as follows:—Ensign, 7th June, 1861; Lieutenant, 14th May, 1862; Captain, 7th June, 1873; Major, 7th June, 1881.

CAPTAIN REGINALD CLARE HART, ROYAL ENGINEERS. *London Gazette, 10th June, 1879:*—"For his gallant conduct in risking his own life to save the life of a private soldier.

"The Lieutenant-General commanding the 2nd Division Peshawar Field Force, reports that when on convoy duty with that force on the 31st January, 1879, Lieutenant Hart, of the Royal Engineers, took the initiative in running some 1,200 yards to the rescue of a wounded Sowar of the 13th Bengal Lancers in a river-bed exposed to the fire of the enemy, of unknown strength, from both flanks, and also from a party in the river-bed.

"Lieutenant Hart reached the wounded Sowar, drove off the enemy, and brought him under cover with the aid of some soldiers who accompanied him on the way."

Captain R. C. Hart, V.C., is the second surviving son of the late Lieutenant-General H. G. Hart, and was born on the 11th June, 1848, at Drewsborough, Co. Clare. He was educated at Marlborough and Cheltenham Colleges; passed into the Royal Military Academy in June, 1866; and was commissioned Lieutenant in the Royal Engineers on the 13th January, 1869. After doing duty for three years in England, he embarked, in October, 1872, for India, and was posted to the Bengal Sappers and Miners. From September, 1874, to March, 1878, he filled the office of Assistant Garrison Instructor at Umballa, subsequently returning to England on sick leave.

In January, 1879, Captain—then Lieutenant—Hart proceeded a second time to India, and serving with the Khyber Field Force in the Afghan War, was at first attached as a regimental officer to the 24th Punjab Infantry, a unit of the 2nd Division. In this capacity he took part in the 2nd Bazar Valley expedition against the Zaka Khel Afridis; and for his distinguished conduct on the 31st January, while on convoy duty, was awarded the Victoria Cross. He afterwards served in the 1st Division of the Force, and was several times employed by the Quartermaster-General's Department in making reconnaissances.

In February, 1881, it was reported that the Ashantis had declared war and invaded the Gold Coast Colony. Lieutenant Hart, receiving his orders only a few hours before starting, accompanied Sir Samuel Rowe, the Governor and Commander-

in-Chief, to the West Coast of Africa, and served on the Special Service Staff of that officer from February to June. In the succeeding month he received his promotion.

Captain Hart was present at the siege of Paris during the Commune war of 1871. *He has been awarded the Silver Medal of the Royal Humane Society; a Medallion from the Mayor, in the name of the City of Boulogne, and a Medal of Honour of the First Class, presented by the President of the French Republic, for saving the life of a Frenchman who was drowning in the harbour of Boulogne-sur-Mer, on the* 27*th July,* 1869. *In accomplishing this feat, Captain Hart received several severe wounds on the head and face, from striking, in leaping from the pier, some sunken piles or rocks. He is also the holder of a* 1*st Class Extra Hythe Musketry certificate, and has passed the final examination at the Staff College. At the present time he is employed on special duty at the Intelligence Department, Horse Guards.*

BREVET LIEUT.-COLONEL EDWARD PEMBERTON LEACH, ROYAL ENGINEERS.—*London Gazette, 9th December,* 1879:—" For having, in action with the Shinwarris, near Maidanah, Afghanistan, on the 17th March, 1879, when covering the retirement of the Survey Escort who were carrying Lieutenant Barclay, 45th Sikhs, mortally wounded, behaved with the utmost gallantry in charging, with some men of the 45th Sikhs, a very much larger number of the enemy.

" In this encounter Captain Leach killed two or three of the enemy himself, and he received a severe wound from an Afghan knife in the left arm. Captain Leach's determination and gallantry in this affair, in attacking and driving back the enemy from their last position, saved the whole party from annihilation."

Lieut.-Colonel E. P. Leach, V.C., is a son of Colonel Leach, late Royal Engineers. He entered the Army on the 17*th April,* 1866, *served at Chatham till October,* 1868, *and proceeded to India in the following December. From March,* 1869, *till February,* 1870, *he commanded a detachment of the Bengal Sappers and Miners at Rawal Pindi. In the succeeding month he entered the Public Works Department as Assistant Engineer, proceeding to Morar, Central India. Appointed, in October,* 1871, *to the Indian Survey, he did duty, in his new capacity, with the Lushai Expeditionary Field Force, receiving at the close of the campaign the thanks of the Secretary of State and the medal with clasp. In November,* 1877, *he returned to England on furlough, and in October of the following year accompanied Mr. Caird, C.B., one of the Indian Famine Commissioners, to India as Private Secretary.*

Serving in the Peshawar Valley Field Force in the Afghan Campaign of 1878-1879, *Lieut.-Colonel—then Captain—Leach accompanied the expeditions into the Bazar and Lughman valleys. Whilst employed upon a survey reconnaissance of the Shinwari country with detachments of the Guide Cavalry and the* 45*th Sikhs, he was attacked by the enemy on the* 17*th March,* 1879, *and severely wounded. For his distinguished conduct on this occasion he received a Brevet Majority, and subsequently the Victoria Cross.*

Major Leach was invalided to England at the close of the year 1879, *but returned to India in the following March. Joining, in charge of the Survey operations, the Kandahar Field Force under Major-General Primrose, he accompanied, in July,* 1880, *the brigade under Brigadier-General Burrows in its advance to the Halmand. He was present at the battle of Maiwand—during which his horse was wounded—and the subsequent siege of Kandahar, and for his conduct was three times mentioned in despatches. Again on the 1st September, 1880, he was present at the crowning defeat of the enemy by Sir Frederick Roberts. At the close of the campaign a Brevet Lieutenant-Colonelcy was conferred upon him, and the medal with clasp.*

SERGEANT PATRICK MULLANE,* ROYAL HORSE ARTILLERY.—*London Gazette*, 17th May, 1879:—"For conspicuous bravery during the action at Maiwand, on the 27th July, 1880, in endeavouring to save the life of Driver Pickwell Istead.

" This non-commissioned officer, when the battery to which he belonged was on the point of retiring, and the enemy were within ten or fifteen yards, unhesitatingly ran back about two yards, and picking up Driver Istead, placed him on the limber, where, unfortunately, he died almost immediately.

" Again, during the retreat, Sergeant Mullane volunteered to procure water for the wounded, and succeeded in doing so by going into one of the villages in which so many men lost their lives."

MAJOR EUSTON HENRY SARTORIUS, THE EAST LANCASHIRE REGIMENT.—*London Gazette*, 17th May, 1881:—"For conspicuous bravery during the action at Shah-jui, on the 24th October, 1879, in leading a party of five or six men of the 59th Regiment against a body of the enemy, of unknown strength, occupying an almost inaccessible position on the top of a precipitous hill.

" The nature of the ground made any sort of regular formation impossible, and Captain Sartorius had to bear the first brunt of the attack from the whole body of the enemy, who fell upon him and his men as they gained the top of the precipitous pathway; but the gallant and determined bearing of this officer, emulated as it was by his men, led to the most perfect success, and the surviving occupants of the hill-top, seven in number, were all killed.

" In this encounter Captain Sartorius was wounded with sword-cuts in both hands, and one of his men was killed."

Major E. H. Sartorius, V.C., entered the Army in July, 1862, being gazetted—after passing out first in order of merit from the Royal Military College, Sandhurst—to an Ensigncy in the 59th Foot. Continuing in that distinguished regiment up to the present time, he became Lieutenant in July, 1865, obtained his company in September, 1874, received a Brevet Majority in March, 1881, and was promoted to a Regimental Majority in July of the same year. In December, 1870, he passed the examination at the Staff College, and subsequently, for a period of four years, served as Instructor in Military Surveying at the Royal Military College, Sandhurst. Proceeding to India to join his regiment, he travelled for a year, en route, in Persia, adding largely to his experiences, and obtaining a great variety of valuable information.

In the Afghan War, Major Sartorius commanded the company of the 59th which escorted the guns of Battery D/2 Royal Artillery, from Quetta to Kandahar, and afterwards served with the regiment in the advance to, and capture of Kalat-i-Ghilzai, in January, 1879. Acting as Assistant Field Engineer, he was present at the subsequent occupation of that place in October, 1879, and was in command of the company which took part in the advance of Brigadier-General Hughes' force to Tazi. At the action of Shah-jui on the 24th October, 1879, he commanded the detachment of his regiment which was present, and for the distinguished service he then performed obtained the Victoria Cross and his Brevet Majority. In addition to being twice mentioned in despatches, his "excellent work and gallant conduct" in connection with the Survey Department received special commendation in the Report of the Proceedings of the Government of India in the Home Revenue and Agricultural Department, bearing date 17th May, 1880.

Major Sartorius has been decorated with—besides the Victoria Cross—the Royal Humane Society's medal for saving, on the 29th June, 1869, the lives of three young ladies at Broadstairs. From the wounds he received at the action of Shah-jui, he has partly lost the use of his left hand.

LANCE-CORPORAL GEORGE SELLAR,* SEAFORTH HIGHLANDERS (ROSS-SHIRE BUFFS).—*London Gazette, 18th October*, 1881 :—" For conspicuous gallantry displayed by him at the assault on the Asmai Heights, round Kabul, on the 14th December, 1879, in having in a marked manner led the attack, under a heavy fire, and, dashing on in front of the enemy up the slope, engaged in a desperate conflict with an Afghan, who sprang out to meet him. In this encounter Lance-Corporal Sellar was severely wounded."

BREVET MAJOR WILLIAM JOHN VOUSDEN,* BENGAL STAFF CORPS. —*London Gazette, 18th October,* 1881 :—"For the exceptional gallantry displayed by him on the 14th December, 1879, on the Koh Asmai Heights, near Kabul, in charging, with a small party, into the centre of the line of the retreating Kohistani force, by whom they were greatly outnumbered, and who did their utmost to close round them. After rapidly charging through and through the enemy, backwards and forwards, several times, they swept off round the opposite side of the village and joined the rest of the troop."

Major W. J. Vousden, V.C., is the only son of the late Captain Vousden, of the 51st (N. B.) Fusiliers. He was educated at Dr. Hill's establishment at Sandwich, and the Grammar School, Canterbury. Entering the Army in 1864, he was gazetted, in the month of January of that year, to an Ensigncy in the 35th Regiment. In October, 1867, he obtained his Lieutenancy, and in due course was admitted to the Bengal Staff Corps. His commission as Captain bears date 8th January, 1876. In both phases of the Afghan War, he participated with his regiment—the 5th Punjab Cavalry—in the heavy and important work which fell to its lot. Besides being employed in numerous minor operations, he served in the Khost Valley expedition, in January, 1879, including the action at Matun on the 7th of the month; took part, in the second campaign, in the advance of the Division under Sir Frederick Roberts on the capital; was present, on the 27th September, 1879, at the skirmish at Karatiga, in which his charger was shot; at the action at Charasiab, on the 6th October, the capture of Kabul on the 8th, and the cavalry pursuit of the enemy on the 9th idem; was with General Baker's brigade in the flank march on the 9th to the 12th December; was present in the actions in the neighbourhood of Kabul on the two succeeding days, earning, by his distinguished gallantry on the 14th, the Victoria Cross; formed one of the beleaguered force in Sherpur from the 15th to the 23rd December, and was present at the action of the 23rd, and in the succeeding cavalry pursuit.

In the cavalry affair on the 14th December, in which Captain Vousden earned his Victoria Cross, the squadron of the 5th Punjab Cavalry, under Captain Carr, with which he was employed, was acting as escort to Battery G/3, R.A. At midday,

Captain Vousden, with about a dozen men, came across on the Bala Hissar road, and in open and level country, a body of Kohistanis, numbering from three to four hundred, making for the bridge over the Kabul River. It is a significant fact, and one which speaks of itself for the gallantry displayed in encountering such stupendous odds, and of the undaunted spirit with which the encounter was sustained, that, in the charge which ensued, six men of Captain Vousden's little band of twelve were wounded, of whom three subsequently died, and that when the enemy dispersed they left no fewer than thirty of their number on the ground, all killed by the sword—of whom Captain Vousden had himself cut down five.

For the services he rendered in the war, Captain Vousden has been twice mentioned in despatches, and has received, besides the Victoria Cross, a Brevet Majority, and the Afghan medal with two clasps.

LIEUT.-COLONEL GEORGE STEWART WHITE,* C.B., THE GORDON HIGHLANDERS.—*London Gazette, 3rd June,* 1881 :—" For conspicuous bravery during the engagement at Charasiab on the 6th October, 1879, when, finding that the artillery and rifle fire failed to dislodge the enemy from a fortified hill which it was necessary to capture, Major White led an attack upon it in person.

"Advancing with two companies of his regiment, and climbing from one steep ledge to another, he came upon a body of the enemy, strongly posted, and outnumbering his force by about eight to one. His men being much exhausted, and immediate action being necessary, Major White took a rifle, and, *going on by himself,* shot the leader of the enemy. This act so intimidated the rest that they fled round the side of the hill, and the position was won.

"Again, on the 1st September, 1880, at the battle of Kandahar, Major White, in leading the final charge, under a heavy fire from the enemy, who held a strong position and were supported by two guns, rode straight up to within a few yards of them, and seeing the guns, dashed forward and secured one, immediately after which the enemy retired."

Lieut.-Colonel G. S. White, V.C., entered the Army in November, 1853, *became Lieutenant in January,* 1855, *obtained his company in July,* 1863, *was promoted Major in December,* 1873, *Brevet Lieut.-Colonel in March,* 1881, *and Lieut.-Colonel in July of the same year. In the Indian Mutiny in* 1857-59, *he was actively employed with the 27th Regiment on the North-West Frontier, and after the conclusion of hostilities, received the medal. His brilliant services in the Afghan War have caused him to be repeatedly singled out for commendation in despatches. Taking part with his distinguished regiment, the 92nd Highlanders, in October,* 1879, *in the advance of the division under Sir Frederick Roberts on Kabul, he commanded the right attack at the action of Charasiab on the 6th of the month—for his gallantry on which occasion the Victoria Cross was subsequently conferred upon him; was present in the pursuit of the enemy on the 8th idem, and the occupation of the capital; commanded the regiment in the expedition to Maidan, under Brigadier-General Baker, in November; served in the operations around Kabul in December, commanding four companies of the 92nd in the brilliant assault and capture of the Takht-i-Shah, and being present at the action on the 23rd; again, at the action of Childukhtean on the 25th April,* 1880, *commanded a wing of the regiment; and after taking part in the memorable march of the relieving force from Kabul to Kandahar, was present at the recon-*

naissance on the 31st August, and the crowning defeat of the enemy on the 1st September.

Lieut.-Colonel White at the present time occupies the office of Military Secretary to the Viceroy of India. In addition to the Victoria Cross, a Companionship of the Order of the Bath and Brevet promotion were conferred upon him for his services in the Afghan War, and he has also received the medal with three clasps and the Kabul-Kandahar bronze star.

* *Portraits and additional particulars of the services of these officers, non-commissioned officers, and men, have not been received in time for insertion in the first edition of this work.*

INDEX TO BIOGRAPHICAL DIVISION.

PORTRAITS AND BIOGRAPHICAL NOTICES OF OFFICERS WHO LOST THEIR LIVES IN THE WAR.

		PLATE		PAGE
Major A. D. Anderson, Staff Corps	*portrait*	I.	*notice*	1
Lieutenant P. E. Anderson, Staff Corps	,,	,,	,,	3
Lieutenant F. C. C. Angelo	,,	,,	,,	4
Surgeon-Major G. Atkinson, M.B.	,,	,,	,,	5
Lieutenant F. M. Barclay, Staff Corps	,,	,,	,,	7
Captain W. B. Barker	,,	,,	,,	8
2nd Lieutenant H. J. O. Barr	,,	,,	,,	10
Major Wigram Battye, Staff Corps	,,	II.	,,	12
Major H. G. Becher, Staff Corps	,,	,,	,,	15
Captain John Beeke	,,	,,	,,	16
Major H. H. Birch, Staff Corps	,,	,,	,,	17
Lieutenant W. H. Bishop	,,	,,	,,	19
Major G. F. Blackwood	,,	,,	,,	20
Surgeon-Major R. H. Bolton	,,	,,	,,	23
Brigadier-General H. F. Brooke	,,	III.	,,	24
Lieut.-Colonel F. Brownlow, C.B.	,,	,,	,,	27
Lieutenant A. Burlton-Bennet, Staff Corps	,,	,,	,,	29
Captain S. G. Butson	,,	,,	,,	31
Lieutenant J. F. M. Campbell, Staff Corps	,,	,,	,,	33
Captain C. A. Carthew, Staff Corps	,,	,,	,,	35
Major Sir P. L. N. Cavagnari, K.C.B., C.S.I., Staff Corps	,,	,,	,,	37
Captain D. T. Chisholm	,,	IV.	,,	42
Lieutenant R. T. Chute	,,	,,	,,	43
Brevet Lieut.-Colonel W. H. J. Clarke	,,	,,	,,	44
Lieut.-Colonel R. S. Cleland	,,	,,	,,	46
Lieutenant Duncan Cole, Staff Corps	,,	,,	,,	48
Lieut.-Colonel J. J. Collins	,,	,,	,,	50
Brevet Major John Cook, V.C., Staff Corps	,,	,,	,,	52
Surgeon-Major H. Cornish, F.R.C.S.	,,	V.	,,	55
Lieut.-Colonel G. B. Crispin, Staff Corps	,,	,,	,,	57
Captain E. W. H. Crofton	,,	,,	,,	59
Captain G. M. Cruickshank	,,	,,	,,	61
Captain F. J. Cullen	,,	,,	,,	63
Lieutenant R. E. L. Dacres	,,	,,	,,	65
Lieut.-Colonel A. G. Daubeny	,,	,,	,,	66
Lieutenant G. G. Dawes, Staff Corps	,,	VI.	,,	68
Lieutenant A. E. Dobson	,,	,,	,,	70
Captain J. Dundas, V.C.	,,	,,	,,	72

INDEX TO BIOGRAPHICAL DIVISION.

	PLATE	PAGE
LIEUT.-COLONEL H. FELLOWES, Staff Corps . . . . . *portrait*	VI.	*notice* 75
LIEUTENANT T. O. FITZGERALD, Staff Corps . . . . . ,,	,,	,, 77
LIEUTENANT ST. J. W. FORBES . . . . ,,	,,	,, 79
CAPTAIN ST. J. T. FROME . . . . ,,	,,	,, 81
LIEUTENANT C. H. GAISFORD . . . . ,,	VII.	,, 82
LIEUT.-COLONEL JAMES GALBRAITH . . . . . . ,,	,,	,, 84
CAPTAIN J. H. GAMBLE . . . . ,,	,,	,, 86
CAPTAIN E. S. GARRATT . . . . ,,	,,	,, 88
CAPTAIN F. T. GOAD, Staff Corps . . . . ,,	,,	,, 90
MAJOR J. GODSON, Staff Corps . . . . ,,	,,	,, 92
THE REV. G. M. GORDON, M.A. . . . . ,,	,,	,, 94
SURGEON H. A. C. GRAY, M.B., C.M. . . . . . . ,,	VIII.	,, 96
LIEUTENANT W. R. P. HAMILTON, V.C., Staff Corps . . . ,,	,,	,, 98
LIEUTENANT EDWARD HARDY . . . . ,,	,,	,, 101
CAPTAIN G. J. HARE, Staff Corps . . . . ,,	,,	,, *
SUB-LIEUTENANT F. H. HARFORD . . . . . . ,,	,,	,, 103
LIEUTENANT C. J. R. HEARSEY . . . . ,,	,,	,, 105
CAPTAIN P. C. HEATH, Staff Corps . . . . . . ,,	,,	,, 106
LIEUTENANT T. RICE HENN . . . . ,,	IX.	,, 107
LIEUTENANT W. F. HENNELL, Staff Corps . . . . . ,,	,,	,, 110
2ND LIEUTENANT A. HONYWOOD . . . . ,,	,,	,, 111
W. JENKYNS, M.A., C.I.E., Staff Corps . . . . . . ,,	,,	,, 112
LIEUTENANT W. N. JUSTICE . . . . ,,	,,	,, 115
SURGEON A. C. KEITH, M.B. . . . . ,,	†	,, 116
SURGEON A. H. KELLY . . . . ,,	,,	,, 117
SURGEON-MAJOR H. KELSALL . . . . ,,	,,	,, 119
CAPTAIN J. A. KELSO . . . . ,,	X.	,, 121
LIEUTENANT F. G. KINLOCH, Staff Corps . . . . . ,,	,,	,, 123
LIEUTENANT S. E. L. LENDRUM . . . . ,,	,,	,, 125
2ND LIEUTENANT E. D. LOS . . . . ,,	,,	,, 127
LIEUTENANT G. H. LUMSDEN . . . . ,,	,,	,, 129
LIEUTENANT H. MACLAINE . . . . ,,	,,	,, 131
CAPTAIN W. H. MCMATH . . . . ,,	,,	,, 135
2ND LIEUTENANT E. S. MARSH . . . . ,,	XI.	,, 138
LIEUTENANT C. A. MONTANARO . . . . ,,	,,	,, 139
CAPTAIN C. S. MORRISON . . . . ,,	,,	,, 141
LIEUTENANT A. R. MURRAY, Staff Corps . . . . . ,,	,,	,, 143
BREVET LIEUT.-COLONEL W. H. NEWPORT . . . . . ,,	,,	,, 144
LIEUT.-COLONEL G. NICHOLETTS, Staff Corps . . . . ,,	,,	,, 146
LIEUTENANT C. NUGENT . . . . ,,	,,	,, 148
COLONEL J. J. O'BRYEN, Staff Corps . . . . . . ,,	XII.	,, 150
MAJOR C. V. OLIVER . . . . ,,	,,	,, 152
2ND LIEUTENANT W. R. OLIVEY . . . . ,,	,,	,, 154
LIEUTENANT E. G. OSBORNE . . . . ,,	,,	,, 155
LIEUTENANT LORD OSSULTON . . . . ,,	,,	,, *
LIEUTENANT W. C. OWEN, Staff Corps . . . . . . ,,	,,	,, 157
LIEUTENANT E. PALMER, Staff Corps . . . . . . ,,	†	,, 158
CAPTAIN E. W. PERRY . . . . ,,	,,	,, 160
OFFICIATING DEPUTY SURGEON-GENERAL J. H. PORTER . . ,,	XIII.	,, 161
LIEUTENANT BROWNLOW POULTER . . . . . . ,,	,,	,, 166
CAPTAIN C. F. POWELL, Staff Corps . . . . . . ,,	,,	,, 168
BREVET-MAJOR L. A. POWYS . . . . ,,	,,	,, 170
CAPTAIN J. J. PRESTON . . . . ,,	,,	,, 172
LIEUTENANT M. E. RAYNER . . . . ,,	,,	,, 174
CAPTAIN R. B. REED . . . . ,,	,,	,, 175
LIEUTENANT T. J. O'D. RENNY, Staff Corps . . . . ,,	XIV.	,, 177
MAJOR W. REYNOLDS, Staff Corps . . . . . . ,,	,,	,, 179

* *Materials for memoirs of these officers have not been received in time for insertion in the first edition of this work.*
† *A portrait of this officer has not been received in time for insertion in the first edition of this work.*

INDEX TO BIOGRAPHICAL DIVISION. 273

		PLATE	PAGE
2ND LIEUTENANT W. P. RICARDO	portrait	XIV.	notice 181
LIEUTENANT J. T. RICE	,,	,,	,, 182
LIEUTENANT S. W. T. ROBERTS	,,	,,	,, 183
CAPTAIN W. ROBERTS	,,	,,	,, 185
LIEUTENANT H. R. ROSS	,,	,,	,, 186
CAPTAIN A. P. SAMUELLS	,,	XV.	,, 188
CAPTAIN E. W. SAMUELLS, Staff Corps	,,	,,	,, 190
CAPTAIN T. A'B. SARGENT	,,	,,	,, 192
CAPTAIN E. D. SHAFTO	,,	,,	,, 194
BREVET LIEUT.-COLONEL A. M. SHEWELL, Staff Corps	,,	,,	,, 196
CAPTAIN H. F. SHOWERS, Staff Corps	,,	,,	,, 198
BREVET MAJOR L. C. SINGLETON	,,	,,	,, 200
CAPTAIN H. F. SMITH, Staff Corps	,,	XVI.	,, 202
MAJOR L. SMITH, Staff Corps	,,	,,	,, 204
SURGEON W. B. SMYTH, A.B., M.B., L.R.C.S.I.	,,	,,	,, 205
CAPTAIN N. J. SPENS	,,	,,	,, 207
LIEUTENANT H. H. S. SPOOR	,,	,,	,, 209
LIEUTENANT F. C. STAYNER, Staff Corps	,,	,,	,, 210
BREVET LIEUT.-COLONEL R. G. T. STEVENSON	,,	,,	,, 212
CAPTAIN E. STRATON	,,	XVII.	,, 214
CAPTAIN S. A. SWINLEY	,,	,,	,, 217
2ND LIEUTENANT B. S. THURLOW	,,	,,	,, 219
MAJOR R. J. LE POER TRENCH	,,	,,	,, 221
BRIGADIER-GENERAL J. A. TYTLER, C.B., V.C., Staff Corps	,,	,,	,, 223
LIEUTENANT E. P. VENTRIS	,,	,,	,, 226
SURGEON-MAJOR J. WALLACE, M.A., M.D., M.R.C.S.	,,	,,	,, 228
SURGEON J. E. WALSH, M.D.	,,	XVIII.	,, 230
2ND LIEUTENANT E. H. WATSON	,,	,,	,, 232
SURGEON G. WATSON, M.B.	,,	,,	,, 233
MAJOR S. J. WAUDBY, Staff Corps	,,	,,	,, 235
CAPTAIN A. A. D. WEIGALL	,,	,,	,, 239
LIEUTENANT C. G. WHITBY	,,	,,	,, 241
LIEUTENANT F. WHITTUCK, Staff Corps	,,	,,	,, 242
LIEUTENANT H. V. WILLIS	,,	XIX.	,, 244
CAPTAIN F. H. WINTERBOTHAM	,,	,,	,, 246
LIEUTENANT N. C. WISEMAN	,,	,,	,, 248
2ND LIEUTENANT F. P. F. WOOD	,,	,,	,, 249
LIEUTENANT I. D. WRIGHT	,,	,,	,, 251
SURGEON-MAJOR J. H. WRIGHT, M.R.C.S., and L.S.A. Lond.	,,	,,	,, 253
LIEUTENANT G. M. YALDWYN	,,	,,	,, 255

PORTRAITS AND RECORDS OF SERVICE OF RECIPIENTS OF THE VICTORIA CROSS.

		PLATE	PAGE
THE REV. J. W. ADAMS, V.C.	portrait	*	notice 259
PRIVATE J. ASHFORD, V.C.	,,	*	,, 259
LIEUTENANT W. ST. L. CHASE, V.C., Staff Corps	,,	XX.	,, 259
GUNNER J. COLLIS, V.C.	,,	*	,, 260
MAJOR J. COOK, V.C., Staff Corps	,,	IV.	,, 52
BREVET-MAJOR O'M. CREAGH, V.C., Staff Corps	,,	XX.	,, 261
CAPTAIN W. H. DICK CUNYNGHAM, V.C.	,,	,,	,, 262
MAJOR A. G. HAMMOND, V.C., Staff Corps	,,	,,	,, 263

* *Portraits and additional particulars of the services of these officers, non-commissioned officers, and men, have not been received in time for insertion in the first edition of this work.*

INDEX TO BIOGRAPHICAL DIVISION.

		PLATE		PAGE
LIEUTENANT W. P. R. HAMILTON, V.C., Staff Corps	*portrait*	VIII.	*notice*	98
CAPTAIN R. C. HART, V.C.	,,	XX.	,,	264
BREVET LIEUT.-COLONEL E. P. LEACH, V.C.	,,	,,	,,	265
SERGEANT P. MULLANE, V.C.	,,	*	,,	266
MAJOR E. H. SARTORIUS, V.C.	,,	XX.	,,	266
LANCE-CORPORAL G. SELLAR, V.C.	,,	*	,,	267
BREVET-MAJOR W. J. VOUSDEN, V.C., Staff Corps	,,	*	,,	267
LIEUT.-COLONEL G. S. WHITE, V.C., C.B.	,,	*	,,	268

* *Portraits and additional particulars of the services of these officers, non-commissioned officers, and men, have not been received in time for insertion in the first edition of this work.*

CHISWICK PRESS :—C. WHITTINGHAM AND CO., TOOKS COURT, CHANCERY LANE.

www.ingramcontent.com/pod-product-compliance
Lightning Source LLC
Chambersburg PA
CBHW082357010526
44111CB00042B/2616